International Directory of

COMPANY HISTORIES

International Directory of

COMPANY HISTORIES

VOLUME 30

Editor

Jay P. Pederson

ST. JAMES PRESS

AN IMPRINT OF THE GALE GROUP

DETROIT • NEW YORK • SAN FRANCISCO
LONDON • BOSTON • WOODBRIDGE, CT

STAFF

Jay P. Pederson, *Editor*

Miranda H. Ferrara, *Project Manager*

Laura Standley Berger, Joann Cerrito, David J. Collins, Steve Cusack,
Nicolet V. Elert, Jamie C. FitzGerald, Kristin Hart, Laura S. Kryhoski,
Margaret Mazurkiewicz, Michael J. Tyrkus, *St. James Press Editorial Staff*

Peter M. Gareffa, *Managing Editor, St. James Press*

Library of Congress Catalog Number: 89-190943

British Library Cataloguing in Publication Data

International directory of company histories. Vol. 30
I. Jay P. Pederson
338.7409

ISBN 1-55862-389-2

Printed in the United States of America
Published simultaneously in the United Kingdom

St. James Press is an imprint of The Gale Group

Cover photograph: Chicago Board of Trade, Financial Trading Floor
(courtesy Chicago Board of Trade)

10 9 8 7 6 5 4 3 2 1

CONTENTS

Company Histories

PREFACE

The St. James Press series *The International Directory of Company Histories (IDCH)* is intended for reference use by students, business people, librarians, historians, economists, investors, job candidates, and others who seek to learn more about the historical development of the world's most important companies. To date, *IDCH* has covered over 4,000 companies in 30 volumes.

Inclusion Criteria

Most companies chosen for inclusion in *IDCH* have achieved a minimum of US$50 million in annual sales and are leading influences in their industries or geographical locations. Companies may be publicly held, private, or nonprofit. State-owned companies that are important in their industries and that may operate much like public or private companies also are included. Wholly owned subsidiaries and divisions are profiled if they meet the requirements for inclusion. Entries on companies that have had major changes since they were last profiled may be selected for updating.

The *IDCH* series highlights 10% private and nonprofit companies, and features updated entries on approximately 45 companies per volume.

Entry Format

Each entry begins with the company's legal name, the address of its headquarters, its telephone, toll-free, and fax numbers, and its web site. A statement of public, private, state, or parent ownership follows. A company with a legal name in both English and the language of its headquarters country is listed by the English name, with the native-language name in parentheses.

The company's founding or earliest incorporation date, the number of employees, and the most recent available sales figures follow. Sales figures are given in local currencies with equivalents in U.S. dollars. For some private companies, sales figures are estimates and indicated by the abbreviation *est.* The entry lists the exchanges on which a company's stock is traded and its ticker symbol, as well as the company's NAIC codes.

Entries generally contain a *Company Perspectives* box which provides a short summary of the company's mission, goals, and ideals, a list of *Principal Subsidiaries, Principal Divisions, Principal Operating Units,* and articles for *Further Reading.*

American spelling is used throughout *IDCH*, and the word ''billion'' is used in its U.S. sense of one thousand million.

Sources

Entries have been compiled from publicly accessible sources both in print and on the Internet such as general and academic periodicals, books, annual reports, and material supplied by the companies themselves.

Cumulative Indexes

IDCH contains two indexes: the **Index to Companies**, which provides an alphabetical index to companies discussed in the text as well as to companies profiled, and the **Index to Industries**, which allows researchers to locate companies by their principal industry. Both indexes are cumulative and specific instructions for using them are found immediately preceding each index.

Suggestions Welcome

Comments and suggestions from users of *IDCH* on any aspect of the product as well as suggestions for companies to be included or updated are cordially invited. Please write:

The Editor
International Directory of Company Histories
St. James Press
27500 Drake Rd.
Farmington Hills, Michigan 48331-3535

ABBREVIATIONS FOR FORMS OF COMPANY INCORPORATION

A.B.	Aktiebolaget (Sweden)
A.G.	Aktiengesellschaft (Germany, Switzerland)
A.S.	Atieselskab (Denmark)
A.S.	Aksjeselskap (Denmark, Norway)
A.Ş.	Anomin Şirket (Turkey)
B.V.	Besloten Vennootschap met beperkte, Aansprakelijkheid (The Netherlands)
Co.	Company (United Kingdom, United States)
Corp.	Corporation (United States)
G.I.E.	Groupement d'Intérêt Economique (France)
GmbH	Gesellschaft mit beschränkter Haftung (Germany)
H.B.	Handelsbolaget (Sweden)
Inc.	Incorporated (United States)
KGaA	Kommanditgesellschaft auf Aktien (Germany)
K.K.	Kabushiki Kaisha (Japan)
LLC	Limited Liability Company (Middle East)
Ltd.	Limited (Canada, Japan, United Kingdom, United States)
N.V.	Naamloze Vennootschap (The Netherlands)
OY	Osakeyhtiöt (Finland)
PLC	Public Limited Company (United Kingdom)
PTY.	Proprietary (Australia, Hong Kong, South Africa)
S.A.	Société Anonyme (Belgium, France, Switzerland)
SpA	Società per Azioni (Italy)

ABBREVIATIONS FOR CURRENCY

DA	Algerian dinar	Dfl	Netherlands florin
A$	Australian dollar	Nfl	Netherlands florin
Sch	Austrian schilling	NZ$	New Zealand dollar
BFr	Belgian franc	N	Nigerian naira
Cr	Brazilian cruzado	NKr	Norwegian krone
C$	Canadian dollar	RO	Omani rial
RMB	Chinese renminbi	P	Philippine peso
DKr	Danish krone	Esc	Portuguese escudo
E£	Egyptian pound	Ru	Russian ruble
Fmk	Finnish markka	SRls	Saudi Arabian riyal
FFr	French franc	S$	Singapore dollar
DM	German mark	R	South African rand
HK$	Hong Kong dollar	W	South Korean won
HUF	Hungarian forint	Pta	Spanish peseta
Rs	Indian rupee	SKr	Swedish krona
Rp	Indonesian rupiah	SFr	Swiss franc
IR£	Irish pound	NT$	Taiwanese dollar
L	Italian lira	B	Thai baht
¥	Japanese yen	£	United Kingdom pound
W	Korean won	$	United States dollar
KD	Kuwaiti dinar	B	Venezuelan bolivar
LuxFr	Luxembourgian franc	K	Zambian kwacha
M$	Malaysian ringgit		

International Directory of

COMPANY
HISTORIES

A.C. Moore Arts & Crafts, Inc.

500 University Court
Blackwood, New Jersey
U.S.A.
(856) 228-6700
(800) 555-9963
Fax: (856) 228-0080
Web site: http://www.acmoore.com

Public Company
Incorporated: 1984
Employees: 2,735
Sales: $187.01 million (1998)
Stock Exchanges: NASDAQ
Ticker Symbol: ACMR
NAIC: 442299 All Other Home Furnishings Stores;
   45112 Hobby, Toy & Game Stores; 45113 Sewing,
   Needlework & Piece Goods Stores

A.C. Moore Arts & Crafts, Inc. is a retailer offering a vast assortment of arts and crafts merchandise, including silk and dried flowers, floral arrangements and accessories, wedding supplies, candles and scents, wicker, stitchery, yarn, unfinished wood products, children's crafts, art supplies, picture frames, stamps and stationery, seasonal items, and fashion crafts (clothing and accessories for decoration and jewelry-making components). Its policy of beating any competitor's advertised price by ten percent is clearly displayed in all its stores; in addition, it offers selected merchandise at discounts of 20 to 40 percent on a weekly basis. A.C. Moore operates 37 stores in the mid-Atlantic and New England states.

A.C. Moore: 1995–97

A.C. Moore was founded by John E. (Jack) Parker, a veteran merchandising executive for F.W. Woolworth, and William Kaplan, a longtime manufacturer of women's handbags. The company opened its first store in 1985 and had 12 stores in 1993, when it lost $225,000 on net sales of $62.5 million after distributing $4 million to shareholders. A.C. Moore's number of stores grew to 16 in 1994, when it had net income of $4.6 million on net sales of $86.4 million. Net income grew to $6.4 million on sales of $100.1 million in 1995, despite no increase in the number of stores. (A.C. Moore's pro forma net income was significantly lower, reflecting adjustment for federal taxation and state on the individual returns of the shareholders rather than on the company before it became a public corporation.)

In 1995 A.C. Moore implemented a plan to build its infrastructure to position the company for rapid future growth. It opened only one store in 1996, but it also leased a new 140,000-square-foot distribution center and office complex in Blackwood, New Jersey, and developed an automated ordering system to electronically link the company with most vendors. A.C. Moore also recruited experienced senior retail executives in the areas of operations, merchandising, and finance and made key additions in other areas, such as buying, information systems, human resources, and real estate. Net income was $6.3 million on sales of $109.3 million in 1996.

A.C. Moore opened eight new stores in 1997. Sales increased to $138.1 million, but net income fell to $4 million, probably because new stores, according to the company, do not on average generate the volume levels of older stores. After reincorporating as a holding company, A.C. Moore completed an initial public offering in October 1997 by issuing 3.1 million shares of common stock at $15 a share and received $42.6 million in net proceeds. The company retired all outstanding bank debt and shareholder loans totaling $28 million. Its long-term debt of $17.7 million at the end of 1996 fell to zero.

A.C. Moore in the Late 1990s

A.C. Moore opened 12 more new stores in 1998 and expanded its distribution center from 120,000 to 250,000 square feet to provide additional space to support the expanding store base. Net income was $3.9 million on net sales of $187 million. The company planned to open at least 18 stores in 1999 and 2000, targeting both existing and new markets within about a 400-mile radius of its southern New Jersey distribution center.

A.C. Moore was described as a shopping destination for baby boomer parents who wanted their children to do something more active than watching television or playing video games on a computer. Chris Reidy of the *Boston Globe* noted that the chain claimed ''to be the one-stop-shopping destination for shoppers who want to design their own T-shirts or buy enough glued Popsicle sticks to keep a pack of unruly Cub Scouts occupied on a rainy afternoon.'' According to a company executive, some 90 percent of the shoppers in the chain's Framingham, Massachusetts store were women, including professionals who had turned to arts and crafts as a way to relieve stress. Features of this store included what the reporter described as ''all the paraphernalia a handy dad needs to build his daughter a dollhouse large enough to shelter a German shepherd'' and staffers able to ''Dick-and-Jane the intricacies of the home-decorating arts to even an ignoramus of macrame.''

A.C. Moore was operating 37 stores, all on leased property, as it entered 1999. Nine were in Pennsylvania, eight in New York, seven in New Jersey, six in Massachusetts, two in Delaware, two in Maryland, and one each in Connecticut, New Hampshire, and Rhode Island. They were typically located in strip shopping centers with convenient parking and were easily accessible from main traffic arteries. The prototype stores ranged in size from 20,000 to 25,000 square feet, with about 80 percent devoted to selling space.

A.C. Moore stores had 26 merchandise areas. Generally, the center contained the floral area, which included a counter for floral arrangement and a ribbon center. The stores also included a customer service area, eight to ten checkout registers, and a room for craft classes.

Each A.C. Moore had a store manager, three associate managers, and a staff of up to 60 full-time and part-time sales associates. Store personnel, many of them arts-and-crafts enthusiasts, assisted customers with merchandise selection and project ideas. The classroom was being used as often as seven days a week for classes for adults and children on a wide variety of craft skills. Typical classes provided instruction in oil painting, cake decorating, advanced stamping, and on making bows, children's beaded necklaces, and memory albums. They were free of charge unless there was an extensive use of materials. The instructors were both sales associates and outside professionals.

A.C. Moore's store sites were being selected on the basis of such factors as location, demographics, anchor and other tenants, parking, and available lease terms. Within a shopping center, the company looked for tenants generating a high rate of shopping traffic, such as specialty value-oriented women's retailers, leading chain supermarkets, discount chains, home improvement centers, and book and domestic superstores.

A typical A.C. Moore store was offering about 65,000 stockkeeping units during the course of a year, with more than 45,000 offered at any one time. The floral-and-accessory category included a wide, seasonally changing assortment of high-quality silk flowers, hand-wrapped flowers, potted plants, green and flowering bushes, dried flowers, assorted mosses, wreaths, containers, and other components to create floral displays. The company's floral designers worked with customers to make any arrangement, free of charge, from silk or dried flowers purchased from the company. A large assortment of pre-made arrangements also was available. This category also included wedding supplies, items used for christenings and baby showers, packaged scents, candles and supplies for making candles, and a wide assortment of wicker baskets. Florals and accessories accounted for 27 percent of the company's net sales in 1998.

The traditional crafts category included a broad range of stitchery kits; yarn; a full assortment of hooks, needles, and other accessories; a wide variety of unfinished wood products; cake- and candy-making supplies; miniatures, including dollhouses and dollhouse furnishings; paraphernalia for making dolls and clothing for dolls, as well as teddy bears and other stuffed animals; children's crafts, including sand art, sidewalk chalk, bead art supplies, children's stitchery kits, and coloring and other books; felt, glitter, and other materials used in the creation of craft projects; and a wide range of books to assist crafters in all categories. Traditional crafts accounted for about 30 percent of A.C. Moore's sales in 1998.

The art supplies and frame category included oil, acrylic, and water-based paints and other art supplies, such as pastels, brushes, drawing pencils, markers, tablets, and art palettes. It also included decorative stamps and stamp pads, fashion stickers, embossing tools, and albums, stencils, and picture frames of all types and sizes. This category accounted for about 28 percent of company sales in 1998.

Fashion crafts consisted of adult and children's T-shirts and sweatshirts to be decorated with fabric art; related accessories; transfers, including pictures to be ironed or sewn on clothing, most of which could be further embellished with glitter and fabric paints; and jewelry-making components, such as beads, sequins, and rhinestones, as well as the tools needed to complete the project. Fashion crafts accounted for about seven percent of company sales in 1998.

Seasonal items included a wide range of merchandise used as decoration for all major holidays and seasons. In addition to Christmas and Easter, holidays resulting in significant sales of seasonal merchandise included Valentine's Day, St. Patrick's Day, and Halloween. Seasonal items accounted for about eight percent of company sales in 1998.

A.C. Moore was purchasing its inventory from more than 500 vendors worldwide. SBAR, Inc. was the leading supplier in 1998, accounting for about 19 percent of the dollar volume of the company's purchases. About 11 percent of its dollar volume, primarily floral and seasonal items, was imported directly from foreign manufacturers or their agents, principally in the Far East. About 57 percent of all merchandise orders were shipped directly from the vendor to the stores. The remaining 43 percent, of which more than 35 percent were floral and seasonal items, were shipped to the stores from the company's distribution center.

Jack Parker, A.C. Moore's president and chief executive officer, and his wife, Patricia, held 27 percent of A.C. Moore's stock during 1999. William Kaplan, the chairman, held 26 percent.

Principal Subsidiaries

A.C. Moore Incorporated; Blackwood Assets, Inc.; Moorestown Finance, Inc.

Further Reading

Kasrel, Deni, ''Region Spawns Two New Retail Chains Via IPOs,'' *Philadelphia Business Journal,* May 22, 1998, p. B6.

Reidy, Chris, ''Rite of Spring,'' *Boston Globe,* April 23, 1998, pp. E1, E7.

—Robert Halasz

ADC Telecommunications, Inc.

4900 West 78th Street
Minneapolis, Minnesota 55435
U.S.A.
(612) 938-8080
Fax: (612) 946-3292
Web site: http://www.adc.com

Public Company
Incorporated: 1935 as Audio Development Company;
    1953 as Magnetic Controls Company
Employees: 8,000
Sales: $1.37 billion (1998)
Stock Exchanges: NASDAQ
Ticker Symbol: ADCT
NAIC: 33421 Telephone Apparatus Manufacturing; 33429
    Other Communications Equipment Manufacturing;
    334419 Other Electronic Component Manufacturing;
    334417 Electronic Connector Manufacturing

ADC Telecommunications, Inc. is a Minneapolis-based supplier of networking products and systems for telephone, cable television, Internet, broadcast, wireless, and private communications networks. ADC's systems and solutions enable local access and high-speed transmission of communications services from service providers to consumers and businesses over fiberoptic, copper, and wireless media. The company is a diversified niche marketer that has chosen to work closely with industry giants as a collaborator, rather than a competitor. Its systems and integration solutions are divided into four groups: broadband connectivity; business broadband; residential broadband; and integrated solutions. It has direct sales offices located in the United States, Canada, Europe, the Pacific Basin, Australia, and Central and South America.

Innovators in Telecommunications and Data Processing: 1930s–70s

Audio Development Company (later renamed ADC Incorporated) was founded by two Bell Laboratory engineers in 1935 as a telecommunications company that created custom transformers and amplifiers for the radio broadcast industry and also audiometers to test children's hearing. In 1941, while participating in a project to develop a sophisticated audio system for Coffman Union at the University of Minnesota, ADC also began to produce jacks, plugs, patch cords, and jackfields, foreshadowing its future involvement in the telephone industry.

Magnetic Controls Company was founded and incorporated in Minnesota in 1953, part of the wave of technological development during the postwar era. The company produced high-quality custom power supplies and magnetic amplifiers and was involved in military and space exploration programs. In 1961, Magnetic Controls merged with ADC Incorporated, and the new company, which used the umbrella name Magnetic Controls Company (ADC's trade name was retained in telecommunications), advanced its most significant innovation, the Bantam jack. This product was an amalgam of miniaturized components and became standard for telephone circuit access and patching. Magnetic Controls launched an ongoing involvement with major space missions in 1962, eventually designing and manufacturing sensors for the Columbia space shuttle.

The 1960s and 1970s ushered in technological advancement in all areas of telecommunications and data processing. Public and private computer use increased, and telecommunications evolved into the computer age, with telephonic digital transmission and the expansion of data communications. As an innovator in these fields, Magnetic Controls grew dramatically. In 1970, when Charles Denny was encouraged by shareholders to quit his marketing executive job at Honeywell and to take over leadership of the company, the company's earnings stood at $6 million. These compounded at 20 percent a year for the next 20 years.

Magnetic Controls Company pioneered yet another industry standard during the 1970s—the digital signal cross-connect product line to access and cross-connect digital telephony circuits. The company also developed specialized test boards for long-distance telephone companies, and designed and manufactured power conversion equipment for major data processing manufacturers. In addition to proliferating new products that addressed the digitalization of the industry, Magnetic Controls

Company Perspectives:

*ADC's mission is to extend its leadership as a global sup-
plier of systems and solutions that enable communications
service providers to serve their customers with high-band-
width connections offering faster, cost-effective and integrated voice, video and Internet/data services in the last
mile of the communications network.*

continued to introduce telecommunications hardware, including
prewired connectorized jackfields and wired assemblies.

A New Focus on Fiber Optics: 1980s

By 1981, Magnetic Controls Company had sales of $61.5
million; by 1983 sales rose to $76.3 million. Nonetheless, the
company was struggling. Although its telecommunications
products were profitable, its magnetics division, which manufactured transformers and power supplies for mainframe peripherals, lost $1.2 million in fiscal 1983. The company made the
decision to sell its magnetics assets in 1984, writing off the
magnetics division as a $3.95 million one-time loss, and moved
forward as solely a telecommunications company.

The company next repositioned itself in the growth industry
of telecommunications—investing in acquisitions, trimming
expenses, and purchasing shares of its own stock. In 1984,
Magnetic Controls Company acquired TMS Systems, Inc., a
private Massachusetts-based company that manufactured telephone call management equipment and software. With TMS
functioning as a separate subsidiary, Magnetic Controls now
sold the TMS product line as well as telecommunications components and local and remote-access test systems. It began
subcontracting assembly work in Mexico and implemented a
computer-based manufacturing resource planning system to
streamline domestic manufacturing operations.

By 1985 the company's focus was decidedly on telecommunications. It purchased Aetna Life & Casualty Company's Fiber
Optic Component division in Westborough, Massachusetts, and
changed its corporate name to ADC Telecommunications, renaming its new subsidiary ADC Advanced Fiber Optics Corp.
The newly named company focused its efforts on manufacturing, selling, and servicing two groups of telecommunications
products: communications connectors and electronics. Rather
than trying to compete with the industry giants in its fields,
ADC's product strategy was to manufacture and sell products in
diversified industries, finding and occupying niches not already
filled. New orders, backlogs, revenues, and operating income
soared to new highs, the increased demand for ADC's products
the result of technological change and deregulation in the $40
billion long-distance telephone service.

ADC's customer base in the early 1980s was a diverse pool
of public telecommunications networks, telephone operating
companies and other common carriers, and private telecommunications networks used by large businesses and government
agencies. IBM, AT&T, the Bell Operating Companies, MCI,
GTE, ITT, Allnet, and Northern Telecom were among the more

well-known companies it served, with no single one representing more than ten percent of net sales. Foreign buyers
accounted for eight percent of revenues; by 1988, they were at
15 percent, with marketing efforts in Europe, the Pacific Rim,
Canada, Latin America, and the Middle East.

In 1988 slightly over half of ADC's business was in public
networks. ADC products were divided into five categories: network management and control products, termination products,
test products, transmission products, and access products—the
last the most significant at approximately 60 percent of sales.
Responding to a demonstrated growth area in new technology,
ADC took steps to become more involved in the fiberization
process of local loops and local area networks (LANs).

ADC narrowly avoided a buyout when the Lodestar Group,
a New York investment fund specializing in mergers and acquisitions, acquired a 6.4 percent stake in the company in 1989.
Shares of ADC were at $16.75, making the market value of the
company $221 million. Instead, ADC acquired Kentrox Indus-
tries, maker of products for high-speed private telecommunications networks, for $31 million and restructured its operations
into three areas: telecom, diversified markets, and operations.

Expansion into the Video Services Industry: 1990s

Beginning the 1990s with a new president—Denny's chosen
successor and former AT&T executive Bill Cadogan—ADC
entered the video services delivery market, acquiring American
Lightwave Systems, Inc., a leading supplier of fiber optic video
transmission equipment for cable operators for $10.7 million,
with an agreement to make payments totaling at least $4 million
over the next three and a half years. ADC also acquired Telinq
Inc. in 1990 and utilized its newly acquired fiber-optics expertise to develop a local loop system with the goal of providing
economical fiber directly to private homes. Fiber products contributed approximately $18 million to ADC's total sales in
1990, having doubled every year since 1987. Cadogan directed
the company to pursue the course of an early follower—rather
than a leader—in the developing industry, while expanding its
fiber division toward a goal of $250 million in sales by 1995.

In 1991 ADC acquired Fibermux, a maker of high-speed,
fiber-optic equipment for local area networks (LANs), for $50
million, $40 million of which was loan money. Fibermux
proved so successful an investment that ADC paid off this loan
in 1993. In 1992 ADC formed a collaborative development
venture with Fulcrum Communications in Birmingham, England, devising a system to carry voice and video signals over
fiber-optic cable to businesses and residences in North America
in a more cost-effective way. ADC also created Networx, a new
transmission platform that integrated cable management and
private networking products, using synchronous optical network and the asynchronous transfer mode (ATM). The cornerstone of Networx was Sonoplex, a multirate, multimedia system
that brought fiber to the customer's work or residence site,
while making use of existing copper lines. In 1991 ADC had
formed a similar partnership with South Central Bell, Mississippi Educational Television, Northern Telecom, IBM, and Apple Computer to create Fibernet, a network linking students at
four high schools in Clarksville, Corinth, West Point, and
Philadelphia, Mississippi, with teachers at Mississippi State
University, Mississippi University for Women, and Mississippi

School for Mathematics and Science to create "electronic class-rooms."

Leading As an "Early Follower" in ATMs

ADC's and its competitors' marketing strategies were dramatically affected in 1992 by workforce reductions and early retirement programs implemented by large local exchange carriers. With sales at $316 million and shares priced at $56.75, ADC had become a leader in a growth field in 1993. The advent of ATM technology and the scrambling of television, computer, and telephone industries to board the information superhighway had wireless telecommunications booming with a growth rate of 25 percent. Seeking to build a stronger relationship with its customers to secure longevity, ADC adopted strategies including simplifying product lines; providing more detailed support materials; and improving ordering, customer service, quality of products, and maintenance support.

The company's products included fiber-optic video, data, and voice transmission systems, and its clients included phone companies, TV broadcasters, and all major cable TV operators. Its new cellular radio switch was undergoing testing by seven large cellular phone operators. ADC continued to market new products, including an Ethernet converter, a coaxial cable delivery option for its Homeworx broadband access system, and a Sonoplex flexible access platform. ADC's Homeworx system was selected by Rochester Telephone Corp. in May 1993 for a six-month video-on-demand trial.

ADC became an "early follower" in the asynchronous transfer mode (ATM) market, announcing a multiyear agreement with Loral Data Systems for an ATM switch. The ATM switch would create the capability of handling the massive flows of simultaneous high-speed digital information that the industry projected would be generated during the latter half of the 1990s and into the 21st century, arising from the blending of the communications, computing, and entertainment industries. The company also landed a coup in March 1994 when Ameritech chose ADC to supply equipment for its $75–$100 million video system, to be developed over the next five years. This $4.4 billion project would bring 70 channels of analog television and 40 channels of digital video to customers, with unlimited program choices and interactive, customer-controllable programming.

A New Era of Leadership: 1994 and Beyond

In 1994, as the Internet began its early growth phase, Charles Denny announced his retirement as chairman of the board and was replaced by Bill Cadogan. The company's revenues had grown to $366 million in 1993, with a market value approaching $1 billion. As ADC Telecommunications, Inc. moved into a new era of leadership, its strategies included a new focus on cable TV and cellular communications, increased international presence, and increased fiber-optic and electronic product offerings in the multimedia market. In 1995 it bought Australian Fiber Optics Research, making inroads into the Australian market. It also increased its presence in China when it sold its digital cable television transmission system to China's Hunan Post & Telecommunications Administration in a two-year deal

worth potentially $14 million. That year, the company's total revenue exceeded $500 million for the first time.

The following year was one of unprecedented deal making for ADC; it acquired seven companies, including Solitra Oy, Da Tel Fibernet, Information Transmission Systems, and the wireless infrastructure equipment group of Pacific Communications Sciences Inc. By 1997, with two more acquisitions under its belt, the company's revenue had exceeded $1 billion, and it was competing with such industry giants as Lucent Technologies, Motorola, and Northern Telecom. Its three-pronged strategy was to sell to phone companies riding the waves of deregulation and Internet growth; to cable TV companies preparing to offer new telephone and data services; and to wireless phone companies. A relatively new market for ADC, wireless operations were in the vicinity of $65 million.

But even though ADC's sales kept growing, its stock price took a sudden plunge in early 1998 as the company reported a net loss of $13.2 million for the first quarter ended January. Analysts attributed the drop to a faltering performance in the company's normally thriving broadband connectivity group. However, throughout the year, ADC continued to reach record year-over-year levels for each quarter's sales and earnings; annual sales growth was 18 percent for a grand total of $1.5 billion by year's end, and earnings per share grew 17 percent. ADC purchased Israeli Teledata Communications Ltd. for $200 million in cash, broadening its international exposure and expanding its product range, and also acquired Princeton Optics, a maker of optical components critical to maximizing available bandwidth within the fiber-optic network.

In planning its course for the next millennium, ADC was focused on being a total solutions provider for the last mile, or local loop, providing the fiber-optic technologies, Internet connectivity and transmission systems, and network software to make high-speed, multiservice communications possible. ADC's strategy was to capitalize on the evolving global communications market and to address key areas of the communications network infrastructure by designing products that enabled its customers to connect physical networks, access network services, transport network traffic, and manage networks.

Principal Subsidiaries

Fibermux Corporation; Kentrox Industries, Inc.; Skyline Technology, Inc.; ADC Broadband Communications, Inc.; Pathway, Inc.; Teledata Communications, Inc.; PCS Solutions, LLC; ADC Broadband Wireless Group, Inc.; ITS Service Company, Inc.; TPO Limited; ADC International OUS, Inc.; ADC OUS Holdings, LLC; Telesphere Solutions, Inc.; ADC Telecommunications Sales, Inc.; Princeton Optics, Inc.; Codenol Technology Corp.; AOFR Americas Inc.; ADC Teledata Communications Ltd. (Israel); Tdsoft Ltd. (Israel); G-Connect Ltd. (Israel); T-Link (Israel); TDC Teledata Communication GmbH (Germany); ADC Telecom Canada Inc.; ADC Europe N.V. (Belgium); ADC Telecommunications Netherlands B.V. (Netherlands); ADC Telecommunications GmbH (Germany); ADC Telecommunications U.K. Ltd.; ADC Telecommunications Australia Pty. Limited; ADC Telecommunications Holdings Pty. Limited (Australia); Teledata Communication Australia Pty. Ltd.; Teledata Manufacturing Australia Pty. Ltd.; Teledata

Holdings Australia Pty. Ltd.; TDC (UK) Limited; Teledata Communications Hellas LLC (Greece); Teledata Communications Do Brasil Ltd. (Brazil); T.D.C. Holdings B.V. (Netherlands); Teledata Communications (Philippines), Inc.; ADC Wireless Systems, Inc.; ADC Wireless Systems Holding Company, Inc.; ADC Metrica (U.K.); Metrica, Inc.; ADC Telecommunicaciones Venezuela, S.A.; ADC de Mexico, S.A. de C.V.; ADC Telecommunications Singapore Pte. Limited; AOFR Pty. Limited (Australia); ADC Mersum Oy (Finland); ADC Solitra Oy (Finland); ADC Mersum U.S., Inc.; ADC Solitra, Inc.; ADC de Juarez, S. de R.L. de C.V. (Mexico); ADC de Delicias, S. de R.L. de C.V. (Mexico); ADC Telecommunications China Limited (Hong Kong); ADC Telecommunications (Nanjing) Co. Ltd. (China); Nanjing ADC Broadband Communications Co., Ltd. (China); ADC International, Inc. (Barbados); ADC Telecommunicaciones Do Brasil LTDA (Brazil); ADC PHASOR Electronics GmbH (Austria); Nanjing ADC Teleco Equipment, Ltd. (China).

Further Reading

"ADC Acquires an LPL Unit," *Wall Street Journal,* July 5, 1990, p. A5.

Alexander, Steve, "Selling 'Bullets' in the Telecommunications War," *Star Tribune,* December 8, 1997, p. 1D.

"Go for the Middle," *Forbes,* April 29, 1991, p. 148.

Karpinski, Richard, "ADC Unveils Transparent LAN Gear," *Telephony,* April 12, 1993, p. 14.

Karr, Albert R., and Christina Duff, "Hiring Levels Remain Low, Belying Late-Spring Optimism for a Rebound," *Wall Street Journal,* August 26, 1991, p. A2.

Lannon, Larry, "ADC Is Eyeing a Strategic Shift," *Telephony,* July 18, 1988, p. 24.

"Magnetic Controls Sees Fall in Fiscal '84 Net on Ongoing Operations," *Wall Street Journal,* March 28, 1984, p. 24.

Slutsker, Gary, " 'I Still Think They're Idiots,' " *Forbes,* July 19, 1993, p. 85.

"Supercom Vendors Ready New Products," *Telephony,* April 19, 1993, p. 26.

Titch, Steven, "ADC Unveils Loop Product Strategy," *Telephony,* February 24, 1992, p. 9.

Van, Jon, "Ameritech Awards Deal in Video Plan," *Chicago Tribune,* March 31, 1994, sec. 3, p. 1.

Wilson, Carol, "ADC Launches Fiber-Coax Platform," *Telephony,* May 24, 1993, p. 11.

——, "ADC Plots Course in Local Loop," *Telephony,* September 17, 1990, p. 9.

——, "ADC Unveils Fiber Product," *Telephony,* June 21, 1993, p. 12.

——, "LECS Confront a Serious People Problem," *Telephony,* March 9, 1992, p. 76.

Yu, Roger, "Bringing It All Together," *Star Tribune,* July 5, 1999, p. 1D.

—Heidi Feldman
—updated by Carrie Rothburd

Advanced Micro Devices, Inc.

One AMD Place
Sunnyvale, California 94088
U.S.A.
(408) 732-2400
(800) 538-8450
Fax: (408) 774-7023
Web site: http://www.amd.com

Public Company
Incorporated: 1969
Employees: 13,000
Sales: $2.54 billion (1998)
Stock Exchanges: New York
Ticker Symbol: AMD
NAIC: 334413 Semiconductor & Related Device
   Manufacturing

Advanced Micro Devices, Inc. (AMD) is one of the world leaders in the microprocessor industry, ranking second behind Intel Corporation. Although AMD's roughly ten percent share of the overall market pales in comparison to Intel's 80 percent, the Sunnyvale, California company is considered a fierce competitor. AMD is considered especially strong as a supplier to the low-end PC market, where it commands a nearly 60 percent share. Nonetheless, AMD's future health seemed dependent on diversification beyond its traditional markets and products. In addition to microprocessors and integrated circuits, the company also produces flash memories, programmable logic devices, and products for networking and communications applications.

Finding Opportunity: 1969–74

In 1968 Jerry Sanders (who had previously worked for Intel founder Robert Noyce) left his position as director of worldwide marketing at Fairchild Semiconductor. By May 1969 he and seven others officially launched Advanced Micro Devices, Inc. The company was incorporated with $100,000 with the purpose of building semiconductors for the electronics industry.

Although the company was initially headquartered in the living room of one of the cofounders, John Carey, it soon moved to two rooms in the back of a rugcutting company in Santa Clara, California. By September of that year, AMD had raised the additional money it needed to begin manufacturing products and moved into its first permanent home, in Sunnyvale. In May 1970, AMD ended its first year with 53 employees and 18 products, but no sales.

The firm initially acted as an alternate source of chips, receiving products from other firms such as Fairchild and National Semiconductor and then redesigning them for greater speed and efficiency. Unlike other second-source companies, however, AMD was one of the first Silicon Valley firms to stress quality above all else, designing its chips to meet U.S. military specifications for semiconductors. At a time when the young computer industry was suffering from unreliable chips, this gave AMD an advantage. The firm began to cater to customers in the computer, telecommunications, and instrument industries who were growing quickly and who valued reliability highly enough to pay for it. AMD avoided producing chips for such inexpensive consumer items as calculators and watches, determining that these were only short-term markets.

Sanders, the driving force behind AMD, also began instituting price incentives, relying heavily on salesmanship to keep the company afloat. To do this, he kept the company decentralized, breaking it into several product profit centers. As a result, engineers and designers were more aware of the business implications of their work than were their counterparts.

A flamboyant leader who flaunted his love of materialism, Sanders used his personality to push his small company into the public eye, giving it a larger presence than its size merited. While attempting to motivate employees through the desire to be as rich as he was becoming, Sanders stressed respect for those low on the company's totem pole. He threw extravagant Christmas parties for everyone in the company and one year held a raffle, awarding $12,000 a year for 20 years to the winning employee—and showed up with a camera crew to record the prize delivery. These practices contrasted markedly with those of AMD's more conservative competitors, including Intel and National Semiconductor, and quickly gave the firm an aggressive reputation.

Company Perspectives:

We at AMD share a vision of a world that is enhanced through information technology, which liberates the human mind and spirit. AMD is a leading supplier of critical enabling technology for the Information Age. In concert with our customers, we empower people everywhere to lead more productive lives by creating, processing, and communicating information and knowledge. We are our customers' favorite integrated circuit supplier.

In September 1972 the company went public, selling 525,000 shares at $15 a share, bringing in $7.87 million. In January of the following year, the company's first overseas manufacturing base, located in Penang, Malaysia, began volume production. By the end of AMD's fifth year, there were nearly 1,500 employees making over 200 different products, many of them proprietary, and bringing in nearly $26.5 million in annual sales. To commemorate its five-year anniversary in May 1974, AMD began what was to become a renowned tradition, holding a gala party, this one a street fair attended by employees and their families, in which televisions, ten-speed bicycles, and barbecue grills were given away.

Defining the Future: 1974–79

AMD's second five years gave the world a taste of the company's most enduring trait, tenaciousness. Despite a dogged recession in 1974–75, when sales briefly slipped, the company grew during this period to $168 million, representing an average annual compound growth rate of over 60 percent. Part of the success of the period was due to the implementation of a 44-hour work week for the company's staff. This was also a period of tremendous facilities expansion.

In 1975 the company received an infusion of cash ($30 million for 20 percent of its stock) from Siemens AG, a huge West German firm who wanted a foothold in the U.S. semiconductor market. In 1976 the company signed a cross-license agreement with Intel. Two years later the company formed a joint venture, called Advanced Micro Computers (AMC), with facilities in both Germany and the United States, to develop, produce, and market microcomputer products. The venture was dissolved a year later, in March 1979, and the company purchased the net assets of the domestic operations of AMC. Also in 1978, the company reached a major sales milestone of $100 million in annual revenue. In 1979 the company's shares were listed on the New York Stock Exchange for the first time under the ticker AMD; that same year, production began at AMD's newly constructed Austin, Texas facility.

Finding Preeminence: 1980–83

The early 1980s were defined for AMD by two now famous corporate symbols. The first, called the "Age of Asparagus," represented the company's drive to increase the number of proprietary products offered to the marketplace. Like this lucrative crop, proprietary products take time to cultivate, but eventually bring excellent returns on the initial investment. The

second symbol was a giant ocean wave. The "Catch the Wave" recruiting advertisements portrayed the company as an unstoppable force in the integrated circuit business. And unstoppable it was, at least for a time. AMD became a leader in R&D investment and by the end of fiscal 1981 the company had more than doubled its sales over 1979. Plants and facilities expanded with an emphasis on building in Texas. New production facilities were built in San Antonio, and more fab space was added to the Austin plant as well. AMD had quickly become a major contender in the world semiconductor marketplace. In 1981, AMD's chips went into space aboard the space shuttle *Columbia*. The following year, AMD and Intel signed a technology exchange agreement centering on the iAPX86 family of microprocessors and peripherals. That same year, in a minor setback, a group of engineers left the company to found Cypress Semiconductor. In 1983, the company introduced INT.STD.1000, the highest quality standard in the industry, and incorporated AMD Singapore.

Weathering Hard Times: 1984–89

In 1984 the Austin facility added Building 2, and the company was listed in a new book entitled *The 100 Best Companies to Work for in America*. The following year, AMD made the *Fortune* 500 list for the first time, and Fabs 14 and 15 began operation in Austin. AMD celebrated its 15th year with one of the best sales years in company history. In the months following AMD's anniversary, employees received record-setting profit sharing checks and celebrated Christmas with musical groups Chicago in San Francisco and Joe King Carrasco and the Crowns in Texas.

By 1986, however, the tides of change had swept the industry. Japanese semiconductor makers came to dominate the memory markets—up until now a mainstay for AMD—and a fierce downturn had taken hold, limiting demand for chips in general. AMD, along with the rest of the semiconductor industry, began looking for new ways to compete in an increasingly difficult environment. In September 1986, Tony Holbrook was named president of the company; the following month, weakened by the long-running recession, AMD announced its first workforce restructure in over a decade. In April 1987, AMD initiated an arbitration action against Intel. Later that year, the company merged with Monolithic Memories, Inc., acquiring the latter's common stock in exchange for over 19 million shares of its own, a trade valued at $425 million. By 1989 AMD Chairman Jerry Sanders was talking about transformation: changing the entire company to compete in new markets, a process which began in October 1988, with the groundbreaking on the Submicron Development Center.

Making the Transformation: 1989–94

Finding new ways to compete led to the concept of AMD's "Spheres of Influence." For the transforming AMD, those spheres were microprocessors compatible with IBM computers, networking and communication chips, programmable logic devices, and high-performance memories. In addition, the company's long survival depended on developing submicron process technology that would fill its manufacturing needs into the next century.

By its 25th anniversary, AMD had put to work every ounce of tenaciousness it had to achieve those goals, growing to be either number one or number two worldwide in every market it served, including the Microsoft Windows-compatible business. AMD became a preeminent supplier of flash, networking, telecommunications, and programmable logic chips as well.

In May 1989, the company established the office of the chief executive, consisting of the top three company executives. In March 1991, AMD introduced new versions of the Am386 microprocessor family, breaking the Intel monopoly. A mere seven months later, the company had shipped its millionth Am386. That year, Siemens sold off its interest in AMD.

In February of the following year, the company's five-year arbitration with Intel ended, with AMD awarded full rights to make and sell the entire Am386 family of microprocessors. Early in 1993, the first members of the Am486 microprocessor family were introduced, and AMD and Fujitsu established a joint venture to produce flash memories, a new technology in which memory chips retained information even after the power was turned off. In July the Austin facility broke ground on Fab 25. In January 1994, computer reseller Compaq Computer Corporation and AMD formed a long-term alliance under which Am486 microprocessors would power Compaq computers. A month later, AMD employees began moving into One AMD Place in Sunnyvale, the company's new headquarters, and Digital Equipment Corporation became the foundry for Am486 microprocessors. In March 1994, a federal court jury confirmed AMD's right to use Intel microcode in 287 math coprocessors, and the company celebrated its 25th anniversary with Rod Stewart in Sunnyvale and Bruce Hornsby in Austin.

From Transformation to Transcendence: 1994–97

In January 1996, the company purchased Milpitas, California-based NexGen, Inc., a smaller semiconductor manufacturer founded in 1989. For fiscal 1998, the company posted net sales of $2.54 billion, a 7.9 percent increase, but also recorded a painful net loss on income of $104 million. In mid-1999, Hillsboro, Oregon-based Lattice Semiconductor Corp. purchased AMD's semiconductor manufacturing unit Vantis Corp. for $500 million in cash.

With Microsoft holding the software market in one fist, and Intel holding the microprocessor market in another, companies like National Semiconductor bowed out of the microprocessor manufacturing business in the late 1990s, refocusing their efforts instead on core competencies. Other companies, according to Kathleen Doler's August 1999 editorial in *Electronic Business*, "lost money six out of . . . nine fiscal quarters." Indeed, AMD reported a 1999 second quarter loss of $162 million. With "68 percent of its revenue [derived] from microprocessors and related products," Doler said, it seemed only prudent that AMD would diversify into other products in order to stay alive in the 21st century.

Principal Subsidiaries

Advanced Micro Devices Inc. Customer Specific Products Division.

Further Reading

Brown, Ken, "Motorola Boosting R&D Through Joint Ventures," *Business Journal—Serving Phoenix & the Valley of the Sun*, July 24, 1998, p. 6.

Bruner, Richard, "AMD, Compaq Hit with Shareholder Suits," *Electronic News*, April 26, 1999, p. 10.

Calabro, Lori, "Closing Time," *CFO, The Magazine for Senior Financial Executives*, October 1994, p. 100.

Dillon, Nancy, "AMD Defies Intel's Monopoly Defense; Chip Maker's Loss Reflects Intel's Strength in Market, but K7 Chip Will Be Test of AMD's Competitive Position," *Computerworld*, July 5, 1999, p. 84.

Doler, Kathleen, "Jerry Sanders' Obsession," *Electronic Business*, August 1999, p. 4.

Dorsch, Jeff, "AMD to Use Leica Inspection/Review System," *Electronic News*, February 15, 1999, p. 26.

Fischer, Jack, "High-Tech Crime Wave Spreading Through Nation," *Knight-Ridder/Tribune Business News*, April 13, 1995, p. 4130273.

Fisher, Lawrence M., "Big Chip Maker Warns on Jobs and Earnings," *New York Times*, March 9, 1999, p. D1.

——, "Falling Chip Prices Bruise Manufacturers—and the Market," *International Herald Tribune*, April 16, 1999, p. 14.

Haber, Carol, "Posting a $32M 3Q Loss, AMD to Profit in 4Q . . . If . . . ," *Electronic News*, October 13, 1997, p. 92.

——, "Turmoil in the Desktop MPU Market: Intel Keeps Chugging As Rivals Bolt and Bleed," *Electronic News*, July 19, 1999, p. 1.

Morrison, Gale, "Sanders Under the Gun," *Electronic News*, April 13, 1998, p. 12.

Niccolai, James, "AMD Forecasts Large Loss; Chip Maker to Trim Workforce by 300," *Computerworld*, March 15, 1999, p. 27.

——, "AMD Posts Loss of $162M; President Resigns; Chip Battle Taking Toll on Intel Rival," *Computerworld*, July 19, 1999, p. 28.

Paul, Lauren Gibbons, "Eliminating the Procurement Middleman; AMD Taps a New Intranet-Based Solution to Buy Nonproduction Goods," *PC Week*, May 19, 1997, p. 135.

Quinlan, Tom, "Big Three of Microprocessors to Unveil New Designs." *Knight-Ridder/Tribune Business News*, October 7, 1998, p. OKRB98280131.

Reinhardt, Andy, and Ira Sager, "Can AMD Snap Its Losing Streak?" *Business Week*, December 8, 1997, p. 83.

Ristelhueber, Robert, "AMD Selling Vantis to Lattice," *Electronic News*, April 26, 1999, p. 1.

——, "The Long Goodbye," *Electronic News*, July 26, 1999, p. 8.

Rutledge, Tanya, "AMD Headquarters Sell for $95 Million," *Business Journal*, February 5, 1999, p. 1.

Schofield, Jack, "Crippling Battle Is on the Cards," *Guardian*, February 11, 1999, p. S2.

Slater, Michael, "Right Speed," *PC Magazine*, September 21, 1999, p. 100.

Takahashi, Dean, "Advanced Micro Devices Mulls Partnership," *Wall Street Journal*, July 29, 1999, p. B6.

——, "AMD Reports Record Loss for 2nd Period," *Wall Street Journal*, July 15, 1999, p. A3.

——, "More Bad News Puts Intel Rival Further Behind," *Wall Street Journal*, June 24, 1999, p. B1.

Takahashi, Dean, and Don Clark, "AMD's Search for No. 2 to Strong CEO Isn't Likely to Attract Many Outsiders," *Wall Street Journal*, July 16, 1999, p. B5.

Venezia, Carol, "Athlon Vs. PIII at 600," *PC Magazine*, September 21, 1999, p. 41.

——, "Performance Tests: Athlon Vs. PIII," *PC Magazine*, September 21, 1999, p. 44.

Willett, Hugh G., "Monopoly 101," *Electronic News*, May 24, 1999, p. 8.

Yates, Christopher, and Peter Coffee, ". . . and Why Intel Built the Chip Set," *PC Week*, June 21, 1999, p. 41.

—Scott Lewis
—updated by Daryl F. Mallett

BELO

A.H. Belo Corporation

P.O. Box 655237
Dallas, Texas 75265-5237
U.S.A.
(214) 977-6600
Fax: (214) 977-6603
Web site: http://www.belo.com

Public Company
Incorporated: 1926
Employees: 6,920
Sales: $1.4 billion (1998)
Stock Exchanges: New York Chicago
Ticker Symbol: BLC
NAIC: 51111 Newspaper Publishers; 51312 Television
   Broadcasting

Originating as a small-town publisher of the *Dallas Morning News* and the *Texas Almanac*, A.H. Belo Corporation has become a diversified media company of national significance. The oldest continuously operating business in the state of Texas, Belo—as it now prefers to be known—owned and operated eight daily newspapers and 17 network-affiliated television stations as of July 1999. Its top three newspapers are the *Dallas Morning News,* the *Providence (Rhode Island) Journal,* and the *Press-Enterprise* serving Riverside, California. Its television stations are strongest in the Southwest and Northwest. The company also owns two regional cable news networks serving Texas and the Pacific Northwest.

Early History to 1920s

A.H. Belo Corporation traces its roots to the *Galveston Daily News,* which was published by Samuel Bangs with a circulation under 200 in 1842, when Texas was still a republic. In 1857, Willard Richardson, who had replaced Bangs as publisher of the fledgling *Daily News,* created the *Texas Almanac.* Ten thousand copies of the first edition were sold. The *Almanac* became a valuable reference book for Texas farmers, ranchers, and businessmen, as well as a voice for the promotion of immigration.

Richardson's editorials advocated the importance of the railroads to the growth of the state of Texas—and to the future of newspaper distribution. By 1865, Richardson had turned the *Galveston Daily News* into the most powerful newspaper in Texas.

Former Confederate Colonel Alfred Horatio Belo joined the *Daily News,* succeeding Richardson as publisher and becoming majority owner of the company, in 1865. In 1881, Belo incorporated the *Galveston Daily News.* Belo expanded the company by starting a new newspaper in 1885 under the recommendation of George Bannerman Dealey, who Belo had hired as an office boy in 1874. The *Dallas Morning News* published its first edition in what was then the prairie town of Dallas, population 18,000. Using the telegraph to communicate across 315 miles, the *Galveston Daily News* and the *Dallas Morning News* issued the first wire-connected publication with joint issues. The *Dallas Morning News* issues were delivered that year on special trains to Fort Worth, Dennison, and Waco to reach a year-end circulation of 5,678 daily and 6,435 Sunday papers. In its early years, the *Dallas Morning News* experienced steady growth in circulation.

Radio and Newspaper Operations in Dallas: 1920s–40s

Dealey's prominence grew with the paper's, and in 1920 he became president. Dealey became a well-known civic leader and visionary, bringing George Kessler to Dallas to devise a city plan, and urging the *Morning News* to take advantage of the sure potential of the new medium that was sweeping the nation: radio. In 1922, WFAA went on the air as the *Dallas Morning News*'s radio service and the first network radio station in Texas. The early broadcasts took place in the library of the *Morning News* office, with a canvas tent used for soundproofing. By 1930, WFAA would become the first superpower radio station in the South and Southwest, broadcasting at 50,000 watts. Nevertheless, the company maintained a decided emphasis on newspaper publishing and did not become seriously involved in broadcast media until the 1980s.

In 1923 the company sold its interest in the *Galveston Daily News,* focusing its newspaper operations entirely on the *Dallas Morning News.* Dealey acquired a majority interest in the company from Col. Belo's heirs in 1926. With partner John F.

Company Perspectives:

In the broadcast industry, there is a great deal of talk about the threat to our business from cable. Yet, consider that the audience reached by one evening newscast in Dallas/Fort Worth, Houston and Seattle/Tacoma exceeds the average audience delivered by CNN nationally Monday through Friday from 5:30 p.m. until 8 p.m. Similarly, the Dallas Morning News, *the* Providence Journal, *and the* Press-Enterprise *deliver almost three million Sunday readers and more than two million daily readers. Only network-affiliated television stations and large newspapers can deliver this mass audience, which advertisers rely upon to sell their products and services.*

Lubben, Dealey incorporated the company, naming it A.H. Belo Corporation in honor of his late employer and mentor. Still linked to the farm-based economy, the *Dallas Morning News* sponsored a ''More Cotton on Fewer Acres'' competition, with participation by over 7,000 farmers. Winners received cash prizes and publication of their farming techniques in a bulletin distributed in the Cotton Belt and overseas in Egypt, India, Brazil, and Mexico.

Moving into Television: 1950s–60s

In 1950 Belo acquired KBTV (later renamed WFAA-TV), and became one of the first television broadcasting companies. Belo moved slowly into the television industry, however, with its primary focus remaining the *Dallas Morning News*. Belo would not buy a second television station until 1968, or a third until 1979. Nevertheless, Belo continued to expand in the 1960s, acquiring News-Texan, Inc., a publisher of seven community newspapers that would later form the Dallas-Fort Worth Suburban Newspapers, Inc.

Newspaper Honors: 1970s

By 1970 the *Dallas Morning News* had a circulation of 239,367 papers daily and 280,696 papers on Sunday—more than twice the circulation of 1940, and over 13 times the population of Dallas when Dealey had returned from his scouting mission in 1885. Seeking to further improve its product, the *Morning News* commissioned a study of the interests of Dallas readers in 1978. As a result of the study, the paper increased its coverage of high interest areas, especially through the development of innovative fashion and entertainment sections. The *Morning News* garnered three Pulitzer Prizes during the 1970s, and its sports coverage was recognized by the Associated Press sports editors in its national ''Ten Best Sports Sections'' list.

Television More Significant: 1980s

A.H. Belo Corporation became a public company in 1981, with its initial offering of 3.9 million shares on the New York Stock Exchange priced at $11.50 per share. In 1983 Belo shed its publishing-only orientation by making the largest broadcast purchase in national history. For $606 million, Belo acquired KHOU-TV (Houston), KXTV (Sacramento), and WVEC (Norfolk, Virginia), all of which were licensed to Corinthian Broadcast Corporation from the Dun & Bradstreet Corporation. To comply with Federal Communications Commission rules regarding the purchase, Belo sold Texas station KDFM-TV and Tennessee station WTVC, recouping approximately $105 million. An asset redeployment plan led to the sale of the company's cable system and its four radio stations, and Belo raised additional capital by selling 4.4 million shares of stock.

It appeared that the acquisition might bring trouble to Belo when the biggest of the four television stations, KHOU-TV in Houston, was hurt by a lagging Texas economy. However, Belo's revenues reached $354 million in 1984, with KHOU-TV and the flagship station WFAA contributing two-thirds of the company's total revenues. Though the company's stock had risen 29 percent (to $42.50 per share) between 1981 and 1983, when it made its intention to acquire the Corinthian outlets public, Belo's stock reached a record high of $55 per share in 1985. The next year, after 40 years with Belo, Chairman and CEO James Moroney retired, and Robert Decherd took the mantle. Dechard was G.B. Dealey's great grandson.

Economic Difficulties: Mid-1980s

Overproduction of oil and overbuilding of real estate struck a blow to the Texas economy in the mid 1980s. Ward Hucy, president of Belo's broadcast division, recognized the danger posed to the earnings of Belo's newly acquired television stations by Texas's lagging economy. Huey instituted cost-cutting measures including layoffs, salary freezes, and the postponement of plans for new transmitter towers and upgraded production equipment. Due to the weak economy in Dallas-Fort Worth and Houston, net earnings continued to decrease in 1986, although both television and newspaper revenues showed increased profits.

Even with financial difficulties, the *Dallas Morning News* took the lead over its local competitor, the *Dallas Times-Herald,* in the 1980s. In 1986, the *Morning News* achieved a new circulation record and won a Pulitzer Prize for a story on housing discrimination that resulted in Senate hearings and national corrective actions. The *Dallas Morning News* circulation grew to 404,812 daily and 618,283 Sunday by 1991.

Belo moved forward in a bold new direction when it formed a partnership in 1989 with Kansas City-based Universal Press Syndicate to create programming based on Universal's roster of comics and columnists. The first Universal Belo project was an animated strip based on the ''Tank MacNamara'' comic, designed for prime-time specials and network sports events. Animation for the strip was created at the California Film Roman studios. The *Dallas Times-Herald* lost all of its Universal columns and cartoons as a result of the new partnership and brought an antitrust lawsuit against the *Morning News.* The lawsuit and its appeal were unsuccessful, but Belo paid a $1.5 million settlement to its competitor.

The Texas economy began to rebound as the 1980s came to a close, and Belo's television ratings soared. In 1989, Belo syndicated ''Mr. Peppermint,'' a Dallas children's program it had aired for 25 years. WFAA's *Texas Country Reporter* was sold in 22 Southwestern markets, and WFAA, after several flat years, saw a 16 percent increase in earnings between 1987 and 1989, when earnings reached $73.3 million. During that same period, KHOU-TV increased its revenues by nine percent to $46 million. By 1990, the formerly troubled KHOU-TV had risen in the ratings from a distant third to number two, giving Belo a number one or two rating for all of its television stations.

Economic Recession: Early 1990s

Just as the Texas economy improved, a national recession began that dramatically impacted newspaper advertising. Newspapers experienced their worst year in a decade in 1990. While the *Dallas Times-Herald* slashed its advertising rates, Belo CEO Decherd held a firm line with rate cards. The *Dallas Morning News* achieved only slight gains in overall advertising, but boosted its circulation by four percent daily and six percent Sunday, posting higher increase rates than those experienced by the *Dallas Times-Herald*. By this time, the *Morning News*'s circulation rates doubled those of the *Times-Herald*.

The war between Dallas's two major newspapers ended in 1991. On December 9th, after 112 years in operation, the *Dallas Times-Herald* published its last issue. Belo acquired the *Herald*'s assets in a $55 million deal, becoming the only major newspaper publisher in Dallas. Twelve other major newspapers also succumbed to the recession, closing their doors in 1991.

The acquisition of the *Times-Herald* caused Belo to change its financial plan in 1992. With circulation boosted in one year to a half million papers daily (a 26 percent increase) and 800,000 Sunday (a 31 percent increase), the *Morning News* was pushing its production capacity. The newspaper recession showed signs of ending, and circulation figures placed the *Morning News* among the nation's most highly read papers for the first time, making national advertising a strong possibility. While other newspapers experienced slow recovery, the *Morning News* used 30 percent more newsprint in 1992 than it had the previous year, publishing a Sunday paper on December 6th that was so large it delayed deliveries by an hour. Decherd adamantly refused to raise the newsstand price from 25 cents, espousing the philosophy that rampant price increases at other newspapers were too aggressive, cutting into reader retention. To manage its growth, Belo invested $41 million in the expansion of its newspaper production plant in Plano, Texas.

The production facility expansion was completed in 1993, and the suburban newspaper operation in Dallas-Fort Worth was restructured into two separate entities, one printing eight community newspapers and the other functioning as a commercial printer. The *Dallas Morning News* won its fifth Pulitzer Prize in eight years, for sport news photography of the 1992 Summer Olympics. Circulation of the *Morning News* held strong at 527,387 daily and 814,404 on Sunday.

Television as well as newspapers were profitable for the company in 1993. Four of Belo's five television stations were rated number one in overall audience delivery, and Belo announced plans to purchase WWL-TV, an affiliate of CBS in New Orleans. Programming activities were placed under the authority of the newly created Belo Productions, Inc. (BPI), an entity that oversaw potential pay-as-you-go cable and television

programs in conjunction with Universal Belo Productions. In 1993, Belo's stock reached $53 per share and sales were $545 million. Net earnings were $51.1 million, 37.3 percent more than in 1992.

Aggressive Acquisitions: 1994–99

Through an aggressive program of acquisitions of television stations, newspapers, and other media properties, Belo's annual revenues increased from $628 million in 1994 to $1.4 billion in 1998. Net earnings rose from $68.9 million in 1994 to $83.0 million in 1997, then dropped to $65 million in 1998 due to higher depreciation and amortization charges as well as severance payments associated with a voluntary early retirement program at the *Dallas Morning News*. Corporate profits in 1998 were also affected by a slowdown in advertising demand in both newspapers and television. During the same five-year period the company's cash dividends increased from $.15 to $.24 a share.

At first Belo acquired television stations, one in 1994 and another in 1995. In June 1994 it acquired the employee-owned New Orleans CBS affiliate WWL-TV for $110 million. The station was previously owned by Loyola University of New Orleans. In February 1995 Belo acquired television station KIRO in Seattle, Washington, for $162.5 million from Bonneville International.

In December 1995 and January 1996 Belo acquired two small newspapers, the 20,000-circulation daily the *Eagle* of Bryan-College Station, Texas, and the *Messenger-Inquirer* of Owensboro, Kentucky, with a daily circulation of 34,000. They were the first in a series of newspaper acquisitions over the next couple of years. Belo acquired its second daily newspaper in Kentucky, the *Gleaner* of Henderson, Kentucky, along with seven weeklies from the Gleaner and Journal Publishing Company, for an undisclosed amount in March 1997.

In April 1996 Belo launched the *Arlington Morning News,* a subsidiary of the *Dallas Morning News,* to compete with the Arlington edition of the Fort Worth *Star-Telegram.* Arlington was one of the fastest-growing urban areas in the state and had desirable income and education demographics for advertisers.

Belo's $1.5 billion acquisition of The Providence Journal Company was completed in February 1997. The deal included nine television stations along with Rhode Island's largest daily newspaper, the *Providence Journal.* In approving the transaction, the FCC noted that while the proposed acquisition was inconsistent with current policy, it would "promote commerce, encourage investment in the broadcast industry, and allow for the free transferability of broadcast licenses." The FCC granted a temporary waiver of its duopoly rules in Seattle, which prohibited ownership of two television stations in one market, and noted that Belo had already agreed to sell one of its two overlapping television stations there. Four Journal Company directors were named to Belo's board of directors following the acquisition. The cash-and-stock deal was financed through a credit and loan arrangement administered by Chase Manhattan Corporation.

However, Belo's plans to swap its Seattle television station KIRO with Fox Television Stations did not materialize. Instead, Belo exchanged KIRO for CBS-affiliate television station

KMOV in St. Louis, Missouri, with Paramount Stations Group in June 1997. Following the transaction Belo owned 15 television stations reaching 12.3 percent of U.S. television households, making it the tenth-largest television operator in terms of viewership and eighth in terms of revenues.

Belo acquired its third major daily newspaper in July 1997, when it assumed majority control of the *Press-Enterprise* of Riverside, California, located in one of the nation's fastest growing counties, for an undisclosed amount. Belo had acquired a 38.5 percent interest in the company in 1996 from Dow Jones & Co. and other minority shareholders. The *Press-Enterprise*, which had been family-owned for 67 years, became Belo's third largest newspaper holding.

In October 1997 Belo acquired KENS television and radio stations in San Antonio from The E.W. Scripps Co. in exchange for $75 million in cash and a 56 percent interest in The Food Network, which had begun broadcasting in 1993. The acquisition made Belo the largest non-network station group affiliated with CBS.

With Belo's string of acquisitions in 1997, net operating revenues jumped to $1.25 billion, almost a 50 percent increase over 1996. However, while the *Dallas Morning News* experienced record advertising growth in 1997, the company nonetheless had higher operating costs and reported net income of $83 million, down from $87.5 million in 1996. The following year was also financially disappointing for the company. Its stock price was down significantly, and net income dropped to $64.9 million on record revenues of $1.4 billion. Belo vowed to take a cautious approach to operations in 1999 in order to improve its financial performance.

Belo's new cable news channel, Texas Cable News (TXCN), began airing on January 1, 1999. The station broadcast from a warehouse located near Belo's headquarters in downtown Dallas. The service debuted in 600,000 TCI and Marcus cable households in Dallas-Fort Worth. Officials said TXCN would be available in several other Texas cities within a year.

Following improved earnings for the first two quarters of 1999, Belo undertook several acquisitions mid-year. In June 1999 it acquired KVUE-TV, an ABC affiliate and the top-rated station in Austin, Texas, from Gannett Co., Inc. in exchange for KXTV, an ABC affiliate serving the cities of Sacramento, Stockton, and Modesto, California, and for cash of up to $55 million. Belo realized a one-time gain of $50 million on the exchange and now owned four Texas television stations in Dallas, Houston, San Antonio, and Austin, reaching 67 percent of the state's television households.

In July 1999 Belo agreed to acquire KTVK, an independent television station in Phoenix, Arizona, from MAC America Communications, Inc. for $315 million in cash. The station had been family-owned since its inception. The agreement also included the rights to operate KASW-TV, the Phoenix WB affiliate, under a local marketing agreement, and a 50 percent interest in the Arizona News Channel, a cable news joint venture with Cox Cable.

Also in July Belo sold KASA-TV, a Fox affiliate located in Albuquerque, New Mexico, and KHNL-TV, an NBC affiliate in Honolulu, Hawaii, along with the rights to operate KFVE-TV, a UPN affiliate also in Honolulu, to Raycom Media, Inc. for $88 million. Raycom was headed by former Belo executive John Hayes. Following the completion of those transactions, Belo's Television Group would reach 14 percent of all U.S. television households.

In the newspaper field, Belo completed the acquisition of the Denton (Texas) Publishing Company, publisher of the *Denton Record-Chronicle* and two free-distribution newspapers, for an undisclosed amount in July 1999. Prior to the acquisition the newspaper had enjoyed 54 years of family ownership. The acquisition strengthened Belo's media holdings in North Texas, where it was competing with the *Star-Telegram* for readers and advertisers.

Belo also announced in July 1999 that it would pay $24 million in cash for a 12.4 interest in the Dallas Mavericks basketball team and a six percent interest in a new sports arena. The minority interest was not expected to affect Belo's finances. Rather, it was a commitment to participate in the local community and to be a long-term strategic partner for the team.

Outlook

Belo continued to be concerned about weak demand in national television advertising, which comprised about half of most television stations' ad revenue. National ad sales were soft due to competition from cable television and a glut of available network advertising time.

Under Robert Decherd's leadership, which was likely to continue for a couple of decades, Belo appeared set to continue its aggressive program of acquisitions. In television it was seeking to increase its coverage of the national market to 20 percent or more. In both television broadcasting and newspaper publishing, Belo was known for strengthening and sharpening local news coverage, while successfully attracting more advertising revenue. Dechard also planned to use state-of-the-art technology to equip Belo's television stations to transmit high-definition television, something the Federal Communications Commission had mandated for all television stations by the year 2006. The great grandson of G.B. Dealey, who published the *Dallas Morning News* on behalf of A.H. Belo and bought the company in 1926, Decherd would thus guide Belo into the new millennium.

Principal Subsidiaries

Newspapers: *Dallas Morning News; Providence Journal; Press-Enterprise; Messenger-Inquirer; Eagle; Gleaner; Denton Record-Chronicle; Lewisville News; Grapevine Sun; Hemet News; Moreno Valley Times.* Television Stations: WFAA; KHOU; KING; KMOV; KGW; WCNC; KENS; WVEC; WWL; WHAS; KOTV; KREM; KMSB; KTVB; KTVK; KVUE; KMSB. Other: Northwest Cable News; Texas Cable News Network (TXCN).

Principal Divisions

Broadcast Division; Newspaper Publishing Division.

Further Reading

"A. H. Belo Completes Purchase of Rhode Island's Providence Journal Co.," *Knight-Ridder/Tribune News,* March 1, 1997.

"A. H. Belo Corp.," *Mediaweek,* February 6, 1995, p. 5.

A.H. Belo Corporation, Commemorating One Hundred and Fifty Years 1842–1992, Dallas: A.H. Belo Corporation, 1992.

"A. H. Belo: Ready to Continue Its Expansion," *Editor & Publisher,* August 17, 1985, p. 13.

"A. H. Belo's Fortune Tied to Texas Economy; Rated Good Longterm Buy," *Television/Radio Age,* July 11, 1988, p. 87.

Alm, Richard, "Media Firm Belo Corp. to Buy Minority Stake in Dallas Basketball Team," *Knight-Ridder/Tribune News,* July 26, 1999.

Alm, Richard, and John Kirkpatrick, "Media Company Belo Corp.'s Stake in Dallas Team Stirs Debate," *Knight-Ridder/Tribune News,* August 12, 1999.

Backover, Andrew, "Dallas-Based Media Firm Buys Denton, Texas-Based Newspaper Publisher," *Knight-Ridder/Tribune News,* June 17, 1999.

"Belo Acquires KTVK and Related Assets," company news release, July 2, 1999.

"Belo Acquires KVUE-TV in Austin, Texas," June 1, 1999, Dallas: A.H. Belo Corporation.

"Belo Acquires Providence Journal Co.," *Editor & Publisher,* October 5, 1996, p. 13.

"Belo Closes on Acquisition of Denton Publishing Company," company news release, July 2, 1999.

"Belo Mulling Sale of Three TV Stations," *Mediaweek,* May 24, 1999, p. 3.

"Belo's $600 Million Deal Highlights 1983 Broadcast Sales," *Editor & Publisher,* January 7, 1984, p. 46.

Beschloss, Steven, "Leaders of the Pack," *Channels,* August 13, 1990, pp. 26–30.

Brodesser, Claude, "Belo Spends Big to Build a Contender in News," *Mediaweek,* October 13, 1997, p. 18.

Brodesser, Claude, and Michael Burgi, "Belo Bellows in Texas Deal," *Mediaweek,* September 8, 1997, p. 6.

"Chairman Says Dallas-Based Belo Is on Track for Financial Goals," *Knight-Ridder/Tribune News,* May 13, 1999.

Consoli, John, "Stockholders OK Providence Sale," *Editor & Publisher,* February 22, 1997, p. 8.

"Dallas-Based A.H. Belo Corp. Acquires CBS Affiliate KMOV-TV in St. Louis," *Knight-Ridder/Tribune News,* June 4, 1997.

"Dallas-Based A.H. Belo to Swap Television Stations," *Knight-Ridder/Tribune News,* February 22, 1997.

"Dallas-Based Belo Corp. Reports Net Income Slide in Fourth Quarter," *Knight-Ridder/Tribune News,* January 28, 1999.

"*Dallas Times-Herald* Folds," *Editor & Publisher,* December 14, 1991, p. 12.

Deener, Bill, "Belo Corp. to Get Austin, Texas, TV Station in Swap with Gannett Co.," *Knight-Ridder/Tribune News,* February 26, 1999.

Downing, Neil, "Providence Journal Co. Shareholders Approve Sale to A.H. Belo Corp.," *Knight-Ridder/Tribune News,* February 20, 1997.

Drummer, Randyl, "Dallas Chain Buys Inland, Calif., Area's Largest Daily Newspaper," *Knight-Ridder/Tribune News,* June 30, 1997.

Dworkin, Andy, "Profits at Dallas-Based Media Company Belo Corp. Outpace Estimates," *Knight-Ridder/Tribune News,* July 29, 1999.

"E. W. Scripps Buys Media Outlets from Harte-Hanks, Trades One to Belo," *Knight-Ridder/Tribune News,* October 16, 1997.

"The FCC Says That the $1.5 Billion Merger of Providence Journal Co. into A.H. Belo Corp. Is So Much in the Public Interest That It Warrants Approval," *Broadcasting & Cable,* March 3, 1997, p. 76.

Hackney, Holt, "A. H. Belo: Turning the Page," *Financial World,* November 9, 1993, p. 20.

Hensell, Lesley, "Belo Brass Dumps Stock Before Drop," *Dallas Business Journal,* October 18, 1996, p. 1.

——, "SEC Said to Be Looking at Belo Officers' Stock Trades," *Dallas Business Journal,* March 7, 1997, p. 3.

Holley, Joe, "Belo the Belt: The Arlington Newspaper War Gets Personal," *Texas Monthly,* July 1996, p. 20.

Kantrow, Yvette D., and Daniel Dunaieff, "Chase Launches 2 Major Loan Syndication Deals," *American Banker,* January 10, 1997, p. 18.

Kirkpatrick, John, and Katherine Yung, "Dallas-Based Publisher Buys Denton, Texas, Newspaper," *Knight-Ridder/Tribune News,* June 18, 1999.

Lenzer, Robert, and Carrie Shook, "Texas Darwinist," *Forbes,* January 26, 1998, p. 42.

Littleton, Cynthia, and Elizabeth A. Rathbun, "Fox Trading for KIRO-TV; Network Will Swap Phoenix, Austin Stations for Seattle," *Broadcasting & Cable,* February 3, 1997, p. 8.

Mendoza, Manuel, "Dallas-Based A.H. Belo Begins Regional Cable News Service," *Knight-Ridder/Tribune News,* December 27, 1998.

Miles, Laureen, "A. H. Belo Corp.," *Mediaweek,* June 6, 1994, p.6.

Moses, Lucia, "E&P's Second Quarter Earnings Scoreboard," *Editor & Publisher,* July 12, 1999.

Moses, Lucia, "Profits Strong Despite Ad Slowdown," *Editor & Publisher,* February 6, 1999, p. 20.

"Newspaper Financial Reports," *Editor & Publisher,* February 19, 1994, p. 14.

Rosenberg, Jim, "Dallas Puts $41 Million into Expansion," *Editor & Publisher,* May 23, 1992, p. 25.

Sacharow, Anya, "A. H. Belo Corp.," *Mediaweek,* January 1, 1996, p. 12.

"Sales, Acquisitions Continue Apace at Station Groups," *Television/Radio Age,* June 8, 1987, pp. 43–44.

Thorpe, Helen, "News Makers," *Texas Monthly,* January 1999, p. 44.

"TV Station Owner A.H. Belo Corp. Has Found a Buyer for NBC Affiliate KHNL Honolulu and KASA, a Fox Affiliate in Albuquerque, N.M.: Raycom Media Inc.," *Broadcasting & Cable,* July 5, 1999, p. 44.

—Heidi Feldman
—updated by David P. Bianco

Aiwa Co., Ltd.

1-2-11 Ikenohata
Taito-ku
Tokyo 110-8710
Japan
(3) 3827-3111
Fax: (3) 3827-2888
Web site: http://www.aiwa.co.jp

Public Subsidiary of Sony Corporation
Incorporated: 1951 as AIKO Denki Sangyo Co., Ltd.
Employees: 10,685
Sales: ¥349.61 billion (US$2.90 billion) (1999)
Stock Exchanges: Tokyo
NAIC: 33431 Audio & Video Equipment Manufacturing;
    334119 Other Computer Peripheral Equipment
    Manufacturing; 335228 Other Major Household
    Appliance Manufacturing

Aiwa Co., Ltd. is a leading manufacturer of audio products, including headphone stereos, minicomponent stereo systems, portable stereo systems, minidisc players, CD and cassette players, and car stereo systems. Nearly 86 percent of company revenues are derived from such audio products. The company also makes and sells visual products, such as VCRs, color televisions, DVD players, and digital satellite television tuners; this sector accounts for about 12 percent of sales. In the "other" category responsible for the remainder of sales, Aiwa is involved in the production of computer peripherals devices, such as modems, terminal adapters, and speakers, and of what the company terms "life amenity products," such as air cleaners and humidifiers. Aiwa manufactures more than 89 percent of its output outside of Japan, with a heavy emphasis on the lower-cost southeast Asian nations of Singapore, Malaysia, and Indonesia. The company is also heavily dependent on overseas sales, with more than 80 percent of total revenues being generated outside Japan, with 43 percent in North and South America, 25 percent in Europe, and 13 percent in areas of Asia outside Japan and in other regions. Although officially an affiliated company of consumer electronics giant Sony Corporation, which owns 50.6 percent of the company, Aiwa prides itself on its independent operation and competes head on with Sony in several product categories.

Early History

Aiwa has somewhat obscure beginnings. The company was founded in June 1951 as AIKO Denki Sangyo Co., Ltd., a maker of microphones. In June 1958 the company's stock was registered for over-the-counter trade. It changed its name to Aiwa Co., Ltd. in October 1959. The following year saw the opening of a factory in Utsunomiya, a town located about 60 miles north of Tokyo. Its stock was listed in the second section of the Tokyo Stock Exchange in October 1961.

A key development came in February 1964 when Aiwa introduced the first Japanese cassette tape recorder, the TP-707. Cassette recorders, players, and decks became the company's core product area, and remained so through the late 1970s. In February 1967 Aiwa established another factory in Iwate. Two years later Sony Corporation purchased a majority interest in Aiwa, which became an affiliated company of Sony. Aiwa nevertheless continued to operate in a largely independent fashion, and its stock remained publicly traded.

During the 1970s Aiwa made an aggressive push into overseas markets. In late 1970 the company formed a joint venture company in Hong Kong called Aiwa/Dransfield & Co., Ltd. The Middle East was identified as a key arena for export growth, and Aiwa in 1973 established a joint venture in Lebanon called Aiwa Sales & Service Co. The company's timing was propitious, as the oil crisis that soon began made the Mideast a more attractive market because of the onset of recession in Europe and North America. By mid-decade Aiwa claimed an approximate 30 percent share of the Middle East tape recorder market. Aiwa also made an early move into overseas production, with the establishment of a factory in Singapore in late 1974. The following year Aiwa opened the Utsunomiya North Factory (the other Utsunomiya factory became known as the South Factory) and its stock was listed on the first section of the Tokyo exchange.

Later in the 1970s the Middle East became a less attractive market as both competition and political instability increased. Aiwa moved quickly to lessen its dependence on the troubled

Company Perspectives:

Known and trusted by customers worldwide, the Aiwa brand is a powerful, competitive marketing tool. This is crucial given that Aiwa's products compete in the standard price range, where most products are sold. Brand image builds trust in a product and clarifies the value it contains. The company has succeeded in popularizing the Aiwa identity, one that has become synonymous with value, through a clearly defined low-cost operations strategy. Aiwa's reputation for price and quality as well as design has helped the company to capture high market shares around the world.

region, targeting Europe and North America for expansion. From 1976 through 1978, the firm established sales subsidiaries in the United Kingdom, Germany, and the United States. By the end of the decade, sales in Europe and North America accounted for 65 percent of all exports, a substantial increase over the approximate 50 percent levels earlier in the decade. In the late 1970s Aiwa also expanded its product line into the area of minicomponent stereo systems, an increasingly popular segment of the audio market; Aiwa's mini systems provided high quality sound and power and such sophisticated features as digital displays in a space-saving small package that included a radio tuner, cassette deck, turntable, amplifier, and speakers. By this time the company was also selling high-priced amplifiers, tuners, and other full-size rack-type audio components. For the fiscal year ending in November 1979, Aiwa posted net profits of ¥244 million (US$1 million) on sales of ¥38.5 billion (US$157.8 million).

In mid-1980 Aiwa ventured into another hot product category, that of headphone stereos (made popular by Aiwa's parent and its Sony Walkman), with the launch of the TP-S30, which featured stereo recording and playback functions. With its increased marketing to the industrialized countries of Europe and North America, Aiwa moved some of its production closer to that important area by opening a manufacturing plant in South Wales in September 1980.

Late 1980s Recovery from Near Bankruptcy

In 1981 Aiwa entered the video area for the first time, when it began production of videocassette recorders in Japan. Unfortunately, following the lead of its parent, Aiwa adopted the Sony Betamax format. Although introduced a year earlier, the Betamax lost out to the VHS format in a battle to determine which would be the industry standard. Compounding Aiwa's difficulties were intense domestic competition and an extremely strong yen, the latter of which made products produced in Japan more expensive in export markets. For the year ending in November 1986, Aiwa was in the red for the first time in eight years, posting a pretax loss of ¥5.17 billion on sales of ¥57.4 billion, forcing it to forego its dividend for the first time in 14 years. Aiwa was teetering on the verge of bankruptcy. Even its pioneering introduction of the first digital audio tape (DAT) system in March 1987 held little promise. Although DAT was initially seen as a threat to the booming CD industry because users could record—not just play—on DAT systems, the technology never really caught on.

Helping to pull Aiwa out of this tailspin was Hajimi Unoki, who was brought in from Sony to become the company's new deputy president. Unoki helped initiate a number of restructuring efforts. Hoping to achieve ¥2.5 billion in annual savings, Aiwa slashed its workforce through voluntary retirements from a high of 3,100 in 1985 to 1,300 by 1988. The company also consolidated its head office facilities, which had been spread among four different locales in Tokyo. In addition, it integrated three of its domestic manufacturing plants, with the Utsunomiya South plant converted to a technology center in early 1989.

Most critically, however, Aiwa aggressively shifted more of its production overseas, to counteract the effects of the strong yen. Production at its plants in Wales and Singapore was increased, with the manufacture of compact disc (CD) players added to the line of products coming out of the Wales facility. An expansion of the Wales facility was completed in March 1989. In Singapore, Aiwa added two more factories in Jurong, with Jurong West opening in February 1987 and Jurong East in September 1988. Through these and other moves, Aiwa increased its overseas production to encompass 50 percent of overall production. By the early 1990s, following the establishment of a new manufacturing base in Johor Bahru, Malaysia, this ratio at times reached as high as 80 percent, by far the highest such figure in the Japanese audiovisual industry. Aiwa returned to profitability and resumed payment of dividends in the early 1990s thanks largely to its shift to lower-cost, lower-wage overseas production—a shift that others in the industry soon imitated. Much of the credit for the turnaround was given to the aggressive Unoki, who was named president in 1989.

1990s and Beyond

By the early 1990s, Aiwa had also expanded its line of products. In mid-1993 Aiwa gained control of Core International Inc., a U.S. maker of computer peripherals. The company also found success—and increased its presence in video equipment—with a line of TV-VCR combination units. The pioneer in this area had been Matsushita Electric Industrial Co., which introduced the first such product in 1983. Aiwa was able to capture a large portion of this market by following with a full line of TV-VCR models, each of which included special features, such as a satellite tuner and a bilingual receiver. According to Shunichi Otaki, writing in the April 1994 issue of *Tokyo Business Today,* this follow-on strategy was a key to Aiwa's prosperity: ''The secret of Aiwa's success lies less in creating new technology than in refining existing technology and delivering new products in a price range that will satisfy today's discount-hungry consumers. This contrasts sharply with the approach of other makers such as Sony, which have always pursued the high end of the market, shunning discounts and straining to create a prestigious brand name.''

While many of its competitors struggled in the early to mid-1990s from the effects of the prolonged Japanese economic downturn, Aiwa remained profitable through the end of the decade. The company continued to shift its manufacturing base outside of Japan, with its overseas production ratio nearing 90 percent by the end of the decade. The increased capacity came from expansions of the Malaysian factory in 1994 and of the South Wales facility in 1995, and from the establishment of two manufacturing subsidiaries in Indonesia—P.T. Aiwa Indonesia in 1996 and P.T. Aiwa Dharmala in 1997. By the late 1990s the company employed more Malaysians than Japanese. Taking this fact a step further, Unoki, in an interview with Claire Leow published in the May 16, 1994, issue of *Business Times,* summarized the dramatic changes he had helped engender at Aiwa during his tenure: "I don't think Aiwa is a Japanese company anymore. In total production, 90 percent will soon be from overseas subsidiaries. In sales, 70 per cent to 85 percent come from overseas. In total employment, 75 percent are non-Japanese." Unoki went on to say that "a company doesn't need to belong to any country. It has to make money. Shareholders put money [in] and look for returns on investment." Aiwa shareholders were in fact rewarded well for their investment, as return on shareholders' equity from 1994 through 1998 was never lower than 11.7 percent and was as high as 20.9 percent.

As Aiwa approached the new millennium, its most successful product area to date had been its minicomponent stereo systems. In the 1990s these systems typically featured an amplifier, tuner, CD player, and dual cassette deck. Aiwa was the clear global market leader in this category, with a 30 percent share. In the United States, Aiwa had captured about half of the market by the late 1990s. While the company continued to find success in its core audio sector, that sector alone in the long run would be unable to keep Aiwa growing. New products were clearly needed. In the Japanese market, Aiwa found success in the late 1990s with a variety of products, including modems and terminal adapters; small, 14-inch to 21-inch "personal-use" color TVs; digital tuners used to receive satellite television broadcasts; and minidisc (MD) players. As was typical of Aiwa products, the TVs, though in the lower price ranges, offered a number of convenient features, such as front panel AV input jacks and onscreen displays. Also typical was Aiwa's approach to the MD, a recordable disc smaller in size than a CD. Introduced in 1992, the MD reached critical mass in Japan only in 1995, at which point Aiwa vigorously entered the category, introducing a line of portable MD players as well as incorporating MD players into minicomponent systems and portable radio cassette decks.

Overseas, Aiwa began a push into the car audio market in 1997 with the introduction in North America of a line of car stereos, speaker systems, and CD changers. Sales were soon expanded to Europe and South America. The car audio products were initially produced on a contractual basis, but in February 1999 Aiwa began direct manufacturing of the products at a company-owned factory in Indonesia. Later in 1999 Aiwa's U.S. subsidiary introduced a line of DVD players, DVD being the latest video technology attempting to supplant the ubiquitous VCR, or at least find a successful place alongside it. By this time the company had also entered the market for what it called "life amenity products," such as air cleaners and humidifiers. Among the products in the prototype stage at the end of the millennium were a personal digital assistant, a portable stereo with a built-in DVD player and video screen, and a small, Internet-centered computer. While still focused on audio, Aiwa appeared to be positioning itself for the long-expected convergence of the consumer electronics and personal computer sectors, which would perhaps take place in the early 21st century.

Principal Subsidiaries

Aiwa Iwate Co., Ltd.; Aiwa Hanaizumi Co., Ltd.; Aiwa Akita Co., Ltd.; Paulownia Co., Ltd.; Aiwa Trading Co., Ltd.; Aiwa Wales Manufacturing Ltd. (U.K.); Aiwa Electronics Malaysia Sdn. Bhd.; P.T. Aiwa Indonesia; P.T. Aiwa Dharmala (Indonesia); Aiwa Singapore Ltd.; Aiwa America, Inc. (U.S.A.); Aiwa (UK) Ltd.; Aiwa France S.A.; Aiwa Deutschland GmbH (Germany); Aiwa International Ltd. (Hong Kong); Aiwa Taiwan Electronics Co., Ltd.; Aiwa Gulf FZE (United Arab Emirites); Aiwa Latinoamerica (Panama) S.A.; Aiwa Nederland B.V. (Netherlands); Aiwa do Brasil Ltda. (Brazil); Aiwa Hong Kong Ltd.; Aiwa Research & Development, Inc. (U.S.A.); Aiwa Digital Technology, Inc. (U.S.A.); Aiwa International (Thailand) Co., Ltd.

Further Reading

"Aiwa Brags Top Spot in Export of Tape Recorders to Mideast," *Japan Economic Journal,* April 22, 1975, p. 7.
"Aiwa Diversifies Mini Lineup with Five New Kinds of Systems," *Japan Economic Journal,* August 12, 1980, p. 34.
"Aiwa Forms Sales Firm in U.S.," *Japan Economic Journal,* May 30, 1978, p. 8.
"Aiwa Will Step Up Exports," *Japan Economic Journal,* March 20, 1979, p. 8.
"Aiwa Works Out Self-Rehabilitation Program," *Japan Economic Journal,* August 2, 1986, p. 22.
Cody, Jennifer, "Aiwa U.S. Unit Expects 40% Rise in Fiscal '94 Sales," *Wall Street Journal,* September 20, 1993, p. A9A.
Dawkins, William, and John Burton, "Aiwa Defends Its Niche in Mini-Audio Price War," *Financial Times,* February 13, 1996, p. 31.
"Giant Rivals Mimic Aiwa's Offshore Success," *Nikkei Weekly,* May 23, 1994, p. 8.
Hanson, Richard C., "Export-Led Recovery for Aiwa," *Financial Times,* January 22, 1980, p. 21.
Leow, Claire, "From Sound of Music to Power of PCs," *Business Times* (Singapore), May 16, 1994, p. 14.
Lo, Joseph, "Aiwa to Push on Despite Tumble," *South China Morning Post,* April 20, 1999, p. 2.
Mitsusada, Hisayuki, "Aiwa Passes Up Glamour for Profits," *Nikkei Weekly,* July 31, 1995, p. 8.
Moffett, Sebastian, "The Road Less Travelled: Don't Look Now, but Some Japan Firms Are Going Home," *Far Eastern Economic Review,* August 29, 1996, p. 63.
——, "Sounds Good: Japan's Aiwa Thrives Even As Its Main Market Shrinks," *Far Eastern Economic Review,* March 28, 1996, p. 53.
Otaki, Shunichi, "Aiwa: A Second-Ranked Player Makes It to the Big Time," *Tokyo Business Today,* April 1994, p. 34.
"Overseas Sales Pay Off for Aiwa," *Nikkei Weekly,* May 12, 1997, p. 8.
Pollack, Andrew, "Aiwa Plans a Production Shift to Japan," *New York Times,* August 6, 1996, p. D3.
——, "Aiwa Weathers Recession with a Tight Focus and Some Luck," *New York Times,* January 11, 1994, p. D6.
Rajendran, Joseph, "Aiwa Forecasts Better Results Despite Depressed Demand," *Business Times* (Singapore), April 8, 1993, p. 2.
Rapoport, Carla, "Aiwa to Boost Overseas Output," *Financial Times,* June 11, 1986, p. 5.
Sahr, Johnny, "Aiwa Chief Looks to 'Beautiful' Future," *South China Morning Post,* May 4, 1999, p. 4.
Thomas, David, "Aiwa Sets Date for Digital Tape Launch," *Financial Times,* February 13, 1987, p. 36.
Velloor, Ravi, and Lim Lay Phing, "Aiwa Aims to Be Tops in Audio-Visuals," *Straits Times* (Singapore), April 27, 1998, p. 42.
Weinberg, Neil, "Good News, Bad News Man," *Forbes,* January 1, 1996, pp. 58+.

—David E. Salamie

Alba-Waldensian, Inc.

---

201 St. Germain Ave. SW
P.O. Box 100
Valdese, North Carolina 28690
U.S.A.
(828) 879-6500
(800) 554-2522
Fax: (828) 879-6595
Web site: http://www.alba1.com

Public Company
Incorporated: 1961
Employees: 750
Sales: $75.24 million (1998)
Stock Exchanges: American
Ticker Symbol: AWS
NAIC: 315111 Sheer Hosiery Mills; 315192 Underwear
& Nightwear Knitting Mills; 339113 Surgical
Appliance & Supplies Manufacturing; 42232 Men's &
Boy's Clothing & Furnishings Wholesalers

Located in Valdese, North Carolina, Alba-Waldensian, Inc. is a highly successful, publicly traded company specializing in the production and sale of seamless knitwear made specifically for medical supplies, such as gauze strips and high-tech, no-slip bandages, as well as women's undergarments and hosiery. With annual sales in 1998 reaching over $75 million, and large production plants in both North Carolina and Tennessee, Alba-Waldensian has made a name for itself in the retail and apparel industry through its ability to profitably corner two separate niche markets due to the company's unique factory knitting-production technique. Because of the differing marketing and production needs of the medical supply industry and that of the womenswear market, the company operates two separate divisions: the Consumer Products Division and the Health Products Division, with the former focusing on womenswear, and the latter, on specialty medical supplies. In addition, the company has a third division, Alba Direct, which distributes and markets Alba-Waldensian's womenswear to retail stores both nationally and internationally.

Early History: Humble Beginnings to Rapid Growth

The company that is today Alba-Waldensian was first created in 1901 by Italian immigrants who had settled deep in the Blue Ridge Mountains of North Carolina. Operating initially in a space hardly large enough to house more than a few machines, the company which eventually became known as Waldensian Hosiery Mills produced knitted women's undergarments and hosiery. By the 1950s Waldensian Hosiery Mills had developed a process by which the company could mass-produce women's stretch panties and bras on special factory knitting machines, which used a circular weave to create the material's desired—and at that time unique—flexibility. While successful, Waldensian Hosiery Mills was for its first few decades a decidedly regional business, with limited reach to a customer base.

Meanwhile, the development of a similar company offered Waldensian Hosiery Mills more than a bit of competition: incorporated as Pilot Fashion Mills in June 1928, this company also produced women's undergarments, and sold their products at prices matching those of Waldensian Hosiery. Pilot Fashion Mills changed its name in 1955 to Alba Hosiery Mills, and continued operating under that name until, at the end of 1961, Waldensian Hosiery Mills and Alba Hosiery Mills merged, forming Alba-Waldensian, Inc. After the merging of the two companies, Alba-Waldensian's focus remained on the production of the stretch knitted material developed by Waldensian Hosiery Mills, and it was this focus which allowed the new company to make its mark. With steady growth throughout the 1960s, Alba-Waldensian went public in 1969, listing its stock on the American Stock Exchange.

For Alba-Waldensian's first five years as a publicly traded company, the business continued to produce womenswear, and focused exclusively on its growth within that industry. In the mid-1970s, however, the company saw an opportunity to put its stretch-knitting technique to use in an entirely separate area: the field of medical supplies. In 1974 Alba-Waldensian introduced its first medical specialty products, and therefore penetrated a new and potentially highly lucrative niche market. The low-tech products initially offered by the company, such as flexible bandages and sterile wound dressings, could be used by a variety of consumers in the medical field, from hospitals and nursing homes to local doctor's offices, with the result being an increased visibility for the company.

Starting in the late 1970s Alba-Waldensian began a series of buyouts and acquisitions which greatly increased its growth in both its divisions. In 1976 the company obtained part of Shelby Seamless Hosiery Mills and, that same year, acquired 50 percent of a company called Alba-Eiser, Inc. The next year Alba-Waldensian acquired the remaining percentage of Alba-Eiser, which was then merged into Alba-Waldensian by 1979. Beginning in 1978 Alba-Waldensian acquired all or part of several businesses for cash: that year, the company bought Commercial Flocking Corporation and 50 percent of Selective Electronic, Inc.; and, in 1983 and 1984, the company acquired W.G. Whitney Corporation and Electric Sok Corporation.

Although the 1980s were far from stable for Alba-Waldensian, with annual sales varying widely from year to year, the company through both its acquisitions and its new focus on the production of medical supplies continued to expand. The company's Consumer Products Division was by now producing a large variety of womenswear under such labels as Some-Body, All Day Long, While You Wait, and Big Beautiful Woman. Placing an emphasis on comfort and affordability, Alba-Waldensian's womenswear labels were by the 1980s carried by such national department stores as J.C. Penney and Sears. Particular attention was paid by the company to the needs of plus-sized women, with the company's hosiery lines specifically marketed to this customer base; one which had traditionally been ignored within the retail industry. The company also began manufacturing hosiery and briefs for the small but growing maternity market, thus further expanding its targeted consumer base.

Alba-Waldensian's willingness to branch out in the 1970's and '80's into previously under-developed fields is what made the company stand out in the apparel industry. The company proved itself as one ready to take a risk in order to fill, or even help create, a niche market. It was unusual to say the least to find a company involved in the production, marketing and manufacturing of women's intimate apparel suddenly making a foray into the very different business of gauze strip and bandage manufacturing; but it was just such a move which caused Alba-Waldensian to become a major player in the retail industry. What tied the company's two quite disparate divisions together was its highly specialized factory-knitting formula: Alba-Waldensian created profits by focusing not on the variety of materials the company could successfully utilize but instead on the amount of products a single manufacturing technique could produce. This way, it mattered not at all if what was being created fit together in any orthodox sense, at least in terms of marketing; what was important was that an abundance of products, in a variety of fields, could be created from one, uniquely developed production technology. Alba-Waldensian had, then, by the end of the 1980's become better known for its material than its designs or styles, though it continued through its womenswear marketing to emphasize comfort and wearability.

Further Expansion: 1990s

In 1992 Alba-Waldensian's Consumer Products Division experienced a great boon through the acquisition of the U.S. operations of Byford Apparel. Byford was a British-based company, begun in 1919 in Leicester, England, which designed and marketed clothing to upscale retail stores. By purchasing Byford, Alba-Waldensian had the opportunity to turn its attentions for the first time to outerwear for both men and women. By the mid-1990s, the company was producing men's socks and sweaters under the Byford label, gaining yet a broader consumer base.

From its inception Alba-Waldensian had always sold its products through distribution to department and specialty stores. In 1994, in order to gain more label recognition for its many apparel brands, the company opened its first outlet store, in the Factory Merchants Outlet mall in Branson, Missouri. While such a progression from distribution to handling its own store was a natural one, the company continued to concentrate its primary efforts on wholesale marketing to other retailers.

Impressive as Alba-Waldensian's growth was in relation to its apparel lines, the company's real growth came in the 1990s from its Health Products Division. In 1994 the company acquired the Pulsatile Anti-Embolism System, which refocused the company's healthcare division by manufacturing products especially geared towards vascular care. A year later, Alba-Waldensian bought Balfour Health Products, which in effect doubled the size of the company's healthcare division. With these two acquisitions Alba-Waldensian now produced a large variety of medical supplies, including anti-embolism stockings (used to prevent blood clots); compression devices designed to improve circulation; sterile wound dressings such as petrolatum and xeroform gauze; and non-adhering gauze strips. Also manufactured by this growing division was net tubing which held dressings in place without adhesive and specialized treaded patient footwear, which prevented patients from slipping on slick hospital floors and could be worn as slippers or socks.

Because of Alba-Waldensian's increased concentration on its healthcare division, which grew exponentially in 1994 and 1995, the company decided to relocate its Health Products Division in a new, separate area. Though the company's headquarters remained in Valdese, its medical products were now designed and manufactured at a large new plant in Rockwood, Tennessee. Alba-Waldensian's North Carolina location was then free to devote itself exclusively to its Consumer Products Division, a separation which, while indicating the continuing expansion of the company, also created a large amount of overhead costs.

Due to a variety of factors, 1996 was a particularly difficult year for Alba-Waldensian. Between the expensive acquisition of Balfour Health Products, and the company's relocation of its healthcare division, the company's profitability fell drastically by year-end, its bottom line in the red by well over $1 million. While the acquisition of Balfour proved eventually to be a fiscally sound risk, the company for the moment was hurting: stockholders were nervous and revenue in both divisions was threatened.

In February 1997, Alba-Waldensian's president and CEO of over five years, Thomas F. Schuster, resigned, declining to elaborate to the press his reasons for doing so. Replacing him was Alba-Waldensian insider Lee Mortenson, who had been on the company's board of directors for over ten years. Mortenson began an aggressive campaign to bring his company back to an acceptable level of profitability, making the slump of 1996 short-lived.

Though 1996 was not a profitable year, the company did strike a couple of deals that year which paid off quite handsomely within a short period of time, helping Alba-Waldensian regain ground both in reputation and financial stability. One such boon was the granting of a patent for what the company called "Comfort Knit" stretch bras and panties which allowed for the creation of the same seamless, wireless shaping found in intimate apparel which utilized more inhibiting, body-constricting materials. Claiming that the "Comfort Knit" material gave shape and flattering contour to a woman's figure without any discomfort, the company soon found the patent to be of great use, and much coveted as well. Indeed, the patent was contested by apparel company I. Appel, a claim which backfired the next year when I. Appel had to pay Alba-Waldensian compensation.

In April 1996 Alba-Waldensian's Byford Apparel line signed a lucrative licensing deal with the Smithsonian Institute. According to the terms of the agreement, Byford created and manufactured men's sweaters and other outerwear under the label "Smithsonian Institution Collection by Byford." The deal came at a serendipitous time for the company, since that year was the Smithsonian's 150th anniversary, and the Institute was receiving—and coveting—much publicity.

Meanwhile, the company continued to develop original and innovative products in its healthcare division, and at the beginning of 1997 was given FDA approval for a compression device created to prevent DVT (deep vein thrombosis). Calling the product PulStar, the company marketed the new device to patients undergoing either prolonged hospital stays or major surgical procedures. Within two decades, Alba-Waldensian had evolved from producing low-tech medical supplies to designing and manufacturing products which were considered revolutionary in their field.

By 1998 Alba-Waldensian was back in the black, with double-digit revenue growth. Part of this growth was attributed not only to the company's medical supply designs, but also its new focus on women's outerwear, which was developed by an offshoot of the company's Consumer Products Division called Alba Design Group. The Alba Design Group signed a licensing deal with Moretz, Inc. under which the former company produced and manufactured women's bodysuits, bandeaus, dresses, and socks using the popular Diahann Carroll label. Because of a renewed consumer interest in intimate apparel in the late 1990s, and Alba-Waldensian's new foray into women's outerwear, the company's Consumer Products Division had sales in 1998 of over $42 million—a record year.

The success of Alba-Waldensian's womenswear was also due in part to the growing development of the company's third division, Alba Direct. Alba Direct's exclusive aim was to bring via telemarketing new clients to the company's Consumer Products Division, a goal which proved more than achievable, as by 1998 the division had obtained clients from as far away as Turkey and Japan.

Though Alba-Waldensian's healthcare division at the end of the decade remained smaller than its womenswear division, the former continued to expand. In 1999 the company's Health Products Division was granted an exclusive three-year contract with a company called Novation, which offered medical supplies to such clients as VHA Inc. and the University Health System Consortium. Within the terms of the contract, Alba-Waldensian became the single supplier for all of Novation's footwear products; a deal which Alba-Waldensian predicted would bring in over $12 million in profits.

Beginning in the mid-1970s Alba-Waldensian began a trajectory of continued growth and expansion which has caused the company to be a leader in two very different fields. Though its path has not been without financial flaws, the end of the 1990s has shown Alba-Waldensian to be a continually powerful presence in the niche industries of intimate apparel and medical supplies.

Principal Divisions

Consumer Products Division; Health Products Division; Alba Direct.

Further Reading

"Alba Announces Novation Contract," *PR Newswire,* January 20, 1999, p. 7335.

"Alba Announces Record Second Quarter Results Up 67%," *PR Newswire,* July 27, 1999, p. 0112.

"Alba Releases President's Comments at Annual Shareholders' Meeting," *PR Newswire,* May 13, 1999, p. 9371.

"Alba-Waldensian, Inc. Receives FDA Approval on a New DVT Prophylaxis Device," *PR Newswire,* January 3, 1997, p. 103.

"Alba-Waldensian, Inc. Receives Patent on Revolutionary New Seamless Stretch Bra," *PR Newswire,* April 3, 1996, p. 403.

"Byford Licenses Smithsonian Institution," *PR Newswire,* April 29, 1996, p. 429.

"Low Margins Push Alba-Waldensian $1 Million into Red During 4th Quarter," *Daily News Record,* March 5, 1996, p. 10.

—Rachel H. Martin

Albertson's Inc.

250 Parkcenter Boulevard
Boise, Idaho 83706
U.S.A.
(208) 395-6200
Fax: (208) 385-6631
Web site: http://www.albertsons.com

Public Company
Incorporated: 1945
Employees: 100,000
Sales: $16.01 billion (1999)
Stock Exchanges: New York Pacific
Ticker Symbol: ABS
NAIC: 44511 Supermarkets & Other Grocery Stores;
44611 Pharmacies & Drug Stores

Albertson's Inc. is the second largest grocery chain in the United States, trailing only the Kroger Company. Following the June 1999 $11.7 billion acquisition of American Stores Company, Albertson's operated more than 2,400 stores in 39 Western, Midwestern, Southern, and Eastern states. The units include combination food-and-drugstores as well as conventional supermarkets (under the Albertson's, Acme Markets, Jewel Food, and Lucky stores names); warehouse stores (Max Food and Drug); and stand-alone drugstores (Osco and Sav-on). Albertson's had small town beginnings but evolved by the late 1990s into a suburban-oriented operation; it also was a predominantly Western chain. The addition of American Stores further altered Albertson's geographic makeup, adding the first two urban markets—Chicago and Philadelphia—and giving it a presence on the East Coast and a nearly nationwide penetration. The company's history turns on the expansion of the one-stop shopping concept upon which it was founded, which led to the growth of larger stores carrying more diverse products and eventually to the jumbo food-and-drugstores that were the key to Albertson's tremendous success.

Early Years

In 1939 Joe Albertson left his position as a district manager for Safeway Stores and—with partners L.S. Skaggs, whose family helped build Safeway, and Tom Cuthbert, Skaggs's accountant—opened his first one-stop shopping market on a Boise, Idaho corner. Albertson thought big from the start—his first newspaper ad promised customers "Idaho's largest and finest food store." Indeed, the store was huge by contemporary standards; at 10,000 square feet it was approximately eight times as large as the average grocery store of that era. The store included specialties such as an in-store bakery, one of the country's first magazine racks, and homemade "Big Joe" ice cream cones. Customers liked what they saw, and the store pulled in healthy first-year profits of $9,000.

Albertson's grew slowly at first. Sales remained constant during the war years, and in 1945 Joe Albertson dissolved the partnership and Albertson's was incorporated. By 1947, the chain had six stores operating in Idaho and had established a complete poultry processing operation. In 1949 the Dutch Girl ice cream plant opened in Boise, and Albertson's adopted the Dutch Girl as its early trademark.

Albertson's expanded during the 1950s into Washington, Utah, Oregon, and Montana. In 1957 the company built its first frozen foods distribution house, which served its southern Idaho and eastern Oregon stores. Albertson's also operated a few department stores during the 1950s, but these were phased out rapidly as the company decided to focus on the sale of food and drugstore items. In 1959 Albertson's introduced its private label, Janet Lee, named after the executive vice-president's daughter. The company also went public in 1959 and with that capital began to expand its markets aggressively.

Albertson's moved into its sixth state, Wyoming, in 1961, and opened its 100th store in 1962. In 1964 the company broke into the California market by acquiring Greater All American Markets, based in Los Angeles. The same year, Albertson turned the position of chief executive over to J.L. Berlin, although Albertson continued to chair the executive board.

Under Berlin's leadership, the company strengthened its Californian position by merging with Semrau and Sons, an Oakland-based grocery store chain, in 1965. This added eight markets in northern California, which Albertson's continued to operate under the name of Pay Less. In 1967 the company purchased eight Colorado supermarkets from Fury's Inc., a

Lubbock, Texas concern. Between these purchases and construction of new units, Albertson's operated more than 200 stores by the end of the decade and annual sales were substantially more than $400 million.

In the late 1960s, Albertson's set several company policies that would secure its snowballing success. One of these was the company's ongoing renovation program. In 1980 Vice-Chairman Bolinder pointed out that "almost every failure of previously profitable supermarket companies can be attributed to stores becoming outdated." Albertson's avoided this pitfall by constantly upgrading its facilities, remodeling and enlarging older stores, and closing those that had become obsolete.

Anticipating the ever increasing competition for profitable operating sites, Albertson's also took care during the 1960s to build a sophisticated property development task force of lawyers, economic analysts, negotiators, engineers, architects, and construction supervisors that allowed the company to stay on top of industry trends. In addition, it expanded its employee training and incentive programs to encourage employees to make a lifetime career with the company.

Combination Format in the 1970s

During its first three decades Albertson's primarily sold groceries, although it did introduce drugstore departments into units where possible. In 1970, however, the company pioneered a unique and exceptionally profitable concept in supermarket design. J.L. Scott, who had become chief executive officer in 1966, announced in 1969 that Albertson's would enter into partnership with Skaggs Drugs Centers, based in Salt Lake City, Utah, and headed by Albertson's former partner, to jointly finance and manage six jumbo combination food and drugstores in Texas. Whereas the average contemporary supermarket was 30,000 square feet or smaller, the combination stores covered as much as 55,000 square feet. In addition, while conventional stores carried strictly grocery items, which have a slim profit margin of one to two percent, the Skaggs-Albertson's combination stores stocked not only groceries but also nonfood items such as cosmetics, perfumes, pharmacy products, camera supplies, and electrical equipment. Banking on the higher profit margin of nonfood items as well as on an aggressive five-year plan, Scott also predicted in 1969 that Albertson's sales would

double within five years. His optimism was not unfounded. By 1974, sales reached $852.3 million, with net earnings of $8.9 million.

The first Skaggs-Albertson's combination stores were opened in Texas in 1970, the year after the New York Stock Exchange began to trade Albertson's shares. In the early 1970s, Albertson's and Skaggs considered merging, but ultimately decided against the move. Albertson's continued its beneficial partnership with Skaggs until 1977, opening combination drug and grocery stores throughout Texas, Florida, and Louisiana.

Along with rapid growth, Albertson's faced some minor setbacks during the early 1970s. In 1972 Albertson's had acquired Mountain States Wholesale of Idaho, a subsidiary of DiGiorgio Corporation. In 1974 the Justice Department filed a civil antitrust suit against Albertson's, asserting that at the time of the purchase Albertson's was the largest retail grocer in the southern Idaho and eastern Oregon market, while Mountain States carried 43 percent of the wholesale grocery market, and that Albertson's purchase created an illegal monopoly.

Robert D. Bolinder, CEO from 1974 through 1976, claimed that the suit was without basis and that Albertson's had in fact preserved competition in the area by acquiring Mountain States. Bolinder still claimed that the Justice Department had misunderstood Albertson's reasons for buying the wholesaler, noting that the subsidiary was not financially integral to the company but accounted for only 3.4 percent of its total sales in 1973. The settlement, in 1977, required Albertson's to divest Mountain States and barred the company from acquiring any retail or wholesale grocery businesses in southern Idaho or eastern Oregon for five years.

Also in 1974, in the Portland, Seattle, and Denver areas, the Federal Trade Commission found fault with Albertson's advertising practices. The company complied with an FTC order requiring that advertised sale items be available to customers and that rain checks be issued when sale items were out of stock, although Bolinder maintained that Albertson's had not violated any laws and emphasized that compliance would not require any change in the company's previously established advertising policies.

In 1976, after chairing the board for 37 years, Joe Albertson became chairman of the executive committee. Warren McCain, who began his career with Albertson's as a merchandising supervisor in 1951, became chairman of the board and CEO. In the same year, Albertson's began to build superstores, which would carry an even higher ratio of nonfood items. A slightly smaller version of the combination store, the superstores ranged in size from 35,000 to 48,000 square feet and featured more fresh foods and perishables. It was during 1976 that the corporation slowly began to phase out its conventional markets. Although a few profitable ones remained open, most were closed or converted into larger stores during the late 1970s and early 1980s. Albertson's also installed its first electric price scanner in 1976. By the late 1980s, 85 percent of Albertson's stores used scanners.

Relying principally on outside distributors, Albertson's successfully penetrated markets located throughout a broad geographic area, but the rapid expansion of its markets during the 1970s called for expansion of company-owned distribution facilities. Two of the company's four full-line distribution facilities were built during this period. The first of these went up in 1973 in Brea, California, and the other was completed in 1976 in Salt Lake City. All Albertson's distribution facilities were built, and operated, as profit centers, contributing a return on investment that equaled or exceeded that of the company's retail stores.

Continued Expansion in the Late 1970s and 1980s

In 1977 Albertson's and Skaggs dissolved their partnership amicably, splitting their assets equally. For Albertson's, the breakup resulted in the formation of Southco, the company's Southern division. Southco assumed operation of 30 of the 58 combination stores formerly run by the partnership. Albertson's continued opening combination stores, concentrating them principally in Southern states, but also opening a few in South Dakota and Nebraska. In 1978 Albertson's strengthened its stronghold in southern California by acquiring 46 supermarkets located in the Los Angeles area from Fisher Foods, Inc.

In 1979 Albertson's took the "bigger is better" concept to the drawing boards again and introduced its first warehouse stores. As inflation drove prices up, Albertson's needed to cut overhead to preserve its profit margin. To this end, it converted, between 1979 and 1981, seven stores into full-line, mass merchandise warehouse stores run under the name Grocery Warehouse. These no-frills stores carried nonfood items but emphasized groceries, with substantial savings on meat and liquor. Although these stores continued to be successful, they did not eclipse the profitability of the more broadly appealing superstores.

The introduction of the combination store and the continuing readaptation of older stores (87 percent of the company's stores were newly built or completely remodeled during the 1970s) allowed Albertson's to prosper despite the economically hostile environment of the late 1970s and early 1980s. In 1983, just after the country's most severe recession since the Great Depression, Albertson's boasted 13 years of record sales. The combination stores, both jumbo and smaller, were in large part responsible for this success. In 1983 these units accounted for only one-third of the chain's 423 stores but were the source of 65 percent of its profits.

Since Albertson's had grown by expanding over a wide geographic area rather than increasing its dominance in a smaller area, it did not hold superior market share in many of the areas where it operated. But it was this diversification, in part, that had allowed Albertson's to weather the economic storms of the 1970s and 1980s so successfully. As it happened, the areas of Albertson's concentration were the areas of relative economic prosperity. In 1981 Albertson's was operating in 17 of the fastest-growing standard metropolitan areas, as identified by the U.S. Department of Commerce. Stores in relatively stable areas helped balance losses in more depressed markets.

Although Albertson's did break into the Nebraska and North and South Dakota markets in 1981, during the 1980s it concentrated principally on increasing its presence in established markets. For example, in an effort to expand its market in Texas, Albertson's modified its advertising strategy. In 1984 Albertson's reentered the Dallas-Fort Worth area, a competitive market that no new firm had entered since Skaggs opened its first store there in 1972. The standard advertising strategy was to offer gimmicks such as double-value coupons and promotional games to attract customers. Albertson's had used such techniques, but chose to approach the Dallas-Fort Worth market with an "every day low-cost" image instead. Store circulars explained, "We won't be advertising weekly specials . . . we'll pass the savings on advertising costs on to you. Tell your friends and neighbors to help us keep prices down." The campaign sparked fierce competition, but the Albertson's units continued to prosper. Although the company traditionally held an upscale profile, it began to extend the new image to other suitable markets.

As Albertson's continued to build larger concentrations of stores, its behind-the-scenes operations continued to grow. In 1982 retail management was reorganized into four operating units/regions: California, Northwest, Intermountain, and Southco. This subdivision allowed each regional director and management team to more effectively focus marketing and retail sales strategies as well as to more closely guide employee and real estate development. Albertson's built another distribution center in the Denver area in 1984 and completed its first fully mechanized distribution center in Portland, Oregon, in 1988. In addition, the Salt Lake City facility was expanded substantially in late 1988 and the Brea, California center was expanded and mechanized in 1989.

Innovation and Improvements in the Early 1990s

The expansion of Albertson's distribution network, combined with new computerized inventory and checkout scanners, enabled the chain to begin to handle its own distribution in 1990. By 1993, almost two-thirds of the items purchased by Albertson's stores were distributed by its own system.

In December 1991 Albertson's announced a five-year expansion plan that called for a $2.4 billion investment in the construction of 250 new stores, the renovation of 175 older stores, and the acceleration of computerization chainwide. By the end of fiscal 1991 (January 1992), more than half of Albertson's stores had computerized time and attendance systems, all of the pharmacies had automated prescription systems, and 96 percent of the stores were equipped with checkout scanners. In 1992 the company acquired 74 Jewel Osco food and drugstores in Texas, Oklahoma, Arkansas, and Florida from American Stores, along with a nonfood distribution center in Ponca City, Oklahoma—all for a total of $442 million. Albertson's had ambitious plans at this time, especially considering that it took the company all of the 1980s to build or acquire 283 stores. Albertson's was targeting its growth for California, Texas, Florida, and Arizona, some of the United States' fastest-growing markets. CEO Warren McCain targeted growth for smaller cities and suburbs where plentiful, inexpensive land allowed Albertson's to maximize profits.

Gary Michael became chairman of the board and chief executive officer of Albertson's on February 1, 1991, and initiated the "Service First" employee award program. The plan recognized and rewarded excellence in customer service. Michael also implemented a quarterly video news program that promoted employee understanding of Albertson's goals and objectives. The employee relations efforts resulted in a 16 percent decrease in the worker turnover rate.

Public relations in the 1990s focused on ''Service First'' and a new advertising theme, ''It's Your Store.'' It was hoped that the slogan would instill in customers a sense of partnership through convenience, quality, competitive pricing, and service. The HOPE (Helping Our Planet's Ecology) line of environmentally safer paper products reinforced Albertson's commitment to the ecosystem.

By January 1992, Albertson's ran 562 grocery stores in 17 Western and Southern states, employing 60,000 workers. The company's 1991 sales and earnings hit record highs for the 22nd year: net income rose 10.3 percent to $258 million and sales grew 5.6 percent to $8.68 billion. Sales surpassed the $10 billion mark in 1993, the year that Joe Albertson died at age 86. Although modern business sensibility had cultivated Albertson's multibillion-dollar success, the solid, small town philosophy of founder Albertson—giving customers quality merchandise at a reasonable price—was at its root.

Number Two Position During the Late 1990s

By the mid-1990s, Albertson's was the number four grocery chain in the United States, with about 800 stores in 19 states and revenues approaching $12 billion. The company continued building its distribution system, with a new, one-million-square-foot center in Plant City, Florida—a facility dedicated to reviving its struggling 74-unit Florida operation—opening in early 1994. By mid-1996, with the opening of a center in Houston, Albertson's had a total of 12 distribution centers. Meantime, in early 1996, Richard L. King, a 28-year company veteran, was named president and COO, with Michael remaining chairman and CEO. Also in 1996, Albertson's introduced Quick Fixin' Ideas. This concept included offering time-starved customers recipes and all the ingredients to make them in one convenient location, as well as offering several prepackaged entrees for heat-and-serve meals (the latter an example of the trend toward home meal replacement). Having been hurt by chains such as Safeway taking business away through their aggressive promotional programs, Albertson's began to put a greater emphasis on advertising and promotion to bolster its longstanding everyday-low-price approach, an approach that some analysts said bored customers. At the same time, Albertson's took steps to improve its customer service and speed up the checkout process.

Albertson's was the object of several class-action lawsuits filed in 1996 and 1997. The suits charged that the company systematically permitted its workers to work ''off-the-clock,'' without paying them. Albertson's was potentially liable for about $200 million in back pay and damage awards. The management contended that the suits, sponsored by the United Food and Commercial Workers, were part of an effort by the union and its allies to unionize the company's stores, only a third of which were unionized.

During the late 1990s, Albertson's continued its ongoing program of store remodeling and achieved some growth through organic expansion. It was through acquisitions, however, that Albertson's vaulted to the number two position in grocery retailing by the end of the decade. At the end of the fiscal year ending in January 1998, Albertson's operated 878 stores in 20 states and had revenues of $14.69 billion. Less than two years later, the company had grown to a nearly nationwide chain of more than 2,400 units in 39 states, with revenues of approximately $33.4 billion, which trailed only Kroger's $43 billion (the latter the product of a May 1999 merger of Kroger and Fred Meyer Inc.).

During the year ending in January 1999, Albertson's made several acquisitions that added some 80 stores to its system and brought the company into five new states: Georgia, Iowa, Missouri, North Dakota, and Tennessee. These included the purchase of Seessel Holdings, Inc., which included ten Seessel's stores in Memphis, Tennessee; Smitty's Super Markets, Inc., which included ten Smitty's stores in southwest Missouri; three Super One stores in Des Moines, Iowa; 14 Bruno's stores in the Nashville and Chattanooga, Tennessee, metro areas; and Buttrey Food and Drug Stores Company, which included 44 stores in Montana, North Dakota, and Wyoming. To gain approval from the Federal Trade Commission for the last of these acquisitions, Albertson's had to divest itself of nine Buttrey stores and six Albertson's units.

In June 1999 Albertson's made its biggest deal ever—valued at $11.7 billion, including $3.4 billion in debt—to acquire American Stores Company, the successor company to Skaggs Drug Centers, Albertson's former combination stores partner. At the time of the merger, Salt Lake City-based American Stores had 288 combination stores, 514 supermarkets, and 783 stand-alone drugstores. To gain FTC approval, Albertson's agreed to divest 145 stores plus four store sites (in overlapping markets in California, Nevada, and New Mexico), in what was believed to be the largest divestiture ever ordered in relation to a retail merger. As with other consolidation moves of the late 1990s, the acquisition was driven by projected cost savings from synergies created by the merged operations. Company officials estimated that $100 million would be saved in the first year, $200 million in the second, and $300 million per year thereafter. Albertson's also announced that it would take $700 million in after-tax charges over a two-year period to cover merger-related costs. Around the time of the completion of the merger, King resigned his executive positions to ''pursue other opportunities,'' with Michael assuming his responsibilities, at least initially.

In addition to increasing the number of units it operated to more than 2,400, the acquisition of American Stores also provided Albertson's with its first freestanding drugstores (under the Osco and Sav-on names) and placed the suburban-oriented company into its first two urban markets, Chicago and Philadelphia. During the five years following the merger, Albertson's planned to spend about $11 billion on capital projects, including building 750 combination stores, 500 drugstores, and 600 fuel centers. The company had been experimenting with some success with fuel centers that had been added to its combination stores, featuring three to six gas pumps and either pay-only kiosks or small convenience stores. Albertson's also planned to remodel about 730 units. An area of possible concern was the meshing of Albertson's mostly nonunion work force with the three-quarters unionized American Stores staff. It was also

---

2525 Dupont Dr
Irvine, Californi
U.S.A.
(714) 246-4500
(800) 347-4500
Fax: (714) 246-4
Web site: http://

Public Company
Incorporated: 19
Employees: 5,972
Sales: $1.26 billi
Stock Exchanges:
Ticker Symbol: A
NAIC: 339115 O
        325412 Pharm
        339112 Surgic

Allergan, Inc. is
pharmaceutical proc
contact lens care pr
products used in the
psoriasis, acne, and
nues is generated b
toxic botulinum ba
Administration-app
trolled blinking, as
ing the temporary e
its products in more
burgeoning sales in
as Brazil, India, an

O

In 1948 Gavin
business in a labor
stores. Stanley Bly,
istry, created the bu

likely that the purch
Albertson's last, as it
abled it to consider fur
truly nationwide chair
pete with the likes of
was rapidly and aggr
sector.

"Albertson's Massive D
    1991, pp. 26–27.
Alster, Norm, "One Man
    38–39.
Baldo, Anthony, "Flemi
    1991, pp. 40–41.
Barrett, Amy, "Albertso
    May 12, 1992, pp. 1
Beauchamp, Marc, "Foo
Berner, Robert, "Alberts
    Posts," *Wall Street J*
Bernstein, Aaron, "This
    Week, March 10, 199
Byrne, Harlan S., "Albe
    Earnings Growth, Hig
    pp. 55–56.
Coleman, Calmetta Y.,
    Checkout Line," *Wa*
——, "Albertson's Plans
    ket Firm to Be Creat
    Street Journal, Augu

Company Perspectives:

Our Mission: To develop a unique level of understanding of our customers in order to implement operational strategies that provide the greatest value for our customers and stakeholders. We will become the partner of choice for ever better health care through the value of our technological innovation, industry leadership, partnering skills and relationships, worldwide infrastructure, research, and manufacturing capabilities.

Our Vision: We're an innovative, technology driven, global health care company focused on eye care and specialty therapeutic products that deliver value to customers, satisfy unmet medical needs, and improve patients' lives.

Contact Lens Care Market Beginning in 1960

In 1960 hard contact lenses first became available. Allergan demonstrated its propensity to take advantage of new technology when it entered the contact lens market that year. Liquifilm, a wetting solution for hard contact lenses, became an important vehicle for Allergan's ophthalmic products.

Allergan began to develop a global outlook in 1964, when it created its first foreign distributorships in Puerto Rico and Iraq. In 1965 Allergan established its first foreign subsidiary in Canada. The company's only competition abroad was Alcon, and Allergan's growth in the international market and the success of its hard contact lens care products combined to bring sales growth of 20 to 25 percent during the 1960s.

Allergan had achieved $10 million in sales by 1970 and was preparing to become a public company. To take the company public, a long-term plan for managing growth was developed. Toward the realization of that plan, Allergan purchased 24 acres from the Irvine Ranch Company and, in 1968, built its Von Karman production facility on that site. In 1971 Allergan went public, erecting its first office building in Irvine, California.

By the mid-1970s, the company had become a major ophthalmic producer, meeting a growing demand for soft contact lens products. Soft contact lenses had become available in 1970, and Allergan became a contractual supplier of soft contact lens solutions to industry giant Bausch & Lomb. Allergan's two lens products were Hydrocare (introduced in 1974) and its enzymatic cleaner. The company's international business flourished because of the success of Allergan's soft contact lens cleaner, which had become the focus of Allergan's European sales since it required no regulatory approval. Allergan established its first manufacturing sites outside the United States in the 1970s, in Puerto Rico and Ireland. The company's operations realized growth of 30 percent in net profits between 1970 and 1975, with total sales reaching $33 million in the latter year.

This period of growth was bolstered by a thriving U.S. ophthalmic market, estimated at a value of $90 million at the manufacturer's level in 1975. Business that year rose by 18 percent (an average increase would be ten to 12 percent), due to price increases and an exacerbated allergy season. In 1975

Allergan held approximately 30 percent of the hard contact lens market and increased its considerable share of prescription ophthalmics by 27 percent.

In 1977 Allergan was reincorporated in Delaware. In 1978 Gavin Herbert, Sr., Allergan's cofounder and chairman, died. Gavin Herbert, Jr., succeeded his father, adding chairman to his titles of president and chief executive officer. Growth continued in the latter half of the 1970s, with revenue rising from $46.4 million in 1978 to $62.6 million in 1979.

Purchase by SmithKline Beckman in 1980

SmithKline Beckman Corporation purchased Allergan for $236 million, and Allergan became a wholly owned subsidiary in 1980. That year, Allergan approached $100 million in sales, a 20 percent increase for the decade. For Allergan, the association with a larger pharmaceutical company was a way to combat its dependence on in-licensing and development. As a subsidiary of SmithKline, Allergan was able to create new products through its first research program. For SmithKline, the purchase of Allergan was the first step in its implementation of a new strategy. In 1970, large profits generated by Thorazine had become a double-edged sword when the patent expired, due to SmithKline's shortsighted lack of investment in research and its failure to develop new ventures. Ten years later, SmithKline's president and CEO Henry Wendt recognized that the company was again becoming dependent on a single product, the anti-ulcer drug Tagamet, with a patent that would expire in 1993.

The purchase of Allergan was Wendt's first step forward in a new strategy to link diagnostic and therapeutic products. In addition, the purchase was to be a catalyst for new partnerships resulting in lucrative research and innovation. Accordingly, SmithKline put Allergan scientists to work, seeking applications of the research knowledge that produced Tagamet to cures for eye or skin diseases.

The potential market for soft contact lenses was enormous. In 1984, according to *Industry Week*, 120 million Americans suffered from a vision problem, but only 12 percent wore soft contact lenses. Two additional factors made soft contacts a lucrative product: a shorter lifespan (soft lens wearers replaced lenses every 15 months or so), and the advent of tinted lenses, used by more than 20 percent of wearers who had no vision problems. Finally, the availability and increased affordability of soft contact lenses for astigmatic wearers caused the traditional ten percent increase in new wearers to jump to 20 percent between 1982 and 1984, according to *Industry Week*.

In 1984 SmithKline strengthened its investment in Allergan—which then held 20 percent of the contact lens solutions market—when it acquired International Hydron, the number two maker of soft contact lenses (behind the industry giant Bausch & Lomb, which held 40 percent of the lens and solutions business). International Hydron became part of Allergan in 1987. At the time of SmithKline's purchase, the contact lens market was reshuffling; some 20 companies had folded in the 1970s, but the remaining 30 businesses were struggling to maintain their positions behind Bausch & Lomb and to take advantage of the unprecedented market potential of soft contacts.

Billion-dollar companies such as Nestlé and Johnson & Johnson began eyeing the market as its potential became apparent.

By 1987, the $500 million contact lens care market was growing at about 20 to 25 percent annually, and Allergan and its competitors were locked in fierce competition. Allergan stepped forward with an innovative new product, Ultrazyme Enzymatic Cleaner, the first weekly enzymatic cleaner that could be used during disinfection. This product was responsive to an increased focus on better lens care, as studies began to demonstrate that unsanitary lenses led to eye problems. Between 1980 and 1989, Allergan's sales increased from $100 million to $800 million.

Allergan employed two strategies to manage this rapid growth: updating its information systems and restructuring its human relations departments. Michael Garrison, who sold computers for General Electric prior to becoming Allergan's director of information management, developed innovative information strategies for Allergan in the late 1980s. These computer-based systems included an in-house voicemail system that linked ophthalmologists directly to Allergan; a million-dollar campaign to provide laptop computers for all 300 U.S. sales representatives to increase territory management; and the donation of computers and communication software to doctors' offices, which made briefs written to support products being considered for FDA approval instantly available for downloading by Allergan researchers.

William C. Shepherd, who would become president of Allergan's U.S. operations and, later, CEO, envisioned a strengthened human resources structure that would enable the company to manage and increase its sales and promote itself as the world's leading eye care company. Supporting 20 percent annual growth and rapid expansion, Allergan restructured its human resources department, utilizing both centralized and decentralized models. Shepherd hired Rick Hilles, who later became Allergan's senior vice-president of human resources, to create and implement this new structure. Hilles divided the company into six strategic operating areas (SOAs) and separated the responsibilities of the human resources department into two separate areas. A decentralized area focused on specific market segments and goals, while a centralized structure provided technological benefits, information flow, research and development, marketing, manufacturing, and overall management. The restructuring was publicly lauded when Allergan received the 1991 Optimas Award.

Going Public: 1989

Allergan again became a public company in 1989, when SmithKline merged with Beecham Corporation, spinning off distribution of Allergan to shareholders. The transition period posed problems for Allergan, which had high costs, inefficient manufacturing systems, gaps in new product development, and large debt. The eye care market was no longer growing at the dramatic pace of the 1980s. Sales had moved away from traditional contact lenses, as disposable lenses and fashion glasses—neither of which were sold by Allergan—took the industry lead. With ophthalmologists spending less, Allergan's diagnostic equipment business also was experiencing little profit.

Allergan's business strategy had become unmanageable because it forced the company to compete over too broad a range of business sectors: from pharmaceuticals to consumer products to diagnostic eye care instruments. In 1990 Allergan was close to a billion-dollar company, but its stock had fallen from $25 a share (at the time of its spinoff) to $15 a share. Investment analysts began to advise investors that Allergan was prime for a takeover, pointing to Nestlé's Alcon Laboratories as a potential purchaser.

Allergan changed its business strategy to reflect market needs in the early 1990s. Under the leadership of president and CEO William Shepherd, Allergan reshaped its operations with a three-pronged strategy: making more money available for research and development, containing costs, and implementing quality. Between 1989 and 1991, Allergan reduced employment by ten percent, consolidated some manufacturing operations, reduced its debt, and improved its cash flow, resulting in the elevation of its price on the stock market. In addition, in 1991 the company's board of directors approved a plan to realign Allergan into market-focus business groups with a regional structure giving the company a global focus on the Americas, Europe, Pan-Asia, and Japan.

With a new focus on specialty pharmaceuticals, Allergan began to emerge as a developer of therapeutic products. In 1991 Allergan acquired Oculinum, Inc. and gained an advantage as the only firm marketing Type A botulinum toxin, a product of the bacterium that causes botulism that had been shown to be safe and effective in treating neuromuscular disorders. Botox, the market name for the substance manufactured by Oculinum, Inc., generated $5 million in sales during its first year. Also in 1991, Allergan researcher David Woodward patented a composition that could be used in treating glaucoma. At that time, most glaucoma treatments inhibited the formation of fluids. The new Allergan composition, a derivative of protoglandin (a fat molecule produced in the eye), helped the eye drain, relieving fluid pressure.

A product generating less excitement was Allergan's first one-bottle contact lens disinfecting solution, UltraCare Disinfectant/Neutralizer. Allergan was late to enter the one-step market, and its solution was considered inferior to its competitors by analysts, according to the *New York Times*. In 1992 Allergan sold its North and South American contact lens business, and in 1993 the company sold its remaining contact lens business.

In 1993 Allergan became involved in a proxy battle, as a result of new rules adopted that year by the Securities and Exchange Commission. The State of Wisconsin Investment Board in Madison rallied support from other institutions to put Allergan's ''poison pill'' shareholders' rights plan to a vote by the holders. Allergan's management position was that shareholder control of the plan would render the board impotent in case of a sudden takeover. Allergan's shareholders, however, passed what became one of the first successful shareholder solicitations by a slight majority (52 percent) at the April 1993 annual meeting.

The early 1990s restructuring improved Allergan's growth, with sales increasing from $762 million in 1991 to $858 million in 1993. Acquisitions marked the years 1994 and 1995. In 1994

Allergan acquired the Ioptex Research global intraocular lens product line. Among the 1995 acquisitions were Optical Micro Systems, Inc., a maker of cataract surgery equipment; Laboratorios Frumtost, S.A., a Brazilian manufacturer of ophthalmic and other pharmaceutical products; and the worldwide contact lens care product operations of Pilkington Barnes Hind. The last of these included the Concept F cleaning and disinfecting system and significantly increased the company's contact lens care product operations in Japan. In late 1995 Allergan launched Azelex cream for the topical treatment of mild to moderate acne of the skin; the product was well received by the market.

Near Merger with Pharmacia & Upjohn in 1996

Increasing competition and acquisition-related costs led to sagging profits for Allergan in the mid-1990s. In early 1996 Allergan entered advanced merger discussions with Pharmacia & Upjohn Inc., but the merger was blocked by AB Volvo, which held a minority stake in Pharmacia & Upjohn. Soon thereafter, Allergan announced a restructuring that included the elimination of about 450 jobs and 1996 pretax charges of about $75 million. The company enhanced its research and development efforts through collaborative agreements in 1996 with SUGEN, Inc., for research into treatments for ophthalmic diseases, such as age-related macular degeneration and diabetic retinopathy, and with Cambridge NeuroScience, Inc., for research into new treatments for glaucoma and other serious ophthalmic diseases. Also in 1996 Allergan received FDA approval for the Alphagan ophthalmic solution for the treatment of open-angle glaucoma and ocular hypertension. By the late 1990s Alphagan was the company's largest selling eye care pharmaceutical product.

In 1997 Allergan expanded its burgeoning skin care line through the FDA approval of Tazorac for the treatment of plaque psoriasis and acne. Also receiving FDA approval in 1997 was Array, a multifocal intraocular lens used to help cataract patients see well over a range of distances—a global market leader since its debut. Although overall sales had surpassed the $1 billion mark in 1995, growth stalled in 1997, with net sales falling slightly, from $1.15 billion in 1996 to $1.14 billion in 1997. With the company's financial performance and stock price continuing to disappoint a number of institutional investors, Shepherd retired at the end of 1997 after 31 years with Allergan. Taking over as president and CEO at the beginning of 1998 was David Pyott, who had been head of Novartis AG's nutrition division, which included the Gerber Products Co. baby food unit. Taking over as chairman was Herbert W. Boyer, a biochemist, member of the Allergan board since 1994, and a founder of Genentech Inc.

Under the new leadership, Allergan began a three-year restructuring effort in 1998 whereby five of its ten plants would be closed and its workforce reduced by 550 people, or nine percent. Allergan subsequently posted a net loss of $90.2 million for the year, due to a restructuring charge of $74.8 million and asset write-offs of $58.5 million. The company in 1998 also contributed $200 million to a new subsidiary, Allergan Specialty Therapeutics, Inc. (ASTI), which was then spun off to shareholders as a dividend. ASTI was charged with conducting research into new pharmaceutical products in the area of retinoids, which held promise for treating such diseases as diabetes and cancer. Allergan retained first crack at any products developed by the quasi-independent ASTI; it had the option to buy the spinoff back, and was likely to do so. Offloading some of its R&D enabled Allergan to increase R&D expenditures without having its earnings-per-share dragged down. Meanwhile, in 1998 the company also entered into a multiyear alliance with the Parke-Davis Pharmaceutical Research Division of Warner-Lambert Company to investigate retinoids for the treatment of metabolic diseases. Among other late 1990s R&D efforts were the attempt to expand the approved uses of Botox to include treatment of migraine headaches, chronic tension headaches, lower back pain, cerebral palsy, and such cosmetic uses as brow furrows; the development of Restasis, a drug for the treatment of moderate to severe dry eye; and the development of Abrevia, a treatment for allergic conjunctivitis.

In April 1999 a seemingly revitalized Allergan announced a $70 million expansion of its R&D campus at the Irvine headquarters and the addition of 300 new research scientists and other professionals. The expansion was slated for completion in 2004. Although the company had been hurt by stagnating sales of its contact lens care lines, which accounted for about 28 percent of overall sales in 1998, large increases in the sales of Botox and of eye care pharmaceuticals, most notably Alphagan, led to an 11 percent increase in overall sales in 1998 and a nearly 17 percent increase for the first six months of 1998. Allergan appeared to be well positioned to thrive in the increasingly competitive pharmaceutical industry.

Principal Subsidiaries

Allergan Australia (Pty.) Ltd.; Allergan France S.A.; Allergan Inc. (Canada); Allergan K.K. (Japan); Allergan Limited (U.K.); Allergan-Lok Produtos, Farmaceuticos, Ltda. (Brazil); Allergan Pharmaceuticals (Ireland) Ltd., Inc.; Allergan S.A. de C.V. (Mexico); Allergan S.A.E. (Spain); Allergan S.p.A. (Italy); Pharm-Allergan GmbH (Germany).

Further Reading

"Allergan Inc.," *Wall Street Journal,* December 7, 1993, p. B4.

"Allergan Pharmaceuticals," *Wall Street Transcript,* March 22, 1976, p. 1.

"Allergan Shareholders Pass Proposal Forcing Vote on Poison Pill," *Wall Street Journal,* April 28, 1993, p. A6.

Altman, Lawrence K., "Botulinum Toxin's Promise As Drug May Rival Its Potential As Weapon," *New York Times,* March 10, 1998, p. F7.

Chen, Ingfei, "Toxin to the Rescue," *Science News,* January 19, 1991, pp. 42–43.

Chernoff, Joel, and Patricia Limbacher, "3 Companies in Proxy Battles," *Pensions and Investments,* April 19, 1993, pp. 1, 34.

"Companies Seek to Test Cancer Drug on People," *Journal of Commerce,* December 1, 1993, p. 5A.

"Composition May Help in Treating Glaucoma," *New York Times,* May 11, 1991.

Crabtree, Penni, "Irvine, Calif.-Based Eye Care Firm Awaits Results of Restructuring," *Orange County (Calif.) Register,* November 15, 1998.

"Drugs and Biotech: New Hope for the Dead?," *Fortune,* November 29, 1993, p. 32.

Filipowski, Diane, "Allergan's Structuring for Success," *Personnel Journal,* March 1991, pp. 56–57.

Greene, Jay, "Allergan's Botox, Made from Toxin, Used to Fight Wrinkles," *Orange County (Calif.) Register,* February 16, 1998.

Knap, Chris, "Irvine, Calif.-Based Allergan May Have New Migraine Remedy," *Orange County (Calif.) Register,* April 21, 1999.

Lev, Michael, "Allergan Gains from a Reduction," *New York Times,* December 5, 1991, p. C8.

Lipin, Steven, and Stephen D. Moore, "Pharmacia & Upjohn's Plan to Acquire Allergan Inc. Is Blocked by AB Volvo," *Wall Street Journal,* May 14, 1996, p. A3.

Marcial, Gene G., "Allergan: Seeing Past the Myopia," *Business Week,* February 5, 1990, p. 78.

McCusker, Tom, "Using Technology to Listen Better," *Datamation,* January 15, 1988, pp. 38–42.

McMenamin, Brigid, "Blurred Vision," *Forbes,* March 23, 1998, p. 142.

"1991 Optimas Awards," *Personnel Journal,* January 1991, p. 53.

Rundle, Rhonda L., "Allergan CEO Shepherd Set to Retire, with Pyott from Novartis As Successor," *Wall Street Journal,* October 6, 1997, p. B7A.

——, "Allergan Opens Eyes with Cataract Ads," *Wall Street Journal,* March 8, 1999, p. B6.

——, "Allergan Plans Job Cuts, Charge of $103 Million," *Wall Street Journal,* September 16, 1998, p. B6.

"SmithKline Beckman Unit to Acquire French Company," *Wall Street Journal,* February 2, 1984, p. 11E.

"SmithKline Plans to Buy Allergan for $259 Million," *Wall Street Journal,* December 7, 1979, p. 14.

"SmithKline: Reducing Its Dependence on Drugs," *Business Week,* November 14, 1983, pp. 211–12.

"Takeover Defenses, One Step Backward in the Proxy Arena," *Mergers & Acquisitions,* September/October 1993, pp. 11–12.

"Tale of a Topnotch Team," *Insight Magazine,* Irvine: Allergan, Inc., March 1994.

Verespej, Michael, "Eye-to-Eye Combat," *Industry Week,* October 15, 1984, pp. 30–32.

——, "Nowhere to No. 2," *Industry Week,* October 1, 1984, pp. 87–88.

Winters, Patricia, "Lens-Care Battle in Sight," *Advertising Age,* October 19, 1987, p. 12.

—Heidi Feldman
—updated by David E. Salamie

Alliant Techsystems Inc.

600 Second Street, Northeast
Hopkins, Minnesota 55343
U.S.A.
(612) 931-6000
Fax: (612) 931-5920
Web site: http://www.atk.com

Public Company
Incorporated: 1990
Employees: 6,110
Sales: $1.09 billion (1999)
Stock Exchanges: New York
Ticker Symbol: ATK
NAIC: 336415 Guided Missile & Space Vehicle Propulsion Unit & Propulsion Unit Parts Manufacturing; 332993 Ammunition (Except Small Arms) Manufacturing; 332995 Other Ordnance & Accessories Manufacturing 334511 Search, Detection, Navigation, Guidance, Aeronautical, and Nautical System & Instrument Manufacturing; 54133 Engineering Services

In 1990 Honeywell Inc. spun off its defense-related business to form a new company, Alliant Techsystems Inc. Alliant quickly became a leading producer of conventional munitions and aerospace and defense systems. As one of the largest manufacturers of low-cost, high-quality munitions in the country, Alliant sells its products to the U.S. Department of Defense and to nations allied to the United States as well as to contractors. The company's aerospace division primarily focuses on solid rocket motors for expendable space launch vehicles, such as those used to propel communications satellites into orbit. Alliant's defense systems division designs and manufactures weapon systems upgrades and works in precision guided munitions development. Alliant operates facilities in more than a dozen states.

Honeywell's Involvement in the Defense Industry: 1941–89

Honeywell's entrance into the defense industry came in 1941, when the war in Europe and Japan's occupation of China led the administration of Franklin D. Roosevelt to begin preparations for the possibility that the United States might be involved in the conflicts. At the time the company—then called Minneapolis-Honeywell—was one of the few U.S. manufacturers with the workforce, facilities, tooling, and expertise to produce precision instruments and controls for the military.

Minneapolis-Honeywell's first military contracts were for an automatic system for releasing payloads at high altitudes for precision bombing. The company's chairman, Harold Sweatt, assigned the company's heating regulator division to develop the system. The company's volume of military business expanded rapidly after the Japanese attack on Pearl Harbor and the U.S. entry into World War II. During the course of the war, the firm turned out turbo engine regulators and complex automatic ammunition firing control devices, among other items, and served as the only U.S. manufacturer of tank periscopes.

At the end of the war Sweatt was determined to keep Minneapolis-Honeywell in the electronic controls business. The most lucrative customer at the time was the Pentagon, which was gearing up for cold war hostilities with the Soviet Union. These circumstances drew Minneapolis-Honeywell even deeper into the stable and lucrative government contracting business. In addition, research dollars provided for Pentagon projects were almost always applicable to commercial projects. The formula worked in reverse as well. Minneapolis-Honeywell purchased the Micro Switch division of First Industrial in 1950. The company's switches were used to operate relays in vending machines and other manually operated devices, but they soon found military applications in battle tanks, artillery, and guided missile systems.

Minneapolis-Honeywell's brief association with the radar powerhouse Raytheon, coupled with their subsequent computer venture, Datamatic, firmly established the company's reputation as a high-technology electronics manufacturer. It led to increased activity in aviation control systems and the company's eventual participation in the manned space program.

In 1964, after shortening its name to Honeywell, the company opted out of the competition for major defense and space projects. Honeywell simply was not in a position to compete economically with such industry giants as Boeing, General

Company Perspectives:

The Alliant way is our commitment to excellence in every-thing we do. As leaders in our field, we want to set the standard for delivering low-cost, high-quality solutions to our customers every time. We will act with integrity, operate safely, and grow the value of our company to our people, our shareholders, and our communities.

Electric, or General Dynamics. Instead, Honeywell concentrated on working as a subcontractor within a narrow range of electronics systems. The company's profitable defense systems businesses, however, created public relations difficulties. Headquartered in the politically liberal state of Minnesota, Honeywell endured a series of protests launched by groups opposed to American involvement in the Vietnam War.

As the war effort in Vietnam wound down during the administrations of Richard Nixon and Gerald Ford, defense budgets were scaled back. This produced less work for Honeywell's defense businesses and later caused the company to reduce its operations. In 1982 Chairman James Renier carried out a corporate downsizing that claimed 3,500 jobs. With this restructuring Honeywell abandoned its adversarial position in the marketplace with regard to IBM and later sold off much of its computer manufacturing assets.

In 1986 and 1988 Honeywell's defense businesses recorded tremendous losses, stemming from huge cost overruns. Unable to collect for the losses and penalized for the late delivery of products under contract, Renier decided to immediately reduce Honeywell's exposure to Pentagon projects. He initially attempted to reposition much of the government defense business toward commercial aviation and flight control markets. In the short run the strategy appeared effective. At this time the company's defense and aerospace operations comprised nearly half of Honeywell's total income and a significant portion of its total profits.

Renier, however, was determined to refocus Honeywell on its core commercial operations. While they made money, its defense businesses—specifically the Defense & Marine Systems division—were not as profitable or promising as other groups in the company. Thus it was felt that defense operations were diluting the company's profitability. In addition, the lessening in tensions between the United States and the Soviet Union raised increasing questions about the long-term viability of involvement in the defense market.

Formation of Alliant Techsystems in 1990

Renier decided to organize the Defense & Marine Systems and Test Instruments divisions along with the Signal Analysis Center into a separate corporate entity. The new entity would operate as an independent subsidiary until it could be sold, preferably to another defense contractor. After several months, however, no company stepped forward with an acceptable bid. Eager to dispense with the low-margin division and to get on with the business of running Honeywell, Renier decided to

distribute shares in the new entity to Honeywell shareholders. To do this, the subsidiary would have to be prepared for life as an independent corporation.

Renier offered the chairmanship of the new company to Toby G. Warson, a former naval commander and CEO of Honeywell's subsidiary in the United Kingdom. Completing the management team were Kenneth Jenson, a former executive in the division, and Dean Fjestul, the head of finance for Honeywell Europe. With his management team in place, it came time to choose a new name. (Renier asked that the new company not use the venerable Honeywell name.) The management eventually settled upon the name Alliant Techsystems. This name was based on the word alliance, which they believed accurately described the relationship the new company hoped to maintain with the U.S. Department of Defense.

After a distribution of one Alliant share for every four Honeywell shares, Alliant began business as an independent company in October 1990. It entered the market with a 50-year history, 8,300 employees, and a position as the Pentagon's 17th largest contractor. Its operations were divided into four main units: precision armament, ordnance, marine systems, and information storage systems. At the time of the company's creation, Alliant consisted of two groups, six divisions, and two operations, representing tremendous bureaucracy and redundancy. One of Warson's first actions as chairman was to consolidate the work functions among the company's various fiefdoms and, in the process, to eliminate 800 administrative jobs.

Within months the operation had been streamlined into a manufacturing and materials arm and an engineering and technology center. Sales were handled by four market groups that were organized in the same fashion as the Department of Defense. In another important move, Warson used the company's entire first quarter operating income to pay for Alliant's restructuring costs and to get it operating under lower debt. Still, Alliant was saddled with a $14 million charge for legal and administrative costs, $30 million in severance payments, a $165 million loan from Honeywell, and a $60 million dividend payment to Honeywell. This brought the new company's debt-to-equity ratio to a precarious 1.4 to one.

Effect of the Persian Gulf War on Sales

With 1989 earnings of $53.8 million on sales of $1.14 billion, it seemed that Alliant was off to a difficult start. But the company gained its independence only three months after the Iraqi invasion of Kuwait. Suddenly, the dynamics of Pentagon work changed drastically. The invasion, coupled with the evaporation of the Soviet military threat because of the collapse of communism, forced U.S. military strategists to focus their combat planning on a new type of enemy, the well-armed third world dictator. Battling this type of opponent did not require nuclear weapons or new weapons platforms.

With the demise of the Soviet military machine, the administration of George Bush increasingly turned to lower-cost improvements in existing weapons systems, those necessary to battle armies such as Iraq's. Alliant was perfectly suited for this approach to modernization. In 1990 Warson told *Industry Week,* ''If you look at the U.S. defense budget, it's clear that the major new weapons systems—for instance the B-2 bomber, the advanced tactical fighters, new tanks and submarines—are in trouble. The Pentagon is looking for ways to enhance existing systems and to improve the performance of the individual soldier. And that's the market we're in.''

Warson noted that budget constraints were likely to preclude the Army from replacing its aging Abrams tanks. Instead, he suggested that the Pentagon would opt to upgrade the weapons by equipping them with the new 120mm ammunition that Alliant made. By and large, the company's products were cheap and effective, and because ammunition, a large part of Alliant's production, had to be continually replaced, the company was assured of a more stable market than airplane, rocket, and submarine builders could enjoy.

As the confrontation in Kuwait became a shooting war and Operation Desert Shield was transformed into Desert Storm, more than 1,300 Alliant workers represented by the Teamsters went out on strike in a dispute over wages, benefits, and the term of another contract. These workers, who manufactured 25mm shells for the Bradley Fighting Vehicle, were quickly replaced by managers struggling to keep production running.

The strike, a notably unpopular one because of the timing, was short-lived, however, as both sides managed to resolve the dispute. Alliant served the war effort well, turning out 120mm uranium-tipped antitank shells, 30mm bullets for the A-10 Warthog and Apache helicopter, and a variety of other ordnance. In addition, Alliant was the sole manufacturer of MK 46 and MK 50 antisubmarine torpedoes, although none were employed during the war.

Alliant continued to gain momentum after the Gulf War was over. Warson carried out a successive wave of consolidations, mostly within the management ranks, dropping a further 800 employees by October 1991. In addition, the number of layers of management was cut from 14 to seven. This enabled the company to compete more efficiently for the dwindling number of Pentagon contracts for new weapons systems.

The one weak spot in Alliant's organization was the company's Metrum Information Storage division. Metrum, Alliant's only nonmunitions unit, manufactured data recording and storage devices. While half of Metrum's sales were to commercial customers, the unit suffered from numerous production setbacks that forced the company to write off millions of dollars. The Metrum division was eventually sold. Still, by 1992 Warson had made tremendous progress in clearing up Alliant's balance sheet. With a manageable debt of $148 million and interest payments under control, it was expected that Alliant would work its debt off the books by 1994.

With a strong financial position, Warson hoped to broaden Alliant's markets by acquiring another company or establishing a joint venture. His first effort in this direction met a swift rebuke. Warson proposed merging the ordnance division of Stamford, Connecticut-based Olin Corporation into those of Alliant, and he had even sealed the $68 million agreement when the U.S. Federal Trade Commission became involved, opposing the sale on the basis that the combination would leave the Pentagon with only one supplier of specialized munitions.

Warson and his colleagues at Olin argued that the market could support only one manufacturer. Far from conspiring to gouge the Pentagon with monopoly pricing, Warson argued that, by preventing the two companies from realizing economies of scale under reduced orders, the Pentagon would in fact be shelling out more for its ammunition. Despite gaining the support of the army for its case, Alliant called off the proposed merger in December 1992.

A New Business Plan for the 1990s

Because the company's business was heavily dependent on military contracts, the continuing decrease in the size of the U.S. defense budget posed a threat to Alliant's profitability. Between 1985 and 1993 the U.S. weapons-procurement budget plummeted by more than half, and further cuts loomed in the future. ''It's important that we manage our business to the realities of the marketplace during this period of rapid change in the defense industry,'' Warson told the *Wall Street Journal* on January 28, 1993. To reduce costs, Alliant shed another 1,700 employees in 1993, dropping the company's total below 4,000. Alliant also scaled back production of its Adam land mine, disposal AT-4 infantry weapon, and MK 46 torpedo. With the savings from these curtailed operations, Alliant hoped to raise profit margins to offset the impact of declining sales, which dropped from $1.1 billion in 1992 to $800 million in 1993.

Alliant ultimately recognized that its continued survival would require strategic shifts as well as organizational restructuring. As the July 13, 1994, *Wall Street Journal* explained, Alliant strove to gain ''entry into new markets'' instead of relying for business predominantly on waning government procurement contracts. In 1993, for instance, Alliant formed a joint venture with the Ukrainian government to dismantle stockpiles of munitions left over from the Soviet Union. In this way the company sought to apply its substantial expertise in munitions handling to an arena that was not dependent on the Pentagon's budget.

As a further effort to widen the scope of its business, Alliant acquired the aerospace division of Hercules Inc. in July 1994. The aerospace operations of Delaware-based Hercules produced rocket motors for space launch and strategic nuclear missiles. This market segment was a new realm for Alliant, but it provided the company with an array of opportunities since the demand for communications satellites was growing rapidly. Such satellites provided mobile telephone services, direct-to-home television feeds, and paging and messaging services. According to the November 10, 1995, *Wall Street Journal,* analysts speculated that more than 350 satellites would be sent into space between 1995 and 2000. Armed with the capacity to manufacture the rocket motors used to launch these satellites—which it had gained by purchasing Hercules—Alliant was ideally situated to capitalize on the boom. Nevertheless, to ensure continued profitability, the company cut its workforce by an additional 20 percent (about 700 jobs) in 1995.

Alliant also began to eliminate units that did not conform to its new strategy. In December 1996 the company sold its Marine Systems Groups—which produced torpedoes, mine-detection equipment, and other naval weaponry—to General Motors' Hughes Electronics. The move enabled Alliant to reduce its debt by an additional $89 million and to concentrate more fully on its profitable rocket technology.

Alliant instituted other changes as well. Instead of continuing to compete head-on with defense industry giants such as Boeing and Raytheon, Alliant began to forge partnerships with them. In June 1995, for example, Alliant was awarded a multi-million-dollar contract from the McDonnell Douglas Corporation to produce solid rocket propulsion systems for the Delta III space launch vehicle. In addition to its 1997 contract with the Lockheed Martin Corp. to manufacture a component of the F-22 Raptor fighter jet, Alliant received a long-term contract from the Boeing Co. in June 1998—worth $750 million—to manufacture solid rocket boosters for Boeing's Delta space launch vehicles.

Of course, Alliant did not abandon its lucrative position in the munitions industry. While the end of the cold war had changed the needs of the U.S. military, the outbreak of bloody regional conflicts in the former Yugoslavia and in various parts of Africa underscored the importance of basic munitions. With the U.S. Congress reluctant to devote vast sums to develop entirely new weapons platforms, the Department of Defense focused heavily on upgrading the capabilities of existing ammunition and electronic warfare and surveillance systems. Alliant strove to meet these needs. The company's low-cost mortar and artillery fuses led the field, and Alliant was also the sole provider of VOLCANO and Shielder antitank systems.

Alliant's strategy of creating new markets while simultaneously bolstering its existing sectors proved to be successful. After a dismal year in 1995, in which Alliant's net income dropped as a result of restructuring charges, the company's sales and profits rose in 1996 and 1997. In 1998 Alliant's net income rose, and the ratio of its total debt to capitalization declined. Sales in 1999 grew 1.4 percent to reach $1.09 billion.

Even more telling was the tectonic shift in Alliant's commercial-to-military sales ratio. In 1995 three percent of Alliant's sales were to commercial clients, with the remaining 97 percent going to the military. Fueled by its burgeoning aerospace sector, 16 percent of Alliant's sales were to commercial clients by 1999, with 84 percent to the military. With a new chairman and CEO in place by January 1999, Alliant's future looked hopeful. Paul David Miller, the company's chief, assured stockholders that Alliant's defense business would remain stable and that its role in solid propulsion would continue to expand.

Further Reading

''Alliant to Cut 30% of Work Force; Posts Loss of $90 Million,'' *Wall Street Journal,* January 28, 1993, p. B4.

''At Military Contractor, Strikers Face Winter's Chill and Neighbors' Wrath,'' *New York Times,* February 16, 1991, p. 10.

Cole, Jeff, ''Re-Entry Mission: U.S. Rocket Makers Rely on Foreign Rivals for New Shot at Space,'' *Wall Street Journal*, November 10, 1995.

''FTC Seeks to Block Merger of Defense Firms,'' *Washington Post,* November 7, 1992, p. C1.

''Honeywell Board OKs Spin-Off of Defense Units,'' *Electronic News,* October 1, 1990, p. 6.

''Honeywell Defense Business Can't Find Buyer; Spin-off Set,'' *Electronic News,* July 30, 1990, p. 27.

''Linkage Plan of Olin, Alliant Is Called Off,'' *Wall Street Journal,* December 9, 1992, p. A4.

Miller, James, ''Alliant Techsystems to Pay $465 Million for Hercules Inc.'s Aerospace Business,'' *Wall Street Journal*, July 13, 1994.

''Precision Pick on Target,'' *Barron's,* June 17, 1991, pp. 44–45.

''Sink or Swim,'' *Forbes,* October 14, 1991, pp. 66–71.

''Toby Warson Dives for Profits,'' *Industry Week,* December 3, 1990, pp. 35–38.

—John Simley
—updated by Rebecca Stanfel

Alltrista Corporation

5875 Castle Creek Parkway, North Drive
Suite 440
Indianapolis, Indiana 46250-4330
U.S.A.
(317) 577-5000
Fax: (317) 577-5001
Web site: http://www.alltrista.com

Public Company
Incorporated: 1993
Employees: 2,000
Sales: $244.04 million (1998)
Stock Exchanges: New York
Ticker Symbol: ALC
NAIC: 326113 Unsupported Plastics Film & Sheet
   Manufacturing; 326199 All Other Plastics Product
   Manufacturing; 327213 Glass Container Manufac-
   turing; 331491 Nonferrous Metal Rolling, Drawing, &
   Extruding; 332115 Crown & Closure Manufacturing

Alltrista Corporation was previously a wholly owned subsidiary of Ball Corporation, which spun it off in 1993. The
company is a manufacturer of plastic and metal products, serving both industrial and consumer markets. Approximately 42
percent of Alltrista's sales derive from its plastics segment,
which produces thermoformed and injection-molded plastic
components. Alltrista's plastics subsidiaries serve a wide range
of markets, including automotive, appliance, manufactured
housing, recreational vehicle, healthcare, heavy trucking, agricultural, material handling, and electronics. The company's
metal products segment consists of two distinct divisions: consumer products and zinc products. Through its consumer products operation, Alltrista manufactures and markets several well-
known lines of home canning products, including Ball and Kerr.
Through its zinc operation, the company is the primary supplier
of zinc penny blanks to the U.S. and Royal Canadian Mints. It
also supplies zinc strip and other zinc products to various
industrial markets.

Under Ball Ownership: 1880–1993

Although Alltrista has only existed as a corporate entity
since 1993, its roots run all the way back to the late 1800s and
the inception of the Wooden Jacket Can Company. The
Wooden Jacket Can Company was founded in 1880 by five
brothers in Buffalo, New York, to produce and sell wood-
jacketed tin containers to hold paint, varnishes, and kerosene.
Eventually, however, their product evolved into tin-jacketed
glass containers, and the brothers—whose surname was Ball—
rechristened the company the Ball Brothers Glass Manufacturing Company. In 1884 the Ball brothers learned that the patent
for sealed glass home canning jars, which had been held by John
Mason, had expired. They began producing their own version of
the jars, imprinted with the Ball name.

In 1887 the brothers moved their jar business to Muncie,
Indiana. In the late 1880s, Indiana was in the middle of a natural
gas boom—which made it an excellent location for Ball, whose
glassmaking operation required great quantities of gas. Soon
after the move, Ball began expanding its business by acquiring
other small companies, including a zinc mill, a rubber manufacturing plant, and a paper packaging operation. The company
continued to expand into the 1900s, further diversifying by
acquiring a metal beverage container company, an aerospace
research firm, a petroleum equipment maker, and a telecommunications division. By the middle of the 1980s, Ball Corporation
had annual sales of more than $1 billion.

In the early 1990s, Ball's management began assessing its
large and extremely diverse portfolio of businesses to determine
what direction the company should take. Its decision was to
focus on its larger businesses and to shed smaller subsidiaries.
The company established Alltrista Corporation, containing the
assets of seven of these smaller subsidiaries. Alltrista was spun
off in early April 1993, giving Ball shareholders one share of
Alltrista stock for every four shares of Ball stock. The company
began trading on the NASDAQ under the ticker JARS.

A New Old Company: 1993

Headquartered in Muncie, the newly formed Alltrista consisted of seven diverse businesses, some of which were more than

Company Perspectives:

Alltrista's vision is a growing, diversified company with businesses that command a leading market position or possess other differentiating characteristics that consistently create value for shareholders, employees, and customers. All resource allocation decisions are focused on this vision.

100 years old. The oldest was the Consumer Products Company, which consisted of the original Ball jar business along with a line of other canning-related products. Despite the corporate name change, Alltrista continued to use the well-known Ball script trademark on its canning products. Another of Alltrista's century-old businesses was the Zinc Products Company, which first produced zinc caps for Ball's canning jars in the 1880s. At the time of the Alltrista spinoff, Zinc Products was a major manufacturer of the zinc penny blanks used to make U.S. pennies. In addition, the company made battery cans, automotive trim, electrical fuse strip, and architectural materials.

Alltrista also held three plastics businesses: Industrial Plastics Company, Unimark Plastics Company, and Plastic Packaging Company. Industrial Plastics manufactured heavy-gauge thermoplastic sheet and thermoformed products, such as molded inner door liners for refrigerators. Unimark Plastics Company, which Ball had purchased in 1978, was a custom injection molder that sold mainly to the medical and consumer products markets. The Plastic Packaging Company produced plastic sheet and containers for use in the food processing industry. Its plastic products featured barrier layers that reduced the oxygen and moisture that could pass through them—making them ideal for shelf-stable, aseptic food packaging applications.

The last two companies in Alltrista's portfolio were its Metal Services Company and The LumenX Company. Metal Services Company was a metal decorating operation that manufactured thin-gauge metal containers for various consumer products, such as canned goods. Alltrista's LumenX Company, which Ball had acquired in the late 1980s, built customized industrial inspection systems that used x-ray and machine vision technologies. LumenX products were used primarily by the automotive and automotive component industries.

Alltrista's president and CEO was William Peterson, who had for 27 years worked in various administrative capacities for Ball. Its senior vice-president and CFO was Thomas Clark, who had previously been Ball's vice-president for corporate planning and development. All seven of the spun-off subsidiaries retained the same management they had had while still under the Ball umbrella.

Divestitures and Acquisitions: Mid- to Late 1990s

When Alltrista was spun off, it was essentially a collection of companies that Ball no longer wanted. Some were profitable, some were not, and there was little coherence among the businesses or the markets they served. Alltrista's management was faced with the task of analyzing the businesses and deciding how to shape the unwieldy, patchwork-quilt company into a whole and profitable business. Because tax laws prohibited any significant divestitures for two years after the spinoff, the company first determined which areas it wanted to grow.

Its first step was to expand the home canning line. In 1994 Alltrista purchased Toronto, Canada-based Bernardin Ltd. Like Ball Corporation, Bernardin had a rich history in the canning products market; since 1881, the company had been producing metal lids for commercial and home canning containers. Alltrista also acquired the Fruit-Fresh brand product line in 1994. Fruit-Fresh, an agent used in canning and preserving to prevent browning and protect flavor, was marketed through Alltrista's Consumer Products division.

The company further grew its Consumer Products division with the March 1996 acquisition of Kerr Group, Inc., one of Alltrista's main competitors in the home canning products market. After completing the $14.6 million acquisition, Alltrista closed Kerr's manufacturing plant in Jackson, Tennessee, and consolidated its operations into Alltrista's plant in Muncie, Indiana.

The year 1996 also marked the end of the IRS-imposed divestiture moratorium, and Alltrista was ready to prune the weak areas of its portfolio. In April, the company made its first move in this direction with the sale of its Metal Services division. Although Metal Services was Alltrista's largest company in terms of sales, it earned little or no profit. Atop that, it had just lost its largest customer in 1995—which was bound to depress its top line.

In 1997 Alltrista's management turned their attention to expanding the Industrial Plastics division. On May 19, the company purchased the Arkansas-based Viking Industries, a producer of large thermoformed plastic products, such as tubs, showers, surrounds, and whirlpools. Viking's primary markets were the manufactured housing and recreational vehicle industries—new markets for Alltrista. The company believed that both industries, and manufactured housing especially, showed great growth potential. The Viking purchase also dovetailed well with Alltrista's existing plastics operation, creating operational synergies. For example, prior to its acquisition, Viking had relied on outside suppliers for the large plastic sheet it used in its thermoforming operations. Alltrista, however, produced the necessary sheet through its Industrial Plastics division—thereby reducing overall cost and improving efficiency.

According to Thomas Clark, who had become Alltrista's CEO in 1995, the sort of operational integration achieved with the Viking purchase was likely to be a hallmark of future acquisitions. ''In the past we have looked at the three plastics businesses as separate organizations and separate activities,'' he said in a December 1997 interview with the *Wall Street Corporate Reporter*. ''We will tend to take a more integrated view in the future.''

The year 1997 also marked Alltrista's second divestiture, when the company sold the line of machine vision inspection equipment produced by its LumenX subsidiary. The following year, the company exited the LumenX business altogether, when it sold the subsidiary's remaining product line—x-ray inspection equipment. Alltrista also initiated plans to close down an unprofitable plastics plant located in Puerto Rico.

Alltrista ended 1997 with net sales of $255.2 million—a 10.8 percent increase over the previous year—and a net profit of $14.8 million. The increase in total sales was primarily attributable to the Kerr and Viking acquisitions within Alltrista's food containers and Industrial Plastics businesses: sales of food containers grew by 39 percent, while Industrial Plastics' sales showed a 62 percent gain. As the year's final milestone, Alltrista moved from the NASDAQ to the New York Stock Exchange on December 31, trading under the ticker ALC.

New Vision: 1998

Alltrista marked its fifth anniversary as an independent company in 1998 by redefining its vision, strategy, and growth goals. The company set its sights high, aiming for $500 million in sales and $50 million in operating earnings by the year 2002. To meet this ambitious goal, Alltrista—which had grown an average of seven percent yearly since the spinoff—would have to double its growth rate in the ensuing years. The new company vision brought with it various other changes. Alltrista reorganized its business into two distinct segments: metal products and plastic products. The metals segment included the zinc operation and the consumer products division, including the home canning products business. Group vice-presidents were named to oversee the two segments.

To help drive growth, Alltrista began seeking new opportunities for its metals division. Already the primary supplier of one-cent zinc blanks to both the U.S. and Royal Canadian Mints, the company tapped European markets in 1998. One of its earliest wins was a three-year contract to supply the Birmingham Mint in Britain with 55 metric tons of zinc blanks for the new unified Euro coins. Alltrista also initiated negotiations with mints in Poland and South Korea to supply blanks for their coins.

The company looked to overseas markets to boost sales of its home canning lines as well. It began preparing to test market its canning jars in Hungary, with the plan to expand into Poland and the Czech Republic if Hungarian sales were promising. Because home canning was far more prevalent in Eastern Europe than in the United States, Alltrista believed that the targeted markets had tremendous growth potential. The home canning products business also expanded its U.S. and Canadian product lines in 1998, introducing a decorative "elite" line of canning jars and closures. In addition, the company added a new housewares line—called Golden Harvest—which included tumblers and other glassware products.

In September 1998, Alltrista moved its corporate headquarters from Muncie to Indianapolis, Indiana. According to Clark, the main impetus behind the relocation was the need to be near a major airport as the company grew more geographically far-flung. Alltrista did not bring its manufacturing business with it to Indianapolis; both the consumer products and plastic packaging operations remained in Muncie.

Triangle Plastics Acquisition: 1999

In March 1999, the company proved itself serious about achieving its growth goal when it announced plans to purchase Triangle Plastics Inc. for $148 million. Triangle was an Iowa-based thermoforming company with 1998 sales of $114 million, a growth rate of around 15 percent, five production facilities, and 1,100 employees. It produced heavy-gauge components for a whole slew of industries, several of which were new to Alltrista. Through its subsidiary, TriEnda Corp., Triangle also manufactured thermoformed materials-handling products, such as plastic pallets. TriEnda—which contributed around 40 percent of Triangle's total sales—had a customer base that included the U.S. Postal Service, and grocery, printing, textile, chemical, and pharmaceutical companies. Alltrista planned to consolidate Triangle's five production facilities with its own plastics group.

The Triangle acquisition, which was completed in late April 1999, made Alltrista the largest industrial thermoformer in North America. It also stood the company in good stead as it worked to quicken its growth rate. "Triangle Plastics is a key step in achieving our goal to grow our company to $500 million in sales with $50 million in operating earnings by the year 2002," Clark said in a March 15, 1999 press release. "To meet this goal we must grow by 15 percent annually, and the Triangle Plastics business fits this criteria." The scope of the Triangle acquisition made investors edgy, however; the company's stock dropped 16 percent in the two weeks after Alltrista announced the purchase.

In May, Alltrista announced that it planned to sell its plastics packaging business to a Missouri-based maker of sheet plastic. As Alltrista positioned its plastics segment to grow in the areas of thermoforming and injection molding, the packaging division—which used different manufacturing processes and served a different market—was no longer a good fit. The division, which had 1998 sales of $28 million, was sold for approximately $30 million.

Looking Ahead

As the 1990s wound down, Alltrista geared up for substantial growth in the new century. The company's main area of focus was expected to be its plastics division, where it planned to add capabilities and new markets to its portfolio by way of both acquisition and internal growth. One potential area of growth in the plastics segment was an expanded geographic coverage, which would allow Alltrista to serve a wider customer base. Another likely rapid growth area was the company's newly acquired Triangle Plastics subsidiary, TriEnda. Alltrista's management believed that there was a growing and largely untapped market for TriEnda's main product—thermoformed plastic pallets for materials handling. In a March 15, 1999 press release, Clark said that only in recent years have plastics begun to displace wood and corrugated packaging and pallets. Noting that plastic pallets account for only four to six percent of the U.S. market, he said, "We are at an early point of plastics penetrating this market, therefore growth opportunities should be significant."

Alltrista also anticipated increased sales in its zinc products division. Part of that growth was likely to be driven by a higher demand for U.S. penny blanks, as well as a continued demand for blanks used to produce the Euro one-cent and five-cent coins. Another avenue of growth in the zinc business was the increasing substitution of zinc for other materials in various industrial applications. The company's sales of battery cans, however, was likely to decline greatly in the coming years, as two of its main buyers of the cans decided to relocate their operations to foreign companies.

Principal Subsidiaries

Consumer Products Company; Bernardin of Canada, Ltd.; Industrial Plastics Company; Triangle Plastics Inc.; TriEnda Corp.; Unimark Plastics Company; Zinc Products Company.

Further Reading

"Alltrista Corporation Launches Expansion Drive; Will Acquire Triangle Plastics Inc.," *PR Newswire,* March 15, 1999.
Jefferson, Greg, "Alltrista Gets Legs," *Indiana Business Journal,* March 29–April 4, 1999.
Koenig, Bill, "Plastic, Metal Products Maker Alltrista Opens Indianapolis Headquarters," *Indianapolis Star and News,* September 15, 1998.
Lauzon, Michael, "Alltrista Corp. Acquiring Triangle," *Plastics News,* March 22, 1999, p. 1.
"President & CEO of Alltrista," *Wall Street Corporate Reporter,* December 2, 1997.

—Shawna Brynildssen

American Banknote Corporation

200 Park Ave., 49th Fl.
New York, New York 10166-4999
U.S.A.
(212) 557-9100
Fax: (212) 338-0740

Public Company
Founded: 1795 as American Bank Note Company
Employees: 3,390
Sales: $336.6 million (1997)
Stock Exchanges: New York
Ticker Symbol: ABN
NAIC: 323110 Commercial Lithographic Printing;
323119 Credit & Identification Card Imprinting,
Embossing, & Encoding

American Banknote Corporation is a holding company with subsidiaries in the United States, Brazil, Australia, New Zealand, and France. Through these, it helps make cashless shopping, banking, and electronic commerce easier and more secure with its transaction cards and systems such as "smart" cards, stored value cards, and credit cards. The company is also one of the world's largest printers of security documents including checks, passports, stock certificates, food stamps, and foreign currency, and it provides printing and storage services for government and private sector organizations. Nearly 75 percent of its sales occur in foreign markets.

In the Beginning: 1795–1968

The two companies that merged to create American Banknote Corporation in 1990, International Banknote and U.S. Banknote Company L.P., could each trace its roots to an early printing company. When the United States was established, the individual states and private banks were responsible for printing currency and stamps. American Bank Note Company, founded in New York in 1795, printed bank notes and stamps for many of the states as well as for private banks. It was not until 1862

that the federal government took over the job of producing money, and American Bank Note soon was printing U.S. currency in denominations of ones, tens, twenties, fifties, and hundreds.

When the United States began printing its own money, American Bank Note had to find other customers. By the end of the century, the company was supplying bank notes for 48 countries, and was also printing stock certificates, bonds, and checks, including the new "traveler's checks" introduced by American Express Company in 1891. The second early predecessor, U.S. Banknote, was founded in New York in 1884, and was soon printing similar types of products.

American Bank Note is credited with introducing a now familiar term to the paper industry. It bought most of its paper for certificates and bonds from Crane & Co., Inc., and liking the texture of the latter, sent Crane an order for "more of that bond paper," to use for its letterhead.

International Banknote on the Scene: 1968–88

In 1968 another player entered the picture. That year, Edward Weitzen became president of B.T. Babbitt, Inc., a nearly bankrupt conglomerate with more than 15 different parts. Incorporated in 1925, B.T. Babbitt had begun as a seller of cleaning products. Weitzen changed the company's name to B.T.B. Corp. and decided to focus on specialty printing. A year later, he acquired American Bank Note Company.

In 1972 Weitzen changed the company's name again, to International Banknote Company Inc., with American Bank Note as its principal subsidiary. He undertook a $55 million capital spending program and by 1981 he had cut long-term debt nearly in half. Its 15 printing plants produced currency for some 70 countries, as well as food stamps for the U.S. government, traveler's checks, airline tickets, stock and bond certificates, driver's licenses, and birth certificates.

The company was also conducting research and development to deter counterfeiting, something it first got involved with in the 19th century when it pioneered using green ink in the printing of money to foil counterfeiters who began using black and white photography.

This time, the company was experimenting with holography, using a technique that created 3-D images by aiming separate laser beams at an object. In the mid-1980s International established American Bank Note Holographics Inc. as a subsidiary of American Bank Note. Its first customers included Visa and Mastercard, Hallmark, and National Geographic, with the company producing a 3-D eagle for the cover of the March 1984 issue. The picture, only 300 millionths of a centimeter thick, was the first holograph to appear in a national periodical. By 1988, ABN Holographics represented almost 30 percent of the company's revenues of $81 million, helping the company move into the black after a net loss of $6.7 million in 1987.

United States Banknote: 1970s–88

U.S. Banknote Company's history followed a somewhat similar pattern. By the mid-1970s, it was a subsidiary of GIT Industries, formerly GIT Realty & Mortgage Investors. Partners Morris Weissman and Stanley Kreitman took GIT private, and in 1981, they and another partner bought the whole company. U.S. Banknote continued engraving and printing stock and bond certificates, added food stamps for the U.S. Department of Agriculture, and received a patent for a new way to place tax stamps on cigarette packs in a carton.

The company also experimented with holography, developing the Holoprint in 1982. U.S. Banknote claimed their technique retained more of the image's color and clarity under poor light, and was better than conventional 3-D holographic images.

In 1986 Weissman and Kreitman liquidated and dissolved GIT and concentrated on security printing. U.S. Banknote Company L.P. became a separate entity, which the two men privately owned and managed. They continued to move the company into related markets, including the annual printing of 700 million federal government payroll checks, and the printing of currency for the Dominican Republic and the Seychelles. With the 1989 purchase of the Los Angeles-based Security Printing Division of Jeffries Banknote Company, U.S. Banknote owned four printing facilities and was the largest security printer in North America, with 1988 revenues of $60 million.

New Company Emerging: 1989–90

In 1989 a proxy fight for control of International Banknote's board was averted when International agreed to merge with U.S. Banknote for $104 million. To avoid an antitrust challenge, U.S. Banknote created Banknote Corp. of America, Inc., which it sold to the French security printing firm François-Charles Oberthur Group. This move gave Oberthur entry into the U.S. market, providing some competition for the new giant.

The merger was completed in 1990, creating the United States Banknote Corporation, the second largest security printer in the world, and the only publicly held one in the United States.

Weissman became chairman and CEO of the new company and Kreitman served as president and COO. The stock traded on the American Stock Exchange under the symbol UBK. The new company had manufacturing plants in New York, Philadelphia, Chicago, Los Angeles, and Singapore, and offices in San Francisco, St. Louis, Pittsburgh, Atlanta, Dallas, Cleveland, Boston, and London, England. It dominated the domestic market for travelers checks and food and postage stamps, and produced all the 3-D holograms for Visa, Master Card, and Euro-Card credit cards. Internationally, it also printed currency for several countries, including Malaysia, Haiti, and Venezuela.

Expanding Internationally: 1991–94

In the United States, companies were shifting from stock and bond certificates to computerized ownership records. To counter the resulting annual loss of six to seven percent of Banknote's business, Weissman and Kreitman looked to diversify, particularly with holograms, and by increasing the company's international business. The breakup of the Soviet Union in 1991, and the resulting start-up stock exchanges, offered Banknote new opportunities. The company quickly signed a contract with Lithuania to print 300 million bank notes, followed by a similar agreement with Estonia, and contracts to print stock certificates for the Central Moscow and Kazakhstan stock exchanges.

Banknote also increased its business with the U.S. government, which was contracting out more of its operations. The company was the sole contractor for food coupons, signed a new five-year contract to print U.S. Treasury checks, and won the job of printing the Elvis postage stamp.

Printing foreign currency and certificates was not the only way Banknote expanded internationally. In 1993 the company bought Brazilian security printer Thaomas De La Rue Grafica e Servicos Ltda., for $45 million. The new subsidiary (ABN-Brazil) was Brazil's largest private check printer and the country's top manufacturer of credit and telephone cards. By the end of 1993, Banknote had reincorporated in Delaware and moved from the American Stock Exchange to the New York Stock Exchange.

Meanwhile, its subsidiary American Banknote Holographics was producing more than 500 million holograms per year for its credit card customers, as well as security applications for customers ranging from Microsoft and Lotus (software packaging) to the state of California (drivers' licenses) to Warner Bros. Inc. and D.C. Comics (Batman products) to the People's Republic of China (national identification cards).

In 1994 the company lost its contract to print postage stamps for the U.S. Postal Service, worth about $24 million, as the Postal Service split up its competitively bid stamp procurement contract among a number of companies. However, a month later, Banknote won a new 20-month contract with the U.S. Department of Agriculture worth $83.7 million to continue to print food stamps coupon books and to develop a new food stamp watermark. In April Ronald Glover, from Dun & Bradstreet Information Services and former head of American Express's traveler's check division, was named president and COO. In May, the company completed a private $65 million bond offering, using the proceeds to repay debt and for capital expenditures, acquisitions, and general corporate purposes.

The company had been working with MasterCard International and Visa International to create a holographic magnetic stripe, and that year it introduced its Holomagnetics technology. The patented system featured an optical magnetic strip containing 3-D images of currency signs. Its first use was on Visa International's new "TravelMoney" card pilot. The card allowed users to obtain cash in worldwide currencies from more than 200,000 Visa/PLUS ATMs. Banknote's revenues for 1994 rose to $208 million, but the company was in the red.

An "Old" Name and New Businesses: 1995–97

In June 1995, its bicentennial year, U.S. Banknote changed its name to American Banknote Corporation. "The new name is in recognition of the sweeping changes taking place at the company," Chairman Weissman said, "changes that reflect the fact that we operate under the name American Bank Note throughout the world."

That year, ABN-Brazil acquired Grafica Bradesco, a security printer whose customers included several major banks in Brazil and signed a $105 million contract with Telebras, Brazil's national telephone company, to continue to produce more than 220 million telephone cards.

Banknote also entered the growing electronic benefit transfer business with the purchase of a 24.5 percent share in TransFirst, Inc., which designed and operated Electronic Benefit Transfer (EBT) and Electronic Parent Locator Network (EPLN) systems. EBT allowed people receiving government benefits to get their payments through automated teller machines using special cards. Banknote also acquired 5.5 percent of the outstanding shares of International Verifact Inc., which had more than a 60 percent share of the Canadian electronic debit payment market. Revenues for 1995 dropped slightly to $206 million, and the company was in the red for a second year.

The company continued making international purchases, buying the Leigh-Mardon Security Group, Australia's oldest and largest security printer, for some $95 million. The new acquisition, with 17 locations in Australia and New Zealand, was seen as providing a base for further expansion into the Pacific Rim markets. The company also won a $13 million, three-year contract from Telstra, Australia's national telephone company, to produce smart cards. One potential customer in the region was a consortium of Japanese companies for which American Banknote Holographics was developing cash value cards and the machines to read them to help prevent counterfeit prepaid cards in the pachinko business in Japan. A popular pinball-like game, pachinko was played in some 18,000 parlors, with players using a card to play a game and win money. Meanwhile, ABN-Brazil purchased Menno, that country's second largest manufacturer of credit cards, and paid $8 million for the printing works of Banco Itau. Banknote also moved into France, with the purchase of Sati, a credit card and check personalization company, for $11.6 million.

Bondholders appeared nervous about the company's diversification into various financial services and its concentration on expansion in Brazil, which accounted for 43 percent of sales. When Banknote attempted to restructure its financing in 1997 with a sale of $225 million in bonds, the sale was first postponed and then reduced to about $155 million, since the market showed little interest.

Banknote's huge domestic debt burden was the problem. Its international operations, which brought in nearly 75 percent of revenue, provided higher margins, good growth opportunities, and the cash flow to service the debt. But those same operations also were subject to greater economic and exchange rate volatility, especially in Brazil.

Trying to Raise Money: 1998

According to *Crain's New York Business*, "interest, depreciation and amortization expenses caused losses of $5.3 million in the first quarter of this year and $6.4 million in the last quarter of 1997." Although Banknote continued its international purchases with the acquisition of two card and check personalization companies in France, its big move in 1998 was the sale of American Bank Note Holographics.

Banknote raised $116 million, less than the $120 million it had hoped to make, which it used for debt reduction. Banknote also sold $70 million in notes. "With this successful tender," Weissman stated, "we are de-leveraging the Company, as planned, and continue to take the necessary steps towards enhancing shareholder value, while emphasizing globally our two primary businesses, transaction cards and printing services." That emphasis was underscored as the company expanded its transaction card business in France with the purchase of two companies, which became part of Sati.

1999 to the Present

Early in 1999, the company announced joint ventures with Gemplus of France to make smart cards and the acquisition of Transtex, the leading supplier of transaction cards in Argentina, Chile, Uruguay, and Paraguay. But new problems soon overtook the company's good news. Banknote and Holographics announced they each would have to restate earnings for portions of 1998 (before and after Holographics' IPO) because of questions regarding overstatement of revenues and net income by Holographics.

The disclosure led to at least 20 class-action suits and delayed the filing of annual SEC reports. The two companies were being investigated by independent auditors, the SEC, and the U.S. Attorney's office in New York. Standard & Poor's put Banknote on watch when it failed to meet interest payments to its creditors.

Holographics got a new president, and Weissman was out as chairman and CEO there, although he kept those positions at Banknote. Securities analysts essentially wrote off both companies. The primary question was whether fraud was involved: were the financial statements deliberately inflated to boost the amount of cash generated through the IPO? By June Banknote indicated the problems could go back as far as 1996, long before the spinoff. In August, the New York Stock Exchange suspended trading in shares of both Banknote and Holographics and indicated it would seek to delist the shares of both companies for failure to meet certain listing standards. Banknote continued discussions with its noteholders regarding a restructuring that would convert 85 percent of the company debt to equity.

Principal Subsidiaries

American Bank Note Company; American Bank Note Company Grafica e Servicos Ltda. (77.5%); American Banknote Australasia Holdings, Inc.; Sati Group.

Further Reading

"American Banknote Agrees to Buy Leigh-Mardon Security Group," *PR Newswire*, April 11, 1996.

"American Banknote Corp. Announces Gemplus Smart Card Joint Venture in Brazil," *PR Newswire*, January 13, 1999.

"American Banknote Corp. Announces IPO of American Bank Note Holographics," *PR Newswire*, May 5, 1998.

"American Banknote Corp. Announces $105 Million Contract with Brazil's National Telephone Company," *PR Newswire*, September 7, 1995.

"American Banknote Corp. Announces Trading in Shares to Be Suspended," *Business Wire*, July 20, 1999.

"American Banknote Corp. to Restate Revenues for the Second Quarter of 1998," *PR Newswire*, January 19, 1999.

"American Banknote Gets into Pachinko," *New York Times*, May 24, 1996, p. D8.

"AmBanknote Acquires 5.5 percent of Verifact," *United Press International*, July 10, 1995.

"Antitrust Will Not Challenge Security Printers Transaction, Says Justice," *Business Wire*, December 29, 1989.

Berreby, David, "All About Currency Printers: The Companies That Make Money from Making Money," *New York Times*, August 23, 1992, p. C10.

Dorfman, John R., "Latent Image," *Forbes*, June 21, 1982, p. 70.

"'Holoprint' Deters Forgeries," *U.P.I.*, November 30, 1982.

"International Banknote Agrees to Merger, Avoids Proxy Battle," *Westchester County Business Journal*, May 29, 1989, p. 1.

"International Banknote Holders Approve Merger," *Westchester County Business Journal*, July 30, 1990, p. 1.

Isidore, Chris, "Printer Tries to Update Image, But Costly Plan Pummels Stock," *Crain's New York Business*, July 20, 1998, p. 4.

"It Ain't Just Stamps: Company Carves Niche in Holography," *New York Newsday*, November 4, 1992, p. 109.

Jones, Stacy V., "Way to Put Tax Stamp on Cigarette Packages," *New York Times*, August 4, 1984, p. A30.

Jordan, John, "American Banknote Holographics Expands Its Operations in Elmsford," *Westchester County Business Journal*, October 19, 1992, p. 11.

Kamen, Robin, "A License to Print Litus Boosts a Firm," *Crain's New York Business*, January 27, 1992, p. 4.

Lelyveld, Michael S., "US Banknote Turning Red Square to Green Profit," *Journal of Commerce*, July 29, 1991, p. 1A.

Leuchter, Miriam, "Banknote's Recovery Linked to Foreign Deals," *Crain's New York Business*, January 17, 1994, p. 23.

Murphy, Patricia A., "The Mess at Holographics," *Credit Card Management*, June 1999.

"New Vulture Target: American Banknote," *Mergers & Corporate Policy*, April 1, 1996.

Pierce, Wadsworth R., *The First 176 Years of Crane Papermaking*, North Adams, Mass.: Excelsior Printing Company, 1977.

Piskora, Beth, "U.S. Banknote Buying Part of EBT Firm," *American Banker*, June 6, 1995, p. 24.

"Smart Bits: American Banknote Wins Aussie Phone Card Job," *American Banker*, October 15, 1997, p. 17.

"Stockholders Approve United States Banknote Name Change to American Banknote Corporation," *PR Newswire*, June 13, 1995.

Suplee, Curt, "National Geographic's New Depth," *Washington Post*, March 6, 1984, p. C6.

"United States Banknote Announces Successful Completion of $65 Million Bond Offering," *Business Wire*, May 5, 1994.

"United States Banknote Completes Acquisition of Brazil's Leading Security Printer," *PR Newswire*, June 23, 1993.

"United States Banknote's Brazilian Subsidiary to Acquire Printing Operations of Banco Bradesco," *PR Newswire*, June 5, 1995.

"U.S. Banknote Holomagnetic Technology Featured in Visa 'TravelMoney' Card Pilot," *PR Newswire*, December 2, 1994.

"U.S. Banknote Names Ron K. Glover As President and COO," *Business Wire*, April 6, 1994.

"U.S. Banknote Wins Food Stamp Contract," *Business Wire*, February 7, 1994.

Zweig, Jason, "From Munis to Money," *Forbes*, February 20, 1989, p. 134.

—Ellen D. Wernick

American Standard Companies Inc.

P.O. Box 6820
One Centennial Avenue
Piscataway, New Jersey 08855-6820
U.S.A.
(732) 980-6000
Fax: (732) 980-6118
Web site: http://www.americanstandard.com

Public Company
Incorporated: 1929 as American Radiator & Standard
    Sanitary Corporation
Employees: 57,000
Sales: $6.7 billion (1998)
Stock Exchanges: New York
Ticker Symbol: ASD
NAIC: 332998 Enameled Iron & Metal Sanitary Ware
    Manufacturing; 332913 Plumbing Fixture Fitting &
    Trim Manufacturing; 333415 Air-Conditioning &
    Warm Air Heating Equipment & Commercial &
    Industrial Refrigeration Equipment Manufacturing;
    336211 Motor Vehicle Body Manufacturing; 339112
    Surgical & Medical Instrument Manufacturing

American Standard Companies Inc. has its roots in the 19th century as a manufacturer of plumbing and heating products. It became the world leader in such staple items as toilets and radiators, diversified into a number of unrelated fields, and then gradually returned to its bread-and-butter industries. In the 1990s American Standard had three core businesses: 1) air conditioning products, which it gained through the 1984 acquisition of The Trane Company; 2) plumbing products, which develops and manufactures bathroom and kitchen fixtures and fittings under the brands American Standard, Ideal Standard, Standard, and Porcher; and 3) automotive products, which develops and manufactures commercial utility vehicle braking and control systems under the WABCO and Perrot brand names. Each of its core businesses occupies the number one

or two position in its market. A fourth segment, the Medical Systems Group, was formed in 1997 to focus on new diagnostic technologies.

Early History

The early history of American Standard is bound closely to the figure of Clarence Mott Woolley, born in 1863 to a wealthy Detroit iron manufacturer. Forced to begin working at the age of 15 after the panic of 1873 wiped out his father's fortune, Woolley by 1886 had become a successful salesman of wholesale crockery and had built personal savings of around $5,000, not an insignificant amount of money at that time. After investigating a number of promising businesses, in 1886 Woolley became a partner in the newly formed Michigan Radiator & Iron Company of Detroit, makers of cast iron radiators for residential and commercial heating systems. The cast iron radiator could be made far more cheaply than its steel predecessor, and Woolley correctly predicted that its advent would mark the beginning of the age of radiant heat.

In 1891 Michigan Radiator merged with the two other leading manufacturers of cast iron radiators, Detroit Radiator Company and the Pierce Steam Heating Company of Buffalo, New York. The merger was an early example of business consolidation and created a firm with yearly net income of $300,000 and a capital base of $8 million. As secretary and head of sales for the new American Radiator, Clarence Woolley, then only 28, soon proved himself an invaluable and tireless promoter of the company's patented advances in radiant heat. An economic downturn, however, nearly snuffed out the new business in the 1890s. As the Depression of the mid-1890s deepened, Woolley recommended pursuing sales contacts he had made with foreign buyers at the 1893 Chicago World's Fair. In 1894 he took the highly unusual step of traveling to Europe to peddle American Radiator products, and, much to the surprise of his skeptical fellow officers, came home with a suitcase full of orders. Thirty train carloads of American Radiator heaters were installed in the new Swiss capital building, and other major orders soon followed. The injection of fresh business kept American alive through the depression's worst years and helped create the company's strong European presence. Over the next 30 years, American added production facilities in many of the major European markets, and by the 1920s about 40 percent of its revenue was generated overseas.

Prospered Under Woolley's Leadership: 1900–20s

In 1902, at age 39, Clarence Woolley was named president of American Radiator. From that date until Woolley's retirement in 1938, American Radiator dominated the world heating market by carefully exploiting four basic strengths, as *Fortune* reported in April 1935. The first was the company's sizable technological lead in cast iron equipment. Although its originally exclusive patents eventually expired, American's head start and great size made it a fearsome competitor. In addition, Woolley saw to it that American spent lavishly on research and development—the second of the firm's strengths. With far more capital than its nearest pursuers, American could afford to maintain its technical advantages even without the benefit of exclusive patents.

The company's two other valuable resources were both vested in Woolley himself. By all accounts, Woolley was a consummate industrial salesman, able to drink with plumbers and sweet-talk corporate executives over dinner. American's sales depended on the support of the master plumbers and builders, who both bought and installed heating systems across the country, and Woolley's sales force knew the concerns and complaints of these men inside out. American's fourth great strength was its president's ability to forecast economic conditions, especially recessions. In 1907, for example, Woolley correctly deduced from soaring raw material prices the imminent arrival of another panic, and kept American's inventories at near-zero levels to avoid having bulging warehouses in a dead economy. In 1915 he laid in an enormous stock of pig iron just before World War I drove up iron prices. It is estimated that this maneuver alone netted American some $2.5 million in savings.

The post-World War I boom economy pushed American's income to around $10 million annually. Flush with success, Woolley built a spectacular new Manhattan headquarters for American; its black brick and gold roof quickly distinguished it as an architectural landmark. Just before the Depression, Woolley planned a merger for American, one that would have been a colossal achievement even in that merger-mad era. His plan was to unite four of the largest building products corporations in the country—H.W. Johns-Manville, Otis Elevator, Standard Sanitary, and American Radiator—into a single immense powerhouse, its unified sales force able to offer the contracting cus-

tomer nearly everything needed. Woolley, however, was able to come to terms only with the Pittsburgh-based Standard Sanitary, the nation's leading supplier of plumbing products. By mid-1929, the merger was concluded; American Radiator & Standard Sanitary Corporation (ARSS) finished that year with income of more than $20 million on sales of $187 million, as well as strong cash reserves with which to face the suddenly grim economic scene.

The Great Depression: 1930s

The Great Depression brought new construction to a dead stop, ruining Woolley's plans for a new conglomerate. The anticipated big profits became big losses. In 1932 ARSS lost $6 million—easily the worst year in the company's history. Although the firm had begun to break even by 1935, it was clear that all was not right in the black and gold tower. The 20-odd companies brought together by the 1929 merger had never been properly consolidated, and antagonism between the American and the Standard affiliates was growing. Friction became such that when one American outfit decided to build a warehouse next to a Standard facility, the latter promptly erected a fence around its property and forced American to put in a separate driveway for its own use.

The hostility was aggravated by American's failure to hold up its end of the sales and profit agreement. American's radiator sales were being seriously challenged by the new forced-air-furnace technique, and what little profit the company managed to make was generated in large part by its numerous European subsidiaries. The company's overall lack of coordination eventually culminated in a confrontation between Woolley and Standard President Henry M. Reed, who pressed the 75-year-old Woolley to step down as chairman of the combined companies. Finally, in 1938, Woolley agreed, and Henry Reed became the new chief executive.

Reed wasted no time in simplifying ARSS's tangled structure. He cut its 25 operating subsidiaries to 12. Top management underwent a similarly drastic winnowing. With a newly unified sales force, American's performance was on the upswing until the outbreak of World War II in Europe, an event that presented a new set of problems. American had always relied on its strong and highly profitable European division for a disproportionate amount of its net income, but with Europe at war, the fate of American's 16 overseas plants was suddenly in doubt. In addition, American's domestic operations were suffering as a result of the growing popularity of ''direct-to-you'' stores, which bought plumbing and heating products in bulk and resold them directly to the consumer. Although direct retailing is now a standard practice, in the late 1930s it caused bitter controversy for those tradesmen and manufacturers who had a vested interest in the older system, in which all equipment was bought and installed by craftsmen. As the nation's largest such manufacturer, ARSS was naturally concerned about this potentially momentous change in its customer mix.

As events unfolded, however, neither World War II nor the direct-to-you stores slowed American's subsequent growth. The company suffered keenly from several years of lost European sales, but, at war's end, the European affiliates were able to reassume their former dominance quickly. As for the direct stores, American generally stuck by its network of plumber-contractors, who did not fare as poorly as some had predicted. American also began to manufacture forced-air heating systems. Over many years, the company wound down its radiator-based business while adding additional forced-air capacity—and its natural counterpart, air conditioning.

Disappointing Performance After Postwar Prosperity: 1945–60

The post-World War II U.S. economy carried building products companies along with it. With the suburbs burgeoning and mortgages easily obtainable, the U.S. construction industry threw up record numbers of new homes across the country, each in need of plumbing and heating fixtures, supplied by ARSS. By the mid-1950s, ARSS was pushing $400 million in worldwide sales and continuing to score steady, if modest, profits. Around 1957, however, American entered a ten-year period of disappointing performance. Affected by rising raw material prices and a strongly unionized labor force, American's earnings per share and dividends drifted downward. From 1955 to 1960 domestic sales at ARSS earned a thin two percent on the dollar. The bulk of corporate profits again were being provided by the company's 20 European plants, which faced a less competitive market than U.S. operations.

Diversification and Expansion: 1960s

Around 1963 ARSS began a program of diversification that would occupy it for the next 15 years. By 1963, in addition to its traditional heating and plumbing lines, the company had branched into industrial controls, plastics, heat-transfer equipment, and nuclear reactor construction. This flurry of activity produced modest results, however; in 1965 sales of $553 million were only marginally higher than they had been in the late 1950s, and profit remained unacceptably low at three percent.

As a result two potential merger partners backed off after concluding that ARSS was too weak to purchase. The most serious of these suitors was Boise Cascade. One of that company's executive vice-presidents, William D. Eberle, joined ARSS as its new president in 1966 and proceeded to turn the company around. In three years, Eberle more than doubled sales while decreasing the company's dependence on the housing market by means of several major acquisitions. American bought Mosler Safe, a maker of security devices for the banking industry; Westinghouse Air Brake Company, a diversified manufacturer of equipment for the railroad, construction, and mining businesses; and William Lyon Homes, a California home builder. Eberle also changed the company's name to American Standard to indicate its movement away from the heating and plumbing niche.

Cutbacks Improved Earnings: 1970s

By 1971 American Standard's sales reached $1.4 billion, its employees numbered some 70,000, and industry analysts judged Eberle's work a mess. By quickly expanding, Eberle had indeed reduced American's dependence on the housing business, but at the cost of massive new debts, a confusing overlay of unrelated businesses, and plummeting earnings. In 1971

Eberle was shuffled out, and his successor, William Marquard, set aside $100 million on the balance sheet to defray the expected cost of undoing Eberle's work. Marquard shut down inefficient plants, reduced employment by 20 percent, and sold off a number of the more extraneous divisions, using the proceeds to reduce debt and raise earnings. Marquard went further, however, easing American out of its original heating business while developing its railroad, truck brake, and mining equipment operations. By keeping only those companies that were efficient and profitable, Marquard built a far sturdier, more lucrative business. Although total sales remained steady at $1.6 billion for much of the decade, earnings per share skyrocketed from 1971's $.11 to $5.25 in 1977.

Strengthened Core Businesses: 1980s

American was not yet finished with its housecleaning. During the 1980s the company completed its long retreat from Eberle's diversified conglomerate to position itself as a relatively simple manufacturer of plumbing and air conditioning products. Under Chairman and CEO William Boyd, American Standard sold the Mosler security business and the various transportation companies. Though generally profitable, these outfits did not mesh well with American's core businesses. American Standard's only major acquisition during the 1980s did mesh, however. In 1983 American Standard purchased The Trane Company, the largest commercial air conditioning products company in the United States. With $833 million in sales, Trane made up some of the volume American Standard had lost to reorganization. By 1988 the once heterogeneous mix of companies at American Standard had been boiled down to three basic businesses: plumbing, air conditioning, and railway brake systems, together producing sales of about $3.4 billion.

Operated As a Private Company: 1988–95

In the October 1987 market crash, American Standard's shares plunged to $35.25. That was when power tool manufacturer Black & Decker began its attempted hostile takeover, eventually making a tender offer of $56 per share in January 1988. After an attempted poison pill defense failed, American Standard was available to the highest bidder. Kelso & Co., an investment banking firm with ties to American Standard's management, bid $78 a share, or 18.6 times American Standard's 1987 earnings. It bought the company in April 1988 in a $3.2 billion leveraged buyout (LBO). Kelso formed ASI Holding Corporation to acquire and merge with American Standard. Egyptian-born Emmanuel Kampouris was named CEO. ASI would change its name to American Standard Companies, Inc. in 1994.

Following the LBO, American Standard's long-term debt amounted to $2.7 billion, nearly 90 percent of the firm's total capital. Kelso supplied $180 million of the firm's equity capital for a 72 percent ownership share. A newly created ESOP (employee stock ownership plan) contributed $50 million, and the remaining $20 million came from 20 of American Standard's officers.

Numerous restrictions were placed on American Standard's ability to raise capital and sell assets. It was saddled with more than $250 million in annual interest payments, which would shrink earnings and possibly push the company into default if there was an economic downturn. To ease the foreign tax burden, about one-third of the LBO debt was placed in heavily taxed countries abroad.

Needing cash, the company was forced to sell its 64-year-old headquarters building in Manhattan for $43 million in August 1988. The company had to raise money to cover $500 million in debt due within two years, not to mention $1.55 billion that had to be repaid within eight years. In June 1988 the company floated an $825 million junk bond offering. It was clear that American Standard's operations would not be sufficient to service the firm's debt. Interest and amortization payments amounted to $325 million a year.

In addition to selling its headquarters building, American Standard was selling several of its businesses. A railway signal business was sold for $105 million. The company's Steelcraft steel door business was being sold for more than $100 million. The railway braking products unit was sold in 1990. Tyler Refrigeration, the number two maker of frozen food display cases, was sold in 1991 to Kelso and a group of Tyler executives. Other businesses were also on the block.

American Standard sought to curb its cyclicality. Periodic recessions affected its bathroom fixture and steel door sales, and the railcar brake and signaling business was coming off a six-year streak of losses. ASI reduced the cyclicality of some of its businesses so it would be less affected by economic downturns. Notably, Trane gained strength in Europe and fortified its replacement business. A new line of color-coordinated luxury bathtubs, bidets, and toilets was also less dependent on new housing starts. Finally, the firm cut factory capacity in its depressed railcar brake business before selling it. In its advertising, ASI appealed to baby boomers who were interested in improving their kitchens and bathrooms at home.

In 1990 American Standard began improving all of its manufacturing processes through Total Quality Management (TQM) and something it called ''demand flow manufacturing.'' Instead of producing in long runs and large batches, demand flow manufacturing lines created a variety of items each day, keyed to direct customer orders. TQM was customer- and employee-oriented. TQM helped American Standard cut its inventories of both finished goods and raw materials, which helped improve the firm's cash position and reduce its dependency on working capital. With the help of Chemical Bank, American Standard undertook a $1 billion refinancing program in 1993. Proceeds from the planned sale of senior subordinated notes and discount debentures would be used to retire higher-cost junk bonds.

All three of American Standard's businesses were weakened by economic conditions in the early 1990s. A U.S. construction slump cut into sales of air conditioners and bathroom fixtures. A European recession affected the company's largest automotive market for its truck and bus brakes.

American Standard's demand flow manufacturing technique enabled the company to cut its inventories by 50 percent between 1990 and 1994. That helped improve cash flow by $60 million a year through savings on interest payments for supplies. An additional $40 million in extra cash flow was generated through refinancing at lower interest rates. The extra $100 million was used to expand the firm's businesses by investing in China, the largest foreign producer of toilets and faucets, and a new joint venture with Rockwell to sell antilock brakes to Mack Truck.

Consistent Growth As a Public Company: 1995–99

By 1994 the company's sales and earnings were growing in all three major business lines. It had acquired 70 percent of Deutsche Perrot-Bremsen's automotive brake business in a joint venture, which helped build up the firm's Belgian-based WABCO Automotive Products Group. Overall sales reached $4.5 billion. A public stock offering was planned, and the company went public in February 1995 with an initial public offering (IPO). In spite of six straight years of reported losses due to interest payments and the cost of switching to demand flow manufacturing, analysts praised the company, and the stock rose 36 percent in the first three months. They liked the fact that all three of American Standard's businesses were making money and that all held the first or second position in market share. Operating income for the first quarter of 1995 was up 43 percent, and sales increased 24 percent. The company was globally diversified, and its management, led by Kampouris, was held in high esteem for adopting demand flow technology.

In 1997 American Standard established the Medical Systems Group as a new business to focus on new diagnostic technologies. Its proprietary diagnostic instrument, Copalis (Coupled Particle Light Scattering), allowed a user to perform multiple tests simultaneously on a single sample. It was approved for use by the U.S. Food and Drug Administration in 1996. Other diagnostic products included noninvasive methods of disease detection, such as the urea-breath test (UBT), and bundling blood virus, infectious disease, and autoimmune serological tests for the in vitro diagnostics industry.

Sales in 1997 reached the $6 billion level after American Standard rejected a $4 billion buyout bid from industrial conglomerate Tyco International Ltd. at the beginning of the year. In 1998 sales reached $6.7 billion. For the five years since American Standard re-emerged as a public company, its sales increased at a compound annual rate of 11 percent (excluding Medical Systems), and operating income (excluding special charges) grew at a compound annual rate of 20 percent. Approximately 50 percent of the company's revenues came from overseas markets. With Wall Street nervous about global diversity as a result of financial crises in several Asian countries, the value of American Standard stock declined significantly in 1998, from a high around $48 to a low around $22. Management and employees owned about 25 percent of the firm's outstanding stock.

Outlook

American Standard's three major businesses continued to claim the number one or number two positions in their markets. The company had several growth-enhancing strategies in place, including its leadership in demand flow technology. The company's manufacturing operations were fully globalized, with 103 manufacturing plants in 34 countries at the end of 1998. That allowed it to shift high-labor content products to low-labor cost regions. As the company continued to retire its outstanding debt, interest payments would take less bite out of the firm's growing operating income. That meant shareholders could begin to look forward to improved bottom-line returns.

Principal Subsidiaries

The Trane Company; Société Trane (France); American Standard; World Standard Ltd. (Hong Kong); Ideal Standard (Belgium); American Standard Medical Systems; DiaSorin-USA; DiaSorin-Europe (Italy); Alimenterics Inc.

Principal Operating Units

Air Conditioning Products: Worldwide Applied Systems; International Unitary Systems (France); North American Unitary Products. Plumbing Products: Americas; Worldwide Fittings; Asia Pacific (Hong Kong); Europe (Belgium). Automotive Products: WABCO Automotive Products Group (Belgium). Medical Systems Group.

Further Reading

"American Radiator & Standard Sanitary Corp.," *Fortune,* March 1940.

"American Standard Sells Subsidiary," *Nation's Restaurant News,* October 28, 1991, p. 64.

Barrier, Michael, "When 'Just in Time' Just Isn't Enough," *Nation's Business,* November 1992, p. 30.

"Brake Business Sold," *Pittsburgh Business Times,* March 19, 1990, p. 9.

Carey, David, "Life After Debt," *Financial World,* October 18, 1988, p. 22.

Clifford, Mark, "Back to Basics," *Forbes,* June 30, 1986, p. 56.

Dowling, Debra, "American Standard Cos. Rejects $4 Billion Buyout Bid," *Knight-Ridder/Tribune Business News,* January 14, 1997.

Glain, Steve, "Top Toilet Makers from U.S. and Japan Vie for Chinese Market," *Wall Street Journal,* December 19, 1996, p. A1.

Goodwin, William, "Chemical Launches American Standard Loan," *American Banker,* April 23, 1993, p. 16.

"Heating Man," *Fortune,* April 1935.

"How American Standard Cured Its Conglomeritis," *Business Week,* September 28, 1974.

Kim, Jonathan, "Bottom Fishing for These Four Depressed Stocks Can Net You Total Returns As High As 29%," *Money,* January 1998, p. 58.

Lippert, Barbara, "After All the Bad Bathroom Ads, American Standard Is a Relief," *Adweek,* June 5, 1989, p. 19.

Lucas, Allison, "Bringing Fun to Plumbing Products," *Sales and Marketing Management,* October 1995, p. 116.

Nuelle, Frances, "The Man Who Put Working Capital to Work," *Chief Executive,* October 1996, p. 40.

"Radiator Maker Starts to Swing," *Business Week,* May 3, 1969.

Reingold, Jennifer, and John Kimelman, "Nerves of Steel: American Standard Has Negative Equity and a Ton of Debt, But Wall Street Loves It, and with Reason," *Financial World,* May 23, 1995, p. 30.

Tully, Shawn, "Prophet of Zero Working Capital," *Fortune,* June 13, 1994, p. 113.

Weber, Joseph, "American Standard Wises Up," *Business Week,* November 18, 1996, p. 70.

—Jonathan Martin
—updated by David P. Bianco

Amerihost Properties, Inc.

2400 East Devon Avenue
Suite 280
Des Plaines, Illinois 60018
U.S.A.
(847) 298-4500
Fax: (847) 298-4505
Web site: http://www.amerihostinn.com

Public Company
Incorporated: 1984 as Chicagoland Concessions, Inc.
Employees: 2,053
Sales: $68.6 million (1997)
Stock Exchanges: NASDAQ
Ticker Symbol: HOST
NAIC: 72111 Hotels & Motels; 56133 Employee Leasing
    Services; 23332 Commercial & Institutional Building
    Construction; 531312 Nonresidential Property Managers

Amerihost Properties, Inc.—known for its fast-growing flag-ship chain AmeriHost Inns—owns and operates more than 90 hotels in 18 states, primarily located in the Midwest. Amerihost traditionally builds its AmeriHost Inn hotels near ''demand centers'' such as office parks, colleges, casinos, and regional outlet malls, in secondary and tertiary markets situated near sizable metropolitan areas. These areas tend to demonstrate a need for hotel rooms, with minimal existing competition. The company considers whether or not the target area has an active economic development program which would suggest long-term potential for lodging demand. Amerihost's holdings include hotels with franchise affiliations, such as Days Inn, Hampton Inn, Holiday Inn, and Ramada Inn. AmeriHost Inn hotels became available for franchising through subsidiary AmeriHost Inn Franchising in 1999. Additionally, the company provides employee leasing and hotel management services to various hotels.

From Kiosks to Hotels: The 1980s

Andrew Torchia and Richard D'Onofrio founded the company, originally incorporated as Chicagoland Concessions, Inc.

in 1984. The following year that name was changed to Amerihost Properties, Inc. Hotel industry veteran Andrew Torchia had formerly headed the office of regional development for Best Western International. He went on with D'Onofrio to form America Pop, a business that sold popcorn and soda from kiosks in the Chicago subways. Torchia and D'Onofrio's kiosk business proved less successful than anticipated, which led to its sale in 1986. Focusing on the hotel industry the pair formed Amerihost Properties, Inc. and in 1987 built their first hotel in Sullivan, Indiana.

In 1988 hotel industry executive Michael Holtz was appointed company CEO and president. His credentials included a Master's degree in Business Administration and a Bachelor of Science degree from Wright State University prior to his 16 years of experience in the areas of hotel operations, management, and renovation. Holtz had been a member of the company's board of directors since 1985, and from 1985–88 served as the Company's Treasurer and Secretary. He was responsible for the development and implementation of all company operations, including hotel development, finance, and management. Concentrating on smaller markets Holtz began building more hotels for Amerihost. He decided that the company could also expand through the purchase and revival of failed hotels. Holtz was confident that his experience would inform and implement a turnaround for previously unsuccessful hotel businesses, but despite 25 hotels in operation and rising revenues, Amerihost lost money in 1993. The company stepped up efforts to expand the AmeriHost Inn brand in overlooked markets in smaller towns and cities. Company executives felt that other brand affiliations were not so important in small-town America. Holtz told Bill Gillette of *Hotel & Motel Management* that ''We're looking for markets not where the population is especially low, but where there are good demand generators. There are probably about 1,500 of those markets out there.'' Holtz explained that they learned early on that hotels in smaller markets do not necessarily benefit from an affiliation with a huge national brand, a realization that prompted the increased hoisting of the AmeriHost flag. ''The savings of that nine percent [national-brand franchise fee] is a significant one,'' according to Gillette's interview with Torchia.

Company Perspectives:

The key to the future success of the AmeriHost Inn hotel brand is consistency in product and service. While the hotel industry is filled with numerous brand names, the traveling public is never sure what to expect when staying at a hotel for the first time, even when staying within the same hotel brand. Many of the major hotel chains have compromised consistency in product and service for the sake of growth. We believe in the importance of consistency and design, and operate our AmeriHost Inn hotels so that our guests experience the same high level of satisfaction at each hotel.

Cost-Effective Angle: The 1990s

The company also cut costs by methodically building identical hotel facilities. In Torchia's words, "we know the cost of every board foot and every brick," adding, "we've never been over budget on a project." Each of its hotels cost about $2.2 million to build, about $20,000 less per room than the amount spent by competitors offering similar accommodations. AmeriHost continued to outperform national franchises in their regional tertiary markets (specializing in towns with a population of fewer than 20,000), while national franchises generally performed better at interstate highway locations. Unlike the franchises which tended to standardize everything including their marketing strategies, Amerihost took a less generic approach and customized its marketing programs for individual locations. Their efforts began to pay off. In 1994 Amerihost reported revenues of $43.3 million, a record-setting accomplishment.

As head of hotel development for Amerihost Properties, Chuck Barcus scouted for 20 towns in 1995 that hosted a steady stream of visitors but lacked modern hotels. He was interested in target towns located near popular attractions. Typically, in such small towns one hotel was enough; a second was overkill. The company preferred markets in which there was little competition, though in areas that were pro-growth. Barcus raced to identify prime locations before competing franchise salesmen from a dozen or so national chains found the good sites. On the average, only one of every 16 communities visited by Barcus was suitable for AmeriHost development. Some of the criteria he used in determining appropriate locations included towns with several developments such as an office park, a factory-outlet mall, a college, or possibly even a prison within four miles.

Unable to compete with the lower pricing at interstate hotel chains (AmeriHost charged between $55 and $65 summer rates and $45 to $55 in winter), the company offered extra services and ambiance: a light breakfast; a standard format two-story wood-paneled indoor pool area; a sauna, Jacuzzi and exercise room; and the latest electronic door locks. Guests at each of AmeriHost's locations were consistently guaranteed these amenities. The company also borrowed a strategy from fast-food king McDonald's. Amerihost encouraged its hotel managers to become a part of their community as a means of building a customer base through referrals. To generate goodwill Am-

erihost typically used only local bank financing, invited town residents to its openings, opened its swimming pools to senior citizens, offered its community rooms for business meetings, and contributed the gift of a night spent at its whirlpool suite for local charity auctions.

Expansion of Wholly Owned Operations: 1997

The implementation of a toll-free reservation system accompanied by a radio and print marketing campaign paid off immediately in increased sales. The company registered the phrase "The joy of relentless consistency," maintaining that the consistently high level of service and quality enabled AmeriHost Inn hotels to receive the American Automobile Association's (AAA) Three Diamond Rating at every hotel. The company implemented a policy of holding monthly meetings at different Amerihost venues, enabling managers to meet with leisure and business guests to determine what they wanted in hotel service and accommodations. The company's extensive market research indicated that guests were most disappointed with the inconsistency of amenities and services available within the same hotel brand. The surveys acted as the foundation of the company's development goals. Amerihost determined that its brand had a 98 percent return rate, suggesting that word of mouth should be recognized as a significant advertising tool.

Amerihost went public in the 1980s but rather than rely solely on Wall Street for financing its rapid expansion of the AmeriHost Inn brand, the company decided to negotiate new investments through joint venture partners. The company's equity interest in each hotel ranged from five to 100 percent. Twenty-three new hotels were opened in 1997, of which 14 were wholly owned. Sacrificing short-term gains, the company saw its revenues fall from $68.3 million in 1996 to $62.7 million in 1997, primarily due to the new construction and start-up costs of the wholly owned operations. During this time the industry as a whole was experiencing significant growth and the long-term outlook appeared positive for AmeriHost Inns. The expansion afforded by joint venture partnerships allowed the company to gain 100 percent ownership of approximately one-half of the AmeriHost Inn hotels open or under construction by the end of 1997.

In June 1998, Amerihost Properties announced that it completed the sale of 26 wholly owned AmeriHost Inn hotels to PMC Commercial Trust—a Dallas, Texas real estate investment trust (REIT) that invested in real estate mortgages in the hotel industry—for $62.2 million, and began negotiating with them for the sale of four additional AmeriHost hotels. Amerihost entered into an agreement to lease back the 30 hotels for ten years at an initial fixed payment of $7.3 million annually. The fixed-rate lease allowed Amerihost to retain the upside earnings growth potential from the hotels, and allowed the company to continue concentrating on AmeriHost Inn brand hotels. A few months later Amerihost announced the purchase of 100 percent ownership of 15 AmeriHost Inn hotels from various joint venture partners, for a combined price of $37 million, including the assumption of approximately $27 million in mortgage debt. Amerihost realized benefits from increased revenue and earnings generated by these hotels as it gained greater flexibility in financing opportunities. The company planned "to sell most of its portfolio to one or several real-estate investment trusts through sale-lease-back agreements,'' according to a *Hotel & Motel Management* interview with Michael Holtz. Its aim was to retain and grow the AmeriHost Inn brand and primarily develop and manage hotels for others. The change in strategy meant that Amerihost would develop and construct for a fee AmeriHost Inns and other-branded properties primarily for REITs. If the property was not an AmeriHost Inn, the company would consider not leasing back the hotel to operate it. Holtz added that ''if it was the home brand Amerihost was developing, it wants control—which means a sale-lease-back agreement with management control.''

In May 1999 Amerihost Properties announced commencement of a Dutch Auction self-tender offer to purchase for cash up to one million shares of its common stock. In a Dutch Auction the company sets a price range, and the stockholders have an opportunity to specify prices within that range at which they are willing to sell shares. That amount represented approximately 16 percent of its outstanding stock. The terms of the tender offer included a purchase price for each tendered share of not more than $4.00 per share, nor less than $3.375 per share net to the seller in cash.

Following the development of a franchising program, Amerihost initiated an aggressive growth campaign, which included the expansion of its concept into larger urban areas. The company planned to continue building approximately ten new, wholly owned AmeriHost Inns per year. Emphasizing quality, the goal was to become a broadly recognized mid-scale name brand, competitive with the larger mid-scale hotel chains.

The company sought franchisees willing to develop multiple properties and expected to have 50 underway in 36 states within the year. Holst told Shannon McMullen of *Hotel Business* that ''We've been receiving inquiries to develop AmeriHost Inn hotels from other parties but were concerned how to do it without compromising quality. That is why we carefully planned the franchising program and will be selective with franchisees.'' Holst explained that the company's AAA three diamond rating demonstrated a high level of quality, which all franchisees must also agree to maintain. The company also added a 100 percent satisfaction guarantee for customers. The majority of the franchised hotels would be newly constructed, with two prototype choices ranging in size from 60 to 120 rooms. Design features included an indoor pool, a meeting room, an exercise room, electronic door locks, in-room coffee service, data ports in guest rooms, in-room on demand movies, and complimentary expanded continental breakfast. The company planned to include franchisees in major decision-making, requiring a 50 percent or more approval from the franchisee community before making changes.

Amerihost's first franchisee was SJB Equities, Inc., a company that became Amerihost's first joint-venture partner in 1989, involved with 14 AmeriHost Inn hotels in Ohio and West Virginia. Management projected a royalty stream of approximately five percent of room revenues, which would generate $40,000 per year per hotel in franchise fees for the typical 60-room hotel. Through franchising, Amerihost hoped to rapidly build the hotel brand, which would eventually be a significant source of recurring, fee-based income. The company outpaced the industry in 1998 with occupancy rates increasing 8.7 percent.

Analysts projected in 1998 that overall profits for the industry would continue to increase for the next several years, and Amerihost executives expressed confidence that its growth trend would continue. In an interview for *Hospitality,* Holtz remained assured of their formula: ''Our standard is the standard, and that is the key ingredient of our concept!''

Principal Subsidiaries

AmeriHost Inn Hotels.

Principal Divisions

Hotel Operations; Hotel Development; Employee Leasing; Hotel Management; Hotel Franchising.

Further Reading

''AmeriHost Franchising Sparks Chain Reaction,'' *Hospitality*, March 1999, p. 43.
Bleakley, Fred, ''Wanted: Towns With Visitors, No Place to Stay,'' *Wall Street Journal,* July 19, 1995.
Comerford, Mike, ''Hotel Chain Sees Room For Growth,'' *Daily Herald*, August 28, 1998, p. 1.
Gillette, Bill, ''Amerihost Builds Own Brand,'' *Hotel & Motel Management*, April 3, 1995, p. 3.
McMullen, Shannon, ''Amerihost Properties, Inc. Rolls Out Franchise Program,'' *Hotel Business*, March 7, 1999.
Roeder, David, ''Amerihost Building Hotels, Name,'' *Daily Herald*, August 30, 1995.
Whitford, Marty, ''Amerihost Switches Portfolio Strategies,'' *Hotel & Motel*, July 6, 1998.

—Terri Mozzone

Ames Department Stores, Inc.

2418 Main Street
Rocky Hill, Connecticut 06067
U.S.A.
(860) 257-2000
Fax: (860) 257-2168
Web site: http://www.amesstores.com

Public Company
Incorporated: 1962
Employees: 36,400
Sales: $2.51 billion (1998)
Stock Exchanges: NASDAQ
Ticker Symbol: AMES
NAIC: 45211 Department Stores

Ames Department Stores, Inc. is one of the largest discount retailers in the United States, with more than 450 stores located in 19 contiguous northeastern, midwestern, and Mid-Atlantic states. The stores sell brand name and other quality merchandise at discount prices, from locations in rural communities, small cities, and suburbs of metropolitan areas. After decades of profitability and steady growth, an acquisition spree in the 1980s—highlighted by the 1988 purchase of 392 Zayre stores—coupled with a downturn in the economy of its core states, drove the company into bankruptcy. After shedding more than half its properties, Ames emerged from bankruptcy in December 1992 and soon returned to profitability. The company has since focused on targeted expansion, most notably the December 1998 acquisition of 155 Hills stores.

Founding and Growth Through Acquisition

Ames was founded in 1958 when two brothers, Milton and Irving Gilman, opened a general store in an old mill in Southbridge, Massachusetts. The Gilmans took the name of their store from the name of its site's old tenant, the Ames Worsted Textile Company. In starting out their business, the Gilmans sought to fill a niche in the retail industry that had hitherto been ignored. They did so by opening a discount store in a rural area where there were no other large, competing stores around. When this formula proved profitable, the Ames company was incorporated in 1962.

Ames expanded steadily, concentrating its growth in the Northeast. In January 1972, 14 years after its founding, Ames made its first major acquisitions: the Joseph Leavitt Corporation and the K & R Warehouse Corporation. Six years later, the company continued its expansion through acquisition when it purchased the Davis Wholesale Company for $1 million, bringing 13 W.T. Grant general stores into the company fold. The purchase of Neisner Brothers, Inc. followed ten months later for $38 million. Neisner Brothers, which was in Chapter 11 bankruptcy and reorganization, operated 32 stores in New York and Florida. Their acquisition brought the number of stores Ames had acquired during the 1970s to 47; the company, however, soon closed ten stores in the New York area.

In each of its acquisitions, Ames bought a struggling company then worked to turn around its operations. In this endeavor, Ames proved largely successful. The company brought in merchandise made by well-known manufacturers and sold it in bright, well-organized settings. Prices were kept low all the time, rather than being set high and then reduced for periodic sales. For advertising, the company relied on direct-mail campaigns sent to carefully selected shoppers who lived near Ames stores. In some cases, this formula succeeded in raising sales by as much as 50 percent.

By 1981, Ames was operating 115 discount stores, in a chain that ran from Maine to Maryland. In addition, the company ran 20 variety stores, most of which were located in Florida. Five discount stores and one variety store had been opened in the last year. All of the company's retail properties were located in small towns or near highways that were easily reached by people living in the surrounding areas. Ames had stuck to its original rural orientation, eschewing heavily industrialized areas and places where one company employed almost all the inhabitants. About 55 percent of the company's sales came from hard goods, and the rest were in soft housewares and apparel.

In order to maintain its policy of offering brand names at discount prices, Ames maintained tight control over its over-

Company Perspectives:

The Ames mission is to provide quality products for family and home at discount prices; provide a convenient and efficient shopping experience; achieve a sustainable competitive advantage; build and sustain strong supplier partnerships.

head and interest payments. These policies enabled the company to establish an unbroken record of profitability since its inception, and eight straight years of growing sales and earnings. Ames ended 1981 with sales of $400 million, nearly one-half of which was accumulated in the last quarter of the year, when Christmas sales enhanced retailers' results.

The company relied on strengthened sales of hard goods such as housewares, automotive supplies, and hardware to power its growth and added departments featuring furniture, flowers and plants, cosmetics, toys, and sports equipment. The quality of Ames's women's clothing and accessories was upgraded, and the company also moved to bring its jewelry sales operations more firmly under its own control. To continue its upward path, Ames began a process of renovating its stores, in hopes of improving its sales per square foot of retail space. In March 1981, the company remodeled its original Massachusetts store, adding 20 percent more display space for higher quality goods and new products. These modifications resulted in a sales increase of 25 percent. After this success, the company embarked on a program to update its other properties, scheduling two more stores for overhauls in the next nine months, and eight others for renewal in 1982.

Ames returned to its policy of growth through acquisition in 1984 when it bought KDT Industries, Inc. for $28.5 million. Like past Ames purchases, this company was an organization in distress. Some of its properties had been sold to pay creditors, leaving 42 King's department stores and $98 million in tax credits. At the end of that year, Ames could look back on a promising pattern of growth, as sales rose more than 25 percent to $822 million, and earnings climbed 43 percent to $28.5 million.

Reassured by these positive results, the company made a riskier purchase the next year, paying $196.5 million in April 1985 for the G.C. Murphy Company, a discount department store chain based in Pennsylvania. With this move, the company doubled its sales, to $1.7 billion, and in one stroke became a powerhouse in retailing. This expansion came at a price, however, as Ames's debt grew temporarily to 80 percent of the company's worth. By purchasing Murphy, Ames moved its operations into 14 additional states.

Within three months of its purchase of Murphy, Ames closed or sold 130 of the chain's unprofitable stores in an effort to make its unwieldy purchase profitable. In addition, the company began the process of converting the Murphy stores to the Ames model, as it reconfigured operating systems, methods, and procedures. This process proved difficult and time-consuming, and it temporarily distracted the company's man-

agement from aggressive growth in its other stores. In the spring of 1986, an error occurred in which the inventories of clothing items intended for wear in the warmer months were shipped out to Ames stores late in the selling season, resulting in forced mark-downs on much of the merchandise, which depressed company earnings for that period.

Despite this setback Ames planned further expansion, plotting 12 percent growth for each year left in the decade. These ambitions were stymied in the following year, as Ames experienced unusually high ''shrinkage''—retailing jargon for losses due to theft and embezzlement of goods, as well as poor inventory control and pricing mix-ups. Ames ended 1987 with $34.2 million in profits.

The Late 1980s Zayres Acquisition

Nine months later Ames agreed to make its largest and most ambitious purchase to date, pledging $800 million to acquire the discount stores division of the Zayre Corporation, based in Framingham, Massachusetts. With this move, Ames doubled its number of stores for the second time in three years to become the third largest U.S. discount store operator. The newly combined companies estimated sales of $5.39 billion in their 736 total stores. For its money, Ames got 392 stores located in the Northeast, the South, and the Great Lakes states. While Ames already operated in many of these areas, its stores were primarily located in rural areas, while Zayre's strength was in urban zones. Although the Zayre purchase enabled Ames to begin operating stores in such promising markets as Florida and Illinois, overall the move was risky. The Zayre properties were sold below their theoretical value as a result of their recent history of large losses. ''I love to buy when its unfashionable and everything is in disarray,'' Ames's chairman told the *Wall Street Journal* at the time.

Because the Zayre name was so well known in the areas where it operated, Ames planned to keep the name for a certain period of time while it converted the stores to the more efficient Ames operating standards, which included a large number of refurbished store properties, lower prices and less reliance on sales to move merchandise, and a smaller selection of goods in some departments. Initially, the company also planned to retain all Zayre personnel, although, ultimately, it estimated that ten to 15 percent of Zayre's unprofitable stores would be closed.

In the first month of 1989, Ames began to implement these plans, closing 77 discount department stores, 74 of which were Zayre stores that had been racking up annual losses of $20 million. To further streamline itself and sharpen its focus on its largest and most recent purchase, Ames sold off its G.C. Murphy properties in August 1989 to E-II Holdings, owned by the Riklis family, for $77.6 million. In this way, Ames hoped to concentrate its efforts on discount retailing, shedding its variety store operations, which fit in less well with the company's overall profile than Ames executives had anticipated. In addition, the sale of the Murphy properties allowed the company to pay off some of the high interest debts incurred in the purchase of Zayre. After these reductions, Ames became the nation's fourth largest discount retailer, with 693 stores in 20 states running from the Northeast, out to Illinois, and then down to the South.

These moves helped Ames to incorporate its new properties more fully into the company. However, the decision on whether to change the name of the Zayre stores still had to be made. Zayre had its own history as one of the oldest and best-known U.S. retail chains. In deference to this heritage and to the brand loyalty of many of Zayre's urban customers, Ames announced in February 1989 that the company would not change the names of 61 profitable inner city Zayre stores. Eight months later, however, on October 26, 1989, it did reopen 254 old Zayre stores as refurbished Ames stores. Improvements included new paint, better lighting, and more attractive displays, as well as a computerized cash register system meant to speed up transactions and improve inventory control. The grand reopening was supported by a multimillion-dollar television advertising campaign featuring the slogan, ''We grew up with better values.'' In addition, the company planned further renovations of these stores in the near future.

Among the most pressing tasks in consolidating Zayre and Ames operations was merging management staffs. The company closed Zayre's Massachusetts office and moved its employees to the Ames headquarters located outside Hartford, Connecticut. Zayre's management corps was cut in half, and the company's 23 regional offices were reduced to seven. This transition was made much more quickly than originally planned, in seven months rather than a year and a half. As a result of this speed, Ames expected to quadruple its savings from this paring down, to $40 million.

Losses in the Late 1980s

Despite this unexpected gain, Ames's profits remained low because sales for the spring quarter of 1989 proved disappointing. The company was forced to post a loss for the first half of the year. As the economy of the Northeast, where nearly half the company's stores were located, further slowed, Ames gradually saw its high hopes for its Zayre stores grow dimmer. Although sales in its old Ames stores rose, returns at its Zayre properties went into a slump, dropping off by 15 percent. By the end of the third quarter, continuing difficulties with Zayre caused a further loss of $7 million, bringing losses at Ames to nearly $28 million for the year.

Growing desperate, Ames opened its stores on Thanksgiving Day, in hopes of boosting sales. Nevertheless, it appeared that Zayre's traditional core of customers was eschewing the remade stores. Zayre shoppers were accustomed to stores open 24 hours a day, a policy that Ames had eliminated as a cost-cutting measure. In addition, Zayre had brought customers into stores with periodic deep discount sales, which were heavily promoted in newspapers and mailed circulars. Along with these items, racks and bins of marked-down items were found in the stores. Ames store policy, however, eliminated deep discounts in favor of steady, everyday low prices, to which it hoped customers would adjust. Although this kept profit margins higher, the company's prices proved uncompetitive in a discount department store bargain war. In addition, Ames switched Zayre's apparel merchandise from inexpensive but fashionable items to basic goods, alienating traditional Zayre customers. The company's elimination of the Zayre credit card and its lack of heavy advertising also cut into sales.

Despite the poor results from the Zayre stores, Ames executives were resolved to stick with their original plan of converting the stores to the traditional Ames model. ''The philosophy is working,'' the chairman of the company told the *Wall Street Journal,* adding, ''It has worked for half our business. It's going to work for the other half.'' This optimism, however, proved ill-founded, as company results continued to worsen. In early 1990 Ames closed an additional 15 of the older Zayre stores, most of which were located near other Ames outlets. When unexpectedly poor sales made it impossible to pay for past purchases, Ames found itself unable to buy needed merchandise from its suppliers. The company ended the year with losses of $228 million.

By late April 1990 Ames was staggering from continued poor sales at its Zayre operations, as well as the debt burden brought on by the large purchase and the costs of converting stores. Manufacturers were refusing to ship the company merchandise, and bankers were refusing to lend it any more money. Finally, on April 25, 1990, Ames was forced to file for bankruptcy, seeking protection from its creditors in Chapter 11 reorganization. Shortly after this, the company's chairman resigned. Stephen Pistner, a specialist in retail corporate turnarounds, replaced him and began the long process of digging Ames out of the hole created by its Zayre purchase. As a result of its bankruptcy filing, Ames suspended all advertising for four weeks, hoping to get the pipeline of merchandise moving again. In addition, the company was able to secure a $250 million loan from a New York bank that allowed it to make essential cash outlays, such as meeting its payroll and paying utility bills.

Among the first steps taken by Ames in this predicament was the closing of an additional 221 stores, a reduction of one-third of its store base. In doing so, the company let 18,000 employees go. Most of the stores, which together had lost nearly $50 million in the previous year, were located in the Midwest and South. Liquidating these properties allowed Ames to raise $210 million from its sold-off inventory. Despite this gain, the company, now being run by a new team of managers, reported a $538 million loss for operations over the first half of 1990. Additional cost-cutting measures were announced in 1991, as Ames continued to work on a plan to pay off its creditors under the watchful eye of the bankruptcy court. In October the company announced that it would close 77 more stores and lay off 4,500 more employees after the holiday season.

In 1992 Ames began to wrap up its negotiations with its creditors in an effort to finalize a plan for reorganization to present to the bankruptcy court. In January the company submitted a tentative plan for reorganization to the court. In March hearings were delayed because disputes over the nature of the company's final payments to creditors remained unresolved. In September, Ames submitted an amended reorganization plan to the court that included an additional set of store closings. In order to help raise $325 million in cash to pay its creditors, Ames elected to shutter 60 stores in 12 states, costing 3,500 workers their jobs.

In December 1992 continuing weak results and large operating losses caused Ames's board of directors to oust Pistner. The company had introduced a policy of offering deeply discounted items to bring customers into stores, with the expectation that, once in a store, people would also buy higher-priced items. Instead, however, the company found that shoppers were "cherry picking" bargains and then leaving, causing Ames to report losses of $91.4 million over its third quarter of 1992. As losses for November continued to mount, despite a relatively high sales volume, the company asked for another delay in the consideration of its reorganization plan. Following Pistner's ouster, Peter Thorner, who had been CFO and executive vice-president, was named president and CEO on an acting basis and began running the company in concert with an oversight committee consisting of three board members.

Emerging from Bankruptcy in 1992

Finally, on December 20, 1992, a bankruptcy judge approved Ames's plan to leave Chapter 11. Ten days later, the company consummated the plan and formally emerged from bankruptcy. The new Ames operated 309 stores in 14 states, a drastic reduction from its peak of 678 stores. To finance its operations, the company had arranged a $210 million letter of credit from its bankers. It planned to use this money to upgrade and replenish the merchandise of its remaining stores.

The key to a company turnaround was a refocus on Ames's traditional customers—people in the lower middle income sector. Also, instead of joining the private label trend, Ames emphasized brand name products. Customer service became a renewed area of focus, as managers worked to ensure that items remained in-stock and on the shelves. The company really began to turn the corner after a new management team was put in place. In 1993 Paul Buxbaum was named chairman, while Joseph Ettore was named president and CEO in June 1994 following the resignation of Thorner. Ettore had been president and CEO of Jamesway Corp., a Secaucus, New Jersey-based discount retailer. Ames returned to profitability in 1994, posting net income of $10.8 million on revenues of $2.12 billion. During 1994 Ames introduced the 55 Gold program, whereby shoppers over age 55 received a ten percent discount on all merchandise every Tuesday; this successful promotion helped to increase sales and store traffic, and aided in the creation of a second core customer—older shoppers. With Wal-Mart expanding rapidly in the Northeast, Ames also worked to modernize stores and their layouts through remodeling, with 52 stores receiving a makeover in 1994 alone.

Ames hit a bump on the road to recovery during the 1996 fiscal year, when weak holiday sales forced it to close 17 of its 307 stores, lay off more than 1,000 people, and take a $20 million charge, which led to a full year net loss of $1.6 million. The company returned to the black in 1997 and had an even stronger year in 1998 when it posted net income of $34.5 million on revenues of $2.23 billion. By this time Ames had recovered sufficiently to risk venturing back into the acquisition realm. In November 1998 the company agreed to acquire Hills Stores Company, a struggling 155-unit discount chain based in Canton, Massachusetts. The total cost of the acquisition, which was consummated in March 1999, was about $330 million. The addition of Hills beefed up the Ames presence in New York, Ohio, Pennsylvania, and West Virginia, and added the states of

Illinois, Indiana, Kentucky, North Carolina, and Tennessee to its territory. Ames became the fourth largest discount chain in the United States, trailing Wal-Mart, Kmart, and Target.

During 1999 Ames remodeled and converted to the Ames format 150 of the Hills stores, spending about $185 million in the process. In April 1999 Ames gained additional units through the $40 million purchase from Caldor Corporation of seven stores in Connecticut and one in Massachusetts, as well as a state-of-the-art 649,000-square-foot distribution center in Westfield, Massachusetts. Caldor was a discount chain being liquidated under Chapter 11 bankruptcy protection. The Caldor stores were converted to the Ames format later in 1999.

Under the leadership of Ettore, who in late 1999 added the title of chairman to his responsibilities as president and CEO, it appeared that Ames had completed its turnaround. By targeting lower middle income and older customers with smaller-size stores (averaging 60,000 square feet versus the 100,000 of the competition), Ames appeared to have carved out a unique niche that allowed it to compete with the national discounters.

Further Reading

"Ames Names Ettore, Jamesway's Ex-CEO, As Its President, Chief," *Wall Street Journal,* June 13, 1994, p. B6.

"Ames Reorganization OK'd; Chairman Pistner Ousted," *Discount Store News,* January 4, 1993, pp. 1+.

Arlen, Jeffrey, "Big Pencil: Ames Moves Up to No. 4," *Discount Store News,* May 24, 1999, pp. A4–A5.

Bulkeley, William M., "Ames to Please: Discounter Rebounds by Targeting a Clientele Below the Wal-Mart Set," *Wall Street Journal,* January 11, 1999, pp. A1+.

Byrne, Harlan S., "Ames Department Stores, Inc.," *Barron's,* October 16, 1989.

Campanella, Frank W., "Small-Town Merchant," *Barron's,* December 28, 1981.

Driscoll, Lisa, "The Fix-It Doctor with a Rough Bedside Manner," *Business Week,* October 29, 1990.

Duff, Mike, "Ability to Adapt Is Ames' Advantage," *Discount Store News,* March 23, 1998, pp. 17+.

Girishankar, Saroja, "Retailer Seeks a New Kind of Customer," *Internet Week,* June 21, 1999, pp. 1, 18.

Hanover, Dan, "Ames Turnaround Is Icing on the Cake," *Chain Store Age,* May 1998, pp. 45–47.

Johannes, Laura, "Ames, Hit by Slow Sales over Holiday, to Close 17 Stores, Lay Off Over 1,000," *Wall Street Journal,* January 15, 1996, p. A5.

King, Resa W., "Now Ames Is a Big-League Retailer," *Business Week,* June 10, 1985.

Klein, Alec, "Ames Department Stores Is Buying Hills, Vaulting to No. 4 in Discount," *Wall Street Journal,* November 13, 1998, p. A4.

Lisanti, Tony, "Ames May Be a 'What Went Right' Story," *Discount Store News,* November 23, 1998, p. 11.

Stankevich, Debby Garbato, "Defying Definition" (cover story), *Discount Merchandiser,* March 1999, pp. 27+.

Thilmany, Jean, "Ames' Gains," *Executive Technology,* May 1999, pp. 14–15.

Tosh, Mark, "Ames Battles Against the Odds," *Women's Wear Daily,* September 20, 1995, p. 6.

—Elizabeth Rourke
—updated by David E. Salamie

Amgen, Inc.

Amgen Center
1840 Dehavilland Drive
Thousand Oaks, California 91320-1789
U.S.A.
(805) 499-5725
Fax: (805) 499-9315
Web site: http://www.amgen.com

Public Company
Incorporated: 1980
Employees: 1,700
Sales: $2.71 billion (1998)
Stock Exchanges: NASDAQ
Ticker Symbol: AMGN
NAIC: 325412 Pharmaceutical Preparation Manufacturing

Amgen, Inc. stands out in the biotechnology industry as one of the only businesses to transform itself from a drug development company into a pharmaceutical manufacturer while simultaneously maintaining steady sales. The largest independent biotechnology company in the United States, Amgen owes its transformation mostly to two gene-spliced drugs, Neupogen and Epogen. The company continues to develop human biopharmaceutical products using proprietary recombinant DNA technology.

A Slow Start in Biotechnological Research: 1980s

Amgen was formed in 1980 by a group of scientists and venture capitalists with a $19 million private-equity placement from venture capital firms and two major corporations. It began operations in 1981 in Thousand Oaks, California, in close proximity to thriving research centers at three nearby universities, among them UCLA and the California Institute of Technology. The company's impressive scientific advisory board included several members of the National Academy of Sciences; its first chairman and CEO was George B. Rathmann, former vice-president for research and development in the diagnostics division of Abbott Laboratories.

Through public stock offerings in 1983, 1986, and 1987, the company raised the capital needed to pursue its research, yet in its first five years, Amgen recorded losses. By 1986 it showed a humble profit, but 96 percent of its revenues that year came not from products, but from interest income and research partnerships with major drug companies. At this time, Amgen had five genetically engineered drugs undergoing human testing, the most promising of which was erythropoietin, or EPO, a synthetically produced hormone that promotes red blood cell production. The drug was targeted for people with kidney disease on dialysis, a process that lowers the kidneys' natural production of EPO. The product proved to be a marvel of genetic engineering: In January 1987, an article in the *New England Journal of Medicine* detailed the positive results of a study involving EPO and 25 kidney-dialysis patients.

Because the worldwide market for patients with kidney failure was about $350 million a year in the mid-1980s, and because there were then fewer than 200,000 kidney-dialysis patients in the United States, Amgen's EPO was accorded "orphan drug" status by the FDA, an exclusive seven-year marketing rights privilege. However, many argued that EPO was not just a drug for those suffering kidney failure; its applications for anemia, a common side effect of certain treatments for cancer, arthritis, and AIDS, were unlimited. The drug could also be used to reduce the need for blood transfusions during surgery.

With those uses in mind, in 1985 Amgen sold Johnson & Johnson the right to market EPO for treatment of anemia in the United States and for all uses in Europe. The previous year, Amgen had formed a joint venture with Kirin Brewery Company, Ltd. of Japan, according Kirin the right to manufacture and market EPO in Japan. Amgen, with rights to the U.S. dialysis market, began building an EPO manufacturing facility near its headquarters even before the company was granted its first patent for its recombinant human erythropoietin, named Epogen. Two days after receiving the patent in October 1987, Amgen filed with the FDA.

While awaiting FDA approval on Epogen, Amgen continued to develop other drugs, including a vaccine against hepatitis B, three products to stimulate the body's disease-fighting system, and two kinds of interferon, or antiviral substances. In 1985

Amgen became the first company to genetically engineer granulocyte colony-stimulating factor (G-CSF), part of the family of substances that compel cells in the bone marrow to produce disease-fighting white blood cells. Researchers were hopeful it would help fight bacterial infections and certain types of cancer, as well as offset the effects of radiation and chemotherapy.

The Race to Market EPO: 1989

As the first company to isolate and patent the human gene responsible for making EPO and to reproduce the drug in large quantities by transplanting the isolated gene into the ovarian cells of hamsters, Amgen had patent rights to genetically engineered EPO. One of Amgen's competitors, Genetics Institute (GI), was the first to isolate a purified strain of the protein and had received a patent on natural, highly purified EPO. The two companies now sued each other for patent infringement in an acrimonious battle due to its high stakes. GI had licensed its patents to Chugai Pharmaceutical Company, which planned to market EPO in the United States through Upjohn Company. Amgen subsequently asked the International Trade Commission (ITC) to block imports of Chugai's EPO, but an ITC judge declined to do so in January 1989.

While Amgen was awaiting the FDA's green light, Johnson & Johnson's Ortho Pharmaceutical Corporation slapped Amgen with a lawsuit over what Ortho claimed would be ''spillover sales'' resulting from non-dialysis use of Epogen. Ortho sought an injunction to delay marketing EPO until a dispute over terms of the two companies' joint venture was settled. At the same time, several U.S. senators were trying to change the orphan drug law and claimed that EPO should not qualify for exclusivity because it had huge money-making potential. Amgen determined that EPO's annual tab for dialysis patients would run $6,000. Medicare would pick up the bill for dialysis patients, most of whom were hit by the huge cost of dialysis itself.

These legal tangles caused further delay in FDA approval of Epogen, which allowed competitors to pull ahead in their efforts to market the drug and meant financial losses for Amgen, which was poised to begin immediate shipments to patients with end-stage renal, or kidney, disease. In March 1989, a federal judge ruled that Ortho and Amgen had to submit a joint application for FDA approval of EPO, suggesting that cross-licensing might be a solution. Meanwhile, GI was nearing the finish line in its own labs.

On June 1, 1989, the FDA approved Amgen's EPO for treatment of anemia in kidney dialysis patients. The next day

Amgen shipped its first batch of the drug to UCLA Medical Center. By the end of June, it had sold nearly $17 million worth of the drug—its first product after nine years in business. Legal wrangles continued, but Amgen had the market to itself. GI's version of EPO awaited FDA approval. Around this time, CEO Rathmann passed his title to longtime CFO Gordon M. Binder, the author of Amgen's deal with Kirin Brewery.

In 1990 the U.S. House of Representatives cleared a measure amending the orphan drug law, but EPO was exempt due to furious lobbying by both GI and Amgen. A federal magistrate ruled that Amgen was infringing on GI's patent, and vice versa; the ruling seemed again to aim at a cross-licensing agreement. Encouraged, GI stepped up its attack on Amgen by asking a federal court to freeze the company's profits on EPO sales, and sought an injunction to stop Amgen from producing the drug. The court's decision held that both companies had valid patents and that each was guilty of infringing on the other's patent. The decision allowed Chugai to use Amgen's patented genetic coding to produce the drug in Japan, then import and sell it. Meanwhile, Amgen's product sales went from $2.8 million in 1989 to roughly $140 million in 1990. In March 1990, a federal judge ordered Amgen and GI to exchange royalty-free cross-licenses on EPO. In a significant setback for Amgen, the judge ruled that GI's product, Marogen, was also covered by the orphan drug status.

An International Market Share with Neupogen

Meanwhile, expectations were great for Amgen's new drug, Neupogen. In clinical studies, G-CSF performed well, and the initial market for Neupogen was calculated to be twice that of Epogen. The hope was that the drug's use would extend beyond chemotherapy patients to include others who would benefit from increased immunization. Since G-CSF was not an orphan drug, many other biotechnology companies were simultaneously racing to bring their version of the product to market. Amgen received the first U.S. patent on recombinant G-CSF in 1989, and FDA approval for Neupogen was issued in February 1991. Amgen retained full domestic marketing rights to the drug, while Kirin Brewery had exclusive license for sales of G-CSF in Japan, Korea, and Taiwan.

In March 1991, Amgen received more good news: A federal court of appeals issued the final verdict in Amgen's ongoing struggle with Genetics Institute over EPO, and the decision favored Amgen. The judge blocked GI from selling its version of the anti-anemia drug, ruling that GI had failed to demonstrate just how it made the purified form of EPO from human urine—the factor by which GI's product differed from Amgen's. Thus, Amgen was given a legal monopoly over domestic EPO sales.

Amgen had shipped about $53 million of Neupogen by May 1991. Total sales for the drug for 1991 exceeded $260 million, and the company became known as a biotechnology leader. Amgen closed 1992 as the first biotech company to top $1 billion in sales and the only one to near the status of independent global pharmaceutical company. In the fall of 1992, Amgen tapped Kevin W. Sharer, president of the telephone giant MCI Communications Corporation, to fill the post of president and COO, and in 1993, Amgen announced an expansion of its research and development investment to nearly double what its 1992 expenditure had been. New research focused on blood-cell growth factors, soft-tissue growth factors, and neurobiology, inflammation, and nucleic acid therapeutics. The company also began exploring growth factors to help heal burns, surgical wounds, bone damage, and other injuries. As of early 1993, Amgen had more than 90 percent of the white blood cell stimulator market in the United States and no competition in the red blood cell stimulator market. Neupogen's growth potential remained considerable. That year, Amgen's revenues reached $1.4 billion, with Neupogen sales increasing 32 percent to provide 52 percent of the company's annual total sales of $719 million.

Throughout 1994, the growth rate of Amgen's products continued to increase. Neupogen sales reached $829 million after the FDA approved its use in bone marrow transplants. Epogen sales also increased 23 percent to reach $729 million once the FDA boosted the target hematocrit level for chronic renal failure. Amgen agreed with Kirin Brewery to develop and market megakaryocyte growth and development factor (MGDF) as a platelet stimulator. It also joined with Amcell Corp. in commercializing certain cell separation products developed by Amcell in a strategic extension of Amgen's clinical research with stem cell factor and Neupogen. In December 1994, Amgen purchased Synergen, acquiring that company's product pipeline, and was awarded a national medal of technology for development of Epogen, the first biotechnology company and only one of five corporations ever to receive this highest presidential tribute for the commercial application of technology.

Throughout this period of growth, Amgen's legal battles continued. In 1991, Amgen was ordered to pay Johnson & Johnson's subsidiary, Ortho Pharmaceutical Corporation, $164 million in damages for selling Epogen in violation of their 1985 EPO marketing agreement during the 19 months it took for Ortho to bring its product to the market. However, in a turn-around case in 1992 Johnson & Johnson was ordered to pay Amgen $90 million for failing to comply with another aspect of the same 1985 agreement. According to the contract, Johnson & Johnson was to develop both a hepatitis B vaccine and interleukin 2, and Amgen was to receive royalties from those products. Johnson & Johnson failed to meet those obligations.

Legal battles claimed much of Amgen's time through 1998. In 1995, the battle between Amgen and GI took another turn. The European Patent Office Board of Appeals had upheld a Kirin-Amgen patent on EPO in 1994. Now a district court in Massachusetts barred GI from asserting its U.S. patent, upholding the 1990 decision in favor of Amgen. The longstanding dispute with Johnson & Johnson's Ortho subsidiary was resurrected again in 1998 when a judge ordered Amgen to pay $200 million to remedy its violation of the sales agreement, while at the same time accepting Amgen's method for calculating "spillover sales" and ordering Johnson & Johnson to pay Amgen's $100 million expenses for the lengthy dispute. But a second dispute with Johnson & Johnson cropped up shortly afterward over whether NESP, (novel erythropoiesis stimulating protein), a new, longer-acting version of EPO, qualified as a new or improved drug. The court eventually awarded all rights to the new version of Epogen to Amgen, making NESP its first big drug success since 1991. Then, Transkaryotic began testing its own rival to Epogen, moving to reopen and challenge a patent infringement suit.

Mapping the Human Genome: 1990s

Bringing new products to market required investments in genomics, which involved mapping and understanding human genetic structure. Amgen's R & D budget increased accordingly throughout the 1990s: from $182 million in 1992 to $663 million in 1998. The company hoped to optimize its potential for developing and delivering product candidates, including those targeting neurodegenerative and inflammatory diseases, cancer support, and endocrine disorders, such as obesity and diabetes.

In 1995 Amgen continued its research on MGDF with Kirin, while on another front the two companies obtained license rights on thrombopoietin (TPO), a platelet stimulator, from Denmark's Novo Nordisk, putting them ahead of Genentech in the race to introduce a TPO product. That year, too, Amgen joined with NPS Pharmaceuticals in developing the latter's Norcalcin to treat hyperparathyroidism in dialysis patients and continued research on the "fat mouse" obesity gene licensed from Rockefeller University. Sales for the year were $1.8 billion.

The year 1996 saw breakthroughs in testing on another Amgen product, Infergen, used to treat patients with chronic hepatitis C. Scientists at Amgen also identified a novel, naturally occurring protein with potential applications in osteoporosis and cloned a gene essential to the growth and proliferation of most cancer cells. The company stepped up clinical development of several new medicines: glia-derived neuro-factor (GDNF) with applications to Parkinson's; recombinant leptin as an anti-obesity drug; keratinocyte growth factor (KGF) for preventing side effects of chemo and radiation therapy; and development with Kirin for NESP (novel erythropoiesis stimulating protein). On the business front, the company enjoyed a solid year financially with revenues exceeding $2 billion, an increase of 15 percent from the year before. Net income increased 26 percent to $680 million. Amgen licensed Yamanouchi Pharmaceutical the right to develop, manufacture, and commercialize Amgen's consensus interferon (CIFN), a novel, non-naturally occurring type one interferon, except in the United States and Canada.

The Goal for 2001

The launch of Infergen in October 1997 set Amgen on track toward achieving its goal of releasing five new products in five years. The company filed and received license applications for Stemgen, a drug that generated the growth of stem cells and led to a faster recovery of blood cells after chemotherapy, and made clinical trial progress on MGDF, KGF, leptin, and NESP. It also in-licensed the worldwide rights to Guilford Pharmaceuticals' FKBP-neuroimunophilins, oral compounds that showed signs of treating neurodegenerative disorders, including Parkinson's and Alzheimer's. Yet despite Amgen's laboratory successes, the year was one of mixed financial results. A significant change in the government's Medicare reimbursement policy led to an unanticipated reduction in the rate of growth for Epogen, which nonetheless brought in $1.1 billion. Worldwide Neupogen sales at $1 billion were also negatively affected by the strengthening of the U.S. dollar, the continued tightening of healthcare budgets in some European countries, and the improved antiviral therapies that reduced the incidence of depleted white blood cell levels in AIDS patients. In 1998 Amgen received further bad news when it was discovered that the standard dose of Epogen could be reduced by a third if injected under the skin rather than being administered intravenously. Far more tragic, though, was the news that a high number of deaths were reported among heart patients who used Epogen.

Still Amgen continued to build upon its foundation in 1998 and 1999. Research and development efforts were driven by internal research, in-licensing, and selective acquisition activities. In 1999 it invested in Abarelix, developed by Praecis Pharmaceuticals to reduce testosterone levels as part of treating prostate cancer. It also applied for FDA approval for an experimental drug to treat rheumatoid arthritis. During this time, Amgen shares rocketed 140 percent by the first quarter of 1999. With sales of its hallmark drugs Epogen and Neupogen, as well as Intergen still rising, and first quarter 1999 earnings up 32 percent, Amgen was prepared to enter the next century as the biggest biotechnology company in the world.

Principal Subsidiaries

Amgen Australia Pty Ltd.; Amgen N.V.; Amgen Canada Inc.; Amgen Greater China Ltd.; Amgen GmbH (Germany); Amgen S.A. (France); Amgen S.p.A. (Italy); Amgen K.K. (Japan); Amgen B.V. (Netherlands); Amgen-Biofarmaceutica (Portugal); Amgen S.A. (Spain); Amgen (Europe) AG (Switzerland); Kirin-Amgen, Inc. (Switzerland); Amgen Limited (U.K.); Amgen Sales Corporation (West Indies).

Further Reading

"Amgen Inc.," *Wall Street Journal,* January 13, 1993, p. B4.
"Amgen Patent Claim on Drug for Anemia Is Rejected by Court," *Wall Street Journal,* May 1, 1990, p. A8.
"Amgen Wins Ruling in Its Patent Dispute," *Wall Street Journal,* April 18, 1990, p. A12.
Andrews, Edmund, "Drug Ruling Is a Setback for Amgen," *New York Times,* March 15, 1990, p. D1.
——, "Rival Seeking to Freeze Amgen Profits on Drug," *New York Times,* January 31, 1990, p. D5.
Armstrong, Larry, "Churning Out Earnings As the Economy Starts to Slow," *Business Week,* July 31, 1989, p. 30.
——, "Two Rising Stars," *Business Week,* April 3, 1992.
"Blood Money," *Economist,* April 20, 1991, p. 86.
Flynn, Julie, "The Hormone That's Making Amgen Grow," *Business Week,* March 16, 1987, p. 96.
Giltenan, Edward, "Bioprofits," *Forbes,* January 7, 1991, p. 10.
Hamilton, Joan, "Amgen Is Hot—And Bothered," *Business Week,* January 23, 1989, p. 40.
——, "A Drug That Could Replace Transfusions—If It Ever Reaches the Market," Business Week, March 27, 1989, p. 60.
——, "The Gene Jockeys Are Finally Seeing Some Green," *Business Week,* July 2, 1990, p. 77.
Jacobs, Paul, "The Cutting Edge: Amgen Faces Hazards to Its Health," *Los Angeles Times,* November 30, 1998, p. C1.
"Leptin in Clinicals for Obesity," *Applied Genetics News,* June 1996.
"Looking for the Biotech Blockbusters," *Fortune,* July 7, 1986, p. 109.
Marcial, Gene, "Biotech Fans Love Amgen's One-Two Punch," *Business Week,* August 13, 1990, p. 104.
Mitchell, John, "Life with Amgen: A Four Part Series," *Thousand Oaks Star,* September 13–17, 1998.
Noah, Timothy, "U.S. Aide Urges Cut in Payments on Amgen Drug," *Wall Street Journal,* June 15, 1990, p. B4.
Palmer, Jay, "Trader," *Barron's,* March 11, 1991, p. 71.
Petruno, Tom, "Amgen: Getting the Worst of Both Worlds," *Los Angeles Times,* February 1, 1993, p. D1.
Pollack, Andrew, "Focus of Attention in Biotechnology," *New York Times,* May 24, 1991, p. D6.
Rundle, Rhonda, "Amgen Inc. Is Expected to Be Awarded $90 Million from Johnson & Johnson," *Wall Street Journal,* September 10, 1992, p. B8.
——, "Amgen Wins Biotech Drug Patent Battle," *Wall Street Journal,* March 7, 1991, p. A3.
——, "FDA Approves Amgen Cancer Drug, but Rivals Loom," *Wall Street Journal,* February 22, 1991, p. B1.
Savitz, Eric, "Fulfilling Their Promise," *Barron's,* September 25, 1989.
Stipp, David, "Genetics Institute, Japanese Firm Seek Injunction Against Amgen in Patent Case," *Wall Street Journal,* January 31, 1990, p. B2.
Teitelman, Robert, "Amgen: Biotech's Next Big Attraction?," *Financial World,* January 26, 1988, p. 12.
"Uncorking the Genes," *Barron's,* May 5, 1986.
Welling, Kathryn, "The Conversion of Paul," *Barron's,* September 7, 1987.
Wyatt, Edward, "What Price Promise?," *Barron's,* April 10, 1989.

—Carol I. Keeley
—updated by Carrie Rothburd

Amway Corporation

7575 Fulton Street East
Ada, Michigan 49355-0001
U.S.A.
(616) 787-6000
Fax: (616) 787-6177
Web site: http://www.amway.com

Private Company
Incorporated: 1959 as Amway Sales Corporation and
    Amway Services Corporation
Employees: 14,000
Sales: $5.8 billion (1998)
NAIC: 32562 Toilet Preparation Manufacturing; 325611
    Soap & Other Detergent Manufacturing

The pioneer of multilevel marketing (MLM), Amway Corporation manufactures and sells its own products as well as brand name products from other companies through a network of three million independent distributors worldwide. Unlike many other MLM firms, Amway offered a broad selection of items, ranging from cleaning products, cosmetics, and vitamins to travel services, discount car purchases, and catalog merchandise. The company's manufacturing facilities include a 3.5-million-square-foot production plant in Ada, Michigan, as well as plants in California, South Korea, and China. Amway products were delivered to distributors in the United States, Canada, and the Caribbean region through 12 Amway Service Centers. The company recorded explosive growth during the 1990s, increasing its revenue volume from $1 billion in 1990 to $7 billion in 1997, largely through international expansion. In 1999 the company formed a new company named Quixtar to sell consumer products at volume discounts through distributors via the Internet. Expectations for Quixtar were high, with some industry observers prognosticating that the new company could eventually eclipse the size of the traditional Amway business.

Origins

Amway's history represents a recent chapter in the long history of direct selling, which began in America's colonial period with unorganized Yankee peddlers selling tools and other items door to door. By the 1800s, direct selling decreased with the advent of mass merchandising, such as department stores and mail-order sales. In the later 19th century and early 20th century, however, some manufacturers found direct sales had advantages over the sales of their products in large stores. They preferred the personal touch, with salesmen making home demonstrations of their products exclusively. By the 1920s door-to-door salesmen were marketing brushes, cooking utensils, and other products. Retail stores fought back with local laws on peddlers. The federal government's regulations of company-employee relations led to the independent contractor solution. As independent contractors, salesmen were no longer employees: they were independent businessmen who bought products for resale. The first network marketing began in 1941 when two men created a mechanism to distribute Nutrilite vitamins. Within this mechanism, in addition to making money in retail sales, distributors earned a bonus on the sales of those individuals whom they personally recruited.

Amway's story began with the friendship between two youths who would become the founders. Jay Van Andel, born in Grand Rapids, Michigan, in 1924, and Richard M. DeVos, born in the small nearby community of Ada in 1926, became friends at Christian High School in Grand Rapids. Their common Dutch heritage of hard work, thrift, and entrepreneurship drew them together.

Both served in the Army Air Corps during World War II. Returning to Michigan after the war, they founded Wolverine Air Service to offer flying lessons. After selling Wolverine and a couple of other small businesses, the two young men bought a schooner and sailed off to see Latin America. The vessel sank in the Caribbean, and the two spent the next six months in South America; when they returned to Michigan, they started the JaRi Corporation to import and sell Caribbean handicraft.

In 1949 DeVos and Van Andel became distributors of vitamins for the Nutrilite Company of California. They enjoyed modest success from their own retail sales and from bonuses earned on the sales force they created in the Midwest. However, increasing government regulations and an internal conflict in Nutrilite led Van Andel, DeVos, and several other leading Nutrilite distributors to start their own venture. In April 1959

Company Perspectives:
Amway has become one of the world's largest direct selling companies by offering anyone the opportunity to have a business of their own.

they created The American Way Association, later renamed the Amway Distributors Association, to protect the independent distributors. They chose as their first product a biodegradable liquid organic cleanser made by a small Michigan firm, the kind of high-demand merchandise that could be easily sold by MLM. By September 1959 the Amway Sales Corporation and the Amway Services Corporation were begun to assist the distributors. Van Andel and DeVos, with the help of their wives and a handful of employees, began operations from offices in their basements. Van Andel created sales literature and supervised new product development; DeVos motivated and trained new distributors.

The company rapidly expanded. The first full year of operations in 1960 resulted in gross sales of $500,000. That figure doubled in each of the next two years, and in 1964 it reached $10 million. Thousands of distributors signed up each month. The expansion was so rapid that as soon as the company moved into new facilities, they were already crowded. In the company history, *Commitment to Excellence: The Remarkable Amway Story,* DeVos noted, ''We were always scrambling, just trying to catch up on back orders, working to train people adequately.''

In 1964 the business underwent a major reorganization. The three divisions—sales, services, and manufacturing—were merged to create the Amway Corporation, with Van Andel as chairman of the board and DeVos as president. Major business decisions were always made jointly by the two founders.

A laundry detergent, SA8, was introduced in 1960. Amway's reputation for selling soap was based primarily on its experience with this product. Other products included a dishwashing liquid, aerosol shoe spray, cookware, hair products, and cosmetics. In 1962 Amway started international growth, with its expansion into Canada. In 1968 the Personal Shoppers Catalog allowed distributors to sell merchandise made by other companies. Catalog sales increased thereafter.

The 1960s also brought some false starts and problems for the new firm. It began marketing underground fallout shelters, for example, in an era when civil defense against atomic warfare was a priority, but gradually consumers lost interest in the shelters. Other short-lived products included 110-volt automobile generators and waterconditioning units. It was not surprising that some items were not successful, however, for by 1968 the company was selling more than 150 products through its 80,000 distributors.

In July 1969 Amway's aerosol manufacturing plant burned completely to the ground. Losses were estimated at $700,000. The next day plans were made for a temporary substitute supplier and a new facility. Six months later the new facility was completed and the company moved in.

Growth and Controversy: 1970s–80s

The 1970s began with a change in corporate structure. Van Andel and DeVos remained board chairman and president, respectively, but four vice-presidents were added to handle the daily burden of a rapidly expanding firm. In addition, 30 regional warehouses were replaced by seven new regional distribution centers in Georgia, Michigan, Texas, California, New Jersey, Washington, and Colorado. Overseas expansion in the 1970s began with Australia in 1971, a choice that was partly influenced by the common culture, language, and economic system. Operations in the United Kingdom began in 1973. Other European operations began with West Germany in 1975, France in 1977, and the Netherlands and the Republic of Ireland in 1978. The Asian market was opened with ventures into Hong Kong in 1974, Malaysia in 1976, and Japan in 1979.

Diversification and acquisitions marked Amway's experience during this time. In 1972 the company purchased Nutrilite Products, Inc., the firm that had introduced Van Andel and DeVos to direct selling. Moreover, to reward and train its key distributors, the company acquired a yacht, Enterprise II, to serve as a floating conference center. A luxury resort and hotel complex on Peter Island in the British Virgin Islands was purchased in 1978, another amenity used to motivate Amway distributors. To house distributors coming to corporate headquarters, the firm bought the dilapidated Pantlind Hotel in Grand Rapids. The hotel, renovated and renamed Amway Grand Plaza Hotel, along with the newly constructed adjoining Grand Plaza Tower, marked a significant addition to downtown Grand Rapids.

Amway's growth was predicated on the success of its independent distributors. Lacking formal control over the distributors, Amway relied on bonuses and incentives to motivate them. As the company grew, distributors built larger and larger sales organizations. Their status and income increased and were marked by achievement levels identified as ''pin levels.'' The first major milestone of a successful distributor was reaching the level of Direct Distributor (DD), thus buying products and literature directly from the corporation instead of from a sponsor or other DD. Soon after Amway's origin, it began recognizing further sales milestones by using the names of jewels in achievement awards. The first Ruby DD was awarded in 1962, followed by Pearl, Emerald, and Diamond, in each instance the award including a decorative pin in which the specific stone was mounted. In 1966 the first Double Diamond level was reached, the Triple Diamond in 1969, Crown in 1970, and the highest level, Crown Ambassador DD, in 1977. By Amway's 25th anniversary in 1984, there were 24 Crown DDs and 15 Crown Ambassador DDs. Almost all of these 39 distributors were married couples; 28 were based in the United States.

The corporation kept in touch with its distributors through a monthly magazine, the *Amagram,* and provided a wide variety of sales literature, audiocassettes, and videocassettes. Although much of the product promotion was done by distributors, Amway also sponsored advertising in magazines, newspapers, radio, and TV. Its advertising costs were much less than other corporations, allowing Amway to introduce new products inexpensively.

Amway's most important legal battle was its successful defense against the allegation that it was engaged in an illegal "pyramid scheme," characterized in part by making money on recruiting new distributors. The Federal Trade Commission (FTC) in 1969 began investigating several companies, including Amway and Nutrilite, filing formal charges against Amway in 1975. Three months of FTC hearings began in May 1977, and a ruling by the full FTC in 1979 declared Amway's MLM plan legitimate. The decision was based on findings that distributors were not being paid to recruit new distributors, that products had to be sold for distributors to receive bonuses, and that the firm was willing to buy back excess distributor inventory. Lawyer Rodney K. Smith in his book *Multilevel Marketing,* after reviewing several cases, concluded, "Amway is not and never has been an illegal pyramid scheme."

In another legal controversy, the Canadian government charged Amway with not paying millions of dollars in customs duties on goods imported from the United States. In 1983, after pleading guilty in the criminal case, Amway paid a C$25 million fine in an out-of-court settlement. *Maclean's,* Canada's weekly news magazine, reported in a November 1983 issue that the fine was "the largest sum that a Canadian court has ever levied and one of the heaviest criminal penalties ever imposed against any corporation in the world." A separate civil case was continued by the Canadian government to collect the duties it should have been paid in the 1970s. Amway again settled out of court, this time in 1989 for C$45 million, 40 percent of the amount the Canadian government tried to collect.

Other serious problems occurred in the first half of the 1980s, when, for the first time, Amway sales declined. Some of the major distributors sold their businesses, and a substantial number of top executives either quit or were demoted or fired. The pyramid allegations surfaced again, not against the corporation, but against certain distributors who advised their sales groups to downplay retail sales, buy Amway merchandise for their own use, and purchase many motivational items, such as tapes and books, from the distributor.

One corporate executive, COO William W. Nicholson, previously a secretary to President Gerald R. Ford and a key player at Amway headquarters since 1984, oversaw the introduction of many new products and services. According to Nicholson, a turning point was reached in 1985 when MCI decided to market its long distance telephone services through Amway. By 1990 Amway was gaining more than 40,000 new clients per month for MCI. Offering its customers discount purchases on new cars was another Amway innovation; by 1988 this service competed with five other discount autobuying services, including the American Automobile Association. Other new items in the Amway inventory included Visa credit cards, prepaid legal services, real estate, and Tandy computers. The increase in high-tech merchandise and services was a dramatic shift for Amway, but the bulk of its sales remained in traditional products such as home care items. According to some analysts, Amway's transition to include more services reflected a general U.S. movement from a goods-and-manufacturing economy toward a service economy.

Not all new ventures worked well for Amway. The Mutual Broadcasting System (MBS), with its hundreds of affiliated radio stations, was purchased in 1977, but inexperience in the field, unfulfilled goals, and lack of profitability, according to DeVos, led to the sale of MBS in 1985. Having retained one satellite division from the original purchase, Amway manufactured and sold satellite dishes for some time, but the last division was eventually sold in 1989.

Probably the most publicized Amway activity in the late 1980s was its failed bid to take over Avon Products, Inc. Amway and corporate raider Irwin L. Jacobs jointly acquired 5.5 million Avon shares, 10.3 percent of the company's stock, in 1989. One week later, without Jacobs's cooperation, Amway offered to buy Avon for $2.1 billion in cash. Although a billion dollars in debt, Avon rejected the bid, citing Amway's evasion of Canadian customs duties and an incompatible corporate culture. In May 1989 Amway withdrew its bid. *Business Week,* in a May 1989 issue, characterized the bid as Amway "flexing its muscles for the first time"; although the bid failed, it was a good indication of Amway's financial strength.

Amway and its founders also became significant sponsors of the arts in the 1980s. In 1982 Jay Van Andel chaired the Netherlands American Bicentennial Commission, while the company sponsored an art exhibit at Amsterdam's Stedelijk Museum. Amway also supported tours of the Hong Kong Children's Choir and the Malaysian Youth Symphony Orchestra. In Grand Rapids, Michigan, the company helped fund an Art Museum, Arts Council, and the Gerald R. Ford Presidential Museum.

Amway also made commendable efforts to be environmentally responsible. Several of Amway's early products were biodegradable, and its SA8 detergent was available in a phosphate-free formula to limit pollution of waterways, and products were concentrated, reducing the amount of packaging that ended up in landfills. After chlorofluorocarbons were reported as hazardous to the ozone layer, Amway modified its aerosol products to delete those compounds. In 1989 Amway was a main sponsor of the two-month-long Icewalk, an expedition to the North Pole, designed to focus attention on environmental issues. In cooperation with the American Forestry Association, Amway also participated in the Global ReLeaf Program, to plant 100 million trees by 1992. In fact, on June 5, 1989, Amway received the United Nation's Environmental Programme's Achievement Award for Excellence, becoming one of two corporations to gain that honor. That same day the firm announced that it would end all animal testing in its research programs and that it would not cooperate with the Cosmetics, Toiletry and Fragrance Association's campaign against the ban on animal testing. In the area of recycling, Amway was named Michigan Recycling Coalition's 1992 Recycler of the Year, for its onsite recycling center and recycling practices in its operations and product development.

Despite the legal battles and occasionally unfavorable media characterizations of Amway, and direct selling in general, the concept was becoming increasingly popular. According to the Direct Selling Association (DSA), total retail sales were approximately $9.7 billion in 1988, up 10.3 percent from 1987, and Amway accounted for about 16 percent of that total. A 1976 Harris poll of U.S. households found that 16 percent of the respondents had tried direct selling. The boom was influenced by shifts in employment trends. First, more women had moved into the workplace and were selling Amway products; in fact, the DSA reported that in 1988, 81.4 percent of all salespeople were women. Moreover, instability in corporate employment had prompted increasing numbers of workers to consider alternative vocations, particularly those in which much of the administrative activities might be handled in home offices.

Amway's European expansion also continued throughout the 1980s, with operations established in Switzerland and Belgium in 1980, and in Spain and Italy in 1986. In 1985 Panama became the first Latin American base of Amway operations, followed by Guatemala in 1986. Amway de Mexico was established in June 1990 with headquarters in Monterrey and distribution centers in Mexico City, Guadalajara, Tijuana, and Juarez. Amway's success depended in part on its ability to adapt its product line to suit local cultures. In Japan, for example, the company began marketing a small induction range made by Japan's Sharp Company, which proved ideal for the small homes of Japan and sold well when demonstrated in the home by Amway distributors. Perseverance and high quality goods resulted in 1988 sales of $536 million for Amway (Japan) Ltd., Amway's largest overseas subsidiary.

International Expansion During the 1990s

Based on rapid international expansion, strong family leadership, and good financial condition, Amway remained a strong force in the 1990s. When Van Andel and DeVos, whose children had begun in the business in the mid-1970s, retired from the company in the early 1990s, all eight of the Van Andel and DeVos children were in leadership positions. Dick DeVos was named president in 1992, and Steve Van Andel was appointed company chairman. Jay Van Andel planned to remain active with the company as senior chairman and member of the policy board.

With the failure of communist economies in Eastern Europe and other nations, Amway's promotion of free enterprise became increasingly noteworthy in the years ahead. During the first half of the 1990s, Amway's territories expanded into Korea, Hungary, Brazil, Portugal, Indonesia, Poland, Argentina, the Czech Republic, Turkey, and Slovakia. In addition to tapping into new, emerging economies, foreign expansion was possibly part of Amway's strategy to offset slowing U.S. sales, prompted, according to one article in an October 1994 *U.S. News & World Report,* by regulatory investigations and media criticism of the company. In 1991, for example, Procter & Gamble won a $75,000 judgment from a group of Amway distributors, who were accused of spreading rumors that Procter & Gamble's products were instruments of Satan. Nevertheless, Amway's overall performance did not suffer; in 1994, sales increased by 18 percent over 1993 to total $5.3 billion. Dick DeVos estimated that 70 percent of 1994 sales came from abroad and predicted that figure would increase to 75 percent by fiscal 1996. In 1994 Amway moved its entrepreneurial business into the Eastern European market and also targeted Vietnam and China as its newest markets.

Japan was probably one of Amway's most successful foreign markets in the 1990s. In a culture where many Japanese businesspeople were accustomed to staying with one company for their entire career, Amway offered new economic freedom. In fact, word of mouth recommendations allowed Amway to operate in Japan without spending any money on advertising up until around 1989. In 1990, over 500,000 Japanese belonged to Amway, making the company one of the largest and most profitable foreign companies in Japan. In 1989 Amway (Japan) Ltd. had over $500 million in sales and $164 million in pretax profits, comprising about one-third of Amway's worldwide business. By the mid-1990s, revenues had more than doubled and the Japanese subsidiary had grown to include 816,000 salespeople. Public offerings of stock in Amway Japan and Hong Kong-based Amway Asia Pacific in 1994 proved a huge success, raising $6.7 billion. DeVos and Van Andel reaped the rewards, more than doubling their net worth in one year. Together, the pair were worth an estimated $9 billion by the end of 1994, vaulting the founders into the exclusive ranks of the ten richest people in the United States, according to *Forbes* magazine.

The strong reception to the public offerings in Asia was indicative of Amway's strength in the 1990s. The company was achieving success not only in Asia, but in markets throughout the world as well, deriving nearly all of its growth from international expansion. Between 1990 and 1996, Amway established 20 new foreign affiliates, increasing the number of countries and territories in which it operated to more than 75. Concurrent with the company's aggressive expansion overseas, sales soared, increasing 300 percent between 1990 and 1996 to reach $6.8 billion. The vibrant growth of Amway's international business, which accounted for more than 70 percent of companywide sales, could not have come at a better time because domestically the company's vitality was beginning to wane. Sales in the United States were flattening by the mid-1990s, unaided by persistent accusations of rumormongering that tarnished the company's image. The strident growth of the company outside North America, however, more than offset its anemic domestic performance, underpinning the seamless transition to the second generation of DeVos and Van Andel management.

Much of the company's success during the latter half of the decade depended on continued growth in foreign markets, but continued growth did not arrive. The foray into China, financed by the 1994 public offering of Amway Asia Pacific, ran into a pernicious obstacle in 1998, when the Chinese government banned direct selling because of concerns it would spawn illegal activity. Eventually, Amway was able to sidestep the prohibition by selling products through sales representatives that did not buy products and resell them, as traditional Amway distributors did. A more crippling blow was delivered by the faltering Asian economy in the late 1990s, the effect of which was readily discernible on Amway's balance sheet. Sales peaked at $7 billion in 1997 before falling 18.5 percent the following year to $5.7 billion. For the first time in more than ten years, Amway posted a decline in sales.

While the company waited for economic conditions in Asia to improve, new areas of growth were explored that hinted at an entirely revamped Amway for the future. In 1998 the company strayed far from its core business by teaming with Virginia-based Columbia Energy Group to sell natural gas and electricity in deregulated markets. Initially, Amway began selling natural gas in Georgia, intending to expand into electricity and to broaden its geographic reach as other states became deregulated. The company's other prominent venture during the late

1990s sparked the greatest excitement, leading some industry pundits to hail it as the boldest move in Amway's history. In September 1999, the company established a new company named Quixtar to sell consumer products on the Internet. With Quixtar, Amway used the same marketing concept as it did in its traditional business: distributors purchased products at volume discounts and earned commissions on the sales and bonuses from the sales of new recruits. Apart from Quixtar's business being conducted electronically, the greatest difference between Amway and its new company was the conspicuous absence of the Amway name. Years of negative publicity stemming from the numerous lawsuits filed by Proctor & Gamble had stained the Amway name, observers contended, prompting Amway to distance itself from a questionable reputation by adopting a new name. Additionally, by excluding the Amway name from its Internet venture, the company hoped to attract younger customers and younger distributors. The expectations for the new business were high, with the most far-reaching predictions calling for Quixtar to eventually supplant Amway's traditional business. President and co-chief executive officer Dick DeVos did not foresee the ultimate elimination of Amway's traditional business, maintaining both companies could coexist well into the future, but his confidence in Quixtar's potential was unequivocal. "Eventually," he informed *Cosmetics International* in June 1999, "Quixtar ought to be larger than Amway," giving Amway a lofty goal to pursue as it entered the 21st century.

Principal Subsidiaries

Nutrilite Products, Inc.; Amway Gesellschaft m.b.H. (Austria); Amway of Australia Pty. Ltd.; Amway Belgium Company; Amway (U.K.) Limited; Amway France; Amway (HK) Limited (Hong Kong); Amway Italia s.r.l. (Italy); Amway (Japan) Limited; Amway (Malaysia) Sdn. Bhd.; Amway Nederland Ltd. (Netherlands); Amway of New Zealand Ltd.; Amway de Panama, S.A.; Amway (Schweiz) AG (Switzerland); Amway De España S.A. (Spain); Amway Asia Pacific Ltd. (Hong Kong); Amway (Taiwan) Limited; Amway (Thailand) Ltd.; Amway GmbH (Germany); Amway de Mexico; Amway Communications Corporation; Amway Hotel Corporation; Amway Global, Inc.; Amway International, Inc.; Quixtar Inc.

Further Reading

"Amway Takes a Bold Step into Cyber-Selling," *Cosmestics International,* June 25, 1999, p. 7.

"Amway Tries Energy," *Crain's Detroit Business,* November 16, 1998, p. 33.

Biggart, Nicole Woolsey, *Charismatic Capitalism: Direct Selling Organizations in America,* Chicago: University of Chicago Press, 1989.

Butterfield, Stephen, *Amway: The Cult of Free Enterprise,* Boston: South End Press, 1985.

Conn, Charles Paul, *An Uncommon Freedom: The Amway Experience & Why It Grows,* New York: Berkley Publishing Group, 1983.

——, *Promises to Keep: The Amway Phenomenon and How It Works,* New York: G.P. Putnam's Sons, 1985.

Cross, Wilbur, and Gordon Olson, *Commitment to Excellence: The Remarkable Amway Story,* Elmsford, N.Y.: The Benjamin Company, 1986.

Eisenstodt, Gale, and Hiroko Katayama, "Soap and Hope in Tokyo," *Forbes,* September 3, 1990, p. 62.

"The $4-Billion Man: Rich DeVos Bet on Capitalism and Won," *Success,* May 1993, p. 10.

Grant, Linda, "How Amway's Two Founders Cleaned Up: Strong Overseas Sales Helped Richard DeVos and Jay Van Andel Add Billions to Their Fortunes," *U.S. News & World Report,* October 31, 1994, p. 77.

Holzinger, Albert G., "Selling America to the Japanese," *Nation's Business,* October 1990, p. 54.

Klebnikov, Paul, "The Power of Positive Inspiration," *Forbes,* December 9, 1991, p. 244.

Morgello, Clem, "Richard Johnson of Amway Japan: Challenging Japan's Sales Culture," *Institutional Investor,* May 1994, p. 23.

Muller, Joann, "Amway Tailors Marketing Approach to Individual Foreign Cultures," *Journal of Commerce and Commercial,* July 8, 1991, p. 4A.

Ruzicka, Milan, "Amway Wins Converts in Former East Bloc," *Journal of Commerce and Commercial,* June 3, 1994, p. 1A.

Shaw, Anita, "Amway: A Global Approach to the Future," *Soap—Cosmetics—Chemical Specialties,* November 1996, p. 66.

Smith, Rodney K., *Multilevel Marketing: A Lawyer Looks at Amway, Shaklee, and Other Direct Sales Organizations,* Grand Rapids, Mich.: Baker Book House, 1984.

Tate, Nancy Ken, "Amway's Green Roots Go Deep," *American Demographics,* April 1991, p. 18.

Vlasic, Bill, "Amway II: The Kids Take Over—Dick DeVos and Steve Van Andel Try to Shed Old Baggage," *Business Week,* February 16, 1998, p. 60.

Xardel, Dominique, *The Direct Selling Revolution,* Cambridge, Mass.: Blackwell, 1993.

—David M. Walden and Beth Watson Highman
—updated by Jeffrey L. Covell

Barnes & Noble, Inc.

122 Fifth Avenue
New York, New York 10011
U.S.A.
(212) 633-3300
Fax: (212) 633-3272
Web sites: http://www.shareholder.com/bks
http://www.bn.com

Public Company
Incorporated: 1894 as C.M. Barnes Company
Employees: 29,000
Sales: $3.01 billion (1999)
Stock Exchanges: New York
Ticker Symbol: BKS
NAIC: 451211 Book Stores; 45411 Electronic Shopping
& Mail-Order Houses

Barnes & Noble, Inc. operates the largest chain of bookstores in the United States. The company revolutionized bookselling by introducing giant, supermarket-style stores with deeply discounted books in the 1970s, and by the late 1990s it operated more than 520 such superstores across the country. Barnes & Noble is also a leading operator of mall bookstores, running the well-known B. Dalton chain, and Scribner's and Doubleday Book Shops. The company also operates, in partnership with Germany's Bertelsmann AG, barnesandnoble.com, one of the top online bookselling operations; both Barnes & Noble and Bertelsmann hold 41 percent stakes in the publicly traded barnesandnoble.com. Barnes & Noble is a leading supplier of books through mail-order catalogs as well. The company sells discounted publishers' remainders and imported books through its catalog, as well as books under its own "Barnes & Noble Books" imprint.

Early Decades

The Barnes family's history in the book business started in 1873, when Charles Montgomery Barnes went into the second-hand book business in Wheaton, Illinois. Barnes soon moved to Chicago, selling new and used books. By 1894 Barnes's firm, reorganized as C.M. Barnes Company, dealt exclusively in school books. In 1902 C.M. Barnes's son, William R. Barnes, became president of the firm, and he continued the business in partnership with several other men. The younger Barnes sold his interest in his father's company in 1917, when he moved to New York. In New York, he acquired an interest in the educational bookstore Noble & Noble, which was soon renamed Barnes & Noble. Though Mr. Noble withdrew from the business in 1929, the name Barnes & Noble stuck.

The company's early business was wholesaling, selling mainly to schools, colleges, libraries, and dealers. Barnes & Noble entered the retail textbook trade somewhat reluctantly. A report in *College Store* magazine recounted that single book customers were tolerated, but that the store's counters and display shelves functioned as barricades against their encroachment. Eventually the store took a building on Fifth Avenue that included a small retail space. The public then "launched a campaign of book buying that soon banished all doubt as to the need for a general retail textbook house in New York." Barnes & Noble opened a large retail store on Fifth Avenue and 18th Street, and this became the company's flagship. The quarters were enlarged and remodeled in 1941, and the store set the standard for college bookstores.

Barnes & Noble served the students of hundreds of New York City schools and colleges, and the store had to operate at top efficiency to accommodate the rush for textbooks at the beginning of each semester. In 1941 the store instituted a "book-a-teria" service that was soon picked up by other college bookstores. A clerk handed the customer a sales slip as he entered the store. Purchases were recorded on the slip by one clerk, money taken by another, and wrapping and bagging done by another. Barnes & Noble installed a telephone service that was quite advanced for the time, with five lines manned by specially trained staff. The New York store was also a pioneer in the use of "Music by Muzak," with the piped-in music interrupted at 12-minute intervals by announcements and advertising. Staff during the textbook rush season sometimes numbered over 300, and the store boasted a stock of two million books.

The successful retail division continued alongside Barnes & Noble's original business of wholesaling to schools and libraries. The company also ran an import and an export division, an out-of-print book service, and published several series of nonfiction books, including the *College Outline Series* of study guides. In 1944 Barnes & Noble began putting out children's educational books after it took over the publishing firm Hinds, Hayden & Eldredge. The company also opened branches in Brooklyn and Chicago, and managed an outlet for used books and publishers' remainders called the Economy Book Store.

Barnes & Noble operated on a grand scale from the 1940s onward. Its wholesale textbook division bought used books from around 200 campus bookstores all across the East and Midwest. The flagship retail store earned a place in the *Guinness Book of World Records* in 1972 as "the World's Largest Bookstore," and Barnes & Noble also claimed this store did the largest dollar volume of any retail bookstore in the country.

But Barnes & Noble began to grow in more ways when it came under the sway of a new young owner, Leonard Riggio. Riggio began his stellar career in the book business at age 18, when he was a poorly paid clerk at the New York University bookstore. Riggio initially studied engineering at night at the university, and in some sense he was unprepared for working with books. He recalled being embarrassed by a customer who asked for a copy of *Moby Dick*—Riggio had never heard of it. Nevertheless, he caught on to bookselling like no one else. In 1965, when he was only 24, Riggio borrowed $5,000 to open his own college bookstore, the Waverly Book Exchange. Though his store was only one-eighth the size of the official NYU bookstore, he soon rivalled his old employer's sales. He offered exceptional service to his student customers, airlifting textbooks to the store if necessary. The success of the Waverly Book Exchange allowed Riggio to buy or open ten more college bookstores over the next several years.

Arrival of Riggio: 1971

When Leonard Riggio set his sights on Barnes & Noble, the venerable bookstore was in a slump. President John Barnes, grandson of the founder, had died in 1969, and the retail and wholesale divisions of the company were purchased by a conglomerate called Amtel, which made toys, tools, and various other products. Business declined under the new management, and Amtel decided to sell. In 1971 Leonard Riggio purchased Barnes & Noble from Amtel for $750,000. He quickly changed the names of his ten other bookstores to Barnes & Noble, and revitalized the old Fifth Avenue store.

The new owner made Barnes & Noble an educational bookstore with a broader focus that included all kinds of how-to and nonfiction books. Riggio believed that more people read books for information than for entertainment, and he changed the setup of the flagship store to give customers easier access to books they might want. He organized the stock into new, more specific categories, for example dividing the traditional category of philosophy into yoga and mysticism. Other sections of special interest books included cooking, Judaica, handyman books, study aids, and dictionaries. Riggio also opened a special children's section in the Fifth Avenue store, which, like the adult sections, emphasized educational books.

Under Leonard Riggio's management, Barnes & Noble expanded to include stores in New York, New Jersey, and Pennsylvania. By 1976, the company leased and operated 21 campus bookstores, and the combined retail and wholesale divisions brought in $32 million in sales. His early success led Riggio to gamble on a new kind of bookstore—the book supermarket. Across the street from the old Fifth Avenue Barnes & Noble, Riggio opened a giant sales annex that sprawled over three buildings. All books at the annex were discounted between 40 and 90 percent, even new books and bestsellers. Shoppers spent hours piling bargains into shopping carts, as Riggio explained to *Publishers Weekly* that he had "set the customer free in an unintimidating atmosphere to roam over a vast space." The prairie-like annex included fiction, textbooks, children's books, reference books, art books, and gift books. Corners were devoted to books on special topics ranging from Latin America to transportation, and huge black and yellow signs directing customers to different categories could be read from 176 feet away. Riggio claimed that most of Barnes & Noble's customers did not intend to read the books they bought, and the casual, warehouse atmosphere of the sales annex was geared to the everyday shopper, not the scholar or bibliophile. It was a marketing technique that worked brilliantly.

Barnes & Noble's thriving sales encouraged the company to grow and innovate. In 1979 Barnes & Noble acquired a chain of retail stores called Bookmasters, and then bought up Marboro Books, Inc., a remainder company with discount retail outlets. Barnes & Noble operated a chain of Supermart Books which serviced drugstore and supermarket book departments, and ran the Missouri Book Co., selling used college textbooks. Barnes & Noble also more than tripled its college store leases in the mid-1980s, increasing from 40 in 1983 to 142 in 1986.

B. Dalton Acquisition: 1986

Total sales grew to about $225 million in 1985, and the next year Barnes & Noble made a major acquisition. For a price estimated at around $300 million, Barnes & Noble bought B. Dalton Bookseller, a bookstore chain with 798 outlets, from Dayton Hudson Corporation. B. Dalton was the second biggest chain bookstore, behind Waldenbooks, and its sales were estimated at $538 million in 1985. The acquisition put Barnes & Noble in the second place spot, and the company continued to acquire chains. In March 1990 Barnes & Noble purchased an upscale chain of 40 bookstores, Doubleday Book Shops, for an estimated $20 million. A few months later, the company became sole owner of a Texas and Florida chain of discount bookstores called Bookstop.

Barnes & Noble had used the name BDB Corp. for the holding company that owned Barnes & Noble, Inc., B. Dalton, and its other businesses. Leonard Riggio was the majority owner, and had a financial partner in a Dutch conglomerate called Vendex. The name of the holding company changed back to Barnes & Noble, Inc. in 1991, and the company reacquired rights to publish under the Barnes & Noble name. These rights had been sold after John Barnes died in 1969.

Opening of Numerous Superstores: Early 1990s

Barnes & Noble, Inc. had grown enormously in the 1980s through acquisitions. The company embarked on a new growth strategy in the 1990s, opening new ''superstores'' at a breathtaking pace. The superstores differed somewhat from the earlier Fifth Avenue ''book supermarket'' Barnes & Noble sales annex. The superstores were large, carrying as many as 150,000 titles, or six times the size of a typical mall bookstore, but they had amenities such as coffee bars and children's play areas, and were designed to be pleasant public spaces where people would browse, read, and mingle. Wide aisles and scattered chairs and benches encouraged customers to linger, and local managers had the autonomy to arrange poetry readings and puppet shows. The discounted (usually by ten to 40 percent) superstore stock was vast, yet the space was as posh and inviting as that of many independent bookstores. Barnes & Noble operated 23 superstores in 1989. Three years later there were 105, and the company intended to open 100 more each year through 1994. On one day in August 1992, Barnes & Noble opened five superstores, and two months later opened three more.

The superstores cost more than $1 million a piece to build, outfit, and stock, and Barnes & Noble lost money by opening so many so quickly. Though sales for 1991 were more than $892 million, Barnes & Noble, Inc. posted a loss of close to $8 million that year. But overall sales continued to rise, and the superstores contributed some impressive revenues. Eighty percent of new superstores contributed to company profits in their first year of operation. A Barnes & Noble superstore on the Upper West Side in Manhattan was expected to bring in $12 million in sales its first year, but it proved so popular with New Yorkers that it actually brought in between $16 million and $18 million. The average superstore commanded a much more modest $3.5 million. The superstores generated on the average twice the sales of mall bookstores, and in 1992 superstore sales rose by 114 percent.

Other booksellers complained about Barnes & Noble's rapid growth, believing that the market could not hold so many bookstores. But Leonard Riggio went on the record repeatedly to dispel claims that his growing chain was predatory. The amount Americans spent on books rose a hefty 12.5 percent in 1992, and Riggio believed the market would continue to grow. But the expansion of Barnes & Noble prompted competitive chains to build more stores too. Waldenbooks planned to more than double the size of its mall stores, from 3,000 to between 6,000 and 8,000 square feet. Borders Inc., a chain of superstores then owned by Kmart, planned to open two new stores a month in 1993.

Going Public: 1993

With its growth so enormous and debt so high, Barnes & Noble, Inc. decided to raise cash by selling its stock to the public. An initial stock offering in 1992 was postponed because of adverse market conditions. Wall Street analysts had been skeptical of the company's ability to sustain its profits, but a year after the first offering was withdrawn, superstore sales had continued to climb. These sales accounted for almost half the company's total revenue, up from 26 percent in 1992, and the company seemed more solid. Barnes & Noble stock began trading on the New York Stock Exchange on September 28, 1993, and demand was so high that brokers were unable to purchase as much as they wanted. The stock had been expected to sell for around $17 a share: it closed at $29.25 its first day. Leonard Riggio retained about a third of Barnes & Noble, Inc., and another third was controlled by his Dutch partner Vendex.

For the fiscal year ending in January 1994, Barnes & Noble reported an 87 percent gain in revenue at its superstores. The textbook area of the company continued to be quite profitable too, and the company ran almost 300 college bookstores across the country. Children's books also sold very well, and Riggio made plans to expand the square footage of the Barnes & Noble Jr. stores that were a part of the superstores. The growth of the Barnes & Noble chain under Leonard Riggio had been spectacular.

In spite of critics' fears that the company's rapid expansion would saturate the book market or set off vicious wars for market share, Barnes & Noble seemed able to keep abreast of what the public wanted in a bookstore, and supply just what was needed. The discount sales annex had been a radical step, eliminating the high-brow atmosphere long associated with bookstores. The superstores managed to combine the savings and huge selection of the discount store with an environment tailored equally well to book lovers, socializers, and bargain hunters. In many ways Barnes & Noble set the standard for its competitors from the early textbook store to the 1990s, by innovating in areas such as store design and marketing of software, and by its pioneering efforts such as providing books for children with disabilities, and offering a literary award to first-time novelists.

During the 1995 fiscal year, Barnes & Noble opened 97 additional superstores, bringing the total to 358. This growth increasingly led to declining sales for mall bookstores, including the company's own. Barnes & Noble had been closing between 50 and 60 B. Dalton stores per year since 1989, but in late 1995 decided to step up its mall closings. The company took a charge of $123.8 million for a restructuring program aimed at developing a core of more profitable mall bookstores (the charge led to a $53 million net loss for the year). During 1995, 69 B. Dalton stores closed and another 72 were shuttered the following year. At the same time, Barnes & Noble expanded the size of many B. Dalton outlets and opened a small number of new, larger B. Dalton stores each year, seeking to place them in locations that offered increased visibility and higher traffic flow. The new and enlarged units performed better than their predecessors, but all mall bookstores continued to be hurt by competition from nearby superstores. By 1998 Barnes & Noble operated more superstores than mall bookstores.

Entering Internet Bookselling: Late 1990s

In 1996 Barnes & Noble bought a 20 percent stake in Chapters Inc., the largest book retailer in Canada, but sold it three years later. For the fiscal year ending in January 1997, revenues soared past the $2 billion mark, reaching $2.45 billion, an increase of more than 23 percent over the previous year. In early 1997 the company entered the burgeoning market for Internet bookselling through a venture with America Online Inc. (AOL), whereby Barnes & Noble became the exclusive bookseller for the more than eight million AOL subscribers. Later that year the company launched its bookselling web site, barnesandnoble.com. These moves came following the emergence of a new competitive threat, namely Seattle-based Internet bookselling upstart Amazon.com, Inc., which had been founded in 1995 and had sales of $147.8 million by 1997—although it had yet to make a profit. The e-commerce battle between Amazon.com and barnesandnoble.com intensified in 1998 when German media behemoth Bertelsmann AG purchased 50 percent of Barnes & Noble's Internet operation for $200 million, a sizable capital fund for the nascent undertaking. For the fiscal year ending in January 1999, barnesandnoble.com saw its sales increase 381 percent, from $14.6 million to $70.2 million; it also developed an in-stock inventory of 750,000 titles ready for immediate delivery, which the company claimed was the largest in the industry. It also claimed to have the world's largest overall selection, with more than eight million new, out-of-print, and rare books available for ordering. In May 1999 Barnes & Noble and Bertelsmann took barnesandnoble.com public, selling 18 percent of the company and raising another $421.6 million for its war chest. The Internet bookseller's joint venture partners retained equal 41 percent shares in barnesandnoble.com. In July 1999 barnesandnoble.com announced the launch of an online "music store," with heavy discounts of as much as 30 percent off retail prices. Here again, Barnes & Noble was following trailblazer Amazon.com, which began selling music online a year earlier.

In March 1998 the American Booksellers Association joined with 26 independent bookstores in suing Barnes & Noble and Borders. The suit claimed that the large chains had violated antitrust laws by using their buying power to demand from publishers "illegal and secret" discounts. Barnes & Noble said it would vigorously defend this and similar actions that were subsequently brought against it. Antitrust concerns of a different nature scuttled Barnes & Noble's attempt to purchase Ingram Book Group, the largest book wholesaler in the United States, a deal that was announced in November 1998. Barnes & Noble was interested in Ingram for its system of 11 distribution centers spread throughout the country. The acquisition of this system would have cut distribution costs and enabled Barnes & Noble to speed delivery of books to its growing legion of online customers. The acquisition, however, drew strong opposition from independent booksellers as well as from Amazon.com. Federal Trade Commission officials ended up siding with the opponents, and recommended in June 1999 that the agency oppose the deal, having concluded that it would stifle competition in both online and offline book retailing. Barnes & Noble soon withdrew its takeover bid rather than enter into protracted litigation.

At the turn of the millennium, the biggest threat to Barnes & Noble's position as the number one U.S. bookseller was clearly Amazon.com, which in mid-1999 had a market value of $18 billion—more than three times the value of Barnes & Noble and barnesandnoble.com combined. In the Internet-crazed world of the late 1990s, the fact that Barnes & Noble held 15 percent of

the total U.S. book market versus Amazon's two percent mattered less than the companies' respective online bookselling shares: 15 percent for Barnes & Noble, 75 percent for Amazon. Part of Barnes & Noble's response to its upstart challenger was to slow its rapid rate of store expansion. In the wake of the failed acquisition of Ingram, it was likely that Barnes & Noble would step up its plans to build new distribution centers from the ground up, to support barnesandnoble.com and potentially give it a competitive edge in its battle with Amazon.

Principal Subsidiaries

Barnes & Noble Booksellers, Inc.; B. Dalton Bookseller, Inc.; Doubleday Book Shops, Inc.; Marboro Books Corp.; CCI Holdings, Inc.; B&N Sub Corp.; B&N.com Holding Corp.; B&N.com Member Corp.

Further Reading

"Barnes & Noble, Educational Bookstore, Celebrates 75 Years of Service," *Publishers Weekly,* February 12, 1949, pp. 901–04.

"Barnes & Noble Encouraged by Software Sales," *Publishers Weekly,* October 26, 1984, p. 69.

"Barnes & Noble Remodels Its Quarters for Efficiency," *Publishers Weekly,* December 6, 1941, pp. 2090–093.

"Barnes & Noble's Revitalization Program," *Publishers Weekly,* September 28, 1970, pp. 69–70.

"Barnes & Noble Stock Soars," *Publishers Weekly,* October 4, 1993, p. 14.

"Barnes & Noble to Buy Doubleday Book Shops," *Publishers Weekly,* March 2, 1990, p. 8.

"BDB Corp. Becomes Barnes & Noble Inc. and Plans to Expand," *Wall Street Journal,* January 9, 1991, p. B5.

Berreby, David, "The Growing Battle of the Big Bookstores," *New York Times,* November 8, 1992, sec. 3, p. 5.

Bhargava, Sunita Wadekar, "Espresso, Sandwiches, and a Sea of Books," *Business Week,* July 26, 1993, p. 56.

Breen, Peter, "Fulfilling Dreams: Why Is Barnes & Noble Trying to Buy Ingram Co. for $600 Million?," *Chain Store Age,* May 1999, pp. 244, 246, 248.

Cox, Meg, "Barnes & Noble Boss Has Big Growth Plans That Booksellers Fear," *Wall Street Journal,* September 11, 1992, p. A1.

——, "Barnes & Noble Cancels Proposal to Offer Stock," *Wall Street Journal,* September 30, 1992, p. A4.

Dugan, I. Jeanne, "The Baron of Books," *Business Week,* June 29, 1998, pp. 108–12, 114–15.

Freilicher, Lila, "Barnes & Noble Success Spawns New Mall Stores," *Publishers Weekly,* August 5, 1974, pp. 43–44.

——, "Barnes & Noble: The Book Supermarket—Of Course, Of Course," *Publishers Weekly,* January 19, 1976, pp. 71–73.

Furman, Phyllis, "Profits, but Little Respect: Despite Stellar Rise, Barnes & Noble Exec Remains Outsider," *Crain's New York Business,* February 26, 1996, p. 1.

Kirkpatrick, David D., "Barnes & Noble's Jekyll and Hyde," *New York,* July 19, 1999.

Knect, G. Bruce, "Independent Bookstores Are Suing Borders Group and Barnes & Noble," *Wall Street Journal,* March 19, 1998, p. B10.

Labaton, Stephen, and Doreen Carvajal, "Book Retailer Ends Bid for Wholesaler," *New York Times,* June 3, 1999, p. 1.

"Literary Supermarket," *Forbes,* May 15, 1976, p. 49.

"Marboro Sells Part of Assets to Barnes & Noble," *Publishers Weekly,* October 29, 1979, p. 28.

McDowell, Edwin, "Book Chain Refinances, Easing Debt," *New York Times,* November 18, 1992, p. D4.

Milliot, Jim, "Barnes & Noble Reports Strong Superstore Sales—Up 114% in '93," *Publishers Weekly,* April 26, 1993, p. 17.

——, ''Superstores Success Spurs New Try at B & N Offering,'' *Publishers Weekly,* September 13, 1993, p. 12.

Munk, Nina, ''Title Fight,'' *Fortune,* June 21, 1999, pp. 84–86, 88–90, 92, 94.

Mutter, John, ''Crown Sells Interest in Bookstop to BDB for $8.3 Million,'' *Publishers Weekly,* June 1, 1990, p. 15.

Prial, Dunstan, ''Barnes & Noble Books an IPO for Web Unit,'' *Wall Street Journal,* August 21, 1998, p. B1.

Reda, Susan, ''Barnes & Noble Forays Open Battle for On-Line Bookselling,'' *Stores,* May 1997, pp. 50+.

Reilly, Patrick M., ''Barnes & Noble Closes Book on Attempt to Buy Ingram, Amid FTC Objections,'' *Wall Street Journal,* June 3, 1999, p. B16.

——, ''Barnesandnoble.com to Join a Crowd of Firms Offering 'Online Music Stores,' '' *Wall Street Journal,* July 7, 1999, p. B2.

——, ''Barnes & Noble Draws Fire over Plan to Buy Ingram Book for $600 Million,'' *Wall Street Journal,* November 9, 1998, p. B10.

——, ''Barnes & Noble Likely to Build Centers for Distribution If Ingram Deal Fails,'' *Wall Street Journal,* June 2, 1999, p. B8.

——, ''Barnes & Noble Sues Amazon.com over Rival's Book-Selling Claims,'' *Wall Street Journal,* May 13, 1997, p. B3.

——, ''Bertelsmann to Buy a 50% Interest in Web Bookseller,'' *Wall Street Journal,* October 7, 1998, p. B8.

——, ''Booksellers Prepare to Do Battle in Cyberspace,'' *Wall Street Journal,* January 28, 1997, p. B1.

——, ''Online Bookseller's Shares Increase by 27% in IPO,'' *Wall Street Journal,* May 26, 1999, p. C19.

——, ''Street Fighters: Where Borders Group and Barnes & Noble Compete, It's a War,'' *Wall Street Journal,* September 3, 1996, pp. A1+.

Reilly, Patrick M., and John R. Wilke, ''FTC Staff Opposes Barnes & Noble's Ingram Bid,'' *Wall Street Journal,* June 1, 1999, p. B3.

Sandler, Linda, and Patrick M. Reilly, ''Barnes & Noble Slows Its Evelyn Wood Pace of Store Openings: A Twist in Bookseller's Plot,'' *Wall Street Journal,* September 2, 1997, p. C2.

Strom, Stephanie, ''Barnes & Noble Goes Public: Vol. 2,'' *New York Times,* September 3, 1993, p. D1.

Stross, Randall E., ''Why Barnes & Noble May Crush Amazon,'' *Fortune,* September 29, 1997, pp. 248, 250.

Symons, Allene, ''Barnes & Noble to Buy B. Dalton: Will Become Largest Chain,'' *Publishers Weekly,* December 12, 1986, p. 17.

Tangora, Joanne, ''Major Chains Set New Software Strategies,'' *Publishers Weekly,* August 24, 1984, pp. 38–39.

—A. Woodward
—updated by David E. Salamie

B/E Aerospace, Inc.

1400 Corporate Center Way
Wellington, Florida 33414
U.S.A.
(561) 791-5000
Fax: (561) 791-7900
Web site: http://www.beaerospace.com

Public Company
Incorporated: 1987 as Bach Engineering
Employees: 5600
Sales: $701.3 million (1999)
Stock Exchanges: NASDAQ
Ticker Symbol: BEAV
NAIC: 336411 Aircraft Conversions; 421860 Aircraft
   Equipment & Supplies Wholesaling; 336321 Aircraft
   Lighting Fixtures Manufacturing; 336360 Aircraft
   Seats Manufacturing

In just a decade, B/E Aerospace, Inc. (BEA) has grown from a tiny maker of airline seats to a leading, full spectrum cabin interiors company. BEA installs seats, lighting, galley equipment (including coffee makers, ovens, refrigerators), and high-tech in-flight entertainment (IFE) systems for the world's airlines. It does not, however, supply overhead bins or lavatories. Refurbishing cabin interiors accounts for more than half of revenue. Although BEA has acquired major names in business jet suppliers, commercial airlines accounted for 90 percent of its revenues.

Obscure Origins

Amin J. Khoury, a chemist with an M.B.A., was in charge of an investment group in the late 1980s looking for businesses in niche markets. Bach Engineering, which had revenues of under $50 million a year making passenger control units for airline seats, seemed an ideal opportunity. The group purchased the company in 1987.

In 1989, the group bought Bach's primary competitor, EECO Avionics, which landed the company a 60 percent mar-

ket share (later to grow to 70 percent). The two acquisitions gave the company its name: B/E Avionics. It went public in 1990. Revenues reached $24 million the next year, and the company acquired Trans Video Systems.

The market for cabin interior products was highly segmented, which made diversification a natural option for BEA. The company set out to compete on the basis of one-stop shopping and unique integrated products. Khoury touted the advantages in service and support this approach gave the airlines, which typically had three or four suppliers of the same type of equipment among their fleets.

In 1992 BEA paid the Pullman Co. $73 million for PTC Aerospace, a maker of airline seats, and its subsidiary Aircraft Products Co., which made equipment for in-flight kitchens. The company changed its name to B/E Aerospace (BEA) after these acquisitions. This was soon followed by the purchase of Britain's Flight Equipment and Engineering Ltd. ($13 million) and its supplier JFB Engineering ($6 million).

BEA continued its growth-by-acquisition strategy in 1993. It bought Aircraft Furnishings Ltd. of Northern Ireland (business and first-class seating) for $7 million, Royal Inventum of the Netherlands (galley equipment) for $33 million, and Acurex Corp. of California (onboard refrigerators) for $63 million in cash and stock. The international nature of the airline industry guided BEA in its selection of acquisitions, particularly as the company would have needed to obtain separate licenses to manufacture cabin equipment in Europe. Approximately half of the company's business was in exports.

BEA promptly integrated its seat-making operations, each of the acquisitions developing a specific type of seat. Its plant in England (formerly FEEL) worked on a unique, convertible coach/business class seat. Its Irish facility (AFL) developed business and first-class seating, while the US (PTC) and English plants worked on the coach and commuter seats.

Revenues reached $200 million in 1993. BEA sold $38 million worth of stock and refinanced $125 million of debt. By this time, BEA controlled 30 percent of the airline seat market, 60 percent of the galley inserts market, and was positioned as a

key player in the emerging in-seat video market, which was
estimated to be worth $200 million a year. At the time, BEA had
installed more in-flight video equipment than all its competitors
combined, including such giants as Sony and Philips. In Air
Transport World, Khoury stressed the importance of designing
electronic and video equipment into the seating itself, which
made BEA's integrated operation uniquely valuable.

BEA created B/E Services Division to upgrade and retrofit
aircraft interiors, located in Seattle, Los Angeles, and London.
B/E Services helped the company weather a downturn in
new aircraft orders prompted by a global recession and the
Gulf War.

At the end of its acquisition binge, BEA had transformed
itself from a tiny niche player to an industry leader. By this time,
BEA was involved in all areas of the cabin except lighting and
lavatories. The company preferred to stay out of markets it
could not lead. In 1995 it controlled 30 percent of the world
seating market, 70 percent of the PCU (headset jacks) market;
85 percent of coffee makers; and 85 percent of refrigeration
equipment. It also had the largest number of in-seat video
installations and ovens.

The height of seat design was incorporated into a new seat
for United Airline's international business class passengers. It
featured a massaging lumbar support, a fold-down footrest, and
headrest extensions to cradle the head during sleep.

Robert J. Khoury became CEO in April 1996. His brother
Amin remained chairman. From 1989 to 1996, the company
spent $290 million on acquisitions. It reduced its employment
by 1,500 and closed 11 facilities.

Great Expectations: 1997

BEA teamed with Harris Corp. in September 1997 to develop LiveTV, a joint venture to bring live television broadcasts
to airline passengers. The market for video entertainment systems on narrow-body aircraft was estimated to be worth $3
billion. Unfortunately, the joint venture encountered difficulty
finding a launch customer willing to invest the huge amount of
capital needed. LiveTV used BEA's BE 2000 video system
coupled with a new antenna and receiver based on U.S. military
satellite applications.

Unfortunately, BEA's top-of-the-line MDDS system encountered some trouble proving its reliability, which resulted in
British Airways canceling its order in the fall of 1997 after two
years of trials. The lost business would have been worth between $155 and $225 million.

MDDS offered video and audio on-demand, in-flight shopping and reservations services, video games and gambling, and
telephony. Reliability problems were not limited to BEA's
experience, particularly among interactive systems. Matsushita
Avionics, Hughes-Avicom International, Interactive Flight
Technologies, and Sony Trans Com were working on competing IFE programs. Some airlines operated advanced IFE systems in a non-interactive mode as an interim measure. Others,
like Delta, Quantas, and El Al, simply installed less ambitious
entertainment services such as Sony's Video Walkman until
interactive IFE could sort its bugs out.

BEA found another MDDS customer in Japan Airlines,
which tested the system on three of its Boeing 747s. At the time,
BEA was already developing the next generation of MDDS
systems, scheduled to become an option on 747s in mid-1999.
Some insiders scolded IFE manufacturers for not solving all the
reliability problems in existing technology before taking it to
the next level.

Alliances for the New Millennium

The market for IFE systems grew more competitive in the
late 1990s. Hughes-Avicom International and Rockwell Collins
demonstrated the viability of strategic alliances in this type of
environment. Within a year of the purchase of Hughes-Avicom
in November 1997, Rockwell Collins was left with a backlog of
about $350 million as airlines ordered its Total Entertainment
Systems by the hundreds. Hughes-Avicom had teamed with
Taiwan's AeroVision Avionics just that July, a move calculated
to strengthen Hughes-Avicom's Pacific presence. BEA looked
for its own partner, seeking both a strategic advantage and a
return on its hefty investment in IFE technology.

In January 1998, BEA confessed to providing aircraft seats
for five Iran Air planes in 1992 and thereby violating the U.S.
embargo. A contractor in France installed the seats. The incident cost more than $4 million in fines and legal fees.

BEA bought several companies in 1998. Puritan-Bennett
Aero Systems (PBASCO), a maker of oxygen delivery systems
and overhead lights, cost $70 million to acquire. The purchase
of Aircraft Modular Products (AMP) for $118 million gave
BEA an entrée into business jet interiors, a fast growing, fragmented market. Market leader AMP supplied Cessna, Gulf-
stream, Dassault, and others. Holbrook, New York-based Aerospace Lighting Corporation, another of the year's acquisition
targets, also specialized in business jets. BEA also bought SMR
Aerospace Inc., an Ohio design firm specializing in cabin
interiors for passenger jets, and paid TI Group plc $25 million
for C.F. Taylor (CFT), a U.K.-based cabin interiors firm and a
major supplier for Airbus. BEA tried to pay for the SMR
purchase through a secondary public offering but canceled these
plans when its share prices fell due to its large debt load.

BEA organized a Flight Structures and Integration Group
comprising its Jacksonville galley manufacturing business and

Seattle design and integration unit, as well as the newly acquired C.F. Taylor. The Interior Systems Group made galley and storage equipment in Florida, oxygen systems and passenger service units in Kansas, ovens in the Netherlands, and refrigeration equipment in California.

In fiscal year 1998, BEA's IFE group had revenues of $81 million. It had installed more than 34,000 video screens to date. These were mostly from its BE2000 and BE2000M product lines. By this time, the BE2000 series was the world's most widely used non-interactive IFE system. The more advanced BE2000M units were achieving some success. United Airlines raised its initial order for the more advanced system to a value of $73 million.

Asian Crisis; Decline and Sell-Off

While United was ordering more and more IFE systems, Delta Airlines and US Airways were contracting BEA to produce premium seating. Nevertheless, BEA could not sustain its pace of rapid growth in the face of the Asian financial crisis, cutbacks in Boeing's widebody program, and its own bank debt. Seven of BEA's manufacturing sites were also closed and 500 of its employees laid off.

Although BEA expected some revenue growth to continue, the company sold Sextant Avionique 51 percent of its IFE business, forming Sextant In-Flight Systems, to be headquartered at existing facilities in Irving, California. (After an initial cash payment of $62 million, the final price of the unit was pegged to operating results.) Sextant Avionique's spectrum of products included flight control and navigation systems, computers, and instruments. As a supplier of avionics (flight instrumentation and controls) and a competitor of Rockwell, which had also begun offering IFE systems, Sextant Avionique seemed a well-suited partner to elevate BEA's reputation for reliability. Guy Baruchel was tapped to head the new joint venture.

United Airlines remained a bright blip on BEA's radar. In February 1999, UAL announced it was ordering $40 million worth of BE2000 IFE systems for the coach class of 36 Boeing 747s. United already had 7,500 BE2000 units in operation; the BE2000M series was installed in all sections of its Boeing 767s.

Such good news may have explained the company's top executives again buying stock in their company. They had previously sold off significant amounts in August 1997. With the world airline fleet growing and new regulations requiring stronger seats, their optimism seemed well placed. BEA spent

$354 million on four major acquisitions in fiscal 1999. The company had a backlog worth $640 million in February 1999.

Principal Subsidiaries

BE Aerospace (USA), Inc.; BE Aerospace Netherlands BV; Royal Inventum, BV; BE Aerospace (Sales & Services) BV; BE Aerospace (U.K.); Holdings Limited; BE Aerospace (UK) Limited; AFI Holdings Ltd.; Fort Hill Aircraft Ltd.; CF Taylor (B/E) UK Limited; CF Taylor (Wales) Ltd.; BE Aerospace Services, Inc.; BE Advanced Thermal Technologies, Inc.; Acurex Corporation; BE Aerospace International Ltd.; Nordskog Industries, Inc.; Burns Aerospace (SARL); Puritan-Bennett Aero Systems Corporation; Sextant In-Flight Systems, LLC (49%); BE Intellectual Property, Inc.; Aerospace Interiors, Inc.; Aerospace Lighting Corporation; SMR Aerospace, Inc.; Flight Structures, Inc.; BE Aerospace Canada, Inc.; BE Aerospace (Canada) Company; BE Aerospace (France) SARL.

Principal Divisions

Seating Products Group; Flight Structures and Integration Group; Interior Systems Group; General Aviation and VIP Products Group; Services Group.

Further Reading

Chuter, Andy, "BA Drops B/E Aerospace As IFE Supplier Lufthansa Technik Signs to Support Tu-204-120," *Flight International,* December 17, 1997.

Flint, Perry, "BE Aerospace Breaks the Mold," *Air Transport World,* September 1993, pp. 77–78, 81.

Martinez, Matthew, "B/E Aerospace Flies with Cash, Not Stock: Wanting to Buy with Stock, Company's Move to All-Cash Deal Is Sign of the Times," *Mergers and Acquisitions Report,* October 12, 1998.

McCaffrey, Thomas P., "The Mid-Sized Firm As a Global Acquirer: BE Aerospace," *Mergers and Acquisitions,* January/February 1995. pp. 34–36.

Sessa, Danielle, "Insiders at BE Aerospace Buy Shares, Leading to Turnaround Speculation," *Wall Street Journal,* March 3, 1999.

Velocci, Anthony L., "BE Aerospace Feeling Pressure to Form IFE Business Alliance," *Aviation Week and Space Technology,* December 7, 1998.

——, "LiveTV Venture Awaits First Customer," *Aviation Week and Space Technology,* November 17, 1997, p. 52.

Winn, Allan, "Keeping Promises," *Flight International,* September 10, 1997.

—Frederick C. Ingram

BISSELL Inc.

2345 Walker, N.W.
Grand Rapids, Michigan 49544
U.S.A.
(616) 453-4451
Fax: (616) 453-2081
Web site: http://www.bissell.com

Private Company
Incorporated: 1883
Employees: 2,500
Sales: $450 million (1999 est.)
NAIC: 333319 Other Commercial & Service Industry
Machinery Manufacturing; 335212 Household
Vacuum Cleaner Manufacturing; 325612 Polish &
Other Sanitation Good Manufacturing

BISSELL Inc. is the number four manufacturer of floor care products, trailing Hoover, Eureka, and Royal. The company is best known for its line of mechanical carpet cleaners, which predate electrical vacuums by 50 years and continue to defy obsolescence; carpet sweepers helped build BISSELL into a diversified homecare company. In the 1980s and 1990s the company built up an impressive and wide-ranging line of deep cleaners. In addition to carpet sweepers and deep cleaning machines, BISSELL Homecare manufactures vacuums, electrical appliances, cleaning agents, and personal care products. The BISSELL Graphics division designs, manufactures, and markets a wide range of specialty tags, labels, clinical research/ study forms, and other printed products. Finally, the BISSELL Healthcare division markets patient-assist, rehabilitation, and orthopedic treatment products.

Building a Better Carpet Sweeper in the Late 1800s

The BISSELL carpet sweeper was developed in 1876 by Melville R. Bissell, who operated a crockery store with his wife, Anna, in Grand Rapids, Michigan. The Bissells received most of their fragile glass and china shipments in crates packed with sawdust, which often spilled onto the floors in their shop. In sweeping up the wood shavings, Bissell kicked up dust that got into his rugs, prompting him to invest in a carpet sweeper. These devices, which had been available since 1858, used floor wheels to drive rotating brushes that swept dirt out of the pile in rugs. Although not perfect, they were infinitely more effective than brooms.

Bissell purchased a model called the ''Welcome,'' but he noted several deficiencies in the design and endeavored to develop a better model. The BISSELL design also used floor wheels to drive a brush, but on an improved reduction gear. The bristles bent slightly as they brushed through the carpet. When they rotated off the floor, they sprung whatever debris was in their path up into a compartment. The dirt could be emptied by simply opening the top of the box and shaking it over a garbage can.

Soon, many of the shop's patrons were asking where they could buy this carpet sweeper, which they had seen work so effectively on sawdust, and Bissell began to wonder if his carpet sweeper was a marketable product. Anna Bissell had no doubt about the product. She eloquently noted that because Americans were clean in mind and body, the carpet sweeper would serve the cause of responsible living while reducing the strain and drudgery of housekeeping.

Melville Bissell could not deny his wife's logic, or the many customers asking about the sweeper. Beginning to see the device as nothing less than a revolution in housekeeping, Bissell cleared a space on the second floor of their crockery store for an assembly shop, where he supervised a small staff of workers. His wife collected brushes from cottage industry homemakers who were enlisted to assemble them.

The Bissells conducted their own sales visits, choosing to distribute their product through housewares retailers rather than through door-to-door salesmen. It took several months, but Anna Bissell succeeded in getting skeptical shopkeepers to purchase and display the carpet sweeper.

The device performed well in in-store demonstrations, and word of mouth quickly established a strong demand for the product. Soon the Bissells were turning out 30 carpet sweepers a day and shipping them to retailers throughout Michigan, the Midwest, and the Eastern states.

Company Perspectives:

Since 1876, BISSELL has been a world leader in manufacturing and marketing a broad line of quality home and floor care products—sweepers, deep cleaning machines, vacuums, and cleaning formulas—which appeal to consumers of all ages, incomes, and lifestyles. Today, these products are welcomed in homes across America, Canada, throughout Europe, and in emerging international markets.

The fiber of how we do business begins with our Mission: ''Quality is defined by our customers, whose complete satisfaction is our goal. Through a Company-wide initiative of continuous improvement, by managing against specific data, and by showing respect for our Associates, we will produce the highest quality products and provide the best service.''

The Bissells stumbled onto an effective new sales tool when a young BISSELL bookkeeper named Claude Hopkins suggested a change in the sweeper's sales brochure. He argued that schematic diagrams and other mechanical details were of less interest to the consumer than the fashion aspects of the product. Hopkins's brochure focused on the ''*golden* maple, *opulent* walnut and *rich* mahogany'' used to make the BISSELL sweeper.

The company's directors feared that Hopkins's approach undersold the technological superiority of the product: every aspect of the sweeper was patented, and the company vigorously sued those who infringed on its design. But they could not deny the fact that Hopkins drastically boosted sales of the carpet sweeper. Inspired, Hopkins drew up a pamphlet promoting a limited edition of the device made from vermilion, a rare and exotic wood transported out of the jungles of India on the backs of elephants and floated to port on rafts. The stunt produced more sales in six weeks than the company had been able to muster in a year. Hopkins, who developed the strategy of promoting the carpet sweeper as a Christmas gift, later joined a Chicago advertising agency, where he built a career as one of the first masters of his art.

Melville and Anna Bissell incorporated their company in 1883 and built a new factory for making carpet sweepers. They also bought out two competitors, the Michigan Carpet Sweeper Company and the Grand Rapids Carpet Sweeper Company, but only to raid them of their managerial talent.

Soon after the new five-story BISSELL plant was completed, it was leveled in a fire. Melville Bissell mortgaged his entire personal fortune, including his home and his stable of horses, to finance a reconstruction. Shortly after production resumed, it was discovered that the factory's entire output was defective. To protect the brand name, Bissell ordered the recall of every defective model, at a cost of more than $35,000.

International Expansion in the Late 19th Century

The BISSELL name had become so well established by 1889, and had such a strong reputation for quality, that few competitors dared to challenge it. But tragedy struck that year

when Melville contracted pneumonia and died at the age of 45. When Anna Bissell took control of the company, she became one of the first female executives in the United States.

After taking over for her husband, Anna decided to build BISSELL into an international brand. The company already had agencies in 20 foreign countries, but its penetration was light. Even though Europeans were more meticulous housekeepers, they had fewer carpet sweepers than Americans.

BISSELL salesmen in England held public demonstrations of the product, gently proving that the carpet sweeper could clean even the most delicate rugs. The big break came when Queen Victoria allowed the BISSELL sweeper to be used in her palace. Following the royal example, thousands of English homemakers ordered their own sweepers. Soon the practice of carpet sweeping became known generically as ''Bisselling.''

First Competition from Vacuum Cleaners in the 1920s

Anna Bissell remained head of the company into the 1920s, when a new threat to the business emerged. Household electrification swept aside gas lights, hand cranks, and foot pedals and paved the way for hundreds of new appliances, including the vacuum cleaner. Bissell, however, remained confident that the public would not overcome its fear of the strange new power source for many years. She recognized electric vacuum cleaners as unforgiving monstrosities that were capable of shredding frail carpets and expensive Oriental rugs. Many models shorted out through misuse, causing terrifying flashes and even fires. BISSELL's greatest asset at this point was the carpet sweeper's well-established position in the retail network. By contrast, vacuum cleaners were sold by door-to-door salesmen, who had reputations as boisterous, imposing cheats.

As better models were developed, vacuum cleaners were accepted in more homes. In addition, vacuum manufacturers gradually eased their way into retail channels, where they made the BISSELL carpet sweeper look ancient by comparison. To avoid losing its place in the market, BISSELL introduced its own electric vacuum cleaner, with motorized brushes and a fan blade for sucking up dust. BISSELL vacuum cleaners, like others on the market, were loud and clumsy and kicked up dust.

Convinced that a market remained for the carpet sweeper, BISSELL continued to make improvements to its product line. Earlier innovations included better bearings and a handle that adjusted the sweeping pressure on the brushes. With a design that debuted in 1928, the cleaner automatically adjusted the height of the brushes to different surfaces.

Melville Bissell, Jr., took control of the company from his mother by this time. During the Great Depression, few people had money to spend on an expensive electric vacuum, so they opted for the BISSELL carpet sweeper. As demand for vacuums weakened, causing many manufacturers to go out of business, BISSELL decided to discontinue building electric models.

Bissell believed that the carpet sweeper had a unique place in the home. Where electric vacuums could be used for heavy duty cleaning, the carpet sweeper would be favored for quick touch-ups, in the same way a broom might be used to sweep up a small mess. To reinforce a peaceful coexistence between the two devices, BISSELL emphasized the ease and convenience of using the carpet sweeper instead of a vacuum cleaner for small jobs around the home, and for cleaning the patio, the pool area, and the cottage. There was a place in every home for the lightweight, inexpensive, and portable carpet sweeper.

World War II naturally curtailed production of consumer products. At BISSELL, the raw materials for making a carpet sweeper, including rubber, aluminum, and wood, were diverted for military production. As a manufacturing organization, BISSELL was melded into the military procurement system and given the task of building a variety of light industrial implements.

After the war, with newfound prosperity and a rapidly increasing standard of living, vacuums became a fixture in every home. In England, the practice of carpet cleaning became known as "Hoovering." The company reestablished its European franchise by building—or in some cases rebuilding—factories and distribution facilities in Britain, France, Germany, Ireland, and Switzerland. To these were added sites in Canada and Australia, making Bissell a truly international name.

Diversification Under Melville Bissell III: 1953–71

Melville Bissell III, a nephew of Melville, Jr., took over leadership of the company in 1953. Unlike his uncle, this Melville Bissell was determined that the Bissell name should stand for more than just mechanical carpet sweepers. He saw the company's market as "floor care" and, later, complete home care. Bissell was aware that the carpet sweeper was effective only for topical dirt. Conventional vacuum cleaners, which BISSELL had continued to avoid, could only brush up dirt in the top quarter-inch of a carpet. A more thorough cleaning, down to the nap of a carpet, would require wet shampooing. He ordered the development of a new product called the Shampoomaster, a nonelectric device that used only water and detergent. The Shampoomaster was manufactured from 1957 to 1967 and during those years was promoted ahead of BISSELL's carpet sweeper.

The company's revenue grew fivefold over this period, but only because of a burst in demand for the carpet sweeper. Sales of the Shampoomaster floundered because few homes were large or consistently dirty enough to warrant shampooing. The device was discontinued, and the company turned back to its traditional carpet sweeper line. In addition, in 1960 BISSELL had introduced the "stick vac," a lightweight vacuum that could be handled like a broom. The BISSELL stick vac competed with similar models built by vacuum cleaner manufacturers Regina and General Electric. BISSELL also acquired the Ohio-based Wood Shovel and Tool Company in 1965. The firm manufactured more than 300 different garden implements, but after only three years all but the company's snow shovel line was spun off.

In 1970 BISSELL purchased a Swiss electric shaver company. But when European currencies were allowed to float in 1973, manufacturing costs skyrocketed. BISSELL sold all of the company's assets, but kept an electric motor technology that was developed into a headlight wiper motor for BISSELL's French

subsidiary RIAM S.A. In 1971 BISSELL entered the printing industry by taking over the Michigan Tag Company, which was renamed BISSELL Printed Products. A second firm, Imperial Business Forms, was acquired by BISSELL, and was followed by two more firms, Atlas Tag & Label and Marion Manufacturing, all of which were later part of BISSELL Graphics.

Refocused on Floor Care Under John M. Bissell in the 1970s

John M. Bissell, a cousin to Melville III, assumed leadership of the company in 1971. Unlike Melville, he believed that the company should not risk losing the business it knew first: floor care. In his mind, the center of that business was the carpet sweeper. Based on that business, BISSELL focused its acquisitions on new ways to protect and grow its floor care business. BISSELL purchased the Penn Champ Company, a manufacturer of aerosol cleaners and fabric shampoo, in 1974. Hoping to provide retailers with an entire family of BISSELL floor care products, the company developed another token line of vacuum cleaners and in 1980 reintroduced the carpet shampoo concept, but as a simple household wet extraction device called The Carpet Machine.

In 1981 BISSELL rolled out a second wet carpet cleaner called "It's Magic." The product contained no pump (the part most likely to fail on such devices), but drew its water pressure from a sink faucet. Although the wet carpet cleaner filled out the BISSELL line, it performed below expectations and was phased out of production.

Resuming its diversification in 1976, BISSELL purchased Venturi, Inc., a manufacturer of plant foods and other organic products. In 1978 BISSELL purchased the Atlantic Precision Works, a manufacturer of kitchen warming trays, and relocated the factory from New York to Grand Rapids. BISSELL later added two other companies to the operation, Slip-X Safety Treads, a bathroom mat maker, and the E&B Company, which made flag poles and clothesline supports. Eventually BISSELL sold off all of these operations.

BISSELL acquired the Fred Sammons Company of Chicago in 1982. Involved in the manufacture of self-help aids for the disabled community, Sammons sold primarily to institutional markets until a new Enrichments line was established for individuals. To support sales of these products, BISSELL created a small network of retail stores under the same name, which it placed in shopping malls. By the early 1990s, Sammons products were sold primarily via direct-mail catalogs.

Expanded Deep Cleaning Offerings in the 1980s

BISSELL's diversification was necessary, not because of weakness in the floor care segment, but because the floor care market had stagnated. John Bissell told the *Grand Rapids Press,* "If we're going to achieve the growth rate we want, we'll have to do it through acquisitions." BISSELL acquired Chicago-based Maxi Vac, Inc., a maker of wet/dry vacuum cleaners, in 1982, boosting its manufacturing and research capabilities in the deep cleaning market. In 1985 BISSELL introduced a three-in-one vacuum cleaner, intended for use on stairs and on the second level of homes, where a heavy vacuum cleaner would be less practical and more cumbersome. In 1992 the company rolled out a new carpet shampoo device called the BISSELL Promax (later renamed Powerlifter because of a copyright battle with Hoover). This was followed a year later by another product with more attachments and capabilities, called the BISSELL Big Green Clean Machine.

The BISSELL Big Green Clean Machine was promoted through the much-maligned but effective medium of the "infomercial." Although the ad harkened back to the sweeper demonstrations of the 1880s, BISSELL risked damaging its good name in such an ad. Nevertheless, the infomercial gave the BISSELL Big Green Clean Machine a more successful launch than other mediums might have. In fact, a smaller version of the device, the BISSELL Little Green Clean Machine, was introduced the same way in October 1993.

Acquisition of the Singer Line in 1996

In 1994 Mark Bissell replaced his father, John, in the positions of president and chief operating officer, with John Bissell remaining chairman and CEO. Two years later Mark Bissell was named president and CEO, with John continuing as chairman. Also in 1996 BISSELL broadened its line of floor care products through the acquisition of the Singer line of upright vacuums and deep cleaners from Ryobi Motor Products. The purchase particularly helped BISSELL gain a more significant presence in the upright vacuum sector, as well as in the lower price end of the market—the company's products generally fell into the upper end.

Within the deep cleaning category, BISSELL already had been successful in the area of canister models (the Big Green) and portable models (the Little Green). In 1997 the company launched its first upright model, the PowerSteamer. BISSELL continued to build up its line of deep cleaners with the late 1997 debut of Steam 'n Clean, the mid-1998 introduction of the Spot Lifter, and the spring 1999 launch of the PowerSteamer ProHeat Plus. The Steam 'n Clean model, at a retail price of less than $150, was the industry's first competitively priced steam cleaner; it also was touted for its compact size, allowing users to comfortably hold it in their hands, and for cutting warmup time from 20 minutes to 30 seconds. BISSELL promoted the new product exclusively through infomercials for the first several months after its launch. The Spot Lifter, retailing for just $59, was a handheld, portable model and was cordless and rechargeable. The PowerSteamer ProHeat Plus, an upright deep cleaner retailing at $299, was said to be the first deep cleaner to contain a heating element.

The Hoover Co. filed two lawsuits against BISSELL in May 1998 alleging patent infringements on certain features of BISSELL deep cleaners and upright vacuum cleaners. BISSELL quickly countersued but the parties reached a settlement in May 1999 shortly after the suits went to trial. The agreement was not disclosed but Hoover stated that the settlement "included an agreement regarding future use of Hoover extractor patents under license."

By the late 1990s deep cleaning machines had clearly replaced carpet sweepers as the core BISSELL business. Although the company held 90 percent of the sweeper segment, that translated into only five percent of overall sales. With its increasingly varied line of floor care products, its emphasis on new product development, and its aggressive marketing and advertising efforts, BISSELL was certain to remain a major player in its industry. It also seemed likely to remain a private company. In mid-1999 Mark Bissell told *HFN—The Weekly Newspaper for the Home Furnishing Network,* "We have a very loyal shareholder base. Our vision is to continue to be a family-held company, and to balance liquidity with the needs of shareholders. . . . I have three kids. My brother has three kids. So there are a lot of Bissellettes running around. We hope that someone from the next generation will rise up from the ranks and run the company."

Principal Subsidiaries

GRAPHICS DIVISION: Atlas Tag & Label, Inc.; ATL East Tag & Label, Inc.; BISSELL Graphics Corp.; Imperial Graphics, Inc. HEALTHCARE DIVISION: AbilityOne Corp.; Am Fab Inc.; Sammons Preston Canada Inc.; Sammons Preston, Inc.; Midland Mfg. Co.; Tumble Forms. INTERNATIONAL: BISSELL Australia Pty Ltd.; BISSELL Ltd. (Canada); BISSELL Homecare Inc. (U.K.); BISSELL Inc.-U.A.E. (United Arab Emirates).

Principal Divisions

Homecare Division; Graphics Division; Healthcare Division.

Further Reading

"Bissell, Inc. Finds Niches—and Grows," *Grand Rapids Press,* June 2, 1985, p. G1.
"The Bustling Business of Bissell," *Michigan Business,* September 1984, pp. 40–42.
Hill, Dawn, "Bissell Aims to Fill Out," *HFN—The Weekly Newspaper for the Home Furnishing Network,* June 17, 1996, pp. 37+.
——, "Bissell Deepens Its Niche," *HFN—The Weekly Newspaper for the Home Furnishing Network,* January 13, 1997, p. 154.
King, Eileen M., "Bissell Counters Hoover Suits," *HFN—The Weekly Newspaper for the Home Furnishing Network,* July 13, 1998, p. 47.
——, "Hoover Takes Bissell to Court: Two Separate Lawsuits Claim Patent Infringement," *HFN—The Weekly Newspaper for the Home Furnishing Network,* June 1, 1998, p. 39.
"More 'Filth' on TV," *Advertising Age,* February 3, 1992, p. 10.
Powers, David Cleary, "Bissell Carpet Sweepers," in *Great American Brands,* New York: Fairchild Publications, 1981.
Rook, Martin, "Bissell: Big-Buck Blitz," *HFN—The Weekly Newspaper for the Home Furnishing Network,* April 7, 1997, p. 139.
"Suits Settled," *HFN—The Weekly Newspaper for the Home Furnishing Network,* May 24, 1999, p. 50.
Zaczkiewicz, Arthur, "Sweeping Success," *HFN—The Weekly Newspaper for the Home Furnishing Network,* June 14, 1999, p. 32.

—John Simley
—updated by David E. Salamie

Blue Bell Creameries L.P.

1101 S. Horton
Brenham, Texas 77834-2807
U.S.A.
(409) 830-2180
Fax: (409) 830-2198
Web site: http://www.bluebell.com

Private Company
Incorporated: 1907 as Brenham Creamery Company
Employees: 2,300
Sales: $225 million (1997 est.)
NAIC: 42243 Dairy Products Wholesalers; 311520 Ice
Cream Manufacturing

Blue Bell Creameries L.P. produces a line of premium ice cream available in 45 flavors, including year round and seasonal flavors. Blue Bell products include frozen yogurt, sherbet, and more than 70 varieties of ice cream snacks, such as Mooo Bars and Country Cones. Homemade Vanilla is the company's best-selling ice cream, as well as the bestselling ice cream in most of the company's distribution areas. Blue Bell prides itself on fresh, quality ingredients and the care that is put into the process of making ice cream. Based in Brenham, Texas, Blue Bell distributes its products in 12 south central and southeastern states. Despite the limited distribution area, Blue Bell represents the third most popular branded ice cream in the United States and produces approximately 100,000 gallons of ice cream each day.

Rural Beginnings: Early 20th Century

Blue Bell Creameries originated in 1907 as Brenham Creamery Company, founded in Brenham, Texas, 70 miles northwest of Houston. The company produced only butter until 1911 when the creamery began to hand-crank two gallons of ice cream each day in an ice cream maker set in a wooden tub filled with ice. All of the major ingredients—milk, cream, eggs, and fresh fruit—were purchased from local farmers and producers. Along with butter, a horse and wagon allowed delivery of the ice cream to the area around the creamery. Though most people made their own ice cream at the time, the creamery's ice cream became popular through word of mouth.

Financial difficulties at the company began in 1916 and continued until E.F. Kruse was hired as manager of the creamery in 1919. Bankruptcy loomed at that time and Kruse left his first paychecks uncashed to ensure the solvency of the company. Under Kruse's conservative management the Brenham Creamery thrived. The company purchased its first motorized vehicle, allowing the company to expand its delivery radius and its business. In 1930 Kruse changed the name of the company to Blue Bell Creamery. The name was taken from the bluebell, a native Texan wildflower that proliferates in the hot Texas summers—high season for enjoying ice cream. In 1936 Blue Bell acquired a refrigerated truck, allowing the company to distribute fresh ice cream longer distances, as well as a continuous freezer, which increased production capacity.

Though Blue Bell is not owned by the Kruse family, it has been operated like a family business. E.F. Kruse brought his sons, Edward and Howard, into the company when they were 13 and 11 years old, respectively. The two made ice cream sandwiches and frozen snacks on a stick and prepared fresh peaches for mixing into an ice cream base. Both proceeded to major in dairy science at Texas A & M University and returned to the company as managers. After a short time in another food company, Ed Kruse rejoined Blue Bell at the request of his father, becoming a salesman in 1951. The same year, E.F. Kruse died and Ed Kruse was selected to take his place, becoming manager of Blue Bell at 23 years of age.

Howard Kruse returned to Blue Bell in 1954 as plant supervisor. He quickly immersed himself in the details and nuances of making quality ice cream. In 1956 Howard was promoted to assistant manager of the company, though he also supervised the plant. In 1958 Blue Bell ceased production of butter and focused solely on the production and sale of ice cream.

In addition to the Kruses, another Brenham, Texas native joined the company at a young age. John Barnhill worked in the Brenham plant for the Kruse brothers and also painted the Blue Bell advertising slogans on drugstore windows where their products were sold. After college, Barnhill rejoined the company in 1960 as its first Houston salesman. In 1962 Barnhill became branch manager of Houston, Blue Bell's first sales and distribution branch outside of Brenham. With the popularity of Blue Bell ice cream growing in Houston, and after 54 years in operation, the

---

Company Perspectives:

From the beginning, we've been cranky about the home-made taste of our ice cream. So cranky, in fact, we have people whose only job (if you call eating our ice cream a job) is to taste every flavor of Blue Bell to make sure it's perfect. But they aren't the only tough judges. Everyone from our Chairman on down is fastidious about the special taste of our ice cream.

Obviously, our preoccupation with taste has paid off because Blue Bell is the most popular ice cream in these parts. Of course, the ultimate taste test is yours, so pick some Blue Bell flavors and give them a try. Once you do, you'll know why we eat all we can and we sell the rest.

---

company achieved the milestone of $1 million in sales in 1963. In 1965 another distribution center opened in Austin and the company began automated production of ice cream.

Cultivation of Country Origins in the 1970s

A banner year for Blue Bell came in 1969 when Howard Kruse developed the company's bestselling ice cream, Home-made Vanilla, and Metzdorf Advertising Agency was hired to develop a country image for Blue Bell. These two events complemented each other as the new advertising strategy emphasized the company's country origins and original hand-cranked ice cream. Howard Kruse intended the new Homemade Vanilla to imitate ice cream made the old-fashioned way, hand-cranked at home. The country image portrayed throughout Blue Bell's advertising history, primarily developed by Barnhill and Metzdorf, continued with the concept of ''The Little Creamery in Brenham.'' Advertising under the new agency fixed the country image by filming in actual Washington County, Texas settings, and using residents of the area in the commercials to exemplify homemade, country-fresh goodness.

Although Blue Bell salesmen in Houston were warned that a country ice cream could not compete in a large city against more than ten different ice cream companies, Blue Bell became the bestselling ice cream in Houston by the mid-1970s. The company's country image became an asset rather than a detriment. In 1977 that country image developed to include a silhouette of a young girl pulling a cow on a rope as the company logo. Homemade Vanilla had become the signature ice cream of the company, a top seller in every market. In 1978 Blue Bell became the first company to package Cookies and Cream ice cream, its second best seller, previously a hand mix of crumbled Oreo cookies and vanilla ice cream available only at local ice cream parlors.

Blue Bell's success relied on the quality of its product being spread through customer word of mouth, like the small town gossip that first spread news of the company's original ice cream. This served the company well in expanding to new markets in Texas as the company focused on market areas near or adjacent to established markets. New branches opened in Dallas in 1978 and in North Dallas and Fort Worth in 1982, as well as in other areas of Texas. By 1984, Blue Bell reached

another sales milestone with $100 million in sales, and by 1988, Blue Bell had opened 13 sales and distribution branches in Texas, outside of the Brenham area.

Blue Bell maintained its own direct store sales and distribution system designed to support a high level of service and product quality. Driver salesmen delivered and restocked freezer cases in grocery stores, convenience stores, and other retail stores to ensure that the company's frozen desserts were fresh and well supplied for their customers. With each branch serving a 75-mile radius, refrigerated trucks maintained a product temperature of 18 degrees below zero to assure product freshness.

Solid Success in the 1980s

The mid-1980s saw a number of internal changes at Blue Bell. Ed Kruse was named CEO and chairman of the board in 1986 and Howard Kruse was made president. John Barnhill became executive vice-president as well as general sales manager and relocated to Brenham. The company also established an in-house advertising department, Blue Bell Advertising Associates, which continued to work with the Metzdorf Agency. The flourishing company required a new corporate headquarters, which was completed in Brenham in 1988, along with a visitor's center. In 1989, 100,000 visitors toured the ice cream plant.

Blue Bell's popularity has been attributed to its production of a high-quality product at a mid-range price. Blue Bell also sought to serve the needs of its customers for dietary ice cream products. In 1989 Blue Bell was the first ice cream company in the country to offer a half-gallon container of diet ice cream sweetened with NutraSweet. The company launched Blue Bell Free, fat free ice cream, in 1991 and Homemade Vanilla Light in 1996. Blue Bell was the first company in the country to develop a line of bite-sized frozen ice cream snacks in 1995.

1990s Expansion Beyond Texas

Blue Bell ventured outside of Texas for the first time in 1989 when branches opened in Oklahoma City and in Baton Rouge. The company credits customer word of mouth as well as a *New Orleans Times-Picayune* newspaper article for its immediately successful entry into the New Orleans market. In three months Blue Bell had attained 33 percent of supermarket ice cream sales in the Baton Rouge-New Orleans area. Oklahoma's Braum's dairy stores gave the company strong competition, but Blue Bell attained a 33 percent market share within supermarket sales in ten months. By the end of 1989 Blue Bell's grocery store sales captured six percent of supermarket sales nationwide and reached $160 million in sales. In Texas grocery stores, Blue Bell continued to experience a high level of product turnover, at 92 times per year compared with the industry average of 35 times.

Throughout the 1990s, Blue Bell utilized the contiguous market expansion plan to introduce its ice cream products into Kansas, Alabama, Missouri, Arkansas, Georgia, New Mexico, Tennessee, and Mexico, as well as new markets in Texas, Louisiana, and Oklahoma. Blue Bell became the bestselling brand of ice cream in Birmingham, Alabama, in less than a month by relying on word of mouth through its loyal customer base from adjacent markets. In less than six months Blue Bell achieved a market share of 44 percent of ice cream sales in Birmingham in 1995.

The company concerned itself with expansion into out-of-state markets while it strove to maintain a high-quality product as well as its image as "the little creamery in Brenham." To accommodate expansion in the northern distribution area, Blue Bell opened a production facility in Broken Arrow, Oklahoma, in 1992, expanded its plant in Brenham, and opened a facility in Sylacauga, Alabama, in 1997 to serve the southeastern distribution area.

Word about Blue Bell ice cream reached far beyond its sales and distribution territory. Betsy Newman, owner of Fruit Baskets of Brenham, began to offer Blue Bell ice cream by courier after her father, a Blue Bell executive, mentioned that the company often received requests for its ice cream from out of state. The ice cream was sent to faraway places for birthdays, weddings, and to employees stationed outside of Texas to work for long periods of time. In addition to the price of the ice cream and sales tax, a delivery of three half-gallon containers cost $15 for dry ice, $16 for the cooler, $36 for shipping, and $11 in administrative fees. Newman averaged six orders per week in 1994.

Blue Bell's humorous television commercials have captured audiences throughout the distribution area. One commercial featured a driver salesman consuming most of the ice cream in his delivery truck his first day on the job. This fit with the company slogan, "We eat all we can and sell the rest." Another commercial featured a character named "Fred" who invited his friends over for homemade ice cream. His friends raved about the ice cream and wanted to know his secret. In a long narrative Fred described the "special recipe," which included vanilla and ostrich eggs from Madagascar. The final act of the commercial showed Fred's real secret, as he filled his home freezer with Blue Bell ice cream.

In July 1996, Blue Bell made the bold move of advertising during the Olympic Games. Shown in 11 south central and southeastern states, the television commercials ran during opening and closing ceremonies, as well as during actual events. A special commercial was produced to underscore the company's country image. Three siblings of retirement age visit the country of their childhood and experience flashbacks to the memories of the old-fashioned country life.

After 90 Years in Business

By the end of 1996 Blue Bell became the third bestselling ice cream company in the United States. With its products available in 14 percent of supermarkets nationwide, Blue Bell held the number three position behind Dreyers Grand and Breyers, both of whom sold their products in 85 percent of the nation's grocery stores. In 1997, the year that Blue Bell celebrated its 90th anniversary in business, company sales grew 17.8 percent.

Blue Bell ice cream products became a market share phenomenon. A 1998 A.C. Nielsen ScanTrack determined that Blue Bell had attained more than 40 percent of supermarket ice cream sales in some of the largest southern markets. The Houston area had always been the company's strongest market, with 66 percent of supermarket ice cream sales. In Dallas the company reached a 60 percent market share, San Antonio/Austin

reached 53 percent, New Orleans/Mobile reached 49 percent, Birmingham/Montgomery reached 42 percent, and Oklahoma City reached 36 percent. With its outstanding market share Blue Bell earned the spotlight in diverse publications that spread beyond its distribution area, such as *Time, Sports Illustrated,* and *Forbes* magazines.

The company continued to grow through its dependable plan of gaining strength in one market and allowing word of mouth to precede the company into the next contiguous market. Consumer requests for Blue Bell ice cream in Memphis led the company to enter that market in 1998. It also entered the Atlanta area, opening two sales and distribution branches there in 1998.

The company continued to invent new dessert novelties. In 1999 Blue Bell launched Rainbow Sherbet Cups, which contained a swirl of orange, strawberry, and lime flavored low-fat sherbet. The Banana Split Country Cones held banana ice cream with a strawberry ice cream center and the ice cream top dipped in chocolate and chopped peanuts. As long as ice cream lovers abounded, Blue Bell could be expected to keep them, and its business, smiling.

Further Reading

"Blue Bell Frozen Novelty Country Cones; Rainbow Sherbet Cups," *Product Alert,* April 26, 1999.

"Blue Bell Inc. Will Buy Plant in Sylacauga," *Birmingham News,* July 5, 1996, p. C1.

"Blue Bell TV Ads Just Playing Games," *San Antonio Express-News,* July 19, 1996, p. E1.

Gallaga, Omar L., "Blue Bell's Cows Come Home: Brenham's 'Little Creamery' Marks 90 Years of Big Sales," *Austin-American Statesman,* August 3, 1997, p. K1.

"Here's the Scoop: Blue Bell Wants Comal Tax Abatement," *San Antonio Express-News,* August 14, 1996, p. E1.

Hicks, Leslie, "Texas' Blue Bell Creamery Plans Ice Cream Ads During Olympic Games," *Knight-Ridder/Tribune Business News,* July 19, 1996, p. 7190103.

Johannes, Laura, "New Texas Rivals Seek to Lick Blue Bell," *Wall Street Journal,* August 3, 1994, p. T3.

——, "Serve This Ice Cream Only with Silver Spoons," *Wall Street Journal,* December 28, 1994, p. T2.

Lofton, Dewanna, "One of Nation's Most Popular Ice Creams Due Here July 20," *Commercial Appeal,* July 8, 1998, p. B4.

Mack, Toni, "The Ice Cream Man Cometh," *Forbes,* January 22, 1990, p. 52.

Mehegan, Sean, "The Marketing 100: Blue Bell: John Barnhill Jr.," *Advertising Age,* June 29, 1998, p. 37.

Murphy, Kate, "Maintaining Local Flavor; Will Too Much Success Spoil Blue Bell Ice Cream?," *New York Times,* February 7, 1998, p. B1.

"Outstanding in the Field," *Houston Chronicle,* September 1, 1996, p. E1.

"Planned Blue Bell Facility To Employ Up to 50 People," *San Antonio Business Journal,* June 28, 1996, p. 3.

Scott, Jonathan, "Cool Arrival for Next Summer: Blue Bell Ice Cream," *Memphis Business Journal,* December 8, 1997, p. 8.

"Slow-But-Sure Philosophy Keeps Blue Bell Thriving," *Austin-American Statesman,* September 29, 1996, p. G3.

Thompson, Doug, "Blue Bell Ice Cream of Texas to Dip into Market in Arkansas," *Arkansas Democrat Gazette,* March 17, 1997, p. D1.

"Welcome to Blue Bell Creamery," Brenham, Tex.: Blue Bell Creamery, 1999.

—Mary Tradii

The Broadmoor Hotel

1 Lake Avenue
Colorado Springs, Colorado 80906
U.S.A.
(719) 577-5733
(800) 634-7711
Fax: (719) 577-5700
Web site: http://www.broadmoor.com

Private Company
Founded: 1918
Employees: 1,600
Sales: $98 million (1998 est.)
NAIC: 72111 Hotels & Motels; 72211 Full-Service
    Restaurants; 721110 Resort Hotels Without Casinos

The Broadmoor Hotel provides luxury accommodations for its guest with 700 rooms and suites, as well as fine dining and entertainment in nine restaurants. A variety of outdoor and indoor activities are available at the hotel, including three golf courses, 12 tennis courts, three swimming pools, and a health spa. The Pikes Peak region offers a variety of tourist attractions as well. Rooms in the 110,000-square-foot meeting and convention facility can accommodate 20 to 1,300 people for banquets or meetings.

The Broadmoor Hotel is the crowning achievement of Spencer Penrose, who attained wealth and status in the Colorado Springs area at the dawn of the 20th century. From its inception the Broadmoor Hotel attracted prominent guests. In the early years John D. Rockefeller, Will Rogers, Jack Dempsey, and Helen Keller visited the hotel, and presidents, movie stars, musical performers, and sports figures have continued to visit the hotel throughout its history.

Prelude to a Luxury Resort

Spencer ''Speck'' Penrose opened the Broadmoor Hotel 28 years after he arrived in Colorado Springs with an almost empty wallet. A marginal business venture in New Mexico prompted Penrose to relocate to Colorado where his Philadelphia childhood friend, Charles Tutt, made him manager of a real estate business in Cripple Creek in 1891. Tutt loaned $500 to Penrose for half ownership in the business as well. In 1893 the two increased their fortune with an investment in the Cash on Delivery gold mine in Cripple Creek, but a violent labor strike in 1894 led Penrose and Tutt to sell the mine. With another business associate they opened a gold processing mill shortly afterward. In 1903, at Penrose's initiative, they backed a young geologist's pioneering method for processing low grade copper ore in Utah, and became enormously wealthy.

After his 1906 marriage to Julie Villiers Lewis McMillan, of Detroit's high society, Penrose turned somewhat away from ambitions of wealth and toward the well-being of the community in which he lived. He determined to make Colorado Springs a tourist destination. Penrose invested in the Pikes Peak Auto Highway Company, which planned to build a toll road to the top of Pikes Peak. Even before government approval of the road, Penrose planned an automobile race, the Pikes Peak Hill Climb. The first race took place in August 1916 and has continued to the present day as the Race to the Clouds. Penrose began Gray Line Tours, which provided car and bus tours to the top of Pikes Peak, and an automobile rental company. Penrose also purchased the Mount Manitou Incline, a steep railway in nearby Manitou Springs.

With tourist facilities in place Penrose addressed the need for hotel accommodations. During World War I America's elite turned toward domestic vacation destinations, and Penrose decided to build a luxury resort which would serve their needs. In 1916 Penrose and several longtime business associates formed the Broadmoor Hotel and Land Company. For $90,000 the company acquired Cheyenne Lake and 18 acres of surrounding land, which included the face of Cheyenne Mountain, an additional 400 acres south of that property, and water rights.

The cost to build the hotel exceeded the $1 million estimate. Architect C.L. Wetmore designed the Broadmoor Hotel to fit into the mountain landscape, with tiers from upper to lower stories of the building and an off-center tower. Two-story wings on both sides of the central building embraced the lake beaches. In keeping with a Southwestern style, the white building was topped with a red tile roof. The company acquired the Broadmoor Greenhouse to provide flowers and plants for the hotel, while the esteemed Olmstead Brothers designed the European style gardens and grounds. Penrose chose the best of everything for the hotel, so it was appropriate that the walls of the hotel have gold in them. When construction began in May 1917, the concrete contained the rubble from gold mining.

Julie Penrose guided the hotel's interior design in an ambiance of understated elegance. Fabrics, carpets, and wall coverings were chosen in the Renaissance style of classic simplicity. The Penroses brought 100 Italian artists from New York and Italy to design the molded plaster ceilings. Ceiling and accent decorations included depictions of classical mythology and the Colorado landscape. Furnishings from European manufacturers managed to cross the war-torn Atlantic Ocean. The Penroses scrutinized every detail of the interior design: the artwork, antiques, chandeliers, and other fixtures. They procured Rosenthal china which carried an ornate ''B'' in the center, as well as Gorhman silver service. An ornamental frieze of clay plaster fired onto the exterior of the main building intimated the ambiance awaiting guests inside the hotel.

Open for Business in 1918

Spencer Penrose used a variety of methods to promote his grand hotel before the opening of the main building in June 1918. Artist depictions of the hotel were featured in advertising as well as the *Preliminary Opening Announcement* which was mailed to travel agents and travel clubs nationwide. Penrose commissioned Maxfield Parrish to paint a picture of the Broadmoor with the hotel to the west of the lake (though it rests on the east side) and Cheyenne Mountain as the backdrop. Advertisements in such periodicals as the *Saturday Evening Post* and *Harper's Bazaar* highlighted the health and beauty of the mountains. The Penroses traveled to the East Coast to promote the Broadmoor Hotel as a luxury resort in the European style as well as the Pikes Peak Region as a tourist destination. When the Broadmoor Hotel opened for business, the cost of $14 per day included three meals with live music at lunch and dinner and access to all hotel facilities.

Amenities at the resort appealed to wealthy families who would spend summers at the resort. These included an elegant ballroom, a swimming pool filled with mountain water, and a spa with Turkish baths. Visitors could canoe or rowboat on Cheyenne Lake which was stocked with trout for fishing. Guides were available for hiking and horseback riding the trails

on the face of Cheyenne Mountain as well as for hunting farther into the Rocky Mountains. Polo fields, tennis courts, bowling greens, and skeet shooting facilities were available for sportsmen. Penrose hired prominent golf course designer Donald Ross for the Broadmoor's 18-hole golf course, the highest altitude golf course of its time at over 6,000 feet above sea level. The terrain at the base of Cheyenne Mountain made for a challenging course as well. The hotel also provided tours to Pikes Peak and a variety of other activities.

The hotel was a success from the beginning and Penrose continued to expand facilities to accommodate dining, sporting events, and leisure activities. The first Broadmoor Roundup rodeo was held in 1920. The event added and changed its offerings every year and led to the creation of the Broadmoor Riding Arena. The rodeo has continued, albeit at another Colorado Springs location, to the present day. The Broadmoor held its first Invitational Golf Tournament in 1921. Women's polo and women's golf tournaments created some controversy in that era. The Cheyenne Mountain Zoo opened in 1926 with an elephant, a camel, and a black bear. Later mountain lions, polar bears, seals, and small, exotic animals were added, as well as a train to travel around the zoo. Carriage rides, boxing matches, and the Jungle Room night club also offered diversions for the hotel guests.

To serve this clientele Penrose employed an Italian chef in Colorado while the maitre d'hotel and 25 waiters came from the best hotels on the East Coast. Julie Penrose's artistic sensibilities ensured that the hotel's entertainment fit the ambiance of the hotel with renowned classical performers and musicians, such as Igor Stravinsky and Sergei Rachmaninoff.

Historical Effects: Prohibition to World War II

Penrose fought the 1919 Prohibition of alcohol financially as well as politically. He purchased the local Manitou Mineral Water Company to provide ginger champagne and sparkling water to hotel guests. Penrose also purchased whole cellars of fine wines and liquor which he occasionally dispensed at private parties. When Prohibition ended in 1933, he displayed his liquor reserve at the new Tavern Restaurant, the hotel's western style bar and grill which also offered local wild game dishes. The Broadmoor Hotel became attractive for its cache of wine and liquor at a time of scarce supply.

By 1933 the Great Depression impacted the number of guests visiting the hotel, however. Though the Penroses did not experience adverse effects from the stock market crash, with little of their wealth invested in stocks, their clientele was affected. Business dropped to the point that employees worked only as needed, sometimes for tips only. Also, the hotel had to close for the winter of 1935. The hotel had been running at a deficit from the beginning, but Penrose had covered the losses from his personal funds. The impact of the Depression on his business associates led to events in which Penrose took complete ownership of the hotel.

When Spencer Penrose was diagnosed with throat cancer in 1931 it impacted the hotel in unexpected ways. Spencer and Julie Penrose traveled a great deal at this time and brought back new ideas for the hotel. Seeing Sonja Henje figure skating at St. Moritz instigated the building of the Ice Palace, completed in 1938.

Travel to Hawaii led to the transformation of the Jungle Room into a Hawaiian village style nightclub with Hawaiian music in 1939.

Penrose's illness impacted the legal arrangements of the hotel. Julie Penrose was independently wealthy, so in 1937 Penrose formed a foundation for charitable purposes as well as for a tax shelter for his businesses. Penrose's death in 1939, at the age of 74, left ownership of the hotel to the El Pomar Foundation. Julie Penrose became president of the foundation, and Charles Tutt, Jr., became president of the hotel and vice-president of the foundation. Tutt had worked with Penrose since his father's death in 1909. Tutt had served as president of the Broadmoor Golf Club and, in the 1930s, as managing director of the hotel.

World War II presented new opportunities and problems for the Broadmoor. As nearby Camp Carson expanded for military training, the Tavern and the nightclub attracted military officers. The hotel housed military officers at a special rate. The war effort also led to staffing problems, which Julie Penrose resolved (while simultaneously making a statement against the injustice of internment) by hiring several Japanese Americans from a camp in southern Colorado. Many continued to work at the hotel after the war.

Postwar Adjustments

After World War II the hotel business became more directed toward conventions and the Broadmoor adapted. The hotel was refurbished while two new wings of guest rooms and a heated outdoor swimming pool were added. In 1950 lobby expansion incorporated ceiling panels in a heraldic design as well as escalators for faster movement of larger numbers of guests.

Charles Tutt, Jr.'s sons, William Thayer and Russell, became involved with the hotel. William Thayer Tutt became vice-president of the hotel in 1946. He was instrumental in bringing the National Figure Skating Championships and National Collegiate Hockey Championship Playoffs to the Ice Palace. After the death of his father in 1961 Thayer Tutt became president of the hotel and supervised continuation of the hotel refurbishment and expansion.

The hotel was expanded with the new South Tower, an addition of 144 guest rooms, meeting facilities, and a new restaurant, the Edwardian-style Penrose Room. The International Center, in the popular hyperbolic paraboloid style of architecture, added a 2,400-seat auditorium and banquet facilities for 1,600 people. Harry Belafonte and his orchestra opened the Center whose performers included such diverse acts as Liberace and Jefferson Airplane. An English-style pub built near the Center, the Golden Bee, was decorated with the paneling and fixtures of an original 19th-century English pub. The main building of the hotel was redecorated in modern furnishings, but with the ornate Baroque style of fabrics and wall coverings.

The hotel and its sports facilities continued to be an attraction. In 1958 a nine-hole course was added, and expanded to an 18-hole course in 1964. The hotel began to host larger national and international golf tournaments. The Ice Palace and local ice ponds became the training site for several winning Olympic and World Championship ice skaters; it was renamed the Broadmoor World Arena as it attained international status. Declining interest in polo initiated the dismantling of the polo field to make room for ski facilities, provided from 1961 to 1991. The indoor swimming pool and spa facilities closed to allow space for administrative offices in the main building.

In 1975 Russell Tutt replaced Thayer as president of the hotel at a time of increased competition in the resort industry. Tutt responded with an update of facilities and services. In 1976 an additional new wing on the west side of Cheyenne Lake added 150 deluxe rooms. Charles Court served continental cuisine, but turned toward American regional dishes in the 1980s. The landscaping was changed from the European style to low-water-use, native Colorado plants. In the area of sports, the Broadmoor added a third golf course and hosted prominent skeet shooting tournaments. Colorado Hall was built in 1982 to provide 18,000 square feet of exhibition and convention space.

The hotel's continual renewal intermixed a sense of the past as well. Historic preservation included restoration of the decorative frieze on the exterior of the main building. The frieze was cleaned and repainted. Julie Penrose's classic simplicity was redesigned into the interior of the original main buildings. Archives were gathered for a future museum and temporarily mounted in the lobby area. The Broadmoor Golf Club had to be razed, but window, tile, and other fixtures were preserved for the new building.

New Ownership 1988

The Federal Tax Reform Act of 1969 required nonprofit foundations to divest half of their for-profit businesses by 1989, and an additional 15 percent by 2004. El Pomar was required to sell majority interest in the Broadmoor Hotel and other businesses in Penrose's empire. The Oklahoma Publishing Company under Edward L. Gaylord acquired 65 percent ownership of the Broadmoor Hotel in 1988, and an additional 15 percent ownership in 1990. Gaylord's interest in the property stemmed from regular childhood visits to Colorado which included stays at the Broadmoor, and his ownership of the *Colorado Springs Sun* newspaper from 1978 to 1986. Gaylord had other family connections to the Colorado Springs community. This satisfied the El Pomar Foundation, which was concerned with maintaining the hotel's traditions and community connections.

Under Gaylord, upgrade and expansion of the hotel continued. At a cost of $20 million a new 90,000-square-foot recreational area opened in 1994 with a fitness center, golf clubhouse, and clay tennis courts. The area held a 33,000-square-foot spa including sauna, massage treatment rooms, and a swimming pool which was contoured to fit the mountain side, and housed under a jeweled and etched glass skylight. An additional $20 million was allocated to 150 new guest rooms and more meeting space. A $7 million renovation of the International Center created a more inviting environment in keeping with the hotel's overall atmosphere. The Broadmoor South guest rooms and lobby were renovated, while the driving range and irrigation system for the golf course were upgraded in 1996.

In October 1995 the Colorado Springs Planning Commission approved zoning for the Broadmoor Resort Community, a gated residential development located on 1,500 acres southwest of the Cheyenne Mountain Zoo. The development would use 300 acres to hold single family homes on ½ to 2½ acre lots and townhomes priced from $350,000 to $2 million. It was expected that the housing development of up to 650 units would accommodate second homes for nonresidents of Colorado. The development was projected to cost $15 million and construction would take 15 years. Community residents would have access to the hotel facilities.

The prominence of the Broadmoor Hotel, as acknowledged by national travel organizations, continued in the 1990s. The *Mobile Travel Guide* gave the Broadmoor a Five Star rating for the 36th year in a row in January 1996. The following autumn the *Official Hotel Guide*, used by travel agents worldwide, classified the Broadmoor under Superior Deluxe accommodations. The Broadmoor was one of only 90 hotels to fulfill the stringent requirements of that prestigious category. The hotel was also honored with the American Automobile Association's Five Diamond Award in November 1996.

Promotions continued to focus on groups in need of meeting facilities in the 1990s. In conjunction with meetings, the mountain setting furnished the possibility for group outings that built teamwork among coworkers and executives. The Action Learning Center was formed to organize challenging outdoor activities, such as rappelling, which required cooperation among participants.

In 1999 the hotel revitalized its retail outlet configuration. The drugstore, espresso bar, and women's boutique were redesigned and a new shoe store was added. A 4,600-square-foot Polo Ralph Lauren store opened in April 1999. The product line included high-end labels not available in department stores, children's clothing, and home accessories. Payment was set like a restaurant, where a bill would be totaled and brought to the patron in a portfolio. A living room style area was included in the store layout for this purpose. Thus, as the Broadmoor prepared for a new century, its allure as a unique world-class hotel continued unabated.

Further Reading

Berozzi-Villa, Elena, *Broadmoor Memories: The History of the Broadmoor Hotel,* Missoula, Mont.: Pictorial Histories Publishing Company, 1993.

"Broadmoor Hotel Earns Superior Deluxe Rating," *Colorado Springs Gazette-Telegraph,* September 8, 1995, p. D1.

"Broadmoor Wins Five Stars from Mobile Travel Guide," *Colorado Springs Gazette-Telegraph,* January 9, 1996, p. D1.

"The Grand Dame of the Rockies—Colorado's The Broadmoor." *Business Travel News,* March 30, 1998, p. 78.

Heilman, Wayne, "Broadmoor Plans Upgrade: Resort to Spend $7 Million This Winter to Renovate Rooms, International Center and to Improve Irrigation on Golf Courses," *Colorado Springs Gazette-Telegraph,* November 29, 1996, p. B11.

——, "Broadmoor Stables Moving from Homes' Path," *Colorado Springs Gazette-Telegraph,* September 6, 1996, p. D1.

——, "These Lots Cost . . . Well, Lots: Broadmoor Plans Exclusive Housing on Mountainside," *Colorado Springs Gazette-Telegraph,* October 6, 1995, p. D1.

Laden, Rich, "Broadmoor Eyes Canyon: Nearly 800 Acres of Scenic Red Rock Area Appeal to Both Developers and Environmentalists," *Colorado Springs Gazette-Telegraph,* April 27, 1999, p. BUS1.

Manuelli, Joe, "Colorado Resort's Facility Off to a Ringing Start," *Travel Weekly,* December 26, 1994, p. 25.

"On Design: A Fitness of Fantasy," *Hotel and Motel Management,* July 5, 1994, p. 18.

Smith, Scott, "Light Feet, Light Hearts: Broadmoor Waltz Club Hopes to Keep Graceful Tradition Alive," *Colorado Springs Gazette-Telegraph,* December 14, 1997, p. LIFE1.

Sucharski, Karen, "Broadmoor Face-Lift Done," *Colorado Springs Business Journal,* April 26, 1996, p. 2.

"Three New Directors Named at Deluxe Corp.," *Colorado Springs Gazette-Telegraph,* November 12, 1996, p. D1.

Turnis, Jan, "Broadmoor Revamps Shops: Polo Boutique First of Changes to Shopping at Posh Hotel," *Colorado Springs Gazette-Telegraph,* April 23, 1999, p. BUS1.

Tutt, William Thayer, *The Broadmoor Story,* New York: Newcomen Society in North American, 1969.

Wengler, Diane, "Hotel's Generosity at Heart of Award," *Colorado Springs Gazette-Telegraph,* April 14, 1996, p. D4.

Zubeck, Pam, "The Broadmoor Gives $100,000 Toward Buying Stratton Land," *Colorado Springs Gazette-Telegraph,* February 18, 1998, p. NEWS3.

—Mary Tradii

Burmah Castrol PLC

Burmah Castrol House
Pipers Way
Swindon
Wiltshire SN3 1RE
United Kingdom
(01793) 511 521
Fax: (01793) 513 506
Web site: http://www.burmah-castrol.com

Public Company
Incorporated: 1886 as The Burmah Oil Company Ltd.
Employees: 20,000
Sales:£2.82 billion (US$4.67 billion) (1998)
Stock Exchanges: London NASDAQ
Ticker Symbol: BMAH
NAIC: 324191 Petroleum Lubricating Oil & Grease
    Manufacturing; 42272 Petroleum & Petroleum
    Products Wholesalers (Except Bulk Stations &
    Terminals); 325188 All Other Basic Organic
    Chemical Manufacturing; 32591 Printing Ink
    Manufacturing; 325998 All Other Miscellaneous
    Chemical Product & Preparation Manufacturing

Originally known as The Burmah Oil Company Ltd., Burmah Castrol PLC is the oldest oil enterprise in the United Kingdom. It is best remembered for having survived in 1975 the most serious crash hitherto in the business history of the United Kingdom and for achieving what was termed by John Davis of *Money Observer,* November 1988, "one of the greatest corporate come-backs of all time." While it once aimed to be a multinational integrated petroleum concern, Burmah Castrol transformed itself in the late 20th century into a firm focusing exclusively on marketing lubricants and specialty chemicals. Through the Castrol brand, the company is the world's leading supplier of automobile and motorcycle lubricants, including engine oils, transmission fluids, and brake fluids. Burmah Castrol's chemical products include those used in foundries and steel works as well as those used in the civil engineering and construction industries; the company is also the world leader in screen printing inks and related products. The company has more than 150 subsidiaries operating in about 55 countries. Approximately ten percent of the company's revenues are derived within the United Kingdom, 27 percent within the remainder of Europe, 31 percent within the Americas, 17.5 percent within Asia, 12 percent within Australasia, and 2.5 percent within Africa.

Burmese and Persian Beginnings

The company derives its name from the centuries-old oil works in Burma—spelled with an "h" in the Victorian era—which in 1886 became a province of the Indian empire. Founded that year in Glasgow by David Cargill, a Scottish-born merchant with lucrative trading interests in Ceylon, The Burmah Oil Company Ltd. introduced new technology into the Burmese operations, such as mechanical drilling at the oil fields and continuous distillation in the Rangoon refinery. The oil fields and refinery were connected by a 275-mile pipeline in 1909. Initially all the oil was sold in Burma, apart from some wax for the United Kingdom, but the company was soon shipping products to mainland India, using its own tankers after 1899.

Following its entry into the subcontinent, Burmah Oil came to the attention of the Committee of Imperial Defence, the United Kingdom's top strategic policy-making body, which alerted the appropriate government departments to the company's vital importance as the only oil company of any size in the British Empire. In 1905 the Admiralty concluded a long-term contract to purchase Burmese fuel oil, as it was beginning to convert its warships to run on oil. Admiralty officials also sought to interest Burmah Oil in acquiring a 500,000-square-mile oil concession in Persia, granted in 1901 to William K. D'Arcy. Since D'Arcy was short of money, the concessions might well have had to be sold into non-British hands. Burmah Oil agreed to the purchase, and in 1908 its drillers struck oil in Persia. The following year it established the Anglo-Persian Oil Company (renamed Anglo-Iranian in 1935 and British Petroleum in 1954), an almost wholly owned subsidiary. Difficulties over refining and transporting the Persian oil proved costly for

Company Perspectives:

At Burmah Castrol, we enhance other people's processes by using our expertise.

Globally, we work in partnership with our customers to develop products, services and applications that meet their specific needs, in their particular environment.

Our solutions are crucial to their success. Success that only comes as a result of collaboration. Of striving to do things better. Of inspiring them and encouraging them. Of winning their trust and confidence. Of becoming a seamless part of their team.

Burmah Oil, and in 1912 the chairman, Sir John Cargill, son of the founder David Cargill, refused to finance Anglo-Persian any further.

Winston Churchill had recently been appointed first lord of the Admiralty, and was seeking reliable sources of naval fuel oil to supplement those from Rangoon. In 1914 the U.K. authorities and Burmah Oil concluded an agreement which overcame their respective problems. The government acquired from the company a majority share in Anglo-Persian, while in turn the Admiralty obtained long-term fuel oil supplies from Anglo-Persian. During World War I, Burmah Oil concentrated on keeping India supplied with kerosene. After 1918 it became more widely known through its newly appointed managing director, Robert I. Watson. Energetic and highly respected throughout the oil world, Watson helped to devise the market-sharing international agreements that supported oil prices during the Depression between the wars and rationalized distribution methods throughout much of the world. In particular, he negotiated the Burmah-Shell agreement of 1928 that created a common distribution system for the subcontinent of India, and acquired for Burmah Oil a four percent shareholding in Shell, of which he became a director in 1929.

Burmah Oil came to the attention of the world in 1942 when Japanese forces overran a poorly defended Burma. To prevent its strategically crucial assets from falling into enemy hands, Watson authorized the destruction of the Rangoon refinery and all the installations at the oilfields. The Allies' reconquest of Burma in 1945 permitted the company to start work again on its devastated properties there. The scale of its efforts was modified, however, by the declared intention of the newly independent republic of Burma to work toward taking over all oil assets. After a short-lived joint venture arrangement, Burmah Oil agreed to an outright sale of its interests in Burma in 1963, obtaining relatively generous compensation since mutual goodwill was maintained to the end.

Diversification Drive: 1957

Its progressive withdrawal from Burma, although not from India or Pakistan, effectively turned the company into an oil investment trust. By the mid-1950s less than a third of its income was derived from trading, the rest coming from its 25 percent stake in British Petroleum (BP) and its four percent

stake in Shell, both earning buoyant profits from their worldwide activities. Consequently in 1957 the chairman, William E. Eadie, launched a policy of diversification, notably in the western hemisphere. Attempts to secure fair compensation from Whitehall for the Burmese assets destroyed in 1942, over and above a nominal *ex gratia* payment, failed, when in 1965 the government of Harold Wilson, by a War Damage Act, blocked the Burmah Oil claim that had been successfully upheld in U.K. courts. By then the company was well embarked on the path of diversification. In addition to some ventures in the United States, Canada, and Australia, in 1962 it had acquired Lobitos Oilfields Ltd., which had production in Peru and Ecuador, and two specialist oil refineries in northwest England. This entry into the rapidly expanding specialized product market was carried further when in 1966 Burmah Oil purchased Castrol Ltd., the United Kingdom's leading independent lubricating oil supplier, which had an unrivaled reputation for marketing skills. Castrol's earnings helped to keep the Burmah group afloat during the difficult period after 1975.

Having ceased to be a fully integrated oil company since its withdrawal from Burma, but finding itself increasingly engaged in overseas exploration and specialist production, the group's strategy in the 1960s was shaped by two quite unforeseen events. First, in 1963 BP and Shell launched a takeover bid, seeking the group's properties in the western hemisphere and the Indian subcontinent, where neither company was well represented, and also feeling alarm at the Burmah group's apparent aspirations to the status of a major oil corporation. The Burmah directors soon beat off the bid, but had to face the urgent need to safeguard the group's future by improving its inadequate return on assets and its depressed share price. Second, the U.K. government in 1965 introduced a corporation tax, which disallowed companies with overseas interests from claiming relief in the United Kingdom on tax already paid to foreign governments, unless they could offset it against domestically earned income. One of those worst hit by this measure was the Burmah group, which consequently had to seek extensive acquisitions at home. Unable to repeat the highly synergistic purchases of Lobitos and Castrol, it bought, among others, the Rawlplug Company Ltd., Halfords Ltd., and Quinton Hazell Ltd., concerned with masonry fixing products, sales of motorists' accessories, and car components, respectively. It also greatly extended one of the former Lobitos refineries, at Ellesmere Port near Liverpool, to provide not only base lubricants for Castrol but also petrol for the large number of filling stations it was acquiring.

This diversification led the group in 1968–69 to reorganize its many subsidiaries into three main divisions. The Burmah-Castrol Company dealt with lubricants and other fuels, while the non-oil activities were divided between Burmah Industrial Products and Burmah Engineering. Nicholas Williams, managing director from 1969 onward and in 1971 chief executive under a part-time chairman, promoted a number of profit-enhancing ventures. The group was already using its offshore expertise, gained in the United States and Australia, to prospect in the North Sea, acting as operator for various consortia. It made the first ever oil strike there in 1966, but had to wait until 1973–74 for a major commercial discovery. In the early 1970s it entered the tanker business, both to transport crude for its own needs and to earn profits by chartering to outside parties. From 1975 it operated the Bahamas terminal, where oil was transhipped from giant tankers into smaller vessels capable of entering the shallower ports in the eastern and southern United States.

To help establish the Burmah group as a major oil enterprise in its own right, and to complement its limited operations in the Western Hemisphere, Williams sought to purchase a large U.S. oil corporation. After unsuccessful negotiations with several companies, including the Continental Oil Company (Conoco), late in 1973 Williams arranged to acquire Signal Oil and Gas Incorporated of Houston, Texas. Signal had plentiful supplies of crude oil, which the group currently lacked for its many refining and marketing ventures. A consortium of U.K. and U.S. banks readily lent the purchase money, secured on the Burmah group's asset base, of which the BP shareholding was the largest single component.

Oil Shocks, Near Collapse: 1970s

The outbreak of the Arab-Israeli War at the end of 1973 and the ensuing fourfold rise in oil prices began a year of grave difficulties for the Burmah group. The new Labour government of March 1974 planned to acquire majority stakes in North Sea operations and to tax oil profits more heavily than before. As delays in the implementation of these plans caused great uncertainty, the stock market prices of oil company shares steadily declined. A fall of about 60 percent in the value of BP shares meant that the lending banks were no longer fully covered under the Signal agreement, which in the closing months of 1974 had to be hastily renegotiated, thereby increasing the interest burden. The group's total borrowings rose from less than half of stockholders' funds at the end of 1973 to almost double a year later, and the board did little to sell off other assets or raise new equity in order to reduce the ratio. Moreover, the consequent reduced world demand for oil products had caused tanker rates to plummet. Thus the group faced substantial losses from this quarter; many of its 42 vessels, acquired at high prices in the earlier boom period, could no longer be chartered out or, if so, only at uneconomically low rates. In December 1974 the Burmah group, faced with a massive cash deficit, requested substantial sterling and dollar loans from the Bank of England.

The Labour government, resisting calls in its ranks for the nationalization of the Burmah group but well aware that the group's financial collapse would set off a calamitous run on sterling, authorized the Bank of England to lend on the security of the BP shares. Early in 1975, however, demands by outside creditors and fuller information regarding the huge tanker losses forced the group to seek an even larger loan from the bank. Under ministerial instructions, the Bank of England insisted on purchasing the BP shareholding outright, at the unduly low price then prevailing, with no profit-sharing agreement on any later resale.

As a further condition of the rescue measures, Williams resigned. The new chairman and chief executive was Alastair Down, formerly deputy chairman of BP. Down, assisted by a handpicked managerial team, had first of all to restore the morale of the 41,000 employees in 300 subsidiaries worldwide. His next task was to determine which assets to retain because of their good cash flows, and which to sell in order to yield essential funds or, as in the case of the 42 tankers, to reduce

losses. Over the next few years, Down and his team sold assets in the United States, Australia, Canada, Ecuador, and the North Sea, totaling no less than £865 million. The largest single group of assets, valued at nearly £300 million, were the Signal and other U.S. subsidiaries. With the full backing of the U.K. government, Down was able to delay selling until a fair offer was received.

Down's achievement in saving the Burmah group was recognized by a knighthood in 1978, the year in which the group returned to profitability after tax. In the following year, it paid its first dividends since 1974. Between 1978 and 1981 it took the U.K. government to court, first to obtain the release of official documents relating to the BP share sale of 1975, and then to recover the shareholding itself, claiming that the sale had been a forced one at an unconscionably low price. The Burmah group was defeated in both lawsuits.

Shifting Away from Integrated Oil Concern: 1980s

This financial recovery allowed the top management to plan in depth the group's future strategy, with the aim of ensuring stable income and long-term growth. Trading profits were coming mainly from lubricants and North Sea production. The North Sea fields were approaching depletion, however, and the group could afford only limited funds for further exploration, which would be very costly. Specialty chemicals therefore provided an alternative source of development. In 1981 the Burmah group launched a bid for Croda International Ltd., a chemical processing company that had lately seen its profits decline. Croda vigorously opposed the bid, and the group withdrew.

On Down's retirement in 1983, his successor, John Maltby, introduced a major rationalization plan. His main objectives were to shed assets that were by then either peripheral or lossmaking, and to concentrate efforts on those assets likely to provide good income and reasonable growth. In 1985 he sold off five tankers, chartering out the two remaining vessels on profitable terms, and in 1986 he disposed of the Bahamas terminal. These sales could only be effected at considerable loss, totaling some £94 million between 1982 and 1987. The group also closed down the Ellesmere Port refinery and disposed of 41 separate businesses, including Rawlplug, Halfords, and Quinton Hazell. In 1986 it sold all of its U.K. exploration and production interests to Premier Consolidated Oilfields PLC, in return for a 25 percent—later almost 30 percent—portfolio (nonactive) investment in the company. Since 1977 it had been transporting liquid natural gas from Indonesia to Japan under an agreement with the Indonesian State petroleum company PERTAMINA, and in 1989 it sold 50 percent of its interest in the scheme to Japan's Mitsui O.S.K. Lines, Ltd. and Nissho-Iwai. The sale provided cash for activities elsewhere while allowing the Burmah group to maintain a stake in this highly profitable operation.

Although most of the group's acquisitions in the 1980s were on a relatively small scale to strengthen its main divisional interests, in 1987 it launched a bid for the Calor group, a specialist supplier of liquefied petroleum gas. This £820 million offer was made jointly with the privately owned Dutch energy group SHV Holdings NV, which by 1989 had a nine percent stake in the Burmah group and a 40 percent stake in Calor. The bid was rebuffed and withdrawn. Despite such disappointments, the group enjoyed a decade or more of sustained recovery, thanks to successive rationalization plans.

By the end of the 1980s, however, the Burmah group appeared once again to have reached a plateau. Turnover in 1989 was only marginally higher than in 1985, but this was the inevitable result of rationalization, which involved the sales of operations.

Focusing on Specialty Chemicals and Lubricants: 1990s

In mid-1990, when Lawrence Urquhart succeeded John Maltby as chairman, the company took the opportunity to restructure. It became Burmah Castrol plc, thereby combining the goodwill and historical associations of the century-old Burmah name with the worldwide reputation of Castrol's products, which contributed more than two-thirds of group earnings. The formerly separate functions of the group were to be merged to create a tighter company structure, eliminate duplication of effort, and speed up decision-making at each level. The chairman and chief executive would oversee head office functions such as finance, shipping, and energy investments. Under him a managing director would be responsible for three international divisions: lubricants, chemicals, and fuels. Eight group directors would report to the managing director, with no fewer than six concentrating on lubricants.

A former director, Roger Wood, in *Accountancy Age,* July 12, 1990, characterized these radical changes as a takeover of the group by its Castrol division, causing it to focus inward, at least as long as the substantial task of integration was underway. Yet the appointment under those changes of one Castrol director solely for the lubricants market in Western Europe and one for the same products in Germany and Eastern Europe suggested that Burmah Castrol was moving ahead of many other British companies in striving to take full advantage of the single European market from 1992 onward, and of the opportunities available in the former Eastern bloc. Other Castrol directors would concentrate on vital lubricants markets in North America, east Asia, and Southern Hemisphere countries.

In October 1990, Burmah Castrol launched a hostile takeover bid for Foseco plc, a U.K.-based company operating internationally and specializing predominantly in metallurgical and construction chemicals. This £259 million (US$496.1 million) acquisition, completed in December 1990, was a major step forward in the expansion of the company's chemicals group. It significantly increased Burmah Castrol's size and improved the balance of the company's business, boosting the chemicals group and correspondingly reducing the weighting of the other groups. With the addition of Foseco, Burmah Castrol had a chemicals group which commanded attention in its portfolio, with a turnover of approximately £650 million.

In 1993 Jonathan Fry was named chief executive of Burmah Castrol; having joined the company in 1978, Fry had previously served as chief executive of both the chemicals and lubricants divisions. As the 1990s proceeded, Burmah Castrol continued to narrow its focus to the marketing of lubricants and specialty chemicals. To this end, the company began jettisoning its gaso-

line station operations around the world. In July 1995 Burmah Castrol sold its U.K. gasoline retailing unit, Burmah Petroleum Fuels Ltd.—which had faced increasing competition from supermarkets that also sold gasoline—to Frost Group PLC for £83 million (US$133.8 million). During 1996 the company divested itself of its gas stations in Turkey, Chile, and Sweden, raising £89 million in the process. Proceeds from the sales were used to cut debt. The disposals left Burmah Castrol with stations in only Australia, Belgium, and the Republic of Ireland.

In July 1997 Burmah Castrol announced a restructuring of its chemicals division, which involved divesting its adhesives operations and focusing on four core chemicals areas: foundry, steel mills, construction, and screen printing inks. Within two years the company had accomplished the former, by selling its U.S. adhesives business, Columbia Cement Co. Inc., and the U.K.-based Industrial Adhesives Ltd. In late 1997 Burmah Castrol announced another reorganization, which was completed in 1998 and involved its Castrol lubricants businesses. As a result of the restructuring, Castrol would no longer be organized along geographic lines but would be divided into four global businesses focusing on a particular customer segment: Castrol Consumer (automobile and motorcycle lubricants), Castrol Industrial (metalworking, food and beverage, mining, and other industries), Castrol Marine (international marine market), and Castrol Commercial (on- and off-road vehicle fleets). Meantime, in February 1998 Urquhart retired, and was replaced as nonexecutive chairman by Fry. Tim Stevenson was named the new chief executive, having previously served as chief executive of lubricants and having joined the company in 1975.

Through the end of the 1990s, Burmah Castrol continued to identify and sell off those operations considered to be outside its core lubricants and specialty chemicals focal points. Among these were the sale of its half-share of the joint venture shipping liquefied natural gas from Indonesia to Japan; its timber treatment business, Protim Solignum International; and its molten aluminum business. Burmah Castrol also sought to build its core businesses through strategic acquisitions. Among the late 1990s additions was Remet Corporation, a New York-based supplier of casting products and services to the engineering industry that was merged into the company's existing investment casting operation, Dussek Campbell Yates. Burmah Castrol also expanded its Fosroc construction chemicals business with the mid-1999 purchases of France-based CIA and Spain-based Holderchem SA. During this same period, the Castrol unit was aggressively expanding its marketing territory to such developing areas as China and Eastern Europe. In late 1999, Burmah Castrol announced that it planned to cut 1,450 jobs during the next few years, aiming at annual savings of £60 million by 2002 and beyond. Despite the relatively mature nature of the company's business sectors, Burmah Castrol appeared to be well positioned for future growth and profitability thanks to its transformation from integrated oil aspirant to tightly focused lubricants and specialty chemicals marketer.

Principal Subsidiaries

LUBRICANTS: Castrol Ltd; Castrol Middle East Ltd; Castrol Offshore Ltd; Castrol (UK) Ltd; Veedol International Ltd; Castrol Austria GmbH; Castrol NV (Belgium); Castrol Croatia d.o.o.; Castrol Marine Oils (Cyprus) Ltd; Castrol (CR) Spol Sro

(Czech Republic); Castrol A/S Denmark; Castrol Oy (Finland); Castrol France SA; The Burmah Oil (Deutschland) GmbH (Germany); Castrol Central & Eastern Europe GmbH (Germany); Castrol Marine Oil GmbH (Germany); Consulta Chemie GmbH (Germany); Deutsche Castrol Vertriebsges GmbH (Germany); Deutsche Castrol-Industrieoel GmbH (Germany); Deutsche Veedol GmbH (Germany); Optimol Oelwerke Industrie GmbH & Co KG (Germany); Tribol GmbH (Germany); Castrol Hellas SA (Greece); Castrol Hungaria Kereskedelmi Kft (Hungary); Castrol Italiana SpA (Italy); Castrol BV (Netherlands); Castrol Nederland BV (Netherlands); Castrol Norge A/S (Norway); Castrol Polska Sp zoo (Poland); SLIL—Sociedade Gestora de Participacoes Sociais Lda (Portugal; 50%); Castrol Romania SRL; Castrol Slovakia Spol Sro; Castrol España SA (Spain); Castrol AB (Sweden); Castrol (Switzerland) AG; Castrol South Africa (Pty) Ltd; Castrol Zimbabwe (Pvt) Ltd; Castrol Argentina SA; Castrol Brasil Ltda (Brazil); Castrol Canada Inc; Castrol Chile SA; Castrol Colombia Ltda; Castrol Mexico SA de CV; Castrol del Peru SA; Castrol Caribbean & Central America Inc (U.S.A.); Caribbean Heavy Duty Lubricants Inc (U.S.A.); Castrol Industrial North America Inc (U.S.A.); Castrol North America Inc (U.S.A.); Castrol (China) Ltd; Castrol Trading (Guangzhou) Ltd (China); Castrol Trading (Shanghai) Ltd (China); Castrol (Shenzhen) Company Ltd (China; 95%); Castrol India Ltd (51%); PT Castrol Indonesia (61%); Castrol KK (Japan); Castrol Korea Ltd; Castrol (Malaysia) Sdn. Bhd. (60%); Burmah Castrol Philippines Inc; The Burmah Oil Company (Pakistan Trading) Ltd (U.K.); Castrol Singapore Pte Ltd; Castrol Taiwan Ltd; Castrol (Thailand) Ltd (49.95%); Castrol Madeni Yaglar Sanayi Ve Ticaret A.S. (Turkey); Castrol (Vietnam) Ltd (60%); Castrol Australia Pty Ltd; Castrol NZ Ltd (New Zealand). CHEMICALS: Burmah Castrol Chemicals Ltd; Foseco plc; Foseco (GB) Ltd; Foseco Holding BV (Netherlands); Foseco Holding International BV (Netherlands). CHEMICALS—CHEM-TREND RELEASANTS: Chem-Trend Industria Inc e CIA (Brazil); Chem-Trend (Shanghai) Trading Co Ltd (China); Chem-Trend A/S (Denmark); Chem-Trend (UK) Limited; Chem-Trend (France) SARL; Chem-Trend (Deutschland) GmbH (Germany); Chem-Trend Korea Limited (60%); Chem-Trend Incorporated (U.S.A.). CHEMICALS—SPECIALTIES GROUP: Dussek Campbell Pty Ltd (Australia); Dussek Campbell Ltd; Dussek Campbell BV (Netherlands); Dussek Campbell (Pty) Ltd (South Africa; 51%); Dussek Campbell Inc (U.S.A.); Yates Investment Casting Wax Inc (U.S.A.); Fosbel Industria E Comercio Ltda (Brazil; 51%); Fosbel International Ltd (51%); Fosbel GmbH (Germany); Fosbel Europe BV (Netherlands; 51%); Fosbel Inc (U.S.A.; 51%). CHEMICALS—FOSROC CONSTRUCTION: Fosroc Guangzhou Ltd (China; 95%); Shanghai Fosroc Expandite Construction and Engineering Products Company Ltd (China; 55%); Fosroc A/S (Denmark); Fosroc SAE (Egypt; 50.65%); Fosroc Ltd; Fosroc International Ltd; Fosroc Hong Kong Ltd (China); Fosroc Chemicals (India) Ltd (90%); Jordanian British Construction Chemicals Company Ltd (Jordan; 70%); PT Fosroc-Foseco Indonesia; Fosroc Korea Ltd; Fosroc Sdn. Bhd. (Malaysia; 70%); Fosroc Ltd (New Zealand); Norwegian Concrete Technologies A.S. (Norway); Fosroc Ltd (Republic of Ireland); Fosam Co Ltd (Saudi Arabia; 50%); Burmah Castrol Chemicals Pte Ltd (Singapore); Fosroc SA (Spain); Fosroc (Thailand) Limited; Al Gurg Fosroc LLC (United Arab Emirates; 49%);

Fosroc Inc (U.S.A.). CHEMICALS—FOUNDRY/STEEL/ALUMINUM: Foseco Pty Ltd (Australia); Foseco Austria GmbH; Foseco SA (Belgium); Foseco Industrial E Comercial Ltda (Brazil); Foseco Canada Inc; Foseco-Morval Inc (Canada); Foseco Foundry (China) Co. Ltd; Shenzhen Foseco-Jinke Non-Ferrous Metallurgical Materials Company Ltd (China; 50%); Foseco (FS) Ltd; Foseco International Ltd; Foseco SA (France); Servimetal SA (France; 65%); Foseco GmbH (Germany); Foseco Industries Asia Ltd (China); Foseco India Ltd (51%); Foseco Srl (Italy); Foseco Japan Ltd (92%); Foseco Korea Ltd; Foseco SA de CV (Mexico); Foseco Nederland BV (Netherlands); Burmah Castrol Chemicals (NZ) Ltd (New Zealand); Foseco Portugal Produtos para Fundicao Lda; Foseco South Africa (Pty) Ltd; Burmah Castrol Chemicals SA (Spain); Foseco Española SA (Spain); Foseco AB (Sweden); Foseco Trading AG (Switzerland); Foseco Aluminum Europa AG (Switzerland); Foseco Golden Gate Co Ltd (Taiwan; 51%); Foseco (Thailand) Ltd (61.25%); Foseco Inc (U.S.A.); Fosven CA (Venezuela; 49%); Foseco Zimbabwe (Pvt) Ltd. CHEMICALS—SERICOL PRINTING: Sericol Australia Pty Ltd; Sericol (Hong Kong) Ltd (China); Sericol Ltd; Sericol International Ltd; Sericol SA (France); Sericol GmbH (Germany); Sericol India (Private) Ltd (67%); Sericol Sp. z.o.o. (Poland); Sericol España SA (Spain); Sericol AG (Switzerland); Sericol Inc (U.S.A.). FOSROC MINING: Willich Fosroc Gmb H (Germany; 50%); Fosroc Ksante Sp. z.o.o. (Poland; 70%); Fosroc Poland Sp. z.o.o.; Willich-Technika Gornicza i Budowlana Sp. z.o.o. (Poland; 50%); Fosroc Stratabolt (Pty) Ltd (South Africa); Witwatersrand Mining Supply Corporation (Proprietary) Ltd (South Africa; 50%); Willich AG (Switzerland; 50%); Fosroc Inc (U.S.A.). FUELS: Burmah Fuels Australia Ltd. ENERGY INVESTMENTS: Burmah Oil Netherlands Exploration BV. CENTRAL MANAGEMENT: Burmah Castrol Australia Ltd; Burmah Castrol Finance PLC; Burmah Castrol Holdings Ltd; Burmah Castrol Overseas Holdings Ltd; Burmah Castrol Trading Ltd; Burmah Castrol France Holdings SA; Burmah Castrol Holdings GmbH (Germany); Cairngorm Insurance Ltd (Guernsey); Burmah Castrol BV (Netherlands); Burmah Castrol N.Z. Ltd (New Zealand); Burmah Castrol (South Africa) Pty Ltd.

Principal Divisions

Castrol Industrial; Castrol Marine; Castrol Consumer; Castrol Commercial.

Further Reading

Barnard, Bruce, "Oil Crisis Doesn't Worry Burmah Oil," *Journal of Commerce,* December 9, 1986.

Beavan, Susan, "Burmah Still Waiting for Its Star to Rise Again," *Times,* October 19, 1983.

Bolger, Andrew, "Growth by Successful Targeting: Andrew Bolger Looks at How Castrol Has Expanded Worldwide," *Financial Times,* June 21, 1994, p. 23.

——, "Preferring a Profits Desert to the Takeover Jungle of Burmah," *Financial Times,* October 20, 1990, p. 8.

Butler, Steven, "Burmah Move Reflects Importance of Castrol," *Financial Times,* July 3, 1990.

Corley, T.A.B., "David Cargill," in *Dictionary of Scottish Business Biography,* Vol. I, Aberdeen: Aberdeen University Press, 1986.

——, *A History of the Burmah Oil Company, 1886–1924,* Vol. I, London: Heinemann, 1983.

——, *A History of the Burmah Oil Company, 1924–1966,* Vol. II, London: Heinemann, 1988.

——, "Robert I. Watson," in *Dictionary of Business Biography: A Biographical Dictionary of Business Leaders Active in Britain in the Period, 1860–1980,* Vol. V, edited by David Jeremy, London: Butterworth, 1986.

——, "Sir John Cargill" and "Sir Alastair Down," in *Dictionary of Business Biography: A Biographical Dictionary of Business Leaders Active in Britain in the Period, 1860–1980,* Vols. I and II, edited by David Jeremy, London: Butterworth, 1984.

Davis, John, "Castrol Fuels Burmah's Rise," *Money Observer,* November 1988.

Dimson, Elroy, and Paul Marsh, "Burmah Oil," *Cases in Corporate Finance,* London: Wiley, 1988.

Hargreaves, Deborah, "An Acquisition with the Right Chemistry," *Financial Times,* April 4, 1991, p. 22.

Joyce, Conor, "Burmah Hides Its Brand Strength Under a Barrel," *Investor's Chronicle,* February 9, 1990.

Marsh, Virginia, "Burmah Castrol Lifts Targets," *Financial Times,* September 9, 1999, p. 24.

——, "Burmah to Buy Remet Casting," *Financial Times,* May 7, 1999, p. 26.

Peel, Michael, "Burmah Considers Non-Core Disposals," *Financial Times,* September 8, 1998, p. 28.

Wilsher, Peter, et al, "Burmah Oil: The Rocky Road from Mandalay," *Sunday Times,* January 5, 1975.

—T.A.B. Corley
—updated by David E. Salamie

Bush Boake Allen Inc.

7 Mercedes Drive
Montvale, New Jersey 07645
U.S.A.
(201) 391-9870
Fax: (201) 391-0860
Web site: http://www.bushboakeallen.com

Public Subsidiary of International Paper Company
Incorporated: 1982
Employees: 1,977
Sales: $485.4 million (1998)
Stock Exchanges: New York
Ticker Symbol: BOA
NAIC: 31193 Flavoring Syrup & Concentrate
   Manufacturing; 311942 Spice & Extract
   Manufacturing; 325998 All Other Miscellaneous
   Chemical Product & Preparation Manufacturing

Bush Boake Allen Inc. manufactures flavor and fragrance chemicals and aroma chemicals for the food, beverage, pharmaceutical, and household products industries. The flavorings, including essential oils, seasonings, and spice extracts, impart a desired taste and smell to a broad range of consumer products, such as snack foods, confections, soft drinks, and alcoholic beverages. The fragrance products appear in soaps, detergents, air fresheners, cleaners, cosmetics, toiletries, and related products. BBA's aroma chemicals are primarily used as raw materials in fragrance compounds. The company, in 1998, had operations in 39 countries. It was 68 percent owned by International Paper Company in 1999.

British Antecedents: 1833–1982

Albright & Wilson Ltd., a British chemicals manufacturer, founded Bush Boake Allen, Ltd. in 1966 by merging W.J. Bush Ltd., A. Boake Roberts Ltd., and Stafford Allen Ltd. These three companies dated back to the 19th century, with the oldest founded in 1833. Bush specialized in liquid flavors, Boake in aroma chemicals and fragrances, and Allen in spices and sea-

sonings. Based in London, BBA had sales of about $90 million in 1978, the year it purchased Monsanto Flavor/Essence, Inc. of Montvale, New Jersey, and Patchogue, New York. Parent Monsanto Company had entered the flavors and fragrances business in 1968, when it purchased George Lueders & Co.

Bush Boake Allen was already a large-scale producer of fragrance synthetics from pinene, a compound derived from sulfate turpentine. The acquisition of Monsanto Flavor/Essence, which had annual sales of about $12 million, gave it access to more synthetic aroma-chemicals technology and rights to "Vellex" malodor counteractants, a product line seen as having great growth potential. BBA had sales of $125 million in 1981.

Union Camp Subsidiary: 1982–94

The following year, Tenneco Inc., which had acquired Albright & Wilson in 1978, sold BBA to Union Camp Corporation, a diversified U.S. manufacturer which made its purchase a wholly owned subsidiary.

Bush Boake Allen had, at this time, 13 manufacturing or compounding facilities on five continents. Its operations were a good fit for Union Camp's own aroma chemicals business, which was based on distilling crude sulfate turpentine into intermediate terpene fractions and aroma chemical precursors. The addition of BBA gave Union Camp greater manufacturing capability to produce a broad range of these chemicals.

With regard to food flavors, local tastes and customs in individual countries as well as a host of different government regulations had to be taken into account. Fragrance markets tended to be more uniform, but considerable creativity was needed to gain acceptance for a new fragrance. Both flavors and fragrances required extensive technical, analytical, and service backup. Bush Boake Allen had testing facilities that included a bakery, small-scale ice cream and soft drink plants, a meat processing operation, and an experimental kitchen, in order to test, as close to true production conditions as possible, the behavior of a particular flavor in the medium for which it was prepared.

A large part of Bush Boake Allen's development activity in aroma chemicals was taking place in London and at a plant in

Widnes, England, where operations began in 1958. Sophisticated instrumental analysis was being employed, including chromatography, mass spectroscopy, and nuclear magnetic resonance in order to isolate and identify constituents of both natural and synthetic materials. This work led to the synthesis of these materials into flavor and fragrance ingredients that could be produced to exacting standards. Although many natural aroma materials were still being employed in compounding flavors and fragrances, pinene-derived synthetic chemicals of the type produced in distillation plants both at Widnes and Union Camp's facility in Jacksonville, Florida, were playing an increasingly dominant role.

Bush Boake Allen's Widnes plant also was producing aroma chemicals from hydrocarbon feedstocks. An expansion of this facility—not completed until 1994—was authorized in 1986 to provide increased production of Lilestralis, BBA's brand name for a non-turpentine, lily aldehyde aroma chemical of perfumery quality for use in a range of toiletry and household products. BBA also was producing, at other locations in England, continental Europe, the Americas, and the Far East, a wide variety of spice products and essential oils (such as citrus and mint) from natural ingredients (such as vanilla and fruit extracts). The BBA division was the largest of Union Camp's chemical group, which had sales of $404 million in 1988.

By this time BBA was the largest processor of turpentine in the world, separating sulfate turpentine into its major components, alpha pinene and beta pinene, at Jacksonville, and then further processing the fractions at Jacksonville and Widnes. Alpha pinene was a source of pine oil used in household cleaners and disinfectants and also was being upgraded into other specialized products. Beta pinene was being used in the production of synthetic aroma chemicals such as geraniol, citronellol, and citral.

During the 1980s Bush Boake Allen expanded its network of flavor and fragrance facilities in order to bring its services closer to local markets throughout the world. It had a presence in 21 countries in 1984 and 23 in 1986. In 1987 it opened new facilities in Jamaica, Japan, and Thailand, and it also acquired Grundy Thompson, an Australian powdered-flavor company. The following year it opened a new facility in Italy. In all, 13 such facilities were opened during the decade, including six in 1988 and 1989, and more were pending for the Middle East, South America, and the Pacific Rim.

Bush Boake Allen greatly broadened its position in the United States by acquiring, in 1990, Chicago-based Food Materials Corp., a producer of flavor compounds and vanilla extract. In 1992 it purchased Texas Laboratories, a leading maker of custom seasoning blends for the snack food and food processing industries with plants in Carrollton, Texas, and Norwood, New Jersey. The purchase price was about $5.9 million. BBA's presence abroad also continued to increase, extending to 27 countries in 1991 and 30 in 1992. The division had record revenues of $336.3 million and record net income of $20.6 million in 1993.

Bush Boake Allen's plans called for further expansion by acquisition and for a greater penetration of two hot markets: Asia and South America. The division was also giving high priority to development of new synthetic musks, improved industrial reodorants, an extended line of dairy flavors, and production of enzyme-modified cheese products with wide application in many processed foods. Union Camp decided that commitment of the necessary funds would be met by selling about 30 percent of BBA's shares to the public.

Public Company: 1994–99

In 1994 5.6 million shares of Bush Boake Allen stock were sold at $16 a share, raising about $84 million in funds for the newly public company, which moved its headquarters from London to Montvale, New Jersey. ''It's a risky move,'' a fragrance industry executive told Matthew Gallagher of *Chemical Market Reporter*. ''This business is very secretive and given the necessity of releasing a prospectus as a part of going public, all sorts of sensitive information is out there for scrutiny''—including sales revenue, market share, profit margin, and corporate strategies.

Bush Boake Allen registered record revenues and net income in 1994, 1995, and 1996, when it was the seventh largest in its industry. Flavors were the company's major sector, accounting for 58 percent of sales in 1996. Of this sum, snack and processed foods, beverages, and confectionery and bakery accounted for 79 percent. Aroma chemicals accounted for 25 percent of the company's sales and fragrances for the remaining 17 percent. Of BBA's fragrances, sales for cleaners and air fresheners accounted for 39 percent, soaps and detergents for 30 percent, and cosmetics and toiletries for 23 percent. BBA was the largest worldwide producer of pine oil. Fine fragrances for colognes and perfumes accounted for eight percent.

Bush Boake Allen earmarked $22.5 million for research and development in 1996. The company's Generessence program allowed researchers to isolate and synthesize totally new aroma chemicals for the exclusive use of the company's perfumers and flavorists. BBA also was engaged in developing several processes intended to enhance its position as an integrated producer of vanilla.

Interviewed for *BUSINESS News New Jersey* in 1997, Bush Boake Allen chief executive Julian Boyden said, ''It takes about as long to develop a good perfumer as it does a good brain surgeon .... You have to be able to identify about 2,000 chemicals by smell and/or taste. It takes about 10 years to build up that skill.'' He added that because fat is the biggest modifier of taste, the popularity of low-fat foods was creating a lot of work in developing low-fat and fat-free foods that would taste as good or the same as foods with more fat in them.

Bush Boake Allen was, in 1997, the world's leading producer of geraniol and Lilestralis as well as pine oil. Hoping to become the premier supplier of aroma chemicals, the company was planning to build an aroma-chemical plant outside of Madras, India, increase geraniol capacity at its Jacksonville plant, and increase its production of petrochemical-based aroma chemicals in Widnes. BBA was the first company to produce aroma chemicals both from terpene and petrochemicals. Widnes had made a shift from turpentine-based aroma chemicals to petroleum-derived ones, such as the ones marketed under the Lilestralis, Abbalide, and Boisvelone trade names, thereby leaving BBA less dependent on turpentine supplies, which varied in quantity according to cyclical production in the paper industry.

Bush Boake Allen's 1997 revenues rose to $491 million, but its net income slipped slightly to $31 million. In 1998, although revenues dropped to $485 million, net income was a record $33.7 million. Interviewed by Peter Landau of *Chemical Marketing Reporter* in early 1999, Boyden said that in the fragrance industry, "the margins have certainly gotten tougher over the last 10 years or so." He said that in the flavor business, the firm's ambition was to build on higher-value compound flavors, such as state-of-the-art spray-dried products. Boyden added, "We're also investing more on the biotech side of our business, looking particularly at dairy flavors at our operation in Wisconsin, developing a range of enhanced dairy flavors, as well as increased natural products from physical separation."

In 1998 Bush Boake Allen opened a major production facility in Istanbul, Turkey, and its first Mexican plant. It had manufacturing and compounding facilities in 15 countries at the end of the year. In addition to the Jacksonville and Widnes plants for aroma chemicals, BBA had a production center for seasonings at Carrollton, Texas, and one for both seasonings and essential oils at Long Melford, England. The company also had 43 laboratories. BBA spent $25.2 million on research and development during 1998.

Bush Boake Allen was constantly creating new compounds in order to meet the many and changing characteristics of its customers' end products. Its flavor products also included essential oils, natural extracts, spice extracts, and seasonings derived from fruits, vegetables, nuts, herbs, and spices as well as ingredients enhanced by enzymes. These were being sold in liquid, powder, and paste forms. Sweet flavors included a full range of fruit flavors as well as flavors such as vanilla, coffee, chocolate, and cola. Savory flavors included meat, cheese, and fish flavors. BBA also was producing flavors for specific applications, principally in the tea, oral-hygiene, and pharmaceutical industries. Bush Boake Allen's range of fragrance products included a line of compounds based on extensive analysis of scents from living plants and flowers, marketed under the Generessence trade name.

Sales of flavor compounds accounted for about 35 percent of Bush Boake Allen's net sales in 1998. Sales of fragrances (excluding the resale of aroma chemicals) accounted for 19 percent, and sales of aroma chemicals, 24 percent. Sales of natural products used as flavoring items in their own right and also as raw materials for fragrances and compounding flavors accounted for the remaining 22 percent. International Paper Company became the majority stockholder of Bush Boake Allen when it purchased Union Camp in 1999.

Principal Subsidiaries

Bush Boake Allen Australia Ltd.; Bush Boake Allen Canada Inc.; Bush Boake Allen (Chile) S.A.; Bush Boake Allen Colombia S.A.; Bush Boake Allen Controladora S.A. de C.V. (Mexico); Bush Boake Allen Espana S.A. (Spain); Bush Boake Allen (Executive Pension Trustees) Limited (U.K.); Bush Boake Allen Industrias E Comercial do Brasil Limitada; Bush Boake Allen Limited (U.K.); Bush Boake Allen (Nominees) Limited (U.K.); Bush Boake Allen Pension Investments Limited (U.K.); Bush Boake Allen (Pension Trustees) Limited (U.K.); Bush Boake Allen Servicios S.A. de C.V. (Mexico); Bush Boake Allen (Works Pension Trustees) Limited (U.K.); GHS Proteins Limited (U.K.); W.J. Bush & Co., Inc.

Principal Operating Units

Aroma and Terpene Chemicals; Americas Region; Asia Pacific Region; Europe Region; International Region.

Further Reading

"A&W, $700M in Sales Now, Eyes New Areas and Businesses, But Remains in What It Knows," *Chemical Marketing Reporter,* January 22, 1979, pp. 5, 24.

Floreno, Anthony, "BBA Broadens Global Reach with Addition of Indian Plant," *Chemical Market Reporter,* November 24, 1997, pp. 1, 15.

——, "Bush Boake Allen Aims for the F&F Big Leagues," *Chemical Market Reporter,* August 11, 1997, pp. 5, 24.

"Interview: Julian Boyden," *BUSINESS News New Jersey,* August 11, 1997, p. 27.

Landau, Peter, "Executive Q&A," *Chemical Marketing Reporter,* February 18, 1999, p. 18.

"Union Camp Sells BBA Stock," *Chemical Marketing Reporter,* March 21, 1994, pp. 7, 18.

—Robert Halasz

Cable & Wireless HKT

Hongkong Telecom Tower
39th Floor
Taikoo Place
979 King's Road
Quarry Bay
Hong Kong
(852) 2888-2888
Fax: (852) 2877-8877
Web site: http://www.hkt.com

Public Subsidiary of Cable & Wireless PLC and China Telecom
Incorporated: 1988 as Hong Kong Telecommunications Ltd.
Employees: 14,233
Sales: US$4.18 billion (1999)
Stock Exchanges: New York Hong Kong Pacific
Ticker Symbol: HKT
NAIC: 51333 Telecommunications Resellers; 51331 Wired Telecommunications Carriers; 51334 Satellite Telecommunications

Cable & Wireless HKT (HKT), formerly Hong Kong Telecommunications Ltd., provides a wide range of communications services in Hong Kong. With eight offices in Asia and two in Canada, HKT has its headquarters in Hong Kong, where it maintains 3.6 million phone lines. Among the products and services offered by HKT are basic telephone services, international telephone services, Internet access, fax and data services, mobile telephone services, multimedia services, satellite links, and telecommunications equipment. The company lost its monopoly on international phone service at the beginning of 1999 and changed its name in midyear to better reflect the company's diverse array of services, particularly in Internet services. HKT is a public subsidiary of Cable & Wireless PLC (54 percent) and China Telecom, the leading telecommunications company in China (11 percent).

Early Years

The origins of HKT date back to the beginnings of Hong Kong's telecommunications history in the 1870s. John Pender, a onetime Manchester cotton merchant, extended his worldwide telecommunications empire to all corners of the British Empire by forming the China Submarine Telegraph Company in 1871. An undersea telegraph cable was put in place in Hong Kong by Pender's company, effectively connecting Hong Kong and Singapore, Britain's main colonies in the Far East, by telegraph to London. Later, in 1873, Pender completed the merger of his Australian, Chinese, and British India companies into the Eastern Extension Australasia and China Telegraph Company to look after the telegraph cable. Several decades later, this company became part of the Cable & Wireless Group.

Domestic telecommunications facilities in Hong Kong became more advanced in 1925 when the Hong Kong Telephone Company took over the interests of Pender's China and Japan Telephone and Electric Company. The company's mandate included providing all the British colonies with local telephone services. Over the next six decades Hong Kong Telephone's line capacity grew to more than 2.5 million, with the company serving approximately six million people.

Telecommunications became increasingly important following World War I, and in 1929 the British companies Marconi Wireless and Eastern Telegraph joined to establish Cable and Wireless (C&W). The company's strategy was to supply telephone and telegraph services in Britain's colonies, and it succeeded in securing an exclusive franchise to provide international communications services in Hong Kong. By 1972 the company's biggest operation was its subsidiary in rapidly growing Hong Kong. Hong Kong Telephone, meanwhile, built a new headquarters in 1972. The company's growth was said to typify the colony's transition from an economy based on manufacturing to one dependent on service industries, which created a demand for telecommunications services. In 1975 Hong Kong Telephone's franchise for domestic service in the colony was extended for an additional 20 years, to expire just ahead of Hong Kong's reversion to China's control in 1997.

Company Perspectives:

We will continue to invest in developing people and technology to reinforce Cable & Wireless HKT's standing as Asia's most successful integrated communications company.

Expanded Services and Growth in the 1980s

In 1981 the Hong Kong branch of C&W was established as Cable & Wireless Hong Kong (later Hongkong Telecom International) to manage its communications services, and in 1984 C&W HK purchased Hong Kong Telephone. Hong Kong Telephone, which had started to develop an all-digital telephone system for the colony and surrounding regions in 1984, boasted one of the most modern networks worldwide. The aim was to give the colony state-of-the-art telecommunications facilities and performance.

In December 1985 the eastern section of the Guangdong microwave project in southern China was opened, for which C&W provided technical assistance. A few months later, in March 1986, the western section opened, effectively linking telecommunications traffic between 25 cities in Guangdong province, which then emerged as an expanding hinterland manufacturing base next to Hong Kong.

In 1986 Hong Kong Telephone started up public facsimile service from Hong Kong to Beijing, Shanghai, Guangzhou, and Shenzhen, a newly created special economic zone. Such facilities were instrumental in helping much of Hong Kong's manufacturing base continue relocating to southern parts of China, then undergoing economic reforms and establishing closer manufacturing links with Western markets. The Cable and Wireless Group had at the time two joint ventures in China. The first, Shenda Telephone Company, of which the group had a 49 percent stake, sold and installed an overhead fiber-optic system that linked Shenzhen City, Shahe, and Nantou. The second, the Huaying Nanhai Oil Telecommunication Service Company, began helping explore for oil deposits in the South China Sea.

Cable and Wireless also signed agreements in 1986 to provide some 1,000 kilometers of digital trunk microwave and five long-distance toll exchanges in the Yangtze Delta region of China, linking 27 cities in Jiangsu and Zhejiang provinces. Another agreement was signed that year with the Guangdong Posts and Telecommunications Bureau to develop a mobile radio telephone and paging service in the Pearl Delta region. The unified system was aimed at allowing local subscribers to use handheld telephones. To complete this contract, Hong Kong Telephone established a nonfranchised operation, Communication Services Ltd. Its function was to introduce new mobile radio telephone and radio paging services, allowing the use of handheld equipment anywhere in Hong Kong and the Pearl Delta region. By March 1987 Communication Services Ltd. had opened 18 retail outlets.

In June 1986 Cable & Wireless also announced plans for an underwater optical fiber cable connecting Hong Kong with Japan and South Korea, to become operational in 1990. As a measure of the group's regional clout, the London-based organization became the first British company to be listed on the Tokyo Stock Exchange. This event underlined the telecommunications group's expanding role in the emerging Pacific Basin region.

In 1988 Hong Kong Telecommunications Ltd. (HKT), also known as Hongkong Telecom, was formed to serve as a holding company for Hongkong Telecom International and Hong Kong Telephone and effectively consolidated the twin international and domestic telecommunications facilities under one umbrella. The first chairman of Hong Kong Telephone was Sir Eric Sharp. A native Briton, Sharp had also been chairman of Cable & Wireless PLC since 1981. Serving as deputy chairman was Brian Pemberton, the London-based joint managing director of the Cable & Wireless Group, with responsibility for the group's activities in the Far East. Day-to-day management of Hong Kong Telephone was put in the hands of Michael Gale, who served as CEO. Gale first joined Cable & Wireless in 1959 and had earlier served as CEO of Hong Kong Telephone.

As of January 1988, HKT had 16,300 employees and was one of the largest employers in the colony. Expansion of specialty services, including nonvoice communications services, was considered a top priority for the new company. For example, Faxline, a support service for Hong Kong's facsimile terminal users, had 26,000 accounts in 1988 and was growing at the time at a rate of 2,000 new users a month. In addition, Datapak, Hong Kong's public data network for communications and networking, was expanding services between host computers and its own central database terminal. One large HKT customer, global computer maker International Business Machines Corporation (IBM), required the establishment in 1988 of a subsidiary data sales service, IBS. Its role was to represent ROLM, a subsidiary of IBM in Hong Kong, providing it with voice and data digital information systems in addition to servicing and consultation services.

Beginning in 1987, satellite communications facilities were provided to HKT through five satellite dishes located at Stanley Earth Station and geosynchronous satellites situated over the Indian and Pacific oceans. With eight permanent and one portable antenna, the earth station proved to be one of the largest commercial satellite facilities in the world. International facsimile transmissions utilizing Hong Kong Telephone's international telephone circuits grew considerably throughout the 1980s. And the creation of the HKT CSL subsidiary in 1990 allowed for the development of sophisticated paging and mobile radio telephone equipment and services.

By the end of the 1980s telephone traffic between Hong Kong and China was becoming increasingly important to HKT. This reflected both the increase in business between the colony and emerging economic centers in southern China and the expanding telecommunications facilities linking the two regions. By 1989, for example, traffic with China accounted for about 20 percent of international traffic revenues for HKT and some 38 percent of traffic volume overall. This compared with 18 percent and 34 percent, respectively, for both revenue producers a year earlier.

Diversification in the Early 1990s

In October 1990, Rt. Hon. Lord Young of Graffham, chairman of HKT, met with Premier Li Peng and Yang Tai-fang, then China's minister of Post and Telecommunications, and announced that China was to spend some US$6 billion by 1995 to expand that country's telecommunications base. By virtue of the new and expanding China business, Young was quoted in the company's 1991 annual report as saying that the "continued development of the Pacific Rim countries, and China in particular, should ensure that the region continues to enjoy strong economic growth.... Telecommunications infrastructures throughout the region are being expanded and modernized to support this growth. Hongkong Telecom is well positioned to benefit from these developments."

In 1991 HKT added Citinet to its portfolio. The service, offering a private switchboard service to subscribers and operated from a central telephone exchange, was taken up by 21,200 account holders in its first year of operation. HKT also introduced radio paging that year, allowing subscribers to carry a credit card-sized pager, complete with Chinese characters, with them for instant access to calls and messages. By 1992 traffic with China continued to underpin the growth in sales at HKT. Chairman Young told shareholders in the company's 1992 annual report, "China's continuing economic development and the integration with the Pearl River Delta area encompassing Macao and Guangdong are also benefitting the Hong Kong economy. We have seen this translated into strong demand for our services, with international calls between Hong Kong and China growing 35 percent."

HKT completed the digitalization of the Hong Kong telephone network in 1993, the first full digitalization of a major urban market. Another world first was the introduction of an underground digital mobile system, designed to supply coverage on underground trains on Hong Kong's Mass Transit Railway. Also that year HKT and its parent company formed a joint venture, Great Eastern Telecommunications Limited, to take advantage of telecommunications opportunities in Asia. In 1994 HKT and the China Ministry of Post and Telecommunications developed a partnership to install undersea cables throughout Asia, and HKT became the biggest mobile telephone operator in Hong Kong.

Major Changes in the Late 1990s

Despite its continued expansion and dominance of the telecommunications industry in Hong Kong, HKT faced a significant new challenge as it entered the second half of the decade—competition. In mid-1995 HKT lost its exclusive franchise to supply domestic telephone services in the Hong Kong region, and three rivals entered the marketplace: Hutchison Communications Ltd., Net T&T Hong Kong Ltd., and New World Telephone Ltd. With the new competition and increasing inflation, HKT announced plans to cut more than 15 percent of its workforce, which amounted to 2,500 staff members, by 1998. The company maintained that the cutbacks would result not from layoffs but through attrition and a reduction in new hiring.

The introduction of competition did not have a negative effect on HKT, nor did it slow the company down. The com-

pany's net profit during the first half of fiscal 1996 increased 15 percent over the same period of fiscal 1995. In 1995 HKT completed its new corporate headquarters, opened offices in Vancouver and Toronto, and announced the formation of subsidiary Cable & Wireless HKT IMS, which would handle interactive multimedia services. The following year HKT launched a new Internet service called Netvigator, thus establishing its early commitment to the Internet, and began offering such services as ISDN (Integrated Services Digital Network) and Caller Display.

In 1997, hoping to increase opportunities in the Chinese market, C&W PLC sold a 5.5 percent stake in C&W to China Telecom, China's government-controlled telecommunications operator. The move was not unexpected. Because Hong Kong was to revert to Chinese rule in July 1997, analysts predicted that C&W PLC would diminish its stake in C&W to increase activity in China, considered a profitable area of growth. China Telecom purchased additional shares of C&W the following year to become the company's second largest shareholder.

Early in 1998 HKT made another significant announcement, that the company would give up its monopoly on international telephone services in 1999 rather than 2006 in exchange for US$865.6 million. As part of the agreement, HKT would be allowed to change the tariffs charged for leasing its telephone lines, possibly resulting in much higher local phone charges for customers. Relinquishing the exclusive rights to offer international services was made less substantial by the fact that customers had had access to numerous international direct-dial (IDD) carriers since deregulation in 1995. IDD rates, according to the *Asian Wall Street Journal*, had dropped by as much as 70 percent between 1995 and 1998 because of the intense competition. HKT's revenues from IDD services already showed signs of decline, and for the fiscal year ended March 31, 1998, according to the company, IDD services contributed 48 percent of total revenue. The previous year IDD calls had accounted for 53 percent of total revenue, and the year before that 56 percent. Still, HKT dominated the telecommunications industry, holding 98 percent of local services and 75 percent of the long-distance arena.

HKT continued to expand its services so that it would not have to rely solely on revenues generated from local and international telephone services. Internet and interactive services grew considerably, with Netvigator the largest Internet service provider in Hong Kong. The company's new interactive television (iTV) service, which offered viewers the opportunity to access the Internet and view movies, signed up about 60,000 subscribers in just a few months. HKT acquired Hong Kong Star Internet Ltd., a subsidiary of Star Telecom International Holding Ltd., in late 1998, thereby joining the region's two largest Internet service providers.

In the highly competitive mobile telephone market, six operators battled for market share. HKT acquired Pacific Link Communications Limited, the Hong Kong cellular phone operations of First Pacific Holdings, in 1998. The acquisition boosted HKT's leadership of the competitive mobile telephone market. For the fiscal year ended March 31, 1998, HKT reported that cellular service revenues increased 28 percent, and HKT continued to dominate the field, boasting more than 860,000 subscribers. According to the *Asian Wall Street Journal,* however, the rise in revenue was due primarily to the purchase of Pacific Link. The publication reported that HKT had lost 30,000 subscribers during the first half of fiscal 1999, bringing its share of the market to 41 percent.

As HKT prepared to enter into full competition in 1999, the company struggled to maintain direction and focus amid great change and a difficult recession. The first half of fiscal 1999 did not bode well; total revenue fell three percent, and the company planned to cut the salaries of its staff of nearly 14,000. "We are now changing from a monopoly situation into a highly competitive market," lamented CEO Linus W.L. Cheung in the *Asian Wall Street Journal.* "If we cannot do something about our costs and efficiency, we will have very little room for maneuver."

As expected, the advent of 1999 brought intense price wars in the long-distance telephone service market. Because of government restrictions, HKT was unable to offer significant discounts. For the fiscal year ended March 31, 1999, total revenues slipped 7.5 percent. IDD services suffered from a 22 percent drop in revenue. The declines, according to the company, were due to severe price competition in international telephone services and mobile services, as well as the recession.

Undeterred by the difficult year, HKT continued to move forward. CEO Cheung wrote in the 1999 annual report, "We have moved from being a monopoly provider of basic telecommunications services to become a competitive, fully integrated communications company." HKT acquired an 85 percent stake in FIC Network Services of First International Computer of Taiwan to strengthen its Internet presence in Asia and upped its stake in Taiwan Telecommunications Network Services from 21.4 percent to 56 percent, thereby expanding its authority in Asian telecommunications markets. The company announced plans to invest US$103.3 million on its interactive television service during 1999 and formed a partnership with Microsoft Corporation to deliver increased services through iTV. HKT had already spent US$180.7 million between 1995 and 1999 developing a fiber-optic network in Hong Kong to accommodate iTV, among other services. In mid-1999 HKT indicated that it would spend US$257.7 million over the following three years to improve its mobile telephone network.

HKT adopted its new name, Cable & Wireless HKT, in June 1999 to signal its diversity of technological products and to further the company's intent to make Hong Kong the Asian center of e-commerce and the Internet. A company press release

indicated that the new name and logo were "part of the Company's strategy to further enhance its position to meet intensified competition on a global scale. The new logo and English trade name can better reflect the scope, dimension and the geographical reach of the various integrated communications services the Company is now offering." HKT's plans for the new millennium included entering China's rapidly growing telephone market, expanding into property development, and continuing to invest in its broad range of telecommunications and Internet services. CEO Leung summed up the company's future in a prepared statement: "Cable & Wireless HKT is a new Company projecting the bold new image we will take into the new millennium, when the borderless infotech and communications industry will reach horizons we cannot even imagine today."

Principal Subsidiaries

Hong Kong Telecom CAS Limited; Hong Kong Telephone Company Limited; Hong Kong Telephone International Limited; Hong Kong Telecom CSL Limited; Hong Kong Telecom IMS Limited; Hong Kong Telecom VOD Limited; Computasia Limited; Monance Limited; Hongkong Telecom Finance Limited; One2Free PersonalCom Limited; Hongkong Telecom Teleservices Limited; Hong Kong Telecommunications (Pacific) Limited; FIC Network Service, Inc. (85%); Telecom Directories Limited (51%).

Further Reading

Granitsas, Alkman, "Hong Kong Is Finally Getting Serious About Opening Its Telecoms Market to Competition," *Far Eastern Economic Review,* August 13, 1998, p. 44.

"Hongkong Telecommunications Ltd.—Introduction to Stock Exchange of Hong Kong Ltd," *Prospectus,* January 29, 1988.

"Hong Kong Telephone: Guide to Customer Services," Hong Kong: Hong Kong Telephone, April 1988.

Kennedy, Sean, "What Is Hongkong Telecom's Net Value?" *Asian Wall Street Journal,* May 6, 1999, p. 4.

Ling, Connie, "Hong Kong: A Wide-Open Telecommunications Market Is Becoming Even More of a Free-For-All," *Asian Wall Street Journal,* June 2, 1998, p. S4.

Mungan, Christina, "Hongkong Telecom Girds for iTV's Next Phase," *Wall Street Journal Europe,* April 1, 1999, p. 4.

——, "Hongkong Telecom Tastes Hard Times," *Asian Wall Street Journal,* November 9, 1998, p. 3.

—Etan Vlessing
—updated by Mariko Fujinaka

▐▐▐*CABLEVISION*

Cablevision Systems Corporation

1111 Stewart Avenue
Bethpage, New York 11714-3581
U.S.A.
(516) 803-2300
Fax: (516) 806-2273
Web site: http://www.cablevision.com

Public Company
Incorporated: 1985
Employees: 15,824
Sales: $3.27 billion (1998)
Stock Exchanges: American
Ticker Symbol: CVC
NAIC: 51321 Cable Networks; 51331 Wired
    Telecommunications Carriers; 51339 Other
    Telecommunications; 443112 Radio, Television &
    Other Electronics Stores; 512131 Motion Picture
    Theaters, Except Drive-In; 711211 Sports Teams &
    Clubs; 71399 All Other Amusement & Recreation
    Industries

Cablevision Systems Corporation is one of the largest cable systems operators in the United States, providing service to about 3.4 million subscribers, primarily in the greater New York, Boston, and Cleveland metropolitan areas. Through its state-of-the-art fiber-optic coaxial cable systems, Cablevision has been expanding its telecommunications offerings beyond cable, into the realms of high-speed Internet access and local telephone service. The company also maintains a strong presence in programming through Rainbow Media Holdings Inc., which is 75 percent owned by Cablevision and 25 percent owned by the National Broadcasting Company, Inc. Rainbow Media owns several cable networks, including American Movie Classics, Romance Classics, Bravo, and the Independent Film Channel. Rainbow also holds a majority interest in the Madison Square Garden arena, the New York Knickerbockers professional basketball team, the New York Rangers professional hockey team, and Radio City Music Hall; as well as interests in

regional sports networks, the Fox Sports Net national network, and regional news networks. Cablevision's other ventures include ownership of the Wiz chain of New York area consumer electronics stores and the Clearview Cinema Group, operator of movie theaters in the northeastern United States. AT&T Corp. holds a one-third stake in Cablevision, but the founding Dolan family maintains control of 80 percent of the voting shares.

Founding by Cable Pioneer

Charles F. Dolan, the founder and chairman of the board of directors of Cablevision, entered the cable television business in its infancy. A maker of industrial films, he became a pioneer of cable television in 1960 when he began wiring hotels in New York City for reception of his cable news service. In 1965 Dolan's company, Sterling Manhattan, won a franchise to operate a cable television system in the southern half of Manhattan. Sterling had wealthy partners—Time, Inc. in particular—and was able to raise money for the cable system through a stock offering, but he was unable to amass enough funds to complete the system. Sterling's debts multiplied until 1973 when Time, having become the owner of 80 percent of the company, decided to liquidate. Time bought the Home Box Office (HBO) channel—the first nationwide pay-TV channel in the United States, which Dolan had founded in 1970—from Sterling, and HBO went on to become the leading pay-TV channel in the United States.

Although Time had lost faith in the marketability of cable service on Long Island, where many free television channels were already offered, Dolan firmly believed that people wanted the commercial-free television with programming alternatives that cable offered. Using part of the $675,000 he received from Time for his Sterling stock, he bought back the Long Island cable franchises from Time and quickly created another cable company, Long Island Cable Communication Development Company. The company offered a free month of HBO to its 1,500 Long Island customers, and was rewarded when over 90 percent of them opted to continue the service for $6.00 a month.

Such early successes enabled Cablevision to begin raising venture capital and attracting more customers. The densely

Company Perspectives:

Cablevision Systems Corporation is one of the nation's leading telecommunications and entertainment companies. Its portfolio of operations ranges from high-speed Internet access and robust cable television packages to championship professional sports teams and national television program networks. Driving Cablevision's success is the company's vision to enrich and enhance the lives of its customers by providing the greatest choice of entertainment, information and telecommunications services possible utilizing state-of-the-art technology.

populated Long Island proved an especially auspicious market. Its proximity to Manhattan made it easy to pick up the microwave signals HBO and other transmitters were still using. Dolan won still more customers by gaining the rights to New York Mets, Islanders, Nets, and Yankees games that were blacked out locally. Cablevision received the highest revenue per subscriber in the United States, partly because Long Island provided an affluent customer base, and partly because of its strategy of selling pay-TV channels in blocks for a lower sum than they would bring individually.

While Cablevision produced significant cash flow, there was little profit due to the capital-intensive nature of the cable business. To keep the company afloat and expanding, Dolan turned to limited partnerships, attracting business magnates such as Hugh Hefner and Milton Friedman as investors. Cablevision slowly expanded, adding systems in Yonkers, New York; New Jersey; and suburban Chicago. By 1980, at about the time the cable industry began receiving significant nationwide attention, Cablevision had 155,000 customers and $14 million of cash flow. It was worth $250 million and had a debt of $45 million. The 50 miles of cable it had owned in 1973 had grown to 4,000 miles.

Formation of Rainbow: 1980

In 1980 Cablevision formed a subsidiary, Rainbow Programming Services, to create cable programming. This programming soon included the American Movie Classics channel, which showed vintage Hollywood films, and Bravo, which showed classic American and foreign films, exclusive Broadway plays, music and dance performances, and educational presentations. In 1983 Cablevision began offering the Newsday Channel, a 24-hour news and information channel produced in conjunction with the New York newspaper *Newsday*. The station did not attract enough viewer support to survive long, however. Cablevision also started Sports Channel, which broadcast New York Nets basketball games, and Islander and Devils hockey games, in addition to Yankees and Mets games. The channel received revenue from advertisers and subscribers, and became one of the cable industry's most successful sports services.

In 1984 Cablevision moved aggressively to win a cable franchise in Boston. It won the bidding with a basic cable fee of $2.00 a month, considered low for the cable industry. The firm planned

to make up for the lost revenue by tiering pay services such as HBO. It ran into construction problems in laying the cable, however, delaying completion of the system—and its capacity for bringing in much-needed revenue—for years. Cablevision was also expanding into New York City, where it won franchises for the Bronx and two-thirds of Brooklyn. Although there were more setbacks—in 1985 Cablevision lost its 47.5 percent stake in a Sacramento cable system when it was unable to pay off a $34 million obligation to partner Scripps Howard Inc.—Cablevision became the 15th largest cable systems operator in the United States in 1986, with 595,000 subscribers.

In 1986, with the price of cable televisions systems at an all-time high, Dolan decided to create a publicly held company with 390,000 of Cablevision's subscribers. The systems going public were in Long Island, Westchester County, New York City, and New Jersey. Systems in Boston and Chicago that had not yet become profitable were not included in the new company until they went into the black. The initial stock price worked out to about $1,700 per subscriber. The stock offering was structured in such a way that it left Dolan with a large percentage of the company's voting rights and control of 75 percent of the board of directors. Dolan received some criticism because the systems he was taking public were believed to have grown about as large as they were going to.

Cablevision's debt stood at about $290 million from acquisitions and the buying out of limited partners. Dolan reportedly wanted to use the $80 million he raised through the offering to pay off part of this debt. Dolan also wanted to spend $25 million on further cable construction in New York City.

In July 1986 Cablevision agreed to acquire two cable systems from Scripps Howard Inc. for $175 million. The systems were also partly held by Dolan, though how much each party owned was not revealed. The systems were located in Fairfield County, Connecticut, and added 120,000 subscribers to the Cablevision system. Later in the year Cablevision acquired the portions of Rainbow Programming Services it did not already own for about $57 million. In 1987 Cablevision bought Adams-Russell Co., a cable TV company based in Waltham, Massachusetts.

Cablevision also expanded its programming services. In December 1986, Cablevision tried again to offer a 24-hour local news channel. News 12, available on all Long Island cable systems, not just Cablevision's, won numerous awards for its news coverage, and became Long Island's premier news service.

In early 1987, Cablevision joined a group of cable operators and investor Kirk Kerkorian in investing $550 million in Turner Broadcasting System Inc. (TBS). The investment in TBS allowed Chairman of the Board Ted Turner to keep control of his company. Cablevision and the other investors desired this because Turner Broadcasting was an important source of programming, and they wanted it to maintain its independence. The group of investors was allowed to name five of TBS's 11 board members.

Increasing its involvement with cable programming, Cablevision bought the Washington Post Company's interests in four of California's Sports Channels in June 1987 for $6 million. At this point, Cablevision had sports channels in Chicago, New York, New England, Philadelphia, and Florida. The firm also increased its expansion out of the eastern seaboard when it bought First Carolina Communication cable systems in Cleveland and Toledo, Ohio.

In 1988 Gulf & Western outbid Cablevision for the rights to Yankees games. To protest, Cablevision dropped Gulf & Western's Madison Square Garden Network, which broadcast the games as part of its regular service. The move angered many of the 400,000 Cablevision subscribers in New York, New Jersey, and Connecticut, who were unable to watch the games. It also upset many cable systems operators, who worried that the controversy would attract unwanted attention from the U.S. federal government. Congress had just deregulated cable in 1987, and as consumers complained about cable service, some lawmakers considered reregulation. Cablevision settled with Gulf & Western in 1989, agreeing to offer the Madison Square Garden Network as an option in its service package, priced and promoted equally to its own Sports Channel.

In 1989 Cablevision and the National Broadcasting Company (NBC) formed a joint venture to market a national cable network as well as regional news and sports networks. They also agreed to offer the first pay-per-view Olympics coverage of the 1992 Summer Games in Barcelona. It was the first time that a broadcast network and a cable system had cooperated in a programming venture, and many industry analysts had doubts that it would work. NBC and Cablevision had competing interests: cable television was a threat to the audiences of NBC's affiliate stations, and cable operators were suspicious of NBC's forays into cable programming. NBC received a 50 percent stake in most of Rainbow's programming services, while Cablevision took 50 percent of NBC's cable venture, Consumer News and Business Channel, and $137.5 million to develop programming for it. The two companies also intended to create a series of regional cable news stations and ten sports channels in addition to the five already operated by Cablevision.

Large Purchases: Late 1980s

Cablevision had borne a high debt load since its inception, having borrowed heavily to lay cable and buy other companies. In the late 1980s the firm's debt increased significantly as it made a number of large purchases. Cablevision bought a regional sports channel in Los Angeles for $18 million. It also bought two cable systems in suburban Cleveland and Long Island from Viacom Inc. for $549 million. Cablevision also received 20 percent of another system under construction in Cleveland and a five percent stake in The Movie Channel and Showtime, two Viacom pay channels. The sale added 120,000 subscribers to the 310,000 Cablevision already had in Long Island and added 75,000 subscribers to the 85,000 it had in Cleveland. Cablevision became the eighth largest cable systems operator in the United States, with over 1.3 million customers in 11 states. But with rising interest payments on its significant debt, Cablevision lost $22.6 million in 1988 on sales of $493 million.

In February 1990 Cablevision announced it would invest $1 billion with three other media companies in Sky Cable, a direct-broadcast satellite service that was to offer up to 108 channels. The plan fell apart in little more than a year, however, due to conflicting interests among the partners.

In the meantime, Cablevision continued to create new programming. It announced plans for a channel that would cover important or sensational court trials. The In Court channel was hampered by a lack of unused channels on most cable systems, as well as a rival channel to be started by American Lawyer Media. Tentative plans to merge the channels were announced before either went on the air. In 1991 the Cablevision and NBC partnership agreed to start a sports-news cable channel. The channel was to be distributed through the Sports Channel America network. Critics pointed out that sports fans wanted to see the games themselves, and that sports news was already covered by a variety of media outlets.

Cablevision and NBC spent $40 million on marketing their pay-per-view Olympics service, and $60 million producing it, but the actual sales were disappointing. The cost of the service to the consumer was high, starting at $95 for weekend coverage, and 160 hours of Olympic coverage was already available on free television. Far fewer subscribers signed up than expected and Cablevision lost $50 million on the venture. Partly as a result of this, Cablevision lost $82.7 million in the second quarter of 1992.

In 1992 Cablevision's debt was more than $1 billion, and the price of its Class A stock declined to the extent that the company canceled a public offering that had been scheduled. But business analysts observed that Dolan continued to think big, and despite its heavy debt, Cablevision continued to grow. In 1991, for instance, Cablevision bought Gateway Cable, a 42,000-subscriber system serving Newark and South Orange, New Jersey. By 1992 Cablevision owned 23 cable systems and had a total of about two million basic subscribers.

Flurry of Acquisitions, Divestments, and Joint Ventures: Mid-to-Late 1990s

The mid-to-late 1990s were marked by a flurry of activity, as Cablevision positioned itself in the center of the convergence of telecommunications, computers, and entertainment. In 1993 Sports Channel America merged with Liberty Media Corporation's Prime Network to form Prime SportsChannel Networks, a collection of regional sports networks that reached about 30 million homes. Through Rainbow, Cablevision owned a 25 percent stake in the new venture. Also in 1993 Cablevision paid about $170 million to gain full control of American Movie Classics, which had been 50 percent owned by Liberty Media. The following year Cablevision launched two new cable channels, Romance Classics and the Independent Movie Channel.

Also in 1994 the company established Cablevision Lightpath as a competitive local exchange carrier and began serving business customers on Long Island. By 1997 the upstart telephone company had more than 1,000 customers in the greater New York City area, with revenue reaching $36.6 million. Continuing to leverage its fiber-optic broadband network, Lightpath in 1998 began offering residential telephone and cable modem Internet access in greater New York and parts of southern Connecticut.

Meanwhile, Cablevision bolstered its presence in the New York sports scene through the early 1995 joint purchase, with ITT Corp., of Madison Square Garden from Viacom Inc. for about $1 billion. Included in the Garden operations were the famous 20,000-seat theater; the MSG Network, a regional sports network; and the National Basketball Association's New York Knickerbockers and the National Hockey League's New York Rangers. In addition, the Garden held the rights to broadcast most of the games played by the Knicks and Rangers, as well as the Major League Baseball's New York Yankees. Also in 1995 Cablevision, through Rainbow, purchased NBC's interests in SportsChannel New York and Rainbow News 12, gaining full control of these operations. In late 1995 James Dolan, son of founder Charles, was named CEO of Cablevision, with the founder remaining chairman.

Increasingly turning to alliances in the rapidly changing, deregulated environment of the late 1990s, Cablevision struck a number of major deals in 1997. In April NBC exchanged its stakes in American Movie Classics, Bravo, the Independent Film Channel, and several SportsChannel sports networks for an overall 25 percent stake in the newly named Rainbow Media. With ITT battling a hostile takeover, Cablevision in June bought most of ITT's stake in Madison Square Garden, paying $650 million to increase its interest (which was held through Rainbow Media) to 89.8 percent. Through a series of 1997 and early 1998 transactions consistent with the general move toward cable clustering, Cablevision transformed its cable systems operations from 2.9 million customers in 19 states to 3.5 million customers in three core clusters—centering around New York City, Boston, and Cleveland—in five states. The company's New York cluster was its most important, and it was substantially beefed up through the acquisition of the New York area cable systems of TeleCommunications Inc. (TCI), which served 829,000 households; TCI thereby gained a 33 percent stake in Cablevision (although the Dolan family maintained 80 percent of the voting shares), while Cablevision also assumed $669 million in debt, adding to its mounting debt load—which reached $4.69 billion by the end of 1997. Despite the debt load, Cablevision had gained a dominant position in the New York cable market—with the exception of Manhattan, where Time Warner held sway—which meshed well with Rainbow Media's exceptionally strong array of Big Apple sports assets.

In December 1997 Cablevision merged its regional sports channels into Fox Sports Net, gaining a 50 percent stake in a new national sports network, which was launched in partnership with News Corp.'s Fox Sports and TCI's Liberty Media. Fox Sports Net began operations with 20 stations in 19 media markets and household penetration of 56 million, enabling it to compete with ESPN, the entrenched cable sports heavyweight. While ESPN broadcast strictly on a national level, Fox Sports Net offered popular coverage of local teams, coupled with national programming, such as news and highlights shows, and national ads. Cablevision pocketed $850 million in the transaction that created the new network. Cablevision rounded out its 1997 dealmaking in December with the $400 million acquisition of Radio City Productions, operator of Radio City Music Hall, the New York landmark and home of the Rockettes. The deal with Rockefeller Group Inc. was handled through Cablevision's Madison Square Garden subsidiary.

Cablevision continued its acquisitive ways in 1998. Taking convergence to the retail level, the company in February paid $80 million to acquire the Wiz, a lossmaking New York City chain of 40 consumer electronics retail outlets. Cablevision viewed the Wiz as a marketing tool to promote its telephone services, cable modems, and such high-tech offerings as high definition TV, the next generation of TV in which the company had also invested. Movie theaters were the next Cablevision venture as the company bolstered its entertainment holdings through the purchase of Clearview Cinema Group in December 1998 as well as the purchase of 16 Loews theaters in March 1999, giving the company about 65 moviehouses in New York, Connecticut, New Jersey, and Pennsylvania. In late 1998 and early 1999 the media reported that Cablevision was in talks to acquire first the New York Yankees and then the New York Mets, but neither deal was consummated. Also in late 1998 Cablevision began selling its cable modem service under the At Home brand, having gained a ten percent interest in the high-speed Internet partnership the previous year, a partnership that included TCI, Comcast Corporation, and Cox Communications, Inc.

By the end of the 1990s, Cablevision was one-third owned by AT&T, following the latter's blockbuster acquisition of TCI in 1999. Speculation was rife that Cablevision itself was an acquisition target, perhaps being eyed by AT&T. It was also speculated that Cablevision and NBC would eventually take Rainbow Media public, an event that would help Cablevision pay down its substantial debt. Despite the company's debt load and the fact that it continued to post net losses nearly every year, Cablevision's strong presence in the New York area market and its wide-ranging but interconnected interests positioned it as a major player in the byzantine world of telecommunications/entertainment.

Principal Subsidiaries

CSC Holdings, Inc.; A-R Cable Investments, Inc.; A-R Cable Services, Inc.; Rainbow Media Holdings, Inc.; NYC LP Corp.; Cablevision of New York City—Master L.P.; Cablevision of NYC-Phase I; Cablevision MFR, Inc.; Regional Programming Partners; Regional MSG Holdings, LLC; Madison Square Garden, L.P.

Further Reading

Binkley, Christina, and Mark Robichaux, "ITT to Sell Its MSG Stake to Cablevision," *Wall Street Journal,* March 7, 1997, p. A3.
Bloch, Jeff, "How High Is Up?," *Forbes,* January 27, 1986.
Burgi, Michael, "Dolans' Hard Row to Hoe: Garden Deal Will Take More Than Fertilizer," *Mediaweek,* February 24, 1997, pp. 4–5.
——, "A Garden of Cable Delight," *Mediaweek,* March 10, 1997, p. 5.
Cauley, Leslie, "Cablevision Gains Control of Home to the Rockettes," *Wall Street Journal,* December 4, 1997, p. B10.
——, "What's Behind Cablevision's Offbeat Buys?," *Wall Street Journal,* February 9, 1998, pp. B1+.
Cauley, Leslie, and Stefan Fatsis, "Cablevision's Talks Over an Acquisition of New York Yankees Are Broken Off," *Wall Street Journal,* November 25, 1998, p. B12.
Chakravarty, Subrata N., "The Convergence Factor," *Forbes,* July 27, 1998, p. 46.
Fabrikant, Geraldine, "Cablevision, Runner of Risks," *New York Times,* November 13, 1986.
Fatsis, Stefan, and Mark Robichaux, "Cablevision's Accord with ITT Yields a Costly Coup," *Wall Street Journal,* March 10, 1997, p. B5.
Furman, Phyllis, "Storm Clouds Loom for Rainbow Cable: Reigning Niche Programmer's New Women's Channel Faces Tight Market," *Crain's New York Business,* January 20, 1997, p. 4.

Gay, Verne, "Divining the Dolans," *Mediaweek,* March 2, 1998, pp. 18, 20–21.

Goldman, Kevin, "Olympics '92: Some Games Have Begun," *Wall Street Journal,* July 20, 1992.

Henderson, Barry, "Oversize Load: Despite Its Latest Deal, Cablevision Still Has Too Much Debt," *Barron's,* June 16, 1997, pp. 15–16.

Kamen, Robin, "Honor Thy Mogul: Charles Dolan Built Cablevision; Can Son Jim Keep It in the Family?," *Crain's New York Business,* September 21, 1998, p. 1.

Kneale, Dennis, "Cablevision to Buy 2 Cable-TV Systems of Viacom," *Wall Street Journal,* August 17, 1988.

Landro, Laura, "NBC Cable Venture Unites Natural Foes," *Wall Street Journal,* February 8, 1989.

Lentz, Philip, "Sports Network Gains Home Field Advantage," *Crain's New York Business,* October 6, 1997, p. 3.

Lesly, Elizabeth, "Cablevision Loses Its Tunnel Vision," *Business Week,* October 20, 1997, pp. 106, 108.

Lieberman, David, "A Cable Mogul's Darning Dance on the High Wire," *Business Week,* June 5, 1989.

Lippman, John, "Fox-TCI Plan Creates First Serious Rival to ESPN," *Wall Street Journal,* June 24, 1997, p. B8.

Roberts, Johnnie L., "ITT, Cablevision Win Garden Auction with $1.08 Billion Cash Bid to Viacom," *Wall Street Journal,* August 29, 1994, p. A3.

Robichaux, Mark, "Cable Channel for Sports News Is Coming to Bat," *Wall Street Journal,* August 28, 1991.

——, "Cable Chief Casts His Eye on Competitors' Turf," *Wall Street Journal,* June 30, 1994, p. B1.

——, "Cablevision May Seek Financial Partner in an Effort to Cut Its Mounting Debt," *Wall Street Journal,* March 24, 1997, p. B10.

——, "Dolan Holds Court for Suitors of Cablevision Systems: Telephone Companies Woo Cable Operator and Purveyor of Programming," *Wall Street Journal,* October 27, 1993, p. B4.

——, "Liberty Will Merge Its Sports Network with Rival Channel," *Wall Street Journal,* January 7, 1993, p. B8.

——, "NBC to Own 25% of a Unit of Cablevision," *Wall Street Journal,* April 1, 1997, p. B11.

——, "Pay-Per-View Games: Down but Not Out," *Wall Street Journal,* August 7, 1992, p. B1.

Sanders, Lisa, "Somebody Heats the Wiz: Cablevision Formulates First Moves in Revival," *Crain's New York Business,* May 11, 1998, p. 1.

Sloan, Allan, "The Man Who Hated Commercials," *Forbes,* October 27, 1980.

—Scott M. Lewis
—updated by David E. Salamie

Cache Incorporated

1460 Broadway
New York, New York 10036
U.S.A.
(212) 575-3200
Fax: (212) 575-3225
Web site: http://www.cache-inc.com

Public Company
Incorporated: 1975 as Atours Incorporated
Employees: 1,500
Sales: $146.8 million (1998)
Stock Exchanges: NASDAQ
Ticker Symbol: CACH
NAIC: 44812 Women's Clothing Stores; 44815 Clothing
    Accessories Stores

Cache Incorporated is a publicly traded company that owns and operates a highly successful national chain of upscale women's apparel and accessories stores. Focusing primarily on formal dresses and fashionable evening wear, Cache's stores compete directly with both small, exclusive boutiques and huge, national department stores, with its prices ranging from $150 dresses to tailored suits for hundreds of dollars. Located mainly in large upscale shopping malls, Cache's stores appeal to a high-income, style-conscious female customer base, providing clothes for both special occasions, such as proms and weddings, and dressy day wear. In 1998 Cache acquired Lillie Rubin, a small national chain of high fashion, high-priced women's apparel, thereby further expanding the company's reach in the niche market of formal attire. With the company's sales in 1998 reaching almost $150 million and stores in more than 30 states, Cache is making its mark as a small but vibrant apparel company, capable of keeping up with the notoriously capricious trends of the retail industry.

Rocky Beginnings: 1975 Through the Late 1980s

Cache was founded in 1975 as Atours Incorporated. Initially located on the East Coast, Atours purchased high-end apparel from U.S. and European vendors, offering customers well-made, trendy day and evening wear. Atours presented an alternative shopping experience to those weary of large, impersonal department stores: the company's stores were kept small, with an emphasis on customer service, the inventory exemplifying a focus on style over quantity. The strategy worked, with Atours going public in March 1981. In July 1983 Atours changed its name to the flashier nomenclature of Cache Inc.

After a strong start, the 1980s proved to be a difficult decade for Cache. With department stores gaining more and more ground in the retail industry and the upscale apparel industry facing increasing competition from both individual designers and upstart small labels, Cache began by 1984 to go into a sales slump. That year, the company lost $1.7 million in sales, and the following year it fared even worse, with a loss of $2 million. By this time Cache owned and operated a chain of 30 separate stores, located primarily in the eastern part of the United States, and, despite the company's vibrant beginnings, such losses proved to be insupportable. Because of the company's back-to-back losses, it was having trouble getting the credit it needed to keep its merchandise updated and well-stocked in all of its stores. Attributing its troubles to rapid growth and a slow-moving inventory, Cache sought protection from its creditors by filing for reorganization under Chapter 11 of the Federal Bankruptcy Code. By taking such action, the company was allowed to continue operations—that is, purchase new merchandise from its many vendors and pay its employees—while simultaneously plot with a team of financial planners a way by which to make itself once again fiscally viable.

Within a year Cache had pulled itself out of the red, without having had to close a single store, and by the end of 1987 was once again experiencing solid growth. By decade's end Cache's stores had expanded throughout the eastern and southern part of the country and, despite the company's few troubled years, was becoming a small but solid presence within the retail industry.

The Early 1990s: Continuing Growth

The late 1980s and early 1990s saw many changes in the retail industry, the most important of which was the explosive growth of large shopping malls. Such malls, if they were upscale in focus, usually were anchored by huge national department stores including Saks Fifth Avenue and Neiman Marcus, with smaller, niche-market stores filling the remaining retail space. Indoor malls offered the consumer more choices than ever before, with a myriad of products and brands presented in a condensed, customer-friendly area. No longer did a customer have to seek out a store for a particular item or product; malls made it possible to offer almost anything one could buy under one roof.

Although this type of product presentation was of an obvious advantage and convenience to the consumer, it made competition all the more intense for those who manufactured and marketed the products, and competition was particularly intense within the apparel industry. Stores like Cache had to effectively manage competition from two separate sources: the large, increasingly powerful department stores and other, smaller boutiques who held a customer base similar to that of Cache's. To flourish, it was necessary for a company to maintain a fine balance between offering merchandise that was of a look and quality similar to that of the company's competitors while simultaneously making that merchandise somehow unique and original, thereby allowing it to stand out in an increasingly flooded market.

By the early 1990s Cache had proved that it could maintain just such a balance, and as the popularity of malls grew, so did the popularity of Cache, with the company's stores gaining a strong presence in upscale malls throughout the eastern part of the United States. Continuing to focus on younger customers interested in trendy, dressy day and evening wear, Cache in 1992 opened 16 new stores nationwide. In 1993 the company's growth continued at the same pace, with the company opening another 16 stores, all of which were located in high-end malls. Internal changes took place within the company that year as well, with Roy Chapman resigning as Cache's CEO. Replacing him was Andrew Saul, a board member who along with his family owned almost 75 percent of the company's common stock.

As of 1993 Cache owned and operated 93 stores and the company's net income had risen to $1.9 million. The company purchased its stock from high fashion vendors from the United States, Western Europe, and Asia, choosing not to maintain its own warehouse, and thus kept overhead lower than it would have been had the company manufactured and stored its own inventory.

Much of Cache's success was due to its presentation: though located within huge malls, the company's stores were kept relatively small—2,000 square feet was the average space of any given store—and were designed as intimate boutiques with a carefully selected inventory, a definite contrast to the sprawling and, to some customers, overwhelming, layout of the larger department stores. This mix of strategic planning in both location and store design proved to be quite successful for the company, and in 1995 Cache experienced record growth, opening 24 new stores in one year.

An Expanding Customer Base: The 1998 Acquisition of Lillie Rubin

By 1997 Cache, which that year had done a record volume of $135.8 million, was looking for ways in which to expand without having to greatly increase the company's overhead costs. Be-

cause of the tough competition within the apparel industry, several of Cache's competitors were not faring well, thereby making it possible for a small but vibrant company like Cache to look at the possibility of growth through acquisition. In 1998 just such an opportunity became available for the company, as an exclusive, small apparel chain by the name of Lillie Rubin declared bankruptcy and began actively seeking a buyer.

Lillie Rubin's stores sold expensive, high-quality apparel and accessories specifically designed as "special occasion" ensembles and appealed directly to high-income women in their 40s and 50s. Lillie Rubin's inventory consisted primarily of sequined, formal evening gowns, tailored pantsuits, and jewelry that was crafted with well-made faux jewels. The conception of the stores' layout was similar to that of Cache's, in that the Lillie Rubin stores presented to the customer a small, low-lighted, and intimate boutique located within a large mall. The Lillie Rubin chains differed from Cache, however, in two important ways: the former had both a higher priced inventory and fewer stores. In addition, competition from large, upscale department stores proved to be more than the small chain could handle, as many department stores, such as Saks Fifth Avenue and Lord & Taylor, specialized in the same type of formal attire found in Lillie Rubin's stock. In an article by Thomas Ryan, writing in *Women's Wear Daily,* the CEO of Lillie Rubin blamed the company's failure on " 'a major slowdown' in business over the past three years caused by the expansion of department stores and mass merchandisers into better-priced apparel; an overall decline in spending on apparel, and a shift away from dressier items as a result of casualization in the workplace."

Lillie Rubin's 1998 declaration of bankruptcy was the business's second Chapter 11 filing in two years, making potential buyers wary of the unstable chain. A plus-sized apparel company called The Forgotten Woman came forward with an offer of $2 million, only to walk away from the deal at the last minute. Several months later Cache entered negotiations with the beleaguered chain, and in August 1998 bought the company for only $775,000.

During the time in which Cache acquired Lillie Rubin, the latter had closed all of its remaining two dozen stores. Within months after Cache's purchase of the company, 12 of the Lillie Rubin stores were reopened. Cache's marketers continued to focus the Lillie Rubin inventory on formal attire, in particular clothing that would be appealing to a more mature clientele, and at the same time attempted to revamp the chain's image into something slightly more stylish and a little less flashy. According to this strategy, the Lillie Rubin stores were updated, making the clothes sophisticated and dressy yet also suitable, in some cases, for day wear—an important trend during the 1990s.

With the acquisition of the Lillie Rubin stores, and the location of some of its own boutiques, Cache had a presence in some of the most expensive malls in the country. Before its failure, Lillie Rubin was to be found in such retail centers as the Galleria in both Houston and Dallas, the Fashion Show in Las Vegas, the Biltmore Fashion Park in Phoenix, Arizona, and, among others, two locations in Los Angeles. During the same year in which Lillie Rubin was acquired, Cache opened four more stores of its own, bringing the number of Cache boutiques around the country to a total of 172 stores. The acquisition of

Lillie Rubin helped Cache round out its presence in the niche market of formal attire, allowing the original Cache stores to continue the focus on a younger, fashion-conscious customer base while also, through Lillie Rubin, establishing recognition with the even more upscale market of formal attire for the slightly older consumer. Although the explosive popularity of the shopping mall had killed many of its competitors, Cache by the end of the 1990s had used such popularity to its advantage and had developed into a steadily growing, vibrant apparel company.

The Late 1990s: Further Plans for Expansion

In 1999 Cache had locations in Puerto Rico and 35 states and owned 184 stores. That year, the company announced an ambitious plan for expansion and began planning to open 150 stores within a five-year period. Because of the company's initial success in reviving the Lillie Rubin chains—a success that exceeded Cache's initial predictions—plans were laid in place to open 100 new Lillie Rubin stores nationwide, as well as an additional 50 new Cache boutiques.

In the late 1990s it became clear to retailers that to remain fiscally healthy and competitive it was necessary in considering expansion to include in the company's plans computer space as well as retail space; the Internet had become an integral part of the consumer environment. Cache made plans to meet this new challenge head on, and in 1999 revealed plans for an internal special-order system by which the company's customers could order merchandise online. By using a system it designed internally, without the aid of a subcontractor or programmer, Cache both maintained control over its online business and saved on overhead. Unlike many special-order systems, Cache's system was almost entirely automatic, requiring very little human, manual manipulation and, therefore, saved the company on labor as well.

Although Cache's beginnings were not entirely free from financial pitfalls, the company since the late 1980s was moving forward at a rapid pace and, with the acquisition of Lillie Rubin in 1998, appeared to maintain not only a steady presence within the apparel industry, but one that had great potential for expansion as well.

Principal Divisions

Lillie Rubin.

Further Reading

''Cache Inc. Requests Chapter 11 Status,'' *Wall Street Journal,* November 13, 1986, p. 5.

Graff, Brett, ''Sold Out,'' *Daily Business Review,* October 20, 1998, p. A1.

''Lillie Rubin Expansion Set in 5-Year Plan,'' *Women's Wear Daily,* February 9, 1999, p. 12.

Moin, David, ''Cache Buys Lillie Rubin Chain,'' *Women's Wear Daily,* August 11, 1998, p. 16.

Power, Denise, ''Cache's E-Commerce Is a Special Order,'' *Women's Wear Daily,* February 17, 1999.

Ryan, Thomas, ''Lillie Rubin in Chpt. 11, Looking for Buyer,'' *Women's Wear Daily,* February 24, 1998, p. 4.

—Rachel H. Martin

Canary Wharf Group Plc

1 Canada Sq.
Canary Wharf
London E14 5AB
United Kingdom
(44) 171-418-2000
Fax: (44) 171-418-2222
Web site: http://www.canarywharf.com

Public Company
Incorporated: 1987 as Olympia & York Canary Wharf
   Ltd.
Employees: 466
Sales: UK£79.6 million (1999)
Stock Exchanges: London
Ticker Symbol: CWG.L
NAIC: 233320 Office Building Construction; 813990
   Condominium Corporations

London landmark Canary Wharf has seen its share of ups and downs. The vast development project—which comprises more than 80 acres of London's Docklands, with more than 13 million square feet of office and commercial space, and also includes One Canada Square, England's tallest building—has not only caused the fall of creator Paul Reichmann, but has also enabled his rise again. The project, approximately 60 percent completed in 1999, is governed by Reichmann-led Canary Wharf Group Plc, which went public in 1998. The IPO valued Canary Wharf at US$3.6 billion—by 1999 the development was valued at US$4 billion, with analysts suggesting that, upon completion, the development may be worth as much as US$12 billion. Linked by subway, light rail, and ferry to London's financial district (the City), Canary Wharf provides office accommodations for more than 25,000 (a number expected to triple upon project completion) and alternative office space for many of the country's national newspapers and financial institutions, among others. In 1999, Citibank announced its intention to move all of its London offices—previously scattered among some 30 downtown locations—to a Canary Wharf tower to be

custom-built for the financial giant. A similar arrangement will provide a home for HSBC Holdings, in a third Canary Wharf skyscraper. In 1999, the company was able to announce a 99.5 percent lease occupancy rate. The company has also begun development of a residential complex next door, in a joint venture with Hotel Properties Ltd. The project, called Canary Riverside, will add approximately 10,000 square feet of residential and hotel accommodations.

Early Docklands Developments

The land on which Canary Wharf rose in the 1990s had seen one form of commercial use or another for more than 800 years. In the 1200s, the area, which became known as the Isle of Dogs because of its use as a royal kennel, was drained to provide pasture and crop land. As the city of London grew in prominence, this Thames-side land was transformed into dockyards. By the 1500s, the Isle of Dogs site had become a prominent merchant harbor: it was from here that many of England's earliest merchant and other ventures set sail. Among these was the sailing of the Mayflower in 1620.

The first of the great docks was completed in 1802. Called the West India Docks, it was one of the world's great civil engineering feats. The entire dock complex reached from the nearby Tower of London to stretch several miles along the Thames, forming the world's largest and busiest port. Dock activity stepped up in the 19th century, as England led the world into the Industrial Revolution and also achieved its highest glory as ruler of the world's oceans. Among the many docks was the site that came to be called Canary Wharf, because it received shipments of bananas and other cargo from the British-controlled Canary Islands. Canary Wharf continued its role as a warehousing area into the mid-1960s.

By the 1930s, the London Docklands was the site of some 55,000 ship movements per year, employing more than 100,000 workers and other employees, while also serving as a vast residential area. Despite heavy bombing during World War II, the Docklands continued to play an important role in the U.K. economy. By the early 1960s, the Docklands handled some 60 million tons of cargo. This proved to be the area's peak, how-

---

Company Perspectives:

The strategy of the Group is to create shareholder value by controlling and actively managing all aspects of the development and operation of the estate, including property development and construction, marketing and leasing and management of its property portfolio. The Directors believe that the Group can, as an active manager, maximise the value and increase the cash flow of its existing properties, creating growth through the development and leasing of its significant property portfolio, and enabling it to return capital to shareholders.

---

ever. By the 1970s, the Docklands had fallen behind in new cargo and container technologies, finding itself bypassed by its competitors. The crushing recession that followed upon the Oil Crisis of 1973 cut deeply into further activity. The Docklands died a slow death, as its facilities were closed. More than 150,000 jobs disappeared over a ten-year period. By 1980, when the last of the docks were shut down, the area—some eight miles long—had become synonymous with urban blight.

Yet the Docklands quickly found new hope. The arrival of the Conservative government, led by Margaret Thatcher, brought a free market approach to the problem. In 1982, the Thatcher government granted the Docklands area Enterprise Zone status. This designation sought to attract investment and development through tax breaks and other allocations. The government also indicated that it would extend the city's public transportation network—and especially the Underground train system—to the largely underserved area.

The first attempt at redeveloping Canary Wharf was announced in 1985, when G. Ware Travelstead was granted control of the Canary Wharf area. Travelstead proposed to build a ten million-square-foot office complex. That project, however, was unable to find funding and quickly collapsed. The Canary Wharf concession was instead bought up by Olympia & York, led by Paul Reichmann and his two brothers.

The Rise and Fall and Rise Again of Paul Reichmann: 1980s to Mid-1990s

In the mid-1980s, Toronto-based Olympia & York was the world's largest real estate agency and the force behind such groundbreaking projects as New York City's World Trade Center and First Canadian Place in Toronto. Originally from central Europe, where father Samuel Reichmann had operated a successful egg business, the Reichmann family had escaped to Tangiers in the years leading up to World War II. From Tangiers, Renee Reichmann, together with her children, helped organize and finance food shipments (via the Red Cross) to the prisoners in the Nazi death camps; the family was also able to rescue more than 1,200 European Jews by providing visas. Following the war, the Reichmanns sent son Paul to study at a northern England Yeshiva and to begin training as an Orthodox rabbi. Paul Reichmann had other plans, however; in the 1950s

he joined brothers Ralph and Albert in Toronto and helped establish a successful ceramic tile importing business.

The brothers Reichmann soon parlayed their growing fortune into other ventures, especially real estate. In the mid-1960s, the Reichmanns set up Olympia & York Developments Ltd. for their real estate holdings. Placed under Paul Reichmann's direction, Olympia & York quickly showed its ambitions, building larger and larger real estate developments. In 1974, the company graduated to the big time, when it won the contract to build the 72-story First Canadian Place tower development in Toronto, the largest skyscraper in Canada. Three years later, the Reichmanns moved into the United States, buying up eight midtown Manhattan skyscrapers for US$340 million. These purchases set the stage for Olympia & York's greatest coup. In 1980, the company was granted the contract to build the three-building, US$1.2 billion World Trade Center.

Paul Reichmann led the company from real estate into other investments. In 1981, the company paid nearly US$540 million for Canadian paper leader Abitibi-Price. This purchase was followed by a US$2.8 billion purchase of control of Gulf Canada. From oil, Olympia & York turned to other liquids, winning a hostile takeover bid for Hiram Walker Resources. That purchase cost the family some US$3 billion. By the mid-1980s, Olympia & York had achieved status as the world's largest real estate developer, as well as a diversified holding group. At that time, the Reichmann family's holdings were estimated at some US$15 billion.

After the collapse of the G. Ware Travelstead project for Canary Wharf, Paul Reichmann led Olympia & York's bid for developing the area. The project was awarded to Olympia & York in 1987, which committed itself to a proposed US$8 billion investment in the development—and included the government's promise to build a strong transportation infrastructure, which would be financed in part by Olympia & York itself. The new company formed to oversee the development was named Olympia & York Canary Wharf Ltd. Original plans called for a single-tower complex. At the last minute, however, Paul Reichmann changed his mind, and decided upon a three-tower design. Construction on the first tower—One Canada Square—began in 1988 and was completed in 1991. By August of that year, the complex of ten buildings, already at four million square feet, welcomed its first tenants, State Street Bank.

Yet, things were already falling apart for Canary Wharf, and for Reichmann. The collapse of the real estate market in the late 1980s and the recession of the early 1990s was not the only factor behind Canary Wharf's huge vacancy burden. The extension of the public transportation system to the complex had seen successive delays, making it difficult for potential tenants to reach the site. Financing further investment in the development had also become difficult for Olympia & York, which had already sunk US$1.6 billion into Canary Wharf. The London development added to Olympia & York's massive US$8 billion debt, and the real estate empire toppled into bankruptcy in 1992. The Reichmann family's US$15 billion fortune was wiped out. Canary Wharf's creditor banks moved in and took possession of the development from Paul Reichmann in that same year. His misfortunes were not over: another high-profile development, a

US$1.4 billion, 30-building development in Mexico City, to be built in partnership with George Soros, was placed on hold in 1994 after the collapse of the Mexican peso.

Canary Wharf's future hung in doubt. Instead of simply selling off the development, however, the creditors decided to continue investing in the project, pumping in an additional US$1.8 billion and bringing the project out of administration (the British term for bankruptcy) in 1993. The operating company was renamed Canary Wharf Group at this time. While construction continued, the complex attempted to lure new tenants with lower lease rates and even free rent periods. Occupancy rates began to rise, aided by the belated opening of the new Docklands Light Railway extension to Canary Wharf, which at last made the project accessible from the London city center. Canary Wharf began to attract new high-profile tenants, including Credit Suisse—which later leased a new, custom-built office building at the site in 1999—and the national newspaper the *Independent*. The working population at the complex swelled to nearly 13,000 as occupancy rates reached 75 percent by 1995.

In December 1995, Paul Reichmann returned to the scene with the surprise offer to buy back the Canary Wharf development. Leading a group of investors, including CBS television's Lawrence Tisch and Saudi prince al-Waleed bin Talal, Reichmann proposed to purchase Canary Wharf for £800 million (approximately US$1.25 billion). Reichmann's former creditors agreed—and Reichmann was given a chance to rebuild his own lost fortune and prestige. As Reichmann told the *Toronto Star*: ''I have to prove I can rebuild and recreate what has been lost by my mistakes.''

Moving Confidently into the Next Century

This is exactly what Reichmann did. Aided by the strong economic recovery of the mid-1990s, and by completion of still more of the project's vital public transportation links—including the expansion of the London City airport, Canary Wharf soon became one of the most sought-after addresses in London. Another factor in the development's revitalized image was the rising importance of networking and other communications technologies, particularly among the financial industry. The old, cramped, and expensive quarters in the city of London were difficult, if not impossible, to adapt to the new technological needs of the country's financial institutions and newspapers, and buildings were often too small to house all of a business's offices. Citibank, as an example, was said to have been operating from some 30 separate buildings. At the same time, Canary Wharf continued to offer lower lease rates, up to 30 percent off the square-foot price in the city. More and more companies began to look at the growing Canary Wharf—and the possibility of moving into custom-designed offices and buildings.

Occupancy rates rose steadily in the second half of the 1990s, as construction continued. By 1998, the complex boasted more than 4.5 million square feet, primarily office facilities, but also growing numbers of amenities such as restaurants, shops, health clubs, entertainment, and other facilities. While some tenants decried the complex as soulless, businesses continued to flock to its offices, raising occupancy rates past 90 percent. In April 1998, Reichmann announced the company's intention to list its shares on the London stock exchange. The company's value at the initial public offering was to be £1.4 billion—high enough to allow the initial investors to recoup their investments, but low enough to encourage the entry of other investors into the company's capital. Nevertheless, the £1.4 billion valuation was considered to be extremely conservative.

Canary Wharf Group went public in April 1999 as Reichmann sold off part of his shares, worth 25 percent of the company. The IPO price of 330 pence (approximately US$5.41) valued the company at £2 billion or US$3.6 billion. Yet even that figure was considered low. By mid-1999, *Forbes* described the complex as having a value of over US$4 billion—and expected that value to rise to as high as US$12 billion by the time of the project's completion early in the next century.

By September 1999, Reichmann had been vindicated. Occupancy rates had soared to 99.5 percent as Canary Wharf became one of the most elite business addresses in London. Meanwhile, more and more residential complexes had begun to rise in the area, making the Docklands not merely a business center, but an increasingly vital part of London itself. Canary Wharf Group had its own plans for residential development: in 1999, the company began construction on the joint-venture Canary Riverside residential condominium and hotel complex with Hotel Properties Ltd.

Principal Subsidiaries

Canary Wharf Holdings Limited; Canary Wharf Contractors Limited; Canary Wharf Finance plc; Canary Wharf Limited; Canary Wharf Investments Limited; Canary Wharf Management Limited; Heron Quays Properties Limited; Heron Quays Developments Limited.

Further Reading

Dalglish, Brenda, ''A Towering Deal: Paul Reichmann Bids for Redemption at Canary Wharf,'' *Maclean's*, September 11, 1995, p. 44.

Grose, Thomas, ''Singing a Different Tune: Paul Reichmann's Canary Wharf Development Has Risen Phoenix-Like from the Ashes of Bankruptcy,'' *Time International*, April 5, 1999, p. 56.

Lenzner, Robert, ''Try, Try Again,'' *Forbes*, June 14, 1999, p. 94.

Lynn, Matthew, ''Will Canary Wharf Fly for Reichmann?,'' *Toronto Star*, March 7, 1999.

Willcock, John, and Garner, Clare, ''Pounds 2bn Float Will Crown the Fall and Rise of Canary Wharf,'' *Independent*, March 2, 1999, p. 10.

—M. L. Cohen

carhartt

Carhartt, Inc.

Three Parklane Boulevard
P.O. Box 600
Dearborn, Michigan 48121
U.S.A.
(313) 271-8460
Fax: (313) 271-3455
Web site: http://www.carhartt.com

Private Company
Incorporated: 1884 as Hamilton Carhartt and Co.
Employees: 2,520
Sales: $307 million (1998 est.)
NAIC: 315211 Men's & Boys' Cut & Sew Apparel
Contractors; 315191 Outerwear Knitting Mills

Carhartt, Inc. is a leading U.S. producer of workwear—overalls, jeans, coveralls, jackets, and other items—favored by those in the construction and farming industries. During the 1990s workwear became fashionable, as popular rap music artists and hip-hop bands started wearing Carhartt clothes. Despite the broader appeal of Carhartt clothing, the company continued to regard its most important customer as the American worker, who preferred Carhartt clothes, even though they were typically priced higher than other work clothes, because they proved durable, comfortable, and easier to clean. In the late 1990s, the company's garments were sold chiefly at smaller retail outlets catering to blue-collar men. However, Carhartt was also available in limited quantities in such department stores as J.C. Penney, Meijer, and Sears. Facing challenges in meeting consumer demand, Carhartt maintained a selective distribution policy in order to handle the growth of the business.

Early History

The company's founder, Hamilton Carhartt, was born in Macedon Locks, New York, in 1855 and was raised in Michigan and Wisconsin, where his father, Dr. George Carhartt, was a physician and surgeon. Although his family distinguished itself mainly in the learned professions, Hamilton Carhartt had an interest in commercial pursuits. He left school in 1882 to enter the furniture business, first in Grand Rapids, Michigan, and then, in 1884, in Detroit.

There Carhartt established a wholesale furniture business under the name Hamilton Carhartt & Co. In 1889, he converted the business from home furnishings into one devoted exclusively to manufacturing apparel for working men. His first products were overalls made of duck—a tightly woven cotton fabric—and denim fabrics for men working on and building the railroads.

In 1905 the business was incorporated as Hamilton Carhartt Manufacturer, Inc.; it was reincorporated as Hamilton Carhartt Cotton Mills in 1910. By this time Carhartt had grown to include two mills in South Carolina and Georgia, as well as plants in Atlanta; Detroit; Dallas; San Francisco; Walkerville, Ontario; Vancouver, British Columbia; and Liverpool, England. The Walkerville plant was devoted to the manufacture of gloves.

By 1925 Carhartt had established a new plant in Paris and had an office and warehouse in New York City. A third mill was operating in Alabama. Hamilton Carhartt Junior—Manufacturer, a subsidiary specializing in young men's working apparel, had operations in Los Angeles and Philadelphia. The company was producing work clothing, overalls, shirts, hunting wear, pants, and shoes.

1920s–30s: Economic Downturns

The Cotton Depression of the 1920s and the Great Depression of the 1930s resulted in Carhartt losing all of its locations except its plants in Atlanta, Detroit, and Dallas. Moreover, the firm sold off its rights to sell in Texas, most of the southern states, and in southern California, Europe, and Canada. Carhartt unsuccessfully attempted to launch a sportswear line during this time.

With the assistance of the people of Irvine, Kentucky, a new plant was completed at the beginning of 1932 for just over $35,000. The new facility employed 20 people when it opened. In 1937 Hamilton Carhartt, age 82, was killed in an automobile accident; his son Wylie Carhartt assumed control of the corporation.

110

Despite economic challenges, the Carhartt firm had a solid reputation for quality clothing. It had built this reputation for durable work and outdoor clothing by using heavyweight 100 percent cotton duck for most of its products. The tightly woven material provided strength and durability as well as wind and snag resistance. All Carhartt duck products also had triple chain stitching over felled main seams. This method locked the seams in place, giving them great strength and making it very difficult to pull them apart. The strength of the fabric was also increased by using double fill yarn, where two yarns were twisted together and used as one.

Keeping it in the Family: 1950s–60s

Wylie Carhartt was succeeded in 1959 as head of the company by his son-in-law, Robert C. Valade, who had begun his career at Carhartt in 1949. During the 1960s Carhartt began to enjoy larger revenues from chain store sales. This enabled the company to repurchase selling rights in territories it had been forced to sell back in the 1930s. Under Valade's leadership Carhartt would grow from sales of $2 million in 1960 to more than $300 million in the mid-1990s.

In 1960 the firm made two significant acquisitions: Crown Headlight of Cincinnati, Ohio, and W.M. Finck & Co. of Detroit, an overalls manufacturer. Following the acquisitions the firm began selling garments under the label of Carhartt Headlight & Finck. Carhartt also acquired E.F. Partridge in Georgia, which effectively gave the company the right to sell garments in the South again. In 1965 Carhartt, Inc., a Michigan corporation, was formed from the merger of Hamilton Carhartt Overall Co., Inc., a Georgia corporation, and W.M. Finck & Co., a Michigan corporation.

Acquisitions and Expansions: 1970s–80s

In 1971 Carhartt established its first contemporary subsidiary, Carhartt South, Inc., to produce jeans, after acquiring a plant in Drew, Mississippi. In 1976 Carhartt formed another subsidiary, Carhartt Midwest, Inc., after purchasing the assets of Shane Manufacturing Co., Inc. The new subsidiary had plants in Evansville, Indiana, and Sebree, Kentucky. In 1978 the acquisition of Gross Galesburg Co. in Galesburg, Illinois, resulted in the formation of a third subsidiary of the same name.

In 1980 Carhartt Midwest expanded into a plant and warehouse in Madisonville, Kentucky. The next year it purchased another plant in Providence, Kentucky, and subsequently closed its Evansville, Indiana, plant. In 1982 Carhartt launched its first national marketing program with national advertising. During the latter half of the decade Carhartt streamlined its organizational structure by merging its subsidiaries with the parent company to form divisions. In 1989 the company built a new distribution center and a new sewing plant on its property in Madisonville, Kentucky. Cutting operations from all plants except Galesburg were then centralized in the former sewing plant at Madisonville. An additional plant was acquired in Edmonton, Kentucky.

Expanding Capacity: 1990s

Carhartt's sales reached a record $92 million in 1990. The firm expanded its capacity in 1992 by purchasing a 64,000-square-foot sewing plant in Glasgow, Kentucky. That year the company's Gross Galesburg division was renamed Muleskins Division and began concentrating its production on sweatshirts. The Muleskins Division was discontinued shortly thereafter.

Work wear was showing signs of becoming a fashion trend in the late 1980s and early 1990s, so Carhartt displayed its outdoor working man's collection for the first time at fashion shows in New York in 1991. The company had been selling its clothes in Japan strictly as fashion items since 1987.

Revenues in 1992 reached an estimated $102 million. Expansion continued in 1993 with the completion of a new 100,000-square-foot distribution center in Glasgow, Kentucky. The firm also purchased an 80,000-square-foot sewing plant in Camden, Tennessee, that began production in mid-July.

Workwear as a fashion trend became very popular in 1993, helping Carhartt toward its 1993 sales goal of $120 million. Top rap and hip-hop groups were wearing Carhartt work clothing on televised videos as well as on CD covers and in performances onstage. Carhartt clothes were even featured in the pages of *Vogue* and *Harper's Bazaar.*

The company was challenged to keep up with demand as trendy urbanites snapped up the firm's limited supply, making it difficult to service the traditional Carhartt market. Mark Valade, Robert Valade's son and vice-president of marketing at the time, told *Sales and Marketing Management,* "We're really having a problem balancing the traditional retailer and the new retailer." All of the firm's manufacturing plants were operating at capacity, and a second distribution center was opened. Still, the company did not have enough product to supply everyone in 1993, and was forced to turn down accounts from department and specialty store chains because it did not have the production capacity to meet demand.

Carhartt's facility in Irvine, Kentucky, which was originally constructed in 1932, was converted to administrative offices and warehousing as the firm embarked on construction of a new 70,000-square-foot sewing plant there.

Further expansion took place in 1994, as Carhartt broke ground on a new central Kentucky cutting center in Glasgow, Kentucky. The company also purchased a 120,000-square-foot sewing plant in McKenzie, Tennessee, from competitor OshKosh B'Gosh, Inc. In 1995 the firm bought a 90,000-square-foot sewing plant in Dover, Tennessee, and a 26,882-

square-foot sewing plant in Marrowbone, Kentucky, in 1996. The McKenzie plant was subsequently closed in 1999.

Internationally, London-based Work in Progress owner Ben Joseph, Carhartt's designated licensee and distributor in the United Kingdom, began promoting Carhartt clothing in England and Ireland in 1995. By 1998 he was also distributing for Carhartt in Europe, with combined revenues reported to be $8 million.

In the fall of 1997 Carhartt introduced a women's line and an Extremes line. Carhartt Extremes was a line of outdoor clothing designed to withstand the harshest weather conditions in wet and cold environments. After testing the women's line the previous fall, the company rolled out its new line of work wear for women at more than 100 stores. It was the first line of Carhartt garments designed specifically for women. Orders met and then exceeded expectations.

The Late 1990s and Beyond

In 1998 Carhartt began construction of the new 350,000-square-foot Robert C. Valade distribution center in Hanson, Kentucky. It opened in May 1999. When Carhartt awarded a contract for the distribution center to a nonunion design-and-build contractor, the company became involved in a dispute with the local building and construction trades council and the AFL-CIO, which threatened to boycott Carhartt products. Although there was never an official boycott, many union members were awaiting the outcome of the dispute before purchasing Carhartt apparel. The dispute was settled in November 1998 when Carhartt agreed to work with appropriate union building and construction trades councils in the construction of future projects, but planned to complete the Hanson facility with the existing contractor and subcontractors. Carhartt had traditionally been a unionized manufacturer, and union workers were a major customer segment. Carhartt had won the AFL-CIO labor management award in 1992.

Carhartt also expanded its marketing efforts in 1997 and 1998 through national sponsorships. It began supporting Professional Bull Riders events in November 1997, and in January 1998 began sponsoring one of the riders, Troy Dunn, who went on to win the title of World Champion in both 1997 and 1998. In the spring of 1997 Carhartt began its role as official national sponsor of Stihl Timbersports. Soon thereafter, Carhartt became a national sponsor of the Future Farmers of America (FFA) as well as the official sponsor of the FFA Home and Community Development Proficiency Award. As a national sponsor of the National High School Rodeo Association, Carhartt supported events all over the country.

Revenues for 1998 reached an estimated $307 million, triple the figure reported in 1992. Wholesale revenues in the United States were about $255 million, while $50 million was credited to Europe and the United Kingdom and $2 million to Japan. However, sales were flat from 1997 to 1998, a fact the company attributed to an unusually warm winter, given a common perception that Carhartt was a seasonal clothing company for fall and winter.

In 1998 Mark Valade became president of Carhartt following the death of his father, Robert Valade. His mother, Gretchen Carhartt Valade, became board chairperson. For the 1998–99 selling season Carhartt introduced a new merchandising concept for stores carrying its products, employing three unique fixtures: a workhorse fixture that expanded from one to two levels of hanging garments, a wall unit, and an accessory fixture. The module was designed to leverage Carhartt's brand power by organizing its full range of apparel and accessories in one easy-to-shop location. New signage was provided to identify the brand and call attention to the company's newer lines. The fixtures were interchangeable regardless of store format, an important consideration since Carhartt apparel was sold in a variety of retail outlets including discount and department stores, farm stores, and uniform outlets. Following a successful test run, the new shop initiative was rolled out to about 100 stores nationwide in 1998, with an additional 90 stores set to come on board in 1999.

In late 1998 the company began focusing on "first layer" clothing, such as T-shirts and jeans, for workers to wear in warmer weather. Even though work clothes had become a popular form of casual wear, all of the company's clothes continued to be designed for workers, especially construction workers. The company's marketing manager visited construction sites throughout the country to find out what workers wanted. Interestingly, he found that workers would often purchase Carhartt clothing for casual dress; then, as the clothes faded or lost their new look, the consumer would then wear the clothes for work.

With the construction of a 200,000-square-foot factory in Penjemo, Mexico, in September 1998, that would employ 500 union workers, Carhartt began making new products outside the United States. However, the company planned to continue making its core products at its existing U.S. facilities.

Further Reading

"Carhartt, Incorporated: A Brief History," Dearborn, Mich: Carhartt, 1998.

Hogue, Leslie, "Work-Wear Fad Builds Carhartt Clothing Brand," *Crain's Detroit Business,* May 3, 1999, p. 17.

"Oshkosh Negotiating to Sell Its Jeans Plant to Carhartt," *Daily News Record,* January 27, 1994, p. 10.

Parola, Robert, "Rugged Carhartt Gets Down to Fashion," *Daily News Record,* April 10, 1991, p. 5.

——, "Workwear Grows New Fashion Muscle," *Daily News Record,* May 19, 1993, p. 4.

Regenstein, Elliot, "Profile in Marketing: Mark Valade," *Sales and Marketing Management,* September 1993, p. 12.

"Shelf Containment," *Chain Store Age Executive with Shopping Center Age,* February 1999, p. 78.

Spevack, Rachel, "Workwear Jumps from Hip-Hop to Mainstream," *Daily News Record,* November 15, 1994, p. 6.

"Work Clothes Maker Reaches Accord with Owensboro, Ky., Trades Council," *Knight-Ridder/Tribune Business News,* November 25, 1998.

—David P. Bianco

Celadon Group Inc.

One Celadon Drive
Indianapolis, Indiana 46235
U.S.A.
(317) 972-7000
(800) CELADON; (800) 235-2366
Fax: (317) 890-8099
Web site: http://www.celadontrucking.com

Public Company
Incorporated: 1986
Employees: 2,323
Sales: $229.9 million (1998)
Stock Exchanges: NASDAQ
Ticker Symbol: CLDN
NAIC: 484121 General Freight Trucking, Long-Distance, Truckload; 484122 General Freight Trucking, Long-Distance, Less Than Truckload; 481112 Scheduled Freight Air Transportation; 483111 Deep Sea Freight Transportation

Celadon Group Inc. is the largest transporter of truckload freight to and from Mexico. The company offers van truckload services of long-haul time-sensitive materials, full truckload services of goods primarily over 10,000 pounds, and flatbed services for larger materials. Its fleet of about 2,100 tractors and 6,000 trailers is managed by a computer satellite system, Qualcomm, which provides instant contact with drivers regardless of their location. Celadon services its customers through four major subsidiaries: Celadon Trucking Services, Cheetah Transportation, Gerth Transport Limited, and Transportacion de Jaguar. Celadon Trucking Services, the largest unit of the company, provides van service from points within the United States and Canada to Mexico. Cheetah Transportation provides flatbed service and Gerth Transportation Limited provides van transportation for Canadian customers. The company's Mexican subsidiary, Transportacion de Jaguar, offers customers border transfer services in and out of Mexico. While Chrysler is Celadon's largest customer, the company has over 4,500 other accounts, including Volkswagen, Fisher Price, and Pier 1. Celadon benefited greatly from the influx in trade created by the North American Free Trade Agreement (NAFTA) passed in 1995. Since its inception in 1986, Celadon has crossed the border into Mexico more than 800,000 times. The company is bonded in the United States, Mexico, and Canada.

Meager Beginnings

Celadon cofounders Stephen Russell and Leonard Bennett had neither employees nor equipment when they started the Indiana-based company, but they did have one major contract— to transport automotive parts to a new Chrysler plant in Mexico. Russell and Bennett named their new company Celadon after reading about celadon pottery, an ancient green-glazed stoneware dating back to the Koryo dynasty (918–1392 A.D.). They hoped their company would be distinctive like the pottery—and it was. Celadon did $8 million in business during its first year and was considered a pioneer of the commerce trail between the United States and Mexico. Russell and Bennett, however, were stymied with their company's success and were unsure what route to take to ensure its future.

By 1990 they had purchased Randy International, an international freight-forwarding company. Freight-forwarders arrange for door-to-door transportation of cargo. They typically buy warehouse space at international locations for wholesale prices and fill that space with consolidated goods from several different customers, who pay retail prices for the space. To pay off expenses related to its expansion into freight-forwarding, Celadon went public in 1994. The IPO put 36.3 percent of the company up for sale and raised about $30 million. After going public, Celadon further expanded its freight-forwarding through a partnership with Jacky Maeder Limited, and in 1995 through the acquisition of U.K.-based Guestair.

Pioneer of the NAFTA Trail

The passing of the National American Free Trade Act in 1995 was a major break for Celadon, which was in a position to capitalize on the explosion in trade between the United States and Mexico. According to the original NAFTA, trucks from

Company Perspectives:

Our strategy is simple. We focus on a niche market and provide truckload services between the United States, Canada, and the Mexican border. Our service is enhanced by a high tractor-to-tractor ratio, the use of well-maintained late model tractors and trailers and round-the-clock dispatch and reporting services.

We have also invested in the area of technological applications to provide a strong platform for enhanced service and future growth. In particular, a satellite communications system that provides competitive advantages in the areas of customer service, driver satisfaction, and reduced maintenance costs. While the long-haul trucking market remains competitive, our strategy is to provide a full-service approach to managing, tracking, and reporting on the transportation of goods across the borders, which allows customers to rely on us to provide many services that were previously performed internally.

Mexico could enter the United States and move freely within the states bordering Mexico, and even as far north as the California-Oregon border. However, the United States blocked NAFTA just as it was about to go into effect. While the United States contended it had "safety concerns," critics claimed the move was politically connected to the powerful Teamsters Union, which worried that allowing low-paid Mexican truck drivers into the country would threaten U.S. jobs. NAFTA was eventually passed, but drivers were prohibited from hauling their loads to their Mexican destinations. Instead, they had to hand off their loads at border-town interchange points, and Mexican truck drivers took over for the final leg of the run.

Celadon quickly adapted to NAFTA's provisions. It cultivated its relationships with over 15 Mexican trucking companies and allowed these companies to drive its trucks to their destinations within Mexico. Many in the industry feared Celadon's trucks would be confiscated in Mexico, but Celadon hauled shipment after shipment without incident. It credited its solid relationships with the Mexican trucking companies for its success. Celadon became known as the primary NAFTA carrier. The company later acquired the Mexican trucking company Transportacion de Jaguar to assist with cargo transfer at the Mexican border.

Bennett, Celadon's cofounder, president, and chief operating officer, had been an adviser to both the United States and Mexico during the NAFTA negotiations. He considered NAFTA as a work-in-progress. In *Directions in Transportation* he explained how Celadon intended to view NAFTA: "You can anticipate the worst or try to visualize the best. Bear in mind that this is a trade agreement, not a transportation agreement. In terms of transportation, we'll learn as we go." Bennett became an expert on NAFTA and gave many speeches on business in a post-NAFTA environment.

Celadon's post-NAFTA progress was not without setbacks, however. In early 1995, the company suffered on Wall Street as

investors reacted to the devaluation of the Mexican peso in 1994. The devaluation made U.S. goods 20 to 30 percent more expensive in Mexico. The company reacted by pulling some of its tractors and trailers off its Midwest-Mexico routes and picking up more domestic business.

In 1995 Celadon became a flatbed transporter when it purchased Cheetah Transportation, based in Mooresville, North Carolina, for $5.1 million. Cheetah was a $25 million flatbed carrier operating since 1984. Cheetah flatbeds, which operated mainly in the Southeast, hauled mostly heavy equipment, building materials, and wire cable. Russell, Celadon's chief executive officer, believed the flatbed industry held a lot of growth potential. In *Transportation and Distribution,* he explained that flatbeds captured only a small portion of the truckload business and that no one company in the flatbed industry had a large percentage of that business. He hoped Cheetah would fill that niche.

While Cheetah proved successful, the freight-forwarding portion of the company's business was losing money. The cost of the merger with Jacky Maeder Limited coupled with a slump in the industry caused Celadon to post losses in 1995.

A Major Acquisition in 1996

In March 1996, Celadon acquired the bankrupt Burlington Motor Holdings in Daleville, Indiana, and became a giant in the truckload industry. Burlington was primarily a domestic carrier, so it opened up new territory for Celadon, which acquired nearly 1,400 tractors and 4,000 trailers from the acquisition. The deal made Celadon one of the ten largest truckload carriers in the United States.

Also in 1996, Bennett left the company to form a distribution and logistics firm in Florida called Enfield Logistics, Inc. Russell and one of Celadon's major stockholders, Hanseatic Corporation, bought most of Bennett's 913,000 shares of Celadon stock. Bennett's $10 million buyout was part of the company's plan to restructure its management and refocus on trucking instead of freight-forwarding. In the *Tribune Business News,* Russell admitted the company "took its eye off the ball" with its expansion into freight-forwarding. He explained that the company planned to refocus on being a truck line into Mexico. Celadon sold the U.S. portion of its freight-forwarding business Harper Group and its South American logistics business, Celsur, to Bennett.

In April 1996, Celadon relocated its corporate headquarters from New York to Indianapolis to consolidate some of its operations that had been scattered around the country. The new headquarters also benefited Celadon's drivers; it included a driver's dormitory, and state-of-the-art truck-washing and fueling facilities.

General Electric in 1997

By 1997 Celadon's missteps into freight-forwarding had taken their toll on the company, which had posted losses for four of the past five years. In an effort to turn the company around, Celadon purchased General Electric Transportation Services (GETS), a unit of General Electric Company, for

$8.5 million. The Fort Wayne, Indiana company had sales of about $75 million and operated 170 tractors. GETS was eventually merged with Celadon Trucking Services, Celadon's largest subsidiary.

Around the same time, Celadon entered into a marketing partnership with West Ex, a Phoenix-based company that provided less-than-truckload (LTL) services in California and the Southwest. Celadon and West Ex hoped to use their LTL services to assist other truckload companies interested in utilizing their fleets more efficiently.

Celadon was back on track once again. In 1997, Russell was elected chairman of the International Trade and Customs Commission of the American Trucking Association. During the same year, Celadon received Carrier of the Year honors from Pier 1, based in Texas, for trucking a significant portion of the company's wicker and pottery out of Mexico.

An Attempt at Privatization

After several years of answering to the public, Russell considered the IPO a mistake for Celadon. "Being a private company, you can focus on the long term without worrying about specific quarterly earnings," he explained in the *Indiana Business Journal* in 1998. Russell also felt Celadon's stock was "unappreciated" on Wall Street.

In 1998, Larendo Acquisition Company, a subsidiary of the New York Investment firm Odyssey, planned to acquire Celadon for $259 million, but backed out because it was unable to secure financing. News of the deal falling through caused a 32 percent drop in Celadon's stock.

In May 1998, Celadon purchased Gerth Transport, a Canadian motor carrier specializing in transportation to and from Mexico, for $19.2 million. The purchase was significant for Celadon; with Gerth under its wing, it could now offer its customers transportation from Canada directly to Mexico.

While the Gerth acquisition strengthened Celadon's market position, driver turnover remained a problem for the company. Celadon tried to improve morale among its drivers with its new "pet program." Under the guidelines of the program, drivers could take a companion cat or dog on the road. Nancy Morris, Celadon vice-president of operations, explained why drivers need companionship in the *Indianapolis Business Journal:* "In many cases, their truck is their home. We want to allow them to have the comforts of home when they're traveling." While Celadon realized that a portion of its drivers will tire of the road and leave each year, it managed to reduce its driver turnover rate from 140 percent to 90 percent.

Celadon also hired recruiters to entice women into becoming truck drivers. Since the truckload industry was male-dominated, the company believed recruiting women could lessen its shortage of drivers. In 1998, about 300 of Celadon's 1,500 truck drivers were women—a high percentage compared to the industry in general, where only 5.3 percent of drivers were women. The company also tried to promote women into upper-level management. Nancy Morris's promotion to vice-president of operations in 1997 made her the holder of the highest executive position attained by a woman in the truckload industry.

Morris joined Celadon the previous year as director of operations and program systems. Prior to this, she worked her way up to upper-level management at North American Van Lines, where she had been employed for 12 years.

The year 1998 also marked the introduction of Celadon's web site, www.celadontrucking.com. Celadon's Internet tracking service, CelaTRAC, enabled customers to track shipment 24 hours a day by accessing the web site and utilizing a variety of search criteria.

New Business and Recognition in 1999

In July 1999, Celadon won the business of Volkswagen de Mexico, which was expected to average $5 million in sales each year for two years. According to the agreement, Celadon would transport automotive parts between the United States, Canada, and Volkswagen assembly plants in Puebla, Mexico, where the "Bug" and other Volkswagen products were assembled.

Around the same time, Celadon signed a letter of intent to acquire all of the assets of Zipp Express Inc., one of the leading truckload van carriers to Mexico, for an undisclosed amount of money. Celadon planned to make the Indianapolis-based Zipp Express a subsidiary. Zipp Express had revenues of $250 million.

Celadon received the Chrysler Corporation's Director's Award in recognition of its excellence in transporting Chrysler products in 1998, and was elected a member of CANACAR, Mexico's trucking association, in 1999. In 1999 Celadon was awarded major contracts in Arkansas, Missouri, and the Carolinas and planned to expand its fleet by 550 new tractors and 1,300 new trailers and hire up to 200 additional drivers. As of 1999, the company still hoped to return to private ownership, but had not found a buyer able to raise the capital to make the acquisition.

Principal Subsidiaries

Celadon Trucking Services; Cheetah Transportation; Gerth Transport Limited (Canada); Transportacion de Jaguar (Mexico).

Further Reading

Bergin, Sarah, "Specialized Truckload Carriers Find Niche Market," *Transportation and Distribution,* December 1996, p. 37.
"Celadon Acquires Transportation Services Operation from GE Industrial Control Services for $8.5 Million," *Business Wire,* August 25, 1997, p. 08251362.
"Celadon, Bennett Agree on $10 Million Buy-Out," *Traffic World,* June 17, 1996, p. 25.
"Celadon Group Inc. Receives Chrysler Corporation's Director's Award," *Business Wire,* August 22, 1998, p. 08271299.
"Celadon Group, Inc. Relocates Corporate Headquarters," *Business Wire,* April 3, 1996, p. 4031216.
"Celadon Group Purchases Freightliner Truck Tractors; Expects Delivery of 100 Tractors in Early 1997," *Business Wire,* November 13, 1996, p. 11131268.
"Celadon Group Reports Development in Burlington Motor Carrier Bid," *Business Wire,* June 26, 1996, p. 6261094.
"Celadon's Len Bennett Creates Enfield Logistics," *PR Newswire,* August 2, 1996, p. 0802DEF002.

"Celadon Trucking: Taking It Step by Step," *Directions in Transportation,* Spring 1994.

Culbertson, Katie, "Celadon's Pet Project Pays Off: Trucking Firm Lowers Turnover by Letting Animals Ride with Drivers," *Indianapolis Business Journal,* February 22, 1999, p. 19.

——, "Russell: Stock Was Undervalued," *Indianapolis Business Journal,* June 29, 1998, p. 3.

——, "Women Rise Through Ranks at Celadon," *Indianapolis Business Journal,* June 8, 1998, p. 7.

Francis, Mary, "Indianapolis-Based Celadon Group Sees Rosy Future with Trucking in Mexico," *Knight-Ridder/Tribune Business News,* April 28, 1977, p. 428B0916.

LeDuc Doug, "Indianapolis Trucking Firm Buys GE Unit That Contracts Hauling," *Knight-Ridder/Tribune Business News,* September 8, 1997, p. 908B0952.

"No Glass Ceiling," *Traffic World,* February 10, 1997, p. 30.

Shultz, John D., "Celadon to Buy Bankrupt Burlington, Will Add 1,400 Tractors, 4,000 Trailers," *Traffic World,* May 27, 1996, p. 41.

——, "Two Mergers Off," *Traffic World,* December 7, 1998, p. 24.

"Specialized Truckload Carriers Find Niche Market," *Transportation and Distribution,* December 1996, p. 37.

"WestEx, Celadon Forge Partnership; Offer Private Carriers Alternatives," *Business Wire,* September 4, 1997, p. 9040119.

—Tracey Vasil Biscontini

Chesapeake Corporation

James Center II
1021 East Cary Street
P.O. Box 2350
Richmond, Virginia 23218-2350
U.S.A.
(804) 697-1000
Fax: (804) 697-1199
Web site: http://www.cskcorp.com

Public Company
Incorporated: 1918
Employees: 5,557
Sales: $950.4 million (1998)
Stock Exchanges: New York
Ticker Symbol: CSK
NAIC: 322213 Setup Paperboard Box Manufacturing;
   322211 Corrugated & Solid Fiber Box Manufacturing;
   322212 Folding Paperboard Box Manufacturing;
   322299 All Other Converted Paper Product Manufacturing; 23311 Land Subdivision & Land Development

Once a broader-based paper and packaging company, Chesapeake Corporation repositioned itself in the late 1990s to be a global specialty packaging firm. The company's major businesses include Field Group plc, the leading folding carton maker in the United Kingdom; Chesapeake Display & Packaging, which specializes in point-of-purchase merchandising services from bases in the United States and Europe; and Chesapeake Packaging Co., a leader in the manufacture of corrugated containers and packaging. A smaller unit, Chesapeake Land Development, is involved in the development of Chesapeake-owned land, including master planned communities and bulk land sales.

Early History

Elis Olsson, a Swedish-born papermaker, was already a recognized pioneer in the industry when he moved his family from Quebec to Virginia in 1918. Olsson had become director of a corporation he organized with the help of a Norwegian shipping financier, Christoffer Hannevig. Olsson had helped to develop the first kraft process mill in Canada. Kraft paper is the heavy brown paper produced from unbleached pulp that is used for such items as grocery bags. Another of Olsson's technical innovations was the first commercial paper mill boiler to use wastewood and bark for fuel. He also engineered the first modern chemical recovery boiler. When Olsson first moved to West Point, the paper industry was in its infancy.

Chesapeake Corporation began via an agreement to lease the assets of Chesapeake Pulp & Paper Company, a subsidiary of Fox Paper Company, based in Ohio. Included with the leased assets was a sulphate mill in West Point that dated to 1914. The company had not proven profitable and the assets were leased with an option to buy, as the original owners wished to withdraw from the operation. Upon his arrival, Olsson quickly invested in plant improvements; pulp and board mills had deteriorated throughout the United States during World War I. Olsson also put his technical skills to use, revamping the tricky sulphate process that produced paper from pine.

Chesapeake was profitable by 1921, but president Hannevig's shipping empire went under and he resigned from the company. Olsson thus sought both financial backing and a new company president. It was hard to find supportive investors in the shaky postwar climate, but H. Watkins Ellerson, president of one of Chesapeake's pulp customer companies, agreed to back the enterprise and serve as president of a reorganized Chesapeake. Olsson became vice-president, but for all practical purposes he ran the company. One of the first decisions of the restructured corporation was to buy the West Point mill instead of leasing. In 1922 bonds were issued to cover the purchase price, as well as the cost of needed plant improvements.

By 1926 Chesapeake was producing kraft paper, market pulp, crude turpentine, and box board on an average of 85 tons a day. It paid its first dividends the same year, a tradition uninterrupted except by the Great Depression. In 1929 Olsson was named president; he remained a leader in the company for the next 30 years, 14 of them as chairman of the board.

The 1930s were a time of growth for Chesapeake, despite the Depression. In 1932 Chesapeake became the second company in Virginia to hire a professional forester and begin a program of reforestation. Reforestation had been a company undertaking since 1922. As orders dropped off during the Depression, salaries and wages were cut. Nonetheless, Chesapeake's earnings reached the million-dollar mark for the first time in 1934. Chesapeake worked with Camp Manufacturing Company to erect and operate a pulp and paper mill in Franklin, Virginia, in 1936. The new mill was named Chesapeake-Camp Corporation at the time; its name later changed to Union Camp Corporation. Chesapeake eventually sold its interest in the mill.

In 1941 the company name was changed to The Chesapeake Corporation of Virginia. Its stock was offered on the New York Stock Exchange for the first time in 1944. During the labor shortage of World War II, Chesapeake maintained its production levels with the help of women—who worked at office jobs, as well as at cutting pulp wood in the forests—and German and Italian prisoners. In 1945 Olsson became company chairman. His son, Sture Olsson, assumed the position of president of the company in 1951.

Entering Packaging in the Postwar Years

Having entered the corrugated container industry in 1946, Chesapeake acquired two box and container companies in 1961: Baltimore Paper Box Company and Miller Container Corporation. Miller went on to become the Roanoke division of Chesapeake Packaging Company. Between 1962 and 1964, Chesapeake invested $21 million into an expansion program that included its second paper machine and a new power plant. In 1967 Scranton Corrugated Box Company, Inc. was acquired. It became the Scranton division of Chesapeake Packaging Company.

In 1968 Sture Olsson resigned as president to serve as chairman of the board; Lawrence Camp was named president and CEO. That same year, Chesapeake acquired the Binghamton Container Company, now a division of the Chesapeake Packaging Company. The company's next major acquisition came in 1977 when it purchased a packaging company that eventually became the Louisville and St. Anthony divisions of Chesapeake Packaging Company.

Decentralization and Restructuring in the 1980s

The 1980s were a time of great growth and change for Chesapeake. During this decade it vaulted to a position as a

Fortune 500 company and instituted a policy of decentralization. Changes commenced with the election of J. Carter Fox as president and CEO of Chesapeake. Only 41 years old at the time, he was the youngest CEO in the industry. Fox had moved up the ranks at Chesapeake. He first worked as a summer maintenance helper while still in school, then joined the company full-time in 1963 as a project accountant. As president and CEO, Fox reorganized the company's management structure. By putting managers in charge of operating units, the company was better able to focus on niche markets. The company was also restructured to reflect its four core business segments—treated wood, point-of-sale displays, table napkins, and brown and white linerboard boxes. Fox also oversaw trimming of the company, unloading unprofitable units such as plywood and sawmill plants.

In 1981 Chesapeake opened its first wood treating plant in Pocomoke City, and a new wastewood-fueled boiler went online at West Point. The new boiler helped to cut oil consumption by about five percent of total energy consumed. Chesapeake's energy program was often ahead of the industry in its utilization of residual and self-generated sources of energy. About this time, Chesapeake wrapped up a $51 million capital improvement program at West Point that was designed—among other advances—to allow the company to bear a greater wood inventory at the mill, thus minimizing its reliance on outside woodyards. In order to meet production demands, the company's sawmill and plywood plants were supplied primarily by contract loggers who harvested wood off private and company-controlled timberlands. These timberlands were in the Blue Ridge Mountains of Virginia and North Carolina, as well as in parts of Maryland and Delaware. In 1982 about 75 percent of the raw material used to produce needed pulpwood and chips came from southern pine. Because the company had experienced four serious wood shortages between 1968 and 1982, management of the woodlands was critical. Decentralization helped to minimize the shortages, as an area manager was designated to oversee and coordinate land management, acquisition, and wood procurement.

Decentralization began in earnest in 1983, when the company was divided into three investment centers. Chesapeake was one of the few pulp and paper companies in the United States to make expansion plans in 1983. The industry was still recovering from the recession and prices for key pulp and paper products were just beginning to bounce back.

In order to utilize the valuable company-owned land in Delaware, Maryland, and Virginia, Delmarva Properties, Inc. was established. Delmarva concentrated on developing various residential, recreational, commercial, and industrial lots on some of the properties too valuable to manage as timberlands. Chesapeake also modernized its West Point mill via a $73 million expansion project; this included a major revamp of the mill's roll handling system to reduce paperwork and order error and make inventory more accurate. The improved system was in place by 1984. Chesapeake acquired its tenth container plant, Color-Box, Inc. of Indiana, that same year. It also purchased a wood-treating plant near Fredericksburg, Virginia. The company's name was shortened during this period to Chesapeake Corporation from The Chesapeake Corporation of Virginia.

In an interview in *Pulp & Paper* magazine in 1984, Chesapeake president and CEO Fox said that the company's small size worked to its advantage. The company could manufacture different special market products to suit individual customer needs. "Only in this way can we hope to successfully compete with some of our competitors who in many cases are much larger firms with far greater financial reserves than Chesapeake," said Fox. Another of the company's advantages, he said, was that "Chesapeake has the closest linerboard mill to the northeastern U.S. market, and we can offer overnight service to the New York City area."

It was during this time that Chesapeake began plumping up its capacity to produce linerboard through expansions and upgrades. It also expanded its production of market pulp. Both these product lines were hard hit in 1982 and 1983. To counterbalance the dip in sales, Chesapeake negotiated a multiyear labor agreement that lowered wages and reduced staff by five percent. The amount spent on capital improvements was justified by the fact that the company had only one mill and had to keep it running efficiently. In 1985 the company acquired Wisconsin Tissue Mills Inc., of Wisconsin and Plainwell Paper Co., Inc., of Michigan. Prices for pulp and linerboard, however, continued to be depressed.

In 1986 Chesapeake completed the conversion of its paper machine at West Point and began production of a new product—corrugating medium. This enabled the company to offer its customers a uniform, high-quality linerboard. The company's new high-speed Tri-Kraft linerboard machine was the first of its kind in North America, using multi-ply technology to produce linerboard and thus producing a sheet with superior strength and uniformity. Start-up costs affected the company's earnings for that year, but ultimately the gamble paid off. When Chesapeake began offering white linerboard instead of the common brown, sales dramatically increased. Companies preferred the white because logos and advertising could be clearly read from them.

In 1987 the company moved its corporate headquarters from West Point to the James Center in downtown Richmond. According to Fox, this was done so that paper-mill staff there could operate as independently as the other decentralized operations. A $160 million expansion was approved to add a fourth paper machine to the Wisconsin Tissue facilities. This project, completed in 1990, boosted that mill's production capacity by more than 70 percent. Chesapeake also acquired Distinctive Printing and Packaging Co., thus expanding its point-of-sale display business.

In 1988 Chesapeake's earnings rose 71 percent, in large part because of the boom in sales of white corrugated boxes. Chesapeake Packaging Company was reorganized to better handle the national sales of point-of-sale display. The company also continued its acquisition of other properties with the purchase in 1988 of a wood-treating plant in Holly Hill, South Carolina, followed shortly by the acquisition of Displayco Midwest Inc.

In 1991 Chesapeake combined with Toronto-based StakeTech to form a $2.5 million venture called Recoupe Recycling Technologies to market a "steam explosion" system of paper recycling. Using basic pressure cooker technology, the system saved water and energy and produced more uniform pulp than other processes. Sales for that year declined a bit; the recession, low demand, and continued pricing pressures were cited. Chesapeake underwent another management restructuring that year, with Paul Dresser becoming chief operating officer.

Pulp market prices dipped in 1992, costing the company some $2 million in the fourth quarter alone. The year was a disappointing one, although the company held a 20 percent share of the mottled white linerboard market that year, a business that was still growing at a rate of seven percent a year. Chesapeake was also doing well in the areas of commercial tissue and point-of-sale corrugated displays.

Increasing Emphasis on Specialty Packaging in the 1990s

Through a detailed reassessment of corporate strategy undertaken in 1992, Chesapeake determined that specialty packaging would be the fastest area of company growth. The company thus began to expand its packaging operations, which accounted for 29 percent of sales in 1993 but would account for almost half by 1998. In addition to the faster growth projected for the specialty packaging sector, that segment of the paper industry was less prone to economic swings and less capital intensive than other industry sectors, particularly the kraft products area. Chesapeake's first major move in building up its packaging operations came in January 1994, when it acquired Lawless Holding Corp., owner of Lawless Container Corp. and six plants in western New York and Ohio. Through this acquisition packaging became, in 1994, the company's largest business segment in terms of sales for the first time.

In April 1994 Sture Olsson retired after 26 years as chairman; Fox added the chairmanship to his duties as president and CEO. Paul A. Dresser, Jr., was named president in April 1995 but resigned a year later, with Fox reassuming that title.

Despite the decreasing importance of kraft products in its overall business mix, Chesapeake felt the full effects of the commodity pricing cycle in 1995 and 1996, with the "up" year of 1995 leading to record net sales of $1.23 billion and net income of $93.4 million, and the "down" year that followed leading to declines in these figures to $1.16 billion and $30.1 million, respectively. During 1996, Chesapeake expanded internationally for the first time, acquiring display and packaging operations in France and Canada and a tissue converting facility in Mexico.

The most dramatic event in the transformation of Chesapeake came in May 1997 when the company sold its West Point kraft products mill, four corrugated container plants, and other related assets to St. Laurent Paperboard Inc. for about $500 million. The exit from kraft products left Chesapeake with two primary sectors—specialty packaging and tissue—along with a much smaller forest products/land development sector. In August 1997 Thomas H. Johnson was named president and CEO of Chesapeake, with Fox remaining chairman. Johnson had previously served as president and CEO of Atlanta-based Riverwood International Corp., a privately held packaging company. In

April 1998 Fox retired, with longtime board member Harry H. Warner taking over as chairman.

Also in 1998 Chesapeake added to its packaging operations through the acquisition of Denver-based Capitol Packaging Corporation, a specialty packaging company; and of Utica, New York-based Rock City Box Co., Inc., a manufacturer of corrugated containers, trays, and pallets, and wood and foam packaging products. Acquisitions as well as divestments continued in 1999. In March of that year—following a bidding war with Shorewood Packaging Corp.—Chesapeake paid approximately $373 million to acquire U.K.-based Field Group plc, a leading European specialty packaging firm. In April 1999 Chesapeake announced that it had signed letters of intent to sell its building products business to a subsidiary of St. Laurent Paperboard Inc. and 278,000 acres of timberland to Hancock Timber Resource Group, a subsidiary of John Hancock Mutual Life Insurance Company. Two months later Chesapeake reached an agreement with Georgia-Pacific Corporation to combine the companies' commercial tissue operations in a joint venture to be managed by Georgia-Pacific and be 90 percent owned by that company and ten percent owned by Chesapeake.

Through these moves Chesapeake would become almost fully focused on one sector—specialty packaging. The divestments would also generate more than $850 million in cash to be used, according to Johnson, "to repurchase Chesapeake stock, continue the growth of our core specialty packaging businesses through strategic acquisitions and alliances, and reduce debt." The rapid transformation of Chesapeake into a global specialty packaging firm appeared to have positioned the company for a period of growth as it headed into the 21st century.

Principal Subsidiaries

Field Group plc (U.K.); Chesapeake Display & Packaging Company; Chesapeake Display & Packaging-Europe S.A. (France); Chesapeake Packaging Co.; Chesapeake Land Development.

Further Reading

Betts, Dickey, "Air-Assisted Separation, New Skim Tank Ups to Yield at Chesapeake," *Pulp & Paper,* August 1982, pp. 86–89.

"Big Recovery in the Making," *Industry Surveys,* May 14, 1992, pp. B75–B79.

"Chesapeake Corporation," *New York Times,* February 20, 1990, p. D4.

"Chesapeake Corporation," *Wall Street Journal,* April 19, 1991, p. A7B.

"Chesapeake Corporation," *New York Times,* June 14, 1991, p. D4.

"Chesapeake Corporation," *Wall Street Journal,* January 13, 1993, p. 4.

Chesapeake World, special 80th anniversary edition, Richmond, Va.: Chesapeake Corp., 1998.

Clark, Barry, "Chesapeake Modernizes Mill with Computerized Roll Handling System," *Pulp & Paper,* March 1984, pp. 62–65.

Dill, Alonzo Thomas, *Chesapeake, Pioneer Papermaker: A History of the Company and Its Communities,* West Point, Va.: Chesapeake Corp., 1987, 424 p.

Glowacki, Jeremy J., "Chesapeake Corp.: Committed to Specialty Markets," *Pulp & Paper,* September 1995, pp. 38–39.

Jereski, Laura, "Recovering," *Forbes,* February 15, 1993, pp. 240–41.

Johnson, Jim, "Paper Giants Launch Joint Venture," *Waste News,* July 5, 1999, p. 1.

Johnson, Stephen S., "Packaging Profits," *Forbes,* January 2, 1995, p. 178.

Jones, Chip, "President Resigns at Virginia's Chesapeake Corp.," *Richmond Times-Dispatch,* March 8, 1996.

Koncel, Jerome, "First Quarter Results Disguise a Bright Future," *Paper Trade Journal,* June 1986, p. 52.

"Long-Log, Tree-Length Requirements Increase," *Forest Industries,* August 1982, pp. 22–23.

Rayner, Bob, "Virginia's Chesapeake Corp. Is Cast As Guerilla Among Industry Gorillas," *Richmond Times-Dispatch,* August 19, 1997.

Slack, Charles, and Lawrence Latane III, "Chesapeake Corp. to Sell $508 Million in Assets to Montreal Paper Firm," *Richmond Times-Dispatch,* April 3, 1997.

Smith, Kenneth, "Chesapeake Producing Multi-Ply Liner on New Management at West Point," *Pulp & Paper,* April 1986, p. 108.

——, "P&P Interview: Chesapeake Looking for Recovery, Record Sales in 1984," *Pulp & Paper,* April 1984, pp. 130–34.

Starkman, Dean, "Georgia-Pacific, Chesapeake Corp. in Joint Venture," *Wall Street Journal,* June 28, 1999, p. B8.

Stipp, David, "Recycling Waste Paper with a Pressure Cooker," *Wall Street Journal,* January 7, 1991, p. B1.

Taylor, Robert, "Redesigned Waste Oil Reclamation System Cuts Chesapeake Fuel Costs," *Pulp & Paper,* December 1983, p. 94.

Wagner, Barbara Hetzer, "Companies with Star Potential," *Business Month,* December 1989, p. 45.

Wuerl, Peter, "Chesapeake Starts Up $73 Million Tri-Kraft Machine at West Point Mill," *Paper Trade Journal,* April 1986, pp. 44–45.

—Carol I. Keeley
—updated by David E. Salamie

CHORUS LINE CORP.

Chorus Line Corporation

4504 Bandini Blvd.
Vernon, California 90040
U.S.A.
(213) 747-8466
Fax: (213) 780-5838
Web site: http://www.choruslinecorp.com

Private Company
Founded: 1975
Employees: 650
Sales: $190 million (1998 est.)
NAIC: 315233 Women's & Girls' Cut & Sew Dress
    Manufacturing; 315232 Women's & Girls' Cut &
    Sew Blouse & Shirt Manufacturing

Founded in 1975 by three men in southern California, Chorus Line Corporation is one of the most successful moderately priced apparel companies in the United States. Begun initially as a retail company focusing exclusively on juniors collections, Chorus Line in the past two decades has branched out to include in its lines designs specifically aimed towards women in their 20s and 30s as well as petite and plus size divisions. Despite being established during a time in which the retail industry was far from stable, Chorus Line in the 1980s and 90s has managed to not only maintain a firm hold in the juniors apparel market, but has continued to grow in both its profitability, which in 1998 topped $190 million, as well as its variety of product. The company's most visible and successful line, a juniors brand called All That Jazz, makes up for more than 60 percent of its sales, but the business also has four other divisions, each of which targets a separate customer base.

Cornering the Juniors Apparel Market in the 1980s

Chorus Line was established by Barry Sacks, Mark Steinman, and Jay Balaban, three Los Angeles-based businessmen who came up with the company's name after realizing their wives all shared a mutual love of dance. In the mid-1970s, there existed a paucity of moderately priced collections designed specifically for adolescent girls: choices were somewhat limited to clothes which were either decidedly styled for children or, on the other end, for adult women—with prices to match. In an increasingly silhouette conscious society, young girls became at an earlier and earlier age interested in fashion—fashion with a trendy, youthful edge—hence opening the possibility for a lucrative niche market, which Chorus Line helped to create.

In the development of All That Jazz, Chorus Line had essentially two goals in view: to appeal to a teenaged, female customer base and to keep prices low. The achievement of the former aim made it necessary for All That Jazz to not only offer stylish, youthful ensembles, but also to keep up with the ever changing trends and whims of the young-adult market. In order to keep costs for the line at a level palatable to middle-class families, Chorus Line had to focus on using inexpensive, mass-produced materials—a difficult objective when those same materials also needed to be durable and fashionable. By using its own design team and producing its collections through locally based factories, Chorus Line by the late 1970s saw both of its initial objectives fully realized, and was gaining a regional reputation as a growing, trendsetting force in the juniors apparel market. One of the most notable things about the company was that, from its inception, it produced collections which were constantly changing in style, but which were also reliably trendy, and therefore made itself continually appealing to the notoriously capricious tastes of the young female customer.

After beginning with an almost exclusive focus on casual, silhouette-conscious dresses, All That Jazz soon branched out, producing pant-suits, more formal dresses, and single pieces such as skirts and casual blouses which could be mixed and matched. By the 1980s Chorus Line started distributing All That Jazz to nationwide department and specialty stores, with the line being picked up by J.C. Penney and Sears.

During this time Chorus Line began to develop other divisions which were meant to complement and mirror the trendy, inexpensive emphasis of All That Jazz. The company's first area of expansion was in womenswear, with the creation of a line called Molly Malloy. Molly Malloy, like All That Jazz, was a line with a decidedly style-conscious edge, but its focus was not so much on trendiness as it was on slightly more conserva-

Company Perspectives:

With its focus on quality, design, up-to-the-moment styling and value pricing, Chorus Line Corporation has become one of the largest apparel companies in the nation.

tive, sophisticated apparel which would appeal to young working women in their 20s and 30s. Chorus Line, seeing the success of both divisions, particularly its original line, expanded All That Jazz to include More Jazz, a collection of plus-size apparel for juniors; Jazz Kids, which toned down the sexiness of All That Jazz in order to appeal to a younger customer base; Jazz Sports, a line which focused on T-shirts and sweatsuits; and Tickets, a collection of dresses and single pieces produced entirely in denim.

Despite Chorus Line Corporation's success and expansion in the 1980s, the company found itself in debt. The retail market was at the time fluctuating a great deal, with start-up companies appearing all over the nation, particularly in southern California, and competition was becoming more than Sacks, Steinman, and Balaban could handle on their own. In 1987 Chorus Line was bought in part by two different investors: Merrill Lynch Interfunding purchased a 45 percent stake in the company, and an East Coast-based investment group headed by Ira J. Hechler bought another 13 percent. The three original partners of Chorus Line maintained control over the design, distribution, and manufacturing of the company's divisions.

Further Growth and Expansion: 1991–94

In 1991 Chorus Line had net sales of over $96 million, making it one of the fastest-growing apparel companies in southern California. Retail insiders were not the only ones to notice the company's success: in 1992, in preparation for the release of the film *Batman Returns,* Chorus Line struck a licensing agreement with LCA Entertainment and Warner Bros. Consumer Products. The deal allowed Chorus Line to design and manufacture dresses, shirts, and pants based on both the Catwoman cartoon character as well as the sensual heroine played by Michelle Phieffer in the Batman film. Predicting that teenaged girls would take their style cues that season from the black-clad film star, All That Jazz put out a collection of revealing body-suits and dresses, all of which bore the Batman insignia. The licensing deal was a first for the company, and sales in the end fell short of those initially predicted, but the partnership between Warner Bros. Consumer Products and Chorus Line proved that the latter had truly come into its own as a nationally recognized clothing manufacturer.

By the early 1990s Chorus Line Corporation's lines were carried by dozens of regional and national stores, from J.C. Penney and Sears to Macy's and Filene's to Dillard's, Foleys, and Carson's. Lesser known regional shops also picked up Chorus Line Corporation's lines, increasing the company's orders at a seemingly exponential rate. To keep up with its increasing expansion, Chorus Line in 1992 moved from its 70,000-square-foot office and manufacturing area into a facility

which included over 100,000 square feet in office space, a piece goods storage area as well as a computerized, round the clock cutting factory, all of which totalled more than 450,000 square feet of space. Possessing a facility of this size allowed the company to continue both its expansion and its commitment to closely managing its collections, from the inchoate stage of marketing and ideas to actual production and manufacturing.

In 1994 Chorus Line saw one of its most eventful and productive years. In February of that year the company financed about $26.5 million to buy back in full the 58 percent of the company owned by Merrill Lynch Interfunding and Ira J. Hechler's investment group. Chorus Line received part of that funding from Nederlanden Capital, and with that deal the original three partners of the company once again owned Chorus Line outright.

That year, too, brought in record revenue for the company, with an increase of over 25 percent from the previous year and sales reaching to $206.3 million. With almost all the company's divisions doing well, Chorus Line hired 125 new employees, bringing the total to over 700.

After developing such a successful distribution and manufacturing company, Chorus Line began looking towards opening its own outlet stores as a new method by which to increase revenue and brand recognition. So, in 1994, after much market analysis and planning, the company opened its first store, located in Goodyear, Arizona. Following quickly on the initial success of that store, Chorus Line opened others in Gainsville and San Marcos, Texas, as well as Camario, California. Eventually the company expanded to 11 stores in all, though most of Chorus Line Corporation's revenue continued to come from its distribution deals with department stores.

One of the most important ingredients behind the appeal of Chorus Line Corporation's lines was price: customers expected the collections from lines such as Molly Malloy and All That Jazz to be available at a cost well below other trendy and fashion-conscious labels. Indeed, the average price of a dress from All That Jazz in the 1990s ranged from around $50 to $80, far below the price of other labels, such as DKNY and Ralph Lauren, which also appealed to the juniors market. As a result of its need to keep production costs down, Chorus Line in the 1990s found it increasingly difficult to use purely domestic resources, which the company had done from its inception. By the early 1990s the company slowly began utilizing foreign, primarily Mexican, contractors for part of its production, and by the middle of the decade approximately 50 percent of the company's mass manufacturing was handled outside the United States. While this change in direction took some business away from local contractors, it also allowed Chorus Line to keep its collections available to the consumer at consistently low prices.

Solving Problems, Preparing for the Future: Mid- to Late 1990s

After a peak year in 1994 Chorus Line began to feel the effects of both the shaky economy of southern California as well as the company's own perhaps too rapid expansion. Just one year after reaching a record number of 750 employees, the company laid off 42 people, and, despite claims of increasing growth, began to downsize its departments and divisions. Among the departments to be most affected was the public relations segment of the company, which was canceled altogether, making it necessary for the company to bring in outside assistance in matters relating to the press and public. To blame for Chorus Line Corporation's slumping performance was the company's phenomenal increase in overhead costs: within a few years the business had opened outlet stores, moved into a new, enormous facility, and expanded its divisions, with negative results.

Around this time Steinman, Sacks, and Balaban developed plans to take the company public, with hopes of a public offering by early 1996. However, because of the business's rocky response to its rapid growth, the plans were scrapped that same year, and Mark Steinman stepped down as president of the company. Replacing him was Andrew Cohen, a retail insider with many years of industry experience. Cohen first began working in the retail business in 1971 when he joined his family's sleepwear manufacturing business, and eventually went on to work for such high-profile companies as Lily of France and Christian Dior. In 1993 Cohen gained the experience which would make him a true boon to a company like Chorus Line: he became president of Esprit Juniors and, later, of Esprit Wholesale, a position which exposed him to all the elements of the frenetic juniors apparel industry.

Cohen's first objective was to increase his company's focus on All That Jazz and Molly Malloy, with an added emphasis in both lines on after-five, more formal dresses. Additionally, Tickets, the company's line of denim wear and its least profitable, was canceled, allowing Chorus Line to concentrate its financial energy on its remaining five divisions.

In 1996 Chorus Line again tried its hand with licensing agreements, signing a deal with Universal Consumer Products Group and Jay Ward Productions which allowed the company to feature cartoon icons such as Bullwinkle on shirts and jackets. Cohen predicted that the deal struck with Universal Consumer Products would bring in over $150 million in revenue.

The late 1990s saw an increase in growth and stability for Chorus Line. Although the company had yet to top its record revenue year of 1994, it continued to increase in profitability, with sales up in 1998 by eight percent for All That Jazz, and 28 percent for Molly Malloy. In addition, the company continued to develop relationships with other retail businesses. In 1998

Chorus Line formed a partnership with ABS, a successful apparel business owned by Allen Schwartz; the partnership had as its aim the production of a line of moderately priced separates and dresses. The line was to be slightly more expensive than either All That Jazz or Molly Malloy, using more costly designs and materials, and was to be called Allen B. Under the terms of the agreement, Allen Schwartz and his team served as the creative end, producing the label's designs and styles, while Chorus Line headed up the line's more pragmatic side of manufacturing and marketing. In addition to the creation of Allen B., the partnership brought Schwartz on board as Chorus Line Corporation's overall creative director.

In 1999 founding partner Jay Balaban, who had been one of the creative forces behind the company's juniors divisions, left Chorus Line, and the company hired three new designers to take his place. With a broad range of retail design experience between them, the three designers—Jose Dias, Beata Beck, and Robert Romero—lent a renewed energy to the company's junior lines, with sales increasing by 18 percent from the previous year.

Chorus Line, despite some internal instability over the years, maintained a solid reputation within the retail industry, one which continued to grow in positive ways. According to Richard Arkin, president of a retail consulting company in California, who was quoted in a *Los Angeles Business Journal* article, Chorus Line was "one of the very best apparel companies in the business," a sentiment that was buoyed by the company's steady popularity.

Further Reading

Ellis, Kristi, "Bullwinkle Joins Chorus Line," *Women's Wear Daily,* May 30, 1996, p. 10.
——, "Chorus Line Kicks Up Dresses," *Women's Wear Daily,* May 6, 1999, p. 11.
——, "Chorus Line Reduces Its Staff Despite 'Most Profitable Year,' " *Women's Wear Daily,* August 22, 1995, p. 8.
Friedman, Arthur, "Chorus Line Forms Firm with ABS," *Women's Wear Daily,* September 8, 1998, p. 8.
Glover, Kara, "Apparel Maker Chorus Line Finds a Niche," *Los Angeles Business Journal,* June 5, 1995, p. 36.
Van Dange, Kim, "Diversifying Gives Chorus Line a Leg Up," *Women's Wear Daily,* November 16, 1995, p. 10.

—Rachel H. Martin

Citigroup Inc.

153 East 53rd Street
New York, New York 10043
U.S.A.
(212) 559-1000
Fax: (212) 527-1181
Web site: http://www.citi.com

Public Company
Incorporated: 1812 as the City Bank of New York
Employees: 173,700
Sales: $76.4 billion (1998)
Stock Exchanges: New York Midwest Pacific London
    Amsterdam Tokyo Zurich Geneva Basel Toronto
    Düsseldorf Frankfurt
Ticker Symbol: C
NAIC: 52211 Commercial Banking; 52212 Saving
    Institutions; 52221 Credit Card Issuing; 52222 Sales
    Financing; 52232 Financial Transactions Processing,
    Reserve, and Clearing House Activities; 52311
    Investment Banking and Securities Dealing; 52312
    Securities Brokerage; 523991 Trust, Fiduciary, and
    Custody Activities; 524113 Direct Life Insurance
    Carriers; 52591 Open-End Investment Funds; 551111
    Offices of Bank Holding Companies

The largest financial services company in the world, Citigroup Inc. combines the international banking of Citibank and the numerous insurance products and non-banking financial services of Travelers Group Inc. Citibank's Visa and Mastercard credit cards and Travelers Bank's credit cards together made Citigroup the number one credit card issuer in the world as of 1999. The company's other well-known subsidiaries include the brokerage Salomon Smith Barney, the insurer Travelers Life & Annuity, the life insurance and consumer lender Primerica Financial Services, and the personal and home equity lender Commercial Credit.

Company Origins

Citicorp has its origin in the First Bank of the United States, founded in 1791. Colonel Samuel Osgood, the nation's first

postmaster general and treasury commissioner, took over the New York branch of the failing First Bank and reorganized it as the City Bank of New York in 1812. Only two days after the bank received its charter, on June 16, 1812, war was declared with Britain. The war notwithstanding, the City Bank was for all intents and purposes a private treasury for a group of merchants. It conducted most of its business as a credit union and as a dealer in cotton, sugar, metals, and coal, and later acted as a shipping agent.

Following the financial panic of 1837, the bank came under the control of Moses Taylor, a merchant and industrialist who essentially turned it into his own personal bank. Nonetheless, under Taylor, City Bank established a comprehensive financial approach to business and adopted a strategy of maintaining a high proportion of liquid assets. Elected president of the bank in 1856, Taylor converted the bank's charter from a state one to a national one on July 17, 1865, at the close of the Civil War. Taking the name National City Bank of New York (NCB), the bank was thereafter permitted to perform certain official duties on behalf of the U.S. Treasury; it distributed the new uniform national currency and served as an agent for government bond sales.

Taylor was the treasurer of the company that laid the first transatlantic cable, which made international trade much more feasible. It was at this early stage that NCB adopted the eight-letter wire code address "Citibank." Taylor died in 1882 and was replaced as president by his son-in-law, Percy R. Pyne. Pyne died nine years later and was replaced by James Stillman.

Stillman believed that big businesses deserved a big bank capable of providing numerous special services as a professional business partner. After the panic of 1893, NCB, with assets of $29.7 million, emerged as the largest bank in New York City, and the following year it became the largest bank in the United States. It accomplished this mainly through conservative banking practices, emphasizing low-risk lending in well-secured projects. The company's reputation for safety spread, attracting business from the largest U.S. corporations. The flood of new business permitted NCB to expand; in 1897 it purchased the Third National Bank of New York, bringing its assets to $113.8 million. That same year it also became the first big U.S. bank to open a foreign department.

Far from retiring or diminishing his influence within NCB, Stillman nonetheless began to prepare Frank A. Vanderlip to take over senior management duties. Stillman and Vanderlip, who was elected president of the bank in 1909, introduced many innovations in banking, including travelers' checks and investment services through a separate but affiliated subsidiary (federal laws prevented banks from engaging in direct investment, but made no provision for subsidiaries).

Expansion in the Early 20th Century

Beginning in the late 1800s, many U.S. businessmen began to invest heavily in agricultural and natural-resource projects in the relatively underdeveloped nations of South and Central America. But government regulations prevented federally chartered banks such as NCB from conducting business out of foreign branches. Vanderlip worked long and hard to change the government's policy and eventually won in 1913, when Congress passed the Federal Reserve Act. NCB established a branch office in Buenos Aires in 1914 and in 1915 gained an entire international banking network from London to Singapore when it purchased a controlling interest in the International Banking Corporation, which it gained complete ownership of in 1918.

In 1919 Frank Vanderlip resigned in frustration over his inability to secure a controlling interest in the company, and James A. Stillman, the son of the previous Stillman, became president. NCB reached $1 billion in assets, the first U.S. bank to do so. Charles E. Mitchell, Stillman's successor in 1921, completed much of what Vanderlip had begun, creating the nation's first full-service bank. Until this time national banks catered almost exclusively to the needs of corporations and institutions, while savings banks handled the needs of individuals. But competition from other banks, and even corporate clients themselves, forced commercial banks to look elsewhere for sources of growth. Sensing an untapped wealth of business in personal banking, in 1921 NCB became the first major bank to offer interest on savings accounts, which it allowed individual customers to open with as little as a dollar. In 1928 Citibank began to offer personal consumer loans.

The bank also expanded during the 1920s, acquiring the Commercial Exchange Bank and the Second National Bank in 1921, the People's Trust Company of Brooklyn in 1926, and merging with the Farmers' Loan and Trust Company in 1929. By the end of the decade, the "Citibank" was the largest bank in the country, and through its affiliates, the National City Company and the City Bank Farmers' Trust Company, it was also one of the largest securities and trust firms.

Surviving the Great Depression

In October 1929 the stock market crash that led to the Great Depression caused an immediate liquidity crisis in the banking industry. In the ensuing months, thousands of banks were forced to close. NCB remained in business, however, mainly by virtue of its size and organization. But in 1933, at the height of the Depression, Congress passed the Glass-Steagall Act, which restricted the activities of banks by requiring the separation of investment and commercial banking. NCB was compelled to liquidate its securities affiliate and curtail its line of special financial products, eliminating many of the gains the bank had made in establishing itself as a flexible and competitive full-service bank.

James H. Perkins, who succeeded Mitchell as chairman in 1933, had the difficult task of rebuilding the bank's reputation and its business (it had fallen to number three). He instituted a defensive strategy, pledging to keep all domestic and foreign branches open and to eliminate as few staff members as possible. Perkins died in 1940, but his defensive policies were continued by his successor, Gordon Rentschler.

As a major U.S. bank, NCB was in many ways a resource for the government, which depended on private savings and bond sales to finance World War II. The bank followed its defensive strategy throughout the war, amassed a large government bond portfolio, and continued to stress its relationship with corporate clients. Unlike its competitors, NCB was so well placed in so many markets by the end of the war that it could devote its energy to winning new clients rather than entering new markets. Sixteen years after Black Tuesday, NCB had finally regained its momentum in the banking industry.

Innovation in the Mid-20th Century

The bank changed direction after the death of Gordon Rentschler in 1948 by moving more aggressively into corporate lending. In 1955, with assets of $6.8 billion, NCB acquired the First National Bank of New York and changed its name to the First National City Bank of New York (FNCB), or Citibank for short.

Citibank used its bond portfolio to finance its expansion in corporate lending, selling off bonds to make new loans. By 1957, however, the bank had just about depleted its bond reserve. Prevented by New Deal legislation from expanding its business in private savings beyond New York City, Citibank had nowhere to turn to for more funding. The squeeze on funds only became more acute until 1961, when the bank introduced a new and ingenious product: the negotiable certificate of deposit.

The "CD," as it was called, gave large depositors higher returns on their savings in return for restricted liquidity, and was intended to win business from higher-interest government bonds and commercial paper. The CD changed not only Citibank but the entire banking industry, which soon followed suit in offering CDs. The CD gave Citibank a way to expand its assets—but at the same time required it to streamline operations and manage risk more efficiently, since it had to pay a higher rate of interest to CD holders for the use of their funds.

The man behind the CD was not FNCB's president, George Moore, nor its chairman, James Rockefeller, but Walter B. Wriston, a highly unconventional vice-president. Wriston, a product of Wesleyan University and the Fletcher School, had worked his way up through the company's ranks since joining the bank in 1946. Having made a name for himself with the CD, Wriston was later given responsibility for revamping the company's management structure to eliminate the strains of Citibank's expansion. Like Vanderlip more than 50 years before, Wriston advocated a general decentralization of power to permit top executives to concentrate on longer-term strategic considerations.

In an attempt to circumvent federal regulations restricting a bank's activities, in 1968 Citibank created a one-bank holding company (a type of company the Bank Holding Company Act of 1956 had overlooked) to own the bank but also engage in lines of business the bank could not. Within six months, Bank of America, Chase Manhattan, Manufacturers Hanover, Morgan Guaranty, and Chemical Bank had also created holding companies.

Citicorp made no secret of its intention to expand, both operationally and geographically. In 1970 Congress—recognizing its error and concerned that one-bank holding companies would become too powerful—revised the Bank Holding Company Act of 1956 to prevent these companies from diversifying into traditionally "non-banking" activities.

Wriston, who was promoted to president in 1967 and to chairman in 1970, continued to press for the relaxation of banking laws. He oversaw Citibank's entry into the credit card business, and later directed a massive offer of Visa and MasterCharge cards to 26 million people across the nation. This move greatly upset other banks that also issued the cards, but succeeded in bringing Citibank millions of customers from outside New York state. The bank failed, however, to properly assess the risk involved. Of the five million people who responded to the offer, enough later defaulted to cost Citicorp an estimated $200 million.

In an effort to gain wider consumer recognition, the holding company formally adopted "Citicorp" as its legal name in 1974, and in 1976 First National City Bank officially changed its name to "Citibank." The "Citi" prefix was later added to a number of generic product names: Citicorp offered CitiCards, CitiOne unified statement accounts, and there were CitiTeller automatic teller machines and a host of other Citi-offerings.

Falling Fortunes in the 1970s and 1980s

Citicorp performed very well during the early 1970s, weathering the failure of the Penn Central railroad, the energy crisis, and a recession without serious setback. In 1975, however, the company's fortunes fell dramatically. Profits were erratic due to rapidly eroding economic conditions in Third World countries. Citicorp, awash in petrodollars in the 1970s, had lent heavily to these countries in the belief that they would experience high turnover and faced the possibility of heavy defaults resulting from poor

growth rates. In addition, its Argentine deposits were nationalized in 1973, its interests in Nigeria had to be scaled back in 1976, and political agitation in Poland and Iran in 1979 precipitated unfavorable debt rescheduling in those countries. Shareholders soon became concerned that Citicorp, which conducted two-thirds of its business abroad, might face serious losses.

In its domestic operations, Citicorp suffered from a decision made during the early 1970s to expand in low-yielding, consumer-banking activities. Although New York usury laws placed a 12 percent ceiling on consumer loans, Citibank bet that interest rates would drop, leaving plenty of room to make a profit. But the oil shock following the revolution in Iran sent interest rates soaring in the opposite direction: Citicorp lost $450 million in 1980 alone. In addition, Citibank purchased $3 billion in government bonds at 11 percent, in the belief that interest rates would continue a decline begun during the summer of 1980. Again, the opposite happened. Interest on the money Citibank borrowed to purchase the bonds rose as high as 21 percent, and the bank lost another $50 million or more.

One investment that did not go awry, however, was the company's decision to invest $500 million on an elaborate automated teller network. Installed throughout its branches by 1978, the ATMs permitted depositors to withdraw money at any hour from hundreds of locations. Not only were labor costs reduced drastically, but by being first again, Citibank gained thousands of new customers attracted by the convenience of ATMs.

Citicorp raised the profitability of its commercial banking operations by deemphasizing interest-rate-based income in favor of income from fees for services. Successful debt negotiations with developing countries cut losses on debts which would otherwise have gone into default. In addition, as a result of the 1967 Edge Act and special accommodations made by various states, Citicorp, until then an international giant known domestically only in New York state, was able to expand into several states during the 1980s. Beginning with mortgages and its credit card business, then savings and loans, and then banks, Citicorp established a presence in 39 states and the District of Columbia. Internationally, the company expanded its business into more than 90 countries. Some of this expansion was accomplished by purchasing existing banks outright.

Wriston, after 14 years as chairman of Citicorp, retired in 1984, shortly after the announcement that Citicorp would enter two new businesses: insurance and information. He was succeeded by John S. Reed, who had distinguished himself by returning the "individual" banking division to profitability.

In May 1987 Citibank finally admitted that its Third World loans could spell trouble and announced that it was setting aside a $3 billion reserve fund. Losses for 1987 totaled $1.2 billion, but future earnings were much more secure. Citibank's move forced its competitors to follow suit, something few of them were able to do as easily—Bank of America, for example, wound up selling assets to cover its reserve fund.

Reorganization in the Early 1990s

As Citicorp entered the 1990s, the United States' biggest bank faced perhaps its most challenging period since its founding. A faltering economy, coupled with unprofitable business loans—particularly in the commercial real estate market—led to serious financial difficulties which threatened the bank's existence. Year-end statistics for 1990 revealed a 20-year low for Citicorp's share price, which eventually fell to $8. Citicorp's ratio of core capital to total assets stood at 3.26 percent, considerably lower than the minimum four percent which regulators instituted as the standard requirement in 1992. The company was operating on an expenses-to-revenue ratio of 70 percent, which prompted immediate cost-cutting efforts in nearly all expendable (non-core) business operations. Third quarter financial statements for 1991 reflected the impact of restructuring charges, asset write-downs, and additions to reserves necessary for coverage of nonperforming loans: Citicorp reported an $885 million loss. For the first time since 1813, shareholders did not receive their 25 cents a share quarterly dividend. Citicorp was in desperate need of reorganization.

Chairman John Reed described this period of great instability as "tough, demanding," and a time of "turnaround." Widely viewed as a slow-moving and analytical visionary, Reed appeared to many to be unable to maneuver the ailing bank out of its mounting difficulties. Critics blamed Citicorp's loan crisis on Reed's efforts during the mid-1980s to expand in the international market and overextend credit to real estate developers, including Donald Trump. Reed silenced his critics, however, with the successful implementation of a two-year, five-point plan aimed at improving capital strength and operating earnings to offset future, but imminent, credit costs.

Of primary importance in the recovery process were cost-cutting measures, growth constraint, and disciplined expenses and credit quality—considered the control aspects of the banking industry. Staff cuts for the two-year restructuring period resulted in the layoff of more than 15,000 employees—including many in senior management positions. Expenses were also trimmed as Citicorp consolidated its U.S. mortgage service and insurance service operations, as well as its telecommunication resources.

Nearly half of Citicorp's third-quarter $885 million loss was affected by the write-down of its $400 million investment in Quotron Systems, Inc. Citicorp bought the stock quotation service for $680 million in 1986 at a time when the company was hoping to expand in the information business. Since the acquisition, Quotron had been losing contracts with major Wall Street firms such as Shearson Lehman and Merrill Lynch. Quotron Systems, Inc. could not compete with the updated technology of its rival, Automatic Data Processing (ADP). In 1992 Citicorp sold two Quotron divisions to ADP, the leader in the computer services market.

To help raise the projected $4 million to $5 million in capital under the five-point plan, Citicorp sold its marginal operations in Austria, Italy, and France; abandoned its efforts in the United Kingdom; and offered $1.1 billion of preferred equity redemption cumulative stock (PERCS). An important factor in the company's recapitalization was investment by Saudi Prince al-Waleed bin Talal, who provided approximately $400 million of the $2.6 billion Citicorp raised in 1991 and 1992.

Although Citicorp relinquished some of its weaker holdings in Europe, it continued to expand and improve operations in the Asian/Pacific region. New branches were opened in Mexico, Brazil, Japan, Taiwan, South Korea, and Australia. Such selective investing produced growth in earnings of up to 30 percent. From September 1991 to September 1992, Citicorp obtained $371 million in net income from consumer banking in the developing world, exceeding earnings in the Japan, Europe, and North America (JENA) unit of global finance.

Uneven Recovery in the 1990s

Citicorp continued its commitment to international core business, capital growth, and credit stability as it cautiously proceeded through a recovery period. Circumstances called for conservative action in the early 1990s to compensate for severe losses. In addition, Citicorp's freedom to make loans was abridged in 1992 when it was placed under regulatory supervision.

Citicorp experienced losses in the value of its real estate holdings in the early 1990s. The company decided to hold on to the nonperforming property in the hopes an economic recovery would boost its value. However, Citicorp sold approximately 60 percent of its holdings in 1993 at a loss. Two years later the other 40 percent had recovered its value.

In 1996 a Citibank employee was accused of helping Raul Salinas, brother of Mexican president Carlos Salinas, sneak out of Mexico funds acquired by illegal means. Further embarrassment from Mexico ensued for Citicorp when its 1998 purchase, Banco Confia, was brought up on charges of laundering drug money. Domestically, Citicorp was faced with rising credit card write-offs as consumer bankruptcy increased in the late 1990s.

In 1998 Citicorp took the lead in mega-banking mergers by joining forces with Travelers Group Inc. Citigroup, as the new entity was called, boasted assets of $698 billion. The merger created the largest financial services firm in the world, what the *Economist* called "a global financial supermarket." With little overlap in service offerings and two separate distribution networks, the two companies hoped to cross-sell to each other's customers. John Reed, chairman of Citicorp, and Sanford Weill, chairman of Travelers Group, agreed to run the new company together.

Despite the Glass-Steagall Act of 1933, which forbade banks from owning insurers and insurers from owning banks, the merger was approved by the Federal Reserve Board. However, Citigroup was required to sell off its insurance businesses, a ruling it hoped would be overridden with new legislation. It stalled the sales while lobbying Congress to modernize the law.

Shares of Citibank and Travelers Group shot up at the announcement of the merger, raising the combined value of the companies by $30 billion. The optimism waned in the months following the merger as cross-selling and creating economies of scale proved difficult to execute. With Travelers still struggling to integrate its recent purchase of Salomon Brothers into its own brokerage business, the merger with Citibank did not proceed smoothly. Rather than cross-selling, the various subsidiaries and divisions moved to protect their own turf. One exception was subsidiary Primerica Financial Services, which sold a range of Travelers products to customers who took the company up on a free financial analysis.

The rift between Citibank and Travelers Group became apparent in late 1998 when Jamie Dimon, likely successor to Citibank's joint chairmen Weill and Reed, abruptly quit. Employees divided along original company lines, with Citibank staff cheering the news as a victory for their man Reed over Weill, who had groomed Dimon to replace him at Travelers. Salomon employees, who had never been fully integrated into Travelers Group before the merger, showed their sympathy for Dimon with a standing ovation on their trading floor. Dimon's loss left a void in the company's leadership, especially because Weill and Reed were both nearing retirement age.

In 1999 Citibank announced a project to simplify its service offerings in an effort to reduce costs. As the bank had grown over the years, its complexity had multiplied to such mind-boggling dimensions that it needed 28 computer systems to handle its back-office records. As an example, Citibank offered 150,000 different kinds of checking accounts in 1999, with variations on how interest was calculated, what fees were charged, and so on. The goal of the new project was to cut complexity by 75 percent and eliminate at least 26 computer systems.

Principal Subsidiaries

Citibank; Travelers Group Inc.; Citibank Mortgage, Inc.; Salomon Smith Barney Holdings Inc.; Travelers Life & Annuity; Travelers Property Casualty Corp. (83.4%); American Health and Life Insurance Co.; Primerica Bank; PFS Investments Inc.; Primerica Financial Services; Commercial Credit Company; Gulf Insurance Company; Citibank Credit Card Marketing; Citicorp Information Resources, Inc.; Citicorp Insurance Services Inc.; Citicorp N.A.; Citicorp Inc.; Citicorp Business Credit Inc.; Citicorp A.G. (Germany); Citicorp (Austria) A.G.; Citicorp Canada; Citicorp Credito, Financiamento e Investimento, S.A. (Brazil); Citicorp Espana S.A. (Spain); Citicorp Copenhagen (Denmark); Citicorp International Limited (Hong Kong).

Principal Divisions

SSB Citi Asset Management Planning Group; Global Consumer Planning Group; Global Corporate and Investment Bank Planning Group.

Further Reading

Citibank, Nader and the Facts, New York: Citibank, 1974.
''Citicorp Battling Back,'' *Economist,* April 25, 1992, pp. 84, 86.
''Citigroup: Fall Guy,'' *Economist,* November 7, 1998.
Cleveland, Harold van B., and Thomas F. Huertas, *Citibank 1812–1970,* Cambridge, Mass.: Harvard University Press, 1985.
Egan, Jack, ''The Fight to Stay on Top,'' *U.S. News & World Report,* December 30, 1991/January 6, 1992, pp. 70–71.
''Financial Mergers: Complex Equations,'' *Economist,* June 5, 1999.
Hutchison, Robert A., *Off the Books,* New York: William Morrow and Company, 1986.
Lee, Peter, ''Is Citi Back from the Dead?,'' *Euromoney,* December 1992, p. 30.
Leindorf, David, and Donald Etra, *Ralph Nader's Study Group Report on First National City Bank,* New York: Grossman, 1973.
Meeham, John, and William Glasgall, ''Citi's Nightmares Just Keep Getting Worse,'' *Business Week,* October 28, 1991, pp. 124–25.
''The Trials of Megabanks,'' *Economist,* October 31, 1998.
''Watch out for the Egos,'' *Economist,* April 11, 1998.

—Edna M. Hedblad
—updated by Susan Windisch Brown

Cobham plc

Brook Road
Wimborne
Dorset
BH21 2BJ
United Kingdom
+44 (0) 1202 882020
Fax: +44 (0) 1202 840523
Web site: http://www.cobham.com

Public Company
Incorporated: 1934 as Flight Refuelling Limited
Employees: 5,300
Sales:£384.1 million (1998)
Stock Exchanges: London
Ticker: FRG
NAIC: 336411 Aircraft Manufacturing; 336413 Other
    Aircraft Parts & Auxiliary Equipment Manufacturing;
    54171 Research & Development in the Physical,
    Engineering, & Life Sciences

From its beginnings as an aerospace job shop and purveyor of some of aviation's first air-to-air refueling systems, Cobham plc has grown to become an indispensable link in the most advanced European military and civil aerospace programs. Cobham is divided into three divisions, Manufacturing, Avionics, and Flight Operations and Services. These divisions market a wide variety of products and services to the aerospace, defense, industrial, and communications industries. In addition to aerial refueling equipment and related services, the company produces or assists among other things in the development of rotary joints, antennas and radar systems, search and rescue equipment, anti-armor weapon launchers, and shallow water diving systems, and also operates a helicopter flight training school.

Audacious Origins

Although best known today for his namesake aerospace firm, Alan John Cobham took a somewhat circuitous route to aviation. He was enthusiastic about geography studies as a child and, as a teenager, he developed a hobby of building large kites.

Nonetheless, at age 15 Cobham apprenticed at a garment wholesalers' firm. A brief stint at farming came three years later, followed by lingerie sales back in London. By this time, World War I had broken out. Unable to enlist otherwise, Cobham used his farming experience to gain a slot in the Army Veterinary Corps. He was sent to France and given the daunting task of tending up to 1,500 ill and injured horses. In spite of the continuing demand for veterinary assistance, Cobham (with the help of a family friend connected to the War Office) managed a transfer to the Royal Flying Corps, where he could work in a field he felt had a more secure future.

In spite of his curtailed education, Cobham passed aviation ground school. He survived flight training in the unreliable machines of the day and became a flying instructor in August 1918. His first assignment was restoring the confidence of aviators who had crashed.

After the war, Cobham landed a brief job scouting potential airfields for the British Aerial Transport Company. He later teamed with two other pilots giving pleasure flights in the Berkshire area. Soon the group was barnstorming as far north as Scotland. In Yorkshire, Cobham met an actress who would become his wife, Gladys Lloyd.

The Berkshire Aviation Company venture faltered in 1920 as the novelty of airplanes wore off, and Cobham found himself selling ladies' clothing again. A promising engagement taking aerial photographs with Airco was curtailed by that company's bankruptcy.

Newly liberated Airco designer Geoffrey de Havilland formed his own aircraft manufacture and hire service with Cobham as his pilot. The first client was Aerofilms, which had received Airco's assets in the liquidation. Cobham helped de Havilland conceptualize his wildly popular "Moth" series of aircraft, a legendary design which helped popularize flying in Britain.

In order to promote de Havillands, Cobham set out upon a series of aerial exploits that included setting a speed record for flying to Africa and back. He toured Europe with the wealthy American Epicurean Lucien Sharpe. He flew to Burma via India to investigate the possibility of air service there. A subsequent trip to Cape Horn, in which Cobham raced a passenger ship on the way back, generated enormous press coverage.

In 1926, Cobham flew to Australia. Tragically, his engineer was killed by a hunter over Iraq. Nevertheless, he returned a hero. A crowd of one million watched him land on the Thames in front of Parliament upon his return. He was knighted at age 32 after this great adventure.

Cobham formed his own company, Alan Cobham Aviation Ltd., in 1927. The firm soon merged with the North Sea Aerial and General Transport Company Ltd., which also was interested in developing intercontinental flying boat service. The new firm was known as Cobham-Blackburn Airlines.

Cobham organized a voyage around the African continent in a Short-Rolls Royce Singapore. After the grueling African trip, he flew around Britain urging local politicians to create new airports. However, government-backed Imperial Airways stole his thunder, establishing its own service to southern Africa. Cobham-Blackburn Airlines closed in July 1930.

Soon after, Cobham joined the board of the new Airstream Company, replacing Neville Shute (Norway), who later became a famous novelist. In 1932, Cobham toured Britain with his National Aviation Days: These air shows introduced thousands of future aerospace professionals to flight. Cobham also founded a Guernsey Islands airline, Cobham Air Routes Ltd., which he soon sold.

A number of engineers had been pondering aerial refueling as a solution to power limitations of the planes of the day. Aircraft expended a great deal of energy climbing to altitude. If they were refueled in flight, they could carry heavier loads and fly longer distances. Cobham began experimenting with the concept, and soon took over the air Ministry's testing as well.

Although a demonstration trip to India ended in disaster in September 1934, Flight Refuelling, Limited soon incorporated on October 29, 1934. Cobham moved his operations to Ford Aerodrome in January 1936. With backing from new partner Imperial Airways, which took a 60 percent stake in the company, Cobham began to consistently work to improve the range of civil aircraft. A variety of configurations were tried.

World War II and Beyond

Flight Refuelling's civil work was halted by the war. Ford aerodrome, where the company had facilities, was first taken over by the Admiralty and then bombed by the Germans. The British government relocated the firm to the Morgan Motor Works where it engineered problems for Bomber Command, for example, the problem of wing icing. It also experimented towing fighters to altitude.

Cobham's suggestions to use in-flight refueling to make possible aerial escorts of North Atlantic shipping were neglected. Late in the war, the firm was called upon to help in a plan to bomb Japan via Burma, using in-flight refueling. Flight Refuelling got an order to convert 600 Lincoln bombers and 600 Lancaster tankers. The plan was canceled when American forces captured an island within flying range of Japan, however.

After the war, the U.S. government expressed interest in using aerial refueling to extend the range of its B-29 bombers, and Cobham landed a contract for US$1.25 million. What really interested the Americans was the prospect of refueling fighter aircraft. The new ''probe-and-drogue'' method allowed just that. FRL also assisted the U.S. Air Force in the historic around-the-world flight of a Boeing B-50A in February 1949. Boeing went on to develop the ''flying boom'' aerial refueling system adopted by the USAF.

Lucrative contracts were scarce after the war. FRL found some success selling pressure fueling equipment. During the Berlin Airlift, FR ferried fuel into the city. Cobham also briefly became involved with another short-lived airline which had bought the name ''Skyways.'' British South American Airways was formed to investigate south Atlantic service, and contracted with FRL for aerial refueling support. FRL also experimented with BOAC crews.

FRL began doing aircraft refurbishment in the 1950s, first on British Meteor jet fighters. The company later converted them into drones, leading it into the aerial target field. The company modified USAF tankers for use in the Korean War.

Sir Alan Cobham bought out his company's other shareholders in 1952. Flight Refuelling went public in 1955, taking the name Flight Refuelling (Holdings) Ltd. It spent the rest of the decade growing internally and making opportunistic acquisitions.

New Leadership in the 1960s

Sir Alan Cobham gradually passed leadership of the company to his son Michael in the 1960s. Michael Cobham was a trained barrister who had joined the company in 1955. He became managing director in 1964, although his father remained rather involved in the business until 1969. His style was less autocratic and more scientific than his father's. Sir Alan Cobham died in 1973.

Michael Cobham took over at a particularly challenging time for the company, as defense work was drying up. Contracts were also being awarded less on the strength of personal persuasiveness, Alan Cobham's strong suit, and more in terms of competitive bids. Management structure became more formal. The company's acquisition strategy would also be more systematic.

In order to survive, Flight Refuelling diversified. It formed Alan Cobham Engineering to provide high pressure fuel systems services to the oil and mining industries. It also began marketing the switch it used in its fueling systems, beginning the company's involvement in electronics. Aviation components became a strong part of the company's business, particularly after it acquired the aviation division of Saunders Valve.

Several R&D projects came to fruition in the mid-1970s. At this time, Michael Cobham delegated the role of managing director to Ken Coates, although Cobham retained a substantial voice due to his 25 percent shareholding. The Cobham board of directors, however, pressed Coates for more rapid growth than had been achieved previously.

FRL had been organized on functional lines, with one sales force for all its different customers. Coates organized the company into three divisions: nuclear and industrial business (which had been losing money) ; military systems; and aerospace components. Improved financial reporting helped the company define its strengths.

The aerospace industry grew rapidly in the late 1970s. However, the company's electronics operation fared poorly in the fast pace of that industry's growth. Nuclear plant components suffered due to inconsistent government policies. The company shifted its efforts in this field toward defense. The flight operations division suffered from defense cuts, but fought back by expanding its range of services beyond aerial towing.

Turnover reached £19 million in 1980. Profits were £3 million. Aerospace components accounted for 40 percent of turnover; military systems, approximately 30 percent. *Management Today* ranked Flight Refuelling, which then had 1,200 employees, Britain's most profitable engineering firm.

Coates aimed to triple FR's business within five years. In 1982, FR entered the vast U.S. components market via its £5.15 million purchase of Stanley Aviation. FR had previously manufactured Stanley pipes under license in Europe. The purchase gave FR a stronger presence with the U.S. military than it could have attained on its own. To reflect its broad range of activities, Flight Refuelling (Holdings) Ltd. was renamed FR Group in 1985. The group acquired Chelton, a leading maker of aircraft antennas, in 1989.

FR had to contend with the vagaries of defense spending, and the recession prompted ''financial discipline'' from the Ministry of Defense. However, the Falklands War brought new demand for the company's services. FRL teamed with Grumman to bid on a huge U.S. Navy contract for inflight refueling. Its aerial target offerings proliferated, culminating in the Advanced Subsonic Aerial Target (ASAT). It also pushed its military wares abroad and looked for new product opportunities.

Air-to-air refueling was another economical way for air forces to extend their reach: a ''force multiplier.'' However, this very power made its export subject to close government scrutiny. Onboard fuel systems were one important export, however; FR shipped half of this production to Europe, where it claimed a 50 percent market share. While British aircraft production was at a near standstill, the company was able to supply about every European aircraft program with some type of component. The company vied to be chosen for a wide spectrum of planes still in the design stages—which resulted in a steady supply of work and a wealth of engineering knowledge in reserve.

During the Persian Gulf War, allied forces discovered first-hand the shortcomings of a dual approach to air-to-air refueling. While U.S. naval aircraft refueled using Alan Cobham's probe-and-drogue system, U.S. Air Force (USAF) planes used an incompatible boom-and-socket method. Operation Desert Storm brought many different forces into play, and the shortage of appropriate tankers added a new level of complexity for military planners. FR subsequently went to work retrofitting USAF tankers with probe-and-drogue refueling pods allowing them to service naval aircraft. FR sent training and support personnel to the Persian Gulf, a trend predicted to continue owing to shrinking military force sizes. FR's annual sales were £185 million (US$296 million) in 1993, when the company had 3,500 employees. Military sales accounted for 70 percent of the total.

Diamond Jubilee: 1994

FR Group renamed itself Cobham plc in November 1994. Its operations had long since expanded beyond its flight refueling core. This also marked the 100th anniversary of Sir Alan Cobham's birth.

In October 1994, FR bought Sargent Fletcher, a U.S. aerial refueling company, for US$11 million. Sargent Fletcher added helicopter refueling capabilities. It bought Comant Industries, a California company making GPS antennas, for US$3.25 million. Comant and the French antenna company Rayan SA were placed under the Chelton subsidiary.

Board member Sir Michael Knight replaced the retiring Michael Cobham in July 1995. Defense spending was tight. Though Knight continued Cobham's course for expansion, broad diversification was not on the agenda. ''We will not make electric kettles,'' he told a *Jane's* interviewer. Cobham aimed to be a leader in all the markets it entered. Acquisitions and internal growth doubled Cobham's size within a few months. Cobham employed 4,000 personnel worldwide in 1996.

Cobham also strived to reduce costs while improving products. Trends in the aircraft industry were for prime contractors to outsource larger assemblies from vendors. The company directed much of its efforts towards upgrades and upgradeable products. The defense contracts it won tended to be for upgrades. In 1996 British Aerospace and Cobham won a contract to refurbish the Royal Air Force's Nimrod maritime patrol aircraft. Their strategy was to extend the life of each plane by replacing high-stress areas of the aircraft such as wing sections. The company was also chosen to manufacture the unmanned aerial vehicle for the British Army's Phoenix artillery surveillance system.

FR Aviation teamed with Bristow Helicopters and Serco Defense Ltd. to establish a joint service military helicopter training school. The joint venture was termed FBS Ltd. The joint service program was expected to save £77 million (US$120 million) over 15 years, largely through the use of newer, more efficient helicopters.

In the late 1990s, Cobham was developing several air-to-air refueling programs. It cooperated with Boeing to retrofit USAF KC-135 tankers with probe-and-drogue systems. Since the cost of converting the Air Force's F-15 and F-16 fighters to this system was prohibitively expensive, Sargent Fletcher created an aerial-refueling tank system (ART/S) that featured an external fuel tank with a probe fitted directly to it. Lockheed Martin chose Flight Refuelling to supply refueling pods for its new KC-130J Hercules tankers.

Cobham continued its growth by acquisition strategy, buying a small maker of lightweight pressure vessels in March 1998. Pressure Technologies Inc. of Baltimore, Maryland, cost the company US$1.3 million (£800,000). Cobham acquired Conax Corporation in May 1998 for US$5.9 million (£3.6 million). Conax, headquartered in St. Petersburg, Florida, made aerospace products such as emergency life support systems. In December, Cobham bought a French maker of communications components, Hyper Technologies SA, for FFr 11.5 million (£1.2 million). The company also stripped off non-core properties.

Annual turnover increased in 1998 from £322.8 million to £384.1 million. Profits reached £63.6 million. About 55 percent came from the military; the rest was civil. Cobham's largest division was Manufacturing, with a turnover of £236.8 million. Avionics had £89.6 million and Flight Operations and Services, £57.7 million.

The group continued to buy businesses in 1999, including certain product lines from Avionics Controls Inc. Chelton bought Flitefone and Bendix King Series III radio product lines from Allied Signal for US$7.7 million (£4.7 million). Cobham spent US$26.8 million (£16.5 million) for ACR Electronics Inc., a Florida firm specializing in marine search and rescue equipment. Cobham bought two other English firms: Credowan Limited, a small microwave components supplier, and the larger European Antennas Limited, which cost £6.75 million.

Cobham's Stanley Aviation and Flight Refuelling subsidiaries worked on the fuel system development for the Boeing X32 Joint Strike Fighter. Cobham also supplied its competitor, Lockheed's X35. Besides the busy military schedules, increased production of Airbus civil airliners and Embraer regional jets helped create record demand for the group's antennas. One area of business that was particularly hard-hit in the late 1990s was Cobham's Westwind subsidiary, which was a long time in recovering from the Asian financial crisis.

Principal Subsidiaries

Alan Cobham Engineering Limited; Carleton Technologies Inc. (U.S.A.); Conax Florida Corporation (U.S.A.); Flight Refuelling Limited; Westwind Air Bearings Limited; Stanley Aviation Corporation (U.S.A.); Chelton (Electrostatics) Limited; FR Aviation Limited.

Principal Divisions

Manufacturing; Avionics; Flight Operations and Services.

Further Reading

Cruddas, Colin, *In Cobhams' Company,* Wimborne, Dorset: Cobham plc, 1994.
Newman, Nicholas, ''Flight Refuelling's Opened Throttle,'' *Management Today,* June 1982, pp. 50–57, 121–29.
Pohling-Brown, Pamela, ''JDSM Talks to . . . Sir Michael Knight,'' *Jane's Defence Systems Modernisation,* September 1, 1996, p. 26.
Reed, Carol, ''FR Group Takes Name of Founding Pioneer,'' *Jane's Defence Weekly,* November 19, 1994, p. 12.

—Frederick C. Ingram

Coborn's, Inc.

1445 East Highway 23
St. Cloud, Minnesota 56302
U.S.A.
(320) 252-4222
Fax: (320) 252-0014

Private Company
Incorporated: 1957
Employees: 4,082
Sales: $480 million (1998 est.)
NAIC: 44511 Supermarkets & Other Grocery (Except Convenience) Stores; 44711 Gasoline Stations with Convenience Stores; 445310 Liquor Stores, Package

Coborn's, Inc. is a supermarket, convenience, and liquor retailer which ranked number 21 in *Corporate Report*'s listing of top 100 private companies in the state of Minnesota. Most of the company's facilities are located in the upper Midwest, with 13 Coborn's supermarkets, ten Cash Wise Food Stores, 15 Little Dukes convenience stores, six stand-alone video rental stores, 14 Coborn's and Cash Wise Liquor stores, 18 pharmacies (mostly in stores), and Coborn's Central Bakery and Central Floral in St. Cloud, Minnesota. In 1999 Coborn's was named one of the ten most generous companies in the United States by *George* magazine.

Beginning with Produce: 1921

Coborn's was founded in 1921 by Chester Coborn who opened a produce market in Sauk Rapids, Minnesota. Within a few years Chester added dry goods and grocery items to the selection, as the company continued to prosper. Having lived through the Great Depression era, Chester resisted the use of borrowed funds to fuel expansion, although he allowed his customers to buy on credit. The small-town business was carefully tended and the company enjoyed steady growth. After his death, Chester's two sons, Chester, Jr., and Duke, continued running the family market. The Coborn brothers purchased a walk-in cooler in 1936, enabling them to enter the meat-

retailing business. Consistent with rural practices of the time, cattle were bought and bartered for, then slaughtered and packaged on the store premises. Chester, Jr., left the business during that period and moved near Walker, Minnesota, to start a resort business. He died in 1959.

Coborn's implemented a cash and carry policy in 1952—no longer extending credit—reflecting the problems involved in offering credit to friends, neighbors, and others who were the company's mainstay. Keeping pace with the times, the company changed from a sole proprietorship to a corporation in 1957. Three years later Duke Coborn died, leaving management of the business to his four sons: Dan, Ron, Bill, and Robert. They soon realized that expansion was necessary in order to provide solid incomes for each of them and their families. The brothers worked on the development of a growth strategy based on demographic studies of niche markets, including markets in surrounding states. They planned to expand by means of acquisitions in areas where they believed they could become the dominant food retailer. Coborn's purchased a supermarket in Willmar, Minnesota, but it failed miserably due to strong competition by larger retailers. Reacting to that situation, Coborn's changed from a conventional supermarket layout to a discount warehouse format, named it Cash Wise, and leased a 30,000-square-foot space to try out the new concept. The format change was inspired by Supervalu's Minnesota-based Cub Foods chain of warehouse stores. Cash Wise became number one in that market within two years. Serving as corporate headquarters, a more modern store was built in Sauk Rapids, which featured the company's first deli, a scratch bakery, and sausage kitchen. Since that time, the company strategy focused on using the traffic flow generated by the grocery business to boost sales for new ventures.

Continual Expansion: 1960s–80s

A second store was opened in Foley, Minnesota, purchased from Red Owl in 1963. Recognizing the potential for marketing near the State College and the St. Cloud downtown area, Coborn's bought an old brick building from the local power company, using the facility for its market. Later, an offsale liquor store was established adjacent to the supermarket. That proved so

Company Perspectives:

Our mission is to operate efficiently, which will allow for future growth and stability. Our business practices will follow the Golden Rule: Treat all *with dignity and respect: We will strive to exceed our customers' expectations by surpassing our competition in all areas of business operations. We will be the preferred employer providing fair and consistent treatment and opportunities for growth, while expecting the employee's best. We will develop effective long-term business relationships that best serve the needs of our customers. We will support the communities we serve with our time, talent, and financial resources. Our future is dependent on working as a team in fulfilling the above commitments and responsibilities to be the best.*

successful that Coborn's decided to locate future liquor stores in or adjacent to the company's supermarkets or warehouse stores. At the Willmar Cash Wise site, Coborn's added a pharmacy, floral department, deli cafe, and a meat/fish department. Another warehouse-format store was opened in Waite Park, Minnesota, with a liquor store that was later relocated across the parking lot to allow room for easy shopper access to the deli/bakery, video, floral, and dry cleaning businesses.

Next in its expansion efforts, Coborn's bought the fixtures and inventory of the Piggly Wiggly grocery store in St. Cloud, reopened the site as its own supermarket, and expanded to include room for a pharmacy. Close in proximity to Sauk Rapids, Little Falls became the location of a 60,000-square-foot building, erected by the company for use as a mall-supermarket/liquor store—and with space to spare, part of the building was leased to White Mart. Later expansion of the site provided room for a pharmacy and a Hallmark store. Coborn's purchased a small supermarket in a strip mall near St. Cloud in Sartell, Minnesota. Within a few years the thriving business justified the construction of a new store directly behind the old one. Following on the successful establishment of the Sartell strip mall business, the company anchored another supermarket in touristy Clearwater, Minnesota, in 1979 and again added a liquor store adjacent to the market.

Complementing its meat and deli-foods operations, Coborn's bought Hunstiger's Sausage Kitchen, making it into a state-of-the-art centralized processing facility. The plant, DBC Foods, supplied all of the Coborn's stores with sausage, smoked meats, and other specialty items as well as deli salads and other prepared deli foods. Their food brand, called Aunt Mabel, was prepared at DBC. Coborn's central bakery was moved to St. Cloud, accommodating all of its stores with daily fresh baked goods.

First Out-Of-State Location: 1985

A great deal of discussion and debate preceded the decision to open a Cash Wise Foods store in a strip center in Mason City, Iowa. It became the first food store with a wine and liquor department inside the store premises, an amenity not legally sanctioned in the state of Minnesota. Another Cash Wise Foods

was established in Hutchinson, Minnesota, located in a building previously occupied by a Pamida Discount Store. The new store was so successful that a newer store was built directly across the street, doubling the size of the first location. Also during this time period, the company moved into Fargo, North Dakota, opening the largest of its stores to date, which included a floral and parcel pick-up department.

Coborn's acquired the Elks Club building in St. Cloud and converted it to a new corporate headquarters, followed by the construction of a 26,000-square-foot warehouse Distribution Center. The company also centralized its dry cleaning operations. Coborn's purchased Top Cleaners of St. Cloud and invested in new equipment to maximize efficiencies which provided cleaning services for Coborn's other dry cleaning operations. In 1986, the company completed its first Little Duke's convenience store in St. Cloud. The convenience store format, offering gas and groceries, was considered a natural extension to the company's supermarket and liquor stores. Dan Coborn explained the company's rationale: ''All the Little Dukes sell gasoline, and the grocery stores bring a lot of cars to the site.'' The company's first car wash introduced at the Little Dukes of Waite Park and was so well received that a second ''touchless'' car wash was added. Prior to 1998, 11 Little Duke's stores were opened, typically on or near existing properties already owned by the company. Always striving for efficiencies, the company implemented a service called Mobile Speedpass, a payment system which worked when customers waved a one-inch plastic transponder (in the form of a key tag) before a sensor on the gas-pump. The customer did not need to carry a wallet or credit cards because gas bills were paid electronically and automatically, allowing the customer to drive away after fueling without ever having to enter the store. Under the system payments were automatically withdrawn from the customer's pre-designated credit card.

Four new stores were purchased from Holiday Foods in 1996. Holiday Stationstores was a retail division of Holiday Companies of Minneapolis, owners of Fairway Foods, a Northfield, Minnesota-based wholesaler. The purchased stores were located in Long Prairie (which included a deli and sit-down eating area), Morris, Mora, and Princeton, Minnesota. Under their agreement, Coborn's made Fairway its primary supplier rather than buying almost equally from Fairway and the Nash Finch Company of Minneapolis. Nash Finch continued as a secondary supplier for the chain. It was expected that the new Coborn's markets would increase sales by 12 percent for the year. Two more Holiday Stationstores were converted to the Coborn's and Cash Wise banners by 1997.

Striving to compete with establishments in the Twin Cities area, Coborn's acquired the Sax Food and Drug Store in Elk River, which featured two entrances and a sit-down deli with glass atriums extending two stories high. Another upscale supermarket followed, newly constructed in Sauk Centre with an attached offsale liquor store complementing the grocery business. Other markets were opened in Owatonna, Moorhead, Brainerd, and Austin, Minnesota; and another North Dakota operation was opened in Bismarck.

Recognizing the great potential for profit in the video rental business, Coborn's upgraded the video rental departments in two of the five stores it acquired from Holiday Companies and several other of their stores were also being considered for the video rental program. Managers increased the number of new releases and modified the pricing to give the customer better value, along with upgrading and refurbishing new signs. Coborn's President Don Wetter said that the reasons for developing multi-dimensional holdings that rotate around the food business had to do with convenience. In his words, "Certainly today, with dual-working family members, they're looking for convenience. The more we can provide in one location, a one-step type of thing, the better the consumer likes it." The company planned to continue evaluating different types of services consumers might appreciate in the food distribution arena, including the expansion of marketing via computers and electronics. Wetter noted in an interview with Mike Killeen of the *St. Cloud Times* that in some parts of the country consumers have already begun shopping via computer, which involved having the goods picked up and delivered to them.

In May 1999, Coborn's was honored by *George* magazine for being one of the ten most generous companies in America. Selected from more than 400 nominees, the award was sponsored by actor Paul Newman and *George,* published by the late John F. Kennedy, Jr., and was meant to honor good citizenship through philanthropy. Other finalists included Bell South, The Home Depot, Kenneth Cole Productions, and MTV Networks. At the award ceremony, John F. Kennedy, Jr., said he hoped the award encouraged "more companies like Coborn's to give back to their communities by investing in and supporting causes that effectively address local, regional, or national problems," according to the *St. Cloud Times*. CEO Dan Coborn said, "The community has been very good to us and it was our responsibility to put something back," adding, "we're not unique in the community by any means." The Coborn family symbolized a heritage of community volunteerism and instilled the same beliefs in the day-to-day operations of its business. Coborn's promoted charitable contributions through: donations to nonprofit agencies and organizations in all communities in which it conducted business; development and promotion of a community leaders volunteer program for employees; initiation of social and human service programs to meet community need;

support for education of youth and scholarship programs; and as a leading contributor to such organizations as United Way. Coborn's provided more than $2 million in annual contributions through direct financial support, in-kind products and services, and human resources, a significant amount considering the notoriously slim profitability margins in the grocery trade.

Confident that a capable management team was in place, Dan Coborn stepped down as CEO of Coborn's in July 1999, after leading the family business for over 37 years. He remained active as a board member. Of the other three brothers, only Bill continued in management, as the company's vice-president and secretary. (Robert had retired in 1989 and Ron had died in 1993.) Nonfamily member and CPA Don Wetter moved up from his position as president to fill Dan's shoes as CEO. He had been with the company since 1974, beginning as a corporate controller. Wetter told Lisa McClintick of the *St. Cloud Times* that his "strengths are in the finance arena." For the future he anticipated numerous mergers and consolidations in the grocery industry. Coborn's, Inc. planned to maintain its family atmosphere, but could be expected to expand its operations in existing stores and continue prudently buying or building new ones.

Principal Divisions

Cash Wise Foods and Liquor; DBC Foods; Little Duke's.

Further Reading

Alaimo, Dan, "Coborn's Upgrading Two Video Sections in Acquisitions," *Supermarket News*, September 2, 1996, p. 39.

Blamey, Pamela, "Meat Study Reveals Data's Value," *Supermarket News*, October 9, 1995, p. 41.

"Coborn's Named One of Ten Most Generous Companies in America," *St. Cloud Times,* May 30, 1999.

McClintick, Lisa, "Coborn's Executive Hands Off Business," *St. Cloud Times*, June 26, 1999, p. 3A.

Sternman, Mike, "Coborn's Caps Conversion of Holiday Units," *Supermarket News,* March 17, 1997, p. 26.

—Terri Mozzone

The Coleman Company, Inc.

2111 East 37th Street North
Wichita, Kansas 67219
U.S.A.
(316) 832-2700
(800) 835-3278
Fax: (316) 832-3060
Web site: http://www.coleman.com

Public Subsidiary of Sunbeam Corporation
Incorporated: 1900 as the Hydro-Carbon Light Company
Employees: 4,700
Sales: $1.02 billion (1998)
Stock Exchanges: New York Pacific Midwest
Ticker Symbol: CLN
NAIC: 33992 Sporting & Athletic Good Manufacturing;
   335129 Other Lighting Equipment Manufacturing;
   333912 Air & Gas Compressor Manufacturing;
   335312 Motors & Generator Manufacturing; 421910
   Camping Equipment & Supplies Wholesaling

The Coleman Company, Inc. is one of the most famous and successful manufacturers of camping equipment and outdoor recreational products. The well-known Coleman lamp was invented by 1909 and the lantern in 1914, and since that time more than 50 million of the lanterns have been sold throughout the world. Coleman is the market leader in lanterns and stoves for outdoor recreational use, and it has created a loyal consumer following for a broad range of insulated food and beverage containers, sleeping bags, backpacks, tents, outdoor folding furniture, portable electric lights, and other recreational accessories. The company's Powermate unit produces portable generators and portable and stationary air compressors. Coleman also makes and markets book bags, backpacks, and related products under the Eastpak and Timberland brand names. Coleman products are sold in more than 100 countries worldwide, with international sales accounting for about one-third of overall revenues. Although its stock is publicly traded, the Coleman Company is controlled by Sunbeam Corporation, which owns 79 percent of the company.

Bright Beginnings

The founder of the company, William Coffin Coleman, was born to a young couple who migrated west to Kansas from New England in 1871. Coleman became a schoolteacher in Kansas and later entered the University of Kansas Law School. Shortly before receiving his degree, however, Coleman ran out of money, and he became a traveling typewriter salesman. Working the southern part of the United States, he found himself in Brockton, Alabama, a poor coal mining community with dirt streets and wood sidewalks.

According to company lore, as Coleman was taking an evening walk down one of the town's streets, he noticed the intense white glow of a lamp in a drugstore window. The lamp, which was powered by gasoline, was so bright that even with his bad eyesight Coleman was able to read under it easily. Since most people at that time used flickering gaslights, smoky oil lamps, or dim carbon filament light bulbs, Coleman immediately saw the lamp as an important step forward.

Coleman arranged to sell this new type of lamp for the Irby-Gilliland Company of Memphis, and traveled to Kingfisher, Oklahoma, to begin his new venture. Unfortunately, he had sold only two lamps at the end of the first week. The lack of sales dismayed him, but he soon discovered that another salesman had previously sold dozens of lamps to the town's shopkeepers. Since the lamps could not be cleaned, they clogged with carbon deposits which snuffed the light out after a short time. The salesman had left a bit too quickly, and the shopkeepers felt swindled.

Unable to sell his lamps, Coleman hit upon the idea of leasing them for $1 per week and servicing them himself. If the lamps failed, the customer did not have to pay. Revenues skyrocketed. In order to remain competitive almost all the town's shopkeepers purchased his lighting service. The business flourished as Coleman reinvested profits and branched out into neighboring communities. Not long afterward, he founded the Hydro-Carbon Light Company.

With the demand for his lamps and lighting service increasing, Coleman received $2,000 from his two brothers-in-law for an eight percent interest in the company. In 1902 requests for

his lighting service were so numerous that he decided to move
the business to Wichita, Kansas, and establish a permanent
headquarters. One year later, Coleman bought the rights to the
Efficient Lamp, improved its design, and began selling it as the
Coleman Arc Lamp. Ever on the lookout for original ways to
market his lamps, Coleman in 1905 arranged for the Arc Lamps
to provide the lighting for a night football game.

Wartime Contributions

By 1909 Coleman had invented a portable table lamp with a
gasoline tank designed as a small fount with a flat base. Bug
screens were later added to protect the mantles during outdoor
use. In 1914 the company developed the Coleman gasoline
lantern for use in inclement weather. When World War I broke
out, the Allies requested U.S. wheat and corn to replenish their
food supplies. Realizing the need for a reliable, bright, and
portable light for farmers carrying out the tasks necessary to aid
the Europeans, the American government declared the Coleman
lamp essential for the wartime support effort and provided Coleman with both money and materials to produce the lanterns.
During World War I, the company made over one million lamps
for American farmers.

The company grew steadily in the 1920s. Although electricity came to the smaller towns across the United States, most
rural areas had to wait. Coleman thus found its largest markets
in rural areas, with ever increasing sales of gasoline stoves, used
both as camp stoves and cook stoves, and lamps and lanterns.
The company also established international operations with a
manufacturing plant and headquarters in Toronto. Locating an
office in Canada was a smart move on the part of Coleman,
since the British Commonwealth gave preferential tariffs and
duties to products made in member nations. By the end of the
1920s the reputation of the Coleman lantern was firmly established, and various accounts of its use were reported: Admiral
Byrd used the lantern on his trip to the South Pole; on Pitcairn
Island the descendants of British mutineers from the *Bounty* and
their Tahitian families illuminated primitive homes with Coleman lanterns; and Coleman lantern-lit runways in the Andes
made emergency landings possible.

The company was not entirely successful in developing new
products and markets. During the late 1920s, Coleman made a
line of waffle irons, coffee percolators, toasters, and electric
irons. Coleman could not, however, compete with Westinghouse Electric Corporation and General Electric Company and
withdrew these product lines quickly. William Coffin Coleman

(known as W.C. to the rest of the company) designed a coffee
maker for restaurants and hotels. Although it brewed excellent
coffee, the machine was complicated to handle and difficult to
clean. It was commercially unsuccessful and the company
halted its production.

Coleman was hit very hard when the stock market crashed in
1929. During the next two years, the Great Depression severely
affected almost every industry in the nation. The demand for
Coleman products declined rapidly, mainly due to the searing
poverty and inability of many people in rural areas to purchase
anything other than food. Inevitably, the company experienced
financial losses, but a good working relationship with a number
of banks helped Coleman to overcome the worst years of the
depression. In 1932 the company's sales totaled a mere $3
million, but a small profit was made.

After Franklin Delano Roosevelt was elected to the U.S.
presidency in 1932, he launched a massive program for rural
electrification, and Coleman was faced with a decline in its
market for gasoline stoves and lights. Nevertheless, Coleman
found two potentially profitable markets, oil space heaters and
gas floor furnaces, and by the end of the decade the company
was the leading manufacturer of both products. At the same
time, Coleman's portable stove and lantern business was making headway in the camping equipment market, and the international operation was beginning to reap significant profits. In
1941 the company reported annual sales of $9 million.

When World War II began, Coleman was called upon to
manufacture products for the various branches of the U.S.
armed services, including 20-millimeter shells for the Army,
projectiles for the Navy, and parts for the B-29 and B-17
bombers for the Air Force. In June 1942 the company was
notified by the Army Quartermaster Corps with an urgent
request—field troops needed a compact stove that could operate
at 125 degrees above and 60 degrees below zero, was no larger
than a quart bottle of milk, and could burn any kind of fuel.
Moreover, the Army wanted 5,000 of the stoves delivered in
two months.

Coleman worked nonstop to design and manufacture a stove
to the Army's specifications. The end product was better than
the Army had requested: the stove could work at 60 degrees
below and 150 degrees above Fahrenheit; it could burn all kinds
of fuel; it weighed a mere three and one-half pounds; and it was
smaller than a quart bottle of milk. The first order for 5,000 units
was flown to U.S. forces involved in the November 1942
invasion of North Africa. Ernie Pyle, the famous World War II
journalist who wrote about the common man's experience in the
war, devoted 15 articles to the Coleman pocket stove and considered it one of the two most important pieces of noncombat
equipment in the war effort, the other being the Jeep.

When the war ended, Coleman's business boomed. Since the
company had been manufacturing products for the armed services during the war, there was an enormous backlog of demand
for its regular products, which had been off the market. Sales
rose to $34 million by 1950, while profits also substantially
increased. At the start of the decade, there were four main
divisions of Coleman products: oil space heaters accounted for
30 percent of sales; gas floor furnaces, 30 percent; camp stove
and gasoline lanterns, 20 percent; and military contracts to

supply Boeing Co. with airplane parts for the B-47 bomber, 20 percent.

Camping and Recreational Product Focus: 1960s–70s

In the early 1950s, Coleman was the leader in sales in each of its civilian product lines. At the end of the decade, however, sales for oil heaters and gas floor furnaces alone dropped a whopping 85 percent, and by 1960 the company suffered an overall loss of 70 percent in sales volume. The U.S. military had also phased out Coleman's contracts for airplane parts. In response, Coleman developed its camp stove and lantern products into an extensive line of camping equipment. The company's portable ice chests and insulated jugs quickly became leaders in the field of outdoor recreation products. Coleman also expanded its line of oil, gas, and electric furnaces to manufacturers of mobile homes, and began designing air conditioning equipment and furnaces for onsite homes.

During the 1960s, Coleman continued to expand its product lines in the field of camping, adding sleeping bags, tents, and catalytic heaters; Coleman soon became the leading manufacturer of camping equipment. Growing along with the mobile home industry, Coleman supplied 40 percent of the specialized furnaces and 50 percent of the air conditioning equipment for mobile homes. Sales grew from $38 million in 1960 to $134 million by 1970, and during the same period net profits increased dramatically from $278,000 to $7 million.

The two leaders of the company were Sheldon Coleman, who replaced his father as chairman of the board in 1941, and Lawrence M. Jones, a longtime employee of Coleman who possessed a doctorate from Harvard University. Sheldon had hired Jones as president of the company in 1964, and the two men collaborated on product development and market strategy. Their joint effort resulted in the manufacture of adjustable backpack frames, a compact cooler, a small backpack stove, canoes made from a petroleum-based substance that created a quieter ride than aluminum, Crosman air guns, and camping trailers. In 1977 Coleman's success continued unabated, with sales reaching $256 million. The company's outdoor recreation business seemed to be recession-proof, and profits from its mobile home products kept increasing.

Ownership Changes: 1980s–90s

For more than three-quarters of a century, Coleman had worked hard to establish and maintain a reputation for high quality products sold at reasonable prices. This reputation paid off handsomely during the 1980s as both profits and sales increased steadily. According to *Fortune,* however, the Coleman family, who owned 25 percent of the company's stock, began withdrawing profits rather than reinvesting for product development and market expansion. Sheldon Coleman, Jr., replaced his father as chairman of the board in 1988, and only one year later he decided to privatize the company in order to reap an even larger profit—the pension plan of the company was overloaded by approximately $30 million.

The new chairman floated an offer of $64 per share for the company's stock. The bid proved too low, and ill-timed as well.

Instead, New York financier Ronald Perelman entered the scene and purchased Coleman for $545 million, or $74 per share, in a 1989 leveraged buyout through his company MacAndrews & Forbes Holdings Inc. Together, Perelman and Jones sold the heating and air-conditioning business, shut down an obsolete factory, and implemented a strategy that improved efficiency and ultimately reduced inventory costs by $10 million.

Through a comprehensive restructuring of its operations, the company increased productivity significantly in 1991, and Coleman's sales reached $346.1 million by the end of the year. In 1992 sales increased to $491.9 million, proof that the company's concentration on manufacturing products in growing recreational markets was paying off. Perelman took Coleman public again during 1992 but retained an 82.5 percent stake in the company. In late 1992 Coleman reacquired the Coleman Powermate line of gasoline-powered electrical generators and high-pressure power washers. The following year the company aimed to bolster its overseas sales through acquisitions. Coleman had encountered difficulty over the years in Europe selling its propane-based camping appliances because Europeans generally preferred products running on butane gas. The purchase of British and Italian camping equipment makers in late 1993 led to the launch of dozens of Coleman brand butane products in Europe.

At the beginning of 1994 Jones retired and was replaced as chairman and CEO by Michael N. Hammes, who had been vice-chairman of the Black & Decker Corporation and president of its worldwide power tools and home products group. Acquisitions continued under the new executive. Added in 1994 were Sanborn Manufacturing Company, whose portable and stationary air compressors were folded into the Powermate division; and Eastpak, Inc., a maker of book bags, daypacks, and related products. The following year Coleman purchased Sierra Corporation of Fort Smith, Inc., maker of portable outdoor and recreational folding furniture under the Sierra Trails brand. In early 1996 the company expanded its Eastpak division by licensing the Timberland brand for a new line of packs. Coleman also acquired the France-based Application des Gaz, a leading European camping equipment maker under the Camping Gaz brand. Meanwhile, the 50 millionth Coleman lantern rolled off the assembly line in 1995.

The company's aggressive pursuit of acquisitions did not come without a cost. By 1996 Coleman had shown tremendous growth since being acquired by Perelman, as revenues reached $1.22 billion, three-and-a-half times the level of 1991—but the company also posted a net loss of $41.8 million. The loss was largely attributed to higher than expected costs related to integrating overseas sales forces following the purchase of Camping Gaz. Another key factor was mounting debt stemming from the string of acquisitions—the debt level having reached $583.6 million by the end of 1996.

On the heels of the announcement of the 1996 loss, Coleman replaced Hammes, installing Jerry W. Levin as acting CEO in February 1997. Levin had previously run the company from 1989 to April 1991 when he became CEO of Revlon Inc., another Perelman-controlled company. Under Levin's leadership, Coleman moved quickly to turn its fortunes around through a number of cost-cutting initiatives. The company closed its administrative headquarters in Golden, Colorado, and a regional headquarters in Geneva, Switzerland. The 7,000-person workforce was cut by ten percent. Four factories, three domestic and one international, were closed. Certain noncore product areas were divested, including power washers and portable spas. Finally, one-third of the company's SKUs were eliminated, greatly streamlining its product offerings.

In March 1998, with the company verging on a turnaround, Perelman sold his 82 percent stake in Coleman to Sunbeam Corporation for $1.6 billion plus the assumption of about $440 million in debt. At the same time Sunbeam announced two other purchases: Signature Brands USA Inc., maker of such household products as Mr. Coffee coffee makers and Health-o-meter scales; and First Alert Inc., a maker of residential safety products, including smoke alarms and fire extinguishers. Charges of accounting irregularities and misleading earnings reports led to the ouster of Sunbeam's CEO, "Chainsaw Al" Dunlap, in June 1998. Soon thereafter, Perelman, who had gained a 14 percent stake in Sunbeam as part of the sale of his Coleman stake, installed a new team at Sunbeam, including naming Levin as CEO. Dunlap had evidently laid plans to sell off Coleman's backpack and compressor businesses, plans that were quickly abandoned once Levin took over at Sunbeam. Nevertheless, with its new parent in extremely shaky financial condition, including being burdened by $2.2 billion in debt, Coleman faced a very uncertain future at the dawn of the 21st century.

Principal Subsidiaries

Application des Gaz, S.A. (France); Australian Coleman, Inc.; Kansas Bafiges S.A. (France); Beacon Exports, Inc.; C C Outlet, Inc.; C M O, Inc.; Camping Gaz do Brasil (Brazil); Camping Gaz Great Britain Limited (U.K.); Camping Gaz (Poland); Camping Gaz Suisse AG (Switzerland); Camping Gaz CS, Spol. SRO (Czech Republic); Camping Gaz GmbH (Austria); Camping Gaz International Deutschland GmbH (Germany); Camping Gaz Hellas (Greece); Camping Gaz International (Portugal) Ltd.; Camping Gaz Kft (Hungary); Camping Gaz Philippines, Inc.; Camping Gaz Italie Srl (Italy); Campiran SA (Iran); Coleman Argentina, Inc. (U.S.A.); Coleman Asia Limited (Hong Kong); Coleman Country, Ltd.; Coleman (Deutschland) GmbH (Germany); Coleman do Brasil Ltda. (Brazil); Coleman Europe N.V. (Belgium); Coleman Holland B.V. (Netherlands); Coleman International Holdings, LLC; Coleman International SARL (Switzerland); Coleman Japan Co., Ltd.; Coleman Lifestyles K.K. (Japan); Coleman Mexico S.A. de C.V.; Coleman Powermate Compressors, Inc.; Coleman Powermate, Inc.; Coleman Puerto Rico, Inc.; Coleman SARL (France); Coleman SVB S.r.l. (Italy); Coleman Taymar Limited (U.K.); Coleman U.K. Holdings Limited; Coleman U.K. PLC; Coleman Venture Capital, Inc.; Eastpak Corporation; Eastpak Manufacturing Corporation; Epigas International Limited (U.K.); General Archery Industries, Inc.; J G K, Inc.; Kansas Acquisition Corp.; Nippon Coleman, Inc.; Pearson Holdings, Inc.; Productos Coleman, S.A. (Spain); PT Camping Gaz Indonesia; River View Corporation of Barling, Inc.; Sierra Corporation of Fort Smith, Inc.; Sunbeam Corporation (Canada) Limited; TCCI Management Inc.; Taymar Gas Limited (U.K.); Tsana Internacional, S.A. (Costa Rica); Woodcraft Equipment Company.

Further Reading

Brannigan, Martha, "For Perelman, Sunbeam Stake Turns a Bit Pale," *Wall Street Journal,* June 4, 1998, p. C1.

Brooks, Rick, and Greg Jaffe, "Sunbeam's Not So Odd Couple," *Wall Street Journal,* March 3, 1998, p. B4.

Coleman Company, *Portrait of the Coleman Company: The First Hundred Years,* Wichita, Kans.: Coleman Company, 1999.

Coleman, Sheldon, and Lawrence Jones, *The Coleman Story: The Ability to Cope with Change,* New York: Newcomen Society, 1976, 28 p.

Doherty, Jacqueline, "Bulletproof Billionaire?," *Barron's,* May 19, 1997, pp. 18, 20.

Dorfman, Dan, "Coleman: No Happy Campers," *Financial World,* April 15, 1997, p. 28.

——, "Coleman Seen Following Marvel As Perelman's Next Disaster," *Financial World,* March 18, 1997, p. 14.

Dumaine, Brian, "Earning More by Moving Faster," *Fortune,* October 7, 1991, pp. 89–94.

Gallagher, Leigh, "Coleman Brass Flexes Muscle and Stakes Out New Terrain," *Sporting Goods Business,* April 1996, p. 28.

——, "Coleman Shutters CO Office in Cost-Cutting Strategy," *Sporting Goods Business,* May 12, 1997, p. 18.

——, "The SGB Interview: Jerry W. Levin," *Sporting Goods Business,* August 7, 1997, pp. 32–33.

Geer, John F., Jr., "Coleman: Hiking Nowhere?," *Financial World,* April 22, 1996, p. 17.

Labate, John, "Growing to Match Its Brand Name," *Fortune,* June 13, 1994, p. 114.

Laing, Jonathan R., "Into the Maw: Sunbeam's 'Chainsaw Al' Goes on a Buying Binge," *Barron's,* March 9, 1998, p. 13.

——, "Now It's Ron's Turn: Sunbeam Shareholders, Beware," *Barron's,* October 12, 1998, pp. 31–32, 34–35.

Lipin, Steven, "Sunbeam Plans $1.8 Billion in Acquisitions: Deals to Include Coleman, First Alert, and Maker of Mr. Coffee Machines," *Wall Street Journal,* March 2, 1998, p. A3.

McEvoy, Christopher, "Acquiring Minds," *Sporting Goods Business,* August 1995, pp. 44+.

Weimer, De'Ann, Gail DeGeorge, and Leah Nathans Spiro, "Chainsaw Al Goes to Camp," *Business Week,* March 16, 1998, p. 36.

Weisz, Pam, "Camp Giant Coleman Goes Electric," *Brandweek,* November 27, 1995, p. 6.

"Will Sunbeam Make the Cut Following Coleman Co. Buy?," *Sporting Goods Business,* March 25, 1998, p. 18.

—Thomas Derdak
—updated by David E. Salamie

Compuware Corporation

31440 Northwestern Highway
Farmington Hills, Michigan 48334-2564
U.S.A.
(248) 737-7300
(800) 521-9353
Fax: (248) 737-7108
Web site: http://www.compuware.com

Public Company
Incorporated: 1973
Employees: 15,000
Sales: $1.64 billion (1999)
Stock Exchanges: NASDAQ
Ticker Symbol: CPWR
NAIC: 51121 Software Publishers; 541511 Custom
    Computer Programming Services; 541512 Computer
    Systems Design Services

Compuware Corporation is the fifth largest software maker in the world. The company's activities include developing, marketing, and supporting systems software products. Historically, Compuware's principal emphasis has been on products designed to improve programmer productivity for International Business Machines (IBM) and IBM-compatible mainframe computers, though the company has been increasingly offering products for PC networks. Compuware operates through two divisions—a product division and a services division. The product division tests, debugs, and maintains large-scale application software. The services division plans, develops, implements, and maintains computer systems for public sector clients and large corporate clients. The company operates out of more than 100 offices in 45 countries around the world.

Early Years

Compuware was established in 1973 by three cofounders: Peter Karmanos, Thomas Thewes, and Allen B. Cutting. According to a *Detroit News* report, Karmanos, Thewes, and

Cutting pooled $9,000 to establish the company. Their original mission statement was: "We will help people do things with computers."

The first office occupied by the fledgling company was located in Southfield, Michigan. Originally, clients came to Compuware for data processing professional services and help with computer installations. In addition, Compuware offered "programmers for hire" to provide additional manpower for specific client projects or to create solutions to particular needs. Unlike other companies specializing in software and computer services for a specific industry, Compuware differentiated itself from competing companies by its emphasis on diverse applications of mainframe computer technology. Karmanos, quoted in the company's 20th anniversary publication, stated: "We were there to help them solve computer problems. . . . We were a resource—a technology resource—to help our customers work smarter and be more productive."

Compuware continued in its original role as a provider of data processing professional services until 1977 when the company entered the software market with a fault diagnosis tool called Abend-AID. The name Abend-AID was derived from the term abnormal end, which referred to unexpected system errors or failures. These types of problems were often caused by faults in computer programs, changes in system environments, or other errors or failures.

Prior to the availability of Abend-AID, computer programmers confronted with abnormal end situations were required to use manual techniques to test and debug programs. The process involved preparing trial transactions through lengthy procedures such as manually creating experimental entries, writing special test programs, and reviewing program logic. Compuware called this process "tedious, time consuming, and error-prone." The Abend-AID program worked automatically. It intercepted system error messages during actual program execution. This enabled programmers to pinpoint precise error locations and identify the cause of the failure. Abend-AID also offered recommendations for necessary corrections.

Because mainframe computers were critical to business operations, time spent correcting problems often had a significant effect on a company's ability to conduct business. Quick remedies helped reduce the amount of downtime associated with computer problems and helped reduce programmer manpower costs. Abend-AID's success in the marketplace enabled Compuware to become established as a major force in the industry.

A New Focus on Software in the Early 1980s

Following the introduction of Abend-AID, Compuware organized a products division to sell Abend-AID and other software packages. Although the company continued to provide services, the percentage of total revenue generated by the services division grew smaller as sales from the products division increased. The company's offerings focused on integrated systems software products designed to improve programmer productivity through program testing, data manipulation, interactive debugging, and fault diagnosis.

Interactive analysis and debugging products were tools to help programmers identify and correct errors in software by evaluating the quality of a program's code and logic. They worked by enabling a programmer to use either test or production data and progress through a program one statement or statement group at a time. Whenever an error was detected, the programmer could stop and make an immediate correction. Using this process, programs could be tested one step at a time until they were free from errors. The first software package in the interactive analysis and debugging product line, MBX Xpediter/TSO, was introduced in 1979. In 1983 Xpediter earned Compuware its first International Computer Program (ICP) award, granted in recognition of $1 million in sales.

File and data management software packages were used to automate test data preparation, thereby insuring the integrity of the data manipulated by programs. Compuware launched its line of file and data management products in 1983. The first offering in the line, File-AID, was originally sold under an exclusive marketing arrangement with another company, but rights to the program were purchased by Compuware in 1992. Using File-AID, programmers had immediate and direct access to the data necessary to conduct tests and analyze production work. Although early File-AID products were designed for IBM and IBM-compatible mainframe computers only, subsequent File-AID products were designed for other types of computers.

CICS-dBUG-AID, designed for use with IBM's CICS (Customer Information Control System) was introduced in 1985. The following year, Compuware introduced MVS PLAYBACK, the company's first product in its automated testing line. PLAY-

BACK simulated an online systems environment that helped computer technicians execute transactions and check data created by manipulation. PLAYBACK streamlined testing procedures by reproducing a real-time environment without requiring that network users staff terminals or even that the communications network be active. Products in the PLAYBACK family offered five phases of testing: the ability to test a single program from a single terminal; the ability to test a single program from more than one terminal; the ability to test the integration of more than one program; the ability to test a program's proficiency at varying production volumes; and the ability to confirm that programming changes made no unexpected consequences in other areas. Subsequent products in the PLAYBACK line permitted the creation of training sessions for network users.

Growth Spurt in the Late 1980s

Compuware entered a phase of rapid growth during the second half of the 1980s. In 1987 *Inc.* magazine ranked Compuware among the fastest growing privately held companies in the United States. Its premier product, Abend-AID, received an ICP $100 million award, and IBM recognized Compuware as a business partner-authorized application specialist. In addition, Compuware expanded its global presence. Following a decision to operate in Europe through wholly owned subsidiaries, Compuware acquired European companies that had been distributing its software products in England, France, Italy, Spain, and West Germany.

To accommodate its expansion, Compuware announced a decision to build new headquarters in 1987. The $20 million facility, located in Farmington Hills, Michigan, provided 165,000 square feet of space in addition to a 4,000-square-foot satellite facility in Southfield, Michigan. When Compuware moved in, it employed 746 people and expected to increase its staff to 995 within a year. The company's annual compound growth rate for the previous five years stood at 34 percent. Software products accounted for 65 percent of revenues; professional data processing services contributed 30 percent; the remaining sales were generated from software developed for specific markets and from educational resources. As the 1980s ended, Compuware broke the $100 million mark in total annual revenue.

More Expansion and Growth in the Early 1990s

The 1990s brought an increased interest in expansion and growth through acquisition. For example, in 1991 Compuware merged with Centura Software in a move aimed at strengthening its interactive analysis and debugging product offerings. Compuware also increased the attention given to smaller computers. Although the company historically had focused on the sale of mainframe programming software, it released a version of File-AID able to test and edit mainframe data files on personal computers (PCs). File-AID/PC enabled program developers to move blocks of data from mainframes to PCs where they could be scrutinized, copied, edited, modified, or printed. The technology provided a means for discovering programming flaws in a quick manner.

Other new products introduced in 1991 included DBA-XPERT for DB2 (a database management program) and Pathvu/2 (an OS/2 version of a previously released interactive analysis and debugging product). Like its mainframe counterpart, Pathvu/2 provided programmers working with COBOL an automated analysis and documentation tool to evaluate the structure of the programming code. To show what was happening within a program and to document missing elements in the code structure, Pathvu/2 created a graphic display of the program's organization. Compuware reported total revenues of $141.8 million in 1991.

In 1992 Compuware established Compuware Japan Corporation. Compuware Japan's main office was in Tokyo, and company officials hoped to add a branch in Osaka. Compuware Japan planned to focus on adapting existing products for Japanese programmers using Fujitsu and Hitachi hardware in addition to IBM mainframe equipment. The following year, Compuware further expanded its presence abroad with the establishment of Compuware Corporation Do Brasil. Brazil was estimated to be the fifth largest IBM mainframe market in the world. Compuware's move followed a policy change relaxing government-imposed import restrictions on computers and software. Company officials expected the Brazilian subsidiary to be well positioned to serve the emerging Latin American market.

Stock Offering in 1992

Compuware's initial public offering of common stock occurred in 1992. The stock was offered at $22 per share and 5.5 million shares were sold by the company. Net proceeds (after underwriting discount and other expenses) totaled $111.5 million. In addition, existing shareholders sold 3.9 million shares of common stock.

Despite the successful stock offering, 1992 also marked the first year since Compuware's inception that the company failed to earn a profit, when it reported a net loss totaled at $23.8 million. According to a published statement, the lack of profitability was attributed to special pretax charges of $52.6 million related to expenses surrounding its acquisition of XA Systems Corporation. XA Systems software products were classified primarily as file and data management tools.

In a move designed to augment its fault diagnosis product line, Compuware purchased the Eyewitness product line from Landmark Systems Corporation in 1993. The acquisition increased Compuware's product line to 27 software products. As of March 1993, Compuware had licensed more than 41,000 copies of its products to more than 5,700 customers around the world. Software license fees and maintenance fees produced 74 percent of the company's total revenues. The remaining 26 percent was generated from professional services.

Compuware's Professional Services Division operated branches in seven locations: Baltimore, Maryland; Columbus, Ohio; Colorado Springs, Colorado; Lansing, Michigan; Toronto, Canada; Detroit, Michigan; and Washington, D.C. Most of the revenue generated from the services division was received from business application programming services. Business application programming services were those in which Compuware's programmers wrote original software to perform a particular function. Other services division operations included analyzing business problems and using computer techniques to overcome them; providing conversion services to organizations switching from one type of computer environment to another; systems planning, a service involved in identifying business objectives and information requirements to make recommendations for hardware and software; and consulting. Although revenues earned by the services division typically carried lower profit margins than did revenues earned by the products division, Compuware stated that it remained committed to providing services to its customers.

Despite its growth and expansion, Compuware's executives insisted that the company's basic mission remained unchanged: to help people do things with computers. They acknowledged, however, that the processing power of computers had changed vastly during the company's 20 years in business.

One significant change within the industry was the expanding presence of PCs. Some industry analysts had criticized Compuware's emphasis on mainframe computer technology. In response, Compuware noted that the 36,000 mainframe computers in operation were running "mission-critical systems" applications that were not suited to PC technology. These included credit card authorization services, airline reservations, and online banking. According to Compuware's data, only 13 percent of mainframe computer operators used software to diagnose faults. Even less used software for debugging, file and data management, and automated testing. Compuware's own analysts felt a sufficient base existed for expansion in the mainframe market.

Nevertheless, in 1993 Compuware turned its attention to the PC arena with its acquisition of EcoSystems Software, Inc. The EcoSystems product line included programs designed to be used in PC networks. The PC market differed significantly from the mainframe market because of the wide variety of computer hardware manufacturers and operating systems employed. Two new products were added to the EcoSystem line during the second quarter of 1994 to help network clients schedule batch jobs and better manage database environments.

Acquisitions Continue in the Mid-1990s

In early 1994 Compuware acquired Uniface Holding B.V. in a stock trade worth $268 million. Uniface, based in Amsterdam, Netherlands, was a supplier of client-server (network) application and development software. According to *Crain's Detroit Business,* industry watchers expected the acquisition to provide Compuware with a strong presence in the PC market at a time when its mainframe software licensing was still growing at a rate of about 30 percent. The acquisition also was expected to give Uniface a greater presence in the North American market. Two additional acquisitions in 1994 were Computer People Unlimited, Inc. and Meta Technologies, Inc., both information technology service firms. Compuware also purchased several product lines from other companies, including Advanced Programming Techniques Ltd.'s Oliver and Simon interactive analysis and debugging software. An indication of Compuware founder Peter Karmanos's growing wealth was his 1994 purchase of the Hartford Whalers, a National Hockey League team, which he later moved to North Carolina and renamed the Hurricanes.

In the fall of 1995 Compuware acquired CoroNet Systems of Los Altos, California, a maker of networked applications management software, and renamed the company's product EcoNet. That purchase was followed quickly by several more, including Icons GmbH of Germany, Technalysis Corp. of Minneapolis, Direct Technology Ltd. of England, and Adams & Reynolds, Inc. of Cleveland. Direct Technology made software testing products; the others were computer service firms. Compuware was increasingly offering products and services that addressed the "Y2K" computer software problem, and revenues from this business segment were growing rapidly as the magnitude of the problem became known. Annual revenues for fiscal 1996 hit a peak of $614 million. Compuware's overall growth had slowed, however, due in part to the lackluster showing of Uniface, and the company reorganized its structure during the year.

In 1997 Compuware purchased Vine Systems, a London, England-based consulting firm, and NuMega Technologies, Inc., of New Hampshire, which provided debugging services and products to Windows software developers. The following March the company acquired UnderWare, Inc., a Boston software defect tracking tools maker. Additional Y2K products also were being introduced by the company during this period. Sales topped $1 billion for the first time in fiscal 1998, with services accounting for nearly two-fifths of Compuware's revenues.

The company had been growing by leaps and bounds, but was still in the same Farmington Hills, Michigan headquarters it had occupied for more than a decade. Karmanos was seeking a new home, and the nearby city of Detroit was bending over backward to lure him to its underused downtown. In early 1999 an agreement was reached for the company to move there. Two new buildings were to be constructed at a cost of $1.2 billion. To lure Compuware downtown, the city had agreed to purchase software and services from the company and provide it with huge financial incentives, including cutting the city's business tax. In April Compuware announced record sales of $1.64 billion for the fiscal year with net income of $350 million.

The company's acquisitions continued in the summer of 1999 with the purchase of Data Processing Resources Corp. of Irvine, California. The $450 million deal would give Compuware 3,400 more employees and greatly broaden the company's service business. Compuware's profits had been growing faster than its revenues, leading *Business Week* magazine to rank it number six on its 1999 list of 50 top-performing companies.

Beginning its second quarter-century in business, Compuware could boast of sales to four-fifths of the *Fortune* 1,000 companies and a 97 percent customer renewal rate. It was purchasing new companies at a rapid clip both to broaden its product line and to boost its presence in the service business. The Y2K problem was providing the company with a temporary surge in income, but it seemed certain that Compuware would be around long after the dust had settled on that particular issue.

Principal Subsidiaries

Compuware Asia-Pacific Pty. Ltd. (Australia); Compuware NV/SA (Belgium); Compuware Asia-Pacific (China); Compuware Nordic Aps (Denmark); Compuware Oy (Finland); Compuware Sarl (France); Compuware GmbH (Germany); Compuware Srl (Italy); Compuware Korea (Korea); Compuware de Mexico (Mexico); Compuware B.V. (Netherlands); Compuware Nordic AS (Norway); Compuware Panama (Panama); Al-Falak (Saudi Arabia); Compuware Asia-Pacific Pte. Ltd. (Singapore); Compuware Southern Africa (South Africa); Compuware S.A. (Spain); Compuware AB (Sweden); Compuware AG (Switzerland); Compuware Ltd. (U.K.); Compuware Corporation Do Brasil (Brazil); Compuware Japan Corporation (Japan); XA Systems Corporation; EcoSystems Software, Inc.; Uniface Holding B.V. (Netherlands); NuMega Technologies, Inc.; Data Processing Resources Corp.; Computer People Unlimited, Inc.; Meta Technologies, Inc.; CorNet Systems; Icons GmbH (Germany); Technalysis Corp.; Direct Technology Ltd. (U.K.); Adams & Reynolds, Inc.; Vine Systems Company, Ltd. (U.K.); UnderWare, Inc.; M.I.S. International, Inc.; MC Squared Corporation; Virtual Innovations, Inc.; Direct Technology Ltd. (U.K.); DRD Promark, Inc.

Principal Divisions

Products; Professional Services.

Further Reading

Britt, Russ, "Leaders & Success: Compuware's Peter Karmanos," *Investor's Business Daily*, June 19, 1997, p. A1.

Child, Charles, "Compuware: Riding the Dinosaur," *Crain's Detroit Business,* February 15, 1993.

Compuware: 20 Years of Helping People Do Things with Computers, Farmington Hills, Mich.: Compuware Corporation, 1993.

Cunningham, Cara A., "Pathvu/2 Taps OS/2 PM Graphics to Analyze COBOL Code," *PC Week,* January 6, 1992.

"Detroit Move Like a Return to Home: Compuware Owner Recalls Roots from Childhood in City," *Detroit News,* April 11, 1999, p. 1.

Doler, Kathleen, "The New America: Compuware Corp.—Giving Clients More Bang from 'Big Iron,' " *Investor's Business Daily,* June 17, 1994, p. A4.

Henderson, Tom, "CompuGrowth: Pete Karmanos Grew Compuware into a Mega-Company—and Defied the Conventional Wisdom in the Process," *Corporate Detroit Magazine,* May 1, 1994, p. 10.

Howes, Daniel, "Compuware Pay Cuts Pay Off," *Detroit News,* July 27, 1994, p. 1.

Jones, John A., "Companies in the News: Compuware Expands from Mainframes to Network Jobs," *Investor's Business Daily,* October 25, 1996, p. B14.

Maurer, Michael, "Compuware Merger Wins Raves," *Crain's Detroit Business,* March 28, 1994, p. 1.

Muller, Joann, "No Way to Treat a Crisis," *Business Week,* July 5, 1999, p. 74.

Olson, Lise, "In Software, Compuware's Got the Program," *Detroit News,* June 26, 1988.

Pachuta, Michael J., "Compuware Expands Its Lines, Buys Software Quality Tools," *Investor's Business Daily,* October 2, 1998, p. B8.

Pallatto, John, "Compuware Moves Data Editor to PCs," *PC Week,* September 30, 1991.

Pepper, Jon, "News Special: The Road to Renaissance—Compuware Considering Shifting Suburban Headquarters to Detroit—Move Would Bring 3,000 Jobs to Downtown Area," *Detroit News,* August 24, 1998, p. A1.

Roush, Matt, and Robert Ankeny, "Compuware to Move HQ to Detroit," *Crain's Detroit Business,* April 12, 1999, p. 1.

"Software Growth: Compuware Corp. Keeps Expanding, Here and Abroad," *Detroit News,* January 28, 1987.

—Karen Bellenir
—updated by Frank Uhle

Correctional Services Corporation

1819 Main Street, Suite 1000
Sarasota, Florida 34236
U.S.A.
(941) 953-9199
(800) 275-3766
Fax: (941) 953-9198
Web site: http://www.correctionalservices.com

Public Company
Incorporated: 1989
Employees: 7,000
Sales: $97.9 million (1998)
Stock Exchanges: NASDAQ
Ticker Symbol: CSCQ
NAIC: 56121 Facilities Support Services; 922140
   Correctional Institutions

Correctional Services Corporation (CSC) provides a full range of juvenile and adult correctional services. Operating 63 facilities with about 13,000 beds in 21 states and Puerto Rico, CSC is one of the nation's largest companies offering jails, prisons, detention centers, and educational and training programs designed for a diversity of individuals, including both first-time offenders and habitual criminals. The company plays an important role in the major trend of local, state, and federal governments contracting with the private sector to take care of its many responsibilities.

Origins and Developments in the Early 1990s

In the 1970s some citizens became bitterly opposed to raising taxes for more government programs. For example, citizens in California, the leading trendsetting state, approved an antitax initiative. Criminal justice Professor Daniel Okada stated the recent "interest in privatization originated with the Reagan administration's agenda to pass along many government responsibilities to the private sector." This international trend set the stage for private prison management firms including Correctional Services Corporation.

James F. Slattery, the founder of CSC, previously had contracted with New York City's Human Resource Department to provide at-risk individuals with residential services and various programs. He also used his expertise as a former real estate executive to help Correctional Services Corporation find good sites for its facilities and meet the requirements of government laws and regulations.

In 1989 Slattery's firm started with two contracts. First, in June it began managing a variety of programs at the Brooklyn, New York Correctional Facility under contract with the Federal Bureau of Prisons. The next month it took over operations at the Seattle Detention Center owned by the U.S. Immigration and Naturalization Service. Under CSC management, this facility expanded from 50 to 150 beds and became the first INS facility to gain accreditation from the American Correctional Association.

In 1994 CSC's annual revenue had increased to $24.3 million. By the mid-1990s other firms were also expanding, but the industry had considerable room for further growth. For example, in 1994 such firms managed less than five percent of all adult prisoners. A 1996 *Business Economics* article reported that over half the states had legalized private management of prisons, a field that was projected to increase 19 percent annually. It was the fastest-growing segment of the nation's security services industry that also included private guards, alarm systems, armored cars, and trained dogs for protection and drug detection.

Florida, for example, began the process of privatizing its prisons and jails when it passed a law allowing the Florida Department of Corrections and county governments to contract with for-profit corporations to operate and maintain correctional and detention facilities. After the 1993 Florida Legislature created the state's Correctional Privatization Commission, Correctional Services Corporation eventually managed nine facilities in its home state.

Expansion and Challenges in the Late 1990s

In 1997 Correctional Services Corporation began planning to operate a new women's prison just east of Oklahoma City in McLoud, Oklahoma. The McLoud Economic Development Au-

144

Company Perspectives:

The Correctional Services Corporation mission is to manage and operate safe, humane and secure correctional facilities that protect the public and provide offenders with training, education and treatment programs designed to reduce recidivism.

thority owned the property, while the Dominion Group built and leased the $20 million facility. This project involving two private firms, a government agency, and banks that provided the financing, illustrated the complexity of such private-public ventures.

Not surprisingly, some criticized the whole concept of privately run prisons. For example, Jenni Gainsborough, the ACLU's public policy coordinator for its National Prison Project, argued in Oklahoma City's July 3, 1997 *Journal Record* that there was a fundamental conflict of interest since private prison firms profited from the long-term operation of prisons, while the "whole point of a prison is to put itself out of business."

In any case, CSC continued to hire well-trained individuals to head its programs. A good example was Louis Robison, who left the Sarasota, Florida public schools after 20 years of service to become the principal and coordinator of CSC's education system. "We are in the business of corrections," said Robison in the January 2, 1997 *Sarasota Herald Tribune*. "My job is make sure that the [CSC] educational program is in place for each one of these young men so that they can leave with high school credits, GED or some type of vocation and take that back into their communities."

Some CSC plans failed. In 1997, for example, the company decided not to bid on a 500-bed women's jail in Broward County, Florida, after being accused of mistreating immigrants and juveniles at two of its detention centers. Also in 1997, CSC submitted a proposal to the state of Arizona to build a prison in Mexico to house up to 1,600 of Arizona's Mexican prisoners. Although supported by Arizona Governor Fife Symington and the state's corrections director as a way to cut prison labor costs and take advantage of the North American Free Trade Agreement, that CSC proposal died on the vine. Nonetheless, the firm continued to grow and prosper.

According to President, CEO, and Chairman James Slattery in the firm's 1998 annual report, "1998 was the best year in the history of our company." Revenue in 1998 was $97.9 million, a huge increase from 1997 revenue of $59.9 million. In the same period, net earnings increased from $3 million to $4.6 million.

In 1998 Correctional Services Corporation began managing or signed contracts to operate several facilities, including the Colorado County Juvenile Boot Camp in Eagle Lake, Texas, a 100-bed secure facility for both males and females involved in a six-month military style program. Others in Texas were the 500-bed Jefferson County Detention Facility for adults; the 872-bed Newton County Correctional Center for adults; and the Dickens County Correctional Center, a 480-bed facility in

Spur, Texas. CSC also began operating two juvenile facilities in Dallas, Texas: the Dallas County Youth Village Secure Program and the Dallas County II (Harry Hines) RTC and Detention Center, each with 96 beds. Outside of Texas, CSC began running or contracted to manage the Bayamon, Puerto Rico Metropolitan Treatment Center for juveniles; the Central Oklahoma Correctional Facility for adult women in McLoud, Oklahoma; the Crowley County Correctional Facility in Olney Spring, Colorado, the company's first all-cell adult facility; the South Fulton County Municipal Regional Jail in Union City, Georgia; the Paulding Regional Youth Detention Center in Dallas, Georgia; two juvenile residential facilities in Crestview, Florida; and the Tallulah, Louisiana Correctional Center for Youth, "the largest privately run juvenile facility in the country," according to the company's 1998 annual report.

CSC financed its expansion by gaining a new $30 million line of credit from a syndicate of banks headed by NationsBank N.A. "We are very excited about this new financing structure," said President/CEO James Slattery in the April 29, 1998 *Business Wire.* "Not only did we nearly triple the size of our bank line, but we have also put together a group of banks which should enable us to further increase our potential borrowings as the need arises."

In August 1998 CSC announced that the American Correctional Association had accredited two large CSC facilities in Florida: the Pahokee Youth Training Center and the Polk County Youth Training Center, each with 350 secured beds. The association's audit had occurred less than 18 months after the two facilities began operating. Cooperation between the company and the Florida Department of Juvenile Justice was cited as a major reason for the early accreditation.

CSC announced in February 1999 that it had contracted with the Nevada state government to operate its 96-bed secure juvenile facility in Clark County. The first such facility to be privatized in Nevada, it was expected to be operational in the second quarter of 2000 A.D. Also in February CSC and Puerto Rico's Administration of Juvenile Institutions agreed not to renew CSC's contract to manage the Bayamon Detention Center in Bayamon, Puerto Rico.

On March 5, 1999 inmates at the Crowley County Correctional Facility in Olney Springs, Colorado, caused about $10,000 in damages in a riot that resulted in some injuries but no deaths. Riot-control teams from four state prisons came to suppress the disturbance. John Suthers, the executive director of the Colorado Department of Corrections, said in a *Denver Post* article that the private prison's "staff was not as well trained as it could have been." After a two-day lockdown shortly after the prison opened in the fall of 1998, the prison's warden admitted that about 70 percent of his guards lacked any prison experience, although all guards received four weeks of training.

The Colorado riot illustrated one of the main concerns many have voiced about private prisons. Critics argued that for-profit prison management firms such as CSC were more interested in making money and thus did not invest in enough security measures and training. Contracting government agencies imposed stricter guidelines in order to prevent such incidents. In addition, courts stated that private prison management firms are liable for any damages at facilities they operate. However, some citizens opposed any private prisons because of such security problems. It was an ongoing controversy in several states that already had or were considering private correctional facilities.

In spite of such concerns, private prisons had become an integral part of the correctional industry in the 1990s. For example, in December 1996 the first conference on private prisons attracted about 120 individuals from financial, insurance, construction, and prison management firms. It was held in Texas, the leading state in privatizing its correctional facilities.

Because of the increasing interest in cost-effective ways to combat crime and make society safer, Correctional Services Corporation faced stiff competition from other firms, including Cornell Corrections, Wackenhut, Management and Training Corporation, and Corrections Corporation of America, acquired by Prison Realty Corporation.

The Merger with Youth Services International

In September 1998 CSC began its merger with Youth Services International, Inc. (YSI). Based in Owings Mills, Maryland, YSI was founded in 1991, and by 1998 operated 27 residential facilities for juveniles and ran several nonresidential programs for about 3,200 youths in 13 states.

''The combination of CSC and YSI creates a company with unmatched capabilities in the delivery of state of the art juvenile services,'' said James Slattery, CSC's chairman and CEO, according to a September 24, 1998 press release. ''The addition of YSI's transitional and academy oriented programs to CSC's secure programs will allow us to offer governmental agencies the broadest spectrum of quality solutions for adjudicated youth, from first time offenders to the most serious habitual offenders. Since many of the facilities of each company are in states not yet serviced by the other, we believe significant new marketing opportunities will become available.''

On March 30, 1999 Correctional Services Corporation and Youth Services International shareholders approved the merger that made YSI a wholly owned subsidiary of CSC. James Irving, vice-president of CSC's Juvenile Justice Division, was named the new president of Youth Services International in May 1999. His 30 years in the corrections industry included being deputy director of the Juvenile Division of the Illinois Department of Corrections and chairman of the Illinois Parole Board. He replaced Timothy P. Cole, who resigned in early 1999 as YSI's chairman, president, and chairman during the merger negotiations.

After the merger, CSC managed 63 facilities, mostly in Texas (21) and Florida (nine), with others in Georgia, Missis-

sippi, Louisiana, Oklahoma, Arizona, New Mexico, Nevada, Washington, South Dakota, Missouri, Iowa, Minnesota, Michigan, Illinois, Tennessee, Virginia, Maryland, Delaware, New York, and Puerto Rico.

In 1999 Correctional Services Corporation continued to pursue new contracts. For example, in Pacific, Washington, CSC sought a contract to build a $30 million detention center for the U.S. Immigration and Naturalization Service. The center was planned to house illegal immigrants from Mexico, Southeast Asia, and other areas for a short time. Reporter Aimee Green in a phone interview said CSC was conducting an environmental impact study due to be completed in 2000. The firm hoped to get the new contract and eventually replace its overburdened 150-bed facility in Seattle.

In 1999 Correctional Services Corporation's prospects seemed positive. Although the general crime rate was declining nationwide, states continued to privatize more of their correctional facilities. In addition, some private prison management firms planned to offer their services in other nations.

Further Reading

Bailin, Paul S., and Stanton G. Cort, ''Industry Corner: Private Contractual Services: The U.S. Market and Industry,'' *Business Economics*, April 1996, p. 57.

Brooke, James, ''With Jail Costs Rising, Arizona Wants to Build Private Prison in Mexico,'' *New York Times*, April 20, 1997, p. 18.

''Correctional Services Corporation Announces American Correctional Association Accreditation of Its Two 350 Bed Youth Training Centers in Florida,'' *Business Wire*, August 27, 1998, p. 1.

''Correctional Services Corporation Completes Merger with Youth Services International,'' *Business Wire*, April 1, 1999.

Fugate, James L., ''Understanding Florida's Private Corrections System'' (letter to editor), *Tampa Tribune*, June 1, 1997, p. 3.

Green, Aimee, ''INS Holding Center May Be Built in Pacific/Corporation Wants to Construct $30 Million Detention Facility,'' *News Tribune* (Tacoma, Wash.), November 15, 1998, p. B1.

Hoppe, Christy, ''Locking in Profits, Private Prison Industry Holds Growing Allure,'' *Dallas Morning News*, December 19, 1996, p. 1D.

Jones, Leigh, ''Seeing Profits in Prisons,'' *Journal Record* (Oklahoma City), July 3, 1997, p. 1.

Kimm, Yvette, ''Louis Robison Named Man of the Year,'' *Sarasota Herald Tribune*, January 2, 1997, p. 2B.

Miniclier, Kit, ''Olney Springs Prison Riot Exposes Problems,'' *Denver Post*, March 16, 1999, p. B1.

Nevins, Buddy, ''Bad Publicity Forces Company to Cede Jail Bid,'' *Sun Sentinel* (Fort Lauderdale), August 22, 1997, p. 4B.

Okada, Daniel W., ''Maybe This Will Work,'' *Infrastructure Finance*, October 1996, p. 9.

—David M. Walden

Coudert Brothers

1114 Avenue of the Americas
New York, New York 10036
U.S.A.
(212) 626-4400
Fax: (212) 626-4120
Web site: http://www.coudert.com

Partnership
Founded: 1853
Employees: 1,000
Sales: $155 million (1998 est.)
NAIC: 54111 Offices of Lawyers

With 25 offices in North America, Europe, Asia, and Australia, Coudert Brothers is an important international law firm that represents multinational corporations, foreign governments, and individual clients. In 1879 it became the first U.S. law firm to open an overseas office—in Paris. Coudert Brothers was also the first foreign law firm to open offices in London (1960), Hong Kong (1972), Singapore (1972), Beijing (1979), and Moscow (1988), although several law firms have larger international practices. Coudert Brothers' attorneys deal with virtually all areas of modern business and commercial law. Unlike some other large law firms, Coudert Brothers receives no more than five percent of its annual revenue from any single client.

Origins: The First Generation

Three sons of Charles Coudert started the law firm of Coudert Brothers. Born in 1795, their father sailed from his homeland of France in 1824. He settled in New York City, where he raised his family. The three brothers, Frederic René Coudert, Charles Coudert, Jr., and Louis Leonce Coudert, were born in New York City in 1832, 1833, and 1836, respectively.

In 1853 Frederic René began his law practice and two years later Charles, Jr., joined him. Then in 1857 Louis came aboard and for the first time the term Coudert Brothers was listed in the city directory.

"Since Papa Coudert's connections lay largely in New York City's French and Spanish populations," wrote Virginia Veenswijk in her history of the law firm, "... from the start Coudert Brothers' clientele was heavily composed of foreign nationals." For example, their first known client was a French physician accused of assault.

By the 1860s the firm represented the Mora family, prominent Cubans in shipping and warehousing who also started their own bank. Building on their father's ties to French leaders, the three brothers gained the French consulate in New York City as their most important early client. They worked on criminal extradition cases that provided little income but built their reputation as French-speaking attorneys.

During the Civil War, the firm worked on cases involving the Union's blockading of neutral shipping from entering the port of New Orleans. In United States v. Mora, Coudert Brothers represented the Mora family that tried to ship goods to the Confederacy. Although the family lost this case, it remained a client of the law firm.

In 1879 the Couderts established a law practice in Paris. Although the Paris office for several decades was a separate business that chose its own partners, the New York and Paris offices remained closely associated and referred clients to each other.

By 1883 the firm employed eight lawyers, making it one of the nation's largest law firms. Its three departments (real estate, litigation, and estates and trusts) represented mostly individuals, unlike New York's other big law firms that based their expansive growth on corporate clients, mainly railroads and banks. For example, New York's Milbank Tweed built a huge practice representing the Rockefeller family and what eventually became Chase Manhattan Bank.

In the late 1800s Coudert Brothers also represented the Roman Catholic Church as it protested the violence and prejudice of American nativists. Although not paid by the church, the law firm gained valuable contacts who helped attract paying clients. The firm also represented William R. Grace, the Democrat who in 1880 was elected as New York's first Catholic mayor. Although Democrats, the Couderts fought the corruption of New York's Tammany Hall.

In 1893 Frederic René Coudert helped represent the U.S. government in an international dispute with Britain that might have led to war. The United States complained that British and Canadian sealing ships had hunted seals in the Bering Straits almost to extinction, and thus had seized some British ships in international waters. An international tribune in France ruled against the United States, for it had jurisdiction only within three miles of its coastline. Although Coudert lost this case, he continued to argue that arbitration was an effective means of settling disputes among nations.

Coudert Brothers, especially its leader Frederic René Coudert, played a crucial role in developing laws regarding international trade and relations around the close of the 19th century. For example, it helped establish rules concerning ocean salvage and navigation.

As improved transportation and communication stimulated international business development in the late 1800s, Coudert Brothers worked on several important cases involving rights of private citizens in claims against foreign governments (United States v. Bayard and Bogardus v. Grace) and differences in foreign currencies (Reynes v. Dumont).

In 1896 Frederic René Coudert accepted President Grover Cleveland's appointment to the Venezuela Commission to help resolve the border dispute between Venezuela and British Guiana.

The Second Generation Takes Over: 1890s–1930s

In 1890 Frederic René Coudert's son Fred Coudert began working at the family law firm. Born in 1871, Fred attended Columbia College like his father before him. Although he earned a Ph.D. in political science, Fred served as a clerk at the family law firm and studied on his own to learn how to be an attorney. Until his death in 1955, Fred Coudert led Coudert Brothers as it continued to make major contributions as an international law firm.

Around the turn of the century the firm represented the governments of Belgium, Russia, Turkey, Venezuela, Italy, France, and others. It also represented some prominent families in either business or personal affairs. For example, the firm served the Jay Gould family and J.P. Morgan, especially after the House of Morgan bought a Paris bank in the 1890s. The French Rothschilds and the Couderts also were close associates, although destruction of the 19th-century records of both the New York and Paris practices prevents a thorough analysis of these relationships. In 1906 the firm represented several insurance companies regarding claims from the terrible San Francisco earthquake and fire.

After the United States annexed Hawaii in 1898 and acquired Puerto Rico, the Philippines, and Guam from Spain as a result of the Spanish-American War, Coudert Brothers played a key role in 17 of the 20 U.S. Supreme Court cases dealing with the rights and responsibilities of these new territories. Known as the Insular Cases, they helped define what it meant to be a growing world power in the early 20th century.

New industries in the early 1900s brought new clients to Coudert Brothers. For example, the firm gained Renault, Michelin, and other manufacturers as clients when the automobile industry was still in its infancy. Coudert Brothers also helped Henry Ford in a major patent case. The silent motion picture industry also brought in fresh business for the New York firm after the turn of the century.

Coudert Brothers' expertise in international law brought new challenges during World War I. For example, it represented the French government when it arranged in 1915 to borrow $500 million from private U.S. banks. The firm also helped the Russian and Italian governments as they sought to purchase U.S. supplies and weapons after they joined the Allied nations in their fight against Germany and the other Central Powers. Meanwhile, Coudert Brothers attorneys consulted with President Woodrow Wilson on how to deal with the Mexican Revolution.

In the 1920s Coudert Brothers and Coudert Frères, the Paris practice, both prospered. As more American elites moved to Paris, Coudert Frères represented various Guggenheims, Vanderbilts, and other prominent individuals regarding their wills and estates. American firms such as General Motors, Western Electric, Du Pont, Frigidaire, 3M, and ITT established French operations with the counsel of Coudert Frères. Meanwhile, the New York office benefited from plenty of estate work, litigation, and representation of U.S. subsidiaries of French companies. By 1929 Coudert Brothers had 11 partners, mostly young men in their 30s. Although Coudert Brothers did well in the 1920s, big New York law firms such as Sullivan & Cromwell, White & Case, and the Cravath firm grew much faster and larger.

During the Great Depression of the 1930s, Coudert Brothers' earnings declined significantly, but the firm remained profitable. Like some other law firms, it represented the increased number of firms declaring bankruptcy. And it also represented new clients in the entertainment and movie industry as it grew in the 1930s. For example, Coudert Brothers successfully defended comedian W.C. Fields when he was accused of torturing his canary in one of his acts. The firm's corporate practice grew slowly, with clients such as Banca Commerciale Italiana and the Buckley family's oil and gas firms.

As war approached in Europe in the late 1930s, Coudert Brothers represented France in its purchase of American airplanes and engines. Many of those planes did not reach France before it was invaded by Germany; they ended up being used by the British in the Battle of Britain. In any case, those purchases stimulated the U.S. aircraft industry, which helped the United States once it joined the Allies after the Japanese attack on Pearl Harbor.

The firm's most controversial litigation occurred during World War II when it represented its long-term client the Banque de France. Many for years mistakenly thought the firm represented Vichy France, a Nazi puppet state, and thus the firm probably lost many clients in the postwar era.

The Third Generation After World War II

By 1944 Alexis C. Coudert, the son of Fred Coudert, was in effect managing the family law firm. The corporate practice had reached a point of equal billing with the firm's litigation practice and soon exceeded estate billings for the first time. In 1946 the firm gained Tiffany & Company as a client. About the same time it took on its first major antitrust and libel cases. In the 1950s the firm represented the Greer estate in a famous case that became the basis of the Simon & Schuster bestseller *The Greer Case: A True Court Drama* and later a TV show starring actor Raymond Burr.

In the mid-1950s Coudert Brothers began a major change in its overall direction. For about a century it had remained essentially a modest-sized law firm working with elite clients, whether individuals or foreign governments. Its practice had brought considerable acclaim but nowhere near the financial rewards of the larger Wall Street firms that represented much larger corporate clients. Consequently, Coudert Brothers, with about 28 lawyers compared to other New York firms with about 80 lawyers, decided for the first time that it had to really expand or die.

In response to more American investment in nations rebuilt with Marshall Plan funds after World War II and to the creation of the Common Market headquartered in Brussels, Coudert Brothers launched its London office in 1960 and its Brussels office in 1965.

With offices in five cities in 1970, Coudert Brothers expanded to 13 offices by the end of the 1970s. In 1972 it opened offices in Hong Kong and Singapore. After leaving as ambassador to the Organization of American States to join Coudert Brothers in 1969, Sol Linowitz promoted the firm's Rio de Janeiro office that opened in 1976. To serve French and Japanese clients desiring to do business in California and other western states, the firm in 1977 started a branch in San Francisco. Then in the winter of 1978–79 Coudert Brothers started offices in Riyadh, Saudi Arabia and Manama, Bahrain. The Rio de Janeiro, Riyadh, and Manama offices later were closed.

In 1979 the government of the People's Republic of China began to seek foreign investors, which resulted in Coudert Brothers being the first outside law firm to operate in China. From 1979 to 1981 three of its lawyers taught a class on international law and foreign trade and investment for public officials in Beijing. "Between seminars and courses for the Chinese on American and international law and articles and seminars for Americans and Europeans on Chinese law," wrote Virginia Kays Veenswijk, "disseminating information took up a major share of everyone's time and energy during the period between 1979 and 1983 when Coudert Brothers was the only law firm with a 'presence' in China."

Starting in 1979, Coudert Brothers also began to represent clients in China. For example, it provided counsel that led to the building of the Great Wall Hotel, oil company investments in off-shore drilling in Chinese waters, and the contracts for the first visit by the Peking Opera to New York City.

All this growth in the late 1970s was exciting for the firm but also resulted in considerable confusion and misunderstandings. However, Alexis Coudert still was at the helm, so the firm held together. But major changes came after he died in 1980. From that point, the firm for the first time in its history was not run by the Coudert family.

Late 20th Century: Family Practice No Longer

In 1984 Coudert Brothers opened an office in Sydney and three years later established an office in Tokyo. The firm in 1986 opened offices in Los Angeles and San Jose and the same year laterally hired 32 attorneys, including the entire antitrust section of Lord Day & Lord. Two years later it was the first Western law firm to start an office in Moscow. Coudert Brothers grew from a total of 122 lawyers in 1987 (53 partners and 64 associates) to 160 lawyers in 1990 (61 partners and 94 associates). That included more women attorneys, which increased from four partners and 42 associates in 1986 to ten partners and 71 associates in 1990.

In the late 1980s the firm's finances improved, gross revenues increasing from $52 million to $120 million from 1986 to 1989. The *American Lawyer* noticed these changes, moving Coudert Brothers from number 99 based on 1986 profits per partner of only $155,000 to number 34 in 1989 based on its $405,000 profits per partner.

A 1991 review of New York law firms found many problems at Coudert Brothers. The author wrote, "Divisiveness has plagued the firm since non-Couderts assumed its leadership," a problem covered in some detail in the firm's history. The review also stated, "High turnover of both partners and associates—as well as somewhat indiscriminate lateral hiring—has weakened the firm's departments and diminished the quality of its work product." Lastly, the firm's management by two committees "receives virtually universal criticism from observers."

On a more positive note, the review found that, "Associates love Coudert" because they received interesting assignments, good training, and enough responsibility without being overworked. Coudert Brothers recruited its associates from mainly Columbia, New York University, Harvard, Fordham, the University of Virginia, and the University of Pennsylvania.

Representative clients listed in the review included IBM, CBS, Time, Royal Dutch/Shell, Allied Chemical, Paine Webber, Chemical Bank, First Boston, Washington Post, Bendix Corporation, Ford Motor Company, Atlantic Richfield, Lanvin Parfums, Fiat, and the Japanese Nippon Electric Company Ltd. Overseas.

In 1994 the firm started a Mexico City office in association with the local firm Rios Ferrer y Guillen-LLarena, S.C. The Denver office opened in 1995. Coudert Brothers opened a Montreal office in 1997 in cooperation with a local firm of over 20 attorneys to assist clients doing business in Canada or Canadian clients that wanted to operate in other nations. To assist its Moscow office, the firm opened branches in St. Petersburg in 1996 and Almaty in 1998. Similarly, to assist clients in central and eastern Europe, it established a Berlin office in 1995 and one in Frankfurt in 1999. In 1998 Coudert Brothers opened an office in Palo Alto to aid clients in Silicon Valley.

The firm's Asian practice expanded with new offices in Jakarta and Bangkok in 1990. After the Clinton administration ended the trade embargo against Vietnam, in place since the communists won the Vietnam War in 1975, Coudert Brothers opened offices in both Hanoi and Ho Chi Minh City in 1994.

The *American Lawyer* in its July/August 1998 rankings of the country's 100 top law firms placed Coudert Brothers number 64, based on its 1997 gross revenues of $141 million. Divided among the firm's 343 lawyers, revenue per lawyer was $410,000. The firm was not listed in the world's 50 largest law firms in the first such ranking by the *American Lawyer* in November 1998.

In 1999 the firm employed about 235 lawyers in New York and its other North American offices, 170 in Europe, and another 120 in Asia and Australia. Although Coudert Brothers pioneered the creation of an international law firm, in the 1990s it faced tough competition in the foreign arena. For example, Chicago's Baker & McKenzie, the world's largest law firm, in 1998 was staffed by 2,300 lawyers, with 80 percent of those individuals based overseas in over 30 countries. Thirteen of the world's 50 largest law firms were based in London. The point was that Coudert Brothers faced major challenges as the new century approached.

Further Reading

Cherovsky, Erwin, ''Coudert Brothers,'' in *The Guide to New York Law Firms,* New York: St. Martin's Press, 1991.
Veenswijk, Virginia Kays, *Coudert Brothers: A Legacy in Law: The History of America's First International Law Firm 1853–1993,* New York: Truman Talley Books/Dutton, 1994.

—David M. Walden

Covance Inc.

210 Carnegie Center
Princeton, New Jersey 08540-6233
U.S.A.
(609) 452-4440
(888) 928-2277
Fax: (609) 452-9375
Web site: http://www.covance.com

Public Company
Incorporated: 1996
Employees: 7,200
Sales: $731.6 million (1998)
Stock Exchanges: New York
Ticker Symbol: CVD
NAIC: 54171 Research & Development in the Physical,
    Engineering, & Life Sciences

Covance Inc. ranks second in size among contract biopharmaceutical research organizations in the United States, providing a wide range of integrated product development services worldwide to the pharmaceutical, biotechnology, and medical device industries. To a lesser extent, it provides health economics and outcomes services to managed care organizations, hospitals, and other healthcare providers, and laboratory testing services to the chemical, agrochemical, and food industries. Covance was created at the end of 1996 as a spinoff of Corning Inc.'s pharmaceutical services business and now has offices in 17 countries.

Predecessor in Life Sciences Research: 1968–87

Covance originated from Corning Glass Works' health and science activities, which were consolidated into a single operating division in 1977. This unit entered the life sciences research field by taking a small stake in Hazleton Laboratories Corp. and then purchasing the rest of the company in 1987 for about $115 million. Hazleton began in 1968 as Environmental Sciences Corp., a manufacturer of equipment for the care of laboratory animals that set up shop in the basement of an old supermarket in Seattle. In 1972 the company acquired Hazleton Laboratories Inc., a contract laboratory founded in 1946 and devoted to toxicological research. Environmental Sciences, which previously had purchased Hazleton's animal research division, took its name and continued to grow by further acquisitions.

By 1982 Hazleton was the largest independent biological testing company and life sciences laboratory in the United States and the largest laboratory equipment manufacturer in the world. Biological research, the main segment of its business, included testing the effect of new drugs, cosmetics, pesticides, and industrial chemicals on animals and chemically analyzing new compounds for the pharmaceutical, chemical, and food industries. It also was testing chemicals for gene mutations and conducting research with monoclonal antibodies. The company's other segments were manufacturing laboratory and medical equipment and breeding rhesus monkeys and beagles for the research departments of chemical and drug companies, government agencies, universities, hospitals, and its own facilities.

Hazleton enjoyed record profits every year between 1972 and 1983. As part of a restructuring program, it sold the equipment manufacturing unit in the mid-1980s. Its chairman described Hazleton in 1986 as the world's leading provider of biological and chemical research services to the pharmaceutical, chemical, food, cosmetic, and biotechnology industries.

Further Acquisitions: 1989–98

In 1989 Corning Glass Works (which became Corning Inc. that year) acquired G.H. Besselaar Associates, a company serving leading international pharmaceutical companies. Besselaar was conducting clinical trials to help new drugs to gain regulatory approval and was following through with post-approval studies and marketing support. Corning Lab Services, Inc., a subsidiary established in 1990 for the parent company's laboratory services segment of its business, included both Hazleton and Besselaar. That year Hazleton acquired Microtest Ltd., a molecular toxicology center in York, England, and Besselaar added locations in Europe, the United States, and Japan to its worldwide network by acquiring two international clinical re-

151

search organizations. Besselaar was the world's largest contract clinical research organization by the end of 1992.

Corning Lab Services expanded its clinical trials expertise with the purchase of Philadelphia Association of Clinical Trials (PACT) Inc. in 1990. In 1991 it added to its roster SciCor Inc., an Indianapolis-based laboratory dedicated to clinical trials of new pharmaceutical compounds. SciCor was known for innovative patient sampling kits and customized data presentation. Corning Lab Services' pharmaceutical laboratory capabilities were expanded in 1992 with the creation in Switzerland of a jointly owned company, SciCor S.A., which was fully acquired in 1994. In 1993 Corning combined Hazleton, Besselaar, and SciCor into a single operating unit, Corning Pharmaceutical Services. Combined, the three businesses offered testing services that supported product development from initial stages to the marketplace.

This segment of Corning's business had revenues of $270.9 million in 1992, $289.7 million in 1993, and $319.5 million in 1994. Its net income came to $266,000, $16.8 million, and $19.6 million in those respective years. The parent subsidiary, Corning Lab Services, was renamed Corning Life Sciences, Inc. in 1994. In 1995 this subsidiary acquired National Packaging Systems, Inc., a pharmaceuticals packaging company. The purchase of Swiss-based CRS Pacamed AG in 1996 expanded the subsidiary's pharmaceutical packaging capabilities to Europe.

Corning Biotechnology Services was founded in 1995 as a majority-owned unit of Corning Life Sciences to offer contract manufacturing of new biological products, such as peptides and recombinant proteins, for biotechnology and pharmaceuticals clients. Armed with a $3 million state low-interest loan and a $500,000 cash gift, this unit located in Research Triangle Park, North Carolina. The plant it opened there in 1997 was the biggest biotechnology facility in the world devoted exclusively to outsourcing.

Corning Pharmaceutical Services, with headquarters in West Windsor, New Jersey, had revenues of $409.2 million and net income of $24.2 million in 1995. In March 1996 the unit purchased Health Technology Associates Inc., a Washington, D.C., consulting firm specializing in conducting cost-effectiveness studies for new drugs. With the rise of managed care, drug companies were increasingly performing cost studies during the initial stages of drug development so that they could decide whether a new treatment would be worth the cost of development.

Corning Inc. announced in April 1996 that its laboratory testing and pharmaceutical services business segments would be spun off to its shareholders at the end of the year, creating two independent companies, which were subsequently named Quest Diagnostics Inc. and Covance Inc., respectively. Covance, the former Corning Pharmaceutical Services, estab-

lished headquarters in Princeton, New Jersey. The company had net revenues of $494.8 million in 1996 and net income of $12.7 million. It increased these figures to $590.7 million and $39.8 million, respectively, in 1997, and $731.6 million and $48.6 million, respectively, in 1998.

Covance, in November 1998, acquired GDXI, Inc., providing centralized electrocardiogram analysis for clinical trials, and Berkeley Antibody Co., providing contract services and custom animal research, antibody production, and applied immunology.

Covance in 1998

The contract services that Covance was providing constituted two lines of business: early development of pharmaceuticals, including preclinical and Phase I services; and late-stage development, including clinical and periapproval, central laboratory, pharmaceutical packaging, and health economics and outcomes services. The first step in the development of new pharmaceuticals involved preclinical research—animal and test tube studies to establish the basic pharmacokinetic effect and safety of a drug, including its toxicity over a wide range of doses. This phase typically lasted six months to three years and, if approved by regulatory agencies, was followed by clinical trials on human beings. During Phase I, research was conducted for six months to one year on about 20 to 100 subjects, usually healthy volunteers in a closely monitored setting.

Phase II, lasting one to two years, began late-stage development. In this phase the drug was being tested on about 100 to 400 carefully selected patients suffering from the disease or condition under study. Phase III, lasting two to three years, involved hundreds or thousands of patients at many hospitals and clinics. Upon completion, a new-drug application would be compiled. This document was, on average, about 100,000 pages long in the United States.

Following regulatory review and approval, the Federal Drug Administration might allow the manufacturer to make the new drug available to a larger number of patients through another application, which would require enrollment and data from thousands of patients. Additional post-marketing reports also were required periodically to monitor the safety and effectiveness data, and additional studies—labeled Phase IV or periapproval—might be undertaken to find new uses for the drug or test new dosage formulations.

Covance served approximately 290 biopharmaceutical companies in 1998, including nearly all of the world's 50 largest pharmaceutical companies and most of the largest biotechnology companies. Early development net revenues from external customers comprised about 33 percent of total net revenues, and late-stage development comprised the other 67 percent. Net revenues attributable to U.S. operations came to about 68 percent of total net revenues. Operations in the United Kingdom came to 16 percent, and operations in other countries accounted for the remaining 16 percent.

Covance had offices in 17 countries in 1998. Major leased quarters were corporate headquarters and a clinical development group in Princeton; West Coast clinical development services in Walnut, California; a periapproval facility in Radnor, Pennsylvania; health economics and outcomes research activities in Washington, D.C.; and clinical and periapproval operations and health economics and outcomes services in Maidenhead, United Kingdom. Other leases included pharmaceutical laboratories in Indianapolis and Geneva, Switzerland, and Covance Biotechnology's facility in Research Triangle Park.

Covance owned preclinical laboratories in Madison, Wisconsin; Harrogate, United Kingdom; and Munster, Germany. It both owned and leased a preclinical laboratory property in Vienna, Virginia. Construction of a new facility in Allentown, Pennsylvania, for the company's domestic packaging operations, was expected to be completed in 1999. Covance also owned a pharmaceutical manufacturing facility in Horsham, United Kingdom, that was renovated to provide pharmaceutical packaging, clinical, and periapproval services. A facility to further enhance Covance's packaging capabilities in Europe was completed in 1998 in Allschwil, Switzerland.

The former Hazleton was now a subsidiary named Covance Laboratories Inc. The former Besselaar was Covance Clinical Services Inc. PACT had become Covance Periapproval Services Inc.; SciCor, Covance Central Laboratories Inc.; National Packaging Systems, Covance Pharmaceutical Packaging Services; Health Technology Associates, Covance Health Economics and Outcomes Services Inc.; CRS Pacamed AG, Covance Pharmaceutical Packaging Services AG; GDXI, Covance Central Diagnostics Inc.; and Berkeley Antibody, a subsidiary of Covance Research Products Inc.

In April 1999 Covance announced that it had reached an agreement to acquire Parexel International Corp., the world's third largest clinical trials company, for stock valued at $671 million. This purchase would have allowed Covance to pass its chief competitor, Quintiles Transnational Corp., in size. During the following two months, however, Covance's stock fell by more than 25 percent on widespread investor disenchantment with the proposed transaction. The merger was called off on

June 25. Wellington Management Co. LLP was Covance's leading stockholder at this time, with 12.7 percent of the shares. Covance's long-term debt stood at $150 million.

Principal Subsidiaries

Covance Biotechnology Services Inc. (78%); Covance Central Diagnostics Inc.; Covance Central Laboratories Inc.; Covance Clinical Services Inc.; Covance Health Economics and Outcomes Services Inc.; Covance Laboratories Inc.; Covance Periapproval Services Inc.; Covance Pharmaceutical Packaging Services AG (Switzerland); Covance Pharmaceutical Packaging Services Inc; Covance Research Products Inc.

Principal Operating Units

Client Relations Group-Europe; Client Relations Group-North America and Asia; Clinical Development Services; Early Development Services.

Further Reading

"Drug Makers Make Covenant with Covance," *New Jersey Business,* December 1998, p. 72.

Goldblatt, Dan, "Pharming Out Clinical Research," *BUSINESS News New Jersey,* July 13, 1998, p. 26.

Holusha, John, "Corning to Spin Off Labs and Drug Unit," *New York Times,* May 15, 1996, p. D4.

Pereira, Joseph, and Robert Langreth, "Covance's Accord to Acquire Parexel Gets Called Off," *Wall Street Journal,* June 28, 1999, p. B6.

Psandya, Mukul, "A Quiet Giant Grows Bigger," *BUSINESS News New Jersey,* April 3, 1996, p. 15.

Tanouye, Elyse, and Laura Johannes, "Covance to Acquire Parexel in $671 Million Deal," *Wall Street Journal,* April 30, 1999, p. A3.

"Thank You, Uncle Sam," *Financial World,* November 1, 1982, pp. 42–43.

—Robert Halasz

Crane Co.

100 First Stamford Place
Stamford, Connecticut 06902
U.S.A.
(203) 363-7300
Fax: (203) 363-7295
Web site: http://www.shareholder.com/crane

Public Company
Incorporated: 1865 as Northwestern Manufacturing
 Company
Employees: 12,500
Sales: $2.27 billion (1998)
Stock Exchanges: New York
Ticker Symbol: CR
NAIC: 32622 Rubber & Plastics Hoses & Belting
 Manufacturing; 326199 All Other Plastics Product
 Manufacturing; 332998 Enameled Iron & Metal
 Sanitary Ware Manufacturing; 332913 Plumbing
 Fixture Fitting & Trim Manufacturing; 332911
 Industrial Valve Manufacturing; 332912 Fluid Power
 Valve & Hose Fitting Manufacturing; 332919 Other
 Metal Valve & Pipe Fitting Manufacturing; 333921
 Elevator & Moving Stairway Manufacturing; 333923
 Overhead Traveling Crane, Hoist, & Monorail System
 Manufacturing; 333911 Pump & Pumping Equipment
 Manufacturing; 333311 Automatic Vending Machine
 Manufacturing; 333319 Other Commercial & Service
 Industry Machinery Manufacturing; 334413
 Semiconductor & Related Device Manufacturing;
 334419 Other Electronic Component Manufacturing;
 336413 Other Aircraft Parts & Auxiliary Equipment
 Manufacturing; 334513 Instruments & Related
 Product Manufacturing for Measuring, Displaying, &
 Controlling Industrial Process Variables; 334519
 Other Measuring & Controlling Device
 Manufacturing; 42131 Lumber, Plywood, Millwork, &
 Wood Panel Wholesalers; 42172 Plumbing & Heating
 Equipment & Supplies Wholesalers

Crane Co. is a diversified manufacturer of engineered industrial products, serving niche markets in fluid handling, aerospace, recreational vehicles and trucks, controls, automated merchandising, and the construction industry. Crane's wholesale distribution business provides the building products markets and industrial customers with millwork, windows, doors and related products, plumbing supplies, valves and piping, and fittings. From its inception in 1855 as a crude bell and brass foundry run singlehandedly by its founder, Richard Teller Crane, the company grew into an S&P 500 firm with international subsidiaries that generate more than $2 billion of sales in fields ranging from heating to wastewater treatment to aerospace to vending machines.

Lightning Rod Beginnings

Crane Co.'s roots extend back to Richard Teller Crane's first effort to cast lightning rod tips and couplings in a foundry that he established in Chicago. Born in Patterson, New Jersey, in 1832, Richard Crane moved into the workforce at an early age. By the age of nine, he worked as a cotton mill operator; by 15 he learned brass and bell foundry and brass finishing trades as an apprentice in a Brooklyn foundry; by 21, he had gained further experience in a locomotive plant and several printing press machine shops. He migrated westward in 1855 to join his uncle, Martin Ryerson, who ran a successful lumber business in Chicago. Ryerson lent his young nephew a corner of the Ryerson lumberyard to launch the makeshift foundry that would become a multinational company over the ensuing century.

Richard Crane built a 14-by-24 foot wooden shed and secured patterns and brass for couplings and copper for lightning rod tips. The sand that he had turned up excavating the furnace served as raw material for molding. After nearly a year as the sole employee—molder, furnace tender, metal pourer, casting cleaner, and salesman—Crane hired two experts from Brooklyn and started a partnership with his brother, Charles, changing the shop name to R.T. Crane and Brother. Markets quickly expanded beyond Chicago to Wisconsin, Kentucky, and Iowa.

The first substantial order came from P.W. Gates & Co., a Chicago manufacturer of mill equipment and freight cars. Gates's supplier had run out of copper and could not fill an

Company Perspectives:

Our Credo: We strive for a dominant presence in niche markets. We generate solid rates of return on invested capital and high levels of cash flow. We use our cash flow effectively to grow and strengthen our existing businesses, and to acquire new businesses. We acquire businesses that fit with our existing businesses and strengthen our position in niche markets. We maintain an incentive compensation plan specifically designed to align the interests of management and shareholders. We do this with one goal in mind: To build shareholder value.

urgent order for journal boxes, the metal containers installed on railroad cars to lubricate axles. After delivering the castings on schedule, Crane won the confidence of Gates & Co. and eventually received all future orders for brass castings.

Following their first big order, the Crane brothers moved to rapidly expand operations and diversify product lines. After building a three-story structure and upgrading production facilities, they began production of engine parts for the emerging railroad business, as well as plumbing and fixtures for new developments in steam power, called ''steam warming'' at the time. In order to fill a $6,000 contract to supply the new Cook County Court House in Chicago with steam heating, Crane designed and manufactured a wide variety of globe and check valves, pipe fittings, steam cocks, branch tees, and hook plates. Their success won the company a similar contract for the newly constructed Illinois State Penitentiary in Joliet, Illinois, which, in turn, won them further credibility and sustained business in the provision of steam heating supplies. With the onset of the Civil War, the company also became a major government supplier of fittings for saddlery, brass fittings, plates, knobs, spurs, and wagon equipment.

By 1865 the Crane brothers completed construction of an industrial-size factory on Jefferson Street, which enabled them to expand all facets of business operations and manufacture a full line of valves in materials ranging from cast iron to malleable iron and brass. That same year, the company was incorporated and renamed the Northwestern Manufacturing Company, reflecting its broadening interests.

In 1866 the company printed its first catalog, which contained products as diverse as fire hydrants, ventilating fans, machine tools, water pumps, bung bushings for beer barrels, and steam engines. The advent of the Bessemer smelting process for iron brought low-cost steel to the United States, further assisting Crane in his development of diverse and durable products.

Crane's entry into the elevator business began in 1867, when the company designed an engine with a safety valve to control elevator speed with heavy loads. From the 1870s until the mid-1890s, Crane provided 95 percent of the hoists used in U.S. blast furnaces. In addition, the company established a presence in passenger elevator manufacturing in 1872, spinning off a separate subsidiary called the Crane Elevator Company that remained a major competitor in the field for over three decades.

With increased focus on industrial manufacturing, it sold its elevator division in 1895 to a joint venture that eventually became the Otis Elevator Company.

The year 1871 literally brought a blaze of change, as the company survived the Chicago fire and helped save the city by providing large steam pumps to displace river water to city mains. That same year, Charles Crane retired from the business and sold his share to Richard, making the original founder sole proprietor once again. To emphasize the family heritage after his brother's departure, Richard changed the name to Crane Brothers Manufacturing Company in 1872.

Late 19th-Century Innovations and Growth

In the late 1880s Richard T. Crane contributed to the rise of industrial automation. He pioneered line production in foundries and invented numerous mechanized systems to increase industrial efficiency in its plants. The company developed a steam-powered conveyor system for moving molds and pouring metal. It also fine-tuned the use of multiple-purpose machines, such as a machine that simultaneously bored cylinders, crosshead guides, and crankshaft bearings for steam elevator engines. Other innovations included oil pumps for the lubrication of engine-driven cylinders, an alarm to signal low water levels in steam boilers, a pipe lap joint that set new standards in the industry, and state-of-the art ceiling plates and pipe hangers.

With increased innovation and business volume, the company expanded rapidly. In 1884 a branch operation was opened in Omaha that proved so successful that another was established in Los Angeles, California, in 1886. Within a few years, branch operations became standard company practice, sprouting up wherever Crane products were in demand. In 1870 a four-story extension was added to the Jefferson Street plant, and in 1881, a second large pipe mill was constructed. By 1880 Crane operated four production facilities employing more than 1,500 workers.

In 1890 the company officially adopted the name Crane Co. Though its name was shortened, Crane's business continued to grow rapidly. A new age of increasingly taller buildings demanded greater numbers of pipes, valves, and fittings for water and steam systems with higher performance standards. In addition, commercial electricity depended on massive steam engines, which in turn required stronger and cheaper fluid control equipment. Anticipating the need for new materials and innovative solutions to remain competitive, Richard T. Crane established a chemical laboratory in 1888. The company developed iron castings of uniform tensile strength, a notable achievement for the period. Before long, the rise of large steam power plants outdated even uniform fittings in cast iron, forcing the company to innovate in steel production. In 1907 Crane negotiated for a German steel innovator, Zenzes, to join its staff and supply his coveted patents. By 1910 Crane was producing valves and fittings with minimum tensile strength of 60,000 psi.

During the first decades of the 20th century, Crane invested in metallurgical research that paid off for the company and the industry at large. Experiments designed to test the effects of high temperatures on various metals culminated in a series of papers published in 1912 that became engineering classics. In addition, a number of Crane quality control procedures became industry standards. Crane's inspection of pipe threads using gauges was adopted by the American Society for Testing Materials, and Crane's practice of tapping and gauging steel flanges eventually served the whole industry as the Pipe Thread Standard.

Crane expanded to East Coast markets with the 1903 acquisition of the Eaton, Cole & Burnham Company in Bridgeport, Connecticut. The company continued to expand its production line, introducing a complete line of air brake equipment, pop safety valves, and drainage fittings, among other products. A 160-acre, electrically powered plant was constructed in Chicago in 1909. After Richard Crane's death in January 1912, his role as president was briefly passed on to the eldest son, Charles R. Crane, and then more permanently transferred to Richard T. Crane, Jr., in 1914.

Among the ventures introduced by the new president was an extensive line of practical, decorative bathroom ensembles supported by acquisitions of sizable pottery and enamelware operations and by unprecedented marketing efforts. The copy for a 1925 advertisement in *National Geographic Magazine* began, "Your personal taste and appreciation of beauty in form and color can be reflected in the appointments of your bathroom." Among other initiatives to corner the rising bathroom market, Crane retained industrial designer Henry Dreyfuss to conceive an entire fixture line.

International Expansion Following World War I

In the years following World War I, Crane established its first operations outside the United States. In 1918 Canadian operations were incorporated as a separate company, Crane Limited, which grew to include Canadian Potteries Ltd., Warden King Ltd., and Crane Steelware Ltd. over the ensuing 20 years. Distribution also expanded to Europe, with the first branch houses established in France in 1918 and in England in 1919. Manufacturing operations were established in those countries in 1925 and 1929, respectively.

While losses during the Great Depression years strained operations, they also prompted replanning and increased efficiency, and served to usher the company into World War II as a reliable and flexible supplier. Although Crane reported its first operating loss in 1931, it rebounded within two years to offer shares on the New York Stock Exchange in 1934. After sustained growth during the next decade, the company was ready to supply the U.S. Navy with valves and fittings for the war effort. From a prewar steel valve production capacity of 6,000 tons per year, Crane increased its capacity to an annual rate of 25,000 tons by mid-1942. By supplying the Navy, the Atomic Energy Commission, and new manufacturers of high-octane fuel using catalytic cracking techniques, Crane gained ample experience in designing and manufacturing a wide range of metal-alloy valves and fittings resistant to corrosion, high temperatures, and extreme strain.

Postwar Growth

Following the war, Crane was able to transfer its war efforts to the peace dividend, meeting increased demands in the petrochemical, chemical, and atomic power industries. With the 1951 acquisition of Hydro-Aire Incorporated, Crane entered the business of precision aircraft products and flow control equipment, supplying filters and valves to all manufacturers of turbine type aircraft

engines. In 1953 Crane developed a household hydronic heating system; it ranked as one of the country's largest manufacturers of residential heating by 1956. In the late 1950s the company shareholders elected a new chairman and chief executive officer, Thomas Mellon Evans, whose strategy was to streamline the distribution network and broaden the industrial product base. A major consolidation of distribution houses and the reorganization of a separate "profit center" resulted in the creation of Crane Supply Company. The October 1959 acquisition of the Chapman Valve Manufacturing Company of Indian Orchard, Massachusetts, significantly expanded domestic valve operations, especially on the East Coast. The following year, acquisition of the 97-year-old Cochrane Corporation in Philadelphia, Pennsylvania, extended Crane's fluid control line to include steam boilers and water, steam, and wastewater treatment equipment. The Cochrane Division became the nucleus of Crane's growing involvement in the business of pollution control.

By the 1960s, Hydro-Aire catered to the space program with production of life-support and coolant pumps. It also expanded its role in the realm of aerospace by taking the lead in antiskid braking systems, fuel and hydraulic pumps, valves and regulators, actuators, and solid-state components.

Expansion continued through the 1960s. In 1961 the Deming Company, a manufacturer of residential and industrial pumps and water systems, was acquired. Four years later, Crane acquired a highly specialized fluid control company, the Chempump Division of Fostoria Corporation, which specialized in leakproof, trouble-free pump systems for exotic or dangerous fluids.

By the mid-1960s Crane had extended its international operations to Italy, with Crane-Orion, Italy; the Netherlands, with Crane Nederland, N.V.; Spain, with the acquisition of that country's largest valve manufacturer, Fundiciones Ituarte, S.A. and the formation of Crane-FISA, S.A.; Australia, with the new valve plant, Crane Australia Pty., Ltd.; and Mexico. Crane Canada Ltd. and Crane U.K. also made significant acquisitions in 1964 and 1966. Through rising space-age technology, Crane expanded beyond terrestrial boundaries, collaborating with the U.S. Space Team and the Brookhaven National Laboratory's test studies of solar energy, among other projects.

Short-Lived Diversifications into Steel and Cement

In an effort to improve its position in the area of building products, Crane acquired Huttig Sash & Door Company in 1968, adding milled wood products, windows, and doors to its line. The 1969 acquisition of CF&I Steel Corporation, a vertically integrated steel company, marked an unprecedented diversification into a major industry beyond its existing areas. CF&I provided everything from iron ore, coal, and limestone to carbon and alloy steel. It represented the largest acquisition in Crane's history and, by 1975, represented the company's single largest business interest. The 1979 acquisition of Medusa Corporation, a cement and aggregates company, added yet another basic materials industry to Crane's list.

In 1980 Crane began a shift in business strategy away from cyclical basic materials businesses toward a diversified mix that would earn higher returns for shareholders. In February 1984,

T.M. Evans resigned as chairman and director of the company, leaving his post to the newly elected Richard Sheldon Evans— son of T. M.—who ushered in a major restructuring effort. On July 13 of that year, the company sold its U.S. plumbing division for approximately $9.5 million. One year later, Crane spun off CF&I Steel to its shareholders, and in 1988 shares in Medusa Corporation were made available to its shareholders as well.

While Crane's restructuring involved substantial paring down, it also called for new acquisitions in light-to-medium manufacturing. In 1985 the company acquired UniDynamics Corporation, expanding diversification in numerous areas: defense and aerospace contracting, fluid controls, vending machines and coin validators, automation equipment, fiberglass-reinforced polyester and laminated panels, and electronic components.

The late 1980s and early 1990s were marked by management efforts to fine-tune the UniDynamics acquisition; several divisions deemed incompatible with the restructuring plan were sold and appropriate acquisitions were made. In February 1987, 12 Crane Supply plumbing, heating, and air conditioning wholesale distribution branches in southern regions of the United States were sold. Substantial additions were made to the company's U.S. valve line, including valve maintenance and value-added services. In April 1992 Crane's Canadian subsidiary, Crane Canada, Inc., acquired certain assets of Jenkins Canada, Inc., a manufacturer of bronze and iron valves, for approximately $4 million.

The Ferguson Machine Co., the largest supplier of intermittent motion control systems in the world, was established as a division of the Defense and Specialty Systems Group of Crane, and in August 1986 Ferguson acquired PickOmatic Systems of Detroit, a leader in cam-activated mechanical parts handling equipment. Crane's Cochrane Environment Systems division acquired Chicago Heater Company, Inc., a designer, manufacturer, and servicer of deaerators and surface condensers, reinforcing Cochrane's market leadership. Additionally, Huttig Sash & Door Company expanded to become the third largest distributor of wood building products in the industry. Pozzi-Renati Millwork Products, Inc. was acquired in February 1988, providing Crane with a strong initial entry into the East Coast market; Palmer G. Lewis Co., a distributor of building material, was acquired in June 1988; and Rondel's, Inc., a distributor of doors, windows, and molding, was acquired in April 1993.

The Crane Co.'s Hydro-Aire Division was augmented in 1990 by the $40 million acquisition of Lear Romec Corp., a manufacturer of pumps for the aerospace industry. In September of that year the diaphragm pump line of the Crown Pump Company was added to Crane's Deming pump line, increasing Crane's share of the industrial pump market. That same year, a Crane attempt to acquire Milton Roy Co., a manufacturer of metering pumps, was halted by an antitrust suit in which Milton accused Crane of a "greenmail" scheme to manipulate the market in order to acquire Milton stock. Milton repurchased all shares held by Crane for $8.2 million.

Surviving Recession: Early 1990s

Downturns in residential construction, in defense spending, and in the aerospace industry, paired with weak economies worldwide, strained key Crane divisions in the early 1990s. Hydro-Aire, the leader in electronically controlled antiskid brakes for the aerospace industry, saw declines in profitability of 13 percent and 18 percent in 1991 and 1992, respectively. The April 1993 sale of the precision ordnance business of Unidynamics/Phoenix to Pacific Scientific Company reflected further reduction in Crane's declining defense business. These losses, however, were offset in part by strong increases in revenues at National Vendors for automated merchandising equipment; at Huttig, which served the residential construction industry; and at Kemlite and CorTec, Crane's suppliers of fiberglass-reinforced panels to the transportation industry. R.S. Evans, Crane's chairman and CEO, noted in the 1992 annual report that "one benefit of a diversified business mix is that a recession rarely cuts across all units with equal impact."

Despite the recessionary trends of the early 1990s, Crane was able to increase total operating profit for 1992 by seven percent and improve productivity, on a sales-per-employee basis, by six percent. During 1992 Moody's upgraded the company's senior debt rating from Baa2 to Baa1, while Standard & Poor's reconfirmed the company's A- credit rating on the $100 million senior notes.

Mid-1990s Acquisition Spree

From the fall of 1993 through the spring of 1994 Crane spent $335 million to make five acquisitions. In October 1993 the company spent $25 million for Jonesboro, Arkansas-based Filon, a fiberglass manufacturer which was integrated into the Kemlite unit. Two months later Crane paid $70 million for Burks Pumps Inc. of Piqua, Ohio, a manufacturer of engineered pumps that complemented Crane's Chempump and Deming pump businesses. Added in March 1994 at a price of $77 million in cash and assumed debt of $17 million was ELDEC Corporation, a Lynnwood, Washington-based maker of aerospace components, including proximity switches and sensing systems, power conversion equipment, fuel flow measurement systems, and integrated modular systems. Crane next won a takeover battle with Tyco International Ltd. for Mark Controls Corporation, a manufacturer of automatic and manually operated valves, specialized electronic and mechanical instruments and controls, regulators, and pneumatic and electronic controllers. Crane acquired Mark Controls in April 1994 for $95 million in cash plus assumed debt of $40 million. The following month Crane, through Huttig Sash & Door, acquired American Moulding and Millwork, of Prineville, Oregon, for $11 million. This acquisition spree increased the company's revenues by 20 percent but also more than doubled its debt, from 27 percent to 60 percent of total capital. Crane's credit rating fell to the bottom of investment grade, Baa3/BBB.

Acquisitions were subsequently put on hold for the remainder of 1994, and only $9.4 million was spent in 1995 to make three minor purchases. Concentrating on consolidating the acquisitions of the previous two years, Crane was able to reduce its debt to total capital ratio to 44 percent by the end of 1995. That year the company posted record net sales of $1.78 billion and net income of $76.3 million.

During the late 1990s Crane continued to perform admirably, with net sales increasing steadily to $2.27 billion by 1998 and net income nearly doubling, reaching $138.4 million by that year. During these boom years in the United States, Crane slowly increased its pace of acquisition, continuing all the while to concentrate on smaller, complementary purchases and to manage the newly acquired companies in a largely hands-off manner. During 1996 Crane completed two acquisitions, the more significant being Interpoint Corporation, a designer and manufacturer of high-density power converters with applications in the aerospace and medical technology industries. Spending $82 million to make five acquisitions in 1997, Crane picked up Sequentia, Inc.'s transportation products business, which produced fiberglass-reinforced plastic panels for the truck body, trailer, and container market—an operation that was integrated into Kemlite; Polyvend Inc., a maker of snack and food vending machines, which was merged into National Vendors; the nuclear valve business of ITI MOVATS, purchased from Westinghouse; MALLCO Lumber & Building Materials Inc., a leading wholesale distributor of lumber, doors, and engineered wood products which was purchased by Huttig; and Stockham Valves & Fittings, Inc., the largest of the 1997 acquisitions.

Crane picked up the acquisition pace in 1998, completing six acquisitions at a total cost of $224 million. Added to the Crane fold were Environmental Products USA, Inc., a maker of membrane-based water treatment systems; Number One Supply and Consolidated Lumber Company, both of which were integrated into Huttig Building Products; Sequentia Holdings, Inc., maker of fiberglass-reinforced plastic panels for the construction and building products markets; Liberty Technologies, Inc., manufacturer of monitoring products and related services for the nuclear power generation and industrial process markets; and Dow Chemical Company's Plastic-Lined Piping Products division.

Beginning in late 1998 and continuing into mid-1999 Crane fought a losing battle to block B.F. Goodrich Co.'s bid to take over Coltec Industries Inc., a maker of aircraft landing gear that Crane itself wished to acquire. Crane attempted to block the takeover through an antitrust lawsuit but eventually reached an out-of-court settlement that left it without possession of Coltec.

At the end of the 1990s Crane continued to find success in its strategy of seeking to dominate selected niche markets. With the company's core businesses lying in manufacturing, Crane's distribution operations seemed increasingly out of place. Huttig Building Products in particular was perhaps a distracting or even detrimental presence in the company's portfolio of businesses as that unit had grown steadily in sales—from about $140 million in the mid-1980s to about $700 million in 1998 (about 31 percent of overall revenues)—but had lower profit margins than the manufacturing lines. Evans told the *Wall Street Journal* in June 1999 that "as Huttig becomes a bigger part of Crane, I think it is holding Crane's overall results down." It was with this in mind that Crane announced that it

was considering the spinoff of Huttig into a separate publicly traded company. Such an occurrence would surely lead to another round of acquisitions, and a further bolstering of Crane's impressive collection of niche manufacturers.

Principal Subsidiaries

FLUID HANDLING: Crane Valves; Crane Nuclear, Inc.; Crane Ltd. (U.K.); Crane Australia Pty., Ltd.; Stockham Valves, Ltd. (U.K.); Stockham Australia Pty., Ltd.; Westad Industri A/S (Norway); Crane Pumps & Systems, Inc.; Cochrane Inc. AEROSPACE: ELDEC Corporation; Hydro-Aire, Inc.; Lear Romac; Interpoint. ENGINEERED MATERIALS: Kemlite Company, Inc.; Sequentia, Inc.; CorTec; Resistoflex; Plastic-Lined Piping Products; Crane Plumbing; Polyflon. CONTROL: Barksdale, Inc.; Powers Process Controls; Dynalco Controls; Azonix Corporation; Ferguson. MERCHANDISING SYSTEMS: National Vendors; National Rejectors, Inc. GmBH (Germany). WHOLESALE DISTRIBUTION: Huttig Building Products; Crane Supply. OTHER: Crane Defense.

Further Reading

"Crane Announces Stock Incentive Plan Vesting," *PR Newswire,* June 11, 1990.
"Crane Co. Acquires Jenkins Canada," Crane Co., April 1, 1992.
"Crane Co. Announces Acquisition and Divestiture," *Business Wire,* April 2, 1993.
"Crane Co. Purchases PickOmatic Systems," *PR Newswire,* August 11, 1986.
"Crane Co. Subsidiary Expands Distribution Network," *PR Newswire,* February 16, 1988.
"Crane Purchases Chicago Heater," *PR Newswire,* June 18, 1987.
"Crane Sells Its U.S. Crane Supply Operation," *PR Newswire,* February 27, 1987.
Goldstein, Alan, "Dateline: Milton Roy Co. Repurchases Crane Co. Shares," *St. Petersburg Times,* February 13, 1990.
Hart, Margaret A., and Alan H. Oshiki, "A Horse of a Different Color," *Chief Executive,* January/February 1998, p. 19.
Jaffe, Thomas, "The Apple Fell Far from the Tree," *Forbes,* September 25, 1995, pp. 73+.
——, "Daddy Dearest," *Forbes,* September 25, 1995, p. 76.
Lipin, Steven, and Paul M. Sherer, "Crane, Seeking to Stop Goodrich Deal, Offers Richer Price for Coltec Industries," *Wall Street Journal,* December 15, 1998, p. A3.
Vanac, Mary, "Rivals' Moves to Block B.F. Goodrich's Bid for Coltec Were Atypical," *Akron Beacon Journal,* July 18, 1999.
Velocci, Anthony L., Jr., "BFGoodrich, Crane Square Off in Battle to Acquire Coltec," *Aviation Week & Space Technology,* January 11, 1999, p. 447.
Voorhees, Rich, "Crane Takes M&A to the Max," *CFO,* September 1994, p. 31.

—Kerstan Cohen
—updated by David E. Salamie

Delta Woodside Industries, Inc.

233 N. Main Street, Suite 200
Greenville, South Carolina 29601
U.S.A.
(864) 232-8301
Fax: (803) 232-6164
Web site: http://www.deltaapparel.com

Public Company
Incorporated: 1983 as Alchem Capital Corp.
Employees: 5,600
Sales: $535.46 million (1998)
Stock Exchanges: New York
Ticker Symbol: DLW
NAIC: 313311 Broadwoven Fabric Finishing Mills;
   31321 Broadwoven Fabric Mills

Delta Woodside Industries, Inc. is a holding company which, through its various operations, is engaged in the manufacture and sale of textile fabrics and apparel. The company operates 16 textile and apparel plants and 26 garment outlet stores. Its 5,600 employees work in seven different states, plus Costa Rica and Honduras. The company has three main businesses that form its core of operations, including Delta Mills Marketing Company, which manufactures woven fabrics for the apparel, home furnishings (drapery linings, bedspreads, lamp shades), institutional (surgical tapes), and industrial (sail cloth and ripstop nylon) markets, Duck Head Apparel Company, which provides medium-priced apparel that is sold in large department stores across the country, and Delta Apparel, which produces knit items, many of which are sold to screen printers and sporting goods stores, under both the Delta Apparel label and under private brand labels. The company has experienced financial problems during the mid- and late 1990s, and has been selling off many of its non-core businesses.

Early History

Delta Woodside was founded by Bettis Rainsford and Erwin Maddrey in 1983. The idea of starting a textile company first occurred to Rainsford when he heard that a mill in his home town of Edgefield, South Carolina, was closing. The shutdown of Edgefield Cotton Yarns, Inc. meant the loss of about 200 local jobs, and the idea of buying the plant appealed to Rainsford, who had returned to Edgefield after law school and dabbled in the nursing home, newspaper, and geothermal energy businesses. Lacking any knowledge of the textile industry, Rainsford hooked up with Maddrey, the former president of Riegel Textile Corp., also in South Carolina. The two men purchased Edgefield Cotton for $4 million, most of which they borrowed.

Following their acquisition of Edgefield Cotton, Rainsford and Maddrey joined forces with Buck Mickel, another local business operator and former vice-chairperson at Fluor Corporation. A company called Alchem Capital Corp. was formed, 50 percent of which was owned by RSI Corp., an outdoor equipment and office supply company controlled by Mickel. Over the next few years, Alchem grew at a steady rate, mostly by taking over mills cast off by larger companies in the struggling textile industry. Alchem's first important acquisition of this period was Woodside Mills, Inc., formerly a division of Dan River, Inc., in 1984. Four South Carolina plants were included with the $31 million purchase of Woodside Mills, whose products included textile fabrics used in the apparel, home furnishings, industrial, and medical markets. These facilities were the Easley Plant in Easley; the Haynsworth Plant in Anderson; and the Furman and Beattie Plants in Fountain Inn.

Alchem completed two important acquisitions in 1985. The company paid Cannon Mills about $4 million for its Maiden Knitting Mills, a circular knitter of finished apparel fabrics. Alchem also purchased Royal Manufacturing Co. that year. Royal, a manufacturer of men's underwear and sportswear with annual sales of about $30 million, was bought from the family of Morris H. Senderowitz, which had founded the company in Allentown, Pennsylvania, in 1910. The acquisition of Royal added four more plants to Alchem's growing collection. In 1986, Alchem made its largest purchase yet, acquiring the Stevcoknit and Delta Fabrics divisions of J.P. Stevens & Co. Stevcoknit, which produced singleknit and doubleknit fabrics, was purchased for $94 million. Delta products (with a history dating to 1903) included lightweight cottons and polyester blends for sportswear and govern-

---

Company Perspectives:

For over 90 years Delta products have been known for quality and value. Delta offers a wide variety of styles to meet the needs of its customers. From the initial design until the product is finally shipped, Delta controls the manufacturing processes to insure that each shirt meets the high quality standards that its customers expect. Time and time again.

---

ment orders, as well as bottomweight fabrics of synthetic fibers for men's wear. The acquisition of these two J.P. Stevens divisions more than doubled Alchem's size, adding 11 plants to Alchem's ten existing facilities, and increasing the company's workforce from 2,500 to 6,000.

Growth and Expansion: Mid- to Late 1980s

Late in 1986, Alchem's name was changed to Delta Woodside Industries, Inc. The company's yearly sales had grown to over $380 million by this time, with earnings of close to $18 million. The following year, Delta Woodside went public, offering two million shares of common stock over-the-counter at $14 a share. At that time, about 25 percent of Delta Woodside's revenue was generated by the sale of unfinished woven fabrics, over 40 percent by finished woven fabrics, another 25 percent by knit fabrics, and the remainder by completed apparel. For fiscal 1987, net sales reached $417 million.

In 1988 Delta Woodside acquired Stanwood Corporation for about $14 million. Stanwood, a manufacturer of knits, underwear, and sportswear, had yearly sales of about $110 million and employed about 3,000 workers. The deal for Stanwood was structured as an exchange of one million shares of Delta Woodside stock for all of Stanwood's assets, which included 1.5 million square feet of factory space at 11 plants in Georgia, Tennessee, and Costa Rica. For the fiscal year ending in July 1988, Delta Woodside's earnings were $27.6 million, up from $21.3 million the previous year, on net sales of $489 million. In October 1988, the company's stock was listed on the New York Stock Exchange for the first time. Toward the end of that year, plans were made to consolidate Stanwood's headquarters into the Royal Manufacturing division headquarters in Greenville, as well as to consolidate Stanwood's dyeing, knitting, and finishing operations into the Maiden facilities. The company also earmarked $20 million for the completion of its new yarn plant in Spartanburg.

The steady flow of new acquisitions continued into 1989. In February of that year, the company paid about $14 million for O'Bryan Bros., Inc. By the middle of 1989, Delta Woodside's vertical integration was generally complete, with company products ranging from commodity yarns to finished apparel. By that time, the company employed about 9,500 workers in its 37 plants. For the year ending July 1, 1989, Delta earned $9.9 million on sales of $569 million. In November 1989, Delta Woodside merged with its longtime affiliate RSI Corp., Buck Mickel's company. This followed the spinoff of much of RSI's business to stockholders. The remaining incarnation of RSI

consisted only of the Harper Brothers office supply operation. The last step of the merger was the amendment of RSI's articles of incorporation, changing the combined company's name to Delta Woodside Industries, Inc. Although the merger was structured in such a way that Delta Woodside was technically merged into RSI, the actual effect of the merger was the purchase of RSI by Delta Woodside at a cost of $1.1 million.

The Early 1990s

Delta's sales and earnings slumped badly in 1990. Including the new office supply operation, the company's sales dropped to $500 million, while earnings sank to $4.4 million. These setbacks were blamed primarily on weak demand in the retail sector, creating pressure throughout the chain of production. In January 1990, the company's 89-year-old Easley Plant was closed as part of a modernization program. The plant's printcloth production was moved to Woodside Mills' Beattie Plant in Fountain Inn, South Carolina. A few months later, Delta purchased the assets of the Shirt Knitting division of Durham Hosiery Mills, Inc. The division, with sales of about $48 million, was added to the company's Duck Head Apparel operation. Its plants (three in Tennessee and one in Georgia) employed about 1,200 people.

As the company entered the 1990s, increasing emphasis was placed on its Duck Head brand apparel line. The clothing was advertised in such publications as *Playboy* and *Sports Illustrated,* and televised ads were featured during college football games. Four retail outlets for "factory second" Duck Head merchandise were added, bringing the total of such stores in South Carolina, Georgia, and Tennessee to seven. In 1991, Delta Woodside benefited from a huge rush of sales attributable to the Persian Gulf War. During the nine-month period ending in March 1991, the company's sales of camouflage and other fabrics to the Defense Department leaped to $49.2 million, well over twice the total for that period the previous year. For the same period, sales in Delta's woven fabrics division grew by 38 percent. These gains were not companywide, however, as both Stevcoknit and Duck Head Apparel showed sales declines for that nine-month stretch.

For the fiscal year ending in June 1991, sales rebounded to $590 million. The biggest gains were made by the Duck Head product line, whose sales reached $61.7 million. The Duck Head line also diversified its products, adding woven and knit shirts, shorts, and women's wear to its original array of casual cotton men's pants. Three-fourths of Delta's net sales for the year were generated by the fabrics division, as was 86 percent of the company's operating profit. In this division, about $313 million in sales came from woven fabrics, while about $128 million worth of knitted fabrics were sold.

Duck Head clothing continued as one of Delta's more important product lines in 1992. Gross sales of Duck Head apparel more than doubled over the course of the year, totaling over $130 million in fiscal 1992, despite the overall sluggishness of the national retail market. Spurred by the Duck Head line, the company's apparel division showed a 69 percent increase in sales and an impressive 267 percent growth in operating profit for the year. As a result of the apparel division's success, a rearrangement in management took place that split the division into two separate management teams, one responsible for Duck

Head operations, the other for Delta Apparel. The fabrics division held steady for fiscal 1992. Sales and profit figures for both woven and knit products, as well as the balance between them, were comparable to those for the previous year. The company continued to supply woven fabrics for casual and tailored pants made by such well-known brands as Levi Strauss, Lee, Haggar, and Farah. While the sale of government products declined by 20 percent for the year (largely due to the war's end), a 25 percent increase in commercial finished cotton business picked up the slack.

As a whole, Delta Woodside's net sales set a company record of $705 million for fiscal 1992. Apparel operations accounted for about 29 percent of sales, closing in on the company's stated goal of 33 percent in the product mix. Net income, at just over $40 million, was also the highest in company history. In mid-1992, Delta's original yarn plant in Edgefield, South Carolina, the company's birthplace, was closed. Shortly thereafter, a new ultramodern plant, also located in Edgefield, went into production. The new plant was named after company cofounder Bettis Rainsford. The Rainsford Plant produced combed cotton and cotton-polyester yarns used in the manufacture of knit fabrics for men's and women's apparel. Much of the yarn was used internally in the company's Stevcoknit operations.

In January 1993, Delta Woodside announced that it had acquired a 100 percent interest in Nautilus International, Inc., the Virginia-based manufacturer of fitness equipment. Nautilus had sales estimated at $18 million in 1992 and employed about 256 people. Delta also purchased 70 percent of the shares of Apparel Marketing Corporation, a New York-based company that held the license to manufacture apparel under the Nautilus brand name. This acquisition gave Delta another recognizable trade name, in addition to Duck Head, under which to market apparel. It also gave the company a solid inroad into the lucrative fitness wear business. Around the same time, Delta announced that it had completed the purchase of a new facility called the Harmony plant at Grecia in Costa Rica, which was set up to employ 210 people. The Harmony plant was acquired for the purpose of manufacturing men's pants under the Duck Head brand name.

The Mid- and Late 1990s

For all of its quick rise to the top of the apparel and textile industry, management at Delta Woodside was not able to continue its unlimited growth and expansion. In 1996 the company lost approximately $62 million, largely due to the unanticipated success of imports on the market which led to a large inventory surplus, numerous closings of unprofitable textile plants operated by the company, and restructuring expenditures because of a comprehensive reorganization strategy. The decline in share price and continuing losses at the company's apparel units led management to the decision to close even more textile plants and to consider the sale of Duck Head Apparel.

In 1998, still reeling from declining sales and profits, management decided to sell its StevcoKnit Fabrics Division, which eliminated almost 1,000 jobs. In the winter of 1999, the company sold off Nautilus to Focus Corporation, a firm in the fitness equipment industry. Other non-core operations were sold off, and even more employees were released to reduce operating costs. By the spring of the same year, a decision was made to spin off both the Duck Head Apparel and Delta Apparel divisions as separate companies, and then sell the entire remaining assets of the firm, Delta Mills, the maker of woven fabrics, to the highest bidder. Although there were prospective buyers, as of the summer of 1999 no purchase had been arranged.

In order to maximize shareholder value, the decision to break up the textile company was clearly the correct one. Yet, the sudden decline and dismantling of what started as a promising company with astute management, well-run operations, and good product lines seemed well worth more study and reflection.

Principal Subsidiaries

Delta Mills Marketing Company; Duck Head Apparel Company, Inc.; Delta Apparel, Inc.; Duck Head Retail Operations; Harper Brothers; Stevcoknit Fabrics Company.

Further Reading

Addis, Ronit, "Iconoclasts," *Forbes*, April 17, 1989, pp. 49–56.

Burritt, Chris, "Say Alchem to Buy Delta, Steveco from Stevens," *Daily News Record*, February 28, 1986, p. 2.

Clune, Ray, "Delta Woodside Sees Turnaround," *Daily News Record*, November 8, 1990, p. 9.

"Corporate Critics Confidential: Textile Industry," *Wall Street Transcript*, June 19, 1989, p. 93967.

"Delta Woodside Industries, Inc.," *Wall Street Transcript*, September 26, 1988, pp. 50–51.

"Delta Woodside Net Down 56%," *Daily News Record*, August 23, 1990, p. 11.

"Delta Woodside Plans Spinoff of Two Units, Sale of Rest of Firm," *Wall Street Journal*, February 9, 1999, p. C15.

"Delta Woodside's Sales to Military Skyrockets," *Daily News Record*, June 13, 1991, p. 7.

Isaacs, McAllister, "Delta Woodside's Rainsford: The Man, the Plant: Quality," *Textile World*, December 1992, pp. 32–38.

Lohrer, Robert, "Delta Woodside Puts Duck Head on Sales Block," *Daily News Record*, October 16, 1998, p. 1.

MacIntosh, Jeane, "Delta Sees Apparel Unit Sales Soaring to $400M," *Daily News Record*, March 20, 1992, p. 2.

Malone, Scott, "Delta Uncertain on Duck Head Sale," *Women's Wear Daily*, February 3, 1999, p. 12.

——, "Delta Woodside to Spin Off Apparel, Mill," *Women's Wear Daily*, February 9, 1999, p. 12.

Meagher, James P., "Delta Woodside Industries Inc.," *Barron's*, August 8, 1988, pp. 93–94.

"Renegades," *Success*, February 1990, pp. 30–31.

Robertshaw, Nicky, "Delta Woodside Industries Going Public," *Daily News Record*, December 4, 1986, p. 2.

Stilwell, Wesley, "Alchem to Acquire Royal Mfg.'s Assets," *Daily News Record*, February 11, 1985, p. 34.

—updated by Thomas Derdak

DePuy, Inc.

700 Orthopaedic Drive
P.O. Box 988
Warsaw, Indiana 46581
U.S.A.
(219) 267-8143
Fax: (219) 267-7196
Web site: http://www.depuy.com

Wholly Owned Subsidiary of Johnson & Johnson
Incorporated: 1903 as DePuy Manufacturing Company
    of Elkhart, Indiana
Employees: 3,220
Sales: $770.2 million (1997)
NAIC: 339113 Surgical Appliance & Supplies
    Manufacturing; 42145 Medical, Dental, & Hospital
    Equipment & Supplies Wholesalers

DePuy, Inc., a subsidiary of Johnson & Johnson, is a designer, manufacturer, and distributor of orthopedic devices and supplies. Through various subsidiaries, the company produces a wide array of products, which are marketed through its global network of sales and distribution offices. The company's oldest business, DePuy Orthopaedics, Inc., manufactures hip, knee, and shoulder replacement systems, as well as environmental protection products and surgical equipment. Through its OrthoTech subsidiary, the company produces and markets orthopedic products for the sports medicine market. DePuy ACE Medical Company makes specialty orthopedic trauma products, including external and internal fixation devices, and bone fracture management and reconstruction products. The company's DePuy Motech/AcroMed, Inc. business is the second largest maker of spinal implant medical devices in the world.

Founding and Early Years

DePuy, Inc. was founded in 1895 by a 35-year-old traveling salesman named Revra DePuy. DePuy's family lived in Grand Rapids, Michigan, at the time of his birth, but soon moved to Canada. While working as a drugstore clerk in Canada, the young DePuy developed an interest in chemistry that would eventually lead him to take classes at the University of Toronto. After graduating from the University of Toronto, DePuy put his chemistry education to work, becoming a traveling salesman for a pharmaceutical company.

It was during his work-related travels that DePuy first visited the tiny community of Warsaw, Indiana. By the time he arrived in Warsaw, the inventive pharmaceutical salesman was ready to start his own business. He had developed plans for a new product—a molded wood-fiber splint for setting broken bones. The fiber splint was designed to replace the wooden splints that were then commonly used to set fractures. DePuy started small, manufacturing the splints in a local hotel where he was living. By 1898, however, the business had outgrown its temporary quarters and moved into its own space in downtown Warsaw.

At the turn of the century, DePuy decided that his business might better flourish elsewhere. In 1901 he moved the operation to Niles, Michigan—taking with him his wife of five years, Winifred Stoner. It was in Michigan, in 1903, that he incorporated the company as DePuy Manufacturing Company of Elkhart, Indiana. Unfortunately, however, the move to Michigan did not accomplish what DePuy had hoped, so in 1904 he and Winifred moved the splint business back to Warsaw. That same year, DePuy modified his original product by fabricating the splints from wire cloth instead of wood fiber.

For the next several years, DePuy grew his business, adding factory workers and hiring a sales staff to carry sample splints to doctors around the country. By 1919 the company had 16 employees, six of whom were traveling salesmen. In 1921 DePuy died, leaving his 25-year-old splint business to his wife, Winifred. In 1924 Winifred remarried, wedding H. Herschel Leiter, a local insurance salesman who had previously worked as a salesman for DePuy. Leiter became DePuy's executive president.

A Series of Owners: 1950s–60s

When Winifred DePuy Leiter died in 1949, her second husband was left as sole owner of DePuy Manufacturing. Not one to stay single long, the 57-year-old Leiter was remarried within six months of Winifred's death to Amrette Webb Ailes. The newly married couple spent less than a year together, however; in May 1950, Leiter passed away. Amrette became the owner of DePuy—a company founded by her former husband's former wife's former husband.

In 1951 Amrette married Harry Hoopes, a Bell Telephone executive. Together, the couple managed to run DePuy successfully, showing a profit each year. By that time, the company had more than 50 employees in the factory and almost 20 salesmen, covering the whole United States. The product line had expanded to include bone plates, screws, and various soft goods, such as rib belts, collars, and braces.

The Hoopes never became extremely involved with the company, preferring to leave the day-to-day operations to DePuy's executive vice-president, Keaton Landis. By the mid-1960s, the couple was ready to get out of the medical device business altogether. They sold DePuy to a group of investors in 1965, and Landis became the company's president. Robert Williams, who had previously been DePuy's national sales manager, was chosen as vice-president.

DePuy's new owners did not hold on to it long. In 1968, they sold the company to Indianapolis-based Bio-Dynamics, a blood diagnostic business. Landis remained president of DePuy, while Williams became vice-president of Bio-Dynamics. A year later, however, Landis became president of Bio-Dynamics, and Williams moved back to Warsaw to take the helm of DePuy.

The ownership shufflings of the late 1960s were not the only changes taking place at DePuy. In 1968 the company expanded into a whole new product line: hip replacements. The impetus for this shift was DePuy's acquisition of exclusive marketing rights for the Muller Total Hip. The Muller Hip was a hip replacement prosthesis developed by Dr. Maurice E. Muller, professor of orthopedic surgery at the University of Berne and a pioneer in total hip arthroplasty. Expanding into hip replacement production, however, required manufacturing space that DePuy did not have. The company's solution was to purchase Kellogg Industries, a corset manufacturing company in Jackson, Michigan. DePuy moved its soft goods operation out of its Warsaw plant and into the newly acquired Kellogg facility—thereby freeing up space for the manufacture of hip replacements.

New Ownership, New Leadership: 1970s–80s

Just four years after being acquired by Bio-Dynamics, DePuy once again found itself under new ownership. In 1974 Bio-Dynamics itself was purchased by Boehringer Mannheim, one of the largest pharmaceutical companies in Europe. The following

year, Boehringer Mannheim formed Corange Limited as a holding company for its group of businesses. Under the restructuring DePuy also became a wholly owned subsidiary of Corange. Being part of a large, well-capitalized company gave DePuy new opportunities for expansion. In 1974 and 1975, the company built a new 61,170-square-foot facility—then added to it over the next several years for a total of 242,110 square feet.

In the years following its acquisition by Boehringer Mannheim, DePuy added substantially to its product line. Between 1977 and 1980, the company began manufacturing a new hip prosthesis called the AML Total Hip System and a new line of implants coated with a porous substance. The substance, called Porocoat Porous Coating, allowed the body's tissue to grow into an implant, eliminating the need for bone cement. DePuy also introduced a total knee replacement system that utilized mobile bearings designed to more closely replicate the biomechanics of a normal knee. This system was the first mobile-bearing knee cleared for marketing in the United States.

In 1984 Robert Williams retired as DePuy's president, and was replaced by James Lent. Lent had spent 18 years at Johnson & Johnson, most recently as president of the company's orthopedic division. When he moved to DePuy, he brought with him two key members of the Johnson & Johnson team. Mike McCaffrey, who had spent 14 years in sales and marketing for Johnson & Johnson, became DePuy's new vice-president of marketing and sales. William Tidmore, a 15-year veteran of Johnson & Johnson's Ethicon division, took over as director of the medical products group.

Lent was an aggressive leader. During the first eight years of his tenure, DePuy showed 20 percent compounded annual growth and introduced a number of new products. Some of this growth was the result of a strategic partnership established in 1989 with the DuPont Company. The joint venture, DePuy DuPont Orthopaedics, combined DuPont's expertise in materials science with DePuy's expertise in orthopedics to develop orthopedic products that used advanced materials.

It was also during the early years of Lent's administration that DePuy began to expand internationally. With a presence already established in Canada and Latin America, the company in 1984 targeted the Italian market through a network of 12 regional importers. The following year saw DePuy's entrance into Japan and New Zealand via wholly owned branch distributorships. In 1986 the company began distributing products in Germany through MEDINORM, an already established maker and marketer of medical products, and DePuy's products began to reach Austria in 1988. That same year, the company purchased a small orthopedic company in Switzerland. The company, Chevalier AG, was a key acquisition because it was to become the base for all of DePuy's European operations.

Acquisitions and Alliances: 1990–96

The beginning of the 1990s was characterized by a series of acquisitions and alliances that served to greatly diversify DePuy's product line. The first of these came in 1990, when Boehringer Mannheim purchased Charles F. Thackray Limited, of Leeds, England. Like DePuy, Thackray had a long history of manufacturing medical devices and instruments. The company had started in the early 1900s as a retail pharmacy, later moving into surgical and orthopedic instruments. In 1963 Thackray began working with the world's foremost pioneer in hip replacement surgery, Sir John Charnley, to produce cemented hip fixation systems. When Boehringer Mannheim acquired the company, it was the United Kingdom's market leader in replacement joints, with sales staff and distributorships in 100 countries. A year and a half after Thackray was acquired by Boehringer Mannheim, it was renamed DePuy International Ltd., becoming the company's international headquarters.

Other acquisitions and partnerships followed in rapid succession. In 1991 DePuy purchased the Rotek Corporation, a medical products manufacturer in Albuquerque, New Mexico. DePuy's relationship with Rotek dated back to the early 1980s, when it had first hired the small company to produce a line of environmental protection products, such as face shields and gowns. After it was acquired by DePuy, Rotek expanded rapidly, moving into a new 20,000-square-foot facility in 1992.

At the beginning of 1992, DePuy announced a new strategic alliance with Genentech, Inc., a San Francisco-based biotechnology company. DePuy and Genentech teamed up to develop orthopedic devices that used Transforming Bone Growth Factor Beta (TGF-B), a protein that stimulated bone tissue growth and regeneration. An orthopedic device, such as a hip implant, that incorporated this protein would likely cause better growth of organic tissue and, consequently, a firmer attachment to the implant.

Also in 1992, DePuy entered the field of arthroscopy instrumentation when it acquired a 20 percent interest in Expanded Optics, a maker of arthroscopes. DePuy received its share in Expanded Optics when Expanded purchased one of DePuy International's subsidiaries—the Thackray-owned Scope Optics. DePuy expanded its presence in the arthroscopy market in 1993, establishing a separate manufacturing operation in Ontario, California, to produce arthroscopy instruments.

The diversification into new markets continued in 1993 and 1994. In 1993 the company broke into the spinal products market in a joint venture with the German company Biedermann Motech. The new partnership, DePuy Motech, broke new ground in the spinal implant market by developing an implant system that provided both anterior and posterior support. Traditional systems had provided only posterior support, which often failed to restore and balance the natural forces in the spine. Within three years, the company was the number three spinal implant producer in the United States, and number four in the world market.

The following year, DePuy gained entry into the trauma market when its parent company purchased the Ace Medical Company. Ace was a Los Angeles, California-based maker of orthopedic trauma products, including internal and external fixation devices. Another 1994 acquisition was DePuy CMW, a bone cement manufacturer based in Blackpool, England. With a more than 30-year history, CMW was the oldest orthopedic bone cement maker in the world.

The year 1996 marked DePuy's entry into still another market—sports medicine. In April of that year, the company purchased Orthopedic Technology, Inc., of Tracy, California. Renamed DePuy Orthotech, the company was a developer and

manufacturer of patent-protected products used to treat sports-related orthopedic injuries. Among its products were knee braces, foot and ankle supporters, tissue fixation devices, and a full line of soft goods.

The first five years of the 1990s had been excellent ones for DePuy. The company had shown steady and impressive growth, posting an average annual increase of 17 percent in sales and 20 percent in profit. In October 1996, DePuy went public, offering 14 million shares of common stock priced at $17.50 per share. After the IPO, Corange and its subsidiaries continued to own a controlling interest in the company.

Acquiring and Being Acquired: 1997–98

DePuy's intention was to use the capital generated in its IPO to grow its business—and it wasted no time pursing that goal. In early 1997, the company purchased almost two million shares of Landanger-Camus, a leading French manufacturer of hip implants and one of the top distributors of orthopedic supplies and devices. The agreement gave DePuy control of 89 percent of the outstanding shares. It also gave them the number one position in the French implant market.

Perhaps the most significant event of 1997, however, occurred in May, when DePuy's parent company, Corange, announced it was to be purchased by Switzerland-based Roche Holding AG for $11 billion. Roche was a holding company for a large, international group of businesses in the areas of pharmaceuticals, diagnostics, vitamins, and chemicals. Its primary interest in Corange was not DePuy; rather, it was the diagnostics and pharmaceuticals businesses operating under the Boehringer Mannheim name.

The Corange acquisition closed in early 1998. Not surprisingly, Roche wasted little time in shedding DePuy, agreeing in July to sell the business to healthcare giant Johnson & Johnson. The $3.5 billion acquisition was finalized in November 1998, making DePuy a wholly owned subsidiary of Johnson & Johnson. To denote its new ownership, the company's name was modified slightly—to ''DePuy, a Johnson & Johnson Company.''

In June 1998, the newly acquired DePuy made its largest purchase to date—the AcroMed Corporation, of Cleveland, Ohio. AcroMed was the second leading maker of spinal implant medical devices in the United States and the third largest globally. The company joined DePuy's existing spinal implant business, DePuy Motech, and was renamed DePuy Motech/AcroMed.

Looking Ahead

DePuy became part of Johnson & Johnson's professional business segment—a group of companies that provided more than 36 percent of J & J's total sales. As part of the largest manufacturer of healthcare products serving the consumer, pharmaceutical, and professional markets in the world, DePuy was positioned to grow in a number of different directions. The combined strength of the Johnson & Johnson and DePuy names, as well as their extensive global presence, was expected to serve as a solid base for further expansion in the orthopedics market.

As DePuy prepared to enter the new century, one of the fastest growing segments of the orthopedic industry was spinal implants. As such, it was likely that the company's spinal products subsidiary, DePuy Motech/AcroMed, would see especially rapid expansion. As of the beginning of 1999, DePuy Motech/AcroMed had received marketing clearance from the FDA for a new spinal device that was designed to facilitate spinal fusion—and further developments in the area of spinal implants were likely to follow.

Principal Subsidiaries

DePuy ACE Medical Co.; DePuy Dupont Orthopaedics, Inc.; DePuy Motech/AcroMed, Inc.; DePuy OrthoTech; DePuy International Ltd.; DePuy Orthopaedics, Inc.

Further Reading

Drawbaugh, Kevin, "Indiana Town Is Hip to Orthopedics Business," *Reuters News Service*, March 13, 1998.

Eckert, Toby, "DePuy Plots Strategy to Survive the Challenges of Managed Care," *Indianapolis Business Journal*, May 19, 1997, p. 14B.

"The History of DePuy," http://www.fwi.com/DePuy/timeline.htm.

Jefferson, Greg, "Johnson & Johnson Spins Wheel of Acquisition," *Indianapolis Business Journal*, July 27, 1998, p. 10.

One Hundred Years of Orthopedic Excellence, Warsaw, Ind.: DePuy, Inc., 1995.

—Shawna Brynildssen

Do it Best Corp.

Do it Best Corporation

P.O. Box 868
Fort Wayne, Indiana 46801-0868
U.S.A.
(219) 748-5300
Fax: (219) 493-1245
Web site: http://www.doitbestcorp.com

Cooperative
Incorporated: 1945 as Hardware Wholesalers, Inc.
Employees: 1,305
Sales: $2.2 billion (1999)
NAIC: 42131 Lumber, Plywood, Millwork, & Wood
Panel Wholesalers; 42132 Brick, Stone, & Related
Construction Material Wholesalers; 42133 Roofing,
Siding, & Insulation Material Wholesalers; 42139
Other Construction Material Wholesalers; 42171
Hardware Wholesalers

Founded in 1945 as Hardware Wholesalers, Inc. (HWI), Do it Best Corporation is one of the largest dealer-owned cooperatives in the United States. From an initial membership of 75 hardware and building and lumber supplies dealers, the cooperative by 1999 had grown to include more than 4,200 member-retailers throughout the United States and 38 foreign countries. Do it Best distributes some 70,000 different hardware and building supplies items from six regional service centers (RSCs). A seventh RSC was scheduled to open in October 1999. In fiscal 1999 (ending June 30) Do it Best reached $2 billion in sales for the first time.

Origins and Dealer-Owned Cooperatives: 1900–45

Hardware Wholesalers, Inc. (HWI) was founded in 1945 by Arnold Gerberding as a member-owned cooperative. It was established to serve independent hardware and building materials dealers. By combining the purchasing power of its members, HWI helped the independent dealer face intense competition from discount stores, warehouse outlets, and big chain operations.

Born in Fort Wayne, Indiana, in 1900, Gerberding went to work for the Pfeiffer Hardware Co. after graduating from high school. After several years he took a job with Schafer Hardware Co. in Decatur, Indiana, at the urging of his uncle, who was the firm's treasurer. Schafer was a small hardware wholesaler that served both hardware and building materials dealers within a 100-mile radius.

Gerberding spent nearly two decades with Shafer, primarily as a buyer. During the 1920s and 1930s, the wholesale middlemen, also known as jobbers, dominated the flow of goods from the manufacturer to the local retailer. The jobbers not only added a layer of expense for the independent retailer, they also controlled the retailers to some extent.

The independent hardware dealers, who were facing growing competition from national catalog and retail chains such as Sears and Montgomery Ward, fought to be competitive by forming associations and using the pooled resources of the group to buy directly from manufacturers. These groups typically tied themselves to a "cost-plus" store that would act as a buyer for the group, then sell merchandise to the associated stores at cost plus a standard handling fee. Using another model, Ace Hardware, formed in 1925, gained combined strength through a franchise of stores that all carried the same name and products.

While working for Shafer, Gerberding developed his own vision for creating a dealer-owned company. Dealer-owned cooperatives had been springing up around the country to break the power of the wholesalers over the independent dealers. The first hardware cooperative wholesaler, Franklin Hardware Co. of Philadelphia, had appeared in 1906. The first truly dealer-owned cooperative was the American Hardware & Supply Company of Pittsburgh, founded in 1920. It was soon followed by others. There were nearly two dozen such cooperatives by the end of the 1930s, but most did not survive.

By the early 1940s Gerberding realized he had to leave Shafer to pursue his vision of establishing a dealer-owned company. Influenced by the ideas of William Stout, head of the American Hardware & Supply Company, and George Hall, founder of the Hall Hardware Company, Gerberding joined the

166

Company Perspectives:

We will continue to adapt to the times, the competition, and the demands of our customers. We will continue to drive down member costs on price-sensitive items, enhance advertising and store design programs, better equip our staff in order to help our members, and more. At the same time, we will continue to hammer away at operating costs so we can provide our members the largest rebates. That's truly our secret for success, along with the quality of our staff.

Auburn Hardware Company of Auburn, Indiana, in 1943 as its general sales manager. Auburn Hardware was one of the wholesale operations that operated on a cost-plus basis.

From 1943 to 1945 Gerberding contacted several area dealers to explore the possibility of creating the organization that became Hardware Wholesalers, Inc. (HWI). He left Auburn Hardware in 1945 and founded HWI on June 28, 1945. A group of independent dealers became the heart of the organizing board of directors of the new company.

The original organizing plan for HWI called for finding 75 dealers to become members. Each member was asked to invest $1,000 by purchasing 20 shares of common stock in the company, with an initial payment of $50 and the balance due upon call from the board of directors. When the meeting to incorporate was held on June 28, 1945, there were 96 subscribers. Nearly half of the new members turned out to be lumber and building materials dealers, with the rest being independent hardware dealers. This mixture became a defining characteristic of HWI and a source of strength for the firm in its early years.

Becoming Established: 1945–55

The directors decided to locate HWI in Fort Wayne, Indiana, not only because that was Gerberding's home town and the home of the businesses of several of the board members, but also because it was the region's rail and truck center. Moreover, Fort Wayne was a rapidly growing community, and it was an ideal place to locate a wholesale distributor to the independent hardware and lumber dealers serving a growing number of homeowners.

An office and warehouse site were selected. Three additional warehouses were added in 1946. All of the early warehouses were small, and the company's equipment was primitive. The company displayed merchandise at various state hardware and lumber shows that were usually held in January and February, and the company's truck did not have a heater.

Acquiring merchandise also posed a problem for the fledgling firm. It faced opposition from the established wholesalers, who would "blackball" merchants and manufacturers who dealt with dealer-owned organizations. Fearing retaliation, some members joined HWI under fictitious names. There was also a shortage of hardware and building materials following the end of World War II. For many years HWI had to deal with

secondary manufacturers, until its growth attracted the interest of the leading companies.

Although faced with many difficulties, HWI saw its revenue increase from $171,069 in 1946 to $546,275 in 1948, and membership increased from 75 to 112 dealers. In 1947 the firm constructed its first warehouse facility in Fort Wayne. From 1952 to 1966 the facility would be expanded through six additions. In 1948 HWI moved its merchandise market from local meeting halls to its new warehouse in conjunction with an open house that allowed the members to see and use the new facility as well as view the increasing range of products. The merchandise markets were held in the warehouse until 1955, when a huge tent was erected on the company's parking lot.

The Second Decade: 1955–66

By 1955 HWI was an established and rapidly growing regional wholesale distribution company. It served more than 200 member hardware and lumber dealers and offered several major lines of hardware products. In 1955 revenues were nearly $3 million, and rebates to members amounted to nearly $170,000.

During the next decade HWI would acquire more major lines of manufactured goods, expand its building materials business, recruit more members, expand its member services, and increase its warehouse space. By 1966 revenues reached $31.5 million, rebates to members were $1.2 million, and the number of members reached 619.

As HWI began to expand beyond the immediate Fort Wayne area, it used commercial carriers to ship products. In 1955 it created its own fleet, initially consisting of two trucks, to make deliveries. The drivers were paid a percentage of the value of products they hauled rather than an hourly wage. As the company began to use larger trucks, an incentive program was introduced, and HWI's drivers were among the best paid in the United States.

In 1964 the company replaced its punch-card system with an IBM computer to handle data. The computer enabled HWI to expand its member services and, perhaps more importantly, offer its members variable pricing based on margins specified by the members themselves.

Expanding Vision: 1967–72

HWI entered its third decade with new leadership. Its founder, Arnold Gerberding, retired on September 30, 1967, at the age of 67. He remained an honorary executive vice-president and consultant to HWI until his death in 1977. The directors appointed Don Wolf, one of their own employees, to succeed Gerberding. Wolf, who worked his way up the ranks of HWI to merchandise and sales manager before his appointment, would lead HWI for the next 25 years.

The 1970s brought more competition for independent hardware and building materials dealers. Established chains such as Sears were expanding their hardware and remodeling departments. Discount store chains such as Kmart, Wal-Mart, and Target, which had appeared in the 1960s, were beginning to flourish. Specialty discount stores that focused on one category of product highlighted another aggressive retail concept. A variety of other retailers were starting to carry housewares and home hardware items.

Perhaps the biggest competitive threat to HWI came from the new lumber, building supply, and hardware cash and carry stores. These giant retail centers were the forerunners of "big box" stores that boasted no-frills, super-discount prices in a warehouse setting. Other competition came from regional buying groups that were growing and seeking to become national in scope, including Ace Hardware and True Value, among others.

In order to meet these competitive threats, Wolf believed that HWI needed to grow beyond a one-warehouse company. The firm preferred to remain independent, although the possibility of merging with another company existed. In order to grow, HWI needed to formalize its planning process and articulate the concepts it stood for. As its basic operating philosophy, HWI adopted the slogan, "Serving others as we would like to be served."

At first the board of HWI resisted the development of regional centers, because it would double HWI's cost of operation and exposure. Financing was also problematic, as HWI did not have a strong cash position at the time. Previous warehouse expansions, which were on a much smaller scale, had been financed by selling bonds to the members. The new facility was ultimately financed by the Lincoln National Life Insurance Company, based in Fort Wayne, through industrial revenue bonds.

Cape Girardeau, Missouri, was selected as the site for the new 300,000-square-foot facility. The city was strategically located to serve the southern and western regions as well as the St. Louis area. Two years before the facility opened in 1971, HWI began recruiting stores in the St. Louis area, so that Cape Girardeau would be immediately profitable when it opened.

HWI grew dramatically in the early 1970s, and a new distribution center was built in Dixon, Illinois, to service the Great Lakes region and, especially, Chicago, Minnesota, and Wisconsin. Again, new members were recruited in the region before the distribution center opened in 1974. In 1977 another distribution center was built in Medina, Ohio, that became HWI's highest volume distribution facility.

To keep up with HWI's growth, additional distribution centers were built in Waco, Texas, in 1980; in Lexington, South Carolina, in 1986; and in Woodburn, Oregon, in 1991. These six large distribution centers—the Fort Wayne warehouse was closed in 1980 following a labor dispute—served more than 3,500 members in the United States and several other countries in the 1990s.

HWI enjoyed dramatic growth throughout the 1970s. Sales reached $455 million by the end of the decade, and the number of members increased to nearly 1,000. Home-building and remodeling, in addition to do-it-yourself maintenance, was the fastest-growing retail market of the decade. Home centers—retail stores that joined hardware with lumber and building supplies—played an important role in HWI's growth in the 1970s and beyond.

By 1976 HWI's merchandise market events had become too large for Fort Wayne, and they were moved to Indianapolis. These three-day events gave members a chance to view new products and take advantage of sales and special deals from vendors. Members could also take the time to meet with HWI staff to discuss areas of concern and new merchandising ideas. Members usually left the events with a six-month marketing plan.

Do it Center Revolution: The 1980s

HWI's sales more than doubled in the 1980s, from $470 million in 1981 to over $1.1 billion in 1990, and membership increased to over 3,000. It was a decade of tremendous growth in the hardware and lumber and building supplies industry, as retail space increased overall by 50 percent. Discount chain stores expanded rapidly, and "big box" stores exceeding 100,000 square feet, such as Home Depot and Builders Square, opened.

HWI's members were able to keep pace, though, and several members more than doubled their number of stores. In fact, most of HWI's growth came from established members selling more products and buying more from HWI. During the 1980s HWI was committed to creating a total retail marketing strategy for its members. Its "Do it Center" program helped "ignite the resurgence in hardware retailing," according to the *National Home Center News,* and HWI was named Hardware Merchandiser of the Year in 1985 by *Hardware Merchandiser* magazine.

The Do it Center concept was developed by merchandising expert Don Watt, who had first impressed CEO Wolf and other HWI people with his presentation at a 1978 industry convention. The Watt Group, headquartered in Toronto, Ontario, was recognized as the leading design and communications group in North America. At the invitation of Don Wolf, Watt attended all 27 of the HWI district meetings in 1979. At each meeting Watt made a one-hour presentation on worldwide marketing trends and modern merchandising. Six months later he returned to HWI headquarters with a two-hour slide presentation that revealed the similarities among contemporary Sears, HWI, Ace, and True Value stores. As a result, HWI retained Watt to develop an innovative marketing concept that would set HWI apart from its competition.

Watt came up with the Do it Center program, which included bright, aggressive colors and signage to create a warm and exciting atmosphere. Floor layouts included "power aisles" that allowed customers to take a short walk and see all of the store's departments. Similarly, employees could easily walk the power aisles to see who needed service. Seasonal and new items were displayed at end caps, the end of shelving units dividing departments.

For some dealers, the new program was too much of a change. However, the concept was tested in 1981, and the results from the first store were good. When four stores were tested, sales in each of the stores increased by 50 percent in the first year. More importantly, the concept was a hit with customers and employees alike. Customers responded positively to features and sales. Employees took pride in working in such an innovative environment, and Do it Centers became a favored place to work.

The Do it Center program was introduced at the fall market in 1982. With many of the dealers remaining skeptical and others wanting to adopt only part of the program, HWI headquarters established strict mandatory guidelines for opening a true Do it Center. Still, it was difficult to convince all of the members, and it was agreed that members who chose not to participate in the program would not be penalized in any way.

Recognition, Growth, and Leadership in the 1990s

HWI's sales nearly doubled again in the 1990s, from $1.1 billion in 1991 to more than $2 billion in fiscal 1999 (ending June 30). At the beginning of the decade HWI was already competing successfully with the big chain discount and warehouse stores. Management guru Tom Peters, author of *In Search of Excellence* and *Liberation Management,* was so impressed with HWI's performance that he changed his keynote address at the Home Center Trade Show at McCormick Place in Chicago in 1989 to focus on the strength and dynamics of such dealer-owned organizations as HWI.

Like many other industries, the wholesale hardware, lumber, and building materials industry was affected by globalization. In the 1990s HWI led international cooperation efforts among dealer-owned firms in the formation of Interlink, a global association of dealer-owned companies. After HWI began working with the two largest dealer-owned organizations in Canada, an organization called Alliance was formed in 1993 to pool buying power and develop programs for members across North America.

Don Wolf stepped down as CEO in 1992 and retired in July of the following year. As part of a planned succession, executive vice-president Mike McClelland became president and CEO of HWI in October 1992. Bob Taylor, who owned five Do it Center stores in Virginia Beach, Virginia, became chairman.

HWI celebrated its 50th anniversary in 1995. ''Serve others as you would like to be served'' continued to be the company's guiding philosophy. When McClelland became president, he added a mission statement: ''We're going to make the best even better.'' That year HWI separated its sales and marketing division into two divisions, with marketing covering advertising, retail merchandising, store design, special events, and communications. Sales would focus on domestic and international sales.

Through its Canadian joint venture, Alliance, HWI had positioned itself as a total North American buying group. McClelland indicated he wanted to eventually form a holding company with the two Canadian partners, Home Hardware Stores and Le Groupe Ro-Na Dismat, and merge into one company with three marketing identities. The group engineered 35 ''common buys'' in the first half of 1995 and entered into 200 ''common alliances'' with manufacturers.

A new store format, Do it Best Vision, was introduced in October 1995. The flexible program allowed smaller retailers with limited resources to buy into Do it Best with varying degrees of financial commitment. Do it Express, which focused on quicker customer service, was introduced in 1996. The company expected that 80 percent or more of its members would choose one of the three available store programs: Do it Center, Do it Best Vision, or Do it Express. In addition, HWI offered

its members three private label brands: Do-it, Do-it Best, and Master Touch.

HWI initially established its web site in May 1996. Later in the year it made its catalog of 61,000 products available on CD-ROM as well. In 1997 HWI contracted with the Internet division of QVC to sell some 4,000 to 5,000 products over the Internet, making them available to an international market. However, none of the firm's private label brands, which members felt gave them a competitive advantage, were offered over the Internet. In May 1998 the firm's INCOM Distributor Supply division debuted a new web site for members. A full-fledged e-commerce site, billed as ''The World's Largest Hardware Store,'' was launched in July 1999. It offered more than 70,000 hardware and building products and featured an online encyclopedia of how-to advice and project tips.

In October 1997 HWI and Our Own Hardware Co., Inc., announced they intended to merge and form a single co-op. At the time HWI had 3,500 members, while Our Own Hardware had 900 members. HWI's annual sales for fiscal 1996 (ending June 30) were $1.6 billion, compared to $218 million for Our Own Hardware. The proposed merger was quickly approved by Our Own's members, and the two co-ops officially became a single buying group effective January 1, 1998. By the end of the year HWI had fully integrated former Our Own members.

HWI officially changed its name to Do it Best Corporation on March 16, 1998. The new name better reflected the co-op's membership, which included hardware stores, home centers, and building supply stores—the entire home improvement retail sector. The Do it Best retail identification program, first introduced in 1996, included the name in HWI's private-brand products, truck fleet, and company web site. HWI had encouraged members to adopt the Do it Best retail identity.

Sales for fiscal 1998 reached $1.9 billion, a five percent increase over fiscal 1997. The firm ended the year with about 4,000 members, including about 900 that joined following the merger with Our Own Hardware. Not counting purchases from new members, sales were relatively flat, reflecting the rest of the industry. In August 1998 the company broke ground for a new distribution center in Montgomery, New York. Scheduled to open in October 1999, the company's seventh distribution center had 360,000 square feet, which could be expanded by an additional 125,000 square feet of warehouse space if necessary.

Toward a New Century

For fiscal 1999 Do it Best reported a 16 percent increase in sales, which topped $2.2 billion. For the future, the company planned to reassert its focus on helping members identify and implement new marketing strategies, as well as to expand its retail development staff for the benefit of its member-retailers. At the end of the century Do it Best had signed up more than 1,000 stores to implement its Do it Best or Do it Center retail designs. After five years the Do it Best Rental Center program had its 500th member join the program. Following Mike McClelland's exhortation to ''make the best even better,'' Do it Best was committed to expanding member services—such as the recently introduced guarantee of 100 percent customer satisfaction with its private label products—and to remaining focused on operating efficiencies.

Further Reading

Cory, Jim, and Cheryl Ann Lambert, ''Efficiency Rules at HWI,'' *Home Improvement Market,* June 1996, p. 36.

''Do it Best Corp. Reports Jump in Sales,'' *Knight-Ridder/Tribune Business News,* July 27, 1998.

''Do it Best Corp. to Open New York Distribution Center,'' *Do-It-Yourself Retailing,* August 1998, p. 33.

''Do it Best Introduces Two New Member Programs,'' *Do-It-Yourself Retailing,* June 1998, p. 23.

''Do it Best Sets Sights on $2 Billion,'' *Do-It-Yourself Retailing,* November 1998, p. 15.

''Hardware Wholesalers Inc. and Our Own Hardware Agree to Merge,'' *Do-It-Yourself Retailing,* October 1997, p. 29.

''Hardware Wholesalers Inc. Changes Name to Do it Best Corp.,'' *Do-It-Yourself Retailing,* April 1998, p. 23.

''HWI and Our Own Hardware to Merge,'' *Home Improvement Market,* October 1997, p. 12.

''HWI Catalog Now on the Internet,'' *Do-It-Yourself Retailing,* October 1996, p. 25.

''HWI Introduces Convenience-Oriented Do-it Express Store Format,'' *Chilton's Hardware Age,* December 1993, p. A-8.

''HWI Separates Sales and Marketing Divisions,'' *Do-It-Yourself Retailing,* April 1995, p. 27.

''HWI Teams up with QVC to Sell Hardware on the Internet,'' *Do-It-Yourself Retailing,* March 1998, p. 19.

Kelly, Joseph M., and Laurie Shuster, ''Flexibility Fuels Do it Best Vision,'' *Home Improvement Market,* June 1996, p. 42.

Lambert, Cheryl Ann, ''HWI Discusses Competitive Strategies,'' *Home Improvement Market,* July 1995, p. 14.

——, ''HWI—Our Own Merger Approved by Members,'' *Home Improvement Market,* January 1998, p. 9.

Lasek, Alicia, ''HWI at 50: Ready for the Next Era,'' *Building Supply Home Centers,* May 1995, p. 22.

Sutton, Rod, and Alicia Lasek, ''HWI Poised for Next 50 Years,'' *Building Supply Home Centers,* May 1995, p. 30.

''True Value and HWI Join Ace in Hardware Cyberspace,'' *Do-It-Yourself Retailing,* July 1996, p. 76.

Wolf, Don, with Michael C. Hawfield, *HWI: People . . . Building a Great American Success Story,* Fort Wayne, Ind.: Hardware Wholesalers, 1995.

—David P. Bianco

Ducati Motor Holding S.p.A.

Via A. Cavalieri Ducati
3 40132 Bologna
Italy
(39) 051-641-3111
Fax: (39) 051-406-580
Web site: http://www.ducati.com

Public Company
Incorporated: 1926 as Società Radio Brevetti Ducati
Employees: 950
Sales: US$281.9 million (1998)
Stock Exchanges: Milan New York
Ticker Symbol: DMH
NAIC: 336991 Motorcycles & Parts Manufacturing

Ducati Motor Holding S.p.A. has the wind on its back. Since its financial rescue by investment firm Texas Pacific Group in 1996 and its initial public offering in March 1999, the famed Italian motorcycle manufacturer has performed a remarkable turnaround, shedding most of its losses while boosting its sales. Ducati produces a range of motorcycles, from its world-famous Superbike racing series to the more recently launched line of cruising bikes designed to place the North American and European casual biker onto a Ducati seat. In an effort to capture some of the marketing flair of rival Harley Davidson, Ducati has also entered the fashion business, producing clothing and other motorcycling accessories—some of which are designed by Donna Karan—which the company sells in its own expanding chain of retail clothing and accessories stores in Italy, New York, London, Capetown, and Sydney. The company's shifting focus—from its traditional performance-before-comfort design—has enabled the Ducati motorcycle to take an increasing place in worldwide motorcycle sales. From just three percent of the international market, primarily in Europe and North America, Ducati expects to build as much as a ten percent share in the early years of the 21st century. The chief architect of Ducati's turnaround is Federico Minoli, CEO since 1996.

Founding a Motorcyling Legend: 1920s

If the Ducati name would later become synonymous with racing motorcycles—and winning races—the company's origins were in another industry altogether. In 1926, Adriano Ducati, together with his brother and other family members, as well as other local investors, founded Società Radio Brevetti Ducati in Bologna, Italy. As the company's name suggests, its initial products were based on patents held by Ducati and destined for the developing market for radio equipment and components. Ducati's first product, the Manens condenser, gave the young company instant worldwide recognition. A string of other successful products followed, making Ducati an internationally recognized name.

By the mid-1930s, the company, despite the worldwide recession, had grown out of its existing facilities. In 1935, the company began construction of its Borgo Panigale factory, on the outskirts of Bologna, a modern production facility that was also designed to attract further industrial and technological investment in Bologna—an early example of the "clustering" found, among elsewhere, in California's Silicon Valley.

While construction continued on the Borgo Panigale plant, Ducati also began developing an international network of production and service facilities, allowing the company to offer its customers faster and more direct distribution and support services. By the end of the decade, the company had opened offices and subsidiaries in Caracas, New York, London, Paris, and Sydney.

World War II put an end to Ducati's glowing radio career. Extensive Allied bombing runs completely destroyed the only recently completed Borgo Panigale factory. By 1944, nothing remained of the Ducati site. While crushing the Ducati family's business, the destruction of the Borgo Panigale plant would nonetheless give rise to a new opportunity—and a new era for the Ducati brand name.

"Vrooming" into the 1950s

As Italy fought, lost—and then, technically at least, won—World War II, Adriano Ducati and his brother began making

171

Company Perspectives:

The future of Ducati is based on our past successes, incorporating a winning combination of Italian style, performance, craftsmanship and leading technology. We are committed to customer satisfaction, offering Ducati enthusiasts the products, accessories and service at a level that their passion and support to the Ducati marque merits. Our company philosophy can be summed up in a few words: Ducati was, is and always will be a leader for technology and innovation. Ducati will continue to incorporate this winning philosophy, a tradition of success and excellence, in its road and racing motorcycles.

plans for the company's postwar future. Reviewing a number of new products, with which the brothers hoped to regain their company's international position, the Ducati brothers made the rather radical decision of switching product focus altogether. Instead of building radio components, the Ducatis began designing for a different market entirely—and by 1946 the first new Ducati product appeared: the "Cucciolo."

The Cucciolo was a small motor designed to be fitted to bicycles. The idea was a quick success, and the Cucciolo soon became one of the biggest-selling motors of its kind in the world. While sold as a kit at first, Ducati soon began marketing its own motorized bike, based on a Capellino frame patent and constructed by Caproni, in Trente. By the beginning of the 1950s, the Cucciolo had graduated from a motorized bicycle to full-fledged status as a motorcycle. With this Cucciolo, the company inaugurated more than 50 years of Ducati motorcycling fame.

The Cucciolo was quickly joined by other motorcycle models. In 1952, the company unveiled its Cruiser, featuring a 175cc engine, electronic ignition, and automatic transmission. The following year saw a more conventional bike, with a small 98cc (quickly increased to 125cc), designed as an affordable, if stripped-down, motorbike. Together with the Cucciolo, these models brought Ducati back to the forefront of the international manufacturing scene, and helped make the company a leading name in cycling.

Yet the company's greatest successes would come with the arrival of the legendary Fabio Taglioni as the company's chief design engineer in 1955. Taglioni brought an avant-gardist approach to motorcycle design, seeking revolutionary solutions for both technical excellence and high performance. Taglioni also understood the need to demonstrate the excellence of his designs, and led the company onto the racing circuit, particularly long-distance competitions including the Giro d'Italia.

Taglioni's influence quickly produced a new generation of Ducati motorbikes. In 1956 the company debuted a four-stroke, 174cc engine, available in touring and sports versions, that could reach speed performances of up to 135 kilometers (approximately 70 miles) per hour. These models, the Tourist,

Special, and Sport models, were joined by the "America" the following year.

By 1958 Ducati had begun producing the 200cc-powered Elite model, which also featured for the first time the Taglioni-designed "Desmodromic" valve gear system. The Desmodromic system would remain an integral feature of the Ducati design through the 1990s, and would provide the launching pad for the company's great racing successes.

Racing Champion in the 1960s

The Desmodromic system paved the way for a new 250cc model, a twin-cylinder cycle specially ordered by racing great Mike Hailwood in 1960. The 250cc engine was soon adapted as a single-cylinder powerhouse for such models as the Diana, Monza, Aurea, and the later GP models, providing speeds up to 170 kilometers per hour. The company would produce still more single-cylinder models, including the famed 250cc, 350cc, and 450cc Scrambler models, which found great success in the United States market. Meanwhile, Ducati was building its reputation among the racing world, with the Mach 250 providing a breakthrough in 1964. This bike was soon followed by the 450 Mark 3D model, introduced in 1968, which pushed the speed limit beyond 170 kilometers (100 miles) per hour. This model was also the first production model to feature the Desmodromic system.

The arrival of the Japanese motorcycles, including Honda, Yamaha, Kawasaki, and Suzuki, soon challenged the Western market leaders and inaugurated a new category of bikes, the so-called Maxi Bike, featuring large-displacement engines of 750cc and more. While Ducati would remain synonymous with high-performance, small-capacity motorcycles, the company raced to join the Maxi Bike competition, producing a twin-cylinder 750 cc engine incorporating the Desmodromic valve system. The new motorcycle would make its debut in April 1972, when it captured first and second place at the Imola 200. This bike would give rise to a new Ducati series, the Supersport, a line that would continue into the 1990s. In 1978 the Supersport captured world attention when Mike Hailwood came out of retirement to capture both the Tourist Trophy and the Formula 1 TT on a 900cc Supersport.

In 1983 Ducati was purchased by the brothers Claudio and Gianfranco Castiglioni, who placed the motorcycle company under their growing Cagiva Group conglomerate. Described as passionate racing fans, the Castiglionis would allow Ducati to remain on the sports bike track, setting the stage for the company's string of 1990s victories. The Castiglionis also expanded the company's line of motorcycles, introducing more models, and adding a wider selection—and higher production volume—of the large displacement motorcycles by then leading the entire market. One of the architects of this new Ducati era would be Massimo Bordi, who joined the company as design engineer in 1983 and who quickly made his mark on the company's racing production.

Inspired by Formula 1 racing, and by the Ford Cosgrove engine design, Bordi set to work designing a new series of high-performance motorcycles. For this, he incorporated the

Desmodromic valve and distribution system to a four-valve, air-cooled motor based on the Cosgrove engine. The result was the "Desmoquattro," which debuted as the heart of the 748 model in the Grand Prix of 1986. Two years later, the 851 model would usher in the era of the Ducati dominance of the Superbike circuit: after winning its first championship in 1990, the Ducati bikes—the 888 in 1991, the 916 in 1994—would go on to win six of the next eight races, firmly establishing Ducati as the category leader.

While Ducati was winning races, it was also losing money. That is, the Castiglioni brothers, in attempts to resuscitate the Cagiva conglomerate, had been draining Ducati's revenues. Production—in the company's now ancient factories—had begun to slow, dipping to a low of just 12,500 motorcycles in 1996. Ducati once again faced financial ruin.

The struggling Cagiva empire caught the attention of Texas Pacific Group (TPG), a U.S.-based buyout specialist. Hiring Federico Minoli, TPG negotiated the purchase of the Ducati business, initially buying 49 percent of Ducati for some $43 million in 1996. Under the terms of the purchase agreement, an additional two percent was placed in a trust held by TPG, which gave the company control of Ducati. In August 1998, TPG bought out the rest of Ducati, paying the Castiglionis $174 million.

Meanwhile, Minoli worked to turn around the famous motorcycle company. One of his immediate moves was to make heavy investments in refitting the company's production lines, adding automation, while also negotiating with the company's suppliers to improve efficiency. Not content simply to increase production levels, Minoli greatly expanded the company's range of models, more than doubling the number of production designs and introducing the Ducati name into new categories. Minoli also replaced most of Ducati's management, putting in place a largely young team. As production levels rose, Minoli set to work streamlining Ducati's distributor model—instituting a two-tiered system of exclusive dealerships, some 40 Ducati-only shops, and some 900 store-in-store shops selling Ducati products in third-party dealerships.

Minoli also worked on revitalizing the Ducati image. Following the Harley Davidson model, Minoli sought to make Ducati as much a lifestyle image as a motorbike. A new line of Ducati-labeled clothing and biking accessories appeared, and the company launched a new, high-fashion ad campaign, selling the ads to such venues as *GQ* and *For Him* magazines. The company also hired Donna Karan to design some of its biking outfits.

The revived Ducati continued to win races and attract new motorcycling fans willing to pay up to $25,000 for a Ducati bike. The company's revenues began to rise, topping US$280 million in 1998, and expected to climb past US$323 million for 1999. With Ducati back on track, Texas Pacific cashed in, taking Ducati public in March 1999 with a listing on the New York Stock Exchange. Two months later, the company opened its first showroom in North America, on New York City's West Side. Featuring the Donna Karan clothing designs, including leather motorcycle jackets with price tags of $1,200 and more, the store also highlighted Ducati's new line of "Naked Sport" motorcycles.

If the rejuvenated Ducati had found fortune as a lifestyle choice, the company remained nonetheless committed to continuing its tradition of building some of the world's fastest racing bikes. The company persevered as a small business in an industry dominated by such powerful names as Honda and Yamaha. After Ducati's public offering, industry rumors began to suggest that a merger might be in store for the famed Italian manufacturer—with Milwaukee's Harley Davidson. The company immediately denied the rumors. But with just three percent of the worldwide motorcycle market, it remained to be seen for how long Ducati could stay independent.

Principal Subsidiaries

Gia.Ca.Moto.

Further Reading

Colker, David, "Naked Motorcycles Travel Comeback Trail," *Greensboro News & Record*, April 2, 1999.

Heller, Richard, "Vroom-Vroom Versus Potato-Potato," *Forbes*, July 26, 1999.

Michaud, Chris, "Ducati Peddles Designer Chic in N. American Debut," *Reuters Business Report*, May 20, 1999.

Putter, Eric, "Ducati," *Dealernews*, November 1997, p. 22.

Tagliabue, John, "Passion Fashion for 2-Wheel Italian Motorcycle Makers Hope to Carve Out Niche in High End of US Market," *Fort Worth-Star Telegram*, May 25, 1999.

—M. L. Cohen

Ducommun Incorporated

111 West Ocean Boulevard, Suite 900
P.O. Box 22677
Long Beach, California 90801-5677
U.S.A.
(562) 624-0800
Fax: (562) 624-0789
Web site: http://www.ducommun.com

Public Company
Incorporated: 1907 as the Ducommun Hardware
   Company
Employees: 1,200
Sales: $170.77 million (1998)
Stock Exchanges: New York
Ticker Symbol: DCO
NAIC: 336412 Aircraft Engine & Engine Parts
   Manufacturing; 336413 Other Aircraft Parts and
   Auxiliary Equipment Manufacturing

California's oldest company, Ducommun Incorporated has gone from repairing watches for prospectors to supplying the world's most advanced aerospace programs, including the space shuttle, military aircraft, and virtually all new civil airliners. The company divested its metals and electronics supply businesses, hitching its wagon to high-tech aviation. Ducommun celebrated 150 years in business in 1999.

Gold Rush Origins

Swiss watchmaker Charles Louis Ducommun came to the United States as a young man. He was swept up in the California Gold Rush in 1849, and left Arkansas on foot, a mule carrying all his possessions. He was 29 years old at the time and smallpox had already blinded him in one eye.

His journey took nine months and brought him to the frontier village of Los Angeles, population 1,600. Los Angeles was gateway to the gold mines of northern California. Ducommun was well-placed to grow along with the city, which incorporated the next year as its population doubled.

Ducommun opened a small shop on Commerce Street and began repairing watches. He soon branched out into hardware and sundries, from pencils to saddles. He associated with the pioneer town's most eminent citizens, including governors. He helped found the city's first bank, the Farmers and Merchants Bank, as well as the municipal water board. He was also known to extend credit to customers hit by hard times such as the drought of 1863. His clock and meteorological instruments kept track of official time and weather for the city. As Los Angeles entered a period of ferocious growth, Ducommun stocked the orange, oil, and construction industries.

Ducommun died in 1896, passing ownership of the company to his sons Charles Albert, Alfred, Emil, and Edmond. They incorporated the business in 1907 as the Ducommun Hardware Company and soon relocated it to a larger store next to the railroad.

Supplying 20th-Century Industries

Ducommun acted as a middleman in the metal industry. This line of business prospered with the coming of World War I. Ducommun supplied regional machine shops making all manner of armaments.

Ducommun began supplying the booming movie industry in the 1920s. In the 1930s, Ducommun supplied legendary aircraft designer Donald Douglas on credit, before he had established himself commercially. Ducommun products also flew with aviation pioneers Lockheed, Ryan, and Lindbergh.

Ducommun provided materials for military aircraft and ships during World War II. The company had 450 employees at the time. The burgeoning civil aviation industry gave the company good prospects after the war. The company had an initial public offering in 1946 and announced sales of $16.5 million for the year. Within a few years, Ducommun was the largest metal materials distributor in the Pacific.

Charles E. Ducommun became company president in 1950, representing the third generation in the company's management. Ducommun grew alongside the nascent space program as the Southern California economy as a whole focused on aerospace.

Ducommun diversified in 1961 when it bought East Coast distributor Kierulff Electronics. It bought specialty fastener distributor R.G. Wallace Co. in the late 1960s.

In the 1970s, Ducommun expanded its geographic range west to Hawaii and east to Texas. Its role also grew in depth. For example, Ducommun's metal service centers were installed with a computer link with client Hughes Aircraft Co. The system was designed to allow Ducommun to handle more of the metals handling functions of its clients. Mills, also looking for competitive advantages, raised their minimum order requirements for economies of scale, making the service center approach even more valid.

Charles Ducommun's descendants left management in 1977, though they remained the company's largest shareholders. Sales hit a new peak of $245 million in 1978; however, a recession was just around the corner.

Decade of Divestiture: 1980s

Revenues were $164.6 million in 1980, with earnings of $3.8 million. Ducommun soon recovered from the recession of 1979–80. By 1983 earnings had doubled: $8 million on sales of $304 million.

In 1981 the company exited metal sales, selling Ducommun Metals Co. to Centaur Metals for $57 million. That same year, Ducommun bought Aerochem and Airdrome Parts, continuing its commitment to aviation. Purchases of Aircraft Hydro-Forming, a supplier of aircraft structures, and Jay-El Products, a maker of switches and keyboards for the aerospace industry, soon followed. In 1983 this segment accounted for ten percent of Ducommun's sales, but a quarter of profits.

However, Ducommun also sought to become a major player supplying the new computer industry. In 1981, its Kierulff subsidiary bought the distribution operation of Texas Instruments, with nine outlets. This made Kierulff a national player. It added several more outlets in the mid-1980s and acquired MTI Systems, a supplier of computer makers in the Northeast, for $6.3 million.

In the early part of the decade, the company's electronics distribution operation grew to become the country's fourth largest. AT&T chose Ducommun's Kierulff unit as a distributor of its PCs through its approximately 30 electronics distribution centers.

In the mid-1980s, chairman Wallace W. Booth, a former Rockwell International executive, focused the company on aerospace at the expense of electronics. President W. Donald Bell, who felt electronics had not been supported adequately, resigned in disagreement with this new direction in 1987. The previous president, David G. Schmidt, had also resigned after a year over clashes with Booth.

The electronics components distribution businesses (Kierulff Electronics, MTI Systems, Ducommun Data Systems) went to Arrow Electronics Inc. of Melville, New York, in January 1988 for $125 million worth of stock. (The additional revenues and efficiencies from the purchase helped Arrow put itself into the black for the first time in four years.)

As Ducommun shed its metals and electronics businesses, gross annual sales fell to $60 million in 1988, down from $360 million in 1980. Ducommun was left with Jay-El Products, Aerochem, AHF-Ducommun, and Tri-Tec Engineering.

The explosion of the space shuttle *Challenger* in 1986 virtually grounded AHF-Ducommun Inc. for a couple of years. This subsidiary made the spacecraft's fuel tanks. A general slowdown in defense spending hurt other parts of Ducommun's aerospace business. Ducommun lost an average of $20 million a year from 1985 to 1989. In 1988 Norman Barkeley, accompanied by a new management team, was brought in to replace Booth. Barkeley's mission: "Survive." By this time, AHF-Ducommun had contracts to supply parts for McDonnell Douglas MD-80 and MD-11 airliners as well as the next generation Advanced Tactical Fighter. In the *Wall Street Journal*, Barkeley attributed Ducommun's subsequent turnaround to "plain old, ordinary grunt work"—elevating prices while cutting costs. Ducommun posted nearly $2 million in income on sales of $74 million for 1990. The company had also cut its long-term debt 75 percent in two years. The ratio of defense to commercial to space work went from a 45-45-10 split to 60-30-10.

Still Pioneering in the 1990s

In 1993, Ducommun-AHF bought a novel piece of equipment that would triple its business in a few years. This digital router used computer files from designers at the aircraft manufacturers to custom shape metal fuselage parts.

The purchase of Brice Manufacturing brought Ducommun into the airline seating business in 1994. The acquisition seemed poised to prosper in the light of FAA regulations requiring sturdier seats on civil airliners. The next year, Ducommun made a brief foray into telecommunications when it bought 3dbm, which it sold to COM DEV International three years later.

Ducommun began trading its shares on the New York Stock Exchange in 1996. With relatively little competition and a sustainable mass, it seemed poised to prosper during the aircraft industry's cyclical recovery. Airline orders poured in from airlines that had postponed new aircraft purchases during the recession. Aircraft manufacturers were outsourcing more of their production. Ducommun won a long-term contract to supply fuselage skins to Boeing's 747 program. Boeing, in fact, accounted for nearly a quarter of Ducommun's business.

Ducommun went on a shopping spree, buying five companies in five years. The acquisitions gave Ducommun a critical role in the production of several diverse aircraft programs, including McDonnell-Douglas fighters, Boeing airliners, and the space shuttle. At the end of his ten-year tenure in 1998, Barkeley saw profits rise to their highest level ever. Ducommun Incorporated posted the highest operating income, $29.8 million, in its history in 1998. Sales were up nine percent to $170.8 million for the year.

Barkeley was succeeded by Joseph Berenato, first as president and CEO, then as chairman. Berenato continued the company's course of growth by acquisition and internal development. Company literature compared the aerospace components Ducommun sold in the late-1990s with the hardware sold to pioneers more than a century earlier.

High valuations of potential takeover targets postponed Ducommun's acquisition plans in 1998 and 1999. The company did purchase American Electronics, Inc., which made satellite components, in June 1998. It bought privately held SMS Technologies in May 1999. The new purchase was to be incorporated into Ducommun's MechTronics of Arizona Corp. subsidiary, a similar operation. SMS would remain in California, however.

Sales for 1998 were $170.77 million and the company boasted above-average profit margins. As it neared the year 2000, Ducommun braced for an anticipated downturn in the commercial aircraft market. Bright spots included the next generation of Boeing 737 aircraft, as well as the C-17 and F-18 E/F military planes. In June 1999, the company received a contract to provide leading-edge wing skins for the A330/A340 line of civil airliners, from Airbus, which was just beginning to outsource more work.

Principal Subsidiaries

Aerochem; AHF-Ducommun; Ducommun Technologies; MechTronics; Brice Manufacturing.

Principal Divisions

Aerospace Structural Components; Electromechanical Avionics Products; Aircraft Seating and Cabin Interiors.

Further Reading

Cole, Patrick E., ''Ducommun Looks to the Heavens for Growth,'' *Business Week,* February 29, 1988, p. 74D.
''Ducommun: 150 Years of Innovation,'' Los Angeles: Ducommun, Inc., 1999.
Gordon, Mitchell, ''New Role: Ducommun Scores As Distributor of Electronic Parts,'' *Barron's,* October 8, 1984, pp. 58–60.
La Franco, Robert, ''Corporate Chameleon,'' *Forbes,* November 2, 1998, p. 220.
Marcial, Gene G., ''Arrow's Fortunes May Be Taking a New Direction,'' *Business Week,* July 18, 1988, p. 128.
''Metal Centers Do a Bigger Job,'' *Business Week,* October 25, 1976.
Veverka, Mark, ''Aerospace Industry's Growth Cycle May Help Ducommun Soar Higher,'' *Wall Street Journal,* January 29, 1997.
Wartzman, Rick, ''Ducommun's Turnaround Is Attributed to Basic 'Grunt Work,' Chairman Says,'' *Wall Street Journal,* March 11, 1991.

—Frederick C. Ingram

Edward **Jones**

Serving Individual Investors Since 1871

Edward Jones

12555 Manchester Road
St. Louis, Missouri 63131
U.S.A.
(314) 515-2600
Fax: (314) 515-2622
Web site: http://www.edwardjones.com

Private Company
Incorporated: 1922 as Edward D. Jones & Co.
Employees: 13,691
Operating Revenues: $1.3 billion (1998 est.)
NAIC: 52312 Securities Brokerage

Edward Jones is one of the world's largest brokerage networks, with more than 4,000 offices across the United States, in Canada, and in England. Almost all Jones offices are one-person affairs, and the firm aims primarily at individual investors who have relatively small accounts. Until the 1980s, Edward Jones offices were found exclusively in rural areas, but the firm expanded into suburbs as well as into big cities, including Chicago and Detroit. Jones takes a consciously low-key and old-fashioned approach to acquiring new accounts, earning its brokers comparisons to milkmen and other vanished service providers of the past. New brokers make 1,000 cold calls before they are allowed to open an office, so they must go door to door cultivating neighborly relations. Jones brokers specialize in low-risk investments, and its customers are usually in the market for the long haul. While the average mutual fund customer buys and sells a fund every three years, Jones customers on average hold on for 20 years. Jones brokers do not sell new stock issues, commodities, or options, preferring established stocks, government bonds, and mutual funds. The average Jones broker handles more than 700 accounts, with an average balance in each of around $50,000. Edward Jones also has an insurance arm, and invests for some corporate clients.

Early Years

Edward D. Jones of Edward D. Jones & Co. was not the same Edward D. Jones remembered on Wall Street as the Jones of Dow Jones. This Edward D. Jones was a broker in St. Louis, Missouri, who opened his own firm in 1922. In 1943 Jones's firm merged with an older investment firm, Whitaker & Co., founded in 1871. The brokerage was nothing out of the ordinary until Edward D. Jones's son Edward Jones, Jr., joined the company in 1948. Jones, Jr., known as Ted, studied agriculture at the University of Missouri, then worked for a while on Wall Street. He had always liked small towns, and was comfortable with farmers and rural people. Up to that point, Jones brokers worked rural territories only as so-called TNT brokers, looking for clients from Tuesday 'til Thursday, before heading back to the St. Louis office. Ted Jones decided that the brokerage would do well to branch into small towns directly, to offer investment services to people that big city firms usually overlooked. Jones, Sr., disagreed with his son, but Ted went ahead anyway, and opened the first Jones branch in 1955 in the tiny town of Mexico, Missouri. When Ted Jones took over as managing partner of the brokerage in 1968, he pressed ahead with his plans to infiltrate rural America. Most offices were in the Midwest, and from the start they followed the Jones pattern still used today: a one-man office, pushing conservative investments.

Even before Ted Jones took over as managing partner, he instituted a broker training program unique in the industry. Jones trained college graduates who had no specific background in the securities industry. While learning the ins and outs of the financial markets, Jones trainees also polished their people skills and learned to hone in on potential investors. Then they were sent to a town where they knew no one. The new broker was required to make 1,000 cold calls, knocking on doors like the storied Fuller brush man or encyclopedia salesman. To reach the quota often took many months of eight- to ten-hour days pounding the pavement. Only after this grueling initiation was completed was the new broker allowed to open an office. It took a particular kind of person, and not your typical broker, to go for the Jones approach. But the scheme apparently built intense company loyalty among Edward D. Jones's scattered crew. Ted Jones commented on his brokers' training in a June 12, 1986 article in the *Wall Street Journal*, ''If it's beneath your dignity, then go work somewhere else.'' But for the brokers who could stand the isolation from co-workers, the small town atmosphere, and the exhausting cold calls, there was money to be made. Jones offices prospered, and the company grew.

The number of Jones brokerages expanded gradually through the 1970s, filling the Midwest. The Jones formula seemed to work in town after town, from Spearfish, South Dakota, to Paris, Illinois. One area Jones tried and failed to penetrate was Florida. The firm made a big push there in the mid-1970s, attempting to recruit brokers from other firms. This did not work, and Jones bowed out of the state. By 1978, Jones operated just over 200 brokerage offices. At that time, the offices were linked by a teletype system, which let them communicate with each other and also keep up with moving stock quotes. However, the network had grown too big for the teletype technology, and brokers had trouble getting their quotes because of tied-up lines. The company therefore switched to using Merrill Lynch's toll-free number for stock quotes for a time, and eventually upgraded to a sophisticated computer and satellite network.

Under New Leadership in the 1980s

Ted Jones stepped down from managing the firm in 1980, and he was succeeded by John W. Bachmann. Bachmann had begun working for the firm one summer when he was in college, and his first position in the head office is variously described as janitor or messenger. When he took over, Edward D. Jones & Co. had approximately 300 offices, still almost entirely in the Midwest. Bachmann launched the company into a rapid expansion. By the mid-1980s, the firm had close to a thousand offices spread across 36 states. The new managing partner did not deviate from the traditional Jones-style training, but was if anything more avid about it than his predecessor. Bachmann was a disciple of the management expert Peter Drucker, who is credited with turning management into an academic discipline. Bachmann engaged Drucker as a consultant in the early 1980s. Drucker apparently liked Jones's structure, which he saw as a strong center surrounded by the relatively autonomous satellites of the one-person offices. Bachmann's vision of the company, fueled by his work with Drucker, went beyond the small-town markets the company had already extensively cultivated. The new managing director realized that there were many Jones-type customers outside small towns—people with low amounts to invest, worried about retirement income, who would enjoy Jones's conservative investment advice and friendly, personal service. These investors were overlooked by the big investment houses like Merrill Lynch and Charles Schwab, who tended to go after wealthy clients first. Thus Bachmann began training new brokers and opening new offices at a furious pace. Beginning in 1981, Jones grew in terms of number of brokers at 15 percent a year all the way into the mid-1990s.

The company made money as it expanded, with a return on equity of typically close to 30 percent, considered quite high in the securities industry. Even as Jones moved into new geographic areas, penetrating big cities such as Atlanta and Chicago, the company clung to its basic strategy, pushing low-risk investments for individual investors. Jones brokers did well. Figures for the late 1980s asserted that many were making over $100,000 a year, but there was some evidence that not all Jones's approved transactions were as low-risk as they should have been. The company was involved in a number of lawsuits and complaints in the mid-1980s, brought by customers who were angry at investments that went sour. In the early 1980s, Jones sold its customers debenture issues for Baldwin-United, an insurance carrier, and these bonds were in default within a year. Other troublesome transactions that Jones pushed were energy partnerships offered by a firm called Petro-Lewis and real estate partnerships offered by one Southmark Corp. These and other ill-fated ventures aggressively pushed by Jones brokers led Matthew Schifrin of *Forbes* magazine to claim in an August 22, 1988 article that Jones made its money by "peddling a good proportion of overpriced junk." Schifrin's article also reported on a class-action suit brought against Jones by 24,600 investors who had lost money in 1983 on limited partnership shares in something called Natural Resource Management Corp. Customers claimed they had been led to expect a 15 percent minimum return. Instead, every $1,000 invested ended up worth only about $50. Jones management, including managing partner John Bachmann, had a big stake in Natural Resource Management, leading to allegations of conflict of interest. Jones settled these complaints out of court.

Another stumble in the mid-1980s was Jones's expansion into the home mortgage market. The firm started to offer its customers home mortgages in 1986, but over two years, the company lost money on these transactions because the one-person offices were overwhelmed with the required paperwork. The mortgage program was discontinued in 1988. In 1987 the firm organized itself as a limited partnership. This made it officially the Jones Financial Companies, L.P., which acted as a holding company for Edward D. Jones & Co. At the time of the reorganization, Jones posted its sales as $268 million.

Expansion Through the 1990s

By the early 1990s, Jones had over 1,500 offices in 45 states across the United States. While the company still had its biggest presence in the Midwest, Jones planned to push into territory where it was underrepresented, including southern California, New England, and Florida. By 1991 Jones offices could be found in every state except Hawaii, Alaska, Delaware, and Massachusetts, and 40 percent of those offices were not in small towns but in suburbs. Managing principal John Bachmann reiterated for the *Wall Street Journal* on February 12, 1991 that "geography doesn't really matter, anyway." Jones was after a particular kind of customer, and that customer could be found just as well in suburban Connecticut as in Sandwich, Illinois. By this time, Jones was an interesting combination of high technology and old-fashioned style. Every Jones office was fitted with a satellite dish, and the isolated brokers tuned in frequently to videos broadcast from headquarters. Some of these leaked to the press in an embarrassing way, giving a glimpse of the seemingly low-key Jones behind the scenes. Just after the Persian Gulf War a Jones principal dressed as "Stormin' Norman" Schwarzkopf, the successful general of that conflict, urged Jones brokers on the satellite broadcast to boost the firms sales with "Operation Bonus Bracket." The presentation stressed that brokers could make more money for themselves and the firm by pushing specific investments which had added fees. The satellite dishes were also sometimes controversial in small towns, where they represented an architectural anomaly. The Edward D. Jones office in Beaufort, South Carolina, was picketed in 1991 by demonstrators who thought the obtrusive satellite dish did not belong in the town's historic business district. Otherwise, the satellite dishes kept Jones brokers in constant touch with headquarters and enabled them to make transactions for their customers in mere seconds. Although the firm still presented an image of down-home conservative advice and one-on-one consultations, it was nevertheless completely modern in the way it did business, and increasingly branching out from its small-town customer base.

By 1994 Jones had penetrated every state except Alaska and Hawaii, with more than 2,600 offices. These offices were in small towns, in suburbs, and to a large extent in big cities, too. The company had over 80 brokerage offices in Chicago, for example. That year Jones also made its first move internationally, opening several offices in suburban Toronto, Ontario, Canada. The move across the border happened after five years of research showed that Canadians matched the Jones investor profile almost perfectly. Jones's typical customer in the mid-1990s was an individual in his or her mid- to late 50s, with grown children and a low or nonexistent mortgage. These people were concerned primarily with investing for retirement. They were baby-boomers—people born just after World War II, and now nearing the end of their working lives. The United States was not the only country that had experienced a postwar baby boom. Canada and Europe had them, too, and so Jones began aiming for customers there. In the mid-1990s Jones discussed extravagant plans, saying it would open 300 to 350 Canadian offices over the next five years, investigate Europe, and think about Mexico. Jones's leader Bachmann told the *St. Louis Business Journal* on July 25, 1994 that he had been approached by Japanese firms interested in a joint venture, but that he was not ready to go to Asia yet.

Jones paused its expansion a bit in 1995 and 1996 to make some internal changes. The firm invested $150 million to upgrade its computer and satellite technology. It had the largest satellite network in the securities industry. It also delved into the Internet, so that by 1997 it had one of the largest client/server systems on the web, and each Jones office had its own home page. Another improvement the company made was to shorten its name from Edward D. Jones & Co. to simply Edward Jones: this was easier to fit on storefront signs. In the mid-1990s Jones also took a second look at some urban markets that had not done as well as expected. Jones had wanted to build a strong presence in Detroit in the early 1990s, but had less than 30 offices in the Detroit metropolitan area by 1996. At the end of that year, Jones started over, announcing it would open over 200 brokerages there over the next several years. By 1997 Jones was back on its expansion tear, hoping to open 100 new offices a month. A large percentage of these new offices were in urban areas. John Bachmann told *Fortune* magazine on October 13, 1997 that his job now was "to see how large and how important we can become" without selling the limited partnership. As Jones became more and more a mass-marketer, it would make it easier to afford national advertising. Other brokerages were competing for Jones customers, so

opening more offices made sense. Merrill Lynch planned in the late 1990s to move into the kinds of rural areas that had long been Jones's mainstay, and banks, too, were increasingly offering some of the investment services that only brokers had handled in the past. Bachmann's plan for Jones was to bring the number of brokerages up to 10,000 by the year 2004.

Edward Jones came to England in 1998, opening its first office in Norwich. A year later the firm had over 50 offices in England, mostly in small towns south of London and in the Midlands. Jones sent some of its most successful U.S. brokers over to England. Here, too, Jones brokers carried on as they did in the United States, beginning with cold calls, knocking on doors, leaving leaflets and business cards, inviting people to investment seminars. Jones planned to have 400 brokers working in England by 2003, and was targeting moves into Ireland and other European Union countries. Jones's rapid expansion seemed to pay off. Revenues grew 25 percent in 1998, up to $1.3 billion, and Jones's return on equity remained the envy of the securities industry. By late 1999, Jones's plan to take on the world with its overseas expansion seemed quite feasible. It had a specific core customer base and a verifiably effective way of reaching new investors. At least in English-speaking countries, Jones was able to move abroad with little change in its basic way of doing business. Saturation of these new markets seemed to present no unusual challenge, and there was every indication that Jones would meet its expansion goals.

Further Reading

Berman, Phyllis, "Door-to-Door in Harpenden," *Forbes*, June 14, 1999, pp. 86–88.

Burns, Greg, "Can It Play Out of Peoria?," *Business Week*, August 7, 1995, pp. 58–59.

Cocheo, Steve, "Is Main Street a State of Mind?," *ABA Banking Journal*, April 1994, p. 52.

Cowell, Alan, "U.S. Concern Solicits British Investment Funds," *New York Times*, June 1, 1999, p. C3.

Desloge, Rick, "Edward D. Jones to Stock New Offices," *St. Louis Business Journal*, August 5, 1991, p. 1A.

Feder, Barnaby J., "The Last-Stand Partnership on Wall Street," *New York Times*, June 21, 1998, p. BU7.

Hansen, Bruce, "Pounding the Pavement," *Memphis Business Journal*, July 8, 1991, p. 1.

Jacobs, Sanford L., "To This Broker, Paris Is in Illinois, New York in Limbo," *Wall Street Journal*, June 12, 1986, p. 1.

McReynolds, Rebecca, "Ed Jones, America's Community Banker," *US Banker*, September 1997, p. 58.

Power, William, "Keeping Up with Down-Home Joneses," *Wall Street Journal*, February 12, 1991, pp. C1, C13.

Power, William, and Siconolfi, Michael, "Edward D. Jones Takes 'Rallying the Troops' to Literal Heights," *Wall Street Journal*, July 12, 1991, pp. C1, C8.

Roush, Matt, "Edward Jones Makes New Expansion Effort," *Crain's Detroit Business*, November 4, 1996, p. 18.

Schifrin, Matthew, "Jonestown," *Forbes*, August 22, 1988, pp. 61–64.

Siconolfi, Michael, "An Alien Saucer Tries to Plop Down in Historic Beaufort," *Wall Street Journal*, June 17, 1991, p. A1.

Teitelbaum, Richard, "The Wal-Mart of Wall Street," *Fortune*, October 13, 1997, pp. 128–30.

Van Allen, Peter, "The One-Horse Broker Is Going Suburban, Too," *American Banker*, April 10, 1997, p. 12.

—A. Woodward

Embers America Restaurants

1664 University Avenue
St. Paul, Minnesota 55104
U.S.A.
(651) 645-6473
Fax: (651) 645-6866
Web site: http://www.embersamerica.com

Private Company
Incorporated: 1956 as Embers Restaurants Inc.
Employees: 1,000
Sales: $16.6 million (1998)
NAIC: 533110 Franchising; 722110 Full Service
   Restaurants

Embers America Restaurants, which began as a single-unit neighborhood restaurant in the mid-1950s, has transformed itself into a unique franchising operation. The Embers America concept links independently owned restaurants but allows franchisees to use their own name and menu items in combination with the Embers logo and proprietary food offerings. Embers targets restaurants along major freeways and secondary highways, ones which travelers often bypass in favor of well-known chains, such as Denny's, Perkins, McDonald's, or Burger King. The company is owned and operated by one of the founding families.

Childhood Friends Building a Business: 1950s–70s

Henry Kristal and Carl Birnberg met as fifth graders, remained friends throughout school, and eventually signed up for the Navy together. Greasy-spoon hamburgers and military food were sorry substitutes for the home cooking they had both enjoyed while growing up in Minnesota.

"We used to write back and forth to each other," Kristal recalled in a 1998 *Twin Cities Business Monthly* article by Brooke Benson. "We'd say, 'wouldn't it be great if there was a place that common people could go and have a good meal for a low price?' That became our goal." They achieved their goal, in 1956, when they opened a 36-seat restaurant in a south Minne-

apolis working class neighborhood; a loan from a local restaurant supplier helped fund the venture.

The restaurant's signature Emberger—a quarter pound of beef topped by a special sauce—sold for 45 cents. A bacon cheeseburger, the Emberger Royal, went for 30 cents more. By comparison, during the period, higher priced restaurants charged $4 to $5 for a steak dinner, a price out of reach for a lot of working people.

The men prided themselves on a quality product. Their hamburgers were larger and leaner than most being sold and were charbroiled rather than fried. Their business was well received. Some customers were drawn back for the burgers, while others sought out the homemade pancakes or other breakfast items which were sold around the clock.

About six months into the operation, Kristal and Birnberg opened a second restaurant, this time across the Mississippi River in St. Paul. The men expanded exclusively in the Twin Cities area until the early 1970s. In 1972, units opened in St. Cloud, Minnesota, and Cedar Falls, Iowa.

A couple years later, the men kicked off the opening of a store in Mankato, Minnesota, with a 100-pound Emberger. Other attention-getting promotions of the era included their television advertising efforts. The 1970s "Remember the Embers" jingle is etched somewhere in the minds of many Midwesterners.

Twenty-six Embers restaurants were in operation by 1978. The men contributed their success to their innovative ways, claiming a number of market firsts. Not only did they up the ante in terms of burger size, wrote Benson, "Kristal and Birnberg swear they were the first to put bacon and cheese on a hamburger." The chain also claimed leadership status in their television advertising and newspaper coupon efforts.

Flames Flickering: 1980s to Mid-1990s

The company's marketing efforts began to go awry in the 1980s, when the business began emphasizing pricing over quality and value. The once healthy lunch and dinner crowds

Company Perspectives:

The Embers America program is truly revolutionary, *as it has never been attempted in the restaurant industry before. We believe the restaurant industry has come full-circle, from mom and pop shops of the past and today's fast food giants to a future that encompasses the best of both worlds. When an independent restaurant operator becomes a franchisee, he or she will discover vastly improved purchasing power and higher quality products, increased brand awareness and marketing power and enhanced growth. These tools will allow them to* fight back *against the industry's giants . . . and win.*

began to thin as advertising focused more and more on discounted breakfast specials such as the $1.99 "Blockbuster Breakfast." The practice also began eroding Kristal and Birnberg's business relationship: the two disagreed about how long to push the discounted meals.

Attention to daily operations began to slip about this time, according to a January 1998 *Star Tribune* article by Dick Youngblood. "Our customer service, at best, was unoffensive—not terrible, but indifferent, mediocre," said Henry's son David Kristal. "So was our ongoing maintenance: Burned out light bulbs remained unchanged for too long, for example, or a tear in the vinyl went unrepaired."

Their once meticulous renovation cycle lapsed as cash flow grew tighter. A belated effort to turn things around by raising prices resulted in the exit of those customers primarily attracted by the discounts. Changes in the market had also put pressure on Embers.

Independently owned businesses faced competition from an increasing number of large chains, such as Applebee's or TGI Friday's, which targeted the family dining market but also sold more profitable beer, wine, and liquor items. Meanwhile, Embers' sales stagnated as costs continued to rise.

"Fortunately, while the profit-and-loss statement was under siege, the relatively conservative management of the recent past left the company with an exceedingly robust balance sheet: There was no debt, and Embers owned most of its 26 restaurants, and the real estate beneath them, in Minnesota, Wisconsin, Iowa, and the Dakotas," reported Youngblood.

As the pressure continued to build on the business his father co-owned, David Kristal was embarking on a different career path. He graduated from Stanford Law School in 1990 and then returned home to work for a St. Paul-based law firm. Kristal gained some notoriety for himself when he and another Winthrop & Weinstine attorney helped a small Atlanta company gain a much sought after contract for the cleanup of New York's World Trade Center after a 1993 bomb blast. The experience also helped Kristal clarify what he liked and did not like about the practice of law.

David Kristal liked the business part of law, the deal-making, he revealed to *Twin Cities Business Monthly*, but not the

research and writing end of the work. Consequently, when his father asked him to come work for Embers in 1993 he agreed—David had worked for the small chain as a cook and waiter during his high school and undergraduate years. Carl Birnberg's son Brad also came on board at the time. The founders hoped the new blood would help shake things up.

The younger Kristal served as vice-president and general counsel for the next two years, but when the gridlock over strategy continued, David went to work for a development firm. While with Minneapolis-based Weisman Enterprises, according to Benson, Kristal helped educational institutions "generate new forms of revenue and develop private public partnerships."

In 1997 things at Embers changed, and Henry asked his son to consider coming back to the company one more time. The Kristals were now sole owners of the floundering business: Henry had bought out his longtime partner. David Kristal recounted to Benson, "I said, I'll come back to the company, but there can be only one decision-maker, one leader." His father agreed but not without some trepidation, for David had his work cut out for him.

Sales peaked in fiscal 1993 at $22.5 million, then fell over the next four years, sinking to $20.7 million in fiscal 1997. The company experienced its first losses in its 40-year history during 1996 and 1997. Now on their own and with David at the helm, the Kristals embarked on an aggressive $5 million rebuilding program to "Rekindle the Embers."

The program, begun in 1997, pumped more than $1.5 million into staff retraining; staff also expanded by about ten percent. Customer service had to be improved, and the Kristals employed a variety techniques to do so. Team building and customer service contests and store level promotions were added to the mix. Employees began going the extra mile for customers, and managers began displaying some entrepreneurial spirit.

About $1 million of the "Rekindle the Embers" funds were targeted for menu revamping. Kristal slashed the number of offerings in about half, from 152 to about 85, by weeding out less popular items and size variations. Embers also cut prices by five to ten percent and upped portion size by as much as 20 percent. Hooks such as a 35 cent desert ("The World's Smallest Hot Fudge Sundae"), Vienna Beef's Chicago Style Hot Dogs, and improved specialty bread items enticed new and former customers.

Embers doubled their ad and promotion budget. Part of the $1.5 million went to a television ad blitz. On the other end of the spectrum, the company sought to strengthen its connections with customers through community support and involvement.

The restaurants themselves received a $750,000 makeover: remodeled interiors and updated signs and exterior awnings. An additional $300,000 was earmarked for new point of service computer equipment—the old equipment was badly outdated.

Taking It to Another Level: Late 1990s

The Kristals rebuilding plan was not limited to rekindling the company. They were positioning themselves to change the nature of how they had been doing business. Seven poorly performing stores were closed, and a plan to move from owner/operator to franchiser was set in motion.

"It's truly revolutionary. It's never been done before," said Kristal in a June 1998 *Minneapolis/St. Paul CityBusiness* article by Dirk DeYoung, about the Embers America concept. Following the example of Ace Hardware stores, the Kristals wanted to created a group of affiliated yet unique restaurants.

In return for a $15,000 initial fee, one percent royalty on gross revenues, and a 6.5 percent royalty on sales increases after the implementation of the agreement, independent restaurants tied themselves to a well established Midwest trademark but retained much of their own identity.

Other franchisers required huge sign-on fees and a cookie-cutter image. Embers franchisees would carry a core group of trademark items, such as Embers America burgers and pancakes, but would sell their own specialty products and use their name in conjunction with the Embers logo. The smaller operations would benefit from their affiliation with Embers in terms of mass marketing, buying, training, and technology.

The concept was not without risk for both Embers and a potential franchisee. First, would the affiliation provide enough financial gain for a small operation to make the upfront cost worth while? Second, would the dilution of their independent status cost them customers? Embers, on the other hand, relinquished direct control over key signature products.

Times had certainly changed for Embers. The company, for example, now transmitted information such as proprietary recipes to franchisees via its Intranet system—a far cry from the days when Henry and Carl kept their recipes in a tin box in the kitchen. Their approach to advertising had changed dramatically as well.

The father-and-son team appeared in television ads both in and outside their market areas to pitch the endeavor. David and Henry touted the Embers "Real American Food" while asking patrons of good family-owned restaurants to call their toll-free number with referrals for the franchising operation. Ad consultants had been wary of the approach and warned that their Dave Thomas-like (Wendy's) spin to their commercials might backfire.

Could they as non-actors convey the intended image? Would the abandonment of their 15-year emphasis on pricing result in another loss of customers? But David said, in a *Minnesota Business & Opportunities* article, that they "wanted to be noticed," so they had to take the risk.

Their gamble paid off. They were noticed. Henry and David became recognizable figures in their target markets. "You've seen the ads: the impish Henry, 66, and the businesslike David, 33, knocking on the door of an ice-fishing house to explain their

new menu and their money-back guarantee of customer satisfaction," wrote Youngblood back in September 1998. Other ads showed a reluctant Henry, in full colonial garb, being urged on by David to introduce the Embers America concept.

Embers' economic outlook appeared to be as upbeat as its ads. The company ended fiscal 1998 with sales of $16.6 million, up 18 percent from 1997 (the figures included the 16 remaining corporate stores). By September 1998, Embers had franchised three restaurants, and three corporate stores were in the hands of longtime managers. (Plans for the first new corporate stores since 1978 were also being tossed around.)

Optimistic View of the Future

Anticipating expansion into other markets, Embers signed on with Todd Daniels Marketing Group, a St. Paul-based firm, early in 1999. The company had depended solely on freelancers during the initial phase of its makeover but now wanted someone to coordinate all marketing activities. In May, Ember's America's growth plan was bolstered by the infusion of $3 million in financing.

The Kristals' franchising goal was to bring in 50 restaurants in about the first 12 months and 1,000 or more over the next five to seven years—the company reported one franchiser had received a sales boost of 30 percent since signing on. As of July 1, 1999, four corporate restaurants and 26 franchise locations were operating in Minnesota, Wisconsin, Iowa, and North Dakota. David and Henry, in the meantime, continued to cut up the airwaves with their offbeat ads.

Further Reading

Benson, Brooke, "Rekindling an Old Flame," *Twin Cities Business Monthly*, December 1998, pp. 52+.

DeYoung, Dirk, "Embers Stokes Franchise Plan," *Minneapolis/St. Paul CityBusiness*, June, 12, 1998, pp. 1, 40.

"Embers America Secures Growth Financing," *Restaurant Finance Monitor*, May 24, 1999.

"Embers Suddenly Hot Stuff Again," *St. Paul Pioneer Press*, April 17, 1999.

Emerson, Dan, "On the Road Again," *Minnesota Business & Opportunities*, January 1999, pp. 46–47, 49.

Franklin, Jennifer, "Embers' Ad Recipe Includes New Firm," *CityBusiness* (Minneapolis/St. Paul), January, 22, 1999, p. 2.

"Once Sagging Restaurant Chain Erases Old Image and Finds New Customers," *Finance & Commerce*, May 15, 1999.

Van Houten, Ben, "Rising from the Embers," *Restaurant Business*, July 1, 1998, pp. 21–22.

Youngblood, Dick, "Embers Owners Fired Up to Turn Chain Around," *Star Tribune* (Minneapolis), January 25, 1998, p. 3D.

——, "Two Entrepreneurial Efforts Are on the Fast Track," *Star Tribune* (Minneapolis), September 27, 1998, p. 3D.

—Kathleen Peippo

Emerson Radio Corp.

9 Entin Road
Parsippany, New Jersey 07054
U.S.A.
(973) 884-5800
(800) 898-9020
Fax: (973) 428-2033

Public Company
Incorporated: 1915 as Emerson Phonograph Co.
Employees: 112
Sales: $158.7 million (fiscal 1999)
Stock Exchanges: American
Ticker Symbol: MSN
NAIC: 421620 Consumer Electronics Wholesaling

Emerson Radio Corp. designs, sources, imports, and markets a variety of consumer electronics products, including television sets, video cassette recorders and players, TV/VCR combination units, home stereo and portable audio products, clock radios, and microwave ovens. These products are mainly sold, and sometimes licensed, under the Emerson and G Clef brand names. Emerson's role in the development of electronic home entertainment is an interesting footnote to American social history in the first half of the 20th century. Its evolution from manufacturer to licenser and outsourcer is an example of the deindustrialization of the United States in the second half of the century.

Fifty Years of Home Entertainment: 1915–65

Victor Hugo Emerson was an early recording engineer and executive who at one time was employed by Thomas A. Edison. In 1915 he established the Emerson Phonograph Co. in New York City. Emerson offered one of the last of the external-horn phonographs for only $3. Its main product, however, was Universal Cut Records, capable of being played laterally or vertically. A wide variety of popular, band, opera, classical, religious, and folk music was offered. Emerson opened factories in Chicago and Framingham, Long Island, in 1920 and described itself as the

third largest record manufacturer. Nevertheless, in December of that year, it went into receivership, a victim of the precipitous sales slump for phonograph music that accompanied the post-World War I recession and the growth of commercial radio.

Emerson Phonograph Co. passed into the hands of Benjamin Abrams and Rudolph Kanarak in 1922. The Romanian-born Abrams, who had been working as a phonograph and record salesman, ran the company with two brothers and in 1924 entered the radio business, renaming the company Emerson Radio & Phonograph Corp. and subsequently selling its record interests. Emerson introduced the first radio-phonograph combination sold in the United States but remained an obscure firm until 1932, when, in the depths of the Great Depression, it introduced a "peewee" radio about 8½ inches long and 6¼ inches wide. Of some 500,000 radios sold between the beginning of December 1932 and the end of May 1933, 300,000 were peewees, and Emerson made half of these, marketing a Universal Compact line priced from $17.95 to $32.50. Emerson still led in the production and sale of this class of radio in 1938, having by then sold more than a million.

Emerson Radio & Phonograph held one-sixth of the U.S. radio market in 1942, when the company converted to military production for World War II. It became a public corporation in 1943, when it offered over 40 percent of its stock to the public at $12 a share. Among Emerson's first postwar products was, in 1947, a television set with a 10-inch tube, retailing for $375. By June 1948 the infant television industry had sold 375,000 sets, and Emerson's price had dropped to $269.50. While this represented a month's salary for most working Americans, it put Emerson at the lower end of the market.

The unquenchable hunger for television enabled Emerson Radio & Phonograph to more than double its sales between fiscal 1948 and 1950. Its net income reached a record of $6.5 million in fiscal 1950 (the year ended October 31, 1950) on sales of $74.2 million. By 1954 radio represented only 15 percent of Emerson's revenue, although the company was credited—or credited itself—with such "firsts" as the clock radio, self-powered radio, and transistorized pocket radio. Emerson also entered air conditioning by purchasing the Quiet Heet Corp. in 1953 and began making tape recorders in 1955.

Company Perspectives:

Emerson Radio's management team continues to respond well to a number of complex challenges and we are ready to advance, with the addition of new products, into new markets abroad and additional distribution channels domestically. Going confidently forward, we will build on the favorable trends developing in our core product line, licensing, sourcing, marketing and distributor arrangements.

In 1958 Emerson Radio & Phonograph paid $6 million to purchase the consumer products division of Allen B. DuMont Laboratories, Inc. This acquisition added to Emerson's products a higher-priced line of television sets, plus phonographs and high-fidelity and stereo instruments, along with the DuMont trademark. By this time, however, almost every existing U.S. household that wanted a TV set had bought one, and many customers were waiting—vainly—for color television instead of buying a replacement set. Emerson's sales dropped from $87.4 million in fiscal 1955 to $73.9 million in fiscal 1956, when it earned a mere $84,852.

Abrams responded with a cost-cutting campaign that consolidated almost all manufacturing operations in a larger Jersey City plant and employed printed circuits for both radio and television output. Net income rebounded, reaching $2.7 million in fiscal 1959 on sales of $67.4 million. In fiscal 1964—Emerson's last full year of independent operation—it earned $2.1 million on sales of $68.2 million.

Trading on the Emerson Name: 1965–90

Emerson Radio & Phonograph was purchased in 1965 by National Union Electric Corp., a diversified manufacturer, for about $62 million in cash and stock. This company continued to produce television and radio sets and phonographs distributed under the Emerson and DuMont names and hi-fi equipment under the Pilot name. (Emerson had acquired the Pilot Radio Corp. from Jerrold Corp. in 1965.) Its line of Quiet Kool air conditioners became a separate National Union Electric division.

Emerson began operating in the red under National Union Electric, with the problem apparently too little volume to cover fixed costs. Between 1967 and 1971 the division lost about $27 million. To alleviate the problem, National Union in 1970 contracted out the manufacturing of the Emerson unit's television sets and some of its other home entertainment products to Admiral Corp., laying off 1,800 employees. Emerson continued to be responsible for design, engineering, and marketing and also imported some of its home entertainment products from the Far East.

In late 1972 National Union Electric announced that Emerson was discontinuing distribution of television sets and other home entertainment products. A license for marketing products under the Emerson name was sold to Brooklyn-based Major Electronics Corp. in 1973. Founded in 1948 by Melvin Lane and incorporated in 1956, this Brooklyn-based company originally made children's phonographs. Subsequently the company diversified into the production and sale of a broader line of low-priced home entertainment products, including stereos, radios, and clock radios. Major also began importing low-cost radios in 1971 and was only manufacturing portable phonographs in 1975. The company moved its headquarters to Secaucus, New Jersey, in 1976 and changed its name to Emerson Radio Corp. in 1977.

The new Emerson profited, its sales rising from $11.5 million in fiscal 1975 (the year ended March 31, 1975) to $49.2 million in fiscal 1978. From a net loss of $870,000 in 1975 the company advanced to net income of $1.5 million in 1978. That year it was importing, assembling, and marketing, primarily under the Emerson name, phonographs, radios, tape recorders and players, compact stereos, digital clock radios, and other low- and medium-priced electronic equipment. It was importing—for assembly in Secaucus or Sun Valley, California—about 60 percent of its components from the Far East, 20 percent from Great Britain, and 20 percent domestically.

In 1980 Emerson Radio dropped its last U.S.-made product—the phonograph line—because labor costs had made it unprofitable. Despite the brutally competitive nature of its business, Emerson Radio raised its sales to $81.9 million in fiscal 1980 and its earnings to $1.6 million. Its strategy was to put its suppliers—chiefly in Taiwan and South Korea—to work imitating Sony and Panasonic audio/video products and then selling them at a lower price. "I think most of the profits we've made have been because of controlling overhead and purchasing," company President Stephen Lane told Thomas Baker of *Forbes* in 1981. "Our travel and entertainment is the lowest in the industry. We take customers to breakfast rather than lunch. We run the company the way you're supposed to."

Emerson Radio started putting out a medical product, Heart Aid, after purchasing 80 percent of near-bankrupt Cardiac Resuscitator Corp. in 1979. The company spent heavily to develop and produce an improved defibrillator-pacemaker and a pacer. It also took an 18 percent share in a developer of computerized axial tomographic (CAT) scanners. This line of products never made money, and Emerson disposed of its holdings in them during 1987–88.

Emerson Radio's consumer electronics business was faring better. The company's reintroduction of television sets in 1983, purchased from South Korea's Goldstar Electric Co. but sold at a higher price level, caused sales to soar from $94.8 million in fiscal 1983 to $181.6 million in fiscal 1984, when net income came to $9.1 million. That year it introduced a product line of video cassette recorders (VCRs). Emerson's other products at this time were portable, clock, and telephone-clock radios; portable cassette player-recorders; modular and compact stereo systems; and stereo rack systems. A compact disc player and microwave oven were introduced late in 1984. In fiscal 1985 sales doubled again, to $357.5 million, and net income rose to $13.3 million. TV sets and VCR's accounted for two-thirds of sales that year.

In 1985 Emerson Radio moved its headquarters to North Bergen, New Jersey, and acquired H.H. Scott Inc., a manufacturer of high-fidelity audio and visual equipment, selling products under the Scott name until 1991, when the line was discontinued. Emerson began importing and marketing compact refrigerators in 1986. It added camcorders, telephones, and answering machines to its product line in fiscal 1988. Personal computers and facsimile machines were subsequently added, with a major 1990 rollout to more than 500 Wal-Mart stores. Sales reached a peak of $891.4 million two years later. Net income, however, was an unimpressive $10.4 million, considering the company's sales volume, while short-term debt climbed to $162.9 million.

Seeking to Survive in the 1990s

The recession that began in 1990 and the entry into personal computers—which eventually proved a $150 million loser—were disastrous to Emerson Radio. The company incurred a loss of $37.5 million in the last nine months of the year. Shares of stock fell as low as $2, compared to a high of $12.75 in 1987. Several shareholder suits charged some Emerson directors and officials with breach of fiduciary duty and self-dealing. Emerson also fell into technical default on its long-term debt, which was $55.4 million at the end of the year, by exceeding its ratio of liabilities to assets.

A Swiss firm, Fidenas Investment Ltd., began purchasing shares of Emerson Radio stock in 1989. By 1992 it held a 20 percent stake—more than that held by Stephen and William Lane—and began a takeover attempt. The Lane brothers, who were seeking to restructure $180 million in debt, conceded defeat in June 1992. Emerson's financial situation worsened, and in fiscal 1993 the company incurred a loss of $56 million on sales of $741.4 million. When it filed for bankruptcy in October 1993, Emerson had been in default on $223 million in debt for the past two years. It emerged from bankruptcy four months later, with Fidenas paying $75 million for a 60-percent stake. Creditors took a ten percent share in the firm, now based in Parsippany, New Jersey.

In order to cut its costs, Emerson Radio in early 1995 licensed the manufacture of certain video products under the Emerson and G Clef trademarks for a three-year period to Otake Trading Co. Ltd. and the sale of these products in the United States and Canada for the same period to Wal-Mart Stores, Inc. As a result, Emerson's net sales fell from $654.7 million in fiscal 1995 to $245.7 million in fiscal 1996. The licensing agreement provided about $4 million a year in royalty income.

Emerson Radio entered the home theater and car audio fields in 1995. It also entered the $900-million-a-year home and personal security market with a carbon monoxide detector and eventually planned to lend its name to burglar alarms, motion detectors, personal alarms, smoke detectors, and safety lights. The company left this field, however, in fiscal 1997. Emerson also announced it would license the Emerson name to more than 250 audio and video accessories made by Jasco Products Co., an Oklahoma firm selling cables, remote controls, and appliance cleaning devices. In late 1996 the company took a 27 percent stake in Sport Supply Group, Inc., the largest direct-mail distributor of sporting goods equipment and supplies to the U.S. institutional market, for $11.5 million.

On the expiration of Emerson's licensing agreement with Otake, this company was replaced by Daewoo Electronics Co.

Ltd., which entered into a four-year agreement with Emerson to manufacture and sell television and video products bearing the Emerson and G Clef trademark to U.S. retailers. Emerson, in 1999, also had five-year license/supply agreements with Cargil International covering the Caribbean and Central and South American markets and WW Mexicana for certain consumer products to be sold in Mexico. In addition, it had a licensing agreement with Telesound Electronics for telephones, answering machines, and caller ID products in the United States and Canada.

After earning net income of $7.4 million in fiscal 1995, Emerson fell into the red the following three years, losing $13.4 million, $24 million, and $1.4 million in fiscal 1996, 1997, and 1998, respectively, on net revenues of $245.7 million, $178.7 million, and $162.7 million. Geoffrey P. Jurick, Fidenas's owner, held 60 percent of Emerson's common stock in December 1998. He had been chief executive officer of the company since 1992 and in 1998 also held the titles of president and chairman of the board.

In December 1998 Oaktree Capital Management, a Los Angeles-based investment firm that held a smaller stake in Emerson Radio, and Kenneth S. Grossman, a private investor, proposed to buy Jurick's holdings in the company for more than $14.6 million. This offer was rejected as inadequate. According to one account, Oaktree's real interest in the company was its stake—now 39 percent, counting warrants—in Sports Supply Group. Emerson announced in August 1999 that it planned to sell this stake to Oaktree for $28.9 million.

Emerson Radio had net income of $289,000 on net revenues of $158.7 million in fiscal 1999 and a long-term debt of $20.8 million at the end of the fiscal year. Some 84 percent of its merchandise in fiscal 1999 was imported, primarily from China, Hong Kong, Malaysia, South Korea, and Thailand. Tonic Electronics (32 percent), Daewoo (22 percent), and Imarflex (12 percent) were its chief suppliers. The company was heavily dependent on two customers: Wal-Mart Stores, which took about 52 percent of its goods in fiscal 1999, and Target Stores, Inc., which took about 24 percent.

Principal Subsidiaries

Emerson Radio (Hong Kong) Ltd.; Emerson Radio International Ltd.

Further Reading

"The Baby Radio," *Fortune,* July 1933, pp. 64–65.

Baker, Thomas, "A Dangerous Dream?" *Forbes,* July 10, 1981, pp. 52–53.

"Benjamin Abrams Dead at 74," *New York Times,* June 24, 1967, p. 29.

Bergman, Robert J., "Emerson Radio Cedes Control, Ends Bitter Proxy Fight," *Wall Street Journal,* June 26, 1992, p. B4.

"Emerson and DuMont Will Phase-Out Home Electronics," *Merchandising Week,* January 1, 1973, p. 15.

"Emerson Radio's Moment of Truth," *Financial World,* August 1, 1982, pp. 22–23.

"Emerson Radio's Plan Would Give Control to a Swiss Company," *Wall Street Journal,* October 4, 1993, p. A9A.

"Emerson Radio to Buy DuMont Laboratories Consumer Products Unit," *Wall Street Journal,* July 7, 1958, p. 13.

"Emerson Rejects As Inadequate Investment Group's Buy-Out Bid," *Twice,* January 7, 1999, p. 5.

"Emerson Turns to New Products," *Record-Bergen County,* December 10, 1995, p. B1.

Fabrizio, Timothy C., and George Paul, *The Talking Machine.* Atglen, Pa.: Schiffer Publishing Co., 1997, pp. 209, 216.

Gault, Ylonda, "Besieged Emerson Tuning New Markets," *Crain's New York Business,* September 10, 1990, p. 6.

"In Tune with Emerson," *Forbes,* June 15, 1954, pp. 22–23.

Marco, Guy A., ed., *Encyclopedia of Recorded Sound in the United States.* New York: Garland, 1993, pp. 248–49.

Mehler, Mark, "Every Which Way Is Up for Emerson," *Financial World,* November 14–27, 1984, pp. 86–87.

Monte, Stevens R., "Emerson Radio Corporation," *Wall Street Transcript,* July 2, 1984, p. 74,453, and September 10, 1984, pp. 75,197–98.

Roberts, Johnnie L., "Emerson Radio, After a Timely Entry into Video, Basks in Electronics Boom," *Wall Street Journal,* June 11, 1985, p. 16.

Ryan, Ken, "Home Theater for the Masses," *HFN/Home Furnishings News,* September 30, 1996, pp. 93, 100.

Smith, Gene, "Personality: Expansion Through Mergers," *New York Times,* July 3, 1966, Sec. 3, p. 3.

"Steady Expansion Seen in Television," *New York Times,* July 11, 1947, p. 23.

Zipser, Alfred R., "Salesman Turns to Cost Cutting," *New York Times,* May 10, 1959, Sec. 3, p. 25.

—Robert Halasz

The Estée Lauder Companies Inc.

767 Fifth Avenue
New York, New York 10153
U.S.A.
(212) 572-4200
Fax: (212) 572-4655
Web site: http://www.elcompanies.com

Public Company
Incorporated: 1946
Employees: 15,300
Sales: $3.96 billion (1999)
Stock Exchanges: New York
Ticker Symbol: EL
NAIC: 32562 Toilet Preparation Manufacturing

Founded in 1946 by Estée Lauder and her husband Joseph, The Estée Lauder Companies Inc. is one of the leading makers and marketers of upscale cosmetics, fragrances, and hair care products in the world. In the U.S. prestige cosmetics category, Estée Lauder Companies has a market share of about 46 percent. The company's main brands—in order of their introduction or acquisition—include the original Estée Lauder line, including skin treatment, makeup, and fragrances; Aramis, a group of men's toiletries (1964); Clinique, a hypoallergenic line (1968); Prescriptives, an upscale line aimed at the urban, multiethnic crowd (1979); Origins, a botanical treatment line designed to appeal to the environmentally conscious consumer (1990); M·A·C, a professional makeup artist line of cosmetics and makeup products (1994); Bobbi Brown *essentials,* a professional beauty line (1995); Tommy Hilfiger fragrances, grooming products, and cosmetics (1995); *jane,* a cosmetics line aimed at young consumers (1997); Aveda, a ''new age'' cosmetics and hair and skin care line (1997); and Donna Karan fragrances and cosmetics (1997). Estée Lauder products are sold in more than 100 countries, with 61 percent of net sales originated in the Americas; 27 percent in Europe, the Middle East, and Africa; and 12 percent in the Asia-Pacific region. The Lauder family owns almost 65 percent of the company's common stock and more than 93 percent of the voting stock.

1920s–50s: Development of an Entrepreneur

Estée Lauder was born Josephine Esther Mentzer in Corona, Queens, New York, in 1908, the ninth child of Rose and Max Mentzer, who had emigrated from Hungary to the United States. Regarding her interest in cosmetics, which originated in childhood, Lauder reportedly recalled: ''I loved to make everyone up. . . . I was always interested in people being beautiful . . . [people] who look like they have a cared-for face.''

Lauder was first inspired to enter the business of cosmetics when her uncle, John Schotz, a chemist from Hungary, established New Way Laboratories in Brooklyn in 1924. Her uncle's products included a Six-in-One Cold Cream, Dr. Schotz Viennese Cream, and several perfumes. Lauder got her start by selling these products in New York City and then, from 1939 to 1942, in Miami Beach as well.

In 1944 Lauder began working in various New York salons and smaller department stores, selling her own product line from behind a counter. Of that original line, three skin creams were her uncle's creations. Lauder also sold a face powder, an eye shadow, and a lipstick called Just Red. Soon the entrepreneur was spending Saturdays selling her products on the floor in Bonwit Teller department store on Fifth Avenue. Lauder's next goal was to get her items into Saks Fifth Avenue. She convinced the Saks buyer that there was a demand for her products after a successful lecture and demonstration at the Waldorf Astoria that prompted customers to line up outside for more product information. One unique aspect of Lauder's products would remain a classic Estée Lauder approach over the years; the fledgling cosmetics dynamo was selling lipsticks in upscale metal cases at a time, just after World War II, when most lipsticks were packaged in plastic.

The year Estée Lauder got started, women's cosmetics was a $7 million business in the United States. The Saks connection helped Lauder achieve a reputation that would allow her to sell her products nationally. Beginning in the late 1940s, Estée Lauder traveled the country, making personal appearances in specialty and department stores and training staff in proper sales techniques. She made impressions on influential people early on, securing a spot in I. Magnin's of San Francisco, a store well-respected in the retail trade. I. Magnin's carried Lauder's products exclusively in

Company Perspectives:

Tastes and styles are evolving on a world scale, greatly influenced by what is happening in America. Improving global economies are making available and affordable products once reserved for a privileged few. The baby boom has come roaring into middle age with money to spend and a determination to fight the effects of growing older. U.S. teenagers have exploded into a major demographic group with a reported $122 billion in spending power. Growing, shifting populations are creating exciting new marketing opportunities.

It really is a new world of opportunity. And the best news for us and for our stockholders is that Estée Lauder has spent the past 50 years preparing for it. We haven't built just a business, we've built a family of businesses. It's a carefully constructed portfolio that gives us balance—in the brands we own, in the markets where we do business and in the diversity a global company needs to protect itself from the ebb and flow of world economies. this balance gives us competitive strength and consumer appeal.

the San Francisco area until the late 1970s. During these early years, Lauder met buyers all over the country and others in the business who would later help her achieve success.

Against the advice of their lawyer, Lauder and her husband entered full-scale into an industry known for extreme market swings and short-lived endeavors. Joseph Lauder worked every day at the small space they had rented, while their oldest son, Leonard, made deliveries to Saks and other stores on his bicycle.

One technique that Estée Lauder pioneered, now standard in the cosmetics industry, was the gift-with-purchase offer. Lauder first began offering free sample items with any purchase to bring the customer back for more. Later, free products were made available to customers who made purchases of a specified minimum dollar amount. Lauder's gift-with-purchase offer gained her a loyal following and helped establish her business. Over the years, however, this practice would lead to markedly low profit margins in the cosmetic industry as a whole and at Lauder's company in particular.

The 1953 Debut of Youth Dew

Early in the 1950s, with $50,000 saved from business profits, Lauder began looking for an advertising representative. After learning that the amount was hardly enough to finance a full-scale campaign, she chose to begin advertising with the help of Saks Fifth Avenue's direct-mail program. The company's advertising budget would soon grow considerably, with the introduction of a new product.

Lauder reunited in the early 1950s with a fragrance executive she had met a decade earlier in order to develop a perfume. Following the examples of Helena Rubenstein and Elizabeth Arden, who had both made their starts in skin care and then moved on to fragrances, Lauder developed a bath oil with a fragrance that lasted for 24 hours. She called the bath oil Youth Dew and introduced it in 1953 at $8.50 a bottle.

With Youth Dew Estée Lauder became an overnight success. "Middle America went bananas for it," stated former employee Andy Lucarelli, as quoted in *Estée Lauder: Beyond the Magic.* Youth Dew sales reached an unprecedented volume of 5,000 units a week in the mid-1950s. Furthermore, sales of skin care products increased due to the popularity of Youth Dew. Thirty years later, the fragrance still had sales of $30 million worldwide.

In 1958, 24-year-old Leonard Lauder joined the company. That year he married Evelyn Hausner, a Vienna-born schoolteacher who would later rise in the company and eventually take over for Estée Lauder herself, making appearances as company spokesperson.

In the early 1960s, Estée Lauder joined Rubenstein, Arden, Revlon, and Cosmetiques in the race to develop a skin care cream like the European products that were becoming popular during this time. Estée Lauder's Re-Nutriv—a careful blend of 25 ingredients—was introduced in a well-orchestrated marketing program typical of most Estée Lauder ventures. Advertisers were careful not to make specific claims regarding the product's ability to revitalize skin or eliminate wrinkles, as such claims could get a cosmetics company into regulatory trouble. A full-page *Harper's Bazaar* ad simply read: "What makes a cream worth $115.00?" The expensive product generated lots of free press for the company.

Estée Lauder Inc. developed an identifiable image in the 1960s. Since the company could not afford color ads, they used black-and-white photos instead. Moreover, in 1971, model Karen Graham began portraying the serene, elegant "Estée Lauder look," a role she would fulfill for 15 years. Graham's identification with Estée Lauder was so successful, many people thought she was Estée Lauder herself.

Through the early 1960s, company sales climbed to $14 million. Lauder had by then gathered a small, talented staff that included Ida Steward, from Bristol-Myers; June Leaman, from Bergdorf Goodman; and Ira Levy, a recent graduate of UCLA—all of whom would remain with the company for decades.

Aramis and Clinique Debut in the 1960s

In 1964 the company introduced Aramis, a trendsetting male fragrance blended from citrus, herbs, and spice to evoke a woodsy scent. Estée Lauder soon met with increased competition, particularly from Revlon, which began to market its own fragrance for men, known as Braggi. Following the deaths of cosmetic leaders Helena Rubenstein and Elizabeth Arden (in 1965 and 1966, respectively), competition heated up between Revlon and Estée Lauder.

The introduction of the Clinique line in 1968 firmly established Estée Lauder's success in the cosmetics industry. Clinique's first national exposure had come via an interview between *Vogue* veteran Carol Phillips and dermatologist Norman Orentreich entitled "Can Great Skin Be Created?" The article, published in the August 15, 1967, edition of *Vogue,* elicited outstanding reader response. Soon thereafter Phillips accepted an offer from Leonard Lauder to join the company and lead the development of the new Clinique line. From the development stage to full-scale introduction, Clinique was designed to be more than just an allergy-tested line of products. Rather, it cultivated an image as a well researched and medically sound line of products produced in laboratories. The first 20 salespeople were given the title of "consultants"; they were rigorously trained and outfitted with white lab coats. Sales counters were brightly lit, products were packaged in clinical light green boxes, and a chart allowed customers to determine which Clinique products fit their particular skin type. As stated in the September 26, 1983, *Business Week,* "Clinique helped fuel a tenfold expansion of the big cosmetics company."

By 1968, sales for privately owned Estée Lauder, at $40 million, financed a move to new corporate headquarters in the General Motors building in 1969. The company was also able to support the Clinique venture, which lost approximately $3 million over the first seven years. Such patient financing became a trademark of Estée Lauder launches. By 1975 the Clinique line had become profitable, prompting competition from Revlon. Through a hasty and ultimately unsuccessful introduction of a product line designed to compete with Clinique, Revlon's Charles Revson made an important discovery. Estée Lauder held a significant influence over department store buyers, who generated customer loyalty through the exclusive sale of her products. Revlon products, on the other hand, were available at lower price discount centers and inspired no such loyalty.

After 12 years with the company, the founders' oldest son Leonard was named president of Estée Lauder Inc. in 1972. Leonard Lauder focused on maintaining good relations with store buyers. His methods ensured a systematic, goal-oriented method of selling company merchandise, coordinating the advertising levels for various product lines and the quality and quantity of store space to be devoted to those Lauder products. Estée Lauder, board chairman, spent mornings working at home and afternoons at the office in the General Motors building. Joseph Lauder oversaw production at the Melville, Long Island, plant.

New Approaches and Scents in the 1970s

The challenge faced by Estée Lauder in the 1970s was to increase its overall presence while building on its respectable reputation. The company's private, family-controlled ownership gave it the flexibility to respond rapidly, when necessary, to industry trends and competition. Through the 1970s, such quick maneuvering was necessary as the company faced increased competition in the fragrance industry. Revlon scored a huge success with the mass-marketed fragrance "Charlie" in 1973, as did Yves Saint Laurent's "Opium," launched in Paris in 1977 and brought to the United States the following year.

During this time, Lauder had been working on a subtler version of its original Youth Dew fragrance. Noting the success of Opium, Lauder launched both Soft Youth Dew and a spicier oriental version called Cinnabar in the fall of 1978. Due to the simultaneous introduction of the closely related products, some questions concerning the company's marketing plans were raised. Both retail buyers and consumers were confused over whether Cinnabar was a version of Youth Dew or a new product. Ronald Lauder commented, as quoted in the September 15, 1978, *Women's Wear Daily,* that the company would continue to market both fragrances and would "probably decide

after Christmas which way to go." While the marketing approach was muddled, the privately owned company proved that it could react quickly in an aggressive market.

A new skin care line in the style of an upscale Clinique was introduced in 1979. The Prescriptives line was promoted as even more high-tech, with one-hour makeup and fashion consultations included as part of the program. When Prescriptives met with a lukewarm reception, the company regrouped to revise the approach. Estée Lauder's other divisions were challenged as well, as competition extended to the relatively slow market for men's fragrances.

In 1978, sales of the Estée Lauder line were approximately $170 million. Clinique sales stood at $80 million, and the Aramis line, which had developed into over 40 products, had estimated sales of $40 million. Men's products, though the lowest in revenue, were growing at a rate of 18 percent a year. Several men's fragrances were launched in lower-priced markets. With the widely successful 1978 debut of Ralph Lauren's Polo, Estée Lauder was prompted to consider launching a new men's product. JHL, named after Joseph Lauder, was introduced in 1982 and, like other Lauder products, was marketed as a more expensive and upscale fragrance. Sales clerks requested business cards from customers in order to send them free samples, and an elegant counter display was developed for promotional items.

In executive changes in 1982 Leonard Lauder, president of the company, was also named CEO. Ronald Lauder, another son of the founders and executive vice-president, became chairman of international operations; the division comprised half the company's sales volume, though less of it profits. The changes did not affect Estée Lauder's active chairmanship or Joseph Lauder's management of the company plants.

The Premier Cosmetics Company of the 1980s

By 1983, Estée Lauder had reached a billion dollars in sales and was recognized as the premier cosmetics company. The company underwent several more executive changes. Ronald Lauder left active management to join the Reagan administration as Deputy Assistant Defense Secretary. Joseph Lauder died in January 1983. The family bought Mr. Lauder's stock for $28 million, at a price the IRS would later charge was undervalued, leaving the company liable for $42.7 million in taxes. The Lauders' lawyer countered that shareholder agreements from 1974 and 1976 controlled the price of the shares, since the stock of the family-owned company could not be sold.

Just as Estée Lauder reached a billion dollars in sales, its closest rival, Revlon—which had watched the Lauder empire grow from infancy—experienced a first-ever drop in sales, to $1.2 billion. While still formidable, Revlon no longer had the guidance of its leader, Charles Revson, who died in 1975.

Unlike Revlon, which touted its large number of product introductions, Estée Lauder took a more careful approach. Clinique added only 12 new products since its inception, most of which were still being sold after 15 years. Estée Lauder's sole product launch in 1983, Night Repair, reportedly had years of research and development invested in it. Night Repair advertising copy claimed that the product was "a biological breakthrough'' which ''uses the night, the time your body is resting, to help speed up the natural repair of cells damaged during the day.'' Dr. Norman Orentreich, the dermatologist consulted in the groundbreaking 1967 *Vogue* interview preceding the introduction of Clinique, offered a different view. As quoted in the September 1984 issue of *Drug & Cosmetic,* Orentreich stated, ''there is no topical preparation affecting the outermost layer of the stratum corneum that the FDA will allow [one] to call a cosmetic that will work.'' Such objections did not impair sales; in fact, Night Repair went on to become a top seller in the Estée Lauder line.

The company's increasing investment in laboratory research and development proved successful, as indicated by the sales of the Clinique line and Night Repair. As reported in the September 26, 1983, *Business Week,* Leonard Lauder stated that ''growth in 1983 R & D expenditures will be twice the company's sales increase.''

In 1990, in a widely reported company change, Robin Burns was brought in to replace Robert J. Barnes as chief executive of the domestic division. Barnes, who held the position for 26 years, remained with the company as a consultant for the international division. Robin Burns started her career as a fabric buyer for Bloomingdale's at age 21 in 1974, joining the staff at Calvin Klein Cosmetics Corporation in 1983. Burns was instrumental to the introduction of the fragrances Obsession and Eternity during her seven-year tenure, turning the $6 million company into a $200 million success story. Leonard Lauder was quoted in the January 12, 1990, *Women's Wear Daily* as commenting that ''Calvin told me, 'No matter what you've heard about her, she's ten times better'.''

Officially taking over the domestic division in May 1990, Burns revived the image of several Estée Lauder fragrances by the end of the year. Hoping to make the company's flagship Estée Lauder line more accessible by implementing changes in its advertising, Burns oversaw production of ads that featured Paulina Porizkova (the model representing the company's entire line starting in 1988), suggesting that a friendlier, less remote countenance would have a wider appeal for consumers. Furthermore, Burns opted to give the company's White Linen scent its own representative, model Paul Devicq.

Similarly, the Aramis line was reinvigorated with a campaign designed to reach a younger male audience. Ad spending was increased by 40 percent, and print ads, traditionally placed in the magazines *Fortune* and *Esquire,* were moved instead to *Rolling Stone, Cosmopolitan,* and *Gentlemen's Quarterly.* Television spots were switched from news programs such as *60 Minutes* to comedy programs such as *In Living Color,* which attracted young people.

The Prescriptives line was expanded in the 1990s with the introduction of All Skins, makeup formulated for working women of different ethnic backgrounds. Nearly all cosmetics companies at the time had been criticized for ignoring large segments of the population for too long. By mid-1992 All Skins was attracting 3,800 new customers a month.

In 1990 the company formed a new corporate division, Origins Natural Resources Inc., which catered to public concern for the environment. Recycled paper was used for product packaging and company correspondence, makeup shades emphasized natural skin tones, and animal products such as lanolin and petroleum-based active ingredients were not used in the makeup formulations. Origins was also offered via freestanding boutiques in Cambridge, Massachusetts, and Soho, Manhattan, which proved to be the new division's top-selling locations.

William Lauder, grandson of the founders, headed the Origins division. In a July 13, 1990, article in *Women's Wear Daily,* he summarized the contemporary Estée Lauder mission: ''We are trying to rewrite the book on how a cosmetics company operates and thinks in the 21st century.'' The company's new approach included gearing more merchandise toward consumers of all economic backgrounds and a commitment to communicating with a growing international audience in addition to a wider variety of American consumers.

In January 1992 Daniel J. Brestle, the president of Prescriptives who had brought that division from a shaky start to $70 million in sales, was named president of Clinique Laboratories USA. The founders' two sons, Leonard and Ronald, continued to play active roles in the executive lineup. Leonard remained president and CEO of Estée Lauder Inc., while Ronald continued as chairperson of both the international and Clinique divisions. Evelyn Lauder, Leonard's wife, oversaw new product development as senior corporate vice-president. By 1992 Evelyn Lauder had gradually taken on Estée's role as company spokesperson as the founder made fewer appearances. Commenting on Estée Lauder's success in the industry in the July 13, 1990, *Women's Wear Daily,* Leonard Lauder summarized the Estée Lauder philosophy: ''We think in decades. Our competitors think in quarters.''

New Ventures and Going Public in the 1990s

In 1993 the company entered into its first licensing venture, signing an exclusive global licensing deal with fashion designer Tommy Hilfiger. Two years later, Estée Lauder's Aramis subsidiary launched the Tommy fragrance for men, which it followed up with Tommy Girl, for women, and Hilfiger Athletics, for men.

In February 1995 Estée Lauder acquired a majority interest in Make-up Art Cosmetics Ltd. (M·A·C), maker of designer cosmetics aimed at professional makeup artists and fashion-conscious consumers; by 1998 the company had gained full control. Estée Lauder also acquired Bobbi Brown *essentials,* a professional beauty line developed by famous makeup artist Bobbi Brown. During this time Estée Lauder also hired a new spokesmodel, actress Elizabeth Hurley, who helped make Pleasures a top-selling fragrance after its debut in 1995.

By late 1995 Estée Lauder herself had stepped aside as chairperson, taking the honorary title of founding chair. Leonard Lauder assumed the chairmanship in addition to his duties as CEO, while COO Fred H. Langhammer added the title of president. Ronald Lauder continued as chairman of Clinique and the international operations.

In part as an estate planning measure and a method for some Lauder family members to cash out portions of their company stakes, The Estée Lauder Companies Inc. went public in November 1995, raising more than $450 million through the IPO.

Secondary offerings over the next few years lowered the Lauder family's stake in the company to about 65 percent of the common stock and 93 percent of the voting stock. Some of the maneuvers by members of the Lauder family in connection with these offerings proved controversial, particularly a capital gains tax-deferral method used in the 1995 IPO which lawmakers outlawed in 1997.

For the fiscal year ending in June 1996 Estée Lauder posted profits of $160.4 million on sales of $3.19 billion, healthy increases over the previous year's figures of $121.2 million and $2.9 billion. Profits and sales increased again in fiscal 1997, reaching $197.6 million and $3.38 billion, respectively. In late 1997 the company returned to the acquisition arena, snapping up Sassaby Inc. and Aveda Corporation. The purchase of Sassaby brought to Estée Lauder the *jane* brand of color cosmetics, a trendy brand aimed at young consumers 13 to 18 years old. Unlike Estée Lauder's typically high-priced products sold primarily in department stores, the *jane* line consisted of mass-market items sold in drugstores, supermarkets, and discounters, such as Wal-Mart—and thereby represented a new marketing channel for the company.

Aveda, purchased for $300 million, was a "new age" brand, consisting of a line of shampoos, cosmetics, and other beauty products positioned within the trendy aromatherapy area. This acquisition marked a major move by Estée Lauder into the hair care segment, where it had only a minor presence through its Origins line. It also represented another new distribution channel, as 85 percent of Aveda's sales came from hair salons. In October 1997 Estée Lauder struck another licensing deal, this time signing an exclusive worldwide agreement with Donna Karan International Inc. to develop a line of fragrances and cosmetic products under the Donna Karan New York and DKNY trademarks.

Prior to the 1997 acquisitions, it had appeared that Estée Lauder was in danger of losing market share because of its near-exclusive focus on the department store channel—a channel that was seeing increasing numbers of customers defect to mass marketers and other outlets. But as with its acquisition of such popular brands as M·A·C and Bobbi Brown *essentials,* the company appeared to be shedding its conservative ways in gaining entrée into the mass market and hair salon channels. To support its brands, Estée Lauder continued to spend massive sums on advertising and promotion, $1.03 billion in fiscal 1998 alone, a figure representing more than 28 percent of sales. It also seemed certain that the company would continue to seek out strategic acquisition targets, such as Stila Cosmetics, Inc., a fast-growing upscale cosmetics company, the acquisition of which was proposed in 1999.

Principal Subsidiaries

Aramis Inc.; Clinique Laboratories, Inc.; Estée Lauder Inc.; Estée Lauder International, Inc.; Estée Lauder Cosmetics Ltd. (Canada).

Further Reading

Appelbaum, Cara, "Just Who Is an Aramis Man?," *Adweek's Marketing Week,* September 30, 1991.

Bird, Laura, "Estée Lauder Pulls Whiz Kid Burns Away from Calvin Klein," *Adweek's Marketing Week,* January 15, 1990.

Bird, Laura, and Laura Jereski, "To Offer Shares, Lauder Lifts Veil of Secrecy," *Wall Street Journal,* September 22, 1995, p. B1.

Born, Pete, "Lauder Readies Origins Brand, First in Decade," *Women's Wear Daily,* July 13, 1990.

Deutschman, Alan, "Nudes for Lauder?," *Fortune,* March 12, 1990.

Duffy, Martha, "Take This Job and Love It," *Time,* August 6, 1990.

Edelson, Sharon, "Lauder's Populist Message," *Women's Wear Daily,* February 7, 1992.

"Estée Lauder Appoints Brestle to Head Clinique," *Women's Wear Daily,* January 27, 1992.

"Estée Lauder Shares to Be Sold in Offering by Lauder Family," *Wall Street Journal,* May 10, 1999, p. B2.

Fallon, James, "Estée Lauder Goes to Oxford," *Women's Wear Daily,* September 6, 1991.

Harting, Joan, "Lauder's Cinnabar Exudes Oriental Mystique," *Women's Wear Daily,* September 15, 1978.

Horyn, Cathy, "Estée's Heirs," *Harper's Bazaar,* September 1998, pp. 486–91, 550.

Israel, Lee, *Estée Lauder: Beyond the Magic,* New York: Macmillan, 1985, 186 p.

Jereski, Laura, "Estée Lauder Family Will Pay Taxes of $40 Million on Controversial Tactic," *Wall Street Journal,* November 26, 1997, p. A4.

Jereski, Laura, and Laura Bird, "Beauty Secrets: Ronald Lauder's Debts and Estée's Old Age Force a Firm Makeover," *Wall Street Journal,* November 8, 1995, pp. A1+.

Kogan, Julie, "What Smell Success?" *Working Woman,* November 1982.

Langway, Lynn, "Common Scents," *Newsweek,* February 6, 1978.

"Lauder and Two Units Suing Printing Company for Fraud," *Women's Wear Daily,* April 16, 1982.

Lauder, Estée, *Estée: A Success Story,* New York: Random House, 1985, 222 p.

"Lauder's Success Formula," *Business Week,* September 26, 1983.

"Launch Fever," *Women's Wear Daily,* August 9, 1991.

Lloyd, Kate, "How to Be Estée Lauder," *Vogue,* January 1973. "Looking for Deep Pockets," *Forbes,* January 21, 1991.

Mirabella, Grace, "Estée Lauder," *Time,* December 7, 1998, pp. 183–84.

Munk, Nina, "Why Women Find Lauder Mesmerizing," *Fortune,* May 25, 1998, pp. 96–98+.

Parker-Pope, Tara, "Estée Lauder Buys Jane Brand's Owner for Its First Venture into Mass Market," *Wall Street Journal,* September 26, 1997, p. B19.

——, "Estée Lauder Sets Deal to Buy Aveda for $300 Million," *Wall Street Journal,* November 20, 1997, p. A10.

Salmans, Sandra, "Estée Lauder: The Scents of Success," *New York Times,* April 18, 1982.

Schwartz, Judith D., "Estée Lauder Uses Bubbling Water to Win Consumers for Time Zone," *Adweek's Marketing Week,* February 5, 1990.

Sloan, Pat, "Burns Reshaping Lauder," *Advertising Age,* November 26, 1990.

Strom, Stephanie, "The Lipstick Wars," *New York Times,* June 28, 1992.

Warren, Catherine, "Estée and Joe," *Women's Wear Daily,* January 7, 1983.

Watters, Susan, "Lauders Fight IRS Ruling over Father's Inheritance," *Women's Wear Daily,* June 14, 1991.

Zinn, Laura, "Estée Lauder, the Sweet Smell of Survival," *Business Week,* September 14, 1992, p. 52.

—Frances E. Norton
—updated by David E. Salamie

Evans, Inc.

36 S. State Street
Chicago, Illinois 60603
U.S.A.
(312) 855-2000
Fax: (312) 855-3150
Web site: http://www.evansfurs.com

Public Company
Incorporated: 1929
Employees: 900
Sales: $92.3 million (1998)
Stock Exchanges: NASDAQ
Ticker Symbol: EVAN
NAIC: 44812 Women's Clothing Stores; 44815 Clothing
    Accessories Stores

Evans, Inc. is one of the preeminent retailers of luxurious fur coats and accessories for women in the United States. The firm's Black Diamond mink, one of its longstanding and most famous trademark furs, is a dark, plush, soft ranch mink that has been sold to privileged women across the country. Although fur sales account for nearly 80 percent of the company's revenues, Evans also sells a wide variety of sportswear, formal and casual dresses, and business suits for women through its retail stores and leased retail locations. The company had experienced continuous growth from its inception during the 1920s, but during the 1960s and 1970s a powerful anti-fur movement exerted a substantial effect not only on its sales figures but also on its strategic plans for growth and development. Compounded by the problem of warm winters, especially in 1997 and 1998, the company plans to sell all of its nine stores in the Chicago metropolitan area, but retain its fur-only stores located in Texas, and Washington, D.C., in addition to the 54 leased departments in retail stores across the country.

Early History

The founder and driving force behind the success of Evans, Inc. was Abraham L. Meltzer, born in 1903 to Jewish immigrants from Europe. Meltzer was raised in the midst of Chi-cago's booming retail industry, a time when famous families such as Field, Carson, Pirie, Scott, and a host of others were making their fortunes selling dry goods to the burgeoning populace of the city. Meltzer grew up with an acquaintance of the city, its environs, and the people who made it work. Having lived a relatively quite and peaceful existence in the city most of his childhood, the young man entered the retail trade during the 1920s and learned what it was like to provide service to those individuals who made large amounts of money in Chicago. As the stock market rose, fortunes were made almost overnight, and those people with more than enough money bought expensive clothing. By the end of the decade, Meltzer had learned enough in the retail trade, and had garnered enough experience as well as capital, to establish his own retail store.

Meltzer's choice of clothing was based on his experience with wealthier customers that he had dealt with throughout the 1920s. For Meltzer, there was a large niche market in Chicago for the sale of fur coats, and the ambitious young entrepreneur believed that he could turn a good profit in selling minks and other luxurious furs to the social elite of Chicago. There was another tangible element in Meltzer's decision to open his own fur store, namely, the harshness of the Midwestern winter. During the decade of the 1920s, and from his memory as a boy growing up in Chicago, Meltzer was well-acquainted with the biting cold temperatures and the bitter wind that swept down from Canada to freeze Chicago nearly every year. Meltzer also knew precisely how warm and practical fur coats could be in the midst of a Chicago snowstorm, and how desirable they were to well-heeled society women from Chicago's Gold Coast and the townhouses along South Michigan Avenue. Incorporating his business in 1929, Meltzer opened a small store at 162 North State Street, the heart of Chicago's retailing sector. The loft where he exhibited his furs during the first years of business was widely regarded to be rather cold during the winter months. Meltzer named his new fur business Evans Furs, Inc.

Within a short time after opening his doors for business, the New York Stock Exchange crashed and the entire country was thrown into the economic difficulties of what has become known as the Great Depression. Through 1930 and 1931, the economy of the nation continued to spiral downward with no solution in sight. Businesses went bankrupt, wealthy individuals and families lost their fortunes, and not a few men overwhelmed with debt took their own lives. When Franklin Delano Roosevelt was elected president in 1932, one of his first decisions was to implement a Bank Holiday, so that all the banks throughout the country could evaluate their prospects of remaining open to serve the public. When the banks finally returned to business, many of them were unable to reopen. Yet this was the first step in rebuilding a banking network with a financial basis that could not be undermined in the future.

Meltzer's fur store, although affected by the difficulties of the Great Depression, nonetheless was able not only to survive but to actually prosper during the 1930s. Forced to lay off some of his workforce, Meltzer devoted more of his own time and energy to supervising his business. To some extent, the fur retail business was recession-proof since those wealthy individuals who had not lost their money in the stock market were able to continue a lifestyle much the same as before the Depression. Furs were still purchased by socialite women for the winter season which involved symphony concerts, opera performances, and charitable fund raising events to help the less fortunate. In 1936 Meltzer decided to move the location of his company to the North American Building at 36 South State Street. The company's headquarters have remained at this address down to the present time.

Within Chicago retailing circles, Meltzer was widely regarded as a marketing genius. He was the first retailer in the entire metropolitan area to use advertising on the radio to sell his furs. Even more innovative was his decision to significantly alter the way fur coats were sold. Before Meltzer, the fur coat retail trade was highly individualized, with fur coats normally made-to-order on a person-to-person basis. A woman was measured for the size of coat that would fit her, she then chose the style and type of fur, the length and lining, and most often the retailer would order the fur and hand make it especially for the customer. Meltzer ushered in a new era in the fur retail trade when he began volume selling. In Meltzer's store, a woman could go in and look at a number of different furs and styles of coats that were already hanging on racks and ready to be taken home (perhaps with a few alterations). Not only did this reduce the price of purchasing a fur coat, but it made it a bit more accessible to upper middle class women.

Evans, Inc. continued its uninterrupted success throughout the 1940s and 1950s. Although America's entry into World War II, and the global conflagration which went on until 1945, hampered the company's ability to expand its operations and sell more fur coats, Meltzer's uncanny ability to draw enough people into his store to buy an extremely high quality, expensive product was nothing less than impressive. In its store on State Street, the company had created an elegant and sophisticated atmosphere where women felt privileged to shop. This atmosphere of rarified luxury, where women were expected to dress properly and even have their hair done before coming in to shop, was what set the standard for fur stores across the country in the late 1940s and throughout the 1950s. During this time, Meltzer began to supply furs and handle fur sales for large department stores on the East Coast, an operation that eventually spread to retailers across the United States. By the end of the 1950s, Evans, Inc. was widely regarded as one of the most elegant and successful of all the furriers in the country. Sales were continuing to increase, and there seemed no end to the profitability of Evans. In 1959 Abraham Meltzer, and his brother who worked for him, were given the most prestigious and coveted award within the fur industry when they were named "Men of the Year."

Change and Transition: 1960s–80s

When Abraham Meltzer retired in 1964, he gave the reins of the company to his son David Meltzer. Even though David was educated in the fur trade, he was not prepared for the developments during the 1960s and 1970s that forever changed the way many people viewed those privileged enough to buy and wear a fur coat. In the mid-1960s, with student unrest on many campuses within the United States, animal rights groups, which had previously been considered fringe organizations whose membership was a radical few, began to attract students to their cause and garner much more attention than previously given them. Not-for-profit and advocacy organizations such as The Fund for Animals, International Fund for Animal Welfare, and the National Wildlife Federation skyrocketed to the forefront of what became known as the animal rights movement.

An offshoot of the animals rights movement was the anti-fur activism that focused on convincing the American and European public that wearing any kind of fur was cruel and malicious to the animal it was taken from. The more radical members of the anti-fur movement engaged in such activities as shooting out the store windows of furriers, pouring glue onto the fur coats of their owners, and throwing paint on women who walked by wearing a fur coat. Even though the entire fur industry stopped using furs designated as threatened by the Endangered Species Act that was passed by Congress in 1973, the damage to the fur industry had already been done. Compounded by a dramatic change in fashion in which younger women regarded the wearing of furs as fit only for grandmothers and matronly types, sales for the entire industry plummeted from $335 million in 1967 to just over $250 million by the mid-1970s.

Evans was not immune from these social movements and trends within the industry, and sales for the company began to drop slowly throughout the late 1960s and 1970s. In the early 1980s, however, David Meltzer became convinced that the only way to increase his company's slumping sales figures was to expand its operations. As a result, the company implemented a major expansion strategy that not only included establishing new Evans stores in the greater Chicago metropolitan area, and other select cities across the nation, but also included the sale of Evans furs in major department stores as well. Soon Evans, Inc. had fur salons in Washington, D.C., New Orleans, Las Vegas, Dallas, and Oklahoma City, and also sold furs in departments stores such as Macy's and Associated Dry Goods affiliates. As David Meltzer looked for innovative ways to increase sales and bring more women into the stores, he decided upon two ideas. First, Evans would expand its product line to include a wider range of women's apparel, and second, the company would also create a less formal, less intimidating atmosphere for purchasing fur coats.

The 1990s and Beyond

Unfortunately, Meltzer's ideas did not work. The expansion strategy cost more money than expected, and sales remained flat. By the late 1980s, Evans, Inc. found itself in serious financial difficulties with continuing criticism from anti-fur activists, prices slashed within the entire industry due to oversupply, and an economy that looked as if it were deepening into a recession. Other furriers were experiencing the same kind of problems: Antonvich International, Inc. filed for bankruptcy and was liquidated; Fur Vault, Inc. was sold to a Korean firm; and Alper-Richman Furs, Ltd. also was forced into bankruptcy and liquidated soon thereafter. As chairman of the board David Meltzer had appointed his son, Robert, to the position of president and CEO in 1988, but removed him as the company's financial crisis deepened. But even closing stores and pulling out of some of the larger department store chains was not enough. Finally, for the first time in its history, the Meltzer family turned to an outside source for direction.

The company's new president and CEO, Leonard Levy, had previously been president at The Fair, located in Beaumont, Texas, which he helped bring out of bankruptcy in two years. But within six months, Levy was let go, supposedly over a personality clash and David Meltzer's consideration of purchasing the leases of 23 fur salons in Lord & Taylor stores across the country, which Levy regarded as imprudent under the company's current financial circumstances. Consequently, David Meltzer again assumed control and direction of the company and, even though Evans, Inc. remained solvent, the firm still needed an extensive overhaul of its operations. Throughout the 1990s, Meltzer cut costs by eliminating staff, closing stores, opening others, and renegotiating leases. Because of these measures, confidence in Evans, Inc. remained high, and creditors either extended the company's line of credit payments, or continued to increase its credit line.

By the late 1990s, Robert Meltzer, who had been removed by his father from the position of president and CEO in 1991, once again assumed those titles. In spite of the fact that fur appeared to be gaining in popularity, Evans was still struggling financially. From 1996 to 1999, the company lost money, and its stock price had fallen to just above one dollar. In the summer of 1999, the management team at Evans decided to sell the remaining company stores in the Chicago area, and concentrate on the leased fur department store operation, located in such major stores as Bloomingdale's, Rich's, Lazarus, Dayton Hudson, Marshall Field's, and others. The company retained its fur-only stores, located in prime retail spots in San Antonio and Austin, Texas, and three within the Washington, D.C. metropolitan area.

As of September 1999, Evans, Inc. was still in the midst of a financial crisis, and a turnaround of the company was required. Whether the management team at Evans would overcome the flat sales endemic to the fur industry, and the ongoing effects of anti-fur activism, was open to question.

Further Reading

Adams, Muriel J., ''Arctic Dream: Evans' Fantasy of Unintimidating Fur Salons,'' *Stores,* March 1988, pp. 14–16.

Collins, Lisa, ''Fur Flies at Stumbling Evans,'' *Crain's Chicago Business,* September 3, 1990, p. 3.

——, ''Why Evans Split with New CEO,'' *Crain's Chicago Business,* January 14, 1991, p. 4.

''Evans Firm Founder Dies in Hospital,'' *Chicago Tribune,* February 15, 1970, Sec. 3, p. 9.

''Evans to Close Three Chicago Area Fur Stores,'' *Women's Wear Daily,* June 15, 1999, p. 8.

George, Melissa, ''Investors Get Skinned at Evans: Furrier Has Another Bad Year,'' *Crain's Chicago Business,* April 26, 1999, p. 3.

Klein, Elizabeth, ''Cold Comfort: Evans Trims Loss by Cutting Costs, Downsizing,'' *Crain's Chicago Business,* July 29, 1991, p. 35.

Ryan, Thomas J., ''Evans to Sell Rest of Chicago Stores,'' *Women's Wear Daily,* July 2, 1999, p. 10.

Wallach, Janet, ''At Evans: Training to Sell 'Better,' '' *Stores,* March 1983, p. 15.

—Thomas Derdak

First Data Corporation

5660 New Northside Drive
Suite 1400
Atlanta, Georgia 30328
U.S.A.
(770) 857-0001
Fax: (707) 857-0404
Web site: http://www.firstdatacorp.com

Public Company
Incorporated: 1971 as First Financial Management
  Corporation
Employees: 33,000
Sales: $5.11 billion (1998)
Stock Exchanges: New York
Ticker Symbol: FDC
NAIC: 522320 Financial Transactions Processing (Except
  Central Bank); 51421 Data Processing Services

In 1995 two of the world's largest financial data processing businesses—First Financial Management Corporation and First Data Resources—merged to form First Data Corporation. This new entity operates in three primary lines of business: payment instruments, merchant processing, and card issuing. First Data is the leading provider of official checks and money orders for banks and savings institutions. Through its subsidiary Western Union, the company also offers money transfer services at 55,000 locations in 168 countries. In the realm of merchant processing, First Data annually processes and settles more than five billion credit, debit, and stored-value card transactions from over two million merchant locations. First Data's TeleCheck subsidiary authorizes more than 2.7 billion check transactions valued at $114 billion each year as well. In its third area of operation, First Data works with more than 1,400 card issuers. The company embosses and issues plastic cards, activates the cards, corresponds with cardholders, and produces and mails billing statements. In addition, First Data has entered the burgeoning field of Internet commerce through partnerships with large online merchants.

Birth of Two Data Processing Companies: 1970s

First Data Resources was incorporated in 1971 and by 1976 had become the data processor for both Visa and MasterCard bank-issued credit cards. American Express, which was itself attempting to build a financial services operation, bought First Data Resources in 1980 to perform processing functions. First Data Resources flourished in this new environment and became the largest bank-processing company in the United States. However, it proved to be an awkward fit with its parent company, and in 1992 American Express spun off the profitable division.

First Financial Management, which was also founded in 1971 and which merged with First Data Resources in 1995, was created as the data processing unit of the First Railroad and Banking Company of Georgia. First Financial was established to process checks by electronically following them through the banking system. By 1983 the operation was reaping $24 million in revenues and had become the largest banking data processor in the Southeast. When First Financial was spun off from its corporate parent in 1983, the company's president promised investors that he would raise First Financial's revenues to $100 million a year within four years. To achieve this stunning rate of growth, First Financial would have to acquire companies rather than develop new ventures from scratch. Thus in 1984 First Financial embarked on a decade-long buying streak.

First Financial's Acquisitions in the 1980s

In March 1984, First Financial paid $2 million for Marion, Illinois-based United Computer Services, Inc., and one month later purchased Financial Systems, Inc. First Financial offered $200,000 for certain assets of First American National Bank-Eastern in May 1984, and in August the company rounded out its first year of acquisitions with the purchase of Financial Computer Services, Inc., for $750,000.

The impetus fueling First Financial's string of acquisitions was the company's agenda to become a major player in the commercial transaction industry. First Financial believed that the future of banking and commerce would be driven by electronic and computerized information, not by cumbersome paper slips and forms. The company's goal was to become the middleman for a wide variety of exchanges in which electronic data was manipulated, acting as a support system for the financial industry of the future.

To attain this status, First Financial continued its rapid pace of acquisitions in 1985, buying four computer data services during the year. In February it paid $135,000 for the assets of the Data One Corporation and in June acquired an interest in Financial Data Services, Inc. for $2.75 million. In the following month Decimus Data Services joined the First Financial family, and in December the company paid $229,000 for Bob White Computing Services.

In making acquisitions, First Financial sought out relatively small entrepreneurial firms that were important because they would help the company increase its list of clients. Because it was cumbersome and time-consuming to win new customers in the financial services field, First Financial found it more economical simply to buy a small company than to individually recruit each of its customers. When First Financial purchased a small firm, the company did not, however, insist that the smaller company's operations be broken down and merged with those of First Financial. Instead, the company left them intact in the same location and with the same management, culture, and individual style. First Financial had a decentralized management philosophy, and although there was ample overlap in its operations, the company did not attempt to institute central marketing or sales operations. Former owners of properties that had been bought were encouraged through stock deals to stay and to work for First Financial, because their ownership in First Financial could be liquidated only over time.

After a brief pause First Financial resumed its acquisitions at the end of 1986, buying the customer base of American Information Services, Inc. for $2.5 million in August. In the following month the company bought American Data Technology, Inc. for $2.2 million, and in October 1986 it acquired Mid-Continent Computer Services for $23 million. These purchases were designed to strengthen First Financial by building up its revenues. In March of the following year First Financial bought Tel-A-Data Limited for $8.2 million and the Confidata Corporation for $500,000. Four months later First Financial also purchased American Automated and its On-Line Terminal Services for $4.3 million.

In the last four months of 1987, First Financial made three purchases that moved it strongly into a new field and nearly tripled the size of its operations. In October 1987 the company bought the National Bancard Corporation (NaBanco) of Fort Lauderdale, Florida, for $48 million. With the acquisition of this company, First Financial moved aggressively into the market for credit card transaction processing. Later that month First Financial added to its holdings in this area when it purchased Endata, Inc., of Nashville, Tennessee. With these moves First Financial became one of the three largest merchant credit card processors in the United States. The company decided to enter this field after its examination of why banks were unable to make money on their credit card operations. First Financial found that banks lost money when they had to collect and manipulate paper credit card receipts from merchants. By installing electronic terminals at cash registers, the company was able to eliminate this step and make credit card transaction processing much more lucrative.

In addition to its credit card operations, First Financial also purchased the First Data Management Company of Oklahoma City at the end of 1987 and Midwest Com of Indiana, Inc., for which it paid $400,000. At the end of the year First Financial reported revenues of $175 million, which yielded profits of $11.6 million. The president had met and nearly doubled his goal of three years earlier.

First Financial built on these strong returns by embarking on further acquisitions in 1988. In February the company continued its expansion into the credit card business by purchasing the processing contracts between retail merchants and Manufacturers Hanover Trust Company. In December First Financial enhanced its computer operations when it bought Appalachian Computer Services, a company based in Kentucky, for $46.5 million. "We're continuing on our path to be a significant financial-transaction company, and this rounds out one of our services," First Financial's chief financial officer told the *Atlanta Business Chronicle*.

By this time First Financial had accumulated more than 25,000 customers, including over 1,500 financial institutions. The total had been achieved through the company's 27 acquisitions, which came, on average, once every three months. First Financial ended 1988 with revenues of $423.7 million, an increase of more than 100 percent over the previous year. Profits reached $29.3 million. Nearly half, by far the largest part, of this income was contributed by First Financial's credit card processing operations.

Early in 1989 First Financial announced that it would branch out beyond its core transaction processing businesses to acquire a Georgia savings and loan association, despite the fact that this industry had been in a severe and protracted slump. The company took the step in order to protect its lucrative credit card processing operations. Concerned that the major credit card companies might one day issue rules that would prevent third-party companies such as First Financial from processing transactions, it decided to buy into the credit card industry in order to gain some say over how the accounts were handled. In order to become a credit card issuer, it was necessary to own a financial institution. By buying Georgia Federal Bank in May 1989 for $234 million, First Financial became the issuer of more than

100,000 credit cards. In addition, Georgia Federal had 11 percent of its deposits in the Atlanta market, where it was the largest thrift institution. Despite its size and strategic importance, Georgia Federal's acquisition by First Financial left the financial community worried about the company's prospects, and First Financial's stock price began to fall.

Developments in the Early 1990s

At the beginning of 1990 First Financial announced that it would switch its stock listing from the over-the-counter market to the New York Stock Exchange. In this way the company hoped to shore up its financial reputation and increase its attractiveness to foreign investors. Just a few days later First Financial also announced that it had reorganized its Financial Services Group into a subsidiary and changed its name to BASIS Information Technologies, Inc. This new entity comprised First Financial's original business operations, which provided check-clearing services to independent local banks, as well as 16 acquisitions that the company had made. With this restructuring along functional lines, the company hoped that BASIS would be better equipped to compete for the business of small financial institutions through its 24 data processing centers around the United States. By the end of its first quarter in business as a separate entity, however, BASIS was reporting only a ten percent profit margin, half of what First Financial executives had predicted.

This news—combined with an announcement that the federal government would investigate the real estate holdings of First Financial's thrift institution and with general jitteriness about the savings and loan industry—forced First Financial's stock price into a steep decline in the spring of 1990. Because the company used its stock to finance acquisitions, the drop in the value of its stock curtailed the number of purchases it could make.

By the start of the summer First Financial's stock price had begun to recover, and the company announced in August that it had finalized its purchase of two Atlanta businesses, Nationwide Credit and Online Financial Communication Systems, which meshed with the company's Microbilt subsidiary. With its purchase of the first company, First Financial entered the debt collection business. With the purchase of the Zytron Corporation in the same month, First Financial enhanced its Endata operations. The company also bought the Electro Data Corporation of Denver and the Bank of Boston's credit card contracts. In December 1990 First Financial announced that it had also acquired the credit card contracts of the Southeast Bank of Florida, which had one of the ten largest merchant contract portfolios. Shortly before this the company had completed its acquisition of the same operations from the Bank of New York, bringing a total of 12,000 new merchant customers to the company's credit card subsidiary. NaBanco, First Financial's credit card subsidiary, had become the nation's largest credit card processing company, with an annual growth rate of 40 percent.

Although First Financial's pace of acquisitions slowed in 1991, its revenues climbed to $1.2 billion. In the following year First Financial made a number of key purchases. In July 1992 the company augmented its credit verification operations by buying TeleCheck Services, Inc., and its subsidiary, the Pay-

ment Services Company, for $156 million. Shortly afterward First Financial expanded its ownership of TeleCheck franchises to 97 percent.

As part of this shift in corporate direction, First Financial divested itself of its savings and loan subsidiary, selling the Georgia Federal Bank and its subsidiary, First Family Financial Services. After a planned sale of this property in the summer of 1992 fell through, First Financial petitioned the Georgia state banking regulators for permission to form a credit card bank, called the First Financial Bank. After transferring Georgia Federal's data processing business to the new subsidiary, the sale of the thrift was completed when First Union Corporation paid $153 million for the property. The move, long urged by the financial community, was expected to lift the price of First Financial's stock.

At the end of 1992 First Financial also announced that it would sell its BASIS Information Technologies subsidiary, the company's original business, which now contributed only ten percent of First Financial's revenues. The move came on the heels of a $150 million lawsuit filed in October 1992 against International Business Machines Corporation (IBM), alleging that IBM had failed to properly implement a new computer system, which had damaged the company's operations. After receiving a cash settlement from IBM, First Financial completed the sale of BASIS to FIServe, Inc. for $96 million in February 1993.

In July 1993 First Financial activated the First Financial Bank as a credit card issuer, making it the sponsoring bank on customer contracts for the NaBanco processing operation. In addition, the company moved more aggressively into the healthcare field, purchasing Hospital Cost Consultants and VIPS, which marketed a Medicare claims processing system. First Financial also took a step into a new industry in 1993 when it purchased International Banking Technologies, Inc. for $47 million. This company had helped extend banking operations to supermarkets by negotiating agreements between grocers and financial institutions. With the move First Financial hoped to introduce its own services to a wider market. By the end of 1993 First Financial's revenues had grown to $1.67 billion.

The paths of First Financial and First Data first crossed in 1994, when each attempted to acquire Western Union Financial Services, the world's leading money transfer company. Western Union was an attractive target for both of these financial services powerhouses. First Financial wanted to acquire Western Union in order to branch out into a new market segment. Although the company had not previously ventured into consumer-oriented operations, Western Union's business was not outside the sphere of First Financial's expertise. After all, First Financial was already experienced in conducting money transactions for commercial customers. "Western Union is one of the most recognized trademarks in the world, with decades of experience in providing reliable services to consumers not currently targeted by our existing businesses," First Financial's president told the *Atlanta Journal-Constitution* on August 30, 1994. First Data, on the other hand, wanted Western Union in order to expand its presence in the consumer transaction market. (First Data had previously entered this market with its MoneyGram business, which it operated in conjunction with

American Express.) First Financial ultimately won the rivals' protracted bidding war, paying $1.9 billion to take control of Western Union.

Merger of First Financial and First Data in 1995

The firms were soon to meet on a less contentious field. In June 1995 they shocked the financial services industry by announcing merger plans, which they intended to accomplish through a stock swap. The information services field was growing more crowded, as computer and telecommunications companies began to offer the same sorts of services First Data and First Financial provided. Merchant processing was "a very concentrated industry and [was] getting even more so," an industry analyst explained to *American Banker*. "There is a lot of logic in the merger." According to the *San Diego Union-Tribune*, First Data and First Financial would be "better able to compete" by joining forces against their competitors in the crowded segment. As Ric Duques, the chairman and CEO of First Data stated in a press release, "our merged companies will have the required resources to meet new demands."

Because of antitrust concerns First Data was required to divest itself of its MoneyGram operation before the merger could be completed. The resulting company, which bore the name First Data Corporation, had net revenues of more than $4 billion and maintained a 30 percent share of the diverse credit card processing market. To streamline itself further, the nascent corporation began to rid itself of divisions that operated outside its core of financial support services. First Data Corporation concentrated instead on three key sectors: payment instruments, merchant processing, and card issuing.

The company continued to grow, but it did so less through acquisitions (as First Financial and the old First Data had done in the past) and more through strategic alliances that bolstered First Data Corporation's market position. In 1996 First Data signed an agreement to perform credit card processing for the entity that came out of the merger of Chemical Bank and Chase Manhattan, which was one of the ten largest credit card issuers in the country. That same year, First Data won a ten-year contract from retail behemoth Wal-Mart Stores, Inc. to provide comprehensive payment and electronic commerce services to all of its outlets. As a result of these partnerships, First Data Corporation's 1996 profits topped $898 million.

In 1997 First Data forcefully entered the realm of Internet commerce. Internet purchasing was expected to increase at astronomical rates, with some analysts speculating that as much as $3.2 trillion might be generated in online sales by 2003. First Data Corporation's partnership with Microsoft in 1997 was intended to keep First Data Corporation firmly at the center of

this new commercial realm. The company formed a joint venture with Microsoft called MSFDC, which was an electronic bill payment company. At the same time, First Data Corporation also continued to develop its traditional operations. The company joined with Chase Manhattan Bank to create a merchant bank alliance named Chase Merchant Service, L.L.C., which offered data processing and related services to merchants for credit, debit, and stored-value card transactions. First Data Corporation's 1997 sales soared to more than $5 billion.

The company continued to pursue online merchants in 1998 and 1999, forging more alliances with leading web businesses. In November 1998 First Data Corporation announced a ten-year marketing deal with iMall, a designer and host of web sites for retail merchants that was acquired by Excite@Home in 1999. First Data Corporation and iMall encouraged retailers to get connected through their joint operation, MerchantStuff.com, which featured the first-ever automated Internet approval and acquisition system for merchants. First Data Corporation also teamed up with Yahoo! Store's 4,000 merchants, as well as barnesandnoble.com, for which it contracted to perform credit card processing for all transactions. With its considerable resources and numerous subsidiaries, First Data Corporation's future looked promising.

Principal Subsidiaries

TeleCheck Services, Inc.; TeleCheck Recovery Services, Inc; Western Union Financial Services, Inc.; Wells Fargo Merchant Services, L.L.C.; BankBoston Merchant Services, L.L.C.; Chase Merchant Services, L.L.C.; Credit Performance Inc.; Paymenttech (48% with BANK ONE Corporation).

Further Reading

Bean, Ed, "An Empire in the Making," *Georgia Trend*, October 1989.

"The Bum Rap," *Georgia Trend*, August 1990.

Fickenscher, Lisa, "First Data, First Financial in Merger to Create $4 Billion Electronic Processor," *American Banker*, June 14,1995.

"First Union Will Buy Georgia Federal," *Atlanta Journal-Constitution*, December 21, 1992.

King, Jim, "First Financial Credit Card Bank Ok'd," *Atlanta Journal-Constitution*, November 26, 1992.

Lee, Shelley, "FFMC Expands at Blistering Pace," *Business Atlanta*, December 1991.

McNaughton, David, "First Financial Plans Bid for Western Union," *Atlanta Journal-Constitution*, August 30, 1994.

Morrison, Cindy, "FFMC Expects to Net a Big One Next Month," *Atlanta Business Chronicle*, November 21, 1988.

Rice, Marc, "First Financial, First Data Agree to Merge," *San Diego Union-Tribune*, June 14, 1995.

—Elizabeth Rourke
—updated by Rebecca Stanfel

Forbes

Forbes Inc.

60 Fifth Ave.
New York, New York 10011
U.S.A.
(212) 620-2200
Fax: (212) 206-5534
Web site: http://www.forbes.com

Private Company
Incorporated: 1917
Employees: 600
Sales: $315.8 million (1998)
NAIC: 51112 Periodical Publishers

Through its namesake magazine, Forbes Inc. has enjoyed a long history as one of the most successful and recognized publishers of financial news and information and ranks as one of the top 15 highest-grossing magazine publishers. The architect behind much of Forbes's growth was Malcolm S. Forbes, who oversaw the company from the 1960s until his death in 1990. Since that time, both Malcolm's son Steve and Casper Weinberger have chaired the company, which in addition to publishing the biweekly *Forbes,* also produces *Forbes FYI, Forbes ASAP,* and *American Heritage.* Privately owned, Forbes Inc. continues to be family-run, with Steve Forbes serving as president and editor-in-chief, Timothy Forbes as COO, Christopher Forbes as vice-chairman, and Robert L. Forbes as president of Forbes Global and Forbes FYI.

Bertie Charles or "B.C." Forbes was born in Buchan, Scotland, in 1880, the son of a tailor and later beer shop owner. Persuaded by a teacher that he had a knack for words, young B.C. landed a job as a type compositor with the *Peterhead Sentinel*, mistakenly assuming that compositors "composed" the news stories that would launch his journalistic career. Eventually, B.C. did get a chance to prove his reporting skills and won a cub reporter's job with the *Dundee Courier and Weekly News,* where he covered everything from murder trials to swimming contests. Forbes's taste for work was insatiable, and he quickly rose to senior reporter, only to leave Scotland for South

Africa in 1902 to assume a senior reporter's position with the *Johannesburg Standard and Diggers' News.* Two years later, B.C. was back in Scotland with a nest egg, a growing interest in business news, and the ability to engage the people who wrote and made the news. Because New York City was, in B.C.'s words, the "greatest newspaper town in the world," it seemed only logical that an ambitious business reporter establish his career there, and in August 1904 Forbes left Scotland for good.

"Devoted to Doers and Doings": 1904–29

By promising to "work for nothing," Forbes convinced New York's *Journal of Commerce and Commercial Bulletin* to hire him as a reporter on the dry goods industry, where he showed an unusual ability to report not just on business news but the personalities behind it. His reputation was growing, and when a London paper offered him a job he turned it down on the condition that the *Journal of Commerce* make him a financial editor. In addition to these new reporting duties, he was also offered the chance to write a regular editorial column for the *Journal,* which soon led to an opportunity to write another column for a rival New York paper (a practice not unheard of in the period). Thus, when newspaper mogul William Randolph Hearst sought to give his *New York American* paper a better financial page it was natural that the prolific Forbes seemed the most likely candidate. As a Hearst writer, Forbes enjoyed even greater readership, more venues in which to print his stories, and real power as the most prominent business journalist of his time.

Though increasingly well paid by Hearst (more than $185,000 a year in today's terms), in September 1917 Forbes decided to leave the position behind to pursue the only journalistic rung he had not yet seized—running his own publication. By relying on his continued income from a column for Hearst's paper as well as loans from the many businessmen he had met as a reporter, Forbes established *Forbes* magazine to profile the "doers and doings" of the growing American business scene. Published every two weeks for 15 cents an issue, the early *Forbes* was largely written by B.C. himself and offered an unusual combination of assertive, biting prose; unabashed cheerleading for business success stories; and a moralistic streak that excoriated companies when they demonstrated corruption or exploitative labor practices.

In the boom years of the 1920s, *Forbes* had the business magazine front to itself, which it served well by popularizing the world of business through revealing glimpses at the personalities behind the numbers and products. To his credit, B.C. Forbes seemed to sense that the great bull market of the late 1920s was getting out of hand, and in the months before the crash of October 1929 he warned his readers that "this is the ideal time to get out of debt," that is, close out their highly leveraged stock portfolios and abandon speculative investing. Forbes thus escaped the terrifying free fall in stock prices in the fall of 1929, but he mistakenly assumed the worst was over and prematurely bought up stocks at their new bargain-basement prices. When stocks continued their descent in the months that followed *Forbes* magazine joined the rest of the country in hard times. Because B.C. himself continued to write for Hearst's paper, however, he could use his still sizable writing income to keep the magazine afloat.

The Great Crash and New Competition: 1929–45

However, the crash was not the only source of trouble B.C. faced as the 1930s began. In 1929 and 1930, respectively, two new competitors, *Business Week* and *Fortune*, joined the business magazine market. Both took a different approach to business news. By publishing twice as often as *Forbes*, *Business Week* embraced a news-oriented approach, and the monthly *Fortune* built a reputation for long, in-depth analyses of corporations. *Forbes*'s highly subjective style and businessman-as-hero slant suddenly seemed less than cutting edge. By 1939, *Forbes*'s advertising had fallen from 1,216 pages in 1929 to 269, and its paid circulation of 102,000 ran a distant third to *Fortune*'s 248,000 and *Business Week*'s 192,000.

To keep *Forbes* afloat, B.C. tried to innovate and diversify. He published books with such titles as *The Salesman's Diary for 1938* and *Daily Pep Pellets*, hired and fired a series of managing editors, and shifted the magazine's focus from financial and stock market stories to a more nuts-and-bolts industrial beat. Though by 1943 B.C. could still claim an income of $50,000 and holdings of half a million dollars, his longtime safety valve, his column for the New York *American*, disappeared when Hearst canceled it.

Postwar Rebirth?: 1945–64

Like the U.S. economy after World War II, things began to look better for *Forbes* magazine as the postwar boom began to take hold. After winning the Bronze Star and Purple Heart in World War II, B.C.'s second oldest son, Malcolm, began to shake things up at the magazine, insisting that it hire its own staff and stop relying on commissioned pieces and scrapping B.C.'s insider's stock tip service in favor of the much more lucrative Forbes Investors Advisory Institute, which by 1950 was generating $51,000 a year in net profit. In 1946, *Advertising Age* reported that *Forbes*'s circulation had leaped by 26,000 in the space of four months, and by 1948 Malcolm had launched the magazine's annual January 1st ranking of U.S. corporations,

which eventually became a profitable source of advertising revenue (and anticipated the *Fortune* 500 list by five years).

Malcolm also made mistakes, however. His attempt at a coffeetable celebration of American history, *Nation's Heritage* magazine, may have been, as it was billed, "the most beautiful magazine in history," but its expensive inks, deluxe coated paper, and hefty newsstand price taxed Forbes Inc.'s coffers and it quickly folded in 1949. While Malcolm's older brother Bruce ran *Forbes* magazine's business operations, in the 1950s Malcolm pursued another quixotic and doomed pursuit that distracted him from his duties at the magazine: running for election to Congress. When B.C. died in May 1954, *Forbes*'s postwar bloom had begun to fade, and with the magazine's ownership now divided between Malcolm, Bruce, and two other brothers (who shared a third of the company's equity) it was unclear who would lead *Forbes* back to battle against *Business Week* and *Fortune*. When a new managing editor, Byron "Dave" Mack, began hiring researchers to verify writers' facts, however, *Forbes* began to become a more reliable source of information, and this seemed to free its writers to write more confidently. *Forbes*'s circulation once again began to climb. By the late 1950s, with Dave Mack shifted to editor and James W. Michaels hired as managing editor, *Forbes* was winning a larger and larger readership among business executives and investors. Between 1954 and 1958 alone, circulation grew by more than 100 percent to 265,000, and in 1957 Forbes Inc.'s revenues stood at an estimated $3.5 million annually.

Malcolm Takes Over: 1964–90

In June 1964, Bruce Forbes, whose advertising and business savvy had helped strengthen *Forbes*'s bottom line, died of cancer at 48. Malcolm stepped into the breach, buying out the 30 percent stake of Bruce's widow to become the majority owner of Forbes's stock. He then pressured his brothers Gordon and Wallace to sell their shares and eventually gained total control of Forbes Inc. His ultimate goal was to make *Forbes* the highest circulation business magazine on the market, and his aggressive, award-winning "Forbes: Capitalist Tool" ad campaign paid immediate dividends. Positioning *Forbes* as the bold and adventurous interpreter of the story behind the news, the message of the new ads was mirrored by Malcolm's own personal promotions: local publicity visits to major advertising markets in which potential *Forbes* advertisers were wined and dined on the family yacht *Highlander*.

By the third quarter of 1966, *Forbes*'s circulation had passed *Fortune*, and by the end of 1967 it stood at 500,000, ahead of *Fortune* by 25,000 but still trailing *Business Week* by 30,000 readers. There were still false steps, however. An Arabic-language version of the magazine folded in 1979, and a weekly *Forbes Restaurant Guide* folded after two years. Moreover, Malcolm had begun buying expensive mansions, ranches, and even a Pacific island to offer getaways for businessmen seeking to live the Forbes life. These projects lost money, however, until Forbes decided to break up his Denver-area ranch into five-acre parcels to be sold to the public through *Forbes* magazine and its newsstand competitors. The stratagem worked, and the Sangre de Cristo ranch eventually returned $34 million for the company on a $3.5 million initial investment. Meanwhile, by the end of 1972 *Forbes*'s circulation had climbed to 625,000

(75,000 higher than *Fortune*), and subscriptions alone were generating $4.5 million a year. Advertising was bringing in $20 million a year by 1976, and the income from the Forbes Stock Market Course and from renting its Manhattan office building further padded the bottom line.

Forbes's competition was only growing fiercer, however. In 1978 *Fortune* switched to a twice-monthly format, which tripled its revenues over the next six years, and a year later a new magazine, *Inc.*, appeared to seize the small business market. By 1984, *Forbes*'s 770,000 circulation trailed *Business Week* by 120,000 and led *Fortune* by only 22,000 readers. Worse, in gross advertising revenue *Business Week* and *Fortune* led with $156 million and $101 million, respectively, with *Forbes* trailing at $84 million. Still, *Forbes* had made enormous progress since 1964: it could boast that "one in five of our readers is a million-aire," and it remained the second most profitable magazine after *Playboy* because it produced no international or regional U.S. editions and maintained only a slim global network of journalists and a comparatively smaller U.S. editorial staff.

In 1982 Malcolm undertook the first of several international "Friendship Tours," in which an army of "Capitalist Tool" motorcyclists and hot-air balloonists descended on such countries as China, Pakistan, Japan, Germany, Turkey, and Spain spreading goodwill and the Forbes name. The same year, *Forbes* launched its notorious "Forbes Richest 400" list, which helped to raise the magazine's net worth to about $250 million (with another $150 million coming from real estate and other property). By 1983, *Forbes* ranked eighth among *AdWeek*'s "ten hottest" magazines (ranked by ad revenue). Since 1970, *Forbes* had expanded from an 18 percent share of the total ad revenues of Big Three business magazines to 33 percent, and it was *Business Week* that bore the brunt. In 1984, it therefore hired a new editor to stave off the *Forbes* threat, but new magazines including *Manhattan Inc.*, *Financial World*, and *Crain's* were making the business newsstand an increasingly crowded, cutthroat place. In 1986, the gloves came off in the business magazine ad wars when *Forbes* ran a confrontational ad under the words "Business Weak."

Steve Forbes and the Technology Challenge: 1990–99

By the late 1980s Malcolm's son Malcolm S. "Steve" Forbes, Jr., who had started at the magazine in 1971, had risen to president and deputy editor-in-chief. He had been giving *Forbes*'s editorial point of view a marked rightward tilt, which was underscored when Casper Weinberger, Ronald Reagan's secretary of defense, was named the magazine's publisher in 1989. In February 1990, Malcolm died in his sleep at age 70, leaving 51 percent of Forbes Inc. to Steve and the rest to his three younger brothers. As his celebrated father was eulogized, Steve reassured the press that the *Forbes* style would not change. For the most part, it seemed to be doing things right. Circulation stood at 735,000, and only *Business Week* sold more ad pages. *American Heritage* magazine, which it had purchased in 1986, had been given a new look under Steve's brother Timothy, and its ad pages grew 20 percent alone in 1989. A German edition, *Forbes von Burda*, had been co-launched with Germany's Burda Publications the month Malcolm died, and plans continued to launch a four-issue-per-year "lifestyle" magazine, *Forbes FYI*, in the fall of 1990. Only *Egg*, a self-styled "hip, urban" lifestyle magazine launched just before Malcolm's death failed to pan out and was shut down in early 1991.

Forbes Inc. worked hard to keep pace with the increasingly global and technology driven business climate of the 1990s. A Japanese edition was unveiled in March 1992; a Chinese edition was announced in 1993; and in 1998 *Forbes Global Business and Finance*, an English-language international edition, was launched under the leadership of former Canadian prime minister Brian Mulroney. Forbes Inc.'s *American Heritage* operations also expanded, entering the custom publishing market in 1993 and starting a quarterly African American history magazine named *American Legacy* in 1996. In the same year, Casper Weinberger was named chairman of Forbes Inc., and in both 1995 and 1999 Steve Forbes launched presidential campaigns that were reminiscent of his father's political crusades of the 1950s.

The challenge of the Internet was the real story, however. Forbes launched a new technology quarterly supplement, *Forbes ASAP*, in 1992, and in the mid-1990s Forbes moved rapidly to establish an online presence, christened "Forbes Digital Tool." As hip, new magazines, including *Wired*, *Fast Company*, *Business 2.0*, *Industry Standard*, and *Red Herring*, vied to become the business magazine for the Internet generation, Forbes opened a news office in Silicon Valley in 1997 and began to run more high technology cover stories. When in January 1999 Jim Michaels stepped down as executive editor after 37 years at the helm, it was no surprise that his replacement, William Baldwin, had built a reputation as a committed technophile.

Principal Divisions

American Heritage; Forbes ASAP; Forbes FYI; Forbes Global.

Further Reading

Forbes, Malcolm, "Cap Weinberger to Become Fourth Forbes Publisher," *Forbes*, October 3, 1998, p. 17.

Donaton, Scott, "Malcolm S. Forbes Jr.," *Advertising Age*, March 1990.

"Greater Expectations," *Forbes*, September 15, 1977, pp. 121+.

Heller, Robert, "The Battle for U.S. Business," *Management Today*, August 1984, pp. 62+.

Jones, Arthur, and Malcolm Forbes, *Peripatetic Millionaire*, New York: Harper & Row, 1977.

Kuczynski, Alex, "Changing of the Guard, and Coverage, at Forbes Magazine," *New York Times*, October 12, 1998.

Levere, Jane L., "Advertising: Forbes Hustles to Build Its Web Brand," *New York Times*, June 9, 1999, p. C8.

"A Magazine of His Own," *Forbes*, September 15, 1967, p. 13.

Motavalli, John, "Clash of the Titans," *AdWeek*, May 22, 1989, pp. 20+.

Winans, Christopher, *Malcolm Forbes: The Man Who Had Everything*, New York: St. Martin's Press, 1990.

—Paul S. Bodine

Fortum Corporation

Snellmaninkatu 13
Post Office Box 1
00048 Helsinki
Finland
358 10 4511
Fax: 358 10 4532 770
Web site: http://www.fortum.com

Public Company (75.5 Percent Owned by the Finnish Government)
Incorporated: 1998 as IVO-Neste Group Ltd.
Employees: 19,003
Sales: Fmk 50.50 billion (US$9.90 billion) (1998)
Stock Exchanges: Helsinki
NAIC: 211111 Crude Petroleum & Natural Gas Extraction; 23331 Manufacturing & Industrial Building Construction; 325199 All Other Basic Organic Chemical Manufacturing; 32552 Adhesive Manufacturing; 32411 Petroleum Refineries; 221111 Hydroelectric Power Generation; 221113 Nuclear Electric Power Generation; 22121 Natural Gas Distribution; 48621 Pipeline Transportation of Natural Gas; 42271 Petroleum Bulk Stations & Terminals; 44711 Gasoline Stations with Convenience Store; 54133 Engineering Services; 56121 Facilities Support Services

Fortum Corporation is an international energy group formed from the 1998 merger of two state-owned Finnish firms: Neste Oy, the nation's main oil and gas corporation, and Imatran Voima Oy, the state power company. Fortum has two primary subsidiaries: Fortum Oil and Gas Oy, which is involved in oil and gas exploration and production, petroleum refining and marketing, and the transmission, sale, and distribution of natural gas; and Fortum Power and Heat Oy, which generates, sells, transmits, and distributes power and heat, through the ownership and administration of hydroelectric, nuclear, and other power plants, as well as steam and heating plants. Other subsidi-

aries are involved in the operation and maintenance of power plants; in the design and construction of power plants, power transmission systems, and other power-related facilities; and in the production and marketing of chemicals, principally adhesive resins and industrial coatings. Though Fortum is a publicly traded company, the government of Finland maintains a 75.5 percent stake in the company.

Beginnings of Neste

In Finland there was never any form of nationalization of existing private industry as occurred in many countries after World War II. State ownership was considered to be a viable way of introducing a new industry in which no interest had been shown by existing companies in the sector.

Before World War II, Finland had no oil refineries. The country was one of the few in Europe that imported all its oil and petroleum products from abroad. When World War II broke out in 1939, Finland was not prepared to cope with the problems that ensued. In September 1939, petrol rationing started in Finland. Fuel and lubricant oils were placed under the control of a special agency called PVa, from the Finnish words for fuel oil storage, under the guidance of the Ministry of Defense. The new agency was led by Colonel Väinö Vartiainen, who was later to play an important part in the early days of Neste. Dr. Albert Sundgren, Finland's only petrochemicals expert, was on the staff of PVa. Earlier he had advocated the establishment of an oil refinery in Finland.

The agency planned to store its fuel oil and lubricant supplies in caves in the granite rocks of Tupavuori, in the township of Naantali on Finland's southwestern coast. A company was to be created to execute the plan.

The storage caves in Naantali were named NKV, from the Finnish words for Naantali Central Storage. After the end of the war, work to complete the caves went on. Responsibility for the NKV project was transferred from the Ministry of Defense to the Ministry of Trade and Industry in June 1947. NKV became a limited company, Neste Oy, and its first general meeting was held on January 2, 1948. The state of Finland was registered as a shareholder with 207 shares, Oy Alkoholiliike Ab, the state-owned alcohol monopoly with 140 shares; and Imatran Voima, the state-owned power company, with three shares.

In the articles of association of the company, it was stated that its purpose was to own and rent storage for liquid fuels and lubricants, and to act as importer, transporter, and manufacturer of these products, as well as trading in them. The beginnings of Neste (Finnish for "liquid") were not very auspicious. In the spring of 1948, Neste purchased an old tanker of 8,896 pennyweight (dwt) from Norway. The ship was a financial disaster. The caves also gave the company problems, when in July 1949 a dangerous fire broke out. The company was in financial difficulties. An agreement between Neste and the government was signed in October 1950, whereby Neste returned some of the less suitable storage space to the state for a remuneration of Fmk 150 million.

Adding Oil Refining in the 1950s

Uolevi Raade, director in the early 1950s of the Department of Industry within the Ministry of Trade and Industry, had become aware of Sundgren's plans for an oil refinery. Raade perceived that a major plan of national importance was waiting for his imagination and will power, and he accepted the challenge. The fortunes of Neste began to change.

Finland had traditionally relied on the services rendered by the major oil companies. They had a strong influence upon Finland's Department of Trade. They tried to make the refinery plans look unfavorable. Raade, however, was known for getting his way. He convinced the minister of trade and industry, Penna Tervo, of the importance of a national refinery. When the plan was brought to the government for the first time in 1951, however, it was not accepted. Raade had to start anew. He finally managed in 1954 to convince Dr. Urho Kekkonen, the influential politician and future president of Finland, of the importance of a national oil refinery. On December 17, 1954, the Finnish parliament authorized Neste to start building an oil refinery with 700,000 tons crude oil capacity.

Raade was named president of Neste on March 1, 1955. Vartiainen remained chairman of the board of directors, and was succeeded by Raade in 1959. Raade nominated Mikko Tanner as technical director. Raade had become aware that Tanner was an excellent engineer when constructing the fertilizer plants of Typpi Oy in Oulu. The managing director up to this time, Eino Erho, was to continue as commercial director of the company. An area near the cave storage reservoirs was selected as the future site of the refinery. The harbor conditions at Tupavuori were considered to be excellent.

The planning of the refinery was entrusted to the U.S. firm The Lummus Company, a specialist in the field. The delivery of

plant and equipment was entrusted jointly to the French company Compagnie de Five-Lille and Germany's Mannesmann. The civil engineering was carried out by Neste itself.

Construction work started at Tupavuori in Naantali in October 1955, and the inauguration of the refinery was held on June 5, 1958. The start-up of production in August 1957 had already shown that no technical problems existed. The guaranteed capacity of 700,000 tons was reached by the beginning of October, and soon it was apparent that the new refinery could reach a capacity of up to 1.2 million tons of crude oil per year.

Neste had planned to refine crude oil from many sources, half of the supply coming from the Soviet Union, and half from Western suppliers. As the company had no intention of forming a retail delivery system of its own, the marketing of products was based on cooperation with oil companies already operating in Finland. The most important of these were Shell, Esso, and Gulf. Shell and Gulf delivered crude oil of their own to be refined by Neste. All prices were tied to international market rates.

Entering Petrochemicals in the 1960s and 1970s

Raade kept up with market requirements. Neste's strategy was to deliver all the motor petrol Finland needed and adjust the production of other derivatives of crude oil accordingly. Thus the company chose a technology that gave maximum petrol output. The bilateral trade between the Soviet Union and Finland guaranteed that increased imports from the Soviet Union would mean new possibilities for exporting Finnish products. In 1960 Neste decided to double the capacity of the Naantali refinery. When the extension was completed and production started in September 1962, a capacity of 2.5 million tons of crude oil was reached.

Raade, however, already had new plans. In November 1962 he presented to his supervisory board a plan to construct a second refinery. He also proposed to purchase the Sköldvik Manor, with an area of 628 hectares near the town of Porvoo, east of Helsinki, as the location of the new refinery. The site had good access to deep waters. This rural area was to be changed into a huge heavy chemical industrial complex within a short time. Later the "green (environmental) movement" became active in opposing Neste as responsible for the change.

In 1963, however, when Lummus and Neste engineers were making plans for the new refinery, the plans received favorable publicity. Finland was living in a climate of industrial growth and was optimistic about the future expansion of technology. The plan to create a new refinery, with capacity equal to that of the enlarged Naantali refinery, was approved in June 1963. Soon Raade demanded that the construction be accelerated. Some of the suppliers had timing problems, and the start-up in spring 1966 was delayed by nearly a year. This did not stop Raade from ordering extensions to the new refinery to be built for start-up in 1968, doubling the refinery's capacity. This new extension started production three months before the planned start-up date. Neste regained some of the reputation it had lost as a result of the earlier delays. Uolevi Raade shared the visions of Sundgren regarding the future of petrochemicals and made careful plans for the realization of his dreams. At the inauguration of the first refinery in Naantali, it was stated in public that petrochemicals were closely associated with the refinery business, and that they would eventually come into Neste's domain. In 1959 Raade had taken Sundgren and two members of his board to Italy to study the activities of ENI and Montecatini. When presenting to the supervisory board his plans for the building of the oil refinery in Sköldvik, Raade told his audience that Neste would continue its development by entering the petrochemicals sector after 1967. Neste started detailed planning for this event, again with Lummus. In 1968 the plan was ready for presentation. The first stage included a plant for producing ethylene. This unit would form an integrated part of the oil refinery in Sköldvik. The second stage would be a plant for producing polyethylene and polyvinyl-chloride (PVC). This production would be carried out by a separate company, formed by Neste and its principal customers. Both units were planned to start production in 1972. In March 1969, a company named Pekema Oy was formed to realize the latter plan. Pekema had eight shareholders, all well-known Finnish industrial companies. Neste was the largest shareholder with 44 percent of the shares. The plant for the company was erected in the vicinity of the Sköldvik refinery. Production started at the beginning of 1972, at the same time as the start of production at Neste's ethylene unit. The company worked for a few years in close cooperation with Neste, but in 1979 the production facilities of Pekema were transferred to Neste and integrated into the company.

At the beginning of the 1970s four industrial companies, one of them Neste, formed a company, Stymer Oy, to produce polystyrene, another basic material for the plastics industry. The facilities of this company were also erected in the vicinity of the Sköldvik refinery. In 1981 this facility too was integrated into Neste. Neste also purchased other outside units that were tied to the refinery and making other chemicals for the plastics industry. Neste was now the dominant petrochemicals producer in Finland.

Few industrial projects in Finland received as much publicity as Neste's plans for a third refinery. Neste had calculated that new refinery capacity would be needed in 1976. After careful study, the company proposed to build another refinery in Lappohja near Hanko. These plans were presented to the supervisory board in October 1970. Helsinki University, whose biological station in Lappohja was considered internationally to be important for the study of wildlife in the Baltic, reacted violently against the plan. A large media debate ensued. "Green values" had become important and politicians were no longer easily converted to Raade's plans. The government assigned an area in Pyhämaa on the Gulf of Bothnia for the planned new refinery. Plans were altered accordingly.

Some doubts still lingered in top political circles. The prime minister, Dr. Mauno Koivisto, told his cabinet that the question should be reconsidered. Against Raade's opinion but with the consent of Tanner, it was decided that new capacity should be added onto the existing refinery.

The final decision was to double the capacity of Sköldvik, later more frequently called the Porvoo refinery, after the town where it is located. As Finland has no oil or gas resources of its own, the small amount of natural gas it required had been provided by imports, mainly from Denmark. But Finnish industry was interested in gas supply on a large scale, such as was found in many countries. The Soviet Union was interested in extending its network of natural gas pipes as far as the border of Finland and in signing a long-term delivery contract. Because of the bilateral trade, Finnish industry was continually looking for new import items from the Soviet Union in order to promote its own exports. In 1971 Finland signed an agreement with the Soviet Union for deliveries of natural gas to Finland. In the same year, Neste became involved in this project. A network for the distribution of natural gas was established by Neste and delivery contracts were drawn up with industrial customers. Gradually the network was enlarged.

Neste had decided in the 1940s that the crude oil should be imported mainly by ships owned by the company. The size of the ships altered according to changing shipping needs. Soviet oil was first imported from Black Sea ports, and later from Baltic ports. Crude oil was also imported from the Persian Gulf. In the early 1970s the Neste fleet had a capacity of over 300,000 pennyweight. After acquiring two supertankers of 260,000 pennyweight each, Neste's fleet consisted in the mid-1980s of 18 tankers, plus five tugs. At the beginning of the 1990s Neste had 19 ships, totalling 419,000 pennyweight. The supertankers had been sold. As a new technical solution, a push barge system was introduced for transporting bitumen.

Neste made a considerable investment in its research facilities. At first, its efforts were mostly directed towards improving the quality of its products. After gaining experience in operating its refineries, Neste was able to develop a variety of products in cooperation with customers without having to modify its plant. The Neste research center was already aiming at an early stage to prepare the company for future investments in petrochemicals. Research into new applications of petrochemicals in wood-based industries produced Neswood, a plastic-impregnated wood, which was employed as flooring at Helsinki Airport.

Eventually Neste Research Center developed into a multiple division for improving technology. When the corporate organization was changed in 1981 to consist of business units with individual responsibilities for results, this included the research and development activities. The technology group included all technical research and development activities within the company. The main activities were research into oil, catalysts, energy, engine performance, bitumen, combustion, and lubrication. Neste Engineering was a separate entity, mainly responsible for planning and directing new projects within the company.

Neste was intended to be an oil refiner, but from the start it was also intended to enter the petrochemicals sector. This happened exactly as Raade had predicted. After starting production of ethylene and after the absorption of the Pekama and Stymer joint ventures into Neste as fully owned operations, Neste added other petrochemicals to its range. The benzine unit opened in 1979. In 1981 the production of many industrial chemicals, such as phenol and acetone, began.

Failed 1980s Diversifications

In 1981 Neste set up a coal trading division. It was soon found, however, that this line of business did not suit the company. In 1985 the coal business was sold to a Finnish coal merchant.

In the same way as in the coal business, Neste planned to enter another area of energy production, and bought Pakkasakku Oy, a company making lead accumulator batteries. The battery market did not, however, fare well in the years leading up to 1990, when half of the shares of Neste Battery Ltd. were sold to the Spanish Grupo Tudor.

Neste still planned to be active in the energy sector on a broad scale. The company had a unit, Neste Advanced Power Systems, which studied applications of solar and wind energy as well as electric vehicle projects. These activities were centered on projects in Scandinavia, the United Kingdom, Greece, and Kenya. Uolevi Raade retired from his position as CEO and chairman of Neste in 1979 at the age of 68. His successor was Jaakko Ihamuotila, until then managing director of Valmet Oy. He kept to the strategy established by his predecessor. Even though initial steps to diversify the company's activities had not been successful, the main part of the strategy, strengthening Neste's position in chemicals, had been achieved by the late 1980s. For 20 years Neste's chemicals division had been the fastest-growing division in Neste. Comprising six business groups, the division produced a wide range of major plastics at sites in Finland, Sweden, Belgium, Portugal, France, and the United States. The petrochemical plants at the Porvoo production complex, together with an ethylene cracker at Sines in Portugal, played a central role in Neste's chemical activities, producing ethylene, propylene, benzene, cumene, phenol, and acetone.

For Neste the international trading of crude oil and petroleum products developed into an important line of business. With offices from Espoo in Finland to London, Houston, Tokyo, and Singapore, the corporation had a network that put it among the foremost international oil traders. The composite materials group, based on reinforced plastics products and semi-finished goods, included sports and leisure goods as well as products for electronics manufacturers and components for the aerospace, automotive, and paper machine industries.

Privatization and Merger in the 1990s

With the breakdown of the Soviet economy and the termination of bilateral trade between the Soviet Union and Finland, Neste entered a new era in the early 1990s. The company had been planning for just such eventualities for some time. Neste had begun reducing its dependence on Russian crude as far back as 1972, when it joined a consortium of Canadian, Swedish, and U.K. companies in a North Sea exploration venture. Other exploration and development ventures followed, all of them in partnership with other oil companies, in the Middle East and North America. In Oman, Neste had a one-third interest in a field, through a partnership with Occidental Petroleum Corp. Neste had entered the U.S. market in 1985, through a 50–50 joint venture with Weeks Exploration Co. of Houston. By the early 1990s its main U.S. producing areas were in east Texas, off the shore of Galveston, Texas, and in Mississippi. By this time, it was quite evident that Neste was no longer dependent on Russian crude. In 1990 the company failed to receive about two million metric tons of crude oil supplies it had contracted from the Soviet Union. Neste had no difficulty making up the short-fall, as its international oil trading operations were dealing more

than three times the amount of crude needed by the company's two refineries.

Neste had entered the service station market in the 1980s through the acquisition of three Finnish petroleum marketing companies. In the early 1990s Neste expanded further into petroleum retailing. In early 1992 Neste increased its ownership of Finnoil Oy from 50 percent to 95 percent, thereby increasing the number of service stations it controlled in Finland to about 900. Neste also established a growing network of service stations in the Baltic states, Poland, Germany, and in the St. Petersburg, Russia, area. St. Petersburg was a particularly attractive market because of its metro area population of eight million people, larger than the five million in all of Finland.

In a prelude to the company's privatization and eventual merger with Imatran Voima, Neste made a series of significant restructuring moves in the mid-1990s. In early 1994 Neste and Sweden's Statoil AS formed a 50–50 joint venture combining the bulk of the two firm's petrochemical and plastics operations. The new entity, Borealis A/S, was headquartered in Copenhagen and instantly became Europe's largest and the world's fifth largest producer of polyolefins, one of the top-selling plastics in the world. In May 1994 Neste and Russia's Gazprom, the world leader in proven natural gas reserves, set up a joint venture called Gasum Oy, with Neste holding a 75 percent stake and Gazprom 25 percent. Gasum gained responsibility for the pipeline that delivered natural gas from Russia to Finland, and for Neste's natural gas supply grid in Finland. Around this same time, Neste altered its divisional structure. The company previously had five divisions: oil, exploration and development, chemicals, gas, and shipping. Following the restructuring it had seven, with the oil division being divided into three new divisions: oil refining, marketing companies, and international trading and supply. As a result of the creation of Borealis, the chemicals division was left with two main areas of focus: adhesive resins and industrial coatings.

Through these moves that refocused Neste on its core oil and energy operations and that reduced its workforce from 12,000 to 8,000, the company improved its balance sheet and profitability, making a partial privatization more likely to succeed. In late 1995, 8.9 million shares of Neste stock were sold through an initial public offering on the Helsinki exchange. The Finnish state was left with an 83.2 percent stake by the end of 1996. In January 1997 Neste and Gazprom formed another joint venture, North Transgas Oy, this one of the 50–50 variety and slated to build a new pipeline that would take natural gas from Russian through Finland then on to the continental European market.

In late 1997 the Finnish government announced plans to merge Neste and Imatran Voima to form an enlarged energy group that would be better able to compete in the rapidly deregulating European power industry. Imatran Voima Oy (IVO) was founded by the Finnish government in 1932 in the town of Imatran, where it built a 100-megawatt hydropower plant (the firm's name translates as ''Imatran's water power''). In its early decades IVO concentrated on building and operating hydroelectric power plants and power transmission systems in Finland. IVO expanded further in the 1960s, building the largest coal-fired power plant in the Nordic countries to that time, and constructing power transmission links between Finland and the

Soviet Union and between Finland and Sweden. In 1965 the company began electrifying the Finnish railway system. IVO entered the nuclear power generation sector in the 1970s, and began selling district heat in 1982. During the 1980s IVO began developing combined heat and power (CHP) plants and expanded overseas in the area of the design and construction of power plants. In the early 1990s IVO launched a new unit dedicated to operating and maintaining power plants on a contractual basis.

Like Neste, IVO had expanded eastward in the 1990s, for example entering into power plant construction projects in St. Petersburg; Eilenburg, Germany; Jawaorzno, Poland; and Chvaletice, Czech Republic. It had built or had plans to build nuclear power plants in Russia and China. In addition, it had operating and maintenance contracts in Malaysia, Thailand, Tanzania, and Indonesia. The 1990s were also marked by the deregulation of the Swedish electricity market, and IVO expanded its operations in that country through a series of acquisitions commencing in 1996. By the time of the proposed merger of IVO and Neste, the still state-owned IVO was the main power company for Finland, and the second largest power firm in the Nordic market, with 13 percent of the overall electricity sales. In addition to its core energy operations, which included energy generation and the supply and distribution of power and heat, IVO's other activities included the operation and maintenance of power plants, the design and construction of power plants and transmission systems, and the manufacture of energy measurement equipment and systems. IVO had revenues of Fmk 13.8 billion (US$2.5 billion) in 1997, a considerably smaller figure than the Fmk 45.7 billion (US$8.2 billion) of Neste. But IVO was much more profitable, posting 1997 operating profits of Fmk 2.59 billion (US$466 million), compared to Neste's Fmk 1.62 billion (US$291 million).

Despite the doubts raised by some analysts as to the wisdom of combining two companies that appeared to have little synergy, the Finnish government pressed ahead, believing that it would be easier to privatize the combined group. In any case, in mid-1998 Fortum Corporation emerged as a new holding company for the combined operations of Neste and IVO (the new company was initially known as IVO-Neste Group Ltd.). In December of that year stock in Fortum began trading on the Helsinki exchange through an initial public offering, with Neste's shareholders also becoming shareholders in Fortum. At year-end 1998, the Finnish government held a 75.5 percent stake. In early 1999 Neste became known as Fortum Oil and Gas Oy, while Imatran Voima's name was changed to Fortum Power and Heat Oy. The operation and maintenance division of IVO was renamed Fortum Service Oy, while IVO's engineering operations became known as Fortum Engineering Oy. Neste's chemical unit was incorporated as Neste Chemicals Oy. The names Neste and IVO also continued as brand names, most publicly in the form of Neste service stations.

The European Commission approved of the creation of Fortum, with a single condition—that the holding in Gasum that it inherited from Neste be reduced. In May 1999 Fortum reduced its stake to 25 percent by selling 50 percent of its shares to several entities, with 24 percent going to the Finnish state and 20 percent to Germany's Ruhrgas Energie Beteilgungs-AG. A number of other deals in 1998 and 1999 further transfigured the nascent

Fortum group. With the chemicals area identified as noncore, Fortum sold its 50 percent interest in Borealis. The following month, Gullspång Kraft AB, a Swedish subsidiary inherited from IVO, was merged with Stockholm Energi AB to form Birka Energi AG, which was 50 percent owned each by Fortum and the City of Stockholm. Birka Energi, operating exclusively in Sweden, was a seller of electricity and heat, and owner and operator of power and heating plants, electricity distribution networks, and district heating and cooling networks.

In June 1999 Fortum and Statoil entered into an agreement to form a joint venture that would combine all the Neste and Statoil retail and direct sales operations and oil terminals in Estonia, Latvia, Lithuania, Poland, and Russia—making the venture the market leader in the region, with 285 service stations and four oil terminals. The venture would not include the Neste stations in Finland nor the Statoil outlets in Norway, Sweden, and Denmark. In July 1999 Fortum sold Enermet Oy, the maker of energy measurement equipment and systems that had been part of IVO, to a private equity fund, then acquired a 30 percent stake in a newly formed holding company, Enermet Group Oy. This move focused Fortum further on its core energy businesses, and was likely to be followed by the sale of Neste Chemicals, which would complete Fortum's exit from the petrochemicals area. On the addition side, Fortum in September 1999 announced that it would acquire Elektrizitätswerk Wesertal GmbH for DM 760 million (Fmk 2.3 billion). Wesertal had been the second largest regional energy utility owned by German municipalities and was purchased from four German administrative districts. Wesertal was primarily involved in the distribution and supply of electricity and gas, but also offered heat, waste disposal, and public transport services.

Principal Subsidiaries

Fortum Oil and Gas Oy; Fortum Power and Heat Oy; Fortum Service Oy; Fortum Engineering Oy; Neste Chemicals Oy.

Principal Operating Units

OIL AND GAS: Oil Retail–Finland; Refining and Wholesale; Base Oils; E&P; Natural Gas; LPGas Trade and Supply; LPGas Distribution; Energy House. POWER AND HEAT: Power Portfolio Management; Power Generation Assets and Operations; Distribution; CHP and Heat Generation and Distribution; P&H, British Isles; P&H, Central Europe; P&H R&D. OPERATION AND MAINTENANCE: O&M Finland; O&M Scandinavia; Maintenance; O&M International. ENGINEERING: Power Plant Engineering; Oil, Gas and Chemicals Engineering; Transmission Engineering. OTHER: Chemicals.

Further Reading

Alperowicz, Natasha, "Neste and Statoil to Form Petrochemical Joint Venture," *Chemical Week*, June 30, 1993, p. 17.
——, "Neste Continues Aggressive Global Expansion," *Chemical Week*, September 18, 1991, p. 8.
Auer, Jaakko, and Niilo Teerimaki, *Puoli vuosisataa Imatran Voimaa*, Helsinki: Imatran Voima, 1982, 302 p.
"Baltic Rim Gas, Retail Businesses Overhauled," *Oil & Gas Journal*, June 7, 1999, pp. 31–32.
Burt, Tim, "Fortum to Sell 50% of Gazprom Joint Venture," *Financial Times*, May 21, 1999, p. 28.

Cragg, Chris, "A Wedding in the North Country," *Energy Economist,* April 1998, pp. 11–13.

"Finland Details State Energy Firms' Merger," *Oil & Gas Journal,* December 29, 1997, p. 23.

"Finnish First," *Economist,* June 2, 1990, p. 76.

"Finland Presses Merger of State Energy Firms," *Oil & Gas Journal,* October 13, 1997, pp. 35–36.

"Gazprom and Neste Plan North European Gas Pipeline," *Oil & Gas Journal,* February 10, 1997, p. 38.

Guttman, Robert J., "Finnish Firms," *Europe,* November 1996, pp. 14–16.

Jackson, Debbie, "Neste Embarks on New Round of Restructuring and Seeks Alliances," *Chemical Week,* April 7, 1993, p. 12.

Knott, David, "Finland's Neste Presses Campaign to Play a Bigger International Role," *Oil & Gas Journal,* May 22, 1995, pp. 17+.

Larsio, Rauno, *Nesteen tie 1948–1973,* Helsinki: Neste, 1974, 92 p.

Madslien, Jorn, "Fortum Seems a Strange Offering," *Corporate Finance,* October 1998, pp. 10–11.

Milmo, Sean, "Neste and Statoil Set Up Shop," *Chemical Marketing Reporter,* January 17, 1994, p. 9.

Neste öljystä muoveihin, Espoo, Finland: Neste, 1982.

Piggott, Charles, "Finland's Fortum Issue Lacks Spark," *European,* November 30, 1998, p. 43.

Sains, Ariane, "Will Oil and Power Mix at IVO?," *Electrical World,* July 1998, p. 29.

"State Oil Company Profiles: Finland," *Oil & Gas Journal,* August 29, 1994, pp. 52+.

Whitcomb, Paulette, "Finns on the Hunt," *Oil & Gas Investor,* November 1991, pp. 40–43.

—Nils Björklund
—updated by David E. Salamie

Friendly's

Friendly Ice Cream Corp.

1855 Boston Road
Wilbraham, Massachusetts 01095
U.S.A.
(413) 543-2400
Fax: (413) 543-3966
Web site: http://www.friendlys.com

Public Companyb
Incorporated: 1935
Employees: 24,000
Sales: $678.10 million (1998)
Stock Exchanges: NASDAQ
Ticker Symbol: FRND
NAIC: 722211 Limited-Service Restaurants; 311520 Ice
   Cream & Frozen Dessert Manufacturing

Friendly Ice Cream Corp. is one of the top names in ice cream on the East Coast of the United States. The company has nearly 700 Friendly's restaurants in 15 states and distributes packaged ice cream products to thousands of retail stores. Friendly was purchased from the Hershey Food Corp. in 1988 by the Tennessee Restaurant Co., headed by fast food wunderkind Donald N. Smith. Since that time it has struggled toward profitability, having shouldered a sizable amount of debt in Smith's leveraged buyout. Friendly was taken public in 1997 to help reduce this burden. The company has also worked to improve its bottom line by upgrading restaurants, developing new products, and expanding its franchise program.

Early Years

In the summer of 1935 two brothers, Curtis and Prestley Blake, decided to go into business for themselves in Springfield, Massachusetts, by opening an ice cream shop. The 18- and 20-year-old Blakes borrowed $547 from their parents to finance the venture, naming their shop ''Friendly Ice Cream'' as a pledge to both themselves and their customers that they would offer warm and caring service. The Blakes made their own ice cream in a two-and-a-half-gallon freezer they had purchased with the borrowed money. The first four days they served the ice cream in cups, but when they decided to offer double-dip cones for a nickel, business began to take off. As the warm weather of that first summer waned, the brothers realized they would need to offer more than just ice cream to keep customers coming in over the winter. After taking a poll of their patrons, they decided to add hamburgers to the menu. By the following summer the Blakes were doing well enough to hire an additional employee, and in 1940 they opened a second shop in West Springfield, Massachusetts.

The United States entered World War II the following year, and in early 1943 the Blakes closed their shops for the duration. Curtis joined the service, while his older brother worked domestically for the war effort. They put signs in the windows of their restaurants announcing that they would be closed ''until we win the war!'' Following the cessation of hostilities, they returned to civilian life and reopened their shops. They expanded again in the late 1940s, with new locations in Longmeadow, Massachusetts, and Thompsonville, Connecticut. By 1951 a total of ten shops were open in the two states. This year saw the introduction of take-home half gallons of ice cream and expansion of the restaurants' menus to include more ice cream products and a variety of sandwiches. The company also built a manufacturing plant in West Springfield to produce ice cream for the growing chain.

Over the next two decades Friendly Ice Cream expanded into other states throughout New England and the Mid-Atlantic region, establishing an especially strong presence on Long Island. The company constructed its corporate headquarters and a new manufacturing plant in Wilbraham, Massachusetts, in 1960. In the late 1960s the Blake brothers took Friendly Ice Cream public with a stock offering. By 1975 the chain had more than 500 restaurants, and that year the company opened a second manufacturing and distribution plant in Troy, Ohio. Restaurant menus had expanded over time to offer breakfasts, chicken, seafood, salads, and more, though ice cream products continued to account for a major share of the company's business.

1979 Purchase by Hershey

Chocolate maker Hershey Food Corp., seeking to diversify, purchased Friendly Ice Cream for $162 million in 1979. By this time Friendly had more than 600 restaurants in 16 states and annual sales of $200 million. Hershey began to aggressively expand the chain, opening more than 100 restaurants within the next five years. In 1984 the company opened its first outlet in Florida, and by the following year, as it celebrated its 50th anniversary, there were 740 restaurants and 34,000 employees. Although annual sales figures had more than doubled since the Hershey buyout, all was not entirely well. Sales growth was mostly due to newly opened restaurants, not increases in per-store sales, and the growing legions of fast-food chains such as McDonald's were cutting into Friendly Ice Cream's business. To catch up, the company began experimenting with new strategies, one of which was a guaranteed five-minute delivery of lunch items on a special menu. The new Express Lunch concept was promoted with a series of television ads.

Despite this and other efforts, Friendly was still not performing as well as Hershey wished, and in September 1988 it sold the company to Chicago-based Tennessee Restaurant Company (TRC) for $375 million. TRC had been founded in the mid-1980s by Donald N. Smith and a group of investors to purchase and manage restaurant chains. Smith was considered a star in the restaurant world, having doubled Burger King's profits while serving as its president from 1977 to 1980 and later heading PepsiCo's restaurant division where he boosted profits 600 percent in two years. Smith was given credit for the success of PepsiCo unit Pizza Hut's popular Personal Pan Pizza concept, as well as the introduction of a successful breakfast menu during an earlier stint at McDonald's. TRC had purchased the 330-unit Perkins Family Restaurants chain in 1985, and the acquisition of Friendly made it the second largest operator of family restaurants in the country. Smith took the title of Friendly CEO and board chairman, in addition to his roles as chairman and CEO of TRC.

TRC immediately began to take stock of the company's strengths and weaknesses and scheduled more than 100 underperforming restaurants for closing within the next year and a half. These were located mainly in Virginia, Florida, and Ohio, with the company's New England stronghold remaining untouched for the most part. The brand name also was changed, with a posses-

sive "s" added to the end. Other changes included layoffs of 60 people at the corporate level, the planned revamping of all of the stores in the chain over the next several years, and folding the company's manufacturing and distribution operations into the newly created Food Service Division. Friendly also began to distribute its ice cream to supermarkets, starting in Albany, New York, and expanding throughout New England. Products ranged from half gallons of ice cream to pies, sundae cups, and cakes. The desserts were grouped in a display that highlighted the company name, which served to cross-promote the restaurants. When frozen yogurt began to take the country by storm, Friendly also added this to its product mix. Looking at other income possibilities, the company opened a firehouse-styled restaurant concept called Company C Rotisserie and Grille in a closed Friendly's in Wyoming, Ohio. The experiment was only a limited success and was not developed further.

Still Struggling in the 1990s

Despite the optimism engendered by Donald Smith's successful track record, Friendly Ice Cream's turnaround was moving slowly. In 1992 *Consumer Reports* ranked the company's restaurants last among 14 family food chains, citing surveyed customers' dissatisfaction with the food quality, service, and atmosphere. CEO Smith acknowledged the chain's problems, telling the Sunday Patriot-News Harrisburg, "The Blake brothers came up with a concept that evolved into something a notch above fast food. When we bought the chain, that image had become blurred." He declared his intention to continue to upgrade the company's reputation. Ongoing renovations to Friendly's restaurants, a program called "Focus 2000," included removal of booths, adding more family-sized tables, hiring additional serving staff, expanding carryout windows, and upgrading dinner menus. In 1994 healthier items such as roasted chicken and baked codfish were added. Typical entrees were priced at between $5.70 and $6.40, which included several side dishes. Sales per restaurant were up, and the company's annual revenues were growing slightly each year. Efforts to expand overseas also were being made, with ventures underway in the United Kingdom and the Far East.

By mid-1997 the company had renovated nearly 90 percent of its restaurants. It was on track to profitability, but the debt load and stiff competition in the marketplace had kept the balance sheet in the red since the purchase by TRC. In July the company announced a new franchise program, selling 34 of its restaurants in Delaware, Maryland, Virginia, and Washington, D.C., to DavCo Restaurants, which agreed to open a total of 100 more locations within ten years. A new limited-service ice cream shop concept, Friendly's Café, was also planned. In November Smith took Friendly public, offering $90 million worth of stock and floating $200 million in senior bond notes in an attempt to reduce the debt load. Unfortunately, in early 1998 the price of fresh cream began to climb steeply, eventually tripling, and Friendly was forced to raise prices for its ice cream products while absorbing much of the increased expense. At the same time, stiff competition in the retail market was causing packaged ice cream sales to flatten out, and the boost in restaurant business that had been seen at renovated outlets also began to drop off. In the latter case, analysts blamed the problems on continuing inconsistent service and a plethora of confusing menu additions. Friendly's stock, which had risen from an opening price of under $18 to more than $26 per share in six months, dropped to less than $5 by the fall.

At the end of 1998, the company announced that it would be closing its Troy, Ohio manufacturing and distribution center, moving those operations to the Wilbraham plant and a new facility in York, Pennsylvania. The move was intended to save shipping costs, as Friendly no longer had restaurants in Ohio and York was much closer to its East Coast stronghold. Friendly also pulled out of ventures it had launched in China and the United Kingdom. In early 1999 the company announced the appointment of a new president and chief operating officer and a new chief financial officer. The stock price was inching upward again, and analysts were applauding the new moves. Friendly rolled out a new product in the spring, the "Cyclone" soft-serve ice cream cone, which could be purchased with a variety of mixed-in additions such as candy, cookie, and fruit pieces. This was the company's first soft-serve ice cream product ever and was brought out in part in response to the success of McDonald's new McFlurry dessert. Friendly announced that it would be the company's largest new product introduction ever, with advertisements to run on both television and radio. Billboard ads and coupons in Friendly supermarket displays rounded out the campaign. The company also announced that it was stepping up the pace of franchise openings, with 25 scheduled for 1999 and 50 to 70 per year to follow.

Halfway through its seventh decade in business, Friendly Ice Cream Corp. continued to struggle to extricate itself from a period of sluggish sales and management difficulties. It was starting to look like CEO Donald N. Smith's goal of reinvigoration might be closer to fruition, as the debt load had been reduced and new measures to streamline operations were taking hold. Competition from the company's rivals was strong, however, and there was still work to be done before the company's health would be fully restored.

Principal Subsidiaries

Friendly Holding (UK) Ltd. (United Kingdom); Friendly Ice Cream (UK) Ltd. (United Kingdom); Friendly's International, Inc.; Friendly's Restaurants Franchise, Inc.; Restaurant Insurance Corporation.

Further Reading

Baily, Steve, and Steven Syre, "Sizable Debt Threatens to Cool Down Proposed Offering by Friendly," *Boston Globe,* October 15, 1997, p. E1.

Bohman, Jim, "Friendly Gets New Face—Restaurant Renovations Boost Sales," *Dayton Daily News,* May 25, 1994, p. 5B.

Bramson, Constance, "Ice Cream: Popular Frozen Yogurt Still Plays Second Fiddle," *Harrisburg Patriot,* September 12, 1990, p. C1.

Carlino, Bill, "Friendly's Eyes Consumers' Vote with Specialty Programs," *Nation's Restaurant News,* September 30, 1996, p. 14.

Carpenter, David G., "TQM As a Driver of Change and Profitability at Friendly's," *National Productivity Review,* September 1, 1995, p. 57.

Cebryznski, Gregg, "Friendly's Launches Soft-Serve Treat in Chain's 'Biggest' Product Introduction," *Nation's Restaurant News,* May 10, 1999.

Geehern, Christopher, "Customer Friendly: Company Stabilized; Considers Going Public," *Sunday Patriot-News Harrisburg,* June 14, 1992, p. F1.

"Hershey to Sell Ailing Friendly," *Newsday,* August 9, 1988, p. 31.

Hopkins, Jan, "Friendly Ice Cream CEO," *CNNfn: Capital Ideas* (television interview), April 29, 1998.

Mans, Jack, "Friendly Creativity," *Dairy Foods,* September 1, 1991, p. 95.

Merritt, Jennifer, "Friendly's Stock Price Takes a Licking on Wall Street," *Boston Business Journal,* October 16, 1998, p. 5.

——, "Friendly's Takes Several Steps to Regroup," *Boston Business Journal,* February 26, 1999, p. 13.

Reidy, Chris, "Friendly's to Try Franchise Route First Deal, with DavCo Restaurants, Aims to Open 100 Stores in Mid-Atlantic States," *Boston Globe,* July 15, 1997, p. E3.

Seligman, Bob, "Friendly's to Sell 100 Units to Help Upgrade Existing Sites," *Nation's Restaurant News,* February 26, 1990, p. 3.

Yoo, John C., "Hershey Sells Off Friendly Ice Cream," *Boston Globe,* August 9, 1988, p. 46.

—Frank Uhle

Gabelli Asset Management Inc.

One Corporate Center
Rye, New York 10580
U.S.A.
(914) 921-3700
(800) 422-3554
Fax: (914) 921-5392
Web site: http://www.gabelli.com

Public Company
Incorporated: 1976 as Gabelli & Co.
Employees: 130
Sales: $138.2 million (1998)
Stock Exchanges: New York
Ticker Symbol: GBL
NAIC: 52312 Securities Brokerage; 52393 Investment
    Advice; 52591 Open-End Investment Funds; 52599
    Other Financial Vehicles

Gabelli Asset Management Inc. is a holding company for subsidiaries engaged in managing mutual funds, offering advisory services to investors and alternative investment products such as risk arbitrage and merchant-banking limited partnerships, and providing brokerage, trading, underwriting, and research services. Although the company was managing assets of more than $16 billion at the end of 1998, its chief asset, to many observers, was its boss, the feisty and indefatigable Mario Gabelli. Dubbed ''Super Mario'' for his awesome record as an investor in stocks, he took Gabelli Asset Management public in 1999 but continued to hold a majority stake in the enterprise.

The son of Italian immigrants, Gabelli was born and raised in New York City's borough of The Bronx. He won a scholarship to Fordham University, where he studied accounting and graduated summa cum laude in 1965 but was unable to land a job as a security analyst. Gabelli emerged with a master's degree from Columbia University's Graduate School of Business two years later and went to work for Loeb, Rhodes & Co., where, he later told a *Forbes* reporter, he discovered, ''Major

moves in the stocks of big companies come once in ten years. So if you want to find stocks that can move a long way, you have to seek out pockets of opportunity. You learn that the greatest gains come from investing in small and medium-sized companies.''

Gabelli was putting into practice the theory of value investing that he learned at Columbia. He rated companies not by earnings but cash flow, analyzing a firm in great detail to calculate what he called private-market value: not the share price at which a stock was selling on an exchange but the price per share someone would be willing to pay in order to buy the whole company. This method would be widely used in the 1980s in leveraged buyouts, in which a public company's managers would buy their company, or at least a considerable part of it, and take it private. The calculations employed were often not the same as the standard valuation measures for public companies.

A Decade of Value Investing: 1976–86

At Loeb, Rhodes, Gabelli researched the farm equipment and auto parts industries and, later, media and broadcasting properties, sectors in which he would continue to specialize. But he left the firm in 1975, he said, when it turned down his idea of publishing a portfolio of small, undervalued stocks. He joined a smaller, research-oriented firm but ran into the same problem and quit in 1976 to form the brokerage house Gabelli & Co. with borrowed funds and money he had accumulated from trading on his own account. By the end of that year he also had formed Gabelli Investors (later Gamco Investors Inc.) to manage money for clients. After sending a memo to a *Barron's* editor touting a company he fancied, Chris-Craft Industries, Inc., Gabelli landed on the cover of this financial weekly. By 1981 Gamco had 81 accounts and was managing about $33 million.

Despite the rocky economy and overall stagnant stock market of the late 1970s and early 1980s, Gabelli made money for his clients each year. Gabelli & Co. in 1977 was a dealer-broker specializing in the shares of companies neglected by the big investment houses because the capitalization of these companies was so small that they could not take a large position without distorting the market for these securities. Gabelli noted that some of these firms had price/earnings ratios of only five, four, and even three to one. Applying the philosophy of value investing, Gabelli found, on investigation, unrecognized worth in such still ignored assets as cellular phone licenses.

While some investors were seeking to get in on the ground floor of a corporation's growth, Gabelli preferred to cash in on a company's "death." During the next few years he invested in or recommended the stocks of more than 50 companies that were taken over by other firms or privatized in leveraged buyouts, enabling him to earn an average annual compounded rate of return of more than 35 percent for his clients. By 1985 he was managing $350 million, two-thirds of it in tax-exempt funds. He stayed fully invested at all times, even when the overall market seemed to be overvalued, focusing on industries in which he was highly knowledgeable, such as broadcasting and auto parts distribution. "I don't need a rising market to bail me out," he told Jeffrey M. Landerman of *Business Week* in 1984.

Gabelli's firm was doing all its own research, usually with the idea of identifying firms that might be candidates for leveraged buyouts: those with characteristics such as a large amount of cash on hand, underlying assets such as real estate, or a large block of stock in the hands of a company founder with no children. He also looked for companies in industries where new competition was difficult and cash flow was high. Once Gabelli selected such a stock, he was willing to wait for years until it appreciated. He began buying Cowles Communications, Inc., for example, in 1977 at $14 a share and eventually became its biggest stockholder. In 1984 the company (now Cowles Media Co.) was privatized at $46 a share, for a total payoff to Gabelli's clients of $33 million. Another media winner was Chris-Craft, whose BHC Communications, Inc. achieved almost a sixfold pretax gain in income over six years in the 1980s and in the 1990s assembled its own network, United Television.

The relentless Gabelli was visiting about 50 companies a year to gain information and meeting the managers of more than 100 other corporations annually, as well as getting together with other portfolio managers to discuss ideas and reading about 20 trade journals, two or three newspapers, and a number of industry and company reports. He also was writing research reports for his brokerage customers and portfolio-manager and other professional-investor clients. "I read annual reports instead of

novels," Gabelli told Jerry Edgerton of *Money* in 1986. As a narrowly focused investor with large holdings in a few companies, he was able to bring influence to bear on company management.

Gabelli's special interest in broadcasting companies took him into cable television in the late 1970s. When cable companies became interested in cellular telephones, he was quick to spot the trend. By the mid-1980s he was investing in some of the 1,400 independent telephone companies in the United States. But he was also a major investor in unglamorous purveyors of basic industrial products—not only auto parts distributors but such companies as SPS Technologies, a producer of industrial fasteners; Greif Bros. Corp., a manufacturer of shipping containers; and Lamson & Sessions Co., a producer of thermoplastic electric-conduit fittings for the construction industry.

Between 1978 and 1985 Gabelli's portfolios outperformed the Standard & Poor's index of 500 stocks each year and more than doubled the results of this S&P index in five of those years. Between 1977 and 1988 Gamco Investors' assets appreciated at an annual compounded rate of 28 percent, a rate exceeded by very few money managers. This money management entity had never lost money over a year and had met Gabelli's objective of ten percent annual return after taxes and inflation in all but two years. Gamco Investors' equity assets, flush with cash invested by company pension funds, reached $1.6 billion in the latter year.

Gabelli Mutual Funds: 1986–97

In addition to brokerage and money management operations, Gabelli in 1986 established his first investment vehicle for the general public, Gabelli Asset Fund. This mutual fund required a minimum investment of $25,000, but only $2,000 for Individual Retirement Accounts (IRAs). By the end of 1988 Gabelli's firm had three mutual funds—two run by Gabelli himself—with combined assets of $650 million. In all, Gabelli Group Inc. (later Gabelli Funds, Inc.)—the parent firm for Gamco Investors and Gabelli & Co.—had $2.5 billion under management from 700 client accounts. Gabelli owned 62 percent of the company. By early 1991 Gabelli Group was overseeing 1,000 institutional and individual accounts, five mutual funds, an arbitrage fund, and several other U.S. and offshore investment partnerships. However, during a disastrous 1990 Gamco's accounts lost 14.1 percent, and three of the four open-end mutual funds lost value, partly because of the fall in share value of telephone companies Gabelli had been touting.

Founded in 1987, Gabelli Growth Fund was first managed by Elizabeth Bramwell, an analyst Gabelli met at Columbia during their student days. Gabelli Growth Fund achieved an annualized return of about 40 percent in 1988 and 1989, better than her boss's own performance. She resigned in 1994 after finding herself locked out of her office for refusing to move from Manhattan to suburban Rye, New York, where corporate headquarters had been established two years earlier. Bramwell said the performance of her fund had slipped vis-à-vis Gabelli's own results partly because she was not being allotted the staff she needed as the fund grew in size. She won $850,000 from Gabelli in an arbitration award regarding compensation allegedly due her.

By this time Gabelli was personally managing seven of the company's 11 mutual funds, with a total of $2.65 billion in assets. He also held an interest in Gabelli-O'Connor, a fixed-income management firm that distributed a small fund family called Westwood, and he controlled Lynch Corp., a publicly held diversified manufacturing holding company in which Gabelli & Co. and Gamco Investors held about one quarter of the shares. In 1994 the Securities and Exchange Commission cited the latter two firms for failing to "establish, maintain and enforce written policies and procedures reasonably designed to prevent the misuse" of inside information stemming from Gabelli's dual position as an investment adviser and as chief executive of Lynch Corp. Gabelli & Co. and Gamco Investors paid $100,000 in civil penalties and agreed to appoint an independent consultant to review the procedures of the two firms and recommend improvements. The SEC did not charge Gabelli or anyone in his employ with actually trading on any inside information that Gabelli might have obtained through his service at Lynch.

In October 1995 the *Wall Street Journal* published an article suggesting that Mario Gabelli's disinclination to delegate authority was resulting in turmoil within his organization, and that while the Gabelli funds were still achieving impressive long-terms results, year-by-year gains were no longer spectacular. The article noted that all seven mutual funds managed by Gabelli himself were performing more poorly in 1995 than the average similar fund, and that all were below the S&P 500 index for the year.

Mario Gabelli refurbished his reputation in 1997, when ten Gabelli equity funds averaged a return of 31.7 percent, the best of any U.S. mutual fund group, earning him the accolade of domestic equity fund manager of the year by Morningstar Inc. These funds included Gabelli Global Interactive Couch Potato, which specialized in entertainment and media stocks and whose lead manager was Gabelli's son Marc. In May 1998 this fund held third position among all funds concentrating on communications companies, with a return of 54 percent in the previous 12 months.

Gabelli Asset Management: 1998–99

By 1998 Gabelli & Co. was a subsidiary of Gabelli Securities, Inc., which was 77 percent owned by the holding company Gabelli Asset Management Inc. In its corporate quarters, Gabelli Asset Management retained its founder's reputation for tightfisted management, with overhead kept to a minimum and a staff so minimal that it did not even include a receptionist. The company earned net income of $57.3 million on revenues of $138.2 million in 1998. It was managing $16.3 billion—of which 88 percent was invested in equities—at the end of 1998 and went public in February 1999, selling six million shares, or about 20 percent of the common stock, at $17.50 a share. Gabelli and other family members continued to control the company and held 97.6 percent of the voting power, partly through ownership of separate Class B shares.

Much of the approximately $96 million in proceeds from the sale of the shares was earmarked to expand and market the offerings of the firm, make acquisitions, and hire talented managers. But Gabelli Asset Management also agreed to pay its founder, in addition to the usual portfolio management fees—averaging more than $20 million annually in recent years—ten percent of the aggregate pretax profits of the firm and a deferred payment of $50 million on January 2, 2002, plus quarterly interest beforehand of $750,000 on that sum. Originally, Gabelli had sought to continue collecting 20 percent of his firm's annual pretax profits. He received a total of $33.6 million in compensation in 1997 and about $42.3 million in 1998.

Not all Wall Street observers thought purchasing Gabelli Asset Management stock a wise investment, despite the founder's spectacular record as a money manager. A Morningstar executive told Richard A. Oppel, Jr., of the *New York Times* that the firm had the potential for strong growth but a history of "wacky promotional schemes" and management "like a cottage industry." A fund industry consultant put the firm's potential weakness more concisely when he said "The company is Mario."

Gabelli Asset Management announced in April 1999 that three of its funds, including "Couch Potato," would henceforth be sold through brokers collecting sales charges, or "loads," as well as directly to investors as "no-loads." Company officials were reported to be gathering data on whether the firm should continue selling its funds directly or exclusively through brokers.

Gabelli Funds, at the end of 1998, was managing 26 mutual funds with $8.2 billion in assets, including three closed-end funds on the New York Stock Exchange. It was managing 975 separate accounts for clients, including corporate pension and profit-sharing plans, endowments, jointly trusteed plans, municipalities, and high net worth individuals, with a total of $8 billion under management, and was serving as subadviser to certain other third-party investment funds. Gabelli Securities, Inc. was providing alternative investment products, consisting primarily of risk arbitrage and merchant banking limited partnerships with $146 million of assets. Gabelli & Co. was a registered broker-dealer and was acting as underwriter and distributor of open-end mutual funds. It was also providing research services. Gabelli Asset Management had offices in New York City and Reno, Nevada, as well as corporate headquarters in Rye, New York.

Principal Subsidiaries

Gabelli Advisers, Inc. (41%); Gabelli Fixed Income, Inc. (including 80%-owned Gabelli Fixed Income, LLC); Gabelli Funds, LLC; Gabelli Securities, Inc. (77%, including Gabelli & Co.); GAMCO Investors, Inc.

Further Reading

Authers, John, "Gabelli's Theory Catches the Mood," *Financial Times,* August 20, 1998, p. 22.

Button, Graham, "In the Boss' Shadow," *Forbes,* November 27, 1989, pp. 238, 240.

Eaton, Leslie, "From Wall St. Guru to Mutual-Fund Empire Builder," *New York Times,* July 16, 1995, Sec. 3, pp. 1, 7.

Franecki, David, "Some Gabelli Funds to Add Sales Charges," *Wall Street Journal,* April 1, 1999, p. C23.

Gould, Carole, "Keeping It All in the Gabelli Family," *New York Times,* May 24, 1998, Sec. 3, p. 7.

Henriques, Diana B., "An S.E.C. Warning to Funds on Inside Information Rules," *New York Times,* December 9, 1994, pp. D1, D6.

"Mario Gabelli's Orphan Asylum," *Forbes,* July 15, 1977, pp. 69–70, 72, 74.

McGough, Robert, "Bramwell Opts to Leave Gabelli Funds Rather Than Relocate New York Office," *Wall Street Journal,* February 11, 1994, p. B3.

Oppel, Richard A., Jr., "Market Place," *New York Times,* February 10, 1999, p. C8.

Rohrer, Julie, "Cashing in at the Wake," *Institutional Investor,* January 1985, pp. 67–68, 71.

——, "What Makes Mario Run?" *Institutional Investor,* pp. 94–98, 101, 103–104.

Schultz, Ellen E., and McGough, Robert, "Gabelli Returns Slip Amid Series of Distractions," *Wall Street Journal,* October 6, 1995, pp. C1, C23.

White, James A., " 'Super Mario' Is Weathering First Setback for His Empire," *Wall Street Journal,* February 15, 1991, pp. C1, C5.

Wyatt, Edward, "Market Place," *New York Times,* April 28, 1998, p. D9.

—Robert Halasz

Gannett Co., Inc.

1100 Wilson Boulevard
Arlington, Virginia 22234
U.S.A.
(703) 284-6000
Fax: (703) 558-4638
Web site: http://www.gannett.com

Public Company
Incorporated: 1923
Employees: 39,400
Sales: $5.12 billion (1998)
Stock Exchanges: New York
Ticker Symbol: GCI
NAIC: 51111 Newspaper Publishers; 51312 Television
  Broadcasting

The largest newspaper group in the United States, Gannett Co., Inc. owns 75 daily newspapers, including *USA TODAY,* the largest-selling daily newspaper in the country. Gannett also owns more than 20 television stations covering roughly 17 percent of the United States. Although the company's focus is primarily on its newspaper and broadcasting properties, it operates a news service and is also involved in commercial printing, telemarketing, data services, and news programming. Headquartered in Arlington, Virginia, Gannett maintains offices in 45 states, the District of Columbia, Guam, and the United Kingdom.

Origins

Gannett was the brainchild of Frank Gannett, who paid his way through Cornell University by running a news correspondence syndicate; when he graduated he had $1,000 in savings. Gannett got into the media business in 1906 when he and several associates bought the *Elmira Gazette* in Elmira, New York, with $3,000 in savings, $7,000 in loans, and $10,000 in notes. They bought another local paper and merged them to form the *Star-Gazette,* beginning a pattern of mergers to increase advertising power that the company would follow throughout its history. Six years later, in 1912, Gannett bought

the *Ithaca Journal,* beginning his toehold in upper New York state. The company gradually built up a portfolio of 19 New York dailies by 1989.

In 1918 Gannett and his team moved to Rochester, New York, a city whose papers would turn out to be among the company's strongest. Many of Gannett's rising executives were groomed at the Rochester papers. The group purchased two newspapers upon their arrival and merged them into the *Times-Union.* The papers' holdings were consolidated under the name Empire State Group. In 1921 the *Observer-Dispatch* of Utica, New York, was acquired. In 1923 Gannett bought out his partners' interests in the Empire State Group and the six newspapers the group then owned, and formed Gannett Co., Inc. Gannett appointed Frank Tripp general manager. Tripp helped run the everyday business of the papers, and the two were close allies for years. The Northeast was Gannett's focus for the next 25 years, and the company expanded aggressively with acquisitions there. Another key executive, Paul Miller, joined the company in 1947, becoming Gannett's executive assistant. By then, the company operated 21 newspapers and radio stations.

The company's role as a leader in technology began in 1929, when Frank Gannett co-invented the teletypesetter. Gannett newsrooms were among the first to use shortwave radios to gather reports from distant sources. In 1938, before color was used much in newspapers, many Gannett presses were adapted for color; with its *USA Today,* the company would continue to be a leader in color use. Other advantages included a corporate plane that helped reporters get to the site of news quickly. Frank Gannett died in 1957, but not before he saw Miller named president and chief executive officer. Miller oversaw the company's expansion from a regional to a national chain in the next decade.

Gannett News Service, as the company became known, was founded in 1942 as Gannett National Service. The wire service subsidiary provided the company's local papers with national stories from Washington, D.C., and 13 bureaus. The stories often featured a local angle or local sources. A television news bureau was added in 1982. Through all these years, Gannett grew by buying existing newspaper and radio and TV stations. In 1966 it founded its first newspaper, *Florida Today.* It was the work of Allen Neuharth, who later was to become the founder of *USA Today.* Neuharth brought the new paper to profitability in 33 months, an incredible feat in the newspaper business, according to analysts. Because the paper was near the National Aeronautics and Space Administration (NASA), it was dubbed "Florida's Space Age Newspaper." The paper was ultimately redesigned to emphasize state and local news and was promoted and sold with *USA Today*, which provided national and international coverage.

Gannett went public in 1967. In 1970 Miller assumed the title of chairman, and Neuharth was promoted to president and chief operating officer from executive vice-president, making him the heir-apparent to the top position in the company. Neuharth went on an acquisition spree, leading the company to its current size and status in the media world. He became chief executive officer in 1973 and chairman in 1979.

1970s: Growth Through Acquisitions

Two notable mergers were those with Federated Publications in 1971 and with Speidel Newspaper Group in 1977. Two years later, Gannett merged with Combined Communications, the biggest such merger in the industry at that time, for $400 million. The Evening News Association joined the Gannett family later when Gannett bought it for $700 million. One near merger was with Ridder Publications. That company's president, Bernard H. Ridder, Jr., was a golfing mate of Miller. Ridder had concluded that the only way his small, family-held company's stock would ever reach its full potential was for Ridder Publications to merge with a big media company. The two talked, but Ridder proved to be more interested in Knight Newspapers because it had less geographic overlap with Ridder than did Gannett. But in 1989 Gannett and Knight-Ridder implemented a joint operating agency to combat the decline in newspaper advertising revenues in Detroit, Michigan. The cooperative venture was the largest ever merging of two competing newspapers' business operations. The arrangement called for the Knight-Ridder's *Free Press* and Gannett's *Detroit News* to divide revenues equally. Since Gannett held more of Detroit's market share before the merger, it took a loss during the venture's first year, 1990.

In 1986 Neuharth retired as chief executive officer, passing the baton to John Curley. Curley had been president and chief operating officer since 1984; he joined Gannett in 1970. Curley took on the title of chairman in 1989. A newsman like most of Gannett's heads, Curley was editor and publisher of several Gannett papers and was founding editor of *USA Today*.

Neuharth continued as chairman of the Gannett Foundation, which was established in 1935 by Frank Gannett to promote free press, freedom of information and better journalism, adult literacy, community problem-solving, and volunteerism. Neuharth spent as freely at the foundation as he had at the company, giving $28 million to various programs in 1989

alone. Despite criticism from some Gannett newspaper executives, Neuharth also oversaw the Foundation's move from Rochester, New York, to Arlington, Virginia, where *USA Today*'s offices were located. Interior design of the charity's new headquarters ran to $15 million.

With expenses rising faster than assets, Neuharth sold the Foundation's ten percent share of Gannett Co. back to the company for $670 million. On July 4, 1991, the philanthropy's name was changed to the Freedom Forum, and its mission was changed to focus on First Amendment and other strictly journalistic issues. Gannett Co. created a $5 million fund to replace money withdrawn from the Gannett Foundation's more community-oriented charities. Other accomplishments of the company in the early 1990s included: increasing the company's use of recycled newsprint to 20 percent of total usage, over 180,000 tons; being named one of the United States' top 20 places for African Americans to work; and becoming the first news service to syndicate a weekly newspaper column dedicated exclusively to gay and lesbian issues.

Neuharth had said in 1982 when he started *USA Today* that it would begin making annual profits in three to five years. By 1990 the paper had had quarterly profits but never a full year of profitability. Between 1982 and 1990, *USA Today* sapped the company of an estimated $500 million. September 1992 marked ten unprofitable years for *USA Today*. But with 6.6 million readers daily, the United States' most widely read newspaper also celebrated record advertising and circulation revenues. *USA Today* executives claimed that had the U.S. economy not been in recession, the paper would have been in the black by 1990. Fortunately, the rest of Gannett's business was strong enough to offset *USA Today*'s annual losses. Curley, the paper's president and publisher, hoped that cost-containment measures, lower newsprint prices, and other savings in the production-distribution process would bring *USA Today* into profitability.

The year 1991 was Gannett's most difficult since the company went public in 1967. The company slipped from second to third in rankings of the top U.S. media concerns as a result of Time Warner's leapfrog to first place. Annual revenues dropped two percent and net income was down 20 percent from the year before. Fifty-five of Gannett's 86 local dailies raised circulation prices, and circulation barely rose.

Yet the national daily newspaper was another demonstration of Gannett's leadership role in the use of technology, as well as journalism. The paper also was an innovator in graphics, especially in the use of color. Media observers credited *USA Today*'s use of color as the spur for industrywide interest in color graphics. The copy for the paper was composed and edited at *USA Today*'s Arlington, Virginia, headquarters, then transmitted via satellite to 36 printing plants in the United States, Europe, and Asia.

$5 Billion in Revenues: 1990s

Gannett's most significant activity during the 1990s took place in the divestiture and acquisition arena, an area that some observers believed the company needed to explore more fully. Critics contended that Gannett, renowned for its financially conservative approach, should loosen its purse strings and adopt a more aggressive acquisition strategy. Confronted with suggestions that the company should purchase a movie studio or a television network, Gannett management demurred, preferring to keep its focus set on its core businesses. ''We aren't complicated people,'' Curley informed the *Wall Street Journal* in late 1995. ''We like newspapers and TV stations. If you run them very well, they can do very well . . . .'' Despite the company's penchant for financial discipline and its steadfast adherence to its existing businesses, the 1990s saw Gannett explore new business opportunities and express more than a modicum of acquisitive might.

Gannett began the process of adding and paring away businesses in 1995. That year, the company shouldered past rival bidders such as Ellis Broadcasting and NBC in its $1.7 billion acquisition of Greensville, South Carolina-based Multimedia, Inc. The acquisition gave Gannett 11 daily newspapers, 50 other newspaper publications, five network-affiliated television stations, two radio stations, and production and syndication control for television shows hosted by Phil Donahue, Sally Jesse Raphael, Rush Limbaugh, and Jerry Springer. The acquisition of Multimedia also ushered Gannett into the cable business, giving the company 450,000 cable television subscribers. As the company delved into the previously foreign territory of operating cable television systems and controlling television programming, it withdrew from two other businesses. In 1996 the company sold its outdoor advertising division to Outdoor Systems of Phoenix, divesting the business to free its resources for the development of its newspaper and broadcast properties and to facilitate the incorporation of the Multimedia properties into its fold. Louis Harris & Associates, Gannett's polling subsidiary, also was sold in 1996, a year that saw the company enter into a joint venture with Knight-Ridder and Landmark Communications to form an Internet service provider called InfiNet, created to help publish newspapers online.

Deal-making continued to predominate at Gannett headquarters as the company entered the late 1990s. The company had exchanged six of its radio stations for a television station in Tampa, Florida, in 1996; in 1998, it exited the business entirely by selling its remaining five radio stations to Evergreen Media. As the company's radio properties disappeared, the number of its television stations increased with the acquisition of three stations in Maine and South Carolina. Before the end of the decade, the company completed two more significant deals, which, in keeping with the trend established in the 1990s, included a divestiture and an acquisition. In 1999, the company sold the cable assets obtained in the Multimedia acquisition. According to company officials, the decision to divest the cable properties was not based on a strategic decision, but represented an opportunity to realize a significant profit. Gannett sold the cable business to Cox Communications for $2.7 billion, a move that the company's treasurer described as ''a grand-slam deal'' in the July 31, 1999 issue of *Editor & Publisher*. In a separate announcement, Gannett revealed that it was acquiring 95 percent of Newsquest plc, the largest regional newspaper publisher in England.

The cumulative effect of the acquisitions and divestitures completed during the latter half of the 1990s lifted Gannett's revenues above $5 billion by the end of the decade. Although the company shied away from headlong leaps into other areas of the media industry—unlike many of its competitors—Gannett's consistent record of financial growth suggested that there was no pressing need to develop into a comprehensive, broadly diversified media conglomerate. For Gannett, the future held no greater prospect than maintaining its stature as the largest newspaper group in the United States, an objective management intended to fulfill by remaining tightly focused and conservative in its leadership during the 21st century.

Principal Subsidiaries

Gannett Direct Marketing Services, Inc.; Gannett News Service; Gannett National Newspaper Sales; Gannett Telemarketing, Inc.; USA Today; Newsquest plc (95%); Gannett Offset; Multimedia Cablevision; Gannett Newspaper Agency (50%); Gannett Media Technologies International; Gannett New Business Product Development; Gannett Retail Advertising Group; Gannett U.K. Limited.

Further Reading

Boulton, Guy, ''Gannett Co., Nation's Largest Newspaper Chain, to Acquire Multimedia Inc.,'' *Knight-Ridder/Tribune Business News,* December 3, 1995, p. 12030214.

Calabro, Lori, ''Douglas McCorkindale: Confessions of a Dealmaker,'' *CFO: The Magazine for Senior Financial Executives,* March 1991.

Case, Tony, ''Two Old Marketplace Enemies End Up the Best of Partners,'' *MEDIAWEEK,* March 15, 1999, p. 18.

Cosco, Joseph, ''Loyal to the Core,'' *Journal of Business Strategy,* March–April 1996, p. 42.

Cose, Ellis, *The Press,* New York: Morrow, 1989.

Crain, Rance, ''Readers Find Newspapers 'Boring . . . Dull,' '' *Advertising Age,* September 14, 1992.

Donaton, Scott, ''Media Reassess As Boomers Age,'' *Advertising Age,* July 15, 1991.

Endicott, R. Craig, ''100 Leading Media Companies,'' *Advertising Age,* August 10, 1992.

Fisher, Christy, ''A Decade of 'USA Today': Color It Red,'' *Advertising Age,* August 31, 1992.

Fitzgerald, Mark, ''Stockholder Proposal Seeks Closing of USA Today,'' *Editor & Publisher,* April 4, 1992, p. 12.

Foust, Dean, ''Patching the Cracks in the House That Al Built,'' *Business Week,* December 16, 1991.

''Gannett: USA's Tomorrow,'' *Economist,* November 25, 1989.

Garneau, George, ''A Flat Year Expected for 1992,'' *Editor & Publisher, the Fifth Estate,* January 4, 1992.

——, ''Gannett Foundation's Revised Mission,'' *Editor & Publisher, the Fifth Estate,* June 8, 1991.

——, ''Newspaper Financial Reports,'' *Editor & Publisher, the Fifth Estate,* August 8, 1992.

Goldsmith, Jill, ''Cox to Buy Gannett Biz for $2.7 Bil.,'' *Variety,* August 2, 1999, p. 25.

Henderson, Barry, ''Gannett to Sell Off Recently Acquired Cable Systems,'' *The Kansas City Business Journal,* September 1, 1995, p. 3.

Kerwin, Ann Marie, ''Advice for the Next Century: Future Role of Newspapers Discussed by Panel,'' *Editor & Publisher, the Fifth Estate,* August 8, 1992.

McClellan, Steve, ''Multimedia Buy Boosts Gannett into Top 10,'' *Broadcasting & Cable,* July 31, 1995, p. 36.

Moses, Lucia, ''Gannett to Shed Cable Business,'' *Editor & Publisher,* July 31, 1999, p. 18

Mott, Frank Luther, *American Journalism: A History, 1690–1960,* New York: Macmillan, 1962.

Powell, Dave, ''Technology and Imagination Are the Stuff from Which Businesses Can Be Built,'' *Networking Management,* March 1991.

Rengers, Carrie, ''Where Gannett Went Wrong,'' *Arkansas Business,* October 19, 1992, p. 22.

Sacharow, Anya, ''The Merger,'' *MEDIAWEEK,* November 27, 1995, p. 12.

—Lisa Collins and April Dougal
—updated by Jeffrey L. Covell

Ghirardelli Ch●colate Company

1111 139th Avenue
San Leandro, California 94578
U.S.A.
(510) 483-6970
(800) 877-9338
Fax: (510) 297-2649
Web site: http://www. ghirardelli.com

Wholly Owned Subsidiary of Chocoladefabriken Lindt & Sprungli AG
Incorporated: 1852
Employees: 300
Sales: $100 million (1998 est.)
NAIC: 311320 Confectionary Chocolate Made from Cacao Beans

Ghirardelli Chocolate Company is one of the leading producers of chocolate in the United States. It was long one of the premier chocolate manufacturers in the West. Its historic factory in San Francisco is now a key landmark in that city, where it functions as an urban mall called Ghirardelli Square. The company's main manufacturing facility is in San Leandro, California. The company has a significant business selling chocolate wholesale. In the 1990s Ghirardelli increased its retail business, selling bagged candies in grocery stores and other outlets, as well as Ghirardelli brand baking chocolate and cocoa. Ghirardelli also operates several ice cream and chocolate stores, mainly aimed at the tourist trade. A family-owned company for over 100 years, Ghirardelli passed through a series of owners in the 1980s and 1990s, and was bought in 1998 by the Swiss confectioner Chocoladefabriken Lindt & Sprungli.

Early Years

Ghirardelli Chocolate Company was founded by an Italian, Domenico Ghirardelli, who was born in Rapello, Italy, in 1817. Domenico's father was a merchant, and he apprenticed his son to a confectioner and spice importer. Domenico learned the

trade, then moved to South America and went into business for himself. He worked for a time in Montevideo, Uruguay, and then settled in Lima, Peru. While in South America, Ghirardelli changed his first name from the Italian Domenico to the Spanish Domingo. Ghirardelli's shop in Lima was next door to that of a cabinetmaker, James Lick. Lick was either a restless or an adventurous fellow. In any case, he decided to leave Peru for California. He landed in San Francisco on January 11, 1848, just 13 days before gold was discovered at Sutter's Mill, precipitating the California gold rush. Lick had brought with him 600 pounds of his neighbor Ghirardelli's chocolate. He soon wrote to Ghirardelli that conditions were ripe in California. He had sold all the chocolate he had with him, and he advised the confectioner to come north. So Domingo Ghirardelli promptly followed Lick to San Francisco. At first he sold chocolate, coffee, liqueurs, and other items to the gold miners, and by 1852 he had established a store in San Francisco. Ghirardelli's company had several locations in its early years, and apparently business was up and down. But by 1885 the company was importing 450,000 pounds of cocoa beans a year, as well as importing and grinding spices and selling coffee, wine, and liquor. Chocolate manufacturing was the mainstay of the business. The equipment needed to sort, blend, roast, and grind cocoa beans took up a lot of space, and the expanding business meant the company needed bigger quarters. Domingo Ghirardelli retired in 1892, leaving the company to his sons, and in 1893 the company purchased a square block in San Francisco bounded by Beach, Polk, Larkin, and North Point Streets. This area luckily survived the earthquake and fire of 1906, and Ghirardelli continued to expand its facilities, erecting new buildings in what became known as Ghirardelli Square. The Ghirardelli site had originally housed the Pioneer Woolen Mill, and Ghirardelli hired the mill's architect to design each of its new buildings. The company built a Cocoa Building in 1900, the Chocolate and Mustard Building in 1911, the Power House in 1915, and finally a clock tower and apartment building in 1916. These were all built of red brick with white trim, and the site is still considered architecturally impressive.

Business boomed during World War I, when the factory operated around the clock producing chocolate for the armed forces. Domingo Ghirardelli, Jr., the founder's eldest son, was president of the company through this period until 1922. That year he stepped down, and his younger brother, Domingo Lyle, became president. The company flourished during the 1920s. Ghirardelli was the largest chocolate factory west of the Mississippi. Besides bulk chocolate and cocoa, the company made retail goods such as instant chocolate malted milk powder. Ghirardelli also did a sizable business in mustard. The company was actually the only mustard manufacturer west of the Mississippi. It sold mustard under the Ghirardelli brand, and also made all the mustard sold under the Schilling brand.

Decline in the 1950s

Domingo Lyle Ghirardelli retained the presidency until 1958, though he worked closely with his brothers and other family members in executive positions. The company's manufacturing plant used large, expensive equipment, and Ghirardelli had three mechanics working full time keeping the machinery in good working order. Ghirardelli imported cocoa beans from all over the world, from the Ivory Coast to Panama, Samoa to Colombia. Each bean had different characteristics, and blending them for the proper taste and color was a sophisticated art. By the 1950s, much of the company's machinery had become antiquated, and the business was exceedingly labor-intensive. As well as using elaborate machinery for processing chocolate, the company also made its own cans and boxes, manufacturing everything it needed for its business except for paper goods. It was clearly no longer an up-to-date factory, but the Ghirardelli family apparently had little initiative to make major changes at that point.

As the Ghirardelli family grew, the number of stockholders increased. By the 1950s there were 40 outside stockholders, and these people generally wanted to be paid a dividend instead of seeing the money reinvested in the plant. The mustard business came to a halt shortly after World War II, when Schilling, Ghirardelli's major customer, was bought up by McCormick, a Chicago-based spice company. Ghirardelli was not making much money, and the management was reaching retirement age. In the early 1960s, the company let word get out that it would consider selling the business.

Ghirardelli had several offers for the company, from scrap dealers or rival chocolate manufacturers, but nothing panned out. Then in 1962 the company received an offer for its land and buildings from Mrs. William P. Roth and her son William Matson Roth. The Ghirardelli family accepted the offer, and the Roths formed the Ghirardelli Center Development Company to renovate the buildings and make them into the block of shops and restaurants now known as Ghirardelli Square. Then in 1963

the Golden Grain Company offered to buy the chocolate company. Golden Grain was another family-run business founded by Italian immigrants, the De Domenicos. Begun as a macaroni maker, the company had gained nationwide appeal with its introduction of Rice-A-Roni. Ghirardelli's machinery was mostly sold to scrap dealers, and Golden Grain started from scratch, constructing a new, modern manufacturing facility in nearby San Leandro, California. Thus Ghirardelli operated as a subsidiary of Golden Grain, in all-new quarters.

Changes in Ownership in the 1980s and 1990s

Ghirardelli was apparently a profitable but small business under Golden Grain. It had strong name recognition, particularly in the West. Under its new owner, the company continued to produce both wholesale chocolate for the confectionary, baking, and dairy industries, and premium retail branded items. By the mid-1980s, the company was doing well, but it only accounted for a little over ten percent of Golden Grain's total sales. In 1986 Quaker Oats, the Chicago-based food conglomerate, acquired Golden Grain, and with it, Ghirardelli. Quaker hung on to Ghirardelli for three years, then announced that the company was for sale. Ghirardelli was bringing in an estimated $35 million in annual sales at the time, but Quaker considered it too small, and not a good fit with its other grocery product lines. However, it took another three years before Quaker could find a buyer. In that time, Ghirardelli redesigned its packaging to give it a more modern and upscale look, and this move was linked to an upsurge in sales. Finally in March 1992 Quaker announced that a Boston investment firm, Thomas H. Lee Company, was buying Ghirardelli. Terms of the deal were not made available, but later disclosures put the price at around $40 million. Annual sales had grown to about the same amount by the early 1990s, though industry watchers also noted that Ghirardelli faced harsh competition from other large chocolate producers such as Hershey and Nestlé. Thomas H. Lee controlled a slew of consumer products manufacturers, including the General Nutrition Companies, Playtex Family Products, and others.

Thomas H. Lee held on to Ghirardelli for only four years. Ghirardelli's president and CEO was Jack Anton, who had led the Thomas H. Lee investment group in the takeover of the company. Anton oversaw great growth in the company's sales during this time. Ghirardelli began opening retail shops, in an effort to find a new market. It had three soda fountain and chocolate shops in San Francisco, and in 1994 Ghirardelli announced it would open more such stores in upscale retail venues in other cities in California and in Chicago. Retail sales accounted for only about 15 percent of the company's total sales, but it seemed the area open for the most growth. Ghirardelli also worked on expanding its presence in grocery stores with branded baking products such as cocoa and chocolate chips. While the company was owned by Thomas H. Lee, its branded products surpassed industrial products in percentage of total sales. By 1994, around 60 percent of total sales were in the branded products division. Total annual sales rose from $37 million in 1992 to about $75 million just two years later. The company pushed to get its products in more grocery stores and other retail outlets in major markets, particularly in big cities in the Northeast and Midwest. In November 1994, Ghirardelli announced that it had forged a distribution deal with the Sam's Club food chain, a grocery chain owned by Wal-Mart. This move helped Ghirardelli reach a national market. By 1994, almost half the company's sales were in markets east of the Rocky Mountains, up from just 20 percent when Thomas H. Lee first acquired Ghirardelli. Ghirardelli had also boosted growth by doubling the number of products it sold, making 125 different food items by 1994. It marketed its baking goods in supermarkets by setting up displays, a recipe center, and a toll free customer support line. With increased marketing and distribution, its grocery sales grew at 50 percent annually in the early 1990s.

In 1996 CEO Anton bought out Thomas H. Lee Company with the help of a Dallas investment firm called Hicks, Muse, Tate, & Furst, Inc. Hicks, Muse was called "one of the most successful LBO [leveraged buyout] artists in the country" by *Business Week* magazine in a July 1, 1996 article. The firm specialized in a "buy and build" strategy, where it bought up small companies in related areas and ran them together. Other food companies it owned in the mid-1990s were Campfire marshmallows, Chef Boyardee, Bumble Bee tuna, and Ranch Style beans. Hicks, Muse paid $65 million for Ghirardelli. Jack Anton continued as CEO, and kept the company on its growth course. Ghirardelli's new chairman was C. Dean Metropoulos, who managed food acquisitions for Hicks, Muse. Hicks, Muse let it be known that it was satisfied with Ghirardelli's present course, which had resulted in annual growth of about 13 percent a year over the past four years. Therefore, the new ownership did not constitute big changes for Ghirardelli. Rather, Hicks, Muse let the company go on with its expansion.

But the relationship with Hicks, Muse was also short-term. In January 1998, Ghirardelli announced that it had been acquired by the Swiss chocolate maker Chocoladefabriken Lindt & Sprungli AG. Jack Anton maintained his position as president, so despite the quick turnover in ownership in the 1990s, there was continuity in management. Lindt & Sprungli was a leading producer of premium chocolates in Europe. Its major markets were Switzerland, Germany, and France. Since 1993, the company had been on an expansion program, and its acquisition of Ghirardelli fulfilled its objective of increasing its share of the North American market. Lindt brand chocolate had more of a presence in the eastern United States than in the West, so its purchase of Ghirardelli gave it better coverage of the entire country. Lindt announced that it was pleased with Ghirardelli's growth, which had averaged 20 percent annually over the five years preceding the sale, and did not anticipate making major changes.

Ghirardelli had sales of over $100 million by the time of Lindt's purchase. It had grown impressively since Quaker let it go. In 1999 the company was still on an expansion track, working on increasing its presence as a national brand by getting more items on supermarket shelves. It rolled out bagged miniature chocolate squares in March 1999, and announced that it was coming up with more premium chocolate items soon, such as chocolate bars in velvet bags and specialty Christmas treats.

Further Reading

Carlsen, Clifford, "Ghirardelli Chocolate Plans National Rollout," *San Francisco Business Times*, April 29, 1994, p. 1.
——, "Ghirardelli Unwraps New Markets, Takes Big Bite," *San Francisco Business Times*, November 11, 1994, p. 3.
Forest, Stephanie Anderson, "Where LBO Means 'Let's Be Offbeat'," *Business Week*, July 1, 1996, pp. 86–87.
"Ghirardelli Thrives on Old World Heritage," *Candy Industry*, August 1994, p. 51.
"Hicks, Muse Buys Ghirardelli Chocolate," *New York Times*, March 5, 1996, p. D2.
Huesmann, Chris, "New Owners to Fund Expansion Efforts at Ghirardelli Chocolate Co.," *Knight-Ridder/Tribune Business News*, March 5, 1996, p. 3050264.
Lawrence, Polly Ghirardelli, *The Ghirardelli Family and Chocolate Company of San Francisco*, Berkeley, Calif.: Regents of the University of California, 1985.
"Quaker Plans Ghirardelli Sale," *New York Times*, January 5, 1989, p. D6.
"Quaker to Sell Chocolate Maker," *New York Times*, March 25, 1992, p. D4.
"Sales Leap 300% After Upscale Redesign," *Packaging*, February 1992, p. 15.
Schnurman, Mitchell, "Hicks Muse Has a Taste for Food Acquisitions," *Knight-Ridder/Tribune Business News*, September 24, 1997, p. 924B0931.

—A. Woodward

G.I. Joe's, Inc.

9805 Boeckman Road
Wilsonville, Oregon 97070
U.S.A
(503) 682-2242
Fax: (503) 682-7200
Web site: http://www.gijoes.com

Private Company
Incorporated: 1952
Employees: 950
Sales: $128.2 million (1998)
NAIC: 45211 Department Stores

A regional retailer with a unique merchandise mix, G.I. Joe's, Inc. sells outdoor apparel and footwear but focuses on two primary merchandise categories: sporting goods and automotive parts. During the late 1990s, G.I. Joe's operated 17 stores with 13 units located in Oregon and four units located in Washington. The company began as an army surplus store in Portland, Oregon, before shaping itself into a retail specialist that emphasized sporting goods and automotive parts. G.I. Joe's attempted to go public in 1999, but dropped such plans when management realized it would have to sell stock at a price considered to be too low. Pending the completion of a stock offering, the company planned to expand into Montana, Idaho, Utah, Nevada, and northern California.

Post-World War II Origins

As a retail enterprise, G.I. Joe's began business in remarkably modest surroundings. The company was started in a field, housed in a canvas tent. The proprietor and founder was Edward M. Orkney, an Army Air Corps pilot who returned to the United States after World War II and bought 2,000 army surplus mummy bags for $1.50 each. In 1951, he pitched a tent in a field in Portland and quickly sold all the sleeping bags, making a sufficient profit to purchase other military surplus merchandise and secure a more permanent site for his business. He relocated to an old building in Portland, stocked his store with army surplus goods, and enjoyed encouraging success. By 1956 the size of his store had doubled and was soon to become the largest retailer of sporting goods and outdoor gear in Portland.

By all measures, Orkney's entrepreneurial debut was a glowing success, his efforts producing a thriving retail enterprise that had evolved into a metropolitan heavyweight in little more than a decade, but G.I. Joe's lacked an enduring strength. Driving the store's growth was the abundant supply of army surplus merchandise that Orkney could profitably offer at sharply discounted prices, a supply that could not last forever. By the 1960s, the stream of military surplus goods had begun to disappear, stripping Orkney of the inventory that had underpinned his success. In response, Orkney transformed G.I. Joe's to keep pace with the changing times. He retained the store's discount merchandise format, but began stocking a variety of different merchandise categories, shaping G.I Joe's into what the retail industry referred to as a "generalist." The store began selling an eclectic array of goods, offering sporting goods, automotive parts, and hardware, among other merchandise categories. By the end of the 1960s, the transition away from surplus military goods had been successfully completed. In 1969 Orkney began expanding the concept, establishing additional G.I. Joe's discount stores in the Portland area.

During the 1970s, expansion occurred at a moderate pace until there were a handful of G.I. Joe's dotting the greater Portland area. As the concept developed into a chain, the breadth of merchandise available in the stores increased, expanding to include housewares, lawn and garden supplies, and apparel. Against the backdrop of this gradual growth, both in terms of physical expansion and in the diversity of G.I. Joe's inventory, a change in leadership occurred midway through the decade. In 1976 Edward Orkney died, leaving behind him a small but thriving business that his son inherited. David Orkney took the helm from his father and pressed forward with his father's legacy by broadening the stores' merchandise categories and presiding over the chain's methodical expansion. A little more than a decade after taking control, however, David Orkney found himself contending with problems his father never had to face. The composition and character of the retail industry was changing, threatening to undermine the effectiveness of G.I. Joe's' merchandising strategy.

Crisis, Change in Format: 1980s

During the 1980s, a new breed of retailer emerged that operated with a concept similar to G.I. Joe's, but on a much grander scale. Discount superstores took the format of offering a diverse array of merchandise at inexpensive prices to an extreme, establishing mammoth retail establishments that occupied the equivalent of a city block and stocking the stores with more than 100,000 different products. Economies of scale, an integral facet of the superstores' strategy, enabled the retail operators to offer their merchandise at extremely low prices, pricing smaller discount retailers like G.I. Joe's out of the market. The dynamics of the discount retail industry had changed, and Orkney responded by distancing his company from its roots as a surplus retailer. During the 1980s, name-brand merchandise began to appear in G.I. Joe's, replacing the discount, low-end goods that had characterized the company's inventory for decades. The shift to name-brand products represented a profound change in G.I. Joe's' merchandising strategy, but it did not provide all the answers to the pervasive trend within the company's industry. By the end of the 1980s, torpid financial growth suggested the need for further alterations to the retailer's formula. The new version of the longtime surplus discounter surfaced in the 1990s, presented as the prototype for the future.

The creation of a "new" G.I. Joe's for the 1990s was prompted by the realization of the company's shortcomings in the late 1980s. The retailer's merchandise selection had become too broad, often to the confusion of faithful customers. Housewares, hardware, automotive parts, apparel, footwear, lawn and garden supplies, sporting goods, home electronics, and CDs represented an overreaching merchandise mix that distracted the chain's focus and made its identity difficult to pinpoint. Annual sales, which hovered above $130 million in 1990, were generated by the company's 13 stores, 12 of which were in Oregon, including six in the Portland area. G.I. Joe's' lone property outside Oregon was located just across the border in Vancouver, Washington, the state where Orkney planned to erect a prototype store free from clutter. At first, Orkney and his management team had considered expanding into northern California, but they decided on the Puget Sound region surrounding Seattle as the focal point for future expansion. "Our game plan in the 1980s," Orkney commented, "was to develop the Oregon market, get extensive advertising coverage, economies of scale—and then look at Seattle."

A Prototype for the Future: 1991

The Seattle store opened in March 1991, its debut marking a turning point in the company's history. In the new store, which measured 57,000 square feet (only marginally larger than the company's other stores), approximately 80 percent of the merchandise remained the same as the Oregon stores, but there was an emphasis on two categories—automotive parts and sporting goods. The combination of automotive parts and sporting goods became the signature merchandise mix of the new G.I. Joe's, giving the retailer its new identity. To furnish this new identity with greater exposure, Orkney announced an ambitious expansion program that promised to double the size of the company during the ensuing decade. Company officials announced G.I. Joe's would open a new store in the Puget Sound area every 18 months, a pace of expansion that would give the company 25 stores by 2002.

The establishment of the new Seattle prototype breathed new life into G.I. Joe's, but one store, no matter the extent of its initial success, could not immediately eliminate existing problems. The $135 million in sales generated in 1991 by the company's 13 other stores was too low according to company officials, at least $10 million below their projections. The disappointment stemming from weak sales led to a change in senior management in 1992, the first since the death of Edward Orkney in 1976. Prior to the management shakeup, David Orkney had presided as chairman, chief executive officer, and president, but in May the company divided the responsibilities of its top executive officer. The new senior executive who assumed day-to-day control over the company's operations was a longtime employee named Norm Daniels. Daniels had joined G.I. Joe's in 1965 at age 16, when he was hired by Edward Orkney to stock the shelves and sweep the floors of the company's original store in Portland. As the company expanded from one store to more than a dozen during the ensuing 25 years, Daniels gradually worked his way up from stock boy. He was serving as vice-president of merchandising and marketing when he earned promotion to the office of president and the new title of COO in May 1992. Chief among his new responsibilities was to spearhead the retailer's transition from a general merchandiser to a sporting goods and automotive parts specialist, a task Orkney believed Daniels was capable of achieving. "We need a retailer at the top," Orkney explained to *Discount Store News* in May 1992, "and Norm Daniels is our best retailer."

In the wake of Daniels's promotion, G.I. Joe's pressed forward with its plans to become a sporting goods and automotive parts specialist. Convinced that the Seattle store was the wave of the future, Daniels aborted plans to establish additional stores and directed the company's resources toward the renovation of its existing stores. In 1993, Daniels announced a five-year plan to remodel and update the 14 stores in Oregon and Washington, devoting $3.5 million to the project. Following the example set by the Seattle store, lawn and garden supplies were eliminated at all stores, coupled with reduced inventories of hardware, housewares, and home electronics. With the space freed by weeding out merchandise that strayed from the retailer's focus, Daniels increased the presence of automotive parts in individual G.I. Joe's, allotting the department nearly an extra 10,000 square feet for a total of 25,000 square feet. Said Daniels: "We want to focus on two major categories: sporting goods and automotive products. We don't want to try and be everything. We don't want to be a department store or mass merchandiser."

The company's efforts to transform from a generalist to a specialist progressed through the mid-1990s with mixed results. The company was consistently profitable during the five-year renovation program, posting annual profits for five of the six years between 1992 and 1997, but annual sales suffered. Midway through the decade sales dropped, their decline attributable to the loss of revenue generated by lawn and garden supplies, housewares, beverages, and home electronics. Following the $8 million drop in sales, the company's annual revenue volume stagnated, resting at a level commensurate with the totals registered during the early 1990s. Spirits at company headquarters brightened, however, after the financial results for 1996 were posted. The company's revamped merchandise mix led to the most profitable year ever recorded by G.I. Joe's, breeding renewed optimism and sparking interest in expansion. "The last couple years we've been focusing on remodeling our older stores," a company official remarked, "but the mood is starting to shift into the expansion mode again."

Embracing Expansion: Late 1990s

G.I. Joe's had not opened a new store since the Seattle store in 1991, which represented a six-year hiatus when the company announced in February 1997 that it was considering opening two new stores in the Puget Sound region. Expansion plans were eventually scaled back, leading to the establishment of one new store south of Seattle before the end of the year, but in terms of significant events in 1997, the addition of a new unit to the chain ran a distant second to an agreement reached later in the year. Daniels, the former stockboy, was about to reach the highest rung of the company's corporate ladder.

In December 1997, a new era in the history of G.I Joe's began. Daniels and chairman Orkney announced they had reached an agreement providing for Daniels's acquisition of Orkney's majority interest in G.I. Joe's. Prior to the acquisition, Daniels sold four stores, company headquarters, and a distribution center to Wilshire Real Estate Investment Trust Inc. and then leased the properties back from Wilshire, obtaining $28.5 million from the sale that may have been used to facilitate the acquisition. As the particulars of the deal were attended to, Daniels announced his plans for the company's future, plans that promised to usher in a period of bold expansion. Daniels discussed establishing three new stores in 1998 and the first half of 1999, making his announcement while displaying a map showing potential sites for more than 40 stores in seven states.

To finance expansion, Daniels announced G.I. Joe's plan to complete an initial public offering (IPO), filing with the Securities and Exchange Commission in late 1998. According to the filing, eight new stores were to be opened during the ensuing four years and ten stores were slated to be remodeled. In another move toward expansion, the company acquired Timberline Direct in late 1998, a purchase that opened new avenues of growth. Timberline Direct, a catalog and electronic commerce firm based in Hillsboro, Oregon, operated three catalog brands distributed to customers throughout the United States and Canada, each focused on outdoor sporting activities. As the acquisi-

tion was reorganized as a division called Joe's Direct, attention turned to the anticipated IPO, the completion of which was in jeopardy. The early months of 1999 found G.I. Joe's facing a market indifferent to public offerings launched by relatively small companies such as G.I. Joe's, forcing Daniels to abort plans for the company's debut as a public company. "We just couldn't price it at what we wanted," Daniels explained.

The cancellation of its IPO left G.I. Joe's facing an uncertain future, clouding the company's plans to spread its presence into Montana, Idaho, Utah, Nevada, and northern California. However, Daniels did anticipate filing for another IPO once the market demonstrated its receptivity to small capital firms. Other aspects of the company's business provided a clearer picture of promising growth, fueling optimism for the future. Looking ahead, the company planned to increase the sales generated by its mail-order and Internet-based business and to push forward with the remodeling of its existing stores, which had proven to increase profitability. Substantial sales growth and a greater geographic presence hinged on the completion of a public offering or securing capital from some other source, an objective that stood high on management's list as G.I. Joe's entered the 21st century.

Principal Subsidiaries

Joe's Direct.

Further Reading

"G.I. Joe's Purchases Timberline Catalog Company," *Aftermarket Business,* November 1, 1998, p. 10.

Goldfield, Robert, "G.I. Joe's Prepared to Capture IPO Market," *Business Journal-Portland,* February 26, 1999, p. 1.

Halverson, Richard, "G.I. Joe's Aims at Upscale Outdoors Niche in Seattle; New Test Unit Emulates Sports Megastores, *Discount Store News,* May 4, 1992, p. 3.

Hill, Jim, "CEO of Northwest Sports Retailer Will Become Majority Owner Soon," *Knight-Ridder/Tribune Business News,* April 29, 1998, p. OKRB98119123.

Hisey, Pete, "G.I. Joe's Enters Seattle with New Look," *Discount Store News,* April 1, 1991, p. 3.

"In Store Focus: G.I. Joe's," *Automotive Marketing,* November 1993, p. 36.

Lustigman, Alyssa, "Soldier's Story," *Sporting Goods Business,* October 1993, p. 42.

Prinzing, Debra, "G.I. Joe's Storms Puget Sound with Refined Product Mix," *Business Journal-Portland,* February 25, 1991, p. 8.

Rose Michael, "G.I. Joe's Field Marshall," *Business Journal-Portland,* May 27, 1994, p. 12.

Szymanski, Jim, "G.I. Joe's May Open Two New Stores in Pacific Northwest," *Knight-Ridder/Tribune Business News,* February 20, 1997, p. 220B1162.

Troy, Mike, "G.I. Joe's New Marching Orders: IPO, New Format, Expand to SW," *Discount Store News,* March 22, 1999, p. 10.

—Jeffrey L. Covell

the good guys! ®

The Good Guys, Inc.

700 Marina Boulevard
Brisbane, California 94005-1840
U.S.A.
(650) 615-5000
(800) 486-4897
Fax: (650) 615-6287
Web site: http://www.thegoodguys.com

Public Company
Incorporated: 1976
Employees: 5,000
Sales: $928.49 million (1998)
Stock Exchanges: NASDAQ
Ticker Symbol: GGUY
NAIC: 443112 Radio, Television, & Other Electronics
Stores

The Good Guys, Inc. is a leading specialty electronics retailer, with more than 60 stores in California, and less than ten stores each in Washington, Oregon, and Nevada. Most of the company's stores operate under the name *the good guys!* and feature a range of electronics, including televisions, video equipment, car and home stereo components, telephones, cellular phones and pagers, and cameras; in the late 1990s, two new formats were introduced, Audio/Video Exposition and WOW! The latter units are jointly operated with Tower Records and offer the full complement of consumer electronics found in a *the good guys!* store, as well as the music, video, computer software, and magazines found in a Tower Records outlet.

One-Man Beginnings

The company was founded in 1973 by Ronald A. Unkefer, who would ultimately become chairman of the board. Unkefer opened his modest television shop in San Francisco's Marina district, a fashionable area frequented by tourists. At first, *the good guys!* was a one-man operation, which led a vendor to ask, "There's only one of you, so how can you be The Good Guys?" The name did not derive from the number of employ-ees, but from a catch phrase Unkefer borrowed from a favorite radio station. As he expanded his staff, he encouraged customers to think of his salespeople as "good guys" who could help them get the best deal on the latest equipment.

Initially, Unkefer did not have ambitions to become a major player in the field of consumer electronics. The Cleveland native had moved to California simply because he wanted to live in the state and run some sort of business. As time wore on and new technologies, such as VCRs and state-of-the-art stereo systems, were introduced, however, he began to see growth opportunities. "It certainly wasn't a grand plan at the time to grow as big as we are now," he reflected in an interview with the *San Francisco Business Times* in 1991, when there were 33 *good guys!* locations. "When I opened up the second store in 1976 I was almost talked into it by a very determined real estate developer." Unkefer's company was incorporated in 1976 as The Good Guys, Inc.

Unkefer decided to launch the second store to help pay his advertising bills at the *San Francisco Chronicle*. The Good Guys! was well positioned to take advantage of the growth in consumer demand for stereo components in the 1970s, and sales increased steadily each year. Unkefer maintained his low-key approach to business—by 1983, there were only four *good guys!* stores in San Francisco. The company continued to expand its product offerings, adding videocassette recorders for consumers eager to create their own home entertainment centers.

In 1985 the company reported net sales of about $71 million, and pretax income of $2.25 million. A year later, Unkefer took his company public to fund further expansion beyond the existing eight stores. The Good Guys had already opened stores outside San Francisco, and was targeting San Jose as the location for its next new store.

The formula for success at The Good Guys was simple and straightforward from the outset. The company used a combination of extensive promotions and advertising, along with competitive pricing and a broad selection (offering 20 percent more models than rival stores). From the early days, customer service was a cornerstone of the company's strategy. The motto at The Good Guys was "Our name is our way of doing business."

224

Expanding Aggressively: Late 1980s

During the late 1980s, The Good Guys kept up an aggressive program of growth and expansion. In 1987 the company made its first foray outside the Bay Area when it opened two stores in Sacramento. By this time, The Good Guys was targeting a decidedly upscale consumer base. According to one retail specialist quoted in *Business Journal—Sacramento,* "It's the type of store in which you would find the owner of a BMW searching for an audio system for his car."

Nevertheless, even yuppie consumers did not prevent The Good Guys from having a bad year in 1986. Earnings dropped by nearly 40 percent from the previous year, and the company's net income fell from $2.2 million to $1.4 million. At one point, the stock plunged $3.125 per share. According to Unkefer, the soft market for durable goods—particularly VCRs—and stiff competition were to blame.

For the balance of the decade, The Good Guys took several steps to boost sales. Feedback from customers revealed that the company's practice of haggling over prices was unpopular and contributed to a "sleazy salesman" stereotype in the minds of consumers. So, in 1987, the company stopped negotiating prices and introduced a lowest-price guarantee. If a competitor offered the same piece of equipment at a lower price, The Good Guys promised to beat that price. The company also instituted a 30-day, no-questions-asked return policy and upgraded its merchandise mix, focusing on higher-end brands.

These fundamental changes produced the desired results. Net income for 1987 was back up, to $2.6 million. By the end of 1988, sales had increased 24 percent and net income was $3.3 million. The company had 17 stores and then opened an 18th in Reno, Nevada, in 1989, the chain's first outside of California. The company retained its impressive sales and income figures through the end of the decade, despite the appearance of arch-rival Circuit City Stores Inc. in San Francisco in 1989. Circuit City opened a store two blocks from one *good guys!* location. The move worked for, rather than against, The Good Guys, however. Company President Unkefer noted in the *San Francisco Business Times* that, "We do better where people can compare," adding that his company offered more upscale merchandise and did not offer appliances.

The Good Guys entered the 1990s flush and prosperous. The company had grown to 30 stores, and sales had increased 51 percent. Net income increased 86 percent over 1989, hitting $7.4 million. The company broke new ground by opening six stores in Los Angeles, a billion-dollar consumer electronics market that was one of the hottest and most competitive in the country. The move brought The Good Guys toe-to-toe with a dozen major competitors, including Circuit City. Unkefer was confident that The Good Guys could hold its own, however, noting that the company's success rested on its dedication to customer service.

Surviving Recession: Early 1990s

But the consumer electronics market has historically been among the first to suffer when recession hits, as it did in California in 1990 and 1991. Analysts predicted difficult times in the wake of a shocking 11 percent, industrywide decline in the sale of color televisions during the second quarter of 1990. The Good Guys did not feel the effects of the recession immediately. Unkefer predicted sales growth of 25 percent per year for the next several years. By the end of 1991, the company had 33 stores and sales of more than $427 million. In addition to such basics as televisions and stereos, *the good guys!* stores now offered fax machines, video cameras, telephones, and answering machines. With the highest sales per square foot of any consumer electronics chain, it looked like the company might emerge relatively unscathed from the recession.

Sales and net income did continue to increase in the early 1990s, but the gains were more modest than they had been in the past. In 1992, for example, same-store sales went up only two percent. "The company's goals in this difficult retail climate are to continue to build market share and maintain our sales momentum," Robert A. Gunst, the company's president and new chief operating officer, said in an interview in early 1992.

A softer market did not curb expansion. *The good guys!* stores grew to number 44 by late 1993, the company's 20th anniversary year. By this time, The Good Guys was well established as one of the top consumer electronics retailers in the country. In keeping with its customer service credo, *the good guys!* stores featured special listening rooms for speakers and onsite installation of car stereos and speakers, cellular phones, and car alarms. The Good Guys was consistently ranked as one of California's top companies. In 1993, sales for the now 48-store chain were $552.4 million, a ten percent increase over the previous year. Net income was $7.6 million.

In a move to further boost sales, reinvigorate growth, and meet consumer demand, the company began selling personal computers in 1993, concentrating on such name brands as IBM, Apple, Compaq, and Packard Bell. With the increase in home offices and advances in information technology, The Good Guys hoped to catch a wave of demand, as it did in the 1980s with home video products. "We feel it is essential for consumer electronics to participate in the information superhighway, and we believe interactive technology is going to be a substantial part of consumer electronics," said Tom Hannah, senior vice-president of stores, in a 1993 interview with the *San Francisco Business Times.* The move was a daring one, given the vagaries of the computer industry and the lingering effects of the state's worst economic problems since the Great Depression. One analyst predicted that the move would ultimately hurt The Good Guys! by diluting the company's focus. After one month, however, The Good Guys reported that computer sales had exceeded projections.

Geographic Expansion and New Formats: Mid-1990s

As The Good Guys entered the mid-1990s, its future seemed to brighten further. In 1994 the company entered the San Diego market with six stores in San Diego. It also repaid customer loyalty with a ''90 Days Same as Cash'' credit plan for holders of a ''Preferred Customer Card.'' To stimulate consumers to buy electronics, The Good Guys! stepped up its targeted direct mail campaign and offered cross-promotions with the California State Lottery and Tower Records, a regional chain.

Expansion continued in 1995 and 1996, along with the introduction of new store formats. In 1995 The Good Guys entered the Pacific Northwest market, opening eight stores in Washington state and three in Oregon, and also opened its second Nevada location. Among the new formats was Generation 21, which offered shoppers a larger, brighter, and more interactive store—development was halted, however, the following year. More promising was the WOW! Multimedia Superstore. Although two of its biggest competitors, Best Buy and Circuit City, had successfully added music and video software to their shelves, The Good Guys had stuck to its line of hard goods. The WOW! concept, however, would change that. The Good Guys teamed with Tower Records, a private Sacramento-based company and a leading retailer of recorded music, to open the first WOW! store in Las Vegas in August 1995. The joint venture 60,000-square-foot store included the full line of consumer electronics found at a typical *the good guys!* store, along with Tower Records' vast selection of music, videos, computer software, books, and magazines. It also included the world's largest slot machine and a café listening bar. A second WOW! store opened in Long Beach, California, in 1996.

In early 1996 founder and chairman Unkefer resigned from the board to pursue other opportunities. Gunst had been named CEO in 1993 and continued to lead the company following Unkefer's departure. The Good Guys introduced its Audio/Video Exposition format in 1996 with the opening of the first such store in Redondo Beach, California. This format featured four ''expo'' rooms in which customers could operate and experience the latest high-tech audio/video equipment within ''homelike settings.'' The thinking behind this concept was that with new digital products being introduced constantly in the mid-to-late 1990s, consumers needed to be educated about the products and have the opportunity to test them out before making a purchase. Gunst told *Discount Merchandiser* in January 1997, ''Our customers are all shopping for products to be used in their homes. So, we've tried to address that need in a more homelike setting that provides packaged solutions to the customers' needs.''

Founder's Return, Restructuring: Late 1990s

Unfortunately for The Good Guys and many other consumer electronics retailers, none of the new digital products as yet had the impact of, for example, the videocassette recorder, a product that many people initially purchased at specialty electronics stores. At the same time, such products as the VCR had become so familiar to most consumers—not to mention so inexpensive—that they had turned into commodities that could be purchased without the intervention of a salesperson; rivals such as Best Buy and Circuit City concentrated on the selling of such commodities. Even worse, VCRs and other mass-market electronics items were increasingly available at general retailers, such as Kmart and Wal-Mart.

In this brutal environment, The Good Guys began losing money in 1996, when it posted a net loss of $6.2 million. Losses continued in 1997 and 1998 and sales were flat. The company began focusing more of its expansion efforts on the WOW! and Exposition concepts, with five of the former and 11 of the latter operating by the end of 1998. With the firm's difficulties continuing into 1999, Gunst resigned in June of that year. Returning at the request of the board of directors as chairman and CEO was Unkefer, who simultaneously spent $4.7 million to take a ten percent stake in the company. In July Unkefer unveiled a restructuring plan aimed at turning The Good Guys around within three years. The company planned to streamline its operations, including some job cuts, aiming at reducing selling and administrative expenses by 20 percent. It also would discontinue its unprofitable home office department, which sold computers, fax machines, and copiers. The company's stores would focus more on innovative high-tech items, most notably wireless communications devices and noncomputer Internet appliances. The Good Guys would thereby emphasize products that required a higher level of customer service than that found at such national retailers as Best Buy and Circuit City. Toward the goal of differentiating the company's stores as a more upscale consumer electronics option, The Good Guys would increase its advertising and marketing budget by more than 20 percent. Finally, until the company returned to the black, all remodeling efforts and store openings were suspended.

This restructuring appeared to have been launched at a critical time for The Good Guys, when a shakeout in the industry was likely. Its success or failure would help to determine whether The Good Guys would be one of the casualties or one of the survivors.

Principal Subsidiaries

The Good Guys–California, Inc.

Further Reading

Carlsen, Clifford, ''Good Times for The Good Guys: Addition of Computers Expected to Reboot Growth,'' *San Francisco Business Times,* November 5, 1993, p. 1.

Emert, Carol, ''Bad Times at Good Guys: Electronics Chain Has Everything Working for It—Except Sales and Profits,'' *San Francisco Chronicle,* May 1, 1999, p. D1.

——, ''Good Guys CEO Discloses Master Plan,'' *San Francisco Chronicle,* July 27, 1999, p. C1.

Glover, Kara, ''Two New Consumer Electronics Retailers Will Enter Super-Competitive Southland Market,'' *Los Angeles Business Journal,* October 22, 1990, p. 6.

''Good Guys and Tower Records Combine Forces,'' *San Francisco Business Times,* May 16, 1988, p. 3.

''Good Guys Become 'Home' Boys with Renovation Strategy,'' *Los Angeles Times,* August 28, 1997, pp. D1, D11.

''The Good Guy!: Unkefer Built Chain by Staying Close to Home,'' *San Francisco Business Times,* October 25, 1991, p. 12.

Groves, Martha, ''Good Guys Comes South,'' *Los Angeles Times,* June 25, 1990, p. 1.

Hill, G. Christian, "Counting on Digital: The Good Guys Chain Hopes New Products Leave Consumers Intrigued—and Confused," *Wall Street Journal,* June 15, 1998, p. R26.

Martin, Patricia, "Good Guys, Another Electronics Retailer, Rides In," *Business Journal—Sacramento,* March 30, 1987, p. 3.

Paige, Earl, "Successful Venture of Good Guys! and Tower Validates 'Big Box' Idea," *Billboard,* June 13, 1998, pp. 79, 83.

Power, Gavin, "Good Guys Reports Best Second Quarter," *San Francisco Chronicle,* April 26, 1994, p. B1.

Ratliff, Duke, "An Adult Toy Store," *Discount Merchandiser,* January 1997, pp. 80, 82–83.

Rechtin, Mark, "Future Bright for Good Guys, Despite Tight Field," *Orange County Business Journal,* September 10, 1990, p. 6.

Scally, Bob, "Good Guys Battles Bad CE Climate," *Discount Store News,* January 6, 1997, pp. 21, 24, 26–27.

——, "Good Guys Founder Returns," *Discount Store News,* June 21, 1999, p. 6.

——, "Good Guys Positions As High-Service Chain," *Discount Store News,* March 9, 1998, pp. 7, 84.

——, "Good Guys Wrestles with Tough Times," *Discount Store News,* February 22, 1999, pp. 6, 70.

Shaw, Jan, "Who's Going to Go Public? Who Else? The Good Guys!," *Business Journal—San Jose,* December 30, 1985, p. 1.

Soltesz, Diana, "The Good Guys! Are Ready to Ride into San Diego County," *Business Wire,* September 23, 1993.

Taylor, Dennis, "Good Guys CEO Resigns After 'Disappointing' Quarters," *San Jose Business Journal,* April 23, 1999, p. 5.

——, "Good Guys Founder Returns to Helm of Troubled Company," *San Jose Business Journal,* June 11, 1999, p. 10.

Veverka, Mark, "Tough Retail Environment Spells Bad News for Good Guys' Outlook," *Wall Street Journal,* January 15, 1997, p. CA2.

"WOW! What a Concept: Good Guys, Tower Awe Shoppers," *Discount Store News,* August 21, 1995, pp. 3, 61.

—Marinell James
—updated by David E. Salamie

Hanson PLC

1 Grosvenor Place
London SWIX 7JH
United Kingdom
(0171) 245-1245
Fax: (0171) 235-3455
Web site: http://www.hansonplc.com

Public Company
Incorporated: 1964 as Wiles Group Limited
Employees: 16,000
Sales:£1.57 billion (US$2.64 billion) (1998)
Stock Exchanges: London New York
Ticker Symbol: HAN
NAIC: 212319 Other Crushed & Broken Stone Mining &
    Quarrying; 212321 Construction Sand & Gravel
    Mining; 324121 Asphalt Paving Mixture & Block
    Manufacturing; 327331 Concrete Block & Brick
    Manufacturing; 32739 Other Concrete Product Manu-
    facturing; 32732 Ready-Mix Concrete Manufacturing;
    327991 Cut Stone & Stone Product Manufacturing

Hanson PLC is an international building materials company with three principal operations. Hanson Building Materials America (HBMA) is the third largest producer of aggregates in the United States, producing more than 100 million tons of crushed rock and sand and gravel for highway, residential, commercial, and industrial construction projects. HBMA also produces concrete pipes, cement, bricks, and asphalt. Hanson Quarry Products Europe is the second largest aggregates producer in the United Kingdom, and leads its market in sea-dredged aggregates, concrete pipes, and concrete blocks. Hanson Bricks Europe is a leading European brick manufacturer. Hanson PLC was a conglomerate until a series of demergers in 1995 through 1997 sliced off the company's retail, industrial manufacturing, chemicals, tobacco, and energy businesses.

Early History

The origins of Hanson go back to 1964. In March of that year a small City (London financial district) merchant bank,

Dawnay Day, floated the Wiles Group on the stock exchange. The group was an animal byproducts, sack hire, and fertilizer business created by George Wiles and based in Hull, Yorkshire. In August 1964 Wiles started to diversify through the acquisition of Oswald Tillotson Ltd., a company operating in the field of commercial vehicle sales and distribution. James Hanson and Gordon White were on the board of Oswald Tillotson Ltd. and held a controlling interest in the company.

James Edward Hanson and Vincent Gordon Lindsay White were both born in Yorkshire and, after war service, started their early careers in their respective family businesses. The Hanson family road-haulage business was 100 years old when it was nationalized in 1948. James Hanson then spent some years in Canada building up a transport business with his brother. In the late 1950s he joined Gordon White—a family friend, whose own family publishing and printing business, Welbecson, was acquired by Wiles in 1965—in a venture importing U.S. greeting cards. Thus, the partnership that underpinned the development of Hanson was already formed when the two men joined first Tillotson and then Wiles.

Between 1965, when James Hanson became chairman of the Wiles Group, and 1969, when the company was renamed the Hanson Trust, further acquisitions were made to develop the group into an industrial holding and management company. Its principal objective was defined by James Hanson as "to expand profitability while achieving careful expansion through acquisitions." The purchase of Scottish Land Development in 1967 for £700,000 took Wiles into the hire and distribution of earthmoving and construction equipment and pumps. In 1968 the group paid £3.2 million for West of England Sack Holdings, which expanded its existing business in that field. In the same year it bought the Butterley Company for £4.7 million, an acquisition that took it into a new field of operations, the manufacture of bricks for house construction.

Hanson was by no means the only company then searching for underperforming and asset-rich companies to target as prospective acquisitions. In 1968 the conglomerate Slater Walker took a large shareholding in the Wiles Group. Hanson and White over the years consistently pointed out the difference between the takeovers made for financial reason—the fast track—and those, like Hanson's, for industrial reasons: ''We are the work horses.''

Expanding Brick-Making Operations: Early 1970s

Between 1971 and 1973 Hanson expanded its brick-making activities with the acquisition of the National Star Brick & Tile Company for £2.1 million, British Steel Brickworks for £2.7 million, and NCB Brickworks for £2.2 million. It also bought a majority interest in a property development company, City and St. James. The changing scope of its activities led to a restructuring of its operations first in 1970, when it sold the commercial vehicle distribution operation, and then again in 1972, when the expansion of brick manufacturing warranted the creation of a separate division.

In 1973 the Bowater Corporation, eager to diversify out of the low profit-making newsprint and pulp activities and fresh from its merger with Ralli International (masterminded the previous year by Jim Slater), made an agreed bid for Hanson. But when the bid was referred to the government's Monopolies and Mergers Commission, Bowater withdrew. This experience, combined with the prevailing uncertain economic climate in the United Kingdom, led Hanson and White to look further afield for development prospects, more particularly because White, ''in disgust at socialism,'' wished to leave Britain. In that year, therefore, White went to the United States. From the 1950s until the mid-1970s, merger activity in the United Kingdom was high and encouraged by governments, particularly the Labour government of Harold Wilson, which established the Industrial Reorganization Corporation specifically to promote mergers such as that of General Electric Company and Associated Electrical Industries Ltd. On the other hand, reference to the Monopolies Commission of mergers that might operate against the public interest sometimes brought a negative response. Even when the commission's verdict was not unfavorable, changing conditions in the period of consideration could lead to the breaking off of the engagement, as happened with Hanson and Bowater. The commission was generally neutral on the matter of industrial conglomerates, although it pointed to the risks of the creation of stock to finance the purchase and to the danger of a failure to increase efficiency after the merger. More damning criticisms of the merger movement and its results in the United States were made by a U.S. congressional report in June 1971.

Entering U.S. Market: 1973

In the United Kingdom the asset-stripping activities of other companies tarnished the public image of the industrial con-

glomerate in the late 1970s. Hanson insisted that it was an industrial management company. In the United States Hanson Industries was formed as a holding company in 1973, with White as executive chairman. His first major acquisition came the following year when, at a cost of $32 million, Hanson Industries bought Seacoast Products, a Florida-based company manufacturing animal foodstuffs, fish meal, and edible oils that remained part of Hanson until 1986.

In the 1970s, against the background of a turbulent world economy shaken by two large increases in world oil prices, Hanson's growth on both sides of the Atlantic was steady rather than spectacular. In the United States in 1976, Hygrade Foods, the second largest seller of hot dogs in ballparks, was acquired, along with other purchases in the food servicing and vending and textile industries. In the United Kingdom, Hanson acquired Rollalong, which manufactured mobile accommodation units. In addition, Hanson purchased two flour milling and cereal companies and also delved, by way of acquisition, into yarn and thread manufacturing.

All these acquisitions fell into what became recognizable as the Hanson pattern. Hanson looked for and bought companies manufacturing basic, low technology products. By introducing a system of centralized and strong financial controls combined with decentralized operating management, Hanson increased profitability both for shareholders and for the holding company, thus building up its resources for more acquisitions. Some acquisitions required further financing with bank debt, to be quickly reduced in part by disinvestment. The diversity of Hanson's portfolio spread the risk with the steady demand for food and other consumer products balancing the upswings and downturns in demand for building industry supplies. The caution of the two founders was well-documented. James Hanson said, ''I've always thought about the down-side risk on a takeover rather than the upside potential—we don't gamble.'' It was this approach, according to White, that led to the decision in 1974 not to buy 51 percent of Avis, the U.S. car rental business. White recalled, ''I told him it could put us straight in the big league but that if it went wrong it would bust us.''

Takeovers and Divestments: 1980s

Hanson's purchase, for £25 million, of Lindustries in the United Kingdom in 1979 was its largest to date and presaged a decade of even greater spending and growth, taking Hanson very definitely into the big league. In 1980 Hanson Industries acquired McDonough, which included footwear manufacturing and retailing and cement manufacturing interests, for an agreed bid of $180 million. In the following year, in what was to become a typical Hanson activity, it recouped $49 million by selling the concrete and cement business. In the United Kingdom there were two major acquisitions in 1982, the Berec Group, manufacturers of Ever Ready batteries, for £95 million and United Gas Industries, makers of gas meters and of gas and electric fires, for £19 million. In the following year Hanson bought United Drapery Stores (UDS) for £250 million and immediately recovered almost three-fifths of the purchase price by selling Richard Shops and some of the other UDS subsidiaries. Allders Stores, a department store chain, and Allders International, which owned and operated duty-free shops at U.K. airports and on ferries and cruise ships, remained part of Hanson until 1989 when it was sold for £210 million.

By 1984, with turnover up to over £2 million, Hanson was increasingly seen on both sides of the Atlantic as a predator, a reputation it enhanced in that year with the acquisition of the London Brick Company for £247 million, making Hanson the world's largest brick manufacturer. At the same time in the United States it paid $535 million for U.S. Industries (USI), stepping in with a brisk offer to replace a management buyout. This acquisition gave Hanson interests in diverse fields ranging from clothes to lighting manufacture, and subsidiaries in office and domestic furniture making as well as heavy engineering. By doubling the size of the U.S. operation, the USI acquisition put Hanson Industries among the top 150 companies trading in the United States. In the following year in the United Kingdom, the attempt to increase its interests in the engineering industry failed when Powell Duffryn successfully resisted Hanson's takeover bid; in the United States Hanson Industries sold the food service management company Interstate United for more than three times the price it had paid in 1978.

The year 1986 was marked by two major acquisitions. In the United States Hanson Industries won control of and paid $930 million for SCM Corporation, a typewriter, food, and chemical concern described by Fortune International as "sluggish." The chemical division, which was the world's second largest producer of titanium dioxide, developed a successful sales and profits record under Hanson. In the two years after the acquisition of SCM, disposal of parts of the conglomerate raised more money for Hanson than it had paid for the purchase. On top of that, 52 percent of the typewriter business Smith Corona was sold by flotation on the New York Stock Exchange in 1989. The Smith Corona sale helped offset the price of SCM, but entangled Hanson in a legal battle lasting more than two years. Investors who bought shares in Smith Corona Corp. claimed that Hanson officials knew of the impending layoffs and falling sales the company announced shortly after the stocks were purchased, and disposed of the property with that knowledge. Hanson and White denied the accusations. Much of the purchase price of Hanson's 1986 U.K. acquisition, the Imperial Group, bought for £2.5 billion after United Biscuits had failed to gain control of the group, was also covered by divestments. Hanson disposed of the Imperial diversifications—the Courage Brewery and off-license chains, Golden Wonder crisps, the hotels and restaurants, and the food interests where the brand names of Ross Young and Lea & Perrins brought a premium price—while retaining the original Imperial tobacco business.

The increasing importance of and value put upon brand names in a multinational business world was reflected in the purchase in 1987 by Hanson Industries of the U.S. conglomerate Kidde, an acquisition regarded at the time in New York as one for which White had, at US$1.7 billion, grossly overpaid; 18 months later Kidde's return on capital was up by more than eight percent, and the acquisition had come to be seen as an "excellent purchase." With over 100 different businesses, including such diverse products as kitchenware and Jacuzzi whirlpool baths, the Kidde acquisition took Hanson Industries into the top 60 U.S. companies. The Hanson investment criteria required that an investment must contribute to profits within one year and pay for itself within four years.

By the beginning of 1989, financial journalists and Hanson watchers were openly speculating about when or where the next

takeover would come. The previous year had, for the first time in the 1980s, passed without a Hanson acquisition while disposals had enriched its war chest, giving the company disposable cash of £12 billion. The 1980–81 recession had been a powerful stimulus to corporate slimming. The increasing application of "hansonization"—the combination of tight financial control with subsidiary autonomy on operational management—had played a part in reducing the number of badly managed candidates for acquisition. Within Hanson, expenditure of more than £500 over budget in the United Kingdom and US$3,000 in the United States required head office authorization.

In August 1989, when Minorco was obliged to admit defeat in its attempt to take over Consolidated Goldfields PLC, Hanson stepped in with a successful bid of £3.5 billion. Following its usual post-acquisition policy, Hanson closed down Goldfields' London head office and sold its South African gold-mining interests and the U.S. aggregates business, Amey Roadstone Corporation, America (ARC).

Continuing Acquisitions: Early 1990s

Despite the worldwide recession in the early 1990s, Hanson continued to be "expansion-minded," as the chairman phrased it in his 1990 letter to the company's shareholders. In May of that year Hanson spent $240 million to buy a 2.8 percent stake (20 million shares) in Britain's largest industrial company, Imperial Chemical Industries (ICI). (ICI's pension fund was one of the largest holders of Hanson stock.) Just two months later, Hanson Industries acquired Peabody Holding Co., the largest coal producer in the United States. After a brief fight over the coal giant with AMAX, Hanson paid US$1.25 billion for Peabody, which upset some U.S. coal officials who resented the foreign ownership. Beazer Plc, one of Britain's largest home construction companies, found itself deeply in debt in a seriously depressed housing market; it also found itself to be a subsidiary of Hanson by the end of 1991.

A 1991 study of Hanson's history of takeovers found that the company made most of its profits by improving the performance of the companies it acquired. The finding refuted accusations that Hanson made most of its money by buying and selling assets. The analysis of the period from 1986 to 1990 showed that, of Hanson's total earnings of £4.16 billion, only 18 percent came from asset sales. During the same period, 55 percent of the company's £821 million pretax profits gain came from the improved performance of Hanson businesses. Despite strong trends in the United States, none of the deals utilized junk bond financing.

But in 1991 external and internal forces came to bear on Hanson's long history of growth through acquisition. The Gulf War and worldwide recession slowed down mergers and acquisitions in the United Kingdom. There were fewer big deals made, but nearly the same number of smaller concerns changing hands. At the same time, Lords Hanson and White began slowly to pass leadership to Derek C. Bonham, who had been with Hanson 20 years, and David H. Clarke, a former director of Smith Corona. Bonham was appointed chief executive of Hanson in early 1992 and Clarke was the president of Hanson Industries, but Hanson and White—as executive chairmen of

Hanson PLC and Hanson Industries, respectively—maintained overall direction.

At that time Hanson PLC had more than $30 billion in assets, $13 billion in revenues, and 70,000 employees, but had neglected some of its core businesses, such as chemicals and coal mining. The company also faced a net deficit of about £1.5 billion, with loans of £9.5 billion and cash of £8 billion. Bonham and Clarke hoped to dispense with many of Hanson's consumer-related companies and make long-term investments in the key businesses.

In April 1992 Hanson sold Ever Ready Ltd. to Ralston Purina Co. for £132 million, generating a £108 million profit. One month later, Hanson and White confounded financial analysts by selling the conglomerate's interest in ICI at a 17 percent pretax profit. The sales fueled speculation on which businesses would next join Hanson's roster. Observers thought Trafalgar House PLC, Pilkington PLC, and Allied-Lyons PLC in Britain, and Solvay & Cie of Belgium were candidates for takeover. In October 1992 the conservative strategy seemed to have been thrown out the window. Hanson announced its hostile £780 million cash bid for Ranks Hovis McDougall (RHM), a move that was quickly repulsed by RHM's board of directors.

Although it seemed that the company had lost its takeover touch, Hanson made one final acquisition in the early 1990s, paying $3.2 billion ($720 million in Hanson stock and the assumption of $2.5 billion of debt) for Quantum Chemical Corporation, the largest polyethylene maker and second largest seller of propane gas (through Suburban Propane) in the United States, in September 1993. The deal, however, increased Hanson's debt-to-equity ratio to 86 percent, a huge leap from the 18 percent of September 1992. It also led in part to the company's first profit decline in 30 years, as aftertax profits fell 33 percent, to $1.5 billion, for the fiscal year ending in September 1993. At the same time, Hanson's stock had underperformed the market for three years running, leading to speculation that the company would be split into separate British and U.S. companies.

Instead, Hanson returned to the strategy of divestiture, selling 15 companies for a total of $800 million by early 1994. Included therein were Beazer's U.S. homebuilding unit, New Jersey-based Hanson Office Products, and its Axelson oil equipment business in Oklahoma. An even more dramatic jettisoning came in May of the following year when Hanson spun off 34 of its U.S. companies into a new public company, US Industries Inc. Among the businesses were Jacuzzi whirlpool baths, Farberware pots and pans, Tommy Armour golf equipment, Rainbow vacuum cleaners, Ames garden tools, and Ertl toys. Also divested in 1995 were Suburban Propane and Cavenham Forest, an Oregon timber company holding 1.1 million acres of forest land. That year also saw the reorganization of Beazer's U.S. building materials operations as Cornerstone Construction & Materials, and the merger of London Brick and Butterley Brick into the U.K.-based Hanson Brick. The year 1995 was also marked by the £2.5 billion takeover of Eastern Group, a U.K. electricity distributor. At this point, Hanson operated within four main business areas: tobacco, energy, chemicals, and building materials.

Demergers: Mid-1990s

Despite the takeover of Eastern Group, it was becoming increasingly apparent that Hanson's days as a conglomerate were numbered. With sales exceeding $17 billion, only very large acquisitions could have any appreciable impact on the company's share price and profits—and there were few of these target companies out there. Furthermore, the trend of the 1990s was away from diversification and toward focusing on core businesses. This was particularly evident in the United States with the breakups of ITT Corp., AT&T Corp., and Minnesota Mining & Manufacturing Corp. Other factors that conspired to lead Hanson PLC in a new direction were the continued poor performance of the company's stock, the death of White in August 1995, and the legacy-mindedness of Hanson, who had announced that he would retire in 1997 at the age of 75.

Despite the signs pointing toward the dramatic, the company's announcement in January 1996 that it intended to split into four businesses still came as a surprise. Several journalists stated that the breakup of Hanson marked the end of the conglomerate era. In any event, on October 1, 1996, the chemicals group—principally consisting of Quantum and SCM—was demerged as Millennium Chemicals Inc., a primarily U.S.-based operation; and the tobacco group was demerged as Tobacco Group PLC, primarily U.K.-based. The energy group was demerged on February 24, 1997, as The Energy Group PLC, which was comprised mainly of the U.K.-based Eastern Electricity and the U.S.-based coal producer Peabody.

This left Hanson PLC as primarily a building materials company. The new Hanson was initially led by Hanson as chairman—replaced following his retirement by Christopher Collins, who had been deputy chairman—and Andrew Dougal as chief executive; Dougal had previously served as finance director. Several businesses outside of building materials were soon sold off: Hanson Electrical, a supplier of wiring accessories; Grove Worldwide, a Shady Grove, Pennsylvania-based maker of hydraulic cranes; Norfolk, Virginia-based Spectrum Construction, a roadbuilding and civil engineering group; Melody Radio, a U.K. radio station; Air Hanson, a small charter aircraft company; and a U.K. commercial property subsidiary.

The disposals were completed in 1998, generating more than £500 million (US$830 million) in proceeds, which were used in part to fund acquisitions, principally in the North American building materials market. The acquisitions actually began in 1997, with the £78 million (US$125 million) purchase of Concrete Pipe and Products, which made Cornerstone Construction one of the largest concrete pipe producers in North America. During 1998 itself, Hanson acquired San Diego-based H.G. Fenton, an aggregates producer, for £52.7 million (US$87.3 million); Becker Minerals, the leading producer of sand and gravel in the Carolinas, for £48.9 million (US$81 million); Condux, the fifth largest producer of concrete pipe in the United States, for £47.2 million (US$78.2 million); and Nelson & Sloan, another San Diego-based aggregates producer, for £22.7 million (US$37.6 million). During its first full year following the demergers, Hanson posted revenues of £1.57 billion (US$2.64 billion) and operating profits of £261.5 million (US$433.2 million).

In January 1999 Hanson announced a new corporate structure, reflecting the company's emergence from its conglomerate past as a unified building materials company. Cornerstone was renamed Hanson Building Materials America; ARC, the U.K. aggregates business, became Hanson Quarry Products Europe; and Hanson Brick became Hanson Bricks Europe. Continuing its North American expansion, Hanson in May 1999 acquired the North American brick group of Jannock Limited for £141.1 million (US$229 million). The group was the second largest brick producer in North America and was soon renamed Hanson Brick America. In January 1999 Hanson made its first significant acquisition in the Asia-Pacific region, with the purchase of a quarrying business in Malaysia.

While North America was likely to continue to be the focus of expansion for Hanson, Europe and Asia were slated for increased attention. Commenting on the company's 1999 half-year performance in the *Financial Times*, Charles Pretzlik stated that "Hanson has reaffirmed its reputation as a solid performer in the sector, and its strategy of expansion in the U.S. has again been vindicated in the face of a dull U.K. market." Although it was a mere shadow of its conglomerate past, Hanson was poised to be a long-term major player within its niche.

Principal Operating Units

Hanson Building Materials America (U.S.A.); Hanson Quarry Products Europe; Hanson Bricks Europe.

Further Reading

Bonte-Friedheim, Robert, and Janet Guyon, "Hanson to Divide into Four Businesses: U.K. Firm's Move Results from Poor Performance of Shares, Analysts Say," *Wall Street Journal*, January 31, 1996, p. A3.

Bowen, David, "Secrets of a Big Game Hunter," *Independent on Sunday*, July 29, 1990.

Campbell-Smith, D., "Much More Than a Predator," *Financial Times*, December 23, 1983.

Dwyer, Paula, and Joseph Weber, "Hanson Looks for a Hat Trick," *Business Week*, March 14, 1994, pp. 68–69.

Fay, Stephen, "The Rise and Rise of Hanson and White," *Business*, March 1986.

Fisher, Mark, "Hanson's US Petro Gamble," *Corporate Finance*, July 1993, p. 5.

Guthrie, Jonathan, "Pin-Stripe Daring Gives Way to Down-to-Earth Dungarees," *Financial Times*, June 13, 1998, p. 22.

"Hanson Assumes Total Ownership of Peabody Holding Co.," *Coal*, August 1990.

"Hanson: A Swansong?," *Economist*, August 5, 1995, p. 58.

"Hanson Finds a True Friend in Need," *Management Today*, August 1991.

"Hanson: Hunter's Return," *Economist*, October 10, 1992.

"Hanson Likes the Look of ICI," *Economist*, May 18, 1991.

"Hanson Offers $1.35 Billion for Bread Baker," *Wall Street Journal*, October 6, 1992.

"Hanson's American Garage Sale," *Economist*, February 25, 1995, p. 70.

"Hanson Sells Its Stake in ICI to Goldman," *Wall Street Journal*, May 11, 1992.

House, Richard, and Lenny Glynn, "Harbingers and Hopes," *Global Finance*, June 1991.

Jenkins, Iain, "How Hanson Tied Itself into Financial Knots," *Global Finance*, August 1996, pp. 28–30, 34–35.

Kimelman, John D., "Hanson: Basic to a Fault," *Financial World*, October 25, 1994, p. 20.

Kochan, Nicholas, "Lord Hanson: Empire Redux," *Worldbusiness*, January/February 1996, p. 42.

Lawson, Dominic, "The Hard Man from Huddersfield," *Spectator*, October 7, 1989.

Lynn, Matthew, "The Hanson Inheritance," *Management Today*, June 1996, p. 30.

Melcher, Richard A., "Can This Predator Change Its Stripes?," *Business Week*, June 22, 1992.

Norman, James R., "Don't Rush Us," *Forbes*, October 14, 1991.

Powell, Scott, "Quality Credits: Hanson's Sterling Efforts," *Euromoney* (Credits Supplement), September 1992.

Rehak, Judith, "End of an Empire," *Chief Executive*, March 1996, p. 27.

——, "Three Years On, the Sum of Hanson's Parts Exceeds the Whole," *International Herald Tribune*, July 10, 1999, p. 15.

Reier, Sharon, "Europe's CEO of the Year: Lord Hanson of Hanson plc," *Financial World*, October 15, 1991.

Rock, Stuart, "Did the Lad Do Good?," *Director*, December 1994, p. 81.

Stonham, Paul, "Demergers and the Hanson Experience, Part One: The Prelude," *European Management Journal*, June 1997, pp. 266–74.

——, "Demergers and the Hanson Experience, Part Two: Demerger Tactics," *European Management Journal*, August 1997, pp. 413–22.

"Studying an ADR: Hanson PLC," *Canadian Shareowner*, May/June 1992.

"Widow Hanson's Children Leave Home," *Economist*, February 3, 1996, p. 51.

—Judy Slinn
—updated by David E. Salamie

HappyKids

Happy Kids Inc.

100 West 33rd Street
Suite 1100
New York, New York 10001-2916
U.S.A.
(212) 695-1151
(877) 832-2118
Fax: (212) 736-0397

Public Company
Incorporated: 1988 as O'Boy Inc.
Employees: 172
Sales: $154.6 million (1998)
Stock Exchanges: NASDAQ
Ticker Symbol: HKID
NAIC: 42232 Men's & Boys' Clothing & Furnishings
    Wholesalers; 42233 Women's, Children's & Infants'
    Clothing & Accessories Wholesalers

Happy Kids Inc. is a custom designer and marketer of licensed and branded children's apparel. Its products include knit tops and bottoms, overalls, shortalls, coveralls, and swimwear (collectively, "playwear") for newborns, infants, toddlers, boys, and girls. Major licensees in 1999 included Nickelodeon's Rugrats cartoon series, AND 1, B.U.M. Equipment, the four major professional sports leagues, and the World Wrestling Federation. The company, based in New York City's garment district, also designs and delivers private-label branded playwear for leading retailers, including the Sesame Street line for Kmart Corporation.

O'Boy: 1988–97

Jack Benun had managed a family apparel manufacturing business before founding a predecessor of Happy Kids in 1979. Other business entities were subsequently formed, all under the common ownership of Benun, his son Mark, and Isaac Levy, who incorporated O'Boy Inc. in 1988. In 1994 O'Boy intro-duced Ocean Pacific, its own branded line of boys' bathing suits and clothing. Prior to and including much of 1995, O'Boy's operating strategy primarily focused on developing, manufacturing, and marketing its own house brands and often concentrated on enhancing sales volume rather than a combination of sales volume and gross margin. This policy, the company came to believe, was a mistake: after earning net income of $703,000 on sales of $74.5 million in 1994, it lost $1.5 million on sales of $79.8 million in 1995. (Net income figures through 1998 reflect the company's status, prior to April 1998, as an S corporation, with shareholders, rather than the company, paying federal and state income tax on profits.)

To leverage its customer relationship, its popular licenses and brand names, and its reputation for quality products and reliable delivery, O'Boy then initiated a new sales strategy, by which customers ordered specific quantities of goods on a fixed-price basis three to nine months in advance of a selling season. By limiting its production of goods to firm orders in hand, O'Boy reduced the inventory risk typically faced by companies in the apparel industry. The company also declined to accept an order unless it met or exceeded O'Boy's gross margin goals.

In 1996 O'Boy began focusing on the development of a diversified portfolio of popular, established, and well-recognized licensed properties and branded private-label arrangements. As a consequence, the company shifted its product mix from lower-profit-margin house brands to higher-margin licensed and private-label apparel. Its focus on playwear products minimized the company's vulnerability to shifting fashions, since the shorts, T-shirts, sweatsuits, and other playwear products O'Boy designed and marketed were the kind of basic day-to-day items that children outgrow long before they go out of style.

O'Boy began creating Sesame Street private-label apparel for Kmart and marketing to specialty retail sporting goods stores such as Champs, FootAction, and The Sports Authority in 1997. It also acquired the licenses to ACA Joe, E.N.U.F. Internationale, and Warner Brothers' Scooby Doo that year. Net sales rose to $90.7 million in 1996 and $106.7 million in

Company Perspectives:

The Company is committed to growing through a strategy of expanding its portfolio of licenses and brands, increasing sales to new and existing customers, and building on its reputation for quality products and superior customer service.

1997. Net income came to $1.5 million in 1996 and $2.7 million in 1997.

Public Company: 1998–99

O'Boy changed its name to Happy Kids in December 1997. Happy Kids made its initial public offering in April 1998, selling about one-quarter of its common stock at $10 a share. The net proceeds of $22.3 million were allotted to pay debt and to repay $2 million in promissory notes to stockholders of the prior private company. These stockholders also received almost 4.3 million shares in the new public company in exchange for their holdings in the separate business entities that comprised the prior Happy Kids and that then became wholly owned subsidiaries of the company.

In 1998 the Licensing Industry Manufacturers Association named Happy Kids licensee of the year in the soft-goods category for its successful marketing of children's clothing under the Rugrats license from Nickelodeon. During the year Happy Kids expanded its portfolio of licensed brands and characters by adding Jim Henson's Kermit the Frog and Friends, World Wrestling Federation, and Arthur, the popular aardvark character that had sold more than 24 million books and was featured in the top-rated preschool program on television. At the end of the year Happy Kids secured two new licenses: for the popular toddler television show ''Teletubbies'' and for Mecca, a popular boys' brand. Happy Kids was making royalty payments ranging between six and 12 percent of net sales.

While about half of Happy Kids' sales was coming from licensed products, the other half was from supplying retailers with private-label brands. These were activewear product lines Sesame Street for Kmart, Canyon River Blues for Sears, and New Legends for Kids R Us, and infantwear product lines First Moments for Kohl's and Lullaby Club for Target. In March 1998 Kmart named Happy Kids ''vendor of the year'' for the Sesame Street private-label program, which was introduced in 1997.

Happy Kids announced in March 1999 that it had signed a three-year licensing agreement with Mudd, a New York City-based juniors' and children's contemporary sportswear company, to design, distribute, and market all of its girls', infants', and toddlers' wear. The new product lines were expected to appear in department stores before the end of the year.

In April 1999 Happy Kids acquired D. Glasgow & Son, a leading designer and manufacturer of children's apparel, for cash and stock valued at $4.9 million, plus the purchase of $2.9

million in inventory. Glasgow licensees included the National Football League, National Basketball Association, National Hockey League, Major League Baseball, and certain Warner Brothers' properties, including Looney Tunes, Looney Tunes Girls, Scooby Doo, and Saban's Power Rangers. Andy Glasgow, president of the acquired company, joined Happy Kids as president of a new Glasgow division.

Happy Kids posted impressive results in 1998, raising net sales almost 50 percent, to $154.6 million, and increasing its net income more than threefold, to $9.6 million. The company's operating margin rose from 7.9 percent to 11.9 percent. Its share price was not rising, however, which was a source of disappointment for Kern Capital Management and other large investors in the company. Potential stock investors remained skeptical since character-based apparel can have a short shelf life. (A planned Godzilla line apparently foundered because the 1998 film reviving this character did not succeed at the box office.)

Happy Kids: Present and Future

Happy Kids' playwear was being designed by more than 50 in-house designers and graphic artists organized in teams dedicated to each of the company's licensed properties and private-label programs. Each team was working closely with licensors, customers, and contract manufacturers, utilizing state-of-the-art CAD systems to design coordinated products featuring textured fabrications and detailed graphics. Happy Kids insisted upon cutting its own patterns and making product samples in-house before assigning a job to a contract manufacturer. To reduce costs, sophisticated company computer systems laid out patterns in a way that maximized fabric yields. Happy Kids also tested manufactured clothes to make sure they looked and fit right.

Happy Kids maintained a sales and marketing staff of 23 people, including its senior management, at the end of 1998. Account teams organized by the company were each led by a sales executive who reported directly to senior management and was responsible for day-to-day customer relationship management and for supervising and monitoring the sales staff, which was being compensated on a salary-plus-commission basis. The sales and marketing staff worked closely with the company's designers and graphic artists throughout the design and production process.

Happy Kids' customers often launched a new product line associated with a new license or private-label relationship in a limited number of stores. If the product proved successful, the company's customers often marketed the product line throughout their retail chains or in a significantly larger number of stores. Happy Kids' design team and sales staff were working closely with its customers to monitor, review, and analyze product launches.

The company's products were being manufactured by more than 75 contract manufacturers. Some 86 percent of its 1998 production came from the Far East, with manufacturers in Thailand accounting for 43 percent and those in Hong Kong for 29 percent. The rest of the production was domestic. Happy Kids was leasing a 130,000-square-foot warehouse facility in New Brunswick, New Jersey, and space in a Long Beach, California, public facility. It maintained showrooms at its corporate headquarters in Manhattan's garment district and in Bentonville, Arkansas, world headquarters for Wal-Mart Stores, Inc.

Happy Kids' sales were highly dependent in 1998 on a few mass-market retailers, with Kmart accounting for 22 percent, Target for 14 percent, and Wal-Mart for 11 percent of net sales. Kids R Us and Price/Costco, as well as Kmart, were the major customers in 1997. The company also was selling to department store chains such as Dayton Hudson, Dillards, Federated Department Stores, and J.C. Penney, mid-tier distributors such as Sears and Kohl's, and specialty retailers such as Champs, FootAction, and Foot Locker. In terms of specific product lines, Rugrats accounted for 20 percent of net sales in 1998; Sesame Street for 18 percent; and AND 1 and B.U.M. Equipment for 14 percent each.

The product line at the end of 1998 consisted of the following: AND 1, basketball apparel for toddlers and boys; B.U.M. Equipment, lifestyle activewear for newborns, infants, toddlers, boys, and girls; Canyon River Blues, activewear for infants, toddlers, boys, and girls; E.N.U.F. Internationale, lifestyle activewear for boys and girls; First Moments, infantwear for newborns and infants; Lullaby Club, infantwear for newborns and infants; New Legends, activewear for toddlers and girls; Rugrats, character-based activewear for boys and girls; Sesame Street, character-based activewear for infants, toddlers, boys, and girls; Scooby Doo, character-based activewear for boys and girls; World Wrestling Federation, character-based apparel for boys.

Coming off a stellar performance in 1998, the company's future remained incongruously uncertain as it approached the new millennium, for in July 1999 Happy Kids received an $11.50-a-share buyout offer from H.I.G. Capital L.L.C., a Miami-based private investment firm that proposed to take the company private.

Principal Subsidiaries

Happy Kids Children's Apparel, Ltd.; Hawk Industries, Inc.; Hot Kidz, L.L.C.; J&B 18 Corp.; O.P. Kids, L.L.C.; Talk of the Town Apparel Corp.

Further Reading

"Happy Kids Purchases Glasgow," *Discount Store News,* June 7, 1999, p. A4.

"Investors Propose $119.3 Million Buyout of Happy Kids," *New York Times,* July 13, 1999, p. C4.

Leder, Michelle, "Wall Street Whims Give Happy Kids a Sad Face," *Crain's New York Business,* September 14, 1998, p. 16.

Reeves, Scott, "Escaping Notice," *Barron's,* March 30, 1998, p. 42.

—Robert Halasz

HEICO

HEICO Corporation

300 Taft Street
Hollywood, Florida 33021
U.S.A.
(954) 987-6101
Fax: (954) 987-8228
Web site: http://www.stockprofile.com/hei

Public Company
Incorporated: 1957 as Heinicke Instruments Co.
Employees: 650
Sales: $95.35 million (1998)
Stock Exchanges: New York
Ticker Symbols: HEI; HEI.A
NAIC: 336412 Aircraft Engine & Engine Parts
    Manufacturing; 336413 Other Aircraft Parts &
    Auxiliary Equipment Manufacturing

HEICO Corporation is a leading supplier of replacement jet engine parts. As such it competes against giant jet engine manufacturers United Technologies Corporation (Pratt & Whitney) and General Electric. The company also manufactures a variety of auxiliary equipment for airlines.

Origins

HEICO was founded in 1957 as Heinicke Instruments Co. The company got its start making products for medical laboratories. In 1974 Heinicke entered the aviation business with its purchase of Jet Avion, which manufactured jet engine parts. Five years later the Securities and Exchange Commission sued the company for misrepresenting its engineering expertise. Heinicke settled the suit and agreed to include more outside representation on its board.

In the early 1980s, Heinicke came under the control of Tyco Laboratories, a New Hampshire-based company that accumulated 46 percent of the company's stock. Tyco, aiming to use Heinicke to expand into the medical supplies market, installed Chester Warner as its CEO. Warner, who replaced previous

president Rolf Franz, was an experienced laboratory products executive who reorganized the company and revitalized its offerings. Heinicke eventually bought back Tyco's shares.

Increasingly stringent FAA safety regulations, and deregulated fares, boosted business in the mid-1980s. Earnings were $7.6 million in 1986 on sales of $46 million. Jet Avion accounted for two-thirds of sales. *Florida Trend* reported that investors who had held the company's stock for the previous ten years could have seen a return of more than 1,000 percent.

The company changed its name from Heinicke Instruments Co. to HEICO Corporation in 1986. This prompted a 1989 lawsuit from Heico Inc., a manufacturing holding company based in Addison, Illinois, which asserted that the change caused "unnecessary confusion in the trade and financial communities." HEICO succeeded in holding on to its new namesake.

HEICO completed a stock offering on the American Stock Exchange in January 1987. Earnings rose to $7.6 million in the fiscal year ending October 31, 1987. However, the company forecast a decline for the next year due to a slow market for jet engine parts.

In October 1987 the company announced that plans to buy All Fab Corp. for $11 million fell through. All Fab, based in Everett, Washington, was an aerospace machining operation. At the same time, HEICO stated it was buying Germfree Laboratories Inc. of Miami. It also authorized a stock buyback.

Ownership Struggles in the 1980s

In 1988 HEICO was a takeover target for H Acquisition Corp., led by Chicago investor George Fox, who offered $75 million, or $30 a share for the company. The investor group led by Laurans Mendelson of Miami subsequently raised its shareholding from 9.9 percent to 13.6 percent of the company.

In 1989 the Mendelson group offered $42 million ($21 per share) for the rest of the company. In February the group planned a proxy fight to gain representation on the HEICO board. By December the group controlled four board seats, one vacated by resigning Chairman and CEO Robert Surtees.

HEICO simultaneously sold its laboratory business to Naperville, Illinois-based Varlen Corp. for $17 million.

United Technologies Corporation sued HEICO in 1989, claiming its Jet Avion subsidiary infringed on patents for the heat and corrosion resistant coatings used in the combustion chambers of its Pratt & Whitney gas turbine engines. These profitable coated products accounted for about a tenth of HEICO's sales.

In September 1992, Herbert Wertheim of Coral Gables, Florida, raised his stake in the company to 10.2 percent and requested two board seats. By this time, his friend Laurans Mendelson had been made chairman and chief executive officer.

As the global aviation industry stalled in the early 1990s, HEICO branched out, forming MediTek Health Corp. to enter the medical imaging field. The venture was short-lived. In June 1996, HEICO sold MediTek to U.S. Diagnostic Labs Inc. of West Palm Beach for $23 million.

Acquisitive in the 1990s

Sales and profits soared in the mid-1990s, buoyed by a recovering aerospace industry. Analysts praised the company's lean operation which allowed HEICO to undersell the big engine manufacturers and earn loyalty among its airline clientele.

HEICO bought Trilectron Industries Inc. in August 1996. The Palmetto, Florida-based company made aircraft ground support equipment such as ground power units and air conditioning units and had sales of about $15 million a year.

HEICO offered $276 million for Figgie International, which made respirators, in 1997, but was unsuccessful. In October 1997, Lufthansa Technik, a subsidiary of Lufthansa German Airlines AG, invested $26 million in Heico Aerospace, buying a 20 percent share in the HEICO Corporation subsidiary.

HEICO continued its acquisitive bent in 1998. It tried to obtain a controlling interest in Teleflex Lionel-Dupont, a French manufacturer of aircraft and aircraft engine components, for stock worth $63 million (FFr 370 million). The French company had annual sales of about FFr 384 million. TLD owned Albret Industrie, ERMA, and Tracma in France; and Devtec and Lantis in the United States. Devtec in turn had subsidiaries in China and Taiwan. However, in September 1998 HEICO announced it would not be able to acquire TLD due to a competing bid.

HEICO paid $15 million for PTM International, a jet engine parts maker based in Miami. McClain International, a private

maker of jet engine parts based in Atlanta, was bought for $41 million. HEICO added another $2.5 million for McClain's headquarters building. Lufthansa provided $9 million to fund the purchase. McClain's annual sales were $11 million. The company was founded in 1962 by a World War II veteran pilot and had 60 employees.

HEICO's revenues rose from $63.7 million in fiscal 1997 to $95.4 million in 1998. South Florida's aviation industry, populated by such firms as GE, B/E Aerospace, and BF Goodrich, soared in the late 1990s. In fact, the region led the nation in the number of aircraft parts suppliers. The industry had been established by companies including Pan Am and Pratt and Whitney; proximity to Latin America had now become an anchor to its success. A slowdown was anticipated, however, based on Boeing's announcement it was cutting aircraft deliveries.

In spite of the pending downturn in commercial aircraft, HEICO continued to buy, trying to dominate more of the supplier chain. In late 1998, the company sold PTM International for £8.8 million and bought Associated Composite Inc. of Miami, which repaired exterior aircraft parts. In December, HEICO bought Washington state-based competitor Rogers-Dierks Inc. in a deal worth at least $15 million. HEICO's Trilectron subsidiary opened its own 113,000-square-foot factory in Palmetto, Florida.

Hitting the Big Board in 1999

Early in 1999, Lufthansa invested an additional $3 million in HEICO's Flight Support Group, bringing its commitment to $38 million. HEICO's Ground Support Group bought Radiant Power from Santa Ana-based Derlan, Inc., a subsidiary of Derlan Industries, Ltd. of Toronto. U.S. Radiant Energy Corporation had sales of about $4 million in 1998, which included backup power supplies and batteries for a variety of on-board applications. The unit was to be incorporated into the Ground Support Group's new Palmetto facility. Radiant was known for its propane- or natural gas-based InfraTek aircraft deicing system, which produced specific wavelengths of radiant heat to remove snow and ice.

After years on the American Stock Exchange, HEICO shares began trading on the New York Stock Exchange in January 1999. A secondary stock offering in February 1999 raised $64 million. Sales were up 43 percent and the company posted record profits in the first quarter of fiscal 1999. Its revenues had grown more than 50 percent annually in the previous five years. Management aimed to attain $1 billion in annual revenues within five years.

HEICO continued its growth by acquisition strategy, announcing in May that its Flight Support Group had bought Miami-based Air Radio and Instruments Corp. The firm was founded in 1983 and employed 30 people. The purchase cost $3.5 million and complemented HEICO's expertise in repairing and overhauling aircraft components. In June 1999 HEICO bought Turbine Kinetics, Inc. and AeroKinetics, Inc. of Glastonbury, Connecticut. Both manufactured jet engine replacement parts. This brought HEICO's product line to 1,200 jet engine parts.

The company also bought a 40 percent interest in privately held R.H. Phillips and Sons Engineers, Ltd., a British firm involved in ground support equipment manufacture. The Chichester, England-based company had been in existence since 1964 and employed 27 people. At the same time, HEICO's Electronics and Ground Support Group created a U.K. subsidiary, Trilectron Europe Ltd. It also opened sales offices in Singapore and India. International sales accounted for nearly half the group's total revenues.

Soon after, HEICO, through its Electronics and Ground Support Group, bought privately held Leader Tech, based in Tampa. Leader Tech was a 20-year-old company that employed 100 people manufacturing circuit board shielding. The purchase enhanced HEICO's own circuit board operations and expanded its high profit electronics offerings.

HEICO's Flight Support Group accounted for 73 percent of revenues in 1998; Ground Support, the remainder. With net sales increasing at a rate of about 50 percent a year, HEICO had validated its investment decisions and secured its role in the future of commercial aviation.

Principal Subsidiaries

HEICO Aerospace Holdings Corp.; HEICO Aerospace Corporation; Jet Avion Corporation; LPI Industries Corporation; Aircraft Technology, Inc.; Northwings Accessories Corp.; McClain International, Inc.; Associated Composite, Inc.; Rogers-Dierks, Inc.; HEICO Aviation Products Corp.; Trilectron Industries, Inc.

Principal Divisions

Flight Support Group; Electronics and Ground Support Group.

Further Reading

Fakler, John T., "Aviation Business Taking Off Despite Stock Lows," *South Florida Business Journal,* October 12, 1998.

"HEICO Feels Good—And It Should," *South Florida Business Journal,* April 18, 1997.

"How the Best Did It," *Florida Trend,* July 1, 1987.

"It's Heico Vs. Heico in Trademark Suit," *Miami Herald,* January 21, 1989.

"Teleflex Lionel-Dupont passe sous pavillon americain," *Echos,* June 9, 1998.

Velocci, Anthony L., Jr., "Market Focus," *Aviation Week and Space Technology,* May 3, 1999.

——, "Weekly Market Performance," *Aviation Week and Space Technology,* August 19, 1996.

—Frederick C. Ingram

Huffy Corporation

225 Byers Road
Miamisburg, Ohio 45342
U.S.A.
(937) 866-6251
Fax: (937) 865-5470
Web site: http://www.huffy.com

Public Company
Incorporated: 1928 as Huffman Manufacturing Company
Employees: 3,702
Sales: $707.6 million (1998)
Stock Exchanges: New York
Ticker Symbol: HUF
NAIC: 336991 Motorcycles, Bicycle, & Parts
   Manufacturing; 33992 Sporting & Athletic Good
   Manufacturing

The largest manufacturer of bicycles in the world, Huffy Corporation is the parent company of four wholly owned subsidiaries that operate in two distinct business segments: consumer products and retail services. Touting itself as "America's First Choice," Huffy Bicycle Company manufactured a complete line of bicycles for adults and children, including an electric scooter that debuted in 1999. Huffy Sports Company ranked as the largest supplier of National Basketball Association (NBA) backboards in North America. On the retail services side of its business, Huffy owned two subsidiaries, Washington Inventory Service and Huffy Service First. Washington Inventory Service employed a national workforce that provided inventory service to retailers. Huffy Service First operated as the only national concern to provide in-store and in-home product assembly and repair services to retailers.

Origins

Huffy grew out of the Huffman Manufacturing Company, which was founded in 1924. Founder Horace M. Huffman, Sr., learned the manufacturing business from his father, George P.

Huffman, who owned the Davis Sewing Machine Company from 1887 to 1925. Taking advantage of the growing automotive industry, Horace Huffman's young company made equipment that could be used in service stations. Working out of a factory on Gilbert Avenue in a noisy section of Dayton, Ohio, near the Pennsylvania Railroad tracks, the first Huffman employees are credited with inventing a rigid spout that could be used to dispense motor oil from 50-gallon drums. The company grew quickly through the 1920s and 1930s and its line of service station equipment expanded. When it incorporated in 1928, the company posted earnings of $3,000.

In 1934 Horace Huffman announced plans to manufacture bicycles after sensing that they would become a popular mode of transportation during the Depression. In the beginning, production rates hovered at 12 bikes per day. Within two years, this rate increased to 200 daily. However, the company was still not producing fast enough to keep pace with its competition and Huffman suffered several setbacks in the beginning. The Firestone Tire and Rubber Company was a primary bike customer, but in 1938 Huffman lost a major portion of the account because it could not match Firestone's demand.

But the solution was not far away. Two years earlier, Horace Huffman, Jr., who was known by the diminutive "Huff," had joined the company on a full-time basis. After short stints as service manager and sales manager, he became works manager and converted the production process to a straight-line conveyerized assembly line. It was just the edge the company needed, and by 1940, bicycle production doubled and sales figures were nearing the $1.5 million mark. Huffman's improved production rate caught the eye of the Western Auto Company, which became a major customer, and also brought Firestone back into the fold.

The outbreak of World War II necessitated a shift in production. The company joined the thousands of other businesses that were vying for government contracts, and was able to secure an order for primers, an artillery shell part. The increased business brought Huffman's sales to nearly $2.8 million in 1942. The following year, the federal government placed an order for 4,000 bicycles. At this point, much of the work was being done by women who were filling the void left by the vast numbers of

---

---

men who had been inducted into the armed forces. The later part of the war proved to be difficult as the production of consumer products in all industries virtually ceased and Horace, Sr., suffered a fatal heart attack in 1945.

Post-World War II Growth and Diversification

The younger Huffman was elected president and immediately had to face the challenge of sustaining production in the postwar period with limited supplies. The government's allocation program, he knew, would not provide enough materials to allow the company to compete at its prewar levels. After attending a seminar on "Work Simplification," Huff taught the procedure to his managers and then held a similar workshop for the company's major suppliers. By meeting the problem head-on, Huffman was able to help suppliers increase their own output and to raise production levels. For two years, the company was able to run two shifts a day without experiencing the traditional slowdown during the winter months. Sales for each of the two years exceeded $10 million.

Then, in 1949, the company ran into the postwar recession. However, two developments allowed the company to survive. First, the Huffy convertible bicycle was introduced and was instantly popular. The bike also brought the name Huffy to the forefront of the bicycle industry. The second development occurred as a result of the company's search for a product that could be manufactured during the winter months. The decision to produce lawnmowers was announced in December 1949.

As a result, the company quickly outgrew its physical plants, and in the early 1950s Huffman acquired a building in Delphos, Ohio, and moved the Automotive Service Equipment division to that location. New facilities were built in Celina, Ohio, to house the bicycle and lawnmower divisions. The Dayton manufacturing plant on Gilbert Avenue was closed and the general offices were moved to Davis Avenue. In 1959 Huffman opened its bicycle plant in Azusa, California.

By 1960 Huffman was the third largest bike manufacturer in the United States. In 1962 Horace Huffman, Jr., was named chairman and Frederick C. Smith became president and CEO. Smith had been materials manager during the crucial postwar period and was credited with strengthening the company's relationship with its suppliers.

In 1964 Huffman expanded its Outdoor Power Equipment division with the acquisition of Diele & McGuire Manufacturing. It was not an entirely successful expansion, however, and the division continued to lose money over the next decade. That same year, the Huffman corporate offices were moved to their current location in Miamisburg.

Huffman went public with its listing on the American Stock Exchange in 1968 and sales reached $42 million the following year. Stuart Northrup, a former Singer Sewing Machine executive, replaced Smith as president in 1972. By 1973 Huffman employed 2,500 workers at five locations.

Throughout the 1960s and early 1970s, Huffman enjoyed continued growth as the market for adult bicycles grew. More and more adults were turning to bikes for exercise and as a means to cut energy costs. Until the end of the 1960s, nearly half of all bicycles in the United States were sold through small independent bike shops that offered personal customer service. In the 1970s, the introduction of mass merchandise retail chains that stocked large quantities of consumer goods and sold them at discount prices opened up a new market for bike sales. Because British-owned Raleigh Cycle was firmly entrenched as the leading supplier to the independent shop owner, Huffman set its sights on the retail chains and developed a ten-speed that required the bare minimum of assembly and service.

The company's growth trend hit a snag in 1974, however, as a new recessionary period brought on an industrywide slump. From its peak in 1973, bicycle sales dropped 50 percent by 1975. Huffman was forced to close its Celina plant for two months and lay off 25 percent of its workers.

Prior to the recession, foreign competition was also putting pressure on U.S. bike makers. In 1972 foreign imports accounted for 37 percent of the U.S. market. The devalued U.S. dollar, however, cut this share to 15 percent by the end of the 1970s. New federal regulations setting safety standards for bicycles also cut into the sale of foreign models. As the industry revived itself toward the end of the 1970s, Huffman decided to take an aggressive marketing stance. Children again became the primary focus of the bike industry and Huffman introduced a new flashy, motocross-style bike called Thunder Trail. Designed to look like a motorcycle with waffle handle-grips, knobby tires, and racing-like number plates on the front, the new models also sported bright, jazzy colors and decals. Not content to settle for what they hoped *might* sell, Huffman held focus groups in shopping centers to determine which features were the most popular. In addition, a greater portion of advertising dollars was spent on television commercials, particularly during the hours when children's programs aired.

The popularity of the Thunder Trail bike made Huffman the number one producer of bicycles in the United States by 1977 and all of the laid-off workers were called back. Net sales for 1977 were $130 million, a 21 percent increase from the previous year.

Although Huffman was still the leading producer of gasoline cans, oil can spouts, oil filters, and jack stands, the Automotive Equipment Division was only accounting for ten percent of the company's sales. Bikes and bike accessories accounted for an overwhelming 90 percent. The Outdoor Power Equipment division, which had been struggling for years in the lawnmower market, was finally sold in 1975. The sale brought in a much needed $10 million in cash. Realizing the need to diversify, Huffman acquired Frabill Manufacturing, a maker of fishing and basketball equipment, in 1977.

Until then, half of Huffman's bicycles were sold under private labels. By the end of the 1970s, however, the company decided to devote more energy to promoting its own brand name. Part of this effort included the decision, in 1977, to change the company name to Huffy Corporation. During this period, Huffy's management also opted not to enter the moped manufacturing field because of doubts about the motorized bike's potential in the United States. Instead, $5 million was spent to expand existing production facilities.

In 1980 Huffy posted its fifth straight year of record earnings and announced plans to open a third plant in Ponca City, Oklahoma. However, despite its strong financial position, Huffy was not immune to the problems that most U.S. businesses experienced in the 1980s. For one thing, production costs were rapidly increasing. In 1982 Harry A. Shaw III was named CEO and immediately embarked on the unpopular road to plant closings and layoffs. Shaw spearheaded the consolidation of all bike manufacturing operations into the Celina plant and sold the Automotive Products Division for cash. Huffy then invested more than $15 million in advanced robotics and new production equipment. The changes resulted in an increase in production capacity by 5,000 bikes a day and a 14 percent cut in production costs. Another $15 million was earmarked to improve computer-generated manufacturing in the bike plant by 1991.

A licensing, sales, and manufacturing agreement with Raleigh Cycle was also cemented in 1982, giving the company the opportunity to tap the high-specification bike market. However, the venture did not prove to be an asset and Huffy sold its rights in 1988.

With bike sales still accounting for 90 percent of the company's sales, the need to diversify was as evident as ever. In 1982 Huffy acquired Gerico, a maker of infant car seats and strollers, and YLC Enterprises, a provider of product assembly services for retail consumer purchases. The former was organized as Gerry Baby Products and the latter as Huffy Service First. Washington Inventory Service, a nationwide inventory taking service, was acquired in 1988. In 1990, Huffy acquired Black & Decker's stake in True Temper Hardware and capital stock in True Temper Ltd. in Ireland for $55 million. A manufacturer of garden and lawn tools, the company claimed approximately 30 percent of the market.

Foreign Competition: 1990s

Buoyed by the completion of its diversification campaign, Huffy entered the 1990s with renewed confidence. As the decade began, the company was collecting nearly half its earnings and sales from its disparate, non-bike businesses, which were beginning to develop their own momentum. Huffy Service First, for instance, had begun to expand its services by assembling gas grills, lawnmowers, and patio furniture for mass retailers in addition to bikes. Diversification engendered its own problems, however, particularly with the newest addition to the Huffy portfolio, True Temper. In an effort to gain market share, Huffy management reduced prices for True Temper lawn and garden equipment, which resulted in a $5 million loss for the division in 1992. Huffy experienced other difficulties during the early 1990s as well, misfiring in its attempt to take advantage of the popularity of mountain bikes. The company introduced a cross-trainer bike in 1992 that represented a hybrid of a road bike and mountain bike, but following an expensive promotion campaign, sales of the crosstrainer were lackluster. The problems with True Temper and the ill-conceived introduction of a crosstrainer paled in comparison to Huffy's overriding problem during the 1990s, however, and that was contending with Asian competitors. Benefiting from lower production costs than their U.S. counterparts, Asian manufacturers enjoyed significant success in the U.S. market during the 1990s, causing considerable havoc for domestic bike producers. Huffy, holding a 30 percent share of the $1.5 billion U.S. market, bore the brunt of the damage stemming from the incursion of Asian producers and saw its profitability sag. The worst period for Huffy arrived in 1995, when the company recorded a crippling $10.5 million loss. For the remainder of the decade, Huffy management devoted itself to curing the ills that led to the devastating loss and implementing measures to ensure that it never happened again.

In the wake of 1995's loss, a rebuilding process began that saw the company reduce its size in some departments and expand into new business areas. Management cut workers' wages, considered new product lines to stimulate profits, and looked to divest underperforming businesses. In 1997, Huffy sold Gerry Baby Products Co., gaining $73 million from the divestiture, and purchased Royce Union Bicycle Co., a Hauppauge, New York-based maker of high-end bikes. The company also acquired bankrupt Sure Shot International, a manufacturer and distributor of basketball goods, organizing the $1.5 million purchase into its Huffy Sports Co. subsidiary. As these transactions were being completed, the company entered a new segment in the bike market, introducing the first Huffy bike motocross, or BMX, model in 1997. At the time of Huffy's entry into the market segment, BMX models represented the only segment in the bike industry recording sales growth. By the end of 1997, the company's financial results revealed the influence of the changes implemented during the previous two years. The news was encouraging. After posting a $10.5 million loss in 1995, Huffy recorded $10.4 million in net income in 1997.

Although Huffy management had directed a remarkable turnaround between 1995 and 1997, the executives still had to contend with the aftereffects of the mid-1990s crisis: their restorative work was not yet completed. One contentious issue stemming from the $10.5 million loss involved Huffy workers at the Celina, Ohio, bicycle plant. When the losses mounted back in 1995, the workers agreed to a 20 percent wage cut to keep production from moving to Huffy's bike plant in Farmington, Missouri. In April 1998, the workers' union met with Huffy management, demanding a 20 percent wage increase and additional raises to compensate for the benefits and wages lost since 1995. The negotiations stalled, with Huffy offering less than the workers demanded. In July, hope for a settlement disappeared entirely when Huffy announced it was closing the Celina plant and laying off all of the facility's 1,000 employees, representing 25 percent of the company's total workforce. Although unpopular in Celina, Huffy management was determined to make the company's bike operations profitable in the long term.

As Huffy exited the 1990s, it continued to pursue the strategy of paring away assets, acquiring new properties, and entering new business areas. In 1998, the company's Washington Inventory Service subsidiary (the second largest inventory counter in the nation) acquired Denver, Colorado-based Inventory Auditors, Inc., with 42 offices operating in 23 states. The acquisition greatly strengthened Washington Inventory Service's position in its industry, since Inventory Auditors ranked third in the industry. The addition of Inventory Auditors, combined with the company's divestitures and efforts to reduce production capacity and increase efficiency, impressed Wall Street, fueling a 25 percent increase in Huffy's stock value during the last six months of 1998. For 1999, the company had further significant changes in store, none more dramatic than the announcement that it was selling True Temper Hardware Co. In February 1999, Huffy sold its garden tools and wheelbarrow business to U.S. Industries, Inc. for $100 million, stripping the company of $123 million in sales. With the proceeds from the divestiture, Huffy planned to reduce its short-term debt and to finance the company's ongoing program of buying back its shares. The last year of the decade also saw Huffy introduce an electric scooter called Buzz that was rechargeable from a standard 110-volt outlet. To strengthen its foray into the electric scooter segment, Huffy reached an agreement in June 1999 with ZAPWORLD.COM to sell the company's stand-up version of an electric scooter, called ZAPPY, through Huffy's distribution channels.

Statistics in the 1990s pointed to a fiercely competitive global market for bike manufacturers in the 21st century, auguring a continuation of the battle between Huffy and foreign competitors in the future. Between 1994 and 1998, comparable retail bike prices dropped 25 percent in the United States largely because of the wave of foreign imports, plunging ten percent in 1997 alone. In 1997 nearly 60 percent of the bikes purchased in the United States were produced by foreign manufacturers who incurred significantly lower production costs than U.S. manu-

facturers. To combat eroding profit margins, Huffy planned to further reduce costs and to eliminate excess production capacity, while developing a more competitive mix of domestic and non-domestic products. For Huffy to maintain its leadership in the industry during the 21st century, much depended on the company's success in overcoming the challenges presented by its overseas competitors.

Principal Subsidiaries

Huffy Bicycle Company; Huffy Sports Company; Huffy Service First; Washington Inventory Service.

Further Reading

"Fifty Years of Growth Took Teamwork," *Huffman Highlights,* Miamisburg, Ohio: The Huffman Manufacturing Company, 1973.

Hannon, Kerry, "Easy Rider," *Forbes,* November 16, 1987.

"Huffy Pedals into First Place," *Sales & Marketing Management,* January 1978.

"Huffy Puts New Spin in the Bicycle Business," *Business Week,* October 10, 1977.

"Huffy Starts to Shift into High Gear," *Money,* October 1993, p. 74.

Jaffe, Thomas, "Huffy Toughs It Out," *Forbes,* May 28, 1990, p. 416.

"Motocross, New Type Bicycle Puts Huffman Mfg. in High Gear," *Barron's,* August 23, 1976.

Troy, Mike, "Features Fill Gap in Bike Sales," *Discount Store News,* March 22, 1999, p. 80.

Wagner, Mike, "Talks Break Off Between Huffy Corp. Management, Workers," *Knight-Ridder/Tribune Business News,* p. OKRB98125030.

—Mary McNulty
—updated by Jeffrey L. Covell

Informix

Informix Corporation

4100 Bohannon Dr.
Menlo Park, California 94025
U.S.A.
(650) 926-6300
Fax: (650) 926-6593
Web site: http://www.informix.com

Public Company
Incorporated: 1980 as Relational Database Systems Inc.
Employees: 3,984
Sales: $734.98 million (1998)
Stock Exchanges: NASDAQ
Ticker Symbol: IFMX
NAIC: 51121 Software Publishers

Informix Corporation is a leading developer of relational database software for computers using the UNIX operating system. Its market, however, is dominated by such competitors as Oracle, Microsoft, and IBM. As a young company, Informix was considered to have emerged at the right time to take advantage of a trend among corporate computer users switching from mainframe systems to networked microcomputers. Yet following a 1988 merger with Innovative Software, the company has experienced a series of troubling setbacks. An accompanying string of reorganizations and leadership changes, the latest in 1999 under newly installed CEO Jean-Yves Dexmier, was expected to help place the company back on track.

Adapting Relational Database Management to UNIX

Originally named Relational Database Systems Inc., this software company was founded by 25-year-old entrepreneur Roger J. Sippl. Sippl's background included a B.A. in computer science from the University of California, Berkeley, and a stint as manager of database research and development at Cromenco, a manufacturer of microcomputers. In 1980 Sippl invested $200,000 in the new company and became its president, chief executive officer, and chairman.

Relational Database Systems was a pioneer in 1981 in distributing fully relational database management systems (RDMS) for multi-user computers through its product line, INFORMIX. RDMS programs link multiple files together and permit the comparison and analysis of the data in these files. RDMS software had existed since the 1970s as customized or proprietary software for mainframe computer systems. Relational Database Systems was one of the first companies to specialize in offering RDMS software packages designed to run on the UNIX operating system used on many microcomputers.

Relational Database Systems quickly became a leader in the new field of UNIX-based database management software. The company gained a technological edge over its competitors by developing its products specifically for workstations and personal computers. Oracle and Relational Technology Inc., other leading RDMS companies at the time, had instead revised software they had originally developed for mainframes and minicomputers.

In the summer of 1985, Relational Database Systems introduced a significant new product, INFORMIX-SQL, a RDMS that featured an ANSI-standard query language that was based on International Business Machines Corporation's (IBM) Structured Query Language (SQL). Although the software was for UNIX, the use of IBM's SQL opened up a potential market of IBM computer users familiar with that query format. The company also introduced INFORMIX-ESQL/C, which offered additional programmable features in the C language.

Also in 1985, the company introduced the first SQL-based RDMS software version for local area networks of DOS-based personal computers. The design of separate "front-end" and "back-end" components of the company's SQL software, developed several years prior, made it most efficient when running on client/server networks. On this type of system, multiple users at individually networked computers could share database files kept on a designated computer known as a server.

The company moved further into providing software for programmers when, in February 1986, it introduced IN-FORMIX-4GL, a programming language designed especially for developing databases. This was its first application-building language to combine the needed fourth-generation application programming features along with SQL, and which further could be used under all versions of UNIX. Later in 1986, it introduced versions of INFORMIX-4GL and INFORMIX-SQL that ran on the VMS operating system of Digital Equipment Corporation's VAX minicomputers and MicroVAC workstations. Also in 1986, the company began development of INFORMIX Datasheet Add-In, a product that added true RDMS capabilities to Lotus 1-2-3.

A Surge in Sales: Mid-1980s

Relational Database Systems had $2.1 million in revenues and $169,000 in earnings in 1983. Over the next three years, the business grew more than tenfold. Revenues in 1986 were $21.1 million, and earnings were $2.4 million. The number of employees grew from 22 in 1983 to 214 in 1986. By the mid-1980s, Relational Database Systems had developed a broad marketing network comprising original equipment manufacturers (OEMs), value-added resellers (VARs), dealers, and distributors. By 1986 OEMs had packaged the company's software products with over 150 different kinds of mid-range computer models and contributed to 22 percent of Relational Database Systems' sales. VARs, which customized the company's software for specific industry markets and also combined it with hardware, accounted for about 13 percent of sales. International distributors were responsible for 13 percent of sales, up 200 percent from 1985.

The company's own direct sales force was significantly expanded through the opening of six regional domestic sales offices between mid-1985 and the end of 1986, and the sales staff increased from 12 to 84 people. Direct sales to corporate end-users made up the largest share—32 percent of the company's revenues in 1986. Another 12 percent of sales were to the government sector.

In August 1986, the company changed its name to Informix Corporation in anticipation of an initial public offering. The company was reincorporated in Delaware under the new name as a holding company, and an operating subsidiary, Informix Software, Inc., was created and headquartered along with Informix Corporation in Menlo Park, California. Informix Corporation went public on September 24, 1986, by selling 969,446 shares at $7.50 per share, raising $6.7 million. The company

raised an additional $2.3 million by selling 330,554 shares to Altos Computer Systems, which put Altos's investment in the company at 23 percent.

Merger-Generated Losses: Late 1980s

In February 1988, Informix made the significant strategic decision to acquire Innovative Software Inc. of Lenexa, Kansas. It was hoped that Innovative's microcomputer software products, and especially its front-end applications, would complement Informix's RDMS software and offer clients integrated office automation software. Innovative, which had 1987 revenues of $18.8 million, had developed a package of integrated software applications for the personal computer called Smart-Ware. Michael Brown, one of the two Innovative founders, became president of the merged Informix, while Sippl retained the posts of chairman and chief executive.

The companies, however, had very different products, markets, corporate cultures, and geographic locations, and were difficult to integrate. Furthermore, the decision to retain dual headquarters led to confusion and inefficiency. Employment increased from 350 to 1,200, while expenses doubled. There was significant turnover in sales and marketing personnel, and two vice-presidents of sales left the company in 1988. Earnings, excluding merger costs of $800,000, steadily declined from $2.5 million in the first quarter of 1988 to the company's first loss of $2 million in the fourth quarter. Furthermore, Informix's accounting methods had to be revised due to criticisms from investors and auditors. To top it all off, in late 1988 Informix was the subject of a class action lawsuit by shareholders charging company officers with inflating the company's stock price. The company ended 1988 with a $46.3 million loss.

Problems in managing the merger contributed to delays in introducing new products. Release 4 of Informix's database engine was delayed from early 1989 to the end of the year. A SmartWare upgrade was also many months late. A new spreadsheet software package called Wingz, which Innovative had begun developing in early 1987, was announced in January 1988, but did not ship until the spring of 1989. Wingz was Informix's first product for Macintosh, and debugging the software took much longer than anticipated. Losses continued in 1989 and 1990.

Despite innovative features and favorable reviews, Wingz never had a reasonable chance of becoming a successful product. It could not compete with Microsoft Corporation's Excel, which held an estimated 70 to 90 percent of market share for Macintosh spreadsheet programs. Likewise, SmartWare II was not a big success because integrated software—a single package that combines word processing, spreadsheet, database management, and other capabilities—never became popular in the United States despite SmartWare's relative success in Europe.

New Management, Corporate Reorganization: 1989

It took a new chief executive with more professional management experience to turn Informix around. Sippl, retaining his post as chairman, turned over the management of the company to Phillip E. White in early 1989. Until then, White had been president of Wyse, and prior to that spent 15 years at IBM before two years as vice-president of sales and marketing at Altos. Sippl eventually gave up day-to-day control as chairman in 1990 and left in 1992, feeling that his start-up company had grown too big for him to manage.

White announced a corporate reorganization in January 1989. He laid off about 200 employees—15 percent of staff—and eliminated the dual nature of the company. Instead he created two product divisions, the Workstation Products Division in Lenexa and the Advanced Products Division at the headquarters in Menlo Park. The Advanced Products Division was responsible for Informix's traditional database, network, and application-development software, while the Workstation Products Division became responsible for Wingz and other office productivity software.

White also took over the presidency of Informix and the management of the Advance Products Division, while former Informix president Michael Brown became president and general manager of the Workstation Products Division. In 1990 White relocated some of the manufacturing operations to Kansas, where labor costs were lower. By the end of 1989, office automation software, developed primarily by the Workstation Productions Division, accounted for 27 percent of Informix's revenues, while database management software accounted for 36 percent. Software development tools, such as INFORMIX-4GL, made up 37 percent of sales.

White's turnaround of Informix proved spectacular. At the beginning of 1990, Informix introduced a new, high-end RDMS product for enterprise-wide use called INFORMIX-OnLine. Designed for online transaction processing, it featured distributed processing, fault tolerance, and multimedia capabilities permitting the storage and retrieval of digitized sounds and graphics. The company returned to profitability in 1991 after losses of $46.4 million in 1990. The following year, sales increased 46 percent to reach $283 million, and net income quadrupled to $47.8 million. Contributing to 1992 sales was a single $26.8 million contract for the Army National Guard and Army Reserves. Informix's stock price, which had fallen as low as $1.31 a share in January 1992, shot up to around $38 a share by the spring of 1993. The market capitalization of the company rose 24 times in the same period to reach $1.2 billion. Manufacturing costs dropped from 13 percent of revenues in 1989 to only five percent in 1993.

Most significantly though, Informix was able to continue growing by taking advantage of the accelerated demand for UNIX-based business software applications among corporations switching from mainframe computers to networks of server-based personal computers and workstations. In 1989 Informix introduced INFORMIX-STAR, software that enabled users of its new INFORMIX-OnLine RDMS to retrieve data from not one but multiple network servers.

Strategic Investments and Partnerships: 1990s

Under White, Informix followed a new strategy of investing in its core databases and software developers' tools while delegating add-on software applications and greater marketing responsibilities to its growing network of about 2,000 value-added resellers. Increasingly, the company shared the costs and

credit for developing new products with other corporate partners. Informix began working with Sequent Computer Systems Inc. on a parallel processing data query product; with Siemens A.G. on a data dictionary; and with Symbol Technologies Inc. on programming tools to aid in the development of applications for wireless networks. Informix also licensed Hewlett-Packard's SoftBench framework for third-party computer-aided software engineering tools. Having learned its lesson from the Innovative merger, Informix did not pursue any more acquisitions, but rather engaged in strategic investments with other companies. As a result of these strategies, Informix was able to maintain operating margins in the early 1990s of over 20 percent.

Meanwhile, Informix began to deemphasize its office automation software in order to concentrate on database management software and programming development tools. Informix also expanded its overseas sales. Its first quarter 1993 European sales increased 48 percent, while Oracle's increased only four percent. In 1993, through 30 overseas sales offices, foreign sales accounted for 58 percent of Informix's revenues, up from 54 percent the year before. The company's lower-end RDMS, INFORMIX-SE, sold through international VARs, did especially well in Europe.

In early 1993, 80 percent of Informix's sales were for software running on the UNIX operating system, and the company claimed to be the world leader in the number of installed RDBSs on UNIX computers. However, having decided to further expand its offerings for other operating systems, Informix increased its marketing efforts for a version of its RDMS launched in 1992 to run on Novell Inc.'s Netware Loadable Module. Informix also began making its INFORMIX-OnLine available for Microsoft's Windows NT server operating system and entered a joint marketing deal with Microsoft for a software package consisting of the INFORMIX-SE Client/Server Software Developer's Kit and Microsoft Windows NT, which began shipping in January 1994. In addition, it began looking into more support for the Macintosh platform, and introduced a new pricing system in December 1993, aimed at setting the software price according to the value that its customers derived from it. This user-based pricing model replaced a pricing structure based on machine class. While emphasizing value to the customers, the new pricing system was also expected to raise revenues slightly on average. Shortly thereafter, competitors began to follow Informix's example in pricing methods.

Informix developed a new product technology in late 1993 called Dynamic Scalable Architecture, the first database management design to combine parallel-processing capabilities, data replication, and connectivity in a single product, while also being adaptable to a user's growing needs. Dynamic Scalable Architecture was first incorporated into INFORMIX OnLine Dynamic Server 6.0, introduced in December 1993. In March 1994, Informix shipped OnLine 7.0, its first true multi-processing database. Codesigned by Informix and Sequent Computer Systems Inc., it featured parallel data query, which automatically splits user queries into several parts which run simultaneously across multiple processors.

In 1995 the company reported record revenue of almost $709 million, a 51 percent growth over 1994, and earnings of

$105 million, an increase of 59 percent. The company's stock hit a 52-week high in February with a newly released version of its so-called relational database management software. In December, the company sealed its leadership position in the object-relational category with the agreement to acquire Illustra Technologies, which offered content management technology.

The following year, Informix entered into two successful partnerships—first with Gemplus and Hewlett-Packard to develop smart cards for secure Internet and electronic commerce applications, and then with Digital Equipment to open the Advanced Technology Center in southeast Asia. Universal Server, the first database to store any kind of information, including graphics, and video, became possible with the merger of Informix's own relational database management software and an Illustra program, which relied on the new object-relational database management technology. Informix began to market the Universal Server and, by year-end, had moved to second place in its industry behind only Oracle. Its share of the database market was now six percent, and its stock hit its all-time high of about $36.

However, the tide turned suddenly in 1997 when the company lost $140 million in its first quarter. Shares plunged 35 percent, and the company was forced to lay off ten percent of its employees. White, soon after replaced by Robert J. Finochio, attributed the loss to the company's failure to close sales on existing products while gearing up for the introduction of Universal Server. Finocchio ordered a refocus on basics, and the building of a new management team to define Informix's marketing mission, but the company's financial woes continued. In August, as shares dropped another 22 percent, it announced that it had booked questionable sales as completed transactions and planned to restate its 1996 financial results. The restatement eventually extended to three and one half years and involved a reduction of more than $250 million in sales and earnings. For 1997, the company suffered losses of $357 million as revenue fell to $662.3 from $727.8 million. Informix's share of the database market dropped to 5.6 percent, and its stock hovered at a low of $4.

In an attempt to move forward, Finocchio trimmed Informix's product line to one main product aimed at the largest corporations—spatial information systems examine relationships between demographic information and geography—and began to focus on high-profit niche markets like electronic commerce, retailing, and media, instead of selling cut-rate database packages. The company was reorganized into two new business units: Data Warehouse Business Unit Group and i.Informix, which focused on web commerce. As the only company in its industry to cover Unix, NT, and Linux, Informix sought to remarket itself, changing its logo and tag line to "The one with the smartest data wins." By the second quarter of

1998, it had once again turned a profit. It expanded its staff to nearly 3,600 and agreed to buy California-based Red Brick Systems Inc. Revenue rose 11 percent to $735 million and net income was almost $58 million for the year.

Finocchio stepped down in 1999, replaced by Jean-Yves Dexmier. Under Dexmier, the company attempted to put the past to rest by paying out $142 million to settle a lawsuit with stockholders concerning Informix's recent losses. Moving forward into the next century, it unveiled its Foundation 2000, a data and content management platform for the Internet and announced its new strategy of going direct to customers rather than focusing on technology for use in developing products for end-users.

Principal Subsidiaries

Informix Software, Inc.

Further Reading

Abate, Tom, "Informix Loses Money and CFO," *San Francisco Chronicle*, May 2, 1997, p. E1.

Angwin, Julia, "Informix Beats Oracle to the Punch," *San Francisco Chronicle*, December 2, 1996, p. B1.

Beckett, Jamie, "Informix Leader Senses Gain After Fill of Pain," *San Francisco Chronicle*, August 18, 1998, p. C1.

Boonruang, Sasiwimon, "Enterprise: Informix Database Market Share Up 25%," *Bangkok Post*, March 3, 1999.

Bozman, Jean S., "Informix Diversifies UNIX Portfolio," *Computerworld*, February 15, 1993, p. 109.

Doler, Kathleen, "Informix to Undergo Restructuring, Delays Its Database Engine," *PC Week*, January 30, 1989, p. 54.

Houston, Patrick, "Backseat Strategist," *PC Week*, July 26, 1993, p. A5.

——, and Karen D. Moser, "Enjoying the Sippl Life," *PC Week*, March 7, 1994, p. A4.

Kaberline, Brian, "Merged Informix Yet to Find Wingz in Software Market," *Kansas City Business Journal*, January 23, 1989, pp. 1, 34.

Karon, Paul, "PC Efforts Stalling Informix's Growth," *PC Week*, December 26, 1988, p. 59.

Kasim, Sharifah, "Informix Sees Prospects with Foundation 2000," *New Straits Times—Computimes (Malaysia)*, August 2, 1999, p. 16.

Lineback, J. Robert, "Sippl Wants to Help UNIX Hook onto the Business Market," *Electronics Week*, March 11, 1985, p. 47.

McCoy, Charles, "Informix Rides High-Tech Wave with UNIX System," *Wall Street Journal*, May 3, 1993, p. B4.

Rauber, Chris, "Prime Times: Database Company Bounces Back," *San Francisco Business Times*, May 21–27, 1993, p. 8A.

Rosenberg, Martin, "Informix: Back on Track?," *Kansas City Star*, April 22, 1998, p. B3.

—Heather Behn Hedden
—updated by Carrie Rothburd

IBM

International Business Machines Corporation

New Orchard Road
Armonk, New York 10504
U.S.A.
(914) 499-1900
(800) 426-3333
Fax: (914) 765-4190
Web site: http://www.ibm.com

Public Company
Incorporated: 1910 as Computing-Tabulating-Recording
Company
Employees: 291,067
Sales: $81.7 billion (1998)
Stock Exchanges: New York Midwest Pacific
Philadelphia Cincinnati Boston Paris Frankfurt Vienna
Tokyo Zürich Geneva Basel Montreal Toronto
Brussels London Amsterdam Lausanne
Ticker Symbol: IBM
NAIC: 334111 Electronic Computer Manufacturing;
334112 Computer Storage Device Manufacturing;
334113 Computer Terminal Manufacturing; 334119
Other Computer Peripheral Equipment Manufacturing;
334613 Magnetic and Optical Recording Media
Manufacturing; 541511 Custom Computer
Programming Services; 51121 Software Publishers;
541512 Computer Systems Design Services (pt);
51421 Data Processing Services; 541513 Computer
Facilities Management Services; 53242 Office
Machinery and Equipment Rental and Leasing (pt);
811212 Computer and Office Machine Repair and
Maintenance (pt); 334418 Printed Circuit/Electronics
Assembly Manufacturing; 33429 Other
Communication Equipment Manufacturing; 54169
Other Scientific and Technical Consulting Services

International Business Machines Corporation (IBM) is the
largest computer maker in the world. Because of its enormous
size, power, and success, and because it sells that most modern
of tools, the computer, IBM has come to symbolize modern life
itself for many. The company's nickname—Big Blue—is a
phrase that may have been originally suggested by IBM's army
of uniformly dressed salesmen, whose dark suits and white
shirts were required by the firm's leader, Thomas Watson, Sr.,
who transformed the Computing-Tabulating-Recording Company (CTR) into a world leader in information technology.

Company Origins

CTR was formed in 1910 by Charles Ranlett Flint. The
so-called "father of trusts" merged two of his earlier creations,
International Time Recording Company and Computing Scale
Company of America, with a third, unrelated entity known as
Tabulating Machine Company. The latter had been founded
some years before by Herman Hollerith, an engineer who invented a machine that would sort and count cards based on the
pattern of holes punched in each.

Hollerith had supplied the U.S. Census Bureau with these
machines for use in the 1890 and 1900 censuses, and the device
was quickly adopted by other organizations in need of rapid
computation. As perfected, the tabulator operated in a simple
three-step manner. Small cards were punched in a variety of
patterns, each one representing a different category of the
subject under survey; the assembled cards were run through a
sorting machine, set to distribute them according to relevant
categories; at the same time an accounting machine kept track
of the results, and, in the later, more sophisticated models,
performed any number of calculations based on those results.

Such a machine found increasing use in a society evolving
rapidly into a largely urban, commercial matrix, where the
ability to monitor and analyze large sums was critical to business profitability. Flint was less interested in Tabulating Machine Company than in the other two members of his new
creation, which in any case got off to a slow start and threatened
to stay that way.

In 1914 Flint hired a new general manager for CTR. Thomas
Watson was already a well-known, if not notorious, figure in
U.S. business. Watson had gone to work for John Patterson at

National Cash Register (NCR) in 1895 and quickly proven himself a quintessential ''NCR man''; bright, aggressive, and loyal, he rose to the position of general sales manager for the entire company in 1910. At Patterson's order, Watson then set up a company whose supposed purpose was to compete with NCR. The company's real purpose, however was to eliminate NCR's competitors. In 1912, along with John Patterson, his former employer at NCR, Watson was convicted of violating the Sherman Antitrust Act on behalf of the company. Shortly after Watson and Patterson were convicted, Patterson fired Watson. Watson was then hired by Charles Flint. Watson never admitted any wrongdoing, and in 1915 the government dropped its case against NCR after the company became famous for its help during a catastrophic flood in its hometown of Dayton, Ohio. The threat of a jail sentence now past, Watson was made president of CTR.

Watson understood immediately that his company's future lay in its tabulating division, and it was there that he committed most of his energy and resources. Scales and clocks were useful items, but the United States would soon be a nation of office workers in need of basic office tools like the tabulator. Watson hired many ex-NCR men and patterned his own well-disciplined sales force along NCR lines—intense competition was combined with equally intense corporate loyalty, and salespeople were courteous, spotlessly dressed, and, above all, understood that CTR sold not a product but a service. A completed sale was just the beginning of the salesman's job; in effect, he had to become a partner in the customer's business, and together they designed a tabulating system for that particular organization.

As was the case at NCR, Watson's sales force became a key factor in his company's success. In a pattern that still holds today, many customers remained loyal because they trusted and to an extent relied upon the CTR salesman's knowledge of their business. Numerous, well-trained, devoted, and well-paid, the CTR sales staff actually dominated the company, ensuring that new technology followed upon the needs of customers and not the reverse. Throughout IBM's history (the company's name was changed to International Business Machines Corporation in 1924) massive and talented sales energy, rather than technological leadership, has kept the company ahead of competitors.

Watson pushed hard in the late 1910s to make CTR the industry leader in tabulating design. He gradually turned back all boardroom challenges to his plans, and by 1925 was both chief executive officer and chief operating officer. In the ten years following Watson's arrival, CTR sales shot up from $4.2 million to a temporary peak of $13 million in 1919, weathered a minor crisis in the early 1920s, and stood poised to ride the booming U.S. economy. The newly named IBM faced some formidable competitors—Remington Rand, Burroughs, and NCR, among others—but from the beginning Watson steered clear of mass-produced, low-priced office products like typewriters and simple adding machines, concentrating instead on the design of large tabulating systems for governmental and private customers. With superior products and a more dedicated sales force, by 1928 IBM was the clear leader in its specialized field and a force in office technology as a whole.

Booming Sales: 1920s–50s

The company was remarkably profitable. In 1928, for example, its profit of $5.3 million was nearly as great as that of giant Remington Rand, though the latter more than tripled IBM's sales of $19.7 million. In 1939, IBM's profit of $9.1 million exceeded that of the next four companies combined, and was an impressive 23 percent of sales.

IBM's business was particularly profitable for several reasons: the company focused on large-scale, custom-built systems, an inherently less competitive segment of the business; IBM's policy of leasing, rather than selling, its machines to customers was very profitable; and IBM maintained cross-licensing agreements dating back to the mid-1910s with its chief competitor, Remington Rand, preventing the two leaders from falling into competitive squabbles. The company required its customers to buy IBM cards for their IBM tabulators. The cards could not be read by any other machine. This last condition made it almost impossible for IBM customers to try other products. With literally millions of such cards already punched, IBM's clients tended to stay put.

The U.S. government filed a suit in 1932 alleging that the IBM-Remington Rand cross-licensing agreement and IBM's exclusive punch card design were anti-competitive. In 1936, after learning that IBM sold nearly 85 percent of all keypunch, tabulating, and accounting equipment in the United States, the Supreme Court ordered IBM to release its customers from all such card restrictions. The Court's decision had little impact on the company's growth, however. Even the Great Depression did not check IBM's progress, as most cash-pressed companies needed more numerical information, not less.

In addition, President Franklin D. Roosevelt's New Deal had created a vast federal bureaucracy in need of the very calculating machines IBM manufactured. In 1935, at the same time the Justice Department was pursuing its case against IBM, the newly formed Social Security Administration placed an order with the company for more than 400 accounting machines and 1,200 keypunchers. The pattern was clear; modern society rested on massive organizations that required machines capable of massive calculations, which were made by IBM. By the end of the 1930s Thomas Watson was enjoying praise for his enlightened employee relations as well as for his ''thinking machines.''

During World War II both private and governmental demand for IBM tabulators increased. The machines were needed to monitor the manufacture and movement of vast resources. Sales boomed, more than tripling to $141.7 million in five years. The war offered IBM another opportunity, less immediately exciting but in the long run of far greater importance. The armed forces needed high-speed calculators to solve a number of military problems relating to ballistics and, later, the development of the atomic bomb. Partly as a result, IBM helped build what might be called the world's first computer, the Mark I. This machine was similar to the first electromechanical calculators built a few years earlier, which used IBM punch cards to work out long arithmetic sums; the Mark I was also capable of retaining a set of rules which could be applied to any later input. Such a memory is one of the essential differences between the calculator and the computer, and the Mark I represented a great step forward. With 765,000 parts and 500 miles of wire, the Mark I still delivered less power than today's hand-held calculator.

Entering the Early Computer Market

Computer design evolved rapidly during the war. IBM joined the partnership building the new Electronic Numerical Integrator and Calculator (ENIAC) at the University of Pennsylvania. ENIAC was useful to the military and gave IBM the experience it needed to proceed with its own electronic machine. When the war ended in 1945, interest in ultra-high-speed calculators died down quickly; few outside the Army needed a room-sized machine designed to analyze howitzer trajectories. Only a handful of scientists continued refining the advances won by ENIAC, eventually creating a more saleable machine called UNIVAC around 1948. When IBM's old rival, Remington Rand, began to market UNIVAC in 1951, it took a significant lead in the new computer business. IBM continued its typically cautious approach. IBM waited until the new product proved its lasting appeal before leaping into the fray. Since it controlled 85 percent of the market for which computers were targeted, and because even electronic computers then still used IBM punch cards, Watson was not especially alarmed by Rand's success.

Heir apparent Thomas Watson, Jr. strongly favored an all-out push into the computer market. By the time he became president in 1952, he had won the power struggle with his father and led IBM into an immense research program designed to surpass Rand. The new president staked his reputation—as well as a significant portion of IBM's assets—on the computer campaign, which had paid off by 1955 with the success of IBM's new 705 general purpose business computer. By the following year Remington Rand had already lost its lead. It was no surprise that IBM came to dominate in computers so quickly, since at that time the computer business was only a small segment of the officeproducts market, which IBM continued to control. The 85 percent of offices using IBM tabulating equipment simply switched over to IBM computers.

In 1949 Thomas Watson's younger brother, Dick Watson, was also brought into the business. The 30-year-old Dick Watson was named president of IBM World Trade Corporation, the parent company's new subsidiary for international sales. In 1949 World Trade had sales of only $6.3 million but operated in 58 countries. In the more important of these countries World Trade set up a subsidiary to market IBM products and even do additional research and development. As the world's industrial powers awoke to the computer age, they found themselves greeted by IBM. It was not unusual for local IBM units to achieve market domination comparable to that of the parent company in the United States. Only in Japan and the United Kingdom were local competitors able to match IBM's presence, forcing the latter to settle for around 33 percent of the market. Barely on the sales map in 1949, World Trade eventually surpassed IBM domestic in total revenue.

Meanwhile, the U.S. computer business filled up with potential rivals. Some of these, like RCA, General Electric, and the newly merged Sperry Rand, were as large as or larger than IBM and should have been able to mount a serious challenge. In every case, however, competitors either lacked an adequate sales organization or were not fully committed to the commercial computer business. RCA, for example, made important contributions to computer technology, but mainly with an eye toward possible applications in its growing television business. Sperry Rand, on the other hand, still controlled the successful UNIVAC machine but was hopelessly behind IBM in sales experience and customer loyalty.

In 1952 the government filed a second, more ambitious antitrust suit against IBM. In 1956 IBM entered into a consent decree which ordered it to divest many of its card-production facilities, sell its machines as well as lease them, submit to certain cross-licensing agreements, and create a subsidiary to compete with itself in the service end of the business. None of these injunctions limited IBM's success, but the 1957 appearance of a small company called Control Data did.

IBM Computer Dominance Through the 1970s

Control Data Corporation (CDC) was a pioneer in niche specialization in the computer world. This tactic seemed to be the only way to compete successfully with IBM. The newcomer made very large, very fast computers for scientific and governmental users in need of maximum crunching power, and after a brief battle, IBM largely ceded the field to CDC. IBM's bread and butter remained the medium to large business computer.

In 1958 Sperry Rand and Control Data brought out the first second-generation computers, which used transistors instead of vacuum tubes. No sooner had IBM met this challenge with its own line of transistorized machines, than it faced the arrival of the industry's third generation—integrated circuitry. Once again IBM lagged in technological change as Honeywell and CDC brought out the first integrated circuit units in the early 1960s, but this time Big Blue's response necessitated a companywide revolution. Integrated circuitry was clearly destined to become the industry standard, and IBM decided to bring out a complete line of such computers. After an unprecedented capital-spending program involving six new plants and many thousands of new workers, the company introduced its 360 line in April 1965. Small, fast, and accompanied by a new set of exclusive software, the 360s were an immediate and lasting success, remaining the worldwide computer leader for more than a decade.

Sperry Rand, GE, Burroughs, RCA, Honeywell, NCR, and Control Data were unable to close the gap between themselves and IBM, which now delivered 65 percent of all U.S. computers. Control Data filed yet another antitrust suit in 1968, charging that IBM had sold ''phantom'' computers to its customers to keep them from placing orders for superior CDC products. The government filed its own suit the following year, supporting CDC's claims and alleging other monopolistic practices. Encouraged by these efforts, IBM's competitors, big and small, filed 22 similar lawsuits in the next few years. IBM beat back every one of them, however, with one exception. The U.S. Justice Department continued its battle for 13 years, until President Ronald Reagan's administration dropped the suit shortly before a ruling was expected.

Niche specialization was clearly the only way to survive in the face of IBM's power. In 1960 Digital Equipment Corporation (DEC) brought out a relatively small, inexpensive computer designed for researchers, effectively creating the microcomputer business. Micros were only a further step in the evolution of the computer, but IBM chose not to enter the market. DEC was soon joined by a host of other micro manufacturers offering a wide range of computers for ever smaller tasks, culminating years later in Apple's marketing of the personal computer for home use. IBM failed to join this race until 1980, at which late date it was unable to dominate the market, as it did mainframes and minicomputers.

In 1971 Tom Watson retired from IBM after suffering a heart attack. His successor, Frank Cary, remained in charge until 1981, at which time John Opel was named CEO. Under these men and IBM's present chairman, John Akers, the 360 line of computers grew into the 370, sales continued to climb, and in the golden year of 1984 corporate earnings reached a staggering $6.6 billion on revenue of $46 billion. With a return on shareholders equity of 25 percent, IBM was the unchallenged favorite of Wall Street and perceived by many in Washington as the only U.S. company able to hold its own against Japanese competition. The firm was profiled in a best-selling book as a paradigm of business excellence.

Losing Ground in the 1980s

The years following were not nearly so kind to IBM. A drop in earnings for 1985 was dismissed as inevitable after the glory year of 1984, but by the end of the decade financial analysts were convinced that IBM was in need of an overhaul. Revenue growth was slow and earnings weak by IBM standards, resulting in a long decline in the company's stock price, and its share of the worldwide computer market had fallen from 36 percent to 23 percent. Chairman Akers responded by cutting his workforce by 32,000 (from a 1985 peak of 405,000) and urged a return to IBM's traditional strength in marketing and customer relations. After a good year in 1990, however, revenue in 1991 fell for the first time since the 1940s and Akers was widely quoted as saying that the company faced a crisis.

By historical standards, he was correct: Big Blue was losing ground. The dip in revenues could be explained as part of the severe 1990–91 recession that took its toll on the entire computer industry, but clearly IBM was no longer the juggernaut it had been during most of its history. Underlying its sluggish growth and net was a fundamental change in the nature of the computer industry, and that was change itself, the continually accelerating rate of technological breakthrough in the world of data process-

ing. So long as computers had remained primarily large and very expensive machines designed for number crunching (mainframes), it was possible for IBM to keep its dominant position by simply building bigger and faster machines.

The increasing power of semiconductor chips changed all of that, however; computers became smaller and were applied to a greatly broadened range of tasks. The mini, micro, and work station technologies all tended to undercut the value of monolithic mains, and independent breakthroughs now tended to focus on software and the crucial problem of networks, the means by which computers communicate with each other and with other forms of data transmission such as telephone and video. Sheer computing power remained important, of course, but it became available in a far greater range of machines at prices that dropped every week.

Given these changes, IBM faced a vastly more complex marketplace both in terms of niches and in the number of its competitors around the world. A wide consensus of observers agreed that IBM's enormous size was a drawback in the quicksilver markets of the 1990s, and in November 1991 Chairman Akers announced the dawn of a new era at the company. Each division of IBM would become a semi-detached business, responsible for its own decisions and bottom-line results. The details of this centrifugal structure transformed IBM into becoming a type of holding company with possibly dozens of discrete operating units under its loose administration. It was hoped that IBM's PC (personal computer) division, for example, would be better able to respond to customer needs and a changing marketplace than when it was forced to take its decisions to company headquarters before acting; and similarly with IBM's mains, minis, software, maintenance, and the many other parts of this $70 billion-per-year corporation.

New Management in the Mid-1990s

Akers had sold the copier division to Kodak in 1988 and followed up in 1991 with the sale of Lexmark, IBM's typewriter, personal printer, keyboard, and supplies business. The divestiture plan had not progressed far, however, when Akers was fired in 1993 and replaced by Lou Gerstner, former CEO of RJR Nabisco. Gerstner scrapped the plan and set about revitalizing the company.

Turning IBM's size and diversity to its advantage, Gerstner expanded the company's small services division, making it a place customers could come for network solutions. By recommending products appropriate for each customer rather than simply pushing IBM goods, Global Services grew rapidly. By 1995 it surpassed Electronic Data Systems (EDS) to become the largest computer services business in the world.

One of the divisions slated to be sold in the divestiture plan was IBM Research, notorious for its long-term research into technologies that never were translated into saleable products. With an $8.9 billion loss in 1993, IBM was searching for costs to cut. Gerstner, however, refused to sell off the division, although he did trim the $6 billion budget by $1 billion. Researchers were also instructed to spend more time working directly with customers, focusing on solutions for real customer problems. The changes led to the resignation of many of the company's scientists. Despite the new focus on the bottom line, the research division continued to lead the industry in patents each year through the 1990s.

By 1994 Gerstner's turnaround strategy was already bearing fruit: The company posted a profit for the first time since 1990. IBM was helped in its recovery in the mid-1990s by the massive growth of the Internet. Although the company abandoned its browser and sold its Prodigy online service, the company benefited from the Internet boom through sales of the big servers needed to run it. IBM also began helping customers move onto the Internet by helping them create web sites and establishing e-commerce.

In the mid-1990s IBM moved into new areas of the computing industry. In 1994 it signed an agreement with Cyrix to manufacture its computer chips. The following year it purchased Lotus Development, a software company best known for its office software, for $3.5 billion. IBM saw the company's Notes groupware, designed to help a company's staff communicate more effectively, as helpful in its foray into networked desktop computing. Remaining at its Boston headquarters, Lotus continued as an independently run subsidiary, with very little interference from IBM. With IBM's resources and distribution network supporting Lotus, Notes users rose from two million in 1995 to 22 million by 1998. IBM benefited by including the Lotus software in a package of applications called eSuite. In 1996 IBM gave a boost to its software planning for networks by purchasing Tivoli Systems Inc., which specialized in creating tools for network management.

By 1996 IBM's recovery seemed solid, with a rise in its market value of $50 billion since 1993. The company's image got a boost in 1997 when its computer Deep Blue won a six-game chess match against World Class Champion Garry Kasparov. The computer, which used huge amounts of parallel processing, could evaluate 200 million chess moves a second, a processing capability the company hoped could be used in such endeavors as weather forecasting and modeling financial data.

IBM continued to expand via new product development and acquisitions through the late 1990s. In 1997 the company bought Unison Software, which specialized in managing computer systems, and in 1998 purchased CommQuest Technologies, a designer and manufacturer of wireless communications chips. Other smaller purchases included a majority holding in site development software company NetObjects in 1998 and NUMA systems expert Sequent Computer Systems in 1999.

The company's shift to providing services had progressed well by the late 1990s. Services accounted for 29 percent of IBM's revenues in 1998 and 39 percent of pretax profits.

Principal Subsidiaries

CADAM Inc.; Lotus Development Corporation; Tivoli Systems, Inc.; IBM Personal Computer Company; Resource Inc.; Compagnie IBM France, S.A.; IBM Canada Ltd.; IBM Credit Corporation; Unison Software, Inc.; WTC Insurance Corporation.

Principal Divisions

IBM Application Solutions; IBM Enterprise Systems; IBM Personal Systems; IBM Programming Systems; IBM Real Estate & Construction Division; IBM Research Division; IBM Systems Integration Division; IBM Technology Products.

Further Reading

"Blue Is the Colour," *Economist,* June 6, 1998.
DeLamarter, Richard Thomas, *Big Blue: IBM's Use and Abuse of Power,* New York: Dodd, Mead & Company, 1986.
Kirkpatrick, David, "IBM: From Big Blue Dinosaur to E-Business Animal," *Fortune,* April 26, 1999, pp. 116–27.
"The New IBM," *Business Week,* December 16, 1991.
Sobel, Robert, *IBM: Colossus in Transition,* New York: Times Books, 1981.
Watson, Thomas J., Jr., *Father, Son, and Company: My Life at IBM and Beyond,* New York: Bantam Books, 1990.

—Jonathan Martin
—updated by Susan Windisch Brown

Ispat International N.V.

Rotterdam Bldg.
Aert van Nesstraat 45
3012 CA Rotterdam
The Netherlands
(31) 10-404-6738
Fax: (31) 10-404-8004
Web site: http://www.ispatinternational.com

Public Subsidiary of the LNM Group
Incorporated: 1976
Employees: 15,000
Sales: US$3.49 billion (1998)
Stock Exchanges: New York Amsterdam
Ticker Symbols: IST US; IST NA
NAIC: 331111 Steel Mills

In just ten years Ispat International N.V. has grown from an obscure fringe company to become one of the top four steelmakers in the world. Led by Calcutta, India's Lakshmi Mittal, registered in the Netherlands but more or less run from the company's London office, Ispat (the Hindi word for ''steel'') is also the industry's first global steel manufacturer, with operations in the United States, Ireland, Mexico, Canada, the Caribbean, Germany, and France. Ispat specializes in low-cost, high-quality steel produced using Direct-reduced Iron (DRI) in the company's minimill-equipped plants. Ispat is also the world's leading supplier of DRI and, as one of the pioneers of the technology, is considered to be years in advance of the rest of the industry. The company's DRI capacity is expected to top ten million tons by the year 2000. The company's global operations enable it to respond quickly to industry movements, using its own shipping fleet to reroute shipments of raw materials and finished product—both flat and long steel—according to market forces. Ispat International is part of the Mittal-controlled LNM Group, which also has steel operations in Indonesia and Kazakhstan. The 46-year-old Mittal, through LNM, controls some 80 percent of Ispat's stock, which trades on both the New York and Amsterdam stock exchanges. Ispat's July 1999 purchase of France's Unimetal will add some 1.5 million tons to the company's production and more than US$800 million to the company's annual sales of US$3.49 billion.

A 21st-Century Carnegie

Lakshmi Mittal was born to be a steel magnate. Growing up in Calcutta, Mittal went to work part-time for his father, Mohan Mittal, owner of several small-scale steel mills in India. By the age of 19, Mittal had already participated in setting up a new mill, while earning a university degree in business and accounting from Calcutta's St. Xavier College. In 1971, at the age of 21, Mittal joined one of his father's mills—a small operation that produced only about 20,000 tons per year—as a trainee. From the beginning, Mittal worked at improving production quality while reducing costs, both necessary components when operating as a private producer in the developing region.

The ambitious Mittal soon chafed under India's tight quota limits on private steel production. Mittal also sought to branch out on his own, if not to leave the family's small steel empire, then to expand it. In 1975 Mohan Mittal agreed to open a new mill in Jakarta, Indonesia, with Lakshmi placed at the head of operations. The mill, at 65,000 tons annual output, was still tiny but gave the young Mittal the launchpad from which to build his own steel empire. In 1976, Lakshmi Mittal formed his own company, Ispat International, giving a clear indication of his intention: that of building the world's first truly international steel producer. As Mittal told the *Wall Street Journal*, ''I always believed in doing something unique, and I felt the opportunities for me in India were limited. Steel has been my strength, and I always wanted to build my steel company, to create the largest global steel company.''

Over the next decade, Mittal greatly expanded production at the Jakarta mill, eventually increasing output to more than 550,000 tons per year. Mittal was also putting into place the technology and strategy that later enabled him to vastly expand his steel empire. The first decision Mittal took was to base the Jakarta plant on the relatively recent electric-arc minimill process. Unlike traditionally, fully integrated steel works, which used huge blast furnaces, minimills were smaller production

Company Perspectives:

Ispat International's philosophy is to channel personal and organisational energies needed to attack and transform global challenges and opportunities into world class performance. Each subsidiary is growth driven and benefits from highly entrepreneurial local management, with proven track records and skills in managing change and integrating diverse cultures. Ispat International's aggressive growth is driven and supported by cumulative experience gained from significant performance improvements at each subsidiary, and its advanced expertise in acquisition management. This is a source of genuine competitive advantage, equipping Ispat International to acquire companies which others would often not even consider.

units providing a lower-cost entry and more flexible setup. Mittal's use of a minimill for his Jakarta plant—and his accountant's urge to reduce costs while maintaining high quality standards—led him next to investigate alternative raw material sources.

Minimills relied almost entirely on scrap steel as raw production material (blast furnaces traditionally used pig iron). Mittal correctly predicted that, with the rising numbers of minimills in the steel industry, prices for scrap steel would quickly rise as well. Mittal began looking for a different type of raw material to feed his steel mill. In the early 1980s, Mittal read of a new potential raw material source, Direct-reduced Iron (DRI). DRI was formed, as its name indicated, directly from iron ore using a special treatment process that allowed for the smelting of iron ore, eliminating the oxygen, without melting. Producing DRI was much less expensive than other raw material processes, giving cost advantages on the order of 40 to 50 percent.

In 1983 Mittal converted his steel works to DRI, buying from the state-run Trinidad & Tobago steel plants, which were among the world's largest producers, for shipping to Jakarta. Over the next several years, Mittal worked on perfecting the DRI process—a non-proprietary process, but nonetheless one that was described as difficult to implement. Using DRI enabled Mittal to cut his raw materials costs nearly in half and to increase production more than tenfold. By the late 1980s, Ispat International's pockets were swelling rapidly.

Forging a Steel Empire in the 1990s

Ispat remained a decidedly minor player throughout the 1980s. But Mittal was developing the strategy that would make him one of the most powerful figures in the global steel industry by the end of the 1990s. Where others in the steel industry found themselves crippled by the recession in the late 1980s, Mittal found opportunity.

Mittal's quest began with his Trinidad & Tobago DRI suppliers. In typical state-run fashion, the Trinidad & Tobago plants were poorly run, loosing more than $80 million per year.

As Mittal described the situation to *Forbes*: ''They weren't paying attention to improving the technology, and they were really not bothered because it was a state-run company.'' As the steel industry—and the global economy in general—collapsed at the end of the 1980s, however, Mittal saw his opportunity. Quietly, Mittal negotiated with the Trinidad mill to take over its lease and operations for ten years—with an option to buy out the mill after five years. The Trinidad & Tobago government agreed, and Mittal and his management team moved in to put order in the house.

It took Mittal only one year to turn the steel plant around and achieve an operating profit. Mittal's formula was also becoming clear: reducing costs, including layoffs, while shipping steel to where Ispat could find the best price. Ispat, however, was not merely content to reduce costs; the company also began intensive investments aimed at modernizing and expanding production. The Trinidad plant not only gave Mittal a new jewel in the crown, it also gave him access to one of the world's largest suppliers of DRI—with production at the time of around seven million tons annually—enabling Ispat to achieve still lower costs. Ultimately, Mittal was able to produce finished steel product at less than the price most of his competitors were paying for their raw stock.

Ispat exercised its option to buy the Trinidad plant in 1994, for the price of $73 million plus the promise of at least an additional $74 million in capital investment over three years. Ispat directly set to work to reduce its costs still further, including employee cutbacks that brought on an extended steelworkers strike. The Trinidad purchase, renamed Ispat Caribbean, by then joined another key component of the emerging Ispat empire. Ispat's revenues grew to $440 million by the end of 1992.

In 1992 Ispat paid the Mexican government $220 million for its Sicarsta steel mills, the country's third largest, but bankrupt, mill built in the 1980s for some $2 billion. The purchase also gave Ispat access to that plant's DRI production; the company also bought shares in the country's DRI mining operations, making Ispat effectively the world's largest DRI producer. Once again, Ispat's management rushed in and began reducing the Mexican plant's costs while boosting production. Ispat quickly turned around the Sicarsta operations, renamed Ispat Mexico, taking production from only 25 percent of capacity to 110 percent of capacity, as expansion continued through the 1990s.

After buying the Trinidad plant, Ispat identified its next acquisition target: Canada's Sidbec-Dosco. That purchase was achieved in 1994. The next year, Mittal and Ispat reorganized. Until 1995, the company had remained part of Mohan Mittal's India-based empire, which had grown beyond its steel core to become one of India's most prominent conglomerates. In that year, Mohan and Lakshmi agreed to break off the younger Mittal's Ispat operations, reforming them into a separate company, which Lakshmi, already living in London, registered in the Netherlands. The Trinidad, Mexico, and Canada operations were grouped under Ispat International, which in turn was placed under Mittal's LNM Group, which also included the original Indonesian operations. The following year, Mittal would add to the LNM Group with the acquisition of the giant Karmet, Kazakhstan steel plant, another money loser, for some $300 million. Mittal again slashed costs—including some

20,000 of the plant's 85,000 workers—and took the plant off its traditional barter system of payments. Once again, Mittal quickly brought profitability to a former state-run operation. At the same time, LNM bought up the former government-run steel mill in Hamburg, Germany. This purchase was soon followed by the acquisition of Irish Steel, the only steel plant in Ireland. The purchase price was entirely symbolic, although Ispat agreed to take on Irish Steel's millions in debt.

While LNM was beginning to diversify its operations, including building a worldwide shipping fleet and entering the fuel industry, Ispat International concentrated on its steady drive to global prominence. In 1997 Ispat, seeking to boost its presence in the German and European long steel market, acquired the ailing wire rod and other long product divisions of Germany's Thyssen AG. The Ruhr Valley plants, renamed Ispat Stahlwerk Ruhrort and Ispat Walzdraht Hochfeld, cost Ispat just $16.4 million.

In August 1997, Ispat blasted into the steel industry's headlines when it placed an initial public offering of 20 percent of its shares (Mittal himself held the remaining 80 percent, through the LNM Group) on the New York and Amsterdam stock exchanges. The IPO, valued at nearly $780 million, was the largest public offering ever in the steel industry. By then Mittal, who had boosted company revenues to nearly $2.5 billion, with profits of some $140 million, had so impressed the industry that the IPO was eight times oversubscribed.

The boost in capital gave Ispat the ammunition for its next acquisition. The company placed its bets on acquiring the Sidor steelworks from the Venezuelan government. However, Mittal's acquisition strategy had started to catch on among the industry. Previously, Ispat had been able to make unrivaled bids for its other acquisitions. In the second half of the 1990s, however, as more and more governments began looking to sell off their often money-losing steel operations, others began to see the opportunity for relatively low-cost entry in the industry. Ispat lost its bid for Sicor, to a consortium of investors who paid $2 billion.

Ispat barely blinked at the loss. Instead, in 1998 it reached an agreement to purchase Inland Steel. Departing from its low-cost acquisition position, Ispat paid $1.43 billion for the East Chicago, Indiana-based steelmaker, one of the world's largest single operations. The Inland acquisition, renamed Ispat Inland,

bolted Ispat International into the world's top ten steel producers; with the addition of LNM Group's holdings, Mittal now found himself in charge of one of a steel empire, with annual production of some 19 million tons. Ispat International's truly global operations were also an anomaly in the traditionally domestic-based and domestic market-focused steel industry.

Ispat's acquisition drive continued in 1999, when the company agreed to purchase the Unimetal and other steel production subsidiaries from France's Usinor conglomerate, adding more than $700 million to Ispat's annual sales. Despite increasing competition for new acquisitions, Ispat remained confident that its carefully planned policy of growth through acquisition could continue into the 21st century. As Mittal himself began to diversify his interests—including joining a U.K.-based satellite television partnership—he also began to groom his most likely successor, son Aditya, aged 24 and a graduate of the Wharton School of Business, who had already taken a key position in the company's all-important mergers and acquisitions team.

Principal Subsidiaries

Ispat Inland (U.S.A.); Irish Ispat Limited; Ispat Caribbean Limited; Ispat Mexicana S.A. de C.V.; Ispat Sidbec Inc. (Canada); Ispat Hamburger Stahlwerke Gmbh (Germany); Ispat Stahlwerk Ruhrort GmbH (Germany); Ispat Walzdracht Hochfeld GmbH (Germany); Ispat Unimetal (France); Ispat Trefileurope (France); Ispat SMR (France).

Further Reading

Adams, Chris, Jonathan Karp, and Lawrence Ingrassia, ''Carnegie's Heir? How Calcutta Business Became a Global Player in the Steel Industry,'' *Wall Street Journal,* March 18, 1998.

''The Carnegie from Calcutta,'' *Economist,* January 10, 1998.

Dolan, Kerry A., ''Carnegie Would Be Jealous,'' *Forbes,* August 23, 1999.

Evans, Richard, ''Showing Its Mettle,'' *Barron's*, November 24, 1997.

Lanchner, David, ''Dragging Steel into the Global Era,'' *Global Finance,* May 1, 1998.

Mehta, Manik, ''Steel's Still-Growing Giant,'' *Industry Week,* January 18, 1999.

Tait, Nikki, and Stefan Wagstyle, ''Gazelle Among the Elephants,'' *Financial Times*, March 19, 1998.

Tomlinson, Richard, ''Metal Guru,'' *Independent,* August 25, 1999, p. 1F.

—M. L. Cohen

Jaco Electronics, Inc.

145 Oser Avenue
Hauppauge, New York 11788
U.S.A.
(516) 273-5500
(800) 966-JACO; (800) 966-5226
Fax: (516) 273-5506
Web site: http://www.jacoelectronics.com

Public Company
Incorporated: 1961
Employees: 540
Sales: $153.7 million (fiscal 1998)
Stock Exchanges: NASDAQ
Ticker Symbol: JACO
NAIC: 334112 Computer Storage Device Manufacturing;
    42169 Other Electronic Parts & Equipment
    Wholesalers; 541512 Computer Systems Design
    Services

Jaco Electronics, Inc. is a marketer and distributor of electronic components and computer peripherals. The company distributes more than 60,000 items from stock, including semiconductors, capacitors, resistors, electromechanical devices, and computer subsystems, for use in manufacturing and assembling such electronic products as computers and data-transmission, telecommunications, and transportation equipment. It also manufactures printed circuit boards under contract and provides a variety of value-added services, including configuring computer systems and other components to customer specifications.

Prosperity, Then Overexpansion: 1961–82

Joel and Charles Girsky founded Jaco (an acronym for Joel and Charles Organization) in 1961 in a two-truck, 400-square-foot Brooklyn garage. The start-up capital of $13,000 came from the life insurance policy of their deceased father. While their competitors were handling a wide range of electronic components, the Girsky brothers decided to distribute only capacitors: small devices used in virtually all electronic equipment to store electric energy and release it in prescribed amounts at selected times.

Jaco, in 1968, established Semiconductors Concepts, Inc., a subsidiary for the distribution and sale of semiconductors, such as transistors and diodes, used to generate, control, or amplify electronic signals in a broad variety of electronic equipment. Also in 1968, Jaco expanded to the West Coast by opening a sales headquarters and warehouse in Chatsworth, California.

Jaco made its initial public offering in 1970, raising $1.2 million by selling common stock at $7.50 per share. Sales rose from $5.1 million in fiscal 1969 (the year ended June 30, 1969) to $8.9 million for fiscal 1971. Net income rose from $285,000 to $382,000 during the same period. The company now was based in Hauppauge, Long Island. By 1970 Jaco Electronics was the largest marketer of capacitors in the United States, and by 1972 the largest in the world. The ten-pound devices it distributed could be found on the desks of over 2,500 purchasing agents and managers of electronic equipment.

In 1972 Semiconductor Concepts, Inc., was marketing semiconductors; Jaco International Ltd., electronic components sold to foreign markets; and Rampart Components, Inc., electronic parts as an exclusive distributor under license from recognized manufacturers. Jaco's customers included industrial giants such as DuPont, Boeing, Lockheed, General Electric, Burroughs, Honeywell, IBM, RCA, Control Data, Chrysler, Westinghouse, and Texas Instruments.

Jaco Electronics was highly valued by its customers for service. Its catalog of capacitors was often referred to as the "bible" of the electronics industry, with military and commercial specifications for more than 50,000 capacitors. A survey found that, without exception, clients interviewed said the company's pricing was competitive and its inventory and delivery schedules superior to the competition. Jaco's managers and personnel were especially praised for their willingness to troubleshoot and solve any problem that might arise in the normal course of operations. "Today isn't soon enough" was the corporate slogan. When Jaco offered, in a trade paper, a free

---

Company Perspectives:

Blending a full line of electronic components, semiconductors, sub-assemblies, and value-added services, Jaco will continue to offer a full-service solution to our customers needs. Jaco is committed to offering established and new technology introduction services to our customer base regardless of size; providing our customers with a high level of speed and efficiency to service their needs by utilizing a well-trained, professional resource team dedicated to service, technology and competitiveness; being the most valuable, viable and innovative partner to our customers and suppliers. Our message is to add value to our suppliers by increasing their market position through adding value to our customers.

---

poster to respondents, more than 20,000 requests were received from around the world.

By the mid-1970s Jaco Electronics had greatly expanded its leased space in Hauppauge and Woodland Hills, California. It earned record net income of nearly $2 million on net sales of $29.5 million in the fiscal year ended June 30, 1974. With the end of the Vietnam War, however, company revenue, highly dependent on military contracts, began to stagnate and the company lost money in fiscal years 1976, 1977, and 1978. After making a profit on record revenues of $64.8 million in fiscal 1980, the company sustained losses in the next three years, having expanded at a time when the electronics industry was caught in a major recession. As a result, the company found itself flooded with inventory and saddled with enormous overhead.

Restructuring and Consolidation: 1982–90

Charles Girsky, who had moved to the West Coast to handle western operations while remaining president of the company, resigned at the end of 1982 to join Integrated Electronics, a firm that assumed control of Jaco's California and Seattle-area divisions, which directed operations in 11 western states. As a result, Jaco's revenues fell from $60.1 million in fiscal 1982 to $29.7 million in fiscal 1983, and in the latter year it sustained a loss of $4.9 million, which included a $1.6 million writedown for the sale of assets in the West. Financial problems also had forced the company to close operations in Boston; Clifton, New Jersey; and Irvine and San Jose, California, in 1982. Only the Hauppauge headquarters and the Dallas-area office now remained in existence. However, the sale of these assets allowed Jaco to remain solvent and provided the opportunity to consolidate its remaining operations.

An emphasis on cost-cutting enabled Jaco Electronics to operate profitably even though its revenues fell to $28 million in fiscal 1985. Two acquisitions of smaller distributors in the late 1980s and the opening of new satellite offices across the United States allowed the distributor to increase its market share. In 1988 it was representing more than 75 electronics manufacturers, selling through its own sales force and independent representatives to more than 8,000 customers. The company also

profited by receiving most of its products from South Korea and Taiwan rather than from higher-priced Japanese manufacturers. In fiscal 1987 capacitors accounted for 49 percent of Jaco's sales; semiconductors for 16 percent; electromechanical devices and motors for 26 percent; and other products for nine percent.

Jaco's semiconductor product line at this time included integrated circuits (multiple combinations of electronic components), microprocessors, transistors, and diodes. Other products distributed, besides capacitors, were relays, fractional horsepower electric motors, and resistors. Jaco's products were being used in computers, data-transmission, telecommunications, and transportation equipment, automatic controls, other receivers of electronic signals, aircraft, missiles, and a broad variety of other equipment. The company also was performing product assembly of fractional-horsepower electric motors, testing components for certain customers, and providing its customers with technical information about the performance characteristics of electronic components.

By the end of the 1980s, capacitors composed only 40 percent of Jaco's sales. Semiconductors accounted for 35 percent in fiscal 1989, electromechanical devices and motors, 18 percent, and resistor products, seven percent. The company's four largest suppliers—AVX, Globe Motors, Kemet, and Samsung—accounted for 53 percent of its sales. Jaco was the leading U.S. distributor of South Korean semiconductors for Samsung, Hyundai, and Goldstar. The company was the 19th largest distributor of electronics components in the nation, distributing more than 60,000 products from over 75 suppliers at prices ranging from $3 per thousand units to about $2,500 per component. Revenues reached nearly $80 million in fiscal 1990.

Jaco Electronics in the 1990s

Jaco Electronics entered the distribution of computer subsystems, including such items as disk and tape drives, floppy disks, and controllers, when it agreed in late 1989 to purchase Dallas-based Quality Components, Inc. for $2.35 million in cash. Quality, which also handled semiconductor lines and had locations in Texas, Oklahoma, North Carolina, and Georgia, listed an estimated $18 million in annual sales but was losing money, It continued as a subsidiary under the name Jaco/QC. In 1990 the parent company was representing more than 115 electronics manufacturers and selling to over 10,000 customers. Military components, which comprised 75 percent of Jaco's sales in fiscal 1987, represented less than 12 percent of its sales in fiscal 1993.

After a sales dip in the recessionary fiscal 1991 and 1992 years (and a $1 million loss in the former year), Jaco Electronics resumed its growth, adding some product lines and expanding its sales force. One Wall Street investor noted with approval in 1993 that more than half of Jaco's sales were coming from capacitors, electromechanical devices, and resistors, as opposed to semiconductors, which were prone to sudden surges and falls in demand.

Jaco's revenues reached a record $167 million and its net income a record $3.9 million in fiscal 1996. Interviewed by Dennis Garabedian for *Long Island Business News,* Joel Girsky described his company's resurgence in these words: "At the end of 1995 the market got fire hot, fire red. Everyone was buying components. Everybody was buying computers. Everyone was adding modems and with the cellular phone business—nobody thought it would end. Basic motivating factors were greed and fear. When you fear that you can't get enough parts to build your equipment, you overbuy to make sure you always have enough. The balloon gets pumped up and up and up, and ultimately it bursts."

Acquisitions were another factor in Jaco Electronics' growth. In 1994 the company entered the contract manufacturing field by purchasing Vermont-based Nexus Custom Electronics, Inc., a producer of printed circuit boards. Jaco began distributing the complete component line of Vishay Intertechnology in 1995 when it added Dale and Sprague, Vishay's two largest subsidiaries, to its roster of suppliers. During 1996–97 it acquired two more suppliers, QPS Electronics and Corona Electronics, Inc.

Despite this surge in business, Girsky pointed out in the *Long Island Business News* that Jaco Electronics—the 19th largest firm in its field—was dwarfed even on Long Island by Arrow Electronics, with about $7 billion in annual revenues, and Avent, with probably over $5 billion. Setting a goal of doubling sales volume every four years, Girsky indicated that further acquisitions were in the works, probably by paying cash to proprietors who were nearing retirement age. He said he preferred to pay in cash rather than stock because Jaco's stock was trading at only $9 a share, below book value. In 1996 the company raised between $17 million and $20 million from a second public sale of stock, using part of the proceeds to reduce its debt to $7 million.

The cyclical nature of the electronics industry was underlined when Jaco Electronics' sales volume fell in fiscal 1997 and 1998. Net income also fell both years, dropping to $1.2 million in 1998. Other electronics distributors were also suffering because of overcapacity and economic problems in East Asia. Shares of company stock were traded for as little as $2.25 in 1998. For future growth, Jaco was looking to expansion in its share of the rapidly growing market for flat-panel display units.

Of Jaco Electronics' $153.7 million in sales in fiscal 1998, passive components, such as capacitors, resistors, and electromechanical devices, accounted for 52 percent, while active components, including semiconductors and computer subsystems, accounted for 48 percent. The company had distribution facilities in Hauppauge and Westlake Village, California, with the former accounting for about 81 percent of inventory in fiscal 1998. There were 14 sales offices. Kemet and Samsung were Jaco's biggest suppliers, each responsible for more than ten percent of the firm's net sales. In October 1998 Joel Girsky owned 15 percent of Jaco's common stock, while Charles Girsky owned 2.4 percent.

Principal Subsidiaries

Corona Electronics, Inc.; Diatel, Inc.; Jaco Electronics Canada, Inc.; Jaco Overseas, Inc.; Miostrom Inc.; Nexus Custom Electronics, Inc.; Quality Components, Inc.; RC Components, Inc.

Further Reading

Agovino, Theresa, "Savvy at Electronics Firm Begins to Put It in the Chips," *Crain's New York Business,* February 20, 1989, p. 19.

Bambrick, Richard, "Jaco to Divest Western Opns. in $5M-$6.5M Deal," *Electronic News,* November 29, 1982, pp. 1, 16.

Elliott, Heidi, "As the Industry Goes, So Goes Jaco," *Electronic News,* September 7, 1998, p. 48.

Ferguson, Bob, "Jaco Electronics Agrees to Buy Quality Components for $2.35M," *Electronic News,* October 30, 1989, p. 38.

Garabedian, Dennis, "Ernst & Young Spotlight on LI's Public Companies," *Long Island Business News,* June 23, 1997, pp. 34+.

Leff, I. Bernard, "Jaco Electronics, Inc.," *Wall Street Transcript,* May 15, 1972, pp. 28,364–28,365.

Welling, Kathryn M., "Not Trendy," *Barron's,* November 29, 1993, pp. 26, 28.

—Robert Halasz

JD Wetherspoon plc

Wetherspoon House
Central Park
Reeds Cresent
Watford
Hertfordshire WD1 1QH
United Kingdom
(44) 1923-477-777
Fax: (44) 1923-219-810
Web site: http://www.jdwetherspoon.co.uk

Public Company
Incorporated: 1979
Employees: 8,600
Sales: £189 million (US$310.4 million) (1998)
Stock Exchanges: London
NAIC: 722410 Drinking Places (Alcoholic Beverages)

JD Wetherspoon plc is one of the United Kingdom's largest and fastest growing chains of publican houses (pubs). Blending a unique formula of unconventional locations—including former automobile showrooms, theaters, banks, and grocery stores—low beer prices, all-day food service, non-smoking areas, and a strict ban on television and music, JD Wetherspoon operates more than 320 pubs in the United Kingdom. Moreover, with as many as 80 new pub openings a year, JD Wetherspoon is also one of the U.K.'s fastest growing companies. The company expects to run from 1,000 to perhaps 1,400 pubs or more, under such names as The Asparagus, The Spinning Mule, The Isaac Wilson (named after a local teetotaler!), and the Shakespeare's Head. The company is also eyeing plans to bring its successful formula to the European continent, starting with Paris. Wetherspoon is the brainchild of chairman Timothy Martin, age 44, who continues to hold 17 percent of the company and an iron rein on operations. Wetherspoon went public in 1979 and trades on the London Stock Exchange.

Trading One Bar for Another in 1979

English-born, New Zealand-raised Timothy Martin was a 24-year-old graduate law student in London in 1979. Martin had passed the bar, but eyed only halfheartedly a career in law. As Martin told the *Independent* in 1999, "I can only to this day read a law book at three pages an hour. A lot of students could read between 10 and 15 times that rate. By the end of the first term, I had a real inferiority complex." Like many a student, Martin sought solace at the end of a day in London's pubs; yet, for Martin, finding a pub he enjoyed proved difficult. Abandoning his own North London neighborhood, Martin began taking a taxi to a pub he had discovered in the Muswell Hill section. That pub had been converted from a former betting shop—a rarity at the time. The pub also featured a selection of regional beers, also rare, as most pubs remained the property of a small number of national brewers, who, of course, imposed their own products on their pubs' menus.

After learning that the Muswell Hill pub's owner was earning £500 per week, Martin found his calling. In 1979 Martin sold his apartment, which he had bought with a 100 percent mortgage. With the London real estate market then in an upswing, Martin was able to pocket a £10,000 profit on the sale. He then secured a £70,000 eight-year mortgage on the Murray Hill location, with an understanding that he would be able to extend the contract when it came due.

In the meantime, Martin began a crash course in pubtending. His first move was to rename the pub, choosing the name JD Wetherspoon after a schoolmaster in New Zealand. "The least likely person to control a pub because he could not control a class," Martin told the *Independent*. Yet Martin's first day as a pub owner proved inauspicious: "I couldn't unlock the doors to let the cleaner in," Martin explained to the *Independent* in 1996, "and by the time the locksmith had opened them it was 11 o'clock, customers were arriving and it was still a mess from the night before."

Nonetheless, Martin's customers stayed—and soon the former betting shop, at 500 square feet only half the size of the usual pub, had become too small. Martin began looking for a new location; yet the country's pubs were more or less locked up by the national brewers, who were equally resistant to selling to the young Martin. Instead, Martin took his inspiration from his own pub, and began looking at other former retail locations for his next pub. In 1981, Martin opened his second pub in a former automobile showroom. Opening pubs in unlikely loca-

Company Perspectives:

Our Motto—CBSM: Cleanliness, Beer, Service and Mainte-nance—is used as a benchmark of excellence throughout our company.

tions—with later pubs finding homes in former banks, grocery stores, and even well-known locations, such as the famed Marquee nightclub and the Half Moon theater—became a Wetherspoon hallmark.

Throughout the 1980s, Martin continued to refine the Weth-erspoon concept. He soon instituted a chainwide ban on music and television, as well as ridding his pubs of games, such as darts and pool tables, that were traditional facets of the English pub. The company would adopt a similar position with the karaoke and bingo nights that its competitors would adopt over the coming decade. Wetherspoon pubs, each with their own name, often taken from a local personality, became known as places were people could talk, and where they could find not only a wide selection of smaller, regional beer labels, but also cheap prices—as much as 50 pence less than competing houses. Wetherspoon was helped also by the Campaign for Real Ale movement, similar to the microbrewery trend in the United States in the 1990s, that encouraged people to buy the regional brands over the dominant national brands.

By 1983 Wetherspoon, with four pubs, had become profit-able, earning £180,000 in net profits. As Martin wrote in the *Independent* in 1996: ''Had I stopped there I could have said this was a successful business. Instead, Wetherspoon went hell for leather for expansion, adding 40 to 50 percent to sales each year.'' In the summer of 1983, Wetherspoon doubled its num-ber of pubs; from there the company began expanding beyond London. Finding locations continued to prove difficult, as the nation's pubs continued to be locked up by the national giants. Martin's choice of unlikely venues helped the company over-come this hurdle. In addition, the passage in 1989 of the British Monopolies and Mergers commission-inspired Beer Orders brought limits on the number of pubs the national brewers were allowed to own. The opening of the market to outsiders enabled Martin to step up the pace of his company's expansion.

Public Publican in the 1990s

By the early 1990s, Wetherspoon had grown to a national chain of more than 40 pubs. Martin had continued to refine his pub concept, including adding non-smoking areas and handicap accessibility; despite the increased potential to purchase exist-ing pubs, Martin continued to seek out unusual locations for his new pubs, often choosing long-derelict buildings. The unusual choice of location could usually be counted on to give the new Wetherspoon pubs a degree of instant notoriety. While expand-ing and refining his pub concept, Martin had also been careful to expand his management team, telling the *Independent*: ''By far the most important thing I've done is to develop a manage-ment team that can compensate for the shortcomings of the founder.''

Yet Martin remained a decidedly hands-on manager, spend-ing more time on the road visiting his pubs than at the com-pany's headquarters. Martin's approach—he claimed to be in-spired by late Wal-Mart founder Sam Walton—proved unorthodox in other ways. For one, he insisted on open commu-nication among his employees, encouraging managers and other staff to speak up with problems and suggestions, even en-couraging them to attend company board meetings. At the same time, Wetherspoon became well-known for its internal promo-tions: any employee, even maintenance personnel, had the op-portunity to rise in the company ranks.

Martin was soon to become one of the U.K.'s wealthiest individuals. In 1992 Martin took Wetherspoon public, with a listing on the London Stock Exchange. Martin's 17 percent of the company placed him among the country's top 200 wealthi-est people. The influx of capital also allowed the chain to go on a vast expansion drive. In just four years, the company had nearly quadrupled its chain, topping 150 pubs by the end of 1996. The company's policy of buying up unusual locations for its pubs had an additional side effect: as former department stores, theaters, supermarkets, and such, the new Wetherspoons were larger than their competitors. Indeed, the company's aver-age store size during most of the 1990s was 4,100 square feet (scaled down to 3,300 square feet in the later part of the decade). This kind of size enabled the company to achieve the economies of scale that allowed it to offer at least one beer below £1, as the company made up the lost margins in higher turnover.

A flurry of pub and restaurant chain takeovers by the U.K.'s brewing giants—which sought entry into the dining-out mar-ket—led to speculation that Wetherspoon too was being eyed as a takeover target. In order to parry that threat, Wetherspoon quickly stepped up the pace of its pub openings, announcing its intention to open an extra 350 pubs through the year 2001, creating some 10,000 jobs. Indeed, the company began to eye even higher goals—such as eventually raising its number of pubs to some 1,000 to 1,500 in the United Kingdom. Weth-erspoon also began looking into exporting its pub concept to the European continent, with Paris as a potential first target.

By late 1998, the company had again doubled its number of pubs, topping 300 locations throughout the United Kingdom. That year would prove somewhat difficult for Wetherspoon—in part because of Wetherspoon's own policy. Its ''no-television'' rule would cause the company to suffer badly during the weeks of the 1998 World Cup, as customers, in the grip of soccer fever, went elsewhere to view the popular sporting event; the company would not recover until late in the year. Nevertheless, Wetherspoon continued to announce aggressive expansion fore-casts, with plans to add another 80 pubs—at a cost of some £100 million—during 1999.

Along the way, Wetherspoon had backed into the lodging industry. Several of its pub purchases were at former hotel locations. The company decided to maintain the hotel opera-tions in addition to its pub activities, forming the Wetherlodges business unit. By the summer of 1999, the company operated three Wetherlodges properties—the 22-room Shrewsbury Ho-tel, the 26-room Golden Acorn, and the 44-room Yarborough. With occupancy rates of close to 100 percent, the hotel addi-tions were a profitable but tiny addition to the Wetherspoon chain, averaging only £800,000 per year. Nonetheless, it pointed the way to a potential future growth area.

After placing all of its pubs on a single, national menu—with prices fixed for all locations—Wetherspoon continued its fast growth pace. By September 1999, the company had topped 350 pubs, and expected to top 400 pubs by year-end. At 44 years of age, company founder Martin remained solidly at the helm of what had become one of the fastest-growing companies in the United Kingdom. Wetherspoon's unique blend of location, service, and price promised continued appeal to the British pub dweller.

Further Reading

Clarke, Hillary, ''The Barrister Who Was Called to the Bar,'' *Independent on Sunday*, January 10, 1999, p. 24.

Larsen, Peter Thal, ''Time to Buy Another Round of Wetherspoon,'' *Independent*, September 16, 1998, p. 21.

Martin, Tim, ''My Only Experience Was Drinking Three Pints a Night,'' *Independent on Sunday*, April 28, 1996, p. 3.

Osborne, Alistair, ''Wetherspoon Lashes Red Tape and Unveils Frothy Profits,'' *Daily Telegraph*, March 13, 1999.

Palmer, Andrew, ''A Brief History of Time, Caterer and Hotelkeeper,'' June 17–23, 1999, http://www.jdwetherspoon.co.uk.

—M. L. Cohen

JPMorgan

J.P. Morgan & Co. Incorporated

60 Wall Street
New York, New York 10260-0060
U.S.A.
(212) 483-2323
Fax: (212) 648-5213
Web site: http://www.jpmorgan.com

Public Company
Incorporated: 1940
Employees: 15,674
Total Assets: $261.06 billion (1998)
Stock Exchanges: New York Amsterdam Frankfurt
    London Paris Swiss Tokyo
Ticker Symbol: JPM
NAIC: 52211 Commercial Banking; 551111 Offices of
    Bank Holding Companies; 522293 International Trade
    Financing; 52222 Sales Financing

J.P. Morgan & Co. Incorporated is a holding company for entities engaged in a wide range of banking activities worldwide, including corporate finance advisory, securities and trading, trust and agency, and other financial services. J.P. Morgan's clients are principally corporations, governmental bodies, and other financial institutions, although the company also offers a variety of banking and asset management services to wealthy individuals and other organizations. J.P. Morgan's principal banking subsidiary is Morgan Guaranty Trust Company of New York, the product of the 1959 merger between J.P. Morgan and Guaranty Trust Company of New York. The J.P. Morgan name re-emerged in 1968 as the holding company of Morgan Guaranty and a number of other subsidiaries.

Early American Banking: The Legendary John Pierpont Morgan

Alternately one of the most admired and most hated men in the United States, the savior of his country and a robber baron, John Pierpont Morgan, the founder of J.P. Morgan & Company, was a legendary financier who wielded national and international power on a spectacular scale. Morgan did not allow publicity to influence his actions in the slightest degree. Indeed Morgan's confidence in his own ultimate success and his unapologetic arrogance are two legacies he handed down to the company that bears his name.

Morgan's father, Junius Spencer Morgan, an American, became a partner in the influential London banking firm of George Peabody and Company in 1854, changing the name of the company to J.S. Morgan & Co. when Peabody retired and he took over in 1864. (Today that firm is Morgan Grenfell.) The firm soon became one of the most important links between London and the rapidly developing American financial community. J.P. Morgan entered his father's banking house in 1854 at the age of 17. In 1857 he was sent to work for the firm Duncan, Sherman & Co. in New York, the New York correspondent of his father's firm. In 1860, Morgan left Duncan, Sherman and founded J.P. Morgan and Company to act as agent for his father's company. In 1864 J.P. Morgan asked Charles H. Dabney to be senior partner in a new firm, which became Dabney, Morgan & Co.

Morgan first drew the attention of the business community in 1869, when he successfully battled Jay Gould and James Fisk, two notorious American financial buccaneers, for control of the Albany and Susquehanna Railroad. In 1871 Dabney retired and Anthony J. Drexel, the head of the Philadelphia investment bank Drexel & Co., became Morgan's new senior partner in a firm called Drexel Morgan & Co.

In 1879, Morgan arranged to sell $25 million worth of the Vanderbilt interest in New York Central Railroad through his father's firm in England. Vanderbilt was impressed enough to give Morgan a seat on the board of directors of New York Central. Six years later Morgan used this position to settle a dispute between the New York Central and Pennsylvania railroads over the New York, West Shore and Buffalo Railroad. It was senseless, Morgan argued, for Pennsylvania and New York Central to engage in a rate war. He suggested that the Pennsylvania should allow the Central to buy the West Shore line and that the Central should turn over control of the South Pennsylvania to the Pennsylvania Railroad. They quickly agreed.

Company Perspectives:

We are committed to offering advice and execution of the highest quality, conducting our business in a principled way, and maintaining the global market presence that helps our clients succeed while enhancing returns for our stockholders.

In 1886 Morgan implemented reorganization plans for both the Philadelphia and Reading Railroad and the Chesapeake and Ohio Railroad. A short time later, he also played a major role in reorganizing the Baltimore and Ohio. After the Interstate Commerce Act was passed in 1887, Morgan helped to convince the country's railroad executives to abide by the law and cooperate with the Interstate Commerce Commission. After the Panic of 1893 Morgan was called upon by the government to reorganize a number of the leading railway systems in the nation, including the Southern, the Erie, the Philadelphia and Reading, and the Northern Pacific. By the end of the century, only two U.S. systems were outside his control.

When Junius Morgan died in 1890, J.P. Morgan became head of the London house. Three years later, in 1893, Anthony Drexel also died, and in 1895 Morgan reorganized the Morgan and Drexel firms. New York-based Drexel Morgan became J.P. Morgan & Co., into which the Philadelphia-based Drexel & Co. was partially merged. At the same time, Drexel, Harjes & Co., Drexel's prominent Paris-based investment banking business, was renamed Morgan, Harjes & Co. At the head now of houses in New York, Philadelphia, London, and Paris, Morgan was a commanding figure in international finance.

At the time, Morgan was still relatively unknown to most of his fellow Americans, but not for long. In 1895 President Grover Cleveland turned to the international bankers for help in stemming the flow of the treasury's gold reserves that had followed the panic of 1893. Morgan, with his connections to the European banking community, helped supply the government with $56 million in gold, much of it from abroad, and profited handsomely on the transaction. The public protest that followed, fueled among other things by Morgan's refusal to reveal his profits to a Congressional investigative committee, contributed to Cleveland's fall from power in 1896.

Although Morgan had now become one of the most vilified men in the United States, his power was only enhanced by the constant publicity. Having organized the railroads and guided the infant Edison Electric Company through its early years, culminating in its merger with the Thomson-Houston Electric Company to create the General Electric Company in 1891, Morgan next turned to the steel industry. In the late 1890s he helped create the Federal Steel Company, the National Tube Company, and the American Bridge Company. The house of Morgan was also instrumental in arranging the takeover of the giant Carnegie Steel Company to form the U.S. Steel Corporation in 1901. A year later, Morgan financed the consolidation of McCormick Harvesting Machine Company, Deering Company,

and three other harvesting machine companies into the giant International Harvester Company.

Also in 1902 Morgan organized the International Mercantile Marine Company, a combination of British and American shipping concerns, to stabilize the shipping trade as his railroad combinations had done. It was one of his rare failures. At the same time, Morgan's image was also sullied in a fight for control of the North Pacific Railroad.

During the panic of 1907, however, government officials and important bankers quickly turned to Morgan for leadership, and the secretary of the treasury deposited substantial government relief funds with J.P. Morgan and its affiliate banks.

As he grew older, Morgan continued to consolidate his influence in a number of fields, particularly banking and insurance. Morgan owned a controlling interest in First National Bank of New York and his bank's future partner, Guaranty Trust Company of New York, and was influential in many other prominent New York banks. He already had a significant voice in the administration of the New York Life Insurance Company when he gained a controlling interest in the Equitable Life Assurance Society in 1909.

It was fear of the power of this "money trust" within the New York banking and insurance community, firmly anchored by Morgan, that instigated a Congressional investigation in 1912 by the Pujo Committee. The committee revealed that if all the Morgan partners and the directors of First National, Bankers Trust, and Guaranty Trust were added together, this group of businessmen held 341 directorships in 112 banking, insurance, transportation, public utility, and trading companies with resources of more than $22 billion.

When J.P. Morgan died in 1913, J.P. Morgan, Jr., known as Jack, became the head of the family business. Jack Morgan continued his father's work, dealing with industry, railroads, banks, and other financial institutions, but he also made his own reputation in government financing. As the most important international banking house in the United States, Morgan became the U.S. agent for the French and British governments during World War I, handling orders for more than $3 billion in war supplies before the United States itself entered the war. Morgan also organized a group of more than 2,000 banks to underwrite bonds totaling some $1.5 billion for Great Britain and France.

Postwar Years

After the war ended, J.P. Morgan & Co. was more powerful than ever. Before the war, the firm's European connections were crucial in bringing capital to a developing America; in the postwar era, however, the United States became a creditor nation and the most important financial market in the world, and Morgan was its leading banker. Continuing to improve its reputation in government financing and the recapitalization of national debts, the bank floated bond issues between 1917 and 1926 totaling nearly $12 billion for Austria, Cuba, Canada, Germany, Belgium, France, Great Britain, and Italy.

When the stock market crashed on October 22, 1929, J.P. Morgan & Co. was again behind a major attempt to avert financial disaster. Five important bankers met in Jack Morgan's office on October 24, 1929 to create a pool to preserve some order in the stock market and stave off disaster. Not only were they unsuccessful, but afterwards J.P. Morgan and the other companies involved were kept under close governmental supervision to determine whether they contributed to the stock market crash.

During the 1930s J.P. Morgan underwent drastic changes. The Banking Act of 1933, better known as the Glass-Steagall Act, required a separation of deposit and investment banking. As a result, the following year J.P. Morgan & Co. left the investment banking business and became a private commercial bank. Three Morgan partners left the bank in 1935 to create a new investment banking firm, Morgan Stanley & Company, to handle the business Morgan had been forced to abandon. Although Jack Morgan continued as head of the commercial bank, by the mid-1930s most of its actual management was left to other partners.

In 1940 J.P. Morgan and Company was incorporated as a state bank under the laws of New York and it began the sale of common stock on the New York exchange. This major change was made because Morgan needed more capital than its distinguished, but not particularly wealthy, partners could provide. With incorporation, Morgan's ties with the still private Drexel & Co. were severed. (Drexel went on to become the Wall Street phenomenon of the 1980s, Drexel Burnham Lambert.)

As a publicly owned, state-chartered bank, Morgan was now permitted to open a trust department, a business private partnerships were prohibited from entering. Formed by Thomas Lamont, Morgan's new chairman, the trust department managed the money of individuals, estates, and large institutions. This department soon became the new center of Morgan's power, managing the pensions and profit sharing funds of some of the largest firms in the country.

Jack Morgan died on March 13, 1943, and his eldest son, Junius S. Morgan II, assumed his position as a director of the firm. Junius, however, remained a figurehead; the operations of the bank were supervised by various partners and department heads. During the late 1940s and throughout the 1950s, Morgan concentrated on its trust and wholesale banking activities.

Mid-Century: Morgan—Guarantee Trust Merger

In 1959 the world financial community was surprised by the announcement of a merger between Morgan and Guaranty Trust. The Guaranty Trust Company of New York traced its roots to two predecessors: the New York Guaranty and Indemnity Company, founded in 1864 and renamed Guaranty Trust Company of New York in 1896, and the National Bank of Commerce, the subsidiary of the Bank of Commerce, which was founded in 1839. New York Guaranty's original business was loaning money against warehouse receipts. It was closely connected with the Mutual Life Insurance Company after 1891, and eventually became a power in financing international trade. It was separated from Mutual Life in 1911, and went on to establish a prominent bond department and to underwrite corporate securities. The National Bank of Commerce was also a commercial bank involved primarily in lending to manufacturers and tradesmen. Both Guaranty and National Commerce had

close ties to J.P. Morgan & Co. J.P. Morgan himself was a director of the National Bank of Commerce from 1875 to 1910, while several Morgan partners were on Guaranty's board.

Guaranty and National Commerce merged in 1929 to increase their strength and position themselves to broaden the range of wholesale services they could offer their customers. After the merger, the new bank, which retained the Guaranty name and charter, became New York's most prominent trust bank as well as one of the largest dealers in government obligations.

J.P. Morgan and Guaranty Trust, both preeminent wholesale banks, primarily served large corporate accounts. Their merger was intended to make Morgan Guaranty not only the principal banker for corporate enterprise, but also the major banker for governments, foundations, and institutions both at home and abroad. In addition, the new bank managed $6.5 billion in trusts, the largest trust business in the world. The merger of Morgan and Guaranty meant that, unlike other major wholesale and commercial banks, the new Morgan Guaranty would have no retail business to fall back on, but the banks' gamble, and the merger, worked.

In 1960 Morgan Guaranty established the Morgan Guaranty International Banking Corporation and Morgan Guaranty International Finance Corporation to further its international expansion. The next year, Morgan Guaranty made its first, and last, attempt to enter the retail banking business. Morgan Guaranty proposed an affiliation with six upstate New York banks, but the Federal Reserve rejected the arrangement in 1962, fearing too great a concentration of power. With this rejection, Morgan Guaranty renewed its commitment to international operations. The three foreign branches that the bank had at the time of its merger had jumped to 26 branches and representative offices by 1978.

In 1969 Morgan Guaranty became the wholly owned subsidiary of J.P. Morgan & Co., a new holding company. Nearly every major bank made similar arrangements at the time, following Citibank's lead, to take advantage of a bank holding company's greater freedom to engage in other financial businesses.

At the end of the 1970s, Morgan's total assets amounted to $43.5 billion. The firm was the largest stockholder in the United States, with more than $15 billion invested in the stock market, and its trust department ranked as one of the top five investors in more than 50 major U.S. corporations such as ITT, Sears, and Citicorp.

Industry Changes: 1980s

The 1980s saw drastic change in banking as major corporations increasingly raised working capital in the securities markets rather than from banks, and the trend towards global banking and universal financial services accelerated. J.P. Morgan began to move back to its origins in investment and merchant banking, including advising clients on corporate restructurings and mergers and acquisitions, and, when possible, securities underwriting and trading. While such securities activities in the United States were severely curtailed by the 1933 Glass-Steagall legislation, J.P. Morgan entered the Eurobond market in

1979, and throughout the 1980s J.P. Morgan Securities Ltd., the firm's London-based securities subsidiary, was among the leading underwriters in that market.

J.P. Morgan continued to call for repeal of Glass-Steagall legislation and for deregulation of the products and services that U.S. banks could offer. While Congress continued to postpone action, in 1987 the Federal Reserve Board allowed certain bank units, including J.P. Morgan Securities Inc., the firm's U.S. securities subsidiary and a primary dealer in U.S. government securities, to deal in commercial paper, municipal revenue bonds, and consumer-related receivables. In 1989 the Federal Reserve gave J.P. Morgan Securities permission to underwrite, within a limit of five percent of total revenues, corporate debt securities, and the firm immediately began to trade and deal in corporate bonds.

During the decade, J.P. Morgan achieved notable success in international corporate finance and mergers and acquisitions advisory. The firm's emphasis on fundamental analysis and innovative financial structures won it a substantial number of complex and high-profile mandates, and in 1989, J.P. Morgan was involved in some of the largest cross-border and U.S. transactions of the year, including the mergers of SmithKline Beckman with the Beecham Group and McCaw Cellular Communications with Lin Broadcasting, and the leveraged buyout of Hospital Corporation of America. This success was marred slightly in 1986 when it came to light that Antonio Gebauer, a senior vice-president, had diverted $8 million in clients' funds for his own use, a scandal that prompted Morgan to tighten some controls.

Beginning in 1982, J.P. Morgan, like most of the international banking community, was severely affected by the inability of Third World countries to service and repay their growing debt obligations. Throughout the decade both banks and debtor nations were involved in the renegotiation and restructuring of existing debt programs. The crisis deepened when Brazil suspended payment of interest on its loans in 1987, and J.P. Morgan placed $1.3 billion of Brazilian debt on a non-accrual basis. It became clear that new solutions to the debt crisis had to be found, and in 1988 J.P. Morgan and the Mexican government offered the first voluntary debt exchange program. However, the environment continued to be highly uncertain, and in September 1989 J.P. Morgan announced that it had added $2 billion to its allowance for loan loss reserves, bringing its reserves to approximately 70 percent of its Third World debt exposure but causing it to post losses of $1.3 billion for 1989.

Ups and Downs: 1990–99

In 1990 the Federal Reserve granted J.P. Morgan permission to deal in equity securities in addition to its corporate bonds and traditional commercial banking activities. After years of petitioning the Fed for this freedom, Morgan rapidly set about becoming one of the world's top investment banks. With its global presence and sterling reputation, it managed to stake out a spot near the top within just a few years. By 1998 it was ranked second in the world in loan syndications and sixth in domestic debt underwriting, global equity underwriting, and worldwide mergers and acquisitions advice.

Morgan's permission to re-enter the securities business after the 55-year hiatus imposed by the Glass-Steagall Act came at a propitious time. Low inflation and interest rates and an improving global economic outlook had spurred investors to buy into higher-yielding assets—first in the U.S. market, then in Europe and emerging markets. For J.P. Morgan, the culmination of this late-1980s/early-1990s market rally came in 1993, when the bank posted record earnings. The trend reversed, however, in early 1994 when the Federal Reserve raised interest rates, causing risk-averse investors to reduce their involvement in many previously active markets. The situation was exacerbated by a sharp devaluation of the Mexican peso, causing investor panic in Latin American emerging markets.

In 1997 J.P. Morgan again fell victim to an emerging market crisis, when the economies of several East Asian nations suffered sudden slowdowns, leaving them unable to repay their foreign debt. Nicknamed "the Asian flu," the crisis resulted in estimated worldwide equity losses of more than $700 billion—at least $30 billion of which was lost by U.S. investors. In addition, the Asian crisis provoked a deceleration in corporate growth in developed nations, as export orders and Asian expansion projects were cancelled. Morgan's earnings reflected the effect of the crisis, showing a seven percent decrease in net profit for the year, due in large part to canceled underwritings in Asia and Asia-related derivatives losses.

Another blow to investors and investment banks was struck in 1998. Near the middle of the year, the struggling Russian economy collapsed, causing the country to default on its national debt. J.P. Morgan said, in an August 28, 1998 press release, that its Russian exposure was approximately $160 million. However, ancillary losses—including missed growth opportunities and depressed revenues from other emerging markets—added up to an estimated $600 million in missed revenues, according to the company's 1998 annual report. The Russian default, following so closely on the heels of the Asian crisis, demanded a reassessment of strategy. Acknowledging the inherent risk in emerging markets, Morgan cut back substantially on its credit exposures to Asia and Latin America by 50 percent and 40 percent, respectively.

Looking at the Next 100 Years

As J.P. Morgan prepared to enter the 21st century, it remained committed to becoming a top investment bank. Toward that end, the company appeared to be stepping away from its traditional role as the stuffy, blue-blooded banker for the wealthy and powerful—by aggressively targeting the more average investor. Morgan also planned to expand its presence in global capital markets and to grow its asset management business. In both these areas, as well as in investment banking and equities, the company's capital strength and long established reputation for high ethical standards promised to prove valuable advantages as markets around the world became increasingly volatile and competition fiercer.

Principal Subsidiaries

Morgan Futures Corp.; Morgan Guaranty International Finance Corporation; Morgan Guaranty Trust Company; Morgan Guaranty Trust Company of New York; J.P. Morgan Investment

Management Inc.; Morgan Holdings Corp.; J.P. Morgan Delaware; J.P. Morgan & Co. Incorporated; J.P. Morgan California; J.P. Morgan Capital Corporation; J.P. Morgan Florida; J.P. Morgan Futures Inc.; J.P. Morgan Overseas Capital Corporation; J.P. Morgan Securities Inc.; J.P. Morgan Services Inc.; J.P. Morgan Trust Company of Delaware; Banco J.P. Morgan S.A. (Mexico); Banco J.P. Morgan S.A. (Brazil); Euroclear Operations Centre (Belgium); JPM Corretora de Cambio, Titulos e Valores Mobiliarios S.A. (Brazil); ICICI Asset Management Company Limited (India); ICICI Securities & Finance Company (India); Morgan Gestion S.A. (Spain); Morgan Guaranty Trust Company (Australia); Morgan Guaranty Trust Company (U.K.); Morgan Guaranty Trust Company (Belgium); Morgan Guaranty Trust Company (Argentina); Morgan Guaranty Trust Company (Brazil); Morgan Guaranty Trust Company (Italy); Morgan Guaranty Trust Company (Hong Kong); Morgan Guaranty Trust Company (Singapore); Morgan Guaranty Trust Company (Germany); Morgan Guaranty Trust Company (Switzerland); Morgan Guaranty Trust Company (Spain); Morgan Guaranty Trust Company (Japan); Morgan Guaranty Trust Company (France); Morgan Guaranty Trust Company (Belgium); Morgan Guaranty Trust Company (Bahamas); Morgan Guaranty Trust Company (Indonesia); Morgan Guaranty Trust Company (Korea); Morgan Guaranty Trust Company (Taiwan); Morgan Guaranty Trust Company (Rome); Morgan Guaranty Trust Company (Philippines); Morgan Guaranty Trust Company (Mexico); Morgan Guaranty Trust Company (Brazil); J.P. Morgan & Cie S.A. (France); J.P. Morgan & Co. Incorporated (China); J.P. Morgan Argentina Sociedad de Bolsa S.A.; J.P. Morgan Australia Limited; J.P. Morgan Australia Securities Limited; J.P. Morgan Benelux S.A. (Belgium); J.P. Morgan Canada; J.P. Morgan Casa de Bolsa S.A. de C.V. (Mexico); J.P. Morgan Chile Ltda.; J.P. Morgan Espana S.A.(Spain); J.P. Morgan Fondi Italia S.p.A.; Futures Hong Kong Ltd.; J.P. Morgan Futures Inc. (Singapore); J.P. Morgan GmbH (Germany); J.P. Morgan Grupo Financiero S.A. (Mexico); J.P. Morgan Holding Deutschland GmbH; J.P. Morgan Iberica S.L. (Spain); J.P. Morgan International Capital Corporation (Singapore); J.P. Morgan International Capital Corporation (Hong Kong); J.P. Morgan International Ltd. (Czech Republic); J.P. Morgan Investment GmbH (Germany); J.P. Morgan Investment Management Australia Ltd.; J.P. Morgan Investment Management (Singapore); J.P. Morgan Investment Management (U.K); J.P. Morgan Investment Management (Germany); J.P. Morgan Investment Management (Japan); J.P. Morgan Nederland N.V.; J.P. Morgan Polska (Poland); J.P. Morgan Securities Asia Ltd. (Singapore); J.P. Morgan Securities Asia Ltd. (Hong Kong); J.P. Morgan Securities Asia Ltd. (Japan); J.P. Morgan Securities Asia Ltd. (Thailand); J.P. Morgan Securities Asia Ltd. (Korea); J.P. Morgan Securities Asia Ltd. (Taiwan); J.P. Morgan Securities Canada; J.P. Morgan Securities Hong Kong Ltd.; J.P. Morgan Securities Ltd. (U.K.); J.P. Morgan Securities Ltd. (Switzerland); J.P. Morgan Sociedad de Valores y Bolsa S.A. (Spain; 50%); J.P. Morgan Sterling Securities Ltd. (U.K.); J.P. Morgan (Suisse) S.A.; J.P. Morgan (Switzerland) Ltd.; J.P. Morgan Trust Bank Ltd. (Japan); J.P. Morgan Venezuela S.A.; Morgan Trust Company of The Bahamas Limited; Morgan Trust Company of the Cayman Islands Ltd.; Societe de Bourse J.P. Morgan S.A. (France).

Further Reading

Allen, Frederick Lewis, *The Great Pierpont Morgan*, New York: Harper & Brothers, 1949.

''J.P. Morgan's Uncertain Future,'' *Economist,* February 14, 1998.

''History, Philosophy, and Character: The J.P. Morgan Legacy,'' http://www.jpmorgan.com/CorpInfo/History/overview.html.

Hoyt, Edwin Palmer, *The House of Morgan*, New York: Dodd, Mead, 1966.

Carosso, Vincent P., *Investment Banking in America*, Cambridge: Harvard University Press, 1970.

—updated by Shawna Brynildssen

Juno Lighting, Inc.

1300 S. Wolf Road
Des Plaines, Illinois 60017
U.S.A.
(847) 827-9880
Fax: (847) 827-9880
Web site: http://www.junoltg.com

Public Company
Incorporated: 1988
Employees: 1,065
Sales: $160.9 million (1998)
Stock Exchanges: NASDAQ
Ticker Symbol: JUNO
NAIC: 3351212 Residential Electrical Lighting Fixture
Manufacturing; 335122 Commercial, Industrial, &
Institutional Electric Lighting Fixture Manufacturing;
335129 Other Lighting Equipment Manufacturing

Juno Lighting, Inc. is an industry leader in the design, manufacture, and marketing of lighting fixtures for commercial, institutional, and residential use, primarily in the United States. Marketing its products primarily through distributors, Juno is the largest independent manufacturer of track, recessed, exit, and emergency lighting in the nation. Architects, interior designers, and custom home builders use the company as a source of style alternatives and value in the marketplace. Juno's top competitors include U.S. Industries, Inc., The Genlyte Group, Inc., and Catalina Lighting, Inc.

Robert Fremont founded the Des Plaines, Illinois-based Juno in 1976. In the early 1950s Fremont had begun traveling the country selling home lighting fixtures for various manufacturers. After working his way up to a position as a vice-president of sales, he decided to quit and start his own company. In 1956 his new business, Halo Lighting, was established in Chicago with help from some of the sales staff that moved with him from their previous employer. Eleven years later Fremont sold the company but remained on as president until the new owners made him a corporate vice-president. He eventually resigned from that posi-

tion, frustrated by the corporate view that emphasized financing and restructuring over marketing and operations. Finally, 20 years after starting his first lighting company, he again decided to organize and operate his own style of business. Fremont then launched Juno Lighting, specializing in high-end business and residential lighting products. He envisioned luminaires that combined beauty, economy, contemporary styling, and flexibility, qualities manifest in what became Juno's flagship, the Trac-Master, a high-quality, stylish track-lighting fixture.

Going Public in 1983

Boosted by a public offering in 1983, Juno acquired Alumitron, a fluorescent lighting company. Fremont developed and introduced the very successful Sloped Ceiling Down-Lights, recessed lights that shine down from a sloped ceiling. In 1988, with $80 million in cash reserves, Juno acquired Indy Lighting, a producer of department store lighting fixtures. Profits from Alumitron were disappointing, leading to its sale in 1990. Further Juno expansion during the 1980s included the purchase of D.W. Barton and Associates, the parent company of Danalite.

Juno's market share grew from 14 percent in 1987 to 20 percent by 1993. Market gains were attributed in large part to low-cost production and direct sales to more than 1,000 of its distributors and showrooms through five U.S. warehouses and one in Canada. Fremont's former company, Halo Lighting, became a division of Cooper Industries, which conflicted with Juno when it introduced a product similar to Juno's patented fixture for sloped ceilings. Juno sued and the companies settled in 1993, with the recognition of Juno's patent. In the following year, Ronel W. Giedt—former president and CEO of Juno's Indianapolis-based subsidiary, Indy Lighting—was named president and CEO of Juno Lighting, Inc. Robert Fremont indicated that the change came about because "the future growth objectives of the company require a separate corporate president and that Giedt's track record with Indy made him the ideal executive for the job," according to *HFD—The Weekly Home Furnishings Newspaper*.

With 40 percent of its assets in cash and equivalents (three times Juno's short term and long term debt combined), the company began plans for constructing a new $17 million plant. Production space was increased by almost 90 percent when Juno's new 524,000-square-foot Des Plaines plant and headquarters opened in 1996—opening on the heels of dismal earnings performance for 1995. Company executives attributed the shortfall to sluggish home and commercial construction, increased material costs, and delayed product introductions. Fremont told Anne Therese Palmer of *Crain's Chicago Business,* ''Juno's underlying strength lies in its ability to develop new, exciting products, utilize effective merchandising and provide immediate service to customers,'' adding, ''They will permit Juno to achieve future sales and profit increases as construction markets improve.''

Juno's product introductions during this period included emergency lighting systems and incandescent down-lighting, which targeted commercial markets. Its commercial clients included Disney, Florsheim, and The Gap. Attentive to energy conservation, a new series of compact fluorescent track fixtures was produced, designed specifically for lighting walls and large display areas for the retail and commercial markets. The fixtures offered a low-profile, low-wattage adjustable incandescent lighting that saved up to 75 percent more energy than comparable incandescents. The cooler operating temperatures benefited the consumer by lowering air conditioning expenses in addition to longer lamp life (12,000 to 20,000 hours), translating into lower lamp replacement costs. Concerned with optimal lighting performance, Juno recommended that consumers use electronic ballasts rather than the magnetic ones that tend to flicker annoyingly and are less energy efficient, heavier, not as long-lasting, and noisier.

Juno had acquired Advanced Fiberoptic Technologies (AFT) in 1997. The purchase was described as a first example of a lighting company acquiring a fiber optics company. The purchase was made with the intention of integrating fiber optic technology into Juno's existing product line, or the development of new products lines for AFT's existing marketplace. AFT's clients included Tiffany's, Walt Disney, and several of the nation's Smithsonian museums. Under AFT's patented process its fiber optic fixtures offered the advantage of generating less heat and ultraviolet rays. The heat reduction was made possible because of the centralized location of a light source that actually blew cooling air.

Strong Reviews: 1997

Juno was spotlighted when it captured the attention of *LJR Great Lakes Review,* a quarterly research report published by a

division of the Lynch Jones & Ryan institutional brokerage. The publication was followed by 300 banks, brokerages, and other institutional clients. Focusing on Midwestern firms, the *Review* typically alerted Wall Street to stocks of mid-sized firms previously undervalued. It was not unusual for a recommended stock to soar following endorsement by the publication. The *Review's* analysts favored Juno despite the previous year's flattened earnings because of the effects of a number of new product introductions by the company. As one of the largest independent producers of specialty lighting, with an estimated 20 percent of the $500 million market, Juno was in a solid position for future growth. analysts expected that the robust U.S. economy, the strong building and remodeling market, and the trend of building larger houses with an emphasis on energy efficient products would combine to ensure an impressive revitalization of revenues for the company. Juno's history was favorable, the new production plant was expected to boost production and cut operating costs, and the company had little debt and $69 million in cash. The stock's 12.9 P/E was well below the estimated annual earnings growth of 15 percent over the next five years and stocks were ''expected to gain 55 percent to $26 for the next 12 months.''

1998: Dissension from Shareholders Following Dim Performance

Despite a strong stock market, Juno's stock continued to trade in the $20 range, inciting action by major shareholders. In 1998, dissident shareholders—led by a shareholder activist group, Lens, Inc. of Washington, D.C., which owned seven percent of Juno Lighting—submitted a shareholder resolution to limit the board to no more than one inside director. Lens, Inc. proposed that Juno's bylaws be amended to require that a majority of the company's directors be independent, also proposing that Lens principal Robert A.G. Monks—known for a 1992 proxy battle with Sears, Roebuck and Company—be positioned as a director. The group also campaigned to redeploy the company's $90 million cash hoard and to develop a succession plan. It was suggested that the company buy back its own stock when shares hit a low of $14.50, but Juno chose not to. The Lens group viewed the cash surplus of 45 percent of company assets at that time as a critical problem, insisting that ''cash doesn't win a competitive rate of return.'' According to *Crain's Chicago Business,* Lens Inc. threatened to ''weigh a proxy contest if it [did not] see 'significant improvement.' '' Juno's director of corporate planning indicated that the company had hired a search firm after agreeing to add two outside directors. In previous unrelated actions, Lens, Inc. pushed for change and was responsible for the departures of CEOs from Waste Management, Inc., Westinghouse, Inc., and Stone & Webster, Inc. Lens principal Nell Minow explained in *Crain's Chicago Business* that small to mid-sized firms deserved greater scrutiny because they were ''more susceptible to a private-company mentality.'' He added that at least five of the company's directors were either executive officers or providers of legal and investment banking services to Juno.

Anxious to get back on track, Juno agreed to comply with terms set forth by Lens, Inc., but they failed to fulfill an April 1998 promise to appoint another two independent directors within 60 days. The company also was searching for a replacement for president and CEO, following the resignation of Ronel Giedt. Joanne Lublin of the *Wall Street Journal* reported that Juno later responded by trying to bar the boardroom door by unveiling a merger and recapitalization plan. Answering to the concern that Juno invest the cash hoard Fremont said, ''I wasn't critical of [Lens's] criticism; we have been unable to use the funds as we should have used them. It has been a board subject for eight years.'' He explained that the problem was a scarcity of attractive acquisition targets. Juno accepted a $25 per share (or $410 million) merger and recapitalization offer from a partnership controlled by Fremont Partners LP, a San Francisco equity fund unrelated to Mr. Fremont. He told Lublin: ''My motives are not to frustrate Lens. My motives are to make sure that Juno does the right thing'' for its shareholders. Unhappy with the price, Lens wrote a letter to shareholders in a campaign effort to defeat the merger plan, blaming the deal on the management-controlled board and proposing a public auction of the company. The Lens principals claimed the takeout value of Juno should have fallen between $30.67 and $34.25 per share. On June 30 Juno announced the merger with Fremont Investors, following majority stockholder approval.

For the six months ending in May 1999, Juno's net sales rose ten percent to $82.8 million, in large part attributable to new products in the commercial area. In July 1999, the company announced that its board of directors had appointed Glenn Bordfeld—who had been with Juno since 1982 and who was serving as president and chief operating officer—as a company director.

Principal Subsidiaries

Advanced Fiberoptic Technologies, Inc.; Indy Lighting, Inc.; Juno Lighting, Ltd. (Canada); Juno Manufacturing, Inc.

Further Reading

Crown, Judith, ''Big or Small, No Place to Hide,'' *Crain's Chicago Business,* March 9, 1998, p. 1.

''Finding Riches in Business Niches,'' *Money,* August 1994, p. 38.

Freid, Carla, ''Up Nearly 25 Percent a Year, A Pro Names Four Mid-Size Stocks to Gain As Much As 55 Percent,'' *Money,* December 1997, p. 183.

''Juno Compact Fluorescent Track Line for Lighting Walls, Big Display Areas,'' *HFD—The Weekly Home Furnishings Newspaper,* September 19, 1994, p. 24.

''Juno Lighting Announces Proration Results,'' *PR Newswire Association, Inc.,* July 8, 1999, p. 6845.

''Juno Lighting's $125 Million Senior Subordinated Notes Rated 'B' by S & P,'' *PR Newswire Association, Inc.,* May 18, 1999, p. 2896.

''Junoesque Prospects,'' *Forbes,* September 27, 1993, p. 180.

Labate, John, ''Juno Lighting,'' *Fortune,* February 21, 1994, p. 99.

''Lens Renews Focus on Juno Lighting,'' *Crain's Chicago Business,* November 16, 1998, p. 1.

''Lighting Specialist Buys Fiber Company,'' *Fiber Optic News,* July 14, 1997.

Lublin, Joanne S., ''Dissident Investors Fight for Board Seats Without Seeking Full Control of Firms, *Wall Street Journal,* June 1, 1999, p. B3.

Palmer, Ann Therese, ''Dimmer Juno Seeks New Markets,'' *Crain's Chicago Business,* July 1, 1996, p. 64.

—Terri Mozzone

King World Productions, Inc.

1700 Broadway
New York, New York 10019
U.S.A.
(212) 315-4000
Fax: (212) 582-9255
Web site: http://www.kingworld.com

Public Company
Incorporated: 1964
Employees: 418
Sales: $683.9 million (1998)
Stock Exchanges: New York
Ticker Symbol: KWP
NAIC: 51211 Motion Picture & Video Production; 51212
   Motion Picture & Video Distribution

King World Productions, Inc. is the world's leading syndicator of first-run television programming. The success of the game shows ''Wheel of Fortune'' and ''Jeopardy!'' and of ''The Oprah Winfrey Show'' catapulted King World to a position of power in the television industry in the 1980s, altering the traditional relationship between television stations and syndicators; in the late 1990s these three shows were the top three syndicated daily shows. The company also found success through the newsmagazine program called ''Inside Edition,'' and a revival of the game show ''Hollywood Squares.'' King World also markets ''The Roseanne Show'' and ''The Martin Short Show.'' The syndication giant, which increasingly became involved in production in the 1990s, was in the process of being acquired by CBS Corporation in late 1999.

''The Little Rascals'' Beginnings

Charles King, the founder of King World Productions, began as a syndicator of radio programs in the 1930s, and was associated with such celebrities as Rudy Vallee and Gloria Swanson. Beset by financial troubles and seeing the money-making potential in television, King redirected his skills into the new medium, working for other distribution companies until 1964, the year he created King World. The first show distributed by King World was ''The Little Rascals,'' a black-and-white slapstick comedy series featuring the characters Alfalfa, Buckwheat, and Spanky. As a syndicator, King bought distribution rights on the reruns and leased them to television stations, keeping one-third of the licensing fees.

When Charles King died in 1973, his company was experiencing difficulties due to the steadily decreasing demand for black-and-white programming, among other reasons. King's children took on the responsibility of reviving King World, with Michael King as president and CEO, Roger King as chairman of the board, and Robert, Diana, Richard, and Karen King in other executive positions. As chief operating officer, Stuart A. Hersch was the only member of the King World board who was not a part of the King family. Through an agreement with Colbert Television Sales, the Kings began selling the game shows ''The Joker's Wild'' and ''Tic-Tac-Dough.'' They enjoyed moderate success with these, but also sought a show that could challenge industry leaders ''Family Feud'' and ''Entertainment Tonight.''

While research into demographics and audience preferences is utilized by virtually all enterprises related to radio and television, King World has been able to capitalize on its research extremely effectively. The company has its own team of researchers and frequently commissions data from outside agencies. This aspect of King World is seen as a pivotal element in its success.

Struck Gold in the 1980s with ''Wheel of Fortune'' and ''Jeopardy!''

Extensive research into the television ratings published by Nielsen and Arbitron indicated that ''Wheel of Fortune,'' which was running on NBC during the day, had potential for high ratings in the evenings despite the fact that three previous attempts to syndicate it had failed. Based on the children's game ''hangman,'' the game show was created by Merv Griffin. With Pat Sajak acting as host, the show enjoyed a small but loyal following. In 1982 King World struck a deal with Griffin to syndicate the game show. Under the agreement, King World

---

Company Perspectives:

King World's shows have been delivering viewers to television stations and advertisers with unprecedented success for over 15 years. Clearly, we will continue to seek distribution opportunities both domestically and abroad. But going forward, we will expand our business by producing or co-producing more new shows and entering new programming genres. In doing so, we will position ourselves to claim an increasingly larger share of the programming pie.

distributed the show to stations for cash and barter, that is, air time to sell to advertisers. King World's Camelot Entertainment was formed to sell the commercial time, initially 30 seconds per episode. For the first season, King World could find stations to carry the game show in a few large cities including Detroit, Providence, Buffalo, and Columbus, but not New York, Los Angeles, or Chicago. Strong ratings, however, came quickly, and the program was soon showing in all the major markets.

One of the most peculiar aspects of the "Wheel of Fortune" story was the flurry of media attention given to Vanna White, a former model who joined Pat Sajak to turn the letters on the game board. Although White hardly said a word during the show, her popularity skyrocketed, with her face appearing on magazine covers and her autobiography becoming a bestseller. While the Vanna White sensation might have seemed arbitrary, it was largely orchestrated by King World. The company produced thousands of promotional spots featuring White, each customized to the local station running "Wheel of Fortune." She was flown to cities across the United States to make public appearances, waving from parade floats and judging look-a-like contests. According to an article in *Marketing and Media Decisions,* "The syndicator has meticulously and shrewdly marketed her, making her into a business and an insurance policy for the continued success of the show."

"Wheel of Fortune" eventually became the most successful television program in syndication history. "Jeopardy!," the second most successful show, followed in September 1984. Another Merv Griffin production, "Jeopardy!" was a revival of a popular 1960s quiz show in which contestants give "questions" to "answers" in a variety of categories. Alex Trebek hosted the new edition. Although it wobbled during its first season, as soon as researchers at King World discovered that the contestant buzzer was annoying audiences, they were able to rectify the situation, and "Jeopardy!" soared in the ratings.

In October 1984, King World Productions went public. At this point, Robert King left the company, selling his piece of it for $1.7 million. With the two most successful syndicated shows on the air, the company could afford to negotiate with television stations from a position of power. The company pressed for three- and four-year contracts with the stations, and if they were refused, they would take the shows directly to the stations' competitors. King World balanced these aggressive tactics, however, by offering customized market research, including a ratings analysis of each station in the market, demo-

graphic statistics, and recommendations for scheduling, earning the company a reputation as a supportive partner. Furthermore, King World financed and produced commercials to promote its programming. In general, this sort of assistance facilitated the cooperation of the stations, but at least one station, WCPX in Orlando, Florida, bristled under King World's negotiating style, and in 1985 they filed suit, claiming the syndicator demanded that they carry other King World programming if they wanted "Wheel of Fortune." A federal judge threw out the suit, citing insufficient evidence.

According to a 1985 article in *Forbes,* the boom in the television syndication industry, which King World was well positioned to take advantage of, was the result of two factors: the rise of independent stations as opposed to networks, and the shorter lifespan of the average network series, which meant fewer shows fit for syndication. At the same time, television syndication was considered by some a risky proposition, with some commentators seeing its rapid growth as a temporary phenomenon. King World needed an unending string of hits in order to continue expanding. Although its first two ventures were undeniably major victories, the chances of accurately predicting audience preference every time, even with the aid of a research staff, were next to impossible.

King World's first disaster was a show called "Headline Chasers" starring veteran game show host Wink Martindale, who first came in contact with King World when it was distributing his "Tic-Tac-Dough." Combining the missing letter aspect of "Wheel of Fortune" with a test of contestants' knowledge of current events, the game show was produced by Merv Griffin, whom Martindale contacted at the suggestion of Michael King. Unlike "Wheel of Fortune" and "Jeopardy!," "Headline Chasers" debuted on network television as a King World production without previous exposure. The company gave the show a long time to get off the ground, but it never did.

Launching "The Oprah Winfrey Show": 1986

In the daytime talk show ratings, the "Donahue" show, starring silver-haired host Phil Donahue and distributed by Multimedia, had held the number one position for 12 years until King World decided to find a personality to challenge Donahue. This type of telecast, like soap operas, is primarily aimed at female viewers. The Kings selected Oprah Winfrey as their challenger. Winfrey had recently moved from Baltimore to Chicago to host "A.M. Chicago" on that city's WLS-TV, and she played a supporting role in the 1986 movie *The Color Purple,* directed by Steven Spielberg. On the eve of the National Association of Television Program Executives conference, where the Kings would be pitching "The Oprah Winfrey Show" to television stations, she received the nomination for an Academy Award for Best Supporting Actress. In September 1986, "Oprah" debuted nationally.

With Winfrey's charisma, born of sincerity and commonsense wisdom, the show overtook "Donahue" in its first year. As Winfrey's popularity grew, she formed her own company—Harpo Productions, Inc.—to produce the talk show starting in 1988. "Oprah" was also a hit with the critics, winning Emmy Awards for Outstanding Talk Show in 1987, 1988, and 1989.

The success of "Wheel of Fortune," "Jeopardy!," and "Oprah" meant tremendous growth for King World. Revenues climbed from $81 million in 1985 to $476 million in 1991, a year when the three major networks lost a grand total of nearly $500 million. King World International was formed to distribute programming around the globe; as of 1992, 26 countries broadcast versions of "Wheel of Fortune." With three shows in the top ten syndicated programs, King World began to take chances when introducing new shows. According to analyst Paul Marsh, quoted in *Broadcasting* magazine in December 1992: "When King World starts a new show it's not like they need to make a lot of capital expenditures or add sales staff. . . . Effectively they get a free swing at the plate every time."

After "Oprah," King World went down swinging with nearly every new program. "Nightlife," a 1986 talk show hosted by standup comedian David Brenner and produced by Motown, did little to dent the ratings of Johnny Carson's "Tonight Show." Industry insiders cited this as a notoriously difficult time slot on the schedule due to the loyalty of Carson's following. The same year, King World brought out the daytime magazine "True Confessions" and the "Rock & Roll Evenings News," neither of which lasted into the next season. "The Laugh Machine," produced by George Schlatter, debuted in 1987 and also yielded disappointing ratings. In March of that year, Roger King was arrested for possession of cocaine, and in September, Stuart A. Hersch resigned from the company. Stephen W. Palley was named to take over the position as chief operating officer.

"Inside Edition" Debuted in 1989

In December 1988, King World purchased the television station WIVB, Buffalo's CBS affiliate, from Howard Publications, Inc., for $100 million. The station had been losing money, and this trend continued after King World acquired it. In 1991 WIVB lost $7.8 million, and the company took action to restructure the debt. In January 1989, King World introduced "Inside Edition," the first show that the company produced on its own. During this time, the news magazine programs that were appearing on every channel were seen as a new breed in the genre: investigative reporting with less bite than the established CBS program "60 Minutes," presented in a more lively, upbeat style. "Inside Edition," then hosted by Bill O'Reilly, did little at first to distinguish itself from the more popular "Hard Copy" or "A Current Affair," but King World tinkered with the format, and the show began to climb in the ratings.

Of all of King World's failed programming, perhaps the most devastating loss was "Candid Camera," a remake of Allen Funt's classic show starring Dom DeLuise, which debuted in 1991. Based on the statistics, the syndicator had high expectations for its performance in the ratings. When plans for the show were announced, King World stock shot up into the mid-30s; when the program failed, the price fell down into the mid-20s.

King World continued to introduce new shows, relying on extensive market research to determine what might succeed. King World's first foray into children's programming was in 1992, with the animated "Wild West C.O.W.-Boys of Moo Mesa," from the creators of the Teenage Mutant Ninja Turtles. In September 1993, the company debuted "The Les Brown Show," a talk show featuring the popular motivational speaker, and the news magazine "American Journal," a spinoff of "Inside Edition" anchored by Nancy Glass (the former lasted only one season, while the latter was canceled following the 1997–98 season).

In March 1994 King World announced an agreement with Winfrey to distribute her show through the 1999–2000 season, an agreement that made her a major King World shareholder. A few months later the company announced that it had reached agreements with television stations and broadcasters renewing "The Oprah Winfrey Show" through the 1999–2000 season and "Wheel of Fortune" and "Jeopardy!" through the 1998–99 season. These agreements would generate up to $1.9 billion in fees, with King World receiving 43 percent of the total.

King World sold WIVB in 1995. The following year, "Inside Edition," by this time being hosted by Deborah Norville, won the prestigious George Polk Award, becoming the first non-network program to be so honored. "Oprah" continued to be honored with awards as well, including 32 Emmy Awards by 1998, having been named Outstanding Talk Show in 1991 and 1992, and in 1994 through 1997. The mid-1990s were also notable for two takeovers of King World that failed to materialize. The company was an attractive target because of its abundance of cash—about $500 million in mid-1995—and absence of debt. Ted Turner, chairman of Turner Broadcasting System Inc., developed a bid to acquire King World but then abandoned it in August 1995 when he encountered opposition from his board. In July 1996 New World Communications Group Inc. was on the verge of acquiring King World but this deal too was scuttled when News Corp. reached an agreement to acquire the 80 percent of New World it did not already own.

In early 1997 King World announced that it was no longer for sale, and was embarking on a program to boost its stock price, which had languished in the mid-1990s because of the potential takeovers and because of concern over the company's overreliance on revenues from its three top properties. The company said it would buy back five million shares of stock (representing 13 percent of outstanding shares) over time, and paid its first ever dividend to shareholders, a special $2-per-share payout which cost the company $74.8 million in cash. In September 1997, amid speculation that she would leave television to revive her film career, Winfrey struck a deal with King World in which she would continue to host "The Oprah Winfrey Show" through the 1999–2000 season, receiving in return a $130 million cash advance against her earnings from the show as well as options that would enable her to purchase as much as five percent of King World's stock. That King World would agree to this astounding compensation package showed how highly the company valued "Oprah," a talk show that had managed to maintain its high ratings even with its focus on more serious topics—not to mention its on-air book club. It had done so despite the increasing competition from numerous upstart talk shows, many of which trafficked in either fluff or sleaze.

Broadening Programming, Pursuit by CBS: Late 1990s

Also in 1997 King World formed a new division, King World Kids, to develop children's programming; an animated show called ''Doodlezoo'' was in the formative stages in the late 1990s. The company also stepped up its development of new adult programs, including ''The Roseanne Show'' and ''Hollywood Squares.'' The former debuted in September 1998, with comedian Roseanne serving as host of the one-hour daily talk show. The former was a revival of a popular game show of the past, and featured comedian Whoopi Goldberg in the ''center square'' (in addition to her role as one of the executive producers), along with a steady stream of guests from the world of entertainment. ''Hollywood Squares'' became a ratings hit while ''Roseanne'' struggled, but both shows survived to see a second season. Scheduled for launch in September 1999 was ''The Martin Short Show,'' a one-hour talk/variety program starring multitalented Martin Short. During this period, King World also began developing network dramatic series, the first of which was ''Murder Inc.,'' a coproduction with NBC Studios sold to NBC in the fall of 1998.

In September 1998, Winfrey and King World agreed to extend ''Oprah'' for two more seasons, through 2001–02. The company paid an even higher price to retain the talk show, shelling out a $150 million advance for a two-year term. ''Oprah'' was simply too important for King World to lose, as it generated 42 percent of the company's overall revenues during fiscal 1998. King World in December 1998 announced that it signed renewals for ''Wheel of Fortune'' and ''Jeopardy!'' through 2003–04.

In April 1999 CBS Corporation said that it would acquire King World for $2.5 billion in stock, a deal that was initially scheduled to be consummated late in that year. CBS eyed King World's syndication business as a way to diversify beyond network programming; it also planned to use the $1 billion in cash that King World had amassed to buy additional radio or television stations. For King World, the deal would allow it to continue to operate as a freestanding unit but one with access to a steady source of capital and to CBS's group of 14 owned stations, representing 32 percent of the United States and a ready platform for King World syndicated shows. During the period in which the takeover was pending, King World announced that Michael King would step down as CEO of the company in September 2000, continuing in an advisory capacity after that date. Until that time, Michael and Roger King would share the chief executive title. In early September 1999, Viacom Inc. reached an agreement to acquire CBS, a deal that delayed the completion of CBS's acquisition of King World.

Principal Subsidiaries

American Journal Inc.; King World Media Sales Inc.; Four Crowns Inc.; Inside Edition Inc.; K.W.M., Inc.; King World Corporation; King World Direct Inc.; King World FSC Corporation (Virgin Islands); King World/GSN Inc.; King World/LR Inc.; King World Merchandising, Inc.; King World Studios West Inc.; Topper Productions Inc.

Further Reading

Duffy, Susan, ''All This and 'Candid Camera,' Too,'' *Business Week,* January 21, 1991.

Fabrikant, Geraldine, ''King World's Chiefs Hope for New Syndication Success with Old TV Standbys,'' *New York Times,* November 10, 1997, p. D11.

Foisie, Geoffrey, ''King World: A Growth Stock Gets Bigger,'' *Broadcasting,* December 7, 1992.

Freeman, Michael, ''King World Pushes Content,'' *Mediaweek,* April 21, 1997, p. 12.

——, ''Mel 1 Takes King 2,'' *Mediaweek,* April 5, 1999, pp. 4–5.

——, ''Squares on a Roll,'' *Mediaweek,* September 21, 1998, pp. 4–5.

Gleason, Mark, ''King World Eyes Comedy Block As Bold New Biz,'' *Advertising Age,* January 18, 1999, p. S3.

''King World on Top of Game Show Hill,'' *Advertising Age,* January 16, 1986.

Lipin, Steven, and Elizabeth Jensen, ''Deal Makers Say King World Might Fetch Less Than Expected in Any Takeover Attempt,'' *Wall Street Journal,* March 22, 1995, p. C2.

Paskowski, Marianne, ''Prize Packagers,'' *Marketing and Media Decisions,* March 1987.

Pope, Kyle, ''CBS Expected to Buy King World for $2.4 Billion,'' *Wall Street Journal,* April 1, 1999, p. A3.

——, ''In CBS-King Deal, Keep an Eye on the Players,'' *Wall Street Journal,* April 2, 1999, p. B1.

——, ''King World CEO Will Quit Next Year but Plans to Keep an Advisory Role,'' *Wall Street Journal,* August 12, 1999, p. B14.

——, ''King World, Not Up for Sale, Plans Stock Moves,'' *Wall Street Journal,* April 15, 1997, p. B19.

——, ''The Talk of TV, Oprah Stays, King World Pays,'' *Wall Street Journal,* September 16, 1997, pp. B1, B14.

Schlosser, Joe, ''The Kings and Eye,'' *Broadcasting & Cable,* April 5, 1999, p. 8.

——, ''Kings High on Short,'' *Broadcasting & Cable,* May 25, 1998, p. 33.

——, ''The Kings: Who'll Stop the Reign?,'' *Broadcasting & Cable,* January 12, 1998, pp. 48–49.

——, ''KW Sees Future in the Stars,'' *Broadcasting & Cable,* August 31, 1998, p. 22.

——, ''KW, WB Square Off over 'Squares,' '' *Broadcasting & Cable,* October 13, 1997, p. 14.

Sharkey, Betsy, and Michael Freeman, ''It's Great to Be a King Again,'' *Mediaweek,* January 19, 1998, pp. 18–21.

Sharpe, Anita, and Eben Shapiro, ''Turner Broadcasting Ends Talks to Buy King World,'' *Wall Street Journal,* August 22, 1995, p. A3.

Swertlow, Frank, ''Ratings Aren't Rosy for Sitcom Star's Talk Show,'' *Los Angeles Business Journal,* November 2, 1998, pp. 3+.

Trachtenberg, Jeffrey A., ''The Other Green Revolution,'' *Forbes,* April 8, 1985.

—Mark Swartz
—updated by David E. Salamie

KOHL'S

Kohl's Corporation

N56 W17000 Ridgewood Drive
Menomonee Falls, Wisconsin 53051-5660
U.S.A.
(414) 703-7000
Fax: (414) 703-6255
Web site: http://www.kohls.com

Public Company
Incorporated: 1988
Employees: 33,800
Sales: $3.68 billion (1998)
Stock Exchanges: New York
Ticker Symbol: KSS
NAIC: 45211 Department Stores

Kohl's Corporation is one of the largest discount department store chains in the United States, with more than 230 outlets, primarily in the Midwest and Mid-Atlantic regions. Targeting middle income shoppers buying for their families and homes, the chain maintains low retail prices through low cost structure, limited staffing, and progressive management information systems, as well as the economical application of centralized buying, distribution, and advertising. This ''Kohl's concept'' has proved successful in both small and large markets, and in strip shopping centers, regional malls, and freestanding venues.

Formed Out of BATUS

Management purchased the chain's 40 stores in 1986 from BATUS Inc., the U.S. division of BAT Industries plc. The parent was formed when James Buchanan Duke, founder of the American Tobacco Co., expanded his U.S. tobacco empire to Great Britain. His encroachment on the British market sparked a trade war, provoking several British tobacco companies to join forces as the Imperial Tobacco Group plc. Imperial succeeded in squelching Duke's British effort, then moved to invade the U.S. market. Taking the threat seriously, Duke negotiated a pact with Imperial Tobacco that formed the British-American Tobacco Co. Ltd. (BAT) in 1902 to manufacture and market the

two companies' blends and brand names. When the U.S. Supreme Court found that BAT was a monopoly, it compelled American Tobacco to annul its territorial agreement with Imperial and divest its interest in BAT. Imperial kept its 33 percent interest in the company until 1972.

Following a tobacco industry trend, BAT began to diversify in the 1960s, purchasing several famous perfume houses. In the 1970s, the company formed a U.S. subsidiary, BATUS Inc., and began to acquire retail department stores. Wisconsin-based Kohl's Food and Department Stores, purchased in 1972, was the British conglomerate's first acquisition in this arena. Within a decade, BATUS had the 19th largest retail holdings in the United States, including Gimbles, Saks Fifth Avenue, and Marshall Field & Co. BATUS invested expansion capital into two of its acquisitions, Saks and Kohl's.

By the mid-1980s, BATUS had more than doubled the number of Kohl's outlets to 34, but the chain was an anomaly in the upscale retail group with its ''value-oriented,'' ''bargain-basement'' positioning. BATUS sold the food segment of Kohl's to Great Atlantic and Pacific Tea Co. (A&P), and began divesting its retail businesses in 1986. That year, Kohl's management team took the chain's 40 stores in Wisconsin and Indiana private. They spent the following three years refining the ''Kohl's concept'': moderately priced, quality apparel for middle-income families.

The concept incorporated several factors. To set itself apart from mass merchandisers and discounters and become a specialty department store, over 80 percent of Kohl's merchandise carried national brand names recognized for quality. Kohl's also prided itself on stocking ''narrow, but deep merchandise assortments,'' especially where advertised specials were concerned. At the same time, Kohl's eschewed the high-end and designer merchandise that characterized upscale department stores. The chain dropped low-volume, low-margin departments such as candy, sewing notions, and hard sporting goods in favor of higher margin goods such as linens and jewelry.

Kohl's was able to price its merchandise more competitively by maintaining a low cost structure. The company kept consumer prices low and margins relatively high through lean staffing, state-of-the-art management information systems, and operating efficiencies that resulted from centralized buying, advertising, and distribution. Promotional and marketing partnerships with vendors also helped hold down overhead. For example, many of Kohl's 200 vendors utilized electronic data exchange (EDI) to submit advance shipment notices electronically, which made ordering more efficient. The chain used aggressive marketing and promotional events to position Kohl's as the "destination store." Once customers arrived, management hoped the stores' convenient layouts, clear signage, and centralized checkouts would encourage high store productivity.

Kohl's most impressive growth spurt began in 1988, when management and The Morgan Stanley Leveraged Equity Fund II, L.P. formed Kohl's Corporation and acquired Kohl's Department Stores. That same year, Kohl's purchased 26 MainStreet department stores from Federated Department Stores, which expanded the chain geographically into the Detroit, Minneapolis/St. Paul, Chicago, and Grand Rapids, Michigan, metropolitan areas. The chain continued to grow internally as well, posting eight to ten percent store-for-store gains in 1989, 1990, and 1991 despite a recessed retail environment. From 1988 to 1992, Kohl's sales increased from $388 million to $1 billion.

Went Public in 1992

Kohl's did not stop there: in 1992 the corporation prepared for further growth by expanding and upgrading its distribution facilities, automating merchandise handling, and making a public stock offering to finance projected openings of 14 to 16 additional stores annually. Kohl's enlisted the help of consultant group SDI Industries of Pacoima, California, to manage the automation and expansion of the chain's ten-year-old distribution center. The center, which supplied Kohl's stores with 98 percent of their merchandise, was expanded to 500,000 square feet, enough capacity to service 120 stores. Automation was achieved at a cost of $9.7 million. Completed in 1993, it encouraged higher productivity and lower turnaround time, and allowed vendors to send advance ship notices electronically and to pre-ticket merchandise. Construction on a second 650,000-square-foot distribution center was underway in Findley, Ohio, in 1993; completed in August 1994, this facility served stores in central Illinois, Ohio, Michigan, Indiana, Kentucky, Tennessee, and West Virginia.

Kohl's advanced toward the 120-store mark with the opening of eight new stores in 1992, expanding its geographical reach to Ohio. The chain added Iowa and South Dakota to its roster in 1993 and opened 11 new stores. Continuing its expansion, Kohl's opened 18 new stores in 1994, and 22 each in the

following two years. Kohl's also continued to tinker with its store format, completing its phaseout of electronics in 1995.

To support a planned expansion eastward into the Mid-Atlantic region, the company built a third distribution center in Winchester, Virginia, which opened in the summer of 1997 with an initial capacity of 350,000 square feet (which was later expanded to 400,000). The Winchester center served Kohl's stores in New York, North Carolina, Pennsylvania, Virginia, Maryland, Delaware, and New Jersey. By 1998 Kohl's had stores in 22 states and the District of Columbia.

During 1999 the expansion emphasis was on the West, particularly Missouri and two new states, Colorado and Texas. To support its westward expansion, Kohl's in 1999 was building a fourth distribution center, a 542,000-square-foot facility in Blue Springs, Missouri, to handle 80 to 100 stores and to service units in Colorado, Texas, Kansas, Missouri, Nebraska, and central Iowa. On the management front, William Kellogg, who had served as chairman and CEO since 1979, relinquished the CEO position to Larry Montgomery in February 1999. Montgomery also continued as vice-chairman, a position he assumed in March 1996, and previously was executive vice-president of stores from February 1993 through February 1996. Also in early 1999 came the purchase of 33 stores previously operated by bankrupt Caldor Corporation. All but one of the stores was in the New York metro area, with the other in the Baltimore area. Kohl's planned to convert the Caldor units to the Kohl's format during 2000. The purchase was funded through the issuance of 2.8 million shares of stock.

From its emergence as a public company in 1992 to 1998, Kohl's nearly tripled its number of stores, while its revenues more than tripled, from $1.1 billion to $3.68 billion. At the turn of the century, Kohl's was moving toward becoming a national chain of between 500 and 1,000 stores. The South appeared to be the next targeted region, as the company in 1999 laid preliminary plans for its entrance into the Atlanta metro area market.

Further Reading

Arbose, Jules, and Daniel Burstein, "BAT Moves Beyond Tobacco," *International Management,* August 1984, pp. 17–20.

"BATUS Battles Chilly Retail Climate," *Chain Store Age General Merchandise Trends,* June 1985, p. 62.

Brookman, Faye, "Kohl's Updates DC," *Stores,* January 1992, pp. 142, 144.

Croghan, Lore, "Kohl's: Discounted Discounter," *Financial World,* November 21, 1995, p. 22.

Duff, Christina, "Kohl's of the Midwest Maps an Invasion of Both Coasts," *Wall Street Journal,* May 12, 1994, p. B4.

Duff, Mike, "The Mid-Tier Titan with Discount Appeal," *Discount Store News,* December 14, 1998, p. 78.

Faircloth, Anne, "The Best Retailer You've Never Heard Of," *Fortune,* March 16, 1998, pp. 110–12.

Faust, Fred, "Kohl's to Enter St. Louis Area with Six Department Stores," *St. Louis Post-Dispatch,* August 12, 1999.

Heller, Laura, "Kohl's to Continue Contiguous Growth," *Discount Store News,* June 7, 1999, pp. 7, 159.

Jagler, Steven, "Kohl's Corp. Marches into the South," *Business Journal-Milwaukee,* April 2, 1999, pp. 1+.

"Kohl's First $1 Billion," *Discount Merchandiser,* March 1993, p. 12.

"Kohl's Way: Narrow but Deep," *Discount Merchandiser,* March 1994, p. 20.

Owens, Jennifer, "Kohl's March to the East Coast," *Women's Wear Daily,* March 12, 1997, pp. 22 +.

"Rain Falls on Gimbels' Parade," *Chain Store Age Executive,* August 1986, pp. 59–61.

Reda, Susan, "Kohl's Expands with Hybrid of Discount Store Efficiency, Department Store Ambience," *Stores,* February 1997, pp. 49–50.

Reese, Shelly, "Hybrid Kohl's Weathers Tough Apparel Climate," *Discount Store News,* May 6, 1996, p. A18.

——, "Kohl's Strives for National Status," *Discount Store News,* April 1, 1996, pp. 3, 104.

Robins, Gary, "Lin Allison Keeps Kohl's on the Leading Edge," *Stores,* August 1991, pp. 54–58.

Rublin, Lauren R., "Taylor-Made Portfolio," *Barron's,* June 22, 1992, pp. 16–20.

Samuels, Gary, "Learning by Doing," *Forbes,* February 14, 1994, p. 51.

Seckler, Valerie, "Stoking Kohl's," *Women's Wear Daily,* June 12, 1996, pp. 10–11.

Tillotson, Kristin, "Minding the Store: Kohl's Comes Up with Winning Mix of Name Brands and Low Prices," *Minneapolis Star Tribune,* February 11, 1994, p. 1D.

Veverka, Mark, "Kohl's Isn't Just for Cheeseheads," *Crain's Chicago Business,* May 22, 1995, p. 4.

—April Dougal Gasbarre
—updated by David E. Salamie

Konica

Konica Corporation

26-2, Nishishinjuku 1-chome
Shinjuku-ku, Tokyo 163-0512
Japan
(03) 3349-5251
Fax: (03) 3349-8998
Web site: http://www.konica.co.jp

Public Company
Incorporated: 1936 as Konishiroku Honten Co., Ltd.
Employees: 4,936
Sales: ¥584.3 billion (US$4.7 billion) (1999)
Stock Exchanges: Tokyo Osaka Nagoya Niigata Frankfurt
    Düsseldorf
NAIC: 333315 Photographic & Photocopying Equipment
    Manufacturing; 334112 Computer Storage Device
    Manufacturing; 334119 Other Computer Peripheral
    Equipment Manufacturing; 333313 Office Machinery
    Manufacturing; 334613 Magnetic & Optical
    Recording Media Manufacturing; 334517 Irradiation
    Apparatus Manufacturing; 334510 Electromedical &
    Electrotherapeutic Apparatus Manufacturing

Konica Corporation produces a wide range of products, mainly within the imaging sphere. Konica manufactures and markets photosensitive products, including color and black-and-white film and paper, and photofinishing equipment and chemicals; cameras and optical products, including compact 35mm and digital still cameras, and plastic lenses; business equipment, including copiers, fax machines, and printers; medical products, including medical imaging film and automatic processors, laser imagers, and imaging cameras; graphic arts and industrial products, including platemaking film, typesetting paper, presensitized plates, color-proofing systems, and image processing systems; and magnetic products, including videotapes and floppy disks. About 45 percent of the company's revenues are generated domestically, with North America accounting for about 25 percent, Europe 17 percent, and Asia and other regions 13 percent. Although it is not the leader in any one industry, Konica remains highly competitive in several.

Late 19th-Century Beginnings

The company was founded in 1873, during the first decade of Japan's industrial revolution, by Rokusaburo Sugiura, who suggested that his employer, the Konishiya apothecary in Kojimachi, Tokyo, begin to sell the new cameras and photographic materials that were being imported from Europe and the United States. The apothecary owners consented and gave Sugiura permission to use the Konishiya name. This was seven years before Kodak was founded.

In 1876 Sugiura changed his name to Rokuemon Sugiura VI to continue the succession of his father's name, moved the business to Nihonbashi, Tokyo, and renamed it Konishi Honten. In about 1880, Rokuosha, a subsidiary company, became a subcontractor for Konishi, producing cameras for commercial applications. By 1882 Konishi had established three factories for manufacturing lithographic materials and equipment, and matte paper for picture mounting and had begun to produce box cameras. By 1890, Konishi expanded camera production from an on-order basis to planned production, and four years later, was producing a variety of studio, field, and folding cameras.

In 1902 a Rokuosha factory was established to manufacture photographic paper and dry plates in what is now Shinjuku, Tokyo. A year later, the company began to market the box-shaped Cherry hand camera, the country's first name-brand camera. Also in 1903, Konishi introduced the Sakura—or cherry blossom, the Japanese national flower—brand name on Japan's first domestically produced photographic paper.

During the next five years, the Sakura brand name was to be found on many new Konishi cameras, including the Sakura Honor Portable, a box camera, and the Reflex Prano, the first Japanese large format single lens reflex (SLR) camera. In 1909 Konishi introduced three new camera models: Pearl, Lily, and Idea, all known for their quality construction.

World War I, which began in 1914, stimulated the Japanese economy and forced many industries to become less dependent on foreign goods. The importation from Germany, for example, of barium compound-coated paper and paper base was barred during the war, and Konishi's Rokuosha developed a method of producing photographic base paper in cooperation with Mitsubishi Paper Company. At the close of the war in 1919, Japan's total industrial production had almost quadrupled that of the 1914 level, and in the same period, the size of the industrial workforce had more than doubled.

A 1916 Konishi catalog reported that the company was exporting the Lily Number 2 camera to Great Britain. This was considered a matter of considerable pride because Great Britain was regarded as the birthplace of photography. During the next ten years, the company developed a variety of new camera models, photographic papers, and processes.

Konishi Honten was renamed Konishiroku in 1921 and reorganized as a limited partnership. On September 1, 1923, the company's headquarters was completely destroyed in the Great Kanto Earthquake. The structure was rebuilt very quickly, and Konishiroku was back in business by the next month.

In 1925 Konishiroku received orders for gun cameras from the Japanese Imperial Navy Command. Rokuosha developed the first domestically produced photographic lens for the navy's gun cameras that year. Known as the Hexar F/4.5—Hexar was taken from the lineage of Rokuemon Sugiura: *roku* means six, or hexa—it was a copy of a lens produced by Thornton, a British company. Although Japanese cameras had included imported photographic lenses up to this time, the Japanese Navy was determined to achieve self-sufficiency in defense matters and had urged the production of such a lens.

In the same year, the company introduced the Pearlette, the first of a well-received line of cameras that would be produced for many years. It was the first metal-bodied camera produced by Konishiroku and was considered innovative, even though it was modeled after Kodak's vest-pocket camera. To publicize the camera and promote photography, Konishiroku formed the Pearlette League, a club for those whose first camera was a Pearlette. The club offered publications, contests, and a variety of other activities.

During the next ten years, Konishiroku introduced a variety of new products. In 1929 it began to market Sakura brand film,

one of the first films produced in Japan. The company introduced its first movie projector in 1931 and its first movie camera in 1935.

Military Production: 1930s–44

In 1936 the company was registered as a publicly owned corporation with the name Konishiroku Honten Company. In 1938, as the likelihood of war increased, the Japanese government placed restrictions on cameras produced for consumers, and Konishiroku directed its major efforts to military products. It developed two types of ultra-compact aerial cameras for the Japanese Army in 1939 and 1940. In 1940, five years after Kodak introduced its Kodachrome color film, Konishiroku unveiled its Sakura natural color, Japan's first color film.

Rokuemon Sugiura VIII, grandson of the company's founder, became president of Konishiroku in 1941. Two years later, the company changed its name to Konishiroku Photo Industry Company, and established a research center. In 1944, under an industrial readjustment order, Konishiroku amalgamated with Showa Photo Industry.

In 1945 the company's Yodobashi factory, warehouse, and research center were damaged by U.S. air raids. At the end of the war, in September, all factories that had been taken over for military production reverted back to the manufacture of consumer goods. Despite a severe shortage of parts, Konishiroku resumed production of several cameras.

Postwar Innovation and Growth

Before the war, Konishiroku had developed and built a prototype of the Rubikon, a general use camera using 35-millimeter film. The camera had not yet been put into production. When war broke out and the company's plants were directed entirely to the manufacture of cameras and optical instruments for military applications, the Rubikon was converted into a camera for taking X-ray pictures and was used for medical applications. After the war, Konishiroku returned the Rubikon to its original design but decided to change its name, as the old name was too much like the Rubicon, the river Caesar crossed on his march to seize Rome. As the name was considered unsuitable in a time so recently removed from war, the name of the camera was changed to Konica—from "Konishiroku" and "camera." Thus was the company's first 35-millimeter camera introduced in 1947.

In 1947 Konishiroku was listed as one of Japan's five leading photographic-lens makers and one of three camera-shutter producers. Konishiroku produced approximately half of all Japanese cameras. Materials such as goat skin for camera bellows, sheet steel for shutters, and piano cord for shutter control were all in short supply, but camera companies were finding substitutes for these materials.

In 1948 *The Dream*, the first Japanese color motion picture, won an award from the Japanese Motion Picture Technology Institute. The film had used Sakura color film. The following year, Japan experienced a deep economic depression. Many small- and medium-sized businesses failed and unemployment was high. Only the Korean War, beginning in June 1950, rescued the economy, with large special procurement orders that stimulated many industries, including those making cameras and optical instruments.

For Konishiroku, the 1950s were a time of growth and continued product refinement. In an effort to increase its U.S. exports, the company established Koniphoto Corporation in Philadelphia, Pennsylvania, in 1956, to market its cameras and photographic materials. That same year, the company won the Deming Prize for Industrial Efficiency for the excellence of its quality-control activities in upgrading productivity. W.E. Deming, a U.S. specialist in statistical quality control, had spurred the development of quality control in Japan in a series of visits to Japan that began in the early 1950s.

In 1962 the company moved Koniphoto from Philadelphia to New York City and opened the Konica European Center in Hamburg as a marketing outpost. The following year, it closed its Yodobashi factory and built a large, state-of-the-art factory in Hachioji, a Tokyo suburb. The first Japanese company to produce X-ray film, Konishiroku had begun its manufacture in 1933 under the Sakura name and produced its first X-ray processor in 1963. The following year, it unveiled Sakura color negative film, the industry's fastest color negative film. In December 1965, after overcoming a variety of technical challenges, Konishiroku introduced the Konica Autoreflex, the industry's first automatic-exposure 35-millimeter SLR.

In 1967 Konishiroku suffered heavy losses caused by the production of defective color film and its inability to increase its market share. Up to this time, members of the company's top management had been selected from the controlling family; but in 1968, a new management team was put in place to turn the company around, and Ryousuke Nishimura became the new president. The new team was successful in slowly diversifying the company into fields that made use of technologies related to cameras and optical instruments and in making the company's products more competitive. Planning for new products became market-oriented, with management collecting appropriate market information before undertaking development of a new product. The new management team also improved employee training and personnel selection, as well as employee-evaluation methods.

Rapid Expansion: 1970s

The 1970s were a period of rapid expansion for Konishiroku. In 1971 the company introduced the U-Bix 480, its first photostatic plain paper copier. By 1978 plain paper copiers would account for 23 percent of the company's total sales. Many of Japan's camera companies had begun to produce small copiers. Their expertise in optics and their existing distribution networks aided this diversification.

Konishiroku celebrated its 100th anniversary in 1973 and began to use the Konica name on more of the products it sold in the European and North American markets. In the same year, the company established a subsidiary called Konishiroku Photo Industry (Europe) in Hamburg to market photographic products. The year 1973 also saw the installation of a new company president, Hiroshi Tomioka.

In 1975, a year of growth and change for Konishiroku, the company introduced the Konica C35 EF, the first of a new generation of compact cameras with a built-in electronic flash. U-Bix copiers were well received, with sales reaching the 50,000-unit mark by 1975. That same year, the company exported its first photographic-paper-making plant to the Soviet Union.

Konishiroku introduced the Konica C35 AF, a camera featuring an automatic focusing system, in 1977. Although more than a dozen camera manufacturers had signed agreements with Honeywell to use its automatic-focus technology, Konica's autofocus camera was the first to reach the market. Coupled with the introduction two years earlier of the Konica C35 EF with its built-in flash, Konica was regaining its reputation as an innovator.

In 1978 Konishiroku moved its headquarters to Tokyo's Shinjuku ward and opened a branch office in Great Britain to market cameras and photographic materials. That same year, the company was one of four Tokyo-based companies accused by Minnesota Mining and Manufacturing Company of dumping color photographic paper in the United States at prices considerably below what they charged in their home markets. In June 1979, toward the end of his tenure as president, Hiroshi Tomioka told *Focus Japan* that because his company "had bought very little equipment during its business slump in the late 1960s, it now has little to lose from carrying out a radical scrap-and-build operation to utilize advanced technologies."

In 1979 Konishiroku established a photo-products marketing subsidiary, Konica Corporation (USA), the first foreign operation to sport the popular Konica name. The company also introduced the Konica FS-1, the camera industry's first motorized, auto-loading, and auto-winding compact SLR camera. Nobuhiko Kawanto became the company's new president that year.

Konishiroku's most notable activity in 1979 was the purchase of its first shares in the U.S.-based Fotomat chain of photofinishing stores, which had experienced a drop in profits the previous year. In an attempt to gain an established channel to the U.S. markets for film and photographic-paper, Konishiroku purchased eight percent of Fotomat. In return, the photofinisher agreed to sell Konishiroku film under the Fotomat name and to purchase its photographic printing paper from the Japanese company. The company increased its stake in Fotomat to 20 percent in 1982, to about 62 percent in 1985, and completed its acquisition in 1986. Fotomat had begun to lose money by 1982, suffering from short-sighted business decisions, overexpansion, and increased competition from mass merchandisers who set up their own photo laboratories and from minilabs, which provide customers with prints in an hour. By 1988, Fotomat had dwindled from a peak of 3,850 kiosks and stores to 1,700 outlets and was reorganized. It also somewhat belatedly recognized the importance of minilabs and began converting many of its kiosks and stores to while-you-wait developing centers.

The price of silver, an essential ingredient in films, skyrocketed in 1980, and Konica, like other film producers worldwide, was forced to repeatedly raise its film prices. Early that year, both Konica and its principle domestic competitor, Fuji Photo Film Company, were investigated by Japan's Fair Trade Commission for conspiring to fix X-ray film prices. That same year,

Konishiroku announced it would go into the audio- and video-magnetic-tape business with Ampex Corporation.

In the early 1980s, Konica obtained exclusive rights to sell Polaroid products in the Japanese market. It also established subsidiaries in both Australia and Canada to market cameras, photographic materials, and magnetic products.

Megumi Ide was named company president in 1983, the same year that Konishiroku introduced the Konica AF3 camera, with the company's own infrared autofocus system replacing the Honeywell autofocus system. The company introduced its first video camera that year, the Konica Color CV, which was touted as the world's smallest and lightest video camera for home use.

Business Machines Division Expansion: 1980s

Konica's business machines division picked up steam in the 1980s. The company acquired a 30 percent interest in Royal Business Machines in 1984 and agreed to sell its plain-paper copiers under Royal's name. The following year, it agreed to start supplying Olivetti with copiers that would be marketed throughout Europe under the Olivetti name. In effect, Konica would end up competing with itself in the European copier market. The company also agreed to export a copier plant to China that year.

The year 1986 saw much activity for Konishiroku. It purchased the balance of Royal Business Machines' stock, and it changed that company's name to Konica Business Machines U.S.A., Inc. It entered into an agreement with IBM to sell that company's high-speed copiers under the Konica name worldwide. Konishiroku introduced a dramatic improvement over conventional floppy discs, the super-high-density 5.25-inch floppy disc and drive system with a ten-megabyte memory capacity, which it had developed and would produce and market in cooperation with Omron Tateisi Electronics Company and Citizen Watch Company. It introduced the Konica Color 7 copier, a reasonably priced, full-color copier that produced copies said to be difficult to distinguish from color photographs.

The company also established two new business division production plants: one in Lüneberg, West Germany, in 1987, for manufacturing plain paper copiers and the other in Maryland, in 1990, for manufacturing copier supplies. Between 1984 and 1989, the company acquired business machine sales agencies in several new locations, including the United States, Australia, Italy, and Belgium.

Japan's leadership in facsimile terminals can be attributed to its strength in copier technology. Konica entered this market a bit late, offering its first facsimile terminals in 1988. It is interesting to note how the Japanese government aided the early demand for facsimile machines. Japan was one of the first countries to allow facsimile machines to be connected to regular phone lines, and the Japanese Ministry of Justice approved facsimile copiers as legal documents when the machine's technology was still in its nascent stage.

Konishiroku introduced a high-quality aspherical plastic pick-up lens for use in compact disc players in 1984, the same year it established Konica Technology, in Sunnyvale, Califor-

nia, a research, development, and marketing subsidiary for high-tech products. It also introduced its first minilab system that year, the Nice Print System-1, the world's first washless print-processing minilab. The revolutionary system required no water hookup and needed only to be plugged in to an electrical outlet to operate. Competitors soon rushed to market similar systems. By reducing space and overhead requirements, these systems led to a dramatic increase in the number of minilabs.

In the 1980s Konishiroku's problems with Fotomat, its inability to capitalize on its washless minilab system, and an increasingly competitive copier market all contributed to Konishiroku's financial difficulties. Between 1982 and 1985, Konishiroku's sales rose 24 percent but its net income for the same period fell by 17 percent. To aggravate the situation, beginning in 1986 the rising yen began to play havoc with Konica's profits. Fluctuating exchange rates narrowed the profit margin of the company's exports.

In 1985 Konica began construction of the Kobe plant, a totally automatic production facility for the design and production of computer peripheral equipment and printers. Konica began to market its first laser printers in 1990.

Change to Konica: 1987

In the fall of 1987, Konishiroku changed its name to Konica Corporation. Although the company had been unifying its product and brand names in European and North American markets since 1973, many people, even in Japan, did not know that Konishiroku produced U-Bix copiers and Sakura film. By unifying its corporate and product names, the company raised its corporate profile worldwide. It also increased its advertising budget, and sponsored athletic teams, such as the U.S. rhythmic gymnastics team, and began to fly a blimp bearing the Konica name in Japan, as did competitors Fuji and Kodak. The company also funded the Konica Gallery, a Japanese gallery in the British Museum that opened in 1990. As Konica claimed just 20 percent of the Japanese film market, such efforts were needed at home as well as internationally.

Konica introduced two important new products in 1987: its first still video system, which recorded images on a magnetic disc for immediate viewing on a television set, and the world's fastest color negative film, the Konica SR-V3200, which doubled the light sensitivity of any film on the market of that time. That same year, the company announced it would become the first Japanese producer of photosensitive materials to set up a manufacturing plant in the United States. In 1989 Konica Manufacturing U.S.A. opened in Whitsett, North Carolina; it produced color photographic paper.

In 1987 Konica's medical products division began to sell a desktop system for analyzing blood, at the rate of 80 patients an hour; an X-ray developing system that cut developing time to 45 seconds, half the time taken by other techniques; and the Konica Direct Digitizer, which enabled the digitization of radiographic images.

Konica was one of seven Japanese companies accused of dumping by the European Community Commission in 1988. The companies were accused of making photocopiers in Europe using mainly Japanese parts in an attempt to avoid an antidumping duty. Konica responded that 40 percent of its copier parts were manufactured locally.

Konica introduced two new cameras in 1989. The Kanpai—Japanese for "toast" or "cheers"—with a voice-activated shutter, was intended for use at parties and other social events and received a favorable market reception. The Konica A4, the world's smallest and lightest fully automatic compact camera, won the European Compact Camera of the Year Award for 1989–90. That year, Konica also introduced the SR-G series of film, a new series of color negative films offering a high level of image quality and speed.

1990s and Beyond

The early 1990s saw the emergence of the single-use, or "disposable" camera. First marketed by Fuji in 1986, Konica began selling its first single-use camera the following year. By 1990 Konica was able to sell seven million of the increasingly popular products, far behind the 30 million sold by Fuji but more than enough for a solid second place. The company introduced several new models of single-use cameras in the 1990s, including the Torikkiri Mini (1992); the Torikkiri Motto Mini Flash Sepia (1997), which produced sepia-toned monochrome prints; and the Konica Issimo (1998), which featured a pop-up flash and the Advanced Photo System (APS). APS had been developed in the mid-1990s by a Kodak-led consortium that included Fuji but not Konica; it offered the ability to select from three photo sizes (4 by 6 inch, 4 by 7 inch, and a panoramic 4 by 10 inch) as photos were taken, and for non-single-use cameras, easy film loading. Single-use cameras came under criticism from environmentalists concerned about the wastefulness inherent in their design. But the photo companies, including Konica, quickly introduced product modifications to facilitate the recycling of various parts of the assembly, and instituted recycling programs at their company-owned photoprocessing laboratories.

Continuing its history of innovation, Konica in 1994 unveiled the ECOJET Nice Print System, the first minilab system to use tablet-form photofinishing chemicals. The system eliminated the need for liquid chemicals, which were expensive and difficult to transport, required a complicated mixing process, and had to be carefully handled by minilab operators. It also reduced both the chemical replenishment rate and the level of effluents. As digital technologies continued to replace analog ones in the 1990s, Konica began marketing in 1998 of the Konica Digital Minilab QD-21 System, an ultracompact, fully digital minilab.

In 1995 Konica introduced the Konica KL-2010, a full-color laser printer. Also that year came the debut of the Konica 7050 digital workgroup document system, which doubled as a 50-copies-per-minute digital laser copier and a 50-pages-per-minute laser printer—the latter when connected to a computer or network. By the late 1990s, through the success of this and other new products, Konica had become the U.S. market leader in high-speed digital copiers. In late 1999 the company stopped producing analog copy machines altogether in order to focus on developing and manufacturing digital models.

Back on the camera front, Konica was increasingly active in the APS scene. In 1996 the company introduced the Konica Super Big Mini MB-S100 camera. The following year Konica brought to market the Konica Revio, which featured a power zoom lens and was at the time of its release the world's smallest and lightest APS camera. Also in 1997 Konica entered the burgeoning market for digital still cameras through the release of the Q-M100. The camera used a memory card able to store from ten to 50 images, depending on the resolution, and was capable of capturing extremely high quality images.

Konica was profitable for most of the 1990s, until posting a loss of ¥3.17 billion (US$25.5 million) for the 1999 fiscal year, which the company attributed to weak domestic and Asian markets. Late in that fiscal year, Konica announced that it would consolidate its U.S. photo printing operations, closing four of its seven film development facilities. This move followed an October 1998 consolidation, whereby 21 photo development subsidiaries in Japan were unified. Konica also announced in February 1999 that it would reduce group employment by eight percent over a two-year period. These developments were evidence of a company committed to protecting its position within highly competitive industries.

Principal Subsidiaries

Konica Marketing Corporation; Konica Medical Inc.; Kyoritsu Medical Co., Ltd.; Konica Business Machines Japan Co., Ltd.; Yamanashi Konica Co., Ltd.; Kofu Konica Co., Ltd.; Konica Denshi Co., Ltd.; Konica Supplies Manufacturing Co., Ltd.; Shinwa Digital Industry Co., Ltd.; Konica System Equipment Co., Ltd.; Konica Gelatin Corporation; Konica Packaging Corporation; Konica Chemical Corporation; Konica Color Photo Equipment Co., Ltd.; Konica Meditech Service Corporation; Nihon ID System Co., Ltd.; Konica Service Co., Ltd.; Konica Engineering Co., Ltd.; Konica Repro Co., Ltd.; Konica Logistics Co., Ltd.; Konica Sogo Service Co., Ltd.; Konica Information Systems Co., Ltd.; Konica Technosearch Corporation; Konica Color Network Co., Ltd.; Konica Color Imaging Corporation; Asia Color Co., Ltd.; Showa Tennenshoku Co., Ltd.; Konica Color Kansai Co., Ltd.; Union Color Co., Ltd. NORTH AMERICA: Konica Headquarters North America, Inc. (U.S.A.); Konica Photo Imaging, Inc.; Konica Medical Corporation (U.S.A.); Konica Manufacturing U.S.A., Inc.; Konica Graphic Imaging International, Inc.; Konica Business Technologies, Inc. (U.S.A.); Konica Supplies Manufacturing U.S.A., Inc.; Konica Technology, Inc.; Konica Capital Corporation I (U.S.A.); Konica Finance U.S.A. Corporation; Konica Canada, Inc. EUROPE: Konica Europe GmbH (Germany); Konica Business Machines Deutschland GmbH (Germany); Konica Graphic Imaging Europe GmbH (Germany); Konica France S.A.; Konica Bureautique S.A. (France); Konica UK Ltd.; Konica Business Machines (U.K.) Ltd.; Konica Nederland B.V. (Netherlands); Konica Austria GmbH; Konica Business Machines Italia S.p.A. (Italy); Konica Business Machines Belgium S.A.N.V.; Konica Czech s.r.o. (Czech Republic). ASIA/OCEANIA: Konica Asia Headquarters Pte. Ltd. (Singapore); Konica Singapore Pte. Ltd.; Konica Hong Kong Ltd.; Konica Manufacturing (H.K.) Ltd. (Hong Kong); Konica (Thailand) Co., Ltd.; Konica Photochem (Thailand) Co., Ltd.; Konica (Dailan) Co., Ltd. (China); Konica Australia Pty. Ltd.

Further Reading

Bounds, Wendy, ''Konica, Partner to Unveil Filmless, Electronic Camera,'' *Wall Street Journal,* August 19, 1996, p. B5.

Janssen, Peter, ''First Shots in a Photo War,'' *Asian Business,* October 1992, p. 56.

Konica Corporation, Tokyo: Konica Corporation, 1989.

Konica's History: The History of Japanese Photography, Tokyo: Konica Corporation, 1987.

Yamada, Toshihiro, ''Camera Obscura: Fuji, Konica, Kodak All Using Shady Practices,'' *Tokyo Business Today,* October 1995, p. 36.

Yamazaki, Yasushi, ''Stiff Competition Seen for Camera Industry,'' *Japan 21st,* February 1992, pp. 107, 109, 111, 113.

—Mary Sue Mohnke
—updated by David E. Salamie

Ladish Co., Inc.

5481 S. Packard Avenue
Cudahy, Wisconsin 53110
U.S.A.
(414) 747-2611
Fax: (414) 747-2963
Web site: http://www.ladishco.com

Public Company
Incorporated: 1905
Employees: 1,130
Sales: $226.77 million (1998)
Stock Exchanges: NASDAQ
Ticker Symbol: LDSH
NAIC: 332116 Metal Stamping; 336412 Jet Propulsion &
    Internal Combustion Engines & Parts, Aircraft,
    Manufacturing

Ladish Co., Inc. is a supplier of high-strength forgings for jet engines and other aerospace and industrial applications. The aerospace market accounts for about 90 percent of sales; jet engine forgings alone account for 70 percent. The company's sales are concentrated in just a few major customers, such as Rolls-Royce, United Technologies (Pratt & Whitney), and General Electric.

Origins

According to the Ladish Co., Inc.'s official timeline, in 1905 Herman W. Ladish bought a steam hammer, setting himself on the track of becoming "Axle Forger to the Industry." Expansion, both in facilities and in product offerings, continued through the 1930s, when Ladish spent $1 million upgrading its plant and began doing its own machining. New products included aircraft brake drums.

During the war years, components for critical U.S. aircraft originated at Ladish's forge, including struts for B-26 bombers and propeller shafts for P-51 Mustangs. The company also supplied engine crankcases. In addition, it developed advanced, high-strength alloys and installed new hammers for forging them.

The company's patented D6 tool steel found its way into early rocket motors. By the end of the 1950s, Ladish had installed the world's largest counterblow hammer. The company was employing about 7,000 people in four plants.

A new plant was added in Kentucky in 1966, as the company continued to supply the space program. Ladish built a factory in Arkansas in 1975 to make industrial supplies. It continued to upgrade its Cudahy forging operation, making it larger and hotter. It produced steel-alloy forgings for use in nuclear equipment and oil wells.

Ladish was forced to contend with a strike in April 1979. While Ladish used alternate employees to keep its production lines moving, its clients such as General Electric searched for alternate sources. At the same time, two critical metals, titanium and cobalt, were in short supply. The strikes at Ladish and at Fafnir Bearing Co., another engine parts supplier, were settled in September.

Changing Hands in the 1980s

In July 1981, Armco Inc. of Middletown, Ohio, announced that it was buying a 53 percent interest in privately owned Ladish after highly secret negotiations. The stock acquisition agreement was originally worth $221 million, later upped to $286 million after ACF Industries of New York made its own offer. ACF already had purchased a five percent interest in Ladish in June. ACF increased its bid to $324 million in cash and stock in August. In preparation for the deal, the rather secretive Ladish revealed that it had sales of $486.3 million in 1980, surprising many analysts. Its earnings were $11.5 million.

This bidding war came at a slow period for the U.S. forging industry. Italy, West Germany, and Japan were beginning to develop considerable competition abroad. At home, Ladish was edged out of the leading independent producer slot by Wyman-Gordon of Worcester, Massachusetts, which posted 1980 sales of $550 million. Like the companies vying for control of Ladish, Wyman-Gordon was also bullish, however, investing $12.5 million in new tooling.

In November 1981, Armco received government approval for its takeover bid, then valued at $286 million worth of stock. Ladish's forging operation tied in nicely with Armco's alloy steel production and promised opportunities for further expansion. But it could not keep its prize acquisition for long. Struggling financially after years of losses in steel, oil-field equipment, and specialty materials, Armco sold Ladish to Owens Corning Corporation in 1985, along with Armco's other aerospace subsidiaries, Hitco (reinforced composites) and Oregon Metallurgical Corp. (titanium), in which Armco had an 80 percent share. The total purchase price was $415 million.

Although the Hitco expertise that initially attracted Owens Corning seemed like a good fit, some analysts wondered how well the other acquisitions, such as Ladish, would work with Owens Corning's existing businesses, centered around the stagnant construction industry. The new businesses gave Owens Corning an entry into the aerospace market, but also exposed it to the vagaries of defense spending.

Within two years, Owens Corning sold Ladish as it came under threat of a hostile takeover. Owens Corning, in fact, divested its entire Aerospace and Strategic Materials Group. An investment group, including members of Ladish management, then bought the company for $236 million. Investment bankers Gibbons, Green and van Amerongen and Salomon Brothers Inc. financed the deal.

Crisis in the 1990s

The early 1990s were catastrophic for the aviation industry. The Persian Gulf War stifled world tourism and a global recession compounded difficulties. Privately owned Ladish experienced its worst losses ever and was losing market share rapidly. In 1992 Ladish closed its Los Angeles forging operation as a result, eliminating 188 jobs. The closing left the company with three facilities, in Wisconsin, Kentucky, and Arkansas.

Payments on the buyback debt ($110 million in junk bonds) forced Ladish into bankruptcy in 1993. It emerged from bankruptcy protection in April. Although just two months in Chapter 11, Ladish suffered a lasting stigma, given the industry's preference for long-term contracts.

Ladish lost between $15 million and $20 million a year in 1994 and 1995, on sales of $122 million and $115 million, respectively. Lagging a few years behind its larger competitors, the company embarked upon a massive competitiveness campaign. After turning to outside consultants for guidance, it initiated many of the employee empowerment measures popular at the time. Ladish kept employees notified of financial and marketing information via e-mail memos and periodic staff meetings. It also started an incentive payment plan.

The company employed "synchronous manufacturing" techniques of controlling work flow throughout its plants. Process improvements included reducing batch sizes. "Process mapping" involved input from all levels of production workers with the aim of removing unnecessary steps. Speaking to *Aviation Week and Space Technology,* a company executive characterized "the speed issue" as the key to improving costs as well as performance. Ladish also attempted to coordinate such improvements across the whole supply chain, from vendors to customers.

Ladish teamed with Paramount, California-based Weber to enter new markets. Weber's 35,000-ton hydraulic press was more than twice the size of any of Ladish's. Weber aimed to capitalize upon Ladish's position in the jet engine forging market. Although in this instance another company brought a unique piece of equipment to the deal, Ladish was already the sole source for several products, such as certain massive rocket engine parts. Ladish had some of the industry's largest presses and hammers.

Kerry L. Woody was named president in 1996. The company employed 1,075 at the time. Annual sales were $162 million, with profits of $2.1 million. During the year, Ladish sold its industrial products division to Trinity Industries for $36.5 million to better focus on its core business. The company bought Stowe Machine Co., Inc. in Windsor, Connecticut, for $9.5 million. That site employed 40, making jet engine components. Rival Wyman-Gordon bought Cameron Forged Products from Cooper Industries, reducing the number of competitors, but making Wyman, already the industry leader, an even larger player. Shortly after Ladish's Kentucky plant flooded in March 1997, the company announced that it was selling its pipe fittings division, which also included a plant in Arkansas.

As a result of Ladish's competitiveness regimen, by 1997 the company was acting like a lean, world-class supplier. Lead times and on-time deliveries improved drastically, and the company handled its raw materials inventories more efficiently as well. In addition, the aircraft industry as a whole was facing a boom time. A thousand employees enjoyed profit-sharing bonuses averaging $2,000 as a result of the improvements. The workforce had been cut in half during Ladish's retooling.

In late 1997, the company announced plans to sell some of its stock on the market to raise capital and to enhance shareholder liquidity. Some shares, given to creditors in its bankruptcy settlement, already had been trading over the counter. The IPO was initially planned for $60 million worth of shares, later increased to $115 million.

The $86 million IPO in March 1998 raised $29 million. Ladish President Kerry Woody told the *Business Journal of Milwaukee* that the company had finally "arrived." A couple of months later, however, one of the major investing groups disbanded, sending share prices tumbling.

Ladish spent $1.6 million to upgrade its 15,000-ton hydraulic forging press in May 1998. By August it was planning a stock buyback and looking for other machining and forging companies to acquire to increase its product line and make its stock more attractive. At this time, the company was practically debt-free and aiming for 40 percent growth by 2000, mostly through acquisitions. Although the Asian financial crisis had begun to affect sales at Boeing and Airbus, sales of helicopters and business and regional jets were increasing. The company also had a steady business in replacement parts.

The booming commercial aviation market in the late 1990s kept suppliers working at full capacity. This led many to focus on improving on-time performance rather than worry about market share, according to a Ladish market survey. Manufacturers also chose to enter longer agreements with fewer vendors.

Ladish announced that it was cooperating with the Chinese aviation industry in 1998. It arranged to buy 1,200 tons of titanium ingot from Sino-Titanium. In July 1998, Ladish teamed with Falk Corp. to build a 30-ton gear for an Army Corps of Engineers hydroelectric power facility.

Concerned the company was being undervalued in the stock market, Ladish management announced that the company was buying back more shares in August 1998, further increased by 50 percent the following May. The company also instituted a poison pill plan in September 1998 to ward off potential takeover attempts.

On December 2, 1998, Boeing announced that it was cutting production 25 percent and laying off 48,000 workers. The worse-than-expected news worried suppliers on all levels of the still recovering aviation industry. To further compound Ladish's difficulties, the firm's 10,000-ton thermal press broke down later that month. The press was down for nearly three months, costing several million dollars in repairs and millions more in lost revenues. Afterward, Ladish was able to boast higher efficiency from the repaired equipment. The company also suffered the loss of partner Weber Metal's huge 38,000-ton press, however, which was down due to a cracked cylinder. The joint venture had just begun to show results, accounting for four percent of Ladish's total 1998 revenue.

Ladish posted profits of about $24 million a year in 1997 and 1998. Annual sales had climbed past $200 million. By early 1999, Ladish was reporting drastically reduced earnings, in part due to its press failure. Earnings continued to fall into the second quarter. As business slowed, Ladish offered its aging workforce retirement incentives. It then brought back apprenticeship programs to deal with a generational shortage of skilled labor. Despite all this, Ladish continued to invest for the future, buying precision machiner Adco Manufacturing of South Windsor, Connecticut. Adco employed about 30 people and was to be folded into Stowe.

Principal Subsidiaries

Stowe Machine Co., Inc.

Principal Operating Units

Advanced Materials and Process Technology Group.

Further Reading

"Aerospace Purchasers Take Broad, Long-Term View," *Purchasing,* October 9, 1997.

Camia, Catalina, and Dale D. Buss, "Owens-Corning to Buy Armco Business in Aerospace Materials for $415 Million," *Wall Street Journal,* August 19, 1985, p. 1.

Gallun, Alby, "Area Aircraft Suppliers Hold Breath for Boeing Cuts," *Business Journal of Milwaukee,* December 14, 1998.

——, "Bucyrus, Ladish Emerge from Chapter 11 Shadow," *Business Journal of Milwaukee,* March 10, 1997.

——, "Firms Face Mass Retirements As Work Force Ages," *Business Journal of Milwaukee,* March 1, 1999.

——, "Ladish Files to Become Public Company," *Business Journal of Milwaukee,* December 29, 1997.

——, "Stock Buyback Plans: Investment Tools or Smoke Screens?," *Business Journal of Milwaukee,* September 14, 1998.

——, "Stock Offering Helps Ladish Take Off," *Business Journal of Milwaukee,* April 13, 1998.

"Ladish Forges Ahead As Aerospace Rallies," *Milwaukee Journal Sentinel,* December 2, 1996.

"Ladish Seeks Close Ties with Rocket Designers," *Space News,* June 2, 1997.

Lank, Avrum, "Stock Sale Could Net Ladish Co. of Cudahy, Wis., $35 Million," *Milwaukee Journal Sentinel,* December 24, 1997.

Mullins, Robert, "Ladish to Sell Fittings Division," *Business Journal of Milwaukee,* March 24, 1997.

Rohan, Thomas M., "A Hush-Hush Deal for a Secretive Company," *Industry Week,* July 27, 1981, p. 17.

Savage, Mark, "Cudahy, Wis.-Based Jet Engine Parts Maker Ladish Co. Plans Stock Buyback," *Milwaukee Journal Sentinel,* August 26, 1998.

Schlesinger, Jacob M., "Owens-Corning to Sell Ladish Unit for $236 Million," *Wall Street Journal,* January 21, 1987, p. 1.

" 'Strategic Buyers' Having Hard Time Finding Good Deals," *Business Journal-Milwaukee,* April 24, 1998.

Velocci, Anthony L., Jr., "Aerospace Suppliers Preoccupied with Possible Cyclical Downturn," *Aviation Week and Space Technology,* May 31, 1999, p. 64.

——, "Ladish Turnaround: Lesson for Industry," *Aviation Week and Space Technology,* June 9, 1997, pp. 70–71.

——, "Survey Highlights Conflicting Priorities Among Suppliers," *Aviation Week and Space Technology,* August 10, 1998, p. 66.

Wetmore, Warren C., "Supplier Strikes Worry Engine Makers," *Aviation Week and Space Technology,* July 23, 1979, p. 22.

—Frederick C. Ingram

Leeann Chin, Inc.

3600 West 80th Street
Suite 210
Bloomington, Minnesota 55431
U.S.A.
(612) 896-3606
Fax: (612) 896-3615
Web site: http://www.leeann-chin.com

Private Company
Incorporated: 1980
Employees: 1,200
Sales: $65 million (1999 est.)
NAIC: 72211 Full-Service Restaurants

Leeann Chin, Inc. is a leading Midwest brand of high quality, quick service Chinese food. The company, which has embarked on a third try at expansion, owned and operated 52 units, located in the Minneapolis/St. Paul, Detroit, Michigan, and Kansas City, Missouri areas, about midway through 1999. The company also operates a 28,000-square-foot production center to pre-prepare and quick freeze products which are then combined with fresh produce at restaurant locations. Founder Leeann Chin continues to oversee recipe and menu development for the company.

Translating Skills into Business Ventures: 1950s–Mid-1980s

Lee Wai-Hing, born in 1933 in Canton, China, learned about the business of food at age 11, when she was working in her father's wholesale grocery market and restaurant. Within a few years her life would change dramatically. In 1949 the communists came to power in her home of Canton. Two years later, the 18-year-old Lee Wai-Hing, now in Hong Kong, married Tony Chin. In 1956, the couple and their small daughter, Laura, immigrated to the United States.

The Chin family, sponsored by Tony's sister, moved to Minnesota. Tony worked at his sister's Minneapolis restaurant, and Leeann altered clothes for upscale downtown department stores. Having earned a loyal following for her work, Chin set up her own business. She did sewing and alterations out of her home while raising five children.

During this time, Leeann treated her sewing patrons to Chinese pastries and appetizers. Impressed with her talent many of them encouraged her to teach cooking or even open her own restaurant. In 1972, Leeann began teaching classes at friends' homes and then through community education programs. "News of the charming cook who held the secrets to such delicacies as stir-fried frog's legs, winter melon soup, and shrimp almond ding quickly spread through the Wonderbread world of the Upper Midwest," according to Nina Shepherd in a 1986 *Corporate Report Minnesota* article. General Mills Creative Learning Center learned of her skills and offered her a teaching position, which she held from 1972 to 1979. (In 1980, General Mills purchased and published her recipes under the title *Betty Crocker's Chinese Cookbook.*)

During the 1970s, Leeann's reputation grew as Minneapolis and St. Paul daily papers published her recipes, and local television shows brought her on for guest appearances. Leeann continued to teach adult education classes in the metropolitan area, but began moving into party, banquet, and reception catering as well. In early 1979, the developers of a mall located in the affluent Minneapolis suburb of Minnetonka asked Leeann to open a cooking school in their building. Seeing too many barriers to success—for example, another cooking school already operated in the Bonaventure Mall—Leeann proposed she open a restaurant. The developers agreed, but she had some other roadblocks to circumvent first.

Neither Leeann's husband nor her in-laws, who were already in the restaurant business, supported the idea. Despite the resistance, Leeann went ahead with the venture. Among the five investors ready to move forward with her were Minnesota banker Carl Pohlad and his friend actor Sean Connery, who had, according to Shepherd, sampled her cooking at a party. The investors' portion, a $165,000 Small Business Administration loan, and Chin's own contribution, came to a grand total of $305,000 in capital.

Company Perspectives:

Each year since 1985, Leeann Chin has been voted the "Best Chinese Food" and the "Best Takeout Food" in Minneapolis.

The company has also won numerous local and national awards for best restaurant design, and Leeann Chin herself was voted Minnesota Entrepreneur of the Year.

While the company is now a rapidly growing restaurant chain, it retains the spirit and the outlook of a small family owned business. The company has always been, and continues to be, actively involved in all of the communities in which it operates, and is a substantial contributor to local civic, neighborhood and charitable causes in these communities.

The 80-seat, buffet-style, Leeann Chin Chinese Cuisine opened in October 1980. Designed by Twin Cities architect John Shea and decorated with Chin's own collection of Oriental art work, the "restaurant has been praised as much for its decor as for its food," observed Shepherd. The food, primarily meats and fresh vegetables, was lightly spiced with garlic, leek, ginger and wine; the restaurant was among the first in the Twin Cities to offer authentic Sichuan (or Szechwan) and Cantonese cuisine.

The endeavor was an immediate hit, grossing $1.5 million in its first year of operation. Behind the scenes another story was brewing. Chin found herself engaged in conflicts with investors over the management and future direction of the restaurant. The disputes led to Chin's near exit from the business. Instead of buying her out as she requested, the investors chose to relinquish their own interest in the operation.

In late 1983, Chin was fully in charge and spent $300,000 on an expansion to 130 seats; 20 more seats were added in 1984. A second restaurant opened in downtown St. Paul in March 1984. Located in a renovated train depot, the new site was just as successful as the Bonaventure location, grossing $1.5 million its first year. Gross sales for the first store were now $2 million.

Meanwhile, Chin's success had drawn the interest of a well-established company. Minnesota-based Dayton's asked Chin to open a takeout operation in the food market area of its downtown Minneapolis department store—nearly one-fifth of the Bonaventure store's revenue was from takeout sales. Chin signed on to create her first takeout store in June 1984. The Dayton's 700 Under the Mall location quickly began seeing an average of 1,000 customers a day.

A Changing Menu: Late 1980s–Mid-1990s

Success carried a new load of burdens. Chin ran a tight operation, and she was stretched to her limits. She needed help. After rejecting a number of possible partnerships, Chin struck a deal with General Mills, Inc. The billion-dollar food company bought her name and the three units in 1985. Chin was appointed president of the Leeann Chin, Inc. subsidiary. The selling price was not disclosed, but the company's fiscal 1985 revenues had been $5 million.

General Mills, which was also developing the Red Lobster seafood and Olive Garden Italian restaurant concepts, believed their financial strength and marketing savvy mixed with Chin's reputation for quality was the right recipe for a successful national Chinese restaurant chain. Competitor Pillsbury had the Quik Wok concept in the works.

General Mills opened additional locations in the metropolitan area and expanded outside Minnesota for the first time. But the effort to crack the Chicago market fell flat, and the company diverted its attention to the other concepts and closed the one buffet and five carryout units located in Illinois. Unlike pizza or burger vendors, approximately 90 percent of the country's Asian restaurants were in the hands of small business owners. Pillsbury's entry into the Chinese restaurant business had nosedived.

Chin, who had no decision-making authority as part of the General Mills operation, was feeling frustrated. After careful consideration, she felt ready to take back the company she founded. When she heard a buyer had stepped forward, Chin asked for the chance to purchase the business. A bank loan and funds from Dimension Capital in Bloomington, Minnesota, financed the deal which was completed in March 1988. Company sales for 1987 had been just over $14 million.

A recession battered the U.S. economy in the early 1990s, but Leeann Chin's company weathered the storm. "Laura Chin, vice president of Leeann Chin Inc., spends part of every day refusing offers from real estate agents and building owners around the Twin Cities. With commercial space in abundant supply and proven tenants a rare commodity, a Leeann Chin restaurant just might be the area's most sought-after retail tenant," reported *Corporate Report Minnesota* in January 1992. Leeann Chin recorded only slightly weaker sales volume while the restaurant industry as a whole dropped eight percent in 1991. The company's figures were helped by new carryout units in the upscale Twin Cities supermarket Byerly's.

Ron Fuller was named president of Leeann Chin, Inc. in January 1993. The former General Mills executive was no stranger to Chin: he had served as the chain's general manager while it was under Big G's ownership. In an August 1996 *Corporate Report* article, Fuller said of his second stint with the company, "[it] was to a point that Leeann realized that a transition needed to be made to professional management."

In early 1994, the $25 million business employed 750 people, operated 20 carryout units, three restaurants, and a catering center. A board of directors was being organized, and Fuller, who had been busy improving operating systems and bringing on new managers, moved to raise private capital.

Three institutional investors, Weston Presidio Capital of San Francisco, Chase Capital Partners of New York, and U.S. Venture Partners in Seattle, pumped in $11 million in 1995. The lion's share was earmarked for the expansion of the Twin Cities and Seattle markets. The company had entered the Seattle market in 1994. Leeann Chin now spent about half her time there.

Fuller had other plans as well. Some of the capital would be used to develop a new concept which he hoped to take national. The Asia Grille by Leeann Chin would feature a full bar and restaurant, food from five Asian countries, a takeout counter, and small oriental market. The national scene included only a few Chinese food chains such as Panda Express and General Mills' China Coast.

But by mid-1996, it was clear that Leeann Chin, Inc.'s second try at expansion was in trouble. Leeann Chin was negotiating a buyout. She wanted to sell her remaining 40 percent stake in the company. The investment firms owned just over 50 percent and Fuller and other managers owned the rest of Leeann Chin, Inc.

According to the Schafer article, tension began to build in the company during the transition of leadership from Chin to Fuller. The new investors, who were cultivated by Fuller, worked closely with him and bypassed Chin. A number of Chin's longtime middle managers departed as operational difficulties compounded during the company's entry into the Seattle market. In addition, Leeann Chin's name was eliminated from the new Asia Grille concept.

Furthermore, Chin's daughter Katie joined the company in October 1995 only to depart in February 1996 over differences with Fuller. Longtime employee and daughter Laura Chin had left in August 1995 to lead the Leeann Chin Foundation. Leeann Chin herself took a leave of absence from her half-time position with the company, beginning in January 1996.

Schafer wrote, "Fuller admits to one goof: opening Seattle supermarket carryout units under the Asia Grille name. They will have to be closed, he says. Yet the company will be profitable in the fiscal year ending this August with roughly $37 million in sales."

At the end of 1996, Leeann Chin's, Inc. owned and operated 25 Leeann Chin Chinese Cuisine and two Asia Grille Express units in the Twin Cities; two additional Asia Grille Express sites in Chicago-area Byerly stores; and three full service Asia Grille restaurants, one in Seattle and two in the Twin Cities. Two more Asia Grille restaurants were being built in Seattle. Ron Fuller resigned as CEO of Leeann Chin's, Inc. late in December, and the company founder returned as head of the board of directors in January 1997.

Third Time's the Charm?: Late 1990s

Stephen A. Finn came aboard as CEO in June 1997. Finn led the Bruegger's Bagel Bakery catapult from 39 units and $28 million in sales to 500 units and approximately $300 million in sales during the period from 1992 to 1997. Previously, he served nine years with Burger King.

Finn planned to succeed where others had failed. In addition to new restaurants and grocery store carryout units in the Midwest, Finn envisioned bottled sauces on grocery store shelves, gourmet kitchen specialty shops, cookbooks, videos, and perhaps a line of cookware and ceramics or a television show.

Finn, in an April 1998 *Corporate Report Minnesota* article by Jennifer Waters said the Asia Grille concept was a "huge strategic blunder" which almost "bankrupted the company" and "set back the brand." The board of directors which had backed Fuller's idea were now realigned behind Leeann Chin's original concept.

"The story here is that the strength of her visions has never gone away," Philip Halperin, a general partner with Weston Presidio Capital told Waters. "And now her visions and her concept have matched up with a wonderful management team."

Finn, unlike Fuller, saw Chin as a pivotal aspect of the expansion drive. "She is the brand, the master chef, the external relations, the teacher," he says. "She is a major asset who will help raise the awareness of the brand and guard against being just a new Chinese restaurant in new markets."

The board of directors dropped the Asia Grille concept entirely in early 1998, having converted express operations to Leeann Chin's units and entered into negotiations to sell the concept itself.

In September 1998, Leeann Chin bottled sauces, Asian Salad Dressing, Imperial Sauces, and Peking Sauce had hit the shelves of Byerly's and Lund's supermarkets in the Twin Cities. (A year earlier, Leeann Chin began opening units in Lund's food stores, following the acquisition of Byerly's by Lund Food Holdings, Inc.)

Leeann Chin, Inc., which had raised $9 million in venture capital in July 1998, had been expected to go public, but market conditions changed all that. Instead, the company would be looking for "a strategic buyer" to allow investors to cash out, according to Finn in an October 1998 *Star Tribune* article. High profile players Planet Hollywood and Rainforest Cafe had been poor performers on the stock market, and the restaurant sector had soured.

Three Leeann Chin units opened in the Kansas City, Missouri, in early 1999, and the first Detroit-area location opened in late April. These areas were demographically similar to the Twin Cities. The Troy, Michigan, unit cost $370,000 to build and equip. The well-dressed new locations served such signature items as Chinese Chicken Salad, Lemon Chicken, and Cream Cheese Puffs.

Broadening the Brand, Building for the Future

Over the years, Leeann Chin had become a household name in the Twin Cities area. Finn hoped she would become just as well known in their new markets. The initial wave of the expansion drive was off to a good start, ahead of schedule in terms of number of units in place and profitability, according to a May 1999 *City Business* article by Jennifer Franklin. Company profits were in the double digit range, and Finn was estimating sales of $80–$90 million by the year 2000.

Finn had 24 new stores, in the Leeann Chin Chinese Cuisine quick service or grocery store carryout formats, on the menu for 1999. Twelve were to be built in the Twin Cities, nine in the Kansas City area, and three in Detroit. Thirty-three more units were planned for 2000. The company's onion and garlic chips, a tie-in with sauce already on the market, would hit retail shelves in 1999. Leeann Chin's third cookbook was slated for publication early in 2000.

"However," wrote Franklin, "Bill Carlino, managing editor for *Nation's Restaurant News*, is skeptical about whether Leeann Chin can go national. 'There has never been a successful national Chinese chain. Every neighborhood has its own Chinese restaurant—a favorite little Chinese place to go. There's no reason to go to a chain.' '' Finn believed otherwise. He was pushing forward, and founder Leeann Chin, whose stake in the company was now down to about ten percent, was out on the road visiting the new restaurants bearing her name.

Further Reading

Barshay, Jill J., ''Entrepreneurs Were Put on Hold by Shutdown of New Offerings,'' *Star Tribune* (Minneapolis), October 19, 1998, p. 1D.

Earley, Sandra, ''Leeann Chin Can Carry Out Expansion,'' *Minneapolis St. Paul CityBusiness*, April 14, 1995, p. 12.

Egerstrom, Lee, ''Green Mill, Leeann Chin to Go Outstate,'' *St. Paul Pioneer Press*, May 12, 1999, p. 3B.

——, ''Leeann Chin Inc. Chief Executive Fuller Resigns,'' *St. Paul Pioneer Press*, January 11, 1997, p. 1G.

Fiedler, Terry, ''Leeann Chin Returning; CEO Departs,'' *Star Tribune* (Minneapolis), January 11, 1997, p. 1D.

Franklin, Jennifer, ''Leeann Chin Expands into New Markets,'' *Minneapolis St. Paul CityBusiness*, April 30, 1999, pp. 1, 33.

Gale, Elaine, ''Laura Chin the Head Cook in New Family Foundation,'' *Star Tribune* (Minneapolis), August 21, 1995, p. 7D.

Johnson, Tim, ''Leeann Chin Inc. Shelves Asia Grille,'' *Minneapolis St. Paul CityBusiness*, April 17, 1998, pp. 1, 43.

Kennedy, Tony, ''Leeann Chin's New Asia Grille to Blend Flavors of Five Asian Countries,'' *Star Tribune* (Minneapolis), June 30, 1995, p. 1D.

''Landlords Hungry for Leeann Chin,'' *Corporate Report Minnesota*, January 1992, p. 14.

''Leeann Chin Inc.,'' *Corporate Report Fact Book 1999*, Minneapolis: Corporate Report, p. 494.

Marcotty, Josephine, ''General Mills to Sell Back Leeann Chin's Restaurants,'' *Star Tribune* (Minneapolis), September 26, 1987, p. 5B.

Morris, Jared, ''Selecting a Successor for Your Family Business,'' *Twin Cities Business Monthly*, May 1994, pp. 32–37.

Randle, Wilma, ''Leeann Chin: Her 'Secret' Is Confidence,'' *St. Paul Pioneer Press*, May 8, 1988, p. 1H.

Schafer, Lee, ''Culture Clash,'' *Corporate Report Minnesota*, August 1996, pp. 18–20.

Shepherd, Nina, ''Journey of a Thousand Smiles,'' *Corporate Report Minnesota*, May 1986, pp. 50–58.

Stopa, Marsha, ''Chinese Restaurant Spreads Roots to Oakland,'' *Oakland Press*, April 28, 1999, pp. C1–C2.

Waters, Jennifer, ''Try, Try Again,'' *Corporate Report Minnesota*, April 1998, pp. 24–27.

—Kathleen Peippo

Loctite Corporation

1001 Trout Brook Crossing
Rocky Hill, Connecticut 06067
U.S.A.
(860) 571-5100
(800) 562-8483
Fax: (860) 571-5465
Web site: http://www.loctite.com

Wholly Owned Subsidiary of Henkel KGaA
Incorporated: 1953 as the American Sealants Company
Employees: 4,200
Sales: $788.9 million (1997)
NAIC: 32552 Adhesive Manufacturing

The manufacturer of Super Glue, Loctite Corporation sells more than 1,000 types of high-technology sealants, adhesives, and coatings, marketing its products to industrial and consumer markets in more than 80 countries. Although Loctite's greatest fame comes from its consumer products, notably Super Glue, the company derives the majority of its sales from industrial customers. Loctite products are used in a variety of industrial applications, ranging from electronics to cosmetics. In 1997, Henkel KGaA, a German manufacturer of chemicals, detergents, industrial adhesives, and cosmetics, acquired Loctite in a transaction valued at $1.2 billion.

Origins

The story of Loctite Corporation begins at Dr. Vernon Krieble's chemistry laboratory at Trinity College in Hartford, Connecticut, in 1953. Krieble's son Robert, who was also a chemist, worked for General Electric Company's chemical business in Pittsfield, Massachusetts. Bob had been working on the development of a synthetic sealant that was labeled ''anaerobic permafil.'' Being anaerobic, the substance would cure only when deprived of oxygen. The problems associated with handling the product puzzled him, and he consulted his father about the chemical's strange behavior. Vernon Krieble discovered that the liquid, when applied to nuts, bolts, and fasteners, would flow into the crevices and harden and lock them together. The

major problem that remained was how to package the product while keeping it aerated; if it was packaged in a sealed container it would harden. The problem was solved after the Plax Company, a division of Emhart Corp., introduced a polyethylene substance that was permeable to oxygen.

Although the original technology was sold by General Electric Company, the Kriebles patented their product as an entire system—anaerobic sealants stored in Plax bottles. The Plax bottles eliminated the need for separate storage devices and aerating devices, such as air compressors, to keep the liquid from hardening. This product became the pilot product of the American Sealants Company which Professor Krieble formed in 1953.

The Kriebleses began cautiously, selling the sealant system to a few companies in the Hartford area. By 1955, however, Professor Krieble retired from Trinity College and was eager to devote time to the commercial development of the product. Krieble convinced a group of Trinity alumni to put up $100,000 to start production. This liquid locknut became known as ''Loctite'' and made its public debut at a press conference in New York City. Despite the initial publicity and sales of $7,000 in 1956, the company remained in the red until 1960 when it reached a profitable sales figure of $1 million. Anticipating growth, the company moved to a production facility in Newington, Connecticut, and established a distribution facility in Australia. A plant in Puerto Rico opened in 1962.

Loctite would prove invaluable for mechanical engineers searching for ways to enhance friction. Despite precise machining, there are generally some inner spaces that are sources of leakage, looseness, and wear in machinery and motors. Kenneth Butterworth described in *The Loctite Story* that ''Loctite liquids flow into all of that surface roughness, then harden because there's no oxygen available. The hardened Loctite keys the two surfaces together.'' Initially engineers were skeptical about this technique for bonding surfaces and worried that its widespread adoption could reduce the need for precise engineering. Business people were also wary, but they were intrigued by the potential for cost reductions.

The fact that Loctite was extremely cheap to produce and eliminated the need for mechanical locking devices, such as lockwashers, helped the company overcome such skepticism.

Company Perspectives:

Loctite is in the business of solving customers' problems. When a customer buys Loctite, they get more than a product—they get a partner who will work side-by-side with them to find innovative solutions to their manufacturing problems. From engineering and testing programs to manufacturing products on the factory floor, Loctite brings a world of expertise and experience to its customers. In a design-through-assembly partnership, no one adds value like Loctite.

Because Loctite competed directly with mechanical locking devices, Krieble priced its product in the same range—although the actual manufacturing cost was much less. The company educated customers about Loctite's usage and potential. The Loctite system also included customer equipment and products required for assembly line applications. As Butterworth noted in *The Loctite Story,* "We don't just sell a bottle of glue, we sell a system and the system can cost one million dollars." The strategy was a huge success in the 1960s, and the Loctite method was used in threadlocking, pipe-sealing, and the development of different strengths and viscosities; sealing machine tool parts (which obviated the need for machines to be built to close finishes, a costly process); and developing a completely bonded assembly for motors used in hand-held power tools for the Black & Decker Corporation.

As its liquid washer grew in popularity, American Sealants changed its name to the Loctite Corporation in 1963. President Vernon Krieble died in 1964 and his son Robert succeeded him, presiding over a line of cyanoacrylate adhesives—better known as Super Glue—and a new anaerobic structural adhesive. By 1965, the company's tenth year, Loctite sales reached $2.8 million with a net income of $260,000.

Late 1960s Diversification

By 1968 the company was poised to enter into the booming automobile market. Foreign automakers embraced Loctite to help stop vibrations in their smaller, higher revving engines. Detroit-based automakers, however, waited seven years to adopt the product and initially used it for threaded and fitted parts, thereby replacing a wide class of locking fasteners prone to loosening. By the mid-1970s, as U.S. automakers began to produce smaller lightweight vehicles, Loctite developed new product lines. Notable among these was 1973's Dri-Loc line of eight products designed for various locking and sealing strengths and for sealing equipment at different temperatures. Other new products followed into the early 1980s, including a new generation microanaerobic adhesive that does not activate until the parts are assembled. This reduced the cost of producing small motors, which could now be built as self-contained units.

Despite being founded on the basic technology of the Loctite product, the company sought to expand its product range and scope throughout its history. The majority of these products were developed by Loctite's engineers. The most significant addition to the Loctite product stable was Super Glue, devel-

oped in the company's labs in Ireland and Connecticut. Basic research and development produced new acrylics, silicones, and urethanes, but Loctite also expanded its industrial product base through several key corporate acquisitions. Most notable among these acquisitions was Permatex, an automotive line acquired in 1972, and Woodhill Chemical Sales Company, purchased in 1974. Permatex's gasket dressings made it a leader in the automotive repair market; Woodhill's product line of adhesives opened up new markets for car and home repairs. It was Woodhill that introduced Super Glue to hardware stores across the country. The two companies were combined into the automotive and consumer division of Loctite in 1974.

The growth of various Loctite product lines as well as corporate acquisitions helped the company expand into international markets. In many cases, successful companies were established separately by Loctite agents; these companies were eventually purchased by Loctite. The company went public in 1980, merging with the International Sealants Corporation. At that time International's sales were $5 million compared to Loctite's $18 million. CEO Kenneth W. Butterworth stated in *The Loctite Story* that the merger of International into Loctite was the most significant in Loctite's history, giving Loctite foreign revenues (accounting for 60 percent of total revenues) and making Loctite a solid transnational corporation.

Although Loctite's sales were hard hit during recessions in the 1980s and 1990s, the company's product diversity and expansion into new markets helped keep its bottom line growing. In addition, as a transnational corporation, Loctite was insulated somewhat from the instability in demand markets that often occurs during a recession; the declining profitability from operations in a recession in one country was buffered by growing markets in other economies. The consumer market remained strong, but because most of Loctite's industrial sales were to overseas firms, the company was particularly vulnerable to fluctuations in the foreign exchange markets. The strong dollar of the early to mid-1980s was particularly devastating because the company lost sales to cheaper imports. Of course, with substantial foreign operations, a stronger dollar meant that foreign profits would translate into larger dollar denominated profits, but this was not enough to offset the domestic decline in sales. Nonetheless, by the late 1980s growth in Loctite's mass of profits was still quite strong.

Loctite's Butterworth looked forward to continued product diversification to fuel future growth. Product diversification led to revenues of $400 million in 1988, only 25 percent of which were derived from the original anaerobic "Loctite" product line. Loctite's diversification also extended geographically. Reliance on foreign sales grew substantially; in 1960 foreign sales accounted for 20 percent the company's sales, while in the early 1990s they represented 60 percent of sales and 80 percent of profits.

Marketing Oriented for the 1990s

Butterworth stepped down as CEO in April 1993, but continued to hold sway over the company as its chairman of the board. Under Butterworth's leadership as chief executive, Loctite recorded robust financial growth and strident international expansion, making encouraging progress during his eight-year reign. During his tenure, sales increased from $240 million to $606 million, while annual earnings swelled from $17 million to $72 million. Internationally, Loctite had equities in companies in 24 countries by the time Butterworth relinquished his title as chief executive, selling more than 1,000 products in 80 nations. Financial and physical growth were hallmarks of Butterworth's legacy, but perhaps his most significant achievement was altering the company's strategy. Since its founding, Loctite had focused on technological innovation, operating on the premise that a product will create a market. Butterworth reversed the company's perspective, maintaining that the market should dictate product development. The transformation meant conferring with customers and addressing their needs with adhesive or sealant products, a market approach that elicited praise from industry pundits. ''He [Butterworth] has helped turn Loctite from a technology-based company into a marketing-oriented company with excellent results,'' an analyst remarked to *Sales & Marketing Management* in 1993, typifying the response to Butterworth's influence on Loctite.

David Freeman, who had been named president of Loctite in 1991, succeeded Butterworth as chief executive in 1993, inheriting a company whose business was divided into three market segments. By far the largest facet of the company's business was its industrial group, which included original equipment manufacture (OEM) and maintenance, repair, and overhaul (MRO) markets. From its industrial customers, Loctite was collecting $490 million in annual revenue by mid-decade, obtaining the remainder of its volume from the consumer market ($190 million) and the automotive aftermarket ($148 million). More than half the earnings realized by the company's three business segments came from international sales, primarily from business conducted in Europe. The importance of adhesive and sealant activity in Europe took on greater significance in late 1996, drawing the attention of all those working at Loctite headquarters in Connecticut. In November, Dusseldorf-based Henkel KGaA announced its intention to acquire Loctite, proposing a takeover that industry observers valued at more than $1 billion.

Henkel, an international manufacturer of chemicals, detergents, industrial adhesives, and cosmetics, was no stranger to Loctite's management. At Loctite's request, Henkel had purchased a 35 percent stake in Loctite to thwart a hostile takeover launched by AlliedSignal during the mid-1980s. In November 1996, the DM 14-billion-in-sales German conglomerate proposed acquiring the 65 percent of Loctite it did not already own, presumably to strengthen its position in the U.S. market. Henkel's adhesives business, which generated DM 2.4 billion, or US$1.5 billion, was nearly twice the size of Loctite's entire business, making for a powerful combination in an industry undergoing consolidation. Unlike the proposed takeover by AlliedSignal, the takeover by Henkel was ''friendly,'' embraced by Freeman and other senior executives who were expected to remain at Loctite once the deal was completed.

Henkel concluded the acquisition of Loctite in January 1997, marking the beginning of a new era for the Connecticut company. Loctite was organized as a Henkel subsidiary with Freeman serving as both chief executive and chairman. Substantial changes were in the offing as Loctite pressed forward under Henkel ownership, highlighted by the decision made in 1999 to abandon the automotive aftermarket business. Loctite sold the business to PBT Brands, Inc., deciding that its resources were

better directed at its core industrial business. Along with the divestiture, the company's corporate headquarters in Hartford, Connecticut, were sold, with the remaining functions of the Hartford site consolidated into Loctite's Rocky Hill, Connecticut facility, which subsequently became the headquarters for all business conducted in North, Central, and South America. As part of the consolidation, Henkel informed Freeman he was being transferred to Dusseldorf, a move the Loctite executive avoided by resigning at the end of May 1999. Freeman's departure left Loctite facing the new century ahead with new leadership. Heinrich Gunn, president of Loctite's European group, became the company's new chief executive. As Loctite entered the 21st century, with Gunn in Dusseldorf alongside Henkel executives, its future role as an elite adhesives and sealant producer was secure, firmly rooted in decades of technological innovation.

Principal Subsidiaries

Loctite Canada; Loctite Mexico.

Principal Divisions

Industrial Automotive; Electronics Industry; Industrial Maintenance; Industrial Production; Medical Equipment.

Further Reading

Butterworth, Kenneth W., *The Loctite Story,* New York: Newcomen Society of the United States, 1988.

Chapman, Peter, ''Henkel Seeks Rest of Loctite in Adhesives Industry Push,'' *Chemical Market Reporter,* November 4, 1996, p. 1.

Cowan, Alison Leigh, ''A Family's Odd Bid to Cash Out,'' *New York Times,* May 26, 1991.

Fattah, Hassan, ''Henkel Makes a $1-Billion Bid to Devour Loctite,'' *Chemical Week,* November 6, 1996, p. 9.

Giragosian, Newman H., *Successful Product & Business Development,* New York: Marcel Dekker, Inc., 1978.

Grant, Ellsworth S., *Drop by Drop: The Loctite Story,* Hartford, Conn.: Loctite Corporation, 1983.

Hulstein, Calvin, ''Assembling with Anaerobics,'' *Chemtech,* October 1980.

Kelley, Bill, ''Sticking to His Guns,'' *Sales & Marketing Management,* July 1993, p. 54.

Kiesche, Elizabeth S., ''Loctite Secures a Grip in a Broader Market; Applying Technology, Marketing Expertise Worldwide,'' *Chemical Week,* March 3, 1993, p. 37.

''Loctite Corporation: Diversification Distances It from Cyclical Woes,'' *Barron's,* October 3, 1988.

''Loctite Corporation Reports 8 Percent Earnings Gains for December Quarter and for 1992,'' *Barron's,* February 1, 1993.

''Loctite Heirs Plan to Sell a Stake,'' *New York Times,* March 21, 1991.

McClenahen, John S., ''Robert Krieble's Capitalist Crusade,'' *Industry Week,* April 6, 1992.

''Super Glue Revamped for 'Everyday' Use,'' *Marketing,* November 3, 1994, p. 7.

Teitelbaum, Richard S., ''A Play on Europe's Recovery,'' *Fortune,* May 16, 1994, p. 30.

''Why Ignore 95% of the World's Market: Loctite Thinks Globally, Profits Locally,'' *Business Week,* October 23, 1992.

Woods, Wilton, ''Sticky Stuff,'' *Fortune,* March 6, 1995, p. 24.

—John A. Sarich
—updated by Jeffrey L. Covell

LUBRIZOL

The Lubrizol Corporation

29400 Lakeland Boulevard
Wickliffe, Ohio 44092-2298
U.S.A.
(440) 943-4200
Fax: (440) 943-5337
Web site: http://www.lubrizol.com

Public Company
Incorporated: 1928 as The Graphite Oil Products
   Company
Employees: 4,324
Sales: $1.62 billion (1998)
Stock Exchanges: New York
Ticker Symbol: LZ
NAIC: 324191 Petroleum Lubricating Oil & Grease
   Manufacturing; 325199 All Other Basic Organic
   Chemical Manufacturing

The Lubrizol Corporation is one of the world's leading suppliers of performance chemicals, including specialty additives for lubricating oils used in various engines, automatic transmissions, and gear drives; as well as specialty products for industrial fluids, fuel additives, process chemicals, and coating additives. North America accounts for about 40 percent of company revenues, Europe, 32 percent, and the Asia-Pacific region, Latin America, and the Middle East, 28 percent.

Early History

The company was founded in 1928 by the Smith brothers (Kelvin, Kent, and Vincent), the Nason brothers (Frank and Alex), and their friend Thomas W. James. The three Smith brothers had all worked at Dow Chemical, a company their father, a professor of chemistry, had helped to establish.

From its beginning the growth of Lubrizol, originally known as The Graphite Oil Products Company, was tied to the expansion of the petroleum and automobile industries. By working closely with manufacturers, or, in the case of shortsighted automobile makers, by staying one step ahead, Lubrizol was able to carve out an unassailable niche for itself. The company's first product, a suspension of graphite in oil called Lubri-Graph, was formulated to prevent car springs from creaking.

After this initial success, the young men addressed a more serious problem. Early automobile engines were lubricated with mineral oil, which meant that the engines overheated frequently, and that their pistons would stick because of the heat or accumulated sludge. When this happened the driver had to pull over and wait for the engine to cool. The chemists at Graphite Oil discovered that by adding chlorine to lubricants the problem of overheating was alleviated. This new product, and later the whole company, was named Lubri-zol, although no one knew what the "zol" stood for (the hyphen was dropped in 1943). Soon auto repair shops and car dealers were ordering the strangely named oil, along with specialty lubricants tailor-made for specific models of engines.

In 1935 Alex Nason traveled to Detroit to promote his small company, but General Motors scoffed at the idea of adding chemicals to oil in order to increase engine performance. At the time, G.M.'s diesel engines became so clogged with impurities that they had to be stripped and cleaned every 500 hours. Eventually the auto manufacturer was convinced of the value of gasoline and lubricant additives, and added Lubrizol products to its list of recommended products for car care.

Focus on Petroleum Additives: 1942

During World War II Lubrizol supplied its products to the military. In order to keep its equipment in optimum running condition the government established scientific tests and rigorous performance standards for all lubricants. After the war, standards for lubricants used in passenger cars were also set. Since Lubrizol had patented important processes and ingredients in the manufacture of high quality lubricants, it profited from the new regulations. In 1942 the company decided to abandon the manufacture of oils and lubricants, and to concentrate solely on petroleum additives such as oxidation inhibitors, detergents, and chemicals to reduce oil breakdown at high temperatures. These additives were then sold to the major oil refineries.

By the 1950s Lubrizol was selling more petroleum additives than any other company in the world, yet it was still a privately held corporation with less than 5,000 employees. There were many factors underlying its success. One factor was the nature of the additive industry. Lubrizol sold its additives primarily to oil companies and, interestingly enough, its only competitors were oil companies. When a company such as Exxon needed an additive it did not manufacture itself, it preferred to buy the additive from Lubrizol rather than a rival oil company. Additionally, Lubrizol's status as an independent company often appealed to nationalized oil industries for political reasons. In the 1960s Lubrizol was the sole supplier of additives to the nationalized oil industry in Peru which was, for ideological reasons, reluctant to deal with the major companies in the petroleum industry.

But Lubrizol's position as a supplier to a handful of huge companies was not without a certain amount of risk. This became apparent in the mid-1950s when Texaco decided to make its own fuel additives. This single corporation had purchased nearly a quarter of Lubrizol's total output, so its defection was painful.

Despite its problem with Texaco the company flourished. It did not, however, expand. The company philosophy was "to grow, but not get big" in the words of one executive. The president at the time, Mr. Clapp, said "Our goal is to increase earnings to shareholders in a business we understand." Consequently, Lubrizol was reluctant to diversify. Until the acquisition of Agrigenetics Corporation in 1985, company policy was to buy companies only as strong as Lubrizol, and there were not many chemical firms that fit this description. In the 1950s the company made its first acquisition, the R.O. Hull Company, which made rustproofing chemicals. This company, which rarely accounted for more than two percent of Lubrizol's sales, was later sold.

Going Public: 1960

In the 1960s Lubrizol continued to watch its revenues steadily increase. In 1960 it became a public company, and by taking advantage of the stock options that the company offered many employees became rich. The company had a good relationship with its employees, in part because salaries were generous and employees were eligible for profit sharing, including those on the shop floor.

Lubrizol's approach to management was distinctive. Job descriptions were flexible, and employees had a high degree of autonomy in deciding what tasks they should do and in what manner. The company's success had always depended on staying at the forefront of research on additives, and technicians historically comprised a high percentage of Lubrizol's workforce. Upper management was also saturated with chemists, although in the 1970s a prominent lawyer joined their ranks. The ordinarily mild-mannered Lubrizol was extremely combative in guarding its patent rights.

Unlike many chemical companies, Lubrizol applauded the country's growing concern with pollution. Lead-free gas and catalytic converters opened up a new demand for lubricants to replace the lubricating action of leaded fuel. Any change in engine design was beneficial for Lubrizol because a new design required new additives, and the company was well-equipped to meet the latest demands before its competitors were able to.

Thriving Amid Oil Crises and Recession: 1970s

By the early 1970s Lubrizol was recognized as an excellent investment. Although ranked by size in the lower 400 of the *Fortune* 500, it was one of the top 40 companies in terms of stock performance. The company seemed impermeable to the various economic problems that arose during the 1970s. For instance, although some of its additives were derived from petroleum products, and many of its products were used in passenger cars, the company prospered as a result of the oil crisis. This was because high gasoline prices encouraged automakers to design new, energy efficient cars, and these design modifications required new fuel additives, transmission fluids, and gear lubricants.

Even the recession had a beneficial effect on Lubrizol, which also made additives used in the production of oils for heavy industrial machinery. During the recession it became imperative for large industrial companies to lower repair costs, and quality lubricants and additives were a good place to start. Lubricants are one of the least likely places for a company to economize. As then president Mastin said, "In relation to these factors (high maintenance costs) the price of superior lubricants is minor, but the benefits are significant."

In the late 1970s Lubrizol started a cautious program of diversification. Its first new purchase (1979) was the Althus Corporation, a maker of lithium batteries. In the early 1980s Lubrizol purchased a biotechnology company that used recombinant DNA for medical uses. Both of these firms were small (200 employees) and financially sound.

Diversification Through Genetic Engineering Plants: Early 1980s

In the early 1980s Lubrizol narrowed its interest in diversification to companies that were perfecting genetic engineering with plants. Using genetic engineering, Lubrizol hoped to develop improved seed oils which could be employed in the manufacture of the additives and specialty chemicals that remained Lubrizol's main product line. In 1985 Lubrizol purchased the Agrigenetics Corporation, one of the leaders in the small field of plant genetics. This company became the first to modify a plant using recombinant DNA when it spliced a bean gene to that of a sunflower.

The purchase of Agrigenetics appeared to be an uncharacteristic move for Lubrizol, especially since Agrigenetics was operating at a loss of nearly $40 million. Agrigenetics was by far the largest acquisition in Lubrizol's history, and one that required the company to go into debt. Industry analysts pointed out, however, that there were only 20 firms capable of developing recombinant DNA techniques for plants, and that corporations who wanted to diversify into this particular field were likely to soon find it impossible to acquire a plant genetics subsidiary. Plant genetics, while risky, provided unlimited possibilities for new technologies, and Lubrizol wanted the patents.

Lubrizol was also interested in moving into this new area because the additives industry was maturing. Around this time, Lubrizol proved itself to be vulnerable to economic trends. Lubrizol had always been able to turn adverse economic conditions to its advantage, but in 1985 the worldwide recession began to cut into demand. Despite the rising concern over maintenance, enough machines and vehicles were out of operation to slightly depress the additives market.

Lubrizol responded to this situation by restructuring the company. There was a shift towards fewer employees in manufacturing and more in the development of specialty chemicals. The workforce was pared down, but this was accomplished through voluntary early retirement plans rather than layoffs.

By 1987 Lubrizol's revenues had surpassed the $1 billion mark for the first time. The following year net income jumped from $81.3 million to $131.2 million. Much of the increase was attributed to an October 1988 settlement of a patent-infringement case filed by Lubrizol against Exxon Corporation, at the time the top two lubricant additives makers, with 30 percent and 25 percent market shares, respectively. The case was set to go to trial when the settlement was reached, by which Exxon agreed to pay Lubrizol $80 million and agreed to stop selling more than 300 products based on Lubrizol processes. The two companies continued to battle in and out of court throughout the 1990s, finally reaching an agreement in March 1999 that settled all intellectual property litigation between the firms, with a payment of $16.8 million from Exxon to Lubrizol.

Refocusing on Additives: 1990s

In June 1991 Lubrizol signed a letter of intent to purchase Amoco Chemical Co.'s petroleum additives unit, but the bid fell through after regulators raised antitrust objections. Lubrizol posted revenues in excess of $1.5 billion for the first time in 1992, but growth soon stagnated because of slackening demand for additives and increasing competition. The company consequently decided to refocus on its additives business, divesting its entire biotechnology holdings from 1993 to 1996.

The late 1990s were a period of consolidation within the additives industry. Emerging out of a series of deals were four main players: Lubrizol; Infineum, a joint venture of Royal Dutch/Shell Group and Exxon which was formed in 1999; the Oronite Division of Chevron Chemical Co., which acquired the viscosity modifiers business of Exxon Paramins; and Ethyl Corp., which had acquired the additives businesses of both

Texaco Inc. and Amoco Chemical during the 1990s. Lubrizol participated in the consolidation trend as well, making six acquisitions during 1998 for a total of $157.8 million. The largest of these were Adibas, the lubricants and fuel additives business of British Petroleum Company PLC; and Carroll Scientific, Inc., a developer and supplier of varnish and wax-based performance additives for the ink market. The latter was an example of Lubrizol's determination to broaden its product base as the growth rate for engine lubricant additives declined.

At the same time, Lubrizol embarked upon a cost reduction program, aimed at reversing the trend toward declining profits. In late 1998 the company announced a three-year plan whereby 12 percent of its workforce would be cut, and the number of production units would be reduced by 20 percent. Lubrizol hoped to lower operating costs by about $28 million as a result of this initiative. Through this restructuring effort as well as additional acquisitions, Lubrizol aimed to maintain its nearly 40 percent share of the additives market well into the new millennium.

Principal Subsidiaries

Lubrizol do Brasil Aditivos, Ltda. (Brazil); Lubrizol Canada Limited; Lubrizol de Chile Limitada; Lubrizol China, Inc. (U.S.A.); Lubrizol Coating Additives Company G.m.b.H. (Germany); Lubrizol Española, S.A. (Spain); Lubrizol Europe B.V. (Netherlands); Lubrizol France S.A. (99.995%); Lubrizol Gesellschaft m.b.H. (Austria); Lubrizol G.m.b.H. (Germany); Lubrizol International Inc. (Cayman Islands); Lubrizol International Management Corporation; Lubrizol Italiana, S.p.A. (Italy); Lubrizol Japan Limited; Lubrizol Limited (U.K.); Lubrizol Metalworking Additives Company, Inc.; Lubrizol de Mexico, S. de R.L.; Lubrizol de Mexico Comercial S. de R.L. de C.V.; Lubrizol Overseas Trading Corporation; Lubrizol Scandinavia AB (Sweden); Lubrizol Servicios Tecnicos S. de R.L. (Mexico); Lubrizol South Africa (Pty.) Limited; Lubrizol Southeast Asia (Pte.) Ltd. (Singapore); Lubrizol de Venezuela C.A. (99.9%); CPI Engineering Services, Inc.; Engine Control Systems, Ltd. (Canada); Gate City Equipment Company, Inc.; Gateway Additive Company; Hyrolec Technical Services Limited (U.K.).

Further Reading

Hall, Matthew, "Lubrizol Invests a Little in Everything," *Ohio Business,* November 1989, pp. 29+.

Kindel, Stephen, "Lubrizol: There's Growth After War," *Financial World,* April 2, 1991, pp. 18+.

Kovski, Alan, "Additives Business Consolidates As Firms Wrestle with Costs," *Oil Daily,* July 15, 1998.

Lublin, Joann S., "Lubrizol and TIAA-CREF Fund Duel over 'Dead-Hand' Takeover Defense," *Wall Street Journal,* March 23, 1999, p. A4.

Ortega, Bob, "Lubrizol Shareholders Call for Repeal of Poison Pill on TIAA-CREF's Motion," *Wall Street Journal,* April 27, 1999, p. A12.

Parker, Susie T., "Lubrizol to Buy Amoco Chemical Unit," *Oil Daily,* June 5, 1991, p. 8.

Reingold, Jennifer, "Stand and Deliver," *Financial World,* June 8, 1993, pp. 28, 30.

Salwen, Kevin G., ''Lubrizol, Already Industry Leader, Gets Raves Even As It's Positioned to Solidify Attractions,'' *Wall Street Journal,* October 26, 1988.

Schiller, Zachary, ''Lubrizol Could Force Exxon to Change Its Oil,'' *Business Week,* November 7, 1988, p. 40.

Schiller, Zachary, and Joan O'C. Hamilton, ''A Biotech Gamble That Went to Seed,'' *Business Week,* September 5, 1988, pp. 88–89.

Siler, Charles, ''Tough and Slippery,'' *Forbes,* May 29, 1989, pp. 42 +.

Teitelman, Robert, ''Seeds of Change: Can Lubrizol's L.E. Coleman Make His New Businesses Bloom Before His Old Ones Wither on the Vine?,'' *Financial World,* October 20, 1987, pp. 50 +.

Villena-Denton, Vicky, ''Lubrizol and Exxon Paramins Setting the Pace for Lube Additive Industry's Globalization,'' *Oil Daily,* March 18, 1991, pp. B-4 +.

—updated by David E. Salamie

Manchester United Football Club plc

Sir Matt Busby Way
Old Trafford
Manchester M16 0RA
United Kingdom
+44 (0) 161 868 8000
Fax: +44 (0) 161 868 8804
Web site: http://www.manutd.com

Public Company
Incorporated: 1878 as Newton Heath
Employees: 550
Sales: £88 million (US$145 million) (1998)
Stock Exchanges: London
Ticker Symbol: MNU
NAIC: 711211 Sports Teams and Clubs; 71131 Promoters of Performing Arts, Sports, and Similar Events with Facilities; 51321 Cable Networks; 72111 Hotels

Manchester United Football Club plc has earned a reputation as England's most financially successful football team. First in its field to be listed on the London Stock Exchange, Manchester has a long and storied history and is famous for commercial exploits that have brought it both detractors and imitators. Its aggressive style and high profile players consistently draw a robust following at home and abroad.

Origins

By the time the predecessor to Manchester United—Newton Heath—was formed in 1878, football, or soccer, had evolved from a game of kicking around animal heads to a gentleman's pastime adopted and improved by working men. Formed in a northern section of Manchester, Newton Heath was comprised of employees at the Lancashire and Yorkshire Railway. The group entered the Division I Football League in 1892.

Beginning with a tentative meeting in 1898, Manchester United players led the unionization of their newly created trade. The Football Association finally allowed for the formation of such a union in 1908, however it ordered all players to resign from it the following year when the union made overtures to join the Federation of Trades Unions. The players' union eventually relented.

Newton Heath was renamed Manchester United in 1902. By this time, business and football had become inseparable. Local businessmen and newspaper publishers sponsored the games while entrepreneurs organized teams as limited companies. Brewer J.J. Davies invested heavily in the Manchester United when it was threatened by bankruptcy. He provided funds to build playing grounds at Old Trafford, which was completed in 1910. The same year, the club, then known as "moneybags United," was reprimanded for questionable financial reporting. The team won a couple of First Division championships before World War I and the FA (Football Association) Cup in 1909.

The club's greatest manager, Matt Busby, was born in Orbiston, a mining village near Glasgow, on May 26, 1909. At an early age, Busby saw football as a way to rise out of the poverty and sectarian strife of his birthplace. But when his family considered immigrating to the United States for a better life, Busby persuaded them to let him work in the mines at age 16 to bring in extra money so they could remain near to football.

Busby rose to prominence in youth soccer leagues and in the mining community. He moved to Manchester in 1926 to play professional football for Manchester City. Ten years later, after injuring a hamstring, Busby transferred to the Liverpool Football Club. He found the atmosphere there much more supportive than at City, and this environment became the basis for his philosophy of managing.

Rebuilding After the Wars and the Busby Babes

Matt Busby was being demobilized from the British Army after leading a football team while in uniform. He was assigned management of Manchester United in 1945, an arrangement brought about by his old friend and long time United staffer Louis Rocca. Manchester United had earlier tried to woo Busby away from City as a player, but were unable to find the funds. The situation at Old Trafford was still dire. Although Manchester United had risen into the First Division in 1938, its reputation had deteriorated between the wars and its playing grounds had been bombed in 1941. The club was also in debt.

To economize, Busby retained older players longer. Manchester United meanwhile fostered a youth soccer program. From the beginning, Busby insisted managers were better placed to make decisions regarding the game than directors and so managed to wrest unprecedented autonomy from the board. Busby, who liked to play football with the ''lads'' himself, had a management approach completely different from his more aloof predecessors.

Football became a £4 million a year industry in the 1940s. Old Trafford was rebuilt and in 1948 Manchester United was valued at £100,000. The team Busby assembled that year cost £7,750 in transfer (signing) fees. Busby was also managing the British Olympic team.

British national pride was at a low ebb in the 1950s, as even the relatively inexperienced Americans defeated Britain in World Cup competition. However, the team Busby created in the 1950s, the ''Busby Babes,'' has been considered one of the greatest of all time and included legendary players such as Duncan Edwards. The league champion team of 1956–57 cost £79,000 in transfer fees. Manchester United developed a trademark, attacking style as Busby imported European playing techniques. Manchester United players also played on the English national team for the World Cup.

After winning the league championship, Matt Busby turned his sights toward European competition. On February 6, 1958, the plane carrying the Manchester United side home from a European Cup match in Yugoslavia crashed on a snowy Munich runway after a refueling stop. Twenty-three were killed in the accident; the team was decimated. With the deaths of some of its best players, England lost its hopes of winning the World Cup. With the tragic news, however, came unprecedented public recognition and sympathy for Manchester United.

For a time Busby, who was himself seriously injured in the crash, swore off football. When he returned, he had to rebuild the team by buying players. The transfer fees he paid set records. He signed Albert Quixall from Sheffield for £45,000 in September 1958 and made several other £30,000 acquisitions in the next few years.

The maximum wage was abolished in 1961 and transfer fees kept climbing. In 1962 the club paid an Italian team £115,000 for Denis Law, then a staggering amount. The teams Busby assembled in the 1960s were full of exuberant, charismatic individuals that played to the ''pop'' spirit of the times and drew crowds of 50,000 at Old Trafford. Players like George Best, who picked up the name ''El Beatle'' abroad, became media stars. The team won the FA Cup in 1963; other championships followed. Manchester United finally won the European Cup, the premier European competition, in May 1968, becoming the first British team to do so. Busby was knighted afterwards.

Along the way, physical violence began to erupt on the field and in the stands, notably at the 1965 FA Cup semifinal against Leeds. At this time, the rival between Manchester United and Liverpool was intense but still good-spirited. Abroad, Manchester United met an alarmingly unsportsmanlike reception at a World Club Championship match in Argentina in 1968.

Sir Matt Busby retired as manager in 1969. Before he did, he bought the lease on the team's souvenir shop. Louis Edwards, a meat trader picked for the board by Busby, had become chairman in 1962. He had also become the owner of Manchester United Ltd.

Wilf McGuinness followed Busby as coach, although Busby retained control of club affairs. McGuinness, who was only 31 years old, did not relate as well to the players as Busby, who returned to coach while searching for a replacement for McGuinness. The next manager, Frank O'Farrell, was himself replaced by Tommy Docherty. As the team's performance faltered, it was difficult for Busby to define his new role as director. The 1970s belonged to Liverpool, not Manchester United, although the Red Devils somehow remained a bigger draw.

Busby was made president in 1980. He resigned a year later after the team gave £2 million contracts to Bryan Robson and Remi Moses. When Busby had started as a player, the maximum wage was £5 a week. Martin Edwards, son of Louis Edwards, was made chairman in 1981.

Ron Atkinson replaced Dave Sexton as manager in 1981. He in turn was dismissed in 1986 and replaced by Alex Ferguson, a successful Scottish manager. Initially, his hands were tied in acquiring expensive players, although in the summer of 1989 Ferguson got approval to spend £8 million on transfer fees. (Martin Edwards had found a buyer for the club in August, Michael Knighton, who was, however, unable to raise the £10 million to complete the purchase.) Despite the spending, the club fared poorly in 1989–90, and Ferguson's job seemed in jeopardy until the next year, when his expensive team started winning.

Red, White, and Gold: The 1990s

In the 1990s, Alex Ferguson's teams managed to recapture some of the glory of the Busby days. Manchester United won the championship of the new Premier League in 1993. (This league was formed by top clubs to give them a larger share of TV revenues.) At the same time, football popularity was at an all-time high worldwide.

When Martin Edwards could not sell the club, he recruited executives who made it the most profitable team in the U.K. It began trading on the London Stock Exchange in 1991. In 1992–93, Manchester United Football Club plc had an operating profit of £7.3 million on a turnover of £25.2 million, thanks largely to merchandising and brand extensions such as Champs Cola, which were worth £5.3 million, up from just £828,000 five years earlier. Besides soda, the club was soon branding lager, wine, even champagne. Selling the brand seemed to observers a more stable source of income than relying on winning games week after week. The club opened a Megastore at Old Trafford in 1994 and spent heavily (£13 million) to upgrade Old Trafford. In July 1993 the club paid a record £3.75 million transfer fee for midfielder Roy Keane.

Sir Matt Busby died on January 20, 1994, after five years with blood cancer. His legacy in Manchester and across Britain was enormous. Many football games across the world observed a minute of silence in his honor, and thousands lined the streets to watch the funeral procession.

By the late 1990s, the club was selling or helping to sell cellular phone service. It was in a 16-year, £24 million deal with electronics maker Sharp and a five-year, £743 million deal with Rupert Murdoch's broadcasting arm BSkyB and the BBC. In 1997 it launched its own television channel, MUTV, in cooperation with BSkyB and Granada Media Group.

BSkyB offered £624 million for the club in September 1998. The bid was upped to £1 billion, but blocked by the Monopolies and Mergers Commission on the grounds that Murdoch was so powerful broadcasting sports worldwide that the deal would be unfair for competition.

Manchester United Football Club plc continued to enter new territory with its commercial exploits. In 1998 the team launched an online store sponsored by Lotus and Sun Microsystems. It also reached out to a large band of supporters in Asia. In the spring of 1999, Manchester United International, a new subsidiary charged with developing the brand abroad, began selling its Manchester United Premium Lager there and opened a huge leisure center in Hong Kong. The club was planning several other complexes in Asia.

Manchester United continued to pay record transfer fees to maintain its winning tradition: £12.6 million for Dwight Yorke in August 1998. Nevertheless, Manchester United Football Club plc seemed like a money-minting machine in the late 1990s. Its very success prompted the keenest criticism from those who felt true football fans were the ones who stayed with their teams through thick and thin. Those with a longer view knew Manchester United had seen plenty of both.

Principal Subsidiaries

Manchester United International Limited; Manchester United Merchandising Limited; Manchester United Catering Limited; MUTV Limited (33.3%); Extramini Limited (25%).

Further Reading

Baird, Roger, ''Strip Tease,'' *Marketing Week,* February 14, 1997.

Bose, Mihir, ''Floating on a Sea of Fantasies,'' *Director,* July 1996, p. 81.

Bowden, Adrian, ''United Conjure Up Their Own Brand of Profits,'' *Investor's Chronicle,* September 30, 1994, p. 51.

Gilbert, Nick, ''The Manchester United Way,'' *Financial World,* February 14, 1995.

Glanvill, Rick, *Sir Matt Busby: A Tribute,* Manchester: Manchester United Football Club plc; London: Virgin Publishing, 1994.

Gorman, Mike, ''Media Choice: Football Programmes,'' *Marketing,* August 3, 1995.

Green, Geoffrey, *There's Only One United: The Official Centenary History of Manchester United,* London: Hodder and Stoughton, 1978.

Hodgson, Derek, *The Manchester United Story,* London: A. Barker, 1977.

Kelly, Stephen F., *Back Page United: A Century of Newspaper Coverage,* London: Macdonald, Queen Anne Press, 1990.

Miller, David, *Father of Football: The Story of Sir Matt Busby,* London: Paul, 1970.

''Professor Sir Roland Smith: Still Running with the Ball,'' *Director,* May 1995, p. 90.

Santoli, Michael, ''Rupert Rallies and Scores,'' *Barron's,* April 19, 1999.

Szymanski, Stefan, ''Why Is Manchester United So Successful?'' *Business Strategy Review* 9, Issue 4 (1998), pp. 47–54.

Tischler, Stephen, *Footballers and Businessmen: The Origins of Professional Soccer in England,* New York: Holmes and Meier, 1981.

Tyrrell, Tom, *Manchester United—The Religion,* London: Kaye and Ward, 1969.

''United's Night,'' *Economist,* May 29, 1999, p. 55.

Walvin, James, *The People's Game: A Social History of British Football,* London: Allen Lane, 1975.

White, Jim, ''United's Hard Sell,'' *Management Today,* February 1999, pp. 32–38.

—Frederick C. Ingram

MANPOWER

Manpower, Inc.

5301 N. Ironwood Road
Milwaukee, Wisconsin 53217
U.S.A.
(414) 961-1000
Fax: (414) 961-7081
Web site: http://www.manpower.com

Public Company
Incorporated: 1948
Employees: 2,015,000
Sales: $8.81 billion (1998)
Stock Exchanges: New York
Ticker Symbol: MAN
NAIC: 56132 Temporary Help Services

The second largest employment services company in the world, Manpower, Inc. provides staffing services through 3,200 offices in 52 countries, serving 250,000 clients worldwide. Fulfilling requests for temporary industrial and office workers is a primary focus for Manpower, but the company has recorded its greatest growth during the late 1990s from technical placements. Worldwide, the company operates more than 200 technical centers devoted to providing temporary technical, information technology, and telecommunications professionals. Manpower derives approximately 75 percent of its sales from international business, primarily from Europe, where the company operates nearly 1,500 offices.

Post-World War II Origins

Manpower was begun in 1948 by Elmer L. Winter and Aaron Scheinfeld, two partners in a Milwaukee law firm who saw the labor shortage that followed World War II as an opportunity to form a temporary agency. A year earlier, Kelly Services, Inc., which would become the second biggest temporary agency, had formed in Detroit. By 1956, Manpower's reputation was established enough that franchising the company name became profitable. In order to set up a Manpower franchise, an

investor paid an initial fee, attended a training course, and then set up an office. The franchisee was responsible for recruiting and placement, as well as paying a percentage of gross earnings to Manpower, while the company provided promotion and management guidance.

Under its founders' charge, Manpower expanded during the 1960s, establishing franchises all over the world, most prominently in Europe, but also in South America, Africa, and Asia. In 1965, Mitchell S. Fromstein, whose small advertising agency had been handling the Manpower account, joined its board of directors. Fromstein's role in the company's development grew as the company grew. Its acquisitions in the 1970s included Nationwide Income Tax Service, Detroit; Gilbert Lane Personnel, Inc. of Hartford, Connecticut; and Manpower Southampton Ltd., which had been one of its franchisees. All of these companies were later sold by Manpower.

In 1976, Parker Pen Co. acquired Manpower for $28.2 million. Like Manpower, Parker was a well-known, family-owned business that had begun in Wisconsin. Where Manpower had enjoyed a meteoric rise in the 1950s and 1960s, however, Parker's sales began faltering in the late 1970s due to its failure to compete with inexpensive writing implements in the marketplace. With Scheinfeld dead and Winter eager to pursue other personal interests, a buyout of all stock was initiated by Fromstein and Parker President George S. Parker. Fromstein bought 20 percent of Manpower's stock and moved up to the position of president and CEO.

When Manpower began, it initially concentrated its efforts on industrial help. Fromstein made changes in this and many other respects. Practicing a managerial style he says he learned from Vince Lombardi, the legendary coach of football's Green Bay Packers, for whom he once wrote speeches, Fromstein is considered responsible for virtually all of the growth and development that Manpower underwent in the 1980s. His innovative approach to the temporary industry included shifting emphasis from the factory to the office, recognizing that automated equipment was revolutionizing the way offices operated, and revising the company's Employment Outlook Survey. The survey, initiated in 1962 to measure the hiring intentions of employers and

Company Perspectives:

Since 1948, Manpower has provided employment opportunities for millions of people around the world. At the same time, we've enabled businesses to remain productive by providing them with quality workers. To do this successfully, we developed a systematic approach to matching worker to work that is unparalleled in the industry. Manpower's Predictable Performance System helps us accurately place people in assignments with more than 250,000 businesses worldwide annually . . . providing our customers with productive workers and our employees with work that matches their skills and abilities.

published quarterly, was revised with the assistance of the Survey Research Center of the University of Michigan. Understanding of and sensitivity to its clients needs became hallmarks of Manpower under the guidance of Fromstein.

Above all, it was Fromstein's commitment to take responsibility for training temporary employees, rather than merely finding places for them to work, which accounted for Manpower's dominance in the industry. In his *Alternative Staffing Strategies,* David Nye writes, ''Manpower is by no means the only [temporary] firm involved in training and testing, but its approach is clearly the most extensive.''

In 1978, when the prospect of a computer that would fit inside an office, let alone on top of a desk, seemed preposterous, Fromstein announced that Manpower would invest $15 million in a computer training program called Skillware. Nye quotes Fromstein: ''The days when a secretary walking into a new office could just flip the 'on' button, roll in a fresh sheet of letterhead, and go are gone.'' An interactive, self-paced program, Skillware enabled Manpower employees to develop competence in a variety of tasks. This approach made temporary employees more valuable to companies because they required less onsite training and made a greater contribution to productivity in a shorter time. Since its inception, Skillware expanded tremendously and was available for 160 software programs in nine languages.

Spurring Growth in the 1980s

The complexion of the job market in the United States and abroad contributed greatly to the ascendancy of the temporary industry in the 1980s. Because the cost of providing benefits rose faster than the cost of providing wages, employers began to see that, even considering the percentage that had to be paid to the temporary agency, hiring on a temporary basis was more economical than searching for, hiring, and training permanent workers. It also proved to be an effective way of testing potential permanent workers. Furthermore, the increase in dual-income families increased the appeal of temporary work to parents faced with the high cost of daycare. The Bureau of Labor Statistics reported that temporary jobs accounted for one percent of the workforce in 1989, doubling the 1980 statistic.

Under Fromstein, Manpower was positioned to capitalize on the situation more effectively than were its closest competitors, Kelly and Olsten Corporation. Total sales were at $300 million in 1976, the year he joined; by 1991 they reached $3.5 billion.

Manpower's rapid growth meant that it was drastically outpacing the pen sales at Parker. For a time, its profits made up for the pen company's losses, but by February 1986 the unbalance had become too great, despite Parker's efforts at reducing its workforce and cutting back on the varieties of pens manufactured. The writing instruments division was sold to a group of investors for $100 million, and Manpower became the name of the parent company.

In 1987, Manpower engaged in an important affiliation with International Business Machines Corporation (IBM). Under the agreement between the two companies, Manpower would provide onsite training and support services (such as a hotline for computer questions) to buyers of IBM systems. IBM benefited from having its users more fully acquainted with its systems, and Manpower benefited from the awareness among these users that its temporary workers were computer literate.

In the same year, Manpower was the target of a hostile takeover in what turned out to be a tangled and complex affair. In August, Antony Berry's Blue Arrow PLC, a British employment-services firm with revenues only one-sixth the size of Manpower's, offered to buy Manpower at $75 per share, for a total of $1.21 billion. Berry, well known in England from his days as a boxer, had terrific success with Blue Arrow since joining them in 1984, taking them from £410,000 (US$725,000) in profits to £30 million (US$55 million). Manpower stock had been at $62.375 at the time of the offer, but excitement over the bid drove the price up to $78, beating the $75 offered by Blue Arrow. In the weeks that followed, Fromstein and Manpower contemplated a return bid on Blue Arrow, considered a joint venture with the Swiss employment firm Adia S.A., threatened to refuse Blue Arrow unless they increased their bid to $90 per share, and publicly denounced Berry's plans for combining the companies, which included implementing an executive search program. This last suggestion infuriated Fromstein, who told the *Wall Street Journal,* ''We aren't blind or deaf. If we thought it was an opportunity, we could have done it years ago.'' Manpower rejected the bid, prompting a shareholder lawsuit on charges that the directors' decision was financially irresponsible.

Three weeks after the initial offer was made, Manpower finally endorsed the Blue Arrow offer at $82.50 per share for a total of $1.3 billion. Under the terms of the sale, Manpower's operations in the United States would continue under the name ''Manpower.'' Fromstein was allowed to stay on as Manpower president and CEO and one of a five-member Blue Arrow board, though by December 1987, he was fired from this position after a long simmering conflict with Berry became apparent.

Fromstein's separation from Manpower, however, was not long-lasting. In spite of his early successes, Berry proved to be an inept manager. His enthusiasm for sports led Blue Arrow into an expensive and unauthorized investment in a yacht for the

America's Cup competition. The stock market crash of October 1987 brought Berry's most substantial impropriety to light. In order to create the funds necessary to purchase Manpower, Berry had secured a loan of $1.3 billion from the National Westminster Bank (NatWest) in England to be repaid from the proceeds of a stock issue. With the bank as underwriters, 38 percent of the shares were purchased by existing Blue Arrow shareholders, leaving the bank the responsibility of selling the rest. According to an article in *Financial World,* potential buyers might have been scared away had they learned of this situation, so NatWest itself purchased 12 percent in order to boost the amount of sold shares to 50 percent, a more respectable figure. Such a purchase was legal, but the underwriters kept it a secret, and once revealed, this was construed as a deliberate attempt to mislead potential investors. A criminal investigation was launched, and by January 1989, top executives at the bank—most notably its chairman, Lord Boardman—were forced to resign and Berry was disgraced on account of his role in the deal and other financial improprieties.

Backed by Manpower's U.S. franchises, Fromstein mounted a successful campaign to regain control of Blue Arrow. Once back at the helm, his first three decisions were to change the name of Blue Arrow to Manpower, sell all businesses that had belonged to Blue Arrow, and to move the company's headquarters back to Milwaukee.

Most Blue Arrow businesses were sold in 1990 and 1991 and the company became a U.S. corporation in 1991. As Manpower entered the 1990s, its major objectives were to continue its policy of staying current with technological advances in the workplace, and to further international expansion into previously inaccessible regions, most notably Eastern Europe.

Swelling Revenues in the 1990s

During the 1990s, Manpower succeeded in achieving much of what it set out to accomplish at the beginning of the decade. The company recorded robust financial growth, exponentially increasing its revenues as the global staffing services industry became one of the fastest-growing business sectors in the 1990s. Manpower's strident revenue growth, which lifted systemwide sales past the $10 billion mark by the decade's conclusion, was propelled by the company's ever increasing expansion rate, particularly overseas—a primary goal when the Fromstein-led concern entered the 1990s.

Significantly, the company's progress during the decade was achieved without the benefit of any major acquisitions. During the 1990s, there were few temporary staffing firms who could make such a claim. The industry was rapidly consolidating, as competitors merged to form global powerhouses, rapidly in pursuit of establishing a worldwide network of staffing offices. Nonetheless, by striking an independent pose, the company saw its lead over all worldwide rivals disappear. Manpower's relegation to the number two position in the world, caused by the 1997 merger of Adia SA and Ecco SA, was symbolic of the company's progress during the 1990s. Manpower took giant strides forward during the decade, but as it did so the pace of rival firms and the changing dynamics of the temporary staffing industry sometimes passed the company by.

Midway through the decade, Manpower's growth began to pick up speed. Coming off $4.3 billion in revenues and a record $83.9 million in net income in 1994, the company began establishing new offices at a frenetic pace, increasing the number of new offices it opened each year from 100 in 1994 to more than 400 by the late 1990s. The spate of new office openings brought Manpower into dozens of new markets, stretching from Milan to Moscow and spreading into Latin America, Asia, and South America. Important alliances were formed as the company fleshed out its global network of offices, highlighted by two partnerships forged in 1996. Manpower signed an exclusive arrangement with Drake Beam Morin Inc., the world's largest executive outplacement company, and formed an alliance with Ameritech to provide call center and help desk agents. Manpower's 50th anniversary marked 50 consecutive years of revenue growth, but during the celebratory year, Adia SA and Ecco SA merged, usurping Manpower as the global leader in its industry.

One year after the merger that created Adecco, Manpower reached an impressive financial milestone. Systemwide sales eclipsed $10 billion in 1998, representing a doubling of revenues during the previous five years, but the towering growth of revenues did not silence all of the company's critics. The emergence of Adecco as the new international leader in the industry prompted some industry pundits to cite Adecco's successes as Manpower's failures, specifically Fromstein's belated entry into the fastest-growing segment of the staffing industry, information technology. During the late 1990s, Adecco derived roughly 20 percent of its revenues from providing information technology temporary workers, nearly twice as much as Manpower collected. Manpower's perceived failure to assume a strong position in a market that was growing 25 percent each year led *Forbes* magazine's Phyllis Berman and Adrienne Sanders to suggest that Fromstein should step aside. Although it was doubtful the criticism of two pundits materially affected Fromstein's mindset, he did remark, ''I'm putting pressure on myself to replace myself,'' as quoted in the January 11, 1999 issue of *Forbes* magazine.

Fromstein retired in 1999, making room for the promotion of Jeffrey Joerres to the posts of CEO and president. A Manpower executive since 1993, Joerres had been credited with spearheading the enormous growth of the company's global accounts, demonstrating a talent that would be instrumental in his efforts to shoulder past Adecco in the 21st century. As Manpower exited the 1990s, it was fast in pursuit of a greater presence in the information technology market. By 1999, the company had established more than 200 offices devoted exclusively to serving technical and information technology staffing needs.

Principal Subsidiaries

Signature Graphics—Milwaukee; Transpersonnel Inc.; Tri Country Business Services Inc.; US Caden Corp.

Further Reading

Berman, Phyllis, and Adrienne Sanders, ''Time to Go?,'' *Forbes,* January 1, 1999, p. 82.
Berss, Marcia, ''You Can Go Home Again,'' *Forbes,* October 1990.

"Case Study: Blue Arrow PLC and Manpower, Inc.," *Buyouts & Acquisitions,* November/December 1987.

Gilbert, Nick, "Manpower Comes Home," *Financial World,* April 30, 1991.

Jensen, Dave, "Temp and Team Spirit," *Management Review,* October 1988.

Kapp, Sue, "Titan of Service," *Business Marketing,* November 1991.
"Market Outruns Offer by Blue Arrow," *Wall Street Journal,* August 5, 1987.

Nye, David, *Alternative Staffing Strategies,* Washington, D.C.: Bureau of National Affairs, 1988.

Sansoni, Silvia, "Move Over, Manpower," *Forbes,* July 7, 1997, p. 64.

Walbert, Laura R., "Menpower Versus Penpower," *Forbes,* December 19, 1983.

"Winter's Tale," *Finance,* September 1969.

—Mark Swartz
—updated by Jeffrey L. Covell

MarineMax, Inc.

18167 U.S. 19 North, Suite 499
Clearwater, Florida 33764
U.S.A.
(727) 531-1700
Fax: (727) 531-0123
Web site: http://www.marinemax.com

Public Company
Incorporated: 1998
Employees: 731
Sales: $291.2 million (1998)
Stock Exchanges: New York
Ticker Symbol: HZO
NAIC: 441222 Boat Dealers

MarineMax, Inc. is the largest recreational boat retailer in the United States, and the leading seller of Sea Ray, Boston Whaler, and other boats made by Brunswick Corporation, which makes up nearly 90 percent of the company's new boat sales and 75 percent of used boat sales, as well as brand names such as Hatteras and Supra ski boats. A conglomeration of major boat dealers, with 47 retail locations throughout the United States, MarineMax sells new and used pleasure and recreational boats, fishing boats, and high-performance boats, as well as related marine products, including engines, boats, trailers, parts, and accessories. The Clearwater, Florida-based company also arranges boat financing, insurance, and extended warranty contracts, provides boat repair and maintenance services, and offers boat brokerage services.

The Bassett Boat Company of Florida: 1944–98

Richard Bassett's family started out in the boat selling industry in Springfield, Massachusetts, back in 1944, and made a decent living selling boats in that small marketplace. More than three decades later, in 1979, the company expanded into Miami and Boca Raton, Florida. In 1991 the company moved its Boca Raton operations and staff. The new multimillion-dollar corporate headquarters, located in Pompano Beach on the water,

contained 16 slips for boats. The Boca Raton facility was retained and used for other purposes. In 1992, Bassett reported total revenues of $45 million.

In 1993 Bassett Boat Company—already one of the largest boat retailers in the United States, with facilities in Springfield and Ludlow, Massachusetts; Wakefield, Rhode Island; and Miami, North Palm Beach, and Pompano Beach, Florida, all handling Sea Ray boats exclusively—began expanding rapidly. That year, when Bill Gardella, Sr., owner of The Rex Marine Center in South Norwalk, Connecticut, closed the doors on his Formula and Regal dealership, Bassett Boat Company leased the then vacant 8,000-foot showroom, relocating its wares from the company's location in Stamford. The move placed Bassett in a major marina located in Connecticut's wealthiest area, along with other boat companies such as The Small Boat Shop, Atlantech Marine Electronics, New England Fiberglass Repairs, Inflatable Boats, Wizard Marine, and Windward Passage Yacht Sales. Additionally in 1993, the company purchased the assets of Boatland of Florida. Boatland, owned by Ed Taggart, brought Bassett two new Sea Ray locations in Stuart and Melbourne, Florida.

In 1994 Richard Bassett stepped down from his position as president in the company his family founded nearly 50 years earlier. He hired Clint Moore, formerly the head of Little Falls, Minnesota-based Larson Boat Co., a division of Genmar Holdings. Previously, Moore had worked for 15 years with the Mercury Marine Division of Brunswick Corporation, then spent two years with Glastron before moving to Larson. While at Larson, Moore increased sales some 25 percent from 1993 to 1994. Moore moved on from Bassett before the inception of MarineMax.

Gulfwind Marine USA: 1967–98

Gulfwind, also known as Outboarder of Sarasota Inc., founded in 1967, meanwhile, was also a major boat dealership and one of the top Sea Ray distributors in its own right. In 1991 the company spent four days in a unique marketing campaign with Sea Ray Boats, offering to pay the new ten percent luxury tax the U.S. government instituted on items worth more than

$100,000, if customers would buy their boats. It worked. The company sold $1.26 million worth of yachts during that period at its three locations in Clearwater, Fort Myers, and Sarasota, Florida. The company, run by president William H. McGill, Jr., reported total sales in 1992 of $20 million.

Putting Heads Together: The Inception of MarineMax, 1998

By 1998, Bassett and Gulfwind were unquestionably the largest dealerships for Sea Ray boats in the United States. But something was missing. By this time, the power boat industry in the U.S. was a $19 billion market, but it was an industry in pain. Sales were down 27 percent from the peak of 1988, when some 790,000 boats were sold. With over 4,000 independent boat dealerships located throughout the United States, and with factors beyond their control, such as economic slowdowns or slumps which affected consumer spending on big-ticket luxury items, something needed to be done to solidify sales and to find a way to free up capital to expand into new types of marketing. In a June 1998 article by Dale DuPont in *Knight-Ridder/ Tribune Business News*, Frank Herhold, executive director of The Marine Industries Association of South Florida, said, "I've thought for some time we need to learn from our friends in the automobile industry. We have to re-engineer the way we go to market."

In an April 1999 article by Scott McCormack in *Forbes*, McGill said, "They say that every boat owner has two great days: the day he bought the boat and the day he sold it. We have to change that or this industry is dead." But how to change it?

Bassett thought he had the answer, so he approached long-time friend McGill and the two began to talk about the industry. Soon, they brought in Louis Del Homme Marine in Texas, Harrison's of California and Arizona, and Stovall Marine of Georgia. The result was MarineMax, Inc., a conglomeration of the different companies, forged into a pooling of interests. Founded in January 1998, the combined company could share finances, databases, customers, facilities, and more.

With McGill as chairman of the board, president, and chief executive officer; Bassett as a director and senior vice-president; and Graham Stovall among the directors, MarineMax, Inc.

was off and running, the largest recreational boat retailer in the United States, if not the world. The creation of MarineMax was reminiscent of CarMax Inc., the Glen Allen, Virginia-based used car dealership division of Circuit City Stores Inc., which turned total revenues of $66.3 million in 1997, and AutoNation Inc., which brought in a whopping $13.92 billion in fiscal 1998. Thus, the potential for explosive growth had already been proven by the automobile concerns.

Other changes MarineMax made in traditional boat selling, according to McCormack, included combining "high, no-haggle sticker prices with luxury service." The higher price charged by MarineMax dealerships reflected an additional 2.5 to 6 percent of the sticker price of the boat to cover the service contract. While that might mean paying more than at another dealership, it included many perks. Why? "At most of the 4,000 dealers scattered along America's waterways . . . service is abysmal," said McGill in the *Forbes* article. "If you break down at sea, well, that's the Coast Guard's problem."

McCormack went on to detail some of the benefits of buying from MarineMax: "If you can't pilot the thing, MarineMax will throw in a free captain for the maiden voyage. He'll keep coming back until you learn how to use the boat. . . . Your boat won't start at 8 a.m. one Sunday morning with the whole family on board? You can page a company technician on call 24 hours a day. If you live in the area, he'll come out to fix the problem. Otherwise, MarineMax arranges for another marina to provide assistance." McCormack also pointed out that MarineMax offered two-year, stem to stern guarantees for all boats over 20 feet, covering maintenance and service costs. In addition, he said, "You won't get charged for small service items like a dead battery or broken canvas snaps."

Going Public: 1998

Following the lead of their car dealership cousins, boat dealerships began going public in order to gain the necessary capital to expand beyond their current market restrictions. The first boat dealership to do so was Travis Boats & Motors of Austin, Texas, a company which was founded in 1979. Travis began buying independent dealers, as well as building new stores, with 21 superstores ranging across the Gulf Coast by 1998. In 1997, Travis posted total revenues of $91.3 million, with a net income of $4 million. Travis went public in June 1996, with an opening price of $9 per share.

MarineMax, Inc. was the second boat dealership to go public, doing so in June 1998, opening at $12.50 per share, and raising $59.8 million during the initial public offering. The company's ticker symbol, HZO, was a play on H2O, for water. MarineMax began acquisitions with the proceeds of its IPO. Notable among the purchases were: Merit Marine of New Jersey; Boating World in Texas; Suburban Boatworks of Warrington, Pennsylvania; Jacksonville, Florida-based Hansen Yacht Sales, Inc., a yacht brokerage operation; Treasure Cove in Ohio for $7.7 million; Cochran's Marine of Minnesota; Skipper Bud's of North Carolina; and Fort Lauderdale-based Woods and Oviatt, Inc., a very well-known brokerage firm in the boating industry. In 1998, the conglomeration reported total revenues of $291.2 million, a 71.6 percent increase over 1997 revenues of all the separate companies combined.

In January 1999, Edward Russell, who started his career as a retail salesman for Gulfwind Marine USA, was promoted from director of sales to president of that company, as well as regional manager for MarineMax. In September of that year, the company opened a new retail facility on the Cuyahoga River near Cleveland, Ohio, described by a company insider as "a critical facility in that region of the country," allowing the company another building block in a north/south corridor stretching from Florida to Maine, and giving customers the ability to buy a boat in Florida and have it serviced in Ohio later in the year.

The company also created "MarineMax University," a program which according to the company "regularly invites just spouses and kids [of boat owners] to the marina to learn how to handle their family boats—everything from docking to programming the navigation system—and to get a look at other, larger, models." The company also sponsored a variety of "getaways" to its customers, "from one-day outings on a Minnesota lake to two-week trips to the Bahamas. Customers cover the costs; the company handles the details, services the boats before leaving and sends along a team of technicians and salespeople."

Thus, as the 21st century approached, the new conglomerate was poised at the top of the food chain in its industry, ready and willing to snap up smaller fish and grow the business exponentially.

Principal Subsidiaries

MarineMax Boat Company of Florida; MarineMax Cochrans; MarineMax Del Homme; MarineMax Gulfwind South; MarineMax Gulfwind USA; MarineMax Harrison's; MarineMax Merit Marine; MarineMax North Carolina; MarineMax Stovall; MarineMax Suburban; MarineMax Treasure Cove; Woods and Oviatt, Inc.

Further Reading

"The Bassett Boat Company of Florida," *South Florida Business Journal*, June 3, 1991, p. 35.

"Boat Dealers Follow Auto Industry's Superstore Strategy," *Knight-Ridder/Tribune Business News*, May 31, 1998, p. OKRB98151065.

DuPont, Dale K., "Clearwater, Fla.-Based Recreational Boat Dealer Raises $59.8 Million in IPO," *Knight-Ridder/Tribune Business News*, June 3, 1998, p. OKRB98154070.

——, "28-Store Boat Dealer MarineMax Goes Public, Hopes to Raise $77 Million," *Knight-Ridder/Tribune Business News*, June 17, 1998, p. OKRB98168332.

"Ed Russell," *Boating Industry*, January 1999, p. 16.

Farrell, Michael, "Dealership Consolidator Sets Public Offering," *Boating Industry*, June 1998, p. 8.

——, "MarineMax Offering Falls Short of Expectations," *Boating Industry*, July 1998, p. 8.

Henschen, Doug, "Bassett Boats Expands in Two Major Markets," *Boating Industry*, May 1993, p. 16.

Johnson, Joan, and Chris Ells, "Boat Dealers: Ranked by Number of Boats Sold in 1995," *Tampa Bay Business Journal*, June 7, 1996, p. 17.

Kurowski, Jeff, "Larson President Joins Dealership," *Boating Industry*, November 1994, p. 10.

——, "MarineMax Acquires Boating World," *Boating Industry*, April 1999, p. 14.

——, "MarineMax Buys Cove Marina," *Boating Industry*, January 1999, p. 9.

——, "MarineMax Buys More Shops, Adds Hattaras Line," *Boating Industry*, November 1998, p. 10.

"MarineMax Initiates Stock Coupon Program—Coupon Program Will Utilize Existing Publicly Traded Common Stock," *Business Wire*, September 13, 1999.

"MarineMax Opens New Cleveland Location," *Business Wire*, September 15, 1999.

"MarineMax Strengthens Florida Presence and Expands Brokerage Operations," *Business Wire*, September 9, 1999.

"MarineMax Reports Record Third Quarter; Revenues Increase 54%; Earnings Rise 42%," *Business Wire*, July 22, 1999, p. NA.

McConnell, Jackie, "Boat Dealers," *Tampa Bay Business Journal*, June 20, 1997, p. 23.

——, "Boat Dealers," *Tampa Bay Business Journal*, March 6, 1998, p. 15.

McCormack, Scott, "Making Waves," *Forbes*, April 5, 1999, p. 76.

"RCG Capital Markets Group to Provide Forum for 16 Undervalued Small-Cap Companies," *PR Newswire*, September 14, 1999.

Spears, Stephen, "Gulfwind Blows off Luxury Tax," *Tampa Bay Business Journal*, May 3, 1991, p. 1.

"*The Sun News*, Myrtle Beach, S.C., Business Briefs Column," *Knight-Ridder/Tribune Business News*, February 12, 1999, p. OKRB990430F5.

—Daryl F. Mallett

MARY KAY

Mary Kay, Inc.

8787 Stemmons Freeway
Dallas, Texas
U.S.A.
(214) 630-8787
(800) 627-9529
Fax: (214) 905-5721
Web site: http://www.marykay.com

Private Company
Incorporated: 1963 as Mary Kay Cosmetics, Inc.
Employees: 500,000
Sales: $1.2 billion (1997 est.)
NAIC: 32562 Toilet Preparation Manufacturing; 325611
  Soap & Other Detergent Manufacturing; 45439 Other
  Direct Selling Establishments

One of the largest cosmetics companies in the United States, Mary Kay, Inc. specializes in the manufacture and direct sale of more than 200 products, including skin creams, cosmetics, fragrances, dietary supplements, and other personal care items. Its direct sales force consists primarily of women who sell full- or part-time through home demonstrations. As of 1999 the company operated in 29 countries around the world.

Company Origins

Mary Kay Ash founded the company that bears her name in 1963, after 25 years of direct selling for other companies, beginning in the late 1930s. A direct sales career allowed her the flexibility she needed as a single mother raising three children.

For many years Mary Kay was a sales representative for Stanley Home Products, presenting "home shows" at the residences of customers. She operated as an independent contractor who purchased merchandise from Stanley and then sold it herself. After a slow first year, the next year she became "sales queen."

She recruited other women as salespeople since Stanley paid a small commission to the recruiter for the sales of each person recruited. She eventually signed 150 women and received a small percentage of the sales of each. When Stanley insisted that she move to Dallas to develop its market but would not pay her any commissions for the sales of the women she had recruited in the Houston area, she reluctantly made the move, but in 1959 Mary Kay left Stanley. Soon afterward, she became a representative for World Gift Company, where she quickly became its national training director. After a disagreement with World Gift, she resigned in 1963.

With no full-time occupation, Mary Kay Ash decided to write a book about direct sales, but it became a book on managing people. She began to think about what a "dream company" might look like, and the book waited 20 years to be written and published. She wrote in *Mary Kay on People Management* that her main objectives became to build an organization where the Golden Rule was the guiding philosophy and to "establish a company that would give unlimited opportunity to women." She also said she based her company on three fundamental principles: God first, family second, and career third.

Mary Kay decided to start a direct sales company since that was the area with which she was familiar; direct sales also would be appealing to women who could sell part-time and follow a flexible schedule. After deciding on a structure, she chose as a product a line of skin care products she had been using for more than a decade.

She had been introduced to the skin care products while she was selling Stanley products at a home party. The hostess, a cosmetologist, was testing these products on her friends. This woman had developed the products from a leather tanning solution her father had formulated, after he noticed how young his hands looked from using the solution every day. Although the cosmetologist marketed the products to her friends, she did not achieve great success in sales and, after her death in 1961, Mary Kay bought the formula from the woman's daughter.

Mary Kay and her husband invested their life savings of $5,000 to rent a small office and manufacture an initial inven-

Company Perspectives:

Our vision: To provide women with an unparalleled opportunity for financial independence, career and personal fulfillment. To achieve total customer satisfaction by delivering the products and services that enhance a woman's self-image and confidence. The principles we live by: Integrity and the Golden Rule must guide every business decision.

Enthusiasm encourages a positive attitude and provides inspiration as we work together to achieve our goals. Quality in our products and services must be a priority in order for us to deliver value and satisfaction to our customers. Service should be prompt and proactive to provide convenience with a personal touch. Praise motivates everyone to reach their full potential. Leadership among our sales force and employees must be encouraged and recognized in order to achieve long-term success. Teamwork allows each person to be valued and appreciated by others while contributing to the Company's success. Balancing our lives with God, family and career in harmony will lead to happy, fulfilled lives.

tory of skin care products. They also recruited nine independent sales representatives.

1963: The First Year

Only a month before the company was to open for business, Mary Kay's husband died, but Mary Kay decided to proceed with the opening. Her 20-year-old son, Richard Rogers, quit his job and for $250 a month ran the financial and administrative operations. His qualifications consisted of two college marketing courses and experience as a sales representative for a life insurance company. Within the year, Mary Kay's son Ben moved his family to Dallas, took a pay cut, and went to work for the family company. Daughter Marylyn joined the company later, becoming the first Mary Kay director in Houston.

Beauty by Mary Kay opened on Friday, September 13, 1963. The products were manufactured by a Dallas company and sold through a network of salespeople, who were called "beauty consultants" and were required to purchase an initial "Beauty Showcase" kit. The beauty consultants were trained in scheduling and conducting Mary Kay parties, or "skin care classes," in private homes. Beauty consultants purchased Mary Kay products at 50 percent below retail and resold them. They also received commissions for sales of salespeople they recruited.

The company tried to differentiate itself from companies that used illegal pyramiding. Unlike pyramid operations, Mary Kay sold its products to all of its consultants for the same 50 percent discount. It also took recruiter bonuses out of company earnings, not out of each sales recruit's earnings.

The company also developed specific guidelines for its salespeople. Emphasis at home parties was on teaching, rather than selling, and the number of guests was held to no more than six. Delivery and payment on the spot were required, and beauty consultants could not purchase from the company on credit. Mary Kay also limited its product line so that salespeople would be knowledgeable about each product.

Unlike many companies, Mary Kay did not limit sales territories. Beauty consultants could recruit other consultants from anywhere in the world. The company also initiated an incentive program that included the use of a pink Cadillac. This famous prize was established in 1967 when a pink Cadillac was awarded to the top sales director. The year after that, five Cadillacs were awarded and the next year, ten. By 1970, the company was awarding 20 Cadillacs. Later, rather than awarding them on a top-seller basis, they were awarded to any sales director reaching a preset sales level. By 1993, 6,500 consultants were driving pink Cadillacs or other complimentary cars.

Annual conventions were held to recognize achievement, a practice that quickly became an important public relations event. Among other programs, the conventions featured workshops for husbands of Mary Kay consultants on how to be supportive of their wives' Mary Kay careers.

In the first full year of operation, sales totaled $198,514 and the company had 318 consultants. Soon, more office space was needed and Mary Kay moved to a three-office headquarters with a training room and warehouse space, for a total of 5,000 square feet. Within two years, Mary Kay had about 850 beauty consultants selling its beauty products.

Expansion in the 1960s and 1970s

After that year, Mary Kay considered franchising to reach a wider market but decided against it because many women would have to turn to men for financing, which would reduce the level of independence that the company had tried to facilitate. Instead, in 1967, the company went public and used the proceeds from the IPO to fund its expansion. Mary Kay Cosmetics was the first company on the New York Stock Exchange chaired by a woman.

For the next decade and a half, sales grew at an average of 28 percent per year. Between 1974 and 1978, however, sales slowed. To revive them, the company increased compensation rates for consultants. Sales rates once again rose and ranged from 29 percent to 82 percent growth for the next four years.

As sales grew, so did the company's need for space, so in 1969 a new 275,000-square-foot manufacturing facility was built in Dallas. A few years later, four regional distribution centers were constructed, and in 1977 a new eight-story headquarters building opened in Dallas. In 1993 the Mary Kay manufacturing facility was the size of three football fields. It also became an FDA-registered drug manufacturing facility, allowing the company to manufacture and distribute over-the-counter drugs such as sunscreen and acne treatment products.

Trouble in the 1980s

The 1980s brought a reduction of growth as employment opportunities for women grew and more entered the full-time workforce. Between 1983 and 1985, Mary Kay's contingent of sales consultants was cut in half to 100,000. Sales fell from

$323 million to $260 million. Fewer women were available to sell the products and fewer were home to buy them.

Mary Kay stock value dropped significantly because of investors' worries about dropping profits. Concerned about how new product introduction and incentive programs were being affected by quarterly disclosure of financial information, Mary Kay and son Richard, Mary Kay's president, decided to take the company private again and bought back all outstanding stock for $315 million. The buyout proved troublesome for Mary Kay because the Internal Revenue Service (IRS) claimed that for 1983–85, Mary Kay owed back taxes since the notes that were issued during the buyout should have been considered equity. Mary Kay contended that its interest payment deductions were proper. The matter was settled in 1991 when Mary Kay, Inc. paid the IRS $3 million.

In 1989 Mary Kay tried to take over its largest rival, Avon Products, but was unsuccessful. Mary Kay then joined forces with other investors to form Chartwell Associates, and this group purchased a 19.8 percent share of Avon. The group also controlled two seats on the Avon board. Avon blocked the Chartwell coalition from purchasing more stock, however. Mary Kay announced that it was withdrawing from the association in early 1991. Shortly after that, however, Chartwell sold most of its shares, leaving Mary Kay and another associate with a three percent share of rival Avon.

Despite tax and acquisition troubles, sales started to rise and climbed to $280 million a year after the company became private again. Mary Kay Ash became chairwoman emeritus of Mary Kay Cosmetics in 1987, and Richard became chairman.

Recovery in the Early 1990s

The sales force also grew, boasting 220,000 in 1991, an increase in large part due to the inducements of larger commissions and bonuses. More consultants, however, were part-timers. Nearly 70 percent of the consultants had other jobs, whereas prior to the buyout, only 33 percent of the sales force held other jobs.

Mary Kay Cosmetics was included in both the 1984 and 1993 editions of *The 100 Best Companies to Work for in America*. In 1993 Mary Kay also became a *Fortune* 500 company. The company surpassed $1 billion in retail sales in 1992, distributing more than 200 products through a sales force of more than 250,000 consultants in 19 countries. By 1993, the company had more than 300,000 salespeople in the United States and abroad selling to nearly 20 million customers. More than half its national sales directors had earned more than $1 million during their Mary Kay careers, and the company was awarding nearly $38 million in prizes every year.

Mary Kay also was responding to growing pressure to improve its environmental practices. In 1989 it was the target of Berke Breathed's satirical "Bloom County" comic strip for testing its products on animals. The company stopped this practice later that year, and it also instituted a companywide recycling program, recycling 11 million pounds of material by mid-1993.

In 1991 Mary Kay expanded its product line to include bath and body products developed as part of its joint venture with International Flavors & Fragrances. These products, along with the 1993 introduction of Skin Revival System, helped the company recover from the slowing sales of the 1980s.

The cosmetics market was highly competitive going into the 1990s, and industry growth was expected to hover only around the rate of inflation. Mary Kay Cosmetics, however, was looking to the overseas market for its greatest growth. It had been steadily adding foreign subsidiaries since 1971 when it opened its first international subsidiary in Australia. Mary Kay opened subsidiaries in Canada in 1978, Argentina in 1980, Germany in 1986, Mexico and Thailand in 1988, Taiwan in 1991, and Spain in 1992.

Beauty consultants in many international markets distributed products made in the United States, but some Mary Kay products were produced in foreign countries for sale in those countries. Some foreign governments required that products be manufactured locally, whereas in other countries the duties on imports were so high that only local production would make the products affordable. Samples of all products were sent to the United States for testing, however.

By 1993, Mary Kay Cosmetics also had representatives in Bermuda, Brunei, Chile, Guatemala, Malaysia, New Zealand, Norway, Singapore, Sweden, and Uruguay. The company was considering foreign expansion options, including acquiring a manufacturing plant in Europe. Mary Kay's most important expansion that year was its entrance into Russia. Within two years, the company's Russian operations were pulling in $25 million in revenues.

Continued International Expansion in the Middle to Late 1990s

The company's expansion into Asia was even more important to the company's growth in the mid-1990s. Mary Kay had developed very successful operations in Taiwan since it began operating there in 1991. By 1995 the company was generating revenues of $29 million there and anticipated even greater growth as Taiwan lowered its duty rate. The company moved into Japan in 1994 and China in 1995. Both countries were difficult to enter: Japan because the company had to reformulate most of its products to meet strict regulations, and China because of the complicated politics that had to be negotiated.

By 1993 Mary Kay had become the bestselling brand of facial skin care and cosmetics in the United States, with wholesale sales of more than $735 million. In addition to its financial success, the company still was considered an outstanding employer, making the lists of both the *Fortune* 500 and *The 100 Best Companies to Work for in America*. Two years later, the company had surpassed $950 million in wholesale sales and was the bestselling skin care and cosmetics brand for the third year running.

In 1995 Mary Kay Ash retired from her position as chairman because of ill health. Although she retained the title of chair emeritus, by the following year Ash had withdrawn entirely from the company's operations. Given Ash's charismatic leadership, many questioned the effect her retirement would have on the company.

Yet in 1996 Mary Kay experienced its tenth consecutive year of record sales, with wholesale sales topping the $1 billion mark. In 1997 Mary Kay was the bestselling brand of facial skin care and color cosmetics in the United States, its fifth consecutive year to achieve that standing. The same year the company expanded into the Ukraine and Czech Republic, and the following year into Brazil.

International operations remained an important source of growth for Mary Kay in the late 1990s. The company's prospects varied widely from country to country. Mary Kay's top-selling international subsidiary, Mary Kay Mexico, saw a 56 percent increase in revenues in 1997 over the year before. In 1998, after ten years in operation, the subsidiary held nine percent of the local cosmetics market. Between 1995 and 1998 the sales force grew 233 percent.

Mary Kay hoped to see similar success with its operations in China, but was thwarted by the Chinese government in 1998. That year China announced a ban on direct sales, sending the burgeoning operations there of Avon, Amway, and Mary Kay into a tailspin. Mary Kay was forced to abandon its traditional sales plan and enter the retail market to continue selling in the country. Despite this setback, the company entered the Hong Kong market in 1999, notwithstanding its reversion to Chinese rule that year.

The company celebrated its 35th anniversary in 1998 with the introduction of a white GMC Jimmy sport utility vehicle to its sales incentive plan. That year Mary Kay was named once again to *Fortune* magazine's list of *The 100 Best Companies to Work for in America.*

Principal Subsidiaries

Mary Kay Cosmetics Inc.; Mary Kay Mexico; Mary Kay Cosmetics Chile S.A.; Mary Kay Cosmetics China; Mary Kay Cosmetics (Japan) K.K.; Mary Kay Czech Republic S.R.O.

Further Reading

Ash, Mary Kay, *Mary Kay,* New York: Harper & Row, 1981, 1987.
——, *Mary Kay on People Management,* New York: Warner Books, 1984.
Byron, Christopher, ''Garbage Time,'' *New York,* April 1, 1991, pp. 16–17.
Farnham, Alan, ''Mary Kay's Lessons in Leadership,'' *Fortune,* September 20, 1993.
Hattwick, Richard E., ''Mary Kay Ash,'' *Journal of Behavioral Economics,* Winter 1987, pp. 61–69.
Ligos, Melinda, ''Direct Sales Dies in China,'' *Sales & Marketing Management,* August 1998, p. 14.
Marchetti, Michele, ''Mary Kay,'' *Sales & Marketing Management,* November 1996, p. 68.
Omelia, Johanna, ''Direct Sellers Expand in Asia/Pacific Rim,'' *Drug & Cosmetic Industry,* September 1996, pp. 58–60.
Ross, Teresa, ''Beautiful Business: Mary Kay,'' *Business Mexico,* December 1998, p. 72.

—Wendy J. Stein
—updated by Susan Windisch Brown

Maxwell Shoe Company, Inc.

101 Sprague Street
Hyde Park, Massachusetts 02136
U.S.A.
(617) 364-5090
Fax: (617) 364-9058

Public Company
Incorporated: 1949
Employees: 149
Sales: $165.92 million (1998)
Stock Exchanges: NASDAQ
Ticker Symbol: MAXS
NAIC: 42234 Footwear Wholesalers; 316214 Women's
    Footwear (Except Athletic) Manufacturing; 316219
    Other Footwear Manufacturing

Maxwell Shoe Company, Inc. designs and makes women's footwear under its own brand names and also makes private label shoes for other companies. Originally a wholesaler of discontinued shoes, the company introduced the Mootsies Tootsies line in 1979 and later made deals to license the Sam & Libby, Jones New York, and Dockers Khakis brand names. The company went public in 1994, at which time Maxwell Shoe still remained under the control of founder Maxwell Blum and his family. In 1997, a year before the Blums sold their remaining shares of Maxwell Shoe, the company branched out into retail via a joint venture with The Butler Group, Inc.

Early Years

Maxwell Shoe Company was founded in 1949, when 24-year-old Maxwell Blum decided to go into the footwear wholesaling business. The decorated World War II veteran, who had recently graduated from Boston University School of Management, started the company in a small warehouse in Boston. Blum purchased discontinued or slow-moving lines of women's shoes from manufacturers and wholesaled them to retailers at low prices. The business proved to be a success, and Maxwell

Shoe grew gradually during the 1950s and 1960s, becoming officially incorporated in 1976.

In 1979, the year that Blum's oldest daughter Betty Ann joined the company, Maxwell introduced its first line of shoes. Drawing inspiration from Maxwell Blum's nickname of "Mutzie," the reasonably priced young women's shoes were given the moniker "Mootsies Tootsies." The new line was a moderate success, but the company's main business continued to be wholesaling discontinued shoes.

In April 1987 Maxwell hired Sperry Topsider President Mark Cocozza to head the Mootsies Tootsies division. Under Cocozza the company began to focus more seriously on sales of its own product line. Maxwell soon introduced infant's and children's shoes for girls called "Little Miss Mootsies," changing the name to "Mootsies Kids" when boys' footwear was added. Offerings initially included casual and party shoes and soon expanded to include oxfords, boat shoes, winter boots, and sandals. The footwear was packaged in eye-catching boxes that featured bold cartoonlike pictures. The company decided against marketing athletic shoes, which had become the leading sales category for the industry, though it had tested athletic designs. Maxwell chose instead to emphasize Mootsies Tootsies' low to moderate price because there were few children's lines in that range. The shoes were distributed to children's shoe stores as well as department and specialty stores.

The company began to manufacture shoes under retail chains' private label names in 1992. This required limited outlay of funds, as Maxwell merely labeled its existing Mootsies Tootsies designs with the name of the company that was marketing the shoes. The new venture was successful and grew in size over the next few years. The company's shoes were being manufactured in Brazil and China, though designed in Massachusetts.

In 1993 Maxwell made its first move to sell upscale women's shoes. Assembling a sample line of 200 shoes, complete with boxes and even mockup advertisements and sock labels, the company wowed women's clothing maker Jones Apparel Group Inc. and was granted a license to manufacture footwear under the Jones New York name. Design of the shoes was handled by Maxwell, but they were intended to accessorize well with clothing manufactured by Jones. Shoes in this line were priced in the $65–$80 range, as opposed to $25–$40 for Mootsies Tootsies. Maxwell went to Italy for the Jones shoes' manufacturing, citing that country's reputation for high quality, fashionable women's footwear. Annual sales of $79 million were recorded for 1993, with net income of $6.7 million. This year also saw Mark Cocozza assume the role of Maxwell Shoe Company president.

Initial Public Stock Offering in 1994

In 1994 Maxwell Shoe made an initial offering of common stock on the NASDAQ exchange, though the Blum family continued to control the company's voting stock. The sale brought in $28.5 million. The company had been growing rapidly since the late 1980s, with five continuous years of 30 percent revenue growth. The year 1994 also saw Maxwell extend its Jones New York shoe line, introducing the Jones New York Sport brand. The company's growth spurt continued during the year, with revenue jumping to $100.9 million. Maxwell boasted a backlog of orders worth more than $40 million at the end of the fiscal year.

In early 1995 several suitors approached Maxwell about purchasing the company, but talks broke off in each case. The retail shoe market slowed down during the year, and the company's sales were nearly even with the previous year, at $101.9 million. Profits declined to $5.8 million.

August 1996 saw Maxwell add a second outside brand name to its stable, purchasing the rights to the trademarks of Sam & Libby Inc. for $5.5 million. San Francisco-based Sam & Libby had seen better days, but Maxwell believed it could reinvigorate the brand, which marketed shoes under several names including Just Libby and New Nineties. Maxwell saw Sam & Libby finding its niche with young professional women who were seeking fashionable footwear, with the Jones New York brand positioned to appeal to older, more established professionals. Sam & Libby shoes were priced at a point midway between Mootsies Tootsies and Jones, retailing at $35 to $50 per pair.

Joint Retail Venture: 1997

In April 1997 the company announced its first move into retail, with plans to form a joint venture with The Butler Group, Inc. called SLJ Retail LLC. Butler owned a chain of mostly mall-based shoe stores called Dolcis, which had shrunk from a peak of more than 500 stores to less than 130. The outlets were spread out over 28 states. Dolcis stores had previously sold their own house brand of shoes, but that segment of the business had been in decline and analysts saw it as a good move for the

company to change its focus to nationally advertised footwear. The stores were converted by December, with 93 bearing the Sam & Libby name and 27 converted into Jones New York outlets. Maxwell owned 49 percent of SLJ, and had an option to expand its stake to 55 percent if the venture was a success. The retail operation was costing the company very little, as Butler was funding the store makeovers. In 1997 Maxwell also licensed the name J.G. Hook to give its private label customers the choice of a brand name other than their own. The company's revenues began to climb again following a period of shoe retailer bankruptcies and consolidations. Revenues for fiscal 1997 hit $134 million with net income back up to $9 million.

In early 1998 founder Maxwell Blum stepped down as CEO and board chairman, staying in touch with the company he had founded as a member of its board. The Blum family sold five million shares of company stock in a secondary offering. Daughters Betty Ann, a co-designer for Sam & Libby, and Marjorie, a sales representative for the New England region, also retired. Both gave up their roles as board members and executive officers of the company as well. Mark Cocozza took on Maxwell Blum's leadership responsibilities in addition to his duties as president.

In August 1998, Maxwell opened a new 220,000-square-foot distribution center in Brockton, Massachusetts. At that time shoes were being made in China, Brazil, Italy, and Spain. The year also saw the company roll out a $2 million national advertising campaign for the Sam & Libby shoe line.

Late in 1998 SLJ Retail announced that it was closing nearly half of the former Dolcis stores, which had already declined in number to 99. The company attributed this in part to locations that were not appropriate for the lines they were selling. The continuing tough retail environment for shoes was also a major factor. The Burton Group's share of the joint venture increased, while Maxwell's ownership dropped to 35 percent. Meanwhile, Maxwell Shoe had made a deal with Levi-Strauss & Co. to market women's shoes under that company's Dockers Khakis brand name. Dockers were to be a casual, moderately priced line of footwear fitting in between the Sam & Libby and Jones New York price brackets. The new shoes were given their debut in New York in December at the national Shoe Expo.

Sales for fiscal 1998 had reached a new peak of $166 million. The Mootsies Tootsies line accounted for nearly half of the total, with Jones New York making up a quarter, private label shoes 13 percent, and Sam & Libby ten percent. Discontinued shoe lines, the company's bread and butter for the first 30 years of its existence, now amounted to only three percent of its revenues. The company's largest customer was discounter TJX Companies, which accounted for about 20 percent of sales. Maxwell had an order backlog of $68 million at the end of the year.

In July 1999 Maxwell sold its license to market the Jones New York brand name back to the Jones Apparel Group, which had purchased shoe maker The Nine West Group, Inc. The deal netted Maxwell $25 million in cash. Though it would bring a reduction in revenue, the company chose to look at the bright side, announcing that it planned to use the infusion of cash to acquire more new brands.

Celebrating a half-century in business, the Maxwell Shoe Company had come a long way from its start as a wholesaler of discontinued shoes. With the growing success of its Sam & Libby and Mootsies Tootsies lines, as well as its private label business, the company was proving to be consistently profitable. Despite the loss of the Jones New York brand name and the disappointing results of the joint retail venture, Maxwell was positioned to grow with its newly acquired Dockers Khakis line and was also actively seeking additional brands to add to its portfolio.

Principal Subsidiaries

The Sprague Co.; Maxwell Retail, Inc.

Further Reading

Berry, Kathleen M., ''The New America: Maxwell Shoe Inc.—Old-Line Shoe Salesman Sings a New Tune,'' *Investor's Business Daily,* October 20, 1994, p. A6.

Brammer, Rhonda, ''Sizing Up Small Caps—Best Foot Forward,'' *Barron's,* September 28, 1998, p. 28.

''CEO Interview: Maxwell Shoe Company Inc.,'' *Wall Street Transcript,* December 12, 1994.

''Maxwell, Loaded for Bear, Hunts for New Acquisition,'' *Footwear News,* September 23, 1996, p. 23.

''Maxwell's Cocozza Takes Baton, Spells Out Growth Opportunities,'' *Footwear News,* May 25, 1998, p. 7.

''Maxwell Slashes 46 Stores, But Gets More Cash,'' *Footwear News,* November 16, 1998, p. 2.

Merritt, Jennifer, ''Hyde Park Footwear Company Kicks into High Gear,'' *Boston Business Journal,* September 11, 1998, p. 1.

''Sam & Libby, Jones Hit the Floor Running,'' *Footwear News,* April 21, 1997, p. 1.

''Sam & Libby Slates 20 Units; Operation's Heart in San Francisco,'' *Footwear News,* February 9, 1998, p. 10.

Smith, Samantha, ''Maxwell Shoe Co. Opens 115 Stores Across the Country,'' *Boston Business Journal,* October 31, 1997, p. 14.

Sohng, Laurie, ''Mootsies Kids Grow with Cocozza,'' *Footwear News,* January 15, 1990, p. 33.

—Frank Uhle

Medtronic, Inc.

7000 Central Avenue, N.E.
Minneapolis, Minnesota 55432-3576
U.S.A.
(612) 514-4000
Fax: (612) 514-4879
Web site: http://www.medtronic.com

Public Company
Incorporated: 1957
Employees: 19,334
Sales: $4.13 billion (1999)
Stock Exchanges: New York
Ticker Symbol: MDT
NAIC: 334510 Electromedical & Electrotherapeutic
Apparatus Manufacturing; 339113 Surgical Appliance
& Supplies Manufacturing; 339112 Surgical &
Medical Instrument Manufacturing

Medtronic, Inc. is the world's leading medical technology company, controlling about 50 percent of the $4 billion global heart-pacing market, which includes pacemakers and defibrillators. The company's products and services also include implantable neurological pain, tremor, spasticity, and incontinence management systems; heart valves; catheters and stents for angioplasty; implantable drug administration systems; surgical instruments; hydrocephalic shunts; autotransfusion equipment; and disposable devices for handling and monitoring blood during surgery. Headquartered in Minneapolis, Minnesota, the company conducts business in more than 120 countries and groups its operations into three regions—the Americas, Europe/Middle East/Africa, and Asia/Pacific.

Early History

Medtronic was founded as an outgrowth of Earl Bakken's part-time work at Minneapolis's Northwestern Hospital. Although much of his time was consumed with graduate studies in electrical engineering, Bakken found time to repair the centri-fuges, electrocardiograph machines, and other intricate electronic equipment at the hospital. Bakken and his brother-in-law, Palmer Hermundslie, surmised that they could make a living at repairing medical equipment. In 1949 Bakken quit school, and Hermundslie left his job at a local lumber company so that they could form the medical equipment repair service they dubbed "Medtronic."

Bakken and Hermundslie initially worked out of a small garage in Minneapolis. During Medtronic's difficult first year, there was one month the business grossed a meager eight dollars. In 1950, however, the partners contracted as sales representatives for the Sanborn Company, the Gilford Instrument Company, and Advanced Instruments, Inc. In the early part of the decade more than half of their sales in the five-state region around Minneapolis came from selling the merchandise of the other companies.

As Bakken gained experience with medical professionals and their instruments, he was called upon to advise them in their experiments. Over the course of Medtronic's first decade Bakken built nearly 100 custom-made—often single-use—devices for medical research. Soon Medtronic was manufacturing several medical research products, including two types of defibrillators, as well as forceps, an animal respirator, a cardiac rate monitor, and a physiologic stimulator.

Advent of the Pacemaker

Medtronic's history became inextricably connected to the history of open-heart surgery. Electrically stimulated pacemaking had taken off in the 1950s when several physicians developed external machines that extended the lives of patients who otherwise would have died. These early pacemakers, however, had several disadvantages. The high-voltage electrodes they used often burned patients' skin, the devices were large and unmanageable, and they had to be plugged into the wall, thus restricting patients' mobility and making power failures life-threatening events.

During the late 1950s Dr. C. Walton Lillehei, a pioneer of open-heart surgery at the University of Minnesota Medical School, was researching a battery-powered device that would conduct a mild electric shock to the surface of a patient's heart in order to combat the heart block that caused fatalities in about ten percent of open-heart surgeries. Lillehei asked Bakken, who worked part-time repairing medical electronics at the school, to design an appropriate device. Within six weeks Bakken returned to Lillehei with the world's first transistorized, battery-operated, wearable pacemaker. By the end of the decade use of the devices had extended beyond the United States to Canada, Australia, Cuba, Europe, Africa, and South America. Bakken's invention was honored by the National Society of Professional Engineers as one of ten outstanding engineering products for the period from 1954 to 1984, and Medtronic earned a reputation as a front-running producer of biomedical engineering devices.

The partnership between electronics and cardiac research continued to advance open-heart surgery—and Medtronic—throughout the 1950s. Dr. Samuel Hunter of St. Joseph's Hospital research laboratory in St. Paul, Minnesota, worked with Norman Roth, an electrical engineer at Medtronic, to create the so-called Hunter-Roth electrode, which required about 70 percent less current than Bakken's pacemaker system. In 1958 Dr. William Chardack and electrical engineer Wilson Greatbatch built the first implantable pacemaker in the United States. The device, which incorporated the Hunter-Roth bipolar wire lead, was first successfully implanted in a human in 1960. By October of that year Medtronic had purchased the exclusive rights to produce and market what was called the "Chardack-Greatbatch implantable pulse generator."

Rapid Growth in the 1960s

The growing company organized its distribution outside the United States and Canada through the employment of the Picker International Corporation of White Plains, New York. Picker specialized in electrical medical equipment sales and had an international network of 72 foreign sales offices. Fourteen Medtronic sales representatives covered the United States and Canada beginning in 1960. The company introduced several products that year, including the Telecor heart monitor; the Cardiac Sentinel, an alarm that automatically summoned aid when a patient's heart rate became critical and stimulated the heart; and the Coagulation Generator, which stanched bleeding during surgery.

The growing product line and increasing demand required that the company move to a new, larger facility in 1961. Despite Medtronic's dramatic sales increases—from $180,000 to more than $500,000 from 1960 to 1962—the company incurred losses during the same period. Expenses, like the appointment of Picker International, the cost of building a new headquarters,

new product research, and attendance at major medical and engineering conventions, increased faster than sales. Early in 1962 the company eased its financial tensions through a bond offering of $200,000 and a $100,000 bank loan. The credit helped Medtronic turn a profit of $17,000 for the first three months of fiscal 1962.

Research continued throughout the 1960s on Medtronic's most important product, the implantable pacemaker. Enhancing the company's pacemaker sales was the introduction of Medicare in 1965, which provided U.S. government funding of healthcare for citizens over the age of 65 and thus increased the use of pacemakers. Among Medtronic's new pacemaker products was an endocardial catheter, a wire lead inserted through the jugular vein to the heart. When pacemakers with this "transvenous" lead were introduced to the market in 1965, they seized a substantial portion of pacemaker sales. In the mid-1960s Medtronic also introduced external and implantable pacemakers that compensated for irregular heartbeats.

New product introductions and pacemaker improvements helped sales surge to more than $12 million by the end of the 1967–68 fiscal year. Profits increased dramatically as well, exceeding $1 million that year. Medtronic established a European Service Center in 1967 to provide technical support for the continent, which generated 80 percent of overseas sales. In late 1969 Medtronic formed its own international division to accommodate direct European sales. In 1970 the company was able to drop its contract with Picker International and control international sales, which accounted for 30 percent of total sales by that time. Direct sales offices were established in 19 countries, and technical centers and manufacturing plants were erected in primary markets.

Medtronic also gained control of its primary North American distributors during the late 1960s and early 1970s. In 1968 the company purchased John Hay & Company, Ltd., a medical sales organization headquartered in Vancouver, British Columbia. The A.F. Morrison Company was acquired the following year, and by 1973 Medtronic accomplished complete jurisdiction over its North American sales with the purchase of the Medical Specialty Company and Corvek Medical Equipment.

Continued Growth through the 1970s

Medtronic reached several milestones during the 1970s. The company surpassed $100 million in annual sales in 1975, and in 1977 Medtronic stock was listed on the New York Stock Exchange. Globally Medtronic commanded a market share of 35 percent in the pacemaker category. By the end of the decade, Medtronic's annual sales exceeded $200 million. The company also began to diversify into other medical fields and regions. In 1976 Medtronic established its Neurological Division, which developed products to help relieve chronic and acute pain. A year later Medtronic founded its Heart Valves Division and launched the Hall mechanical heart valve. The company also established a headquarters in Latin America, as well as one in Europe. Manufacturing facilities in Puerto Rico, Canada, and France followed. By the end of the decade Medtronic had made its first major acquisition, Medical Data Systems, an Ann Arbor, Michigan, nuclear imaging company.

Medtronic remained primarily a pacemaker company, however, and cardiovascular products developed for the diagnosis and treatment of heart disease included a nuclear-powered pacemaker. Medtronic's pacemakers were also made smaller, more resilient, and more reliable during the decade. The company consolidated pacemaker production vertically through the creation of Micro-Rel, Inc., a manufacturer of hybrid circuits, and the acquisition of Energy Technology—later renamed Promeon—a producer of lithium batteries. Other cardiovascular equipment developed in the 1970s helped physicians diagnose patients instantaneously and monitor them by telephone. Cardiovascular products contributed the bulk of Medtronic's sales.

Despite the company's success, the 1970s was not a trouble-free decade for Medtronic. Like many U.S. companies, Medtronic was affected by high inflation during the late 1970s. Tougher regulatory policies instituted by the U.S. Nuclear Regulatory Commission and the Food and Drug Administration also increased research costs through requirements for tougher clinical and follow-up testing. In 1976 Medtronic was forced to issue its first major product recall after the company discovered a technical flaw with the Xytron pacemaker. Medtronic's U.S. market share subsequently fell from 60 percent to 40 percent.

Medtronic experienced several leadership changes during the 1970s. In 1974 Bakken gave up the day-to-day responsibilities of the presidency to become chairman of the board. Thomas E. Holloran replaced him for two years, followed by Dale R. Olseth, who was elected president and chief executive officer.

Diversification in the 1980s

In the 1980s Medtronic sought to expand its product line further while keeping its strong emphasis on pacemakers. Routine reinvestment of more than eight percent of annual revenues during the decade fueled research and development of new and improved medical devices, and by 1981 annual sales reached another milestone—the $300 million mark. William R. Wallin was named president and CEO in 1985, and diversification became a corporate goal.

Computer technology helped Medtronic develop pacemakers that catered to a patient's particular requirements. The Spectrax SXT, a programmable pacemaker that could be reprogrammed after the initial implantation without performing surgery, led the market soon after its release in 1981. In 1985 the Activitrax pacemaker was the first such device to automatically adjust the rate of heart stimulation in accordance with the rate of activity. After its introduction to the market in 1986, the Activitrax quickly claimed 20 percent of the pacemaker category. That same year Medtronic solidified its position in this market for ''rate-responsive pacing'' with the purchase of Biotech of Bologna, Italy, and Vitatron of Dieren in the Netherlands. Breakthrough products in the late 1980s included CapSure steroid leads, which were designed to ease tissue inflammation, and Synergyst pacemakers, which united dual chamber and rate-responsive pacing.

Medtronic expanded into the fields of cardiac surgery and vascular therapies in the late 1980s through new products and acquisitions. Among the product lines new to Medtronic were tissue heart valves, coronary angioplasty catheters, and tissue heart valves. Among the companies Medtronic acquired were Johnson & Johnson Cardiovascular, which produced the industry leading Maxima membrane oxygenator, a device used during open-heart surgery to reoxygenate blood, and Versaflex Delivery Systems, Inc., a company that made coronary angioplasty catheters. The company also began to develop neurological and drug delivery services, including the SynchroMed Drug Delivery System, the first implantable and programmable drug delivery system. Neurological devices introduced in the late 1980s included the Selectra and ComfortWave electrical nerve stimulators, used to treat sprains and back pain. La Jolla Technology, Inc., another producer of electrical nerve stimulators, was acquired in 1987 to strengthen Medtronic's position in this industry.

Medtronic's rapid growth and expansion, however, was not without setbacks. In 1983 Medtronic voluntarily recalled a new pacemaker lead when it recorded relatively high failure rates in clinical tests. These disadvantages resulted in slowed pacemaker sales, and in 1985 Medtronic reported its first year without an increase in sales and earnings. Medtronic was also involved in expensive patent litigation with such large medical manufacturers as Eli Lilly & Co. and Siemens AG during the decade.

Despite a few bumps in the road, Medtronic was able to increase its annual sales from $300 million in 1981 to $755 million in 1988 through numerous acquisitions and the development of new technologies. By the end of the decade, Medtronic had moved beyond its position as a pacemaker manufacturer and had become a major medical technology corporation.

Continuing Expansion in the Early 1990s

In 1991 William W. George became president and CEO, succeeding Wallin, who became chairman of the board, and Medtronic's total sales exceeded $1 billion. Medtronic had developed six primary areas of expertise by the early 1990s: bradycardia pacing, tachyarrhythmia management, heart valves, and cardiopulmonary, interventional vascular, and neurological devices. In 1992 the company's international sales contributed 40 percent of total revenues, justifying new facilities and expanded operations in Japan, China, and Eastern Europe, as well as increased focus on such developing nations as India and China and on countries in Latin America and Africa.

Continuing with its diversification strategy, Medtronic acquired a number of companies during the first half of the decade, including TUR, a German pacemaker manufacturer; Bio-Medicus, Inc., the world's largest maker of centrifugal blood pumps; PS Medical, Inc., a maker of shunts, devices designed to prevent fluid buildup in the brain; and DLP, Inc., which developed cardiac cannulae used in surgery. These acquisitions helped solidify Medtronic's lead in the area of medical technology and advanced the company's presence in new fields. In 1995, according to the *Star-Tribune,* Medtronic had a 49 percent share of the conventional pacemaker market, 32 percent of the implantable defibrillator market, and 75 percent in nerve-related devices.

Medtronic stepped up its product development cycles and continued to feed its research and development budget—the company spent about 11 percent of total revenues on research and development in 1995, up from 9.4 percent in 1990—to survive in the increasingly competitive medical technology marketplace. The Thera line of pacemakers took about 27 months from final design to market introduction, about half the pacemaker design cycle of the mid-1980s. Medtronic's focus on product development resulted in a number of pioneering devices during the first part of the decade, including the PCD defibrillator, the Jewel implantable cardioverter-defibrillator, implantable Transvene taccharrhythmia leads, the Model 9790 pacemaker programmer, and additional models of the SynchroMed Drug Delivery System, including one for the treatment of chronic spasticity.

Accelerated Development in the Late 1990s

In the second half of the decade, Medtronic adopted an increasingly aggressive expansion strategy to survive in the medical product field, which had been consolidated into a handful of large medical technology companies. The pacemaker category, Medtronic's core business, was expected to slow in growth, and the company intended to stave off declining profits through diversification. Medtronic's revenues exceeded $2 billion in 1996, and the company continued its acquisition and new product introduction efforts. In 1995 Medtronic added Micro Interventional Systems, Inc., a developer of catheters designed to treat stroke victims, to its neurological division. A year later the company acquired Synectics Medical AB of Sweden, which made systems for gastroenterology, urology, and sleep apnea; InStent, a stent manufacturer; and AneuRx, a maker of endovascular stented grafts. Between 1996 and 1998 Medtronic introduced a number of new products, including the Micro Jewel II, an implantable cardioverter-defibrillator; the Wiktor Prime coronary stent, designed to support the walls of a coronary artery; and the Activa Tremor Control System, which helped treat tremors associated with Parkinson's disease.

Amid the flurry of sales growth—during the second quarter of fiscal 1997, Medtronic's pacemaker sales grew nine percent, implantable defibrillator sales increased 27 percent, and its neurological product sales grew more than 60 percent—the company's vascular operations, which included catheters and stents, were not doing as well as the company had hoped. Although the coronary stent market was growing rapidly, Medtronic was unable to successfully market stents, and as a result the company was forced in early 1998 to take its first business-related charge since 1985. The company also announced plans to close eight manufacturing plants and downsize its staff by 600 employees.

Medtronic was also losing market share in the defibrillator category to strong competition, particularly from Guidant Corp., which offered a technologically advanced dual-chamber defibrillator that grabbed about 25 percent of the U.S. defibrillator market soon after its introduction in 1998. Medtronic was the leader in the $1.8 billion global defibrillator industry, which was growing at the breakneck rate of about 30 percent a year, but according to Sanford Bernstein & Co.'s Kenneth Abramowitz, as reported in the *Wall Street Journal,* in the United States Medtronic held some 40–45 percent of the market, while Guidant had a share of 45–50 percent. Medtronic fought back in mid-1998, however, by acquiring Physio-Con-

trol International Inc., a maker of external defibrillators, in its largest acquisition to date.

Medtronic's problems were relatively minor in comparison to its outstanding growth in 1998. Medtronic acquired Avecor Cardiovascular, Inc., to expand its cardiac surgery operation, and Midas Rex LP, a maker of pneumatic instruments for neurological surgery. Through its acquisitions Medtronic grew by 45 percent in 1998. Medtronic also opened a new pacemaker manufacturing facility in Europe in that year and was honored as one of the 100 best companies to work for by *Fortune* magazine.

As Medtronic entered its 50th anniversary year in 1999, the company showed no signs of slowing down. Among the new products introduced by the company were the Medtronic.Kappa 700, a series of pacemakers designed to adapt automatically to patient needs; the InSync stimulator, a device used to treat heart failure; and the Gem implantable defibrillator series. By the close of fiscal 1999, which ended in April, Medtronic had acquired two more companies. Sofamor Danek Group, Inc., the leader in spinal disorder treatment and cranial surgery, significantly boosted Medtronic's neurology division, and according to *Health Industry Today,* the purchase of Arterial Vascular Engineering, Inc., increased Medtronic's market share to a commanding 40 percent of the $3.5 billion global market in coronary stents.

Medtronic reported that fiscal 1999 represented the company's 14th consecutive year of increased revenues, with nearly one-third of its revenue attributed to operations in Europe, Africa, and the Middle East. Not only was Medtronic enjoying increased sales but the company was also leading the pack in terms of product development. According to the U.S. Patent and Trademark Office, Medtronic was issued the most medical device patents in the world from 1969 to September 1998; to remain competitive in the aggressive medical device industry, Medtronic planned to invest nearly $500 million in research and development in fiscal 2000.

As Medtronic approached the new millennium, the company continued to strengthen its four primary product platforms: cardiac rhythm management, neurological and spinal surgery, vascular devices, and cardiac surgery. In August 1999 Medtronic acquired Xomed Surgical Products, Inc., the leading manufacturer of surgical products used to treat ear, nose, and throat problems. Its acquisition, according to Medtronic, would position the company as the global market leader in the ear, nose, and throat category. Medtronic planned to release numerous new products and technologies in fiscal 2000 to continue its leadership position in the medical technology field.

Principal Subsidiaries

Medtronic Europe S.A. (Switzerland); Medtronic International, Ltd. (Hong Kong); Medtronic of Canada, Ltd.

Further Reading

Alexander, Steve, ''New Product Machine,'' *Star-Tribune* (Minneapolis-St. Paul), June 5, 1995, p. D1.

Barshay, Jill J., ''Medical Devices,'' *Star-Tribune* (Minneapolis-St. Paul), September 22, 1998, p. D1.

Burton, Thomas M., "Medtronic's Stock Price Falls 10% on Warning of Earnings Shortfall," *Wall Street Journal,* August 7, 1998, p. B5.

Dubashi, Jagannath, "Change of Pace," *Financial World,* March 17, 1992, pp. 26–27.

Lau, Gloria, "Companies in the News—Device Maker Medtronic Inc. Steps Up Defibrillator Efforts," *Investor's Business Daily,* July 21, 1998, p. A33.

Medtronic Beginnings, Minneapolis: Medtronic, Inc., 1993.

Moore, Michael P., "The Genesis of Minnesota's Medical Alley," *University of Minnesota Medical Bulletin,* winter 1992, pp. 7–13.

Nelson, Glen D., M.D., "A Brief History of Cardiac Pacing," *Texas Heart Institute Journal,* vol. 20, 1993, pp. 12–18.

Sherer, Paul M., "Medtronic Has Fans, but Doubters, Too," *Wall Street Journal,* December 31, 1998, p. C1.

The Story of Medtronic, Minneapolis: Medtronic, Inc., 1997.

Toward Man's Full Life, Minneapolis: Medtronic, Inc., 1990.

—April Dougal Gasbarre
—updated by Mariko Fujinaka

The Mersey Docks and Harbour Company

Maritime Centre
Port of Liverpool
Liverpool L21 1LA
United Kingdom
(44) 151-949-6000
Fax: (44) 151-949-6338
Web site: http://www.merseydocks.co.uk

Public Company
Incorporated: 1970
Employees: 1,211
Sales: UK£180 million (US$298.2 million) (1998)
Stock Exchanges: London
Ticker Symbol: MDK.L
NAIC: 488310 Port Facility Operation

The Mersey Docks and Harbour Company is the United Kingdom's second largest port operator, controlling the Port of Liverpool on the River Mersey, and Medway Port, on the River Medway. In the Port of Liverpool alone, Mersey handles more than 30 million tons of cargo per year, with a growing emphasis on high-margin cargo such as fruit, containers, and grains, while also serving as an important port for oil shipments (from Shell Oil), lumber, and steel. The Port of Liverpool's location also makes it a primary hub linking England and Ireland, both for cargo shipments and for passenger ferry and other passenger transport vessels. In the late 1990s, Mersey started an extensive £60 million investment program, including a vast expansion of existing light direct rail-linked industrial and warehousing facilities, new roll-on roll-off facilities, and participation in the construction of an office tower—Liverpool's first since the 1980s—and hotel complex. Mersey Docks and Harbour Company is also the U.K.'s leading harbor management and consulting company, through its overseas port management subsidiary, Portia Management Services Ltd. Mersey also operates its own shipping subsidiaries, BG Freight Line Holding B.V., based in the Netherlands, and Coastal Container Line Inc. Mersey Docks and Harbour Company is led by Chairman Gordon Waddell.

CEO Trevor Furlong has announced his intention to retire in the year 2000, naming Peter Jones, current head of the Port of Liverpool division, as his replacement.

Mersey Beaten in the 1960s

When the Beatles, Gerry and the Pacemakers, the Searchers, and others brought the name Mersey to the world's attention in the 1960s, the Port of Liverpool on the River Mersey had already left its best days far behind. The Liverpool harbor had played a major role in the United Kingdom's industrial development, and served as one of the country's principal ports during the 18th and 19th centuries. Less gloriously, the port also played a principal role in the 18th century slave trade, functioning as one of the largest slave ports. By the time of the abolition of slavery in the United Kingdom, however, the Liverpool port had already turned to industrial activities, and became a primary port of call in the rapidly developing industrial economy, as well as a key player in the U.K.'s rise to dominance on the world's oceans.

At the height of the port's activities, the Port of Liverpool served more than 20,000 ships per year; Liverpool also became one of the United Kingdom's chief centers of shipbuilding activities, and provided the base for such shipbuilding and shipping giants as White Star Lines, who sailed the Titanic, and Cunard, which still remained in operation in Liverpool in the 1990s. The importance of Liverpool and the Mersey shipping route was recognized in the 1850s, when the British government created the Mersey Docks and Harbour Board to oversee port activities in 1857.

Liverpool continued to play a major role in the country's industrial growth and development. Yet by the 1890s Liverpool had already begun to fade as a major port. The chief cause behind the harbor's slump was the shallow river basin. As shipbuilding technology increased, and especially with the switch to iron and steel shipbuilding techniques, the ships themselves were growing larger, with greater and greater displacements. By the turn of the century, the ships were simply too big to dock in Liverpool; larger vessels were forced to anchor at the harbor's deep water points. Cargo shipments became increasingly difficult to bring to shore; more and more shippers turned away from Liverpool, in favor of the United Kingdom's deeper and more modern docks.

Liverpool declined through the first half of the century. Its northern location, however, protected it from the Nazi bombing raids of World War II, and this fact helped bring new activity to the port. Yet the renewed activity lasted only for the duration of the war. With the end of hostilities, Liverpool slipped once again into its now-minor port status. By the end of the 1950s, the United Kingdom's shipping focus had moved from its west coast to the eastern coast—closer to the U.K.'s newly developing European Community trading partnerships. Meanwhile, fewer and fewer cruise ships were using the harbor; even Liverpool's own Cunard ended its Liverpool departures by the middle of the 1960s.

Conditions deteriorated still further, sparking a violent dock workers' strike in 1967. Over 9,000 workers joined the picket lines. In the end, the workers won out, and the government introduced the National Dock Labour Scheme of 1967. The principal highlight of the scheme: guaranteed lifetime employment contracts for all dock workers.

The National Dock Labour Scheme came into play at a time when new technologies and manufacturing methods were producing more sophisticated cranes and cargo handling systems, reducing the number of laborers needed. With dwindling cargo activity and shrinking revenues, the Mersey Docks and Harbour Board could ill-afford to maintain the level of its workforce. Yet, under the National Dock Labour Scheme, the board had no choice.

By the end of the 1960s, the Mersey Docks and Harbour Board was sinking fast. The government finally released the money-losing body, selling it to the private sector in 1970—one of the first of Britain's nationalized businesses to be privatized—while listing the Mersey Docks and Harbour Company on the London stock exchange. The new company entered business without its debts—as the government forgave it more than £100 million. The British government, meantime, kept a 20 percent share of the company.

Mersey's fortunes seemed to be picking up in the first years of the new decade. But the Arab oil embargo and a resulting worldwide recession swiftly ended any cause for optimism. Mersey Docks and Harbour staggered through the rest of the decade, watching harbor activity dwindle to next to nothing. Nonetheless, the company had not quite given up, putting into place, in the late 1970s, a modernization effort designed to make the Port of Liverpool once again a major competitor on the U.K. and international shipping scene. Mersey also began to explore other activities, launching its Portia harbor management subsidiary in 1978.

Rebuilding in the 1990s

By the mid-1980s, Mersey Docks and Harbour Company had succeeded in raising its cargo handling tonnage to ten million tons per year. More efficient handling technology and facilities also enabled the company to improve its margins on its revenues. At last, in 1989, the Conservative government, led by free market economy disciple Margaret Thatcher, relieved Mersey of the National Dock Labour Scheme. The abolition of guaranteed lifetime employment enabled Mersey Docks and Harbour Company to trim its payroll. By 1990, the company had cut out some 600 Mersey dockyards jobs—with the government providing severance pay funding.

The slimmer port company began looking for expansion. In the early 1990s, the British government began the process of privatizing the rest of its ports and harbors. One of the first of the new wave of harbor privatizations was that of Medway Port, on the River Medway, which was bought up by a group of venture capitalists, who promptly fired its union dock workers and replaced them with non-union and contract workers. The Medway management also forced the fired workers to sell back their shares—at only £2.50 per share. Yet several months later, in 1993, Medway Ports agreed to be acquired by Mersey Docks and Harbour Company, for the price of £37.25 per share. Moreover, it was learned that the former Medway chief executive had privately purchased some 100,000 shares in the months prior to the Mersey acquisition.

The dock workers sued Mersey for unfair dismissal. In a surprise settlement, Mersey agreed to pay £10,000 to each of the 270 workers (this settlement did not address the share price issue). Meanwhile, the former Medway chief executive—along with the rest of Medway's top management—resigned from their positions, leaving Mersey in the difficult position of having no one at the helm of its newly acquired subsidiary. Mersey faced more problems later in the year, when its bid for a £20 million expansion project was turned down in favor of a larger real estate development project which, according to Mersey, would restrict its ability to expand the Port of Liverpool's operations.

By then, however, Mersey had already begun to look farther afield for its own expansion. With its Portia subsidiary taking a leadership role in international harbor management, Mersey began to bid for operations contracts of foreign ports. Portia meanwhile had achieved a substantial position around the world, leading to port operations consulting contracts in Argentina, Bangladesh, Kazakhstan, Malaysia, Russia, and South Africa, among others. The company also announced its interest in acquiring other U.K. port operations, as they became privatized.

Mersey faced a different kind of labor problem in 1995. When union stevedores at another company operating out of the Port of Liverpool went on strike, 600 of Mersey's dock workers refused to cross the picket lines. Mersey in turn fired its union workers, who promptly set up their own picket lines to demand back their jobs. The result was a highly publicized battle between strikers and management that lasted more than two years. After strikers rejected an early offer from Mersey, which included back pay compensation and the restoration of some jobs, Mersey held firm. The strike finally ended when the workers capitulated, accepting a £10 million settlement in back pay.

The failure of the strike was said to spell the end of the United Kingdom's once powerful industrial unions, especially as Mersey Docks and Harbour Company revealed that the strike, while embarrassing for the company, had not had a great impact on its revenues—or on its profits. Indeed, during the strike, the company was able to announce a new record in annual cargo handling, topping 30 million tons for the first time in 1997. The end of the strike, meanwhile, meant that Mersey could turn its full attention to its ambitious plans for development of the Liverpool port.

In 1998, the company announced a £60 million development effort, including £35 million to be spent on two new roll-on roll-off facilities, as well as construction of an office tower and participation in construction of a four-star harborside hotel. The company also launched construction of a vast new industrial and warehousing site, the Liverpool Intermodal Freight Terminal (LIFT), which, with 860,000 square feet of new warehousing and light industrial plant facilities, ranked as one of the United Kingdom's largest private-sector industrial construction projects. Mersey also announced its intention to bring cruise ships back to Liverpool, planning to dredge the harbor to provide new deep-water berths for cruise ships and passenger ferries.

The company hoped to attract more than 500,000 passengers to the harbor by the turn of the century. At the same time, Mersey continued to boost its own moves abroad. After forming a partnership with Rolls Royce subsidiary Clarke Chapman to win, in 1996, a $155 million contract to oversee the development of and provide management operations for a new private port in Argentina, Mersey took part in a consortium bidding for construction and management contracts for a new port in Chile.

The company's African operations were also boosted in 1999, as the company started construction of a grain terminal at Kenya's Port of Mombasa.

Mersey Docks and Harbour Company had raised tonnage to nearly 35 million tons per year, despite a temporary loss of business while its Shell Oil facility was under renovation, and despite the difficult economic climate following the crash of the Asian stock markets in the late 1990s. With revenues rising to £180 million, and profits at a healthy £52 million, Mersey clearly had the wind at its back in more ways than one: in 1999, it started operation of a £2.5 million windmill power generating farm built on its sea wall.

Principal Subsidiaries

Portia Management Services Ltd.; BG Freight Line Holding B.V. (Netherlands); Coastal Container Line Inc.; Medway Ports Ltd.; Mersey Docks Property Developments Ltd.; Mersey Docks Property Holdings Ltd.; Neptune Insurance Ltd.; Portia World Travel Ltd.; Sheerness Produce Terminal Ltd.; Woodside Business Park Ltd.

Further Reading

Gribben, Roland, "Mersey Wins £100 Million Port Contract in Argentina," *Daily Telegraph*, October 1, 1996.
Hellier, David, "Vincent Resigns at Mersey Docks: Former Medway Chief Quits," *Independent*, April 14, 1994, p. 33.
Osborne, Alistaire, "Mersey Docks on the Alert for Buying Opportunities," *Daily Telegraph*, February 16, 1999.
——, "Mersey Plans New Generation in Windmills," *Daily Telegraph*, August 18, 1999.
Potter, Ben, "Sound Value on the Mersey Beat," *Daily Telegraph*, February 16, 1999.
Shah, Saeed, "Mersey Docks Beats Forecasts," *Times*, August 18, 1999.
Yates, Andrew, "Cruise Liners to Return to Liverpool's Pier Head," *Independent*, January 15, 1998, p. 26.

—M. L. Cohen

Metso Corporation

Fabianinkatu 9 A
Post Office Box 1220
00101 Helsinki
Finland
(0) 20 484 100
Fax: (0) 20 484 101
Web site: http://www.metsocorporation.com

Public Company
Incorporated: 1999
Employees: 23,000
Sales: Fmk 21.97 billion (US$4.2 billion) (1998)
Stock Exchanges: Helsinki New York
Ticker Symbol: MX
NAIC: 33312 Construction Machinery Manufacturing;
    333131 Mining Machinery & Equipment
    Manufacturing; 333291 Paper Industry Machinery
    Manufacturing; 333293 Printing Machinery &
    Equipment Manufacturing; 333612 Speed Changer,
    Industrial High-Speed Drive, & Gear Manufacturing;
    336211 Motor Vehicle Body Manufacturing; 334513
    Instruments & Related Product Manufacturing for
    Measuring, Displaying, & Controlling Industrial
    Process Variables; 54199 All Other Professional,
    Scientific, & Technical Services

Metso Corporation, a leading worldwide manufacturer of forestry, pulping, and paper machinery, is the product of the mid-1999 merger of Valmet Corporation and Rauma Corporation. The company operates under the Valmet name in the areas of pulping and paper machinery; Metso's Timberjack unit is the world's leading maker of forest machines, with a global market share approaching 30 percent. Metso's other principal operating units are Neles Automation, a leading supplier of process automation and flow control equipment and systems; Nordberg, the world's leading designer and supplier of crushing, pulverizing, and screening systems for rock and similar materials, with principal customers in the mining, quarrying, and civil engineering sectors; and Valmet Automotive, a manufacturer of specialty cars

on a contractual basis and the only automaker based in Finland. Metso derives 49 percent of its sales within Europe, 30 percent from North America, 15 from the Asia-Pacific region, four percent from South America, and the remaining two percent elsewhere. The company has manufacturing operations in 12 countries and offices in a total of 40 countries.

Valmet's Interwar Beginnings

Although Valmet was not incorporated until 1950, its story begins in the interwar period. After World War I, the Finnish government found it feasible to open industrial plants to make arms for the national defense forces. These factories—an airplane factory, a rifle factory, and a factory for manufacturing artillery guns—were run by separate boards of directors, each responsible to the Ministry of Defense. The factories' output was dependent on the national budget, and all orders for production came from the Ministry of Defense within the framework of the budget, decided by the national diet.

When the war between Finland and the Soviet Union ended in September 1944, the Finnish army had to be demobilized and all orders for arms from the arms factories were canceled. The defense factories found themselves in difficulties, as they were ordered to maintain their levels of employment and find new products to manufacture. The first solution to this almost impossible situation came from the articles of armistice which demanded that Finland deliver goods to the Soviet Union as war reparations. Finnish industries were obliged to fulfil this obligation, as were the government-owned arms factories. These factories were consequently transferred from the Ministry of Defense to the Ministry of Trade and Industry. At the same time, two small navy repair yards were transferred. It was apparent that the organization of the factories had to change. A law was passed, giving special status to the corporation about to be formed, as a compromise between a limited company and a state office. The new organization was named the State Metal Works (in Finnish, Valtion Metallitehtaat, shortened to VMT). Its governing bodies consisted of a large supervisory board, composed mainly of politicians, and a board of directors, consisting of executives from within the corporation. Lieutenant General Leonard Grandell, formerly an experienced officer in the General Staff, was temporarily nominated chairman of the board and chief executive officer. The final choice of chief executive officer was Yrjö Vesa, then deputy managing director of one of Finland's major enterprises in the shipbuilding and machinery industry, the Wartsila group. On February 15, 1947, he was appointed chairman and CEO of VMT.

VMT was assigned a large part of the war reparation program, mainly machinery that could not be supplied by existing private industries. The airplane factory had a particularly large engineering staff, as it had been producing airplanes of its own design. This engineering talent was utilized for the design of many of the items demanded by the Soviets. Very few of the items included in the reparations program, however, were suited for the commercial market.

Formation of Valmet: 1950

Experience soon showed that the form under which VMT operated was not flexible enough for commercial transactions. The Finnish government had to present to the parliament a bill requesting that the group be made a joint stock limited company. The articles of association were approved on November 15, 1950. The name Valmet Oy (Valmet Corporation) was given to the new company. The shares were held by the state, represented by the Ministry of Trade and Industry. The share capital was Fmk 1 billion.

Much of the structure of the old defense works was retained in the organization of the new corporation. The army and navy officers who had been in charge of the different factories remained and were nominated managing directors of divisions within the group.

The most important task was to find products suitable for the different divisions and with good sales potential. After experimenting with many different products, Rautpohja Works, the former artillery gun factory in Jyväskylä, Finland, developed skills in papermaking-machinery production and dropped most of its other activities. Those that were maintained included heavy plate work, such as sluice gates for hydroelectric power plants and overhead cranes. Tourula Factory, the former rifle factory, had problems in finding suitable items for its existing machinery. After trying out many kind of consumer goods, which were later abandoned, Tourula finally switched to agricultural-tractor production. Jyskä Factory, the former artillery ignition fuse factory, specialized in making tools, bolts, and nuts on its automatic lathes, previously used for ignition fuses. The manufacturing of kilowatt-hour meters was also introduced. The airplane factories continued on a decreased scale to manufacture training aircraft for the Finnish Air Force, but diversified into the production of

diesel locomotives. The straddle carriers demanded by the Soviet Union as war reparation continued to be produced, initially for sale to the Soviet Union, which seemed to have a huge demand for this kind of carrier, used in sawmills. The company's aeronautical expertise turned out to have other applications, and a department was created to supply equipment for industrial and office air conditioning. The instrument department of the airplane factory developed gradually into a versatile production unit for industrial control equipment.

The shipyards had more problems because they were equipped only for small ships, as included in the war reparation program. Gradually, standard ships for the maritime market were included in the program, but the size of the building beds was a limiting factor. The Soviet Union remained by far the biggest market for the yards.

Overcoming Various Problems: 1950s–70s

In 1953 financial problems started to haunt the newly founded company. To find solutions, the advisory board nominated a committee to study the situation, later to be followed by a state committee, nominated by parliament. The recommendations of this committee included a total reconstruction of the company and a change of top management. It was found that the company was under pressure from heavy debts, coming from overvaluing on their books the material inherited from the former defense factories, from selling ships at a loss to the Soviet Union, and from the excessive overhead costs of the organization. As a result of the need to strengthen the financial base of the company, the Bank of Finland and the National Pension Fund joined the company as minority shareholders.

In the spring of 1954, the chief executive, Yrjö Vesa, was released from his position as were the divisional managing directors. All industrial divisions were to report directly to the new CEO. In July of the same year an elderly industrialist, Baron G.W. Wrede, was nominated chief executive officer of Valmet. Even though his time with Valmet was short—he died on February 17, 1958—he and his staff managed to change the company into a commercially viable enterprise. During this time, the main operational divisions were established at the various factories.

After the death of Baron Wrede his deputy managing director, Aarne Härkönen, was nominated CEO. The operation of Valmet continued along the lines already established. The papermaking-machinery division strengthened its position by extending its sales to China, Italy, Poland, and the Soviet Union in addition to the home market. Important features of the early days of the Valmet machines were the differential drives and pick-up presses, the first of their kind in Europe. The first agricultural tractors, developed in the early 1950s, were small machines of only 20 horsepower. In 1956 Valmet launched a standard size 33-horsepower diesel-powered tractor, which was well received in the domestic market. The airplane factory developed into a supplier of diesel locomotives for the Finnish railroads, and also maintained departments for industrial trucks, air conditioning, and instrumentation. The shipyards, mainly supplying the Soviet market, had problems. The crisis of the 1950s had made Valmet careful not to accept orders at loss prices, and although the Soviet orders were large, there were long discussions over pricing. The latter part of the 1950s left

Valmet's Helsinki yard without orders, simply because of disagreements on price. Fortunately for Valmet, the sudden boom in shipbuilding, caused by the Suez crisis in 1956, came to its rescue and the yards were kept open.

At the end of the 1950s, Valmet's management decided that the company had to strengthen its main divisions in order to survive when free trade seemed to be the environment of the future. The Valmet paper machines had a good share of many markets, but U.S. manufacturers still seemed to have the upper hand. They sold their machines the world over, even to Finland, while Valmet had not yet managed to export to the United States. To penetrate the North American market, Valmet and Tampella, another Finnish company in the field of papermaking machines, combined their efforts. The contracts for joint deliveries to two big companies, Boise Cascade in Louisiana and Eurocan in British Colombia, were the starting points.

After years of intensive marketing, Valmet became a worldwide market leader in papermaking machines. Many companies in the industry in other countries were assimilated into the Valmet group during this process. Another reason for the success was Valmet's research and development activity within this division. The company managed to invent new and superior products, such as new headbox and former designs. Its superior manufacturing techniques, which had already advanced in the artillery gun factory before Valmet was formed, also contributed to its success. Valmet developed a new material for suction rolls as well as a revolutionary machine for drilling the many holes required for these rolls.

Agricultural tractor production caused problems for Valmet as the market consisted only of the Finnish farming industry, and even there competition from major international competitors was fierce. Valmet had to find export markets or other means of increasing the weight of the division. As Valmet had experienced some success in exporting tractors to Brazil, the company found it advisable to enter that country as a locally based manufacturer to reinforce its position there. Thus Valmet do Brasil was established in 1960. Soon it developed into the second largest tractor factory in Latin America. Valmet was inspired by this success to try its luck in other markets. The most important step came in the 1970s when Valmet reached an agreement with the Swedish company Volvo to combine the efforts of the two companies in manufacturing agricultural tractors, leading eventually to Valmet's becoming the sole manufacturer of tractors in Scandinavia.

The airplane factory in Tampere, which had gradually developed into a diesel locomotive factory, was continuing to change shape. After the electrification of the Finnish state railroads had begun, locomotive manufacturing decreased. The making of equipment for increasing international container traffic became more important. By skillful development of harbor transport and loading equipment, based on the old straddle carriers for sawn timber developed for the Soviet war reparations, Valmet became a world leader in the modern business of large-container moving machinery. Only Japanese companies in the Far East were able to challenge Valmet in this field.

The airplane factory in Tampere never completely ceased its original business of building airplanes, but it changed its mode of operation. In 1958 the decision to equip the Finnish air forces with French jet trainers of the Fouga Magister type led to a long period of employment for Valmet's skilled workmen, building the planes under French license. Most of the airplane production was transferred to the Kuorevesi Factory. The little factory, established during World War II and hidden among dense Finnish forests, far from any city, thrived again. When the Fouga planes were built, the activity continued as Swedish Draken fighters and later English Hawk fighter trainers were assembled. The name of the Kuorevesi Factory was consequently changed to the Valmet Airplane Factory, and the old airplane factory in Tampere was renamed Valmet Tampere Works.

The instrument department of the Tampere Airplane Factory had been developed gradually into a versatile unit manufacturing control equipment for process industries. In 1973, the division received a new factory building in the vicinity of the Tampere Works and was renamed Valmet Instrument Factory, having an independent status equal to other divisions within the Valmet group. The factory had a prominent position as designer and supplier of pneumatic process control equipment. Its main customers were paper and pulp mills and power plants but other types of industry were also served. When electronics replaced the pneumatic control systems, Valmet gradually adapted its systems accordingly.

The shipyards had already been a major cause of financial problems for Valmet. In the early 1960s, Valmet's top management found that new problems were looming around the corner. The orders for the Soviet Union were unprofitable, and Härkönen, then president and chief executive officer, presented to the supervisory board a plan to cut down on Valmet's shipbuilding activities. It was based on the fact that Helsinki was a harbor, providing considerable ship repair work for a yard. Maintaining a yard for repair without new shipbuilding, however, was not feasible. Repair work was not steady, and new work evened out the flow. Therefore it was decided to concentrate all Valmet's shipbuilding activities in Helsinki and devote the Pansio Yard in Turku to other activities. Meanwhile, the Tampere Works had a problem in not having sufficient space available for its air conditioning activities. These were now transferred to Pansio. The former yard was thus divided into two units: a factory, fully specialized in industrial as well as office-building air conditioning, and a heavy steel manufacturing unit, making steel building frames and bridges as well as assisting the shipbuilding division. The structural change was intended to stop losses in Valmet's shipbuilding division and allow possibilities for growth in other, more promising lines of activity.

Aarne Härkönen, president and CEO of Valmet, died on October 19, 1964. Olavi J. Mattila, then secretary of state for trade policy in the Ministry of Foreign Affairs, was nominated CEO. His term was to start at the beginning of 1965. Under his leadership, the structural changes at Valmet continued. The group was to consist of the following independently led divisions, which eventually became separate subsidiary companies: Valmet Paper Machinery; Valmet Tractors; Valmet do Brasil; Valmet Transportation Equipment; Valmet Instruments; Valmet Defence Equipment (later renamed Valmet Aviation Industries after other defense articles, such as assault rifles, were transferred to another company, in which Valmet did not have a majority holding); and Valmet Shipbuilding.

Valmet Shipbuilding was reestablished with the construction of a large modern shipyard unit in Vuosaari, east of Helsinki. The new management did not accept the decision of its predecessors to cut down on shipbuilding and thus reversed the strategy. However, the large new Vuosaari shipyard, completed in 1974, was only temporary. In 1986, under new management, Valmet and the Finnish engineering company Wartsila, the largest shipbuilder in Finland, agreed to form two new companies: Valmet Paper Machinery Inc., in which Wartsila became a minority shareholder by transferring its paper manufacturing units to the new company, and Wartsila Marine Industries Inc., a shipbuilding company into which Valmet came as a minority shareholder, transferring its yards to the new company. Soon after the takeover, Wartsila Marine closed the Vuosaari yard, ending Valmet's direct involvement in shipbuilding, although the company maintained a 30 percent stake in Wartsila Marine.

Meanwhile, in 1968 Valmet entered the field of automobile production through a joint venture with Saab-Scania AB of Sweden, with the partners establishing a car plant in Uusikaupunki, Finland. Production of the Saab 96 began in November 1969.

Restructuring, Flotation: 1980s

Valmet experienced another financial crisis in 1981. Mattila retired as CEO and was replaced by Matti Kankaanpää, formerly managing director of Valmet Paper Machinery and, since 1980, of Valmet, under the leadership of Mattila as chairman. The crisis was solved by changes in structure and dropping of unprofitable divisions. The company concentrated on its main lines of activity, with emphasis on becoming leaders or at least prominent players in each of these fields of activity. This policy led to many acquisitions and in some cases to divestments, such as the manufacturing of rolling stock and of elevators.

To improve the public image of the company and erase the image of state-owned enterprise, Kankaanpää decided to make Valmet a public company by floating it on the Helsinki Stock Exchange. In late 1988 Valmet acquired nearly 10,000 new shareholders, many of them employees of Valmet. This reduced the Finnish State's ownership position from 100 percent to 80 percent.

In 1989 Wartsila Marine went bankrupt, forcing Valmet to take a Fmk 360 million writeoff on its stake in the company. This in turn led to a pretax loss of Fmk 267.8 million (US$67 million) for the year.

Prelude to a Merger: 1990s

A recessionary climate in the early 1990s led to additional losses: Fmk 290 million in 1990 and Fmk 692 million (US$152 million) the following year. Valmet soon returned to profitability, but, in anticipation of additional stock offerings aimed at further reducing the state's stake, the company made a number of restructuring moves. In 1992 Valmet gained full control of the Uusikaupunki auto assembly plant, then in September 1995 changed its name to Valmet Automotive. In April 1994 Valmet sold its Transmec transportation division, with the exclusion of the power transmission unit, and its tractors division to Sisu, a Finnish machinery and engineering firm, for Fmk 600 million

(US$107.8 million). The following January the company merged its Valmet-Tampella unit with its paper machinery operations to form the Paper and Board Machinery group. Twelve months later Valmet completed its exit from the field of aviation with the sale to the Finnish State of its stake in a firm involved in aircraft parts manufacturing and aircraft maintenance. Valmet also completed one major acquisition during this period, paying Fmk 725 million (US$144 million) for Atlas Converting Equipment plc, a U.K. maker of converting machinery used in the packaging and paper industries for paper, film, and aluminum foil handling.

Through these moves, Valmet achieved additional operational focus, emerging with five main groups in its organizational chart by the late 1990s. In addition to the Paper and Board Machinery, Converting Equipment, and Power Transmission groups, the two other groups were: Automation, a producer and servicer of process automation systems for the paper and other industries; and Valmet Automotive, which continued to assemble cars, particularly specialty models, on a contractual basis. In the automotive sector, Valmet began production of the Porsche Boxster in September 1997 and of the Saab 9-3 Convertible in early 1998. Meantime, in a reflection of the company's growing international profile, Valmet stock was listed on the New York Stock Exchange for the first time in May 1996. Further stock offerings reduced the Finnish State's stake in Valmet to 58.6 percent in 1994 and to 20 percent in June 1996. For 1998, Valmet's last full year of operation before its merger with Rauma, the company posted net sales of Fmk 11.65 billion (US$2.3 billion) and net income of Fmk 675 million (US$133 million).

Brief History of Rauma

The history of Rauma Corporation began in 1942 with the founding of Rauma-Raahe Oy from a combination of several sawmills and timber companies. In 1945 Rauma-Raahe entered the shipbuilding arena with the purchase of a shipyard in the town of Rauma, located on Finland's west coast, where ships had been built since at least the 16th century.

Rauma-Raahe was involved in the first large merger in Finnish business history, when Repola-Viipuri Oy and Lahti Oy merged with the company in 1951 to form Rauma-Repola. The new firm continued its involvement in the timber processing and shipbuilding industries, but also expanded during the 1950s into the manufacture of pulp industry and metallurgical machinery. In 1970 Rauma-Repola diversified further through the acquisition of Lokomo Oy, a firm founded in 1915 and headquartered in Tampere, Finland. This purchase broadened Rauma-Repola's array of industrial machinery to include crushers, excavators, road graders, cranes, and forest machines.

During the late 1980s and early 1990s, Rauma-Repola made a number of major acquisitions, which both strengthened and broadened the company's existing business groups. These purchases also formed the backbone of the Rauma Corporation that emerged in the 1990s. The acquisition of U.S.-based Jamesbury in 1988 built upon the previously acquired Neles of Finland; the two firms were merged as Neles-Jamesbury, a leading maker of industrial valves and control systems. Also purchased in the late 1980s were Nordberg Inc. of the United States and France's

Bergeaud, which combined under the Nordberg name to comprise a global power in the rock crushing equipment for the mining and construction industries. Timberjack Corporation, a leading North American producer of timber harvesting machinery, was added in 1989 in a deal worth about US$120 million. Finally, Rauma-Repola, through a series of transactions ending in 1991, gained full control of Sweden-based Sunds Defibrator Industries AB, one of the leading makers of pulp machinery in the world. By this time, Rauma-Repola had exited from the shipbuilding industry.

On January 1, 1991, Rauma-Repola merged with United Paper Mills Inc. (UPM), a Finnish forest products company, to form Repola Corporation, a private company. A new subsidiary was created, Rauma Corporation, which housed the combined operation's metals and engineering operations and which operated independently of its parent with its own board of directors and executive board. Rauma was comprised of four main business groups: Timberjack, Sunds Defibrator, Nordberg, and Neles-Jamesbury. Rauma-Repola's forest products activities were subsumed within a new UPM unit, which was also set up as a subsidiary of Repola. In June 1995 Repola sold about 25 percent of Rauma through an initial public offering, with Rauma's stock being listed on the Helsinki and New York stock exchanges.

The following May, two of Finland's three biggest forestry groups, Repola and Kymmene Corporation merged to form UPM-Kymmene Corporation, the number one forestry firm in Europe. Wishing to focus on its core forest products operations, UPM-Kymmene reduced its stake in Rauma to 34.5 percent by the end of 1998 through secondary offerings. In 1997, meanwhile, Neles-Jamesbury's name was changed to Neles Controls. Rauma reported net income of Fmk 418 million (US$82 million) on sales of Fmk 10.32 billion (US$2.03 billion) for 1998.

Emergence of Metso, 1999

In November 1998 the boards of directors of Valmet and Rauma proposed a merger of the two companies, in yet another consolidation move, this one creating the world's largest supplier of pulp and paper equipment. The merger was approved by shareholders in January 1999 and by the European Union one month later. It closed on July 1, 1999, with the new company initially called Valmet-Rauma Corporation; it adopted the name Metso Corporation on August 24 of that year—"Metso" being the Finnish word for wood grouse, a bird familiar to Finns and symbolic of the company's ties to nature and the environment. Metso stock was listed on both the Helsinki and New York stock exchanges, and the company's two largest initial shareholders were UPM-Kymmene, with a 14.7 percent stake deriving from its interest in Rauma, and the Finnish State, with an 11.6 percent interest deriving from its stake in Valmet. Pertti Voutilainen, who had been chairman of Rauma, was named the first chairman of Metso; Matti Sundberg, president and CEO of Valmet, became CEO of Metso; and Heikki Hakala, president and CEO of Rauma, began serving as president of the newly merged company.

Metso began its existence with three main business groups. The Fiber and Paper Technology group included the Valmet paper machinery unit, the Valmet fiber processing machinery unit (formerly, Rauma's Sunds Defibrator unit), and a service unit providing paper and pulp machinery service. The Automation and Control Technology group comprised Neles Automation as well as the automation activities of Valmet. The Machinery group included the Timberjack and Nordberg operations of Rauma and the Valmet Automotive contract car manufacturing unit. Through the elimination of overlapping operations in the areas of corporate administration and distribution networks and from the benefits of economies of scale in procurement and component production, Metso hoped to saved approximately Fmk 400 million (US$80 million) per year. The company planned to reduce its personnel by about 2,000 persons, or about nine percent of its workforce, during 1999 and 2000.

Principal Operating Units

Fiber and Paper Technology (Paper Technology; Fiber Technology; Service); Automation and Control Technology; Machinery (Timberjack Forest Machines; Nordberg Crushing Systems; Metso Machine and Component Manufacturing; Valmet Automotive Car Manufacturing).

Further Reading

Björklund, Nils G., *Valmet: Asetehtaiden Muuntuminen Kansainvaliseksi Suuryhtioksi*, Jyväskylä, Finland: Gummerus, 1990, 355 p.
Brown-Humes, Christopher, "Finnish Units Form Biggest Forestry Group in Europe," *Financial Times*, September 12, 1995, p. 25.
——, "Long Courtship Guarantees Steady Union," *Financial Times*, September 12, 1995, p. 29.
——, "Repola to Float Stake in Engineering Subsidiary," *Financial Times*, June 2, 1995, p. 16.
Burt, Tim, "Orders Tumble at Valmet and Rauma," *Financial Times*, December 31, 1998, p. 24.
——, "Rauma and Valmet Announce Merger," *Financial Times*, November 18, 1998, p. 33.
Causey, James E., "Wisconsin's Beloit Corp., Foe End Their Patent Disputes," *Milwaukee Journal Sentinel*, March 18, 1998.
"Further Structural Changes Sought to Improve Profitability," *Timber Wood Products*, December 12, 1998, p. 10.
Kennedy, Carol, "A Green Business Goes Back to Its Roots," *Director*, December 1991, pp. 54–57.
"Lars Nasman," *World Paper*, June 1, 1995, p. 54.
Lewis, Jane, "Valmet Aims for Unified Look," *World Paper*, July 1, 1994, p. 26.
Tessieri, Enrique, "Birth of a Healthy Giant: Repola to Be Finland's Largest Quoted Company," *Financial Times*, November 15, 1990, p. 44.
"Timberjack: Serving All Segments of the Forest Products Industry," *Wood Technology*, October 1, 1990, p. 107.
"Valmet and Rauma to Merge," *Pulp & Paper*, January 1999, p. 21.
"Valmet's Orders Grow," *World Paper*, September 1, 1995, p. 28.
Virtanen, Olli, "Finland Picks Valmet for First Partial Privatisation," *Financial Times*, August 3, 1988, p. 21.

—Nils G. Björklund
—updated by David E. Salamie

Mettler-Toledo International Inc.

Im Langacher
P.O. Box MT-100
CH-8606 Greifensee
Switzerland
(+44) 1-944 22 11
800-786-0038
Fax: (+44) 1 944 24 70
Web site: http://www.mt.com

Public Company
Incorporated: 1945 as Einzelfirma E. Mettler
Employees: 7,000
Sales: US$936 million (1998)
Stock Exchanges: New York
Ticker Symbol: MTD
NAIC: 333997 Industrial Scales Manufacturing

Mettler-Toledo International Inc. is the world's leading manufacturer of precision weighing instruments and other precision analytical instruments for the laboratory and industrial/retail markets. The company holds leading positions in most of its product categories, including a leading 38 percent of the global laboratory balance market; the leading shares of the U.S. and European industrial and food products weighing instruments markets; and the top three global market positions in such analytical instruments markets as titrators, automatic lab reactors, thermal analysis systems, pH meters, electrodes, automated synthesis products, and moisture analyzers. Mettler-Toledo is also the world leader in metal detection systems for the cosmetics, chemicals, food processing, pharmaceutical, and other industries. Based in Greifensee, Switzerland, Mettler-Toledo trades on the New York Stock Exchange.

Mid-20th-Century Balancing Act

Mettler-Toledo built its global leadership position both through internal growth and a long history of acquisitions, enabling the company to strengthen its core market areas while expanding into diversified markets. Although parts of the company, including its Toledo line, established in 1901 as the Toledo Scale Company in the United States, predate the company, Mettler traces its official origins to 1945 and the invention of the single-pan analytical balance by company founder Erhard Mettler. The company was established as Einzelfirma E. Mettler, in Küsnacht, Switzerland. With the introduction of its scale, the company broke the less accurate two-pan weighing mold, using Mettler's so-called "substitution principal" to achieve more accurate measurements. Large-scale production of the unit began in 1946. From the start, the company looked toward the international market for its sales.

Mettler continued to refine its technology, introducing, in 1952, the Mettler Mikrowaage ("Microscale"), capable of measurements to 0.000001 grams. Several years later, the company would be able to increase the accuracy of its measurements still further, bringing measurements to the seventh place after the decimal point. At the same time, the company began marketing a range of precision scales for weight measurements from 0.1 grams to 0.01 grams.

The company's increasing sales brought it to its first expansion moves in 1952, with the opening of the Stäfa, Switzerland production facility, which would undergo a series of extensions and remain in use into the 1990s. Two years later, the company's increasing international presence, in particular in the United States, led it to open its first international subsidiary, Mettler Instrument Corp., in Hightstown, New Jersey. This international expansion would be followed by the company's move into Giessen, Germany, in 1957. From there, the company expanded throughout Europe, and later throughout much of the world, to place its subsidiaries and its products closer to its clients. This would form the basis of the company's sales strategy, centered around a locally based sales staff. In the late 1990s, the company's sales staff would account for some 50 percent of its total payroll.

After more than a decade of strong internal growth, Mettler prepared for its first acquisition. In 1962 the company acquired Dr. Ernst Rüst AG, a maker of high-precision mechanical scales, which had been founded just three years before. The newly added division would be renamed as Mettler Optic AG.

Mettler also made its first moves at expanding its product categories, introducing a thermal-analyzer, the TA 1, in 1964. By the end of the decade, the company had delivered more than 100 units of this product.

In 1965 Mettler opened a new assembly facility, in Uznach, which initially employed just three people for the assembly of the company's precision balances. At the company's Stäfa production facility, Mettler was preparing the rollout of a new product group, the FP line, an apparatus for melting point determination. Initial production was 100 units; the product line would retain a key place in the company's catalog, while undergoing successive technological improvements in the coming decades. The FP line was joined by the TM line of temperature analysis instruments, introduced in 1968, as well as the PE line of precision balances, the company's first scales to incorporate emerging electronic technology. By then, Mettler also had moved into new facilities, with the construction of the first building of its Greifensee campus, which would remain the company's headquarters through the end of the century.

Diversification in the 1970s

The company took a new step toward a diversified product line with the 1970 introduction of its DV and DK lines of automated titration systems. At the same time, Mettler strengthened its core scales component with the acquisition of balance manufacturer Microwa AG. The following year, another acquisition, of August Sauter KG, of Albstadt-Ebingen, in Germany, added that company's specialized industrial and retail scales, as well as more than 500 employees to the Mettler payroll. By then, Mettler had taken its place among the world's leading manufacturers of specialized scales and other analytical apparatus.

Advances in micro-electronics technology made possible the next step in Mettler's history: the conversion to electronic systems. In 1973 Mettler debuted its PT1200 scale, the industry's first fully electronic precision balance. With a capacity of 0 to 1,200 grams, the PT1200 had a sensitivity to 0.01 grams. The new balance proved immediately successful upon its official 1974 launch. The success of the PT1200, and its successors, enabled the company to open an additional production facility, in Uznach, with an initial floorspace of 2,100 square meters. The company continued to refine its electronics technology, and in 1979 rolled out its DeltaRange, which was awarded the IR100 Award and voted one of the most significant technical achievements for the year.

In 1980 Mettler's shares were bought up by Swiss giant Ciba-Geigy. Mettler was added to Ciba-Geigy's industrial division. The purchase enabled the company's founder to retire, while ensuring Mettler the resources for future growth. Mettler would continue, however, to operate independently and to continue its own development.

By then, Mettler had begun to expand beyond its original laboratory market to produce balances and other equipment for the industrial and retail, especially food retailing, markets. In 1982 the company presented its first electronic precision balance for industrial applications, the Sauter MultiRange. The company also introduced its PE precision scale, which featured an extremely compact form. A new product line was launched in 1985, when Mettler, in a collaboration with Ciba-Geigy, introduced its first automated lab reactor, the Mettler RCI. The company also moved into the Asian market, opening a joint venture operation in China, where it began production of laboratory equipment in 1987.

Acquiring Independence in the 1990s

The second half of the 1980s was marked by three significant acquisitions. The first took place in 1986, when Mettler acquired fellow Swiss company Ingold Firmengruppe and its line of laboratory and industrial-use electrodes and sensors. Next, in 1987, Mettler took over Garvens Automation GmbH, near Hanover, Germany, and that company's dynamic checkweighers, dosage control, and other processing systems. Whereas these acquisitions would bring Mettler into new product territories, Mettler's next major acquisition would bring the company something else: a new name.

In 1989 Mettler acquired the Toledo Scale Corporation, based in Worthington, Ohio. Toledo, which had been founded in 1901, was then the largest producer of industrial and food retailing scale systems in the United States. The acquisition would lead Mettler to capitalize on Toledo's strong brand recognition. Following the acquisition, Mettler changed its name to Mettler-Toledo AG. The company also restructured, placing its European subsidiaries under the Mettler-Toledo name.

Mettler-Toledo continued its product line expansion when it acquired the rheology and laboratory automation systems from Contraves AG in Zurich in 1990. Another acquisition made that year brought the laboratory balance production of Ohaus Corporation into the Mettler-Toledo group of products. After launching the micro-scale Mettler MT5 in 1991, with sensitivity to 0.000001 grams, the company introduced the Mettler UMT2, a fully automated balance capable of reading weights from 0.0000001 grams to two grams, in 1992. On a larger scale, Mettler-Toledo inaugurated new production facilities in Albstadt and Giesen, in Germany, as well as new quarters in Schwerzenbach, in Switzerland.

In 1993 Mettler-Toledo reorganized its Swiss operations into a more vertically integrated structure under the Mettler-Toledo AG structure. At the same time, the company delineated its balance line into three categories: Basic, Standard, and Professional. In that same year, Mettler debuted two new products: the TA8000 thermal analysis system and the AT 10005 mass comparator.

In 1996 Mettler-Toledo regained its independence from Ciba-Geigy after a management buyout, assisted by AEA Investors, a New York-based investment group, worth US$402 million. The following year, AEA Investors brought Mettler-Toledo to the public, listing the company on the New York Stock Exchange. The listing gave the newly independent Mettler-Toledo the capital to increase its acquisition drive, as the company set out to complete its product offering and consolidate its leadership position in its various markets. An important acquisition was the 1997 purchase of the United Kingdom's Safeline Ltd., the leading manufacturer of metal detection systems destined for the food, pharmaceutical, cosmetics, chemicals, and other industries requiring security testing procedures for their packaged products.

The year 1998 saw three more important acquisitions. The first took place in July 1998, with the purchase of Illinois-based Bohdan Automation Inc., a maker of laboratory automation and automated synthesis equipment. The move marked a further enhancement of Mettler-Toledo's position in the growing laboratory automation markets, especially in the synthesis reactor product category. At the end of 1998, Mettler-Toledo was able to boost this segment still further, as it announced the acquisitions of two drug and chemical compound automated discovery and development systems manufacturers, Applied Systems, of Annapolis, Maryland, and Myriad Synthesizer Technology, based in Cambridge, England. By then, Mettler-Toledo had elected a new company chairman, Robert Spoerry, who had been serving as company CEO since 1993.

Mettler-Toledo continued on its acquisition march in 1999. In February of that year, the company announced its intention to acquire French industrial and retail scale manufacturer Testut-Lustrana. The move pointed the way to a further consolidation of the highly fragmented laboratory equipment market. In April 1999, Mettler-Toledo completed the acquisition of full control of its Chinese joint venture partnership, which, combined with company-owned production facilities in Shanghai, would enable the company to expand its sales throughout the Asia-Pacific region.

With 46 percent of sales in Europe and 43 percent of sales in the United States, Mettler-Toledo had become one of the most global of laboratory equipment manufacturers. Its growing operations in the Asian region, which provided some 11 percent of company sales, gave it a strong foothold there, despite the region's economic difficulties in the late 1990s. By then, industrial products had risen to become the company's largest product area, with 49 percent of annual sales, as compared with just 38 percent for sales of laboratory products. Mettler-Toledo looked forward not only to extending its products to the full range of laboratory analytical equipment and apparatus for retail and industrial applications, but also to the consolidation of its industry—with itself in the leader's position.

Principal Subsidiaries

Mettler-Toledo Ges.m.b.H. (Austria); Mettler-Toledo B.V. (Belgium); Mettler-Toledo Finance Ltd. (Bermuda); Mettler-Toledo Industria e Commercio Ltda (Brazil); Safeline do Brasil Limitada (Brazil); Mettler-Toledo Inc. (Canada); Changzhou Electronic Scale Limited (China); Mettler-Toledo Instruments (Shanghai) Ltd. (China); Mettler-Toledo International Trading (Shanghai) Corp. (China); Ohaus International Trading (Shanghai) Ltd. (China); Panzhihua Toledo Electronic Scale Ltd. (China); Xinjiang Toledo Electronic Scale Ltd. (China); Mettler-Toledo d.o.o. (Croatia); Mettler-Toledo spol. s.r.o. (Czech Republic); Mettler-Toledo A/S (Denmark); Mettler-Toledo Analyse Industrielle S.a.r.l. (France); Mettler-Toledo Holding (France) SAS (France); Mettler-Toledo S.A. (France); NS Mettler-Toledo I SAS (France); NS Mettler-Toledo II SAS (France); NS Mettler-Toledo III SAS (France); Ohaus S.a.r.l. (France); Safeline SA (France); Garvens Automation GmbH (Germany); Mettler-Toledo (Albstadt) GmbH (Germany); Mettler-Toledo GmbH (Germany); Mettler-Toledo Holding Deutschland GmbH (Germany); Mettler-Toledo Management Holding Deutschland GmbH (Germany); Ohaus Waagen Vertriebsgesellschaft m.b.H. (Germany); Safeline GmbH (Germany); Hong Kong Mettler-Toledo (HK) Ltd.; Mettler-Toledo Kereskedelmi Kft. (Hungary); India Mettler-Toledo India Private Limited; Mettler-Toledo S.p.A. (Italy); Mettler-Toledo K.K. (Japan); Mettler-Toledo (Korea) Ltd.; Mettler-Toledo (Malaysia) Sdn. Bhd.; Mettler-Toledo S.A. de C.V. (Mexico); Ohaus de Mexico S.A. de C.V.; Gelan Engineering B.V. (Netherlands); Gelan Holding B.V. (Netherlands); Gelan International B.V. (Netherlands); Gelan Metaaldetectiesystemen B.V. (Netherlands); Mettler-Toledo B.V. (Netherlands); Mettler-Toledo Holding B.V. (Netherlands); Cargoscan A/S; (Norway); Mettler-Toledo sp.z.o.o. (Poland); Mettler-Toledo AO (Russia); Mettler-Toledo (Singapore) Pte. Ltd.; Mettler-Toledo Spol s.r.o. (Slovak Republic); Mettler-Toledo d.o.o. (Slovenia); Mettler-Toledo S.A.E. (Spain); Mettler-Toledo AB (Sweden); Mettler-Toledo GmbH; Mettler-Toledo Holding AG; Mettler-Toledo Logistik AG; Mettler-Toledo Pac Rim AG; Mettler-Toledo (Schweiz) AG; Microwa Prazisionswaagen AG; Pivott Instrumente AG; Mettler-Toledo (Thailand) Ltd.; Bohdan Europe Limited (U.K.); Mettler-Toledo Ltd. (U.K.); Mettler-Toledo Myriad Limited (U.K.); Ohaus UK Ltd. (U.K.); Safeline Limited (U.K.); Safeline Holding Company (U.K.); ASI Applied Systems Inc. (U.S.A.); Bohdan Automation Inc. (U.S.A.); Hi-Speed Checkweigher Co., Inc. (U.S.A.); Mettler-Toledo Chemistry Systems Holding Inc. (U.S.A.); Mettler-Toledo Inc. (U.S.A.); Mettler-Toledo Process Analytical Inc. (U.S.A.); Ohaus Corporation (U.S.A.); Safeline Inc. (U.S.A.).

Further Reading

''Balance Basics,'' April 1999, p. 28.
''Batch Plant,'' *Glass,* August 1996, p. 342.
''Mettler Toledo Acquires Two Companies,'' *Instrument Business Outlook,* December 1998.
''Mettler Toledo Gets the Balance Right,'' *Cosmetics International,* April 10, 1999, p. 13.
''Mettler Toledo Set to Jump Swiss New Equity Pipeline,'' *Euroweek,* January 8, 1999, p. 20.

—M. L. Cohen

Morton's Restaurant Group, Inc.

3333 New Hyde Park Road
New Hyde Park, New York 11042
U.S.A.
(516) 627-1515
Fax: (516) 627-1898
Web site: http://www.mortons.com

Public Company
Incorporated: 1978 as Morton's of Chicago Inc.
Employees: 3,612
Sales: $189.8 million (1998)
Stock Exchanges: New York
Ticker Symbol: MRG
NAIC: 72211 Full-Service Restaurants

Morton's Restaurant Group, Inc. owns and operates Morton's of Chicago, a high-end steakhouse restaurant chain aimed at a business clientele, and Bertolini's Authentic Trattorias, a smaller chain offering Italian specialties in a casual dining atmosphere. At the end of 1998 Morton's Restaurant Group owned and operated 43 Morton's of Chicago and 12 Bertolini's units. All Morton's of Chicago restaurants were similar in style, concept, and decor, and were located in retail, hotel, commercial, and office building complexes in major metropolitan areas and urban centers. Catering primarily to business-oriented clients, Morton's of Chicago had an average per person check of about $65 in 1998. The Bertolini's restaurants offered white tablecloth service, with an average per person check of about $20. Morton's Restaurant Group also held a minority of stock in two other restaurant chains, Mick's and Peasant.

Arnold Morton's Concept: 1978–87

Born into a family of Chicago restaurateurs, Arnie Morton was director of food and beverages for Playboy's clubs and resorts in the 1960s. Known, according to William Rice of the *Chicago Tribune,* as the man who "pinned the tails on the bunnies," Morton found corporate management stultifying af-

ter Playboy founder Hugh Hefner moved to California. He left in 1973 to open a discotheque and several restaurants in the Chicago area. In 1978, with Klaus Fritsch as his partner, he opened Morton's, a Chicago steakhouse that was to serve as the prototype for the Morton's of Chicago chain.

Ted Kasemir, an employee, later recalled to Rice of Morton's, "There wasn't much room for a kitchen, so he kept the menu short and simple enough to be done by a broiler cook instead of a chef." Instead of aging and cutting the meat on the premises, Morton "bought meat that was cut and aged. Then he glamorized the front, gave it a classy, clublike feel." The aging process involved two to three weeks at 34 to 36 degrees Fahrenheit in climate-controlled rooms.

By the time a Morton's of Chicago restaurant opened in Washington, D.C., in October 1982, the chain had developed an elaborate "presentation" of the menu during which a server wheeled a cart to the diner's table and held aloft, for inspection, raw cuts of beef wrapped in cellophane, a raw chicken marinating in the wrap, a live Maine lobster crawling across its tray, and various other items, including gigantic specimens of Idaho potato and steamed asparagus. All items were a la carte.

Washington Post restaurant reviewer Phyllis C. Richman was not impressed. While conceding that the new Morton's was "playing to a packed house" and offering "a good show," she wrote of the steaks that "despite their highly touted aging, they have little flavor."

By 1987 there was another Chicago-area Morton's steakhouse and seven more in other cities, including Philadelphia, Dallas, and Boston. Entrees at the Boston unit, which opened in 1987, included prime rib, veal and lamb chops, and swordfish steak, as well as chicken, lobster, and the usual two-inch-thick steaks. That year, when Morton's of Chicago had sales of more than $15 million, the chain was sold for a reported $12.4 million to Lexington Investment Co., a venture capital firm, and Alex. Brown & Sons, a Baltimore brokerage house. Fritsch stayed on as president of the enterprise.

Company Perspectives:

Morton's Restaurant Group was founded with the mission of identifying, acquiring and growing time-tested restaurant groups which are clearly distinguished in their market niches. This mission was refined to focus on two interrelated strategies: expanding and replicating the continuing success of our Morton's of Chicago *steakhouse restaurants and* Bertolini's Authentic Trattorias; *providing Morton's Restaurant Group with the means to transition our company to new levels of competitiveness and growth.*

Quantum Restaurant Group, 1989–96

Morton's Steak Houses was sold in 1989 for $9 million in equity to Quantum Restaurant Group, Inc., a company recently founded by Allen J. Bernstein with venture capital from Castle Harlan, a private New York City merchant banking firm. Quantum's first acquisition, in December 1988, had been an 89 percent stake in Peasant Restaurants Inc., an Atlanta-based, 14-unit restaurant firm, for $11.6 million. The Peasant chain began in 1973, when Stephan Nygren and Richard Dailey turned a Mexican restaurant on Atlanta's Peachtree Street into the Pleasant Peasant, a continental New York bistro. Dailey's Restaurant followed in 1984, and a unit later opened in Washington, D.C. Peasant Restaurants included a diner-style sister chain, Mick's, which was founded in 1984 and consisted of four units in 1989.

Quantum Restaurant Group was not profitable in its early years. Although restaurant revenues rose from $50.2 million in 1989 to $78 million in 1991, a variety of nonoperating expenses raised its negative net income to $20.6 million in the latter year. The company made its initial public offering of stock in 1992, its first profitable year. One of the two new Morton's that year was a unit in Beverly Hills—named Arnie Morton's of Chicago so as not to be confused with the celebrity-studded, West Hollywood "Mortons" opened in 1980 by Arnold Morton's son Peter. Reviewing Arnie Morton's in the magazine section of the *Los Angeles Times*, Charles Perry called the three-pound double porterhouse (actually half T-bone, half sirloin strip), "the most satisfying steak I've had in years."

Morton's of Chicago made its New York City debut in October 1993, locating in midtown Manhattan. "Are we too snooty, too myopic, too chauvinistic . . . too *rigid* for *Second City* brassness?" *New York* restaurant critic Gael Greene asked rhetorically. This transplanted Midwesterner gave the new Morton's a mixed review but called the three-pound porterhouse "spectacular. Really rare, fire-glazed, tender but not too, bursting with flavor. As is the sirloin. And our two-and-a-half-pound lobster ($38.95) is cooked to a perfection rarely found in a steakhouse."

Another sophisticated city with a tradition of fine dining, San Francisco, received its own Morton's of Chicago a year later. *San Francisco Chronicle* food editor Michael Bauer—another transplanted Midwesterner—turned thumbs down on some of the side dishes, expressed outrage at the prices, and sneered at the food presentation. However, he called the steaks "better than I've had since my father sold his butcher shop in Kansas. Beef lovers will swoon over the buttery tenderness of the double-cut filet ($27.95), the richly marbled rib eye or even the melt-in-your mouth quality of the brochette ($19.95) skewered with onions and peppers."

There were 10 Peasant and 25 Mick's restaurants in 1994, when Quantum Restaurant Group—which now wholly owned both chains—shifted to lower prices for the former, with most entrees in the $7 to $16 range. Chefs were recruited and trained to replace kitchen managers in executing Peasant's new culinary strategy. The chain, although remaining Atlanta-based and -oriented, opened a Philadelphia unit in 1994. The Mick's chain also was concentrated in the Atlanta area, but there were other units in Baltimore, Memphis, Miami, Minneapolis, Nashville, Philadelphia, and Washington. In December 1993, Quantum launched a new chain, called Bertolini's Authentic Trattorias, that featured northern Italian food at midscale prices. The original Bertolini's had opened in Las Vegas in 1992 and the second in Atlanta in September 1993. Four more opened in 1995.

Peasant and Mick's were proving to be Quantum Restaurant Group's black hole, sucking out the profits earned by Morton's of Chicago. In 1995 Quantum put the two chains on the block and took a pretax charge of $15.5 million related to the closing of certain Mick's and Peasant restaurants. As a result, the company lost $13.9 million during the year. In 1996 the two chains lost $11 million on revenues of $54.4 million, but Quantum nevertheless registered net income of $1.8 million.

Morton's of Chicago remained Quantum's high-end restaurant chain. Billing at an average rate of about $65 per person in 1996, the 34-unit Morton's was the most expensive major restaurant chain in the world. It also had the severest operating controls, with the emphasis on complete consistency for its business-oriented customers. Bernstein, who started out in the business as the owner of 17 Wendy's units, was using fast-food principles not only to manage cost and quality but to recruit and train managers, chefs, and serving staff.

All Morton's of Chicago units were designed to be, in the words of one manager interviewed by Glenn Collins of the *New York Times* in 1996, "a timeless place of refuge," with no windows, dark-wood furnishings, photos of celebrities, Leroy Neiman prints, and canned music featuring Frank Sinatra. A large, mahogany-paneled boardroom was set aside for business meetings by corporate clients. While the emphasis was on beef, Morton's also offered fresh fish, lobster, veal, and chicken. All units featured an open display kitchen where steaks were prepared. Each had a fully stocked bar with a complete line of name brands and an extensive premium wine list, offering about 175 selections.

The prime aged beef—at a wholesale price of over $14 a pound—was shipped from Chicago, lobsters from New England, smoked salmon from Seattle, swordfish from New York's Block Island, and cheesecake from New York City's borough of The Bronx. Chefs were trained to prepare and present every dish to exact company specifications, with the same ingredients and recipes. A color-photo display depicted the desired presentation of each dish. Each Morton's of Chicago monitored inventory, sales, and profits with a point-of-sale computer system similar to those used by the fast-food chains. If supplies were suddenly found to be running low, Morton's deployed couriers, air carriers such as Federal Express, and even taxicabs to make sure all the 500 kitchen items, sauces, and garnishes were available to diners. Downtown units remained open Sundays, despite little business, in order to cater to visiting out-of-town businesspeople. Nine Morton's were serving lunch as well as dinner in 1998.

Morton's Restaurant Group, 1996–99

Quantum Restaurant Group renamed itself Morton's Restaurant Group in 1996. The company announced in early 1997 that it was selling 19 Peasant and Mick's restaurants, for $6.8 million in cash and notes, to Gregory M. Buckley, former president of Quincy's Family Steakhouse. Morton's retained a 20 percent stake in the two chains and kept the Washington units for itself, but closed, sold, or otherwise disposed of these by the end of the year. The transaction allowed Morton's to concentrate on its eponymous steakhouse chain, which now was accounting for 85 percent of its revenues. The first overseas Morton's opened in Singapore in 1998, followed by another in Toronto. Bernstein was hoping eventually to establish 60 to 70 Morton's units outside the United States.

Bertolini's opened another restaurant in 1996, one in 1997, and two in 1998. Like the steakhouse chain, it was being run on the principle of uniformity, with each unit offering the same menu, ingredients, ambience, and level of service. During 1998, however, Morton's Restaurant Group identified several underperforming Bertolini's units and authorized a plan for the closure or abandonment of certain ones. In early 1999 the company closed the units in Westbury, New York, and Contra Costa, California.

The revenues of Morton's Restaurant Group peaked at $193 million in 1996, just prior to the sale of underperforming Peasant and Mick's restaurants. Net income rose from $1.8 million in 1996 to $6.9 million in 1997. The company lost $1.9 million in 1998, after taking a pretax charge of $19.9 million for a writedown of Bertolini's assets. Despite this setback, Morton's high operating income—$24.5 million in 1998—attracted investors, who bid the stock as high as $25 a share in 1997 and 1998, compared to the $10 per share at which the company went public.

Alcoholic beverages accounted for about 32 percent of Morton of Chicago's revenues in 1998. The on-premises private dining and meet facilities referred to as "boardrooms" and available in all but the Chicago Morton's accounted for about 18 percent of the chain's sales. During the year dinner service accounted for about 67 percent of Bertolini's revenues and lunch for about 33 percent. Alcoholic beverages accounted for about 20 percent.

FMR Corp. was Morton's Restaurant Group's largest stockholder in May 1999, with 12.8 percent of the shares. Bernstein held 6.3 percent of the shares. Several investment and venture capital firms held six percent or more of the stock. The company's long-term debt was $40.3 million at the end of 1998.

Principal Subsidiaries

Bertolini's Restaurants, Inc.; Italian Restaurants Holding Corp.; Morton's, Inc.; Morton's of Chicago, Inc.; Porterhouse, Inc.

Further Reading

Bauer, Michael, "Steaks Are Right, Service Is Rote," *San Francisco Sunday Examiner & Chronicle,* February 5, 1995, Datebook section, p. 38.
Bernstein, Charles, "Ex-Le Peep Exec Bernstein Behind Peasant Acquisition," *Nation's Restaurant News,* May 22, 1989, p. 4.
Collins, Glenn, "A Big Mac Strategy at Porterhouse Prices," *New York Times,* August 13, 1996, pp. D1, D4.
Gabriel, Frederick, "By Trimming the Fat, Morton's Is Attracting Investor Stakes," *Crain's New York Business,* March 3, 1997, p. 4.
Greene, Gael, "To Sirloin with Love," *New York,* November 8, 1993, p. 72.
Hayes, Jack, "Pleasant Peasant Scales Prices, Hires Exec Chefs," *Nation's Restaurant News,* August 15, 1994, pp. 1, 107.
——, "Quantum Leaps, Launches New Bertolini's," *Nation's Restaurant News,* December 6, 1993, p. 3.
Janofsky, Michael, "On the Menu, Steak Bucks Trend," *New York Times,* January 25, 1993, pp. D1, D4.
Konig, Susan, "A Fast-Food Strategy for a High-End Menu," *New York Times,* September 20, 1998, Sec. 14 (Long Island), p. 15.
Perry, Charles, "Chicago Chops," *Los Angeles Times Magazine,* December 20, 1992, p. 58.
Rauscher, Susannah Vesey, "Peasant Restaurants Sold," *Atlanta Journal-Constitution,* January 4, 1997, p. C1.
Rice, William, "Check, Please," *Chicago Tribune,* Sec. 5, pp. 1, 4.
Richman, Phyllis C., "Morton's of Chicago," *Washington Post Magazine,* February 13, 1983, pp. 26–27.
Rosenberg, Hilary, "The Operators at Castle Harlan," *Institutional Investor,* April 1993, pp. 57, 63.
Santangelo, Mike, "He's the King of Fine Dining," *Newsday,* April 28, 1997, p. C7.

—Robert Halasz

National Geographic Society

1145 17th Street NW
Washington, D.C. 20036-4688
U.S.A.
(202) 857-7000
Fax: (202) 828-6679
Web site: http://www.nationalgeographic.com

Non-Profit Organization
Incorporated: 1888
Employees: 1,200
Sales: $500 million (1998)
NAIC: 511120 Periodical Publishers; 511130 Book
    Publishers; 512110 Video Production

Founded as a club of distinguished gentlemen devoted to promoting the study of geography, the National Geographic Society is the largest educational society in the world and the publisher of one of the world's most widely circulated magazines, *National Geographic,* as well as *National Geographic Traveler* and *National Geographic Adventure.* The company is also involved in book publishing, education, public service projects, and television production, but its flagship magazine remains its crowning achievement. Thanks in large part to the efforts of three generations of the Grosvenor family, *National Geographic* has become a staple of American mass culture. The Society's trustees in recent years have included such notables as Supreme Court Chief Justice Warren Burger, Lady Bird Johnson, Air Force General Curtis LeMay, astronaut Frank Borman, and businessman J. Willard Marriott, Jr. Having embraced new media and new techniques in publishing, the Society has brought the far corners of the world to the doorsteps of millions of Americans. Frank Luther Mott, an eminent journalism historian, observed that *National Geographic* has compiled "a fabulous record of success, especially since the magazine is founded on an editorial conviction that rates the intelligence of the popular audience fairly high."

Eminent Origins in the 1880s

The National Geographic Society was founded in January 1888 in Washington, D.C., by a group of eminent citizens who wanted to promote geographic research and the popular distribution of the results of such research. The charter members of the Society included Alexander Graham Bell; Bell's father-in-law, lawyer Gardiner Greene Hubbard; explorers John Wesley Powell and A.W. Greeley; and scholar George Kennan, uncle of future ambassador to the Soviet Union George F. Kennan. Hubbard was one of Bell's early financial backers and had served as the first president of the Bell Telephone Company, the forerunner of AT&T. He was elected to serve as the Society's first president.

The first issue of *National Geographic* appeared shortly after the Society's founding and was published intermittently until January 1896, when monthly publication began. The early magazine bore little resemblance to the readable, eye-catching *National Geographic* of later years. Its articles were written in a dry, academic style and bore titles such as "Geographic Methods in Geologic Investigation" and "The Classification of Geographic Forms by Genesis," and there were no illustrations. It is not surprising, then, that circulation remained limited, with less than 1,000 subscribers and negligible newsstand sales.

Gardiner Greene Hubbard died in 1897 and was succeeded as president by his famous son-in-law. When Alexander Graham Bell took the helm, he found the National Geographic Society in a precarious financial state, largely because its magazine had failed to provide a strong revenue base. He soon realized that *National Geographic* needed two things: a change in editorial policy that would make it a popular scientific magazine rather than a scholarly journal, and a full-time editor who would manifest the changes he sought. Bell hoped to fill both needs in 1899 when he wrote to his friend, historian Edwin Grosvenor of Amherst College, to ask if either of Grosvenor's sons might be interested in assuming editorship. Gilbert H. Grosvenor, then a 23-year-old prep school teacher in New Jersey, accepted.

Having grown up in Istanbul while his father researched his two-volume history of the Turkish capital, Gilbert Grosvenor had become fascinated with foreign lands and peoples at an early age—but he later confessed that he was also drawn to the job by his desire to be near Bell's daughter Elsie, whom he later married.

Grosvenor proved to be the catalyst behind the immensely successful popularization of the magazine. After studying such classic examples of travel writing as Darwin's *Voyage of the Beagle* and Charles Dana's *Two Year's Before the Mast*, Grosvenor concluded that *National Geographic* articles could be made more readable without sacrificing their educational value. Grosvenor then mandated some stylistic changes for the magazine, including eliminating academic jargon, keeping sentences short and punchy, and replacing scholarly formality and detachment with engaging first-person narrative.

Grosvenor also introduced photographs into the magazine, a step that would gain *National Geographic* more recognition than its newly accessible style. He knew well the impact that photographs would have; his father's history of Istanbul, published in 1895, was the first scholarly book published in the United States to make extensive use of photoengravings. Though some critics considered it vulgar to run photos in an academic work, the book sold well. Gilbert Grosvenor encountered much opposition from more conservative trustees of the National Geographic Society when the changes that he wished to make became known. He had, however, the firm backing of Alexander Graham Bell, which afforded him the time to prove the editorial merits of his innovations. Skyrocketing circulation (by 1906 the magazine could boast of 11,000 regular subscribers) confirmed his abilities.

Opposition from within the Society's board softened, too. In one incident in December 1904, Grosvenor faced a challenge when the next month's issue was about to go to press with 11 pages blank for want of copy. In that day's mail, however, he found an unsolicited packet containing the first photographs ever taken of the Tibetan capital of Lhasa. Awed by the photos and desperate for material, he used them to fill the blank pages. He later wrote that he expected to be fired for running an 11-page pictorial spread, but several days after the issue appeared, he was elected a trustee of the Society. Grosvenor ran *National Geographic*'s first color photos in 1910. The magazine remains a pioneer in the journalistic use of photography.

Alexander Graham Bell retired as president of the National Geographic Society in 1903, although he remained a contributor to the magazine and an influential member of the organization until his death in 1922. He was succeeded by a series of short-term chief executives: W.J. McGee served briefly, followed by Grove Karl Gilbert. Willis Moore served from 1905 to 1909. Henry Gannett, a charter member and chief geographer of the U.S. Geological Survey, succeeded Moore and served until his death in 1914. Gannett was succeeded by O.H. Tittman, who resigned in 1919. He was followed by John E. Pillsbury, who served less than a year before his death in December 1919. In 1920 the entire National Geographic Society and its expanding operations became Gilbert Grosvenor's responsibility when he succeeded John Pillsbury as president. Grosvenor remained editor of the magazine, which continued the readable, relatively upbeat style that he had created.

In these early years the Society began its sponsorship of high-profile exploratory, archaeological, and naturalistic expeditions. In 1906 it contributed $1,000 to the Arctic expedition led by Commander Robert E. Peary, with whom the Society had a longstanding professional relationship. In 1909 Peary became the first to reach the North Pole, and the National Geographic Society has basked in this triumph ever since. Another of its early successes was Yale archaeologist Hiram Bingham's 1912 expedition to Peru, during which the Inca capital of Macchu Picchu was excavated.

As president of the Society, Grosvenor continued its sponsorship of extraordinary expeditions. The Society provided financial support for Commander Richard E. Byrd's various Arctic and Antarctic voyages between 1925 and 1930, during which he became the first person to fly to the North and South Poles. Byrd was aided by a special compass designed by Albert Bumstead, the Society's chief cartographer, which used the sun for navigation, since magnetic compasses would not work at the poles. In 1935 the Society and the U.S. Army Air Corps co-sponsored *Explorer II*, a helium balloon that set an altitude record for an occupied balloon that stood until the dawn of the Space Age. In 1939 the Society and the Smithsonian Institution co-sponsored an expedition to southern Mexico during which archaeologist Matthew Sterling uncovered a Mayan stela, an inscribed tablet, that was the oldest known human artifact from the New World.

National Geographic reached the mass readership that its founders had sought, with a circulation of 500,000 at the end of World War I, and the Society continued to expand its activities. In 1922, after receiving a request for geographical information from the National Education Association, the Society launched a weekly publication designed for classroom use, *Geographic School Bulletins*. During World War II, the Society opened its photographic and cartographic archives to the United States military. Its vast library of photographs of foreign countries provided intelligence about infrastructure in enemy-held territory and also helped unveil camouflage when compared with the military's own reconnaissance photographs. The Society's maps of distant lands, which it had been accumulating since creating its own cartographic department in 1916, also proved valuable. After the war, the Society received a grateful letter from Fleet Admiral Chester Nimitz, one of the war's heroes, who reported that a National Geographic map of the South Pacific saved him considerable difficulty in 1942 when the crew members of the B-17 in which he was flying used it to get back on course after losing their bearings in a storm near Guadalcanal. Further, President Franklin Roosevelt asked the Society for a map, and was so impressed with the encased set that was given him that he later asked for and received a similar set to give to Prime Minister Winston Churchill. Churchill was so pleased with his maps that after the war, when the Society asked him to return the original set for a new and updated set in order to place the originals in the Society's museum, Churchill politely refused.

The Space Age

After the war, with so much of the Earth's land mass already explored and mapped, the Society turned part of its attention to the last remaining frontier: outer space. It co-sponsored with the California Institute of Technology the ambitious Sky Survey, which would produce the Sky Atlas, the first comprehensive photographic map of the heavens. Work on the Sky Survey began in 1949 and was completed in 1956, using the 48-inch "Big Schmidt" telescope at Palomar Observatory in California.

Almost concurrently, the Society also began its long and successful association with marine explorer Jacques-Yves Cousteau. The Society sponsored a number of Cousteau expeditions in the 1950s, including the 1956 dive during which he took photographs of the Romanche Trench in the Atlantic Ocean, the deepest point at which photographs had ever been taken. During another National Geographic-sponsored expedition in the mid-1950s, Cousteau shot footage for his Oscar-winning documentary *The Silent World*.

Gilbert Grosvenor retired in 1954 after 34 years as president of the National Geographic Society and 55 years as editor of *National Geographic*. He then became chairman of the Society and was succeeded in his former positions by his old friend and longtime assistant editor, John Oliver La Gorce. La Gorce served for three years, then retired and became vice-chairman of the Society. He was succeeded by Grosvenor's son, Melville Bell Grosvenor. Although his father remained the unquestioned sage of the board of directors, the title of CEO was given to the younger Grosvenor.

As editor of *National Geographic*, Melville Bell Grosvenor expanded the magazine's use of color photography and put a color photo on the cover for the first time. As CEO of the National Geographic Society, he expanded the Society's book publishing operations and also led it into the increasingly ubiquitous medium of television. Film shot by National Geographic photographers had appeared on television since 1955, but always on network programs. Then, in 1958, Grosvenor and longtime staffer Luis Marden decided to produce the Society's own television programs. Three years later, the Society formed its documentary film department. The first Society-produced television special, "Americans on Everest," aired on CBS in 1965.

Gilbert H. Grosvenor died in 1966, and the next year his son retired and became chairman of the Society. In 1970, Gilbert M. Grosvenor, Melville's son, assumed the leadership position at *National Geographic*. He had joined the staff straight from Yale after winning the National Press Photographers Award for coverage of President Eisenhower's tour of Asia in 1951. Before long, Grosvenor became the center of controversy by enacting a subtle shift in *National Geographic*'s editorial policy, easing it away from the uniformly upbeat tone and avoidance of sensitive topics that his father and grandfather had maintained. Under Gilbert M. Grosvenor, the magazine ran major stories on racial turmoil in South Africa, communism in Cuba, and social conditions in Harlem. Although the board of trustees publicly endorsed Grosvenor's editorship, some directors of the Society were scandalized, and conservative media critics accused *National Geographic* of contracting "a bad case of radical chic." Grosvenor became president of the Society in 1980, leaving the post of editor to his longtime assistant Wilbur Garrett.

Grosvenor took charge of an organization that was, in some ways, the envy of the publishing industry. In 1980 *National Geographic* boasted 10.7 million subscribers and a circulation of well over 30 million. That year, the Society announced a profit of $3 million on revenues of $217 million, yet the Society continued to refer to its annual profit as a "surplus" and its subscribers as "members," genteel terms used by nonprofit organizations. The Society retained its not-for-profit status and accompanying tax exemptions even though it published one of the bestselling magazines in the world and ran successful book publishing and television production operations. When the Society erected a new headquarters building in Washington, D.C., in 1981 at a cost of $30 million, it paid in cash.

The 1980s would not prove entirely kind to the Society, however. It fielded much criticism for a 1981 cover in which two Egyptian pyramids were digitally manipulated to appear closer together, a technique it promptly abandoned. Circulation figures and advertising revenues from *National Geographic* remained flat throughout most of the decade. Slowdowns in the economy and increased competition from other popular science magazines presented the greatest threat of decrease in readership since the Great Depression. The Society's television operations received a boost in 1985 when it signed an agreement with cable station WTBS to produce a weekly documentary series, "National Geographic Explorer."

Gilbert Grosvenor had always focused on emerging technologies that could affect the Society's long-term future. In 1981 he speculated openly about the possibility of putting *National Geographic* and publishing books on video. In 1990 the Society published a multimedia software package called "GTV" in collaboration with Lucasfilm and Apple Computer. "GTV" was designed for use in middle schools and provided interactive lessons in U.S. history. Moreover, the Society was publishing its own catalog of merchandise and exploring the possibility of cooperative ventures, particularly with the catalog and retail firm The Nature Company, hoping to use merchandising as a new source of revenues.

New Horizons at the End of the Century

By the mid-1990s, the Society had sold more than four million home videos. Its for-profit subsidiary, National Geographic Ventures, was producing educational materials in a variety of formats, including a Disney Channel television program called "Really Wild Animals." The group was planning to air the National Geographic Channel on cable and satellite in cooperation with NBC. It also ran the Society's web site and online store, and had established theaters and exhibits at national parks.

One plan to issue *National Geographic*'s entire back catalog on CD-ROM drew criticism from authors' rights groups, however, since no additional royalties were to be paid to writers and photographers for reuse of the work. The set, released on 30 CD-ROMs, retailed for $199.

Upon the retirement of Gilbert M. Grosvenor, Reg Murphy, formerly editor or publisher of the *Baltimore Sun, San Francisco Examiner,* and *Atlanta Constitution,* moved up to president and CEO of the Society in May 1996. Also during this time, in January 1994, Bill Allen became only the eighth editor in *National Geographic* magazine's history.

The Society began placing *National Geographic* on newsstands in 1998, breaking a century of its ''members only'' tradition. The group had actually tested some issues at the newsstand previously, and had recorded good sales figures in foreign retail outlets. Single-copy sales were expected to account for only a small fraction of total sales. The flagship's sister publication, *National Geographic Traveler,* introduced in 1984, had been sold at newsstands for seven years.

National Geographic Adventure, the Society's answer to *Outside* magazine, the leader in the burgeoning adventure travel category, debuted in April 1999. Initially a quarterly, *Adventure* was expected to be produced monthly by 2001. John Rasmus was the first editor at *Adventure;* he had previously held that position at *Outside* and *Men's Journal.*

As the National Geographic Society entered the 21st century, it boasted three magazines, programs for television and home video, an expanded web site, and two freestanding retail stores in Washington, D.C. Under development were new cable and international television channels and a new magazine. The Society was also seeking partners to capitalize upon the *National Geographic* brand name via toys, software, and other consumer goods. The Society's magazines were selling record levels of advertising and new foreign language versions surpassed expectations abroad. The Society commemorated the millennium with a seven-part series on global issues.

Principal Subsidiaries

National Geographic Ventures.

Further Reading

Adams, Mark, ''Geographic Shifts,'' *Mediaweek,* June 26, 1995, p. 18.
Behr, Peter, ''Geographic: The Wealth of Knowledge,'' *Washington Post,* December 7, 1981.
Conaway, James, ''The Geographic's Founding Family,'' *Washington Post,* December 19, 1984.
Granatstein, Lisa, ''Looking for *Adventure,''* *Mediaweek,* July 20, 1998, pp. 17–18.
Gremillion, Jeff, and Lisa Granatstein, ''2000: A Space Odyssey,'' *Mediaweek,* February 2, 1998, p. 14.
Grosvenor, Gilbert H., *The National Geographic Society and Its Magazine,* Washington, D.C.: National Geographic Society, 1957.
Hays, Constance L., ''Seeing Green in a Yellow Border,'' *New York Times,* August 3, 1997, Sec. 3.
Kerwin, Ann Marie, ''Two New Titles Join Ranks of Adventure Travel Books,'' *Advertising Age,* March 8, 1999, p. 22.
Ringle, Ken, ''Around the World in 25 Years,'' *Washington Post,* February 4, 1990.
Sawyer, Kathy, ''Change at the Geographic,'' *Washington Post,* July 17, 1977.
Trueheart, Charles, ''Garrett, Grosvenor and the Great Divide,'' *Washington Post,* May 7, 1990.

—Douglas Sun
—updated by Frederick C. Ingram

NCR Corporation

1700 South Patterson Boulevard
Dayton, Ohio 45479
U.S.A.
(937) 445-5000
Fax: (937) 445-1682
Web site: http://www.ncr.com

Public Company
Incorporated: 1900 as National Cash Register Company
Employees: 33,100
Sales: $6.51 billion (1998)
Stock Exchanges: New York
Ticker Symbol: NCR
NAIC: 333313 Office Machinery Manufacturing; 334111 Electronic Computer Manufacturing; 334119 Other Computer Peripheral Equipment Manufacturing; 51121 Software Publishers; 541512 Computer Systems Design Services; 811212 Computer & Office Machine Repair & Maintenance; 339944 Carbon Paper & Inked Ribbon Manufacturing; 323110 Commercial Lithographic Printing; 323116 Manifold Business Form Printing

When National Cash Register Company was formed during the last two decades of the 19th century, it had one product—cash registers. Today NCR Corporation, as it is now known, develops and markets a wide range of computer and terminal systems; office automation products; automated teller, data warehousing, and telecommunications services; semiconductor components; software; and business forms and supplies. Among NCR's claims to fame are its introduction of bar code scanning in 1974, its position as a world leader in paper roll products for cash registers, and the fact that fully 40 percent of the checks issued around the globe are cleared with NCR equipment.

Origins

NCR's first years were shaped in large part by John Henry Patterson, who was president from 1884 to 1921. Patterson's early emphasis on sales, his initiation of business practices that became standards for other companies and industries, and his pioneering efforts in industrial welfare made NCR a role model for other companies during the late 1800s and early 1900s.

While running a dry goods operation in Ohio during the early 1880s, Patterson found he was losing money because not all sales were being reported by his clerks. When Patterson learned of a device called a cash register, he ordered two from James and John Ritty, who had recently established a Dayton, Ohio-based company called National Cash Register. In 1882 the Rittys sold part of their company and renamed it the National Manufacturing Company.

Patterson, meanwhile, was reaping such financial rewards from the use of his cash registers that he bought stock in the Rittys' company. He eventually joined the board of directors and suggested that the company use nationwide marketing techniques to sell its cash registers. Patterson's ideas met with opposition, and in 1884 he bought additional stock and took control of the company. Once president, Patterson again named the company National Cash Register Company and moved quickly to change NCR's emphasis from manufacturing to sales. His interest in sales led to the concept of quotas and guaranteed sales territories for agents. Patterson also provided his agents with sales seminars, training brochures, and scripted sales pitches, and required them to wear white shirts and dark suits. All of these practices were new at the time but soon became widespread at other companies.

Cash register sales responded almost immediately to Patterson's techniques. Sales more than doubled to 1,000 machines a year by 1886, while by 1888 the number of NCR employees had grown from 12 to more than 100. About this time Patterson also began to produce various forms of printed advertising. Beginning in the late 1880s, prospective customers were inundated with weekly or monthly advertising circulars and direct-mail letters describing products. Employees' publications were introduced to bolster communication and enthusiasm about meeting sales quotas. *Output*—the first employee newspaper—listed sales, discussed the benefits of cash registers, and printed encouraging words from satisfied customers.

Company Perspectives:

With over 100 years of experience meeting the needs of consumer-oriented businesses, NCR partners with businesses to transform transactions into relationships.

Poor economic conditions in the 1890s affected many companies in the United States, including NCR. Between 1892 and 1897 the company's production was reduced and employees worked scaled-down weeks. The company also looked more closely at the manufacturing side of business: a system of interchangeable parts for cash register models was introduced, streamlining production and trimming overhead.

In 1894 NCR constructed a new and larger "safety-conscious" facility in Dayton with the aid of bank loans. The following year Patterson hired Thomas J. Watson, who rose quickly through the sales ranks to become a sales manager in New York and later became part of an inner circle of Dayton executives. It was Watson who led the campaign to reduce competition, including a massive advertising blitz as well as an adamant defense of patents. By 1897 NCR's competition had been reduced to three companies, down from more than 80 a decade before.

In 1900 NCR reported the sale of its 200th cash register. It now employed a record 2,269 people. That same year the company was chartered as a New Jersey corporation for the purpose of selling stock. Construction of a ten-building facility began in 1906, and overseas operations, which had been established in the 1880s, were growing as well. In a company publication, NCR boasted that its sales force extended from Norway and Alaska to New Zealand and China, with nearly 1,000 agents in more than 270 offices.

First Electric Cash Register in 1906

In 1906 a young inventor named Charles F. Kettering gave the company its first electric cash register. Kettering, who had been hired just two years earlier, also developed NCR's Class 1000 machine, a low-cost redesigned register that remained in production for nearly 40 years with only minor changes. Kettering left the company in 1909 to join the automotive industry.

Spurred by the success of Kettering's cash register and the Class 1000 machine, sales continued to climb throughout the early 1900s. By 1911 NCR had sold a million machines. The company's aggressive battle to secure patent rights and fend off competition led the American Cash Register Company to file an antitrust complaint based on the Sherman Antitrust Act, a federal law prohibiting the monopolistic restraint of trade or commerce. In 1912 the government brought NCR to trial and presented 32 cases of alleged trade interference. The following year Patterson, Watson, and 20 other officers were found guilty of trade restraint and unlawful monopoly in three of those cases. (The decision would be reversed two years later by a higher court.) In 1913, however, Watson left the company after a falling out with Patterson.

The Dayton Flood of 1913 brought more attention to NCR. Under Patterson's leadership, the company responded to the flood by suspending all operations and providing relief shelter in company facilities.

Shortly thereafter, during the early stages of World War I, NCR continued to make cash registers while involved in wartime production contracts with the government. By 1919 the company was operating almost solely on a wartime production basis.

The 1920s marked NCR's gradual entrance into its accounting machine era. NCR already had proved its dominance in the cash register field, having controlled more than 95 percent of that market prior to the outbreak of the war. In 1921 NCR announced its Class 2000 itemizer, which provided 30 totals and embodied what the company believed were the best features of all previous registers. John Henry Patterson passed the reins of the company presidency in 1921 to his son Frederick Beck Patterson, who also assumed the duties of the chairman of the board after his father's death a year later.

Frederick Patterson exercised voting control over NCR after the death of his father, while comptroller Stanley C. Allyn and director John H. Barringer led the company's first major diversification drive. NCR's profits rose from $2.8 million in 1921 to $7.8 million in 1925. Because of its success, the company went public with stock sales for the first time.

The 1920s were good years for office equipment firms. After 1925 competitors made inroads into the cash register market, while NCR failed to introduce new products. Sales flattened for NCR, and by 1928 Remington Rand topped the list of business machine companies, taking in $59 million to second-running NCR's $49 million. Young IBM was fourth at the time with $19 million reported in sales.

Struggling During the Great Depression

In attempts to hasten the diversification drive, NCR purchased the Ellis Adding-Typewriter Company in January 1929. That same year the company announced the Class 3000, NCR's first hybrid machine, which represented an advance in the area of payroll, billing, and accounting operations. The promise of the new machine was dampened by the Depression later that year. Sales and earnings plunged while the company began a four-year process of cutting the number of its employees in half. With NCR nearly bankrupt by 1931, New York bankers Dillon, Read and Company, who had set up the 1925 stock sales, were ready to invade the company. In response, NCR's board of directors sought out Edward Deeds to take control of the company, and Frederick Patterson agreed to step down as chairman in 1931. Patterson remained as president until Deeds assumed that additional post in 1936; it was Deeds who turned things around for NCR.

Joining the company at the beginning of the century, Deeds had been put in charge of engineering and construction for a new factory. By 1910 he had become vice-president. Deeds left NCR for Delco in 1915 and later helped found the Wright

Airplane Company with Orville Wright, Charles Kettering, and H.E. Talbott. Deeds's success by 1931 was evident, as he sat on the corporate boards of 28 companies.

Shortly after Deeds took control, the company purchased the Remington Cash Register Company, whose assets strengthened NCR's position. In 1934 the company moved back into the black. Despite broad price fluctuations, by mid-decade sales were stabilizing and overseas operations were expanding in Great Britain, Europe, Central America, South America, and the Middle East and Far East. By the end of the decade NCR was third in the business machine field behind Remington and fast-climbing IBM. NCR in 1939 earned $12 million less than it had the year prior to the Depression. In 1940 Stanley Allyn assumed the post of president, while Deeds continued to serve as chairman and chief executive.

Effects of World War II and Its Aftermath

World War II had a significant impact on NCR, as well as on other data processing and business machine companies, spurring the conversion from office tabulating equipment to data processing. By the time the United States entered the war in 1941, NCR's expansion into Central America and South America in the 1930s had gained importance, helping to offset the wartime reduction or elimination of operations in Japan, Germany, and Australia. For the next few years the sale of rebuilt machines was the only business NCR continued in countries directly involved in the war. By 1942 the U.S. War Production Board halted the manufacturing of all cash registers to conserve metal.

Wartime contracts for such items as bomb fuses and rocket motors covered NCR's overhead during the war, while reconditioning of machines provided modest profits. The company's in-house electronics research program, established prior to World War II, was utilized by the U.S. Navy during the war years. NCR built a computerlike device to calculate bombing navigational data. It also worked on a secret operation to assist the Navy in breaking the German ENIGMA communication cipher. Dubbed "the Bombe," the mechanism was actually a high-speed electromechanical decrypting machine; about 120 Bombes were built during the course of the war.

By the war's end a pent-up market for cash registers and accounting machines resulted in a hiring surge for NCR in Dayton. Business boomed after the war. Between 1946 and 1949 NCR reestablished itself in war-torn areas of the United Kingdom, West Germany, and Japan. Improvements and expansion continued into the early 1950s, with a rebuilt plant in Australia, a new factory in Toronto, and new office buildings in Hawaii and Mexico.

Entering the Computer Business in the 1950s

NCR continued its electronics work after the war and in 1952 secured a defense contract for a bombing navigational computer. That same year the company entered into a stock purchase agreement with Computer Research Corporation, which became its electronics division the following year. Development of a computer designed for scientific work had limited impact, and the company's role in the computer industry remained conservative in the mid-1950s. But the 1956 introduc-

tion of the Post-Tronic, an electronic posting machine for banking, was successful. Sales of the Post-Tronic eventually passed the $100 million mark before the machine passed out of use near the end of the 1960s.

With NCR on the edge of a new era, the aging Deeds retired as chairman in 1957 and was succeeded by Allyn. Robert S. Oelman, who had been instrumental in procuring wartime contracts as a company vice-president, became president. Later that year NCR announced the 304, a general purpose computer based on solid-state technology. A few years later, in 1960, NCR's first "small" computer—the 390, manufactured by Control Data Corporation (CDC)—made its debut.

In the early 1960s NCR increased its development of computers, as well as peripheral devices and software. In 1962 Oelman became chairman of the board, and R. Stanley Laing was named president two years later. Mid-decade saw NCR continue to operate under a split sales strategy, targeting its old customer line as well as new customers in the data processing market. NCR's computer-related products were successful, but its innovations still remained conservative; the company's marketplace continued to revolve around banking and retailing.

By the end of the 1960s NCR often was referred to as one of the "Seven Dwarfs" because of its relative position of inferiority to IBM. Joining NCR in these ranks were General Electric (GE), RCA, Burroughs, UNIVAC, CDC, and Honeywell. With GE and RCA bowing out of the computer field in the early 1970s, the five remaining companies became known as the BUNCH, an acronym made up of the first letter of each name.

NCR announced its third generation of computers in 1968 with the introduction of the Century Series, which included a variety of business applications and allowed NCR to market its wares to a broader customer base. NCR's failure to take advantage of new conditions calling for terminals and software cost it some market share and resulted in a trend of declining profits from 1969 to 1972.

The first half of the 1970s marked the greatest transition period in the history of NCR as it attempted to move full force into the computer market. The period was marred by a number of setbacks that were worsened by an inflationary economy and poor business climate. Labor costs to produce older technology products were enormous, and the company also had marketing problems. Layoffs followed declining earnings, and the company was hit by a three-month strike at its Dayton plant in late 1971. The strike idled 8,500 production and maintenance employees, sharply reduced equipment deliveries, and cost the company millions of dollars in lost orders.

In 1971 NCR entered into a cooperative agreement with CDC to establish a computer peripherals company. The following year NCR established its microelectronics division. Declining profits continued through 1972, and the company posted its first net loss since 1933.

With revenues on shaky ground, William S. Anderson was named president in 1972 and chairman of the board in 1974. Anderson, who had been successful in heading up NCR's Far East operations and NCR Japan, was the first president to come from outside the parent company. His success in Japan was due in part to the revamping of the company's marketing organization there, and as president, Anderson quickly moved to modify NCR's marketing structure through a similar "vocationalizing" system. The branch manager system, in which a branch manager was responsible for sales from a number of different industries, was replaced by a system whereby a district manager oversaw one major marketing area and marketing personnel were trained to specialize in a single vocational area. Areas of specialization included retail, finance, commercial business, industrial, medical, educational, governmental, and media. In 1974 NCR reported that its computer business was finally out of the red. That same year the company's name was changed from National Cash Register to NCR Corporation.

Growth in the Late 1970s

NCR began making great strides in the computer field after naming Charles E. Exley, Jr., president in 1976. A 22-year veteran of Burroughs Corporation, Exley oversaw the introduction of a new series of computers and related equipment during the later part of the decade. NCR's 1976 announcement of the 8000 series was well received, and improvements were made throughout the remainder of the decade.

NCR's push into computers resulted in strong earnings, while the company began a series of smaller company acquisitions that boosted expertise in factory data systems, microcards, and IBM-compatible data systems. In fewer than five years NCR revamped its entire product line. During this time the company withdrew from the mainframe computer arena and moved closer to its traditional core industries such as banking and retailing. In 1979 the company passed the $3 billion revenue mark.

NCR came into the 1980s strong, posting its first double-digit increase in revenues in 1980, but growth stalled in 1981, and earnings dropped. Product lines besieged by bugs in the late 1970s resulted in user lawsuits being filed against NCR in the early 1980s. In 1980 a lawsuit was filed by Glovatorium, a small Oakland, California dry cleaning firm. Glovatorium, a first-time computer user, had purchased an NCR Spirit/8200 system to do routine accounting, but the system failed to work. NCR defended its case on the grounds that contracts with Glovatorium had contained limitations of liability and disclaimers. The California judge ruling in the case in 1981 said NCR had targeted first-time computer users and was under a special obligation to be fair in dealing with the user. Punitive damages totaling $2 million were awarded along with compensatory damages for breach of warranty and intentional misrepresentation. The following year NCR agreed to a $2.6 million settlement with Glovatorium.

In 1983 Exley was named chief executive officer, and in the following year he became board chairman. Under his leadership, NCR underwent a corporate restructuring process, made a push back into personal computers, began reemphasizing fiscal control, and started a long-term plan of repurchasing its own stock. The Tower family of microcomputers, which was introduced in 1982, became one of the keys to NCR's success in the mid-1980s. By 1986 the company was again posting double-digit increases, while most of the computer industry was suffering from a market recession.

NCR's revenues had grown to $6 billion by 1988, as the company developed customized products that generated significant indirect sales. Meanwhile NCR's microelectronics division became a leading producer of semiconductors, and the company surpassed IBM as the largest worldwide supplier of automatic teller machines (ATMs). Personal computers and the Tower microcomputers also saw significant sales gains in the emphasis switch from mainframes to distribution processing.

In 1988 Gilbert P. Williamson was promoted from executive vice-president to president, while Exley remained chairman and CEO. The following year overall sales began to dip, although foreign sales were rising. The company closed out the decade as the last thriving member of the BUNCH that had avoided a merger or sellout of interests.

NCR expected to keep its products on par with the computer industry's powerhouses. In late 1989 it announced that it was jumping into the market for microcomputers that were based on a powerful new microchip. The announcement helped NCR land an agreement with Businessland, Inc. to begin selling the new line in 1990.

According to Exley, NCR entered the 1990s with a goal to "reach all markets." The company had operations in nine countries, with products sold in more than 120 countries. NCR expected continued success in the ATM and semiconductor markets and expanded sales in technology and information processing markets. The company also expected indirect sales to increase, with a number of NCR-manufactured products being sold bearing other companies' labels.

NCR looked for benefits from the implementation of "concurrent engineering," to keep its operations on a par with Japanese competitors through a more timely and less costly manufacture of products. Concurrent engineering eliminated a number of independent steps of production, some of which had been contracted out, and replaced that system with one in which design engineers and manufacturing personnel collaborated in a closer working environment, thereby reducing the time needed to correct glitches. NCR had introduced concurrent engineering in 1987 in its new Atlanta, Georgia plant, and by the 1990s the concept was implemented to some degree in all of NCR's manufacturing facilities.

The 1990s started with great promise for NCR. As the result of an April agreement with California-based Teradata Corporation to develop parallel-processing computer technologies, NCR received 1.4 million shares of Teradata stock. In May the J.C. Penney retail chain announced that it would buy $45 million worth of workstation systems from NCR; two months later, NCR negotiated a $10 million contract to automate the branch offices of the Fleet Norstar Financial Group.

Hostile Takeover by AT&T in 1991

Then NCR ran into a formidable adversary, the American Telephone & Telegraph Company (AT&T). Seeking to bolster its failing computer division, AT&T issued a bid for NCR in December 1990, placing the purchase price at $90 a share, or $6.1 billion. The bid was met with instant hostility by NCR and over the next five months the tug-of-war was played out in the media. NCR Chairman Charles Exley publicly expressed his disdain at the thought of helping AT&T become profitable in the computer field and vowed to quit if the takeover were successful. AT&T countered with a proxy fight to unseat the NCR board of directors. Both sides hired high-powered advisers—takeover lawyer Martin Lipton and Chemical Bank for AT&T, and investment bankers Goldman-Sachs for NCR.

NCR fought hard by taking out full-page newspaper advertisements to turn public opinion its way and by asking the FCC to investigate AT&T's bid. In the end, AT&T agreed to pay the $110 per share, or $7.4 billion, that NCR was demanding, stipulating, however, that payment be made in AT&T stock. The merger was completed in September 1991. In July NCR announced plans to create a new division to market computer products to telephone companies. NCR's market position was slowed by the hostile takeover and subsequent adjustment period. Exley retired in February 1992 and Gilbert Williamson, NCR president, succeeded him as CEO. Elton White, executive vice-president, moved into the president's spot.

Incorporating NCR, with its superior product development capabilities and focused marketing plan, into AT&T, whose computer products were not as sophisticated but whose market was universal, proved to be a challenging task. To counter the market drop, a restructuring of NCR occurred almost immediately. In August 1992, even before the merger was completed, plans to close NCR's Cambridge, Ohio plant were announced. In November NCR's Workstation Products Division was split into smaller groups that would function as independent corporations. A number of AT&T employees and products were moved into the division at this time. That same month, AT&T announced that 120 workers would be released from NCR's Network Products Division in St. Paul, Minnesota.

Despite the internal upheaval caused by the hostile takeover bid, NCR continued to develop new products. A pen-based notepad computer, the NCR System 3125, was introduced in June 1991. The computer was the first of its kind to use an electronic stylus instead of a keyboard. The alliance with Teradata was solidified in December when NCR purchased the company for $520 million in AT&T stock. Ironically, Teradata's biggest customer had been AT&T.

In early 1993, after initially keeping a ''hands-off'' attitude toward NCR, AT&T installed one of its executives, Jerre Stead, as NCR CEO. Stead's casual, ''open-door'' approach was one that clashed with NCR's conservative corporate culture, and his desire to broaden NCR's focus and step up the company's production of PCs was not popular in all quarters. In 1994 NCR also was renamed AT&T Global Information Solutions (GIS).

Under AT&T's management NCR/GIS was not performing up to par, however, and Stead jumped ship in 1995. The company found a replacement in Lars Nyberg, a Swede who had successfully turned around the fortunes of Philips Electronics N.V.'s computer division. Nyberg immediately began to make serious changes, announcing a restructuring that included the layoffs of 20 percent of the company's workforce. NCR was reportedly losing almost $2 million a day for AT&T, and Nyberg also made the decision to get out of the PC business, in which NCR seemed to have few prospects for long-term success. The company also dropped the unpopular GIS name and became known as NCR once again.

In early 1996 AT&T announced that it would spin off NCR as part of a massive realignment, issuing to its shareholders NCR stock worth nearly $4 billion, or about half of what it had invested in the company four years earlier. NCR became independent in January 1997, and its stock resumed trading on the New York Stock Exchange. Nyberg continued his efforts to restore NCR's fortunes and reorganized further during the year, cutting another 1,000 jobs and reconfiguring the company's structure into five large divisions from 130 smaller ones. He also sold three of the company's manufacturing plants to Solectron, Inc., who would continue to make computer hardware for NCR at the facilities. Two acquisitions were completed as well, those of Compris Technologies, Inc. and Dataworks, companies that made software for the food service and retail sectors. The company posted a small profit in 1997, its first in five years.

NCR's fortunes were on the upswing in part because of the company's focus on the relatively new field of data warehousing. Sifting through the vast amounts of data generated when millions of consumers used ATMs or made purchases, businesses could discern patterns that allowed narrow targeting of product pitches to individual customers. NCR had half of the market in this field, and analysts estimated that most *Fortune* 1000 companies would double the size of their data warehouses within the next several years. NCR was also the top maker of ATMs worldwide, with about 27 percent of the international market.

As it continued to fine-tune operations in 1998, the company eliminated 5,200 more jobs and also repurchased $200 million worth of stock. Revenues for the year dropped by one percent but earnings increased more than 15fold, to $122 million. NCR also acquired half ownership of Stirling Douglas Group, Inc., a maker of software for retail businesses, and announced a partnership with Microsoft to develop advanced data warehousing systems. In early 1999 NCR's board approved a further $250 million stock buyback. Freed from the stranglehold of AT&T, NCR appeared to be making a remarkably swift recovery and was positioned for further growth with its command of the expanding data warehousing and ATM markets.

Principal Subsidiaries

NCR Nederland NV (Netherlands); NCR Australia Pty. Ltd.; NCR Canada Ltd.; NCR France, S.A.; NCR GmbH (Germany); NCR Japan Ltd.; NCR Espana, S.A. (Spain); NCR (Switzerland); NCR Ltd. (U.K.); NCR Danmark A/S (Denmark); NCR Argentina SAIC; NCR de Mexico, S.A. de C.V.; Data Pathing, Inc.; Compris Technologies, Inc.; International Investments, Inc.; National Cash Register Co.; North American Research Corp.; Old River Software, Inc.; Quantor Corp.; Sparks, Inc.; Microcard Corp.; NCR Overseas Trade Corp.; Scott Electronics Corp.; Dataworks; Stirling Douglas Group, Inc. (50%).

Principal Operating Units

Retail; Financial; National Accounts Solutions; Systemedia.

Further Reading

Allyn, Stanley C., *My Half Century with NCR,* New York: McGraw-Hill, 1967.

"AT&T Bares Its Teeth," *Business Week,* December 17, 1990.

"AT&T Buying Computer Maker in Stock Deal Worth $7.4 Billion," *New York Times,* May 7, 1991.

"AT&T Deal for NCR Final," *New York Times,* September 20, 1991.

"AT&T to Buy Teradata Corp. in Stock Swap," *Wall Street Journal,* December 3, 1991.

Bernstein, Mark, "John Patterson Rang Up Success with the Incorruptible Cashier," *Smithsonian,* June 1989.

Beyerlein, Tom, "Foreign Sales Vital to NCR," *Dayton Daily News,* November 25, 1996, p. 1A.

Boudette, Neal, "New-Look NCR Picks Up the Pace," *PC Week,* March 1991.

Byrne, Harlan S., "NCR Corp.: Ringing Up Profits," *Barron's,* December 7, 1998, p. 22.

Celebrating the Future, 1884–1984, Dayton, Ohio: NCR Corporation, 1984.

Crowther, Samuel, *John H. Patterson, Pioneer in Industrial Welfare,* New York: Doubleday, Page & Company, 1923.

Davis, L. J., "When AT&T Plays Hardball: NCR Was on a Roll, Its Strategy Was Paying Off, So Why Did It Have to Be Sold?," *New York Times Magazine,* June 9, 1991.

Dillon, Jim, "AT&T GIS—What Went Wrong?," *Dayton Daily News,* July 27, 1995, p. 2A.

——, "Rebirth of a Company Series: NCR—The Company," *Dayton Daily News,* November 24, 1996, p. 1A.

Dillon, Jim, and Laura Bischoff, "After Almost Four Years of Struggle, NCR Corp. and Its Chief Executive Lars Nyberg Are . . . Sittin' Pretty," *Dayton Daily News,* January 24, 1999, p. 1F.

Drummond, Mike, "Under a Microscope—Proponents, Critics Grade NCR on Its Performance and Speculate on Its Future," *Dayton Daily News,* February 8, 1998, p. 1F.

Keller, John J., "Why AT&T Takeover of NCR Hasn't Been a Real Bell Ringer," *Dayton Daily News,* September 20, 1995, p. 1A.

"A Lawyer's Switch to Aid a Hostile Takeover," *New York Times,* April 21, 1991.

McClellan, Stephen T., *The Coming Computer Industry Shakeout,* New York: John Wiley & Sons, 1984.

Miller, Annetta, "Does This Deal Compute?," *Newsweek,* May 20, 1991.

"NCR Arrives First with a Powerful Pen-Based Computer," *New York Times,* June 30, 1991.

"NCR Planning New Sales Unit," *New York Times,* July 31, 1991.

"NCR to Buy Data Company for $520 Million," *New York Times,* December 3, 1991.

"Raising Computers to the Power of Two," *U.S. News & World Report,* May 20, 1991.

"Rocky Road Ahead for AT&T-NCR Merger," *PC Week,* May 13, 1991.

Teresko, John, "Charles Exley: After Burroughs, NCR and AT&T," *Industry Week,* February 17, 1992.

Upbin, Bruce, "Too Little and Probably Too Late," *Forbes,* October 5, 1998.

Zuckerman, Lawrence, "NCR to Build Its Comeback with Care," *Cincinnati Enquirer,* October 27, 1996, p. I1.

—Roger W. Rouland
—updated by Frank Uhle

Patrick Industries, Inc.

1800 S. 14th Street
P.O. Box 638
Elkhart, Indiana 46515
U.S.A.
(219) 294-7511
Fax: (219) 522-5213
Web site: http://www.patrickind.com

Public Company
Incorporated: 1961 as Merv Lung Building Company
Employees: 1,722
Sales: $453.51 million (1998)
Stock Exchanges: NASDAQ
Ticker Symbol: PATK
NAIC: 42131 Lumber, Plywood, Millwork, and Wood
Panel Wholesalers; 321918 Other Millwork; 321999
All Other Miscellaneous Wood Manufacturing; 44419
Other Building Material Dealers

Patrick Industries, Inc. is a manufacturer and supplier of building materials and equipment. Through its subsidiaries, the company manufactures a broad range of products, including decorative vinyl and paper panels often used as wallboard, cabinet doors, countertops, extruded aluminum products, drawer sides, pleated shades and mini-blinds, wood adhesives, and laminating machines. The company also operates a nationwide wholesale building materials distributorship, which supplies prefinished wall and ceiling panels, particleboard, hardboard siding, passage doors, roofing materials, hardware, insulation, and other building supplies. Patrick's main markets are the manufactured housing industry and the recreational vehicle industry, which together account for approximately 80 percent of its total sales. The company also markets certain of its products to other markets, including the furniture manufacturing, automotive aftermarket, and marine industries.

Founding and Early Growth: 1959–69

Patrick Industries began its corporate life in 1959 as a small building supply distributorship in northern Indiana. The founder, Mervin Lung, was a hardworking entrepreneur who had already dabbled in several different jobs and industries. Lung had jumped into the world of work immediately after graduating from high school, first helping remodel homes, then later purchasing two small, local businesses. Eventually, he sold both of his businesses and took a job with an aircraft and auto parts manufacturer in South Bend, Indiana. He also continued to take on home remodeling projects on the side. This side business of remodeling led Lung to create the company that would become Patrick Industries. A shrewd and resourceful businessman, Lung realized that he could make money by wholesaling his excess building supplies to other remodelers. Working from a barn in which he stored his supplies, he began selling off his extra wood paneling, trim, and other building materials. He named his fledgling enterprise the Merv Lung Building Company.

The idea proved successful. Soon, Lung quit his job in South Bend and moved his wholesaling business into a larger facility in nearby Elkhart, Indiana. In 1961, he incorporated. Although Lung started out selling supplies to other home remodelers, his focus soon shifted to a different customer base. The north central region of Indiana, where Lung's business was located, had become a major hub for the rapidly growing recreational vehicle and manufactured housing industries. Capitalizing on his proximity to the two thriving industries, Lung began catering to the production needs of area manufacturers. Targeting industrial scale customers allowed him to order supplies in bulk from building supply sources—then warehouse and resell the materials as required. Lung soon expanded his business to target makers of RVs and manufactured housing across the nation.

As Lung grew more familiar with his markets, he became keenly aware of the cyclical nature of the RV and manufactured housing industries. Sensitive to interest rates, availability of financing, and general economic conditions, both industries' sales tended to fluctuate substantially and unpredictably. This made it virtually impossible for manufacturers to stock a consistent level of inventory. Consequently, they often found themselves without the materials necessary to complete new production orders, and had to rely on rush deliveries. Lung frequently had to scramble to meet very short delivery deadlines for customers who needed materials right away.

Company Perspectives:

Patrick's astounding growth has been accomplished through strong customer affiliations, continued growth within existing divisions, enormous investment in new equipment and facilities, targeted acquisitions that complement the company's original markets, and quality products and services.

Lung began looking for ways to stabilize these irregular ordering methods and inventory levels. The solution he devised was to locate distribution centers near his customers' manufacturing plants. This allowed him to fulfill orders immediately and consistently without incurring high shipping expenses. Lung's first step toward implementing his plan came in 1963, when he built a new distribution and sales center near Valdosta, Georgia. Georgia's manufactured housing industry was one of the largest in the nation; by 1968, 15 percent of Lung's total sales were coming from his Valdosta facility. Encouraged by the initial success of his plan, Lung decided to open more strategically located distribution centers—in Kansas, Pennsylvania, Texas, Florida, and North Carolina. In another foresighted move, Lung linked his remote facilities together via a computer network. This allowed the corporate offices to monitor inventory levels and coordinate deliveries nationwide. Lung's concept, the just-in-time (JIT) method, would eventually become common practice in many industries—but in the mid-1960s, it made the Merv Lung Building Company a standout among its competitors.

Other milestones arrived in 1968 as well. The first came when Lung took his building supply company public. Before making an initial public offering, he renamed the nine-year-old company Patrick Industries and adopted a Shamrock as the company logo. The Celtic-themed identity was an homage to the "Fightin' Irish" of the University of Notre Dame, which was located in neighboring South Bend, Indiana, and which Lung faithfully supported. The second occurred with the company's first two acquisitions. Using capital generated from the public offering, Lung led Patrick into new markets with the purchase of Mobilcraft Wood Products, Inc. and Midwest Laminated Plastic Products Inc. Mobilcraft was a maker of wood cabinet doors and drawer fronts. Midwest Laminated Plastic Products—subsequently renamed Midwest Laminating—manufactured furniture and cabinet components using laminated particleboard and plywood. Both companies already served Patrick's two major markets.

Whereas Patrick's initial business base had been distribution, the purchases of Mobilcraft and Midwest Laminating moved the company into manufacturing as well. Lung's hope was for Patrick to achieve a higher profit margin on its newly acquired manufacturing operations than it traditionally had on its distribution business.

Rapid Diversification: 1970–95

The early 1970s were boom years for the manufactured housing industry. Interest rates started to fall in the spring of 1970 and continued to decrease steadily for two years. Would-

be homeowners took advantage of the opportunity, and sales of manufactured homes—one of the most affordable options for first-time buyers—rose accordingly. Between 1970 and 1973, the number of shipments of manufactured homes rose from 401,190 to 579,960, an increase of almost 45 percent. As a primary supplier to the factory-built housing industry, Patrick was well-positioned to benefit from the surge in sales. The 1970s, however, were anything but good for Patrick's other main market, the RV industry. The OPEC oil embargo of 1973 and the resulting hike in gas prices made the notion of "recreational" driving all but obsolete. As a result, sales of RVs plummeted, forcing several manufacturers out of business.

As Patrick entered the 1970s, Lung began looking for ways to further broaden the company's product portfolio and command a greater presence in the manufactured housing supply chain. In 1972 the company formed a new division: Custom Vinyls. The division produced laminated panels by applying decorative vinyl or woodgrain paper to plywood or gypsum substrates. The finished panels were most commonly used as interior walls in manufactured housing and recreational vehicles. The following year, Patrick acquired Nickell Enterprises, a manufacturer of drawer sides, drawer bottoms, and shelving. In 1977 the company built a new cabinet and door manufacturing and distribution center in Woodburn, Oregon.

By 1980 the manufactured housing industry was suffering hard times. The falling interest rates of the early 1970s had reversed, climbing to alarming highs by the end of the decade. Consequently, shipments of manufactured homes fell to 221,091 in 1980—a decrease of 45 percent in ten years' time. Patrick's sales and income reflected the market slump, declining steadily as the 1970s wore on.

Despite the market downturn, Patrick Industries continued to expand and diversify. In 1980 the company entered a new field with the acquisition of the Elkhart, Indiana-based ILC Products, which it renamed Patrick Metals. The new subsidiary was a manufacturer of aluminum extrusion products—such as windows and doors—for the RV and manufactured housing industries. Also in 1980, Patrick purchased Conroth Distribution, a network of building supply distributorships that carried other manufacturers' products. Like Patrick, Conroth served the manufactured housing, recreational vehicle, and marine industries.

In 1989 Mervin Lung's son, David, became president of Patrick Industries. The 42-year-old David had grown up working in his father's business. In 1970, after graduating from college, he joined the company full-time and in 1985, after having worked in various departments, became vice-president of administration. While David assumed the president's position, Mervin Lung continued to be active in the company, serving as its chairman and CEO.

The year 1991 brought the formation of a new Patrick division—Sun Adhesives. Sun was developed primarily to produce the wood glues and sealants Patrick used in its laminating and cabinetry operations. In addition, the company developed and marketed other adhesives products for use in a variety of industrial markets. Patrick's decision to produce its own glues was significant in that it was the company's first step toward vertical integration. A second such step came in 1994, with the acquisition of Harlan Machinery Co., of Boulder City, Nevada.

Harlan, a producer of laminating presses and other woodworking machinery, had previously been one of Patrick's major equipment suppliers. David Lung explained the rationale behind the acquisition in a 1997 interview with the *Wall Street Corporate Reporter*. ''[The acquisition] allows us to develop equipment by experimenting without upsetting our current production,'' he said. ''In turn, we give our customers a better product for the money down the road, without disrupting our production and service to our customers.''

Patrick expanded again in 1995, with the purchase of U.S. Door. The Phoenix, Arizona-based company manufactured wooden cabinet doors for the manufactured housing and RV markets, as well as the furniture industry. The new subsidiary was renamed Patrick Door and began operating as a division of Patrick's Mobilcraft division.

By the midpoint of the decade, Patrick was generating around $360 million in sales—almost double its sales just five years earlier. Almost half of the company's total sales came from products manufactured by its laminating operations—specifically, the prefinished wall panels made by Custom Vinyls. Patrick's distribution business accounted for another 35 to 37 percent, and the company's wood and aluminum products made up the rest of the pie. Approximately 70 percent of Patrick's total sales were made to customers in the manufactured housing industry.

Patrick's string of acquisitions throughout the 1980s and early 1990s had been designed to build the manufacturing segment of the company's business and to strengthen its position as a supplier to its two key markets. However, many of Patrick's newly purchased manufacturing operations had ''crossover'' product lines—products that could readily be used in other industries. The countertops, shelving, and cabinet doors produced by Midwest Laminating, Mobilcraft, and Custom Vinyls, for example, had applications in the furniture and cabinetry industries. The manufacturing processes used by Patrick Metals could be used to produce running boards, ladders, and other accessories for the RV, automotive, and marine industries. Demand in these industries, while affected by general economic conditions, did not tend to fluctuate as dramatically as in the manufactured housing and RV markets. Therefore, by diversifying into these more consistent industries, Patrick could help reduce vulnerability to the cyclical nature of its two major markets.

Improvements and Expansions: 1996–99

Throughout the second half of the 1990s, Patrick invested heavily in improving its existing facilities and building new ones for various subsidiaries. In May 1996, the company opened a new $7 million manufacturing facility for its Woodburn, Oregon operation. The new plant contained a laminating and a cabinet door manufacturing division, as well as administrative offices and a distribution center. Also in 1996, the company opened a new 90,000-square-foot plant in Fontana, California. The facility, Patrick Moulding, manufactured mouldings and trim that were wrapped in vinyl or furniture-grade woodgrain papers.

The following year, Patrick started another major project to expand and consolidate the distribution and manufacturing operations of its Charlotte, North Carolina Custom Vinyls plant. In August 1997, Patrick added a new product line to its growing portfolio with the acquisition of United Shade, Inc. United Shade, based in Elkhart, manufactured window shades and blinds for vans, RVs, and manufactured housing.

That same year also saw the addition of a new Patrick division: Patrick Thermoforming Resources. The new plant, which was built in Goshen, Indiana, produced thermoformed plastic bath products, including tub surrounds, tubs, showers, and sinks. It served as a supplier to Patrick's two core markets, as well as other industries. The following year, Patrick acquired Woodtek, L.L.C., a manufacturer of wood products, for $2.6 million.

At the end of 1998, Patrick had sales of $453.5 million and net profit of $9.3 million. Of total sales, approximately 35 percent derived from the company's distribution business. Laminated products made up 40 percent of the total, with wood products, adhesives, shades, thermoformed products, and laminated equipment making up the remainder. The company operated 16 warehouse and distribution centers and 26 manufacturing plants located in 14 states. Manufactured housing and recreational vehicle producers remained Patrick's two largest markets; in 1998, the two industries combined provided more than 80 percent of the company's total sales.

Looking to the Future

With its upgraded and enlarged facilities, Patrick's manufacturing capability was enhanced, allowing the company to handle larger industrial orders. This meant higher production at lower operating cost and a more consistent flow of inventory. It also paved the way for future growth in the company's product lines and markets. Patrick expected to grow both through internal expansion and through acquisitions. Specifically, the company anticipated purchasing or opening subsidiaries that strengthened its presence in the RV and manufactured housing markets and offered the possibility of diversification into other industries as well. Another key point in Patrick's strategy for the coming years was overseas opportunities. With an existing sales presence in Canada, Mexico, South America, and Asia, the company's management was looking for ways to expand into other foreign markets.

As Patrick prepared to move into the 21st century, it remained heavily dependent upon market conditions in the manufactured housing and recreational vehicles industries. At the beginning of 1999, both industries were on an upturn. The quality of manufactured housing had improved steadily since the industry's early days, making it an attractive option for a wider range of homeowners. As a result, the manufactured housing market had increased its share of the single-family housing market, claiming approximately 30 percent in 1998, according to the Manufactured Housing Institute. Demand in the RV market was also up, as favorable economic conditions and increased discretionary income allowed consumers to spend more for recreational products and activities. If the manufactured housing and RV markets remained strong, it was likely that Patrick would continue to see growth in its sales and profits.

Principal Subsidiaries

Harlan Machinery Company, Inc.; Patrick Door, Inc.; Patrick Mouldings, L.L.C.

Principal Divisions

Mobilcraft Wood Products; Midwest Laminating; Nickell Enterprises; Custom Vinyls; Sun Adhesive; Patrick Thermoforming Resources; Patrick Metals; Conroth; Patrick Distribution.

Further Reading

Kurowski, Jeff, ''Patrick Industries Establishes Impressive RV/MH Growth Curve,'' *RV Business,* September 1, 1996, p. 13.

''Patrick Industries,'' *South Bend Tribune Business Biography*, January 31, 1999.

''President and COO of Patrick Industries, Inc.,'' *Wall Street Corporate Reporter*, October 23, 1997.

Smith, Bruce, ''Wall Street Analysts Are Bullish on Patrick Industries,'' *Indianapolis Star/The Indianapolis News*, May 15, 1995, p. 17.

—Shawna Brynildssen

Peapod, Inc.

9933 Woods Drive
Skokie, Illinois 60077
U.S.A.
(847) 583-9400
(800) 573-2763
Fax: (847) 583-9494
Web site: http://www.peapod.com

Public Company
Incorporated: 1989
Employees: 240
Sales: $69.26 million (1998)
Stock Exchanges: NASDAQ
Ticker Symbol: PPOD
NAIC: 5411 Grocery Stores; 5431 Fruit and Vegetable
   Markets; 7375 Information Retrieval Services

Peapod, Inc. is the largest and most successful Internet supermarket in the United States, providing people with the ability to shop online for their groceries. The company offers its customers a wide variety of product choices, from fresh vegetables to frozen meat to bagels and cream cheese, all delivered to the doorstep in a quick and efficient manner by stores affiliated or in partnership with Peapod. Peapod's membership has grown to approximately 100,000 people, each of which can place an order either by fax, phone, or email after reviewing the most current products and prices by logging on to the company's web site. Currently, the company provides its services in a select number of metropolitan locations throughout the United States, including Long Island, New York; Chicago; Boston; San Francisco and San Jose, California; Austin, Dallas, and Houston, Texas; and Columbus, Ohio. In addition to the online services Peapod provides, the company has grown into one of the leaders in the field of marketing research, and offers its targeted media and research services to large and well-known consumer goods corporations interested in unique promotions and advertising for point-of-purchase sales.

Early History

The founders of Peapod, Inc. are two brothers, Andrew B. and Thomas L. Parkinson. Andrew graduated with a B.A. in Economics from Wesleyan University, while his brother Thomas graduated with a B.A. in Design from the same school, and then went on to earn an M.A. in Industrial Design from Pratt Institute. After school, Andrew worked with Kraft and Proctor & Gamble in a variety of product and brand management positions, learning the marketing techniques of the most successful corporations within the food products industry. Thomas also worked at Proctor & Gamble, but in sales management positions where he learned the importance of up-to-date computer technology for the growth of a company in the climate of contemporary business practice. Not satisfied with their respective positions, and fully confident they could build their own successful company, the two men decided to take the plunge and combine the world of the Internet with the food products industry.

In 1989 the Parkinson brothers established a test pilot program designed to last four years while involving 400 households in Evanston, Illinois, a suburb just north of Chicago. With a small amount of start-up money, they arranged for people to purchase grocery products over the Internet, and then delivered those groceries to the homes of their customers. They christened their company Peapod, Inc. In forming their firm and in devising a strategic plan, both Thomas and Andrew were well aware of other people's failed attempts at the same kind of online supermarket service. In 1988, Prodigy, the largest of the online consumer-oriented firms, ran a similar pilot program in nine cities across the United States. However, after a three-year period, Prodigy management decided to cease its attempt due to its inability to attract a large enough subscriber base to make the effort worthwhile.

Yet the Parkinson brothers had carefully studied Prodigy's foray into the online supermarket service and concluded that the large company had repeated the fatal mistake of many other firms that had tried to establish the same business. All of the companies, including Prodigy, concentrated primarily on the telemarketing aspects of the business, and used most of their money to reach out to customers. What they had failed to do was pay adequate attention and provide the necessary funding for the fulfillment aspects of the business. According to the Parkinsons, once these companies had taken an order and transmitted it to the retail grocery store, they considered their job done. But the retailer still had to fill the order, and then contract a third party to deliver the goods. As a result, when customers started to complain that their orders were not filled properly, or delivered days late, none of the parties involved accepted responsibility for the mistakes. In addition, having three parties involved in the service increased prices to such an extent that customers thought it too expensive.

The notion of controlling the entire process, from taking online orders, to transmitting them to grocery retailers, to delivering the goods themselves, was therefore the driving force behind the vision of the two brothers. Not surprisingly, from its inception Peapod guaranteed the satisfaction of every customer order and, in order to learn every detail about the fulfillment side of the business, Thomas and Andrew took it upon themselves to personally pick up and deliver customer orders during the first two years of the company's existence. By the end of that period, the two brothers were more convinced than ever that quality fulfillment and customer satisfaction were the inextricably interwoven ingredients that would make Peapod successful where others had failed.

As Peapod started to grow, its services began to attract women. According to most demographic surveys of online services, approximately 75 percent of those who shop and buy are male. But Peapod marketed its services primarily to women, since it had discovered that women most often made decisions about household purchases. Soon, Peapod's online services were inundated by career women who not only cared for their house and family, but were entrepreneur's themselves with no time to squeeze the cantaloupes in the local grocery store. These women found that it was easier to make a few computer keystrokes than to run to the food mart at midnight to pick up the bare necessities of milk, butter, cereal, and soda. By the end of 1992, Peapod had over 5,000 loyal customers in the Chicago and San Francisco metropolitan areas.

Growth and Expansion During the 1990s

By the beginning of October 1994, Peapod had tripled its revenues over the previous 12 months. The company had arranged exclusive agreements with Jewel Food Stores and with Safeway Food Stores, in Chicago and San Francisco respectively, to fill hundreds of orders per day for its customers. By this time, the Parkinson brothers had hired full-time employees called ''shoppers'' who worked next to Jewel and Safeway store staff. Nearly 40 such shoppers were working at each of the seven Jewel stores in Chicago and three Safeway stores in San Francisco. One of the reasons the system worked so well was the sophisticated evaluation of the efficiency of Peapod's shoppers, tracking the number of each item chosen by every shopper, how quickly the shoppers filled orders, and the number of mistakes when the order was completed. Deliveries were then made according to a 90-minute window the customer had chosen. Outstanding work was rewarded with additional incentives, while inefficient work was improved upon.

The cost of such service was not cheap. Customers paid a startup fee of $29.95, a monthly service fee of $4.95, plus a fee of $6.95 for delivery and a five percent fee of their total grocery bill order. Although this system of Peapod's was quite expensive to implement and maintain, the Parkinson brothers were correct in their assessment that consumers were more than willing to pay more for efficient and timely service. Over 80 percent of the people who initially tried Peapod's online service decided to keep it. By the end of 1995, Peapod had expanded its customer base to over 10,000 people in Chicago and San Francisco, and had over 450 employees shoppers and drivers filling orders and making deliveries.

Peapod, Inc. was growing by leaps and bounds. The company's 1995 revenues had doubled to just over $16 million, and its 1996 revenues skyrocketed to over $30 million. Over 1995 and 1996, Peapod was adding approximately 2,000 subscribers a month to a total customer base that had already reached 27,000, with new partner stores including Kroger in Columbus, Ohio, Safeway Stores in San Jose, California, Stop&Shop in Boston, Massachusetts, and plans to negotiate partnerships with more stores in the near future. The founders of Peapod had clearly reached out to a large section of the U.S. population— young, time-starved married couples with demanding dual careers and children that required time to raise. Rather than spending time shopping twice a week sometimes at their local grocery store, these couples had decided to pay more and shop less—the typical Peapod customer ordered once every ten days—for the opportunity to spend more time with their family.

Preparing for the Future

By the end of 1997, the company was operating in Chicago, San Francisco, San Jose, Boston, Columbus, Austin, Dallas, and Houston. At the time, Peapod counted over 100,000 subscribers in its customer database. Part of Peapod's unrivaled success to this point consisted in its ability to provide simple access to shopping categories that people had come to rely upon. For example, a person could choose items from menus on the Peapod web site organized in three categories, including narrow categories such as potato chips, broad categories such as snacks, or brand names such as Jay's. Food items were also sorted by cost per ounce or cost per pound, and by the current items on sale. In addition, what pleased a great many customers was their ability to add personal comments to any order they made, including statements about their desire for only ripe avocadoes, and whether they would accept alternatives if such avocadoes were not available. Peapod's marketing research indicated that this service alone accounted for a significant number of repeat customers.

In 1998 the Parkinson brothers reached a major strategic decision and implemented a warehouse distribution network unlike anything the company had known before. Not losing any time, during the autumn of that year a dedicated warehouse facility was opened by Peapod on Long Island, New York. By consolidating its fulfillment operations into a single large warehouse, Peapod reduced its reliance on third party pickers, namely local distributors and supermarket chains. The intention was to enhance control over the service quality, lower costs from the order fulfillment, and consequently reduce consumers' costs in order to increase membership. Yet the company did not do away with third party participation entirely, since it had reached an agreement with Giant Food and Edward's supermarkets to provide certain product procurement and inventory management services in the greater New York metropolitan area. In January 1999, the company opened a 70,000-square-foot warehouse, termed a "consumer direct center," and consolidated 12 separate fulfillment locations at various supermarkets and groceries throughout the Chicago metropolitan area. Peapod reached an agreement with Jewel/Osco to provide its warehouse in Chicago with product replenishment in the same way that it handled more traditional retail supermarkets and groceries.

Total revenues for 1997 reached $56 million, while 1998 revenues increased to just over $69 million, an increase of nearly 22 percent. By the end of 1998, the company had surpassed its one-millionth order via the Internet, which was widely regarded by industry experts as an impressive, even

unique, achievement. By the summer of 1999, Peapod counted some of the most prestigious and successful companies in the United States as its retail partners, including Jewel/Osco in Chicago, Safeway Stores in San Francisco/San Jose, Kroger in Columbus, Stop&Shop in Boston, Tom Thumb in Dallas, Randalls in Austin and Houston, and Edwards Super Food Stores in New York. In March 1999, Peapod finalized a product alliance with Walgreen Company, the largest U.S. drugstore chain, to supply the firm's San Francisco warehouse distribution center with a variety of over-the-counter beauty and health products which would be sold via the Internet.

Peapod's future appeared promising. As more and more time-starved people sought ways to make their lives easier and more convenient, the Internet provided them with the opportunity to do so. In turn, Peapod, the largest and most successful online grocery provider, would no doubt continue to use its sophisticated and efficient order fulfillment and delivery services to help people shop for groceries in the most cost-effective manner possible.

Further Reading

Chandler, Susan, "The Grocery Cart in Your PC," *Business Week,* September 11, 1995, p. 63.

Fox, Bruce, "For Peapod, Fulfillment Is the Key to Success," *Chain Store Age Executive,* October 1994, p. 33.

Liebeck, Laura, "Peapod Goes National," *Discount Store News,* August 24, 1998, p. 4.

Reese, Shelley, "Peapod Demonstrates Potential of On-Line Grocery Shopping," *Stores,* January 1997, p. 48.

Smith, Ann, "Peapod, Inc.," *Progressive Grocer,* January 1999, p. 9.

Wallace, David, J., "Logging on for a Loaf of Bread," *Advertising Age,* October 10, 1994, p. 20.

—Thomas Derdak

P.H. Glatfelter Company

96 South George Street
York, Pennsylvania 17401
U.S.A.
(717) 225-4711
Fax: (717) 225-6834
Web site: http://www.glatfelter.com

Public Company
Incorporated: 1906
Employees: 3,833
Sales: $705.1 million (1998)
Stock Exchanges: New York
Ticker Symbol: GLT
NAIC: 32211 Pulp Mills; 322121 Paper (Except
   Newsprint) Mills; 322232 Envelope Manufacturing;
   322233 Stationery, Tablet, & Related Product
   Manufacturing; 322299 All Other Converted Paper
   Product Manufacturing

P.H. Glatfelter Company, a producer of engineered papers (such as tobacco papers and sophisticated filter papers) and specialty printing papers, was founded in 1864 in the rolling hills of south central Pennsylvania. Since the early 20th century it has been an industry leader in uncoated printing paper, used largely in hardback versions of novels and other trade books. Other Glatfelter products have included high-quality recycled paper for trade and reference books, and thin, flax paper for cigarettes as well as lightweight religious and financial publications. An increasingly global manufacturer, Glatfelter in 1998 acquired Schoeller & Hoesch Group, a maker of engineered papers based in Germany and the world's leading producer of papers for the tea bag industry. Overall annual production capacity at all of the company's mills worldwide is approximately 600,000 tons. Guiding the company over the years has been an old-fashioned business philosophy emphasizing long-term goals and fiscal conservatism.

Pennsylvania Roots

Spring Grove, the original home of P.H. Glatfelter Company, was established in 1747 along the Codorus Creek some ten miles north of the Pennsylvania-Maryland border. To the west of the town were the Blue Ridge Mountains, and to the east, beyond the larger town of York (where the company relocated in 1999), flowed the wide Susquehanna River. The town's original name, Spring Forge, reflected its early industry, an iron forge, which during the American Revolution manufactured supplies for the Continental Army. The forge was in operation until 1851, when Jacob Hauer bought the buildings and converted them into a paper mill.

Some 20 miles southeast, near the Maryland town of Gunpowder Falls, another paper mill, called Loucks, Hoffman & Company, began operations in the 1850s. It was here in 1856 that 19-year-old Philip H. Glatfelter began his first job in the paper trade. Glatfelter—whose wife, Amanda, was the sister of Jacob Loucks—worked in the firm for seven years, and in 1863, at the height of the Civil War, Glatfelter decided to go into business on his own.

By this time Hauer had died, and his Spring Paper Mill was being sold at an orphan's (probate) court. A printed announcement of the sale mentioned a "tract of land containing about 101 acres . . . a large stone paper mill, a frame machine house, stone stock house, and four tenant houses." The mill itself had two Burnham water wheels propelled by the Codorus Creek, four large-capacity engines, and a 62-inch cylinder paper machine. Glatfelter learned about the mill from Loucks, whose second wife, Mary, was the daughter of Jacob Hauer. On December 23, 1863—one month after President Lincoln's famous speech at nearby Gettysburg—Glatfelter bought the property for $14,000.

Glatfelter's new paper business, initially called Spring Forge Mill, began operations in July 1864 with a daily capacity of 1,500 pounds. Its first product was newsprint, which Glatfelter made from a pulp of rye straw mixed with a smaller amount of straw and rags collected from various cotton gins along the region's railway lines. This pulp material was retrieved in

Company Perspectives:

Vision Statement: The P.H. Glatfelter Company will become a recognized world leader in the production of highly specialized and engineered papers. We will create value for our customers by understanding their needs and by helping them to achieve their business objectives. We will create value for our shareholders through differentiating our business from others within the paper industry as measured by the generation of superior financial results.

Our pursuit of these objectives will be unrelenting and will be conducted with unfailing integrity while striving to provide rewarding challenges and opportunities to our employees, and upholding our responsibility to the global environment as well as to the communities in which we reside.

spacious railcars known as barns. Because at the time Spring Forge itself did not have a railway line, "barns" returning from the cotton gins could get no closer than Jefferson and York, some five and ten miles, respectively, from the mill. When the town changed its name in 1882 to Spring Grove, the company thus became the Spring Grove Mill.

For the first 25 years newsprint continued to be the company's main product, and during this period it made impressive gains in production. From the initial capacity of 1,500 pounds per day, the mill was able to expand to 3,500 pounds in 1873, 60,000 in 1885, and 110,000 by 1895. This increased capacity was made possible by the company's investment in new, modern facilities. In 1874, for example, the mill was moved farther north along the Codorus Creek, and next to it the company constructed a new building costing $200,000 and containing an 82-inch paper machine. Two years later Spring Forge celebrated the opening of its rail line, which ran through the mill's new site.

In 1880 Glatfelter entered into an agreement with Pusey and Jones Company of Delaware to build a 102-inch fourdrinier machine, allowing the mill to produce a considerably wider roll of paper. Named after Henry and Sealy Fourdrinier, who patented an early form of the machine in England in 1806, the fourdrinier machine fed pulp onto a continuous wire belt, shook it to remove excess water, and then pressed and dried the pulp into paper. Glatfelter's new fourdrinier machine was until 1887 the largest in the world, and the extremely wide paper rolls made by the machine helped him gain new customers. In 1887, when the *Philadelphia Public Ledger* began operating two 94-inch printing presses, Spring Grove Mill was the only business in the country that could supply the paper. The mill also produced paper for a variety of other newspapers in Pennsylvania and Maryland, including the *Philadelphia Evening Telegraph*.

High-Quality Paper: Late 19th Century

Soon Glatfelter also changed his pulp-making methods, which would result in a better quality paper. Prior to 1881 the mill mechanically separated the fibers of the raw materials, probably with the use of a grinder. This process, acceptable for newsprint and other paper intended for temporary use, had a number of drawbacks. Mechanical separation tended to fragment and shorten the fibers, thus lessening their ability to bind and make strong paper. Moreover, fragmentation left considerable debris in the pulp, and various remaining chemical constituents caused the paper to grow yellow with age. Even when new, such paper did not have a "high whiteness" and was difficult to bleach.

As a result, Glatfelter began to take note of a new chemical method called the soda process, which enabled a high-quality paper to be made from wood fibers. It was developed in 1851 by Englishman Hugh Burgess, who a few years later immigrated to the United States to set up a paper mill in Pennsylvania. In the soda process, wood chips were boiled in a caustic alkali at a high temperature and pressure; afterward, the separated fibers were washed in water and then bleached. In 1881 Glatfelter built a giant soda-process mill, which was used to make pulp from jack pine, poplar wood, and straw. Straw, however, came to be used in decreasing quantities. By 1885 this new production helped the company surpass $500,000 in total sales, and four years later the number of employees reached 110. With its new pulp-processing method, the company in 1892 was able to make one of its most important changes—the suspension of newsprint production and the subsequent focus on high-quality paper for books, lithographs, and business forms. For this purpose, another soda-process pulp mill was installed in 1895, and by the turn of the century the company had become an industry leader of high-quality uncoated printing paper.

The founder's son, William L. Glatfelter, entered the business in 1887 after graduating from Gettysburg College, and that year he began a long apprenticeship under the guidance of his father. He had already worked at the mill for 19 years when, in 1906, the business was incorporated as P.H. Glatfelter Company. The following year the founder died, and the reins to the company were handed to his son.

President of the company from 1907 to 1930, William Glatfelter oversaw a tremendous increase in production, as well as continued advances in chemically processed wood pulp. In 1918, in order to manage the mill's growing need for wood, he established Glatfelter Wood Pulp Company, a wholly owned subsidiary, with more than 10,000 acres of timberland in southern Maryland. Additional timberland in Maryland and eastern Virginia would eventually boost the acreage to 107,000.

William Glatfelter was responsible for instituting a number of other major projects, many of which were completed in the early 1920s. A new basin for storing up to 50,000 tons of coal—the fuel used to fire the company's high-pressured boilers—was constructed during this period, as was a large indoor loading room, where newly manufactured paper was placed on waiting railroad cars. A tachometer, which measured rotational speed, was attached to all of the company's machines, thus providing a more accurate way to monitor production. Most spectacular was the new fourdrinier paper machine, installed in 1922, which was capable of making rolls of fine paper 170 inches wide. This giant paper machine, designed by Glatfelter engineers and housed in a new building, was the world's first fourdrinier to have an easily replaceable wire belt. Perhaps reflecting these changes, Spring Grove's Main Street, where the company's office building was located, was first paved in 1922.

Surviving Great Depression

In 1928, just a year before the great stock market crash, annual production at P.H. Glatfelter Company had reached 50 million pounds, and the number of employees stood at 300. That year, in keeping with the company's policy of "maintaining a modern, efficient mill," P.H. Glatfelter II, William's son, introduced a new, ten-year modernization program, which included the installation of an even larger, 190-inch fourdrinier machine. As a result, the outlook for the company seemed especially bright, but just two years later conditions noticeably changed for the worse. By 1930 the country was quickly falling into an economic crisis, and sales at P.H. Glatfelter Company and other paper concerns were plummeting. William Glatfelter, moreover, unexpectedly died in April. Unlike many other firms, P.H. Glatfelter Company managed to survive the Great Depression of the 1930s, and its new president, P.H. Glatfelter II, was even able to complete his modernization program, at a cost of some $2 million. As part of this program, one of the company's pulp mills was refurbished, and its capacity was doubled. When the economy picked up again during World War II, P.H. Glatfelter Company added, among other improvements, new equipment for bleaching paper.

P.H. Glatfelter II, president until January 1, 1970, guided the company through the postwar economic boom and started a new effort at reforestation and environmental stewardship. In 1947 the company set aside 600 acres of land near Fairfield, Pennsylvania, to create the state's first tree farm. Between 1950 and 1962 it spent $1.6 million to build a wastewater treatment plant, and a new 400-ton boiler was installed in 1963 to more efficiently burn a pulp byproduct called black liquor. During this time there were also millions of dollars spent on capital improvements for increased production. For example, the company's seventh and eighth paper machines were added in 1956 and 1965, respectively, and between 1964 and 1968 capital expenditures alone were nearly $40 million.

An especially ambitious project was the P.H. Glatfelter Dam, completed in 1965 along a stretch of the Codorus Creek about five miles south of Spring Grove. The dam created a 15-billion-gallon reservoir called Lake Marburg, which was intended to guarantee a reliable water supply for the Glatfelter mill farther downstream. In addition, the reservoir was eventually surrounded by a newly created 3,326-acre Codorus State Park, which included a public swimming pool, and provided opportunities for camping, hiking, horseback riding, and boating. The project cost some $10 million, split equally between P.H. Glatfelter Company and the Pennsylvania Bureau of State Parks.

Bergstrom and Ecusta: 1979, 1987

P.H. Glatfelter II retired in 1970 and his son, P.H. Glatfelter III, became president, a position he held for a decade. An early challenge for the new president was Hurricane Agnes, which hit the eastern seaboard in June 1972 and created severe floods in Spring Grove. According to P.H. Glatfelter III, the flood "caused more damage and financial loss to the Company than any other single event." Among other notable developments

during his tenure was the 1973 decision by Glatfelter employees to join the United Paperworkers International Union, and in 1977 the company received the Isaac Walton League of America Clean Water Award. The company entered a new product line in 1979 with its purchase of Bergstrom Paper Company, a leading manufacturer of recycled printing paper, with mills in Neenah, Wisconsin, and West Carrollton, Ohio. The West Carrollton mill was sold in 1984, but during the 1980s the company rebuilt all three paper machines at the Neenah plant.

Thomas C. Norris, named president in 1980, was the first person outside the Glatfelter family to run the company. His experience with P.H. Glatfelter Company stretched back to 1958, when he took a part-time job in the paper mill at the age of 19. Like his predecessors, Norris oversaw a program of new capital expenditures, including the rebuilding of two paper machines at Spring Grove. Even more significant was the company's 1987, $220 million purchase of Ecusta Corporation, located in Pisgah Forest, North Carolina, which made extremely thin flax paper for the tobacco industry. The purchase of Ecusta doubled the number of Glatfelter employees from 1,700 to 3,400 and provided, along with uncoated and recycled printing paper, a third major underpinning of the company's sales. Uncoated printing paper, however, remained its core product, which by the early 1990s made up some 30 percent of all paper used in the United States for hardcover trade books. Among the many well-known books printed on Glatfelter paper were Norman Mailer's *Harlot's Ghost* (1992), Steven King's *Four Past Midnight* (1990), and Alexandra Ripley's *Scarlett* (1991), the sequel to Margaret Mitchell's *Gone with the Wind,* which in 1936 used Glatfelter paper for the original printing. *Great Books of the Western World,* a multivolume publication of classics, was printed with recycled paper from the Neenah mill.

P.H. Glatfelter Company headed into the 1990s with an exceptionally strong financial base, secured by its remarkable lack of debt. Although P.H. Glatfelter Company had occasionally borrowed money—for example, $179 million in 1987 to complete its acquisition of Ecusta—even this loan was paid off in just two years. The company's strength was also found in its emphasis on specialized, high-quality paper, which was much less affected by recurring business cycles than large-volume, "commodity" paper products. In 1988 Glatfelter's chief financial officer, M.A. Johnson II, explained, "Our emphasis is on profit, not on volume. That's why we continue to be a niche company, one that is competing in areas where we're not banging heads with people who are commodity-oriented." Starting in the mid-1980s, the company expressed considerable self-confidence in its financial strength by its repurchase of millions of outstanding shares of Glatfelter stock.

With its financial security and its emphasis on specialty products, P.H. Glatfelter Company was able to profitably weather the declining market conditions for paper, which, beginning in 1990, were spurred by industry overproduction. Glatfelter's record sales of $569 million in 1988, $598 million in 1989, and $625 million in 1990 tumbled to $567 million and $540 million, respectively, in 1991 and 1992. Even so, the company still posted a respectable net profit of $56.5 million in 1992, down from a high of $92.9 million in 1989. The company's good health was credited to its old-fashioned, conservative business philosophy, as well as to the able guidance of President, CEO, and Chairman

Thomas Norris, who in 1992 was one of only 11 corporate leaders given *Financial World*'s Silver Award for "superior business leadership and achievement."

Mid-to-Late 1990s Difficulties

Glatfelter received a huge blow in late 1992 when Philip Morris Co. announced that it would single-source its domestic cigarette paper from Kimberly-Clark Corp. Glatfelter's Ecusta Division thus lost its largest domestic tobacco paper customer. Overall company revenues thereby dropped to a lower level for the two years following, running at $473.5 million in 1993 and $478.3 million in 1994. During 1994's fourth quarter, Glatfelter attempted to sell Ecusta, but the offers that came in were considered to be below market value. The company subsequently decided to take a one-time charge of $128 million to write down the value of Ecusta, leading to a net loss of $118.3 million for 1994. This followed a barely profitable 1993, when earnings stood at $16.2 million.

Glatfelter rebounded some in the mid-1990s, but continued to be buffeted by difficult market conditions through the entire second half of the decade. Overcapacity in the tobacco paper sector and increased competition in the area of specialty papers forced prices down, depressing both revenues and earnings. Glatfelter's tobacco paper business was particularly vulnerable as cigarette liability lawsuits and subsequent settlements were forcing cigarette makers to raise prices and to pressure their paper suppliers to lower their prices. In 1998 Glatfelter responded to these pressures by announcing layoffs at Ecusta's Pisgah Forest facility, with head count reduced by about 215, generating annual savings of approximately $8.4 million.

Glatfelter also looked overseas for a potential boost, acquiring Schoeller & Hoesch Group from Deutsche Beteiligungs AG in January 1998 for about $158 million. Schoeller & Hoesch, with sales of $173 million, was headquartered in Gernsbach, Germany, where it owned and operated a paper mill. The company also held a 50 percent controlling interest in a paper mill in Odet, France, and owned other production facilities in Wisches, France; the Philippines; and Summerville, South Carolina. Schoeller & Hoesch was founded in 1881 as a pulp producer, then evolved into a leading producer of engineered papers; it was similar to Glatfelter in its focus on maintaining leading positions in a number of niche growth markets. At the time of the acquisition, Schoeller & Hoesch was the world's number one maker of tea bags, with global market share in excess of 30 percent. The German firm also held 19 percent of the European market for cigarette papers, 24 percent of the European market for metalized label paper, and 25 percent of the global market for overlay paper. One of the unique aspects of Schoeller & Hoesch was its pulp mill in the Philippines, which processed abaca fiber, a versatile fiber with a broad range of applications.

As a result of this acquisition, Glatfelter's revenues reached a record $705.1 million in 1998. Its debt load was also substantially increased, however, leaving its debt-to-capital ratio at 45 percent—not unusual by industry standards but high for the conservative-minded company. Glatfelter was likely to pay down this debt before seeking additional acquisitions. In order to further enhance its international visibility, Glatfelter in late 1998 moved its stock from the American Stock Exchange to the New York Stock Exchange. In a change-filled year, Norris announced in June that he intended to retire in 2000. George H. Glatfelter II, who had been senior vice-president, was named the new president and CEO, with Norris remaining chairman until his retirement. Another historical development came in September of the following year when the company relocated its headquarters from Spring Grove to York, Pennsylvania. Glatfelter's executives were thereby separated from the facilities in the company's founding town, enabling them to focus on the company's entire worldwide operations and leave management of the Spring Grove mill and the Glatfelter division to the appropriate managers.

Principal Subsidiaries

Balo-I Industrial, Inc. (Philippines); Ecusta Australia Pty. Limited; Ecusta Export Trading Corp. (Barbados); Ecusta Fibres Ltd. (Canada); Glatfelter Investments, Inc.; Glatfelter of Nevada, Inc.; Glenn-Wolfe, Inc.; Mollanvick, Inc.; Newtech Pulp Inc. (Philippines); Papcel-Kiew (Ukraine); Papcel-Papier und Cellulose, Technologie und Handels-GmbH (Germany); Papeteries de Cascadec S.A. (France; 50%); Papierfabrik Schoeller & Hoesch Auslandsbeteiligungen GmbH (Germany); Papierfabrik Schoeller & Hoesch GmbH & Co. KG (Germany); PHG Tea Leaves, Inc.; PHG Verwaltungsgesellschaft mbH (Germany); S&H Verwaltungsgesellschaft mbH (Germany); Schoeller & Hoesch N.A., Inc.; Schoeller & Hoesch S.A.R.L. (France); Spring Grove Water Company; The Glatfelter Pulp Wood Company; Unicon-Papier-und Kunststoffhandels GmbH (Germany).

Principal Divisions

Glatfelter Division; Ecusta Division.

Further Reading

Abelson, Reed, "P.H. Glatfelter Co.," *Fortune,* June 5, 1989, p. 176.

Briggs, Rosland, "Spring Grove, Pa.-Based Tobacco Paper Company Rolls Toward Recovery," *Philadelphia Inquirer,* May 12, 1999.

Cauffiel-Zinn, Jan, "The P.H. Glatfelter Company," *Barker* (inhouse magazine of P.H. Glatfelter Company), Spring/Summer/Fall/Winter 1989, pp. 12–13.

"CEO Interview: George H. Glatfelter II," *Wall Street Transcript,* July 19, 1999.

"Cigarette Paper Producers' Uncertain Future," *Pulp & Paper,* May 1999, p. 23.

Cochran, Thomas N., "P.H. Glatfelter Co.," *Barron's,* August 29, 1988, pp. 32–33.

Finchem, Kirk, "P.H. Glatfelter: Returns to Growth After Losing Key Customer," *Pulp & Paper,* December 1996, pp. 42–43, 45.

Henriques, Diana B., "A Paper Company That Loves Itself," *New York Times,* December 23, 1990, p. F12.

Lipper, Mark, *Paper, People, Progress: The Story of the P.H. Glatfelter Company of Spring Grove, Pennsylvania,* Spring Grove, Pennsylvania: P.H. Glatfelter Company, 1980.

Morris, Kathleen, and Elicia Brown, "1992 CEO of the Year Silver Award Winners," *Financial World,* March 31, 1992, p. 34.

P.H. Glatfelter Co., Spring Grove, Pa., 1690–1940: 250 Years of Papermaking in America, Stroudsburg, Pa.: Lockwood Trade Journal Co., 1940, p. 88.

—Thomas Riggs
—updated by David E. Salamie

Premium Standard Farms, Inc.

423 W. Eighth Street, Suite 200
Kansas City, Missouri 64105
U.S.A.
(816) 472-7675
Fax: (816) 843-1450
Web site: http://www.psfarms.com

Wholly Owned Subsidiary of Continental Grain Company
Incorporated: 1988
Employees: 2,200
Sales: $295 million (1997 est.)
NAIC: 11221 Hog & Pig Farming

The third largest hog farmer in the United States, Premium Standard Farms, Inc. (PSF) oversees two hog operations—one in Missouri and the other in Texas—that represent the most comprehensive, technologically sophisticated pig farms in the country, guiding the animals from birth to slaughter to individually packaged pork products. PSF established its first pork production operation in Missouri, where the company built state-of-the-art feed mills, hog barns, genetic engineering facilities, and processing and packaging plants, endeavoring to bring vertical integration to the pork industry. To pay for the equipment and facilities, PSF relied on its majority owner, investment bank Morgan Stanley & Co., which invested and raised roughly $500 million to make PSF the elite pork producer in the United States. Expansion carried the company into Texas, where a pork production operation equal to the size of the Missouri operation was established, but depressed hog prices and soaring corn prices during the mid-1990s led to the company's collapse. In July 1996, PSF declared bankruptcy, emerging from court protection two months later. In 1998 the company's long-term prospects were given a boost when Continental Grain Company, a massive agribusiness and financial services conglomerate, acquired a majority interest in PSF. Following the acquisition, PSF was incorporated into Continental Grain's operations, which included pork production facilities already owned by the company.

Origins

From the start, the realities of PSF's business belied its ambitious aspirations. The company began business in the basement of a building that was later home to the Snappy Convenience Store, carrying a payroll of three people. It was a modest start for a company plotting to revolutionize the pork production industry, but PSF's founders were wholly determined to do just that, no matter the extent of the climb that lay ahead. Dennis Harms and Tad Gordon were motivated by a vision, convinced industry preeminence awaited a hog producer who used state-of-the-art technology to produce superior quality pork in an efficient manner. The pair theorized that customers would welcome the same consistency and quality in pork that characterized the product produced by the chicken industry. They envisioned a hog farm employing the latest technology and supported by vertically integrated operations, which would give them control over every aspect of the pork production process, from the artificial insemination of the sows to the packaging of a pork chop. By controlling the breeding, raising, slaughter, and packaging of pigs, Harms and Gordon believed they could deliver consistency and quality to customers and achieve greater profitability through the advantages wrought by vertical integration. But the financial requirements for creating a comprehensive, technology-driven enterprise were heavy. The essential necessity for turning a dream into reality was capital, and a substantial amount of it.

Prior to founding PSF in 1988, Harms was employed as a grain salesman, a profession that provided little experience in securing the substantial start-up money PSF would need. Gordon's previous professional experience, however, was suited perfectly to fulfill the company's most pressing need. Gordon was a Wall Street investment banker, schooled in the particulars of high finance and familiar with the most powerful merchant bankers in the country. From his perspective, Gordon saw a highly fragmented pork industry that lacked the technological sophistication prevalent in the chicken industry, a promising business opportunity begging for a properly equipped, new contender for market dominance. It was a perspective he shared with acquaintances working on Wall Street, as he tried to

---

Company Perspectives:

Our commitment to total quality is shaping the future of food production. Food production has entered a new era, and Premium Standard Farms is leading the way with new methods that manage all aspects of pork production, from the farm to the dinner table. The unique Premium Standard Farms process is based on standardization throughout our organization. Because we manage all aspects of production, we are able to guarantee the highest quality, premium taste and superior value. Since 1988, Premium Standard Farms has been combining the best science and technology with the best people in agribusiness, resulting in consistently leaner, more nutritious and more flavorful fresh pork and pork products. We see tomorrow's challenges as opportunities for growth as we continue to supply our customers with the very best pork.

---

convince investors to financially support the concept he and Harms had created. As Harms concentrated on setting up operations at the junction of U.S. Highway 136 and U.S. Highway 65, welcoming the arrival of the first pig in July 1989, Gordon pitched the PSF vision on Wall Street. The unusual partnership of a grain salesman and a Wall Street investment banker was made stranger when New York City-based Morgan Stanley & Co. agreed to financially support the fledgling Missouri hog farm. PSF entered the 1990s with the resources to actualize Harms's and Gordon's vision.

According to the vice-chairman of Morgan Stanley, Bob Niehaus, the venerable investment bank agreed to financially support PSF's assault on the pork industry because it saw "the industry was fragmented and the opportunity was there for a consolidator with the right formula." Morgan Stanley's merchant banking division believed Harms and Gordon had articulated the right formula, and the money came pouring in. With a steady stream of cash, Harms and Gordon began building facilities for a fully integrated, state-of-the-art pork production operation in northern Missouri, aiming to create an 80,000-sow farm capable of carrying swine from birth to individual packages of pork displayed at retail locations. Futuristic hog barns were constructed, facilities with "biosecurity" standards that required individuals to shower, scrub down, and wear special, germ-free suits before entering to prevent disease. Feed mills were constructed, a packing plant was built, and computers were put into service, armed with software that monitored a pig's development from birth until it reached the slaughter weight of 250 pounds at 11 months. The pigs moved through a series of buildings, fattening as they progressed through PSF's scientifically based development program, ending their one-way journey after passing through Harms Way (named in honor of Chief Executive Officer Dennis Harms) and into the packing plant. With Morgan Stanley's financial support, Harms and Gordon built other facilities. A Genetic Improvement Facility was erected, headquarters were expanded—sporting what one visitor described as a "magisterial entrance" that included a waterfall, and an elaborate employee training center was established. By the early 1990s, what had started as a dream was rapidly turning into reality.

Between 1991 and 1996, Morgan Stanley, the majority owner of PSF, invested or raised more than $500 million to fuel the company's drive to become the largest hog farmer in Missouri and one of the largest in the country. As the early 1990s progressed, PSF climbed the industry rankings, blossoming into a national force. By 1994, the company was prepared to expand upon its original operations in Missouri and establish additional hog operations elsewhere.

Mid-1990s: Financial Disaster Looms

In early 1994, PSF acquired National Hog Farms of Texas, an 18,000-sow farm located in the Panhandle of Texas. Later in the year, the company opened what it touted as the U.S. meat industry's most advanced pork processing facility. The 300,000-square-foot operation, located in Milan, Missouri, was capable of processing more than 1.7 million hogs annually, the targeted capacity of the company's Missouri hog operations. The capacity of the company's Missouri operations, which was reached in early 1995, was the same capacity Harms and Gordon planned for hog operations in Texas, an expansion project that was under way by early 1995. The company had 53,000 acres set aside in Texas, intending to spend $250 million to develop another pig farm capable of producing what one industry observer described as "cookie-cutter" hogs. In the spring of 1995, contractors began the exhaustive task of establishing the infrastructure for the Texas farm. Roads were built, foundations were poured, and a network of water and sewer lines was buried beneath the soil. Before the work was completed, however, the entire project came screeching to a halt. On May 1, 1995, the contractors were told to stop working, informed by PSF that work would resume in two weeks. Shortly thereafter, the contractors were told the postponement was indefinite. The rapid pace of PSF's expansion had collapsed, its sudden stop signaling the outbreak of profound problems for the ambitious company.

As became readily apparent when construction activity ceased in Texas, PSF's strident expansion had been ill timed. The company had invested hundreds of millions of dollars in new equipment and facilities and launched an aggressive foray into Texas, positioning itself to capture a sizable portion of the U.S. market and the international pork market. Meanwhile, conditions within its industry deteriorated. In 1994 and 1995, hog prices plummeted to levels averaged during the mid-1970s. Exacerbating depressed hog prices was the inflated price of corn, the animal's staple feed, which rose to a record high in the mid-1990s. All competitors in the pork industry suffered from the deleterious conditions, but perhaps none more than PSF. The company was highly leveraged, financing much of its aggressive growth through $420 million in junk bonds, and consequently was highly vulnerable to the depressed market conditions. It became increasingly difficult for the company to make the interest payments on its mounting debt, as losses piled up. Between January 1995 and September 1995, PSF registered $66 million in losses, more than twice the amount recorded during the same nine-month period in 1994. By the end of 1995, losses for the company neared the $100 million mark. As PSF entered 1996, the company's future existence was seriously in doubt.

In attempting to determine what had gone wrong at PSF, industry observers did not have to scrutinize the pork producer's operations long. Costs had spiraled out of control, propelled by the company's desire to create a pork production enterprise that would serve as the model for all others to follow. ''They built a Rolls-Royce when a Chevrolet could have gotten them there,'' one competitor remarked. For its part, the company conceded that the aggressive expansion program had backfired, becoming hobbled by debt when hog prices plunged and the price of corn rose. ''We tried to do too much too soon too fast,'' offered a vice-chairman at Morgan Stanley. By May 1996, PSF, which had grown to become the fourth largest pig farmer in the United States, could no longer pay the interest on its debt. In July 1996, the company filed for bankruptcy, seeking protection from creditors while it restructured its operations and resolved the problems that had led to its collapse.

A Second Start in 1996

While management grappled with the formidable task of preparing for PSF's survival, several industry analysts theorized that the company's long-term health depended on its acquisition by a larger parent company who could incorporate the hog operations into its existing business. Of more pressing importance to PSF's reorganizers in the summer of 1996 was emerging from bankruptcy, a process that was accelerated by the company's early development of a restructuring plan, which was approved by investors, lenders, and other parties prior to filing for Chapter 11 protection. Restructuring permitted PSF to convert some of its debt into equity, enabling the company to achieve a greater distinction between the $246 million in assets and the $237 million in liabilities it registered when filing for bankruptcy. The restructuring process also led to an ownership change in the company. Under the arrangement, Putnam Investments, a company whose fund held a sizable percentage of PSF's junk bonds, became the largest shareholder in the Missouri and Texas hog operations, replacing Morgan Stanley as PSF's largest shareholder. Two months after filing for bankruptcy, PSF had completed its reorganization, emerging as a going concern in September 1996. Shortly after the company's second start, the public learned of PSF's new senior executive, the individual whose responsibility it was to steward the fortunes of what continued to rank as the country's fourth largest hog farmer. Robert Manly, formerly the executive vice-president of Virginia-based Smithfield Foods Inc., was announced as the president and CEO of PSF.

Following the severe disappointment of 1996, PSF forged ahead, seeking to make its second assault on the pork industry an enduring one. There was evidence that the company was progressing successfully during the late 1990s. The $250 million in annual sales recorded when the company declared bankruptcy had grown to $295 million by 1997, sparking a modicum of optimism about the company's future. More encouraging news arrived in 1998, when PSF allied itself with a much larger partner and bolstered its chances for long-term success.

In May 1998, Continental Grain Company, one of the world's largest grain concerns, acquired a majority interest in PSF. Continental Grain, with interests in financial services and a number of agribusiness pursuits, entered the pork production business in 1985, maintaining pork production facilities near PSF's operations in Missouri. Following the acquisition, Continental Grain's Missouri pork operations were incorporated into its new 51 percent-owned subsidiary. In addition to Continental Grain's pork operations, PSF also gained the services of its parent company's vice-president and general manager of pork operations, John Meyer. Meyer was named CEO of PSF, working alongside Manly, who remained as president of PSF and assumed responsibilities for the day-to-day operation of the company. Together, Meyer and Manly hoped to carve a legacy of success for PSF, which, having weathered an overly ambitious start in business, boasted the equipment and facilities to dominate its industry.

Further Reading

Davis, Mark, ''American Heart Association Certifies Some Pork Products,'' *Knight-Ridder/Tribune Business News,* December 3, 1997, p. 1203B1033.

Fircloth, Anne, ''Those Pigs at Morgan Stanley,'' *Fortune,* October 14, 1996, p. 36.

Gilmore, Casey, ''Hog Farm Stalls Plans for Expansion,'' *Kansas City Business Journal,* June 9, 1995, p. 1.

''Management Team Named at PSF,'' *Feedstuffs,* June 29, 1998, p. 7.

Mansur, Michael, ''Settlement Appears Near in Missouri Lawsuit Against Hog Producer,'' *Knight-Ridder/Tribune Business News,* July 16, 1999, p. OKRB991970BA.

Marbery, Steve, ''Continental Grain to Buy Majority of PSF,'' *Feedstuffs,* January 12, 1998, p. 1.

——, ''PSF Faces Debt, Environmental Hurdles,'' *Feedstuffs,* January 8, 1996, p. 1.

——, ''PSF Fails to Meet Payments, Goes Private,'' *Feedstuffs,* May 6, 1996, p. 1.

——, ''Smithfield Exec to Head PSF,'' *Feedstuffs,* October 21, 1996, p. 1.

Smith, Rod, ''PSF Completes Restructuring; to Continue Growth,'' *Feedstuffs,* September 23, 1996, p. 1.

——, ''PSF Files for Chapter 11; Seeks 'Fresh Start,' '' *Feedstuffs,* July 8, 1996, p. 1.

—Jeffrey L. Covell

PremiumWear, Inc.

5500 Feltl Road
Minnetonka, Minnesota 55343-7902
U.S.A.
(612) 979-1700
Fax: (612) 979-1717
Web site: http://www.premiumwear.com

Public Company
Incorporated: 1887 as Northwestern Knitting Company
Employees: 265
Sales: $42.45 million (1998)
Stock Exchanges: New York
Ticker Symbol: PWA
NAIC: 315211 Men's & Boy's Cut & Sew Apparel
Contractors; 315212 Women's, Girls', & Infants Cut
& Sew Apparel Contractors; 315999 Other Apparel
Accessories & Other Apparel Manufacturing

PremiumWear, Inc.'s core business is the designing, sourcing, and marketing of apparel as a licensee of the "Munsingwear" brand for the promotional products/advertising specialty industry. The company re-entered the "green grass" professional golf shop market in January 1998 using its "Page & Tuttle" brand. The company is what remains of one-time underwear king Munsingwear, Inc.

Comfortable Underwear Yields Big Business: 1880s–1960s

George D. Munsing left New York in 1886 to establish a textile factory in Minneapolis, Minnesota, along with two associates from the Massachusetts Institute of Technology, Frank H. Page and Edward O. Tuttle. While superintendent of Rochester Knitting Works, back in New York, Munsing had experimented with knit fabrics and ribbing and hit on a process to plate silk on wool, thus creating an itchless material. The company's first products were knit underwear for women and men. Patent attorney Amasa C. Paul served as president of Northwestern Knit-

ting Company, incorporated on February 15, 1887. Munsing was vice-president.

Munsing was concerned primarily with the technological aspects of the business; consequently, the areas of manufacturing and merchandising were neglected at first. The fledgling company sometimes failed to meet shipping deadlines, which resulted in cancelled orders. Furthermore, the retail customers they served were provided little information about the range of products the company was capable of producing. The investment of a number of prominent Minneapolis businessmen helped the company stay afloat during the difficult early years.

Patents helped Northwestern establish a foothold in the industry. Munsing's plated, elastic knit fabric was patented in 1888 along with patents for knit undershirts and drawers. A patent for a crocheting machine, used for trim or finish, followed in 1891. "The turning point in the firm's fortunes, however, came with the production of the union suit in the early 1890s, making the business 'the first knitting company in the United States to make and market knit union suits in a large way,'" wrote Marcia G. Anderson in "Munsingwear: An Underwear for America."

The one-piece, cream-colored garment became the company's signature product. Early print ads showed families gathered around the fireplace: men, women, kids, all wearing their union suits. The new product was manufactured out of the company's Lyndale Avenue plant in Minneapolis. Northwestern moved there in about 1890 or 1891 following a number of relocations. The firm would go on to manufacture its products there for nearly a century.

In 1894 Munsing left the company; the other founding partners were gone as well by this time. Northwestern put its merchandising efforts in overdrive and grew rapidly over the next two decades. New products were added, and the manufacturing plant was enlarged. Big long underwear orders for U.S. troops fighting in World War I gave the company widespread recognition.

By 1917, the company was producing 30,000 garments a day. One-tenth of all U.S. made union suits were produced by

Company Perspectives:

Throughout history, the Munsingwear name has stood for quality and innovation. Whether it's been the creation of a new fabric, the development of a new manufacturing process or the introduction of never-tried-before sales or marketing techniques, the company will continue to be successful based on a tradition of satisfying customer needs and responding to market changes.

Our mission is simple: To be a leading provider of branded knit and woven shirts to the Special Markets and Golf industries through total commitment to quality in people, value in products and excellence in service to our customers while delivering superior return to our shareholders.

the Minneapolis company and its predominantly female workforce. Incidentally, the company was recognized for its humane working conditions during a time when factory work often was performed under deplorable conditions.

Munsing returned to the company he helped found in 1919, this time as a research specialist. That year the company was renamed Munsingwear Corporation. Munsing stayed with the business until his death three years later.

Around this time, Munsingwear established a design department; it was one of the first apparel makers to do so. Offerings grew broader as the industry began its move to modernize styles. The 1922 price list included 102 styles of underwear made in various models of wool, cotton, silk, knit, and woven fabrics, and fashioned for all age ranges.

In 1923 the company changed its name to Munsingwear, Inc. and began selling stock on the New York Stock Exchange. The Minneapolis-based company was the world's largest producer of underwear under a single trademark. Three presidents had led the company during its rise. F.M. Stowell, who started out as a shipping clerk, guided Munsingwear from 1913 to 1932.

During the 1930s, the company sold sleep-and-lounging garments, hosiery, knit coats, pull-ons, and foundation garments for women, as well as its traditional underwear. Munsingwear introduced the elastic fabric girdle to the market in 1932.

Significant manufacturing facilities joined the growing company during the 1940s and 1950s. Among them were the Vassar Company of Chicago, which was, in 1958, combined with Hollywood-Maxwell Company of California to form the Hollywood Vassarette Intimate Apparel Division.

Along the way Munsingwear continued to seek out innovations in fabrics and design. The company introduced nylon tricot to its women's line in 1947 and patented the nylon reinforced neck band in shirts in 1950. Trademarks also were being established. In 1955 Munsingwear put the penguin logo on its knit golf shirts. "Stay-There" foundations with "Ban-Lon" appeared in 1958.

In the 1960s, through its David Clark subsidiary (a company purchased in 1941), Munsingwear produced apparel for NASA's Gemini and Apollo programs. Using new fabrics and manufacturing techniques, the company added swimwear and men's and boys' products during the decade, and in the 1970s introduced cross-country ski wear.

Times Change, Munsingwear Does Not: 1970s–80s

In 1974 sales were $104 million. Men's and boys' wear provided 57 percent of revenue, women's apparel 37 percent, and the David Clark subsidiary six percent. The men's and boys' division had grown about 11 percent a year from 1968 to 1974. Munsingwear's Grand Slam knit sport shirt was estimated to be the largest selling golf shirt in the world. The Vassarette Division, on the other hand, had lost ground. A new generation of women had abandoned the foundations and other garments worn by their mothers and grandmothers.

Net earnings began to slip in the second half of the decade, but the company hung on to its top 20 ranking among the country's 15,000 clothing manufacturers. From 1932 to 1979, Munsingwear and its five presidents had weathered the Great Depression, union strife, World War II, expansion of operations into new regions, the advent of sales to foreign countries, rapidly changing fashions, and an oil embargo. The industry in which they operated was highly fragmented and highly competitive.

Ken Johnson wrote in a 1975 *Corporate Report Minnesota* article, "The fact that Munsingwear has survived, profited and grown for many years should, therefore, not be taken lightly. Its success is a tribute to establishing brand names associated with quality, style and a reasonable price, and the ability to keep costs under control."

Sales continued to rise slowly during the last years of the decade, but net earnings had begun to slide. Ray Good, a former executive vice-president with food giant Pillsbury Co., came on board as president in October 1979. Munsingwear's massive Minneapolis plant, a city landmark, was shut down two years later.

"The closing of the Minneapolis factory, a decision made by the directors in spite of appeals from Mayor Fraser and the local textile union, was a shocker, not only to the 400 employees laid off but to the city's many elderly residents. They remember with nostalgia the winters of childhood in the one piece 'union suit,' which made life cozy," wrote Evadene Burris Swanson for *Hennepin County History*.

Good viewed the plant as a major drain on the company, which was being crippled by heavy short-term debt, overcapacity, and money-losing operations. But the shutdown and other measures, including licensing deals, technological upgrades, a bumped-up ad budget, and a cut-back product line, failed to prevent a flow of red ink. Munsingwear lost $3.8 million on $134 million in sales in 1980.

Designer jeans and logoed sport shirts had flooded the market, backed by sophisticated advertising creating "must have" brands. Manufacturers had moved in droves to cheaper offshore production. Munsingwear steadfastly remained production oriented, operating its own fabric plants and manufacturing facilities. The company did not even have a marketing department, according to a 1981 *Corporate Report Minnesota* article by William Souder.

"The company has had three straight years of deficits and has changed presidents more frequently than styles: three in the last two years," wrote Eleanor Johnson Tracy for *Fortune* in September 1984. President number three, George K. Hansen, a seasoned apparel executive, put the Munsingwear house in order well enough to bring the company back to profitability. But when Hansen decentralized operations, creating a holding company structure, and then tapped into the junk bond market to acquire three apparel companies, weakness in Munsingwear's two main divisions became apparent.

The men's and Vassarette divisions, which produced half of total sales, were missing delivery dates and carrying big excess inventories. In addition, the company's traditional customers, the department stores, thought the apparel supplier had weakened the brand by selling products with the Munsingwear label in mass merchandising channels.

Drastic Measures: 1990s

By the end of the decade, debt-ridden Munsingwear was on the brink of closing its doors. "Munsingwear's revolving-door management has been blamed for the bulk of the company's woes. The firm has lost more than $50 million in the past three years, analysts have stopped following it and its own accountants earlier this year expressed concern about whether the company could stay in business," wrote Ann Merrill in a 1990 *Minneapolis/St. Paul CityBusiness* article.

Charles Campbell, hired in 1989 to head the company's men's apparel division, was named president and CEO one year later. Considered an apparel turnaround king by some in the industry, he began by trimming down the company and then led Munsingwear through a Chapter 11 reorganization in 1991.

The company, which once had more than 3,000 employees worldwide, six divisions, and $200 million in sales, held only its men's activewear line with the Grand Slam, Munsingwear, Penguin Sport, and Penguin Club labels. Campbell's plan for the new and much smaller company was to build on its golf shirt legacy.

Robert Sharoff quoted Campbell in a 1992 *Daily News Record:* "Munsingwear practically invented the golf shirt in the country. At one time, we had a very big presence on the pro circuit. I have a picture in my office of Bing Crosby, Bob Hope, Jack Nicklaus and Arnold Palmer standing arm in arm, and all four are wearing Munsingwear shirts. We decided to get back into that business."

Campbell had moved Munsingwear from a production-driven to a marketing-driven concern, with few remnants of the past. Munsingwear no longer sold its original product, underwear, in any shape or form. The legacy ended when the men's underwear business was licensed to Fruit of the Loom in 1991; the famous union suit had gone by the wayside back in 1969. Munsingwear reported its first full-year profits in six years in fiscal 1992. Campbell left the company to head another apparel concern in 1993.

The company produced mixed results over the next several years, losing $2.3 million on sales of $51.5 million in 1995. The next year, Munsingwear sold its trademarks for cash and exited the retail and pro shop markets. Included among the labels sold to Miami-based Supreme International Corp. were all Munsingwear brands and the Penguin and Grand Slam names.

Renamed PremiumWear, Inc., the company continued to operate its special markets business, which it entered in 1994. PremiumWear licensed back the Munsingwear and Penguin trademarks for use on apparel made for that segment. PremiumWear's 1996 sales in the special market area were $27 million, up 75 percent from the previous year.

The multibillion-dollar advertising specialty market handled merchandise for business promotions and employee incentives. PremiumWear sold to distributors and dealers, which in turn supplied companies and institutions with apparel bearing their logos or names. The company sold to the much smaller uniform market via giants such as Cintas Corp., which supplied uniforms for a wide range of workers, including those in the retail, medical, and restaurant businesses.

The overhaul was led by retired Wolverine World Wide Inc. (Hush Puppies) CEO Thomas D. Gleason, who had joined the board in mid-1995. The company had a net worth of $13 million at the time, with approximately the same amount of debt, and could not compete in apparel arenas requiring heavy design and advertising spending and frequent inventory replacements.

Tightly Focused Future

The company had reluctantly exited the growing golf apparel business when it sold its trademarks in 1996, but then re-entered the segment in January 1998. PremiumWear placed its "Page & Tuttle" line—named after two of the company's original co-founders—in 500 of the country's approximately 15,000 golf club shops. The PGA and LPGA player-endorsed line competed with brands such as Ashworth, Ralph Lauren's Polo, Izod, and Nike. But the golf shop segment did not require the level of design and marketing expenditures inherent to other retail apparel. The pro golf shop segment had been growing by five to ten percent over recent years, while the rest of the apparel market had remained relatively flat.

The promotional products/advertising specialty end of the business grew by 22 percent in 1998, and the company netted $1.5 million on about $42.5 million in total sales. The company expected the industry as a whole to continue to grow at a double-digit pace. PremiumWear planned to offer its new more upscale "Page & Tuttle" brand to its special market customers beginning in 1999. The company further tightened its focus in 1999 with the closure of its North Carolina cut-and-sew operation. Production done at that plant was scheduled to be outsourced offshore.

Further Reading

Anderson, Marcia G., "Munsingwear: An Underwear for America," *Minnesota History,* Winter 1986, pp. 152–61.
Beulke, Diane, "Heads Roll As Munsingwear Tries for Another Comeback," *Minneapolis/St. Paul CityBusiness,* October 21, 1987, pp. 1, 27.

''Betting on the Bang Theory,'' *Corporate Report Minnesota,* December 1979, p. 65.

Feyder, Susan, ''PremiumWear New Golf Shirt Won't Include the Penguin,'' *Star Tribune* (Minneapolis), January 9, 1998, p. 1D.

Hillbery, Rhonda, ''A Better Kind of Bankruptcy,'' *Minneapolis/St. Paul CityBusiness,* November 25, 1991, pp. 11, 18.

Johnson, Ken, ''The Munsingwear Fit,'' *Corporate Report Minnesota,* February 1975, pp. 29–30.

Merrill, Ann, ''Campbell Tailors a New Munsingwear,'' *Minneapolis/St. Paul CityBusiness,* September 17–23, 1990, pp. 1, 22.

——, ''Munsingwear Sews Up Deal to Supply Sears with Shirts,'' *Minneapolis/St. Paul CityBusiness,* January 6–12, 1992, pp. 1, 15.

''Munsingwear a Supreme Buy: Miami-Based Company Has Big Plans for Branded Golf Labels,'' *Daily News Record,* May 24, 1996, p. 1.

''Munsingwear Falls Deeper into Red,'' *Daily News Record,* April 9, 1996, p. 9.

''Munsingwear Reduces Loss in 4th Quarter to $298,000,'' *Daily News Record,* March 13, 1995, p. 2.

''Munsingwear: Scoring on Comeback Course,'' *Daily News Record,* May 11, 1992, p. 10.

''Munsingwear Selling Marks for China, Vietnam, Macao,'' *Daily News Record,* July 2, 1996, p. 10.

''Munsingwear Shows $1.2 Million Profit in Year,'' *Daily News Record,* February 19, 1993, p. 2.

Peterson, Susan E., ''Campbell Will Leave Munsingwear to Become CEO of Crystal Brands, a Larger Competitor,'' *Star Tribune* (Minneapolis), July 16 1993, p. 1D.

''PremiumWear Has Strong Quarter,'' *Daily News Record,* March 2, 1998, p. 11.

''PremiumWear, Inc.,'' *Corporate Report Fact Book 1999,* p. 377.

''PremiumWear Names James Murphy General Manager of Golf Division,'' *PR Newswire,* July 28, 1999.

''PremiumWear Net Skyrockets in 4th Quarter, Year,'' *Daily News Record,* April 9, 1999, p. 12.

''PremiumWear to Close N.C. Plant,'' *Star Tribune* (Minneapolis), April 27, 1999, p. 3D.

Souder, William, ''Munsingwear on the Mend,'' *Corporate Report Minnesota,* August 1981, pp. 47–51, 134–40.

Swanson, Evadene Burris, ''Don't Say 'Underwear,' Say 'Munsingwear,' '' *Hennepin County History,* Winter 1987, pp. 3–19.

Trachtenberg, Jeffrey A., ''The Minnow and the Basses,'' *Forbes,* February 25, 1985, p. 75.

Tracy, Eleanor Johnson, ''Stodgy Munsingwear Changes Its Underwear,'' *Fortune,* September 3, 1984, p. 67.

Youngblood, Dick, ''Smaller Is Better,'' *Star Tribune* (Minneapolis), January 26, 1998, p. 1D.

—Kathleen Peippo

The Prudential Insurance Company of America

751 Broad Street
Newark, New Jersey 07102
U.S.A.
(973) 802-6000
(800) 353-2847
Fax: (973) 802-3128
Web site: http://www.prudential.com

Mutual Company
Incorporated: 1873 as Widows and Orphans Friendly
    Society
Employees: 105,000
Total Assets: $279.42 billion (1998)
NAIC: 524113 Direct Life Insurance Carriers; 524114
    Direct Health & Medical Insurance Carriers; 524126
    Direct Property & Casualty Insurance Carriers;
    524298 All Other Insurance Related Activities; 52599
    Other Financial Vehicles; 523930 Financial Planning
    Services

The Prudential Insurance Company of America is one of the largest diversified financial institutions in the world and, based on total assets, the largest insurance company in North America. Along with its primary business, insurance, the company also operates in securities, investments, residential real estate, employee benefits, home mortgages, and the corporate relocation industry. In 1999 Prudential was in the process of reorganizing as preparation for a transition to demutualization and public ownership, pending regulatory approval, in 2000.

A Major Innovator in Life Insurance: 1870s–1900s

A Yale dropout named John F. Dryden established the forerunner of Prudential in 1873, naming it the Widows and Orphans Friendly Society. Two years later, influenced by the British Prudential Assurance Company, Dryden changed his company's name to The Prudential Friendly Society (the company settled on its current name in 1877). When Dryden visited British Prudential at this time, he was impressed by several key elements, including the British company's offering of low-cost industrial insurance for laborers; the fact that agents collected premiums each week from customers at home; and that the company served not the wealthy or middle class, but the working class. Unable to find backers in his native New England or New York to build the company he envisioned, Dryden crossed the Hudson to Newark, New Jersey, and convinced several Newark citizens to purchase $30,000 of capital stock.

The first prospectus of the company succinctly set forth its aims: Relief in sickness and accident for people of meager means, pensions for old age, adult and infant burial funds—all goals which corresponded closely to the needs of the diverse ethnic groups then immigrating to the United States. Yet the company's first directors failed to recognize Dryden's vision or organizational talents. As a result, Newark real estate broker Allen L. Bassett was installed as president. His tenure was short-lived, however, and Noah Blanchard, a tanner, took the helm. In 1881, when Blanchard died, the directors finally elected John Dryden president by one vote. He served in that position for 30 years. During those years, he led Prudential to several major innovations and established a corporate culture that marked Prudential for generations.

Under Dryden's leadership, Prudential enjoyed explosive growth. In 1885, it reported 422,671 policies in force; by 1905 it had 6.49 million. Assets grew from $1.03 million in 1885 to $102.38 million in 1905. Prudential expanded to neighboring states, and, in 1909, opened its first international branch in Toronto, Canada. In 1896, the company's advertising department created Prudential's longstanding logo and slogan: the Rock of Gibraltar accompanied by the words, ''The Prudential has the strength of Gibraltar.'' Both were chosen to express the solidity of the products the company offered. The company's image was further bolstered by the outcome of a New York state legislative committee investigation under Senator William W. Armstrong in 1905. While the major companies of the day became targets of the investigation into violation of customer interests, Prudential emerged relatively unscathed.

When Dryden died in 1911, his son, Forrest Dryden, followed him as president. Under Forrest's leadership, the company continued its rapid growth.

Mutualizing and Surviving: 1910s–30s

However, control of the company became and remained a problem during Forrest Dryden's term. Its huge resources and conservative investment philosophy made Prudential's assets look appealing to potential purchasers. Tired of fending off corporate suitors and raiders, the board took its first steps to make the company mutual and sell the company to its policy-holders.

Later in Forrest's tenure, World War I drained the company with its heavy claims. Then, as a result of the 1918–19 influenza pandemic, Prudential paid out over $20 million for flu-related deaths. Shortly afterward, Forrest Dryden brought scandal to the firm because of a conflict of interest he had due to certain stocks he held. By the time he resigned in 1921, company totals exceeded $5.6 billion, an increase of $3.6 billion in ten years. Corporate assets rose from $259 million in 1911 to $830 million in 1922. Edward D. Duffield became Prudential's next president.

During Duffield's term, Prudential stayed much the same. While the company innovated by offering group insurance coverage to home office staff in 1924 and started group health in 1925, the Great Depression strangled most growth. Mortgages valued at $1.5 billion in 1931 bottomed at $787 million in 1935, even though the value of policies in force grew $1.5 billion between 1930 and 1935. In 1938, when Duffield died suddenly, he left a company still tremendously successful, but no longer a leader in the industry.

Franklin D'Olier followed Duffield as president. While D'Olier recognized the problems Prudential faced with its conservative managerial corps, he never succeeded in attending to them. A larger crisis demanded his attention: Hitler's actions in Europe and the U.S. commitment to World War II. D'Olier helped organize the New York regional civil defense and later served on the Strategic Bombing Survey Commission. However, in 1942, Prudential finally converted to a mutual company, completing the process started in 1915, and, in 1928, it entered the market for major medical coverage, group credit insurance, and group insurance in multiple employer-collective bargaining units. The group sales department was the brainchild of Edmund Whittaker, an actuary who had joined the company in 1928, and who conceived of actuaries as the "engineers of insurance."

A New Era of Decentralization in the 1940s

In 1946 Prudential entered a new era. Carroll M. Shanks took office as Prudential's seventh CEO. At 40, he was the youngest president since Dryden. Shanks had joined Prudential in 1932 and was known for his unorthodox methods; during his 15 years as president, he remade the company, leading Prudential into a bold decentralization that stunned the industry.

Within months of Shanks taking office, resignations or early retirements were announced down to the level of middle management. Next, in 1948, he opened regional home offices across the nation, each with its own senior vice-president in charge and with total responsibility for the region. Newark retained the corporate senior officers, actuaries, and evaluation and staff departments, but each vice-president handled local sales, investments, general management, and issues from policy to claims.

The reorganization dealt with many of the company's problems. It attacked the excessive specialization that separated workers and stymied activity; it cut the many levels between the president and operating employees; it eliminated layers of red tape and provided new opportunities for energetic and creative managers. Each regional home office occupied a striking modern office building that dominated its city and told the region that Prudential had arrived in style and strength. Quickly the regional home offices helped Prudential establish a new national presence. Corporate policy called for the regional office to invest its dollars in the local community. With the inception of each of the eight home regional offices, Prudential's sales jumped and investment income rose sharply. In 1948, the first regional sales office in Los Angeles boosted revenue in that region by 20 percent. Group pension sales totaled $44 million in 1945, and, by 1955, exceeded $194 million; group life sales exceeded $589 million in 1949, a record for both Prudential and the industry.

As regional leaders exercised their autonomy, they created a multitude of new products, many tailor-made to their regional markets. Shanks adapted the best innovations to the national scene. Prudential set up employee security programs that combined group life and health insurance. In addition, it changed major medical insurance in the 1950s when it revised the method for computing the deductible. The company also underwent internal change. In 1951 Prudential's district agents voted to go on strike, the first formal job action by a white collar union in the nation. The American Federation of Labor led the workers for three months as they negotiated for improvements and succeeded in obtaining recognition of the union as their bargaining agent.

Investment Strategies for the 1960s

Under Shanks, Prudential also revised its investment strategies. Shanks consistently looked for niches where Prudential could risk a small amount yet increase its average return much above that of its competitors. In 1950 the Prudential began buying common stocks and, by 1964, had three percent of its assets in stock on which it realized $75 million in capital gains. The strategy was successful; by 1962, the life insurance industry averaged a return of 4.4 percent on all invested assets. Prudential averaged 4.7 percent, producing an additional $60 million in income for the company. After 1958, Prudential ceased to buy bonds in the market and instead negotiated separate loans with corporations for higher rates on which the corporations received more rapid, less costly, and more flexible financing. In 1956, Shanks created a commercial and industrial loan department to seek out small business loans.

When Shanks retired in 1960, the Prudential board named Louis R. Menagh, Jr., as chief executive officer. At 68 one of the oldest to win the post, Menagh had worked his way to the top from a position as clerk. Menagh retired in October 1962, and the board named Orville E. Beal president. Beal had headed the regional home office in Minneapolis, Minnesota, and was committed to Shanks's bold vision.

In 1964, Beal led Prudential in selling its first group variable annuity policy. These annuities were invested entirely in common stocks and were, thus, a much more attractive hedge against inflation than prior annuities based on bonds, mortgages, and similar investments. In 1967, Prudential surpassed the Metropolitan as the world's largest insurance company; total Met assets amounted to $23.51 billion while Prudential announced $23.6 billion. In 1968, it established PIC Realty Corporation as a wholly owned subsidiary that owned and leased commercial real estate through joint ventures with established real estate developers. Prudential shared additional profits as a principal in real estate development.

Beal stepped down in 1968, the same year the company abandoned its original pay-by-the-week policies, closing an important chapter in the company's history. He turned his leadership role over to Donald MacNaughton, who led the company through some of its most expansive innovations. MacNaughton particularly addressed issues of corporate social responsibility. When Newark suffered terribly after one of the worst urban riots in U.S. history, MacNaughton pledged to use Prudential's resources to help with the problems of urban centers and gave $50 million to Newark. He convinced the insurance industry to pledge $1 billion in help to U.S. cities, an amount later increased to $2 billion. In his nine years as CEO, MacNaughton developed an array of new products for the company and plunged it into the international marketplace, well ahead of most of the competition. In 1969, Prudential celebrated total assets of over $25 billion; when MacNaughton retired in 1978 reported assets were $35.8 billion.

Opportunities Amidst Inflation and Stagflation: 1970s

When the New Jersey legislature revised insurance laws in 1967, it broadened the operations of life insurance companies, permitting them to offer fire and casualty coverage, individual variable annuity plans, direct investment in real estate, investment management services, mortgage investing, and to own or lease business or communication equipment. Prudential took advantage of these new opportunities; inflation was corroding the pay checks of U.S. workers and fewer customers wanted policies that pledged fixed payments. Instead Prudential aimed its sites at the new middle-class consumer, aiming to meet all their insurance needs.

In 1970 Prudential entered the property and casualty insurance business. Unable to secure the necessary state licenses, and without a sufficiently large body of trained and certified agents, the company contracted with Kemper Insurance to provide "shell" companies in 26 states. Homeowners insurance policies had traditionally been written for three to five years, and

corporate profits suffered from inflation. Instead, Prudential wrote all its policies at current rates. To minimize losses, it carefully selected the geographic regions it entered. However, the retraining costs of certifying 30,000 agents were great. By 1972, Prudential dropped its contract with Kemper and continued in the casualty and fire field through its subsidiary Prudential Property and Casualty Insurance Company.

MacNaughton continued the search for higher returns in a period of inflation and stagflation. In 1973 Prudential formed Prudential Reinsurance Company, insuring other insurance companies against extraordinary losses. In 1974 Prudential purchased CNA Nuclear Leasing, renaming it Prudential Lease. In its first year, contracts grew by 88 percent and returned 16 percent on equity. Prudential Reinsurance gave Prudential its first entrance into the international market.

In 1976 Prudential acquired Hanbro Life Assurance Ltd. of Britain and entered the European Common Market. MacNaughton developed many more product lines between 1973 and 1978. PIC Realty Canada, Ltd. owned and developed property in Canada. Prudential Health Care Plan operated health maintenance organizations. Pru Capital Management provided administration and management services to Prulease. Le Rocher, Compagnie de Reassurance, wrote reinsurance in Europe. Pru Funding offered long-term loans and operation leases for Prulease. Pru Supply contracted to supply fossil fuels or other inventories. Prudential General Insurance Company provided group casualty and property protection, and Pru Service Participacos, a wholly owned Brazilian subsidiary, provided services to another Brazilian property and casualty company.

MacNaughton retired in 1978 and was succeeded by Robert Beck, who had joined Prudential in 1951 as an agent. Beck attacked the problem of the continuing lapse rate on life insurance policies by entering new markets. The company formed Dryden and Company and Gibraltar Casualty Company to sell coverage of unusual and difficult insurance risks to the surplus lines market. Prudential also formed additional subsidiaries to market group and commercial property and casualty insurance. In 1979 Prudential signed with Sony Corporation to form Sony-Prudential to sell life insurance in Japan. Beck also led Prudential in another investment opportunity; PRUCO formed a subsidiary, P.G. Realty, to purchase, sell, and operate farmlands in Nebraska. Later, other subsidiaries were formed to operate farm lands in Florida.

Beck's most controversial acquisition came when he purchased the Bache investment and brokerage house in 1981. With Bache, Prudential could sell money market funds, mutuals, tax shelters, real estate partnerships, as well as stocks and bonds, all hedges against inflation. Prudential-Bache hired George L. Ball, former president of E.F. Hutton & Company, as its chair and CEO. Ball, a Wall Street star known for his aggressive and innovative tactics as a broker, led the brokerage firm on an expensive, but ultimately failed effort to break into the top levels of Wall Street investment banks for the next nine years.

Unprecedented Growth and Scandal: 1980s

Throughout the 1980s, Prudential continued to search for ways to maximize income from its investments. In 1981, the company formed Property Investment Separate Account, a vehicle to enable pension funds to invest in real estate. It also developed several successful investment initiatives: SMALLCO invested in firms under $200 million, and MIDCO in firms between $75 and $460 million in capital. Beck led Prudential in a continued effort to diversify, opening health maintenance offices in Oklahoma, Atlanta, Georgia, and Nashville, Tennessee. New life insurance subsidiaries were formed in Texas, Arizona, and Illinois. The company also formed the Mircali Asset Management firm to manage global investments for other institutions.

In September 1986, Robert Beck retired. His successor as CEO and chairman of the board, 54-year-old Robert C. Winters, had joined Prudential in 1953. Winters took over after several decades of unprecedented growth in the company. Prudential's assets had more than doubled since 1978. After many years of spinning off a seemingly endless line of subsidiaries and holding companies, the company now took time to evaluate and integrate the gains of earlier years. A new corporate strategy needed to be articulated to make sense out of the recent period of expansion, one that gave form to future plans.

In 1987 the company reorganized its Prudential Realty Group into four new firms: Prudential Property Company, Prudential Acquisition and Sales Group, Prudential Mortgage Capital Company, and the Investment Service Group. Prudential offered its customers virtually every variety of insurance known, both for individuals and groups. That year, it acquired Merrill Lynch Realty and Merrill Lynch Relocation Management and offered customers a nationwide system of real estate brokers. Prudential sold its shares in Sony-Prudential to Sony. It formed a Prudential Life Insurance Company Ltd. in Japan, which offered a full range of individual life policies. Other subsidiaries were formed or acquired to sell policies in Spain, Italy, South Korea, and Taiwan.

The October 1987 panic on the market cost Prudential $1 billion in paper value and marked at least a temporary end to runaway leveraged buyouts and massive mergers and acquisitions. The managers at Prudential had made millions for the company in the heady days of LBOs. From one financial package put together to help sell a company, Prudential earned $200 million on an investment of $650 million.

There was, however, a negative side to the boom years of the market. Many of the sophisticated financial packages Prudential crafted were initially tax havens for its customers. But when the 1986 tax reform act eliminated the rationale for the many tax shelters, customers quickly abandoned them. In addition, the packages designed by the financiers were often so sophisticated that neither the customers nor the agents marketing the devices could understand them, and many of the innovations tried by Prudential faltered. Prudential pumped $2.4 billion into Bache Group, for example, with continual losses. In 1989, a difficult year for Prudential, Bache lost $48 million. In November 1990, Prudential-Bache announced that it was cutting back on its investment banking operation by about two thirds, having made the decision to reorganize the firm to focus on its strengths in the retail brokerage business. In early 1991, with losses totaling more than $250 million and amid lawsuits relating to selling real estate limited partnerships, Ball resigned. Hardwick

Simmons, former president of Shearson's Private Client Group, took over leadership of Prudential Securities Inc., renamed as part of its restructuring.

During Simmons's first year in charge of Pru Securities, the firm launched an aggressive ad campaign and enjoyed record earnings. In 1993 profits reached nearly $800 million. Yet Simmons had also to deal with the private lawsuits of angry investors who had lost hundreds of millions of dollars in limited partnerships sold by Pru Securities brokers, several potentially damaging class action suits, and an SEC investigation. The cause of his trouble: some $6 billion of limited partnerships sold in the 1980s to more than 100,000 investors now valued at only a fraction of their original selling price. In response to the negative publicity, Prudential retreated behind a shield of secrecy, but with probes into the limited partnerships by state securities regulators expanding, the company accepted various settlements, including public censure in 1992. Prudential remained under scrutiny for the next several years for "churning," inducing policy holders to trade up to more expensive policies without explaining the costs. The investigation, concluded in 1996, and involving regulators from 45 states, assessed Prudential a $35 million fine and set up a restitution plan for 10.7 million policyholders. The settlement, approved by a New Jersey district court judge in 1997, led to an eventual payment in excess of $2 billion.

The problems at Prudential Securities coincided with a downturn in profits for the brokerage firm. Profits at Prudential Mortgage dropped, too, with a decline in mortgage lending activity and a rise in interest rates. Sales of life insurance to individuals diminished as well. Prudential's reinsurance business and property and casualty units had been hard hit by several natural disasters, including Hurricane Andrew. In 1994 insurance operations lost $907 million as a result of the Northridge, California earthquake. The board took advantage of Winters's retirement in late 1994 to bring in new "outsider" management in an attempt to resolve its problems. Arthur Ryan came from Chase Manhattan, where he had overseen the marketing of mutual funds and insurance. Before that, he had led a large sales operation at Control Data. With $300 billion in assets, Prudential also began to take steps to boost efficiency, bringing in Coopers & Lybrand, McKinsey, Deloitte & Touche, and other consultants. It announced plans to shed its reinsurance and mortgage units and to liquidate its $6 billion real estate portfolio. Real estate divestitures began in 1997 with the sale of the company's property management unit and its Canadian commercial real estate business. The following year, it sold Prudential Center complex in Boston.

The Move to Go Public in the Year 2000

In 1998, Ryan went before New Jersey's insurance commissioner to lobby for passage of a law that would allow a mutual insurance company to sell shares to the public. Under Ryan's plan, the company would change its corporate structure so that it could raise money by selling stock. Detractors of the plan, such as the insurance director for the Consumer Federation of America, argued that it would enrich management via stock options, while causing policyholders to lose out in the form of lower dividends. In 1999, in preparation for becoming a stock-owned firm, Prudential undertook another reorganization, dividing its businesses into international, institutional, and retail units. The firm's life, property/casualty, mutual fund, and investment products fell within the retail unit, while group life, 401k and other employee benefit products became part of the institutional unit.

To focus on insurance and financial products, Prudential divested some of its business, including healthcare operations, which it proposed to sell to Aetna for $1 billion. In late 1998, it had announced its intention to pull out of unprofitable Medicare markets, dropping coverage for about 20 percent of its seniors in the SeniorCare program by refusing to renew Medicare-risk contracts in northern and southern California; Maryland; Washington, D.C.; New York; New Jersey; and parts of Florida. Also in 1999, Prudential began rapid global expansion; early that year, it opened a mutual fund company with Mitsui Trust & Banking Co. in Japan, acquired a license to open an office in Poland, and launched new insurance companies in Argentina and the Philippines.

Prudential ranked as the largest life insurer in terms of assets in the United States in 1998. It placed second in net premiums written that year and occupied sixth place in annuity sales during the preceding three years. About 55 percent of the company's earnings came from the sale of insurance, which grew by 21 percent in 1998, while 45 percent came from its investment and securities businesses. As it approached the 21st century, Prudential faced competition not only from a host of domestic giants, including Citigroup, MetLife, and Merrill Lynch, but from the overseas financial service titans as well.

Principal Subsidiaries

Gifford Fong Associates, Inc.; Merrill Lynch Mortgage Corporation; PIC Realty Canada, Ltd,; PRUCO, Inc.; PRICOA International Bank, S.A. (Luxembourg): The Prudential Life Insurance Company, Ltd. (Japan); AMODA, Sdn. Bhd. (Malaysia; 40%); HSG Health Systems Group Limited (Canada); Jennison Associates Capital Corp.; PRICOA Vita S.p.A. (Italy); PRUCO, Inc.; PRUCO Life Insurance Company; Premisys Real Estates Services, Inc.; PRUCO Life Insurance Company of Illinois; Prudential Fund Management Canada Ltd.; Prudential of America General Insurance Company (Canada); Prudential Overseas Funding Corporation N.V. (Netherlands Antilles); U.S. High Yield Management Company; Prudential Realty Securities II, Inc.; Prudential Special Equity Fund (Luxembourg; 47%); PruServicos Participacoes, S.A. (Brazil); Tesseract Corporation; The Prudential Insurance Company of Korea, Ltd.; The Prudential Insurance Company of New Jersey; The Prudential Investment Corporation; The Prudential Life Insurance Company of Arizona; The Prudential Real Estate Affiliates, Inc.; Prudential Mutual Fund Management, Inc.

Further Reading

Carr, William H. A., *From Three Cents a Week ... The Story of The Prudential Insurance Company of America*, Englewood Cliffs, N.J.: Prentice Hall, Inc., 1975.

Eichenwald, Kurt, "Prudential-Bache Chief Quits After Big Losses," *New York Times*, February 14, 1991, p. D1.

Fifty Years the Prudential: The History of a Business, Charged with Public Interest, Newark, N.J.: The Prudential Insurance Company of America, 1927.

Hawkins, Chuck, "Pru Securities Isn't Secure Yet," *Business Week*, September 7, 1992, p. 82.

Miller, Theresa, "Pru's Focus on Distribution," *Best's Review Life/ Health Edition*, February 1999, p. 49.

Sheehan, Robert, "That Mighty Pump, Prudential," *Fortune*, January 1964.

Spiro, Leah Nathans, "What Does Prudential Really Owe?" *Business Week*, February 2, 1998, p. 117.

—Thomas J. Heed
—updated by Carrie Rothburd

Rag Shops, Inc.

111 Wagaraw Road
Hawthorne, New Jersey 07506
U.S.A.
(973) 423-1303
Fax: (973) 427-6568

Public Company
Incorporated: 1984
Employees: 1,150
Sales: $90.6 million (1998)
Stock Exchanges: NASDAQ
Ticker Symbol: RAGS
NAIC: 442299 All Other Home Furnishings Stores;
    45112 Hobby, Toy & Game Stores; 45113 Sewing,
    Needlework, & Piece Goods Stores

Rag Shops, Inc. operates specialty retail stores that sell competitively priced craft and fabric merchandise to consumers who create decorative accessories and sew. Each store offers such craft items as silk flowers, wicker, picture frames, wood products, stitchery, yarn, wearable art, and art and craft supplies. Fabric items include apparel and home decorative fabrics, trimmings, patterns, and sewing notions. Rag Shops stores— known individually under the name ''Rag Shop''—are located in shopping centers; most are in New Jersey or Florida.

Rag Shops Through 1991

The company's origins go back to 1952, when Stanley Berenzweig founded a distribution business called Mobile Fabrics in his Paterson, New Jersey garage. In 1963 he opened his first Rag Shop retail store. A second fabric store had opened by 1980. There were nine in 1983, when Rag Shops added craft items to its product line, and 20 by the end of 1986. By this time crafts and related items had proven so successful that they accounted for about 45 percent of net sales.

Rag Shops' net sales grew from $19 million in fiscal 1987 (the year ended August 27, 1987) to $57.8 million in fiscal

1991, the year the company went public. Annual net income grew from $284,000 to $2.3 million over that period. The company collected $8.8 million in 1991 by the public sale of one-third of its common stock at $6.25 a share. At the end of the fiscal year there were 44 Rag Shops, of which 21 were in New Jersey, 13 in Florida, five in Pennsylvania, four in New York, and one in Maryland. The company's expansion strategy was to grow by expanding within areas from which it already was attracting customers and into contiguous areas, thereby capitalizing on preexisting advertising and name recognition.

Each Rag Shop store was offering about 15,000 fabric and crafts products in 1991. Custom picture framing also was offered in 33 of the stores. The company was selling a wide variety of seasonal merchandise, with special emphasis on the Easter, Halloween, Christmas, and back-to-school seasons. Through their purchases, customers could make many finished products for personal use, gifts, home beautification, and seasonal decoration. Fabrics, for example, could be made into career, leisure, children's, bridal, and special occasion fashions, or draperies, upholstery, and quilts for home use. The company's craft items could be used to create needlepoint and stitchery, personalized hand-painted apparel, floral arrangements, and dolls.

Rag Shops' marketing and merchandising strategy emphasized the sale of multiple products for use by the customers to create a single project. To assist customers in making their own selections and to encourage their purchase of several products, the company's stores displayed finished models incorporating a variety of merchandise in close proximity to where the components were sold. Each of Rag Shops' stores offered at least three craft or sewing classes every week. During each class, participants completed a project using materials purchased from the store at which the class was offered.

Rag Shops had a preferred-customer mailing list of about 540,000 persons to whom it sent direct-mail pieces at least 12 times a year, with a monthly calendar of promotions emphasizing special sale items, seasonal products, and other currently popular merchandise. Fashion shows held periodically at many of the company's stores also were an effective method of attracting customers and generating the purchase of fabrics, patterns, notions, and related merchandise necessary for the customer to create the featured apparel. These shows were later replaced by instructional demonstrations of merchandise held at the sites of charitable organizations, conventions, and schools.

Rag Shops was reported to be placing significant emphasis on home fabrics at this time because the recession was causing people to stay home more and redecorate. The company was planning to spend nearly $2.5 million during the year to promote this category through such means as direct-mail pieces, flyers, and twice-a-year storefront displays dedicated solely to decorative fabrics. Some stores were moving their home fabric departments to the front, and certain locations added recessed lighting and new carpets in fashion colors. The shop-at-home service available at some Rag Shops was to be expanded.

The average Rag Shop store was 7,500 square feet at this time, although one store was as large as 18,000 square feet. The company's 51,000-square-foot leased distribution center in Paterson was later expanded to 85,000 square feet. Corporate headquarters were located in leased space in Hawthorne, New Jersey.

Mixed Results: 1992–97

The number of Rag Shop outlets reached 54 at the end of fiscal 1992. Net sales increased to $73.6 million, and net income reached a record $3 million. A retail performance index by Management Horizons, an industry consultant, ranked the company seventh, with a 31 percent annual revenue growth and a 60 percent average annual profit growth. Rag Shops had been ranked one of the nation's top 200 small companies by *Forbes*.

Rag Shops President Donald G. Hunt told Loretta Roach of *Discount Merchandiser* in November 1993, "Our real growth has taken place in the craft/fun type fabrics. We're pulling back in apparel type fabrics that require the home sewer to sit at the sewing machine, buy a pattern and spend time, which has become a precious commodity now, with so many double wage-earner families. We've moved to home decorator fabrics, crafts, and fun-type fabrics.... We now do a complete decorator fabric business, from draperies to quilting."

Rag Shops had 61 stores at the end of fiscal 1993. The standard store size of 8,500 square feet was slowly being updated to 10,000 or 12,000 square feet, with wide aisles, shopping carts, and displays that invited browsing and creative ideas. New Jersey and Florida remained the focus of store siting. Hunt explained, "There are economies associated with being able to operate stores in clusters. It cuts down on your advertising costs around the markets. It gives you name dominance, and name recognition in these markets and allows you to saturate TV with special promotions."

The home craft category now represented 65 percent of Rag Shops' business. A prototype layout called for new fixturing that would allow the stores to expand their crafts holdings without using more space. Crafts workshops were being held throughout the day, and on Saturdays the stores offered a free workshop for children. Store displays, situated in close proximity to the merchandise used, were showcasing completed projects. Wearable art was one growing category. This included jewelry-making items, stitchery products, fabric painting, yarn, appliques, and other accessories.

Although net sales increased to $84.2 million in fiscal 1993, net income fell to $2 million in what proved to be the beginning of an extended decline in profitability for Rag Shops. New stores accounted for all of the company's sales growth, with sales per square foot actually decreasing from $174 to $166. Accordingly, after the number of Rag Shop outlets reached 66 in early 1994, company management began focusing its efforts on improving the strength of existing stores and increasing sales per square foot of retail space.

The number of Rag Shop outlets peaked at 69 in fiscal 1995, including one in Rhode Island and one in Connecticut. Net sales reached $89.5 million in fiscal 1994 but declined to $86.1 million in fiscal 1995 and $83.8 million in fiscal 1996. Net income declined to $767,000, $542,000, and $520,000, respectively. Company executives took ten percent salary cuts in late 1996 as they sought ways to improve sales. At Rag Shops' annual meeting in January 1997, however, the company reported that sales were increasing for the first time in more than three years, owing in large part to a change in emphasis on its product line, improved technology, and a new marketing strategy.

Rag Shops was opening prototypes of what Michael Aaronson, who became president in 1995, called "bigger, lighter, brighter" stores, with up to 15,000 square feet of selling space, including a 12,000-square-foot outlet in Edgewater, New Jersey, and a 15,000-square-foot unit in Vero Beach, Florida. The additional space was allowing the stores to carry a wider selection of merchandise. More fabrics—such as drapes and slip covers—were to be carried for home decorating than for clothing. Bar-code scanners, installed to monitor sales and inventory accurately, were now in place in 23 stores and were expected to be in all units by midyear. This was expected to free employees from time-consuming inventory control and allow some suppliers to automatically replenish the company's merchandise.

Rag Shops had been mailing circulars to about a million customers 14 times a year. In September 1996, however, it converted from direct-mail marketing to newspaper advertising. The company's new marketing plan called for the chain to place inserts into Sunday newspapers 24 times a year and rely on in-paper advertising the other 28 Sundays each year, thereby reaching three million readers every Sunday. Net sales for Rag Shops in fiscal 1997 climbed to $86.5 million, but net income dropped to $207,000 because of increased expenses attributed to automation and marketing as well as increased payroll costs. Company executives expressed confidence, however, that the enterprise was moving in the right direction.

Rag Shops in 1998

For fiscal 1998 Rag Shops reported net income of $942,000—the first annual increase since 1992—on record sales of $90.6 million. The company paid off its long-term debt of $554,000 during 1998 and tested an automated store-ordering system to help executives do a better job of targeting merchandise. The installation of this system, completed in all stores by March 1999, also would enable individual stores to adapt their stock to local demographics and sales patterns. Speaking to shareholders at the annual company meeting in January 1999, Aaronson said that Rag Shops hoped to grow at a rate of six to eight stores per year for the next three years. At the end of fiscal 1998, there were 66: 33 in New Jersey, 19 in Florida, seven in Pennsylvania, six in New York, and one in Connecticut.

Rag Shops' construction of larger new stores had many practical advantages, Senior Vice-President Evan Berenzweig—son of the chain's founder—told Mike Duff of *Discount Store News* in April 1999. "Most of our customers are women, and a lot of them are mothers," he explained. "They have strollers and shopping carts they want to use, and we have wider aisles to accommodate them. We want to give them an opportunity to get in and out of the store fast." He added, "If you want to identify one macrotrend, it's [being] fast. We want to have product available and fast checkout and fast crafts. Of course, we have craft customers who spend a tremendous amount of time on their projects, but if we want to appeal to more people we have to have crafts that people can do fast."

As seen from the entrance, the new stores were divided evenly between fabrics and crafts. In the past, fabrics had been displayed in the front and crafts in the rear, which was at variance with the chain's sales breakdown, now two-thirds craft items and only one-third fabrics. "We discovered," Berenzweig said, "that, almost comprehensively, our fabric customer is a craft customer, but that's not necessarily true the other way."

Crafts and fabrics were being divided by a promotional aisle that included seasonal and value items, and—in the larger stores—bigger items such as rattan furniture. The front section of both the crafts and fabrics sides also featured seasonal goods. The crafts side also included a growing selection of arts supplies and children's crafts as well as more established crafts segments. On the other side apparel fabrics were given priority, with home-oriented material in the rear and along the walls. Vignettes above fabric displays showed potential uses for the fabrics and included items from the crafts side of the store. By combining items from its various departments, Rag Shops was advertising the breadth of its product line.

A total of 59 of Rag Shops' 66 stores were offering custom framing at the end of fiscal 1998. In the larger stores, framing was being done on the premises instead of at an offsite shop. The chain also was turning out both pre-made and custom-arranged bouquets from its straw flower collections, with selections adapted to local characteristics. Each store had a craft teaching room used for paid instruction, since the company had found that free programs did not attract the quality of teacher needed. This room also was being used for children's parties at which the children were encouraged to make a present for themselves.

Stanley Berenzweig, still chief executive officer of Rag Shops, and his wife, Doris, owned some 43 percent of the company's stock. A share of common stock traded at between $2.12 and $3.75 in fiscal 1998 and was trading at about $2 a share in the summer of 1999. Book value was $5.10 a share and the company had no long-term debt.

Principal Subsidiaries

Mobile Fabrics, Inc.; The Rag Shop, Inc.; RSL, Inc.

Further Reading

Coleman-Lochner, Lauren, "Rag Shops' Strategies Paying Off," *Record-Bergen County,* January 23, 1998, p. B1.

DeMarrais, Kevin G., "Crafting a Comeback," *Record-Bergen County,* January 24, 1997, p. B1.

Duff, Mike, "Rag Shops Plans Slow-Grow Success," *Discount Store News,* February 8, 1999, p. 6.

——, "Rag Shops Takes 'Fast' Track in Rags-to-Riches Story," *Discount Store News,* April 5, 1999, pp. H26–H27.

Geller, Adam, "It's in the Bag," *Bergen Record,* Business Sec., January 28, 1994.

Roach, Loretta, "A Spark of Creativity," *DM/Discount Merchandiser,* November 1993, pp. 88, 90.

Wendlinger, Lisa D., "Rag Shops to Riches: '90s Goal," *HFD/Home Furnishings Daily,* January 7, 1991, pp. 38, 191.

—Robert Halasz

NORMARK Corporation

Rapala-Normark Group, Ltd.

10395 Yellow Circle Drive
Minnetonka, Minnesota 55343
U.S.A.
(612) 933-7060
Fax: (612) 933-0046
Web site: http://www.rapala.com

Private Company
Incorporated: 1960 as Rapala Company
Employees: 50
Sales: $52 million (1998 est.)
NAIC: 42191 Sporting & Recreational Goods & Supplies
   Wholesalers; 33992 Sporting & Athletic Good
   Manufacturing

Rapala-Normark Group, Ltd., through its subsidiary Normark Corporation, markets high quality fishing, hunting, and outdoor sporting goods. Two avid anglers founded the company to distribute a single lure, the Original Floating Rapala, which became the top-selling fishing lure in the world. Many of the company's other products, such as the Rapala Fillet Knife, have earned the respect of outdoor enthusiasts and significant market share as well.

Fabricating Finnish Fishing Lure: 1930s–50s

The Normark story, technically speaking, begins in Finland during the 1930s, with Lauri Rapala. It was a period of widespread economic depression, and Rapala pieced together a living for his family by working as a lumberjack in the winter and a farm hand or commercial fisherman in the summer—hard work either way.

In hope of boosting his fishing income and as well as cutting down on the time and effort spent rebaiting hooks, Rapala began playing with the idea of an artificial lure. He already knew that in schools of minnows the wounded ones, those which wobbled when they swam, were the most likely targets of larger fish. He attempted to duplicate the motion in an artificial minnow. After much trial and error, the undertaking finally paid off.

The lure he produced in 1936 was fabricated from cork, covered with colored tin foil claimed from candy and cheese packets, and sealed with the celluloid backing of photographic film. "This first lure still exists today—it's black on top, gold along its flanks, white on the bottom—just like the minnows of Lake Paijanne," wrote Stephen Dupont in *Crafting of a Legend: The Normark Story.*

The lure dramatically increased Rapala's trout and pike catch. Encouraged, he continued to refine his invention, switching, for example, from cork to pine bark for the body. His luremaking endeavor was sidetracked, however, when Finland was invaded by its towering neighbor to the East. Rapala went off to war for six years, first fighting the Soviet Union and later Nazi Germany.

Once at home, Rapala found that postwar vacationers to Lake Paijanne had heard about his lure and were eager to buy one. A family business emerged. Rapala's four sons, Risto, Ensio, Esko, and Kauko, helped with production, and wife Elma handled the packaging and bookwork. Gradually, the men fabricated devices to mechanize what had been entirely handmade. An old spinning wheel was adapted as a sander and a circular saw was constructed to shape the wood. Lauri continued to be a stickler for accuracy: the action of each of the 1,000 lures they produced during the year was tested in a tank of water or in the lake.

The Rapala family lures made their way to North America by various means during the 1950s. Athletes participating in the 1952 Helsinki Summer Olympic games picked up the lure from a shopkeeper who had begun stocking them following a vacation to Lake Paijanne. Finns who immigrated to or were visiting the United States also helped to create a Rapala lure pipeline.

Minnesota Connection: 1960s

Ron Weber, a Minneapolis-based fishing tackle sales representative, had heard rumors of a prolific "Finlander plug," and, as an avid angler, he was eager to try one. During a frustrating Canadian fishing trip in the summer of 1959, Weber's fishing partner pulled out an unfamiliar lure and tied it on his line. "Suddenly, where there were no fish, there were fish galore," wrote Dupont.

Company Perspectives:

A lightweight lure that no one knew how to use, with a name no one knew how to pronounce. The back room of a south Minneapolis bait-and-tackle shop. A beat-up metal desk. And lots of enthusiasm.

What began as a simple dream in 1959 has evolved into one of the fishing tackle industry's most influential organizations. Based in Minnetonka, Minnesota, with companies in 12 countries and distribution in more than 130 countries, the Rapala-Normark Group is the world's largest fishing lure company, as well as one of the world's largest premium fishing tackle distributors.

Fishing tackle companies have come and some have all but disappeared since 1959, but the Rapala-Normark Group endures.

On his way back to Minneapolis, Weber stopped in Duluth, which was both his home town and home to numerous Finnish immigrants. The Finnish owner of an outdoor clothing store had some Rapalas behind his counter and sold Weber a few. After trying them out for himself, Weber wrote to Lauri Rapala and asked for 500 of his lures. Rapala first had to have the letter translated. Next, he sought help from Helsinki's Foreign Trade Department on how to proceed. In early 1960, Weber received his order.

As the Rapalas tended to matters on their end, Weber convinced his friend and sporting goods storeowner Ray Ostrom to help distribute the lure. Initially named the Rapala Company, the part-time business operated out of Ostrom's store—the men renamed the company Nordic Enterprises before settling on Normark, or ''north land,'' in 1965.

Weber and Ostrom first test-marketed the lure in Minnesota and Wisconsin. Sales were initially slow; the $1.95 price induced sticker shock in retailers accustomed to selling lures for less than a buck.

Even though the Rapala was twice as expensive as popular lures such as the Johnson Silver Spoon, the Jitterbug, and the Lazy Ike, it was well positioned for the changing fishing tackle market. Early Normark sales rep Bill Cullerton, Sr., said in *Crafting of a Legend*, ''The timing was perfect. With new mono line and lighter fishing tackle, the industry needed lighter lures.'' Sales began to pick up.

Normark, now armed with an exclusive North American distribution contract from Rapala, turned to the news media to spread the word about the lure. During the 1960s, Ostrom cultivated relationships with local and national sports and outdoor reporters. The company would also finance fishing films targeting sportsmen's shows and fishing clubs. The company's greatest exposure, however, was generated by a 1962 *Life* magazine article.

A *Life* reporter, in the Twin Cities to cover the newly formed Minnesota Vikings, met Ostrom at a dinner party given by the outdoor editor for the *Minneapolis Tribune*. Ostrom, who just happened to have a couple lures in tow, sparked the reporter's interest in Lauri Rapala's story. ''A Lure the Fish Can't Pass Up,'' hit the news stands in an issue adorned by Marilyn Monroe, shortly after her death. Millions bought the magazine and orders barraged Normark.

Weber and Ostrom could fill only a fraction of the three million requests. Tales of a Rapala black market and a Rapala rental market surfaced, as did copycat plugs. Storeowners paid retail prices just to put the product on their shelves. Weber and Ostrom dropped their other enterprises and devoted themselves full-time to marketing the lure.

The amazing demand for the lure compelled Weber to go to Finland to ask Rapala to increase production. Rapala was overwhelmed: ''There's so many of you and so few of us.'' Weber responded with an offer to finance a small factory.

Once the production problem was solved, Weber set his sight on growth. Two models of a new Rapala lure, the Original Finnish Jigging Minnow, joined the Original Floating Rapala in the U.S. market in 1963. Since the new lure was also intended for ice fishing, Weber and Ostrom began carrying a Finnish-made ice auger.

The company's sales climbed steadily. In 1965 the national trade magazine *Sporting Goods Dealer* named Normark Importer of the Year. The hot-selling Rapala lure was tops in pulling in contest winning fish as well, according to *Field & Stream* magazine.

Once again capitalizing on their knowledge of fishing, in 1967 Weber and Ostrom brought out a fillet knife, one modeled after a well-worn butcher's knife. Weber had to convince Finnish knife maker Lauri Marttiini to take on the task of fabricating the very thin, flexible blade he envisioned. When the Rapala Fish 'N Fillet Knife hit the market, it quickly became a popular item, producing more than 40 percent of Normark revenue for a time.

Throughout the 1960s, U.S. anglers embraced Lauri Rapala's lures, which now included a sinking model called the Countdown. ''Normark Corp. has received some 20,000 voluntary letters testifying to the Rapala's fish-catching ability,'' wrote Schara. Back in Finland, the lure vitalized the region. A branch of Finland's largest bank was established in Rapala's home town, and the president of Finland honored Rapala for his contribution to the economy.

Casting a Wider Net: 1970s

In 1970 Normark and Rapala Oy, the Rapala family company, introduced its first salt water lure, the Rapala Magnum. The feat reflected the level of interdependence the two businesses had developed. ''Weber and Ostrom not only marketed and distributed Rapala lures, they astutely interpreted the needs of American anglers and communicated those needs to the Rapala brothers,'' wrote Dupont. Normark relayed information about species of fish the Rapalas had never seen and clued them into the peculiarities of a market which revolved around producing new and improved products year in and year out.

As demand increased, Lauri's sons upgraded the production facilities with state-of-the-art equipment. Ever mindful of their father's concern with accuracy, each new product, even just size variations of an established lure, faced rigorous design and manufacturing standards.

Meanwhile, Normark broadened its mission to include customer education. *How to Fish a Rapala by the Book* and *How to Clean a Mess of Fish Without Making a Mess of the Fish* advised anglers on how to get the best results from their Normark and Rapala products. Angling tips from professional fishermen filled other books and pamphlets. (Keeping up with the times, educational video tapes were added in the late 1980s, and a web site was established in the 1990s.)

Normark also added compasses, rod racks, clothing, and a variety of knives to the product mix during the 1970s. In 1977 orange-handled Finnish-made Fiskars scissors caught the imagination of homemakers as well as outdoor enthusiasts, helping Normark go on to capture a majority of the U.S. scissors market. The company was the leading scissors seller in North America for about a decade.

Normark's cross-country ski venture proved to be less successful. When introduced in the early 1970s, the Norwegian imports appeared to be a sure winner, but growing competition from downhill ski makers, a couple seasons with meager snowfall, and a shift toward more high-tech gear sideswiped the operation. (Normark exited the business and restructured around 1980, a period of general economic recession in the United States.)

The company succeeded in turning around another one of its operations. Weber and Ostrom purchased the National Expert Bait Company in 1968. The 36-year-old Minneapolis-based lure manufacturer produced high quality spoons, a product which complemented the Rapala line. Interestingly enough, the decision to purchase the manufacturer was also influenced by the Cold War. Weber and Ostrom feared that any aggression against Finland by the U.S.S.R. would cut off their supply of product.

The new lure line lacked the luster of the Rapala. After a decade, Weber made some dramatic changes in the operation. The business was renamed the Blue Fox Tackle Co., relocated to prime Minnesota fishing country, and revived with smart new lures, ones which catered to an industry increasingly fascinated with a scientific approach to fishing.

In 1979 a line of spinner baits designed in conjunction with noted bass angler Roland Martin gave Blue Fox entry into the Deep South. The company followed with the Super Vibrax spinner and Pixee Spoons which gained admirers among salmon and trout anglers in the Pacific Northwest and Alaska.

Changing Times: 1980s–90s

During the early 1980s, many industries experienced flat or falling sales. The fishing tackle business was no exception. Weber and the Rapala brothers hoped to animate the sluggish industry with a new product. The Shad Rap, a project which was shelved when Lauri Rapala died in 1974, was tapped for production. Unfortunately, a potential problem surfaced. If the lure was a big hit, the Rapala brothers would not be able to keep pace with demand. Normark, through its longtime ad agency Car-

michael Lynch, executed an ad campaign which turned the weakness into a strength.

"Beg One, Borrow One or Steal One," proclaimed Shad Rap ads. "When word spread among fishing tackle circles about the Shad Rap's ability to catch fish, as well as its unavailability, all hell broke loose," wrote Dupont. Normark had to allocate lures among retailers. Shad Rap backorders hit a million, and lure rental and black markets surfaced. Normark had prepared to ward off knockoffs by means of new packaging which featured Lauri Rapala's image and the phrase "Hand Tuned, Tank Tested."

Times were good. Combined sales for Normark and its affiliated companies in Canada, Great Britain, Sweden, and Finland had hit the $40 million mark. (Weber and Ostrom held stock in the foreign operations as individuals, but not through Normark Corporation.) Ostrom retired from Normark in 1984, leaving the company in the hands of cofounder Weber.

Weber and his new management team faced a number of challenges during the later half of the 1980s and into the early 1990s. The marketplace had changed: angler numbers had dropped and mass merchandisers replaced the independent bait-and-tackle shop as the primary point of purchase. Normark worked to both satiate giant retailers' voracious appetite for product and maintain customer loyalty.

The company's product portfolio gained new accessories, including blade sharpeners, fillet gloves, and digital scales. The Rapala Fishing Club, established in 1988, offered angler members opportunities to share fish stories and fishing tactics as well as field test new lures.

The period was also marked by the entry of a new generation of Rapalas into leadership positions. Jarmo Rapala, the first professional businessman to lead Rapala Oy, broadened the company's international presence and tightened the relationship with Normark. In 1990, Weber and Rapala moved to consolidate the two companies as Rapala-Normark Group Ltd.

Lure introduction, of course, continued amid all the changes. Breaking from the traditional balsa wood lure, the first hard plastic Rapala was introduced in 1989. Bass and walleye anglers loved the Rattlin' Rapala, and the way was paved for additional plastic offerings. Blue Fox products also created some excitement in the market during the later half of the 1980s thanks to a line of fish scents and a soft plastic lure, the Foxee Jig.

By 1991 Normark had sold more than 150 million Rapala brand lures in the United States, and the offerings continued to grow during the first half of the decade. The Rapala Husky Jerk, another plastic rattler launched in 1996, created the next sensation. Southern bass anglers, walleye, northern pike, and inshore saltwater anglers all took to the suspending jerkbait, according to Dupont, while the *Wall Street Journal* took note of its widespread success. In 1997 the Risto Rap, a deep diving castable lure—one developed by Ron Weber's son Craig, a Normark employee since his teenage years—was honored by the American Sportsfishing Association.

Future Catches

The 225-millionth Rapala lure was expected to be produced sometime in 1999. Jarmo Rapala credited the lure's continuing success to its versatility. "It's as effective on Florida bass as it is on tarpon located along the west coast of Africa," he said in an early 1999 company news release.

In addition to racking up impressive sales over the years, Rapala lures continued to bring in world record fish, 61 as of March 1999, the most for any lure. Continued commitment to quality and innovation carried on by a new generation will most likely keep anglers pulling in record catches well into the next millennium.

Principal Subsidiaries

Normark Corporation.

Further Reading

Anderson, Dennis, "Finn's Knifes a Steel Deal," *St. Paul Pioneer Press*, April 29, 1983.

——, "One Man's Passion," *Star Tribune* (Minneapolis), May 9, 1999, p. 18C.

"Buy a Rapala, Get a Big Fish Free," Minnetonka, Minn.: Normark Corporation, June 8, 1999.

"Cashing in on the Cold," *Corporate Report Minnesota*, December 1973, pp. 26–28.

Cothran, Thomas C., "The Rapala Lure: the Customers Always Bite," *Corporate Report Minnesota*, November 1984, pp. 72–73.

Dupont, Stephen, *Crafting of a Legend: the Normark Story*, Minnetonka, Minn.: Normark Corporation, 1998.

"The Fishing Lure of the 20th Century?" Minnetonka, Minn.: Normark Corporation, March 1999.

Peterson, Susan E., "Don Addy Tackles the Top Spot at Normark Corp.," *Star Tribune* (Minneapolis), July 6, 1992.

Schara, Ron, "Finnish lure Is Hottest Fishing Item in U.S., *Minneapolis Tribune*, May 11, 1969, pp. 4–5.

——, "Hooked by Rapala," *Star Tribune* (Minneapolis), October 11, 1995, p. 10C.

——, "Luck Isn't All That for Lure Makers," *Star Tribune* (Minneapolis), August 13, 1997, p. 8C.

——, "Lure of the Rapala Spurs Angler," *Star Tribune* (Minneapolis), September 4, 1991, p. 1C.

—Kathleen Peippo

Red Wing Shoe Company, Inc.

314 Main Street
Riverfront Centre
Red Wing, Minnesota 55066-2337
U.S.A.
(651) 388-8211
Fax: (651) 388-7415
Web site: http://www.redwingshoe.com

Private Company
Incorporated: 1905
Employees: 2,500
Sales: $300 million (1998 est.)
NAIC: 316213 Men's Footwear Manufacturing; 316214
    Women's Footwear Manufacturing; 316211 Rubber &
    Plastics Footwear Manufacturing; 316219 Other
    Footwear Manufacturing

Red Wing Shoe Company, Inc. manufactures durable and comfortable footwear tailored to the needs of specific occupational and recreational activities, from farming to hunting and hiking. The company's brands include Red Wing, Irish Setter, Vasque, and WORX. The Sweasy family of Red Wing, Minnesota, solely own Red Wing Shoe. Until the 1970s, Red Wing's reputation rested primarily on a wide variety of footwear marketed as "work shoes," emphasizing their practical applications in the workplace. By the mid-1980s, however, as U.S. workers moved increasingly out of industrial and agricultural sectors into service related jobs, the company's scope changed. Under the direction of a new president, William J. Sweasy, and a new generation of management, the company's emphasis shifted from "work shoes" to "shoes for work," a slight semantic change that underscored the company's new commitment to innovative lines of lighter, more comfortable footwear developed to accommodate new work-oriented and recreational needs. By the end of the 1990s, Red Wing sold more than three million pairs of shoes and boots per year, through a worldwide network of more than 4,200 dealers. Within the U.S. market, this network included about 400 Red Wing Shoe Stores (of which about 160 were company owned). About 15 percent of overall revenues were generated from sales outside the United States, in more than 100 countries worldwide.

Early History

Red Wing traces its history to 1905, when German immigrant Charles Beckman closed his retail shoe store and organized the Red Wing Shoe Company with 14 other investors. The young company initially manufactured 110 pairs of shoes per ten-hour day. The brand's steady growth stemmed from the booming industries of farming, logging, mining, blacksmithing, and railroading that represented largely untapped footwear markets. Red Wing tailored its shoes to the demands of specific customer groups, offering a wide range of shoe sizes and widths to ensure fit, and a constantly growing line of specialized products with different capabilities.

Red Wing innovation in its early years reflected efforts to shod diverse markets. In 1908, the brand offered welt-constructed shoes featuring a leather strip attached to the shoe upper and sewn into the sole. The enhanced comfort and durability of the shoes particularly appealed to farmers, Red Wing's primary customers at the time. Continued demand justified the construction of a four-story factory with a daily output of 450 pairs, four times the 1906 capacity. Then in 1912, the company added the black and brown "Chief" line, commonly known as "the farmer's shoe." In addition to the traditional welt construction of earlier farming shoes, the Chief featured specially tanned, manure-proof leather for longer durability.

Numerous other shoe designs ensured the company's continued success. Red Wing began fulfilling military needs with the onset of World War I, manufacturing in 1918 the regulation Munson U.S. Army Last, designed to "fit all feet" with maximum comfort and durability. After the war, the Munson remained a top seller and influenced other popular shoe designs for over 50 years. In the 1930s, Red Wing moved into a steel toe line designed to provide added toe protection in high risk jobs. That line retained its popularity and developed into several models, one of which even became popular during the punk counterculture fad of the 1970s. Also in the 1930s, the company developed an oil-resistant, highly comfortable design named the "Oil King" boot and adopted primarily by oil field workers.

For slightly more elite circles of the era, Red Wing also introduced a men's dress or riding boot dubbed the "Aristo," which served as a model for a women's line of shoes and boots.

Meanwhile, the company's early decades were also marked by significant management changes. In 1911 Beckman retired, with stockholder C.H. Boxrud taking over as president. J.R. Sweasy, who had joined the company as a "cost man" in 1914, was elected general manager in 1918. Two years later Sweasy gained control of the company through stock purchases. After Boxrud died in 1921, Sweasy became president of Red Wing Shoe.

The development of rubber added significantly to Red Wing's success in its early decades. In the early 1930s, Sweasy introduced the rubber cord sole to replace the leather norm. His gamble with the new material proved both lucrative and trendsetting. The Gro Cord soles and Goodyear heels used in Red Wing shoes set the standard for a shoe industry that grew to depend almost exclusively on synthetic materials.

In addition to durability, lowered costs figured into Red Wing's new materials. During the Great Depression, synthetic materials helped produce an extremely cost-effective shoe. Model No. 99, named after its price of 99 cents, kept the factory in production during the financial downswing.

Red Wing continued to grow at a healthy rate, and after World War II the company reached national and eventually international markets. War mandated unprecedented volume, as the U.S. government contracted hundreds of combat shoes manufactured to regulation specifications in 239 different sizes and widths. By 1949, when William D. Sweasy took over as company president following the death of his father, Red Wing had proven its reliability in meeting urgent demand under tight supervision. Sweasy turned that strength to civil ends, introducing a company reorganization to place greater responsibility on department heads and develop teams of management specialists in every department. Sweasy also initiated a new distribution strategy in which Red Wing retail stores would open on the West Coast and move east over time.

Reorganization paid off quickly. Record profits were achieved in 1952, largely attributable to the No. 877 Irish Setter Sport Boot, which continued to assure Red Wing a strong position in the competitive boot market. The Irish Setter's landslide success was partly responsible for Red Wing's introduction of its Vasque outdoor division in 1965. That division capitalized on the hiking boot craze of the 1970s and went on to include lightweight hiking boots and walking shoes in the 1980s and 1990s. Meantime, Arlo "Ole" Jensen became company president in 1972, with Sweasy becoming chairman of the board.

Shifting Focus, New Products: 1980s

After continued growth through the 1960s and 1970s, Red Wing responded to trends in market research, changing many of its marketing strategies and brand lines. In an October 1, 1984, *Footwear News* article, Tom McConnell, Red Wing product manager, identified three trends affecting the company: a shift from a rural to a metropolitan workplace; the replacement of a blue-collar workforce with a gray-collar or service-related one; and rising numbers of women in the workforce. To service these new markets, Red Wing changed its emphasis and its motto, from "work shoes" to "shoes for work." While the company would continue to offer work and sports boots, product development and marketing efforts in the 1980s increasingly focused on those markets promising the most growth, including footwear for such professions as computer operators, food service technicians, health care workers, and security personnel.

Red Wing's shift in marketing strategy was paralleled by a new corporate tone prompted by an increasingly younger generation of management. In 1984 William J. Sweasy, Jr., assumed the role of president after Jensen retired from the post. Sweasy represented the third generation of his family to serve as a Red Wing executive; his father, William Sweasy, remained CEO. The 33-year-old president ushered in an era of active strategic planning, greater communications, increased line diversity, and new personnel. "Before, the upper management team operated intuitively; they shot from the hip, so to speak," noted one company spokesperson in a 1986 *Footwear News* article. The article emphasized that overall company spirit was not critical of the old management, but favored the new approach in light of changed and emerging business opportunities. In August 1989, William Sweasy, Jr., became the first company executive from outside the Twin Cities area elected to chair the Better Business Bureau of Minnesota, representing an honor for Red Wing Shoe Company and its new leader.

New management style and brand image also brought new products to Red Wing. Special attention was paid to women's comfort footwear. While more than 40 million women held jobs involving substantial standing or walking in the mid-1980s, Tom McConnell told *Footwear News* that "most resources have simply remade men's styles on a scaled-down last." In response, Red Wing introduced Lady Red Wings, incorporating safety toes and lightweight urethane soles in a more feminine, less cumbersome line of shoes. McConnell projected sales of approximately 250,000 pairs, retailing at $40 and up.

In the 1980s, Red Wing also developed its Vasque Outdoor Footwear division, which produced aesthetically appealing walking shoes under the Vasque brand name. While earlier walking shoes had often sacrificed cosmetics for hi-tech features used in running shoes—rubbers, bottoms packages, heel counters, and lacing systems—Red Wing emphasized casual, multipurpose walking shoes in attractive designs. Art Kenyon, divisional manager for Vasque in 1988, told *Footwear News* "the consumer today really is concerned with cosmetically fine footwear, boots that can function and still look nice." In the early 1990s, Vasque also benefited from the renewed popularity of hiking boots, sales of which had been declining since the 1970s. Despite the downward sales trend, Vasque had continued to create heavy hiking boots for wilderness excursions as well as a variety of lighter styles for casual walkers and fashion customers. Discussing the company's ready position at the time of the hiking boot resurgence, Kenyon—who had by 1991 become president of Vasque—observed: "We came from the mountain down to the mainstream," adding that "the others came up from the gymnasium," in reference to competition from such athletic footwear companies as Nike, Reebok, and New Balance. In 1990 Vasque introduced Kids Klimbers, a line of hiking footwear for children, featuring a "variable fit child growth system" to accommodate quickly growing feet for an extra six months on average, and also incorporating children's tastes into shoe design. The division's hiking boot product line became the fastest-growing segment of the Red Wing Shoe Company during the early 1990s. In 1993 Vasque launched its first line of sports sandals, responding to a popular trend during that time.

In the work shoe arena, Red Wing also explored new directions. Following the demands of consumers who often wore athletic shoes outside the workplace, the company introduced steel toe athletic shoes—two safety-style athletic shoes in black and white. In addition, the company moved toward work shoes made from lighter materials and softer leather. "Our consumers are saying, make it soft but tough," explained Andy Thompson, advertising and promotions manager of Red Wing, in a 1988 *Footwear News* article. Red Wing also developed a group of barnyard acid resistant shoes geared for the farm industry and a "decathlon" sole made from a durable, lightweight, shock resistant, and oil resistant material.

Red Wing's new products were supported with new marketing initiatives. Lady Red Wings appeared in a TV ad campaign that was second only to Acme Boot Co. in terms of market saturation, according to McConnell. Premiering in October 1984, the commercials were computer animated to lend a contemporary feeling to the new line. Red Wing also ran a series of print advertisements featuring a top model in *McCall's, Women's Day,* and *Mademoiselle* magazines and promoting the image of an up-to-date, attractive, and fashionable Red Wing clientele.

In the late 1980s, the company began a restructuring of its retail division in order to gain exposure and market penetration. In May 1986 Wes Thies, retail division manager, outlined a twofold strategy in *Footwear News.* The company's object was to expand the existing specialty store concept and to introduce three prototypes geared to various consumer demographics. The first prototype was aimed at smaller markets with populations between 30,000 and 60,000. The units were designed with a sales area in front and shoe repair shop in back and targeted Red Wing's blue-collar consumers.

Red Wing also emphasized the use of a company newsletter as a marketing tool. The "Red Wing's Shoe News & Views," published monthly, helped a 40-member sales staff communicate product news and company policies with over 6,000 stores.

While the Red Wing newsletter addressed retailers, the company moved to develop more effective means of communicating brand awareness to the public. With the advent of desktop computer power and database marketing, age-old advertising techniques were losing their effectiveness. Stan Rapp, president of CRC Consulting Group in New York, told attendees of the 1992 All-Industry Marketing (AIM) Conference that marketing efforts had to be increasingly individualized as mass advertising rapidly became obsolete. He noted that shoe companies needed to micromarket and draw consumers into a feedback loop by fostering two-way, relationship marketing. In its own variation on such techniques, Red Wing launched a television campaign in the early 1990s in which it sought to foster a relationship with consumers by providing a toll-free number. The commercial claimed that "our shoes don't wear out," providing consumer testimonials and toll-free purchasing information. In addition, all customers were sent a note thanking them for their business and a form to rate their salesperson. After six months, each customer received another form to rate the shoes' performance, strengthening a personalized, two-way marketing dynamic.

Red Wing's efforts to adapt to changing markets also included greater emphasis on international growth. By 1990 several brands were being distributed in over 80 countries. Despite the intricacies of dealing with currency fluctuations and of identifying elusive, foreign trends, the market for U.S. footwear exports offered substantial growth potential for Red Wing. Palmer Beebe, one executive instrumental in setting up Red Wing's international department, moved on to run Team America, an export business handling footwear for a consortium of U.S. companies. "U.S. footwear is underexported," Beebe claimed in a July 1991 *Footwear News* article.

Red Wing faced pressing issues regarding employee health insurance as it entered the 1990s. With medical costs skyrocketing, the company confronted several challenges. In 1992 the company encountered astronomical expenses for worker's compensation insurance, a burden that prompted Red Wing—and other Minnesota companies—to look at other states with cheaper policies for future expansion. Even though Red Wing earned a 25 percent discount in 1992 for the job-classification quoted rate, for a positive safety record, premiums still increased 41 percent from 1988 to 1992. In an effort to ease such burdens, the 1992 state legislature changed some benefits and gave broad authority to the Department of Labor and Industry to cut overall costs by 16 percent. Later that year, Rich Chalmers, vice-president of human resources at Red Wing, collaborated with Ron Schiemann, a Minnesota entrepreneur, to conceive a healthcare purchasing group designed to improve the delivery of healthcare and reduce costs for ten employers, including Red Wing Shoe, Riedell Shoes Inc., and the City of Red Wing. According to the plan, participating employers would be self insured for a given dollar amount, beyond which reinsurance would take effect. The Chalmers/Schiemann plan was just one of several healthcare measures that Red Wing considered to best cover its employees.

1990s and Beyond

In 1988 Red Wing Shoe Company moved its company headquarters to the company owned St. James Hotel/Riverfront Centre, located on the Mississippi River in downtown Red Wing (the St. James Hotel had been built in 1875 and renovated in 1977). In 1991 Sweasy, Jr., added the CEO position to his title of president.

As a whole, the U.S. shoe manufacturing industry produced only one-fourth as many shoes in 1994 as it did in 1968. Bucking this industry trend, Red Wing Shoe continued throughout the 1990s to make most of its shoes and boots in the United States. Some products were made in Mexico and China, with the entire Vasque line produced overseas. When the company sought to expand its production capacity in the early 1990s, however, the company looked outside of the City of Red Wing. In 1994 Red Wing Shoe added to its two production facilities in its namesake city through the purchase of shoe factories in Potosi, Missouri, and Danville, Kentucky. The Potosi plant was earmarked for production of a new Red Wings for Women product line, which was established in 1994. At mid-decade, Sweasy, Jr., handed the presidential post to Joseph Goggin, remaining chairman and CEO himself. Goggin had been with the company for nearly 30 years, serving as chief financial officer prior to becoming president.

In 1999 Red Wing Shoe restructured into brand-centered divisions in order to better focus on its customers and to aid the company's international expansion efforts. The Red Wing division offered premium work-oriented footwear, including steel toe, rugged work, work casual, service, and women's wear product lines. The Irish Setter division centered on hunting and sports boots, while Vasque focused on the footwear needs of hikers and backpackers. A fourth division, the WORX brand, had been launched in 1998 and offered a line of moderately priced work shoes and boots. The WORX line was produced overseas, and the lower price of the line allowed the company to pursue different markets and distribution channels than that of the flagship Red Wing brand, the handling of which was limited to protect the trade areas of existing dealers. The WORX brand could thus be distributed to a wider range of retailers, sold via mail order, and sold directly to companies.

Also in 1999 the Vasque division entered into a strategic alliance with Marmot Mountain Ltd. that, according to Red Wing Shoe, "will share key operational, logistical, delivery and information-support systems . . . [to] create broader opportunities in global brand development, increased customer service levels, and progressive information systems solutions." That year also saw Red Wing Shoe open a flagship retail store in the Mall of America, located in Bloomington, Minnesota, and the largest shopping mall in the United States, boasting of 43 million visitors a year. The company hoped to educate and ultimately convert shoppers to its premium shoe and boot brands through this store, which featured a multimedia interpretive center with information on the company's history, products, and manufacturing process. Roger Bunn, vice-president and general manager of retail at Red Wing, hoped the store would result in Red Wing converts. He told the *Minneapolis Star Tribune,* "We feel very strongly that one of the hidden benefits of buying Red Wing boots is the construction, the craftsmanship, the fact that we control all processes in Red Wing. We're not real sure that most of the buying public is even aware of those benefits. We needed to find a way to send out the message that there's a reason why to buy the boots."

At the turn of the century Red Wing Shoe offered more than 180 styles of shoes and boots and 120 shoe sizes and widths for men and women. The company's two factories in Red Wing produced about 10,000 pairs of shoes daily, with about 12,000 pairs produced in the plants in Missouri and Kentucky. With its new divisional structure in place, Red Wing Shoe seemed likely to continue its successful promotion of high quality footwear.

Principal Subsidiaries

S.B. Foot Tannery; St. James Hotel/Riverfront Centre.

Principal Divisions

Red Wing Brand; Vasque Brand; Irish Setter Brand; WORX Brand.

Further Reading

Francis, Lorna R., "Strong Gains Reported in Steel Toe Athletics; Work and Safety Shoes," *Footwear News,* November 14, 1988, p. 4.

——, "Work and Safety Shoes Make Nick in Fashion Scene; Boot Industry," *Footwear News,* November 3, 1986, p. 26.

"Health Care Relief Plan to Unfold in Red Wing," *Business Dateline,* July 13, 1992, sec. 1, p. 1.

Howard, Tammi, "Footwear Sources Jump on Newsletter Bandwagon; Marketing Tools," *Footwear News,* May 26, 1986, p. 12.

——, "Red Wing Giant Waking Up to Get Place in the Sun; Marketing; Shoe Industry," *Footwear News,* May 26, 1986, p. 52.

——, "Red Wing Shifts Marketing to Service-Related Fields," *Footwear News,* October 1, 1984, p. 17.

"How the Once Ugly Duckling Was Turned into a Swan; Walking Shoes," *Footwear News,* April 11, 1988, p. S2.

Marvin, Patrice Avon, and Nicholas Curchin Vrooman, *Heart and Sole: A Story of the Red Wing Shoe Company,* Red Wing, Minn.: Red Wing Shoe Company, 1986, 293 p.

Meyers, Mike, "Proving a Negative Positively Impossible, Especially When It's About NAFTA Impact," *Minneapolis Star Tribune,* May 31, 1993, p. D1.

Moore, Janet, "A Giant Step for Red Wing Shoe," *Minneapolis Star Tribune,* July 26, 1999, p. 1D.

Myers, Greg, "These Boots Are Made for Walkin'," *Corporate Report Minnesota,* December 1996, pp. 24, 26–29.

"Red Wing Shoe Co. Attributes 87 Years of Success to One Word: Service," Red Wing, Minn.: Red Wing Shoe Company, Inc., 1992.

Rooney, Ellen, "Vasque to Celebrate Silver Anniversary," *Footwear News,* October 9, 1989, p. 15.

St. Anthony, Neal, "Worker's Comp Irks Blue-Collar Employers; Above-Average Rates Frustrate Companies," *Minneapolis Star Tribune,* November 30, 1992, p. D1.

Seckler, Valerie, "Micromarketing Puts Focus on Individuals; Footwear Marketing," *Footwear News,* May 18, 1992, p. 2.

Sicherman, Al, "Sole Asylum: A Tribute to Red Wings, the Shoes That Work," *Minneapolis-St. Paul Magazine,* May 1994, pp. 54+.

Underwood, Elaine, "The Competition Is Stepping Up for Hiking Boots," *Chicago Tribune,* September 9, 1991, p. C6.

"Vasque Debuts Line of Kids' Hiking Boots; Red Wing Shoe Co. Vasque Outdoor Footwear Div.," *Footwear News,* November 12, 1990, p. 23.

Wanger, Diane, and Bob Wanger, "Servicing the Feet of America," *Leather,* July 1996, p. 19.

Watters, Susan, "Makers Hedge Dollar Bets to Build Export Business; Fluctuating Foreign Currency Deters U.S. Footwear Companies from Exporting," *Footwear News,* July 8, 1991, p. 30.

Wilner, Rich, "Resources Set to Put Sport Sandals in Overdrive," *Footwear News,* November 9, 1992, p. 1.

Youngblood, Dick, "If the Shoe Fits, in All Likelihood It's a Red Wing Product; Work Boot Is Key to 93-Year-Old Minnesota Company's Success," *Minneapolis Star Tribune,* April 20, 1998, p. 2D.

—Kerstan Cohen
—updated by David E. Salamie

Restoration Hardware, Inc.

15 Koch Road
Corte Madera, California 94925
U.S.A.
(415) 924-1005
(888) 243-9720
Fax: (415) 927-9133
Web site: http://www.restorationhardware.com

Public Company
Incorporated: 1980
Employees: 2,200
Sales: $209.4 million (1998)
Stock Exchanges: NASDAQ
Ticker Symbol: RSTO
NAIC: 44413 Hardware Stores; 44211 Furniture Stores;
   442299 All Other Home Furnishings Stores; 454110
   Mail-Order Houses

Restoration Hardware, Inc. sells over 5,000 assorted items to restore old homes and provide its customers with replicas of traditional furniture, cabinets, lighting, bath items, tools, gardening equipment, books, clothing, amusements, and other miscellaneous merchandise. The company sells these pricey items in over 70 retail stores in its main California market and 24 other states, Washington, D.C., and Vancouver, Canada. Customers also can order from a colorful catalog. Unlike many firms, Restoration Hardware does not use market research but relies mainly on the judgment of founder Stephen Gordon to decide what to sell. If he likes it, the stores sell it. This fast-growing chain appeals to educated and successful baby boomers seeking to recreate a nostalgic home environment based on traditional family values.

Origins and Early History

Stephen Gordon, Restoration Hardware's founder, was born in 1951 in Plattsburgh, New York. Although raised in a middle-class family, he was inspired by successful families that vaca-tioned in the nearby Adirondacks. During the Vietnam War, he attended Drew University and participated as a campus radical, while harboring ambivalent feelings about the establishment. "I had such conflict," recalled Gordon in the January 25, 1999 *New Yorker*. "Part of me had this incredibly ambitious side that I was afraid of expressing."

After graduating with a B.A. at Drew University and an M.A. in psychology from Humboldt State University, Gordon became a counselor in Eureka, California. In 1979 he left his psychology career to restore a rundown home in Eureka. To return the Victorian home to its former splendor and transform it into a bed and breakfast, Gordon searched diligently but in vain for good quality furnishings and accessories. "Nearly impossible to find," said Gordon in the March 12, 1999 *Salt Lake Tribune*. His frustration after looking through antique and hardware stores led him to start his own business. First, he worked out of his library to provide items to others hoping to fix up historic homes.

Then in 1980 Gordon opened in Eureka his first retail store specializing in hard-to-find items that tended to be rather expensive. He sought out not only hardware items but also any older products that he felt were interesting. David Brooks in the *New Yorker* said, "Gordon has ransacked his childhood tactile memories and turned them into nostalgic inventory." For example, he sold replicas of a chair his third-grade teacher had used.

"Early on, Stephen Gordon perceived that customers wanted more from him than an assortment of hardware," according to a company fact sheet. "They were looking for a way of life. . . . Tradition that wasn't stodgy, a hip outlook without being trendy."

Making shopping fun was part of Gordon's plan from the beginning. Hence, he chose items such as Moon Pies, described in his catalog as a "sinfully delicious American treat for generations," the metal Slinky toy made in the 1940s, and glass marbles complete with a rule book on the traditional children's game.

Gordon organized his stores much differently than most retail outlets, where many varieties of a single product were located in one section. Instead, Gordon's stores had several rooms or areas centered on different themes: living room, garden area, library, bedroom, bath area, and foyer and hardware rooms.

After his Eureka store proved successful, Gordon in 1985 opened two stores in the San Francisco Bay area. "If we could make it in Eureka, where disposable income isn't king," said Gordon in a company chronology, "I knew there was opportunity." In 1989 he followed up with three more stores in the Bay area.

Major Growth in the 1990s

After running stores in California in the 1980s, Gordon with the help of outside investors opened new stores in southern California, Phoenix, and Portland by 1995. With only five stores in operation in 1994, Restoration Hardware's retail sales were $4.2 million. The same year, Gordon finally began delegating part of the firm's management by hiring Thomas Christopher, a former executive for Pier 1 Imports and Barnes and Noble, as executive vice-president, chief operating officer, and director. Thomas Low, formerly with Home Express, was hired as Restoration Hardware's senior vice-president and chief financial officer in 1995. Revenues jumped to $13.2 million in 1995.

In 1996 Restoration Hardware opened its first store east of Phoenix in the new Somerset North mall in Oakland County in metro Detroit. "We're tickled pink to get into the Somerset project—it's a special place to be," said Thomas Christopher in the May 19, 1996 *Detroit News*. "I've always had great success in the Detroit market [previously working for Pier 1 Imports and Barnes & Noble] . . . I've had my sights on getting a Restoration Hardware in Detroit since I joined the company. Our customer is a homeowner, over age 35, with a college degree and a fairly good household income. If you look at the demographics of (the Detroit) market, Oakland County most closely matches the profile."

The firm in 1996 also opened new stores in the Town Center Plaza near Kansas City; Woodland Hills near Los Angeles; the Old Orchard Shopping Center in Skokie, Illinois; Virginia; and Texas. When Restoration Hardware in 1996 opened its first Denver store in the Park Meadows mall, Mary Beth Jenkins, a Denver retail consultant, said in the July 3, 1996 *Denver Post* that the firm "is a new, cutting edge tenant, and the fact that Denver will add this to its list of retailers puts it on the map." Restoration Hardware in October 1996 opened its 15th store in the Galleria in St. Louis. The firm tripled its 1995 revenues to reach $39.7 million in 1996.

In 1997 Restoration Hardware opened 21 new stores, including several in the South and East. Most featured about 5,000 specific items displayed in 7,500 square feet of space. Revenues for 1997 were $97 million, with 41 stores in operation at the end of the year. Founder Steve Gordon in the February 1997 *Home Improvement Market* said, "If I was forced to describe Restoration Hardware as home fashion or interior design shops, I would say home fashions in a corny sort of way."

On June 19, 1998 Restoration Hardware began selling its common stock for $19 a share on the NASDAQ using the symbol RSTO. The firm's initial public offering raised almost $75 million.

The company in 1998 also began offering its products through catalog sales. Marta Benson, a 1984 philosophy graduate from Wesleyan College who headed Restoration Hardware's catalog division, said in the January 25, 1999 issue of the *New Yorker* that, "I'm proud of being a merchant." After seeing the movie *The English Patient,* Benson said she thought "it was so moving and so beautiful, and I thought, all I do is sell stuff. But I'm reconciled to it, because I'm selling stuff that has meaning."

According to the *New Yorker* author, that same message of Restoration Hardware's social meaning was captured in a 1998 video made for possible investors. Using images from the 1940s and 1950s, the video proclaimed, "Lurking in our collective unconscious, among images of Ike, Donna Reed, and George Bailey, is the very clear sense that things were once better made, that they mattered a little more." But with postwar prosperity, Americans became obsessed with consumption and big stores selling plastic merchandise. The video continued, "The retail environment came to reflect this mentality—more square footage, more, more, more. Then, one day, the generation used to having everything recoiled, and became the generation searching for something."

In 1998 Restoration Hardware acquired The Michaels Furniture Company of Sacramento, California, formerly an independent vendor. "For a number of years, we both admired and successfully sold the Michaels brand of Mission furniture in our stores," stated Restoration Hardware's 1998 annual report. Michael Vermillion had started his company over 25 years earlier by hand making furniture in his garage. The two firms planned to introduce a new line of jointly designed furniture in 1999.

In 1999 Restoration Hardware opened an East Coast distribution center/warehouse in the Marshfield Business Park in Essex, a Baltimore suburb. The firm leased 276,000 square feet from UPS Properties for seven years. The new facility started with 40 employees but planned to have 100 in six months.

As the 1990s ended, Gordon continued many of the hands-on tasks he had assumed from the company's beginnings. For example, he continued to write most of the descriptions found on cards by each store item and in the catalog. For his miniature Allagash River Canoe, priced $39 in the summer 1999 catalog, Gordon wrote, "There are few memories as dear to me as those associated with my first week-long canoe trip on the Allagash

River in Maine. . . . Our small-scale replica is beautifully executed and true to form. Ply the rivers of your mind.''

Gordon sometimes featured historical details on his product descriptions. For example, he wrote how Willis Alfred in the early 1900s created the Winged Weeder tool to make gardening easier for his four daughters. Gordon told how *The Hardy Boys* series of mystery novels, popular when many baby boomers were growing up, had been started back in the 1920s.

Restoration Hardware's appeal in these and other items was not just usefulness and rugged quality, but also a strong sense of family togetherness and nostalgia. ''Memory-provoking stocking stuffers,'' said a customer in the December 21, 1998 *Business Week*.

Restoration Hardware found success in selling to both men and women. Unlike most housewares stores, men accounted for about 30 percent of Restoration Hardware's sales. Analyst Dave Ricci at Chicago's William Blair & Company noted in *Business Week* that ''other stores are focused on tabletop or kitchen. That's not as appealing to men. Restoration Hardware combines tabletop with nickel-plated hammers.'' In 1998 furniture and lighting brought in 43 percent of the firm's sales. Other categories were discovery items, books, and accessories (23 percent), hardware and housewares (17 percent), bath and bedroom (nine percent), and garden and other items (eight percent).

On January 30, 1999 Restoration Hardware operated 15 stores in California and 50 others in New York, Florida, Texas, Utah, Arizona, Oregon, Alabama, Colorado, Connecticut, Georgia, Illinois, Kansas, Louisiana, Massachusetts, Michigan, Minnesota, Missouri, New Jersey, North Carolina, Pennsylvania, Tennessee, Virginia, Washington, the District of Columbia, and Vancouver, British Columbia.

In 1999 the firm's finances showed mixed results. After two quarters ending on July 31, 1999, Restoration Hardware recorded $114 million in net sales, up 57.7 percent from the same period in 1998. However, its stock price had declined—from over $36 a year earlier to about $8.50 on August 12, 1999. That caused several brokers to downgrade their assessment of Restoration Hardware, thus no longer recommending that investors buy the firm's stock.

However, Stephen Gordon, Restoration Hardware's CEO and chairman, intended to expand the chain to about 95 stores by the end of 1999. Thomas Christopher, who replaced Gordon as president of Restoration Hardware in 1998, predicted the chain would peak at 200 stores. ''While we've evolved, we haven't strayed from our roots,'' said Gordon in a company chronology. ''We're a home furnishings store with a hardware heart.''

Further Reading

''Blame Boomers for Boom in Renovation,'' *Salt Lake Tribune*, March 12, 1999, p. B2.

Brooks, David, ''Acquired Taste,'' *New Yorker*, January 25, 1999, pp. 36–41.

''The Business of Bliss, It's Hip! It's Hot! It's Hardware!,'' *House & Garden*, March 1997, pp. 32, 36.

Chaplin, Heather, ''Past? Perfect!,'' *American Demographics*, May 1999, pp. 68–69.

Faust, Fred, ''Fixture Mixture Hardware Store Puts Its Handle on the Galleria,'' *St Louis Post-Dispatch*, October 9, 1996, p. 8C.

Lambert, Cheryl Ann, ''Witty & Whimsical Hardware,'' *Home Improvement Market*, February 1997, p. DPR18.

Marsh, Ann, ''Not Your Dad's Hardware Store,'' *Forbes*, January 26, 1998.

Massingill, Teena, ''Corte Madera, Calif.-Based Restoration Hardware Tries to Keep Up with Growth,'' *Knight-Ridder/Tribune Business News*, February 9, 1999.

Neuborne, Ellen, et al, ''Welcome to Yuppie Hardware,'' *Business Week*, December 21, 1998, p. 94.

O'Brien, Dennis, ''Calif. Retailer to Open Warehouse, Distribution Center . . .,'' *Sun* (Baltimore), July 9, 1999, p. 3C.

Parker, Penny, ''New Mall's Opening Moved Up Park Meadows Set to Debut Aug. 30,'' *Denver Post*, July 3, 1996, p. A1.

Preddy, Melissa, ''Shops at Somerset: Prestige, Demographics Are the Drawing Cards,'' *Detroit News*, May 19, 1996, p. C1.

Steinhauer, Jennifer, ''New Stock Is Fueled by Nesting Boomers,'' *New York Times*, June 21, 1998.

—David M. Walden

R.H. Macy & Co., Inc.

151 West 34th Street
New York, New York 10001
U.S.A.
(212) 695-4400
Fax: (212) 629-6814
Web site: http://www.macys.com

Wholly Owned Subsidiary of Federated Department
Stores, Inc.
Incorporated: 1919
Employees: 56,300
Sales: $8.5 billion (1998)
NAIC: 45211 Department Stores; 44815 Clothing
Accessories Stores

R.H. Macy & Co., Inc.—better known as Macy's—is a subsidiary of Federated Department Stores, Inc. and operates through two department store groups: Macy's East and Macy's West. The groups, in turn, operate approximately 187 stores located in 21 states. Macy's stores target the middle-to-higher-priced market, offering women's, men's, and children's clothing and accessories; housewares; home furnishings; and furniture. The company also maintains two direct-to-customer retail operations: a mail-order catalog business called Macy's By Mail, and an e-commerce web site, macys.com.

The Macy Family: 1858–96

Rowland H. Macy made his fifth attempt at opening a retail store in Manhattan in 1858. His previous four attempts with similar stores had failed resoundingly, culminating, with the demise of his shop of Haverhill, Massachusetts, in his bankruptcy. Although Macy's store was situated far north of the traditional retail market, the store on Sixth Avenue near Fourteenth Street sold a healthy $85,000 worth of merchandise within one year.

Macy instituted a cash-only policy not only for customers but for himself as well. No Macy's inventory was purchased on credit, and no Macy's credit account was issued until well into the 1950s. This was unusual in a day when most stores routinely sold on credit. The new store benefited from the founder's advertising and promotion skills as well as his product line instincts. By 1870, when sales broke $1 million, a stable clientele could purchase not only dry goods, but items like men's hosiery and ties, linens and towels, fancy imported goods, costume jewelry, silver, and clocks.

Macy's son was not interested in the retail business, so Macy passed ownership into other hands. In 1860 he hired his cousin Margaret Getchell to do bookkeeping at the store, and she subsequently married a young Macy's salesman, Abiel T. LaForge. Macy increased LaForge's responsibilities, and eventually chose him as heir to half his store. The other half went to Macy's nephew, Robert M. Valentine.

Valentine and LaForge became the proprietors when the founder died unexpectedly in 1877 on a buying trip in France. LaForge died soon after. Valentine bought LaForge's share, and attempted to continue the family succession by bringing in LaForge's relative, Charles Webster. When Valentine died, Webster married his widow, and brought in his brother-in-law, Jerome B. Wheeler. In 1887, however, Webster bought Wheeler out, becoming the sole proprietor of a thriving business, which he felt he could not perpetuate singlehandedly.

Searching for a partner, Webster approached the Straus family, who for 13 years had leased space in Macy's to operate a chinaware department, the store's most profitable section. In 1887 it generated almost 20 percent of the store's sales. The Strauses eagerly accepted Webster's offer, the partnership culminating many years' work and launching the family into a social role comparable to that of the Rothschilds in Europe. Lazarus Straus, the family's patriarch, emigrated in 1852 from Germany to the United States, dissatisfied with Germany's collapsed 1848 revolution. After several years as a peddler, he was able to send for his wife and four children. The family developed a successful general store in Talbotton, Georgia, then moved to New York City in 1867 after the end of the Civil War. Lazarus Straus bought a wholesale chinaware-importing firm and brought his sons Isidor, Nathan, and Oscar into the business, renaming the company L. Straus and Sons.

Lazarus Straus died only a year after buying into Macy's but his sons carried on the business. Under the new partnership, Macy's matched and outpriced its rivals, including A.T. Stewarts, Hearn's, and Siegel & Cooper. Macy's sales rose to $5 million within a year, and subsequently continued to grow by ten percent annually. The Straus brothers introduced their odd-price policy, now used virtually everywhere in U.S. retailing. Charging $4.98 instead of $5.00, the store motivated consumers to buy in quantity in order to accumulate substantial savings. Following in Macy's footsteps, the Strauses brought in line after line of new merchandise—Oriental rugs, ornate furniture, lavish stationery, bicycles, even pianos. They also instituted the store's depositor's accounts, in which shoppers could make deposits with the store and then charge purchases against them. This, in effect, provided Macy's with interest free loans, and was a forerunner of installment buying and layaway plans.

The Straus Family: 1896–1918

In 1896 Charles Webster sold his half interest in Macy's to the Strauses, ending the founding family's line of ownership. Jesse, Percy, and Herbert Straus, Isidor's sons, urged their father to relocate the store to its Herald square location at 34th Street and Broadway in 1902. The giant new store cost $4.5 million, but funds were easily raised on the Straus family's good name, built upon the success of Macy's and the independently operated Abraham & Straus, acquired in Brooklyn in 1893.

No modern convenience was lacking in the Herald Square store. It was equipped with newly designed escalators, pneumatic tubes to move cash or messages, and an air exhaust system that provided the store with a constant supply of fresh air. Macy's spacious building had ample fitting rooms, accommodation desks, an information counter, and comfortable restrooms. Macy's had a fleet of comparison shoppers who checked out other stores' prices to be sure Macy's merchandise was competitively priced. Sales pushed to $11 million within a year of the move. Called the world's largest store, Macy's Herald Square thrilled tourists and locals alike.

After his father's death, Isidor Straus had emerged as the family patriarch, and remained, among the sons, the most interested in the store. Nathan gradually developed more as a philanthropist than a businessman, and Oscar, after taking a law degree, disregarded the business in favor of politics. Isidor and his wife, Ida, were among the passengers on the ill-fated voyage of the *Titanic*. After their deaths in 1912, Isidor's sons Jesse, Percy, and Herbert bought out Nathan's interest in Macy's and ceded their interests in Abraham & Straus to Nathan. Nathan, thus, became the sole owner of Abraham & Straus.

As it did most of its products, Macy's sold books at substantially below their wholesale price—25 percent below. In 1909 a book publishers' association sued Macy, charging that the price-cutting hurt their copyright value. The Strauses countersued, claiming that the group constituted an illegal trust under the Sherman Antitrust Act. The publishers responded by cutting Macy off completely. The Strauses, however, obtained stock through other channels—wholesalers, transshippers, or other retailers who had overstocked; they even cut deals directly with authors. The U.S. Supreme Court decided in Macy's favor in 1913, but the controversy made it even tougher for the store

to acquire well-known brands in any product line, prompting Macy's to develop its own private labels.

Postwar Expansion

When World War I ended in 1918, sales were up to $36 million, twice that of 1914. Macy's began its expansion into other cities, acquiring substantial interests in LaSalles & Koch Co. in Toledo, Ohio, in 1923, and Davison-Paxon-Stokes Co. in Atlanta, Georgia, in 1925. In subsequent years the balance of stock in both companies was acquired. In the 1920s Macy's began the tradition of sponsoring New York City's Thanksgiving Day parade. The public relations impact of the event went national when two major television networks began to cover the parade in 1952. Just before the Great Depression, Macy's bought L. Bamberger & Co. of Newark, New Jersey, a division that would later lead a renaissance for Macy's. In the 1940s, it added stores in San Francisco, California, and Kansas City, Missouri. By the late 1940s, Macy's was not only the world's largest store but the United States' largest department store chain.

Jack I. Straus, Jesse's son, became chairman of Macy's in 1940. He had grown up with the store, having been present at age two at the Herald Square opening. He realized that the family line was thinning, and began training and promoting outsiders into the top executive positions in the firm. Over the years the Strauses would gradually lessen their holding in the company, but the family remained at the helm of Macy's until the 1980s, when Edward S. Finkelstein, a manager hired by Macy's in 1948, led the company into an entirely new phase.

Straus passed the chairmanship of Macy's on to Robert (Bobby) Weil, his sister's son, as the 1940s ended. Weil beefed up Macy's advertising campaign, billing the store as the "community" store. Nevertheless, as the postwar economy picked up, New Yorkers no longer craved the bargains that were Macy's stock in trade, and did more shopping at other stores. Macy's stock fell from $3.35 per common share in fiscal 1950 to $2.51 in fiscal 1951. Further problems lay ahead.

In 1931 the Federal Fair Trade Law had allowed suppliers of certain products to specify a minimum retail price in order to stabilize the depression-era economy. With the exception of Korvettes, Macy's competitors—Abraham & Straus, Gimbel Brothers, Bloomingdale's, and B. Altman—abided by these minimums. In 1952, however, Schwegmann Brothers, a New Orleans, Louisiana, drugstore chain, contested the law and won its case. The reversal of the 20-year-old practice of price fixing undercut Macy's strategy. Macy's had undersold its competitors with its six percent-less-for-cash policy, but now that fixed minimum prices were not protected by law, all retailers could lower their prices without fear of being sued by suppliers.

Weil decided to combat this by cutting Macy's prices even further. The huge Herald Square store proved to have several weaknesses—while no one could match the giant's prices across the board, Gimbel could undersell Macy's in pharmaceuticals; Gertz of Long Island, New York, in books; and Bloomingdale's, in stationery and menswear. In 1952 Macy's posted the first year of loss in its history. Its battle plan was outmoded; Macy's fumbled in directions it had previously ignored, instituting charge accounts and catering more to its suppliers.

The Finkelstein Years: 1960s–85

While the flagship store struggled with image problems, a renaissance began in another division: Bamberger's of New Jersey. David L. Yunich took the helm of the decaying urban store in Newark in 1955. During his eight years of guidance, Bamberger's mushroomed, opening in suburbs all over New Jersey. The chain's annual sales rose from $82 million to $500 million, its profits being among the highest in the nation and topping even those of the mammoth New York division. Herbert L. Seegal and his protegé Finkelstein came to Bamberger's in 1962 to step up its growth, using new customer-oriented merchandising. Instead of buying whatever suppliers offered, Bamberger's bought the top of the line in any new group of goods, and featured that in the most glamorous displays Bamberger's customers had ever seen. The technique garnered notice not only within Macy's but from top executives of other chains as well. The store began its push out of New Jersey to the south and west in 1968, and by the 1980s had three times as many stores as in the late 1960s. Bamberger's of New Jersey's sales for the fiscal year ending July 31, 1981, were $799 million; with Macy's California and New York divisions, it formed a powerful triad generating 86 percent of Macy's sales.

Macy's had acquired the old O'Connor, Moffat Co. store as its first California outpost in 1945. It was renamed and made Macy's flagship in San Francisco's then posh Union Square. Like other urban retail centers, however, Union Square and its surrounding complement of chic shops, including I. Magnin, Liberty House, the Emporium, Bonwit Teller, Gumps, and a host of others, fell victim to urban decay in the 1960s. Finkelstein was sent to bail out Macy's California in 1969. Macy's upgraded its image, aiming its product lines at a more well-heeled buyer. The transformation of California's 12 stores helped Macy's surpass most of its competitors, leaving it as one of the top three retailers, along with the Emporium and I. Magnin.

Finkelstein was brought back to the East in 1974 to work on the Herald Square store. He trimmed off such departments as pharmaceuticals, major appliances, sporting goods, and toys in which the store could not compete. Macy's put an end to its concentration on household durable goods, departments that got heavy competition from Korvettes and Sears as well as local department stores. In place of the discontinued departments, inventories were increased and presentations were refined in certain departments, including linens and domestics, furniture, menswear, and jewelry.

Finkelstein remodeled about 35 percent of the space in New York's 16 stores, including the Herald Square store, which benefited from the installation of the Cellar in 1976. Macy's basement, which had been a no-frills depository for bargain merchandise, was transformed into a sparkling esplanade of airy specialty shops offering gourmet foods, yard goods, stationery, baskets, and contemporary housewares. Geared to a trend-conscious consumer, the cross between a European boulevard and a chic suburban mall also offered frequent cooking demonstrations, an old-fashioned apothecary, and a pottery shop complete with a working potter at the wheel. The Cellar caused such a stir that Bloomingdale's hastily installed a similar group of boutiques, although Bloomingdale's management claimed its conception predated the Cellar's opening. The revitalized Macy's had its biggest holiday season ever in 1976, and increased its annual earnings greatly from the previous year.

The chinks in Macy's formidable front were minor; competitors claimed that Macy's modern image was tarnished by its refusal to accept major credit cards. In addition, Macy's as a corporation lacked diversity. It operated only department stores, while most other similarly sized operations had diversified into specialty stores. Macy's eventually began development of such stores in the early 1980s.

In 1978 Finkelstein was promoted from president to chairman of Macy's New York division. The Macy's Miracle, as it was called, gained momentum as annual sales soared between the years 1979 and 1982. In 1982 corporate sales gains of 20.1 percent topped the industry, and Macy's surpassed its major competitors in operating profit per square foot.

While other stores were consolidating departments under fewer buyers, Macy's added more buyers, encouraging them to find unique products. Stores were overstocked by ten percent to 20 percent, so that unpredicted buying surges could be accommodated. It hired many executives for its training program, up to 300 per year in larger divisions. In 1984 Macy's had its theretofore best year. Sales rose 17.2 percent to $4.07 billion from 1983's $3.47 billion, which was up 16.4 percent from the previous year. At each of its 96 stores, Macy's averaged after-tax profits of $2.31 million. During 1984 Macy's common stock soared in value. The year 1985 was tough for most retailers, including Macy's. For the year, sales were $4.37 billion, up 6.4 percent from the previous year, but net income dropped almost 15 percent from $221.8 million to $189.3 million. The increase in sales was small compared to steady gains of 12 percent to 17 percent in the previous four years. Sales costs had risen, due to an increased advertising push, and to new staff training programs.

By 1984 Macy's bulky inventories had gotten out of hand. Inventories were 35 percent larger than in 1983. Prices were slashed, but the store could not seem to get rid of its excess. The store continued to build stock instead of eliminating it, miscalculating the buying force of the public; other stores were reducing their inventories. Finkelstein had attempted to expand his private-label lines; he kept the prices too high, however, to attract buyers. Finkelstein's vigilant management had never slipped before; the uncharacteristic miscalculation worried analysts. Wall Street began to waver in its praise. Macy's had the second best year in its history in 1985, but the radical drops were not taken kindly in an institution that had been on a steady rise for over a decade.

Mergers and acquisitions abounded in the retail industry in 1985. A company with a weak profit record was a likely target because that performance pushed its stock value down, and a change in management could improve it. Although Macy's ten-year profit history was phenomenal, the recent questions from analysts were pushing Macy's stock prices down, and Finkelstein worried about a hostile takeover. In addition, he felt that his best executives were being lured to other stores. Rapid growth and subsequent compensation had satisfied his players over the past ten years, but now the store approached a plateau. Finkelstein had to do something to restore the company's vitality.

Finkelstein's solution was to lead the top 350 executives in a leveraged buyout of Macy's, at $70 per share, not much above a recent market high. He saw ownership and the subsequent share in profits as a way to motivate employees. Some shareholders objected, and one even filed suit, but the offer was sufficiently attractive that they eventually agreed. As for the Straus family, patriarch Jack was outraged, but in effect he had relinquished ownership long ago. In 1924 the Straus family had total ownership; by the 1960s, it was down to 20 percent; and by the 1980s, the family held only about a two percent interest in the chain. Its attachment to the store could not stop management from executing the biggest takeover of a retailer at that time and the first leveraged buyout of a major retail chain.

Losing Ground: 1986–90

The year after the buyout, Macy's stores did so well that the chain could almost report a net profit, despite the debt service on the heavy borrowing needed to fund the buyout. In 1988 Macy's added further to its debt, however, by purchasing Federated's Bullocks and Bullocks-Wilshire and the I. Magnin chains. The $1 billion expenditure weighed heavily on company finances, but a confident Macy's stocked stores with merchandise in anticipation of a strong holiday season in 1989. The economic recession of the late 1980s, however, had lowered consumer demand for the entire retailing industry, and sales during the holidays proved disappointing. Moreover, when a troubled major competitor, the Campeau retailing empire, ran huge sales to increase its cash flow, Macy's had to follow suit. Burdened with an overstocked inventory that was selling too slowly, coupled with high spending on expensive promotions, Macy's saw its earnings for the holiday season drop 50 percent.

Factoring companies that finance manufacturers' shipments to retailers tightened credit for those who did business with Macy, but the company was able to show that it was managing its cash flow through financial maneuvering that allowed Macy's to get additional monies from major stockholders. In addition, the company sold two subsidiaries, Macy Credit Corp. and Macy Receivables Funding Corp., to General Electric Capital Corp. for $100 million, relieving the company of $1.5 billion in debt. Several months later, Macy's completed the sale of its equity interest in the Valley Fair Shopping Center in San Jose, California.

The company, however, still had $4 billion in long-term debt, and in early 1990 rumors of bankruptcy started to circulate. The rumors persisted throughout the year and on December 4, 1990, Finkelstein took out a full-page ad in the trade journal *Women's Wear Daily* to quash them once and for all. Once again the store looked forward to holiday sales to boost cash flow, and once again there were heavy promotions and discounting to spur consumer demand. But the recession had persisted, consumer confidence was low, and sales were again below expectations. Sales throughout 1991 continued to be slow and Macy's sustained further losses. Still another disappointing holiday season made it increasingly difficult for Macy's to service its debt. To further cut its deficit, Macy's bought back $300 million of its bonds for less than 50 percent of their face value.

Bankruptcy: 1992–94

Despite Macy's efforts, the poor retail climate combined with ineffective merchandising, diminishing public image, and lack of management focus led to further revenue losses. In early 1992 the company announced an indefinite delay in paying its suppliers. A last minute effort by investor Laurence Tisch to buy $802 million of outstanding stock did not win creditor support. The final blow came on January 27th when Macy's declared bankruptcy. By April, Finkelstein had been replaced by Myron E. Ullman III and Mark S. Handler.

The new co-executives devised a five-year business plan that included reducing the advertising budget from over four percent of sales to under three percent, fewer one-day sales, more focused promotions, fewer private-label items, improved customer service, and a new computerized inventory management system. Store expansion continued, however, and in August 1992, a new department store was opened in the Mall of America in Minneapolis, the company's first in Minnesota. Later in the year a new Bullock's department store was opened in Burbank, California, and new I. Magnin stores replaced existing department stores in Phoenix and San Diego.

By early 1993, the plan had begun to demonstrate its effectiveness as Macy's showed its first profit—$147.7 million—since filing for bankruptcy. Moreover, sales during the 1992 holiday season were better than expected, reaching $1.2 billion, while revenue was 3.8 percent higher than the previous year. Even with these promising results, however, Macy's continued to rid itself of unprofitable operations. In March 1993 the company announced that it would close 11 stores with low growth potential. The latest store closings included five department stores in Connecticut, New Jersey, and California, and six I. Magnin specialty stores in Seattle and cities in California.

Continuing its marketing strategy of reaching out to consumers in new ways, Macy's announced in June 1993 that it was planning to start a 24-hour television home shopping channel. Orders and customer service would be provided by the Home Shopping Network Inc. That month brought more promising news—sales of $1.34 billion for the quarter were 5.8 percent higher than the same period the previous year. In addition, sales in stores open at least one year increased 3.1 percent. Macy's cash flow was $28.5 million in the quarter, exceeding the requirements of its bank loans by about $6.5 million. Industry analysts reported that the strategy of increasing productivity and cutting costs, in spite of the continued poor economy on the coasts, was beginning to pay off for Macy's.

Under Federated's Ownership: 1994–99

In January 1994, Federated Department Stores made a move to acquire Macy's when it bought almost $5 million of Macy's debt from Prudential Insurance Company. Headquartered in Cincinnati, Federated owned several department store chains, including Abraham & Straus, Jordan Marsh, The Bon Marche, Rich's/Goldsmith's, Stern's, Lazarus, and Macy's major competitor, Bloomingdale's. For seven months, Macy's officials resisted Federated's efforts to purchase it, hoping to instead turn the company around on their own. However, the company's efforts to climb out of bankruptcy were proving inadequate;

despite cost-cutting measures and new marketing initiatives, it was unable to return to profitability. In July 1994, the company yielded to Federated, agreeing to be acquired and filing a joint reorganization plan. After bankruptcy court approved the reorganization in December 1994, the companies completed the merger, bringing Macy's out of its three-year bankruptcy.

The Macy's-Federated merger created a true retail giant. The combined companies laid claim to more than $13 billion in revenue, 11 department store chains, and more than 300 stores in 26 states. It was not long after coming under Federated's ownership that Macy's felt the first tremors of change. Federated began rolling several of its smaller chains into the two large Macy's East and Macy's West divisions to streamline operations and avoid intercompany competition. As an initial move in this direction, Federated consolidated its Jordan Marsh chain into Macy's East. The following year, the company phased out its 130-year-old Abraham & Straus chain in January, converting most stores to Macy's, Bloomingdale's, or Stern's. Nine of the former A&S stores joined the Macy's East division.

On the West Coast, as well, retail institutions were vanishing as a result of the Macy's-Federated union. In 1994, Macy's West discontinued its I. Magnin business, a chain of 12 stores that dated back to 1876. While rich in history, I. Magnin was not proving financially successful. The following year, another famous name disappeared from the retail scene, when the company converted all 21 Bullock's locations to Macy's. Federated also bulked up Macy's presence on the West Coast with the 1995 acquisition of Broadway Stores, Inc., an 82-unit chain headquartered in Los Angeles. The majority of the newly acquired Broadway stores were converted into Macy's.

In 1997 and 1998, Federated began major renovations on Macy's East flagship store at Herald Square in Manhattan and Macy's West flagship store at Union Square in San Francisco. The company also explored two new avenues of retailing: mail order and online sales. Macy's East began the company's first-ever mail order catalog, Macy's By Mail, while the West division tackled cyberspace by launching macys.com.

By the middle of 1999, Macy's East operated a total of 87 stores, occupying a total of 23.8 million square feet. Macy's West consisted of 100 stores, totaling 20.1 million square feet.

As a Federated subsidiary, Macy's was part of a strong and growing organization, with a healthy bottom line. Building on Federated's strength, Macy's was likely to remain a cornerstone of department store retailing for years to come.

Principal Operating Units

Macy's East; Macy's West.

Further Reading

Barmash, Isadore, *Macy's for Sale,* New York: Weidenfeld & Nicolson, 1989.

Chakravarty, Subrata N., "Survivor on 34th St.," *Forbes,* August 6, 1990, p. 10.

"Macy Shows Gain in Sales, Cash Flow," *New York Times,* June 12, 1993.

Macy's New York 125th Anniversary: 1858–1983, New York: R.H. Macy & Co., Inc., 1983.

"Macy's Plans to Close Additional 11 Stores with Layoffs of 1,500," *Wall Street Journal,* March 2, 1993, p. B4.

Moore, Martha, and Dale Dallabrida, "Macy's on Sale: Locations, Cachet Catch Rivals' Eye," *USA Today,* January 6, 1994.

Neuborne, Ellen, "A Retail Giant in Store: Federated to Acquire Rival Macy," *USA Today,* July 15, 1994, p. 1.

Peterson, Thane, "Macy's Is Trimmed in Red," *Business Week,* December 30, 1991, p. 48.

Pomice, Eva, "Macy's Hopes for Santa Claus," *U.S. News and World Report,* December 3, 1990, pp. 60–62.

"R.H. Macy Shows Profit for Five Weeks, Its First Since Bankruptcy-Law Filing," *Wall Street Journal,* February 2, 1993, p. B3.

Silverman, Edward, and Christine Dugas, "End of an Error: Decision to Take on Heavy Debt Cost Macy's Its Independence," *Newsday,* July 17, 1994, p. A72.

Strom, Stephanie, "Home Shopping to Get Work for Macy Channel," *New York Times,* June 8, 1993, p. D5.

Trachtenberg, Jeffrey, *The Rain on Macy's Parade: How Greed, Ambition, and Folly Ruined America's Greatest Store,* New York: Times Business, 1996.

Zinn, Laura, "Prudence on 34th St.," *Business Week,* November 16, 1992, p. 44.

Zinn, Laura, and Christopher Power, "It's Too Soon to Write Macy's Obituary," *Business Week,* December 17, 1990, p. 27.

—Elaine Belsito
—updated by Shawna Brynildssen

Tobacco Company

R.J. Reynolds Tobacco Holdings, Inc.

P.O. Box 2866
Winston-Salem, North Carolina 27102-2811
U.S.A.
(336) 741-5500
(800) 372-9300; (800) 565-5214
Fax: (336) 741-5511
Web site: http://www.rjrt.com

Public Company
Incorporated: 1879 as R.J. Reynolds Tobacco Company
Employees: 8,000
Sales: $5.7 billion (1998)
Stock Exchanges: New York
Ticker Symbol: RJR
NAIC: 312221 Cigarette Manufacturing

R.J. Reynolds Tobacco Holdings, Inc., is the holding company for R.J. Reynolds Tobacco Company, one of the largest cigarette manufacturers in the United States. As of 1999, the company held a 25 percent share of the cigarette market and sold four of the ten most popular cigarette brands in the nation: the premium brands Winston, Camel, and Salem; and the discount brand Doral. Mired in litigation throughout the mid- to late 1990s, R.J. Reynolds, along with other major U.S. tobacco companies, agreed to pay $206 billion in a settlement reached with the federal government in 1998. In 1999 the company was divested from RJR Nabisco.

Early History

The company's founder, Richard Joshua Reynolds, son of prosperous tobacco manufacturer Hardin W. Reynolds of Patrick County, Virginia, sold his part interest in a tobacco business he had with his father and in 1874 moved 60 miles south to Winston, North Carolina, in the heart of the bright leaf, or flue-cured, tobacco area. Reynolds invested $7,500 in land and built and equipped a small factory there to manufacture flat plug chewing tobacco. During the first year of operation Reynolds produced 150,000 pounds of tobacco that sold primarily in the Carolinas and Virginia. In 1879 the R.J. Reynolds Tobacco Company was incorporated in North Carolina. Reynolds faced stiff competition from manufacturers in Winston and its neighboring city of Salem. Reynolds, along with his brother William Neal Reynolds, who joined the firm in 1884, controlled the company. Initially Reynolds sold his products to jobbers who distributed chewing tobacco for him under their own brand names. In 1885 he introduced his own brand, Schnapps, which became popular.

In the 1890s there were several significant changes in the Reynolds Tobacco Company. In 1890 the company issued its first stock, with R.J. Reynolds owning nearly 90 percent of the company. He was elected president, with his brother serving as vice-president. In 1892 a sales department was created along with a systematic national advertising program.

Reynolds was one of the first companies to introduce saccharin as a sweetening agent in chewing tobacco. The company also adopted many labor-saving devices and had a 400 percent production increase between 1892 and 1898. In 1894 Reynolds began to experiment with smoking tobacco to compete with James Buchanan Duke's profitable brands and also because of his desire to turn scrap tobacco into a paying product. In 1895 the company introduced its first smoking tobacco brand, Naturally Sweet Cut Plug. In 1898 the company's assets were valued at more than $1 million.

Due to considerable expansion in the late 1890s, Reynolds was in need of large amounts of capital. Reluctantly, he turned to his rival Duke for help. In 1898 Duke's American Tobacco Company established a subsidiary, Continental Tobacco Company, in an effort to monopolize the nation's chewing tobacco business. In April 1899 Reynolds sold two-thirds of his stock to Continental, but retained his position as president of the R.J. Reynolds Tobacco Company. Reynolds tried to maintain his independence in Duke's tobacco trust and reportedly told friends that "if Buck Duke tries to swallow me, he will get the bellyache of his life." Duke let Reynolds have his independence as long as he acquired chewing tobacco companies in the Virginia and Carolina area for the trust. Reynolds gobbled up ten companies, but by 1905 he demonstrated his independence from the trust by producing five brands of smoking tobacco. In late 1907 he introduced Prince Albert smoking tobacco, a unique mixture of burley

Company Perspectives:

R.J. Reynolds' operations are guided by three key goals that we seek to accomplish while acting always in a responsible and ethical manner: We will continually strive to meet the preferences of adult smokers better than our competitors by developing, manufacturing and marketing distinctive, high quality tobacco products, and by developing technologies that have the potential to reduce the health risks associated with smoking. We will deliver an attractive return to shareholders in terms of significant, sustainable dividends and long-term growth in earnings and cash flow by strengthening our brands, aggressively managing costs and seizing growth opportunities as they arise. We will provide an open work environment where RJR employees can fully express their creativity and competitiveness to improve the company's performance and profits.

and flue-cured tobacco. Prince Albert achieved instant success with the slogan "it can't bite your tongue."

The tobacco trust, like most trusts during the first decade of the 20th century, proved to be unpopular. In 1911 a U.S. Circuit Court ordered the dissolution of the American Tobacco Company. American was forced to divest itself of all Reynolds stock. R.J. Reynolds and members of his family reacquired some of the company's stock. In actuality the trust years were good to Reynolds. He expanded facilities, hired aggressive new managers, and increased production and sales almost fivefold during the trust period. By the time he reacquired control of the company in 1912, the R.J. Reynolds Tobacco Company was the smallest of the big four tobacco manufacturers, but it was quick to expand.

Soon after achieving independence from the trust, Reynolds instituted a plan to get the company's stock into the hands of friendly investors. A company bylaw encouraged Reynolds' employees to buy company stock, and the board of directors approved lending of surplus funds and profits to employees for the purchase of "A," or voting, stock. By 1924 the majority of the company's voting stock was in the hands of people who worked for the company. Soon all tobacco businesses began to emulate the Reynolds stock purchase plan.

As early as 1912 R.J. Reynolds considered the production of cigarettes because of the great success that the Prince Albert brand had experienced. By July 1913 Reynolds had manufactured the company's first cigarette. Reynolds decided to produce three different cigarette brands simultaneously to see which one had the greatest public demand. He personally selected the blend—Turkish tobacco, burley, flue-cured—and the name of the brand that proved most popular, Camel. The Camel brand became an instant success because of its blend, pricing, and advertising. Camels sold for ten cents a pack, which undersold Liggett & Myers' popular Fatima. Reynolds spent more than $2 million in 1915 in an aggressive national advertising campaign. In 1919 the famous slogan "I'd walk a mile for a Camel" appeared. Reynolds also instituted the idea of selling cigarettes by the carton. Profits soared from $2.75 million in 1912 to nearly $24 million in 1924, largely because of the

phenomenal sale of Camels. By 1924 the R.J. Reynolds Tobacco Company's net profits surpassed the nation's largest manufacturer, the American Tobacco Company.

The company prospered under R.J. Reynolds's paternalistic leadership and continued to do so for decades after his death in 1918. William Neal Reynolds assumed the presidency after his brother's death and remained in that position until 1924 when he was elected chairman of the board of directors, with Bowman Gray, Sr., appointed president. This ensured the perpetuation of R.J. Reynolds's management philosophy and provided a continuity of leadership from people inside the company. Before R.J. Reynolds's death he had begun the process that led to the company's listing on the New York Stock Exchange—preferred stock in 1922 and common in 1927.

William Neal Reynolds retired as chairman in 1931 to be replaced by Bowman Gray, Sr. Under Gray's direction the company in 1931 introduced moistureproof cellophane as a wrapper to preserve freshness in cigarettes—an innovation that other companies soon adopted; began to manufacture its own tinfoil and paper from factories in North Carolina to reduce dependence on foreign supplies; and developed a new sales policy that concentrated on mass sales based on brand name recognition and customer loyalty. Reynolds during the 1930s invested heavily in a series of advertising campaigns that emphasized the pleasure derived from smoking. By 1938 the company produced 84 brands of chewing tobacco, 12 brands of smoking tobacco, and one primary brand of cigarette, Camel.

After Gray's accidental death in 1935, S. Clay Williams directed the company until 1949. During the 1940s R.J. Reynolds faced shortages of materials and personnel because of World War II, and immediately after the war there were labor problems that included accusations of communist sympathies against certain union leaders. Labor relations improved by the early 1950s, however, as the company became agreeable to many union-advocated reforms, including the desegregation of its workforce.

In 1948 a major antitrust suit against the tobacco industry went to trial. Several R.J. Reynolds officers were convicted and fined on charges of monopolistic practices, although they strongly asserted their innocence. The company itself also was convicted. The company's misfortunes continued. In 1949 Reynolds introduced a major new cigarette brand, Cavalier. The public did not accept the brand, which lost $30 million in five years.

The innovative John C. Whitaker assumed the presidency in 1949. During his tenure Reynolds rebounded and prospered. Technical advances increased the amount of tobacco suitable for cigarette manufacturing, which helped the company's output double from 1944 to 1958. Reynolds instituted an active merchandising campaign by using display racks of cigarettes in supermarkets. In addition, company bylaws that had resulted in concentration of stock in the hands of employees were gradually eliminated, making the shares available more widely.

A major factor in Reynolds's growth during the 1950s was the introduction of Winston and Salem cigarettes, from which the company received huge profits. Winston, the company's first filter-tipped cigarette, appeared in March 1954 to compete directly with Brown & Williamson's Viceroy. With catchy advertising phrases such as "Winston tastes good like a cigarette should'' and ''It's what's up front that counts,'' the cigarette was quickly accepted, with 40 billion sold in 1954. By 1956 Reynolds began marketing Salem, the industry's first king-size filter-tipped menthol cigarette. It too made tremendous profits. Nevertheless, Camel retained its leadership as the industry's bestselling cigarette until the early 1960s. All cigarette manufacturing was centralized in 1961, when a massive modern factory opened in Winston-Salem.

During the 1950s the tobacco industry experienced for the first time critical attacks centering on the issue of smoking and health. In 1952 an article entitled ''Cancer by the Carton'' appeared in *Reader's Digest*, and the next year the Sloan-Kettering Cancer Institute announced that its research showed a relationship between cancer and tobacco. The development of filter-tipped cigarettes was in part a response to health concerns. The board of directors also responded by appointing a diversification committee in 1957 to study possible investment in nontobacco areas and to consider expansion of tobacco operations overseas.

Diversification: 1960s–70s

Alexander H. Galloway became president in 1960 and, along with Chairman Bowman Gray, Jr., led the company into a period of unparalleled growth and diversification. The corporate diversification strategy initially focused on acquisitions in food-related industries. Reynolds bought Pacific Hawaiian Products in 1963 and spent $63 million for Chun King in 1966. All nontobacco companies were placed under the direction of a subsidiary—R.J. Reynolds Foods—that was created in 1966. By the late 1960s, diversification had expanded into nonfood areas. In 1969 the company bought Sea-Land Industries, a containerized shipping business, and adopted a new corporate name—R.J. Reynolds Industries. Aminoil, a domestic crude oil and natural gas exploration firm, was purchased for $600 million in 1970. Businesses later added to the R.J. Reynolds Industries portfolio were Del Monte in 1979 and Heublein in 1983.

Tobacco, however, continued to be the mainstay of Reynolds. In 1968 R.J. Reynolds International was established to develop foreign tobacco markets. Two years later all tobacco operations became a subsidiary of R.J. Reynolds Industries. In the 1960s the smoking and health controversy had intensified. In 1964 the U.S. Surgeon General issued a report linking smoking with lung cancer and heart disease. The U.S. Congress in 1965 passed the Cigarette Advertising and Labeling Act, which required tobacco companies to place health warnings on cigarette packs. Cigarette advertising was banned from radio and television after 1971. The federal cigarette tax was doubled in 1983.

In addition to governmental pressure, Reynolds faced intense competition, primarily from Philip Morris, as marketing strategy focused on luring customers away from competitors instead of attracting new smokers. By 1976 Philip Morris's Marlboro surpassed Winston in domestic sales. In 1977 Reynolds introduced the Real brand cigarette to appeal to the back-to-nature movement, but its sales were disastrous, and by 1980 the so-called ''Edsel of cigarettes'' was discontinued. Reynolds actively engaged in the domestic tar wars of the late 1970s. Several promising new low-tar brands, such as Doral and Vantage, were marketed in an effort to improve tobacco's health image. In 1983 Reynolds began manufacturing the novel 25-cigarette-per-pack Century. Most consumers, however, preferred the traditional 20-per-pack cigarettes. By 1983 Philip Morris had replaced Reynolds as the leader in domestic sales.

Reynolds's strategy in the 1980s centered on developing new foreign markets for tobacco products to offset lower domestic demand and sales. In 1980 Reynolds was the first U.S. company to reach an agreement with the People's Republic of China to manufacture and sell cigarettes there. In September 1980 the company announced an ambitious $2 billion, ten-year construction and plant modernization plan. By 1986 the ultramodern Tobaccoville factory just north of Winston-Salem began production.

Refocusing the Company in the 1980s

Leadership at Reynolds underwent significant changes during the diversification period. For the first time in the company's history several persons from outside the corporation were brought into major management positions. J. Paul Sticht, originally an executive from Federated Department Stores, who joined Reynolds in 1972, and his protégé J. Tylee Wilson led Reynolds into a period of extensive growth. By 1980 Sticht and Wilson had developed a new direction for the company. Reynolds began to divest itself of noncomplementary companies and concentrate efforts on strengthening existing subsidiaries through acquisition of tobacco and food-related businesses. In 1984 Reynolds sold Aminoil to Phillips Petroleum for $1.7 billion. In one of the largest acquisitions ever, Reynolds purchased Nabisco Brands, Inc. in 1985 for $4.9 billion, which raised the corporation's nontobacco earnings to 40 percent of its total. The next year the conglomerate officially changed its name to RJR Nabisco, Inc.

Tumultuous changes followed. F. Ross Johnson, who came over from Nabisco in 1985, was appointed president and chief operations officer. By 1986 he had forced Wilson out and assumed the position of chief executive officer. He continued Wilson's policy of returning the company to its core business by selling off more than half the corporation's subsidiaries. Johnson also moved corporate headquarters from Winston-Salem to Atlanta. In 1987 Reynolds began to test-market a smokeless cigarette, Premier, in response to mounting pressure to make smoking more acceptable. Premier was a colossal failure.

At a meeting of the board of directors on October 19, 1988, Johnson proposed a massive leveraged buyout. Johnson headed a group of company executives who wanted to buy Reynolds stock for $17 billion by borrowing against the corporation's assets through bank loans and the issuance of high-yield junk bonds. Once the new company became private, unprofitable parts would be sold. Ultimately, the new and leaner company would issue stock and become public, with the Johnson group to realize huge profits. The directors, alienated by Johnson's proposal, opened the door to other bidders. In November 1988 they accepted the $24.88 billion offered by Kohlberg Kravis Roberts & Co. (KKR), an investment firm specializing in leveraged buyouts, instead of a higher bid from the Johnson group. This was the biggest leveraged buyout in U.S. history. RJR Nabisco Holdings Corp. was set up at this time as the parent company of RJR Nabisco, Inc.

Johnson resigned in February 1989. A month later KKR selected Louis Gerstner, Jr., former president of American Express, as chief executive of RJR Nabisco Holdings. He immediately began cutting costs to reduce the massive buyout debt. There was an 11.5 percent personnel cutback in tobacco operations; the practice of overstocking retailers with cigarettes was eliminated; corporate headquarters were moved to New York; and Del Monte and parts of Nabisco were divested in 1990. Attempts to target selected groups with new cigarette brands, such as Uptown for blacks and Dakota for blue-collar urban women, failed in 1990. RJR, however, did penetrate the Soviet market that year.

Under Gerstner, in the early 1990s, RJR Nabisco had focused on increasing the efficiency of its existing operations, rather than on making acquisitions. By 1991 it had reduced its debt to about $17 billion from $25 billion at the time of the buyout. Early in 1991 the company went public once again with a new issue of stock, although KKR continued to own a majority of shares. By early 1995 KKR had sold all its remaining shares. Later that year, RJR Nabisco unexpectedly named Steven F. Goldstone, an attorney with no corporate executive experience, as CEO.

Splitting up Tobacco and Food Businesses: Late 1990s

Also in 1995, RJR Nabisco placed 19.5 percent of Nabisco on the stock market. Asserting the company had not gone far enough and that Nabisco needed to be divested completely, investor Carl Icahn, along with Bennet LeBow, attempted a takeover of RJR Nabisco. Although the pair's plan to spin off Nabisco fully was popular on some fronts, their lengthy proxy fight was unsuccessful. After preparing for another such fight, Icahn sold all of his 19.9 million shares in March 1997 for $730 million.

R.J. Reynolds' image suffered in the mid-1990s after the American Medical Association concluded that children were attracted to the company's advertising campaign featuring cartoon character Joe Camel. Tired of fighting litigation from the Federal Trade Commission regarding the campaign and of increasing pressure from the public, R.J. Reynolds dropped the Joe Camel cartoon ads in 1997.

When incriminating industry documents became public in the mid-1990s, R.J. Reynolds and competitors Philip Morris and B.A.T. Industries were sued by dozens of state attorneys general for costs associated with treating tobacco-related illnesses. Although the trio agreed to a settlement in 1997, the deal disintegrated during the Congressional approval process. In the meantime, the tobacco companies raised cigarette prices significantly, in anticipation of a large settlement payout. Finally, late in 1998 the cigarette makers agreed to pay states $206 billion. Although the final amount was less than what they had agreed to before, R.J. Reynolds and rivals did not win protection from private class-action suits, a condition for which they had lobbied strongly.

In March 1999 the Federal Trade Commission dropped its Joe Camel suit against R.J. Reynolds, saying the 1998 tobacco settlement had accomplished the goals of their litigation. The settle-ment required R.J. Reynolds to abandon cartoons in advertisements, billboard advertising, and branded merchandise sales.

R.J. Reynolds' international operations suffered in the mid- to late 1990s. The company reduced its staff by ten percent in 1997 in an effort to apply the saving to the international business. However, R.J. Reynolds Tobacco International remained weak, and the company sold it to Japan Tobacco, Inc., for $8 billion in May 1999. Terms of the sale included trademarks of R.J. Reynolds Tobacco International and international rights to Camel, Winston, and Salem brands.

At the same time, RJR Nabisco spun off the domestic tobacco business through a stock distribution to RJR Nabisco shareholders. Goldstone explained the split by saying, "Cookies and cigarettes do not share distribution or marketing or even the same sales force. They are very, very different businesses." The divestiture still left the food business, as a subsidiary of the original holding company, vulnerable to tobacco-related lawsuits. In July 1999, R.J. Reynolds named Andrew Schindler president, CEO, and chairman of the newly independent company.

Principal Subsidiaries

R.J. Reynolds Tobacco Company; Arjay Equipment Corporation; Arjay Holdings; R.J. Reynolds Finance S.A. (Switzerland); R.J. Reynolds (Portugal) Limitada; R.J. Reynolds Scandanavia; R.J. Reynolds Tobacco Co. Gmbh (Germany); R.J. Reynolds Tobacco (Hong Kong) Ltd.; R.J. Reynolds Tobacco (England) Limited.

Further Reading

Anders, George, "Back to Biscuits: Old Flamboyance Is Out As Louis Gerstner Remakes RJR Nabisco," *Wall Street Journal*, March 21, 1991.
Burrough, Bryan, and John Helyar, *Barbarians at the Gate: The Fall of RJR Nabisco*, New York: Harper & Row, 1990.
Dobrzynski, Judith H., "Running the Biggest LBO," *Business Week*, October 2, 1989.
Durham, Richard, and Howard Gleckman, "Big Tobacco's Hard Line Won't Soften Congress," *Business Week*, April 20, 1998, p. 46.
"FTC Drops Its Complaint Against Cartoon Camel," *Marketing News*, March 1, 1999, p. 51.
Lesly, Elizabeth, "Why Is a Lawyer Running RJR Nabisco?" *Business Week*, December 18, 1995, p. 38.
Purdum, Todd S., "Filling the Pantry at Reynolds," *New York Times*, June 16, 1985.
"RJR Nabisco: Lawyers at the Gate," *Economist*, March 13, 1999.
Salmans, Sandra, "Reynolds: Smoking Still Pays," *New York Times*, April 12, 1981.
Serwer, Andrew E., "From Icahn, with Love," *Fortune*, March 31, 1997, p. 163.
Sloane, Leonard, "Durable Tobacco King: Reynolds Still Faces Marketing Challenge," *New York Times*, May 20, 1973.
Tilley, Nannie M., *The R.J. Reynolds Tobacco Company*, Chapel Hill: University of North Carolina Press, 1985.

—Charles C. Hay III
—updated by Susan Windisch Brown

Rogers Communications Inc.

---

333 Bloor Street East
Toronto, Ontario M4W 1G9
Canada
(416) 935-7777
Fax: (416) 935-3538
Web site: http://www.rogers.com

Public Company
Incorporated: 1920 as Famous Players Canadian
    Corporation
Employees: 10,010
Sales: C$2.84 billion (US$1.83 billion) (1998)
Stock Exchanges: Toronto Montreal Alberta Vancouver
    New York
Ticker Symbol: RG
NAIC: 513322 Cellular & Other Wireless
    Telecommunications; 513112 Radio Stations; 51312
    Television Broadcasting; 513211 Cable Networks;
    51339 Other Telecommunications; 51112 Periodical
    Publishers; 53223 Video Tapes & Disc Rental

The largest communications company in Canada, Rogers Communications Inc. functions as a holding company for two main wholly owned subsidiaries—Rogers Cablesystems Limited and Rogers Media Inc.—and for the 51-percent-owned subsidiary Rogers Cantel Mobile Communications Inc. The publicly traded Cantel, which is 33 percent owned by a joint venture of AT&T Corp. and British Telecommunications PLC, is Canada's largest wireless telephone company and the only company licensed to provide digital cellular, paging, and wireless data services nationwide. Cantel serves more than 1.7 million cellular subscribers and owns a national network covering approximately 93 percent of the Canadian population. Rogers Cablesystems is Canada's largest cable company, serving more than 2.2 million subscribers, or 27 percent of the nation's cable subscribers; it operates 29 cable systems clustered in four main urban markets: Toronto, Ottawa, the Guelph to London corridor in Ontario, and Vancouver and the lower mainland of British Columbia. The Cablesystems unit also of-

fers a high-speed Internet access service via cable (Rogers@Home) and runs the country's second largest chain of video rental stores (Rogers Videos). Rogers Media's operations include broadcasting, publishing, and new media. In broadcasting, Rogers Media owns and operates 19 radio stations, one television station (CFMT-TV), and a home shopping service (The Shopping Channel); and owns minority interests in a pay-per-view television network (Viewer's Choice Canada Inc.), and in two specialty cable programming services (Outdoor Life Network and CTV Sports Net). The publishing operations are handled within Maclean Hunter Publishing Limited, which Rogers Communications acquired in 1994 and which produces 16 consumer magazines and 45 business publications; it is best known for *Maclean's,* Canada's English-language weekly news magazine, with a readership of 2.3 million. Rogers' new media activities center around investments in leading Internet brands, such as Quicken Canada and Electric Library Canada.

On three notable occasions, Edward S. Rogers, Jr., challenged conventional wisdom while orchestrating the development of his company, refusing to heed the advice of those purporting to know better. Each instance proved to be instrumental to the growth of Rogers Communications and greatly contributed to Rogers's personal success, helping him earn the epithet most sought after by entrepreneurs: self-made billionaire. First, Rogers decided to enter the FM radio broadcasting business, which raised the eyebrows of disbelieving critics who declared that FM radio would never be popular. Next he made the decision to enter the cable television business, while onlookers proclaimed that consumers would never pay for television. Then, in the mid-1980s, Rogers set his sights on the nascent cellular telephone business, but the board of directors of Rogers Communications rejected his proposal. Rogers reacted characteristically: he went ahead anyway, using his own money to help launch the venture. By the turn of the millennium, despite all the pessimistic predictions, Rogers Communications was one of the largest communications companies in the world.

Early History

Rogers inherited some of his pioneering and entrepreneurial spirit from his father, Edward S. Rogers, Sr., who in 1921 was the first Canadian to transmit a radio signal across the Atlantic.

At the time only 21 years old, Rogers went on to become much more than a historical footnote by inventing the radio amplifying tube, a device that revolutionized the radio industry by eliminating the need for cumbersome, leak-prone acid batteries, enabling consumers to operate their radios on alternating current. Rogers's invention led him to found CFRB (Canada's First Rogers Batteryless), which became the most popular radio station in the country, and Rogers Majestic Corporation, a manufacturing concern devoted to producing his invention. Rogers moved on to break ground in another direction in 1931 when he was granted the first license in Canada to broadcast experimental television, but eight years later, when Edward S. Rogers, Jr., was five years old, the elder Rogers died of overwork and a bleeding ulcer, leaving no one in charge to supervise his various business interests. The Rogers estate floundered and the popular CFRB station was lost.

The younger Rogers, who preferred to be called Ted, was affected deeply by the death of his father. He followed his father's footsteps in his first big business deal, purchasing radio station CHFI-FM in 1960 while studying for a law degree at Osgoode Hall Law School. Rogers used a life insurance policy as collateral to take out a $63,000 loan and paid $85,000 for the station, an intrepid move considering that only five percent of the Toronto market possessed FM receivers at the time. Undaunted by critics who dismissed the FM concept, Rogers plunged into the FM radio broadcasting business, establishing Rogers Radio Broadcasting Limited as the owner of CHFI. To help promote the station, Rogers, then 26 years old, approached Westinghouse Canada and convinced the company to manufacture inexpensive ($39.95) FM radios, which he then sold or gave away to listeners. Two years later, a year after earning his law degree, Rogers purchased CFTR-AM, then went on to win other radio licenses, initially using money from his parents' estate and later soliciting financial assistance from the Bank of Montreal and Toronto business leaders.

Entering Cable Broadcasting: Mid-1960s

By the mid-1960s, Rogers was ready to steer the Canadian communications industry in a new direction. While his father had shown himself to be an ingenious engineer, the younger Rogers was carving his niche in the communications industry as a marketer, transforming existing but little-used technology into widely sought-after services. His entry into FM radio broadcasting had proved to be an insightful move, the first of his successful efforts to broaden the appeal of existing communications technology, but when he was awarded Canada's first cable franchise in 1965 his abilities produced success of a much higher magnitude. Competing against industry stalwarts such as Gulf & Western and CBS for the first rights to broadcast cable, Rogers emerged victorious, registering one of the several key licensing coups that would carry him to the top of the communications industry.

After slightly more than a decade in the cable business, Rogers had established a formidable presence, constructing a cable network that had few rivals. In 1978 he made an aggressive move to bolster his company's position further when he acquired Canada's second largest cable company, Canadian Cablesystems Limited, in an unfriendly takeover. At the same time, Rogers began collecting cable franchises in the United States. The following year he took his company public as the largest cable operator in Canada. Another leading cable company, Premier Communications Limited, was added to Rogers's stable of cable properties in two transactions during 1979 and 1980, extending the company's coverage to British Columbia, where Premier served three urban centers. In 1981 Rogers targeted UA-Columbia Cablevision Inc. as his next acquisition, offering his family's five radio stations, owned by a private company named Rogers Telecommunications Ltd., and his extensive cable television interests for a loan to secure UA-Columbia's 450,000 cable subscribers. Rogers bid $152 million for 51 percent of UA-Columbia, teaming up with United Artists Theater Circuit Inc. to beat out competing bids offered by Knight-Ridder Newspapers and Dow Jones. When the deal was concluded in November, Rogers Communications' cable properties served 1.75 million subscribers, making the company the largest cable operator in North America.

Rogers Communications' frenetic growth slowed during the early 1980s after the acquisition of UA-Columbia, as an economic recession inflated interest rates to 20 percent between 1982 and 1983. Saddled with $750 million in debt it had assumed to finance its growth, Rogers Communications staggered through the early and mid-1980s, divesting assets and abandoning plans to expand into Europe. "We sold off everything we could, just to keep afloat," Rogers reflected later to *Forbes*. "It was like flying a plane, and you're just tossing stuff out of the plane just trying to keep above the trees." The company paid its price for two decades of aggressive expansion, losing more than $100 million between 1982 and 1987, but the losses, although severe, were of secondary importance to Rogers. More important was securing commanding control over emerging communications technologies, even if that goal was achieved through lackluster financial performance.

The Move to Cellular: Early 1980s

Prompted by recent developments in cellular telephone technology, Rogers began exploring the possibility of entering the business in 1982. In February of the following year he approached the company's board of directors, who, considering the financial condition of the struggling company at the time, rejected his proposal to obtain a cellular telephone license. Rogers persevered, looking elsewhere for financial support. Assistance was obtained from the Belzerg family of Vancouver-based First City Financial Corporation and Philippe de Gaspee Beaubien of Montreal-based Telemedia Inc. Rogers then invested $2 million of his own money to launch the venture, which was incorporated in May 1984 as Rogers Cantel Mobile Communications Inc. Over the next four years, after investing an additional $5 million, Rogers bought out his partners to become the sole owner of Cantel, giving his company a third leg to stand on.

The future of the communications industry, as Rogers and others perceived it, entailed all communications services being transmitted via a single wire into businesses and individual residences, preferably by one company with broad communications capabilities. As a result, Rogers Communications sought to become a communications conglomerate capable of bundling telephone, television, and paging and wireless services in one monthly bill to consumers throughout Canada.

One important branch of the communications field was missing from this growing empire, however: Rogers Communications did not maintain a stake in providing telephone service. Rogers attempted to fill this void in 1985 by making a bid for CNCP Telecommunications Limited, a subsidiary of Canadian Pacific Limited, but the attempt was rejected. Four years later Rogers tried again, but first he made an uncharacteristic move by selling his U.S. cable properties to Houston Industries, Inc., in February 1989 for $1.58 billion. Instead of using the money to support an aggressive expansion program, he plowed the money back into Rogers Communications, with $525 million earmarked for refurbishing the company's cable operations and another $600 million dedicated to strengthening Cantel, which by this point had captured more than 50 percent of the Canadian mobile telephone market.

Unitel, Maclean Hunter, and the Early 1990s

One month after Rogers Communications sold its U.S. cable properties, Rogers made another bid for CNCP Telecommunications to end what he referred to in an interview with the *Globe and Mail* as ''Soviet-style communications monopolism.'' This time around Rogers was successful, acquiring a 40 percent stake in the company from Canadian Pacific Limited and spawning a new business arm for Rogers Communications, which was later named Unitel Communications Holdings Inc. In June 1992 Unitel received permission from the Canadian Radio-Television and Telecommunications Commission to compete against the telephone companies in the public long-distance market, making the company one of the largest of the long-distance companies in the country, trailing only Bell Canada.

Unitel, however, proved to be a drain on Rogers Communications' profits, losing a total of $600 million between 1992 and 1995. Rogers Communications had experienced its fair share of losses, sacrificing annual earnings for market share and for financing entry into new business areas, leading Rogers to casually note in a 1994 *Maclean's* interview, ''All this company has to do to make money is stop growing.'' Nevertheless, more than $500 million in losses racked up between 1990 and 1994 were cause for concern, and by 1995 Rogers was beginning to pin some of the blame on Unitel, confiding to Rogers Communications shareholders that year, ''Our policy is to be in long-distance, but not necessarily in Unitel.'' Earlier, the company's interest in Unitel had been dropped to 32 percent after AT&T

signed on as a partner in January 1993 when it purchased a 20 percent stake.

Despite mounting losses, Rogers Communications concluded a pivotal deal in 1994 when it acquired Maclean Hunter Limited for an enormous $2.5 billion. Financed largely by bank loans, the acquisition of Maclean Hunter, a cable and publishing conglomerate, gave Rogers Communications a 62 percent stake in Toronto Sun Publishing Corporation, which owned the *Toronto Sun,* the *Financial Post,* tabloids in Edmonton, Calgary, Toronto, and Ottawa, and nearly 200 other publications, including *Maclean's, Chatelaine,* and *Canadian Business.* These properties were organized in late 1994 under the newly named Maclean Hunter Publishing Limited, which was set up as a subsidiary of the newly created Rogers Multi-Media Inc. (soon renamed Rogers Media Inc.), which was a direct subsidiary of Rogers Communications. Rogers Media was also responsible for Rogers Broadcasting Limited, which included Maclean and Rogers radio stations, in addition to Rogers' television stations and other broadcasting interests.

Maclean Hunter's numerous cable properties ranked the company as Canada's fourth largest cable operator. With 700,000 cable subscribers in Canada (compared to Rogers Communications' 1.9 million), Maclean Hunter also owned U.S. cable systems in Florida, New Jersey, and the Detroit area that served more than 500,000 subscribers. The Canadian cable systems were folded into Rogers Cablesystems, while the U.S. properties were quickly sold off. Other Maclean Hunter properties that were sold in 1995 and 1996 included several radio stations, magazines in the United States and Europe, and some printing operations. To gain regulatory approval, Rogers also had to divest Maclean Hunter's CFCN-TV, which was sold to Shaw Communications Inc. in September 1995. Maclean's paging operations were subsumed by Rogers Cantel. In 1996 Rogers sold off several additional operations acquired with Maclean Hunter, including printers Davis & Henderson Ltd. and Transkrit Corporation and the 62 percent interest in Toronto Sun Publishing. All told, the divestments of Maclean Hunter properties generated nearly $3 billion, much of which was used to pay down Rogers' massive debt.

Alliances Key Strategy in the Consolidating Late 1990s

Despite the divestments, Rogers' debt continued to increase, nearing $5 billion by 1996, then hitting $5.6 billion in 1997. Throughout the mid-1990s and into the late 1990s, the company also continued to post losses every year. Like other players in the cable and cellular industries, Rogers was spending massive sums on capital expenditures ($800 million in 1996 alone) to build up a customer base of cable and cellular subscribers which would hopefully pay off handsomely in the long run. Ted Rogers had viewed the acquisition of Maclean Hunter as a step toward turning his company into the Time Warner of Canada, a media conglomerate controlling both content and the networks that deliver the content. But the mounting debt, a falling stock price, the prospect of continued losses for several more years, and increasing competition for Rogers Cantel from such newcomers as Clearnet Communications Inc. and Microcell Telecommunications Inc., forced the founder's son to at least temporarily pull back from his vision. This situation led to the divestment of Toronto Sun Publishing and its impressive content collection. Rogers Communications also gave up on the money-losing Unitel operation, taking a $99 million writedown to bring the value of its investment to zero. In late 1996 Rogers sold cable systems serving about 303,000 subscribers in Ontario to Cogeco Cable Inc. for $350 million.

In addition to asset sales, Rogers increasingly turned to alliances in an attempt to secure a significant position in the rapidly consolidating, deregulated communications world of the late 1990s. In April 1996 Rogers entered into partnership with RadioShack Canada Inc. to open and operate about 100 shopping mall stores across Canada which would sell Cantel products and services along with RadioShack products and accessories. In November of that year Rogers Cantel and AT&T entered into an alliance whereby Cantel would cobrand its wireless services as "Cantel AT&T," and Cantel would gain access to AT&T's services, technology, and marketing—a potential leg up over Cantel's phone company rivals and the wireless newcomers.

By this time, Rogers Communications had also entered the local telephone business through an entity called Rogers Network Services, which was renamed Rogers Telecom Inc. in 1997, and had become an Internet service provider through the cable-based Rogers WAVE. In April 1997 Rogers joined with At Home Corporation in a venture through which it began offering high-speed cable Internet access under the name Rogers@Home. In support of its Internet ventures, Rogers began replacing its cable systems with upgraded two-way cable, which was available to 78 percent of Rogers Cablesystems customers by year-end 1998.

In June 1998 Rogers Communications exited from the local phone market by selling Rogers Telecom to Calgary-based MetroNet Communications Corp. for $600 million in cash and 12.5 million nonvoting shares of MetroNet worth an initial $400 million. The company used the cash to pay down debt. Also in 1998 Rogers Cantel began a turnaround, thanks to streamlining, reducing costs, improving customer service, and introducing new simplified rate plans.

Rogers stepped up its alliance strategy in 1999, entering into deals with some of the biggest names in communications. In a deal announced in July and closed the following month, Microsoft Corporation paid C$600 million (US$400 million) for a 9.2 percent stake in Rogers Communications. The deal provided Rogers with much needed cash for paying off debt and funding capital projects, in return for the company agreeing to use Microsoft's software in a minimum of one million set-top boxes for digital television. Rogers also deepened its relationship with AT&T in 1999. Earlier in the year AT&T had entered into a joint venture with British Telecommunications PLC (BT) that combined the two companies' international operations. In August this joint venture spent C$1.4 billion (US$934 million) for a 33 percent stake in Rogers Cantel, providing Rogers Communications with another opportunity to pay down debt. Cantel, AT&T, and BT also said that they planned to work together on the next generation of wireless technology and would develop global calling plans for a single set fee. The deal reduced Rogers Communications' stake in Rogers Cantel to 51 percent.

The late 1999 deals helped to reduce the combined debt of Rogers Communications and Rogers Cantel from C$5.1 billion to C$3.1 billion, moving Rogers closer to having investment grade debt—rather than junk bond level—and paying dividends (the company had paid only one dividend in its history, in 1979). Aligning itself with AT&T, BT, and Microsoft positioned Rogers for eventually being able to offer its customers a bundle of long distance and wireless telephone services, paging services, cable television, and Internet access. The company appeared to be poised to be a major force in the converging world of 21st century communications.

Principal Subsidiaries

Rogers Cantel Mobile Communications Inc. (51%); Rogers Cablesystems Limited; Rogers Cablesystems Ontario Limited; Rogers Media Inc.; Maclean Hunter Publishing Limited; Rogers Broadcasting Limited.

Further Reading

Bank, David, "Microsoft Agrees to Pay $400 Million for 9.2% Rogers Communications Stake," *Wall Street Journal,* July 13, 1999, p. B7.

Blumenstein, Rebecca, and Solange De Santis, "AT&T, British Telecom to Buy Stake in Canada Wireless Firm Rogers Cantel," *Wall Street Journal,* August 6, 1999, p. B4.

Brehl, Robert, "Ted Rogers Pledges Turnaround by Five Years," *Globe and Mail,* May 26, 1998, p. B1.

——, "Ted Rogers' Troubled Neighbourhood," *Globe and Mail,* January 10, 1998, p. B1.

Brehl, Robert, and Lawrence Surtees, "MetroNet Grabs Rogers Unit," *Globe and Mail,* May 21, 1998, p. B1.

"Bust It Up, Guys," *Canadian Business,* December 12, 1997, pp. 33–34.

Dalglish, Brenda, "Rogers Reconnects with Investors," *Globe and Mail,* January 16, 1999, p. B1.

——, "Up in the Air: Long-Distance Competition Squeezes New Phone Companies," *Maclean's,* May 8, 1995, p. 50.

Dalglish, Brenda, and E. Kaye Fulton, "Cable Booster: Ted Rogers Wins Federal Approval for His Maclean Hunter Bid," *Maclean's,* December 29, 1994, p. 44.

Dummett, Ben, "Rogers' Free Spending Perturbs Critics," *Globe and Mail,* August 4, 1997, p. B9.

Enchin, Harvey, "It's Official: CRTC Okays MH Takeover," *Globe and Mail,* December 20, 1994, p. B1.

——, "Rogers Writes Off Unitel," *Globe and Mail,* August 10, 1995, p. B1.

——, "Sun Sale Hardly Dents Rogers' Debt," *Globe and Mail,* August 3, 1996, p. B3.

Enchin, Harvey, and Stacey Young, "Rogers Pledges to Put Financial House in Order," *Globe and Mail,* August 31, 1996, p. B1.

Evans, Mark, "Rogers Sells $1.4-Billion Cantel Stake," *Globe and Mail,* August 6, 1999, p. B1.

"Famous Players Canadian Corp.," *Financial Post,* June 5, 1965, p. 35.

Fisher, Ross, "Ted's Team," *Canadian Business,* August 1989, p. 28.

Garneau, George, "Maclean Hunter Agrees to Be Bought by Rogers," *Editor & Publisher,* March 19, 1994, p. 50.

Hawkins, Chuck, "A Cable Mogul with a Live-Wire Idea," *Business Week,* July 4, 1988, p. 39.

Jackson, Basil, "Building Hustle Ahead As Movies Try Comeback," *Financial Post,* September 12, 1962, p. 36.

Jenish, D'Arcy, and Warren Caragata, "Cable Gets Zapped: A Wave of Consumer Protest Prompts Rogers to Rethink the Launch of New Channels," *Maclean's,* January 16, 1995, p. 26.

Mahood, Casey, ''Microsoft Takes a Stake in Rogers,'' *Globe and Mail,* July 13, 1999, p. B1.

Marion, Larry, ''The Legacy,'' *Forbes,* July 6, 1981, p. 81.

Mason, Todd, ''Houston Industries Splurges on Cable TV,'' *Business Week,* September 12, 1988, p. 40.

Meeks, Fleming, ''This Will Be a Very Political Issue,'' *Forbes,* February 19, 1990, p. 80.

Munk, Nina, ''Ted Rogers' New Apartment,'' *Forbes,* April 24, 1995, p. 42.

Newman, Peter C., ''The Ties That Bind,'' *Maclean's,* February 21, 1994, p. 34.

Noble, Kimberley, ''Bill and Ted's Joint Adventure,'' *Maclean's,* July 26, 1999, p. 36.

Osterland, Andrew W., ''Cable's Other Ted,'' *Financial World,* October 25, 1994, p. 36.

Partridge, John, ''Rogers Gives His Rival More Reasons to Worry,'' *Globe and Mail,* April 3, 1989, p. B1.

Rowan, Geoffrey, ''Rogers Empire Strives 'to Secure the Fortress,' '' *Globe and Mail,* May 11, 1996, p. B1.

Stoffman, Daniel, ''Great Connections,'' *Globe and Mail,* August 18, 1989, p. P37.

Surtees, Lawrence, ''Rogers Hooks Up with AT&T,'' *Globe and Mail,* November 14, 1996, p. B1.

Wells, Jennifer, ''Rogers in Retreat: What Comes Next After Selling the Sun?,'' *Maclean's,* May 20, 1996, p. 36.

Willis, Andrew, ''Mr. Rogers' Stubborn Streak Pays Off Big,'' *Globe and Mail,* August 6, 1999, p. B11.

—Jeffrey L. Covell
—updated by David E. Salamie

Royal KPN N.V.

Maanplein 5
2516CK Den Haag
The Netherlands
(31) 70 332-44-43
Fax: (31) 70 332-44-85
Web site: http://www.kpn.com

Public Company
Incorporated: 1989 as Koninklijke [Royal] PTT
    Nederland
Employees: 36,073
Sales: NLG 17.72 billion ($9.3 billion) (1998)
Stock Exchanges: Amsterdam Frankfurt London New
    York
Ticker Symbols: KPN
NAIC: 51331 Wired Telecommunications Carriers; 51333
    Telecommunications Resellers; 513332 Cellular and
    Other Wireless Telecommunications

Royal KPN N.V. is a Dutch telecommunications provider—the leading telephone service provider in the Netherlands—and is aiming to take a leading position in the international telephony and related services industries. The company's latest form was realized in 1998, following the break-up of parent company PTT Nederland, a government-owned monopoly overseeing the telephone and postal services. (PTT's other major holding, the Dutch postal service, became known as the TNT Post Group.) KPN serves more than eight million fixed-line customers and more than two million mobile telephone customers in the Netherlands. KPN is also active in Internet services, with its PlanetNet and XS4all services making it the country's largest Internet provider, while its corporate networking services and services for third-party telephone carriers also dominate in its Dutch domestic market. On the international front, KPN is a founding member of the Unisource alliance, with members Telia of Sweden and Swiss Telecom, and has entered a partnership with the U.S. telecom giant AT&T. KPN has also been expanding internationally through the acquisition of partnerships in foreign fixed-line and mobile telephone systems in Hungary, Ireland, and the Czech Republic, operating a European partnership with Colorado-based Qwest, and pursuing expansion in the Asian market. Led by former PTT Nederland CEO Wim Dik, who announced his departure in mid-1999, KPN was the subject of takeover rumors as it neared the 21st century.

A Post-Telegraph Monopoly in the 19th Century

The history of KPN may be traced through the history of Dutch communications, a system which until the 1990s was controlled by the government. Although postal services had long been in place in the collection of city-states that later became the Netherlands, it was not until the end of the 18th century that the Dutch postal services were reformed into a single, national system, modeling its organization after the system developed by the French. This system, officially established in 1799, provided the foundation of what would soon become known as the PTT Post.

The Dutch postal service inherited a variety of postal tariffs, and collection and delivery methods. In 1807, however, the Post was placed under the administration of the Ministry of Finance. This body passed the country's first Postal Act, a series of regulations providing for a more standardized collection, carrying, and delivery system, while also establishing a single rate system—based on distance and weight—for the entire country. Yet the Post was still not conceived of as a public service; instead, it was expected to operate more along the lines of a tax collection service, providing funds for the national treasury.

A shift in the vision of the Netherlands' postal services came in the mid-19th century. The passage of the Postal Act of 1850 established the postal service as a service in the public interest. While remaining under the finance ministry, the Post shed its role as tax collector to become a public service. The Postal Act of 1850 further codified the postal service's domestic monopoly and created a simplified postal rate structure. Two years later, the postal service began the implementation of a nationally organized network of postal service facilities; every town would receive its own post office and a system was established for the collection and delivery of letters. By the 1870s, the Post's network of post offices covered most of the country.

393

Company Perspectives:

KPN will further exploit growth opportunities on the Dutch market in the area of fixed and mobile telephony with a view to maintaining and expanding its strong market position. It will pursue this goal by focusing on portfolio innovation, customer retention and continual efficiency improvement.

In the meantime, the Netherlands had begun to install its first telegraph transmission networks. In 1852, the country formally organized its telegraph utility, the Rijkstelegraaf, under the Ministry of the Interior, which assumed responsibility for installing a roadside network of telegraph poles and cables. Use of the telegraph as a communication means remained relatively limited, however.

The postal system and the telegraph service, which was soon to add the newly invented telephone, operated as separate government agencies until the 1880s. Given the limited growth of the telegraph in the Netherlands, it was decided that the two services should be joined into one agency, under a single ministry in 1886. Combining the two services offered the pragmatic benefit of allowing both to operate from the postal services' national network of post offices. With the addition of telephone services, this agency would become known as the PTT (for Post, Telegraph, and Telephone) and would remain a state-run monopoly for more than 100 years.

Growth of the Telephone System in the 20th Century

The combination of postal services with the country's telegraph and telephone systems was never wholeheartedly performed. Even though the two services were available through the same offices—the network of post offices created by the postal service—operations remained more or less separate, with each branch retaining its own personnel and culture. For the most part, the two services operated in parallel, each with its own personnel, budget and finances, and infrastructure.

The Depression era forced the PTT to modernize. The introduction of more efficient sorting systems enabled the PTT to cut back on the number of its delivery rounds; instead of the three deliveries per day, PTT postmen now performed only two. The growth of the telephone network, and the rising number of telephone users, was also slowly changing the communication habits of the Dutch commercial and private user, who would soon reach for the telephone, rather than the pen.

The difficult economic climate presented an opportunity for the PTT, in that government allowed the agency to operate more and more as a commercial enterprise. Unlike other government agencies, which were provided for in the national budget, the PTT was given a more corporate status, enabling the company to make the necessary capital investments and take writeoffs on its balance sheet, rather than depend on government approval for each investment. The PTT was also given its own press and publicity departments, enabling the agency to compete for consumer attention. While most of Europe's postal services and

telephone companies remained under government control, the PTT's relative independence allowed it to present a more modern appearance to consumers, who were treated also with original postal stamp designs.

The Nazi takeover of the Netherlands during World War II would interrupt the PTT's independent activities, as the Germans seized control of the country's communications systems. With the Liberation, the PTT was faced with rebuilding its telephone infrastructure. By the end of the 1940s, the agency was reporting heavy losses, especially from its postal services. In this way, the PTT was no different from most of its government-run counterparts in other countries. Telephone services, nevertheless, would provide a means to maintain a positive balance sheet for PTT, as the telephone quickly imposed itself as a mainstay in the postwar home. The PTT's telephone monopoly allowed the government-run service to maintain relatively high rates. As in most of its European counterparts, the telephone service charged by the minute for all calls, including local ones.

Expanding Services and Privatization in Mid- and Late 20th Century

Through the 1960s and 1970s, the PTT continued to improve the quality of its phone lines and telephone transmissions. The telephone industry was by then preparing to enter a new era of innovation. The use of telex equipment and facsimile machines, joined later by electronic messaging systems, and Internet-based voice and video communication technology, as well as portable telephone systems freed of dependence on a physical telephone wiring system, threatened a drastic transformation of traditional communication systems. While the telephone industry was facing a time of great change, the postal world was also changing; the arrival of dedicated express mail and other courier services, led by such companies as Federal Express and United Parcel Service in the United States, and Australia's TNT, presented new challenges to traditional postal services.

By the 1980s, the era of government-run, monopoly services had reached the beginning of the end. Restructuring was quickly becoming a necessity, not only to enable the PTT to compete in a rapidly transforming marketplace, but also to give the consumer more options—and potentially lower rates. During the 1980s, the PTT focused on expansion activities, buying up interests in domestic cable and television networks and moving toward international expansion of its telecommunications services. In 1989 the PTT was finally privatized.

That year, the PTT was reorganized as a private business, PTT Nederland N.V., under the direction of CEO Wim Dik. Under the new structure, the postal service, renamed PTT Post, joined the larger telecommunications industry sister company, PTT Telecom, as an independently operating subsidiary. Despite no longer being a government agency, the new PTT remained nonetheless wholly owned by the Dutch government. The change, however, allowed the company to pursue its own growth strategy into the 1990s, unhampered by the slower governmental decision-making process. Privatization also enabled the company to seek new international partners, some of which had balked at the prospect of pursuing projects with a government agency.

Partnering would prove essential if PTT Telecom—with its relatively small Netherlands market—was to be able to compete on an international scale. The coming of telephone deregulation in the European market—scheduled for the late 1990s—would also present PTT Telecom with new opportunities. In 1992, PTT Telecom joined with Sweden's telecommunications monopoly Telia to form the Unisource alliance. This partnership quickly gained more weight with the addition of Swiss Telecom in 1993. By the following year, Unisource had reached an international cooperation agreement with AT&T to form the joint venture Uniworld. Launched in 1996, Uniworld targeted commercial customers with integrated data-voice telephone packages. Uniworld also gave PTT Telecom a position in the Far East, as a member of WorldPartners with AT&T, Japan's KDD, and Singapore Telecom.

In 1994 PTT Nederland went to the stock market, as the Dutch government sold off some 30 percent of its shares on the Amsterdam exchange. The public listing of the postal-telecommunications business marked the largest offering ever in the Netherlands, and also the world's first public listing of a post office. Interest in the new shares was high; with most investor attention going to PTT Telecom, nearly twice as large as the NLG 5 billion-per-year PTT Post. Two years later, PTT Nederland offered another 25 percent of its shares, effectively ending the Dutch government's control of the country's post and telecommunications services. At that time, PTT Nederland took listings on the New York, London, and Frankfurt stock exchanges as well.

The public offering not only enhanced PTT Telecom's profile in the telecommunications industry, it also gave the company maneuvering room in the rapidly changing telecommunications landscape. This would prove especially necessary, as PTT Telecom faced the end of its domestic telephone monopoly, as well as competition for the Netherlands' mobile telephone customers. With the increase in capital, PTT Telecom began an international expansion drive. In 1994, the company bought a 30 percent interest in Bakrie Electronics Company (BEC) of Indonesia, partnering with that country's telephone monopoly to build and operate new telephone networks.

The Eastern European market would also be targeted by PTT Telecom as part of its international expansion. In partnership with Swiss Telecom and AT&T, PTT Telecom bought up a 27 percent share in SPT, the Czech telecommunications provider. Moreover, PTT Telecom's partnership in the Pannon GSM digital mobile telephone network brought the company to Hungary. PTT Telecom also began building a fixed line and mobile telephone infrastructure in Ukraine, in partnership with other providers.

In 1995 PTT Post stepped out of the shadows of its larger sister company when it reached an agreement to acquire the struggling TNT for some NLG 2.7 billion. The purchase, which placed PTT Post roughly on the same revenue footing as PTT Telecom, set the stage for the next evolution of the former state-run monopoly. In 1998, PTT Nederland announced that it was splitting into two entirely independent, publicly listed companies, Royal KPN, which contained the company's telecommunications activities, and TNT Post Group (TPG), which took over the company's postal, logistics, and express mail services wing, including both companies' shares of the GDEW partnership. Both KPN and TPG retained listings on the Amsterdam, New York, London, and Frankfurt stock exchanges.

After boosting its role as an Internet service provider in the Netherlands, with the acquisitions of XS4all and Capital Online, making it the country's largest ISP, KPN continued its international and domestic expansion in 1999. In June of that year, KPN agreed to acquire Telecommunications Services & Networks (TS&N) from Origin Nederland, strengthening KPN's telephone and telecommunications services, including voice, data, and PCX management services for such large corporate clients as Philips, among others. One month later, KPN paid $510 million for the purchase of a 51 percent stake in the former Bulgarian state-owned telecommunications provider BTC. The purchase, made in partnership with Greek telecommunications provider OTE, also gave KPN ownership of a national GSM mobile telephone license in Bulgaria. Despite its expansion efforts, KPN remained a relatively small player in the highly competitive global telecommunications business. The retirement announcement of KPN chief Wim Dik in 1999 fueled industry opinion that KPN itself would become a takeover candidate early in the new century.

Principal Operating Units

Fixed Line Telephony; Mobile Telephony; Telecommerce; Corporate Networks; Carrier Services; Business Communications.

Further Reading

Dickey, Allan, "Public Services at Private Prices," *Eurobusiness*, March 1994, p. 57.
Hastings, Phillip, "Rush to Repackage," *Financial Times*, June 17, 1999.
"Hitting the Mail on the Head," *Economist*, April 30, 1994, p. 69.
Resener, Madeleine, "How the Dutch Did It," *Institutional Investor*, April 1995, p. 66.
"TNT Sale May Signal Industry Trend," *Logistics Management*, January 1997, p. 26.
Woodford, Julian, "KPN," *Utility Week*, January 23, 1998, p. 24.

—M.L. Cohen

Royal Packaging Industries Van Leer N.V.

PO Box 25
Amsterdamseweg 206
1180AA Amstelveen
The Netherlands
+31 20 543 0600
Fax: +31 20 543 0700
Web site: http://www.vanleer.com

Public Company
Incorporated: 1919
Employees: 17,000
Sales: NLG 3.84 billion (US$2.37 billion) (1998)
Stock Exchanges: Amsterdam
NAIC: 422130 Containers, Paper & Disposable Plastics, Wholesaling; 421840 Containers, Industrial, Wholesaling; 322215 Paper Plates Made from Purchased Paper or Paperboard; 332439 Drums, Light Gauge Metal, Manufacturing; 326199 Drums, Plastics Manufacturing

Royal Packaging Industries Van Leer N.V. is one of the world leaders in industrial and consumer packaging. Van Leer's steel drum sales place it as the leading global manufacturer of these industrial containers. Van Leer's industrial products include steel, plastic, and fiber drums, intermediate bulk containers and other container products, as well as container closure systems, industrial films and sheeting, and metallized holographic papers. On the consumer side, Van Leer manufactures food packaging products including plastic tubs, containers, and covers, molded fiber products, including egg boxes and other protective enclosures, and tableware, including the Chinet brand of disposable dishes; much of the company's consumer products business is in the sale of printed consumer packaging products.

Van Leer's operations are divided into its two primary product segments, each with its own strategy. Representing the oldest part of Van Leer's business, its industrial products seg-

ment serves many of the world's leading oil and chemical companies. The highly competitive marketplace, and limited overall market growth prospects, have led Van Leer to focus on developing more efficient product capacity and technology. The company's entry into the consumer packaging market came with its acquisition of Unilever's 4P consumer packaging unit in 1992. Through 4P and other subsidiaries, including the Chinet brand, Van Leer has gained a leading position in the worldwide consumer packaging and printed consumer packaging markets.

A publicly traded company since 1996, Van Leer has had difficulties realizing shareholder value in a market with limited organic growth opportunities. After building scale through acquisitions—which doubled the company's sales—Van Leer itself became an acquisition target in 1999. At the end of July of that year, Van Leer announced that it had reached an agreement to merge its operations into those of Finland's Huhtamaki, creating the world's eighth largest packager. The merger, to cost Huhtamaki an estimated $1 billion, was expected to be completed by the end of 1999. The company would then be named Huhtamaki Van Leer, with annual sales of more than 2.8 billion Euros.

Packaging in the Post-World War I Era

Bernard van Leer started up a small factory outside of Amsterdam in 1919 at the age of 36. Van Leer's initial production revolved around small cans, boxes, cartons, and other packaging items for the local market. Van Leer, however, proved to be a shrewd businessman; he soon extended the company's production facilities into the industrial packaging arena. A breakthrough for the company came in 1925, when Van Leer received an order for 10,000 steel drums from the Shell Oil Company.

This order would soon lead Van Leer to focus solely on industrial packaging products and, specifically, on the production of steel drums and drum closure systems. In 1927 Van Leer adopted a new closure system to improve the reliability of its steel drums when it purchased a license to fit its drums with the U.S.-developed ''Tri-Sure'' closure system. Van Leer quickly built a reputation for the quality and reliability of its steel drums. American Flange, the company that originally developed the Tri-Sure system and continued to hold patent and trademark rights, would become a Van Leer subsidiary in 1988.

Another factor in the company's success was its early recognition of the need to look beyond its domestic market. With global customers such as Shell, the company reasoned that, rather than shipping its drums around the world (which amounted to shipping air, as it were), Van Leer should produce its steel drums in the same locations as its customers. Thus began the company's international expansion, bringing Van Leer to every continent, with more than 40 subsidiaries operating in 15 countries by the 1950s.

At the time of Bernard van Leer's death in 1958, the company, which remained wholly owned by the van Leer family, was posting NLG 340 million in sales per year and had grown to an operation employing 5,500. Bernard van Leer was succeeded by son Oscar van Leer, born in 1914. Under Oscar van Leer, the company saw strong growth and became a diversified, internationally operating packaging company.

Ownership—and net profits—of Van Leer would, however, gradually be transferred from the van Leer family to the Van Leer Group Foundation, which in turn attributed the company's profits to the Bernard van Leer Foundation, a charitable trust established by the company's founder to aid children throughout the world, particularly in Van Leer's countries of operation. The Van Leer Group Foundation, set up by Bernard van Leer's own children, would maintain 100 percent control of the company until the mid-1990s.

Diversification in the 1970s

The strong growth of the global petrochemicals industry in the 1950s and 1960s, as automobile use achieved its true dominance of the world transportation market, contributed to Van Leer's own growth during the period. The company's international success, and the work of the Bernard van Leer Foundation, received accolades at home, when the company was awarded the prestigious title of ''Royal'' by the country's royal family, a title normally reserved for Dutch companies at least 100 years old. Van Leer adopted the name of Royal Packaging Industries Van Leer in 1969.

The company's close relationship to the petrochemical market—through its continued focus on steel drums and steel drum closure systems—enabled it to achieve steady growth through the 1960s. But it also left Van Leer vulnerable to downturns in the oil industry. Such was the case in the early 1970s, when the Arab Oil Crisis transformed the world's oil markets. The crisis hit Van Leer hard; by 1975, the company posted the first loss in its history.

Under Oscar van Leer, the company determined that this loss would be its last. To protect itself from the fluctuations of its primary markets, the oil and chemical industries, Van Leer decided that it needed to diversify its operations, bringing the company into new product areas and new industrial markets. Van Leer entered the plastics market, particularly in the production of plastic and fiber-based drums, and in the manufacture of industrial strength films, such as the company's Valeron brand. The company's diversification efforts involved more than adding new products, but also prompted the company to step up its research and development activities, leading Van Leer to introduce a number of product innovations to the packaging industry.

The company's diversification moves were successful. The company once again posted profits by 1976. By 1979, when Oscar van Leer retired, the company's net sales had grown to NLG 1.3 billion. Oscar van Leer would be followed by Willem de Vlugt, considered the architect of the company's success in the 1980s and 1990s.

By the 1980s, the company had grown to an internationally operating grouping of subsidiaries. The company began taking steps to streamline its organization, bringing greater efficiency to its operations, while grouping its many subsidiaries as Business Units. The Business Unit model would come to define the company's organization in the early 1990s, as Van Leer reorganized around 30 or so Strategic Business Units, each of which acted as an umbrella for a number of Business Units, based on geography and/or product compatibility. Strategic Business Units were expected to coordinate product category and geographic market strategies, guiding production and distribution, while providing budgetary oversight. At the same time, the Strategic Business Units and the Business Units were encouraged to operate independently, adapting their strategies to their specific markets.

Van Leer had by then expanded into the world's largest market, the United States. The company's U.S. implantation began in the early 1980s both through production plant construction and through a number of strategic acquisitions. Two significant acquisitions of the time were those of Keyes Fiber Company (later renamed The Chinet Company) and the steel drum business of Inland Steel, which became known as Van Leer Containers Inc. In 1988 Van Leer acquired American Flange and the rights to its Tri-Sure closure system; Van Leer thus became an important supplier to its own competitors.

Mergers and Acquisitions in the 1990s

By the 1990s, organic growth in the industrial packaging market was becoming difficult to achieve. Although Latin America and the Asian region represented some growth potential, the overall market seemed to have reached maturity, while remaining highly fragmented. Van Leer's initial response was to expand its own product lines beyond industrial packaging to the consumer packaging market, which had not yet seen its peak in market growth. In 1992 Van Leer acquired Unilever's 4P consumer packaging operations, worth some NLG 1 billion per year. The purchase would raise Van Leer's sales to more than NLG 3.8 billion for 1993 and establish the company among the world's top ten packaging companies.

The 4P purchase gave Van Leer the momentum to pursue internal growth and market expansion through a two-pronged strategy. The first continued Van Leer's long history of international presence, as the company stepped up the construction of new foreign production facilities. The second part of the company's strategy took Van Leer on the acquisition trail, as the company began a series of purchases and takeovers to complement its existing operations.

To finance its expansion drive, Van Leer went public in 1996, taking a listing on the Amsterdam stock exchange. In the transaction, the Van Leer Foundation sold off some 35 percent of its holding, reducing its participation in the company to 65 percent. With the cash inflow from the stock offering, Van Leer was able to step up both its building of new plants and its acquisitions of related companies.

Among the company's purchases was that of Uniflex Packaging Company Ltd., of Thailand, a consumer goods flexible packaging producer, renamed Van Leer Packaging (Thailand), in 1997. In that same year, the acquisition of Nyman Manufacturing Company, based in Rhode Island, complemented the company's Chinet tableware activities. A year later, the company added another U.S.-based company, Sirco Systems, LLC, a knock-down steel drum maker based in Birmingham, Alabama. Meanwhile, Van Leer had traveled to New Zealand, adding a molded fiber packaging plant in Auckland, and to Russia, adding a steel drum plant in Vologda.

At the same time, Van Leer scored a number of major new contracts, including a 1997 contract with Dow Corning to supply that company's worldwide steel drum and pail needs, as well as International Bulk Containers and other packaging products. The following year, Van Leer added contracts to supply Castrol with European steel and plastic drum requirements and to supply steel drums for Esso's international operations.

These activities helped the company raise its revenues to NLG 4.75 billion for 1997. The company also was posting steady profit growth, reporting NLG 122 million for that year. Yet Van Leer's expansion moves in the Asian market exposed it to that region's economic collapse in 1998. The company also was affected by a similar crisis in Latin America. The company's sales slipped back to NLG 4.5 million for the year, and profits barely climbed to NLG 132 million. At the same time,

Van Leer's stock had long been dwindling, sliding to a low of NLG 17 per share by the beginning of 1999.

In 1998 Van Leer was said to be "desperately" searching for a new large acquisition—on the scale of its 4P acquisition—to return the company to a strong growth track. Yet acquisition candidates in the packaging market had become scarce; between the large, top ten businesses such as Van Leer, and a myriad of small concerns, there seemed little opportunity for the type of takeover Van Leer needed to boost its revenues to double-digit growth.

In May 1999, Van Leer announced that it was involved in a new, large-scale acquisition: the company was being taken over by Finnish packaging producer Huhtamaki. Clashes over this move would lead to the sudden departure of Willem de Vlugt from the Van Leer leadership. By the end of July 1999, the proposed takeover had transmuted into more of a merger than an acquisition. The two companies would join operations, maintaining headquarters in Finland and The Netherlands. The proposed company, to be named Huhtamaki Van Leer, would become the world's eighth largest consumer and industrial packager, with revenues of more than 2.8 billion Euros per year. The Van Leer Foundation would remain a principal shareholder in the new entity, with 14.6 percent of shares equaling that of its Finnish counterpart, the Finnish Cultural Foundation. Approval of the merger was expected to come before the end of the year.

Principal Subsidiaries

American Flange & Manufacturing Co. Inc. (U.S.A.); The Chinet Company (U.S.A.); Nyman Manufacturing Co. (U.S.A.); 4P North America, Inc. (U.S.A.); Leopack B.V.; Leotech BV; Euro Papier Recycling B.V.; Es + Es Verpakkingen B.V.; Tri-Sure Japan Ltd.; Inpack Industries B.V. (India).

Further Reading

"Finnen bevoordelen Van Leer Foundation," *De Telegraaf-I,* July 23, 1999.
"Van Leer Agrees to Offer by Rival," *Financial Times,* July 23, 1999.
"Van Leer lijdt geen pijn in Zuid-Amerika," *De Telegraaf-I,* August, 26, 1998.
"Van Leer topman loopt weg na diepgaand conflict," *De Telegraaf-I,* May 22, 1999.
"Van Leer zoekt wanhopig naar overnamekandidaten," *De Telegraaf-I,* March 18, 1998.
"Wat does Van Leer," *De Telegraaf-I,* May 5, 1999.

—M.L. Cohen

Russell Corporation

755 Lee Street
Alexander City, Alabama 35011-0272
U.S.A.
(256) 500-4000
Fax: (256) 500-9036
Web site: http://www.russellcorp.com

Public Company
Incorporated: 1902 as Russell Manufacturing Company
Employees: 15,737
Sales: $1.18 billion (1998)
Stock Exchanges: New York Pacific
Ticker Symbol: RML
NAIC: 315211 Men's & Boys' Cut & Sew Apparel
    Contractors; 315212 Women's, Girls', & Infants' Cut
    & Sew Apparel Contractors; 31321 Broadwoven
    Fabric Mills; 315191 Outerwear Knitting Mills;
    313311 Broadwoven Fabric Finishing Mills

From humble origins in a small Alabama town in 1902, Russell Corporation has evolved into a leading manufacturer and marketer of activewear, athletic uniforms, knit shirts, licensed athletic apparel, sports and casual socks, and woven fabrics. Vertically integrated, Russell is involved in the entire process of converting raw fibers into finished apparel and fabrics. The company's three principal brands are Russell Athletic, which is the largest producer of athletic team uniforms in the United States; Jerzees, known for its popularly priced fleece and lightweight activewear; and Cross Creek, maker of knit golf wear and other casualwear.

Early 20th-Century Founding

Founder Benjamin Russell was only 25 when he bought six knitting machines from R.A. Almond in 1902. Russell, a struggling lawyer in Birmingham, Alabama, was anxious to return home to Alexander City and open his own business. With borrowed money, he incorporated Russell Manufacturing Company in 1902, remaining its president until he died in 1941. Russell's knitting machines, 12 sewing machines, and 12 em-

ployees were crammed into a 50 by 100 foot wooden building. Because of the lack of electricity, Russell Manufacturing Company relied on steam for power. At the end of the first year of production, the company was turning out 150 items of clothing per day. Though first year profits were disappointing, the entrepreneurial young owner envisioned his plant expanding into all aspects of the garment making business.

Russell's dream was slowly realized, and profits grew steadily in the following years. Six years after opening his plant, Russell acquired spinning frames, allowing the company to produce its own yarn. Several years later, it could bleach its own cloth. Electricity came to the plant in 1912, and two years later a second yarn plant went into operation.

Demand for cloth and yarn shot up dramatically during World War I, during which time the company expanded and prospered. When the war ended, the ensuing recession left the company unaffected because the demand for yarn continued. In response, the company added workers and plants. Also at this time, the Russell Mill School was established for educating the children of employees as well as for adult programs. The company's fourth yarn plant began operation in 1921, and in early 1927 a weaving operation was installed. By the end of the year Russell Manufacturing Company could dye its own cotton and yarn, coming close to realizing Benjamin Russell's ambition of making his company a completely vertical or "fiber to fabric" operation.

Moving into Athletic Wear and Screen Printing: 1930s

Until 1932, however, fabric still had to be sent to other U.S. plants for finishing. Despite the company's losses during the Great Depression, Benjamin Russell decided to expand his business. The worst year of the Depression, 1932, turned into a milestone year for the 30-year-old company; it acquired full finishing operations, thereby becoming one of the few fully vertical fabric factories in the world. That same year Benjamin Russell's son, Benjamin C. Russell, established an athletics division called the Southern Manufacturing Company. Its first products were football jerseys sold to a sporting goods distributor in New York. In 1938 the company's first screen printing developed for the printing of names, numbers, and designs on

---

Company Perspectives:

We are building a brand new Company. Russell's future is about transforming a manufacturing-driven organization into a world-class consumer marketing Company that will compete successfully on a global basis. Everything we do is about fulfilling this goal.

---

athletic uniforms. In 1960 the Southern Manufacturing Company was renamed the Russell Athletic Division. No one in 1932 would have guessed that this unobtrusive sideline would alter the company's identity from that of a domestic fabric manufacturer to a global leader in the sportswear industry.

Civilian textile manufacturing declined during World War II because of enormous government clothing contracts that strained the company. By war's end, machinery was badly in need of repair because replacement materials had been difficult to obtain during the war years. In addition the company's founder, Benjamin Russell, had died at the outset of World War II. His son Benjamin C. Russell took over the helm during the difficult but prosperous war years but died prematurely of pneumonia in 1945. Another Russell son, Thomas Dameron Russell, succeeded to the helm. By the time he stepped down as president 23 years later, the company had become a leading manufacturer of athletic and leisure wear and exited the fashion clothing manufacturing business.

In the 1950s sporting and leisure wear had not yet caught on with the general public. With two domestic recessions, the company was hard hit by falling sales and growing competition, and expansion was temporarily impeded. Changes in the clothing industry, however, helped Russell rebound. By the early 1960s, T-shirts had become acceptable garb for both sexes. In the late 1960s the unisex trend in clothing strengthened while leisure clothing became popular in the early 1970s. These trends served to Russell's advantage. In 1966 a new sewing plant was established in Montgomery, Alabama (the first Russell plant to be built outside of Alexander City). Four years later, the Athletic Division had expanded so much that a separate plant became necessary. The company went public in 1963. The firm, whose name had altered in 1962 to Russell Mills, Inc., would be a public stockholding company in which the Russell family and other insiders would continue to own approximately 32 percent of the stock.

Modernization and Expansion in the 1970s and 1980s

In 1968 Eugene C. Gwaltney became president of Russell Mills (which in 1973 would alter its name to Russell Corporation). That year company sales stood at $51 million. During Gwaltney's term in office, plant expansion continued. The company's screen printing facilities were enlarged, and it acquired a yarn manufacturing plant in northeast Georgia in 1977. In the mid-1970s Russell opened a new distribution center in Alexander City. All operations at this ultramodern facility, such as storage retrieval, shipping, and goods reception, were fully automated and consolidated. At the same time, new buildings went up to house operations including data processing, personnel, and secu-

rity. By 1981, with the consolidation of knitting into one plant, Russell could boast the most modern knitting facilities in the world. Expansion into Florida and south Alabama took place after 1982, the year Eugene Gwaltney was elected chairman of the board and was succeeded as president by Dwight L. Carlisle.

In 1989 the Russell Corporation test and evaluation mill was constructed at a cost of $6 million. This was an innovative facility in which new machinery was evaluated before purchase, avoiding the interruptions in operations implicit in tests during the production process. By 1990 the company owned and operated 13 sewing plants outside of Alexander City and employed 15,000 workers. Since 1976 sales revenues had increased by 13 percent annually. With the acquisition of two subsidiaries, Quality Mills in North Carolina and Cloathbond Ltd. in Scotland, in 1988 and 1989 respectively, the company had become a global contender in the sportswear industry.

According to market analysts, a key to the company's success was its aggressive technological modernization. In a five-year period ending in 1992, the company invested more than half a billion dollars in capital expenditures which translated into approximately 15 percent of annual sales—far higher than the industry's average of eight percent. In addition, the company spent at least three percent of sales revenues on print and television advertising. In both 1980 and 1990 *Textile World* cited Russell Corporation as the "Model Mill" of the year. Another reason for the company's success was research and development. In 1992 an innovative new material that prevented pilling, NuBlend, was introduced in Russell's Jerzees line of sportswear and won accolades from the leisurewear industry. Partly because NuBlend was the preferred fabric for screen printers, Russell held the top market share in the fleece screen printing business at 30 percent.

Under president and CEO John C. Adams, who succeeded the retiring Carlisle in 1991, approximately 80 percent of Russell Corporation's early 1990s sales were derived from its principal divisions: Athletic, Knit Apparel, Fabrics, and its major U.S. subsidiary, Cross Creek Apparel, Inc. (formerly Quality Mills). The company had become the top manufacturer of athletic uniforms in the nation. In 1992 Russell was awarded a five-year contract to serve as the exclusive producer and marketer of athletic uniforms for most Major League Baseball teams. The contract also stipulated that the company held the exclusive right to manufacture and market replicas of major league uniforms, T-shirts, and shorts. This put the company in an advantageous position in relation to its main rival, Champion, Inc., the supplier of uniforms to the NBA teams. The Knit Apparel Division produced the Jerzees brand of activewear, which had been introduced in 1983, and included T-shirts, fleece, knit shorts, and tank tops, which were sold to specialized retailers and large merchandisers such as Wal-Mart. Cross Creek produced the Cross Creek Pro Collection, featuring casual knit shirts and rugbys, which were sold mainly in golf pro shops, and Cross Creek Country Cottons, which were purchased by screen printers and embroiderers for resale. The remainder of Russell's revenues were derived from the Fabrics Division, which manufactured and marketed lightweight cotton material for sale to clothing manufacturers, and from its European subsidiary, Russell Corp. UK Ltd. in Scotland. This subsidiary had been acquired in 1989 under the name Cloathbond, Ltd.; it was a vertical establishment that manufactured and marketed a full line of Russell clothing, from the cotton fiber to the finished product, for the European market. This international expansion helped the company approach $1 billion in sales in the early 1990s. In 1992 alone, Russell's international sales increased 40 percent over 1991.

In April 1993 Gwaltney retired as chairman of Russell, ending a 41-year career at the company. Adams then served as chairman, president, and CEO. Later that year Russell paid $35 million to acquire The Game, Inc., a maker of licensed sports headgear and apparel, with a leading position in the marketing of such products for colleges and universities. The name of the acquired entity was changed to Licensed Products Division in 1994. That year Russell acquired Fort Payne, Alabama-based Desoto Mills, a finisher/manufacturer and marketer of sports and casual socks under the Desoto Players Club, Athletic Club, Performance Club, and Player Performance brand names. Russell also acquired the trademarks and licenses of Chalk Line, Inc. in 1994, a year in which the company's revenues exceeded $1 billion for the first time.

Major Restructuring in the Late 1990s

Although sales and net income reached record levels in 1996, in part because of the impact of the Summer Olympics which were held in Atlanta that year, Russell's fortunes turned south in 1997 when both sales and net income fell. The decline was caused by intensifying competition as industrywide overcapacity and price-cutting by rivals forced Russell to lower its own prices, all of which hurt the company's results. Particularly troubled was the Licensed Products Division, which Russell dissolved in 1997, dividing its operations among the other divisions. In 1997 Russell also ended its licensing deals with the professional football, basketball, and hockey leagues.

In early 1998, as the company's troubles continued, Adams retired; stepping in as chairman, president, and CEO was John "Jack" Ward, former CEO of the Hanes Group and senior vice-president of Sara Lee Corporation. Within months of Ward's arrival, Russell announced a major restructuring. Over a three-year period, the company planned to eliminate about 4,000 jobs, or 23 percent of its workforce; close about 25 of its 90 plants, distribution centers, and other facilities; and move most of the final assembly of garments abroad, to Mexico, Honduras, and elsewhere in the Caribbean basin. The company expected to take charges of $100 to $125 million during the restructuring period. Russell hoped these efforts would result in annual savings of $50–$70 million. Part of these funds would then be used to bolster the marketing and advertising of Russell's brands, including tripling the advertising budget to $25 million per year. Russell also established a second headquarters in Atlanta in February 1999, a move designed to make travel more convenient and to aid in recruiting efforts, particularly of marketing aces who did not relish the idea of living in the small town of Alexander City.

Finally, in January 1999 Russell reorganized into six strategic business units as part of its transformation from a manufacturing-driven organization to a consumer-oriented marketing corporation. Each of the units was self-contained, with full responsibility and accountability for results; each included such functional areas as manufacturing, sales, marketing, finance, information systems, and human resources. Three of the units centered around a major Russell brand: Russell Athletic, Jerzees, and Cross Creek. Fabrics and Services focused on

quality woven fabrics, as well as housing some central service functions operating companywide. Russell Yarn was established as a supplier of yarn for the manufacture of Russell textiles and apparel. The International Division was charged with marketing all Russell branded products outside the United States and Canada; it conducted business in 50 countries in all.

Restructuring charges led Russell to post a fiscal 1998 net loss of $10.4 million on revenues of $1.18 billion. Results for the first half of 1999 also showed a net loss—of $12.9 million—but the restructuring had resulted in a decrease in selling, general, and administration costs of 13 percent. Russell had also increased its offshore apparel assembly to 55 percent of total capacity, a substantial increase from the 17 percent mark before the restructuring was launched. Russell had far to go before it could be considered ''turned around,'' but it appeared that the company was well on its way.

Principal Subsidiaries

Cross Creek Apparel, Inc.; DeSoto Mills, Inc.; Russell Corp. UK Ltd.

Principal Operating Units

Russell Athletic; Jerzees; Cross Creek; Fabrics and Services; Russell Yarn; International.

Further Reading

Bernstein, Andy, ''John Adams: The SGB Interview,'' *Sporting Goods Business,* September 22, 1997, pp. 26–27.

Ebenkamp, Becky, and Terry Lefton, ''Russell Shows Some Muscle,'' *Brandweek,* May 10, 1999, p. 1.

Hagerty, James R., ''Russell's New CEO Is Looking to Make Rivals Sweat: Stock Price Bulks Up on Plans for a Trimmer Athletic-Gear Company,'' *Wall Street Journal,* August 5, 1998, p. B4.

Leibowitz, David S., ''Finding Value in Small Town America (Russell and Dean Foods' Stocks),'' *Financial World,* February 2, 1993, p. 86.

Lloyd, Brenda, ''Russell Corp. to Cut 4,000 Employees and Close 25 Facilities,'' *Daily News Record,* July 24, 1998, p. 1.

——, ''Russell Sees Sales Hitting $1.1B, Increase in Earnings for Year,'' *Daily News Record,* April 28, 1994, pp. 5+.

McCurry, John, ''Adams Retires, Russell Names Ward As CEO,'' *Textile World,* May 1998, pp. 24+.

——, '' 'New' Russell Stresses 'Global,' '' *Textile World,* March 1999, p. 20.

Miller, Andy, ''Russell Hopes to Score with Baseball Apparel,'' *Atlanta Constitution,* January 21, 1992, p. D1.

''Russell Corp. Says It Will Cut 4,000 Jobs, Shift Work Abroad,'' *Wall Street Journal,* July 23, 1998, p. A6.

''Russell's All Star Line-up: Managing for the Distance; Russell Manufacturing Tops Technology Curve,'' *Textile World,* June 1990, pp. 40–64.

Saunders, Thomas B., ''A History of Russell Corporation,'' Alexander City, Ala.: Russell Corporation, 1990.

Smarr, Susan L., ''Looking at the Big Picture,'' *Bobbin,* February 1990, pp. 60–64.

''TW's 1996 Leader of the Year: John C. Adams,'' *Textile World,* October 1996, pp. 36–38, 40, 43–44, 46.

Welling, Kathryn M., ''Out of Fashion Buys: An Analyst Cottons Up to Selected Apparel Stocks,'' *Barron's,* July 9, 1990, pp. 12–13, 28–29, 50.

—Sina Dubovoj
—updated by David E. Salamie

Salton, Inc.

550 Business Center Drive
Mount Prospect, Illinois 60056
U.S.A.
(847) 803-4600
Fax: (847) 803-1186
Web site: http://www.saltoninc.com

Public Company
Incorporated: 1943
Employees: 219
Sales: $305.6 million (1998)
Stock Exchanges: New York
Ticker Symbol: SALT
NAIC: 335211 Electric Housewares & Household Fan
    Manufacturing; 335221 Household Cooking Appliance
    Manufacturing

Salton, Inc. is a leading manufacturer of small electronics, principally for the kitchen. It has a roster of strong selling items, including the George Foreman Grill, the Juiceman juice extractor, and the Breadman bread machine. It markets appliances under a variety of other well-known brand names such as Toastmaster, White Westinghouse, Farberware, Block China, and its own Salton line. The company sells its goods both in department stores and in mass market outlets such as Kmart. It also has had key success selling appliances through television infomercials: half-hour programs that demonstrate a product, usually with a celebrity spokesperson. The company has kept abreast of changing tastes by bringing out new products quickly, catching fads and then moving on to the next. Salton experienced enormous growth in the 1990s, with sales growing at over 60 percent annually between 1996 and 1999. Company headquarters are in suburban Chicago, but almost all its manufacturing is contracted in Asia.

Entrepreneurial Beginnings

Salton got its start in 1943 as the brainchild of inventor Lewis Salton. Salton left his native Poland shortly after the German invasion in 1939 and settled in New York, where he was soon employed as an engineer for RCA Corporation. He worked long hours and often got home after supper, to be faced with cold leftovers. Salton's wife dutifully ran to the kitchen to warm his food in the oven, but the engineer decided there must be a better way. He invented a heated serving cart on wheels. Now his supper could stay warm, and be easily rolled out to him as soon as he got home. Salton raised enough money to begin manufacturing his hot tray, and began going from store to store in New York trying to get a buyer. All along, Salton had a bigger idea in mind. He wanted to sell enough hot trays to finance what he thought would be really useful and a big money-maker: an industrial tape dispenser. However, the hot tray held its own, and the Salton Tape Dispenser never made it off the drawing board. Lewis Salton recalled in an interview with *Advertising Age* in the July 12, 1982 issue, that on one visit to a department store buyer, his business suddenly took off. "I left the cart on the floor and walked into the buyer's office and described it to him," he told *Advertising Age*. "As I did, a saleslady walked in and asked the price of it. I told her $49.95. She came back and said, 'I just sold two.' " In an hour, Salton had an order for 60 hot trays.

Business was up and down at first, but in the 1950s the Salton Hotray became a staple in many U.S. homes. Two factors influenced early sales. Products like the Salton Hotray existed in Europe, and imports in the 1950s helped create a demand. Then Salton scored influential free advertising with a *Ladies' Home Journal* feature on the device. Stressing the convenience of the product, the article concluded with a woman declaring she would rather be without her front door than without her Salton Hotray. After the article appeared, sales tripled.

Salton followed the success of the hot tray with a bun warmer in 1963. The company focused on convenience products that saved time in the kitchen or allowed consumers to make things easily at home that they would otherwise buy ready-made. Consequently, Salton manufactured an ice cream maker, a peanut butter grinder, a yogurt maker, a coffee grinder, a personal fan, and other such products. But sales of the core product, the Salton Hotray, began to drop off in the 1970s as microwave ovens became prevalent. Microwave ovens were the ultimate quick cooker and food warmer, and the simple hot tray could not compete.

Under New Owners in the 1980s

By the early 1980s, Salton had developed into a worldwide company, with branches in the United Kingdom and in South Africa. Sales stood at about $8 million annually by 1983. However, the Hotray had dropped off in sales steadily since at least 1978. Headquartered at its manufacturing facility in the Bronx and still partially overseen by Lewis Salton as vice-chairman, the company was stagnating. In 1980 the company was purchased by Bromaine Holding Company, a South African conglomerate that had already bought the rights to Salton U.K. and Salton South Africa. Bromaine brought in a new president for the firm, and then another and another. In two years, Salton ran through three top executives, and it was clear the company lacked direction. Salton needed to develop new products to stay atop the fickle home appliance market, but it lacked cash to develop them. By 1982 Salton's research and development team numbered only three people. The company seemed to be going nowhere, and in 1983, Bromaine decided to sell Salton. The buyer, for an undisclosed amount, was the British firm Marley Ltd. Marley was on a buying spree in the United States, picking up two other housewares firms, Ingrid Ltd. and Max Klein Plastic Products. Marley planned to infuse cash into the dormant company, and redevelop the dwindling hot tray market. The new leadership also planned to work on the specialty coffee maker business. Lewis Salton ceased his association with the company he had founded at this point. He signed a non-compete agreement and began a new company. In 1985 Salton's headquarters moved to the Chicago area.

New Start in the Late 1980s

Marley's fleet of housewares companies was subsequently bought by Sevco, Inc. The consolidation of these businesses was tricky, and apparently never worked. Sevco filed for bankruptcy in 1990, claiming that costs incurred in the acquisition and consolidation of its businesses had driven it under. Salton got out from under its parent in 1988 in a leveraged buyout orchestrated by Leon Dreimann. Dreimann had been head of Salton's Australian arm, and he had a clearer idea of where the company should go than any of its recent owners. He became chief executive officer in 1987, and in 1988 wangled the buyout of the firm, using only $2.5 million in venture capital. Dreimann acted quickly to get Salton back on the right track. He renamed the firm Salton Housewares, and switched its manufacturing suppliers from European firms to much less expensive producers in Hong Kong and Taiwan. In 1989, Salton Housewares merged with another small appliance manufacturer, Maxim, and the name changed again, to Salton/Maxim. The company was doing sales of around $10 million annually in the late 1980s, and after the Maxim merger, it jumped to $18 million. Then the company began to grow quickly, fueled in two ways. It began acquiring key brands, and it marketed products very successfully using television infomercials.

Salton/Maxim's first infomercial success was the Sandwich Maker, in 1990. The Sandwich Maker was a product that had long been a staple in Dreimann's native Australia, but it had not been sold in the United States. It was a small counter-top grill that cooked a sandwich while pinching the two bread slices together, so the filling was neatly enclosed. Salton/Maxim first ran a test infomercial for the Sandwich Maker in Florida. Dreimann recounted in a June 1997 interview with *Adweek* that the Sandwich Maker infomercial initiated an enormous interest in the small appliance. One Florida retailer called and asked for an entire shipping container of 6,000 units. The company did not have that many on hand. The contractor who made the Sandwich Makers insisted on selling Salton/Maxim at least 20,000 units, and Dreimann took the risk. Driven by the infomercial, the 6,000 units destined for Florida sold out immediately. When the company took the infomercial national, the rest of that initial order sold out, too. Over the next 15 to 16 months, Salton/Maxim sold over three million Sandwich Makers, and sales leaped from $18 million to $52 million.

Salton/Maxim was suddenly a hot company. Buoyed by the sudden success of the Sandwich Maker, Dreimann decided to take the firm public. The company made an initial public offering in October 1991, selling just over 40 percent of the company, or 2.3 million shares, at $12 a share. Just after the company went public, it suffered a series of setbacks, so that key products it expected to have on the shelf for Christmas were delayed. Salton/Maxim's stock price plunged as a result. Several groups of stockholders sued, arguing that the prospectus for the public offering was misleading. The company eventually settled the suits in 1994 by issuing $900,000 of new stock to the disgruntled investors. As it turned out, the stumble after the public offering was an aberration.

Growth and Acquisitions in the 1990s

Salton/Maxim actually had a very effective formula for marketing its products. Interest in the Sandwich Maker virtually ceased by the end of 1991, but the company was able to pick up on a new fad, juice extractors. Interest in this product was driven by an infomercial narrated by Jay Korditch, an ex-football player who swore that juicing fruits and vegetables had helped him overcome cancer. Korditch advertised the Juiceman brand juicer, and Salton/Maxim did brisk sales of its own similar appliance. After six months, the juicing craze seemed to end. But then Salton/Maxim's Dreimann took an unusual step. Though his own company had warehouses full of unwanted juicers, Dreimann advocated buying the Juiceman brand juicer. Since Juiceman was the leading brand, Dreimann gambled that it might outlast the fad. He proved correct, and the Juiceman became one of Salton/Maxim's staple products. Salton/Maxim also bought Breadman in 1994, another market-leading popular kitchen item sold through infomercials. Salton/Maxim began a steady series of its own infomercials, finding that even if sales through the ads themselves only broke even, retail sales usually jumped. Another 1994 acquisition was distribution rights for a line of products marketed by Ron Popeil, a noted infomercial salesman. Popeil's products included an Automatic Pasta Maker and Popeil's Automatic Food Dehydrator. Salton/Maxim also acquired Block China, a noted supplier of tableware and glassware, in 1996.

After going on this acquisition streak, Salton/Maxim allowed itself to be 50 percent acquired in 1996 by Windmere-Durable Holdings, Inc., a manufacturer of kitchen and personal care appliances. Windmere had produced many of Salton/Maxim's appliances at its Hong Kong factory since the early 1980s. The alliance gave Salton/Maxim needed cash, and provided the company access to Windmere's mass market distribution channels. Salton/Maxim also licensed the White Westinghouse brand name for small kitchen appliances in 1996.

Salton/Maxim continued its strategy of marketing innovative products through both infomercials and mass marketers. It had a big hit in the late 1990s with its George Foreman Grill. Salton made the grill as a joint venture with Foreman, a former heavyweight boxing champion. The countertop grill, endorsed by a celebrity, advocated as a cooker that reduced fat, produced sales of approximately $200 million within four years. Total company sales in the late 1990s rose precipitately, from about $99 million in 1996 to $182 million in 1997 to over $305 million in 1998. By 1998 roughly half the company's sales were brought in by products marketed through infomercials.

Salton/Maxim decided to end its alliance with Windmere in 1998, and it bought back the half of its stock that company had owned. Shortly after, Windmere had a financial shock that almost brought it to collapse. Other small appliance makers also had troubles in the late 1990s, including Sunbeam and Hamilton Beach/Procter Silex Inc. Salton/Maxim seemed far and away the best run and most profitable of all the companies in its niche. Shortly after buying its shares back from Windmere, Salton/Maxim agreed to buy Toastmaster for around $53 million. Toastmaster was a well known brand of small household appliances with sales of about $100 million.

In 1999 Salton/Maxim changed its name officially to Salton, Inc. The public company, which had been sold on the NASDAQ, moved to the prestigious New York Stock Exchange that year. Salton announced that it would expand its presence in infomercials, and push into Internet sales. The company had a strong roster of top brands, with its new Toastmaster, the continued blockbuster George Foreman Grill, the Breadman, the Juiceman, White Westinghouse and a slew of coffeemakers, waffle irons, shower radios, and assorted other home gadgets. The company continued to bring out new items, hoping to ignite fads. These ranged from a modest bagel slicing machine to a high-priced kitchen computer with video, CD, cable television, and Internet and e-mail access from the countertop. Salton had grown from a modest company with one principal product to a comprehensive kitchen and home electronics distributor. Perhaps most importantly, Salton had proved inimitable in its marketing know-how. Its surge of growth in the 1990s was extraordinary. Yet it was possible its expansion would continue, as the company held on to its formula of quick rollouts of new products and highly effective advertising.

Principal Subsidiaries

Toastmaster Inc.

Further Reading

Bernard, Sharyn, ''Windmere Alliance with Salton/Maxim to Create Synergies,'' *HFN*, March 4, 1996, p. 6.

Bernard, Sharyn, and Kehoe, Ann-Margaret, ''Salton to Buy Block China,'' *HFN*, June 10, 1996, p. 1.

Brown, Erika, ''Ooh! Aah!'' *Forbes*, March 8, 1999, p. 56.

Dworman, Steven, ''Salton-Maxim Solutions,'' *Adweek*, June 30, 1997, p. S14.

Murphy, H. Lee, ''Salton Maxim's Stock Plunges,'' *HFD*, December 23, 1991, p. 56.

Norris, Floyd, ''A Battered Stock Follows the Fads,'' *New York Times*, June 22, 1992, p. D8.

Osterland, Andrew, ''Putting a Gizmo in Every Kitchen,'' *Business Week*, May 31, 1999, pp. 94–96.

Ratliff, Duke, ''Salton/Maxim Buys Juiceman,'' *HFD*, January 17, 1994, p. 143.

Ryan, Dick, ''Ingrid Parent Closes Salton Deal,'' *Retailing Home Furnishings*, September 5, 1983, p. 21.

Thau, Barbara, ''Toastmaster/Salton Merger Completed,'' *HFN*, January 18, 1999, p. 34.

Zotti, Ed, ''Ideas Brew in Inventors' Kitchens,'' *Advertising Age*, July 12, 1982, p. M10.

—A. Woodward

Sam Ash Music Corporation

278 Duffy Avenue
Hicksville, New York 11801
U.S.A.
(516) 932-6400
Fax: (516) 822-8443
Web sites: http://www.samash.com
        http://www.samsontech.com

Private Company
Founded: 1924
Employees: 1,000
Sales: $260 million (1998 est.)
NAIC: 45114 Musical Instrument & Supplies Stores;
    44312 Computer & Software Stores; 33431 Audio &
    Video Equipment Manufacturing

Sam Ash Music Corporation is the second largest musical instrument retailer in the United States. The private, family-held company trails closely behind industry leader Guitar Center, Inc., a public company with 1998 revenues of $391.7 million. The company operates approximately 30 discount superstores across California, Connecticut, Florida, Illinois, New Jersey, New York, Ohio, and Pennsylvania. Sam Ash also sells sheet music, recording equipment, electronics, videos, computers, software, and vintage guitars, and also offers custom-built instruments and music clinics. All of the stores feature rooms in which customers are encouraged to try out instruments.

Family Founded: 1924

Violinist Sam Ashkynase immigrated to the United States at the turn of the 20th century, along with his wife Rose. A performer, he was often on the road in order to make a living for himself and his small family and decided, after re-evaluating his career, to change the situation. Rose pawned her diamond engagement ring for $400. With the money, the two of them leased a tiny 500-square-foot shop in an out of the way, run-down area of Brooklyn in 1924. There they sold wind-up phonographs, sheet music, and the occasional violin.

Deciding that Ashkynase was too difficult to pronounce, the couple shortened their last name to Ash. Over the next 18 years, with their sons, Jerome and Paul, they struggled to make the store a success, living in the three rooms behind the store. The two boys ran the odd errand as they grew up, but eventually joined in the day-to-day operations, all of them working 14-hour days, seven days a week. Ash soon gained a reputation as a vendor who was willing to do just about anything for his customers, from a midnight repair of something to delivering products across town.

They survived the Great Depression through sheer willpower, and managed to scrape together enough money to move to a larger, better shop on a main thoroughfare in Brooklyn. The business began to prosper, and the Ashes were finally able to maintain a comfortable living.

Changing of the Guard, Expansion: 1956

Sam Ash died suddenly in 1956 and his wife and sons took over the business. Almost immediately thereafter, the boys began looking for ways to grow the business, launching an aggressive expansion campaign. The two opened a satellite store on Long Island, and then grew into a huge, five-storefront megastore on Manhattan's famous "Music Row," more commonly referred to in the real world as West 48th Street. Nearly 25 years after opening, the Music Row shop was one of the "most impressive" the company owned, according to Lisa Josefak's October 1996 article in *LI Business News*, "grown to a complex housing nine store fronts with individual shops dedicated to live sound guitars, pro-keyboards, home keyboards, sheet music, string, brass, wind, and wood instruments, drums, computers and recording. 'We take up both sides of the street,'" Jerome said.

Another store was opened in Hempstead, New York, in 1961. That was followed three years later by an opening at Huntington Station. In 1966, three more stores were added, in King of Prussia, Pennsylvania, and Miami Lakes and Margate, Florida.

Samson Technologies Corp.: 1980

In 1980 the brothers made a commitment to furthering technology in the music performance industry with the founding of

---

Samson Technologies Corp. From the beginning, this Syosset, New York-based subsidiary was dedicated to making wireless technology problem-free, easy-to-use, and accessible for everyone. In the early 1980s, Samson was among the first to introduce dependable VHF systems that helped popularize the use of wireless in different performance and public speaking applications. Later, the company's Broadcast Series broke new ground with a synthesized receiver in a solid-metal, 19-inch rackmount format which, for the first time, offered wireless users the choice of ten selectable VHF channels.

As various sound and transmission systems evolved, the Samson web site declares, the company never lost sight of the small but critical details that made wireless user friendly. One example was handheld transmitters that included a full complement of on-board controls, and a choice of microphone elements so performers could always have sound when they went to wireless transmissions. Attacking the problem of residual noise head on, Samson pioneered the use of dbx Noise Reduction in wireless. This critically acclaimed technology significantly eliminated noise without artificially coloring the signal, a major concern for musical performers. The company also utilized its long-term experience to create a new and unique line of microphones specifically designed for wireless, including QMIC, a high-output microphone designed to keep feedback to a minimum. Samson also created Microprocessor True Diversity circuitry, which scanned incoming signals at over 200,000 times a second to ensure the best possible reception under the most adverse conditions. By 1998 the privately held subsidiary of Sam Ash had posted total revenues of $37 million and employed 75 people.

Branching out into New Areas of Music: 1988–90

In 1988 the company created the Sam Ash Professional Division to manufacture and sell household audio and video equipment, including audio recorders; radio and television broadcasting and communications equipment; and computers and software. The division was conceived to meet the needs of recording studios, broadcasters, and post-production houses. By 1995, it boasted 12 employees and was bringing in $7 million in total revenue. The company also opened the Sam Ash Music Institute in New York in 1990, an accredited school featuring classes in recording and synthesis.

By October 1996, the company had 13 stores, spread across New York, New Jersey, Connecticut, Florida, and Pennsylvania, and was generating nearly $190 million in annual revenue. In November of that year, both Sam Ash and Guitar Center, the two largest chains of music stores in the United States, opened stores in Cleveland. The opening of the Sam Ash store brought the total number of stores in the company's stable to 14, extending its reach further into the heartland of America. Agoura Hills, California-based Guitar Center, meanwhile, was up to 28 stores, and planned to open an additional seven at that point.

According to Stan Bullard, in a November 1996 article in *Crain's Cleveland Business*, a ''study by *Music Trade* magazine cited in Guitar Center's SEC filing said the music instrument industry's sales are increasing by 7 percent annually. The nation's five largest music products retailers have just 8 percent of the $5.5 billion market in the United States.'' Presumably then, there was plenty of room for Sam Ash to grow, both via acquisitions and the opening of new retail stores. That year, the company was a finalist in the 1996 LI Entrepreneur of the Year Awards, ''for demonstrating excellence and extraordinary success in such areas as innovation, financial performance, and personal commitment to their business and community.''

In June 1997, Mackie Designs Inc., a manufacturer of sound mixers for the music industry, filed a lawsuit against Sam Ash, its subsidiary Samson Technologies, and German studio electronics firm Behringer Spezielle Studio-Technick GmbH, for breach of contract, unfair competition, and copyright, trademark, and patent violations. In the lawsuit, Mackie was seeking $327 million in damages caused by the alleged manufacture and sale of Mackie products by the defendants, violating a 1993 dealer agreement with Mackie. The main defendant in the suit was Behringer which, Mackie said, had ''a history of copying other companies' products and selling them as its own,'' citing an instance of Behringer manufacturing and selling a product based on one manufactured by California-based Aphex Systems, Ltd. (Aphex successfully sued and won damages of $1.187 million). According to the suit, when Behringer decided to enter the mixer market, it formed a ''copying partnership'' with Sam Ash in order to manufacture ''knockoffs'' of various Mackie products. In July 1998, Sam Ash and Samson Technologies returned a lawsuit to Mackie, alleging defamation by the Woodinville, Washington-based console manufacturer, alleging that Mackie ''engaged in a concerted campaign to defame the reputation, business, and character'' of the companies by taking ''the unusual step of publishing its complaint on the Internet before trying its weak case in a court of law,'' stated a press release by Sam Ash. The company believed that the Mackie suit ''was an unfair attempt to damage the business of Samson and Behringer and reduce competition in the industry.'' Samson went on to posit ''that the purpose of the lawsuit [was] to obtain discovery of the trade secrets that have made Behringer products strong competition for Mackie.''

Rapid Expansion, West Coast Stores: 1998

In February 1998, the East Coast music retailing giant expanded to the West Coast with the opening of stores in Westminster, Cerritos, West Hollywood, and Canoga Park, California, bringing the total number of Sam Ash stores to 19 across the United States. In September, the company stepped up its expansion rather rapidly, opening ten new stores throughout the country over the next 12 months. Four were opened in Chicago during the fourth quarter of fiscal 1998, with another three going to Los Angeles and Orange County, California, early in 1999, joining the four stores already in that area. Three additional stores were opened in northern California and along the East Coast. The new stores expanded the company's existing store base from 20 to 30. Total sales for 1998 jumped 28.7 percent to $260 million.

In the late 1990s, the company's Samson Technologies subsidiary teamed up with *Riverdance—The Show*, the hit, sold-out Irish music, song, and dance extravaganza which toured the United States, Great Britain, and Australia in three separate productions. Samson, through its Handheld Audio in Great Britain distributor, provided nearly 60 UHF Series 4, UHF Synth Series 5, and UHF Synth Series 6 systems to mike vocals and instruments and stage, as well as the taps on the dancer's shoes, using microphones embedded in the heels, in conjunction with beltpack transmitters cleverly concealed on the dancer's bodies.

In August 1999, Sam Ash snapped up Manny's Music Store, a New York store which was touted as a "haven for musicians." At the end of 1999, the company was still privately held, and still run by numerous members of the Ash family, including Sam Ash's sons, Jerome (chairman) and Paul (president); Jerome's three sons, Sammy (senior vice-president), David (COO), and Richard (CEO).

Principal Subsidiaries

Sam Ash Professional Division; Samson Technologies Corp.

Further Reading

Bullard, Stan, "Local Music Store Scene Tunes up for New Players," *Crain's Cleveland Business*, November 18, 1996, p. 1.
Feldman, Amy, " 'They're Good Brothers and They Love Each Other," *Forbes*, August 2, 1993, p. 118.
"Hicksville, N.Y.-Based," *Billboard*, September 12, 1998, p. 65.
Josefak, Lisa, "Sam Ash Music Is Upbeat About Business," *LI Business News*, October 14, 1996, p. 16.
MacFarquhar, Neil, "Manny's, Haven for Musicians, Is Sold to a Chain-Store Rival," *New York Times*, August 4, 1999, p. B2.
"Sam Ash Music Corp.," *Billboard*, February 7, 1998, p. 43.
Verna, Paul, "Mackie Sues over Knockoffs," *Billboard*, July 5, 1997, p. 34.
——, "Sam Ash, Samson Sue Mackie," *Billboard*, July 4, 1998, p. 40.

—Daryl F. Mallett

Samuels Jewelers Incorporated

2914 Montopolis Drive #200
Austin, Texas 78741
U.S.A.
(512) 369-1400
Fax: (512) 369-1527
Web site: http://www.samuels-jewelers.com

Public Company
Founded: 1956 as Barry's Jewelers
Employees: 1,007
Sales: $81 million (1999)
Stock Exchanges: OTC
Ticker Symbol: SMJW
NAIC: 44831 Jewelry Stores

Samuels Jewelers Incorporated owns and operates one of the largest chains of jewelry stores in the country, with 116 stores located in malls from California to Texas. Known until 1998 as Barry's Jewelers, the company manages stores under five different names: A. Hirsh & Son, Hatfield Jewelers, Mission Jewelers, Schubach, and Samuels Jewelers. With stores primarily in the western part of the country, Samuels Jewelers offers customers a broad array of merchandise, with diamonds and gemstones comprising the majority of the company's sales. Samuels Jewelers also specializes in watches and high-fashion gold jewelry, and competes directly with both high-end jewelry stores and discount chains. Samuels Jewelers has a troubled financial history, with the company filing for bankruptcy twice in five years; nonetheless, the company is committed to remaining a significant force within the jewelry industry.

Beginnings of a Regional Chain: 1956–Late 1970s

Samuels Jewelers was originally founded as Barry's Jewelers in 1956. Started by David Blum and Gerson Fox in Los Angeles, California, the company started out as a single store which within a few years grew into a small, regional chain. Barry's Jewelers continued to flourish throughout the next several years, with stores concentrated primarily in southern California. Blum and Fox focused on offering their customers good service with a high-quality inventory at prices competitive to other chains. At the time, chain jewelry stores were just beginning to make a mark within the industry, and Barry's Jewelers soon grew to regional prominence in the western area of the country, opening dozens of stores within two decades.

In 1977 a company called Unimax bought Barry's Jewelers from Blum and Fox. Unimax retained the two founders to continue overseeing the business, and within five years Barry's Jewelers had expanded to 54 stores, with locations in malls across the West. At the end of 1982 Blum and Fox bought back Barry's Jewelers from Unimax, and began an aggressive campaign of expansion which was to last almost ten years.

Rapid Growth: 1980s

Beginning in 1982 Barry's Jewelers began to take advantage of an economic climate of looser credit standards and consumers who were spending more freely. In part due to the rapid expansion of indoor shopping malls in the 1980s Barry's Jewelers became one of the fastest-growing jewelry chains in the country. The company opened several new stores of its own, and also acquired two other jewelry chains, Mission Jewelers and Samuels Jewelers. Barry's Jewelers bought Mission Jewelers from Zale Corporation, and in doing so added 60 new locations to the company's roster, as well as expanded the company geographically, with the Mission Jewelers stores being centered primarily in the Southwest. The acquisition of Samuels Jewelers, which was purchased by Barry's from the Canadian company Peoples Jewelers, was also a boon for the company, as Samuels was a well-respected, if small chain which had been in operation in the western regions of the country since 1891.

In 1986 Barry's Jewelers went public, and between that year and the next grew to 104 stores, becoming one of the fastest expanding jewelry chains in the country. Within a period of eight years the company had expanded from 54 to a total of 228 stores, the vast majority of which were located within malls, and had acquired a number of small but fiscally healthy chains. By 1990 Barry's Jewelers counted among its divisions not only

Samuels Jewelers and Mission Jewelers, which were the company's two strongest acquisitions, but also the stores Gold Art Creations, Hatfield Jewelers, which operated out of Los Angeles, A. Hirsch & Son, Schubach, and Ringmaker. All the stores specialized primarily in precious gemstones, watches, and gold jewelry, but inventory also varied slightly from chain to chain, with certain stores focusing more on modern, fashion-conscious jewelry while others emphasized a more classic image. Barry's Jewelers' divisions, in other words, were not operated as if a single entity, with a centralized system of control: each division had its own management, marketing, and accounting team, which helped the divisions maintain a unique identity. Having the company's divisions maintain such independence, however, proved to be disadvantageous to the company in the long run.

A vitally important part of Barry's Jewelers' rapid growth was due in part not only to a retail economy conducive to the expansion of chain stores, but to the company's own willingness to extend in-house credit to customers who had little or no credit history. Flexible credit became an essential element to Barry's Jewelers' customer service, and allowed a customer who would otherwise be unable to afford pieces in a certain price range to have access to that merchandise through credit. Such methods of purchase were of course a risk, both for the company and to the customer's financial well-being, but the practice ensured the company a larger customer base and, perhaps most importantly for a store trying to survive within the highly competitive jewelry market, also virtually guaranteed loyal, repeat customers. By decade's end, when Barry's Jewelers had reached its peak point of expansion, credit accounted for almost 72 percent of the company's sales in all its divisions.

Turn for the Worse: Early 1990s

After almost a decade of phenomenally successful growth and acquisitions, Barry's Jewelers in 1990 began to be troubled by financial threats on several fronts. The company's growth had stretched its overhead to the limit, and, with so much of the company's sales coming from consumer credit, Barry's Jewelers found itself in a vulnerable position, overly dependent on the fulfillment of debt from customers with shaky or nonexistent history. The company began to have increasing difficulty paying its many vendors and, with rumors circulating about the business's instability, weakened investor confidence caused the company's stock to fall from a high of $9 a share to $1.50 a share.

As a brief recession set in at the beginning of the decade, many of Barry's Jewelers' customers who had utilized the company's in-house credit were unable to pay back their debts, and had to default on their bills. Had the company not relied so heavily on credit, these defaults probably would not have made much more than a dent in the business's financial well-being. Additionally, in 1991 Barry's Jewelers had a devastating holiday season, which was by far the most important selling period for a jewelry business, and the company fell far short of its targeted Christmas and Hanukkah revenue predictions. By the end of the year Barry's Jewelers had losses of over $29 million, bringing into question the company's future viability.

Besides facing bad consumer debt and increasingly poor sales, Barry's Jewelers had a new, unforeseen competitor in the early 1990s: home shopping networks. Home shopping networks were a threat to the more traditional retail industry for several reasons, the two most important of which were price and convenience. Because labels did not have to showcase their merchandise in actual retail space, overhead costs were much lower for home shopping merchants than other retailers, allowing the former to keep prices far lower than those of their competitors'. In addition, with products being sold on television, the consumer did not have to plan a specific trip to make a purchase; it was all right there in the customer's own home, making both impulse and planned purchasing easier.

In February 1992, after a further loss in overall sales, Barry's Jewelers began planning a financial restructuring caused, according to the company, by ''a depressed retail market and deterioration in its (the company's) financial condition.'' The company filed for Chapter 11 bankruptcy protection, and worked out a plan with its investors under which the business's vendors would continue to be paid while the company plotted a new financial strategy. While most businesses remain under Chapter 11 for at least half a year, Barry's Jewelers was able to emerge after only four months, and by June was operating on its own again.

The restructuring resulted in several changes, with the company's bondholders receiving financial and managerial control of the business. The company was also able to obtain a $103 million line of credit which allowed continuing payments to vendors, thereby keeping inventory well stocked and up to date throughout the restructuring process.

Though Barry's Jewelers came out of Chapter 11 in a short period of time, the company was forced to downsize, and closed 68 of its poorest selling stores. The stores were sold to small regional chains and independent jewelers at a fraction of their actual worth, but the sales were necessary to both meet the company's debts and aid in the maintenance of Barry's Jewelers' more lucrative locations.

One of the more important alterations which came about as a result of Barry's Jewelers financial difficulties was not fiscal but structural: the company after 1992 made significant moves towards centralizing their financial and managerial operations, with the aim of making the company's divisions more unified and less heterogeneous in both presentation and style of management. The company changed its policies of allowing each of its divisions to autonomously handle its marketing and credit operations, creating several new managerial positions which operated directly from the company's headquarters in Monrovia, California. In addition, founder David Blum's son-in-law, Terry Burman, who was a longtime employee of Barry's Jewelers, was named the company's new CEO. The new management team, which included people recruited from well-established businesses such as Gumps and Tiffany, was in charge of the marketing, merchandising, loss prevention techniques, and accounting for all the company's divisions, and had the aim of making Barry's Jewelers' operations more cost-effective across the board.

The company also placed a new emphasis on employee training: with home shopping networks taking an increasing number of customers away from traditional retailers, good, reliable customer service became one of the most important ways in which to attract and retain a solid consumer base. The company's new training program included workshops, weekly meetings, and video instruction for each of the company's divisions, giving Barry's Jewelers' employees a thorough and up-to-date knowledge of the products they were selling.

By the middle of the decade Barry's Jewelers was again making a profit, pulling in a revenue of $114 million in 1994, and by 1995 the company was operating 162 relatively profitable stores in 16 states. At this time the company began focusing on a new phenomenon which was sweeping through the retail industry: the increasing popularity of the superstore. Instead of opening new stores, the traditional method of expansion for chain retailers, Barry's Jewelers concentrated on converting some of its more successful locations into superstores. A superstore carried 50 to 60 percent more inventory than a typical jewelry boutique, and offered the customer a broader selection of high fashion jewelry. Superstores also competed directly with discount chains and home shopping networks, emphasizing value and quantity as well as customer service.

Continuing Struggle: 1995–99

Though Barry's Jewelers by 1995 had constructed ambitious plans for growth and increased profitability, with intentions to open 21 new stores and convert more of their existing boutiques into lucrative, competitive superstores, the company was again ailing by the end of 1996. Even with a new $100 million line of credit from the Bank of Boston, the company found the competition from discount chains and other stores too intense, and, after another poor holiday season, had lost $6.8 million by 1997. Such a loss caused the company to default on some of its bank agreements as well as close 11 more stores.

In May 1997 Barry's Jewelers again filed for Chapter 11 protection, listing liabilities of over $134 million. Restructuring, both financial and organizational, was again in order: Randy McCullough, the former president of Silverman's Jewelers, became the company's new CEO and, after Barry's Jew-

elers emerged from bankruptcy later that year, board members made the decision to change the company's name to Samuels Jewelers.

The new name arose from the fact that Samuels Jewelers was the business's most successful and, to the consumer, easily recognizable division. Not only was the company name changed: plans were laid to change all the company's divisions to Samuels Jewelers, which would further condense operations at the ailing chain. After the company reestablished itself for the second time, it moved its headquarters from California to Austin, Texas, where many of Samuels Jewelers' stores were located. The company's divisions now included, besides Samuels Jewelers, Hatfield Jewelers, Schubach, A. Hirsch & Son, and Mission Jewelers, making a total of 115 stores across the West.

In 1999 things began to look up for Samuels Jewelers. The company had a better than expected Christmas season and also made its first acquisition since emerging from Chapter 11 in 1997. That year, Samuels bought the small but successful Silverman's Jewelers, of which McCullough used to be the president. Silverman's Jewelers operated 17 stores in nine states, and by acquiring the company Samuels Jewelers once again proved itself to be competitive within the jewelry industry.

Principal Divisions

Hatfield Jewelers; Mission Jewelers; Schubach; A. Hirsch & Son.

Further Reading

"Barry's Jewelers Inc. Announces Distribution of Plan and Disclosure Statement and Intent to Change its Name to Samuels Jewelers Inc.," *Business Wire*, July 20, 1998, p. 07200328.

"Barry's Uses Chapter 11 to Finalize Restructuring," *Jewelers Circular Keystone*, April 1992, p. 18.

Glover, Kara, "Barry's Jewelers Shines After Price Cuts, Revamp of Retail Operations," *Los Angeles Business Journal*, October 17, 1994, p. 15.

"Samuels Jewelers Inc. Announces Merger with Barry's Jewelers Inc.," *Business Wire*, October 5, 1998, p. 1314.

"Samuels Jewelers Inc. Announces the Acquisition of Silverman's Jewelers Inc.," *Business Wire*, July 23, 1999, p. 0233.

Shuster, William George, "Barry's Closes 70 Stores in Major Restructuring," *Jeweler's Circular Keystone*, June 1991, p. 9.

——, "Helzberg, Barry's Aim for Growth," *Jewelers Circular Keystone*, April 1996, p. 140.

——, "Three Who Came Back," *Jewelers Circular Keystone*, June 1995, p. 298.

—Rachel H. Martin

See's Candies, Inc.

210 El Camino Real
South San Francisco, California 94080
U.S.A.
(650) 583-7382
(800) 915-7337
Fax: (650) 875-6825
Web site: http://www.sees.com

Wholly Owned Subsidiary of Berkshire Hathaway, Inc.
Incorporated: 1922
Employees: 250
Sales: $288 million (1998 est.)
NAIC: 31320 Confectionary Chocolate Made from Cacao
   Beans; 445292 Confectionary Stores, Packaged, Retail
   Only

See's Candies, Inc. is a leading U.S. candy company, with a particularly strong customer base in the West. It manufactures its candy at two plants in California, and sells its more than 120 varieties through some 200 retail See's Candy shops. About two-thirds of See's shops are located in California, with most of the others found west of the Rocky Mountains. See's also sells its candies through Bloomingdale's in New York City, and markets overseas, particularly in the Pacific Rim countries. See's has changed little since its founding in 1921, retaining the black and white logo designed in the 1930s on its packaging and maintaining an old-fashioned decor in its numerous shops. See's candies are made without preservatives, and freshness is one of See's biggest selling points. Customer loyalty is intense. Owned by the See family until the early 1970s, the company since then has been operated by Berkshire Hathaway, the conglomerate controlled by one of the United States' richest men, Warren Buffett. In 1999 See's celebrated its 75th year in business.

Early History

See's Candies was founded by Charles A. See, a Canadian immigrant to Los Angeles. See was raised near Gananoque, Ontario, where his parents ran a summer resort called Tremont Park. See went to college to learn pharmacy, and eventually ran two drugstores in the mining town of Timmins, Ontario. When See's businesses were both destroyed in a summer forest fire, he left pharmacy and became a chocolate salesman. One of the most successful Canadian candy companies was a chain of shops called Laura Secord. See studied Secord, and determined that he could begin a similar chain. But he chose to leave Canada, and start over in California. In 1921, See took his wife and two children and his 65-year-old mother, Mary See, to Los Angeles, which was then a thriving town in the midst of great growth. See soon found a business partner, James W. Reed, and together they opened the first See's Candy Shop. Mary See was evidently a great home confectioner, and her son used many of her recipes. More than that, Mary See became the symbol of the new company, and the image of the grandmotherly See was used in much advertising to embody the old-fashioned, homemade qualities of See's candy. The company incorporated in 1922, with James Reed, Charles See, and other See family members as the officers and stockholders.

In the 1920s, before large-scale refrigerated distribution was available, there were dozens of small candy makers like See's across Los Angeles. Despite local competition, See's seemed to immediately distinguish itself, and only a few years after its founding, the company had more than ten shops in the city. The See's production facility had a growing number of employees, who worked in the kitchen, packed candies, and made deliveries. The company began an innovative marketing program in the late 1920s, using distinctive Harley-Davidson motorcycles for deliveries. The motorcycles were fitted with a large sidecar embossed on all sides with the black and white See's logo. The neat black and white motif was woven throughout the See's company. Employees wore white uniforms piped in black, and the store fronts too were painted crisp white, with the See's name in black on the awnings and in the windows.

By the end of the 1920s, the company was flourishing, and had begun building a $100,000 candymaking factory on Los Angeles's West Washington Boulevard. But See's was deeply affected by the stock market crash in 1929 and the ensuing Great Depression. To keep going, See's had to reduce the prices of its candy sharply. The per pound price had been about 80 cents in the late 1920s, and Charles See dropped it to just 50 cents so that he could maintain sales. The company rented the buildings for its shops, and See also pleaded with his landlords to accept a reduced rent. Nevertheless, the company went ahead with its ambitious construction plans, and built the expensive new facility. Though the upfront cost of the new plant was high, the modern factory was more efficient than See's old one, and so it eventually saved the company money. Another way the company weathered the Depression was to initiate a bulk ordering plan. See's brought in clubs and charities by offering them a reduced price on orders of 50 pounds or more. Then the groups could resell the candy at a profit, for fundraising.

In the mid-1930s, the company began looking at expansion beyond Los Angeles. In spite of its belt-tightening, See's was doing well. The small chain had grown to about 30 shops. Charles See went on an exploratory trip to San Francisco in 1935, and in 1936 the company opened its first store there, on Tenth Street. This first shop also comprised a production plant and business offices, to use as headquarters for planned expansion in the area. By the end of 1936, See's had nine shops in San Francisco, and the company formed a subsidiary to run them.

World War II and After

World War II brought an end to the Depression, though it did not alleviate difficulties at See's Candies. Because sugar, butter, and other ingredients were rationed, and many imported ingredients were scarce, the company could not get enough raw materials to produce all the candy it could sell. It would have been possible to substitute some lower-quality ingredients for the restricted items, but the company instead chose to make a limited amount of candy with its tightened supplies. Consequently, its stores were open only a few hours each day, and customers had to wait in line, hoping to get in before the shop was sold out.

Founder Charles A. See died in 1949, and the presidency of the company passed to his son Laurence. See's was in good shape after the war, as California's economy was growing rapidly. Released from wartime rationing, the company could make as much candy as it needed, and newly affluent customers continued to favor the black and white shops. Under Laurence See, the company embarked on a new marketing plan. It began opening See's Candy shops in shopping malls. Malls were a new phenomenon, filling in for older downtown shopping districts as the population of California increasingly moved into suburbs. Over the first ten years of Laurence See's leadership,

the company expanded rapidly. By 1960, the company had 124 shops spread across California. See's had two manufacturing plants, one in southern and one in northern California, and the company as a whole employed approximately 1,000 people.

Between 1960 and 1970, See's began expanding into neighboring states. President Laurence See was choosy about new locations for See's shops, carefully checking demographics to find growth areas or places similar to other See's markets. See's moved into Phoenix in 1960, just as that city was experiencing a great influx of population from northerly states. In addition, See's opened other shops in Portland, Oregon, and Seattle, Washington. Both these cities were growing, and shared many characteristics with San Francisco, one of See's most important markets. By 1971 the See's chain had grown to over 150 shops across the western states and in Hawaii. The company had a product line of more than 60 varieties of candy.

Under New Owners in the 1970s

Laurence See, founder Charles See's eldest son, died in 1969 at the age of 57. The presidency of the company then passed to Harry See, Laurence's younger brother. Though Harry had been actively involved with the company for many years, he had other interests, such as a vineyard he owned. Not long after Harry took over, the See family announced that the company was for sale. The candy industry in the early 1970s was comprised of many small companies, with few of them making annual sales of more than $50 million. See's sales for fiscal 1971 were just over $28 million. Candy consumption was rising annually, though only by a very small percentage, and lots of competition meant companies had to maintain their profitability by controlling costs. Though See's was not particularly large, it was a leading company. Its competitors were other well-known national brands, including Hershey Foods Corporation, Tootsie Roll, Russell Stover Candies, and Fanny Farmer Candy.

The investor who decided See's Candies was a golden opportunity was Warren Buffett. Buffett was a graduate of Columbia's business school who began investing in little-known stocks just out of college. By the time he was 35, he was a multimillionaire. His specialty was picking undervalued stocks. Later he began buying up whole companies, and See's was one of his first purchases. The actual buyer of See's in 1972 was Blue Chip Stamps, a trading stamp company that was controlled by Buffett through Berkshire Hathaway. Blue Chip offered $35 a share for the See family's portion of the company, which amounted to approximately 67 percent. Blue Chip soon acquired the rest of the outstanding stock, and See's was no longer a family-owned company. Yet it was See's unpretentiousness that made up much of its appeal, and the new owners had no intention of altering the company. The new president was Chuck Huggins, who maintained that job through the 1990s. Huggins worked hard to assure both customers and employees that the new See's would not be different from the old See's. The company did update by adding new quality control and research and development departments. But the candy remained the same, and marketing continued to focus on the image of Mary See and her old-fashioned charm. Also, Buffett's Berkshire Hathaway had deep pockets, and it was able to provide stable financial backing for See's expansion. Blue Chip Stamps folded into parent Berkshire Hathaway in 1978, and at that time Berkshire Hathaway had immense holdings in the insurance industry, and Warren Buffett was one of the wealthiest men in the United States. Under Berkshire Hathaway in the 1970s, See's established more stores in its key Western markets, and also moved into new territory in Texas.

Changing Conditions in the 1980s and 1990s

In many ways See's was the same company it had always been. Its image had not changed despite its becoming part of a large, modern conglomerate. For example when the company discontinued a low-selling flavor, maple walnut creams, in the 1980s, hundreds of customers wrote in to express their dismay. See's president Huggins not only reinstated the flavor, but he replied to each customer's letter and enclosed a gift certificate. Yet the company had modernized behind the scenes. The company had always prided itself on the freshness of its product, which was all preservative-free and had a shelf-life of only several weeks. By the late 1980s See's manufacturing facilities were using highly automated, state-of-the-art packaging machinery to print out on each box the date and location where it was filled. The large, visible imprint made it easy for customers to see that they were getting a fresh product, and helped the company maintain a high level of quality control. Sales and profits moved predictably in the 1980s. Though new competition cropped up, especially in premium chocolates such as Godiva and designer lines such as Bill Blass, See's had a loyal customer pool. In 1984 See's sold over 27 million pounds of chocolate, and donated approximately 80,000 pounds to charities.

The company continued a slow geographic expansion, picking just a few areas east of its core market. In the early 1980s, See's operated more than ten stores across Texas and had a small string of shops in the St. Louis area. It opened a shop in Knoxville, Tennessee, and several more in Colorado. By the late 1980s, though, See's decided to pull out of these markets. Its products could not compete on price with candies that were made in the Midwest, and the Texas and Colorado economies softened with a downturn in the energy industry.

By the early 1990s, See's instead was moving ahead with plans to sell its candies abroad. See's had had stores in Hong Kong since the 1960s, but international distribution was tricky for the company, since the chocolates had to be kept refrigerated and then needed to be sold within a few weeks. See's moved its products to Hong Kong by air. It had its own refrigerated storage unit at the San Francisco airport, and the flight was met in Hong Kong by a refrigerated truck. The company received constant inquiries about operations in Asia, and in the early 1990s it opened a shop in Tokyo and made plans to bring See's to Singapore, Taiwan, South Korea, the Philippines, and China. See's also announced in 1993 that it planned to open stores in Canada and Mexico.

By the mid-1990s, See's had grown to a $235 million company. In the boxed chocolate category, See's was second only to Russell Stover, and led two other venerable brands, the Midwest-based Fannie May, and Fannie Farmer. The product line had grown to approximately 130 items by 1996. One change was that some of the new products were non-chocolates, such as licorice, lollipops, peppermints, and sourballs. Yet 15 percent of See's sales were its truffles, a particularly rich chocolate candy. By 1998, sales had grown to $288 million. The company seemed firmly entrenched in its core West Coast market. Sales had continued to go up without a significant stretch into new markets. Two-thirds of See's stores remained in California, where its manufacturing plants were also located.

Further Reading

"Blue Chip Makes an Offer for Remainder of See's," *Wall Street Journal*, February 8, 1972, p. 7.

"Blue Chip Stamps Extends See's Candy Tender Offer," *Wall Street Journal*, March 20, 1972, p. 10.

"Blue Chip Stamps Plans to Purchase Privately 67.3% of See's Candy," *Wall Street Journal*, December 22, 1971, p. 11.

Burstiner, Mary, "See's Candies Sweet on Foreign Expansion," *San Francisco Business Times*, October 15, 1993, p. 1.

"Comeback for Candy Makers," *Financial World*, November 10, 1971, pp. 6–7.

"Freshness Codes Enhance See's Candies' Quality Reputation," *Packaging*, June 1989, p. 76.

Gregg, Judie, and Morris, Marlene, "A Day at Mary See's," *Los Angeles*, June 1985, pp. 184–189.

Henderson, Janice Wald, "A Sweet Tradition," *Bon Appetit*, December 1993, p. 30.

Kragen, Pam, "CEO of See's Candies Tours Southern California Malls," *Knight-Ridder/Tribune Business News*, May 23, 1996, p. 5230404.

Stein, Ben, "Buffing Buffett," *New York*, September 11, 1995, pp. 42–44.

—A. Woodward

BRITAIN'S OLDEST BREWER

Shepherd Neame Limited

Faversham Brewery
17 Court Street
Faversham, Kent ME13 7AX
United Kingdom
01795 532206
Fax: 01795 538907
Web site: http://www.shepherd-neame.co.uk

Private Company
Incorporated: 1698 as Faversham Brewery
Employees: 930
Sales: £58.68 million (1998)
NAIC: 31212 Breweries; 72241 Drinking Places
(Alcoholic Beverages); 42281 Beer & Ale
Wholesalers; 72111 Hotels & Motels

Shepherd Neame Limited has the distinction of being among the oldest British brewers as well as the 15th oldest registered company in the world. It operates the Faversham Brewery, which has been brewing continuously over the same artesian well since 1698. "Shep's" brews 50 million pints a year and exports three million. Bishop's Finger, Spitfire, and Master Brew are among its beer brands. The firm controls about 370 pubs in the southeast of England, where it also operates hotels.

Origins

The water at Faversham, in Kent, contains calcium and naturally lends itself to ale production. By the 17th century, the town was supplying this region one of its favorite beverages. Although 1698 is the traditional date given for the founding of the Faversham Brewery, evidence suggests that it was merely moved at that date and had been in thriving existence for 20 years. The predecessor to Shepherd Neame was founded by Captain Richard Marsh, a member of the militia. After his death, Marsh's daughter Silvester sold the property to Samuel Shepherd, a brewer and eminent citizen who had served as the town's mayor.

Shepherd took ownership of the brewery in 1742. Under Shepherd, the business also acted as an agent for London brewers and began acquiring its own local pubs. Shepherd's son Julius inherited the family business in 1770 after being active in the management for 15 years. He continued to acquire pubs, and in 1789 bought a Boulton and Watt steam engine to replace horses as the company's grinding and pumping muscle. The purchase prompted a progressive new name: the Faversham Steam Brewery. In spite of such entrepreneurial drive, in the early 19th century the brewery felt the negative effects of unrest among agrarian laborers (their jobs threatened by new threshing machines) and high levels of taxation due to the Napoleonic wars.

Victorian Expansion

Giles Hilton became a partner in the brewery after marrying a niece of Julius Shepherd's. Geographic expansion was a major concern during this time, and the firm acquired pubs as far away as Dover. Finding suitable tenants and maintaining ale houses accounted for a considerable amount of the partners' time.

The firm encountered financial trouble and had to mortgage a £3,000 piece of property in 1847. Hilton, who had diverse business interests, then withdrew from the partnership, making the brewery's position even more precarious.

Although John Henry Mares does not appear to have been experienced in brewing, he invested £5,000 in the venture, becoming a 25 percent partner, and pressed it to expand its brewing capacity. Its beers were proving increasingly popular around Kent, and when the railroad belatedly came to Faversham in 1858, Shepherd & Mares would capitalize upon the more convenient access to the London market.

Henry Shepherd, Sr., died in 1862, leaving his less capable son in the partnership. After the death of John Mares in December 1864, the firm therefore relied heavily on the young (28-year-old) Percy Beale Neame, who had only joined the firm that October.

The investments in capacity undertaken during Mares's tenure tripled production within a few years. A final round of investment came in 1869 as the company built a new headquarters at 17 Court Street. The company's property in the 1870s (boom years for England) included 115 pubs, some with cottages attached. The company also owned ten of its own rail cars for delivering beer. Its network of suppliers had similarly expanded; it supplemented its local purchases with hops from as far away as Bavaria.

Yeast became an important side business for Shepherd Neame. Another byproduct of the brewing process, spent grains, were sold to farmers as feed. Together, they accounted for about £2,000–£3,000 of turnover per year in the early 1870s.

The end of the 1870s saw another great depression, although Shepherd Neame & Co. continued to make money due to the strong pound. Private brewers such as pubs which brewed their own ale suffered much of the brunt of the decline in beer drinking which accompanied the availability of new diversions competing with the pub experience. The temperance movement also had an effect on sales. At the same time, competition intensified due to the newly increased capacity of rival brewer W.E. and J. Rigden. Unpaid bills and unreturned casks remained persistent problems.

Neame became sole proprietor of the firm in 1877. Three sons followed him into the business. Around the end of the 19th century, Harry Neame, the oldest son, began buying malt and barley from as far away as Spain and California. The brewery began purchasing barley in cooperation with Rigden. At this time, Shepherd Neame's annual turnover was £88,564 with profits of £19,132. There were 60 breweries in operation in Kent; Shepherd Neame would be the only survivor 100 years later.

Percy Neame died in 1913, leaving control of the company with his oldest son, Harry. He was not a sole proprietor, since a new business entity, Shepherd Neame Ltd., had been created, its shares allotted to the elder Neame's ten children as well as the head brewer, C.L. Graham. Harry Neame became chairman and managing director.

World Wars I and II

Although production rose until World War I, profits faltered, probably mostly due to higher taxation under a Liberal government. Beer sales increased during World War I on account of the troops stationed in the area. However, mobilization made both brewery personnel and pub tenants scarce. The firm therefore began employing women in bottling operations with good results. Neame family representation in management was thinned as Alick and Arthur Neame both died during the war, though not of service-related injuries.

Shepherd Neame shared in the booming economy immediately after the war and erected new buildings to bolster capacity. One piece of business the company declined was an offer to cater ferry service. Although the British economy faltered in the 1920s, Shepherd Neame survived rather well.

The brewery suffered a steep decline in barrelage in the 1930s, resulting in cutbacks in most areas with the exception of motor transport, seen as crucial to developing business. Shepherd Neame also invested in mechanized bottling equipment and bought a few pubs. The company earned between £50,000–£60,000 per year in the 1930s. Family and executive shareholders in the private enterprise were well rewarded.

Harry Neame's son Jasper became managing director and chairman early in World War II, when dozens of personnel were either consigned to the armed forces or served part-time in civil service units at home. Shepherd Neame supplemented the meager income of its employees serving in the military. The company also had to contend with falling bombs: several stores and pubs were damaged.

Beer was not rationed like sugar or gasoline; in fact, production was increased for morale. In order to save money on transport costs, brewers were assigned geographical areas to supply. Shepherd Neame did meet great difficulty in finding an adequate supply of barley. The firm bought its own hop fields in Kent in order to remedy a similar situation.

Postwar Problems—and Profits

After the war, although demand for beer fell, labor remained scarce. In fact, money and raw materials were scarce as well. Wartime rationing of mechanical supplies continued. Shepherd Neame responded by buying many more pubs in order to provide more outlets for Shepherd Neame's products. The company avoided coastal areas in order not to suffer the vagaries of the tourist trade. The rival Rigden brewery (then known as George Beer and Rigden) was acquired by Fremlins of Maidstone in 1948. In the next couple of decades, brewers would emerge as very attractive takeover targets due to the value of their real estate holdings. Shepherd Neame also had to contend with natural forces. In late January 1953, floods overran the brewery and damaged some of the company's pubs.

Shepherd Neame felt compelled to renovate its pubs to make them more attractive to a public confronted by a widening array of leisure options. Increasing motor vehicle use in the 1960s added to this mobility. Breathalyzers, introduced in 1967 to monitor drunk driving, made snacks and other non-alcoholic attractions even more important. Food service became one of the company's new specialties.

During the 1960s, the company modernized its 1930s era bottling operation, a feat which took seven years to accomplish. It also began offering beer in kegs. Shepherd Neame recognized the growing popularity of lagers by signing distribution agreements with Carlsberg and Hürlimann, a Swiss brewer. Another change was the end of horse-drawn ale carts.

Jasper and Laurie Neame had become joint managing directors in September 1951. When Jasper died in 1961, his brother retained his post and Kenneth Johnston succeeded him as chairman. Profits rose sharply in the middle of the decade, reaching £93,000 one year. The firm's real estate continued to appreciate as well. With the sale of the Cobb Brewery to Whitbreads in January 1968, Shepherd Neame remained the last independent brewery in Kent.

Laurie Neame died in December 1970 and Kenneth Johnston retired as chairman in the spring of 1971. In their wake came Colin (also vice-chairman) and Robert Harry Beale (''Bobby'') Neame. The company bought an innovative computer system after Stuart Fraser Beale Neame, a ten-year IBM veteran, joined management. Profits exceeded £100,000 in 1971.

Shepherd Neame was becoming a modern brewery, both in terms of production and marketing. It had installed a laboratory and begun advertising on television. The company replaced its wooden, copper-lined fermenters with new stainless steel ones, and particular attention was given to streamlining the production process, which shrank the workforce to about 200.

The British government, wanting to break up an oligarchy, ordered Whitbreads to sell off pub houses in 1972. Shepherd Neame bought 32 of them, a major expansion. The purchases produced decidedly good results. The company bought another 33 houses in the next eight years. It also invested in upgrading existing ones.

Expanding Throughout the 1980s and 1990s

Shepherd Neame bought 46 pubs in the 1980s. Perceiving a need for moderately priced hotels in the Southeast, the company acquired three Invicta Inns. It installed new fermenters to accommodate increased demand for lager. Once a rarity in Britain, by this time it accounted for 40 percent of pub sales. More new fermenters were installed in 1995.

Shepherd Neame began bottling wine from vineyards at its farm, the first English brewer to do so. However, the company sold much of this land in 1982 when hop production failed due to falling prices and disease. By the mid-1990s, Shepherd Neame had withdrawn from all its farm-related enterprises such as using spent grain and yeast as livestock feed. The mad cow disease crisis helped bring this to an end. The vineyard was also shut down, and the land leased out.

In 1988 Shepherd Neame bought Grants, founded in Dover in 1774. Nine years later the firm's Morella Cherry Brandy would win Shepherd Neame its first royal warrant. The brandy was a favorite of Queen Victoria's and had been marketed under the priceless slogan ''Keep it near, keep it handy.'' Other new products in the 1990s were Kingfisher beer, which Shepherd Neame licensed from Bangalore to sell in Indian restaurants. It developed its own Sun Lik beer for Chinese restaurants.

Profits were £3.6 million on sales of £26.7 million in 1990. As the brewing industry in Britain consolidated, Shepherd Neame launched a new massive round of acquisition. It bought 33 houses from Allied in 1990, 22 from Bass and Courage in 1991, and followed this by another 60 leased (and later bought) from Whitbread.

Colin Neame stepped down as vice-chairman in 1984. The loss of him and other experienced managers prompted the company to create a technical board of outside professional talent. The company was restructured in July 1999, and Johnathan Neame, a qualified barrister, became managing director.

As its bottle washing equipment reached obsolescence, Shepherd Neame stopped reusing returnable bottles. Its new disposable packaging gave longer range exports new viability without the problem of returning the empties. A new long-necked half liter bottle was introduced to compete against nitrogenated cans. The success of these bottling innovations kept plants busy around the clock, as Shepherd Neame shipped to 12 countries. Its Bishops Finger brand became the bestselling British import in Sweden. Shepherd Neame began selling Bishops Finger in Calais to compete with the cheap beers British vacationers took back home with them. When it proved wildly successful there, the company began expanding its domestic distribution.

Triumphant Tricentennial

The problem of cheap imports from France, where duties were a fraction of those in the United Kingdom, was a recalcitrant one for Shepherd Neame. One of every three pints of beer consumed in Kent was estimated to have been bought across the Channel. Shepherd Neame fought against increasing taxation with high profile advocate Cherie Booth, wife of prime minister Tony Blair. The company won a judicial review; however, the House of Lords refused to override an Appeal Court decision not to refer the case to the European Court. The campaign did succeed in bringing the issue into the political arena, and Shepherd Neame gained an estimated five times the value of its legal fees in free publicity.

Principal Subsidiaries

USBN Limited (50%); Pubco PLC (20%).

Further Reading

Barker, Theo, *Shepherd Neame: A Story That's Been Brewing for 300 Years,* Faversham, Kent, and Chesterton, Cambridge: Shepherd Neame Ltd. and Granta Editions, 1998.
Gwyther, Matthew, ''End of the Hereditary Beerage,'' *Management Today,* February 1999, pp. 40–46.
Kennedy, Carol, ''The Great Survivors,'' *Director,* December 1993, pp. 50–54.

—Frederick C. Ingram

The Singer Company N.V.

2 Chinachem Plaza
26th Floor
68 Connaught Road
Hong Kong
(852) 475 8607
Fax: (852) 475 3652
Web site: http://www.singer-nv.com

Public Company
Incorporated: 1863 as Singer Manufacturing Company
Employees: 3,800
Sales: $1.26 billion (1998)
Stock Exchanges: New York
Ticker Symbol: SEW
NAIC: 333298 Sewing Machines (Including Household-
    Type) Manufacturing

The Singer Company N.V. is the number one maker and seller of consumer and industrial sewing machines in the world, not to mention the oldest. With distribution into more than 150 countries worldwide and ownership of 1,500 retail outlets, Singer boasts of having one of the best-known brand names in the world. Throughout the late 20th century, however, Singer has struggled to maintain profitability, and the original sewing operations have weathered several incarnations as a private and a public company.

Company Origins

Isaac Merritt Singer was born in Pittstown, New York, in 1811, and ran away from his immigrant parents at the age of 12 to join a troupe of traveling actors. Singer remained an actor until 1835. During the following years he worked at various jobs while he invented things on the side. By 1850, Singer had gone to Boston with a patented device for carving wood-block type he hoped to sell to type manufacturers.

In Boston, Singer became interested in a prospective client's sewing machine repair business. The first patent for a sewing machine had been granted in England in 1790, but because of their unreliability none of the machines since then had been commercially successful. The first sewing machine with an eye-pointed needle, invented in 1846 by Elias Howe, seemed on the verge of capturing the public interest, but it, too, required frequent repairs. Singer quickly set to work to invent a reliable machine.

Singer finished his machine in 1850 and was granted a patent for it in 1851, the same year he established I.M. Singer and Company. The machine was an immediate success, prompting Howe to file suit against Singer for patent infringement. In 1854 Singer hired a young lawyer named Edward Clark to defend him; Clark agreed to take the case in exchange for a third of Singer's business, and eventually the two men became equal partners in the company, Singer running the manufacturing side and Clark the financial and sales side.

Clark stymied the lawsuits brought against Singer and then brought the manufacturers together to pool their patents by creating the Singer Machine Combination, the first patent pool in the United States. The combination, which lasted until 1877, when the last patent ran out, licensed 24 sewing machine manufacturers to make the machines for $15 a machine, with Singer and Howe receiving $5 each for every machine sold domestically.

Expansion in the 19th Century

With Clark supervising the day-to-day operations, I.M. Singer and Company began to grow rapidly. Until the late 1850s the price of a sewing machine limited its market to commercial interests like professional tailors and harness manufacturers. But at that time, Clark introduced the first consumer installment payment plan. This plan, combined with an aggressive marketing strategy, enabled the young company to survive the business panic of 1857 and gave Singer the decisive lead in sewing machines for more than a century.

In 1863 Clark and Singer dissolved their partnership and the company was incorporated as Singer Manufacturing Company after Singer's rather sordid personal life (which eventually resulted in 24 children by four women) came to light. Both

---

Company Perspectives:

Singer is one of the most widely recognized and respected brands in the world. The company is the largest manufacturer and seller of sewing machines and a leading marketer of consumer durables for the home.

Clark and Singer retained some stock in the company but sold the rest to their employees. Clark continued as president of the company until his death in 1882; Isaac Singer, who had fled to Europe, died in England in 1875.

For the next 70 years, the business was led by three men: F.G. Bourne, who was president from 1873 to 1905; Douglas Alexander, who led the company from 1906 to 1949; and Milton Lightner, who served from 1949 to 1958. These men increased Singer's role as the United States' first multinational company. Singer had begun manufacturing in Scotland in 1867 and in Canada in 1873. By the 1880s, the company's extensive European operations were exporting sewing machines to Africa and soon after the turn of the century Singer was selling its product in the South Pacific. The one setback during this growth and expansion occurred in 1917, when the company's Russian holdings were seized during the Bolshevik Revolution. In 1918 Singer acquired the Diehl Manufacturing Company to make sewing machine motors.

Throughout the 1920s and 1930s, Singer's profits rose steadily as it convinced more and more people around the world that a Singer sewing machine was indispensable. By the end of World War II, however, the sewing machine market had matured in the United States. To make matters worse, within a few years European manufacturers were offering zig-zag machines (which Singer had decided in the 1930s would not find a market in the United States) and, suddenly, highly competitive Japanese manufacturers began to flood the market. In the United States alone, Singer's market share had halved, to only one-third, by the late 1950s.

Singer had hired a lawyer, Donald P. Kircher, to supervise the company's legal affairs in 1948. In 1955 Kircher was appointed Lightner's assistant, and in 1958 he was made president. Hired to help turn Singer around, Kircher began a complete reorganization of the company: plants were modernized, manufacturing procedures automated, products upgraded, and merchandising improved. By 1963 Singer's share in the U.S. sewing machine market had increased to 40 percent.

Diversification in the 1950s and 1960s

Under Kircher's direction, Singer also began an ambitious overseas construction program. Besides spending large amounts of money to revamp company facilities in Scotland, Brazil, France, West Germany, and Italy, Kircher also started building new factories in Australia, Mexico, and the Philippines. In addition, Kircher reaffirmed the strategy of looking toward underdeveloped regions of the world for the company's largest markets.

Kircher also began a domestic diversification program. One of his first decisions was to purchase Haller, Raymond & Brown, Inc., a leading electronics research firm and Singer's first step into the electronics industry. He also bought three companies in 1960 and 1961: two knitting-machine makers and a carpet-tufting-machinery maker. Initially, this diversification strategy was also successful. Between 1958 and 1963, Singer's sales almost doubled, to $1.2 billion (between 1952 and 1956 sales had risen only 12 percent, from $325 million to $364 million). In 1963 Singer dropped the "Manufacturing" from its name to better reflect the nature of its business.

Kircher's plan also included a more aggressive acquisition and diversification policy. The first important purchase, in 1963, was of Friden, Inc., a manufacturer of office equipment and calculators. The second one, of General Precision Equipment Corporation (GPE), was made in 1968. General Precision gave Singer access to three markets: industrial products (such as gas meters), defense electronics, and aerospace. But GPE and Friden were only part of Kircher's grand plan. Altogether, Kircher bought 22 manufacturing firms with products ranging from audio to aerospace equipment.

In 1958, 90 percent of Singer's total sales came from sewing machines; by 1970, this portion was reduced to 35 percent, and Kircher's diversification strategy seemed to work. Singer's sales exceeded $1.9 billion, 40 percent from business abroad.

Losses in the 1970s

But Kircher, described by subordinates as autocratic and imperious, had overreached himself. Although the company reported $2.6 billion in sales for 1974, one Wall Street analyst estimated that Singer's debt had reached $1.1 billion—a staggering price for its acquisition program. Combined with a collapse in the aerospace market and a glut in office equipment in the late 1960s, it is not surprising that Singer reported a $10.1 million loss in 1974. The single bright spot that year was Singer's original sewing machine operation, which accounted for 54 percent of company sales.

While Kircher was confined to a hospital bed in 1975, the board of directors looked for someone to replace him. They hired Joseph Flavin, who had worked at IBM and at Xerox, where he was an executive vice-president. Forty-seven years old when he became Singer's president, Flavin immediately took a $411 million write-off to eliminate the company's money-losing ventures, including a home-building concern, a printing operation, a telecommunications firm, an Italian household appliance plant, and a West German mail-order house. This write-off was the largest of its time and reduced Singer's book value by 50 percent. Flavin then planned to revitalize the company's sewing machine operation and develop its power tool and aerospace businesses.

Over the next few years, Singer also concentrated on developing high-technology electric components, including air conditioning and heating systems, gas meters, thermostats, electrical switches, dishwashers, and auto dashboards. The company made the guidance system for the Trident missile and navigation equipment for airplanes and ships, and Singer electrical instruments played an important role in NASA's Apollo lunar modules.

Flavin managed to reduce the company's $1.1 billion debt by 55 percent after he became president, but in 1979 he took a $130 million write-off on the sewing machine business, which in North America and Europe had fallen off drastically. This move involved the restructuring of Singer's North American and European operations; its oldest factory in Europe, near Clydebank, Scotland, was one of the casualties. Flavin also replaced 80 of his top 200 managers. All these changes were made in the middle of a headquarters move from New York City to Stamford, Connecticut.

In 1980 Singer's aerospace and marine divisions' operating profits increased by 34 percent, to $36 million, due in large part to Singer's role as the nation's leading manufacturer of aircraft simulators, including the one used to train space shuttle astronauts. In addition, this division won a large contract for helicopters from the Defense Department in 1981. Encouraged by these results, management decided to create SimuFlite, a new venture that provided ground school and flight simulation training for corporate pilots.

Continued Problems in the 1980s

Foreign manufacturers like Bernina, Pfaff, and Viking, along with inexpensive imports from Japan, began to cut deeply into what little was left of Singer's sewing machine market during the early 1980s. That and the belief among top officials at Singer that the sewing industry in the United States was finally drying up led the company to abandon its century-old core business. In 1986 Singer spun off its sewing machine division as a separate company called SSMC Inc. Singer also got rid of all 1,600 company-owned stores and service centers, either by closing them or making them independent.

Although Singer had become a $2 billion-a-year defense conglomerate, it was beset by endless problems and an enormous debt. Its stock price was driven down by the announcement of a $20 million loss in July 1987, which it attributed to development costs for several new aerospace products. Then, that fall, Chairman Joseph Flavin died unexpectedly. Therefore, to no one's surprise, Singer became a prime takeover candidate. The buyer was a surprise, however: Paul Bilzerian, a somewhat obscure corporate raider best known as a greenmailer. For $50 a share—some $15 below what Singer's investment banker, Goldman Sachs, had expected it to sell for—Bilzerian walked away with Singer.

Despite a staggering debt load, Bilzerian at first promised not to strip Singer of its most productive assets, planning only to sell off its defense electronics business. But only months later, prime assets began to go. Between July and October 1988 Bilzerian sold eight of Singer's 12 divisions, for about $2 billion, which tidily covered his debt.

But, in December 1988, Bilzerian was indicted—for non-Singer-related activities—and in May 1989 he was convicted of nine counts of securities and tax violations. More troublesome for the company itself, however, was the multitude of suits filed against it after mid-1988 by former employees regarding pension benefits; stockholders disillusioned by Bilzerian's dealings; buyers of divisions who claimed they were overcharged; and the federal government, which sought treble damages of $231 million for Defense Department overcharges dating back to 1980. Renamed the Bicoastal Corporation in 1989, the company agreed to pay $55 million to the federal government in 1992 to settle the fraud charges.

Rebounding: Early 1990s

Meanwhile, SSMC, the original sewing machine business, defied predictions and managed to stay in business. In 1989 Semi-Tech Global purchased SSMC and began to turn the company around. SSMC reclaimed its heritage by renaming itself The Singer Company. Then, in 1991, the company offered shares to the public on the New York Stock Exchange. Semi-Tech Global retained control of the company with ownership of 50 percent of the shares. Two years later, Semi-Tech Global sold its interest in Singer to Semi-Tech Corp., owner of 43 percent of Semi-Tech Global.

Also in 1993, Semi-Tech Global acquired G.M. Pfaff AG, the second largest sewing machine manufacturer in the world. Founded in 1862 in Germany, the company had a history almost as long as Singer's and had built a comparable international reputation. Although Pfaff sold its machines mostly through its own retail stores in Germany, its international sales were handled through mass merchants, independent dealers, and distributors.

In the early 1990s Pfaff was operating at a loss, and Semi-Tech Global purchased 72 percent of the company's shares, thus gaining control of the company. Semi-Tech cut staff, outsourced and relocated much of the company's manufacturing, and sought growth primarily in developing countries. In addition, Semi-Tech Global hired Singer to manage the company. Within the next few years, Singer and Pfaff were cross-sourcing each other's products and had created efficiencies in research and development by working together to design new products.

In the mid-1990s Singer began selling other consumer durable products, hoping to cash in on widespread respect and awareness of its brand. New products included televisions, videocassette recorders, and home appliances. The company focused its sale of this new line in developing countries, where it had established distribution networks and, unlike most manufacturers and retailers in these countries, offered credit plans. For example, Singer met with a great deal of success in Mexico, where it focused its efforts on working-class consumers unused to the idea of credit but unable to buy a major appliance like a sewing machine without it. Singer's sales in Mexico quintupled between 1988 and 1993 and showed no signs of diminishing. It also held its repossession rate to about two percent.

Despite success in such developing countries as Mexico, Singer was reporting losses by the late 1990s. Although the company could still claim profits of $29 million in 1996, in 1997 Singer lost $238 million on revenues of $1.1 billion. Revenues had declined 19 percent from the previous year, stemming from the economic crisis in Asia, an economic slowdown in Brazil, and weak sales in the United States. A new president and chief executive officer, Stephen H. Goodman, took charge in early 1998.

In an effort to eliminate redundancies and thus reduce costs, Singer acquired Pfaff in 1997 for $157.5 million. Thus Singer's management of Pfaff became permanent when it purchased Semi-Tech Global's 80.5 percent interest in the company. Singer consolidated the two companies' marketing and distribution operations, shared their manufacturing plants, and reduced their combined overheads. As part of this reorganization, Singer eliminated almost 6,000 jobs, cutting 5,531 from manufacturing and 437 from marketing. The company projected this 28 percent cut would result in savings of $104 million a year.

Although revenues were up in 1998, to $1.26 billion, Singer still reported a loss of $207 million. The continued economic downturns in Asia and Brazil affected the company's performance, as did a decline in the industrial sewing market. Singer initiated a restructuring program in 1998 that included projected property sales of approximately $260 million. That year the company sold $37 million worth of property. In 1999 Singer continued with the program by selling its Taiwan operations for $58.6 million. On September 13, 1999, Singer announced that it was voluntarily filing for reorganization under Chapter 11 of the U.S. Bankruptcy Code. The company's stock continued to trade on the New York Stock Exchange at the NYSE's discretion.

Principal Subsidiaries

G.M. Pfaff AG (80%); Singer Nikko (Japan; 50%); Singer (Thailand; 48%).

Further Reading

Brandfon, Ruth, *Singer and the Sewing Machine: A Capitalist Romance,* London: Barrie & Jenkins, 1977.

Cooper, Grace Rogers, *The Sewing Machine: Its Invention and Development,* Washington, D.C.: Smithsonian Institution, 1976.

Siegle, Candace, ''Sewing It Up,'' *World Trade,* May 1994, pp. 122–24.

''Singer Merges and Trims,'' *Apparel Industry Magazine,* January 1998, p. 13.

—updated by Susan Windisch Brown

Skyline Corporation

2520 Bypass Road
P.O. Box 743
Elkhart, Indiana 46515
U.S.A.
(219) 294-6521
Fax: (219) 293-0693
Web site: http://www.skylinerv.com

Public Company
Incorporated: 1959
Employees: 3,500
Sales: $664.8 (1999)
Stock Exchanges: New York
Ticker Symbol: SKY
NAIC: 321991 Manufactured Home (Mobile Home)
Manufacturing; 321992 Prefabricated Wood Building
Manufacturing; 336214 Travel Trailer & Camper
Manufacturing

Skyline Corporation designs and produces manufactured housing and recreational vehicles (RVs). Approximately 80 percent of the company's total sales are derived from manufactured homes, which are sold under several different trade names. Skyline makes two basic types of manufactured housing: single-section mobile homes and multi-section homes. Single-section homes, which range from 36 to 80 feet in length and 12 to 18 feet in width, are often located in designated mobile home parks. Because their size makes them easy to move from place to place, they are considered "mobile homes." Skyline's multi-section homes, however, are larger and more closely resemble site-built homes. Buyers typically place these homes on traditional lots, and rarely, if ever, move them. Almost 70 percent of the homes produced by Skyline are multi-sections. The company's recreational vehicle segment manufactures three types of towable RVs—conventional travel trailers, fifth-wheel trailers, and park models—as well as a line of slide-in truck campers. They are sold under the "Nomad," "Layton," "Aljo," and "WeekEnder" trademarks. Skyline operates 25 manufacturing plants in 12 states

and distributes its products through a national network of manufactured housing and RV dealers.

1950s: A New Spoke in an Industry Hub

Skyline Coach, the predecessor to Skyline Corporation, was established in 1951 in Elkhart, Indiana. Its founder, Julius Decio, started the business to produce mobile homes, which were commonly called "house trailers" at the time. The business Decio chose was by no means an uncommon one for Elkhart and its surrounding communities. For 20 years, the city—located in northern central Indiana, just a few miles from the Michigan border—had been a major hub for the mobile home industry. The area's mobile home business had begun in 1933, when a local merchant decided to try replicating a contraption he had seen at the Chicago World's Fair that looked like a tent on wheels. Setting up shop in Elkhart, he began building "house trailers," which resembled rudimentary recreational travel trailers. The trailers' affordability and mobility made them a good option during the Great Depression, when many families traveled across country looking for jobs and a better life.

The success of this first mobile home manufacturer led others to start similar businesses, and gradually the region became a major source of house trailers. During the Dust Bowl of 1937 and 1938, people began using house trailers not just to travel in, but as actual homes. In response, manufacturers modified their products to make them more closely correspond to traditional homes, increasing the size of the units and adding more amenities. By the end of World War II, mobile homes had evolved into something much different from their travel-trailer predecessors. Larger and more elaborate in design, they were no longer meant to be towed, camper-style, across the country by families on the move. Rather, they had become an alternative and more affordable type of house, typically stationed in one place. There were, however, a number of manufacturers still producing the early smaller trailers, primarily for use as recreational vehicles. After the war, these manufacturers essentially split off from the mobile home industry to form the RV industry.

It was into this newly bifurcated industry that Julius Decio entered when he began building house trailers in a friend's "welding garage." His early efforts met with success, and the business was profitable from its first year in operation. In 1952, Decio's 22-year-old son, Art, returned to Elkhart from Chicago, where he had just graduated college. Art quickly took an active role in his father's business, working as a division manager in the plant and helping to build the fledgling company. In 1956, he became Skyline's CEO.

The company expanded geographically under Art Decio's capable leadership, targeting emerging mobile housing markets in retiree states, such as Florida. Another important facet of the new CEO's administration was a movement toward near-total reliance on third-party suppliers for materials. Whereas many mobile home manufacturers at that time produced some of their own cabinets and building supplies, Art Decio preferred to order virtually everything from outside sources. By having suppliers deliver inventory on a "just in time" basis, Skyline was able to minimize the need for warehouse space, reduce waste, and better control inventory.

1960s: Diversification and Acquisition

Decio kicked off the 1960s by taking Skyline public. At the time of its initial public offering, the company boasted an impressive string of profitable years and no corporate debt. Skyline's second milestone of 1960 was to diversify its business by opening a travel trailer and RV plant in Elkhart. This reunion of the mobile home and RV industries made sense on several levels for the company. Since the industry split in the early 1950s, both the RV and housing segments had remained well represented in northern Indiana. Dozens of RV manufacturers—and the second- and third-tier suppliers supporting them—had production facilities in the region. In addition, many of the materials required to produce mobile homes corresponded with the materials needed to produce RVs. Therefore, Skyline's addition of an RV division allowed for certain inventory and cost efficiencies.

Skyline also used the proceeds from its 1960 IPO to expand its mobile home business via acquisition. In 1962, the company acquired Homette Corporation and Layton Homes Corporation. The following year, Skyline bought Buddy Mobile Homes, and in 1966, added Academy Mobile Homes to its growing portfolio. The company also changed its name from Skyline Coach to Skyline Corporation.

Mid-1970s: Market Downturn

During the 1960s and early 1970s, low interest rates and a generally stable economy had combined to keep the manufac-

tured housing business in high gear. According to the Manufactured Housing Institute, the industry hit an all-time high in 1972, reporting shipments of more than half a million units. In 1973 and 1974, however, interest rates began to climb, and housing sales began to plunge. Shipments of manufactured homes declined by 42 percent in 1974 and another 35 percent in 1975. The RV industry, likewise, fell on hard times in the 1970s. The OPEC oil embargo of 1973 and the resulting hike in gas prices put the brakes on recreational driving. This, combined with the rising interest rates, caused RV sales to fall off.

Already contending with bleak market conditions, Skyline and other producers of manufactured housing were confronted with still another hurdle in 1976. Concerned about mobile homes' safety, Congress enacted legislation that set stricter standards for their construction. Officially changing the product's name to "manufactured housing," the government required all mobile homes to meet stringent manufacturing, fire, electricity, and safety codes. The tougher requirements—and the costs associated with compliance—spurred a wave of closings and consolidations in the manufactured housing industry. Despite the odds against it, Skyline managed to remain solvent and successful throughout the industry slump, never once posting an annual loss. In 1978, the company expanded again, purchasing Country Vans Conversion.

1980–98: Market Swings

The market for RVs improved in the early years of the new decade; between 1980 and 1984, the number of vehicles shipped increased by more than 80 percent. The market for manufactured housing was slower to rebound, however, with sales remaining at levels much lower than they were in the early 1970s. Skyline continued to show improved earnings and remained debt-free—but to do so, it had to trim costs and streamline operations. In 1983, the company had 28 operational and six idle manufactured housing plants. Just four years later, cost-cutting measures had reduced that number to 23 operational and two idle plants. Skyline also hedged against further economic downturns by amassing cash reserves. In 1987, one-fourth of the company's pretax income came from interest.

The 1990s ushered in better interest rates than consumers had seen in more than a decade, and sales of manufactured housing picked up immediately. Although Skyline's sales also improved, the company was unable to keep pace with its competitors and consequently surrendered part of its market share. Management attributed the market share loss to a lack of capacity in areas where the manufactured housing markets were expanding fastest. In an April 1996 interview with *Investor's Business Daily*, Decio cited Georgia and Texas as two such rapid-growth markets, pointing out that Skyline did not have a strong manufacturing presence in either state. "Even though we're a national company, at certain times we can't keep up," he said.

To bolster output and remedy the situation, Skyline initiated an aggressive expansion plan. In 1994, the company upgraded its manufactured housing plant in Sugarcreek, Ohio, and its RV plant in McMinnville, Oregon. The following year, Skyline laid out another $10 million to renovate four more facilities—in Indiana, Pennsylvania, Florida, and Louisiana. In addition to boosting production, the upgrades were designed to allow all facilities to manufacture a wider range of products. The expansion program paid off; between 1992 and 1995, net income improved by more than 50 percent.

In 1997, Skyline's sales of manufactured housing fell slightly, and the resulting dip in total sales broke the company's five-year record of modest but steady annual increases. A major reason for the decline was an exceptionally harsh winter, which slowed housing sales in some parts of the United States. Another factor was a general softening in the demand for manufactured housing nationwide, which led many of Skyline's dealers to reduce their inventories. The company's RV division had a better year, however. RV sales increased by more than 14 percent over 1996 sales, reversing the previous year's RV industry slump.

The year 1998 saw a flip-flop in the fortunes of Skyline's two business segments. The market for manufactured housing improved in the second half of the year, driving up Skyline's housing sales. In addition to the overall market improvement, the housing segment benefited from a stronger demand for multi-section homes, which commanded higher prices than single-section homes. On the other hand, Skyline's recreational vehicle sales decreased in 1998, despite the fact that, industry-wide, demand for the vehicles increased.

1999 and the New Century

Skyline appeared to have both its business segments on track in 1999. The market for manufactured housing remained relatively steady through the first half of the year. More significantly, consumer demand for multi-section homes continued to grow, pushing the company's housing dollars up despite a slight decrease in actual units sold. As its quality continued to improve, manufactured housing was expected to become an attractive option for a wider range of homeowners.

Skyline's RV business also appeared to be on the upswing as 1999 progressed, showing gains both in units sold and in sales income. This increase was due in large part to overall favorable economic conditions and increased discretionary income, which allowed consumers to spend more for recreational products and activities.

Since its inception in the 1950s, Skyline had been more of a tortoise than a hare, taking few risks and growing slowly and sure-footedly. As the company prepared to leave the 20th century behind, it showed no signs of altering that approach. Because demand in both of Skyline's major markets was so closely tied to economic cycles, it was impossible to predict how the company might fare in the future. So long as the general economy remained strong, however, it seemed likely that Skyline would thrive.

Principal Subsidiaries

Skyline Homes, Inc.; Homette Corporation; Layton Homes Corporation.

Further Reading

Cooksey, Bill, ''Mobile Homes Firm Speeds Up,'' *Shreveport Times*, June 22, 1994, p. 1.
Goldenberg, Sherman, ''Northern Indiana: The Manufactured-Housing Industry,'' *Indiana Business*, May 1, 1987, p. 46.
Jones, John, ''Companies in the News: Skyline Keeps Up Manufactured-Home Sales in RV Slump,'' *Investor's Business Daily*, April 11, 1996, p. A18.
Magary, Don, ''Skyline's Art Decio: Life Is Not Just Business,'' *RV News*, November, 1996.

—Shawna Brynildssen

Smith & Wesson Corporation

2100 Roosevelt Avenue
Post Office Box 2208
Springfield, Massachusetts 01102-2208
U.S.A.
(800) 331-0852
(413) 781-8300
Fax: (413) 747-3677
Web site: http://www.smith-wesson.com

Wholly Owned Subsidiary of Tomkins PLC
Incorporated: 1857 as Smith & Wesson, Inc.
Employees: 1,300
Sales: $125 million (1999 est.)
NAIC: 332994 Small Arms Manufacturing; 336991
   Motorcycle, Bicycle, & Parts Manufacturing; 51121
   Software Publishers

Smith & Wesson Corporation is the world's leading manufacturer of handguns. Among the company's best known products over the years have been the .22 rimfire revolver (Model 1), which became a worldwide success in the mid-1800s; the .38 special revolver (Model 10), a 20th-century model used extensively by police forces; the .44 Magnum revolver made famous by Clint Eastwood in his *Dirty Harry* movies; and the line of .357 Magnums, which, according to the company, became the most popular line of revolvers of all time. Smith & Wesson also sells handcuffs, bicycles designed for law enforcement use, and law enforcement software and systems, such as the Automated Suspect IDentification System and Identi-Kit software, through which an electronic composite drawing of a suspect can be matched against a database of mug shots to identify and rank possible suspects. Apparel and other nongun products affixed with the company logo are sold through several company-owned retail outlets in the United States. Smith & Wesson was purchased by U.K. conglomerate Tomkins PLC in 1987.

Mid-19th-Century Origins

The history of Smith & Wesson begins in the 1850s with a partnership between Horace Smith and Daniel B. Wesson.

Smith was born in 1808 in Cheshire, Massachusetts. His father, a carpenter, moved the family to Springfield, Massachusetts, four years later, taking a job in the U.S. Armory. After finishing his public school education at age 16, Smith joined his father at the Armory as a gunsmith's apprentice. He gained expertise in the manufacture of guns through the 18 years he spent at the Armory. In the 1840s Smith worked for a number of gun manufacturers and spent three years running his own gunmaking concern. In 1851 he patented an improvement on the breech-loading rifle. He next took a position at Allen, Brown & Luther, a rifle barrel manufacturer based in Worcester, Massachusetts. It was there that he met Wesson.

Born in 1825 in Worcester, Wesson worked on the family farm and attended school until the age of 18. He then apprenticed himself to his eldest brother, a gunsmith. After completing his apprenticeship in 1846, Wesson worked as a journeyman gunsmith before taking over his brother's business after his death in 1850. Soon thereafter, he joined Allen, Brown & Luther.

This was still the era of the muzzle loaders, firearms that had to be reloaded with loose powder, ball, and primer. Through their partnership, Smith and Wesson played a key role in the ending of the muzzle-loading era. They formed their first partnership, the Smith & Wesson Arms Company, in 1852, working to perfect a lever-action pistol with a metallic cartridge and a new repeating action, for which the partners received a patent in February 1854. According to Smith & Wesson historian Roy G. Jinks, "The fire power of this lever action pistol was so impressive, that in 1854 when the gun was reviewed by *Scientific American,* it was nicknamed the Volcanic since its rapid fire sequence had the force of an erupting volcano."

The repeating action of the pistol was not entirely successful and when the Norwich, Connecticut-based company encountered financial problems, Oliver Winchester stepped in as a new investor. The factory was moved to New Haven, Connecticut, and the company name was changed to Volcanic Arms Company. In 1855 Smith retired while Wesson accepted a position as superintendent of the company. Wesson soon departed as well. The company later adapted the 1854 patent to rifles, creating the Winchester repeating rifle, which became world famous. In 1866 this firm changed its name again, to the Winchester Repeating Arms Company.

Meanwhile, in 1857 Smith and Wesson joined in a new partnership and began manufacturing the first Smith & Wesson revolver (''Model 1'') in Springfield, Massachusetts. This revolver was based on a patent the partners had received in August 1854 for a central-fire metallic cartridge, which contained not only powder but also a lubricant located within the case between the powder and the ball. The revolver included what was called a ''rimfire'' cartridge (later known as the .22 rimfire), featured repeating action and an open cylinder, and was manufactured with interchangeable parts. Its unique design helped make it an enormous success, including its adoption by U.S. military authorities. When demand exceeded the capacity of the firm's small, 25-person workshop, Smith & Wesson built a new factory in central Springfield on Stockbridge Street near the Armory, and expanded its workforce to 600. Improving on the original model, the company soon introduced the Model 2, which featured a .32-caliber cartridge.

Late 19th-Century Growth

During the Civil War, demand for Smith & Wesson revolvers increased further and helped establish the company as one of the top gunmakers in the United States. Following the war, however, sales fell to just a few guns per month as the ensuing depression hit Smith & Wesson hard. To drum up new sales, the partners established sales agencies in England, France, and Germany. They also exhibited their wares at the international exhibition in Paris in 1867, resulting in large contracts with several European and South American countries, as well as Japan and China. The Russian government alone placed an order for 200,000 revolvers. With a larger international market secured, the company proceeded to introduce its first large caliber gun, a .44-caliber revolver, the Model 3. This gun proved popular around the world and in the American West.

In addition to making improved models based on their own inventions, Smith and Wesson also purchased patents from other inventors. One of the most important of these was a design by William C. Dodge that automatically emptied shells from a gun—a patent Smith & Wesson bought in 1869. In July 1873 Smith sold his interest in the company to Wesson and retired. He died 20 years later, leaving no direct descendants. Wesson carried on as the sole principal for ten years before bringing his two sons on board as partners in 1883. Four years later, Wesson patented a safety revolver designed to prevent accidental firing. Smith & Wesson in 1899 introduced its most famous revolver, the .38 Military & Police, also known as the Model 10—a gun popular with law enforcement officials for nearly the entire 20th century. After Wesson died in 1906, the company he cofounded

continued to be owned and managed by members of the Wesson family well into the 20th century.

New Models and War Contributions in the First Half of the 20th Century

The early decades of the 20th century were marked by the introduction of the N frame line of revolvers. This line featured a new larger frame, and first appeared in 1908 with a .44-caliber S&W Special cartridge. The N frame revolver received international notice during World War I, when Smith & Wesson supplied 75,000 N frame revolvers to the British government. The 1930s saw the debut of the K-22 Outdoorsman, a model designed for the competitive shooter, and the .357 Magnum, a more powerful handgun designed for law enforcement officers. The .357 marked the debut of the Magnum line, which became famous later in the century.

During World War II, Smith & Wesson supplied arms to the United States and its allies; by 1941 the company was entirely dedicated to war production. By war's end, the company had supplied more than 1.1 million .38 Military & Police revolvers.

In 1946 C.R. Hellstrom was named president of Smith & Wesson, becoming the first person outside the Wesson family to run the company. Three years later Smith & Wesson completed construction of a new and much larger factory in Springfield. Among the first new models to roll off the assembly lines were Model 39, the first U.S.-made 9mm double-action pistol, and Model 29, the legendary .44 Magnum.

Bangor Punta/Lear Siegler Era, 1965–87

By the mid-1960s Smith & Wesson reigned as a leading maker of handguns, with an emphasis on revolvers used in law enforcement, and had also begun to sell handcuffs. It was still largely in the hands of the Wesson family, with some stock selling over the counter. For the year ending in June 1965, the company posted earnings of $1.5 million on sales of $10.4 million. During 1965 Smith & Wesson introduced Model 60, an all stainless steel revolver. Late that year, the firm's era of independence came to an end with its acquisition by Bangor Punta Alegre Sugar Corp., a conglomerate based in Bangor, Maine, with operations in railroads, textiles, foundry equipment, sewage disposal systems, yacht manufacturing, commercial finance, grain elevators, and other areas. Bangor Punta paid about $22.6 million to gain control of Smith & Wesson.

Under Bangor Punta ownership, Smith & Wesson expanded its product line into areas related to handguns and handcuffs in the 1970s. For the law enforcement market, Smith & Wesson began selling riot control equipment, night vision apparatus, breath-testing instruments, police car lights, and sirens. Another new law enforcement product was the Identi-Kit software program which helped investigations create facial composite drawings of suspects. In the sporting market, Smith & Wesson began offering its dealers a full line of products, including ammunition, holsters, and long guns. By the late 1970s about 25 percent of the company's sales were for nongun products.

The 1970s was a period of slow or no growth for the U.S. firearms industry, which faced a host of problems, concisely summarized in a 1978 *Business Week* article: ''skyrocketing product liability costs, highly restricted export markets, burgeoning labor and materials costs, an aging plant and skilled labor force, foreign gunrunning scandals, the recurring threat of federal gun controls, diminishing hunting grounds and shorter hunting seasons, stiff competition from imports, and, recently, competition from foreign companies manufacturing firearms in the U.S.'' While Smith & Wesson was not immune to these problems, it was, according to *Business Week,* ''the envy of the industry,'' because of its grip on the law enforcement market and its efficient, modern plants. The company was also highly profitable, posting operating profits of $18.4 million on sales of $84 million for the year ending in September 1977.

In the early 1980s Smith & Wesson began making 9mm semiautomatic pistols for the U.S. military and for law enforcement agencies seeking more powerful weapons to do battle with heavily armed criminals. In January 1984 Santa Monica, California-based Lear Siegler Corporation acquired Bangor Punta, giving Smith & Wesson a new parent. Under the direction of Lear Siegler, whose primary holdings were in the manufacture of aerospace and automotive parts and systems, Smith & Wesson divested numerous noncore areas in order to concentrate on its main areas of strength: making and selling handguns, handcuffs, and police Identi-Kits.

In spite of the divestments, Smith & Wesson was a company on the decline in the early to mid-1980s. Its entry into the semiautomatic handgun market was the move of a follower, not a market leader. The U.S. units of two foreign gunmakers, Austria's Glock GmbH and Italy's Beretta SpA, had led the introduction of semiautomatic weapons into the U.S. market. With overall sales of guns remaining flat, the new competition not only ate away at Smith & Wesson's market share, they also cut into its sales. It was also becoming clear, as summarized by Charles E. Petty writing in *American Rifleman,* that the quality of Smith & Wesson guns was on the decline. Although sales had surpassed the $100 million mark by the early 1980s, growth slowed by the mid-1980s and profits were down. For the fiscal year ending in June 1986, the gunmaker reported operating profits of $14.1 million on sales of $116.1 million. The profits figure represented a decline of 41 percent from the level in 1982.

Tomkins Era, 1987 On

It was in this troubled state that Smith & Wesson would once again see its ownership change hands. In December 1986, leveraged buyout specialist Forstmann Little & Co. led a group that took Lear Siegler private in a $2.1 billion LBO, with a new holding company created called Lear Siegler Holdings Corporation. As was typical of 1980s LBOs, the new holding company quickly sought to sell off noncore assets to pay down the debt incurred in the buyout. Smith & Wesson was one of the companies identified as noncore, as Lear Siegler Holdings intended to concentrate on its aerospace and automotive operations. Among the firms bidding to acquire Smith & Wesson was fellow firearms maker Sturm Ruger & Co. Prevailing in the end, however, was U.K. conglomerate F.H. Tomkins PLC (later simply Tomkins PLC), which paid $112.5 million in June 1997 to purchase Smith & Wesson.

Tomkins saw in Smith & Wesson ''a company with a good name and market position with a strong potential for growth

through management achievement,'' according to Robert Muddimer, as quoted in *American Rifleman.* Muddimer, who was installed as interim president of the gunmaker, said that Tomkins' initial goal was ''to enhance quality, and to service the market in terms of quality and accuracy with a blend of new technology and traditional gunsmithing arts.'' In recognition of the company's problems with the quality of its products, Tomkins set out to make improvements by modernizing the design and manufacturing process through the addition of computer-aided design equipment and a host of high-tech manufacturing apparatus. Tomkins also instituted a much more rigorous testing process. Already by mid-1989 the new equipment and programs had helped significantly lower the rate at which guns were being returned for warranty repair. For automatic pistols, the return rate had fallen from 6.3 percent to a record low of 1.2 percent, while only two percent of Smith & Wesson revolvers were being returned for service, halving the previous rate of four percent.

Although Tomkins was clearly aware of the declining quality of Smith & Wesson guns prior to its purchase of the company, the British firm came to believe that Forstmann Little had misled it about a jamming problem in a line of L-frame .357 Magnum revolvers. In 1994 Tomkins sued Forstmann Little for damages and indemnification.

Meanwhile, the Tomkins-led Smith & Wesson was showing a renewed vigor in the area of product development. In 1988 the company launched an improved, third-generation line of semiautomatic pistols. With interest in gun ownership increasing among women, Smith & Wesson introduced the LadySmith line of handguns in 1989. Under the leadership of Ed Shultz, who became president in 1992, Smith & Wesson introduced the Sigma Series of pistols. Debuting in March 1994, the Sigma Series was the company's first line to feature plastic frames. Glock sued Smith & Wesson over the design of the Sigma, alleging patent infringement and other charges, leading to a 1997 settlement whereby Smith & Wesson agreed to make a multimillion-dollar payment to Glock and to slightly modify the Sigma pistols.

In January 1998 Smith & Wesson began selling bicycles designed specifically for police work. During the late 1990s the company also opened up eight retail stores around the United States, selling apparel and a variety of other nongun products affixed with the company logo. This latest diversification away from guns came at a time when gun sales remained stagnant. Americans already owned approximately 230 million guns, which last for a long time, dampening demand. Other reasons given for the sales stagnation included a decreasing interest in hunting and falling crime rates, the latter of which might have been resulting in decreased demand for self-protection weapons. At the same time, the gun industry was under an increasing legal assault, with more and more municipalities suing gun manufacturers alleging negligence in the manufacturing, marketing, and distribution of guns. These suits were somewhat similar to the largely successful suits brought against the tobacco industry in the late 1990s. The potential for large liability judgments, along with increasing calls for stiffer federal gun control measures, gave added impetus to Smith & Wesson's and other gunmakers' moves to diversify. For its part, Smith & Wesson aimed to increase its sales of nongun products to 50 percent of overall sales, which would be a substantial increase over the 18 percent level of the late 1990s. Despite the seeming turnaround engendered by Tomkins, Smith & Wesson's future was shrouded by the potential for increased gun control measures and liability judgments.

Further Reading

"Bangor Punta Plans Bid to Buy Stock of Smith & Wesson," *Wall Street Journal,* October 7, 1965, p. 19.

Barrett, Paul M., "Attacks on Firearms Echo Earlier Assaults on Tobacco Industry," *Wall Street Journal,* March 12, 1999, pp. A1, A6.

——, "Gun Industry Seeks to Shut a Trade Group," *Wall Street Journal,* June 7, 1999, pp. A3, A6.

——, "Uneasy Gun Makers Add Gentler Product Lines," *Wall Street Journal,* March 25, 1999, pp. B1, B10.

Carr, Robert E., "Women's Market Is Not Gun-Shy: S&W," *Sporting Goods Business,* March 1989, p. 29.

Fried, Joseph P., "Gun Marketing Is Issue in Trial Against Makers," *New York Times,* January 6, 1999, pp. A1, B7.

Fuhrman, Peter, "A Conglomerate of His Own," *Forbes,* February 27, 1995, pp. 106+.

Furchgott, Roy, "Packing Heat—and a Big Wheel, Too," *Business Week,* March 9, 1998, p. 6.

Hull, Jennifer Bingham, "Lear Siegler Inc. Agrees to Buy Bangor Punta," *Wall Street Journal,* December 13, 1983, p. 2.

Humphreys, Noel D., "Dangerous Deal: How a Fast Sell-Off Haunts an LBO Firm," *Mergers & Acquisitions,* November/December 1994, pp. 39+.

Jinks, Roy G., *History of Smith & Wesson: No Thing of Importance Will Come Without Effort,* North Hollywood, Calif.: Beinfeld Publishing, 1977, 290 p.

"Lear Siegler Holdings Says It Will Sell Units, Posts Loss for Quarter," *Wall Street Journal,* February 19, 1987.

Maines, John, "Can Females Be Friends with Firearms?," *American Demographics,* June 1992, pp. 22+.

Maremont, Mark, "A Raider's New World," *Business Week,* June 15, 1987, pp. 49–50.

O'Connell, Vanessa, and Paul M. Barrett, "Firearms Firms, Amid Rising Litigation, Take Steps to Reduce Criminal Gun Use," *Wall Street Journal,* July 22, 1999, p. B10.

Petty, Charles E., "Inside Smith & Wesson," *American Rifleman,* August 1989, pp. 46–49, 85–86, 94.

Stevenson, Richard W., "Smith & Wesson Is Sold to Britons," *New York Times,* May 23, 1987, pp. 33, 35.

Taylor, Roger, "Too Big for Its Own Good?," *Financial Times,* January 17, 1998, p. FTM5.

Thurman, Russ, "S&W and Glock Settle Suit," *Shooting Industry,* June 1997, p. 62.

"Why the Firearms Business Has Tired Blood," *Business Week,* November 27, 1978, pp. 107, 110, 112.

Widem, Allen M., "Smith & Wesson Aims Its Mace at the Public," *Advertising Age,* May 31, 1984, pp. 3, 53.

—David E. Salamie

SPS Technologies, Inc.

101 Greenwood Avenue, Suite 470
Jenkintown, Pennsylvania 19046
U.S.A.
(215) 517-2000
Fax: (215) 517-2032
Web site: http://www.spstech.com

Public Company
Incorporated: 1903 as the Standard Pressed Steel
    Company
Employees: 5,983
Sales: $716.6 million (1998)
Stock Exchanges: New York
Ticker Symbol: ST
NAIC: 332722 Bolt, Nut, Screw, Rivet, & Washer
    Manufacturing

SPS Technologies, Inc. is a leading international company producing both stock and specialty fasteners and fastening systems for automotive, aerospace, and industrial sectors. It also makes precision tools such as thread roll dies, drills, and metal cutting tools. For airplanes, helicopters, and satellites, SPS designs and manufactures instrument and distribution panels, armament controls, turbine lockplates, and other items. The firm's Specialty Materials and Alloys Group provides superalloys and ceramic cores used in gas turbines, medical prostheses, and other products. SPS is also the leading U.S. manufacturer of magnetic materials used for a wide range of applications, including assemblies for cars, aircraft, power supplies, electrical components, and telecommunications. After numerous acquisitions in the 1990s, SPS operates facilities in Pennsylvania, Utah, California, Ohio, Michigan, Tennessee, Illinois, Nebraska, and New York. Its overseas plants are located in England, Ireland, China, Canada, India, Brazil, Australia, Mexico, and Singapore.

Early Years: 1900–45

An industrial accident in Philadelphia resulted in Howard T. Hallowell starting a new company. In 1900 an overhead shaft hangar made of brittle cast iron broke at the American Pulley Company where the young draftsman worked. Hallowell designed a better hangar made from pressed steel, which was patented in 1901. In 1903 Hallowell and Harald F. Gade, a Norwegian engineer, along with their friends and relatives, started the Standard Pressed Steel Company in a rented Philadelphia plant to make the improved hangars.

In 1906 the firm began making socket set screws and soon a new plant was added just for the many screws, bolts, and other threaded items needed for the company's products. In these early days skilled craftsmen did the best they could with calipers and scales to make precision parts, but it was the increased demand from World War I that caused the firm to greatly improve the accuracy of its manufactured items. During the war, the company operated three plants close to each other in Philadelphia.

In 1920 the Standard Pressed Steel Company moved its operations to one site in Jenkintown, a Philadelphia suburb that remained the firm's headquarters in the decades ahead. Workers at the plant needed many work benches, so the company started making not only work benches but also other shop equipment, such as shelves and cabinets, that were sold to other companies. Thus was born the new line of SPS products. Also in the 1920s, the firm's Unbrako Socket Screws were used by many manufacturers, and the company strengthened its distributor network.

The company in the 1930s slowed down due to the general business decline but learned some valuable lessons. For example, to meet the needs of radio manufacturers that wanted low inventory, Standard Pressed Steel learned how to operate on a strict schedule to make sure its customers received the parts they needed just in time to start production lines.

Other developments in the Great Depression included purchasing the Steel Factory Stool and Chair Business from Philadelphia's Metal Products Company. The company also redesigned its Unbrako Socket Head Cap Screws so their outer surfaces were rougher. That simple change made it easier for workers with greasy hands to handle the screws.

The firm in 1930 started selling its Unbrako Screws to customers in England. In 1937 the firm began making those screws in Coventry, England, which led to the founding of Unbrako Socket Screw Company Ltd. By the late 1930s the busy firm destroyed its older buildings in Jenkintown and built a modern plant, a good move that prepared them for the demands of World War II.

The call for military parts and supplies helped SPS grow during World War II. In fact, SPS established a new company, The Pennsylvania Manufacturing Company, to meet the government's demands for building complex machinery that was sent to the Picatinny Arsenal during the war years. Meanwhile, SPS facilities in Jenkintown ran 24 hours a day and employment peaked at over 3,000 workers. It made 30-caliber and 50-caliber armor-piercing bullet cores and also airframe bolts and other aircraft parts as the nation increased its production of warplanes. In 1941 the firm set up the nation's first commercial machinery to test the fatigue of its fasteners. That led to more dependable bolts and screws and other threaded products.

Post-World War II Expansion

Following the 1949 recession, growth of the nation's economy brought more orders to the firm, especially after the Korean War started in 1950. Sales grew from $14 million in 1949 to $34.7 million in 1951, the year Howard T. Hallowell became the chairman of the board, while his son H. Thomas Hallowell, Jr., took his place as president.

In the 1950s the firm acquired the Cooper Precision Products Company of Los Angeles; the Cleveland Cap Screw Company; the Columbia Steel Equipment Company in Fort Washington, Pennsylvania; the Nutt-Shell Company; The Detroit Diamond Company that made special kinds of nuts; and International Electronic Industries in Nashville, Tennessee.

Also in the 1950s the company bought 46 acres in Santa Ana, California, and built a modern 260,000-square-foot facility that was quite similar to the Jenkintown plant. To produce metric products for the growing European market, the company in 1959 organized Unbrako Schrauben in Koblenz, Germany; full production began the following year. By the early 1960s it had other overseas production or distribution facilities in Mexico City; Melbourne, Australia; Japan; and Shannon, Ireland. In 1962 company sales topped $100 million from selling its products in 52 countries. It employed a total of over 7,500 men and women in seven nations.

Much of this growth came as firms like Boeing, McDonnell Douglas, and Lockheed built more military and commercial planes in the postwar era. For example, each Boeing 747 frame required about 500,000 stock fasteners.

In 1978 the company changed its name to SPS Technologies, about the same time new opportunities arose with NASA and the space shuttle program. The firm created high-strength bolts, nuts, and shear pins used in the shuttle's boosters and fuel tanks. Because of the extremes in space flight, the company designed its shuttle fasteners from special nickel and cobalt alloys that could withstand temperatures from −423 degrees to 750 degrees Fahrenheit and had tensile strength of 260,000 pounds per square inch. Since each shuttle needed hundreds of SPS bolts and some shuttle bolts cost up to $600, the shuttle program from the 1970s to the 1990s provided SPS with new and lucrative markets.

In the early 1980s SPS sales and earnings dropped, in part from fewer aircraft orders and the general recession. In 1983 sales declined to $212 million from a record $341 million in 1981. Earnings dropped to just $313,000 in the recession year of 1982.

According to a 1984 *Forbes* article, "To break the cyclical nature of its business, SPS diversified its way out of trouble, with only mixed success." One useful new product was the SPS Joint Control System that featured hand operated wrenches with sensors and a microcomputer that gave users a warning when the tension limit neared, thus saving customers money by preventing broken nuts.

In 1979 SPS acquired an automated materials handling firm. For the next five years, however, it lost money on that diversification attempt. Yet, it was not hurt as much as expected by advanced adhesives that some used instead of fasteners. In fact, adhesives sometimes were used to coat fasteners and thus enhance their usefulness.

In any case, employment in the fastener industry by 1984 had declined to 52,000 workers from its peak in the mid-1960s of 68,000 workers. Foreign competition from inexpensive Asian products hurt this U.S. industry, but it was also part of a general decline in the number of Americans employed in manufacturing.

Business in the 1990s

In the late 20th century fewer and fewer people worked in manufacturing industries that relied on automation and high-tech solutions to improve their productivity. An SPS Hi-Life Tools plant in Shannon, Ireland, illustrated the process. With new software supporting a workforce reorganization, the plant in the early 1990s became much more efficient. Before the change, the plant often failed to get orders because typically it took 14 weeks from receiving an order to dispatch. By 1993 the firm was able to "engineer, manufacture and deliver a part to the U.S. in 10 days, and even faster for specials," according to an article in *Computer Weekly*. With that kind of performance, SPS Hi-Life Tools sent 70 percent of its orders to the United States. Such improvements in the early 1990s helped transform the United Kingdom's manufacturing sector that seemed doomed in the 1980s.

After a loss of $800,000 on net sales of $319.1 million in 1993, the firm's finances improved during the rest of the decade. Sales grew steadily, reaching $485.9 million in 1996, $588.6 million in 1997, and $716.6 million in 1998. Net earnings likewise increased, from $22.3 million in 1996 to $32.5 million in 1997 and $44.6 million in 1998.

Numerous acquisitions fueled SPS's growth in the late 1990s. For example, in 1996 SPS acquired all or most of the outstanding stock of three firms: Flexmag Industries of Marietta, Ohio, that manufactured flexible bonded magnets; Swift Levick Magnets of Derbyshire, England, another magnet manufacturer; and Mecair Aerospace Industries based in Pointe Claire, Quebec, Canada, a firm that produced fasteners and other parts for aircraft and power generating systems.

SPS acquisitions in 1997 included the following firms that strengthened the SPS fastener segment: Postkey, Ltd. in Nuneaton, England, a supplier of tooling services; Greer Stop Nut, Inc., a manufacturer of nylon locking nuts located in Nashville, Tennessee; and Mohawk Europa Limited, a Shannon, Ireland firm that made cutting tools for the metalworking, automotive, and aerospace industries. In addition, SPS gained three companies that aided its materials business: RJF International Corporation's Bonded Magnet Business in Cincinnati and Marietta, Ohio; Lake Erie Design Company in Wickliffe, Ohio, which made ceramic cores used in gas turbines and medical prosthesis products; and Magnetic Technologies Corporation, a firm based in Rochester, New York, and Rochester, England, that made subassemblies for photocopiers and printers.

In 1998 SPS acquired the following five firms. Greenville Metals, Inc., in Transfer, Pennsylvania, manufactured master alloy ingot and shot, foundry additive products, and a variety of induction alloys. It also converted and refined scrap for different customers. In Waterford, Michigan, Terry Machine Company made specialty fasteners for the auto industry. Howell Penncraft in Howell, Michigan, produced high-speed tool steel and carbide products used for metal forming. The fourth firm, Nevada Bolt & Manufacturing Company, based in Las Vegas, made nonstandard bolts and nuts from steel and special alloys. Chevron Aerospace Limited in Nottingham, England, was acquired for $54.9 million. It produced various aircraft parts, such as structural assemblies, avionic panels, and turbine lockplates.

In 1999 independent testing demonstrated the high quality of an SPS Technologies product. Minnesota-based Polaris Industries Inc. requested an engine fastening system that could endure high levels of vibration and stress. Unbrako Engineered Fasteners, part of SPS Technologies, provided its products that were sent to an independent lab for fatigue testing. The SPS fastener outlasted a competitor's product by at least 500 percent. "There was just a phenomenal amount of difference between the lives of the two studs," said Polaris's Steve Weinzierl in the May 6, 1999 *Machine Design*. The bottom line was that the SPS item saved Polaris about $8.2 million on warranty expenses. That was the kind of high quality product that SPS Technologies relied on to ensure its success as it approached its centennial in 2003.

Principal Subsidiaries

Terry Machine Company; Chevron Aerospace Group Ltd. (England); Postkey, Ltd.; Mohawk Europa Limited; Howell Penncraft, Inc.; Cannon-Muskegon Corporation; Lake Erie Design Co., Inc.; Greenville Metals, Inc.; Arnold Engineering; Flexmag Industries; Swift Levick Magnets; Magnetic Technologies Corporation; National-Arnold Magnetics; Greer Stop Nut, Inc.; JADE Magnetics Limited (China); Mecair Aerospace Industries, Inc. (Canada); Metalac S.A. Industria e Comercio (Brazil); Nevada Bolt & Mfg. Co.; Standco Canada Ltd.; Unbrako Mexicana, S.A. de C.V. (Mexico); Unbrako Products Pte., Ltd. (Singapore); Unbrako Pty. Limited (Australia); S.P.S. International Limited (Ireland); SPS Technologies Limited (England); SPS/Unbrako K.K. (Japan); Precision Fasteners Limited (India); Shanghai SPS Biao Wu Fasteners Company Limited.

Principal Operating Units

Aerospace Fasteners Group; Automotive Fasteners Group; Industrial Fasteners Group; Chevron Aerospace Group; Precision Tool Group; Specialty Materials and Alloys Group; Magnetic Materials Group.

Further Reading

"Fasteners Join in Harsh Environments," *Machine Design,* May 6, 1999, pp. 93–94.

Green-Armytage, Jonathan, "Reaping Success," *Computer Weekly,* December 9, 1993, p. 32.

Hallowell, H. Thomas Jr., *SPS—Its First Sixty Years: A Brief History of Standard Pressed Steel Company,* New York: Newcomen Society in North America, 1963.

"Staying Alive," *Forbes,* April 9, 1984, p. 145.

—David M. Walden

Stagecoach Holdings plc

Charlotte House
20 Charlotte St.
Perth
Tayside PH1 5LL
United Kingdom
(44) 1738-442-111
Fax: (44) 1738-643-648
Web site: http://www.stagecoachholdings.com

Public Company
Incorporated: 1980
Employees: 32,000
Sales: £1.55 billion (US$2.49 billion) (1999)
Stock Exchanges: London
Ticker Symbol: SGC.L
NAIC: 485113 Bus Services, Urban & Suburban; 485210
    Bus Line Operation, Intercity; 487110 Buses, Scenic
    & Sightseeing Operation; 48551 Charter Bus Industry;
    482111 Passenger Railways, Line-Haul

Stagecoach Holdings plc has ridden the deregulation of the United Kingdom's bus and rail routes to become one of the country's leading public transportation providers. Led by Chairman (and cofounder with sister Ann Gloag) Brian Souter and CEO Mike Kinski, Stagecoach has pursued an aggressive expansion-by-acquisition policy, helping to consolidate the British transportation market. But Perth, Scotland-based Stagecoach has also launched itself on the international scene, where it holds prominent positions in Sweden, Australia, New Zealand, Finland, Italy, Portugal, and—through the 1999 acquisition of Coach USA, a leading transport provider based in Texas—the United States. Stagecoach has also entered the Hong Kong and Chinese transportation markets through a position in Road King Infrastructure of Hong Kong and operations of Hong Kong's Citybus franchise. In total the company and its 30 subsidiaries run a fleet of more than 12,000 buses and other vehicles. Stagecoach has also diversified into other transport sectors, including the U.K. rail franchise South West Trains; the acquisition of train leasing company Porterhouse; and a 49 percent position in Virgin Rail, the railroad company set up by Virgin Records magnate Richard Branson. Stagecoach also owns an airport—Scotland's Prestwick Airport. Stagecoach's acquisition of Coach USA gives it a major foothold in the estimated US$40 billion public and school bus markets.

Rags-to-Riches in the 1980s

Ann Gloag and younger brother Brian Souter grew up in Perth, Scotland's council flats (the equivalent of the United States' housing projects). The Souters' father was a driver for the local community's bus lines. Buses played a large role in the Souters' lives. Brian Souter would later recall playing with buses on the floor of the family's home. As Ann Gloag—who had already made a 20-year career as a nurse before founding Stagecoach—said, as related by *Time International*: "Buses were what the family knew. My father, my husband and my brother had all worked on them."

The rise of the Thatcher era spelled a wave of deregulation and privatization of industries that had formerly been government controlled. Among the first industries to be privatized was the public transportation sector, and specifically the United Kingdom's bus routes. Gloag and Souter were quick to recognize the potential of this newly opening market. In 1980, using their father's £25,000 severance paycheck, Gloag and Souter bought two small buses. Just days after the bus line deregulation was enacted, the brother-sister team were ready to begin operations. They called their company Stagecoach, and offered redline service between Dundee and London.

Stagecoach was not the only new bus operator to ply the United Kingdom's roads. But the brother-sister team hit upon a service formula that kept customers coming back: offering sandwiches (prepared by their mother), blankets, and tea, while also charging lower fares than their competitors. Soon after the company started operations, it was able to add a second route, between Glasgow and London. By the mid-1980s, Stagecoach operated along a growing number of Scotland's roadways.

If privatization had opened the way for Stagecoach, the deregulation of the busing industry in the middle of the decade brought the company its greatest opportunities. The breakup of the formerly government-run National Bus Company into its regional subsidiaries created 70 independent bus companies,

431

which were generally sold to their management. While content to be government employees, many of the new bus line owners were uncomfortable in this position, or were otherwise eager to cash in on the growing interest in private bus companies.

Stagecoach was quick to recognize the potential opportunity of the National Bus Company breakup: Souter and Gloag embarked on their own acquisition tour, making nearly 40 acquisitions between 1985 and 1999. Among the first acquisitions were those of Cumberland Motor Services and United Counties Omnibus, both made in 1987 and both counted among the company's largest purchases. The fast-growing company continued to stretch its holdings throughout the United Kingdom. In 1989, Stagecoach took another leap forward when it bought East Midland Motor Services. At the same time, the company became one of the first bus lines to operate a global strategy: in 1989, the company entered Africa, buying a 51 percent stake in United Transport of Malawi. Further African expansion followed with the purchase of Kenya Bus Services in 1991.

The company's strategy proved simple and highly effective. New acquisitions were placed through rigorous cost-cutting measures, including drastic reductions in management levels as the subsidiary operations were placed under parent Stagecoach's control. The company was also careful to position its own people in key management positions, assuring a cohesive strategy. The company's acquisition drive itself helped improve profit margins, as the company began to realize economies of scale. Stagecoach also made shrewd use of the real estate acquired through its acquisitions. Many of the former National Bus Company regional subsidiaries had operated from depots and offices in downtown locations. Stagecoach quickly sold off these valuable properties, moving operations to less expensive locations. With the cash gained, the company was able to return to the acquisition trail.

At the same time as Souter and Gloag were buying up the United Kingdom's bus routes, they were careful not to neglect passengers. Bus lines added to the Stagecoach family were quick to see fare reductions—often drastically undercutting their rivals, and even operating for limited times for free. These practices, which included hiring away conductors from other local companies, were to bring negative repercussions to the company as it rapidly became one of the largest players on the U.K.'s public transport scene. Under frequent investigation by the country's Monopolies and Mergers Commission, Stagecoach was found to have acted, at least in one instance, in a manner that was "predatory, deplorable and against the public interest." Yet, in the deregulated, highly competitive public transportation market, none of Stagecoach's activities were illegal.

Moreover, for whatever aggressiveness Stagecoach brought to bear on its rivals, the company was careful to treat its

passengers well. When a bus company was added to the Stagecoach stable, its fleet was usually outfitted with an array of new buses, allowing Stagecoach to claim one of the youngest bus fleets in the country. Apart from lower fares, Stagecoach also added other services (although the hot tea and sandwiches seemed to have fallen by the wayside). As its network of bus companies grew, the company began innovating with hub-and-spoke style express coach services, which were much appreciated by the company's passengers. Stagecoach also began operating open-top buses on some of the company's more scenic commuter routes; these buses proved popular with passengers, both commuters and sightseers alike. In addition, where other companies avoided sparsely populated—and expensive—rural routes, Stagecoach began introducing new routes. But these were quick to provide linkups into the company's other lines, bringing yet more passengers on board.

"Public" Public Transport in the 1990s

Stagecoach continued its acquisition drive into the 1990s, buying up more and more bus lines staggering with the economic recession. Among its early 1990s purchases were two prominent Scottish bus operators, Fife Scottish and Bluebird Buses, acquired in 1991. The following year, Stagecoach formed its Stagecoach South subsidiary, combining a number of its southern England operations into a single, cost-effective entity. The company made a similar move in western England, after buying up Western Travel in 1993. This operation was renamed Stagecoach West. Meantime, Stagecoach moved to a new continent, with the purchase of New Zealand's Wellington City Transport. Through the rest of the decade, Stagecoach continued to build its position, both in New Zealand and in Australia, making it a prominent player in that region.

The year 1993 also marked a new milestone for Stagecoach. Having reached annual sales of £100 million, the company went public, taking a listing on the London stock exchange. The listing made millionaires out of Souter and Gloag, who soon numbered in the country's top 100 wealthiest people. Access to new capital enabled Stagecoach to continue its growth-by-acquisition campaign. The deregulation of the London bus industry opened the country's most important market: Stagecoach established its presence with two key purchases, those of the South East London & Kent Bus Company Ltd. (Selkent) and East London lines, in 1994. In that same year, Stagecoach strengthened its position in the northern regions of Scotland and England, making a number of important acquisitions.

The company was well on its way to becoming the leading coach bus operator in the United Kingdom. Additional lines in Cambridge in 1995, and in Exeter and Manchester in 1996, firmly established the company's leadership position. But Stagecoach was also boosting its foreign position, first with the start-up operation of Portugal's Rodoviaria Lisboa in 1995, and then with the £230 million purchase of the formerly state-run Swedish bus operator, Swebus, in 1996. That purchase, the company's largest to date, forecasted Stagecoach's future expansion on the European continent, as more and more countries studied privatization of their bus routes.

By 1996 Stagecoach had swelled to annual revenues of more than £1 billion per year, with operations in nine countries, and a 17 percent share of the United Kingdom's bus market. With acquisition opportunities becoming rare in the U.K. bus sector—and with large-scale purchases likely to bring the company fresh difficulties with the Monopolies and Mergers Commission—Souter and Gloag now looked to diversify their operations. The privatization of the country's train system opened up a new route to Stagecoach. In 1996 the company bought the rights to operate South West Trains (SWT), which enabled the company to offer bus-rail linkup services to its southern region and London operations. In the same year, Stagecoach paid £825 million for Porterbrook, a rolling stock leasing company which owned some 30 percent of the country's passenger railroad vehicles.

By 1997 Stagecoach's operations of SWT were being called into question, as the company faced a high rate of daily cancellations and continued passenger dissatisfaction. While the company pledged to turn operations around, Stagecoach nevertheless found itself threatened with the loss of the SWT franchise and the possibility of fines for substandard services reaching into the millions of pounds. Stagecoach was also chafing under shrinking expansion possibilities in the United Kingdom. As Souter told *Investor's Chronicle* in 1997: ''We don't intend to make any more U.K. acquisitions. The U.K. has moved very quickly. We got in early when there was still a bob in it. But we want value for shareholders and are getting out of a market that is overpriced.''

Stagecoach's U.K. railroad ambitions were also being thwarted, when it lost its bid to operate the West Coast Mainline and ScotRail railroads, which went to National Express and Virgin Rail. In response, in 1998 Stagecoach turned to new sectors for development. After losing a bid to chief U.K. competitor FirstGroup to run Hong Kong's main bus franchise, Stagecoach nonetheless found entry into the rapidly developing Chinese market. In 1998 the company made the surprise purchase of a 22 percent stake in Road King Infrastructure, a Hong Kong-based toll road builder, with operations chiefly on the Chinese mainland. The following year, Stagecoach achieved its ambition, when it took over operations of Hong Kong's Citybus operations, which, with 1,200 buses and more than 4,000 employees, gave Stagecoach the number two position in the city's bus market. Meanwhile, the company was preparing to abandon its money-losing operations on the African continent. When Ann Gloag stepped down from day-to-day operations, the company hired Mike Kinski as CEO.

Stagecoach took another turn in 1998, when it purchased, for £41 million, Scotland's Prestwick Airport. This acquisition looked to be short-lived, however; by the summer of 1999, the company was rumored to have been offered some £80 million for Prestwick. Stagecoach's flagging interest in airports quickly found an explanation: in June 1999, the company announced its intention to acquire Coach USA, the largest passenger coach service in the United States.

Based in Houston, Texas, Coach USA had taken an early lead in consolidating the charter and tour bus industry in the United States. Founded by venture capitalist Steven Harter in 1995, and run by CEO Lawrence King, Coach had rapidly built a fleet of some 3,500 sightseeing buses, as well as an equal number of taxis and other vehicles. After going public in 1996, the company went on a buying spree, making more than 50 acquisitions across the country, with particular emphasis on Texas, Florida, and the Midwestern and Eastern regions. By the time Coach entered into talks with Stagecoach, the U.S. company was posting revenues of more than US$800 million. The acquisition agreement with Stagecoach, which left King in place as the head of the U.S. operation, cost the U.K. operator more than US$1.8 billion, including the assumption of some $600 million in Coach's acquisition-induced debt.

Principal Subsidiaries

National Transport Tokens Ltd.; A1 Service Ltd.; AA Buses Ltd.; Circle Line Coach & Omnibus Ltd.; Magic Bus; Stagecoach Bluebird, Stagecoach Burnley & Pendle; Stagecoach Busways; Stagecoach Cambus; Stagecoach Cheltenham District; Stagecoach Cirencester; Stagecoach Coastline Buses; Stagecoach Cumberland; Lakeland Experience; Coachline; Stagecoach Darlington; Stagecoach Devon Ltd.; Stagecoach Devon Ltd.; Stagecoach East Kent; Stagecoach East London; Stagecoach East Midland; Stagecoach Fife Buses; Stagecoach Glasgow Ltd.; Stagecoach Gloucester Citybus; Stagecoach Graphics Ltd.; Stagecoach Grimsby Cleethorpes; Stagecoach Hampshire Bus; Stagecoach Hants & Surrey; Stagecoach Hartlepool; Stagecoach Kingston upon Hull; Stagecoach Lancaster; Stagecoach London Ltd.; Stagecoach Manchester; Stagecoach Midland Red; Stagecoach; Selkent (South East London & Kent Bus Company Ltd.); Stagecoach (South) Ltd.; Stagecoach South Coast Buses; Stagecoach Stroud Valleys; Stagecoach Swindon & District; Stagecoach Transit; Stagecoach United Counties; Stagecoach Viscount; Stagecoach West Ltd.; Stagecoach Western Buses; Sussex Bus Ltd.; Island Line Ltd.; Porterbrook Leasing Company Ltd.; South West Trains Ltd.; Stagecoach Supertram; Stagecoach Aviation Group Ltd.; Glasgow Prestwick International Airport Ltd.; Stagecoach Australia Pty Ltd.; Stagecoach New Zealand; Stagecoach Wellington; Fullers Group Ltd.; Stagecoach Portugal; Swebus AB; Stagecoach Finland Oy Ab; Citybus Ltd. (Stagecoach Asia Ltd. subsidiary); Coach USA, Inc.; Road King Infrastructure Ltd. (22%); Virgin Rail Group (49%); Kwoon Chung Buses (25%); Sita Buses (Sogin-Gruppo Fs) (35%).

Further Reading

Flanagan, Martin, ''A Cultural Revolution in Buses,'' *Scotsman*, March 20, 1999.

Gibson, Helen, ''Boom Times for Buses,'' *Time International*, October 21, 1996, p. 52.

Harrison, Michael, ''Bus Firm That Took the Fast Route to Trouble,'' *Independent*, March 15, 1997, p. 10.

Nag, Arindam, ''Britain's Stagecoach Buys Ticket to Ride US Market,'' *Reuter's Business Report*, June 14, 1999.

Stevenson, Tom, ''Stagecoach Offers an Exciting Ride,'' *Independent*, October 10, 1996, p. 26.

Yates, Andrew, ''Souter Eyes Wider Stage,'' *Investor's Chronicle*, February 14, 1997.

—M. L. Cohen

STARCRAFT🔾

Starcraft Corporation

2703 College Avenue
P.O. Box 1903
Goshen, Indiana 46527-1903
U.S.A.
(219) 533-1105
Fax: (219) 533-7180
Web site: http://www.starcraftcorp.com

Public Company
Incorporated: 1903 as Star Tank Company
Employees: 550
Sales: $53.09 million (1998)
Stock Exchanges: NASDAQ
Ticker Symbol: STCRC
NAIC: 811121 Automotive Body, Paint, & Interior
   Repair & Maintenance

Starcraft Corporation is an aftermarket "upfitter" (or customizer) of vans, sport utility vehicles, and pickup trucks, targeting various segments of the automotive conversion market through its various subsidiaries and product lines. Its flagship subsidiary, Starcraft Automotive Group Inc., specializes in higher-end conversion packages that offer a variety of safety and luxury features, while also offering similar, but more affordable, conversion packages marketed under the trade name Imperial. The Starcraft Automotive plant also manufactures shuttle buses, which are marketed under the Starcraft trade name. Through its Tecstar subsidiary—a joint venture with a Michigan-based engineering company—Starcraft upfits vehicles directly for General Motors. Starcraft sells its custom vehicles through a network of approximately 500 automobile dealers in the United States and 18 other countries. In the United States, each of Starcraft's dealers is an authorized dealer for General Motors, Ford, or Chrysler. The company's National Mobility vehicles, converted for use by the handicapped, are distributed through automotive dealerships and mobility centers, and its shuttle buses are marketed to nursing homes, churches, and hotels through a network of independent bus dealers.

Early History

The forerunner to Starcraft Corporation, the Star Tank Company, was founded in 1903 in Goshen, Indiana, a tiny town near the Michigan border. Its founder, Arthur Schrock, first began the business to manufacture metal feeding and watering tanks for livestock. In the 1920s, however, Schrock broadened his manufacturing operation to include aluminum boats, and the company was renamed Star Tank and Boat. In the mid-1960s, the company diversified yet again, entering the recreational vehicle industry with a line of fold-out campers that were sold under the trade name Starcraft. The Schrock family sold the business to a conglomerate in 1969.

In 1977, the company entered a new and rapidly growing market, when it began customizing vans through a newly formed subsidiary, Starcraft Van Conversions Corporation. To convert a vehicle, the company took incomplete van chassis, obtained directly from major automotive manufacturers, and added a variety of customer-chosen features, which might include anything from curtains, to specially built seating, to coordinating upholstery and interior decor.

The vehicle conversion industry had started in the early 1970s and had gathered steam steadily through the middle of the decade. When Starcraft joined the fray in 1977, young, recreational users comprised the main market for the vehicles. Starcraft bucked that trend, however. The company targeted an older market, offering an upscale luxury product for middle and upper income buyers.

The company's sales of conversions increased steadily through the 1980s, driven by the growing demand for custom luxury vans. Moreover, the Starcraft name became well-known for high quality in design and implementation. In 1987, Star Tank and Boat's management team acquired the company in an expensive leveraged buyout that left it heavily in debt. The following year, the new management sold off the company's boat-building business, Starcraft Power Boats, to Brunswick Corporation, one of the nation's largest boat and marine engine producers. The financial picture did not improve, however, and in November 1990, Starcraft filed for Chapter 11 bankruptcy protection. The company was auctioned by the bankruptcy court

Company Perspectives:

Our commitment, with utmost integrity, is to continually improve quality, innovation, safety, service and value. Our focus is to exceed the expectations of our customers, associates, community and shareholders. We will remain the worldwide manufacturer of choice in custom, automotive-related products.

and purchased by Kelly Rose, an entrepreneur from northern Indiana, and his partner Stephen Kash.

Coming up Roses: 1991–94

Rose was a resident of Elkhart, Indiana, a city just northwest of Goshen. In 1977, he had cofounded an electronics supply business in Elkhart that catered to the van conversion industry. By 1990, however, he had sold his interest in the electronics company and was ripe for a new challenge. As soon as Starcraft filed for bankruptcy, Rose knew he wanted it. ''I wanted to buy Starcraft badly,'' he said in a September 1994 interview with *Indiana Business Magazine.* ''There's no other company that enjoys as much of an elite reputation,'' he explained. Rose enlisted Kash, who worked in the conversion business in Elkhart, as a partner and made the purchase. Simultaneously, he sold Starcraft's recreational vehicle business to a third-party RV company.

Rose made major changes at Starcraft, hiring new upper-level management and restructuring its production process. Sinking more than $2.5 million into capital improvements, he converted the company's manufacturing floor into team-centered production lines. A firm believer in employee empowerment, Rose also implemented a more bottom-up style of management. Striving to give his employees the tools they needed to be successful, he instituted ''Starcraft U''—a series of classes on business skills, which were held in onsite classrooms.

Under Rose, Starcraft's fortunes quickly reversed. For the 49 weeks ending December 29, 1991, the company posted a $1.3 million profit on sales of $43.5 million. The numbers for 1992 were even more encouraging: a $2.9 million profit on $57.4 million in sales. In 1993, Rose took the company public in an offering that generated approximately $13 million.

1994: Diversification and Innovation

Since it had begun converting vehicles in the late 1970s, Starcraft had established a reputation for its high-end custom vans. The market for these luxury vans was particularly strong through the boom years of the 1980s, when discretionary income was high and consumer spending grew steadily. By the early 1990s, however, consumer confidence in the economy was growing shaky, and the spending spree was drawing to an end. As consumers grew more cautious in their buying habits and more sensitive to price, the market for more affordable vehicles outstripped the luxury market. To respond to the market shift, in 1994 Starcraft purchased Imperial Industries, Inc., a

maker of lower-priced conversions. With the inclusion of the Imperial line, Starcraft was positioned to offer a full line of vehicles that fit a wide range of budgets. In 1995, the company built a state-of-the-art, 110,000-square foot factory in Goshen for its newly purchased subsidiary.

Starcraft caught national media attention in the mid-1990s with the introduction of the Integrated Seat Belt, a new safety feature for its custom vans. The IBS was a new belt designed to prevent seat-back failure during rear-impact collisions. In addition to the conventional lap belt and shoulder harness, the IBS incorporated a second belt that ran through the seat back. In lab and crash tests, the system held the seat back in an upright position during impact, preventing crash-test dummies from slamming backward. IBS was named one of the 100 most technologically significant new products of 1994 by *R&D Magazine* and was featured in 1995 on a nationally televised segment of *Inside Edition.*

Starcraft had sales of $81.6 million in 1994, and profits of $3.8 million, an increase of 13 percent over 1993. Unfortunately, it would be the last increase in profits for several years to come, as a trend was beginning that would prove seriously detrimental to the van-conversion industry. Sport utility vehicles were taking over the automotive market.

Mid-1990s Market Downturn

The movement toward sports utility vehicles and pickup trucks had been gathering momentum for several years. Since Ford first introduced its Explorer in 1990, SUV sales had skyrocketed, growing 130 percent by 1996. By the middle of the 1990s, consumer obsession with the boxy SUVs had drawn buyers away from full-sized vans, which were the bread and butter of the conversion industry.

Not surprisingly, as sales of van conversions were faltering, sales of SUV and pickup conversions were climbing. Starcraft addressed this trend by opening a new manufacturing operation—Starcraft Southwest—to specialize in conversion pickups and sport utility vehicles. Based in McGregor, Texas, Starcraft Southwest marketed its products under the trade name Lonestar. In 1995, it began developing special conversion packages for the Ford Explorer and Ford Windstar minivan. The following year, the company was asked to develop luxury conversions for the Jeep Grand Cherokee and the Plymouth Voyager, marking the first time it had ever worked with Jeep and Plymouth. Starcraft also worked with GMC to develop a new conversion package for the Jimmy sport utility vehicle.

Already reeling from the effects of the SUV craze, the conversion industry was further hurt by a shortage of key chassis. GM's production of full-size vans decreased by 22 percent in 1995, significantly curtailing the number of van chassis available for conversion. The following year, all three major automakers cut back their production of light trucks, limiting the number of chassis available to fill orders for minivans, SUVs, and pickup trucks. This chassis shortage was worsened by an extended General Motors strike in the spring of 1996.

In October 1996, faced with declining sales and the need to trim costs, Starcraft announced its plan to consolidate its Imperial and Starcraft manufacturing operations. Imperial was moved into Starcraft's 650,000-square-foot facility in Goshen, thereby reducing overhead and allowing for integration of engineering and production.

Such cost-containment strategies could not counterbalance the effect of the market slump. Net earnings declined by 27 percent in 1995, then plummeted 96 percent in 1996. Still, Starcraft fared much better than its competitors, remaining profitable and debt-free while most conversion companies slid deep into red ink. By the end of 1996, there were approximately 100 van upfitters in the United States; just ten years earlier, there had been more than 2,000.

1997–98: New Markets

In early 1997, Starcraft began looking for new income sources to offset the shrinking sales of its van-conversion business. Its first such effort was the acquisition of National Mobility Corp., an Elkhart, Indiana-based manufacturer of modified vans for the disabled. Founded in 1992, National Mobility specialized in making minivans wheelchair accessible by lowering the rear floor and installing fold-out ramps. Most of the company's sales were made to taxi fleets, government agencies, and private transit companies that served healthcare organizations. Once the National Mobility acquisition was complete, Starcraft established a new retail division to handle the subsidiary's products and began selling them through a dealer network.

The market for van conversions continued to decline in 1997. In addition, the demand for SUV and pickup truck conversions had also fallen off. As a result, Starcraft decided to close its Texas operation, and the company's Goshen plant took over manufacture of the vehicles previously sold under the Lonestar name. Starcraft closed out 1997 with total sales of $99 million, a decrease of 12.5 percent over 1996. The company posted a net loss of $11.3 million for the year.

Starcraft expanded its product line again in 1998, when it began producing shuttle buses. The buses, which were marketed under the Starcraft name, ranged in length from 20 to 35 feet and contained seating for 12 to 25 passengers. Starcraft offered a range of features on the vehicles, including interior and exterior storage compartments, wheelchair lifts, and various seat types and arrangements. The primary markets served by the company's new enterprise were nursing homes, churches, and hotel resorts.

A second 1998 initiative took Starcraft into the taxicab market. In the early part of the year, the company partnered with GM's Chevrolet division to convert Venture minivans into taxis. To convert the vans, Starcraft replaced their sliding side doors with hinged ones, added temperature controls in the passenger area, and installed a plexiglass shield behind the driver's seat. The first converted Venture taxis were shipped to New York City in February for a trial period, and another batch went to Chicago for a similar trial. The endeavor proved successful, and in April of that year both the New York and Chicago Taxi Commissions approved the Starcraft Taxicab Minivan, opening the door for Starcraft to further penetrate the cab market in those two cities.

Starcraft formed a second partnership in 1998 with a Troy, Michigan-based engineering firm that specialized in building show cars and engineering prototypes for General Motors. The joint venture, named Tecstar, Inc., was formed to win a three-year contract with Chevrolet to upfit its 1999 S10 Xtreme pickup. Under the contract, Tecstar would add ground effects, wheels, and badging to the standard S10 trucks, and Chevrolet would then market them as factory vehicles. The arrangement marked a change in the way Starcraft had historically marketed and sold its products. "This is a significant event for Starcraft, enabling us to participate directly in the OEM market for the first time and benefit from the marketing expertise and national advertising strength of Chevrolet," Rose said in a February 17, 1998 press release. "The Xtreme program," he added, "has brought Starcraft into the Tier 1 automotive business." Tecstar leased a manufacturing facility in Shreveport, Louisiana, near the GM plant that produced the S10. In the fall of 1998, Tecstar won another General Motors contract, this one to outfit two new versions of the Chevrolet Tahoe. The company leased 100,000 square feet of production space in Grand Prairie, Texas, near the Arlington, Texas GM plant that produced the Tahoe.

Starcraft's total sales for 1998 were $53.1 million, down 26.5 percent from 1997. For the second year in a row, the company posted a loss, albeit a smaller one than in 1997. The loss was primarily attributable to the continuing slowdown in the vehicle conversion market; during 1998, the company's conversion sales declined 27 percent. Conversely, Starcraft's National Mobility sales grew 39 percent.

1999 and Beyond

After a losing first quarter, Starcraft turned to profitability in the second and third quarters of 1999. The two good quarters pulled the company's bottom line closer to the black. For the nine months ended June 27, 1999, Starcraft showed only a $208,000 loss, as opposed to a $3.2 million loss for the same time period in 1998. Starcraft's management cited diversification and cost-containment efforts as key reasons for the company's improved performance. As Starcraft drew near its centennial, no imminent turnaround was expected in the vehicle conversion industry. Thus, the company recognized the need to continue developing and nurturing new businesses and products. It was hoped that this diversification strategy would continue to offset flagging sales in vehicle conversions and ultimately lead Starcraft back to a position of financial strength.

Principal Subsidiaries

National Mobility Corporation; Starcraft Automotive Group, Inc.; Tecstar, Inc. (51%).

Further Reading

Couretas, John, "Van Plans Vary As Upfitters Cope with Slumping Market," *Automotive News*, September 14, 1998, p. 20.

Erickson, Arden, "Believing in the Team Make Starcraft Work," *Elkhart Truth*, March 16, 1993.

Kerfoot, Kevin, "Starcraft Corp. Expanding in Goshen," *Indiana Manufacturer*, June 1, 1995, p. 1.

Kurowski, Jeff, "Starcraft's Set to Survive," *South Bend Tribune*, February 27, 1997, p. B7.

"Van Converters Diversify Due to Shrinking Market," *RV Business*, May 1, 1998, p. 12.

—Shawna Brynildssen

Stepan Company

22 West Frontage Road
Northfield, Illinois 60093
U.S.A.
(847) 446-7500
Fax: (847) 446-2853
Web site: http://www.stepan.com

Public Company
Incorporated: 1928
Employees: 1,400
Sales: $610.45 million (1998)
Stock Exchanges: New York
Ticker Symbol: SCL
NAIC: 325613 Surface Active Agent Manufacturing;
    325199 All Other Basic Organic Chemical Manufac-
    turing; 325211 Plastics Material & Resin Manufacturing

Stepan Company has carved out a highly specific niche market for itself by producing and supplying specialty and intermediate chemicals that are sold to other companies to make a wide variety of end products. The company's three core business segments include: surfactants which are used in detergents for cleaning clothes, carpets, floors, and fine fabrics, as well as shampoos, toothpastes, and a host of other personal care products; polymers which are used in manufacturing plastics, refrigeration, and building materials; and specialty products, which are used in a range of flavoring, food, and pharmaceutical items. The company's production of surfactants generates the most sales, approximating $500 million by the end of 1998, with polymers and specialty products providing the balance. Management at the company has long held the strategic objective of continually expanding its manufacturing base, which has resulted in the establishment of production facilities in The Philippines, Canada, Columbia, Mexico, Germany, and France.

Early History

Stepan Corporation was founded by Alfred Stepan, Jr., descended from a long family line living in London, England.

When his father relocated from London to the United States during the late 1890s, he got a job at the age of 13 as an office boy at Roessler and Haslacher, a chemical firm in New York City that was later acquired by Du Pont. Alfred's father developed into one of the preeminent chemical research scientists in the early part of the 20th century, and Alfred himself was destined to follow in the footsteps of his father.

After graduating from the University of Notre Dame, Stepan attended the law school at Northwestern University in Evanston, Illinois. One year of law school was enough for the ambitious young man, however, and he decided to plunge into the chemical business. With $500 borrowed from his mother, Stepan went into business as a jobber of cleaning solvents and refrigeration gas in 1932. Naming the firm after his own family name, he initially worked out of a $2 dollar a month office in downtown Chicago. For three years Stepan worked as a salesman, selling his products to companies located throughout the metropolitan area. In 1935, however, young Stepan began working as a manufacturing chemist making ''fishy oils and fatty acids'' for tannery companies.

It was a short step into the specialty chemicals industry. By the time the United States entered World War II in December 1941, Stepan Corporation was firmly established as one of the fastest growing manufacturers of surface-acting agents, which were made for use in detergents and disinfectants, perfumes, soap, bubble bath, and pesticides. When the war ended in 1945, Stepan Corporation enhanced its reputation as a specialty chemicals manufacturer by concentrating more and more on specialty chemicals for consumer products. By the end of the decade, the firm was rapidly becoming a leading supplier of aromatic chemicals, fragrances, and flavors that were used in the perfume, cosmetics, and household industries.

Growth and Expansion: 1950s–60s

During the 1950s, the company under the direction of its founder focused on building a reliable customer base in the detergent industry. Alfred Stepan, Jr., was convinced that the industry was recession-proof, since hospitals and large corporate buildings would always purchase cleaning agents. Over the decade, Stepan succeeded beyond his expectations by carving out a niche that served nearly 2,000 customers, including almost all of the large *Fortune* 500 consumer products companies. From 1955 onward, sales began skyrocketing, and the owner plowed more and more capital into research and development. In 1958 Stepan Corporation made an initial public offering of stock on the New York Stock Exchange. Now even more capital was available for the company to expand its product line and its manufacturing facilities.

In 1964 Stepan made a decision to enter the rich citric acid market, but rather than use sugar beets as a base, he concentrated on making citric acid from blackstrap molasses at half the price. This significant effort cost the company a great deal in manpower, capital, and tons of blackstrap molasses. By the time Stepan realized that his venture was not going to be profitable, the company had lost more than $2.5 million in 1967, and per-share profits had declined precipitously from $1.67 in 1964 to a mere 12 cents by 1967. Incredibly, Stepan, Jr., turned the company around immediately. The owner refocused on the production of specialty chemicals for the consumer products industry; concluded an agreement with a British firm to become the exclusive manufacturer and marketer of a versatile new urethane foam; developed a chemical additive that doubled the life of an ordinary pair of blue jeans; and expanded the firm's research facility in Maywood, New Jersey, so that it could become one of the leaders in the field of aromatic chemicals. The turnaround was so dramatic that by the end of the decade sales amounted to over $25 million and earnings increased to an all-time high of $1.69 per share.

Alfred Stepan, Jr., was not only successful in business but in his personal life as well. Although one side of his family had been deeply involved in chemistry, the other side of his family was drawn to the arts, and a number of Stepan's ancestors had been closely associated with some of the more famous opera houses in Europe before immigrating to the United States. Stepan was therefore immersed in the operatic tradition and, while a prominent businessman in Chicago during the 1950s, was asked to serve as president of the Lyric Opera in Chicago.

The Lyric Opera, through mismanagement and unanticipated misfortune, had fallen on difficult financial times. When Stepan became president, he immediately reorganized the management structure of the opera, and initiated the fundraising drive that brought the opera house back to financial stability.

Transition and Change: 1970s–80s

In 1973 Alfred Stepan, Jr., stepped aside and relinquished the day-to-day operations of the company to his son F. Quinn Stepan. The new president of Stepan had been raised by his father within the chemical industry, spending most of his school vacations working in the firm's plants and laboratories, and even taking business trips with his father around the country. Having graduated with a degree in chemistry from the University of Notre Dame, Quinn went to work full time in 1961 selling surfactants for the company. After receiving an M.B.A. from the University of Chicago in 1963, the young man worked in a variety of positions and, in 1967, was promoted to vice-president in change of corporate development. In 1969, he was appointed vice-president of the Industrial Chemicals Division. As the head of corporate development, the younger Stepan was instrumental in shaping the company's growth during the late 1960s and early 1970s. Under his leadership sales increased 18 percent a year since 1968, and by the end of fiscal 1973 the firm's profits had increased an impressive 30 percent over the previous year. Even more impressive was the fact that the company's sales figures had skyrocketed from $25 million in 1968 to $65 million by 1973.

When Quinn assumed the post of president in 1973, he had already developed a strategic five-year growth plan that included the acquisition of numerous companies within the industry. In 1972, Stepan purchased the surfactants operation of Allied Chemical; the urethane foam systems division of Diamond Shamrock; the Presto Chemical Company, a manufacturer of gel coating, mold release agents, and pigment dispersions; and Westbrook-Marriner, a producer of lanolin. In 1973 the firm bought Armstrong Cork's urethane foam systems business. These strategic acquisitions not only increased Stepan's sales of urethane from $1.5 million to over $10 million, but the purchase of Allied Chemical's surfactants operation increased Stepan's market share significantly. Soon after he became president, Quinn Stepan also implemented a comprehensive reorganization plan for the accounting, purchasing, manufacturing, and engineering departments.

By the end of fiscal 1985, under the leadership of Quinn Stepan, the company reported record-high sales of $235 million. Approximately 70 percent of this figure was accounted for by the firm's strong presence in the surfactants market. Clearly, the growth through acquisitions strategy that Quinn Stepan implemented during the early 1970s was not only increasing revenues, but enlarging the firm's manufacturing capacity and consequently expanding its market share in the specialty chemicals industry. During the mid-1980s, the company made a series of acquisitions that strengthened its traditional core business while simultaneously diversifying into process chemicals production. In June 1985, Stepan purchased Westvaco's specialty surfactants division, estimated to be worth over $20 million. The purchase included a manufacturing facility located in Georgia, which made anionic surfactants that were used in industrial and agricultural products.

The purchase also enabled Stepan to enter a new market, since the facility produced defoamers for pulp and paper mills as well. One of the added benefits of the transaction was that it gave Stepan a strong presence in the Southeast, complementing the company's other regional manufacturing facilities in Illinois, California, and New Jersey. Along with the purchase of Westvaco's specialty surfactants division, the company also purchased the designs, technology, customer lists, and inventory of polyurethane coating resins and polyether polyols of another small firm for a wide variety of urethane applications. Although this agreement did not include the acquisition of any plant or equipment, it was widely regarded within the industry as a highly successful purchase, since it was estimated to add approximately $4–$5 million to Stepan's sales figures.

The 1990s and Beyond

The decade of the 1990s was a good one for the company. In 1992, sales amounted to just over $435 million, and by the end of fiscal 1997 sales increased to $581 million. The compounded annual growth rate in sales for these years was approximately six percent, not a dramatic figure, but nonetheless indicative of well-administrated, well-organized, thoughtful management. Yet Quinn Stepan, still in full control of the firm's direction, had set a sales goal of $1 billion by the end of the year 2000, and in order to reach this goal he decided not only to increase the capacity of all Stepan's current manufacturing facilities, but to make a concerted attempt to expand operations and enter the European market. In 1998 non-U.S. sales accounted for 16 percent of the company's total revenues, so the growth through acquisitions strategy that worked so well in the United States was implemented in western Europe. The grand strategy, according to Quinn Stepan, was to garner half of the company's sales from internal growth and the other half from acquisitions, both domestically and internationally. The core areas that Stepan intended to concentrate on included laundry and cleaning, personal care emulsion polymerization surfactants, agricultural surfactants, urethane systems, and food emulsifiers.

Stepan Company continued to search for niche markets that complemented its own product line, and those markets that strategically placed it in potential strong growth situations. Although the company's billion-in-sales goal was a lofty one, and perhaps unattainable by the end of 2000, the firm nonetheless was well-positioned for achieving such a landmark in the not too distant future.

Further Reading

Floreno, Anthony, ''Jobs & People,'' *Chemical Market Reporter,* March 29, 1999, p. 34.
''He Started on Sales Trips Early in Life,'' *Chemical Week,* November 14, 1973, p. 48.
Levy, Robert, ''The Turnaround Specialist,'' *Dun's Review,* October 1968, p. 92.
Morris, Gregory, ''Koppers and Stepan-Reichhold Join Aristech in Expansion Race,'' *Chemical Week,* October 16, 1996, p. 13.
''Stepan Company,'' *Soap & Cosmetics,* February 1999, p. 66.
''Stepan Company,'' *Soap & Cosmetics,* May 1999, p. 54.
''Stepan Eyes Specialty Surfactants and Overseas Markets for Growth,'' *Chemical Market Reporter,* March 9, 1998, p. 5.
Trewhitt, Jeffrey, ''Stepan Steps Out in Surfactants, Urethanes,'' *Chemical Week,* July 3, 1985.

—Thomas Derdak

Suburban Propane Partners, L.P.

240 Route 10 West
Whippany, New Jersey 07981
U.S.A.
(973) 887-5300
(888) 752-9024
Fax: (973) 515-5994
Web site: http://www.suburbanpropane.com

Public Company
Incorporated: 1928 as Suburban Propane Gas Co.
Employees: 3,217
Sales: $667.3 million (fiscal 1998)
Stock Exchanges: New York
Ticker Symbol: SPH
NAIC: 454312 Liquefied Petroleum Gas (Bottled Gas) Dealers

Suburban Propane Partners, L.P., a publicly traded limited partnership, is the third largest marketer of propane fuel in the United States serving more than 700,000 retail and wholesale customers in over 40 states. Found in the extraction of both crude oil and natural gas, propane is a gas liquefied under pressure and distributed in tanks and cylinders for reconversion to a gas under normal air pressure. Suburban Propane also sells propane-related appliances and services.

Independent Company: 1928–82

The company was founded in 1928 as Suburban Propane Gas Co. by Mark Anton because the New Jersey home where he lived was beyond the range of gas lines. Anton found that he could obtain propane from a nearby Phillips Petroleum Co. plant that considered the gas a useless byproduct of the oil-refining process. He marketed propane to other New Jersey homeowners who wanted gas for cooking and heating. Anton established an office in Belleville, a gas well in Boonton, and plants in Belvidere, Farmingdale, and Livingston. At the end of 1945 the company went public as Suburban Propane Gas Co.,

the first publicly owned company whose sole purpose was to distribute propane. It purchased Phillips' 13 liquefied petroleum gas properties in the United States. The following year it had revenues of $5.5 million and earnings of $600,000 on sales of 14 million gallons of propane.

But Anton had more ambitious plans. He wanted to organize vertically, producing the propane Suburban sold and manufacturing the tanks that held the liquid plus an array of gas-burning appliances. Accordingly, Suburban Propane Gas acquired a manufacturing plant in Tennessee that produced gas heaters, another in Pennsylvania that made gas ranges, and a third in Charlotte, North Carolina, that manufactured propane tanks. During the 1950s the company purchased a small gas field near Pearsall, Texas, and established a plant there to produce butane, propane, and natural gasoline. Revenues reached $47.1 million in 1960.

Anton retired in 1963 and was succeeded as chief executive officer of Suburban Propane Gas by his son, Mark J. Anton. The company had 129 sales, service, and distribution stations in 19 states, all but one of them east of the Mississippi. Its subsidiaries now included Frio-Tex Oil & Gas Corp., controlling about 67 natural gas wells in Texas and selling LP gases (including butane and a mixture of butane and propane), and Plateau, Inc., producing and distributing petroleum products in New Mexico. That year, however, the company sold its unprofitable manufacturer of gas ranges. Suburban Propane Gas was, in 1965, the world's largest independent retail distributor of liquid petroleum gases, marketing more than ten percent of this product in the United States. It was supplying bottled gas to more than 500,000 homes in 26 states and thousands of industrial plants and commercial and institutional enterprises.

By 1968 Suburban Propane Gas's non-propane activities were accounting for about one-quarter of the company's revenues and earnings. The purchase in 1967 of additional properties in Crockett County, Texas, brought the number of its Frio-Tex natural-gas wells to 175. A pipeline was delivering propane and butane to two plants—one wholly owned, the other partly owned, by Suburban—for conversion to liquids. Suburban's manufacturing subsidiaries were producing gas-fuel appliances as well as propane tanks. The company was also producing miniaturized "Dyna-Trail" central heating systems for the rec-

Company Perspectives:

It is the mission of Suburban Propane to: lead the industry in customer satisfaction by offering the highest level of total value; treat all employees fairly and create a work environment that offers challenge, opportunity and rewards; maintain the highest level of safety standards for the well-being of our employees, customers and communities. Accomplishing our Mission will result in profitable growth and provide a fair return to our shareholders.

reational vehicle industry. Plateau was operating an oil refinery in New Mexico and marketing some of the production to more than 70 gasoline stations under the Plateau brand.

Suburban's anchor gas distribution business was now operating in 28 states. Service to industries and farms was growing more rapidly than home use. For farmers, LP gases were fueling grain dryers, cotton gins, tobacco curers, weed burners, tractor engines, and poultry brooders. Industries were using propane to power forklift trucks, for heating at construction sites, for plaster drying, and to thaw coal and iron shipments. Suburban was meeting most of its gas needs from more than a dozen suppliers, including many of the major oil companies. Its revenues reached a record $96.6 million, and net income a record $5.5 million, in fiscal 1970 (the year ended September 30, 1970).

Suburban Propane Gas's revenues grew every year in the 1970s and its operating income every year except fiscal 1975. With the purchase in 1971 of Vangas, Inc., a California-based propane marketer active in seven western states, the company was providing propane to 600,000 customers in 32 states. It also had 268 gas wells in operation, held about 40 percent of the market for recreational vehicle heaters, and owned nine cable television (CATV) franchises serving 12,000 customers: a business it entered in 1970 and then divested at a profit by late 1974. The company, which disposed of the propane tank plant about the beginning of the decade, also again began producing gas cooking ranges, but only for recreational vehicles, in 1971. It also had begun making combination heater-air conditioners for space use in buildings. But propane distribution still accounted for 72 percent of revenues in fiscal 1972.

Suburban Propane Gas acquired a second oil refinery in Utah in 1975. The Iranian revolution of 1978 created a world oil shortage and a consequent run-up in oil prices that enabled the profits from Suburban's petroleum refining and marketing division to surge from the 171 retail service stations it now owned or controlled in five western states. Conversely, high gasoline prices depressed the recreational vehicle industry, and in 1979 Suburban wrote off its inventory of RV propane heaters. The manufacturing division turned its attention to a line of solid-fuel furnaces and heaters for the home and a fireplace insert with thermostatic controls. The exploration and production division purchased a Colorado oil and gas drilling and well service firm in 1980 and entered the onshore deep drilling business in 1981 with the purchase of a Texas company. In fiscal 1981 sales reached a record $850.9 million.

Downsized Division: 1982–95

A Canadian businessman named Samuel Belzberg and two of his brothers attempted to take over Suburban Propane Gas in late 1982, raising their holdings in the company to about 12 percent of the stock. Anton and six other top corporate executives, in collaboration with the Bass family of Fort Worth, Texas, then offered $45 a share, or $238.5 million, for the company, which would be 80 percent owned by the Basses and 20 percent by the executives. In January 1983, however, Suburban was purchased by National Distillers and Chemical Corporation for about $275 million.

Now simply called Suburban Propane, the division stopped making heaters and also left the gasoline service station business. The largest U.S. retail marketer of LP gases, Suburban Propane was distributing the product in 44 states in 1986 through company-owned service centers and offices. Sales of 744 million gallons that year were partly through about 500 bulk storage stations. The company also owned a refrigerated storage facility in California and underground storage facilities in Mississippi and Texas. Through its exploration subsidiary, Suburban had partial ownership of about 600 oil and natural gas wells. It was also still engaged in contract drilling in Texas and well servicing in Colorado, owned and operated a gas processing plant in Texas, and operated and held partial ownership in other gas processing plants in Texas and Oklahoma.

National Distillers and Chemical Corporation changed its name to Quantum Chemical Corporation in 1987. Between 1984 and 1989 the Suburban Propane unit purchased smaller companies distributing a total of 400 million gallons of propane a year. Propane marketing sales rose from $571.6 million in fiscal 1985 to $677.7 million in fiscal 1988, when $113 million was registered in operating profit. The following years were less lucrative, however. In 1988 Suburban sold all its interests in oil and gas wells, gas processing plants, and contract drilling. That year it lost its position as the nation's top-ranking retail LP gas distributor and no longer was selling any LP gas but propane. In fiscal 1992 Suburban Propane had $641.6 million in revenues and operating profit of $51.2 million.

Public Partnership: 1996–99

Hanson PLC, a British-based conglomerate, acquired Quantum Chemical in 1993. Hanson concentrated on mending Quantum's finances and its troubled petrochemical sector, the chief source of its business. By the end of 1995 Suburban had fallen to third place among retail propane distributors. It had sales of $633.6 million in fiscal 1995 (compared to $677.8 million in fiscal 1994) and net income of $30.2 million.

In December 1995 Hanson announced it would sell a 62 percent interest in Suburban Propane through an initial public offering, retaining the other 38 percent. The Hanson subsidiary was first restructured as Suburban Propane Partners, L.P., a master limited partnership. A total of 18.75 million units were then sold at the end of February 1996 at $20.50 per unit, with proceeds to the partnership of $359.6 million. This sum was earmarked for intercompany payables of Quantum Chemical. The partnership's long-term debt at the end of 1995 (adjusted to reflect the initial public offering) was $425 million.

A January 1996 *Wall Street Journal* column by Linda Sandler questioned whether the new partnership would be a wise investment. One securities analyst called the propane market a ''cutthroat business'' in which big companies such as Suburban were unable to raise prices for fear of being undercut by countless small ''mop-and-pop'' firms. With the total propane market stagnant, any gain in market share apparently would have to come from acquisitions. Suburban Propane had a $300 million bank line for this purpose, according to Mark Alexander, a Hanson executive who was appointed chief executive of the partnership. It was serving more than 700,000 customers in 41 states at this time but held less than seven percent of the U.S. market for propane.

During fiscal 1996 Suburban Propane Partners acquired 17 propane distributors at a total cost of $31.7 million, with the emphasis on operations active on the East and West Coasts and around the Great Lakes. ''We're in every auction process,'' Alexander told Ellen Simon of the *Newark Star-Ledger* in December 1996. ''Whenever there is one, we will bid. We'll only bid rational prices. So we don't win many. If the competition wants to overpay, so be it. We'll be there to pick up the pieces.'' Alexander went on to say, ''This company should double in size in five years. In ten years, it should be a full-service organization.'' Suburban purchased ten more propane distributors in fiscal 1997 and 1998 at a total cost of $5.7 million.

Hanson sold its stake in Suburban Propane Partners in October 1996 to Suburban Propane GP, Inc., a wholly owned subsidiary of Millennium Petrochemicals Inc., which had formerly been Quantum Chemical Corporation. Millennium sold its share in the partnership—now 26.4 percent—for $75 million in May 1999 to Suburban Energy Services Group LLC, a new entity owned by senior management of the partnership. This firm replaced Millennium as general partner of Suburban Propane Partners.

Suburban Propane Partners sold 71 percent of its propane to retail customers and 29 percent to wholesale customers or for hedging activities in fiscal 1998. Retail customers consisted of residential customers (27 percent), commercial customers (18 percent), industrial customers (ten percent), agricultural customers (five percent), and other retail users (11 percent).

Suburban generally was making retail deliveries of propane to customers' storage tanks by means of bobtail and rack trucks. The partnership also was delivering propane to retail customers in portable cylinders. Propane also was being delivered to certain other bulk end users, such as industrial, agricultural, and utility customers, in larger trucks called transports. Among Suburban's suppliers of propane were its own storage facilities in Elk Grove, California, and Hattiesburg, Mississippi. In its wholesale operations, Suburban Propane Partners principally was selling propane to large bulk end-users, such as industrial, agricultural, and utility customers.

Principal Subsidiaries

Suburban Propane L.P., and its subsidiary, Suburban Sales and Service, Inc.

Further Reading

Anton, Mark J., *Suburban Propane Gas Corporation,* New York: The Newcomen Society in North America, 1982.

Cole, Robert J., ''Group Bids for Suburban Propane,'' *New York Times,* December 9, 1982, p. D5.

''Cool Weather to Heat Up Suburban Propane Results,'' *Barron's,* October 31, 1974, pp. 32–33.

''New Uses for LP Gas Fuel Suburban Propane,'' *Barron's,* August 31, 1964, p. 21.

Sandler, Linda, ''Hanson Will Benefit from Suburban Propane Partnership Sale, but Will Investors Do As Well?'' *Wall Street Journal,* January 15, 1996, p. C2.

Scott, Robert D., Jr., ''Propane Gas Distributors,'' *Wall Street Transcript,* January 29, 1973, pp. 31,667–31,668.

Simon, Ellen, ''Propane Chief Faces Pressure,'' *Newark Star-Ledger,* December 3, 1996, pp. 43–44.

''Suburban Propane Gas Corporation,'' *Wall Street Transcript,* January 19, 1980, pp. 60,320–60,321.

''Suburban Propane—Income Plus Growth,'' *Financial World,* September 1, 1965, pp. 13–14.

Zelkind, Michael A., ''Suburban Propane Gas,'' *Wall Street Transcript,* April 14, 1969, pp. 16,354–16,355.

—Robert Halasz

SUCCESSORIES

Successories, Inc.

2520 Diehl Road
Aurora, Illinois 60504
U.S.A.
(630) 820-7200
(800) 621-1423
Fax: (630)953-2110
Web site: http://www.successories.com

Public Company
Incorporated: 1990
Employees: 464
Sales: $52.8 million (1998)
Stock Exchanges: NASDAQ
Ticker Symbol: SCES
NAIC: 454110 Mail-Order Houses; 453998 All Other
  Miscellaneous Store Retailers (Except Tobacco
  Stores); 51113 Book Publishers

Successories, Inc. is an enormously successful direct mail-order catalog firm with numerous retail stores that specializes in designing, assembling, and marketing a diverse line of self-improvement and motivational products. Successories makes many of its own proprietary designs, including such items as desktop art, audio tapes, wall decor, books, mugs, greeting cards, and personalized awards and gifts, but also markets and sells motivational products manufactured by other firms. A good example of the company's product is a framed picture with a boat in the middle of the sea and the caption reading: "RISK: You cannot discover new oceans unless you have the courage to lose sight of the shore." One of the cornerstone's of the company's success lies in its ability to customize products to fit the needs of individual customers. Since 1990, the company has sold its product line to a wide range of customers, including many *Fortune* 500 firms, entrepreneurs, schools, athletic organizations, mid-sized and small companies, and a host of individuals. Successories has 36 retail locations, including 31 stores, and five kiosks in malls, located in 13 states across the country.

Early History

The CEO, chairman, and founder of Successories is Arnold M. "Mac" Anderson. Anderson graduated with a B.A. in communications from Murray State University, and from that time onward the young entrepreneur was on a fast track to success. Rather than working for others, Anderson was talented and confident enough to think he could start his own firm, and he did exactly that a few years after graduating from Murray State. The first of his entrepreneurial endeavors involved establishing a refrigerated food products business, which he dubbed Orval Kent Food Company, that marketed its product line to supermarkets and groceries across the United States. Anderson was partial owner of the company and its vice-president of sales. The young man expanded the company's customer base and doubled its sales figure within two years. Yet Anderson soon grew restless in his position of vice-president and began to look for new entrepreneurial opportunities where he could manage the entire operation. Without wasting any time, in 1980 Anderson established McCord Travel Agency, a start-up firm specializing in commercial travel and incentive programs for corporations. McCord Travel grew at an impressive pace, and by 1985 the company was large and successful enough for Anderson to sell it to Helen Curtis. With money in his pocket and the entrepreneurial spirit burning within him, Anderson began to search for another business opportunity.

It was not long before he found one. Anderson had been ruminating for some years as to how his employees could be best motivated to achieve the goals set for the companies he managed. What kind of message or inspiration could be devised to heighten the sense of responsibility and commitment in the workplace? Anderson concluded that his employees were much like athletes in training for an upcoming competition—employees needed encouragement and motivation, as well as means to more positive thinking, more often than not provided by coaches to athletes on the playing field. Finally, Anderson concluded that a business which sold inspirational sayings and motivational plaques, for example, could establish a niche in a marketplace looking for unique ways to celebrate human achievement. Not long after he had sold his travel agency,

Company Perspectives:

We believe motivation originates with attitude, grows in response to goals, and endures when reinforced through exposure to insightful ideas in your environment. Successories is dedicated to helping individuals and organizations realize their full potential. Our goal is simple . . . to help you reach yours!

Anderson established Successories, Inc., a trade name under which he designed and marketed personal and business products that celebrated the human spirit and promoted positive thinking.

By 1988 Anderson had established a small but thriving mail-order catalogue firm with a customer base of over 400,000. Anderson hired a small group of in-house designers that created proprietary art works and designs which could be used in an extremely wide variety of product lines, including wall posters, honorary plaques, coffee mugs, T-shirts, and desktop decorations. Successories wall decor product line included highly professional photographs of dramatic scenes on quality paper stock with inspirational and motivational captions such as: "Attitude is a little thing that makes a BIG difference," and "Success is a journey, not a destination." The designers provided groupings of wall decor products, which included a uniform appearance with similar though not identical visual themes, similar color schemes, and unique lettering and border design. Each print was made the same size, and then framed in an aluminum or cherry wood finish. All of this added up to a distinctive trade product.

Before long, Successories had started to manufacture other products as well, such as motivational books and audio tapes featuring inspirational speakers Zig Ziglar, Les Brown, Anthony Robbins, Wayne Dyer, and others, and hats, motivational rocks and crystals, key rings, pocket medallions, and lapel pins. Medallions were made of round brass disks with inscriptions such as "No goals, no Glory," and "Do it Right." Motivational rocks and crystals were either etched or engraved with similar pithy sayings. As Successories grew, and catalogue sales continued to increase, Anderson made sure that the company's most successful product lines included one or two new items in each quarterly publication of the catalogue.

Growth and Expansion: 1990s

Successories grew at a steady but unspectacular pace and, in order to expand its operations and customer base, Anderson decided to open retail locations. Beginning in 1991, the company established retail stores and small kiosks in malls. Opening a kiosk in a large mall was a rather innovative strategy at the time, since most companies were inclined to conduct their retail operations through permanent store locations. Kiosks were small self-contained retail displays, measuring 10 by 12 feet, and situated in the center aisle of a large, enclosed mall. The four sides of the kiosk were used for displaying products and selling them. The cost/benefit of opening a kiosk, as opposed to

a permanent retail store, was very positive, due to the extremely low expense of establishing, furnishing, and stocking such a location. Within a short period of time, the company had numerous retail stores as well as kiosks located in huge shopping malls across the United States.

Although the company stores and kiosks were selling products at a brisk rate during the early 1990s, Anderson wanted to expand his operations and increase sales revenues. In order to achieve his goals, the founder of Successories decided to implement a highly sophisticated and comprehensive franchising program. Management, led of course by Anderson, devised a strategy that included company-owned stores and franchise stores located in different demographic areas: company-owned stores were to be situated within large metropolitan areas with at least one million residents, while franchise stores were to be situated in areas where the population was less than one million people. By operating numerous company stores in close proximity to one another, the intention was to increase efficiency and profitability. Through this "cluster" approach, management at Successories thought that the organizational and distribution efficiency gained by providing its product line to a number of retail stores at the same time within a highly localized area would enhance marketing efforts and thereby increase sales. In contrast, in an area where the population demographics suggested establishing a single franchise store, a franchise owner/operator it was assumed would have the ability to organize and manage a more efficient operation than the company itself, due to the lower overhead costs and capital required for opening and maintaining a single retail store.

With its expansion strategy in place, and Anderson still providing Successories with its vision and direction, the company began to grow rapidly. Company retail stores, kiosks, and franchise retail stores were opened in numerous states throughout the country. In 1992 Successories reported revenues of $5.7 million, mostly due to catalogue sales. By 1993, however, revenues had jumped to over $13 million, and by 1994 revenues had doubled to nearly $30 million. More and more of the company's sales came from its retail stores and franchise network. By the end of fiscal 1995, Successories counted 51 company-owned locations and 41 franchise locations in 17 states. The company also opened retail stores in Australia, Bermuda, Canada, The Netherlands, Ireland, New Zealand, Saudi Arabia, Malaysia, South Africa, and the United Kingdom. Revenues had skyrocketed to just over $44 million, with approximately half of the total amount derived from sales within company-owned and franchise retail stores and kiosks.

The years 1996 and 1997 continued the success of the early part of the decade for the company. The company reported approximately 200 retail locations throughout the United States by the end of fiscal 1997. Half of these locations were company-owned retail stores and franchise stores. The other half came as somewhat of a windfall to Successories when management reached an agreement with Waldenbooks. Waldenbooks acquired and began to immediately operate 100 brand-new Successories kiosks in malls during the autumn of 1997. In addition, management had reached important distribution and advertising agreements with major firms, including contracts to distribute its products through direct-mail catalogs published by British Links Golf Classics, and a host of office supply catalogs such as Office Depot, BT Office Products, and Viking Office Products. At approximately the same time, Successories reached an agreement with major mass merchandisers such as Office Depot and Wal-Mart to sell its Winners Collection proprietary products. In a rather unusual agreement, Successories reached an accord with Frontier Corporation of Rochester, New York, to provide motivational and inspirational messages on prepaid phone cards manufactured by Frontier.

The Shift to Franchising

Outwardly, it seemed as if Successories was destined to continue growing and reaping ever larger profits. Sales for the company had increased to over $56 million in 1996. Yet quite surprisingly and unexpectedly, even to management, sales remained at precisely the same figure for 1997. In order to correct what looked like the beginning of a downward trend for the company, Anderson once again asserted his personality and implemented a comprehensive reorganization of the firm. The president and CEO was replaced with a more results-oriented person who was a specialist in the field of marketing. Most importantly, the decision was made to convert all of Successories' company-owned retail stores to franchise stores. The plan was to reduce the operating costs associated with providing the support necessary for company-owned stores.

Although revenues dropped to $52.8 million for fiscal 1998, the changes Anderson and his new management team had implemented were enabling Successories to regain some of the ground it had lost. In early 1999, the company reported that domestic sales from its Successories catalog had increased almost 25 percent. An even more encouraging sign was the increase in 1998–99 holiday sales volume over the previous year, amounting to an impressive 300 percent. Looking for a quick infusion of capital investment to help the company maintain its position within the highly competitive marketplace for motivational products, management reached an agreement with the investment firm of Corbin & Company for the latter to purchase approximately 18.4 percent of the company's outstanding shares. Thus, in a relatively short span of time, management at Successories made the changes necessary for the company to improve its financial health.

As long as Successories, Inc. remained under the leadership and direction of founder Mac Anderson, it was clear that he would take the necessary steps to allow for the company's continued growth and expansion. But the market for motivational and inspirational products was highly saturated, and the success of the company's reorientation and restructuring was yet to be seen.

Further Reading

"Aiming for Impact," *Supermarket Business,* July 1998, p. 73.

Elson, Joel, "Ya Gotta Have Heart," *Supermarket News,* March 2, 1998, p. 51.

"Making a Statement," *Supermarket Business,* October 1997, p. 61.

Murphy, Lee, "Successories Sees Partners As Key," *Crain's Chicago Business,* August 4, 1997, p. 20.

"My Life Is Miserable. You've Made a BIG Difference," *Forbes,* March 24, 1997, p. 40.

—Thomas Derdak

Sun Country Airlines

Sun Country Airlines

2520 Pilot Knob Road
Suite 250
Mendota Heights, Minnesota 55120
U.S.A.
(651) 681-3900
(800) FLY-N-SUN; (800) 359-6786
Fax: (651) 681-3970
Web site: http://www.suncountry.com

Private Company
Incorporated: 1982
Employees: 1,200
Sales: $250 million (1998 est.)
NAIC: 481111 Scheduled Passenger Air Transportation

Sun Country Airlines, operated solely as a vacation charter service for most of its history, became a scheduled carrier on June 1, 1999, offering nonstop flights to and from Minneapolis/ St. Paul, Milwaukee, and Detroit to major U.S. cities and international destinations. The company, owned by Milwaukee-based leisure travel mogul William E. La Macchia, Sr., competes head-to-head with industry giant Northwest Airlines, while it continues to operate some charter flights in conjunction with wholesale tour operators.

Pilots Take Off: Early 1980s

Sun Country Airlines, the brainchild of former Braniff International pilots, took flight in January 1983. Following the shutdown of Braniff in 1982, Ken Sundmark sought out Bob Daniels, his former neighbor and cofounder of Mainline Travel Inc. Sundmark proposed they establish a charter service, combining the assets of Mainline and the airline expertise of the now unemployed Braniff crew. "They needed outside financing, and they also needed a reliable market, something more steady than the topsy-turvy world of post-deregulation scheduled services," wrote Peter Reed in a February 1987 *Corporate Report Minnesota* article.

Mainline, which owned MLT Vacations Inc., had already toyed with the idea of owning its own plane to serve its vacation travel market and willingly signed on for the ride. Mainline's principle owners, Daniels and MLT CEO Warren Phillips, retained 51 percent of ownership. Eleven Braniff pilots, two cabin attendants, an attorney, and a financial consultant shared the remaining 49 percent.

Sun Country Airlines was incorporated in July 1982 but implementation of service was delayed by higher than expected start-up costs. Airport facilities, fuel suppliers, maintenance contractors, and airplane lessors all required large deposits on their goods and services. MLT committed additional funds, in the form of a letter of credit for the deposit on the airplane and a cash loan of $250,000, to get Sun Country's inaugural flight from Sioux Falls to Las Vegas, in the air. At first, Sun Country flew just one aircraft, a Boeing 727-200.

The company quickly became profitable, within six weeks according to the Reed article, and was able to pay back MLT's loan within eight months. Net income was $180,413 for the first fiscal year and $1.47 million for fiscal 1984. Headquarters were less than glamorous. Sun Country operated out of an old freight building. That space and the rented hanger had once been Braniff's—the defunct airline frequently housed planes overnight at Twin Cities International, then flew them out as charters.

During the early days and from the top on down, Sun Country employees had multiple roles to perform. Company executives flew aircraft. Flight attendants acted as receptionists and baggage handlers in a pinch. Pilots updated manuals and even pitched in to clean the company's aircraft.

In addition to sharing the workload, Sun Country's employees shared the knowledge that they were responsible for the financial health of the business—the fate of Braniff and other airlines was still fresh in their minds. Sundmark, Sun Country vice-president of finance, gained his financial know-how while serving as a representative of the Air Line Pilots Association. Peter Reed wrote, "Sundmark's formula for Sun country's success is simple: 'Cost control, cost control, cost control.'"

To survive, Sun County and every other airline had to keep its seat per mile cost down. The seat-mile measurement was tied to a number of factors. Key among them was the number of seats being filled. During the first three-and-a-half years of operation Sun Country's average load exceeded 90 percent, thanks to MLT. The travel company purchased seats from Sun Country, packaged the air travel with hotel and a variety of other services, and then sold the packages via travel agencies. Consequently, Sun Country had no marketing costs, and by leasing its aircraft, terminal, and office space, the tiny airline kept debt service costs off its books.

Sun Country, unlike other U.S. charter companies, depended primarily on vacation travel business; other charters gained revenue by seizing opportunities to fly military, cargo, and summer vacation charters to Europe. Although Sun Country had remained profitable from the start, their business was highly seasonal, concentrated around the Midwest's peak tourist season, January through mid-April.

Attempting to balance the seasonal flux of revenue, Sun Country added new destinations and flights originating from cities with different travel patterns. The Dallas/Fort Worth area, for example, generated a travel market to Las Vegas even during the summer months. More importantly in terms of revenue growth, Sun Country increased capacity during winter months by leasing additional planes from a British carrier whose peak times occurred during the summer. Sun Country began with one additional 727 in December 1983, upped it to two planes during the next two years, and moved to three during the 1986–87 winter travel season. In January 1986, to accommodate growth, Sun Country moved into a new facility. In June, the company leased its first wide-bodied plane, a DC-10, which offered larger capacity and longer flight time than the 727s.

Turbulent Air, New Ownership: Mid-1980s to Mid-1990s

As Sun Country operating officers pushed to keep the airline growing, the majority owners at Mainline were increasingly concerned with the small charter service's ability to compete in an increasingly tough market. Major airlines had begun discounting fares, placing them in line with what Mainline paid for Sun Country seats. In that light, Phillips and Daniels struck a deal with NWA Inc., parent company of Northwest Airlines, to sell both Mainline Travel and Sun Country Airlines.

Members of the Braniff ownership faction felt the deal overvalued Mainline and undervalued Sun Country—$22 million and $5.5 million, respectively—and sued to block the purchase. A compromise deal was reached but rejected by two of the shareholders. The sale of Mainline was completed in 1985, but NWA dropped the bid for Sun Country. Sun Country eventually tried to force the dissenting shareholders to sell their shares to the company; the matter was tied up by litigation for several years. In late 1988, Midwest banker B. John Barry purchased majority ownership of Sun Country from the original investors.

Publicity shy Barry, who owned 12 Minnesota and Wisconsin banks with combined assets of $530 million, maintained a low profile over the next several years. The Gulf War changed all that. Thanks largely to military charters, Sun Country's revenue increased by 38 percent to $109 million, and net income more than doubled to $9.7 million for the 12 months ending June 30, 1991.

Sun Country's bottom line had also been aided by a decline in the number of charter companies. About 15 carriers had been in operation during the mid-1980s, but only a handful remained viable, including American Trans Air (Indianapolis), Tower Air Inc. (New York), and Key Airlines Inc. (Georgia). Sun Country was the third largest charter airline in the United States.

Historically, Sun Country had expanded conservatively, a practice which had helped the airline weather the industry downturn. The company had no long-term debt. Barry, encouraged by the year's growth, pushed forward with an aggressive expansion plan. He intended to add two DC-10s and four or five 727s to the aircraft already in service.

While the military charters had produced a good-sized blip on Sun Country's revenue screen, MLT continued to be a very important customer. The small carrier was also closely tied to MLT's sister company Northwest Airlines. Sun Country leased both airport facilities and a number of its planes from Northwest. (The Sun Country hanger had been purchased by NWA at the time of the MLT deal.) However, the relationship between the two companies was changing. In late 1990, NWA had notified Sun Country that it would not be renewing its lease on the facility or on some of its planes. (Significantly, Northwest Airline had begun operating its own quasi-charter service which it sold via Mainline; discounted tour seats and vacation packages were booked on regularly scheduled Northwest flights.)

The changes in climate with NWA factored into Sun Country's declining numbers in 1992. When NWA chose not to extend its DC-10 lease agreement with Sun Country, the smaller operation was forced to pump out dollars for repair and maintenance costs associated with the return of the aircraft sooner than anticipated. Also eating into Sun Country's profitability was a rebound of competition in the charter industry. A drop in aircraft leasing prices had encouraged start-up companies to join the fray. Sun Country, on the other hand, was still carrying higher rates. Moreover, a price war among the major carriers forced fares downward in all categories. On a positive note, passenger numbers remained solid, and NWA decided to extend the facility lease after all.

Even as Sun Country grew, charter demand fell, as more large airlines offered comparable service. Sun Country launched its own vacation travel package program late in 1995. Doug Iverson reported in December 1995 for *Knight Ridder/Tribune News* that some industry observers speculated the "move could be the beginning of a major rift" between Sun Country and NWA. "In the past, Sun Country flights to 12 cities were marketed through MLT. Since Northwest was essentially getting a cut, observers believe the airline didn't fight back and allowed cheaper flights to such destinations as Detroit, Chicago, Cleveland and Newark."

In early March 1996, Sun Country moved into direct competition with Northwest by offering discounted summer fares to locations such as Boston and J.F.K. in New York. Sun Country hoped Twin Cities travelers, who, according to American Express Domestic Airfare Index, paid 25 percent more than the national average for flights, would flock to their gates. Northwest, which controlled 80 percent of the Twin Cities air market, was quick to respond to the challenge. The giant airline slashed its fares. Sun Country had to reduce its fares, thus putting their profit margins in jeopardy.

In August Sun Country announced that it had lost 50 percent of its MLT business for the 1996–97 winter vacation season. The airline said that the cut-back was related to the reallocation of resources to scheduled flights. The business with MLT had been producing 25 percent of the charter company's annual revenue of more than $200 million.

Travel Mogul at the Helm: Late 1990s

Mark Travel Corporation owner Bill La Macchia purchased Barry's majority interest in Sun Country in the spring of 1997. La Macchia's Funjet vacation package firm had been doing brisk business with Sun Country since the mid-1980s. At the time of the sale Sun Country employed 1,000 people and operated flights from 23 cities. Privately held Mark Travel, based in Milwaukee, generated annual revenue of about $600 million.

Sun Country was on the slide when La Macchia took over. Operating profits which had been about $9.57 million in 1994, fell to $2.1 million in 1995, and plummeted again in 1996. Barry's venture in scheduled service had nosedived, scuttled by the combination of a meager marketing effort and Northwest's aggressive response to the competition.

"They got beat up terribly," La Macchia said of Sun Country's initiative against Northwest, in an April 1997 *Star Tribune* article by Tony Kennedy. "My focus is not scheduled service. I'm in the package business." (Barry retained some shares and remained on the board of directors as did founding pilot and CEO John Skiba. The Barry family and Skiba had been the only stockholders prior to the sale.)

La Macchia's son, Bill, Jr., called back from a nine-year stint of working in the Las Vegas hotel and casino business, was named COO of Sun Country. Six months later he was promoted to president. "Since then, La Macchia has steered the privately held company out of crisis and driven its growth by booking travel directly rather than relying on charter sales to wholesale

tour operators," wrote John Rosengren and Paul Duncan for *Corporate Report* in February 1999.

The turnaround was aided by a 15-day strike by Northwest pilots in late August 1998. Seizing the opportunity, Sun Country added seats and new business destinations, and backed the effort with a $1.5 million advertising campaign. Bookings tripled and bolstered a traditionally slow period. The airline maintained pre-strike prices in an effort to earn the good will of frustrated Northwest travelers. Sun Country ran a two-for-one post-strike promotion hoping to bring back customers gained during the Northwest walk-out, but the bigger player countered with its own two-for-one ticket special.

In January 1999, Sun Country was offering 81 nonstop flights to 23 domestic destinations plus winter travel flights to five Caribbean Islands. The majority of the 2.6 million travelers the airline had carried in 1998 had been vacationers. The charter business still brought in more than 80 percent of sales, but the La Macchia's were positioning themselves to change all that. Sun Country planned to alter the scheduled service to charter service ratio to 60/40, respectively.

The new plan was a far cry from the course La Macchia, Sr., had chartered when he took over the struggling airline. The change in mindset was due to "economics," according to Sun Country marketing director Lori Barghini. "As a charter we don't have the option of doing anything to our schedule," she said. "And charter operators want to fly on a Friday or a Sunday. We have to fly every day to make a profit."

La Macchia was used to making a profit. Mark Travel's estimated fiscal 1998 net profit was $20 million. *Leisure Travel News* had named La Macchia one of the 25 most influential tour and travel industry executives on three different occasions. He had deep pockets. "I could probably support the needs of Sun Country for a long time," La Macchia said in an April 1999 *Star Tribune* article by Kennedy, "but we have to make a profit. The community has to support Sun County to enjoy a competitive market."

After putting $41 million on the table for 75 percent of Sun Country's stock, La Macchia saw net losses of $11.7 million in fiscal 1997. It was more than he had expected. Eager for total control, he purchased the remaining Sun Country shares in the summer of 1998. Now the profits and losses were all in La Macchia's hands.

La Macchia was going head to head with the nation's fourth largest airline, and Northwest had a history of driving small carriers out of the market. Sun Country, according to Rosengren and Duncan, faced some internal barriers to success as well. The airline lacked a frequent flyer program, was viewed as a vacation airline by business travelers, contended with already cramped terminal conditions, and had limited listing in the central reservation system used by travel agents.

Aware of its internal weaknesses, Sun Country had a frequent flyer/loyalty program in the works and tapped into Mark Travel's sophisticated computer resources for its reservation system. The existing Hubert H. Humphrey charter terminal at Twin Cities International was receiving a makeover, and a new terminal, with Sun Country as the anchor tenant, was scheduled to open in 2001.

Determining to Fly High in the Future

Sun Country positioned itself as an underdog fighting giant Northwest. Playing off of ex-wrestler Jesse Ventura's unexpected victory in the 1998 Minnesota's governor's race, a billboard read: ''Jesse Did It—Why Can't We?'' The billboard campaign was just one piece of a multimillion-dollar marketing push. Print ads featured a mail-in coupon offering a chance to win a year of free travel. Company president Bill La Macchia, Jr., appeared on the small screen pedaling his family business door-to-door. Radio ads emphasized low fares and cultivated a connection with the flying public.

With about 500 daily flights and 410 planes, Northwest badly outgunned Sun Country, which had just 15 planes and flew a maximum of one time per day to the 15 cities it served. Eric Torbenson wrote on the eve of scheduled service, ''La Macchia Sr. knew going in that he couldn't compete on price, nor on the number of flights. He hopes to win over Twin Cities travelers with great service. With just a few more than 1,200 employees company-wide, compared with 50,000 at Northwest, Sun Country feels the camaraderie of its flight crews will help set it apart from Northwest.''

As the low airfare battle with Northwest heated up during the early summer, La Macchia made some other moves. Mark Travel purchased Trans Global Tours and strengthened its position in the Twin Cities market. The Twin Cities-based vacation charter business ranked second to NWA-owned MLT Inc. Sun Country announced the addition of state-of-the-art Boeing 737-800 series aircraft to its fleet beginning in January 2001, and that it would become a signatory carrier in Seattle, thus receiving a terminal location comparable to the larger airlines.

But these victories were small in comparison to the risks it faced in its fight with Northwest. In April 1999, La Macchia told the *Star Tribune* he was willing to spend up to three years building the Sun Country business, but his task was daunting. No other larger carrier had successfully bridged the gap from charter to scheduled airline. La Macchia, however, was determined to give it his best shot.

Further Reading

Causey, James E., ''Mark Travel Corp. Owner to Buy Twin Cities Airline,'' *Knight Ridder/Tribune Business News*, April 17, 1997.

Iverson, Doug, ''Minnesota's Sun Country Airlines Challenges Northwest with Air Fare Cut,'' *Knight Ridder/Tribune Business News*, March 8, 1996.

——, ''Sun Country Airlines Aims to Outshine Northwest with Latest Low Fares,'' *Knight Ridder/Tribune Business News*, May 31, 1996.

——, ''Sun Country Airlines Begins to Offer Packages Similar to Major Customer,'' *Knight Ridder/Tribune Business News*, December 20, 1995.

Kennedy, Tony, ''Bill La Macchia: Sun Country Money Man,'' *Star Tribune* (Minneapolis), April 25, 1999.

——, ''Competition Promises to Make Summer Air Fares a Breeze,'' *Star Tribune* (Minneapolis), April 24, 1999.

——, ''Sun Country Airlines to Be Sold,'' *Star Tribune* (Minneapolis), April 16, 1997, p. 1D.

——, ''Sun Country Loses Charter Business,'' *Star Tribune* (Minneapolis), August 8, 1996, p. 1D.

Kurschner, Dale, ''Financial Situation Gets Cloudier at Sun Country,'' *Minneapolis/St. Paul City Business*, October 23–29, 1992, p. 12.

——, ''Sun Country Takes Off,'' *Minneapolis/St. Paul City Business*, October 28, 1991, pp. 1, 21.

——, ''Sun Country to Construct Headquarters,'' *Minneapolis/St. Paul City Business*, December 30, 1991, pp. 1, 16.

Maler, Kevin, ''MAC Clears Sun Country Improvements for Takeoff,'' November 25–December 1, 1994, p. 8.

Reed, Peter, ''The Little Airline That Did,'' *Corporate Report Minnesota*, February 1987, pp. 68–72.

Rosengren, John, and Paul Duncan, ''Up, Up, and Away,'' *Corporate Report* (Minnesota), February 1999, pp. 24–29.

''Sun Country Airlines,'' *Corporate Report Fact Book 1999*, p. 577.

''Sun Country Airlines Becomes Signatory Carrier,'' *PR Newswire*, July 6, 1999.

Torbenson, Eric, ''St. Paul-Based Airline Buys Tour Company,'' *Knight Ridder/Tribune Business News*, June 23, 1999.

——, ''Sun Country Aims to Be Jesse Ventura of the Skies,'' *St. Paul Pioneer Press*, May 6, 1999, p. 1B.

——, ''Sun Country: Little Airline That Could?'' *St. Paul Pioneer Press*, May 30, 1999, p. 1A.

Ylinen, Jerry, ''Court Dispute Focuses on Control of Innovative Charter Airline,'' *Travel Weekly*, July 20, 1987, p. 35.

——, ''Shareholders Appeal Ruling to Force Sale of Sun Country Stock,'' *Travel Weekly*, December 14, 1987, p. 14.

—Kathleen Peippo

We're the dot in .com™

Sun Microsystems, Inc.

901 San Antonio Road
Palo Alto, California 94303
U.S.A.
(650) 960-1300
(800) 801-7869
Fax: (650) 969-9131
Web site: http://www.sun.com

Public Company
Incorporated: 1982
Employees: 26,300
Sales: $11.72 billion (1999)
Stock Exchanges: NASDAQ
Ticker Symbol: SUNW
NAIC: 334111 Electronic Computer Manufacturing;
51121 Software Publishers; 541512 Computer
Systems Design Services; 51421 Data Processing
Services

Archrival of Microsoft Corporation, Sun Microsystems, Inc. focuses on network computing rather than desktop mainframes, designing and manufacturing its own software and hardware. A 1980s start-up company, Sun generated in excess of $10 billion in sales during the late 1990s, recording astounding success with its own computer chip, SPARC, and own operating system, Solaris. Sun pioneered the use of shared software and hardware components among competing workstation manufacturers in order to create industry standards. After making a reputation for itself as a designer of high-powered workstation computers and servers, Sun expanded its talents, positioning itself as an Internet and electronic-commerce specialist during the latter half of the 1990s. The company's seminal achievement was the introduction of Java technology, the first universal software platform that enabled developers to write applications once to run on any computer. The company maintained offices in 150 countries, selling its products and services to the telecommunications, manufacturing, education, financial, and government markets.

Founding

Sun began as a computer project designed by Andreas Bechtolsheim while he was a graduate student at Stanford. His computer was a modification of a relatively new kind of computer, the workstation, which, like the PC (personal computer), can be utilized by single users. The workstation, however, provides users with more power. Workstations are designed for network integration and equipped with high-resolution graphics, and are fast enough to handle demanding engineering and graphics tasks. Unlike the first workstations, which had been introduced to the market only the previous year by Apollo Computer, Bechtolsheim's workstation used off-the-shelf parts, thus making it more affordable.

Bechtolsheim not only shunned custom-made hardware, but also broke with the industry tradition of adhering to proprietary operating system software. Instead, he hoped to enable different workstations brands running on a common operating system to share data. AT&T's UNIX operating system was the obvious choice; it could operate on a wide variety of computers and was already very popular among scientists and engineers because it enabled users to perform several tasks on screen at once. He began selling licenses for his computer, called the Sun (which stood for Stanford University Network) at $10,000 each in 1981.

Within a year Bechtolsheim's project attracted the interest of Stanford M.B.A. graduates Vinod Khosla and Scott McNealy, each of whom had some experience in the computer business. They were named president and director of manufacturing, respectively, of Sun Microsystems, Inc., upon its founding in February 1982. Bechtolsheim, who was the brains behind the hardware, became vice-president of technology. One of the first people the founders hired was Bill Joy, a Berkeley Ph.D. well known for his design of a popular version of the UNIX operating system. His task was to design the company's software.

Sun's use of standard hardware components and standard operating system software produced short-term payoffs for the fledgling company. Sun's workstations, unlike those of industry pioneer Apollo, operated on UNIX and from the outset networked easily with the hardware and software already on the market. In addition, although Sun's design could easily be cop-

Company Perspectives:

Sun was founded with one driving vision. A vision of computers that talk to each other no matter who built them. A vision in which technology works for you, not the other way around. While others protected proprietary, stand-alone architectures, we focused on taking companies into the network age. As a result, we've become the dot in .com, providing systems and software with the scalability and reliability needed to drive the electronic marketplace.

ied, the strategy of using existing technologies allowed Sun to enter the market quickly with a low-priced machine. Sales grew rapidly as a result. Within six months of incorporation the company became profitable.

Sun's first workstations, the Sun-1 and Sun-2, were instant successes, achieving $8 million in sales the first year, 80 percent of which came from sales to the university market. Sun's founders, however, had their eyes on the mainstream technical market, dominated at that time by the major computer companies. Sun's first big success in this area was the contract it signed in its second year with ComputerVision, a major CAD (computer-aided design) systems supplier that had decided to drop its proprietary hardware in favor of a new platform for its software products. ComputerVision had decided to sign a contract with Apollo, but, aggressively courted by Sun executives, the company reversed its decision and accepted a counteroffer made by Sun. Thus, Sun established its reputation as a serious player in the computer business and simultaneously earned the envious wrath of its competitors.

Growth in the Late 1980s

Expanding rapidly, Sun moved out of its original location in Santa Clara to a larger building in Mountain View, which became its new headquarters. In January 1984 Sun opened its first European sales office. In that same year Sun established a subsidiary, Sun Federal, to serve the government market. By 1991 Sun Federal was shipping more than half the workstations ordered by local, state, and federal government. Sun's informal corporate culture attracted engineers from the top universities. At the same time Sun hired additional managers who had experience working at other leading computer companies. Also in 1984 McNealy took over as president, as Khosla realized his dream of being able to retire as a millionaire before the age of 30.

During this period Sun continued to promote open systems. In 1984 it began broadly licensing Joy's design of a distributed file system software, called NFS (Network File System), that allowed data to be shared among many users in a network regardless of processor type, operating system, or communications system. NFS soon became an industry standard. Sun was so successful with this strategy that in 1984 Apollo was forced to abandon its exclusive design and instead produce a system that operated with standard software.

Between 1985 and 1989 Sun was the fastest-growing company in the United States, according to *Forbes* magazine, with a compound annual growth rate of 145 percent. It had become a public company with its successful initial public offering in 1986. The following year Sun surpassed Apollo in sales, and by the close of that year it had become the leader in workstation sales. Only six years after incorporation Sun achieved $1 billion in annual sales. Part of the reason for Sun's stupendous early success was the fact that the product in which it chose to specialize, the workstation, was becoming popular just at the time Sun entered the market. Furthermore, because it was a workstation industry pioneer, it established strong relations with the most sought-after clients and the most important software developers. Sun's corporate strategy also enabled it to offer its new customers the latest technology, while its competitors had to support established clients reluctant to scrap their outdated computer systems. Industrywide, sales of workstations rapidly displaced those of minicomputers, and the large computer companies that sold these had to compensate by offering workstations as well.

Debut of SPARC: Late 1980s

In the increasingly competitive market for workstations, where the speed of the computer is an important factor, Sun developed an even faster workstation in the late 1980s. Based on a different kind of microprocessor, this new product utilized RISC (reduced instruction set computing) architecture. RISC was simpler yet quicker than the then prevailing CISC (complex instruction set computing) architecture. As had been the case with the workstation itself, Sun was not the first company to design a RISC-based computer (IBM had introduced a model in 1986). Sun made improvements on it, however, and designed its own RISC architecture called SPARC (scalable performance architecture); it soon dominated the market of RISC-based workstations. In April 1989 Sun introduced its SPARCstation 1, a small, low-cost desktop computer with expanded capabilities. SPARCstation 1 employed new levels of integration and miniaturized the essential electronic components. By the end of the year Sun could claim to be the world's largest supplier of RISC-based computers, with the SPARCstation the most popular workstation on the market.

As Sun was not a manufacturer of its own processors or computer chips, in 1987 it licensed Bechtolsheim's SPARC design to a few silicon chip manufacturers, which then began to produce them for Sun's needs. Then, in keeping with its tradition of the "open system," in July 1988 Sun announced that it would offer its RISC design for license to other computer makers in recognition that for RISC to succeed it needed to become a pervasive presence in the marketplace. By licensing SPARC it stimulated low-cost, high-volume production of SPARC systems and thus increased the number of third party applications available. In 1989 licensing of SPARC was turned over to a new coalition of computer companies called SPARC International, an independent testing organization founded in nearby Menlo Park, California. McNealy hoped SPARC would produce the same kind of phenomenal growth for workstations that IBM brought to PCs a decade earlier when it permitted others to copy its standard PC hardware and software designs. In April 1991, however, Sun told its dealers it would prefer that they not sell SPARC clones. Sun claimed that small dealers would have difficulty succeeding against Sun in selling "clones" and were thus encouraging the smaller outfits to sell complementary "compatible" products, whereupon competitors charged hypocrisy in Sun's call for "open systems." Although it did not at first entirely convince other workstation companies to copy Sun's SPARC design, Sun was singlehandedly making SPARC one of the international standards. By 1992 all its new workstations were based only on SPARC.

As Sun was developing its SPARCstation computer, it was also making moves to ensure the presence of improved software to take advantage of it. In 1987 Sun signed an agreement with AT&T to develop an enhanced version of the UNIX operating system to make it the software standard for workstations. AT&T even took a 19 percent equity investment in Sun in 1988 (which it sold off in 1991 upon the NCR acquisition). The product that emerged in late 1989 established a de facto high-end UNIX standard (System V Release 4.0). It was at this time that competing computer manufacturers were settling on UNIX as a universal operating system, and RISC-based hardware proved the obvious supporting standard because of its speed in handling the complexities of UNIX and its suitability for the demands of the new user interfaces and applications software. Sun Microsystems, with its RISC-based SPARCstation and involvement in upgrading UNIX, was well-positioned to take advantage of the trend. "Sun is the strongest candidate to carry the UNIX banner. It has momentum. If it can keep up the recent good work, it can continue to dominate the workstation market," wrote technology consultant Richard Shaffer in *Forbes* in 1990.

Despite the success of the SPARCstation, the year of its introduction, 1989, marked a temporary financial setback for Sun. It lost money during the difficult product transition period by launching the new SPARCstation 1 while at the same time trying to support two older product lines using different technologies. Meanwhile, it was encountering difficulties managing the chaos resulting from its explosive growth. Problems included rapid personnel hiring and training, communications problems, and reorganization pains. A new management information system did not accurately forecast parts needed to fill orders, and demand for SPARCstation 1 was misjudged. That year Sun also temporarily lost its market lead in workstation shipments when Hewlett-Packard purchased Apollo and combined their market shares.

Things improved rapidly the following year. The company reduced its product families from three to one, the SPARC systems. The SPARCstation 2, released in November 1990, had the power of a minicomputer. The financial outlook improved, with revenues up by 40 percent over the previous year, and for the first time in a long while Sun was spending less than it was taking in. By the end of 1990 Sun claimed more than a third of the total market share of workstation shipments, leaving Hewlett-Packard a distant second at 20 percent. Sun held a similar share of the world market of RISC technology with its SPARC product line. As the market continued to grow, Sun aimed at expanding at a similar rate, maintaining the same market share. Meanwhile, its stock doubled from a low of $14 in August 1989 to $37 in July 1990.

At the beginning of the 1990s Sun further widened its market objectives for its workstations beyond engineers, software developers, and chip designers, targeting commercial

users such as insurance companies, brokerages, airlines, and publishers. In the spring of 1990 Sun announced a new line of low-end products designed to capture an increasing share of the vast commercial computing market, which was dominated by minicomputers and high-end PCs. Sun became the first workstation producer to introduce a low-end system for under $5,000. A month later the company announced the first color workstation for less than $10,000. It also began distributing its products through respected PC resellers. Sun was able to persuade software publishers to adapt over 2,800 programs for SPARC computer systems by 1991, including such major programs as Lotus 1-2-3, WordPerfect, and dBase IV, thus substantially broadening Sun's commercial market. By the end of 1992, when over a third of Sun's sales were to commercial as opposed to technical markets, there were more applications for Sun workstations than for any other UNIX workstation.

Business strategies in 1990 included streamlining the organization into two core management groups. Custom job-shop manufacturing was eliminated, allowing high volume from a single, elegantly designed product line to permit Sun's manufacturing system to attain economies of scale. More of the working capital and investment risk was pushed onto outside contractors that produce the printed circuit boards, boxes, and screens, leaving Sun with the relatively simple tasks of assembly and testing. It stayed out of the lucrative high-end of the workstation market to build on volume and market share in the lower end. By the close of 1990 Sun was one of the top ten computer hardware companies in the country, but unlike most of the others, it sold only workstations and servers: it did not sell PCs, minicomputers, or mainframes.

Sun had in the past attempted to build a critical mass for its technology and establish a de facto standard in hardware. In September 1991 it aimed at a similar broadening of its influence in operating system software when it announced plans to make the Sun OS operating system, a version of UNIX, run on more computers than just its own, including those running on Intel microprocessors. It was at this time that Kodak sold its UNIX software unit, Interactive Systems, to Sun. Interactive supplied UNIX System V release 4.0 for Intel-based computers, and thus the purchase of Interactive endowed Sun with needed expertise in the arena of Intel-based UNIX systems. Interactive had already previously agreed to install Sun's operating system, Solaris 2.0, onto Intel X86 architecture. With more computers using Sun's operating system, it would become easier to link Sun workstations with others in a network, and more software could be written for Sun's operating system. Sun needed a constant flow of new programs to keep its workstations sales booming, particularly now that it was facing challenges in hardware.

In 1991 Sun followed IBM and Apple by becoming a hybrid software-hardware company. This new strategy was an attempt to offset shrinking profit margins on hardware by selling software. A reorganization of the company transferred its software-selling operations to two new subsidiaries, SunSoft and Sun Technology Enterprises. SunSoft sold Sun's operating system to computer manufacturers, while Sun Technology Enterprises supplied software for SPARC machines, such as networking, printing, imaging, and PC emulation products. At the same time other core businesses and functions were also reorganized into subsidiaries.

The largest of these was Sun Microsystems Computer Corporation, which McNealy headed in addition to his post of CEO of the parent company. Each subsidiary was set up as a separate profit and loss center having its own management to oversee product development, manufacturing, marketing, and sales.

By 1991 Sun's product line was beginning to show its age as competitors brought out machines superior in both price and performance. In the early 1990s the workstation market competition grew increasingly fierce, as it was one of the few areas of the computer industry still enjoying sales growth of more than 20 percent annually in 1991. One of the reasons for this growth was the RISC technology and the recent emphasis on serving the general business computing market. As Sun was trying to enter the office market, however, office computing companies such as IBM, Apple, Compaq, Digital Equipment, and Hewlett-Packard were pursuing the technical market, and Sun's move into the broader commercial computing market put it into competition with the bigger computer manufacturers on their home turf. Sun also reversed itself by moving into the high-end of the workstation market, where performance speeds were essential, using multiprocessors (two or more processors chained together) and special software. It introduced its first multiprocessor, the SPARCserver 600NO series, and new operating software for it in 1991.

By mid-1992, Sun had 21 subsidiaries around the world providing sales, service, and technical support, and overseas sales accounted for more than half of its revenues. Manufacturing was carried out at three sites: Milpitas, California; Westford, Massachusetts; and Linlithgow, Scotland. In February 1992 Sun became the first U.S. company to establish a significant presence in Moscow. Sun forged an agreement with a group of 50 Russian scientists, including the Russian scientist who had developed supercomputers in the Soviet Union, to work as contractors with the company.

Introduction of Java: 1995

Sun's tenth anniversary marked the conclusion of a decade of remarkable success, but not all industry experts were willing to bet that the company's second decade of business would be as successful as the first. With the enormous growth rate of the PC market and the proliferation of competitive workstations being offered by other manufacturers, Sun faced a difficult road ahead, industry pundits explained, and would be hard pressed to sustain its growth rate throughout the 1990s. The experts were wrong. Sun recorded prolific growth in the years following its tenth anniversary, demonstrating enviable success by focusing on high-end servers priced from $500,000 and up. The most significant facet of the company's business, however, was the introduction of a new product in the mid-1990s that forced analysts to quickly change their opinion about Sun's growth potential. In mid-1995, Sun introduced Java, a brand name that stood for a programming language and a set of components and tools that allowed users to write software across any computer and operating system. The potential for Java was vast, exuding the universality McNealy had preached for years. In essence, Java represented a self-sufficient computing system, emulating all the functions of the computing device, regardless of the underlying operating system.

Following the introduction of Java, McNealy found a more receptive audience to his vision of a computer world based on networks supported by powerful, high-end servers, a vision that ran counter to the approach taken by Microsoft's founder Bill Gates. McNealy reveled in his attacks against Microsoft, both in the press and in court, as he fought against ''Wintel,'' the duopoly held by Microsoft's Windows and Intel's processing chips. ''The PC is just a blip,'' McNealy remarked in an interview with *Business Week* in 1999, dismissing the significance of the PC revolution led by Microsoft. ''It's a big, bright blip, but just a blip. Fifty years from now, people are going to look back and say: 'Did you really have a computer on your desk? How weird.' '' McNealy envisioned network computing as the future, a future in which the billions of computer chips in products ranging from refrigerators and telephones to smart cards and door locks would all be connected in a network.

By 1998, Sun's revenues had increased to $10 billion and its net income, after more than doubling since the mid-1990s, had reached $763 million. In keeping with McNealy's posture as an industry renegade, Sun operated as the only major hardware and software vendor without a cooperative relationship with Microsoft. Because of the company's independent stance, its corporate structure was reorganized in 1998 to better contend with competitors such as Microsoft. ''Our goal,'' Sun's chief operating officer explained to *Electronic News* at the time of the reorganization, ''is to align the organization more tightly and streamline internal processes so that we achieve greater operation efficiency and provide a unified face to the customer.'' The five companies that had operated as autonomous businesses were stripped of their independence and restructured into seven divisions focused on market segments and industries.

As Sun pressed ahead with turning McNealy's vision into reality, forging alliances with other companies ranked as a primary objective. To succeed in the long-term, the company needed to lead a counterrevolution and convince other computer manufacturers and electronics companies that the future was networks. Following America Online's acquisition of Netscape Communications, Sun signed a three-year alliance with America Online that bolstered Java's presence on the Internet. In 1999, Sun signed Java technology licensing agreements with Sony, Motorola, Ericsson, Samsung, Alcatel, Nortel, OpenTV, BEA Systems, Siemens-Nixdorf, and Scientific Atlanta. The last year of the decade also marked the introduction of a new software technology called Jini, which served as the cornerstone of McNealy's dream to link a vast array of electronic devices. Launched in January 1999, Jini technology eliminated many of the problems associated with connecting computers and other devices, such as printers, copiers, and fax machines, to a network.

As Sun prepared for the 21st century, much of the company's long-term success depended on the widespread acceptance of McNealy's iconoclastic perspective. Toward this end, there were positive signs supporting the Sun vision. Tele-Communications, Inc., for example, was planning to use Java to deliver telephone service, bill-paying, and other services through television set-top boxes. Java also was attracting interest from manufacturers of consumer devices such as wireless telephones, smart cards, and video game consoles. Although the company had its fair share of critics, its ability to record robust growth while exploring alternative approaches to computing earned the respect of many. "If you want to know where the computer industry is going," an analyst informed *Business Week,* "ask Sun." Another analyst commented to *Business Week,* "There have been times when Sun seemed way out of sync, yet two or three years later, we see the rest of the industry moving in their direction." Whether or not McNealy's blueprint for the future would prevail remained a question to be answered in the 21st century.

Principal Subsidiaries

Sun Microsystems Computer Corporation; SunSoft, Inc.; Sun Technology Enterprises, Inc.; Sun Express, Inc.; Sun Microsystems Laboratories, Inc.; Java Software; Sitka Corp.; SunPro Inc.; SunSelect.

Further Reading

Alsop, Stewart, "Warning to Scott McNealy: Don't Moon the Ogre," *Fortune,* October 13, 1997, p. 171.

Coffee, Peter, "Memo to Sun's CEO: Stay on That Message," *PC Week,* June 29, 1999, p. 26.

Fisher, Susan E., "Vendors Court Reseller Partners As Workstations Go Mainstream," *PC Week,* July 30, 1990.

Gaudin, Sharon, "Java Critics: Sun's Reorg Falls Short," *Computerworld,* April 27, 1998, p. 4.

Goff, Leslie, "The Rise of Sun; Fledgling Company Envisions Open System Leading to Better Technology, Lower Prices," *Computerworld,* August 23, 1999, p. 68.

Hof, Robert D., "Where Sun Means to Be a Bigger Fireball," *Business Week,* April 15, 1991.

——, "Why Sun Can't Afford to Shine Alone," *Business Week,* September 9, 1991.

Hutheesing, Nikhil, "Suntel Inside," *Forbes,* December 14, 1998, p. 54.

Markoff, John, "The Smart Alecks at Sun Are Regrouping," *New York Times,* April 28, 1991.

McNealy, Scott, "The Killer App.," *Forbes,* December 1, 1997, p. S152.

Moeller, Michael, "Sun Gathers Forces; Reorganization Is Aimed at Presenting a Consolidated Front," *PC Week,* April 27, 1998, p. 17.

Morrissey, Jane, "Sun Negotiating for Interactive Unix Technology," *PC Week,* September 23, 1991.

"Sell 'em Cheap," *Economist,* May 11, 1991.

Shaffer, Richard A., "The Case for Sun," *Forbes,* April 16, 1990.

Sun Microsystems: The 10-Year Success Story, Mountain View, Calif.: Sun Microsystems, Inc., June 1992.

"Sun Power," *Business Week,* January 18, 1999, p. 64.

"Sun Revamps for 'New Era of Growth'," *Electronic News,* April 27, 1998, p. 12.

Taschek, John, "This Just In: The World Revolves Around Sun," *PC Week,* January 4, 1999, p. 48.

Wrubel, Robert, "Top Gun Once More," *Finance World,* October 2, 1990.

—Heather Behn Hedden
—updated by Jeffrey L. Covell

Superior Uniform Group, Inc.

10099 Seminole Boulevard
Seminole, Florida 33772-2539
U.S.A.
(727) 397-9611
Fax: (727) 391-5401
Web site: http://www.superioruniformgroup.com

Public Company
Incorporated: 1920 as Superior Surgical Manufacturing
   Company
Employees: 1,800
Sales: $160.71 million (1998)
Stock Exchanges: American
Ticker Symbol: SGC
NAIC: 315239 Women's & Girls' Cut & Sew Other
   Outerwear Manufacturing; 315225 Men's & Boys'
   Cut & Sew Work Clothing Manufacturing

Superior Uniform Group, Inc. is the second largest maker of uniform and service apparel, behind Cintas Corporation, in the United States. Superior's products are sold to five distinct marketplaces: employee identification; cleanrooms; healthcare; security/public safety; and corporate identification. The company's products include corporate I.D. wear as well as career apparel and accessories for the hospital and healthcare, hotel, fast food, transportation, industrial, and commercial markets. Superior stocks approximately 6,500 styles in addition to offering special custom order services. The company markets its products through sales presentations, catalogue sales, trade advertising/shows, and conventions. It competes with national and regional manufacturers and also with local firms in most major metropolitan areas.

Early History

Superior Surgical Manufacturing Company was founded in 1920 as a family business that initially focused on manufacturing and distributing apparel products for hospitals and other institutions within the healthcare industry. In addition to clothing, the company also sold medical instrument kits, restraints, operating room masks, and gauze sponges.

It was business as usual until the 1960s when the company underwent significant changes. Following its initial public offering in 1968, Superior acquired companies which allowed for further diversification of product lines. Several new factories were opened throughout the southeastern region of the United States, which greatly increased production capabilities. The company's sales force was expanded and divided into regional territories, with sales management centers located in Atlanta, Chicago, Dallas, Los Angeles, and New York. Additional sales facilities and showrooms were then placed strategically throughout the country. In 1979, Superior moved its headquarters from Huntington Township, New York, to Seminole, Florida, relocating over 80 key employees and their families.

Earnings rose steadily until a slight slowdown occurred in 1986, but the company experienced an upswing after issuing an innovative sales catalogue and following a licensing agreement with Disney. The agreement allowed Superior to manufacture and sell hospital sleeping garments for children. The company's Looney Tunes designs featured six major Disney characters, designed to make a child's hospital stay more pleasant. Superior overcame the period of recession and was soon back on track.

As a result of increased sales in the healthcare sector and a continued focus toward efficiency, Superior Surgical finished 1990 with record results. Sales were up over eight percent, while earnings were reported up 27 percent to $4.01 a share. Realizing the growing awareness to environmental issues, Superior began making operation room garments that could be reused. The firm issued its newest Health Care Catalog, and the publication was a tremendous factor in increased sales and shareholder equity. In the words of a *Miami Herald* analyst's report, "It seems every time we look at this (Superior Uniform) stock, its price is near all-time highs." Along with achieving new stock highs, the company increased its dividend. Superior continued to post outstanding results. Earnings for the quarter ended Sept. 30, 1993 were 84 cents per share, up from 69 cents the year earlier. The company expected 1993 to be a record year. Superior was focused at that time on the recently enacted

---

Company Perspectives:

The mission of Superior Uniform Group, Inc. is to enhance our long term profitability by maintaining a leadership position in understanding and serving the uniform/career apparel industry, as we market, manufacture, and sell a brand line of proprietary products. We are committed to: providing customer satisfaction in product quality, value and service; maintaining our reputation for creativity, reliability and integrity; and offering employees opportunities for growth and self-development in a secure and stable work environment.

Occupational Safety and Health Administration (OSHA) regulations, which were intended to protect healthcare personnel from blood-borne pathogens. Superior reacted quickly in designing and manufacturing a complete line of reusable protective apparel, linen collection systems, and accessories designed to comply with OSHA regulations while helping hospitals and other healthcare facilities reduce waste and disposal costs.

Alterations in the 1990s

Until 1990 Superior had one large warehouse, where every morning employees would receive a stack of orders. They would roam the entire warehouse picking items, which were then delivered to a consolidated packing station. The company was shipping 80 percent of its orders (for which it had inventory) within two weeks, a time frame that became unacceptable for many customers who were demanding shorter lead times. Superior decided to overhaul its warehouse and distribution system. Managers organized six modules of five employees and the warehouse was divided into six sections. Each team became responsible for one section and the processing of an order—from the placing of new merchandise on the shelves to the staging of orders for shipping. Each module was given its own packing station with a label printer and a computer terminal which was online to the company's main computer in Seminole, Florida. The teams became familiar with a particular section of goods, where specific products should be placed, and how to work more efficiently as a small, integrated group. The new system enabled the company to ship 99.3 percent of its orders the same day, and simplified the invoice processing. Following the success of the modular set-up in the distribution center, Superior began implementing modular systems throughout the company.

In response to high employment rates and a forward-looking focus, Superior invested heavily in streamlining efficiencies through technology. Approximately two percent of annual sales ($12 million over five years) was spent "de-skilling" operations and modernizing equipment. The automated contoured seamer was introduced, for example, reducing the training cycle from 20 weeks to two weeks, saving almost $3,200 per operator. Prior to that innovation, each day an operator was away from the job the company lost a day of production. With an average absenteeism rate of about four percent, the de-skilled automated operation—expensive in the short run—was anticipated to pay off in seven to ten years. The company implemen-

ted other technologies from programmable sewing machines to weaving machines for garment ties. Superior relied on the expertise of equipment suppliers, including Atlanta Attachment Company, Juki America Inc., and Scovill Fasteners Inc. to update and innovate for them, easing its dependence on vast inhouse electronic and mechanical workers.

Company officials anticipated potential long-term problems in finding skilled operators. They considered the possibility of producing offshore, but decided that for the most part high start-up costs and the initial poor quality of workmanship (attributed to training an entire plant of unskilled operators) made it prohibitive—noting problems incurred by some competitors in the industry. It was decided that the company should continue producing the majority of its items domestically and to concentrate investment in equipment with a long-term payback. Superior did, however, enter into seven joint ventures in three Central American countries, Guyana, Honduras, and El Salvador. Shortly thereafter, a plant was added in Mexico. Three of the plants were Catholic missions that provided employment for the needy, according to Cedrone of *Bobbin*. Benstock explained that the move to offshore production on a limited basis was necessary for competitive reasons. Others were selling items below cost and officials at Superior did not want to lose business on a number of products. The company relocated part of its production, but did not make heavy investments, or build new plants.

Other heavy equipment investments during this period included the addition of three GERBERcutters from Gerber Garment Technology, Inc. and a Satellite Plus system (which allowed micro-scheduling of groups of operators as opposed to entire departments) from Leadtec, a division of Willcox and Gibbs. The installation of the GERBERcutters coincided with the consolidation of Superior's cutting operations at the company's 180,000-square-foot Eudora, Arkansas plant. The equipment enabled the cutting of 150,000 yards of fabric each day by three modular teams of six employees.

In 1996 Superior completed the construction of one of the most innovative distribution centers for apparel in the world, locating it in Eudora. Borrowing technologies from many different industries, it took over three years to design, plan, and construct the $10 million facility. Controlled by a central management system, conveyors were designed to tie into robotics pulling, tilt tray sorting, and vision verification.

Going to Court: 1996

In 1996, Superior pleaded guilty to one count of giving the government false information and was required to reimburse the government $6.5 million, said Charles Wilson, U.S. attorney for the Middle District of Florida, according to the *Miami Herald*. The probe had focused on a nine-year contract between Superior and the Veterans Affairs Department that ended in 1992. The plea bargain settled allegations that the Pinellas County company knowingly overcharged the Department of Veterans Affairs, the General Service Administration, and other government agencies for medical items and for clothing, the federal authorities said. The settlement resolved potential criminal and civil cases against Superior. The false information involved prices for various medical and veterinary supplies from Fashion Seal Uniforms, a division of Superior, according to court documents. Beginning with the announcement of the government's investigation, the company experienced a downward spiral in its share prices. As part of the settlement, Superior started a training program in ethics and compliance for its employees. The training included supplying employees with a toll-free telephone number to ensure that employees could report any suspicious activity. Superior continued to pursue business with the government, but on an open-order rather than a contractual basis.

Ted Jackovics of the *Tampa Tribune* reported that Superior planned to implement changes in its product line. CEO and Chairman Gerald Benstock told him that "he is not satisfied with the way the company is performing," and stated plans to shift from manufacturing surgical uniforms to acquiring companies that focused on embroidered sportswear. As the company turned toward producing more non-healthcare-related items it became necessary to reconsider changing the company name. In 1998, Superior Surgical Manufacturing Company was legally changed to Superior Uniform Group, Inc. Executives were hopeful that the name-change would attract more attention to its core leisure wear.

In 1998 Superior acquired Sope Creek, a Marietta, Georgia company that specialized in embroidered golf, resort, and corporate logo apparel. Other acquisitions were being sought in the resort and corporate image lines, which Benstock had targeted as a "fragmented industry," made up of a multitude of cottage businesses. Executives hoped that the company's sales representatives would encourage such existing corporate accounts as Publix and Winn-Dixie, which already bought uniforms from the company, to order casual wear for their workers. Superior executives also had plans for tapping into the corporate identification programs of its 20,000 accounts. Superior's Fashion Seal Uniforms division introduced Fashion Max Scrubs, a line made of a patented permanent finish that wicked moisture away from the wearer's skin. Garments reputedly enhanced evaporation to keep the body cooler, while prohibiting bacterial growth and resisting stains. Also during this time, Fashion Seal and Universal Laundry Bags (another Superior division) offered a full line of cleanroom apparel, laundry bags, stands, and accessories for use in the healthcare and linen supply industries.

Positioning for the Future

Cintas Corporation of Cincinnati, which continued to acquire smaller companies, was the industry leader in uniform production and sales. Striving to remain competitive in the ever consolidating industry, Superior (still considered a medium-sized competitor) followed its Sope Creek buy with the purchase of the 50-year-old Empire Company for approximately $9.1 million, plus the assumption of certain liabilities. The Portland, Oregon company operated as a supplier of uniforms, corporate I.D. wear, and promotional products, with customers largely located in the Northwest. Company executives continued to evaluate the market and to seek additional acquisitions in order to complement and expand the company's existing units.

Members of the Benstock family were well-represented on the board, including Gerald Benstock as well as his sons Michael and Peter. A *Florida Trend* article quoted Alexander Paris, Jr., a market analyst with Barrington Research Associates in Chicago: "It's a nice small-cap company, good for the long-term, patient small-cap investor." He noted the advantages in having Benstock, his son and son-in-law running the company, "There's a high level of insider ownership, so it's run like a private company."

Principal Divisions

Superior Surgical International; Sope Creek; Universal Laundry Bags; Lamar Caribbean Sales; D'Armigene Design Center; Fashion Seal Uniforms; Worklon; Martin's Uniforms; Appel Uniforms.

Further Reading

"Apparel Firm Will Repay Government $6.5 Million," *Miami Herald,* April 3, 1996, p. 5B.

"The Bobbin Top 40," *Bobbin Magazine,* June 1998, p. 1.

Booker, Stacie Kress, "Dressed to Work," *Florida Trend,* June 1998, p. 26.

Cedrone, Lisa, "A Superior Outfit," *Bobbin Magazine,* September, 1992, p. 60.

Cohen, Sarah, "Florida Uniform Maker, Superior Surgical Can't Predict Upturn," Knight-Ridder/*Tribune Business News,* May 6, 1996, p. 5060422.

"Earnings Look Strong for Superior Surgical," *Miami Herald,* December 14, 1992, p. 36BM.

Goldfield, Robert, "Uniform Merger: Perfect Fit for Portland Employer," *Business Journal—Portland,* May 7, 1999, p. 1.

Hundley, Kris, "Seminole, Florida-Based Superior Surgical Changes Name to Superior Uniform Group," Knight-Ridder/*Tribune Business News,* May 10, 1998, p. OKRB9813021C.

Jackovics, Ted, "Superior Seeks to Broaden Appeal," *Tampa Tribune,* May 9, 1998, p. BF1.

"Superior Surgical Gets Boost from the Mouse," *Miami Herald,* June 29, 1987.

"Superior Surgical," *Miami Herald,* May 27, 1991, p. 28BM.

"Superior Uniform Group Announces Its Acquisition of The Empire Company," *PR Newswire,,* April 5, 1999, p. 3999.

"Superior Uniform Group Introduces Fashion Max Scrubs," *Laundry Today,* February 1999, p. 20.

"Uniform Manufacturer Likely to Grow Again," *Miami Herald,* September 26, 1994, p. 40BM.

—Terri Mozzone

TMP Worldwide Inc.

1633 Broadway
New York, New York 10019
U.S.A.
(212) 977-4200
Fax: (212) 247-0015
Web sites: http://www.tmpw.com
            http://www.monster.com

Public Company
Founded: 1967 as Telephone Marketing Programs
Employees: 4,100
Sales: $406.8 million (1998)
Stock Exchanges: NASDAQ
Ticker Symbol: TMPW
NAIC: 54181 Advertising Agencies

TMP Worldwide Inc. is the world's largest Yellow Pages advertising agency as well as a leader in the field of recruitment advertising. Its offerings include monster.com, a web site that in 1999 was carrying more than 140,000 job advertisements and contained a database of more than a million resumés. Both Yellow Pages and recruitment clients place small advertisements that are distributed to thousands of media outlets. TMP Worldwide's astonishing growth in the 1990s was fueled by the acquisition of more than 100 companies, including 45 between the beginning of 1996 and the end of 1998.

Yellow Pages Specialist in the 1980s

The company was founded in 1967 by Andrew J. McKelvey as Telephone Marketing Programs, a specialist in placing advertisements in Yellow Pages telephone books. By 1980 the New York City-based company also had offices in Chicago, Los Angeles, Miami, Toronto, London, and Milan. Its gross annual billings had reached about $35 million, which, at 15 percent commission, came to more than $5 million in revenue. Telephone Marketing Systems was placing ads for clients such as Ryder Systems and Econo-Car in the nation's 5,700 directories. The company also held a three-year consulting contract with the French government.

Telephone Marketing Programs had $67.5 million in gross billings and $10 million in gross income in 1983, all stemming from Yellow Pages advertising. "We saw a tremendous opportunity to consolidate in the early 1980s," McKelvey later told Hugh Pope of the *Wall Street Journal.* "We learned how to buy agencies, how to merge them, and our market share grew steadily. The average agency doesn't want to go into Yellow Page advertising. They want to make award-winning commercials. But what we do is just as creative."

In 1985, when Telephone Marketing Programs ranked 67th among U.S. advertising agencies, its gross billings were $103.3 million and its revenues $15.3 million. TMP now had seven major offices and six sales units nationwide. In 1986 it opened TMP Japan Inc. in Tokyo as a joint venture. In France, it was in the initial phase of making advertisement placements by electronic delivery.

Telephone Marketing Programs was benefiting from a proliferation of new Yellow Pages directories as a result of the government-mandated breakup of the American Telephone & Telegraph Co. (AT&T). This was forcing advertisers to expand their budgets for directory advertising, and largely as a result, Yellow Pages revenues rose 19 percent to nearly $7 billion in 1985. To accommodate national advertisers unwilling to spend more money, however, TMP, in an effort to target the best buys for its clients, was beginning to survey customers in a variety of markets to determine which directories they used and how often they used them.

By the end of the 1980s Telephone Marketing Programs was the largest advertising agency in the Yellow Pages field. In 1989 its gross billings reached $270 million and its gross income climbed to $40.5 million, of which all but $3 million was in the United States. The company now had 17 offices. It gained 22 clients in that year, including giant firms such as Avis, Coca-Cola, CVS, Hitachi, and SmithKline-Beecham, while losing only seven. The company's billings and earnings reached $501 million and $59.7 million, respectively, in 1992. By 1994 it commanded a 40 percent share of the Yellow Pages market, including such major clients as General Motors and Ryder Trucks.

Recruitment Advertising Player: 1993–95

TMP Worldwide entered the field of recruitment advertising in 1993, when it purchased Chicago-based Bentley, Barnes &

Company Perspectives:

The company's philosophy of front-line employee empowerment continues to be instrumental in the success of TMPW's client-agency relations. This philosophy has also helped TMP Worldwide become the world's largest recruitment advertising agency, a top 10 Web publisher, and the world's 14th largest advertising agency overall.

Lynn, an agency with about $50 million in annual capitalized billing, of which recruitment advertising accounted for roughly 75 percent. TMP sold the agency's consumer division to Ayer Inc. in 1994.

Paul Austermuehle, a Bentley, Barnes vice-president who was made president, said the following year that TMP's advanced Yellow Pages technology had helped his agency discover new revenue streams. TMP's heavy investments in computerization and technology, for example, enabled a longtime Bentley, Barnes client to meet a Clear Air Act mandate by reducing the number of commuters who were driving to and from work without passengers. "We're only just now discovering how to make the best use of all the things our TMP marriage provides," Austermuehle told Ylonda Gault of *Crain's New York Business.*

Like Yellow Pages advertisements, recruitment, or classified advertising was an unglamorous, labor-intensive part of the advertising business neglected by many name agencies because of relatively low profit margins. TMP Worldwide followed the Bentley, Barnes purchase with seven other acquisitions of agencies specializing in recruitment in the following year. These included Deutsch Shea & Evans, Merling Marx, and Chavin & Lambert of New York City and Rogers and Associates of Santa Clara, California. The additions raised TMP's recruitment billings to about $125 million a year and made it the third largest recruitment agency in the United States and the nation's 19th largest advertising agency overall. In 1994 the company lost $2.5 million on commissions and fees of $86.2 million.

Founded in 1981, Rogers & Associates was the second largest advertising agency in Silicon Valley, with California offices in Los Angeles, San Diego, and San Francisco as well as Santa Clara, plus offices in Chicago, Dallas, Miami, and Tampa. Curtis Rogers became president of TMP Worldwide's new recruitment division, while his partner, Steve Schmidt, was appointed president of the parent company's interactive/new media division, with responsibility for "Career Taxi," a web site enabling clients to create an online brochure for attractive prospective job applicants.

By early 1995 TMP Worldwide's roster of acquired recruitment agencies had reached 12. Of TMP's 70 offices, 25 were focusing on recruitment advertising. TMP's billings in 1995 included $200 million from classified recruitment advertisements in newspapers and other publications. Its acquisitions that year included two competitors in the Boston-area recruitment ad business: Adion and the Haughey Group. TMP's 2,500 recruitment advertising clients at the end of 1995 included Cigna, Nike, Dean Witter Reynolds, and Gateway 2000.

Adion founder Jeff Taylor became head of TMP Interactive, which was put in charge of the "Monster Board" recruitment web site Taylor created in 1994. He later told Rex Crum of *Boston Business Journal,* "I knew the business [of Monster Board] was bigger than New England, but almost all the ads and job seekers were from New England. By selling, I was able to utilize the infrastructure of TMP and grow the business." At the end of 1995 Monster Board was listing more than 7,000 positions from U.S. and Canadian employers, receiving resumes from 48 countries, and registering 15,000 "hits" a day.

TMP Worldwide was not ignoring its core Yellow Pages business, which among its 2,100 clients in 1995 included Ford Motor Co., MCI Communications, Hallmark Cards, Pizza Hut, and United Van Lines. Its gross Yellow Pages billings of $425 million in 1995 accounted for 30 percent of the total billings in this field by U.S. agencies—three times the share of its nearest competitor. An important 1995 acquisition was the purchase of Dallas-based GTE Directories Corp.'s Yellow Pages business and assets from U.S. West. By contrast, TMP held only a seven percent share of the recruitment advertising market. TMP had net income of $3.2 million on commissions and fees of $123.9 million in 1995, marking an end to at least four years of deficits.

Publicly Owned Powerhouse: 1996–99

TMP Worldwide spent more than $25 million to acquire 12 companies in 1996 and, at the end of the year, had acquired 36 companies since the beginning of 1994 with estimated total gross annual billings of about $350 million. The company made its initial public offering in December 1996, raising $80.5 million by offering a majority of its outstanding Class A shares of common stock at $14 a share. This sum almost exactly matched the company's long-term debt at the end of the year and enabled it to borrow more money for more acquisitions. McKelvey remained president and chairman of TMP and continued to hold 60 percent of the company, including all the Class B shares, which had 10 times the voting power of the Class A shares.

TMP Worldwide registered commissions and fees of $162.6 million in 1996. It lost $52.4 million after taking a charge of $52 million for issuing stock to existing shareholders of TMP's predecessor companies in exchange for their shares in these companies. By July 1997, when TMP sold 2.4 million more shares to the public, its stock was trading at $22.25 a share.

TMP Worldwide's overseas acquisitions included the 1996 purchase of the recruiting firm Neville Jeffrees Australia Pty Limited for $25 million. TMP had purchased eight companies in 1997—including Belgian and Dutch recruitment agencies—at a total expense of $18 million by July, when it landed Austin Knight, the largest such agency in Great Britain, with 1996 gross billings of £134.4 million (about $210 million), commissions and fees of £29.3 million (about $45 million), and 24 offices worldwide. Collateral lines of business brought its annual revenues to more than £70 million (about $110 million). Its clients included Sony Electronics, British Gas, Schweppes, Nestlé, and Yahoo! TMP now had a presence in 11 countries and 80 offices worldwide. Other 1997 acquisitions included the British companies MSL Group and Lonsdale Advertising, and a U.S. agency, Johnson Recruitment Advertising. TMP's 1997 revenues came to $329.5 million and its net income to $10.7 million.

By this time TMP Worldwide was placing the advertisements of all its print clients online at web sites that included not only Monster Board but Online Career Center, the Internet's earliest career site; MedSearch, the main online classified-ad service for the healthcare industry, and Be the Boss, a site promoting opportunities in franchising. Founded in 1992 by Bill and Susan Warren, Indianapolis-based Online Career Center continued to be run by Bill Warren.

By late 1998 Monster Board was listing 50,000 job postings and receiving more than two million visitors a month, making it the Internet's top job-search site. Prospective employees paid nothing, while the cost to employers began at $175 for 60 days. The service was available in five countries. In January 1999 Monster Board, Online Career Center, and MedSearch combined to form Monster.com. During the second quarter of 1998, Monster.com had an operating profit of $455,000 on revenues of $10.7 million. Monster.com's revenues for the first quarter of 1999 reached $20.1 million. In May 1999 it was serving 42,000 clients, listing 204,000 jobs, holding more than 1.3 million active resumes, and recording 7.6 million "hits" per month. It was planning to introduce, in July 1999, Monster Talent Market 1.0, a service to connect job searchers with contractors, consultants, freelancers, and small business owners.

TMP Worldwide had made 14 acquisitions in 1998 by mid-October of that year. Among these was Stocking Advertising and Public Relations, one of the oldest agencies in the Washington, D.C., area, with annual revenue of $11 million. TMP paid for the purchase with stock valued at $14.5 million. The company had gross billings of $1.4 billion in 1998, including about $794.2 million for recruitment advertising and about $485.2 million for Yellow Pages advertising. Commissions and fees came to $406.8 million, including $48.5 million in Internet revenue. Net income was $4.2 million.

TMP Worldwide's list of 17,000 clients in 1998 included more than 80 of the *Fortune* 100 companies and about 400 of the *Fortune* 500. The company maintained 71 offices in the United States and 46 abroad. Its long-term debt was $118 million at the end of the year. McKelvey held 37.2 percent of TMP's shares in March 1999. The company's growing Internet business was not lost on investors, who bid its stock to a peak of $93 a share in the spring of 1999.

TMP Worldwide's ravenous appetite for acquisitions showed no sign of slowing in 1999. In January it announced the acquisition of three European recruitment agencies: the German firms Bonde & Schmah and PMM Management Consultants and the French company Sources, SA. The latter purchase, combined with TMP's other operations in France, put the company into a leadership position in the recruitment advertising industry in that country, according to McKelvey. Also in January 1999, TMP Worldwide acquired Morgan & Banks Limited, its biggest acquisition to date, for more than 5.1 million shares of TMP stock. This Australian company was providing permanent recruitment of personnel ranging from mid-level executives through clerks and was also engaged in temporary contracting and human resources consulting.

TMP Worldwide entered the executive search field in March 1999, when it agreed to buy LAI Worldwide Inc., a firm based in New York City, for more than $80 million in stock. According to Joann S. Lublin of the *Wall Street Journal,* McKelvey told an interviewer, "We are [now] going to be a big player at the upper end ... starting with [college] internships running through the whole gamut ending with CEOs." LAI was merged with TASA Worldwide, TMP's executive search division, with Robert L. Pearson, LAI's chief executive officer, to run the operation jointly with Michael Squires, TASA's president.

During the first quarter of 1999, temporary contracts accounted for 30 percent of TMP Worldwide's sales; recruitment advertising for 24 percent; search and selection, 22 percent; Yellow Pages, 13 percent; and Monster.com, 11 percent. McKelvey indicated that the company name would probably be changed to TMP.com when the bulk of its revenue was coming from the Internet. He said that he believed recruitment advertisements, Yellow Pages ads, and executive searches eventually would converge on the Internet and that TMP wanted to acquire businesses promoting online advertisements to Yellow Pages advertisers.

Principal Subsidiaries

McKelvey Enterprises, Inc.; Worldwide Classified Inc.

Further Reading

Crum, Rex, "Monster of His Dreams," *Boston Business Journal,* November 6, 1998, p. 3.

Dougherty, Philip H., "A Yellow Pages Specialist," *New York Times,* May 29, 1980, p. D15.

Edwards, Paul L., "Exec Looks Forward to Yellow Pages Growth," *Advertising Age,* May 19, 1986, p. 74.

Gabriel, Frederick, "Stock Soars As Ad Firm Employs New Lines to Provide Growth," *Crain's New York Business,* June 2, 1997, p. 4.

Gault, Ylonda, "No Glamour, Just Gains," *Crain's New York Business,* September 5, 1994, pp. 3, 31.

Hodges, Jane, "IPO Provides TMP Chief with More Fuel for Growth," *Advertising Age,* January 6, 1997, p. 29.

Hyten, Todd, "Recruitment Ad Firms Sold to TMP Worldwide," *Boston Business Journal,* January 5, 1996, p. 3.

Kontzer, Tony, "Valley's 2nd-Largest Ad Shop Sold," *Business Journal-San Jose,* February 27, 1995, p. 1.

Kramli, Beth, "TMP Worldwide Announces Agreement to Acquire Austin," *Business Wire,* July 21, 1997.

Lublin, Joann S., "TMP Worldwide Agrees to Acquire Exec-Search Firm," *Wall Street Journal,* March 12, 1999, p. B2.

Pope, Hugh, "Yellow Pages Agency TMP Steps into Spotlight with Global Moves," *Wall Street Journal,* January 16, 1997, p. B11.

Schaff, William, "The Value of TMP's Monster," *Informationweek,* May 17, 1999, p. 154.

Schoettle, Anthony, "On-Line Employment Sites Search for Niche," *Indianapolis Business Journal,* October 26, 1998, p. 9A.

"U.S. Agency to Create Recruitment Ad Giant," *People Management,* August 7, 1997, p. 10.

—Robert Halasz

TNT Post Group N.V.

PO Box 13000
1100 KG Amsterdam
The Netherlands
(31) 20 500 60 00
Fax: (31) 20 500 70 00
Web site: http://www.tntpost-group.com

Public Company
Incorporated: 1752 as Statenpost
Employees: 101,582
Sales: NLG 16.33 billion (US$8.7 billion) (1998)
Stock Exchanges: Amsterdam Frankfurt London New York
Ticker Symbol: TPG
NAIC: 492210 Delivery Service; 491110 Postal Delivery
   Services

The Netherlands' TNT Post Group N.V. (TPG) is helping to redefine postal services. The first publicly traded postal service in the world, TPG offers mail, express mail, and logistics services on a worldwide basis. The combination of the former Dutch postal service and the express mail and logistics activities of TNT Worldwide has created the world's fourth largest mail services provider, behind Federal Express, UPS, and DHL, worth more than NLG 16 billion (nearly US$9 billion) in annual revenues. TPG's business activities include domestic mail services and direct mail services in The Netherlands; international mail and international express mail services, principally in Europe and Asia; and worldwide logistics operations with a focus on supply chain management. Formed from the breakup of the former Dutch postal and telecommunications monopoly, the PTT Nederland, TPG's shares joins sister company Royal KPN's shares on the Amsterdam, Frankfurt, London, and New York stock exchanges. The company is led by chairman and CEO A.J. Scheepbouwer.

Birth of a Postal System in the Mid-18th Century

The formation of The Netherlands' post office system coincided with the evolution of that country from a collection of loosely federated cities into a single national entity. Prior to the mid-18th century, each of the various cities operated their own postal services. The federalization of the region—which at one time included much of Belgium—into a more cohesive gathering of states under Stadhouder Willem III also encouraged the consolidation of the region's postal facilities. In the first half of the 18th century, ownership of postal services was transferred from a city level to a state level. In 1752 The Netherlands officially established a new postal service, called the Statenpost, which granted regional monopoly status to each of the state-run post offices.

The new entity placed the Dutch mail services on a more equal footing with the postal systems of other countries. It was not until the end of the 18th century that the Dutch postal services were reformed into a single, national system, modeling its organization after the system developed by the French. This system, officially established in 1799, provided the foundation of what would soon become known as the PTT Post.

The Dutch postal service inherited a variety of postal tariffs and collection and delivery methods. In 1807, however, the Post was placed under the administration of the Ministry of Finance. This body passed the country's first Postal Act, a series of regulations providing for a more standardized collection, carrying, and delivery system, while also establishing a single rate system—based on distance and weight—for the entire country. Yet the Post still was not conceived of as a public service; instead, it was expected to operate more along the lines of a tax collection service, providing funds for the national treasury.

A shift in the vision of The Netherlands' postal services came in the mid-19th century. The passage of the Postal Act of 1850 established the postal service as a service in the public interest. While remaining under the finance ministry, the Post shed its role as tax collector to become a public service. The Postal Act of 1850 further codified the postal service's domestic monopoly and created a simplified postal rate structure.

Two years later, the Post marked its entry into the modern era of postal services delivery, when it issued its first postage stamp. That same year also saw the institution of a nationally organized network of postal service facilities—now, every town received its own post office and a system was established for the collection and delivery of letters. The postman quickly became a national fixture, delivering mail as much as three times a day. The postal service rapidly extended its network of post offices. New services, including delivery of postcards and packages, also were introduced. By the 1870s, the Post's network of post offices covered most of the country.

A new communication technology would soon join the postal service. By the mid-1850s, The Netherlands had begun to install its first telegraph transmission networks. In 1852, the country formally organized its telegraph utility, the Rijkstelegraaf, under the Ministry of the Interior, which assumed responsibility for installing a roadside network of telegraph poles and cables. Use of the telegraph as a communication means remained relatively limited, however.

The postal system and the telegraph service, which was soon to add the newly invented telephone, operated as separate government agencies until the 1880s. Given the limited growth of the telegraph in The Netherlands, it was decided that the two services should be joined into one agency, under a single ministry in 1886. With the addition of telephone services, this agency would become known as the PTT (for Post, Telegraph, and Telephone) and remain a state-run monopoly for more than 100 years.

Separation in the 1990s

The combination of postal services with the country's telegraph and telephone systems was never wholeheartedly performed. Even though the two services were available through the same offices—the network of post offices created by the postal service—operations remained more or less separate, with each branch retaining its own personnel and culture. For the most part, the two services operated in parallel, each with its own personnel, budget, finances, and infrastructure.

The Depression era forced the PTT to modernize. Where mail previously had been sorted by hand, the government agency introduced mechanized systems, especially with the introduction of the Marchand Transorma, a machine capable of sorting mail to 400 different destinations, placed into service in 1931. A more efficient sorting system enabled the PTT to cut back on the number of its delivery rounds—instead of the three deliveries per day, PTT postmen now performed only two. This cutback produced still more economies, encouraging the PTT later to cut back the number of daily deliveries to one.

The economic climate presented another opportunity for the PTT, as the government allowed the agency to operate more and more as a commercial enterprise. Unlike other government agencies, which were provided for in the national budget, the PTT was given a more corporate status, enabling the company to make the necessary capital investments and take write-offs on its balance sheets, rather than to depend on government approval for each investment. The PTT also was given its own press and publicity departments, enabling the agency to compete for consumer attention. While most of Europe's postal services and telephone companies remained under government control, the PTT's relative independence allowed it to present a more modern appearance to consumers, who were treated also with original postal stamp designs.

The Nazi takeover of The Netherlands during World War II interrupted the PTT's independent activities, as the German occupier seized control of the country's communications systems as well. With the Liberation, the PTT was faced with rebuilding its telephone infrastructure. By the end of the 1940s, however, the agency was presenting heavy losses. In this way, the PTT was no different from most of its government-run counterparts in other countries.

The agency performed its first analysis of postal usage, identifying national traffic trends and postal processing rates. This analysis led to more cost-cutting steps, including the scaling back of the post office network, in which many of the smallest offices were closed and the number of daily deliveries was reduced, as a single daily delivery became standard. At the same time, the agency began raising its postage and telephone rates. Telephone services provided a means to maintain a positive balance sheet when the telephone quickly imposed itself as a mainstay in the postwar home. Yet the PTT's postal arm continued to represent a financial burden, in part because its personnel were considered civil servants and granted all of the benefits of this status.

By the late 1960s, the PTT was faced with the need for still more cost-cutting measures. The decision was made to reorganize operations, in particular, to consolidate sorting, culling, canceling, and other handling activities into larger-scale facilities. The process of concentration began in the 1960s and continued through the 1970s, with the opening of 18 "mail interchange" processing facilities. Advancements in automating, sorting, and handling systems enabled fewer processing centers to handle increasingly large volumes of mail. An important improvement in the PTT's mail system came with the introduction of the postal code (known as the zip code in the United States) in 1977. The four-digit, two-letter postal code system allowed automated equipment to sort mail down to the individual delivery round, whereas the previous system could only automate sorting to a citywide level. This improvement finally enabled the PTT to reduce its delivery schedule to a single delivery per day. The number of processing facilities could also be reduced, down to 12. The great volumes of mail being processed in these facilities enabled the PTT to operate at a profit.

Innovation also was coming to the telephone industry— soon to become known as the telecommunications industry. The use of telex equipment and facsimile machines, joined later by electronic messaging systems and Internet-based voice and video communication technology, as well as portable telephone systems freed of dependence on a physical telephone wiring system, threatened a drastic transformation of traditional communication systems. While the telephony industry was facing a time of great change, the postal world also was changing: the arrival of dedicated express mail and other courier services, led by such U.S. companies as Federal Express and United Parcel

Service and Australia's TNT, presented new challenges to traditional postal services.

The era of government-run, monopoly services had reached the beginning of the end. Restructuring was quickly becoming a necessity, not only to enable the PTT to compete in a rapidly transforming marketplace, but also to give the consumer more options—and potentially lower rates. During the 1980s, however, the PTT focused on expansion activities, buying up interests in domestic cable and television networks and moving toward international expansion of its telecommunications services. It was only in 1989 that the PTT was finally privatized.

In that year, the PTT was reorganized as a private business, PTT Nederland NV, under direction of CEO Wim Dik. In the new structure, the postal service, renamed PTT Post, joined its larger telecommunications industry sister company, PTT Telecom, as an independently operating subsidiary. Despite being no longer a government agency, the new PTT remained nonetheless wholly owned by the Dutch government. The change, however, allowed the company to pursue its own growth strategy into the 1990s, unhampered by the slower governmental decision-making process. Privatization also enabled the company to seek new international partners, some of which had balked at the prospect of pursuing projects with a government agency.

One such partnership was established in 1992, when PTT Post joined its time-sensitive mail and freight services with those of Australia's private TNT and the government-owned post offices of Canada, France, Germany, and Sweden in the partnership GD Express Worldwide (GDEW). TNT, which, since its founding in 1946 had expanded to become one of the world's top four express mail and freight delivery businesses, took on a 50 percent ownership of GDEW. Before long, PTT Post bought out GDEW's public post office partners, so that GDEW became a de facto joint venture with TNT.

Faced with the imperatives of the commercial business world, PTT Post, led by Ad Scheepbouwer, underwent a restructuring during the first half of the 1990s, reaching profitability as early as 1993. One important move PTT Post made was to franchise some 1,600 of its smaller post offices, while placing the others under a joint venture operation with the Postbank, a subsidiary of Internationale Nederlanden. The reorganization also led PTT Post to cut some 1,000 jobs. At the same time, the subsidiary began making its first expansion moves, buying up a number of small domestic and international courier and express mail delivery services. PTT Post also was making moves into a new area, that of logistics.

In 1994, PTT Nederland went to the stock market, as the Dutch government sold off some 30 percent of its shares on the Amsterdam stock exchange. The public listing of the post-telecommunications business marked the largest offering ever in The Netherlands and also was the world's first public listing of a post office. Interest was high in the shares; nonetheless, most investor attention went to PTT Telecom, nearly twice as large as the NLG 5 billion-per-year PTT Post. Two years later, PTT Nederland offered another 25 percent of its shares, effectively ending the Dutch government's control of the country's post and telecommunications services. At that time, PTT Nederland took listings on the New York, London, and Frankfurt stock exchanges as well.

The following year, PTT Post stepped out of the shadows of its larger sister company when it reached an agreement to acquire the struggling TNT for some NLG 2.7 billion. The purchase, which placed PTT Post roughly on the same revenue footing as PTT Telecom, set the stage for the next evolution of the former state-run monopoly. In 1998, PTT Nederland announced that it was splitting into two entirely independent, publicly listed companies: Royal KPN, which contained the company's telecommunications activities, and TNT Post Group (TPG), which took over the company's postal, logistics, and express mail services wing, including both companies' shares of the GDEW partnership. Both KPN and TPG retained listings on the Amsterdam, New York, London, and Frankfurt stock exchanges.

Among the first activities of the newly independent TPG was to reorganize its operations into two distinct units, PTT Post and TNT Worldwide, while shedding the noncore activities inherited from the TNT acquisition. The company also concentrated on the expansion of its mail handling facilities, including the opening of a state-of-the-art sorting facility in Liege, Belgium, an international road hub and depot in Duiven, The Netherlands, and the opening of six new Netherlands-based sorting facilities replacing the 12 facilities that had been in existence since the early 1980s. While expanding its infrastructure, TPG also continued consolidating its international presence, acquiring Jet Services, an express service based in France and operating throughout most of Europe, and in 1999 acquiring Italy's Tecnologistica, with logistics operations in Italy, France, and Germany.

TPG ended its first year as an independent company on the upswing. Not only had its operating revenues swelled to more than NLG 16 billion, with profits of more than NLG 820 million, but the company's PTT Post subsidiary received a new distinction, as it was granted the right to add the moniker Koninglijke (Royal) to its name. To commemorate the occasion, the Royal PTT Post issued a special postage stamp, marking its 200th anniversary. As one of the world's largest postal and express mail services, with a steadily building position in international logistics, TPG had taken center stage in a rapidly changing postal industry.

Principal Operating Units

Koninglijke PTT Post; TNT Worldwide.

Further Reading

Dickey, Allan, ''Public Services at Private Prices,'' *Eurobusiness,* March 1994, p. 57.
Echikson, William, ''Privatization: Posts with the Most,'' *Business Week,* August 17, 1998, p. 18.
——, ''This Postal Service Plans to Put Its Stamp on the World,'' *Business Week,* April 27, 1997, p. 19.
Hastings, Phillip, ''Rush to Repackage,'' *Financial Times,* June 17, 1999.
''Hitting the Mail on the Head,'' *The Economist,* April 30, 1994, p. 69.
Resener, Madeleine, ''How the Dutch Did It,'' *Institutional Investor,* April 1995, p. 66.
''TNT Sale May Signal Industry Trend,'' *Logistics Management,* January 1997, p. 26.
Woodford, Julian, ''KPN,'' *Utility Week,* January 23, 1998, p. 24.

—M. L. Cohen

Tweeter Home Entertainment Group, Inc.

10 Pequot Way
Canton, Massachusetts 02021
U.S.A.
(781) 830-3000
(800) 893-3837
Fax: (781) 830-3223)
Web site: http://www.twtr.com

Public Company
Incorporated: 1972 as New England Audio Company,
  Inc.
Employees: 1,400
Sales: $232.29 million (1998)
Stock Exchanges: NASDAQ
Ticker Symbol: TWTR
NAIC: 443112 Radio, Television & Other Electronics
  Stores

Tweeter Home Entertainment Group, Inc. owns five small chains of retail stores that sell video and audio equipment in the middle to high-end price range. Having grown from a single location called Tweeter, etc. into a chain of 19 stores, in 1996 the company began acquiring similar chains around the country with the goal of becoming a national retail presence. Tweeter went public in 1998 and has continued to grow since that time. The company's marketing strategy emphasizes competitive prices, knowledgeable staff, carefully designed store environments, and the placement of its outlets near electronics discount megastores like Best Buy and Circuit City. A key to Tweeter's success is its guarantee that if a lower price is advertised elsewhere within 30 days of a purchase, Tweeter will automatically mail a refund check directly to the customer.

Beginnings

Tweeter was founded in 1972 when Boston University dropout Sandy Bloomberg and his cousin Michael opened a stereo shop near the B.U. campus called Tweeter, etc. Sandy Bloom-

berg's original goal may have been simply "to meet girls" as he once put it, but the store was a success and expanded to other New England locations over the next few years. Tweeter, which took the corporate name of New England Audio Company, Inc., was helped in its growth by refinements that were taking place in home stereo gear in the early and mid-1970s. The company developed a reputation for selling the higher-end brands of audio equipment and offering a well-trained and friendly staff. In the early 1980s Tweeter experienced further growth when it capitalized on the home video boom, with VCRs and camcorders leading the way. The company also was selling and installing car stereo equipment. By 1986 there were 13 Tweeter, etc. stores.

The late 1980s saw Tweeter's revenues begin to drop as sales for more expensive home audio and video equipment slowed and competition from cut-price chains became strong. In 1990 the company hired Jeff Stone, an executive vice-president for Bread & Circus supermarkets, to take the positions of president and chief operating officer. Stone's services had been sought for some time by Sandy Bloomberg, and he was finally hooked with the offer of an equity stake in the company. Stone quickly took action to improve Tweeter's situation—securing loans, trimming staff, training store managers to better understand their roles in the business as a whole, and updating Tweeter's corporate strategy. He directed the company to set clear-cut future goals, something it had not done previously.

Despite the positive changes Stone had implemented, Tweeter's sales were still being hurt by the general perception that its prices were too high. In 1993 senior Tweeter management met in Vermont at a special retreat to mull over the company's problems and work out solutions to them. They looked at customer surveys that showed that the public gave the company good marks for its quality of merchandise, knowledgeable staff, and first-rate service department, but still considered price the most important factor in deciding where to shop. To address this, the executives came up with Tweeter's Automatic Price Protection guarantee. Although the company had already been refunding the price difference to anyone whose purchase was advertised cheaper elsewhere, this required the customer to spot the ad and bring it in to Tweeter for a refund. The program took this to a new level: Tweeter would monitor

Company Perspectives:

Tweeter Home Entertainment Group is a specialty consumer electronics retailer whose niche is in the better quality audio, video and mobile electronics product categories. Our differentiation in the marketplace is created through the quality of our product offerings and is a result of our totally customer focused and customer friendly organization.

We are dedicated to providing our customers with a unique shopping experience through unparalleled customer service, a professional, thoroughly knowledgeable and friendly sales force and through state of the art store environments.

its competitors' local ads and automatically issue refund checks to customers when a product was advertised for less within 30 days of a purchase. The company even included its own advertisements in the plan.

The program was started in August 1993 and was a rapid success. Some critics pointed out that Tweeter's higher-end product mix did not especially overlap with the widely advertised wares of "entry-level" audio/video retailers like Circuit City, Lechmere, Nobody Beats the Wiz, and others, but the company maintained that 75 percent of its inventory also was sold by these competitors. Tweeter was able to offer reasonable prices in part because it belonged to a cooperative of small audio retailers who purchased goods from wholesalers in bulk and thus obtained better prices than each could individually. The company expected the increased sales volume generated by interest in the new policy to far outweigh revenue losses from the automatic refunds. Tweeter had been issuing $3,000 to $4,000 in refunds monthly through its previous program, and it anticipated this figure to roughly double. Within the next three years the company issued more than 30,000 checks, most for $20 or less.

In conjunction with the automatic refunds, Tweeter cut back on newspaper advertising and increased its television and radio promotions, budgeting $500,000 for publicity in the months following the start of the refund program. The company's fortunes were buoyed by the price guarantee plan, the rebounding U.S. economy, and consumer demand for new products like home theater systems. Tweeter remained focused on home and mobile audio/video gear, choosing not to sell computers and telecommunications equipment like many of its larger competitors.

Growth in the Mid-1990s

The company had held steady at 13 stores between 1986 and 1993, but now began to expand again, opening its 14th and 15th outlets by August 1994. That year saw record revenues of $43.5 million, up from $35 million in 1993 and $25 million in 1990. This occurred despite the entry in early 1993 of "big box" electronics retailer Circuit City into the New England market. Tweeter was better able to fend off this destabilizing influence than low-end electronics retailers such as Fretter, Lechmere, and Nobody Beats the Wiz, given its significantly differentiated and

higher-margin product lineup. Within several years both Fretter and Lechmere would be belly-up, while Tweeter kept on expanding, boasting 18 locations in Massachusetts, Rhode Island, Connecticut, and New Hampshire by the summer of 1995.

The company paid special attention to the design of its stores. A newly opened Tweeter outlet in Boston featured a turquoise facade, a split-level purple, blue, and turquoise interior with surround-sound and home-theater listening rooms, and other specially designed areas for display of large-screen televisions and outdoor listening systems. The 7,000-square-foot store had cost an estimated $500,000 to set up. In early 1996 the company opened a new store in Burlington, Massachusetts as a cooperative venture with music retailer Strawberries. Both companies' outlets shared a common interior space while maintaining separate outside entrances.

In May 1996 Tweeter's parent company purchased the 13-store electronics retail chain Bryn Mawr Stereo & Video, based in King of Prussia, Pennsylvania. Bryn Mawr, founded in 1965, offered knowledgeable service and much the same product mix as Tweeter and had stores in Pennsylvania, Maryland, Delaware, and New Jersey. Just prior to the $8.7 million acquisition, Bryn Mawr also had begun to offer Tweeter's automatic refund program. New England Audio announced that both chains would be expanding, opening as many as 20 new stores within three years. Tweeter intended to enter both Maine and upstate New York as part of this plan. Company executives expected to boost Bryn Mawr's per-store sales dramatically, as they stood at less than half what the company was achieving at Tweeter. Bryn Mawr sales staff were to be retrained, and advertising was to shift to broadcast, rather than print, media. Results were swift, with Bryn Mawr sales jumping 37 percent in the first full quarter of New England Audio Company ownership. Tweeter management felt that the time was right to pursue such acquisitions, as the owners of many small chains of stereo shops founded in the 1960s and early 1970s were reaching an age at which they were considering selling out and retiring.

In 1997 New England Audio made its second acquisition, this time buying the Atlanta, Georgia-based HiFi Buys chain. HiFi Buys' ten stores were larger, at about 15,000 square feet versus 7,000 for Tweeter, and focused more on lower-priced products. New England Audio announced that it would shift the chain's merchandise toward Tweeter's and Bryn Mawr's more expensive mix, institute the same automatic price difference refund guarantee, and again favor broadcast advertising over print. HiFi Buys would retain its name. The $19.7 million purchase put the combined total of stores among the three chains at 45, Tweeter having opened three new outlets since the Bryn Mawr acquisition. Funding for this growth had come from the private equity market, where the company had gone first in late 1995. Some $37 million had been raised by this method.

1998: Initial Public Offering and More Acquisitions

Seeking further capital for expansion, the company made an initial public offering of stock on the NASDAQ in July 1998. It put 2.7 million shares on the market and raised $46 million, some of which went to the investors who had funded earlier acquisitions. New England Audio Company's name was changed to Tweeter Home Entertainment Group, Inc. in the process. Revenues for 1998 increased to $232 million from the previous year's $132 million, with consolidated income from HiFi Buys stores accounting for much of the increase. Same store sales also grew companywide by 12.5 percent. Tweeter was expecting further revenue growth to be spurred by DVD video disc players and digital television sets. Tweeter, etc. had been the first chain to sell the latter, and the company anticipated an explosion in sales as high-definition digital broadcasting made older televisions obsolete over the next ten years. The company also took a stand against the DIVX video disc format in which Circuit City had invested, refusing to stock DIVX players in its stores. The company's position was validated by the marketplace when in 1999 Circuit City announced that it was abandoning DIVX, killing the controversial rent-with-the-option-to-buy digital movie format. Tweeter did not necessarily consider such giants as Circuit City and Best Buy to be its enemies, however. It was company policy to locate new stores near these less service-oriented, entry-level stores, with the expectation that many customers would be drawn away from them by Tweeter's better-trained staff, higher-quality goods, and automatic price-difference refund guarantee.

In February 1999 Tweeter finalized its next acquisition, spending $8.2 million to buy Home Entertainment of Texas, Inc. Home Entertainment had seven stores, four in Houston and three in the Dallas area, and Tweeter anticipated enlarging and adding to the chain's locations. The purchase had come about in part because Tweeter and Home Entertainment management had become acquainted through meetings of their common buying cooperative.

Tweeter expanded further westward just a few months later when it acquired DOW Stereo/Video Inc. of San Diego, California. DOW operated nine stores that focused more on the lower end of the market, and Tweeter intended to upgrade DOW's product mix to match the rest of its subsidiaries. The company also planned to relocate and remodel several of DOW's stores and eventually expand the chain to Orange County. DOW had annual sales of $38 million, and analysts considered it a bargain for the $5.5 million Tweeter had paid. Company executives announced that Tweeter had now finished its first round of acquisitions and would focus on fully integrating the new chains into its corporate structure before making further purchases. By July 1999 the company had a total of 73 stores in 13 states and expected to open as many as 24 more within the next fiscal year. In August Tweeter announced the formation of a joint venture with Cyberian Outpost, Inc. to market electronics products on the Internet.

As Tweeter neared the end of its third decade in business, the company's successful combination of guaranteed low prices, knowledgeable sales staff, and carefully designed and located stores were propelling it to success in every market it entered. The introduction of digital television, digital video discs, and the still growing home theater market also were helping to fuel its growth. The company's track record was solid, its management was seasoned, and its prospects for continued success looked bright.

Principal Subsidiaries

Tweeter, etc.; Bryn Mawr Stereo & Video; HiFi Buys; Home Entertainment of Texas; DOW Stereo/Video.

Further Reading

Donker, Peter P., "Tweeter Confident in Auburn Site," *Telegram & Gazette* (Worcester, Mass.), March 16, 1999, p. E1.

Drummond, Mike, "DOW Stereo/Video Being Sold to Tweeter of Massachusetts," *San Diego Union-Tribune*, May 19, 1999, p. C1.

Goldgaber, Arthur, "Electronics Chain Caters to Technophiles," *Investor's Business Daily,* December 28, 1998.

Hyten, Todd, "Tweeter, Etc. Going Public in Two Years," *Boston Business Journal*, May 26, 1995, p. 3.

——, "Tweeter, Strawberries Combine Stores in Burlington," *Boston Business Journal*, February 2, 1996, p. 3.

Lunt, Dean, " 'It's Yours to Fix'—Retail Tactics Hit Right Note," *Patriot Ledger* (Quincy, Mass.), July 27, 1996, p. 21.

——, "Tweeter Etc. Parent Buys PA-Based Stereo Chain," *Patriot Ledger* (Quincy, Mass.), May 17, 1996, p. 26.

McCloy, Andrew P., "Tweeter Etc. Parent Company Acquires Atlanta-Based HiFi Buys," *Boston Business Journal*, March 14, 1997, p. 3.

Nutile, Tom, "You Really Can't Beat These Prices," *Boston Herald*, August 17, 1993, p. 1.

Reidy, Chris, "Sound Strategy—With Plans to Acquire Texas Firm, Tweeter Continues Push to Become National Audio, Video Electronics Player," *Boston Globe*, December 10, 1998, p. B16.

——, "Tweeter Still Sound," *Boston Globe,* August 15, 1994, p. 16.

Scally, Robert, "Tweeter Enters California As Best Buy Expands There," *Discount Store News*, June 7, 1999.

Sit, Mary, "Tweeter Etc. Offers Price Protection Program," *Boston Globe,* August 17, 1993, p. 35.

Syre, Steven, and Charles Stein, "Huge Appetite for Retail Stocks Propels Tweeter," *Boston Globe,* March 2, 1999, p. D5.

"Tweeter to Pull DIVX from DOW," *Consumer Multimedia Report,* May 31, 1999.

—Frank Uhle

UL Underwriters Laboratories Inc.®

Underwriters Laboratories, Inc.

333 Pfingsten Road
Northbrook, Illinois 60062-2096
U.S.A.
(847) 272-8800
Fax: (847) 272-8129
Web site: http://www.ul.com

Nonprofit Company
Incorporated: 1901
Employees: 5,258
Sales: $351.5 million (1997)
NAIC: 541380 Testing Laboratories (Except Medical,
    Veterinary)

Underwriters Laboratories, Inc. (UL) and its subsidiaries around the world evaluate products, materials, and systems for safety and compliance with U.S. and foreign standards. In 1998, more than 14 billion UL Marks appeared on new products worldwide. The UL staff has developed more than 600 Standards for Safety, 80 percent of which are approved as American National Standards. Testing and service fees from clients support the independent, not-for-profit organization.

A Testing Laboratory: 1894–1904

At the 1893 World's Columbian Exposition in Chicago, people flocked to the Palace of Electricity. They stared awestruck at the dazzle created by 100,000 Edison light bulbs. Chicago fire insurance authorities were more concerned about the fires that kept breaking out, igniting the cheap jute covering the structure. Were they caused by the network of electric wires and hook-ups, by this new "alternating current"? Why were the new fire alarm systems having such problems? They turned to William Henry Merrill, an electrical inspector, to help them.

Merrill set up a laboratory near the fairgrounds, above Fire Insurance Patrol Station Number One. The lab's mission was to increase fire prevention by testing new electrical devices that could cause fires and investigating everything that affected the spread of a fire. According to *This Inventive Century*, UL's

centennial publication, the one room held "a bench, table, chairs and a few electrical measuring devices purchased for the grand sum of $350." With the financial support of the Chicago Board of Fire Underwriters and the Western Insurance Association, the lab became the Underwriter's Electrical Bureau.

Merrill's first test was conducted on an asbestos paper used as an insulation material, which the manufacturer claimed was nonabsorbent and noncombustible. The lab's report, issued on March 24, 1984, found, in fact, that the paper did absorb water, but could not be made to burn. Although not appropriate as insulation, it was fire resistant. In the lab's first year, Merrill and his staff of two completed 75 tests; in the first five years, they performed 1,000 tests—checking sockets, switches, wires, and a variety of supposedly noncombustible materials. In 1898 they published the first list of "approved fittings and electrical devices," including flexible electrical cord and a snap light fixture. The approved products also received distinctive labels, indicating they had been inspected and certified free from reasonable safety hazards by Underwriters Laboratories. Thus was born the UL Mark.

In 1900 the lab moved into larger quarters, and in 1901 it was chartered in Illinois as Underwriters Laboratories, Inc., taking its name from its new sponsor, the National Board of Fire Underwriters. Its purpose, according to the charter, was "to maintain laboratories for the testing of appliances and to enter into contracts with the owners and manufacturers of such appliances respecting the recommendation thereof to insurance organizations."

In 1903 the National Board appropriated money to build a fireproof building north of the Chicago River, which would serve as UL's home for the next 75 years. That same year, the Laboratories began fire performance testing on wire windows and fire doors, moving beyond fittings and electrical devices, and UL wrote its very first Standard, "Tin Clad Fire Doors and Shutters." The company's early motto was "Fire is servant, not master," and in 1904 UL approved its first automatic fire sprinkler.

Testing Consumer Products for Safety: 1905–26

By 1905, UL had a budget of $300,000 and had published 7,500 reports. That year, UL issued its first label for a fire extinguisher and Merrill expanded his lab's services beyond simple testing of products. To ensure that the ''listed'' fire extinguisher continued to meet safety requirements, he initiated regular inspections at the manufacturer's plant. That practice soon was widened to include follow-up, onsite inspection of all approved consumer products. By 1907, UL inspectors were operating in 67 cities.

The beginning of the 20th century saw the introduction of a huge variety of new electrical appliances. UL listed the ''Autophone,'' a motor-driven phonograph with a $\frac{1}{6}$ horsepower motor in 1907, and the first ''modern'' vacuum cleaner in 1909. Some inventions failed UL tests for years until one finally was safe and durable enough to meet UL's requirements. An electric iron was introduced in 1912 and became very popular. But the early models frequently started fires when the current was on. Not until 1926, after rigorous, reasonable testing of the Steam-O-Matic, which had an automatic temperature control, did UL list its first flat iron. In 1913 UL tested the first security devices and replaced the word ''approved'' with ''Listed'' and ''Inspected.'' For consumer products, UL testing focused on three basic questions: What is the shock hazard? What is the fire hazard? What is the danger of physical injury? By testing for safety, UL helped allay public suspicions and fears of electricity.

Testing Building Materials, Airplanes, Automobiles, and Other Risky Things: 1906–20s

The 1906 San Francisco earthquake, which destroyed 25,000 buildings, served to further expand UL's activities, as UL helped the National Board of Fire Underwriters to develop building codes. UL also helped develop early National Electrical codes, and its engineers would help establish, and its research would be used by, numerous industry councils to develop safety codes. UL sought to help determine to what standards materials should be held. In the process, its engineers explored how a fire behaved, how fast a building would burn, and what effect a major fire would have on the structure and materials. To find those answers, it created massive furnaces.

In 1907 UL began testing roofing materials, directing the flames from 36 burners on a mock-up of a complete roof and dropping red hot discs on the material. Most roofs at that time were made of wooden shingles, but in 1916 UL gave a time rating for three kinds of roofing. In 1924 tests began on a new roofing material: asphalt.

In 1910 testing began on building columns, which were becoming important factors in building construction as more of the new skyscrapers were erected. A 1919 report presented landmark findings on the effect of fire on building columns, and the following year UL's Standard Time-Temperature Curve became

a U.S. standard. That curve made it possible to give a fire rating to just about every type of construction. Also in 1920, UL began testing floors and ceilings, using two new horizontal test furnaces. In 1922 UL introduced the 25-foot-long Steiner Tunnel to determine how fast a controlled flame spreads. During ten-minute tests, engineers were able to calculate the surface burning characteristics of different products, and the Steiner Tunnel set its own standard as a testing mechanism.

Twenty-two years after establishing his lab, Merrill became the organization's first president who was a full-time UL employee. This occurred when UL became self-sustaining from the income generated by the testing fees paid by manufacturers and direct support from the insurance industry ceased. Merrill quickly established industry councils for burglary protection, casualty, electrical products, and fire protection to develop safety codes.

That same year, UL went international, opening an inspection office in London to check British products being exported to the United States. Over the next 80 years, UL would open more foreign inspection offices and develop partnerships with certifiers in other countries, ensuring that products coming into the United States met U.S. safety standards.

From safety matches (1908) to gasoline pumps (1911) to auto safety glass (1914) and locks (1915) to wooden ladders (1915) and x-ray machines (1915), UL tested and certified products beyond the direct danger of fire and electricity. In the early 1920s, UL tested and registered airplanes, issuing air worthiness certificates to 35 private and commercial planes (including a seaplane). Those certificates were required to get insurance. For two years (1921–23) UL also registered and ''Marked'' pilots. One example from the UL ''Rules of the Air'' registered pilots had to follow was: ''Airplanes shall always give way to balloons and airships whether fixed or free.'' UL's efforts helped support the establishment of the Civil Aeronautics Board in 1923, as the federal government assumed responsibility (and regulation) of air safety.

Also during the 1920s UL engineers continued to work with automobile manufacturers to test the parts that went into cars, from headlights to fuel systems to steering wheel locks. By 1924, UL had tested 700 automobiles. In 1923 Merrill died, and Dana Pierce became president. Pierce was president for 12 years and continued to expand the organization. UL opened a lab and office on the West Coast and another lab in Illinois, which tested high explosives and toxic gases. Consumer products Listed during Pierce's tenure included the first hot-water heater for home use, several coffee percolators, portable electric saws and drills, the Pianola player piano, waffle irons, and electric dishwashers, heating pads, and fans. UL also tested the first household refrigerators, issued the first radio Standard, and increased its work with electric motors and safes and vaults.

Continued Growth: 1930s–60s

Alvah Small became UL's third president in 1935, and the following year UL re-incorporated as a nonprofit corporation in Delaware. Small introduced a fleet of mobile labs, using specially equipped cars, to test products in the field. In 1941 UL began formal testing of the combustibility of plastics. With the introduction of engineered plastics in 1957, this became a major research area for the organization.

During World War II, UL tested fireplace flues and vents for temporary wartime housing and developed systems for protecting windows from bomb explosions. In 1948 Curtis Wellborn was named president. He oversaw a major expansion program, opening new facilities in Northbrook, Illinois, and Santa Clara, California, and initiating new international activities. These included the testing of European-made products in testing centers in Europe with follow-up onsite inspections.

In 1954 UL won a landmark Internal Revenue Service decision upholding its nonprofit status. Although the issue continued to be raised periodically in future decades, the decision that UL was a nonprofit organization testing for public safety has not been overturned.

One area of intensive testing during the early 1950s was televisions and their imploding picture tubes. UL had received the first submittals of TVs for testing in 1939 and, after the war, many more appeared on the scene. UL worked with manufacturers to develop protective shields and glass laminates so that the picture tube glass would not shatter. Televisions also were tested for radiation, the temperature of control knobs, overheating, stability, and durability. The latter test involved putting a 50-pound weight on the top of the set and checking that the television still operated properly. TVs earned the Mark only after passing more than 45 tests.

The introduction of new types of office machines posed new safety concerns. In 1953 UL Listed the first mainframe computer and in 1955 it certified the printed wiring (circuit) board. In 1959 UL Listed the Xerox 914 copier, which churned out six copies a minute. That year, Merwin Brandon became the organization's fifth president and UL continued to grow. In 1967 UL helped establish the Consumer Advisory Council.

In the fire protection area, UL continued to monitor and inspect fire hoses, extinguishers, and sprinkler heads. It tested and Listed smoke detectors, issuing the first Standard in 1960. The organization also began certifying that fire pumpers delivered a stream of water at 1,000 gallons a minute and would not tip when a full crew of firefighters was on board. In 1985 UL again turned to a fleet of mobile labs to test aerial and ground ladders on fire trucks.

Boats and Foreign Subsidiaries: 1970s–80s

UL established its Marine Department in 1970, which became the recognized testing agency for the U.S. Coast Guard. UL began testing the buoyancy and strength of life vests in 1971 and soon moved to boats, testing some 210 types of components, from hull arrangement to lights to fuel lines.

The 1970s saw the first Standard for automatic garage door openers (1973), as well as the Listing of video game systems and videotape recorders (1975), microwave ovens (1977), the personal computer (1978), and the automatic teller machine (1979). One ATM test ensured that a skilled burglar using sophisticated tools could not penetrate an ATM within 15 minutes. Also in 1979, UL Listed the electronic grocery scanner, its

first effort at evaluating lasers, and moved its headquarters from Chicago to Northbrook.

During the 1980s, UL issued its 500th Standard, the first separate Standard for telephone equipment, and opened the first UL-operated inspection centers outside the United States. Its international activities continued to grow with its Far East subsidiaries, UL International Ltd. and UL International Services, Ltd., responsible for testing products in Hong Kong and Taiwan. UL also helped companies meet international quality assurance standards by introducing an ISO (International Organization for Standardization) 9000 Registration program.

An Increasingly Global Presence: The 1990s

In 1990 Tom Castino became UL's eighth president and accelerated the organization's shift from being the provider of the U.S. national product safety mark to becoming, in his words, "the leading provider of worldwide product certification and management system registration services." Instead of concentrating primarily on ensuring that products coming into the United States met UL and U.S. safety standards, Castino wanted to focus on developing a high level of global acceptance so that manufacturers with plants in various countries would be able to more easily test for UL Listings and/or certification by other countries' authorities.

In 1993 UL received accreditation as a certification organization by the Standards Council of Canada. Now UL could test and certify to Canadian standards and codes for products sold in Canada, not just for those exported to the United States. UL established a special UL Mark for Canada. That same year, the organization created a new subsidiary in Japan to provide more service to its Japanese customers. By 1994, more than one-third of UL activity represented work for clients outside the United States.

UL entered into strategic agreements with foreign testing and certification organizations, making it possible for UL to conduct a single set of tests after which a product could receive certification for the United States, France, Brazil, or Mexico. In Asia, the Hong Kong laboratory of UL International Ltd. gained accreditation by the China National Accreditation Committee for Laboratories, and in the United Kingdom, UL's subsidiary received accreditation by the United Kingdom Accreditation Service. In Denmark, UL bought the Danish national testing and certification organization, Demko, when the government moved to privatize state-owned enterprises. In 1998 UL organized itself on a geographic business unit basis to provide local, full service around the globe.

But the focus on global acceptance did not mean that UL had stopped its efforts at home to meet the safety demands of emerging technologies. The organization established its first U.S. subsidiary, EMC Technology Services, Inc., to address the product design phases and testing needs of electromagnetic compatibility compliance (EMC). UL built additional testing chambers and acquired C&C Laboratory, Inc., a California-based EMC testing and services company, and made it part of the new subsidiary.

In 1999 UL expanded its monitoring services to include Internet privacy, with the Better Business Bureaus hiring UL to monitor compliance with the BBBOnline privacy seal program. UL also developed a new service to test and recognize software components and worked on the development of the 1998 Standard for Software in Programmable Components, which included requirements for the functioning of operating systems and application software.

For more than 105 years, from insulation to the Internet, Underwriters Laboratories, Inc. helped to make a safer world. Despite the introduction of more complex materials, systems, and products, it continued to follow William Merrill's principles: "Know by test, and state the facts. Testing for Public Safety. Our only function is to serve, not to profit."

Principal Subsidiaries

UL International Ltd. (Hong Kong); UL International Services, Ltd. (Taiwan); UL International Services, Ltd. (Singapore); UL Japan Co., Ltd.; Demko A/S (Denmark); UL de Mexico, S.A. de C.V.; UL India Private Ltd.; UL International Italia S.r.l.; UL International (U.K.) Ltd.; EMC Technology Services, Inc.

Further Reading

"About UL—Who We Are and What We Do," Underwriters Laboratories Inc., 1999, http://www.ul.com/about/index.html.

"After ISO 9000," *Electronic Business Buyer,* October 1994, p. 48.

"Better Business Bureaus Hire Underwriters Labs," *American Banker,* August 18, 1999, p. 18.

Bezane, Norm, *This Inventive Century: The Incredible Journey of Underwriters Laboratories 1894–1994,* Northbrook, Ill.: Underwriters Laboratories Inc., 1994.

Flock, Jeff, "UL Safety Labs Celebrates 100th Anniversary," Cable News Network, Transcript #211-4, March 26, 1994.

Ritter, Jim, "Test Fires Help UL Plan for the Real Thing," *Chicago Sun-Times,* October 8, 1996, p. 11.

Sutton, Larry, "Safety Stamp Born in L.I. Lab," *Daily News* (New York), December 15, 1996, p. 1.

"UL Acquires Danish Demko," *Flame Retardancy News,* August, 1996.

"UL Launches Software Component Recognition Program," *M2 Presswire,* August 10, 1999.

"A World of Difference Between UL 'Listed' and UL 'Registered'," *Code Authority,* Underwriters Laboratories Inc., 1997, http://www.ul.com/auth/tca/v6n1/difference.htm.

—Ellen D. Wernick

United Defense, L.P.

1525 Wilson Boulevard, Suite 700
Arlington, Virginia 22209-2411
U.S.A.
(703) 312-6100
Fax: (703) 312-6148
Web site: http://www.uniteddefense.com

Wholly Owned Subsidiary of Iron Horse, Investors,
  L.L.C.
Incorporated: 1994 as United Defense, L.P.
Employees: 5,400
Sales: $1.22 billion (1998)
NAIC: 336992 Armored Military Vehicles & Parts
  Manufacturing

United Defense, L.P. manufactures armored vehicles for U.S. and allied military forces. Its armored troop carriers and medium/light tracked combat vehicles are generally fabricated out of aluminum. The company also manufactures naval missile launchers and guns. United Defense has operations in 15 states and six foreign countries.

Origins

One of the antecedents of United Defense, L.P., Food Machinery Corporation (FMC), was a maker of agricultural equipment that began defense work in 1941, when it built the first amphibious landing craft for the U.S. Marines.

Over the years FMC produced some of the most enduring military equipment, such as the M113 Armored Personnel Carrier, used by the Army since the 1960s. The Navy became a client, purchasing the Mk45 naval gun system, which would be in use for another 40 years.

The M109 Self-Propelled Howitzer, the most widely used field artillery vehicle, was introduced in 1974. During the 1970s the company began developing the Bradley Fighting Vehicle, a troop carrier/fighting vehicle, which began production in 1981.

FMC's rival BMY Combat Systems, a unit of Harsco Corp., began upgrading the Army's Paladin howitzers in 1991. After the cost for each vehicle tripled, the Army awarded a new production contract to FMC Corporation.

Consolidation in the 1990s

A wave of consolidation swept through the defense industry in the 1990s. Between 1993 and 1997, there were 20 mergers among large defense contractors. The Pentagon encouraged this trend as a means of saving costs.

FMC's flagship product, the Bradley, was not well received overseas, which left the company vulnerable when the U.S. Department of Defense halved its annual orders to 200 vehicles per year, which it had been buying at a cost of $1 million each. FMC began planning its exit from the business. Defense sales accounted for a quarter of FMC's 1993 sales and 43 percent of income.

Harsco Corp., based in Camp Hill, Pennsylvania, also wanted to rely less on defense. It subsequently made a major metals acquisition. FMC and Harsco began discussing the possibility of merging their defense businesses in 1992. Their joint venture, United Defense, L.P., was formed in January 1994 out of FMC's Defense Systems Group and Harsco's BMY Combat Systems Division. FMC held a 60 percent stake in the new company; Harsco, 40 percent.

The deal reduced the number of combat vehicle makers to two: United Defense, maker of aluminum troop carriers, and General Dynamics, which specialized in tanks made of steel. Harsco brought lean and flexible manufacturing capabilities to FMC's technical expertise. Not included in the joint venture was a separate Harsco division which made trucks for the Army.

United Defense was based in Arlington, Virginia, and started with about 6,000 employees. It had annual sales of $1.6 billion in 1996, of which its armament systems division contributed $400 million a year. Parent FMC Corporation employed 17,000 people worldwide in its Performance Chemicals, Industrial Chemicals, and Machinery and Equipment divisions.

Besides pushing for consolidation, the Pentagon encouraged cooperation among competing firms. United Defense began

Company Perspectives:

Our vision is to protect freedom worldwide by supporting U.S. and Allied security needs.

To make this vision a reality, United Defense will provide soldiers, sailors, airmen, and marines with the finest combat capability in the world. We will focus on serving six major markets: Combat Vehicle Systems, Fire Support, Combat Support Vehicle Systems, Weapons Delivery Systems, Amphibious Assault Vehicles, and Combat Support Services.

producing missile launchers in cooperation with Lockheed Martin. United Defense provided the mechanical systems while Lockheed Martin created the electronics. In 1997, United was granted a $1 billion contract to develop the Crusader field artillery system in collaboration with General Dynamics. The project originally involved another two contractors.

Iraq's Russian and French artillery outperformed that of the U.S. Army during the Persian Gulf War, although the United States had more advanced missiles, tanks, and helicopters. The Crusader was designed to fire faster and farther than existing U.S. artillery pieces—ten rounds per minute to 25 miles. Crusader was fully automated, not dependent on the numerous manual tasks traditionally associated with firing artillery. Like the M109A6 Paladin, the Crusader used two vehicles—one carrying the gun plus an ammunition carrier.

Business was scarce for surviving defense firms. The *Wall Street Journal* reported that in the ten years since 1987, a quarter of the country's four million defense jobs were eliminated. United Defense employed 5,700 at ten sites in 1997. Its Minnesota plant employed 1,600 in 1997, half its mid-1980s level. Union manufacturing jobs were cut by 75 percent, to under 500. The Crusader program brought 250 mostly engineering jobs.

United Defense lost a multibillion-dollar contract to produce amphibious assault vehicles for the Marine Corps, a longtime client for whom FMC had developed the concept between the wars. The setback signaled to FMC executives it was time to leave the business entirely and concentrate on its core strengths of herbicides, insecticides, and food additives.

New Owners in 1997

FMC and Harsco began looking for bids in May 1997. By the summer of 1997, defense contractor General Dynamics and investors The Carlyle Group were vying to purchase United Defense from FMC and Harsco. General Dynamics offered $1 billion but raised antitrust flags since this deal would have left it the only armored vehicle manufacturer in the country. General Dynamics officials countered that the market was so small this was allowable, and the company could save taxpayers money by consolidating operations. In addition, despite its calls for cooperation and consolidation, the Pentagon preferred to have at least two sources for military equipment to ensure supplies in wartime.

FMC and Harsco ultimately accepted a lower offer from Carlyle, indicating their unease with the prospect of an antitrust fight from Republican Senator Arlen Specter, whose home state Pennsylvania would have lost jobs in the event of a United Defense/General Dynamics merger. In October 1997, through its Iron Horse subsidiary, Carlyle acquired United Defense, L.P. from FMC and Harsco for $880 million, later adjusted to $863.9 million.

Carlyle intended to grow the business, then either sell it or hold a public offering, typical of its modus operandi. (Interestingly, it had already bought and sold the electronics division of rival bidder General Dynamics.) Carlyle was an investment trust formed in 1987. It owned a dozen other companies at the time of the acquisition, including several defense firms. (Holdings included waste recycler GTS Duratek Inc. and Baker & Taylor, a major book distributor.) Its properties had combined annual sales of $5 billion.

Carlyle's chairman, Frank C. Carlucci, had been Secretary of Defense under Ronald Reagan and was also a director at General Dynamics. The firm stated Carlucci had separated himself from involvement in the bidding process to avoid a conflict of interest. Carlyle specialized in undervalued companies affected by changes in government policy. According to the *Washington Post,* between 1990 and 1996, Carlyle averaged annual returns of more than 32 percent.

After the acquisition, sales and profits fell at United Defense due to fewer domestic and foreign shipments. Some aspects of United Defense's business, such as U.S. government contract work and the Crusader program, showed improvement. Gross profits were $59.2 million on sales of $1.22 billion in 1998. Exports accounted for $230.3 million of sales in 1998, up from $89.1 million in 1997.

The Future of Defense Procurement: 2000 and Beyond

After experiencing some quality problems in the late 1980s, United Defense set out to systematically improve its communications with suppliers. By the late 1990s, this resulted in more dependable and better quality deliveries and made the company's own receiving and inspection operations more efficient. On the design side, Electronic Product Definition software allowed United Defense to link its engineers around the world. Only the newest software could handle the complexity of the company's products, whose parts numbered in the tens of thousands.

Simulation-based acquisition took communications between Army purchasers and defense contractors to a new level. Simulation Modeling for Acquisition, Requirements and Training (SMART) was a joint Army/industry plan for reducing development costs. This concept integrated industry and government product development teams (IPTs). The new level of cooperation introduced soldiers into the development process and allowed trainers to be trained before systems were deployed. United Defense president and CEO Tom Rabaut pressed for more commonality among systems in various projects and more reuse and interoperability of components.

Rabaut warned of two obstacles to advancement in military technology. He complained the low burden of proof of the new Civil False Claims Act (a new law to encourage whistle-blowers) scared technology entrepreneurs away from defense contracts, ultimately denying the Army the opportunity to bene-fit from the latest innovations. Rabaut also found it alarming that the U.S. Department of Defense seemed to be moving in a socialistic direction, while other industries across the world were becoming more privatized. He was referring to depots in particular, where the Defense Department maintained its own equipment. He argued this work should be in the private sector, since so little new equipment was being purchased.

The Bradley Fighting Vehicle was no longer in production at the end of the century, but BFV derivatives were and United Defense was upgrading existing vehicles. The company was also busy developing the next generation Crusader Field Artil-lery System, designed to replace the M109A6 Paladin, and was hoping to land a $20 billion Crusader production contract in 2000. The company was also developing a Composite Armor Vehicle and a Grizzly minefield-breaching vehicle.

Principal Subsidiaries

FMC-Arabia (Saudi Arabia; 51%); FMC-Nurol Savunma Sanayii A.S. (Turkey; majority owned).

Principal Divisions

Armament Systems Division; Ground Systems Division; Inter-national Division; Paladin Production Division; Steel Products Division.

Further Reading

Boatman, John, "United We Stand . . . ," *Jane's Defense Weekly,* May 20, 1995.

"Carlyle Beats Out Dynamics for United Defense," *Wall Street Jour-nal,* August 27, 1997, p. A3.

DeMeis, Rick, "Electronically-Linked Teams Design the Defense Sys-tems of the Future," *Purchasing,* May 7, 1998.

Gilpin, Kenneth N., "Military Contractor Sold to Buyout Firm," *New York Times,* August 27, 1997, p. D2.

Litsikas, Mary, "United Defense Teams with Suppliers to Boost Qual-ity," *Quality,* April 1997, pp. 74–76.

Machan, Dyan, "The Strategy Thing," *Forbes,* May 23, 1994.

Mintz, John, "Area Firms in Bidding War for Army Vehicle's Maker," *Washington Post,* August 14, 1997, p. E01.

Pasztor, Andy, "General Dynamics May Have to Rethink Game Plan—Failure to Acquire United Defense Makes Firm's Goal Appear Riskier," *Wall Street Journal,* August 28, 1997, p. B4.

Pearlstein, Steven, "Carlyle Group to Buy Military Contractor; United Defense Makes Weapons, Transports," *Washington Post,* August 27, 1997.

Peters, Katherine McIntire, "Unique Partnership Yields Results," *Gov-ernment Executive,* April 1998, p. 69.

Peterson, Susan E., "Bringing in the Big Guns: Crusader Artillery System Carries Hopes of United Defense," *Minneapolis Star Tri-bune,* May 26, 1997, p. 1D.

——, "Carlyle to Acquire United Defense for $850 Million; Fridley Plant to Have New Owners; Deal Likely to Close in About 90 Days," *Minneapolis Star Tribune,* August 27, 1997, p. 1D.

—Frederick C. Ingram

U.S. Can Corporation

900 Commerce Drive
Oak Brook, Illinois 60523
U.S.A.
(630) 571-2500
Fax: (630) 573-0715
Web site: http://www.uscanco.com

Public Company
Incorporated: 1983
Employees: 3,200
Sales: $710.24 million (1998)
Stock Exchanges: New York
Ticker Symbol: USC
NAIC: 332431 Metal Can Manufacturing

U.S. Can Corporation is one of the leading world manufacturers of steel and plastic containers for automotive products, personal care and household items, paint, plastic and industrial supplies, and custom and specialty products in both the United States and in Europe. The company is the leading supplier of aerosol cans throughout the United States, with a 50 percent share of the market. In Europe, U.S. Can is the second largest manufacturer of aerosol cans. The company is also proud of the fact that it supplies approximately one-half of all the one-gallon paint cans sold across the United States. During the past five years, U.S. Can Corporation has focused on developing an international network of sales offices and manufacturing facilities, and has opened new company locations in the United Kingdom, France, Spain, Italy, and Germany.

Early History

U.S. Can Corporation was the dream of William J. Smith, its founder and longtime chairman, president, and chief executive officer. After graduating from Syracuse University, Smith began his lengthy career in the packaging business by joining American Can Company, one of the three dominant firms in the industry which included American Can, Crown, Cork & Seal, and Ball Corporation. After working a number of years in a variety of both employee and managerial positions at several manufacturing facilities within the company, Smith had worked his way up to assume the title general manager of general packaging. Within two short years, Smith had been promoted to senior vice-president of technology at American Can. This position brought with it diverse and far-reaching responsibilities, including the departments of research and development, engineering, manufacturing technology, and productivity. Experience gained from supervising and managing these departments provided Smith with a comprehensive knowledge of the packaging industry. By the time he was promoted to executive vice-president in 1981, Smith was more than able and willing to manage the company's paper sector, which at that time increased its sales to approximately $1.3 billion. At the same time, Smith was appointed chairman of American Can's operating committee, a position that propelled him into the airy, upper echelons of high management, and placed upon him responsibilities and duties much the same as a chief operating officer.

Upon reaching the near top of American Can Company management, there was not a great deal of corporate ladder left to climb. After having surveyed his status within the company, Smith decided to retire in 1983. Yet the experienced and talented manager was unable to remain away from the business world for long. In the same year, Smith made the major commitment to establish his own company. Drawing from his years of experience in the packaging business, and a host of contacts on which to gather a management team around him, Smith arranged to purchase the paint and manufacturing operation of The Sherwin-Williams Company. Sherwin-Williams had a long history in the packaging business, specifically in manufacturing and supplying one-gallon containers for the paint market. Smith's idea was to acquire this operation and use it as a cornerstone to establish a packaging business to supply containers for a wide array of industries, including personal care, household, and automotive markets. Smith named his company U.S. Can Corporation, hoping to capitalize on the familiarity of American Can throughout the packaging industry.

From its inception, U.S. Can concentrated on aspects of the packaging business that Smith knew best, namely, manufacturing the containers used for house paints. The paint industry amounted to sales in the billions of dollars, and the largest segment of that comprised the millions of gallons of house paint. Within the first few years of its existence, U.S. Can was manufacturing nearly one out of every five paint containers, in sizes that ranged from pints to gallons. At approximately the same time, Smith and his management team decided to manufacture aerosol containers for the household and consumer products markets. Aerosol containers were used for an ever growing number of products, including shaving gels, hair care products, cleaning fluids and sprays, and food products such as whipped cream. By the time the company reached the end of the 1980s, sales figures had increased to well over the $100 million mark, and the road ahead was laden with more and more opportunity.

Growth and Expansion: Early 1990s

By 1992, the company had reached over $400 million in sales. Much of this dramatic increase in sales was due to the burgeoning demands for aerosol containers. The company was manufacturing aerosol containers for a broad customer base and, due to the promising projections within the market, expanded its manufacturing capacity for both consumer product aerosol containers, and household and automotive aerosol product containers. A new manufacturing facility was built in Horsham, Pennsylvania, with a large-diameter production line in order to accommodate the needs of consumers who purchased large-size containers of household and automotive products, mostly sold in mass-market discount stores where economy packaging provided the public with more produce for their money. Simultaneously, another facility was built in Green Bay, Wisconsin, this time with a small, 45mm diameter production line in order to meet the growing needs of consumers who purchased small, more compact personal care packaging that reflected the needs of a more mobile society and general public. Both of these facilities were operational by the end of fiscal 1996. In addition, U.S. Can made a commitment to the growing demand for barrier packaging with the aerosol industry, where the product was separated from its propellant within the container. Many personal care product firms were moving in this direction, especially in the shave gels, hair care, saline solutions, and food products markets. Responding to this need, U.S. Can revamped its manufacturing line in Racine, Wisconsin, and began to capture a large part of the market for this specific type of container.

In 1994 U.S. Can created its Custom and Specialty Group so that it could manufacture an almost endless variety of metal container products as the need presented itself. Within two years, this Group had five plants manufacturing a wide range of metal containers, including such items as embossed containers for Liz Claiborne Cosmetics, a rather uniquely designed tin container for Fossil, Inc. watches, newly designed canisters for collectible plates by Lenox Corporation, and innovative Flex-Seal canisters for Republic of Tea, Inc.

In addition to the company's expansion of manufacturing facilities, Smith and his management team were convinced that a strategic acquisitions program would enable U.S. Can to capture ever greater shares of targeted markets. With this strategy in mind, the company acquired Alltrista Corporation's metal services division to enhance the company's metal processing operation. The new acquisition complemented U.S. Can's facility in Brookfield, Ohio, that was quickly developing into one of the leading cutters and graders of metal for products that ranged from oil filters to pictures frames, as well as becoming a leader in precision coating and lithography. In 1996, the company acquired CPI Plastic, Inc., one of the leading suppliers of resealable injection-molded pails and drums. This acquisition was made to strengthen the operations and expand the scope of the Paint, Plastics, and General Line division of U.S. Can.

The single most important development during this period of time, however, was the company's expansion into the international market. U.S. Can reached a multi-year contract with The Gillette Company to manufacture barrier aerosol containers to a facility in Reading, England, operated by Gillette. Shortly afterward, U.S. Can built its own fully integrated aerosol container manufacturing facility in Merthyr Tyfil, south Wales. With a sure foothold in the European container market, the company entered and won a bid ordered by the European Union for the aerosol container operations that was available and due to be divested because of the CMB/Crown, Cork & Seal merger. In one swoop, U.S. Can completed the purchase from Crown, Cork & Seal of five aerosol manufacturing facilities across Europe, including locations in the United Kingdom, France, Germany, Spain, and Italy. As a result, the company catapulted to the rank of number two in the aerosol container market in Europe, and was well positioned to capitalize on a fast-growing market. Approximately half of the European aerosol market was in personal care products dominated by the U.S. firms of Gillette, Procter & Gamble, and S.C. Johnson, all of whom U.S. Can was already supplying with aerosol containers.

Transition and Change: Late 1990s

Unfortunately, the heady period of unlimited expansion and growth came to an abrupt end in 1997. U.S. Can lost its single largest and most important customer, S.C. Johnson & Sons, Inc., a personal and household products company based in Racine, Wisconsin, to its strongest competitor, Crown, Cork & Seal. To make matters worse, S.C. Johnson and Crown, Cork & Seal reached a five-year supply contract, which essentially eliminated U.S. Can from winning any short-term bids. Debt began to mount as a result, and the company soon found itself overwhelmed with debt equal to approximately 85 percent of its capital. Management's first reaction was to close as many manufacturing facilities as possible, dramatically par down its workforce, and begin a strategy of selling off divisions or businesses which were not bringing in enough revenue. By the end of 1997, the company reported a loss of $32 million on sales of just over $738 million.

Recognizing the need for a new management team, founder and longtime President and CEO William Smith decided to retire at the age of 71. Smith remained on the board and assisted in the search for a talented leader that could improve the waning fortunes of the company. The board of directors acted quickly and decided to hire Paul W. Jones. Jones had a long history of management experience, including a lengthy stay at General Electric Corporation where he held many different managerial and executive positions. In 1989, he was hired by Greenfield, Inc., a well-known manufacturer of industrial cutting tools based in Augusta, Georgia, to return the company to profitability and financial security. The company was laden with debt, and unable to turn a profit when Jones arrived on the scene. Jones immediately implemented a comprehensive and far-reaching reorganization strategy, including paying down the company's debt, selling off non-strategic divisions, and initiating an acquisitions plan. Within nine years, Jones had almost rid Greenfield of all its debt, acquired over two dozen companies, and took the company public with a highly successful IPO. To top it off, Jones then arranged for Greenfield to be sold for over $1 billion to Kennametal, Inc., one of the most respected and successful firms within the field of industrial manufacturing.

When Jones arrived at U.S. Can, he immediately set about to work in the same fashion as he had at Greenfield. Non-core businesses were sold off, including the company's metal pail business, the metal services division, and its standalone machine shop. Management at U.S. Can was also restructured, and new high-level executives where brought in to help Jones turn the company around. The continuing restructuring plan reduced costs and also enhanced manufacturing capabilities in strategic areas, such as aerosol containers. Three major facilities were closed in 1998, including an assembly plant in Green Bay, Wisconsin, a manufacturing facility in Alsip, Illinois, and a custom and specialty manufacturing plant in Columbiana, Ohio, while other facilities in Illinois, Georgia, Ohio, and Maryland increased their manufacturing capacities to offset the closings.

The most significant change, however, occurred when the new management announced a revised plan to forge a stronger presence in the European and South American aerosol markets. Not only did U.S. Can improve its management and enlarge the manufacturing capacities of all its European operations, but the company also purchased an interest in Formametal, S.A., one of the largest aerosol can manufacturing firms in Argentina. Double-digit growth rates were predicted for the aerosol markets in both Europe and South America over the next ten years, and Jones had been astute enough to place U.S. Can in a position to take advantage of this development.

Jones's presence at U.S. Can, along with his reputation as a turnaround specialist, calmed fears that the company would continue its downward spiral. Nonetheless, the challenges before Jones and his management team would be difficult to overcome, especially within the predominantly slow growth market that U.S. Can now found itself.

Further Reading

"Aerosol Services," *Chemical Market Reporter,* January 18, 1999, p. 24.

Demetrakakes, Pam, "Proactive Packaging: New Technologies Allow Packaging to Be More Than Just a Barrier," *Food Processing,* February 1999, p. 90.

"Food Industry Pushes Hygienic Standard," *Paperboard Packaging,* May 1999, p. 20.

"Interview with Paul W. Jones," *Wall Street Reporter Magazine,* June 1998, p. 38.

Murphy, H. Lee, "U.S. Can CEO Must Prove Mettle in Firm's Turnaround," *Crain's Chicago Business,* May 4, 1998, p. 10.

Neff, Jack, "All Dressed Up, No Place to Go," *Food Processing,* May 1999, p. 120.

"Steel Containers Provide Lasting Durability," *Modern Materials Handling*, April 30, 1999, p. 117.

—Thomas Derdak

U.S. News and World Report Inc.

1050 Thomas Jefferson St., N.W.
Washington, D.C. 20007
U.S.A.
(202) 955-2000
(800) 234-2450
Fax: (202) 955-2049
Web site: http://www.usnews.com

Private Company
Incorporated: 1933 as United States News
Employees: 500
Sales: $330 million (1999 est.)
NAIC: 51112 Periodical Publishers

U.S. News and World Report Inc. (USN&WR) publishes a weekly newsmagazine of the same title. It is the nation's third leading weekly newsmagazine, behind *Time* and *Newsweek.* Major sections of the magazine include Outlook, a quick take on national and international events of the week; U.S. News, often supplemented with national surveys and interviews with newsmakers; World Report, an analysis of events worldwide, especially as they affect the United States; Business, with an emphasis on data-analysis of economic trends along with profiles of business leaders and coverage of major business developments; Science & Ideas, featuring forward-looking reporting on science and health topics; and News You Can Use, a mix of practical information and enterprising stories. USN&WR also publishes annual guides to the best colleges, best graduate schools, best hospitals, best mutual funds, and other subjects. USN&WR is owned by Mortimer Zuckerman, whose media holdings also include the *Atlantic Monthly*, the *Daily News* (New York), and *Fast Company.*

Early History: 1933–84

In 1933 journalist David Lawrence founded a weekly newspaper he called *United States News.* As the title implied, it was devoted to domestic news. It was the successor to the newspaper the *United States Daily,* which Lawrence had founded in

1926. In 1940 *United States News* was recast as a magazine. Following the end of World War II, Lawrence founded a new magazine in 1946 called *World Report,* which covered international affairs. As domestic and world affairs became more intertwined in the post-World War II years, the two magazines *United States News* and *World Report* were merged to create *U.S. News & World Report* in 1948. Lawrence served as editor of the magazine until his death at 84 in 1973.

In 1962 USN&WR became an employee-owned company. The magazine developed a family atmosphere for its employees. It provided an analytical approach to the news and did not offer any entertainment features such as became commonplace among its competitors.

Diversification and Change: 1980s

In the early 1980s USN&WR diversified into computer-based publishing and a satellite transmission network. The magazine considered itself a pioneer in the technology of magazine production and distribution. It helped fund the Atex editorial computer system and led the industry in the use of digital scanning and satellite transmission of copy to printing plants around the country.

In 1981 USN&WR entered into a $200 million joint venture with Boston Properties, Inc. to develop 3.5 acres of land it owned in Washington, D.C. The land had been acquired by founder David Lawrence. Under the terms of the 50–50 venture, USN&WR would supply the land and Boston Properties the development. The head of Boston Properties was Morton Zuckerman, who had recently purchased the *Atlantic Monthly* in 1980. By 1984 a new 160,000-square-foot headquarters had been built for USN&WR on the property, with plans calling for such developments as a new Hyatt hotel, condominiums, and more office space. USN&WR eventually experienced a cash shortage from expenses associated with its diversification and liabilities associated with its profit-sharing trust.

USN&WR ended 1983 with a paid circulation of 2.1 million, making it the third most widely circulated weekly newsmagazine behind *Time* (4.6 million paid circulation) and *News-*

Company Perspectives:

U.S. News & World Report *is a weekly national newsmagazine devoted largely to reporting and analyzing national and international affairs, politics, business, health, science, technology, and social trends. And, in a NEWS YOU CAN USE section, it provides practical advice on how to live smarter and better.*

---

week (three million paid circulation). Revenues for 1983 were estimated to be $150 million, up ten percent from 1982.

In December 1983 an unidentified bidder offered $100 million to purchase the magazine, four times the appraised equity value of the outstanding shares. With 60,000 shares outstanding, the employee-owned company had seen the value of its shares increase in the past three years to $420 per share. A subsequent appraisal in early 1984 put the value at $625 a share, or a total of $38 million. In 1980 shares were valued at $152 a share.

In February 1984 the directors announced the company was for sale and that bids would be considered. In addition to the magazine and real estate, the company operated a typesetting service, newsletters, and a radio programming business. As financial information about USN&WR became public, it appeared the company was in weak financial condition and burdened by its Washington, D.C., real estate venture. Instead of earning net income between $5 million and $8 million, it appeared that USN&WR's pretax profits were about $4 million before extraordinary items or profit-sharing, and that net income was around $2 million. One analyst had pegged net income at $7.5 million early in the bidding process.

Investment banker Morgan Stanley & Co. was hired to advise management on the sale. It set a minimum bid of $100 million for the company. Morgan Stanley also screened potential bidders by examining their financial condition. Final offers were due by May 11, 1984.

By June 1984 it was announced that USN&WR would be acquired by Morton B. Zuckerman. In acquiring the magazine, Zuckerman outbid nine other competitors, who reportedly included United Marine Publishing Inc. (publisher of *Inc.* and *High Technology*), Hearst Corporation, Family Media Publishers (publisher of *Ladies Home Journal*), and Gannett Company, among others. Zuckerman would later acquire the *Daily News* in 1993, and in 1995 he helped launch *Fast Company,* a new business magazine.

Zuckerman was a wealthy real estate investor and developer who owned Boston Properties Inc. His previous business arrangement with USN&WR to develop its 3.5-acre real estate holdings in downtown Washington, D.C., may have helped with his winning bid. Many of the other publishers who were considering purchasing USN&WR were not experienced with the business of real estate development. Zuckerman graduated from Harvard Law School and taught for nine years at Harvard Graduate School of Business. At the time of the acquisition

Zuckerman said he had no plans to radically change the magazine's editorial direction. The sale was completed in October 1984 for a purchase price of $176.3 million.

Valuing the Employee-Owned Company

As a result of the acquisition, employee shareholders received $2,842 a share for their holdings. Less than ten years earlier, in 1975, an employee retired and sold his stock back to the company for $65 a share. At the time he and other employees were satisfied with the price; but following the sale of the company in 1984, some 220 former USN&WR employees filed a $100 million suit against the company, several former directors, and the magazine's appraisers, American Appraisal Associates Inc. The plaintiffs claimed they were entitled to almost $100 million from USN&WR and its profit-sharing plan, which represented their share of the proceeds of the sale.

At USN&WR, most of the employee-owned stock was held in a profit-sharing plan, with the remainder held by individual employees through a stock bonus plan. Technically, the employee ownership structure was not an employee stock ownership plan (ESOP), but the same valuation methods could be applied to both. Appraisers could choose to value employee-owned stock using a minority basis, which would be the value of the stock if only a minority interest in the company were available, or a control basis, which would be the value of a controlling interest. At issue was whether employees who sell back their minority shares should receive the same price a purchaser would pay for control of the company.

While the U.S. District judge's opinion on a pre-trial motion indicated he thought some defendants may have run afoul of legal requirements, in June 1987 he ruled that the company's directors acted "in an entirely appropriate manner" and that the appraisals were "perfectly reasonable and acceptable."

Hiring Senior Editorial Staff

After the sale to Zuckerman, USN&WR hired several top editors to improve its senior editorial staff. Zuckerman commissioned Harold Evans, former editor of the *Times* of London, England, to develop an editorial plan for the magazine. Richard C. Thompson was hired away from *Business Week* and named publisher, while James C. Mason was also lured from *Business Week* and named associate publisher. Mason would leave the magazine in 1986, and Thompson assumed a part-time schedule in 1991.

In March 1985 Zuckerman selected Shelby Coffey of the *Washington Post* to succeed Marvin Stone, who had been associated with USN&WR for more than 25 years, as editor of USN&WR. Stone had resigned in January 1985 and was expected to be appointed to a position with the U.S. Information Agency. Within a year Coffey stepped down and was replaced by David Gergen. In July 1986 Michael Ruby was named to the new position of executive editor to assist Gergen. Ruby was formerly assistant managing editor of *Newsweek.*

In August 1988 senior writer Roger Rosenblatt was named to replace David Gergen as editor. After two years at USN&WR, Gergen wanted to expand his horizons. Among other things, he had been appearing as a regular analyst on ''The MacNeil-Lehrer News Hour'' on public television. Under Gergen USN&WR's circulation rose to 2.362 million, the highest in the magazine's history. By comparison, *Time* had a circulation of 4.7 million and *Newsweek* 3.2 million.

New Ways to Deliver Information: 1990s

In 1991 USN&WR created a new section, ''Outlook,'' to provide a new look and a faster review of the week's news in the magazine. In May 1991 USN&WR launched a new magazine, *Family Fun,* in association with Jake Winebaum, a former senior executive at USN&WR. *Family Fun* was aimed at parents with children from ages 3 to 15 and focused on family activities, such as vacations, entertainment, and at-home education. Winebaum was the magazine's publisher, and USN&WR provided production and advertising sales support. Within a year, *Family Fun* was sold to Walt Disney Co., with Winebaum continuing as the magazine's editor and publisher.

USN&WR spun off several book publications from its news pages. In 1991 a team of USN&WR reporters wrote *Triumph Without Victory: The Unreported History of the Persian Gulf War,* which was co-published by Random House and Times Books. Other books included *America's Best Hospitals,* published by John Wiley & Sons, and *Letters for Our Children: Fifty Americans Share Lessons in Living,* which was based on a 1994 magazine feature and published by Random House in 1996.

In 1992 USN&WR beat *Time* and *Newsweek* for the most ad pages for 1992. USN&WR had 2,170 ad pages compared to 2,100 each for *Time* and *Newsweek*. USN&WR publisher Thomas R. Evans boasted that USN&WR had a 34 percent share of the newsweekly ad market, up from 23 percent in 1985 when USN&WR was acquired by Zuckerman.

In 1993 USN&WR celebrated its 60th anniversary. With electronic delivery of information the apparent wave of the future, the magazine became available on CompuServe Information Service. It had negotiated to be on America Online, but lost out to *Time*. After two years on the CompuServe Information Service, USN&WR introduced in 1995 a comprehensive web site (www.usnews.com) that included a digital version of the magazine. The web site also featured video and sound feeds, hotlinks to other sites, daily live sound bites, regular news updates, interactive educational games, and more. In 1994 USN&WR had created a new video and multimedia production division, U.S. News New Vision. It also experimented with a new cover wrap to boost single-copy sales, which had fallen 14.5 percent between comparable periods in 1993 and 1994. Overall circulation remained 2.28 million.

Capitalizing on the reputation of its popular annual guide to colleges, USN&WR in 1995 launched its first CD-ROM product, *The U.S. News Complete College Adviser*. It was designed to help students select a college and guide them through admissions applications and financial aid forms. USN&WR's Colleges and Careers Center web site was introduced in January 1997. That was followed in 1998 by the *U.S. News Getting into College Kit,* which included a video, a guidebook, and a CD-ROM.

Fast Company, a new business magazine aimed at an audience younger than *Business Week,* was launched under the auspices of USN&WR in 1995. It was overseen by Zuckerman, Fred Drasner (president and CEO of USN&WR), and two former editors of the *Harvard Business Review*.

The late 1990s were marked by several top editorial changes at USN&WR. In 1996 James Fallows was hired as editor, replacing husband and wife coeditors Michael Ruby and Merrill McLoughlin. Fallows brought in several top editorial managers and staff members, which caused several others to leave the magazine.

In 1997 USN&WR moved its business operations, including personnel, finance, and circulation, from Washington to New York City. The magazine's editorial offices remained in Washington. The move reflected Zuckerman's desire to run all of his media holdings from the *Daily News* building on West 33rd Street in Manhattan.

As part of an orderly management transition, Thomas Evans was promoted from executive vice-president and publisher to president and publisher of USN&WR. Drasner, former president and CEO, retained his CEO title and would oversee overall strategic business direction. Eric Gertler was named executive vice-president. Harold Evans was named editorial director of all of Zuckerman's publications, effective early 1998.

In October 1998 Drasner relinquished his CEO title and was succeeded by *Daily News* associate publisher Ira Ellenthal, who was also named group publisher for USN&WR, *Atlantic Monthly,* and *Fast Company*. Drasner remained CEO and copublisher of the *Daily News* as well as cochairman of the company's executive committee, which was responsible for overseeing all of the group's magazines. Eric Gertler, who had recently been promoted to COO, was given the additional title of president. Then in 1998 editor James Fallows resigned. He was replaced by Stephen Smith, a veteran of both *Time* and *Newsweek*. In 1999 Smith rehired many of the editorial staff that had departed when Fallows was hired.

Outlook

USN&WR's paid circulation was holding flat at 2.2 million, but in the first half of 1998 circulation of *Fast Company* jumped 86 percent to 254,555. While USN&WR was not likely to catch *Time* or *Newsweek* in terms of circulation, it could be expected to remain competitive in terms of advertising revenue. The magazine had a new, experienced editor, and Zuckerman had several other ventures that would presumably keep him too busy to make too many changes at the number three newsmagazine.

Further Reading

''Aid to Fledgling Magazine,'' *New York Times,* April 4, 1995, p. D8.

Alsop, Ronald, ''U.S. News Suitors Will Be Weeded Out; Morgan Stanley Studies Their Finances,'' *Wall Street Journal,* March 16, 1984, p. 15.

Dougherty, Philip H., ''Associate Publisher Leaving U.S. News,'' *New York Times,* October 10, 1986, p. D17.

Elliott, Stuart, ''People: Thomas R. Evans; Richard Thompson,'' *New York Times,* September 16, 1991, p. D9.

"Evans Named 'U.S. News' President," *Mediaweek,* February 17, 1997, p. 3.

Granatstein, Lisa, "Ellenthal Succeeds Drasner at Zuckerman's Mag Group," *Mediaweek,* October 12, 1998, p. 10.

Hevesi, Dennis, "U.S. News and World Report Sets Change in Editor's Post," *New York Times,* August 11, 1988, p. D17.

Huhn, Mary, "Zuckerman Plans Biz Book," *Mediaweek,* April 3, 1995, p. 5.

Jones, Alex S., "Putting a Value on U.S. News," *New York Times,* March 16, 1984, p. D1.

Lipman, Joanne, "Magazines," *Wall Street Journal,* February 12, 1992, p. B5.

"Magazine's Business Moving to New York," *New York Times,* April 15, 1997, p. B8.

"Michelle Faurot (Becomes President of U.S. News New Vision)," *Folio: The Magazine for Magazine Management,* September 15, 1994, p. 71.

Reilly, Patrick M., "Two Publishers Plan to Launch Parents Magazines," *Wall Street Journal,* March 4, 1991, p. B3.

Schwadel, Francine, "U.S. News Publisher Is Considering Offers from Several Bidders," *Wall Street Journal,* June 8, 1984, p. 11.

Singer, Martin M., "U.S. News Tries to Boost Sagging Sales," *Folio: The Magazine for Magazine Management,* November 15, 1994, p. 27.

Steptoe, Sonja, "Suit Against Magazine Highlights Debate on Valuing Employee-Owned Companies," *Wall Street Journal,* September 16, 1986, p. 31.

Swett, Clint, "Technology Talk Column," *Knight-Ridder/Tribune Business News,* May 17, 1995.

"U.S. News & World Acquisition Price Cut 3.4% by Zuckerman," *Wall Street Journal,* July 30, 1984, p. 22.

"*U.S. News & World Report* Gets the Crown," *Folio: The Magazine for Magazine Management,* February 1, 1993, p. 13.

"A *U.S. News & World Report* History: 1933 to the Present," August 10, 1999, http://www.usnews.com/usnews/misc/history.htm.

"U.S. News Buyout of Stock Was Proper, Federal Judge Rules," *Wall Street Journal,* June 23, 1987, p. 47.

"U.S. News Chooses Coffey As Its Editor," *Wall Street Journal,* March 19, 1985, p. 47.

"U.S. News: Fact Sheet," August 10, 1999, http://www.usnews.com/usnews/misc/fact.htm.

"U.S. News Goes Online," *Folio: The Magazine for Magazine Management,* November 15, 1993, p. 14.

"U.S. News Is Expected to Announce Today Which Bidder It Chose," *Wall Street Journal,* June 11, 1984, p. 43.

"U.S. News Is Seeking 'Indications of Interest' in Acquiring Company," *Wall Street Journal,* February 21, 1984, p. 12.

"U.S. News Is Sold to Zuckerman; Developer Pays $168.5 Million," *New York Times,* June 12, 1984, p. D5.

"U.S. News May Not Be Such a Catch After All," *Business Week,* May 7, 1984, p. 32.

"U.S. News Names Ruby to a Top Editor's Position," *Wall Street Journal,* July 28, 1986, p. 22.

"U.S. News Retains Morgan Stanley & Co. After Suitor's Offer," *Wall Street Journal,* January 10, 1984, p. 42.

"U.S. News Scouts Ways to Raise Cash," *Business Week,* January 9, 1984, p. 38.

"Zuckerman Will Buy U.S. News," *Business Week,* June 25, 1984, p. 40.

—David P. Bianco

Vinson & Elkins

VINSON & ELKINS L.L.P.

Vinson & Elkins L.L.P.

2300 First City Tower, 1001 Fannin
Houston, Texas 77002-6760
U.S.A.
(713) 758-2222
Fax: (713) 758-2346
Web site: http://www.velaw.com

Partnership
Founded: 1917
Employees: 1,837
Sales: $255 million (1997)
NAIC: 54111 Offices of Lawyers

One of the world's major law firms, Vinson & Elkins L.L.P. (V&E) employs over 600 attorneys at its headquarters in Houston and branch offices in Austin, Dallas, London, New York, Singapore, Beijing, Moscow, and Washington, D.C. Although it offers expertise in most legal specialties, V&E historically and in the 1990s continues to be famous for its oil and energy practice. *Petroleum Economist* in June 1999 ranked it as the top law firm for knowledge of U.S. law and best overall service to the energy sector. Other sources rank Vinson & Elkins as one of the major law firms in corporate finance, mergers and acquisitions, and equity offerings. The firm serves a diverse group of over 3,000 clients, ranging from all sizes of companies to states, foreign nations, cities, and individuals.

The Partnership's Early Years

William A. Vinson was born in 1874 in North Carolina to devout Presbyterian parents. In 1887 the Vinsons moved to the small town of Sherman, Texas, where William graduated from Austin College in 1896. He studied the law as an apprentice to a local judge and soon began practicing law in his home town. In 1909 he moved to rapidly growing Houston, where he practiced in different partnerships before teaming up with James A. Elkins.

Elkins was born in Huntsville, Texas, in 1879. His family lived next to James Baker, who moved to Houston to found the law firm Baker & Botts. After graduating from high school, Elkins was tempted to play professional baseball but chose the law instead. He earned an undergraduate degree in law in Austin, then returned to Huntsville to practice. Between 1907 and 1910 he maintained law practices in Huntsville and Houston. In 1917 he moved his young family to Houston to form the partnership Vinson & Elkins.

In 1917 Jesse H. Jones, president of Houston's National Bank of Commerce, asked V&E to become the bank's general attorneys, thus loosening the close ties the bank previously had with Baker & Botts, Houston's largest law firm at the time.

Another early client of the new firm was Prairie Oil & Gas Company, a Standard Oil subsidiary that retained the firm so it could do business in Texas. Years later Vinson & Elkins helped Prairie, through several mergers, become Magnolia Petroleum Corporation.

The completion of Texaco's huge building in 1915 was just one sign of Houston's growing oil industry. Although Vinson & Elkins received some work from such giant oil firms, in reality they usually represented mostly small independent oil companies, taking a risk that their clients would eventually prosper. In a chaotic legal climate where land, oil, and natural gas claims were often quite confusing and agreements were scribbled on paper scraps or just done by word of mouth, the law firm beginning in the 1920s kept many of its lawyers busy researching land titles as the Texas oil industry boomed.

In 1924 Elkins and Vinson, along with other V&E partners and some friends, invested their money to start the Guaranty Trust Bank, which after two other name changes became the First City National Bank in 1956. Following the example of Baker & Botts that in the late 1800s helped establish a bank, V&E and Guaranty Trust maintained reciprocal positive relations. V&E provided legal services to Guaranty, while the two firms referred clients to each other. Judge Elkins in the 1920s and 1930s bought shares in several other banks and became one of the state's prominent bankers. V&E attorneys often became board members of those banks and thus the law firm gained more influence and clients. Elkins helped start the Texas Bankers Association.

Company Perspectives:

Since our firm was founded, it has attracted an outstanding and diverse group of attorneys as well as an international clientele. Our clients include the governments of sovereign nations and of North American states, cities and municipalities, public and private companies, financial institutions, entrepreneurs, and individuals and families.

Lawyering During the Great Depression and World War II

New Deal legislation resulted in numerous new federal rules and regulations and agencies to enforce them. Thus Vinson & Elkins faced new challenges helping their clients adjust to the new legal atmosphere. Elkins himself made numerous trips to Washington, D.C., on behalf of the firm's clients.

At first Elkins favored increased federal involvement because of the economic crisis, but by the middle of the 1930s he warned corporate clients of the increased power of unions backed by Communists and the New Deal. "Elkins's common position . . . was that the New Deal was a radical, anti-capitalist, centralizing force from the left, one inspired by Moscow and spearheaded by labor unions sanctioned by the federal government," said author Harold Hyman.

Elkins, the undisputed head of the law firm, was just one of many lawyers who opposed much of the New Deal. Many corporate attorneys, for example, fought the new Securities and Exchange Commission (SEC) that required public corporations to file annual disclosure statements about their finances and other activities.

Like many other law firms, Vinson & Elkins endured the loss of several lawyers who served in the military during World War II. Within a few weeks after Pearl Harbor, six of its 52 attorneys either volunteered or were drafted. In the firm's history book, one V&E attorney recalled that, "The firm was stripped of all its junior members and was left to the older lawyers, who managed to keep it afloat."

Yet at the same time federal wartime regulations increased client demands on Vinson & Elkins. For example, one lawyer in 1943 complained how the War Production Board demanded that V&E client Pure Oil produce three million cubic feet of gas for a war plant, while the Public Works Administration directed how the gas was to be refined, and the Office of Price Administration set the selling price.

Vinson & Elkins played a crucial role in helping Houston expand from about 375,000 residents in 1941 to over 480,000 in 1946. During the war and the economic boom in the 1950s, V&E's lawyers provided legal services to assist companies building new subdivisions.

Post-World War II Challenges

In 1951 Vinson died after years of illness. Obituaries noted his contributions to insurance law, redrafting the Texas code of civil procedures, successful business investments, and serving as a director of numerous industries, and his dedication to the Houston Public Library and the First Presbyterian Church.

Growth in the postwar era led to moves to new facilities. In 1960 the firm moved its offices from crowded spaces in the Esperson Building to the newly constructed FCNB Building, a 32-story highrise occupying an entire block in downtown Houston. In spite of new offices, the firm remained firmly under the control of founder Elkins. Hyman said Elkins's "combative resistance made adaptation to change difficult at V&E." For example, the firm in the 1940s and 1950s had a few attorneys working in tax law, but Elkins delayed the growth of that field.

In 1971 the law firm opened its London office. That practice created in 1994 a new multinational partnership that included both English solicitors as well as American attorneys.

In 1981 Vinson & Elkins moved to the high rise First City Tower, where it remained in 1999. It also opened new branches, including the Dallas office in 1986. Compared to its other offices, the Dallas branch often recruited experienced attorneys as lateral hires from competing law firms. By the late 1990s the Dallas branch included over 100 attorneys.

In 1984 V&E accepted a contingency fee case that many firms had turned down. The firm represented Houston-based Energy Transportation Systems Inc. in its antitrust lawsuit against a group of railroads. The jury decided on a $1.035 billion verdict against the railroads. Eventually Energy Transportation Systems settled for $350 million, of which about $101 million was paid to Vinson & Elkins. Partners, associates, paralegals, and other staff members received large bonuses, but the "ETSI award had a potentially corrosive effect in the Firm," according to Harold Hyman, referring to some conflicts over who should receive how much. However, Vinson & Elkins survived this challenge of dealing with prosperity, which was not true of some other law firms.

In the mid-1980s Vinson & Elkins diversified to some extent. For example, a health industries section was created within the firm to take advantage of new opportunities as healthcare expanded much faster than the general U.S. economy.

Practice in the 1990s

Based on its work since the early 1970s representing clients with business interests in the former Soviet Union, Vinson & Elkins established its Moscow office in 1991. Several other U.S. law firms started Russian offices at about the same time, since the collapse of the Soviet Union opened up new opportunities for foreign businesses. However, some of those firms later withdrew because of the unstable government, high operating costs, and even food shortages.

Expansion continued in the late 1990s. For example, Vinson & Elkins in 1997 created its Beijing office in the People's Republic of China. By 1999 that office was staffed by five V&E attorneys fluent in Mandarin. V&E in 1999 was the only Texas law firm to have an office in Singapore.

In 1998 V&E opened its New York office, which by 1999 included 13 attorneys experienced in several aspects of business law and litigation. Those fluent in Spanish represented clients in Mexico, Brazil, Chile, Argentina, Uruguay, Venezuela, and other Latin American nations.

A 1994 survey by the market research firm Global Research examined approximately 400 corporate law firms. Of all the U.S. firms, Vinson & Elkins was the only Texas firm to rank in the top ten for quality, which pleased Vinson & Elkins' managing partner, Harry Reasoner.

In 1998 V&E served clients in 98 mergers and acquisitions worth over $38 billion. Some of those 1998 clients were Halliburton Company, in its $8.1 billion acquisition of Dresser Industries; Capstar Broadcasting Corporation, in a $4.1 billion merger with Chancellor Media Corporation; and Occidental Petroleum Corporation, in its $2 billion acquisition of Equistar Chemicals. Other merger/acquisition clients included KN Energy, Enron Corporation, Meridian Industrial Trust, Seagull Energy Corporation, BMC Software, Prime II Management, Neste Oy, Lomak Petroleum, Houston Industries, Concentra Managed Care, International Home Foods, Core Laboratories, and Associated British Sugar.

The firm in 1998 also counseled clients in over 60 offerings in the debt and equity markets, raising a total of over $14.5 billion. Several clients in this area were again oil or energy firms, such as Northern Natural Gas Company, Belco Oil & Gas Corporation, Pool Energy Services Company, Nuevo Energy Company, Seven Seas Petroleum, and Wainoco Oil Corporation. Clients in other industries included Electronic Data Systems Corporation, Hastings Entertainment, Southwest Airlines, Continental Airlines, and First Sierra Financial. This corporate finance practice led the *American Lawyer* in April 1999 to rank Vinson & Elkins as one of the nation's top law firms in this area.

Although Vinson & Elkins had diversified, its oil and energy practice in the 1990s remained crucial. In an interview in the September 1996 *Petroleum Economist*, the head of the energy team stated that his firm's "most important competitive advantage [in that field] is its broad experience in the industry over a long period of time. Energy is the basis on which the firm was founded . . . and continues to be its largest area of practice."

In 1998 Vinson & Elkins' energy lawyers accounted for over 160 of the firm's 560 attorneys. The firm was involved in energy projects all over the world. For example, in a 1998 interview in the *Petroleum Economist*, the periodical was told that "Vinson & Elkins has been involved in Asia since signifi-

cant discoveries were made in Indonesia in the 1970s, and our lawyers have recently played significant roles in energy projects in China, India, the Philippines, Vietnam, Indonesia, Bangladesh and Papua New Guinea."

The *American Lawyer* in its July/August 1998 issue ranked Vinson & Elkins as the 20th largest law firm in the United States, based on 1997 gross revenues of $255 million. Divided among the firm's 509 lawyers, that resulted in about $500,000 per lawyer, more than most of the magazine's top 100 law firms.

In November 1998 the *American Lawyer*, in cooperation with London's *Legal Business*, published its first survey of the world's largest law firms. Vinson & Elkins ranked number 42 based on its 554 attorneys, with only four percent of that number stationed overseas. Ranked according to 1997 annual revenue, V&E was number 24.

The high fees charged by such large law firms as Vinson & Elkins led some to seek alternative sources of legal services. For example, paralegals known as document processors occasionally used commercial legal software programs to provide those with limited incomes access to 70 kinds of documents, ranging from wills to uncontested divorces and adoptions. Some bar associations argued that this approach oversimplified what often were complicated matters and also might be a form of practicing law without a license. In any case, new technology made information much more accessible as the Information Age rapidly advanced. The days of professionals, whether lawyers, doctors, or scientists, being the only ones with special knowledge and training, seemed long gone. Professionals including the attorneys at Vinson & Elkins thus faced new challenges as the 20th century ended.

Further Reading

"Big Accounting Firms Lure More Tax Lawyers from Law Firms," *Wall Street Journal*, February 3, 1999, p. 1.

"Cheap Computer Services Compete with Lawyers," *Omaha World-Herald*, December 26, 1994, p. 5.

"Energy Finance Poll Results," *Petroleum Economist*, June 1999, pp. 2–8.

Hyman, Harold M., *Craftsmanship and Character: A History of the Vinson & Elkins Law Firm of Houston, 1917–1997,* Athens, Ga.: University of Georgia Press, 1998.

"Vinson & Elkins," *Petroleum Economist*, September 1996, p. 98.

"Vinson & Elkins," *Petroleum Economist*, June 1998, p. 91.

—David M. Walden

VISX, Incorporated

3400 Central Expressway
Santa Clara, California 95051-0703
U.S.A.
(408) 733-2020
Fax: (408) 773-7200
Web site: http://www.visx.com

Public Company
Incorporated: 1987
Employees: 238
Sales: $133.8 million (1998)
Stock Exchanges: NASDAQ
Ticker Symbol: VISX
NAIC: 339112 Surgical & Medical Instrument
   Manufacturing; 334510 Laser Equipment,
   Electromedical, Manufacturing

VISX, Incorporated is the leading designer, manufacturer, and marketer of laser vision correction systems. The company, which was founded in 1986, manufactures laser systems to treat vision problems such as nearsightedness, farsightedness, and astigmatism. VISX was the first company to be awarded FDA approval for systems used to perform Photorefractive Keratectomy (PRK), a procedure in which the cornea is reshaped to correct the patient's vision. VISX systems are also used to perform Laser Assisted in-Situ Keratomileusis (LASIK), a similar procedure that uses an instrument called a microkeratone to fold back a layer of the cornea so a laser can be used to reshape it. LASIK has become the procedure of choice among ophthalmologists because it can be used to treat higher levels of nearsightedness and offers a shorter recovery time. A typical PRK or LASIK procedure lasts about 15 to 40 seconds and consists of about 150 laser pulses, each of which lasts several billionths of a second. A patient visit is usually 30 minutes, including postoperative dressing. Patients may experience mild discomfort for 48 to 72 hours after the procedure. VISX has more patents than any other laser vision system correction company—over 140 and at least 70 more pending.

The company's revenues stem from its global sales of laser systems, service and parts sales, and license fees collected from ophthalmologists. VISX markets its lasers to ophthalmologists who then market the procedures to the public. Its revenues were just under $134 million in 1998 for an operating income of $59 million. Both the company's corporate headquarters and its manufacturing centers are located in Santa Clara, California.

The Beginning in 1986

In the early 1980s, researchers discovered that IBM's new excimer laser, which was initially used to etch computer chips, could be used for laser vision correction surgeries. The excimer laser used an ultraviolet beam of light that was so fine 200 pulses were needed to cut through a single strand of human hair. The laser used ''cold light'' that did not damage the surrounding tissue the way other thermal or ''heat'' lasers did.

Doctors Charles Munneryn and Stephen Trokel founded VISX in 1986, after designing a laser vision correction system with an excimer laser and a computerized workstation. Munnerlyn and Trokel sold their system to ophthalmologists, who used it to perform Photorefractive Keratectomy (PRK) on patients with low levels of myopia, more commonly known as nearsightedness. PRK was usually performed on one eye at a time. Numbing drops were applied to the eye so the procedure was painless. The ophthalmologist used an instrument called a speculum to hold the eye open. He or she then removed the epithelium—the layer of protective skin covering the cornea. While the patient fixated on a red, blinking light, the ophthalmologist used the laser to reshape the cornea by removing microscopic layers of tissue.

VISX hoped to eventually win the approval of the Food and Drug Administration (FDA), so it could market and sell its system in the United States. Once it gained FDA approval, the company planned to tap into the huge market of vision correction—the one out of two people worldwide suffering from vision problems.

In 1987 the first eye was treated with VISX technology and the company was incorporated. In 1989 VISX went public and began to market its laser systems overseas.

Company Perspectives:

VISX is committed to the continued development of technology designed to enable millions of individuals worldwide to eliminate or reduce their need for corrective lenses by taking advantage of innovative ophthalmic procedures, including Photorefractive Keratectomy (PRK).

However, VISX and another company, Taunton Technologies Inc., had been disputing bitterly for several years regarding patents for the excimer laser and the system itself. While no one can obtain a patent on laser surgery in general, inventors can file patents on the parts and designs used in the system. Taunton Technologies was founded in 1986 by Dr. Francis L'Esperence, who believed he had a right to some patents regarding the system used to perform the surgery. The two companies eventually resolved their disagreements through a merger. VISX was acquired by Taunton in 1990. After the merger, Taunton adopted the VISX name.

Pillar Point Partners in 1992

Despite the potential of the VISX system, the company was having trouble acquiring the patents and finances it needed to gain FDA approval. After negotiating for about a year and a half, executives from VISX met with executives from Summit Technology Inc., its main competitor, in 1992 on a golf course in Half Moon Bay in California. The two competitors worked out an agreement to ''pool'' their patents and raise enough revenue to move toward gaining FDA approval. They named the patent-pool agreement Pillar Point Partners after Half Moon Bay's most prominent feature, the Pillar Point. The two companies agreed to sell the excimer laser systems for about $500,000 and charge ophthalmologists an additional licensing fee of $250 per eye for each surgery they performed.

In 1993 VISX submitted its first application to the FDA for approval of its excimer laser system to perform PRK. The FDA recommended conditional approval in 1994, around the time the company shipped its 200th system overseas.

Significant Advances in the Mid-1990s

In 1995 VISX received FDA market approval for PRK with its system. In March 1995, the company upgraded its system and introduced its new STAR Excimer Laser System, which could treat about 90 percent of Americans with mild to moderate levels of myopia. The FDA approved this system in 1996.

In the same year, the U.S. Navy purchased a STAR System to treat nearsighted military personnel. The system was installed at the Navy Medical Center in San Diego, California. Before purchasing the system, the Navy performed clinical studies on military personnel who had undergone the PRK with the system. The studies measured combat activities of these personnel, such as rifle shooting accuracy, before and after the surgery. The results were promising. After the surgery, military personnel were able to shoot just as accurately as they had before the surgery while wearing corrective lenses.

Around the time of the Navy purchase, VISX launched its web site, www.visx.com, to provide consumers, ophthalmologists, and others in the eyecare industry with information about laser vision correction surgery. The interactive web site included testimonials from patients who had undergone the surgery as well as a referral network for people considering laser vision correction surgery.

In April 1997, the STAR system received FDA approval to treat higher levels of myopia and hyperopia, more commonly known as farsightedness. The system could also be used to treat astigmatism, an eyesight disorder where an incorrect curve of the eye prevents focusing. Astigmatism affects about 28 million Americans. The approval of the STAR system to treat astigmatism made the headlines in all of the major U.S. print and broadcast media. To treat astigmatism and higher levels of myopia, ophthalmologists used the VISX system to perform LASIK, in which they fold back a layer of the cornea and then use a laser to reshape the tissue. Patients who had undergone LASIK healed more quickly and returned to normal vision sooner than those who had undergone PRK.

Word of the STAR system spread fast. In May 1997, the U.S. Department of Veteran Affairs signed a two-year contract with VISX that allowed certain branches of the United States military to purchase the STAR system. The U.S. Air Force purchased its first System under this contract, which was installed at Wilford Hall Medical Center, Lackland Air Force Base, San Antonio, Texas.

FTC Charges in 1998

The year 1998 was a difficult one for VISX. In March, the Federal Trade Commission (FTC) charged VISX with price-fixing and patent fraud. The price-fixing charges stemmed from the agreement VISX had made with Summit Technology in 1992, in which the two companies combined their patents. The FTC wanted Pillar Point dissolved because it determined that, by working together, VISX and Summit were able to inflate their prices because no other company could compete with their combined patents and finances. The FTC also believed that without the partnership VISX and Summit would be unable to force doctors to pay the $250 per eye licensing fee. In a competitive environment, physicians would be able to shop around for the best deal.

VISX countered that Pillar Point was created to enable the technology to be marketed, not to eliminate the competition. ''We've spent $52 million bringing this to market, and there's no way we could sell these lasers for $500,000 and ever recoup what we've put into it,'' Mark Logan, Chairman and CEO of VISX explained in the *Knight Ridder/Tribune Business News.* ''If it weren't for the $250 fee, we'd have to sell these systems for $3 million each and have a very small market, which isn't good for anyone.'' VISX eventually ended the Pillar Point partnership on its own. The company insisted the dissolution had nothing to do with the FTC charges, and that its partnership with Summit was not amicable. In June 1998, VISX and Summit dissolved Pillar Point and settled all pending disputes. VISX paid Summit $35 million, which caused its stock to drop.

The FTC patent charges proved to be more serious, however. The complaint charged that Dr. Trokel, cofounder of VISX, withheld information from the Patent Office about previous patents that had been filed by other researchers. The complaint also accused Dr. Francis L'Esperance, the founder of Taunton, with falsifying a notebook to take credit for others' inventions. VISX had to pay a substantial litigation charge from the patent suit. As of 1999, the suit remained in the appeals process and was expected to take several years before a final decision was reached. However, the patents remained valid until the situation was resolved, which enabled VISX to solidify its position as a market leader.

In 1998 the FDA approved VISX's new STAR S2 Excimer Laser System, which offered patients smoother ablations—removal of layers of the cornea. The STAR S2 achieved this smoothing capability through a seven-beam laser system that resulted in nearly flawless results. VISX marketed the STAR S2 internationally as the VISX STAR S2 Smoothscan.

Logan commented on the STAR S2 in articles carried over *Business Wire*: "We have listened to our customers and believe the STAR S2 offers tremendous advantages. Unlike single-beam scanning lasers, the System's seven scanning beams cover a larger area of the cornea and allow procedures to be completed quickly and efficiently."

A Clear Outlook for the Future

As of 1999, VISX had the only system with FDA approval in the United States for correcting all three major refractures: nearsightedness, farsightedness, and astigmatism. However, the company's competitors were taking strides to gain similar approvals. Summit Technology was advancing technologically, and Bausch and Lomb planned to introduce its own laser system. Nidek, a privately held Japanese firm with its own laser system to treat myopia, waived its licensing fee in an effort to gain market share. Despite the competition, however, VISX could be expected to remain a market leader well into the future.

Further Reading

Aragon, Lawrence, "Pillar Point Receives Laser Patents from VISX, Summit," *Business Journal,* June 22, 1992, p. 4.

Barlas, Pete, "VISX Getting Tough in Fight for Its Royalties," *Business Journal,* August 7, 1995, p. 3.

Barrere, Michelle, "VISX Gets Approval for Excimer Laser," *Ophthalmology Times,* April 15, 1996, p. 26.

Borzo, Greg, "Royalty for Eye Surgery May Drop," *American Medical News,* July 6, 1998, p. 23.

Bray, Hiawatha, "Rival Firms Celebrate FDA Approval of Laser Eye Surgery Treatment," *Knight-Ridder/Tribune Business News,* April 26, 1997, p. 426B1033.

Delevett, Peter, "Recent FTC Allegations Against VISX May Involve PTO," *Business Journal,* April 20, 1998, p. 5.

——, "VISX Sees the Lawyers Coming," *Business Journal,* April 13, 1998, p. 1.

"FDA Approves New VISX STAR S2 Laser Excimer Laser System," *Business Wire,* March 24, 1998, p. 3241093.

Hertz, Beth Thomas, "VISX Gets Panel's OK on Hyperopia," *Ophthalmology Times,* September 1, 1998, p. 1.

"Laser Vision Centers Say FDA Approval of Astigmatism Will Have Positive Impact; Company Says Majority of U.S. Laser Fleet Affected," *Business Wire,* April 25, 1997, p. 4250027.

Ray-Durpree, Janet, "Nation's Two Eye-Surgery Laser Firms Accused of Price Fixing," *Knight-Ridder/Tribune Business News,* June 28, 1996, p. 6280221.

Rosenberg, Ronald, "FDA Approves VISX, Inc. Plan to Use Laser Equipment for Astigmatism," *Knight-Ridder/Tribune Business News,* January 16, 1997, p. 116B1143.

Sabbagh, Leslie B., "LASIK Safer Than PRK in High Myopia," *Ophthalmology Times,* December 1, 1998, p. 1.

"Summit, VISX Sign Consent Agreements," *Ophthalmology Times,* August 15, 1998, p. 52.

"VISX and U.S. Military Sign Two-Year Contract; United States Air Force Orders VISX STAR Excimer Laser System," *Business Wire,* May 14, 1997.

"VISX Announced Expansion of Patent Portfolio," *Business Wire,* February 12, 1997, p. 2121050.

"VISX, Inc. Comments on Recent Drop in Share Price," *Business Wire,* August 1, 1996, p. 0811053.

"VISX Launches Excimer Laser Correction Web Site," *PR Newswire,* August 19, 1996, p. 0819PHMO11.

"VISX Philosophy Differs," *Health Industry Today,* February 1, 1996.

"VISX Reports Record Sales and Earnings," *Business Wire,* October 14, 1998, p. 0294.

—Tracey Vasil Biscontini

The Walt Disney Company

500 South Buena Vista Street
Burbank, California 91521
U.S.A.
(818) 560-1000
Fax: (818) 840-1930
Web site: http://www.disney.com

Public Company
Incorporated: 1938 as Walt Disney Productions
Employees: 117,000
Sales: $22.97 billion (1998)
Stock Exchanges: New York Pacific Midwest Tokyo
Ticker Symbol: DIS
NAIC: 51312 Television Broadcasting; 513112 Radio
    Stations; 51321 Cable Networks; 711211 Sports
    Teams & Clubs; 71311 Amusement & Theme Parks;
    51211 Motion Picture & Video Production

A colossal force in the entertainment industry, The Walt Disney Company is best known for bringing decades of fantasy and fun to families through its amusement parks, television series, and many classic live-action and animated motion pictures. Beginning in 1984, a pivotal juncture in the company's history, Disney enjoyed an enormous creative and financial renaissance, due to the leadership of CEO Michael Eisner; the success of such subsidiaries as Touchstone Films, Hollywood Pictures, The Disney Studios, Buena Vista Distribution, The Disney Channel, and Buena Vista Home Video; the sales of Disney consumer products through The Disney Stores and a multitude of licensing arrangements; and a recommitment to excellence in the making of original feature-length animated films. Under Eisner's reign, Disney acquired Capital Cities/ABC in 1996, a $19 billion deal that increased the company's stature enormously. Adding to the theme parks, cruise ships, professional sports teams, and dozens of other businesses owned by the company, the acquisition of Capital Cities/ABC gave Disney the power of broadcasting and the ability to meld entertainment content with programming. During the late 1990s, the company was aggressively building a presence on the Internet and adopting a concerted approach to international expansion.

The Birth of a U.S. Icon

Walt Disney, the company's founder, was born in Chicago in 1901. His appeal to the greater United States is said to have had roots in his humble, middle-class upbringing. Disney's father, Elias, moved the family throughout the Midwest seeking employment. Young Disney grew up in a household where hard work was prized: feeding the family's five children left little pocket change for amusement. Walt Disney began working at the age of nine as a newspaper delivery boy. His father instructed him and his siblings in the teachings of the Congregational Church and socialism.

Drawing provided an escape for Disney, and at the age of 14 he took his work on the road and enrolled at the Kansas City Art Institute. His art was temporarily put on hold when he joined the Red Cross at age 16 to serve as an ambulance driver at the end of World War I. In 1919 he returned to the United States and found work as a commercial artist. Together with Ub Iwerks, another artist at the studio, Disney soon formed an animated cartoon company in Kansas City.

In 1923, following the bankruptcy of this company, Disney joined his brother Roy in Hollywood. By the time he arrived on the West Coast, word came from New York that a company wanted to purchase the rights to a series of Disney's live-action cartoon reels, ultimately titled *Alice Comedies*. A distributor named M.J. Winkler offered $1,500 per reel, and Disney joined her as a production partner.

A series of animated films followed on *Alice*'s heels. In 1927 Disney started a series called *Oswald the Lucky Rabbit,* which met with public acclaim. The distributor, however, had the character copyrighted in its own name, so Disney earned only a few hundred dollars. It was while pondering the unfairness of this situation on a California-bound train that Disney first thought of creating a mouse character named Mortimer. He changed the name to Mickey Mouse, drew up some simple sketches, and went on to make several Mickey Mouse films with his brother Roy, using their own money.

On the third Mickey Mouse film, Disney decided to take a bold step and add sound to *Steamboat Willie*. The cartoon was synchronized with a simple musical background. The process provided some of the first technical steps in film continuity: music was played at two beats a second and the film was marked every 12 frames as a guide to the animator, and later an orchestra.

Film distributors laughed at Disney's idea. Finally one, Pat Powers, released *Steamboat Willie* in theaters. Audiences loved what they saw and heard, and suddenly Disney was a hit in the animation business. In 1935 the *New York Times* called Mickey Mouse "the best-known and most popular international figure of his day." Meanwhile, Disney suffered criticism from observers who judged him to be a cartoonist of only mediocre ability. (Iwerks was responsible for the actual design of Mickey Mouse and the other characters.) Disney was, however, given credit for his ability to conceptualize characters and stories.

The Mickey Mouse projects brought in enough cash to allow Walt Disney to develop other projects, including several full-length motion pictures and advances in Technicolor film. Disney's first full-length film, *Snow White and the Seven Dwarfs*, opened in 1937 to impressive crowds and led to a string of Disney hits, including *Pinocchio* and *Fantasia* in 1940, *Dumbo* in 1941, *Bambi* in 1942, and *Saludos Amigos* in 1943.

Around 1940 Disney decided to tackle live-action films, first with *The Reluctant Dragon* and to a greater extent with 1946's *Song of the South*. Meanwhile, during World War II, Disney lent his characters to the war effort, making shorts, including one in which Minnie Mouse showed U.S. homemakers the importance of saving fats. After the war, Walt Disney Productions was back in business with live-action features including *20,000 Leagues Under the Sea. The Living Desert* was released in the early 1950s by Disney's new distribution company, Buena Vista, to tremendous box office success.

Taking on Television: 1950s

During the 1950s, as Americans began to spend more time at home watching television for entertainment, Disney's studio took full advantage of the small screen revolution. In 1954, the "Disneyland" television series premiered. The show included an introduction by Walt Disney and incorporated film clips from Disney productions with live action and coverage of Disneyland. Some four million people tuned in each week. Disney also made a national folk hero out of Davy Crockett when he devoted a three-part program to coverage of his life. Within a matter of weeks, U.S. boys could not live without coonskin caps and other Crockett merchandise, all of which earned Disney a fortune. Crockett's popularity led to the era of the Disney live-action adventures that included the 1950s hits *The Great Loco-motive Chase, Westward Ho, Old Yeller,* and *The Light in the Forest.*

In October 1955 "The Mickey Mouse Club" debuted on the ABC television network. The hour-long show aired at 5 p.m. weekdays and made television history. Six years later, his groundbreaking Sunday night color TV show "Walt Disney's Wonderful World of Color" (later changed to "The Wonderful World of Disney"), began its 20-year run on NBC. At the same time, Disney was making stars out of Fred MacMurray, Hayley Mills, and Dean Jones in such movies as *The Shaggy Dog, The Absent-Minded Professor, Pollyanna,* and *The Parent Trap.* In 1964 Disney's *Mary Poppins* became one of the top-grossing films of all time.

Disney required professionalism of his staff and demanded the highest-quality Technicolor available, and as a result his live-action films topped competitors in both creativity and technical standards. He also had his hand in several other projects, including Audio-Animatronics (automatically controlled robots) and a Florida amusement complex that eventually became Walt Disney World, complementing California's vacation hot spot, Disneyland.

On December 15, 1966, Walt Disney died of lung cancer. Shortly after Disney's death, his brother Roy issued an optimistic statement pledging that Walt Disney's philosophy and genius would be carried on by his employees.

But no one could match Walt Disney's keen story sense or enthusiasm, and the studio foundered through most of the 1970s despite several strong CEOs, including E. Cardon "Card" Walker, who had joined the company as a traffic boy in 1938. The studio did manage a few successes during this period, including *Blackbeard's Ghost,* with Dean Jones and Suzanne Pleshette, and the 1969 release *The Love Bug,* which became the year's biggest box office hit and the second highest grossing film in Disney history after *Mary Poppins.* Other popular releases of the late 1960s and early 1970s included *The Jungle Book, The Aristocats, Bedknobs and Broomsticks,* and several live-action features.

But a run of box office disappointments followed in the mid-1970s before *The Rescuers* proved successful. *Pete's Dragon,* an experimental film combining human and animated characters, followed. Progress was slow but steady for the Disney studio in the late 1970s and early 1980s as well. The studio released three new live-action movies: *The World's Greatest Athlete, Gus,* and *The Shaggy D.A. Return from Witch Mountain,* a sequel to the popular mystery-fantasy *Escape to Witch Mountain,* premiered in 1978. A risky science fiction venture titled *The Black Hole* cost $20 million to produce but was lost in the amazing success of *Star Wars,* an all-time science fiction box office recordbreaker that became one of the most popular films ever released in the United States. CEO Ron Miller brought in new directors and younger writers who produced such films as *Watcher in the Woods* and the computer-generated *Tron,* but achieved only mild success in the face of competition from other movie studios.

In 1983, beginning with the release of *Mickey's Christmas Carol,* Disney's fortunes finally began to look up. A string of successful movies followed, including the Arctic adventure

Never Cry Wolf and a production of Ray Bradbury's *Something Wicked This Way Comes.* That same year the company also began marketing a family-oriented pay-TV channel called the Disney Channel, which quickly became the fastest-growing channel on cable television.

Corporate raider Saul Steinberg attempted a hostile takeover of the company in 1984. Disney ultimately bought Steinberg's 11.1 percent holding in the company for $325.4 million. A number of lawsuits were filed by shareholders against both Disney and Steinberg's Reliance Group Holdings, charging that Disney's managers had attempted to secure their positions and had lowered the value of the stock. The suits were settled in 1989 when the two companies jointly agreed to pay shareholders $45 million.

The Eisner Era Begins: 1984

Shortly after their purchase of 18.7 percent of Disney's stock, the Bass family of Texas supported the Disney board's hiring of Michael Eisner from Paramount Pictures to be Disney's new CEO and Frank Wells to be president.

Eisner, responsible for such Paramount blockbusters as *Raiders of the Lost Ark* and *Beverly Hills Cop,* immediately began to emphasize Touchstone Films, a subsidiary devoted to attracting adult movie audiences. Commentators began to note that Eisner, like Walt Disney, had the ability to predict and deliver movies people wanted to see. The 1985 release of *Down and Out in Beverly Hills* helped Touchstone build momentum, which it increased with *Outrageous Fortune, Tin Men, Ruthless People,* and other hits. In Eisner's first four years as CEO, Disney surged from last place to first in box office receipts among the eight major studios.

Eisner also set out to take full advantage of expanding markets such as cable television and home video. Disney signed a long-term deal with Showtime Networks, Inc., giving the cable service exclusive rights to Touchstone and other Disney releases through 1996. In addition, Eisner bought KHJ, an independent Los Angeles TV station; sought new markets for old Disney productions through television syndication; and began to distribute such TV shows as "The Golden Girls."

Certain Disney classics, including *Lady and the Tramp* and *Cinderella,* were released on videocassette during the late 1980s. Eisner protected the value of the films by limiting the availability of the tapes. He also scheduled the re-release of many other films for the late 1980s and early 1990s, by which time a new generation of children would be ready to see the films in the theater once again. Disney's revenues soon began to increase, averaging an improvement of approximately 20 percent annually during the second half of the 1980s.

In 1989 Disney-MGM Studios Theme Park opened near Orlando, Florida, on the grounds of Walt Disney World. Despite its name, the park was not a collaboration between the two studios; Disney purchased the rights to include attractions based on MGM films. Euro Disney, of which Disney owned 49 percent, opened outside of Paris, in Marne-la-Vallée, on April 12, 1992; and Tokyo Disneyland, licensed though not owned by Disney, regularly drew phenomenal crowds in a powerful consumer market. Plans were made to open a second Disney-MGM Studios park, on a site adjacent to Euro Disney, in the mid-1990s.

In the early 1980s the parks were responsible for about 70 percent of the company's revenue. Although they continued to be a crucial part of the company, the theme parks found competition with Disney's newer projects, including hotel expansions, home video distribution, and Disney merchandising, which together in 1991 garnered an impressive 28 percent of fiscal revenues. Virtually as important, perhaps more so given their unrealized potential, were Disney's international operations—evident not only in Japan and France, but throughout much of Europe, the former Soviet Union, South America, and China—which contributed 22 percent of total revenues in 1991.

Meanwhile, Touchstone remained healthy. Hollywood Pictures, Disney's newest film-producing arm, also began making more films in the late 1980s. Disney continued to score hits with *Three Men and a Baby, Good Morning Vietnam, Who Framed Roger Rabbit,* and others. Most importantly, production costs, though constantly rising, were held by Disney in 1989 to an average of $15 million per movie, compared to an industry average of more than $23 million.

Taking a Roller-Coaster Ride: 1990s

The 1990s, termed the "Disney Decade" by the company, promised to witness perhaps the most dramatic changes and accomplishments of Disney's more than half-century history. The combined talents of Eisner, president Frank Wells, and studio chairman Jeffrey Katzenberg caused a rush of excitement as the decade began. By the second quarter of 1991, the studio, under Katzenberg's strong leadership, had surpassed the theme parks in profitability, leading the company to commit to a record-high 25 new films in 1992. By far the greatest highlight of 1991 was Disney's 30th feature-length animated film, *Beauty and the Beast.* Amid a troubled year and a depressed economy, during which corporate net income plummeted by 23 percent and Disney, despite the success of its studio, experienced its first year with no growth since 1984, this film—nominated for best picture and winner of Academy Awards for best original score and best original song—provided much welcomed relief. *Beauty,* like its 1989 Oscar-winning predecessor *The Little Mermaid,* shattered previous records for the most successful opening of an animated film. It quickly became the highest-grossing picture of its genre.

Although Disney was notorious for undercutting its Hollywood competitors, it, too, was forced to pay exorbitant amounts for top creative talent. Both Bernard Weinraub, in a *New York Times* article, and Eisner, in the company's 1991 annual report, reported that Disney was going to try to stem the flow of high production costs for big-budget films and instead offer films with appealing storylines and engaging characters. According to Ron Grover, Katzenberg himself began pushing for such a redirection in early 1991. Presumably, films like the modestly budgeted 1990 sleeper *Pretty Woman* were expected in the future.

Disney's next forays—its creation, for example, of Hyperion Press and Hollywood Records for stakes in the publishing and adult music industries—were expected to further strengthen its reputation as an entertainment giant. Yet, here too, it became increasingly cautious. In August, the company revealed that its Imagineering division, responsible for theme park design, was laying off up to 400 of its employees. Further news that Euro Disney's profitability for its first year was in serious doubt indicated to some that Disney might be struggling. However, Disney's overseas investment was less than $200 million, ''a fraction of the total,'' according to Stewart Toy. ''And whether or not there's a profit, Walt Disney gets 10 percent of ticket sales and 5 percent of merchandise sales.''

As the Disney Decade continued to unfold, and speculations of mergers and other high-level behind-the-scenes negotiations repeatedly surfaced, one fact remained clear. According to Joe Flower, author of *Prince of the Magic Kingdom: Michael Eisner and the Re-Making of Disney,* the Disney name ''remains the company's largest resource, an asset that would be difficult if not impossible for any other company to build or buy. While Disney may suffer setbacks in particular areas, and may even abandon some businesses, it was likely that, all things considered, the company would continue to grow faster and more safely through the next decade than the average American company.''

During the latter half of the 1990s, Disney did indeed grow at a prolific rate, but by the decade's end there was little cause to celebrate. The remainder of the Disney Decade was pocked with troubling developments that shook the foundation of the Disney empire, prompting some experts to suggest the previously unimaginable: that the omnipotent Disney name was losing its market appeal. The tumultuous period began with tragedy, when Frank Wells died in a helicopter crash in 1994. The fatal accident left Eisner without his most trusted aide and left Disney without a president, a title Katzenberg reportedly coveted. Two days after the helicopter crash, Katzenberg approached Eisner about the job, but his bid to become president was rebuffed. Katzenberg responded by leaving Disney, departing on decidedly unfriendly terms. An acrimonious feud between Eisner and Katzenberg erupted that became litigious. Upon his departure, Katzenberg was given the equivalent of ten year's pay, but the former studio head wanted considerably more cash. He filed a lawsuit against Disney, demanding $580 million in compensation.

Against the backdrop of a sordid legal battle, whose ugly details became the stuff of headlines, Eisner prepared to add a new dimension to Disney's operations. In 1994, Eisner attempted to buy the NBC television network from General Electric Company, but the deal fell through because General Electric, reportedly, wanted to retain ownership of 51 percent of the network. Eisner pressed ahead, determined to buy a television network. His search ended in 1995 when Disney announced its head-turning merger with Capital Cities/ABC, a $19 billion deal that gave Disney control over television stations, radio stations, cable networks, and legions of other properties. Applauded by industry pundits as a strategically sound move, the acquisition of Capital Cities/ABC married the vast content collection controlled by Disney to the expansive broadcasting capabilities of the ABC network, exponentially increasing the might of what, after the transaction was completed in 1996, stood as a more than $20 billion entertainment conglomerate.

The late 1990s saw Eisner steer Disney in several other strategically important directions. The growth of the Internet presented the company's chairman and CEO with another opportunity to disseminate Disney's entertainment content to the public. In 1998, Disney acquired Starwave, which maintained ESPN.com and Mr. Showbiz, as well as other web sites, and purchased 43 percent of Infoseek, acquiring the rest of the Internet search engine company in 1999. In January 1999, the company launched the GO Network Web portal. Other additions to the company's operations in 1998 included the opening of the 540-acre Animal Kingdom park in Florida, the Disney version of a zoo, and the launching of an 875-stateroom cruise ship christened the *Disney Magic,* to be followed by the debut of a sister ship, the *Disney Wonder,* in 1999. Eisner also acquired two professional sports clubs, the Mighty Ducks of Anaheim, a professional hockey team, and Major League Baseball's Anaheim Angels. Concurrent with the numerous acquisitions he presided over, Eisner endeavored to expand Disney's geographic reach. During the late 1990s, the company collected roughly 20 percent of its revenue from overseas business—too low of a percentage from Eisner's viewpoint. China and India were considered to be high-growth markets.

The scope and scale of Disney's properties by the late 1990s represented an impressive list of businesses that few companies in the world could equal. The additions to the Disney portfolio during the latter half of the decade turned an already sprawling empire into a multifaceted entertainment conglomerate of mind-boggling proportions, but no matter the size of a company, success depended on execution. As it became evident during the court proceedings to resolve Katzenberg's lawsuit, Disney's massive revenue-generating, profit-making engine was sputtering inefficiently. The details delineating the company's problems were divulged because of the nature of the Katzenberg case. Eisner, who had the opportunity to settle his former studio chief's compensation claim for $100 million, decided not to give in without a fight, believing the demand for as much as $580 million was preposterously high. It was a decision he later regretted. In court, Eisner learned that Katzenberg had negotiated a contract with Wells during the 1980s. A passage in the contract, as published by the *Financial Times* on June 4, 1999, read: ''It is, of course, obvious but nonetheless worth pointing out that many of these pictures still have substantial revenues forthcoming from ancillary markets which continue to accrue to Jeffrey's benefit .... Of course, [these] will continue 'forever' in the sense that even if he should leave one day, there would be an arbitrated amount as to future income from the pictures.'' The inclusion of the word ''forever'' in the contract struck a crippling blow to Eisner's hope of leaving the courtroom victorious.

Because the amount of Katzenberg's claim depended on the future profit potential of certain facets of the Disney enterprise, company lawyers were inclined to paint a bleak picture of the company's financial health at the end of the 1990s and its prospects for the years ahead. Despite the incentive to underestimate the company's financial might, it became obvious to onlookers that all was not right in the Magic Kingdom. The theme parks were performing well, but nearly every other aspect of the company's business suffered from disappointing results. ABC was at the top of the list, hobbled by low ratings and rising costs, including the $9.2 billion spent for ABC and ESPN to acquire the rights for the NFL through 2008. Internationally, the company was not making headway, notoriously evident in two cinematic failures. *Mulan,* the Chinese-themed animation film, generated a paltry $1.3 million during its run in China. The release of *Hercules* in India fell decidedly flat and actually led to a loss of $14,000. On the whole, the last year of the decade signaled a depressing end to the 20th century for Disney. For the first nine months of 1999, excluding the income gained from an asset sale, operating income was down 17 percent, net income dropped 26 percent, and earnings per share fell 27 percent.

The Katzenberg compensation claim was settled for a reported $200 million, although both parties refused to divulge the amount. More significant to industry observers than the exact dollar amount of the settlement was the information revealed during the proceedings, prompting some analysts to cast a wary eye toward the entertainment behemoth. Some critics charged that Eisner's autocratic leadership inhibited efficiency and progress, but the most threatening diagnosis struck at the company's fundamental strength. Some industry experts contended that "age compression," the theory that youths of the late 1990s emulated teenage behavior at an earlier age than in decades past, was draining the strength of the Disney name. Rebellion against the wholesome Disney image was the result, reducing the size of Disney's target audience. "They've never gotten past the problem that their core audience is girls 2 to 8 and their moms," a former, unnamed, Disney executive explained in the September 6, 1999 issue of *Fortune* magazine. Sociological intricacies aside, the future financial health of Disney depended on the ability of the company to reap the rewards inherent in its operations, on its effectiveness in churning out profits from a powerful entertainment machine that looked good on the outside but internally was suffering. The continued attraction of the Disney name in the 21st century represented the foundation upon which the company's return to soaring profits would be built.

Principal Subsidiaries

ABC, Inc.; A&E Network (37.5%); Anaheim Sports; Buena Vista Home Video; Buena Vista International; Buena Vista Internet Group; Buena Vista Pictures Distribution, Inc.; Buena Vista Television; Childcraft Educational Corp.; The Disney Channel; The History Channel; Disney Consumer Products International, Inc.; Disney Development Co.; The Disney Store, Inc.; EDL Holding Co.; Euro Disney S.C.A. (49%); E! Entertainment Television (39.5%); ESPN (80%); Fairchild Publications; Hyperion; Infoseek Corporation; KHJ-TV, Inc.; Lake Buena Vista Commu-nities; Lifetime Entertainment Services (50%); Miramax Films; Reedy Creek Energy Services, Inc.; Touchstone Films; Touchstone Television; Walt Disney Attractions; Walt Disney Imagineering; Walt Disney Pictures and Television; WCO Parent Corp.; WED Transportation Systems, Inc.

Principal Divisions

Broadcasting; Creative Content; Theme Parks; Resorts; Sports.

Further Reading

Beard, Richard R., *Walt Disney's Epcot,* New York: Abrams, 1982.

Birnbaum, Steve, *The Best of Disneyland,* Boston: Houghton Mifflin, 1987.

"Disney Merges Television Production Arms," *MEDIAWEEK,* July 12, 1999, p. 3.

"Disney Profit Jumps 30%," *New York Times,* April 28, 1992.

"Disney Trimming Theme Park Staff As Par Gears Up," *Variety,* August 3, 1992.

"Eisner's Mousetrap," *Fortune,* September 6, 1999, p. 106.

Flower, Joe, *Prince of the Magic Kingdom: Michael Eisner and the Re-Making of Disney,* New York: John Wiley & Sons, 1991.

Grover, Ron, *The Disney Touch: How a Daring Management Team Revived an Entertainment Empire,* Homewood, Ill.: Business One Irwin, 1991.

Holliss, Richard, *The Disney Studio Story,* New York: Crown, 1988.

Holstein, William J., "Mickey's Net Loss," *U.S. News & World Report,* June 21, 1999, p. 48.

La Franco, Robert, "Disney's Problems Go Well Beyond One Big Lawsuit," *Forbes,* July 5, 1999, p. 50.

Leebron, Elizabeth, *Walt Disney: A Guide to References and Resources,* Boston: G.K. Hall, 1979.

Maltin, Leonard, *The Disney Films,* New York: Crown, 1984.

Parkes, Christopher, "Inside the Magic Kingdom," *Financial Times,* June 4, 1999, p. 6.

Taylor, John, *Storming the Magic Kingdom: Wall Street, the Raiders, and the Battle for Disney,* New York: Knopf, 1987.

Thomas, Bob, *Walt Disney, an American Original,* New York: Simon & Schuster, 1976.

Toy, Stewart, Patrick Oster, and Ronald Grover, "The Mouse Isn't Roaring," *Business Week,* August 24, 1992.

"Walt Disney Co.," *Discount Store News,* June 21, 1999, p. 26.

Weinraub, Bernard, "2 Titans Clash and All of Filmdom Feels Shock Waves," *New York Times,* April 13, 1992.

—Cindy Pearlman and Jay P. Pederson
—updated by Jeffrey L. Covell

The Woolwich plc

Watling St.
Bexleyheath
Kent DA6 7RR
United Kingdom
(44) 181-298-5000
Fax: (44) 181-298-4783
Web site: http://www.woolwich.co.uk

Public Company
Incorporated: 1847 as The Woolwich Equitable Benefit
    Building and Investment Association
Employees: 6,000
Total Assets: £33.63 billion (1998)
Stock Exchanges: London
Ticker Symbol: WWH.L
NAIC: 52211 Commercial Banking; 551111 Offices of
    Bank Holding Companies; 522292 Mortgage Banking;
    52222 Sales Financing

The Woolwich plc is one of the United Kingdom's leading financial services providers, with over £30 billion in assets. A former building society, The Woolwich joined most of the United Kingdom's other building societies in converting to bank status in 1997. Shedding its mutual status, The Woolwich went public on the London stock exchange and took a place on the country's prestigious FTSE 100 index. The Woolwich remains largely centered on its mortgage and other lending products; despite seeing its market share slip back from 7.5 percent to around three percent, The Woolwich remains one of the United Kingdom's largest mortgage providers. The company also offers traditional personal banking services, as well as domestic, automotive, and even pet insurance services. In the late 1990s, The Woolwich has been developing its investment services, including offshore investment facilities through its Woolwich Guernsey subsidiary. The Woolwich also operates lending subsidiaries in France and Italy. Despite its moves to diversify its product portfolio, The Woolwich has become the subject of takeover speculation in the rapidly consolidating U.K. financial services market.

Industrial Revolution Solution

The Woolwich was born out of the new economic and social realities of mid-19th-century England. The Industrial Revolution and the rise of the working class, which began swelling the country's urban centers, had brought the need for new housing initiatives. The first building societies made their appearance in the late 18th century, as workers—chiefly artisans—grouped together to pool their resources in order to buy land and build their homes. Group members generally drew lots to determine who would have the next home built by the group. These societies were generally called "terminating societies," given that, once the last member in the group had his home, the society was disbanded.

By the mid-19th century, the urban landscape had been dramatically transformed by a huge workforce of factory workers. The building society concept underwent its own development to reflect the changing workforce and their economic position. Where the terminating societies rarely had more than 20 or 30 members, the building society had many more, and functioned more as a lending organism than a direct home builder. Toward the middle of the century, the building society began to operate not only as a lender, but also as a savings facility, offering interest on members' secured savings. These building societies were meant to stay.

One of the earliest of such "permanent" building societies was The Woolwich. In 1847 five local businessmen decided to pool resources and open a lending and savings facility in order to aid in the development of the community. The Woolwich Equitable Benefit Building and Investment Association was founded in August 1847 with the express purpose of providing lending for people seeking to buy or build homes and secure savings services for its members. The appeal of the building society, apart from its ability to provide mortgages to the largely underpaid industrial workforce, lay precisely in its cooperative nature, during a time that saw the first stirrings of the union movement and a growing demand for democracy.

The explosive growth of the industrial workforce provided fuel for the rapid expansion of the building society movement.

Company Perspectives:

Our Business: The Woolwich aims to be the most effective provider of diversified personal financial services in the U.K. Offering a wide spectrum of solutions to customers' lending, investing and protecting needs, it also possesses the vision and the determination to be the best.

By the end of the 19th century, the United Kingdom counted more than 1,700 societies. Many of these societies proved to be less than ''permanent''; however, legislation provided in the Building Society Act of 1874 helped secure the importance of the building society, giving the movement a stronger basis with which to face the often drastic economic fluctuations of the era.

Leader in the 20th Century

The Woolwich prospered in the late 19th century; known by then as The Woolwich Equitable Building Society, the group was able to move to expanded headquarters, while remaining in the town of Woolwich. The society's biggest growth came shortly into the 20th century. The end of World War I saw a new level of optimism for the victorious United Kingdom. A boom in housing and other development provided the basis for The Woolwich's growth. In 1923, the building society decided to expand, opening its first branch office in London's Cheapside.

The rapid growth in new building and housing developments in the late 1920s and early 1930s enabled The Woolwich to continue its own rapid expansion. By 1933, The Woolwich, with an assets portfolio of some £38 million, could claim to be the third largest building society in the United Kingdom. Reflecting the building society's new prominence, The Woolwich opened a new headquarters building—Equitable House—on Woolwich's General Gordon Square in 1935.

The building society would not have long to enjoy its new headquarters. With the declaration of war in 1939—and the beginning of the German bombings of London—the company moved to temporary headquarters in the Pilgrim House in Westerham, in the Kent countryside. With a large part of the British male population engaged in the military effort, The Woolwich, like most of its financial and industrial counterparts, began taking on female employees for the first time. Despite the war, The Woolwich continued to expand, opening its first branch office outside of England, in Edinburgh, Scotland, in 1941.

The end of the war brought a fresh wave of construction as the country recovered from the damage caused by the German bombs. Another force driving the growth of the housing market in general and The Woolwich in particular was a new trend in housing. The nation's returning soldiers now sought to build and own their own homes, a development found elsewhere in much of the Western nations, encouraged in part by the shift of emphasis from the extended family to the nuclear family. The building boom inspired a fresh growth spurt in The Woolwich, which reached assets of £100 million in the mid-1950s.

By the 1960s, The Woolwich began to expand through most of England and much of the United Kingdom as well, opening branches on most of the country's ''high streets.'' The Woolwich was also reinventing itself as a modern financial services provider, although still focused on its core mortgage lending product. At the end of the 1960s, the building society had put into place its first mainframe computer system, using an IBM 360/30, at a new administration center in Bexleyheath, Kent. The country's great building wave was drawing to a close: by the start of the 1970s, more than half of all families in the United Kingdom had bought their own homes. Woolwich's mortgage products had proved highly popular, enabling the company to establish itself on a fully national scale.

Conversion in the 1990s

The economic recession of the 1970s, brought on by the Arab Oil Crisis, would devastate the British economy, plunging the country into a long period of gloom. Consolidation of the still highly fragmented building society industry became the order of the day. By the mid-1990s, the number of societies had dwindled to just 80 survivors. Of these, The Woolwich remained in its top three position, behind Halifax and Nationwide.

Part of Woolwich's success in surviving came from its early implementation of networking technologies, which linked all of the society's branches to the Bexleyheath mainframe. The first in the industry to realize such a network, the society benefited not only from cost reductions, but also from a more modern image. Image provided another factor in The Woolwich's growth: the launch of a mid-1970s advertising campaign contributed the highly popular phrase ''I'm with The Woolwich.'' More and more people in the United Kingdom were able to say just that.

In order to fuel its growth, The Woolwich became one of the first building societies to look for external financing. In 1983, the society went to the public market to raise capital, issuing certificates of deposits on the London Money Market. The influx of capital enabled the company to step up the industry's consolidation, as it swallowed four smaller building societies. The society's acquisition drive culminated in its merger with the Gateway Building Society in 1988, making The Woolwich one of the industry's true heavyweights, with assets totaling some £13 billion. By then The Woolwich had also begun to diversify its operations beyond its traditional mortgage lending product.

The so-called Big Bang deregulation of the financial industry in 1986 set the stage for The Woolwich to enter into a new array of financial services markets. In 1989 The Woolwich launched its first subsidiary operation, Woolwich Independent Financial Advisory Services Limited, which, as its name implied, brought the building society into the financial planning market. The company also began developing a real estate arm, Woolwich Property Services, which grew to a national chain with nearly 170 branch locations by the late 1990s, including the 1991 takeover of the U.K. real estate operations of the Prudential Corporation. Meanwhile, in 1989, The Woolwich left its headquarters in the Equitable Building at Woolwich to establish new headquarters in its Bexleyheath locations.

From Bexleyheath, The Woolwich rolled out other subsidiaries as it diversified its product portfolio. In 1990 the company launched an offshore banking and investment vehicle, Woolwich Guernsey, which principally served the United Kingdom's large expatriate community, and also opened Woolwich Life, a joint venture with the Royal & Sun Alliance Insurance Group to provide life insurance, mortgage endowments, critical illness coverage and savings bonds to the mortgage market; Woolwich held 90 percent of the joint venture, to Royal & Sun's ten percent. Woolwich Unit Trust Managers Limited was launched in 1991, offering unit trust services to customers at Woolwich's branch locations. By then, The Woolwich had already ventured overseas, starting up Banca Woolwich in Italy, principally as a mortgage loan distributor through third parties. In 1991 the building society bought out the 20-branch strong residential mortgage lender Banque Immobilière de Crédit from Midland Bank, renaming the operation Banque Woolwich SA.

Public Bank for the 21st Century

Despite calling itself Banca in Italy and Banque in France, The Woolwich was still a building society back home in the United Kingdom. Yet the society was rapidly heading towards its largest transformation yet. In the meantime, in the early 1990s, the society continued to expand, buying up the struggling Town and Country Building Society in 1992. That same year, the society changed its name to Woolwich Building Society, dropping the longheld ''Equitable.''

Another piece of The Woolwich portfolio was added in 1993, when the surveying operations of Ekins The Woolwich and the separate Woolwich Property Services were combined to form Ekins—The Woolwich Surveying Services Limited, one of the largest specialist residential surveyors in the United Kingdom. The last piece of the diversified Woolwich portfolio was added in 1995, when the society formed The Woolwich Insurance Services Ltd. joint venture with Legal & General Group, offering personal insurance products including homeowners, automobile, and pet insurance policies underwritten by Legal & General.

Woolwich was clearly heading toward a change in its status. By the mid-1990s, growing numbers of the United Kingdom's building societies were making the move to convert to full-fledged bank status. One of the earliest ''converts'' was Abbey National, which converted to a shareholder-held public status in 1989. Many of Woolwich's major competitors, including Halifax and Alliance & Leicester were also said to be preparing a conversion.

Woolwich announced that it too would be converting from a mutually held building society to a publicly held banking corporation in January 1996, with its public offering on the London stock exchange slated for 1997. In preparation for the change, the society named a new chief executive officer, to replace the retiring former CEO Donald Kirkham. The job was to go to Peter Robinson, who had risen to the top of the society's organization over a 23-year career, and who had been handpicked to take over the CEO spot by Kirkham himself. Yet within three months of his appointment, Robinson was forced to resign amid allegations that he had misused his executive position, including using society resources for his personal gain. Robinson was replaced by John Stewart as CEO.

The Woolwich conversion did not take place until 1997, with the delay as a possible result of its executive troubles. By the time The Woolwich finally went public, however, those problems seemed far behind, as the listing, worth some £3 billion, generated an enthusiastic welcome—and a total market capitalization of more than £5.5 billion. The Woolwich's conversion from building society to bank placed it among the top ten British financial institutions, and granted the company instant FTSE 100 status as one of the United Kingdom's blue-chip companies. It also created shareholders of the former building society's 3.5 million members—who voted to abandon mutuality for free-market capitalism. By the end of 1997, however, the unsteady worldwide market—including the economic collapse of many of the Asian economies—had drained off some of The Woolwich's share strength. At the same time, the company's decision to open a number of customer service centers, effectively cutting out many of the third-party mortgage brokers through which The Woolwich had sold many of its mortgages, resulted in the company losing a large portion of its market share. By 1998, the company's market share had slipped from 7.5 percent to just 3.1 percent.

The company's share price nevertheless rebounded, aided by The Woolwich's decision to shed its money-losing real estate division, selling the chain of estate agencies for £23 million. The company also managed to win back some of its market share by rolling out new products, including subprime loan packages and a new mortgage package, the Open Plan Borrowing, combining mortgages, personal loans, and customer savings in a single vehicle. The new package was a quick hit with Woolwich customers, accounting for 45 percent of the company's new mortgages.

In 1999 The Woolwich further boosted its range with two joint ventures. The first was a partnership with home shopping retailer Littlewoods. Dubbed Littlewoods Financial Services, the venture began marketing home insurance, personal loans, and credit cards to Littlewoods' 3.5-million-strong customer base in October 1999. Initial offerings were to be based on The Woolwich's products and brand names; with plans to launch Littlewoods-branded financial packages by the end of the year 2000. A second joint venture was also set to debut at the end of 1999, as The Woolwich and U.S.-based Countrywide Credit Industries set up the Global Home Loans partnership for the U.K. market, beginning operations in September 1999.

The Woolwich had successfully expanded beyond its former mortgage lending core, while vowing to remain an independent operation. Yet industry analysts remained skeptical of the company's long-term independent status, considering The Woolwich to be too small to compete with the industry giants and too large to take a comfortable position as a niche player. While The Woolwich insisted on its intention to remain independent—and was quietly buying back shares from its member shareholders—the company admitted that it would be interested in a possible acquisition to boost its size.

Principal Subsidiaries

Littlewoods Financial Services (50%); Woolwich Surveying Services Limited (Ekins Surveyors); Woolwich Independent Financial Advisory Services Limited; Woolwich Insurance Services Limited (90%); Woolwich Life Assurance Company Limited (90%); Woolwich Unit Trust Managers Limited; Global Home Loans (50%); Banca Woolwich SpA (Italy); Banque Woolwich SA (France).

Further Reading

Beugge, Charlotte, ''Woolwich Sells 167 Agencies,'' *Daily Telegraph*, November 11, 1998.

Hickey, Bernard, ''Woolwich Aims for Independence,'' *Reuters*, June 22, 1999.

Lodge, Steve, ''Woolwich Will Not Be the Last,'' *Independent on Sunday*, January 14, 1996, p. 22.

''Outlook: Woolwich,'' *Independent*, February 18, 1999.

Oziel, Clelia, ''Woolwich H1 Profit Leaves Market Cold,'' *Reuters*, July 29, 1999.

''Woolwich Debuts in Style on London Exchange,'' *Reuters Business Report*, July 7, 1997.

—M. L. Cohen

Wyant Corporation

100 Readington Road
Somerville, New Jersey 08876
U.S.A.
(908) 707-1800
(877) 326-1650
Fax: (908) 707-1526
Web site: http://www.wyantcorp.com

Public Company
Incorporated: 1971 as Hosposable Products, Inc.
Employees: 500
Sales: $67.12 million (1998)
Stock Exchanges: NASDAQ
Ticker Symbol: WYNT
NAIC: 322291 Sanitary Paper Product Manufacturing;
   325612 Polish & Other Sanitation Good
   Manufacturing

Wyant Corporation, a New York corporation based in New Jersey, manufactures and distributes disposable wipers and sanitary paper products and systems through IFC Disposables, Inc., a U.S. subsidiary, and manufactures and distributes sanitation products and systems, including janitorial chemicals, to commercial and institutional markets in Canada through Wood Wyant Inc., a Canadian subsidiary.

Hosposable Products: 1971–90

The company was founded and incorporated in 1971 as Hosposable Products, Inc., with Leonard Schramm as president and chief executive officer and Sidney Schramm, his father, as chairman of the board. Each of them owned 23.6 percent of the stock. Hosposable produced disposable incontinence pads and adult diapers for use by hospitals, nursing homes, and other institutions providing services to the sick and elderly. Its (leased) office and plant were in Jersey City. During 1972, the company's first full year, about 83 percent of its net sales of $726,943 were made to government agencies, especially federal

agencies. Hosposable added the production of infants' disposable diapers for sale to an agency of the U.S. Department of Defense in 1973 and, later, also aimed the product at the civilian market, but this business segment never became a significant source of revenue and was eventually dropped.

In 1975 Hosposable Products, through Bridgewater Manufacturing Corp., a new subsidiary, purchased the machinery, equipment, and inventory of Blessings Products, Inc. of Bound Brook, New Jersey, for about $500,000. This acquisition enabled Hosposable to substantially expand its production of underpads and to broaden its product line to include disposable washcloths and draw cloths for sale to the same class of institutions. The company's net sales rose to $7.8 million in 1977, but net earnings were extremely slender in this period, with a peak of $185,209 in 1976. By 1977 government agencies accounted for only about one-quarter of Hosposable's business, in part because the company found that such contracts were not proving lucrative. By contrast, Hosposable was now making a significant proportion of its sales to American Hospital Supply Co., a national distributor of equipment and supplies to hospitals.

By 1984, when Hosposable Products became a public company, it was no longer sited in Jersey City. Its products were being manufactured at leased plants in Bound Brook, which also served as corporate headquarters, and in Fresno, California. The company's disposable underpads, draw sheets, and diapers continued to consist of multiple layers of absorbent paper wadding or fluffed cellulose sandwiched between a top sheet of nonwoven fabric—rayon at the time—and a bottom layer of polyethylene sheeting, all bonded together with an adhesive. The fabric layer had the soft, supple characteristics of bed linen and was permeable. The polyethylene sheeting provided a barrier against penetration by liquids and other discharges not absorbed by the wadding.

These products were being sold mainly to large distributors for eventual use, under private labels, primarily by hospitals, nursing homes, other healthcare institutions, and government agencies. About nine percent of the company's sales in 1984 were being made to retail chains selling to individual consumers, generally under their own private labels. American Hospital Supply accounted for 52 percent of the company's sales in 1984, but its share declined markedly in subsequent years.

Hosposable Products' net sales in 1982 came to $11.9 million (a figure not topped until 1987), but its net earnings amounted only to $38,000. In February 1984 the company made its initial public offering, receiving about $1.4 million in net proceeds by the sale of 400,000 shares of common stock at $5 a share. Sidney and Leonard Schramm each retained 11.7 percent of the shares. Some of the proceeds of the sale were used to retire about $530,000 in bank debt. Some of it also went for the purchase, for about $2.6 million, of an air-laid plant and machine installed at Bound Brook in 1986. A $2.3 million bond issued by the New Jersey Economic Development Authority also made this purchase possible.

Using this air-forming plant, Hosposable Products began making nonwoven fabrics for various industry uses in January 1987. Production reached about 2.3 million pounds in 1988 and was being sold to converters producing a wide range of consumer and industrial products, mostly for dusting, wiping, and cleaning. By 1989 some of this raw material was being used by the company itself. This new venture was not immediately profitable, however. After earning $570,000 in 1986 the company lost $294,000 the following year, primarily because of the start-up costs of the new machinery and high costs of purchased raw materials. Hosposable Products, on sales of $14.3 million, lost $464,000 in 1988, an outcome it blamed on the escalating price of purchasing raw materials. The company was profitable again in 1989. In 1990 its net income passed $1 million for the first time, on sales of almost $19 million.

Controlled by Wyant: 1990–99

Wyant & Co. Ltd., a privately owned Canadian sanitation firm, purchased a large block of Hosposable Products stock in 1990 and received an option to purchase twice that amount. Wyant was in existence by 1971, when it had net income of $201,000 Canadian on net sales of $9.1 million. (The Canadian dollar was at virtual parity with the U.S. dollar at the time.) Wyant and Hosposable Products also entered into an agreement whereby Wyant agreed to purchase 72 hours of production per week of Hosposable's air-laid product for six years and to pay $1.9 million for Hosposable's product, research, development, sales training, market information support, and advertising suggestions over a six-year period.

Wyant, in early 1991, exercised its option by purchasing the Schramms's stock and thus raising its share of Hosposable Products to 41 percent. Leonard Schramm remained president of the company, however, until fiscal 1996. Also in early 1991, Hosposable Products purchased IFC Nonwovens, Inc., a Tennessee-based corporation with a manufacturing plant in Jackson, Tennessee, for $4.7 million. This company was producing a broad line of disposable, industrial, and ''clean room'' wiping products, some of which utilized air-laid nonwoven fabric being supplied by Hosposable. This company became a Hosposable subsidiary, IFC Disposables, Inc. IFC Disposables accounted for 30.5 percent of the parent company's net sales of $27.1 million in 1991.

In 1993 Hosposable Products described itself as a manufacturer of plastic-resin and paper-based products produced by air-laid processing technology and equipment. These, besides the aforementioned products, included airline inflight service-cart covers. In December 1993 the company received $5.3 million in 20-year bonds from the New Jersey Economic Development Authority to finance both the acquisition of additional air-laid production equipment and the $3.7 million purchase of a warehouse facility in Branchburg, New Jersey. The Branchburg property, which had a Somerville mailing address, replaced the Bound Brook facility and also became Hosposable's corporate headquarters.

Net sales for Hosposable Products continued to increase annually, reaching $34.5 million in 1994. Net income reached $1.2 million in 1993 and was slightly above $1 million in 1994. Net sales rose in 1995 to $40.5 million, of which private-label sales accounted for 18.6 percent, compared with only 2.5 percent in 1994. The company lost $209,000, after taking a $550,000 writedown of IFC property. Sales reached $42.3 million in 1996, but Hosposable lost more than $1 million after paying $550,000 in fees associated with the impending acquisition of Canadian operations of G.H. Wood + Wyant Inc.

This completed transaction, effected in 1997, brought the newly named Wood Wyant Inc., a Canadian manufacturer and national distributor of a broad range of industrial and institutional sanitation products, under the Hosposable corporate umbrella. In addition to the former Wyant & Co., Wood Wyant consisted of the former G.H. Wood & Co. This privately held Canadian manufacturer, marketer, and distributor of janitorial products and sanitary supplies was the leading supplier of sanitary supplies and equipment in Canada, with annual sales of about $40 million, when it was sold in 1987 to Ecolab Inc. Ecolab sold it to Wyant & Co. in 1993. The combined Wood and Wyant operations adopted, in 1994, a primary focus on washroom and floor care programs within the healthcare, education, industrial, and office channels of distribution, with account managers providing customers with cost-effective solutions to sanitation problems.

Hosposable Products was renamed Wyant Corporation in 1997. Wyant consisted of three segments: IFC, Wood Wyant, and Wyant Health Care Division, the original segment of the Hosposable business. The Health Care Division introduced branded and private-label adult briefs in 1997 to further expand its line of incontinent care products in this growth market. Also in 1997, IFC transferred its manufacturing operations from Jackson, Tennessee, to Brownsville, Tennessee. With the addition of Wood Wyant, net sales of the consolidated company rose to $94.9 million in 1997. There was a net loss of $360,000.

In 1998 Wood Wyant acquired six Canadian businesses. Two of these, H.A. Perigord Co. Ltd. and Professional Sanitation Products Ltd., were distributors of sanitation products purchased for a combined $3.1 million in cash and stock. Four were related businesses, based in British Columbia: Fraser Valley Industrial Chemicals Inc., a manufacturer of janitorial chemicals; Furnel Distributors Ltd.; Midway Furnel Sanitary Supply Ltd.; and Midway Supply Ltd. The latter three were distributors of sanitation products. Wood Wyant paid $2.6 million in cash and stock for these acquisitions. Wyant Corporation's sales were $67.1 million in 1998.

In early 1999 Wyant agreed to sell the Health Care Division to Paper-Pak Products, Inc. of LaVerne, California, for about

$15.5 million, including the assumption of $3.5 million in debt. Net sales of this division came to $36.5 million in 1998, and net income, after two unprofitable years, to $1.6 million. Wood Wyant, in May 1999, agreed to purchase certain assets and the operating business of the Atlantic Sanitation Division of Cassidy's Ltd. Based in Dartmouth, Nova Scotia, this division was a leading provider of sanitation products and services to the commercial and institutional markets in the Canadian provinces of Nova Scotia, New Brunswick, and Prince Edward Island.

Wyant Corporation in 1998

Wood Wyant was manufacturing and distributing a broad range of industrial and institutional sanitation products in Canada in 1998, including paper hand towels, bathroom tissue, related sanitary paper products, janitorial chemicals, waste receptacles, and cleaning equipment and systems. It was the only dedicated national distributor of a full line of sanitary paper products, janitorial chemicals and equipment, and sanitation supplies to institutional markets in Canada. It was servicing some 20,000 customers through a direct sales organization supported by customer service centers located across Canada.

Wood Wyant's manufacturing operations included the conversion of base paper and the manufacture of janitorial chemicals. Base paper was being converted into paper hand towels and bathroom tissue. Janitorial chemicals were being developed and manufactured from raw materials produced by chemical suppliers, which were then blended in large tanks and packed into shipping containers for sale by Wood Wyant.

Wood Wyant's major facility was an owned 149,500-square-foot manufacturing and distribution plant in Pickering, a borough of Toronto. It also had smaller leased manufacturing plants in Scarborough (also a borough of Toronto) and Abbotsford, British Columbia. The latter two were chemical plants with total production in 1998 of about 2.9 million liters (49 percent of capacity).

Wood Wyant also had 14 leased distribution facilities/service centers in the provinces of Alberta, British Columbia, Manitoba, Nova Scotia, Ontario, and Quebec. It maintained a policy of next-day delivery of all core stocking products from its major service centers. The principal customers were in the healthcare and education (including schools, universities, and colleges) segment but also included industrial entities and distributors. U.S. customers accounted for less than eight percent of sales. Wood Wyant's corporate headquarters was in Montreal.

IFC's manufacturing operations, at leased quarters in Brownsville, Tennessee, included the conversion of various materials into wiping products. Specialized machinery was cutting, folding, or winding various materials into finished products, which were then packaged and placed into shipping containers. These products were being sold to some 683 distributors and brokers located in 44 states by both a direct sales organization and independent brokers. IFC accounted for only 6.5 percent of Wyant's sales in 1998.

The Wyant Health Care Division, prior to its sale to Paper-Pak in July 1999, was manufacturing products—principally disposable underpads and adult briefs—for protection against incontinence, some of it for sale as private-label brands by major customers. The division's air-laid fabrics were being used as components of wiping products manufactured by IFC and also were being sold in roll form to converters and manufacturers producing a wide range of healthcare, consumer, and industrial products. Manufacturing facilities were in Branchburg and Fresno. Most division sales (other than intercompany transactions with IFC) were being made to distributors that, in turn, sold its products to institutional users such as hospitals and nursing homes and to industrial users. Other sales were to private labelers selling to retail individual/chain stores. The retail chains usually sold the products under private label.

Wyant Corporation had long-term debt of $3.9 million in 1999. A Wyant family voting trust held 55 percent of the company's common stock. Wyant & Co. held 37 percent of its preferred stock, which was convertible to common stock on a share-to-share basis. Two Wyant family members were on the seven-person board of directors.

Principal Subsidiaries

Bridgewater Manufacturing Corp.; IFC Disposables, Inc.; Wood Wyant Inc. (Canada).

Further Reading

"Wyant Corporation Common Stock to Be Transferred to NASDAQ Smallcap Market," April 1, 1999, http://www.wyantcorp.com/english/contents/press/april_1_1999.htm.

"Wyant Corporation Completes Sale," July 21, 1999, http://www.wyantcorp.com/english/contents/press/july211999.htm.

"Wyant Corporation Reports Acquisition," *PR Newswire,* May 31, 1999, p. 0092.

—Robert Halasz

Ziebart International Corporation

1290 East Maple Road
Troy, Michigan 48083
U.S.A.
(248) 588-4100
(800) 877-1312
Fax: (248) 588-0718
Web site: http://www.ziebart.com

Private Company
Incorporated: 1959 as Ziebart Corporation
Employees: 200
Sales: $150 million (1997 est.)
NAIC: 53311 Lessors of Nonfinancial Intangible Assets
   (Except Copyrighted Works); 811121 Automotive
   Body, Paint, & Interior Repair & Maintenance;
   811122 Automotive Glass Replacement Shops;
   811198 All Other Automotive Repair & Maintenance

Ziebart International Corporation, which offers a wide range of services and products for cars and trucks, is perhaps best known for its rustproofing and auto protection services, its primary line of business for its first 30 years. In the 1990s the company began focusing on expanding its products and services. As a result, its franchised and company-owned retail locations offer a range of professional detailing services, appearance protection services, car accessories, and truck and van accessories in addition to rust protection. In 1998 Ziebart entered into a co-branding agreement with Speedy Auto Glass and began offering auto glass replacement in many of its locations.

1950s–80s: Beginnings and Expansion Through Franchising

In 1954 Kurt Ziebart, a master mechanic from Germany, living in Detroit, Michigan, developed a scientific process called rustproofing, the first successful method of protecting an automobile from corrosion. Using Ziebart's chemical method, car owners could protect the metallic body of their vehicles from rust caused by rain, snow, and ice. The first store, bearing the proprietary Ziebart name, was opened on Harper Avenue in Detroit in 1959, to rustproof automobiles. The system proved popular, particularly in the Great Lakes states, where the salt mixture sprayed on the roads during the winters caused rusting, as well as in coastal areas where the salt air encouraged rust. The company was soon establishing franchised locations, primarily in the Midwest, throughout the 1960s.

In 1969 Ziebart opened its first international operation in Windsor, Ontario, across the border from Detroit. The following year Ziebart was bought by Swedish immigrant E. Jan Hartmann, who developed Ziebart's operations through its master franchise system into the Pacific Rim, the Middle East, Australia, Europe, and Mexico. Ziebart expanded overseas by finding a corporation within each country that had the ability to become a master franchisee for the country. The master franchisee would then be responsible for establishing locations through subfranchising.

The Mexican master franchise was given to Praxis Corporation in 1993, and average sales for the first location in Monterrey were twice the U.S. average. The first German location was also opened in 1993. By this time, Ziebart manufactured its own rust protection chemicals, paint sealants, fabric protectors, and various cleaners and polishes. It distributed most of its products worldwide from its warehouse in Detroit. The company also operated a separate Canadian warehouse for its Canadian locations.

Product Diversification in the 1990s

In 1990 Ziebart had more than 1,000 locations in 40 countries and more than $100 million in worldwide dealer sales. The company had also acquired Tidy Car in 1989, which included about 200 detailing locations in the United States, Canada, Sweden, and Denmark. Detailing was a type of deep cleaning that restored a vehicle to like-new condition. Ziebart eventually expanded the Tidy Car locations to include accessories and Ziebart protection services.

The year 1991 was good for growth at Ziebart Tidy Car, with revenues increasing by 12.5 percent. Tidy Car was the largest franchise system of automotive detailing services in the United

Company Perspectives:

Ziebart has circled the globe with success for nearly four decades. We've launched and nourished hundreds of individual entrepreneurs and master franchise organizations. In more than 40 countries across six continents, people have recognized the Ziebart name for two generations. Vehicle owners know that Ziebart stores are the premier places on earth where, under one roof, they can find everything they need to help keep their cars and trucks beautiful, and exciting to drive.

States. Ziebart began testing the possibility of combining the new Tidy Car franchises with the traditional Ziebart locations. It conducted market tests in six cities that combined detailing services with accessories and protection products. During the test Ziebart and Tidy Car products were offered to owners of the separate franchises. The test proved successful, and toward the end of 1991 more than 400 franchises had the opportunity to convert to a joint Ziebart Tidy Car franchise. By October nearly 60 percent had either made the change or were in the process of converting. Some 70 Canadian Ziebart-only franchises remained unchanged.

Ziebart recognized that consumers were spending more on their cars and trucks and keeping them longer. The company also noted that people were generally too busy to maintain their vehicles themselves, so they were willing to spend money on high-quality professional services such as those that Ziebart offered to protect their investment in their cars and trucks. In fact, new vehicle purchases in 1992 were down about ten percent, and analysts observed that owners were keeping their vehicles for an average of more than seven years. With the trend of consumers driving older cars came the demand for services such as Ziebart's to keep cars looking like new.

In 1992 Ziebart introduced ChipFix, a detail service that restored paint surfaces that had been chipped or dinged, as part of its product diversification strategy. The ChipFix system could match more than 25,000 colors. ChipFix was priced at $89 and $100, making it much cheaper than a full paint job. Moreover, the process could be completed in a few hours. After being test marketed, the new service was launched in the late spring of 1992. At the time Ziebart Tidy Car operated 700 locations in more than 40 countries.

By 1992 about two-thirds of Ziebart's revenues came from protection services, with detailing accounting for about seven percent of sales. The company's marketing efforts stressed one-stop shopping for car care and the high quality and durability of its products and techniques that had been proven over the past 30 years.

When Mississippi River flooding paralyzed rail and truck traffic in 1993, Ziebart developed a special marketing campaign for its Tidy Car division in the Midwest. The program offered a ten percent discount ($10 off the standard $100 price) to power-wash mud from car-engine compartments and remove mildew and odors from vehicle interiors.

In 1994 Ziebart's employees purchased the company through an employee stock ownership plan (ESOP). The franchise support system was expanded, and Ziebart's line of products and services broadened. The following year, Ziebart offered new Ziebart TidyCar franchises that would focus on detailing and installing bolt-on accessories. The company planned to offer these franchises for less than the cost of the original rustproofing franchises. About 65 percent of the new franchises' business was projected to be detailing, cleaning, and protectants, with the remaining 35 percent being auto and truck accessories.

Sales of Ziebart's core service, rustproofing, fell by 25 percent during 1996 and 1997. During the 1980s rustproofing had accounted for 80 percent of Ziebart's revenues, and by the mid-1990s it was accounting for less than 30 percent of the company's business, even though market research indicated that most customers associated Ziebart with rustproofing. The rise of auto leasing and better grades of metal being used in car production were among the factors contributing to a decline in the demand for rustproofing. Ziebart's business was also being affected by increased competition from the automotive aftermarket as well as from automakers themselves, who were starting to offer consumers such options as lighted running boards, an add-on that Ziebart had been offering as well. Franchise sales were flat for 1996–97, and the number of franchise locations was holding steady at around 600.

The company felt that detailing offered good prospects for growth. Detailing was estimated to be a $1 billion per year market and was highly fragmented. Ziebart estimated it was the largest detailing operation in the United States with about two percent of the market. In the auto accessories market, the challenge was to offer the newest, most popular accessories and to jettison them in favor of other accessories when the trends changed. In 1997 the hottest accessories were remote starters, which allowed drivers to warm up or cool off their vehicles before getting into them, and Ziebart promptly began offering these. Some franchisees supported Ziebart's diversification strategy, while others gave up their franchises because they felt that consumers associated Ziebart exclusively with rustproofing and that company efforts were going too far afield.

At the end of 1997 Ziebart introduced a new marketing slogan—''Survival Gear for Cars''—as part of an already-running ad campaign featuring Adam West, star of the 1960s television series ''Batman.'' A newly expanded line of products and services was marketed under the slogan, and Ziebart was offering such products and services as sunroofs, window tints, auxiliary lighting, sound barriers, keyless entry and electronic alarm systems, remote car starters, paint renewal, and fabric protection. ''Survival Gear'' also included a range of professional detailing services, appearance protection services, rust protection, accessories, and truck and van accessories. Ziebart positioned itself to offer services and products for long-term car owners as well as individuals who kept their cars only for a couple of years. Services included cleaning, restoring, and renewing the paint finish; rust protection; installing underbody sound barriers to reduce noise levels; and spraying Ziebart's patented bed liners to protect truck beds and cargo areas. For a vehicle's interior Ziebart locations could apply the company's own chemical formulations to restore interior fabric and protect it from permanent spills, dirt, and stains.

While Ziebart's primary market was the individual car and truck owner, the company also serviced wholesale accounts, mainly car dealerships and fleet owners such as municipalities, utility companies, and even floral shops. Favorable market forces included higher car prices, which prompted owners to treat their vehicles as valuable investments that required care and protection.

Co-Branding and Franchise Standards in the Late 1990s

In 1998 Ziebart initiated a co-branding arrangement with Speedy Auto Glass, whereby Ziebart would offer the installation of Speedy Auto Glass at its stores, and Speedy would offer Ziebart products in its outlets. The co-branding plan between Ziebart and Speedy called for the opening of 150 new Ziebart stores within Speedy facilities and 225 new Speedy stores within Ziebart's franchise and company-owned operations. Speedy Auto Glass was a Canadian-based company that entered the U.S. market in 1984, and was the leading supplier of replacement auto glass in Canada as well as a leader in the western United States. Speedy had an established position with insurance companies and an established relationship with North American glass distributors. It had a strong franchise that was geographically compatible with Ziebart's and operated some 300 corporate stores and 200 franchise outlets in North America. The co-branding arrangement was part of Ziebart's strategy to add ''need'' products and services to its line of ''want'' products and services. Auto glass was considered a ''need'' product, because people needed to replace a cracked windshield or broken glass, while many of Ziebart's other products were used to upgrade vehicles and were classified as ''want'' products or services.

Once the auto insurance networks were notified that Ziebart stores would be offering glass replacement, business began coming in without any advertising or marketing efforts. ''It's an insurance-driven business,'' noted one franchisee whose business increased 20 percent after taking on Speedy Auto Glass replacements. Ziebart dealers were given extensive training in glass replacement at Speedy's Seattle headquarters.

Over the years Ziebart developed an excellent reputation for its franchise operations and franchise support, earning recognition from such publications as *Entrepreneur, Success, Franchise Times,* and *Income Opportunities,* as well as numerous awards from the International Franchise Association for outstanding performance. Ziebart's franchise support included sophisticated marketing programs as well as sales and technical support. The company's worldwide training team conducted detailed, hands-on technical and business training for franchise operators. Moreover, the company produced an extensive plan that set franchise standards; potential franchisees were required to work in an existing Ziebart store before being given their own franchise. Once in business, franchisees had access to a well-staffed support hotline. Ziebart also provided information services support and equipped its stores with point-of-sale computer applications.

Ziebart also valued its advertising program, seeking to create high visibility television, radio, and print advertisements. In the late 1990s, the ads were designed to increase awareness in, and drive sales for, Ziebart's ''Survival Gear for Cars'' marketing campaign. Franchisees were supplied with merchandising materials for their stores, including signs, brochures, and other promotional materials. Each year Ziebart held an International Dealer Conference to encourage communication among its widespread franchisees and to provide information about new products, services, and marketing plans. Celebrating 40 years in business as it approached a new century, Ziebart could be expected to continue anticipating and meeting the wants and needs of car owners, and to grow its franchise operations in the process.

Further Reading

Cunningham, Dwight, ''Flood's Impact Hitting Here, Even If You Can't See Water,'' *Crain's Detroit Business,* July 19, 1993, p. 3.

Geisler, Jennie, ''To Boldly Go Where No Other Specialty Retailer Has Gone Before,'' *Aftermarket Business,* October 1, 1993, p. 20.

Roush, Matt, ''Customers Picked Ziebart's New Slogan,'' *Crain's Detroit Business,* December 22, 1997, p. 13.

''Ziebart and Speedy Tie a Ribbon on Bigger Cut of Auto Aftermarket,'' *Successful Franchising,* February 1999.

''Ziebart Debuts Detailing Franchises,'' *Aftermarket Business,* March 1, 1995, p. 31.

''Ziebart Franchises Marry Accessories, Detailing into One,'' *Aftermarket Business,* October 1, 1991, p. 5.

''Ziebart's Service Does Away with Dings,'' *Aftermarket Business,* May 1, 1992, p. 7.

—David P. Bianco

INDEX TO COMPANIES

Index to Companies

Listings in this index are arranged in alphabetical order under the company name. Company names beginning with a letter or proper name such as Eli Lilly & Co. will be found under the first letter of the company name. Definite articles (The, Le, La) are ignored for alphabetical purposes as are forms of incorporation that precede the company name (AB, NV). Company names printed in bold type have full, historical essays on the page numbers appearing in bold. Updates to entries that appeared in earlier volumes are signified by the notation **(upd.)**. Company names in light type are references within an essay to that company, not full historical essays. This index is cumulative with volume numbers printed in bold type.

INDEX TO INDUSTRIES

Index to Industries

CONSTRUCTION

CONTAINERS

DRUGS/PHARMACEUTICALS

ELECTRICAL & ELECTRONICS

ENGINEERING & MANAGEMENT SERVICES

ENTERTAINMENT & LEISURE

FOOD PRODUCTS

FOOD SERVICES & RETAILERS

HEALTH & PERSONAL CARE PRODUCTS

HEALTH CARE SERVICES

HOTELS

INFORMATION TECHNOLOGY

MATERIALS

TOTO LTD., III; 28 (upd.)
Toyo Sash Co., Ltd., III
Tuscarora Inc., 29
Ube Industries, Ltd., III
USG Corporation, III; 26 (upd.)
Vulcan Materials Company, 7
Walter Industries, Inc., III
Waxman Industries, Inc., 9

MINING & METALS

A.M. Castle & Co., 25
Alcan Aluminium Limited, IV
Alleghany Corporation, 10
Allegheny Ludlum Corporation, 8
Aluminum Company of America, IV; 20 (upd.)
AMAX Inc., IV
Amsted Industries Incorporated, 7
Anglo American Corporation of South Africa Limited, IV; 16 (upd.)
ARBED S.A., IV, 22 (upd.)
Arch Mineral Corporation, 7
Armco Inc., IV
ASARCO Incorporated, IV
Battle Mountain Gold Company, 23
Bethlehem Steel Corporation, IV; 7 (upd.); 27 (upd.)
Birmingham Steel Corporation, 13
Boart Longyear Company, 26
British Coal Corporation, IV
British Steel plc, IV; 19 (upd.)
Broken Hill Proprietary Company Ltd., IV, 22 (upd.)
Brush Wellman Inc., 14
Carpenter Technology Corporation, 13
Chaparral Steel Co., 13
Christensen Boyles Corporation, 26
Cleveland-Cliffs Inc., 13
Coal India Limited, IV
Cockerill Sambre Group, IV; 26 (upd.)
Coeur d'Alene Mines Corporation, 20
Cold Spring Granite Company, 16
Commercial Metals Company, 15
Companhia Vale do Rio Duce, IV
CRA Limited, IV
Cyprus Amax Minerals Company, 21
Cyprus Minerals Company, 7
Daido Steel Co., Ltd., IV
De Beers Consolidated Mines Limited/De Beers Centenary AG, IV; 7 (upd.); 28 (upd.)
Degussa Group, IV
Dofasco Inc., IV; 24 (upd.)
Echo Bay Mines Ltd., IV
Engelhard Corporation, IV
Fansteel Inc., 19
Freeport-McMoRan Inc., IV; 7 (upd.)
Fried. Krupp GmbH, IV
Gencor Ltd., IV, 22 (upd.)
Geneva Steel, 7
Gold Fields of South Africa Ltd., IV
Handy & Harman, 23
Hanson PLC, 30 (upd.)
Hecla Mining Company, 20
Hemlo Gold Mines Inc., 9
Heraeus Holding GmbH, IV
Hitachi Metals, Ltd., IV
Hoesch AG, IV
Homestake Mining Company, 12
The Hudson Bay Mining and Smelting Company, Limited, 12
Imetal S.A., IV
Inco Limited, IV
Industrias Penoles, S.A. de C.V., 22
Inland Steel Industries, Inc., IV; 19 (upd.)
Ispat International N.V., 30
Johnson Matthey PLC, IV; 16 (upd.)

Kaiser Aluminum & Chemical Corporation, IV
Kawasaki Steel Corporation, IV
Kennecott Corporation, 7; 27 (upd.)
Kerr-McGee Corporation, 22 (upd.)
Klockner-Werke AG, IV
Kobe Steel, Ltd., IV; 19 (upd.)
Koninklijke Nederlandsche Hoogovens en Staalfabrieken NV, IV
Laclede Steel Company, 15
Layne Christensen Company, 19
Lonrho Plc, 21
The LTV Corporation, 24 (upd.)
Lukens Inc., 14
Magma Copper Company, 7
The Marmon Group, IV; 16 (upd.)
MAXXAM Inc., 8
Metaleurop S.A., 21
Metallgesellschaft AG, IV
Minerals and Metals Trading Corporation of India Ltd., IV
Minerals Technologies Inc., 11
Mitsui Mining & Smelting Co., Ltd., IV
Mitsui Mining Company, Limited, IV
National Steel Corporation, 12
NERCO, Inc., 7
Newmont Mining Corporation, 7
Niagara Corporation, 28
Nichimen Corporation, IV
Nippon Light Metal Company, Ltd., IV
Nippon Steel Corporation, IV; 17 (upd.)
Nisshin Steel Co., Ltd., IV
NKK Corporation, IV; 28 (upd.)
Noranda Inc., IV; 7 (upd.)
North Star Steel Company, 18
Nucor Corporation, 7; 21 (upd.)
Oglebay Norton Company, 17
Okura & Co., Ltd., IV
Oregon Metallurgical Corporation, 20
Oregon Steel Mills, Inc., 14
Park Corp., 22
Peabody Coal Company, 10
Peabody Holding Company, Inc., IV
Pechiney, IV
Peter Kiewit Sons' Inc., 8
Phelps Dodge Corporation, IV; 28 (upd.)
The Pittston Company, IV; 19 (upd.)
Placer Dome Inc., 20
Pohang Iron and Steel Company Ltd., IV
Potash Corporation of Saskatchewan Inc., 18
Quanex Corporation, 13
Reliance Steel & Aluminum Co., 19
Republic Engineered Steels, Inc., 7; 26 (upd.)
Reynolds Metals Company, IV
Rio Tinto plc, 19 (upd.)
Rouge Steel Company, 8
The RTZ Corporation PLC, IV
Ruhrkohle AG, IV
Saarberg-Konzern, IV
Salzgitter AG, IV
Sandvik AB, IV
Schnitzer Steel Industries, Inc., 19
Southwire Company, Inc., 8; 23 (upd.)
Steel Authority of India Ltd., IV
Stelco Inc., IV
Sumitomo Metal Industries, Ltd., IV
Sumitomo Metal Mining Co., Ltd., IV
Tata Iron and Steel Company Ltd., IV
Teck Corporation, 27
Texas Industries, Inc., 8
Thyssen AG, IV
The Timken Company, 8
Titanium Metals Corporation, 21
Tomen Corporation, IV
Ugine S.A., 20
Usinor Sacilor, IV

VIAG Aktiengesellschaft, IV
Voest-Alpine Stahl AG, IV
Walter Industries, Inc., 22 (upd.)
Weirton Steel Corporation, IV; 26 (upd.)
Westmoreland Coal Company, 7
Wheeling-Pittsburgh Corp., 7
Worthington Industries, Inc., 7; 21 (upd.)
Zambia Industrial and Mining Corporation Ltd., IV

PAPER & FORESTRY

Abitibi-Consolidated, Inc., 25 (upd.)
Abitibi-Price Inc., IV
Amcor Limited, IV; 19 (upd.)
American Pad & Paper Company, 20
Asplundh Tree Expert Co., 20
Avery Dennison Corporation, IV
Badger Paper Mills, Inc., 15
Beckett Papers, 23
Bemis Company, Inc., 8
Bohemia, Inc., 13
Boise Cascade Corporation, IV; 8 (upd.)
Bowater PLC, IV
Bunzl plc, IV
Caraustar Industries, Inc., 19
Champion International Corporation, IV; 20 (upd.)
Chesapeake Corporation, 8; 30 (upd.)
Consolidated Papers, Inc., 8
Crane & Co., Inc., 26
Crown Vantage Inc., 29
Daio Paper Corporation, IV
Daishowa Paper Manufacturing Co., Ltd., IV
Dillard Paper Company, 11
Domtar Inc., IV
Enso-Gutzeit Oy, IV
Esselte Pendaflex Corporation, 11
Federal Paper Board Company, Inc., 8
Fletcher Challenge Ltd., IV
Fort Howard Corporation, 8
Fort James Corporation, 22 (upd.)
Georgia-Pacific Corporation, IV; 9 (upd.)
Groupe Rougier SA, 21
Honshu Paper Co., Ltd., IV
International Paper Company, IV; 15 (upd.)
James River Corporation of Virginia, IV
Japan Pulp and Paper Company Limited, IV
Jefferson Smurfit Group plc, IV
Jujo Paper Co., Ltd., IV
Kimberly-Clark Corporation, 16 (upd.)
Kruger Inc., 17
Kymmene Corporation, IV
Longview Fibre Company, 8
Louisiana-Pacific Corporation, IV
MacMillan Bloedel Limited, IV
The Mead Corporation, IV; 19 (upd.)
Metsa-Serla Oy, IV
Mo och Domsjö AB, IV
Monadnock Paper Mills, Inc., 21
Mosinee Paper Corporation, 15
Nashua Corporation, 8
NCH Corporation, 8
Oji Paper Co., Ltd., IV
P.H. Glatfelter Company, 8; 30 (upd.)
Packaging Corporation of America, 12
Papeteries de Lancey, 23
Pope and Talbot, Inc., 12
Potlatch Corporation, 8
PWA Group, IV
Rayonier Inc., 24
Rengo Co., Ltd., IV
Riverwood International Corporation, 11
Rock-Tenn Company, 13
St. Joe Paper Company, 8
Sanyo-Kokusaku Pulp Co., Ltd., IV

TOBACCO

TRANSPORT SERVICES

UTILITIES

WASTE SERVICES

NOTES ON CONTRIBUTORS

Notes on Contributors

BIANCO, David P. Freelance writer.

BISCONTINI, Tracey Vasil. Pennsylvania-based freelance writer, editor, and columnist.

BODINE, Paul S. Freelance writer, editor, and researcher in Milwaukee, specializing in business subjects; contributor to the *Milwaukee Journal Sentinel* and the *Baltimore Sun*.

BROWN, Susan Windisch. Freelance writer and editor.

BRYNILDSSEN, Shawna. Freelance writer and editor based in Bloomington, Indiana.

COHEN, M. L. Novelist and freelance writer living in Paris.

COVELL, Jeffrey L. Freelance writer and corporate history contractor.

DERDAK, Thomas. Freelance writer and adjunct professor of philosophy at Loyola University of Chicago.

FUJINAKA, Mariko. Freelance writer and editor living in Paso Robles, California.

HALASZ, Robert. Former editor in chief of *World Progress* and *Funk & Wagnalls New Encyclopedia Yearbook*; author, *The U.S. Marines* (Millbrook Press, 1993).

INGRAM, Frederick C. South Carolina-based business writer who has contributed to *GSA Business, Appalachian Trailway News*, the *Encyclopedia of Business*, the *Encyclopedia of Global Industries*, the *Encyclopedia of Consumer Brands*, and other regional and trade publications.

MALLETT, Daryl F. Freelance writer and editor; actor; contributing editor and series editor at The Borgo Press; series editor of SFRA Press's *Studies in Science Fiction, Fantasy and Horror*; associate editor of Gryphon Publications and for *Other Worlds Magazine*; founder and owner of Angel Enterprises, Jacob's Ladder Books, and Dustbunny Productions.

MARTIN, Rachel H. Denver-based freelance writer.

MOZZONE, Terri. Minneapolis-based freelance writer specializing in corporate profiles.

PEIPPO, Kathleen. Minneapolis-based freelance writer.

ROTHBURD, Carrie. Freelance technical writer and editor, specializing in corporate profiles, academic texts, and academic journal articles.

SALAMIE, David E. Part-owner of InfoWorks Development Group, a reference publication development and editorial services company.

STANFEL, Rebecca. Freelance writer living in Helena, Montana.

TRADII, Mary. Freelance writer based in Denver, Colorado.

UHLE, Frank. Ann Arbor-based freelance writer; movie projectionist, disc jockey, and staff member of *Psychotronic Video* magazine.

WALDEN, David M. Freelance writer and historian in Salt Lake City; adjunct history instructor at Salt Lake City Community College.

WERNICK, Ellen D. Freelance writer and editor.

WOODWARD, A. Freelance writer.